2012/13

3 0132 02108998 7

THE GUIDE TO

MAJOR TRUSTS
VOLUME 1

THIRTEENTH EDITION

Tom Traynor, Jude Doherty
& Lucy Lernelius-Tonks

Additional research by:
Denise Lillya

DIRECTORY OF SOCIAL CHANGE

Published by
Directory of Social Change
24 Stephenson Way
London NW1 2DP
Tel: 08450 77 77 07; Fax: 020 7391 4804
Email: publications@dsc.org.uk
www.dsc.org.uk
from whom further copies and a full publications catalogue are
available.

Directory of Social Change Northern Office
Federation House, Hope Street, Liverpool L1 9BW
Policy & Research 0151 708 0136; email: research@dsc.org.uk

Directory of Social Change is a Registered Charity no. 800517

First published 1986
Second edition 1989
Third edition 1991
Fourth edition 1993
Fifth edition 1995
Sixth edition 1997
Seventh edition 1999
Eighth edition 2001
Ninth edition 2003
Tenth edition 2005
Eleventh edition 2007
Twelfth edition 2010
Thirteenth edition 2012

ISBN 978 1 906294 54 0

British Library Cataloguing in Publication Data
A catalogue record for this book is available from the British
Library.

Cover design by Kate Bass
Text designed by Kate Bass
Typeset by Marlinzo Services, Frome
Printed and bound by Page Bros, Norwich

Contents

Introduction

This edition

Welcome to the thirteenth edition of *The Guide to the Major Trusts Volume 1*. Since the last edition of this book was published in 2010, the UK and the rest of the world has gradually moved out of the worst recession in living memory, although the economic situation remains uncertain. Austerity measures put in place by the government have now filtered down to grassroots level, with all charities and voluntary and community groups likely to be affected in some way by funding cuts from local authorities and other sources. Grant-making trusts and foundations have also been hit by the economic downturn over the past few years; however, they continue to provide valuable support to thousands of charities across the UK. As reported in the previous edition of this book, many of the funders featured here continue their efforts to try to mitigate some of the effects of these straitened times on their beneficiaries by maintaining levels of grantmaking where possible. We are confident that the information contained in this book will continue to help to support many successful fundraising strategies.

The purpose of this book has always been to get inside the policies and practices of the largest trusts and foundations in the country, and to explain what they are doing with their money, open them up to public scrutiny, encourage transparency and provide information for charities that are seeking funding for their valuable work. In doing this, the book has had considerable success. As well as being a practical and useful resource for those seeking grants, it has also been an independent review of the work of the larger trusts and foundations. As such, it has enabled readers to compare and contrast grantmakers and how they operate.

We continue to see improvements in the way in which trusts report their activities and the impact that their funding has on the charities they support. The annual reports and accounts of many of the funders in this book now contain a more detailed level of analysis than ever, and new reporting requirements such as statements on public benefit seem to have given some impetus for more funders to consider their objectives, achievements and performance in greater depth.

During the research for the last edition of this book it was interesting to read about trusts' individual responses to the financial crisis of 2008/09 in their annual reports. Many of them were hit hard, and collectively the value of the assets of the trusts featured last time fell by around £4 billion on

pre-recession levels. One of the most surprising things this time was how few of the trusts and foundations featured here commented in any great detail on the financial crisis beyond an acknowledgement that the economic climate remains tough. The focus of their discussions was generally based on how they may have changed their grant-making criteria or tightened up their application processes – the discussions focused on operational responses rather than financial impact. This may demonstrate that the funders here are moving on and adjusting to the new economic reality, and it perhaps should be encouraging to know that the collective value of the assets of these trusts and foundations has increased by £3.7 billion since the previous edition (to just under £36.7 billion). The result of this is that their collective income has also increased by £19.5 million (to just under £3.33 billion) – a modest increase, but an increase nevertheless. However, total grants have fallen since the previous edition.

The trusts in the edition gave almost £2.14 billion to organisations during the latest year for which financial information was available: in most cases the 2009/10 financial year. This is a decrease of £272.4 million, or 11%, on the amount represented in the previous edition. Given the recent recession and the current difficult economic climate, this may not be surprising, although naturally there are those that have reduced their funding significantly more than others, and many have actually increased their grantmaking since last time. Figure 1 shows the percentage of the 400 trusts contained in this book and the variance in their assets, income and grants compared to the previous edition:

Figure 1

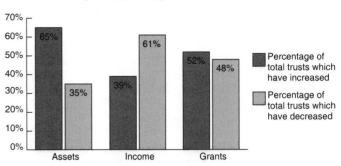

Top 400 trusts compared to 2010/11 edition

As figure 1 shows, the value of the assets of 65% of the trusts and foundations featured here increased since we

Top 25 trusts (excluding Big Lottery Fund and Awards for All)

	The Guide to the Major Trusts Volume 1 – 2010/11	Total grants		The Guide to the Major Trusts Volume 1 – 2012/13	Total grants
1	The Wellcome Trust	£598.5 million	1 (1) ^	The Wellcome Trust	£551.5 million
2	The Football Foundation	£82.1 million	2 (5)	Comic Relief	£58.2 million**
3	The Garfield Weston Foundation	£55 million	3 (4)	The Leverhulme Trust	£53.4 million
4	The Leverhulme Trust	£48.5 million	4 (8)	BBC Children in Need	£41.7 million
5	Comic Relief	£47 million*	5 (2)	The Football Foundation	£40.5 million
6	The Gatsby Charitable Foundation	£40.9 million	6 (3)	The Garfield Weston Foundation	£34.2 million
7	The Wolfson Foundation	£39.2 million	7 (6)	The Gatsby Charitable Foundation	£33.1 million
8	BBC Children in Need	£36.8 million	8 (17)	The Monument Trust	£32 million
9	The Henry Smith Charity	£26.7 million	9 (7)	The Wolfson Foundation	£28.2 million
10	Lloyds TSB Foundation for England and Wales	£23.7 million	10 (12)	Esmée Fairbairn Foundation	£27.6 million
11	The Prince's Charities Foundation	£21.9 million	11 (9)	The Henry Smith Charity	£24.9 million
12	Esmée Fairbairn Foundation	£21.5 million	12 (10)	Lloyds TSB Foundation for England and Wales	£23.4 million
13	Wales Council for Voluntary Action	£21 million	13 (16)	The Sigrid Rausing Trust	£21.3 million
14	Arcadia	£18.4 million	14 (15)	The Tudor Trust	£19 million
15	The Tudor Trust	£17.8 million	15 (20)	Paul Hamlyn Foundation	£18.7 million
16	The Sigrid Rausing Trust	£17 million	16 (18)	The City Bridge Trust	£16.8 million
17	The Monument Trust	£16.3 million	17 (-)	Age UK (formerly Help the Aged and Age Concern)	£16 million
18	The City Bridge Trust	£15.5 million	18 (13)	Wales Council for Voluntary Action	£14.8 million
19	The Jack Petchey Foundation	£14.5 million	19 (24)	The Northern Rock Foundation	£12.4 million
20	Paul Hamlyn Foundation	£13.4 million	20 (23)	The Coalfields Regeneration Trust	£12.1 million
21	The Shetland Charitable Trust	£11.7 million	21 (22)	The Trust for London (formerly the City Parochial Foundation)	£10.4 million
22	City Parochial Foundation	£11.5 million	22 (21)	The Shetland Charitable Trust	£10.3 million
23	The Coalfields Regeneration Trust	£11.5 million	23 (-)	The Robertson Trust	£9.7 million
24	The Northern Rock Foundation	£10.5 million	24 (-)	J Paul Getty Jr Charitable Trust	£9.5 million
25	The Wolfson Family Charitable Trust	£10 million	25 (-)	Allchurches Trust Ltd	£8.3 million
	Total	**£1.23 billion**		**Total**	**£1.13 billion**

* £12 million in the UK   ** £19.7 million in the UK   ^ figures in brackets show position in the previous edition

last researched this book, although just 39% saw an increase in their income. And while collectively the total grants represented here fell by £272.4 million, just over half of the trusts actually increased their grantmaking. It should be noted, however, that a significant proportion of this £272.4 million reduction in overall grants is due to a £184 million drop in funding from the Big Lottery Fund (BLF) compared to the previous edition. (The BLF's income actually increased since the previous edition, despite a 10% reduction in its share of the income from the National Lottery, introduced by the coalition government following the 2010 election.)

In each of the three years from 2010 to 2012, the BLF transferred £172 million to the Olympic Lottery Distribution Fund to help to fund the London Olympics 2012. This arrangement was put in place by the Department of Culture, [Olympics,] Media and Sport in 2007, with the total amount diverted from the BLF up to and including 2013 budgeted at £718 million. For more information on DSC's campaign to have this money returned as promised, visit our Big Lottery Refund campaign at: www.biglotteryrefund.org.uk. BLF's annual report and accounts for 2010/11 state, however, that the general reduction in funding during that financial year, which corresponds with most of the fall in grants seen here, were due to a small number of large commitments slipping into the next financial year (BLF 2011, p.42).

Other significant reductions in grants came from large funders including: the Wellcome Trust, which gave £551.5 million in 2009/10 compared to £598.5 million in 2007/08; the Football Foundation, which gave £40.5 million in 2009/10 compared to £82.1 million in 2007/08; and the Garfield Weston Foundation, which gave £34.2 million in 2009/10 compared to £55 million in 2007/08. It should be noted, however, that these decreases in funding are not necessarily due to the recession or the continuing challenging economic climate.

The Wellcome Trust, for example, saw the value of its assets increase by a staggering £708.8 million since the last edition, although conversely a relatively small decrease in income of £27.8 million. A decrease in grants of £47 million since the last edition simply reflects routine regular fluctuations from year to year, and with funding from this huge trust typically exceeding half a billion pounds each year, relatively small decreases of around 8% can distort the overall picture. In the case of the Garfield Weston Foundation, the grant figure of £55 million in the previous edition of this book was unusually high, as the foundation gave a substantial grant of £10 million to Oxford University for the New Bodleian Library and accounted for a further £15 million to be paid over the next two years. Since the previous edition of this book, the foundation's assets and income have actually increased by £365.2 million and £17.3 million respectively, and the total amount given in grants described here is comparable with the amount given before the recession (£38 million in 2005/06).

As figure 1 shows, 52% of the trusts and foundations featured here have increased the value of their grants since the last edition. These include the Monument Trust, whose grantmaking has increased by almost £15.7 million on the figure in the previous edition – this increase reflects a general trend of substantially increasing the value of the total grants it makes as a result of the trust benefiting from the substantial estate of the late Simon Sainsbury. Other trusts which have shown an increase in funding in this edition include: the Leverhulme Trust, which has given around £6.8 million more this time; the Esmée Fairbairn Foundation, which saw an increase of over £6.1 million; and the Paul Hamlyn Foundation, with an increase of almost £5.3 million. It should also be noted that the Lloyds TSB Foundation for Scotland is again featured here after being omitted from the previous edition while it suspended its grantmaking during a dispute with Lloyds Banking Group. The foundation has reached a successful outcome which has secured its funding from the group and has now resumed its funding activities.

There are 17 trusts which are new to this volume, including: the Pendragon Charitable Trust; the Castanea Trust; the Michael Cowan Foundation; the Cleevely Family Charitable Trust; and Summary Limited. It should be noted, however, that some of the recently registered trusts featured here had little or no financial information available at the time of writing and may prove to have a grant-making capacity lower than would normally make them eligible for inclusion. They are featured here as they appear to have the potential to make significant grants in the future, although this may prove not to be the case. Each of the newly registered trusts were contacted for more details on their financial situation, although the responses to these enquiries were disappointing.

As we can see from the Top 25 table, the top 25 trusts and foundations gave around £200 million less overall than the top 25 featured in the previous edition. As in previous editions, however, fluctuations either way are significantly influenced by the variations in the giving of the very largest in this guide; so when taking into account the decrease from the Wellcome Trust, the Football Foundation and the Garfield Weston Foundation, for example, the decrease in grants from the top 25 perhaps looks less significant. In fact, the £1.13 billion given by the top 25 here is significantly more than the top 25 gave in the eleventh edition of this guide (£958.9 million), before the recession.

The current environment

In summer 2011 we surveyed the trusts and foundations in this book and asked them a variety of questions, including:

▹ Did you receive fewer, about the same or more applications than the previous year?
▹ How are you reacting to any increase in demand from applicants?

▹ What are the most common mistakes applicants make when they apply to you for funding?

We had a response rate of 30%, which was around three times more than for the survey conducted for the last edition, when recession-related survey fatigue may have been taking its toll. The 120 responses drew some interesting results and comments.

Of those that responded, 49% received fewer or about the same number of applications compared to the previous year, with 51% receiving more applications.

Figure 2

No. of applications received during the last financial year

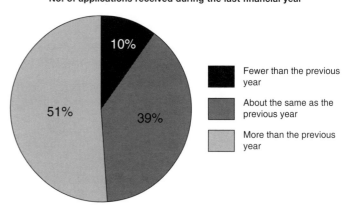

Fewer than the previous year

About the same as the previous year

More than the previous year

Given the prevailing narrative around the difficulties in obtaining funding from trusts and foundations due to, amongst other things, increased competition, then these figures can be seen as encouraging. However, there will be many reasons why almost half of the trusts and foundations who responded to this question have received fewer or about the same number of applications compared to the previous year: potential applicants may be discouraged from applying, for example, because they believe there has been a dramatic drop in the general funds available; many charities may have shifted their focus towards engaging in the procurement process and tendering for contracts; and, quite simply, post-recession, there are fewer charities to actually make applications.[1] Just over half of the respondents received more applications than the previous year, although whether the overall number of applications being made to trusts and foundations increased is unclear.

We also asked those that received more applications than the previous year how they were reacting to this increased demand. The main themes of the comments that were offered were that they were tightening up their application criteria and being more rigorous when assessing the applications they received. A number of those that responded said they were maintaining their overall levels of grantmaking but reducing the size of individual grants; a few stated that they were in a position to increase the amount of total grants given. Inevitably, a number of them stated that they have been unable to sustain previous levels of grantmaking, as reflected in figure 1. In addition to this we asked each trust to tell us what the most common mistakes were that applicants made when applying for funding. Overwhelmingly, the main theme was applicants clearly not

---

[1] Figures from the Charity Commission show that the total number of registered charities in 2008 was 168,354. The following year after a period of recession this figure had dropped to 160,515. There was a slight increase in 2010 (162,415); however, by 2011 the number of registered charities had again fallen, to 161,649 (Charity Commission 2011).

reading the trusts' guidelines, or choosing to ignore them and submitting ineligible applications. As a new feature of this edition of the guide you will find within the trusts' individual entries the full comments of those that replied.

In the last edition we highlighted surveys carried out by the Association of Charitable Foundations (ACF 2009), the results from which seemed to confirm our own research in that trusts and foundations were 'cautiously optimistic' about their long term funding prospects, and from the Charity Commission (2009), in which 14 out of 19 large grant-making trusts said at the time that the economic downturn had had little or no effect on them, but they had, however, been more cautious in their approach to grantmaking. Our research two years on shows that trusts and foundations were right to be cautiously optimistic about their future funding prospects as they have proved to be resilient, although there have undoubtedly been other difficulties elsewhere in the wider voluntary and community sector. As noted above, many of their previous and potential beneficiaries have not been so fortunate.

The evidence continues to suggest that while the economic climate remains challenging, grant-making trusts and foundations continue to try to at least maintain their levels of funding where possible. Potential applicants, however, need to ensure more than ever that their approaches are rigorously researched and targeted at the right funders. Trusts and foundations still report that they receive a significant number of ineligible applications which are wasting valuable resources on both sides.

To illustrate the point, in our summer 2011 survey we also asked all of the trusts and foundations in this book: how many applications did you receive in the last financial year? How many of these were ineligible? How many of the applications you received resulted in a grant being awarded? Out of the 400 trusts and foundations, 79 were able to provide all three of these figures. The total number of applications received by these 79 trusts was 67,437,[2] and these can be broken down as follows in figure 3:

Figure 3

Breakdown of the total number of applications received by the 79 trusts and foundations responding to the question

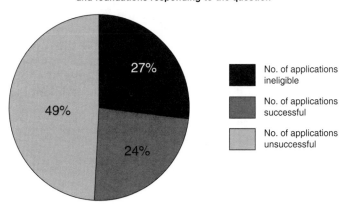

■	No. of applications ineligible
■	No. of applications successful
■	No. of applications unsuccessful

Even though this only represents less than a quarter of the funders here, it provides an interesting picture for fundraisers. Roughly speaking, around a quarter of

applications were ineligible and a quarter were successful, with about half of all applications received being unsuccessful. Clearly ineligible applications are a significant issue, which is why DSC continues to campaign for an end to ineligible applications by providing detailed information on the policies and practices of trusts and foundations and making key recommendations to potential applicants, namely:

▌ Read the guidelines provided by the trust (not doing so being the most common reason for applications being ineligible given by the trusts who responded to our survey).
▌ Do your research; make sure you apply to the right funders.
▌ Seek clarification if there is anything you are unsure of in the guidelines or application process.
▌ Do not send blanket appeals: funders can tell if an application is a general mail-merged appeal sent to many organisations without due regard for their individual policies and funding priorities.
▌ Make sure that your application is clear, concise and jargon-free.

If we just look at the applications received which met the trusts and foundations' guidelines and basic eligibility criteria, this figure is 49,133.[3] Figure 4 shows how these applications fared:

Figure 4

Breakdown of the total number of eligible applications received by the 79 trusts and foundations responding to the question

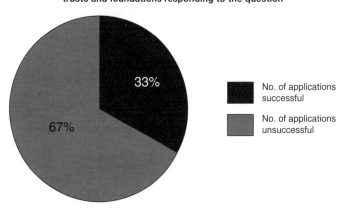

■	No. of applications successful
■	No. of applications unsuccessful

As we can see, one in three applications to the trusts and foundations in our sample were successful. Compared with data from our research in previous years, the number of unsuccessful applications has risen slightly, but it could be argued that this is to be expected given that over half of the respondents to our 2011 survey stated that they had seen an increase in applications.

In conclusion, our research suggests that funding from grant-making trusts and foundations remains stable despite the recent recession and the prevailing economic challenges. Funders are continuing their efforts to mitigate the worst effects of the financial crisis on the charities that rely on their funding to help support some of the most disadvantaged members of society. The austerity measures imposed by the current coalition government and the

---

[2] Some trusts appear to have included applications from individuals as well as organisations. Significantly, this does not include applications to the Big Lottery Fund or Awards for All.
[3] 16,105 applications were successful; 33,028 were unsuccessful.

proposed Welfare Reform Bill, however, make the likelihood of an increased demand on trusts and foundations' finite resources in the future almost inevitable. We shall see how this plays out in the next edition of this guide.

As we also saw in the previous edition, sources of funding have ceased to exist, but new sources are created on a regular basis. Grant-making trusts and foundations exist to give money to other organisations. But the need to put forward a strong case for why your charity or your beneficiaries should receive some of it has never been greater.

DSC policy and campaigning

Over the years DSC has campaigned on a number of fronts for better grantmaking. We believe that funders have a responsibility that extends far beyond providing funding. The way funders operate and develop their programmes has a huge impact on the organisations, causes and beneficiaries which their funding supports, as well as on the wider voluntary sector. Transparency is a key principle for us: by providing information about funders in this book and other DSC publications we have sought to open up their practices to greater scrutiny. Clearer and more accessible information enables fundraisers to focus their efforts effectively, and encourages open review and discussions of good practice. Our Great Giving campaign has grown out of these long-established beliefs.

We have identified some specific campaigning areas that we wish to focus on as part of an overall campaign for better grantmaking.

1) A clear picture of the funding environment
We think that to enable better planning and decision making from funders and policymakers, more comprehensive information is needed about where money is going and what it supports. Many of the funders in this book are leading the way, although some fall short in terms of the level of detail they provide about their activities and effectiveness.

2) Accessible funding for campaigning
Financial support for campaigning is vital to the role organisations play in achieving social change. Greater clarity from grant-making trusts is needed so that campaigning organisations can find the support they need more easily.

3) An end to hidden small print
DSC is asking all funders to provide the terms and conditions which govern the use of the funds at the outset when people apply and to be open to negotiating terms when applicants request it.

4) No ineligible applications
We know that most funders receive applications that do not fall within the funder's guidelines. Clearer guidelines can help, but applicants also need to take more heed of funder guidelines and target their applications appropriately.

DSC has always believed that clear and open application and monitoring processes are essential for both funders and fundraisers to produce more effective applications and better eventual outcomes. The availability of such information has come a long way since the first edition of this guide. However, an important element of the funding process often remains hidden from wider scrutiny.

The detailed terms and conditions which set out what the applicant is required to do to obtain and retain the grant are too often unavailable until the point at which a formal offer of a grant is made. For an applicant, seeing these terms and conditions for the first time only when there is an offer of money on the table is not helpful. Even if negotiating the conditions is an option, the balance of power is still squarely with the funder. If the funder is not willing to negotiate, the applicant is faced with a difficult decision: should any conditions conflict with their organisation's values or the wider needs of their beneficiaries, they then face a dubious choice between accepting conditions which may threaten their independence, and turning down much needed funding.

We surveyed the largest charitable, corporate and government funders to find out more about the availability and accessibility of their terms and conditions, which culminated in a research report, *Critical Conditions* (DSC 2009). This research found that many trusts and foundations were demonstrating what we consider good practice – 72% of those that responded said they made their terms and conditions publicly available, and there were a number of good examples. However, nearly half of trusts that responded stated that their terms were non-negotiable, a stance that we consider not to be in the best interests of funders or applicants. Overall these findings compared favourably to the central government funders that responded. By comparison these funders appeared to be less transparent and more averse to negotiating. They also tended to have more complicated and lengthy terms.

However, in late 2009 DSC asked similar questions of a much larger sample of trusts and foundations, and the results paint a different picture. In this research only half of respondents said their terms and conditions were publicly available, and a solid majority said they were non-negotiable. The proportion of those which said their terms were not publicly available at all was three times greater than in the *Critical Conditions* survey. Some of the variation is accounted for by the fact that the larger sample contained a far greater number of smaller trusts and foundations that do not have any terms and conditions at all (49% of respondents to this survey said they had terms and conditions, compared with 86% in the *Critical Conditions* report). Nevertheless, this further research broadly suggests that there is room for improvement from trusts as regards the transparency of their funding terms and conditions.

Some may argue that providing more information at the beginning of the application process could make things more time consuming and costly, but DSC believes the benefits of greater transparency should take precedence. It is crucial that fundraisers have access to all the information they need to make an informed decision about whether to apply. It is also vital that such information is publicly available so that funders and others can make comparisons and share good practice. Further, in this age of digital communication, there is an ever-increasing expectation that all the relevant information, guidance and application forms will be available online. A link to a web page or a short document outlining the detailed terms and explaining their place in the application process is easy to provide and need not cost anything. Clear instructions should be provided for the fundraiser about the importance of the terms and conditions, why they are necessary and what they mean, along with exhortations to read them thoroughly.

Again the onus is not entirely on the funder – fundraisers have a responsibility to inform themselves as fully as possible and to ask for relevant information if it isn't available or is not clearly presented by the funder. Reading and evaluating the criteria, guidance and detailed terms and conditions is part of making a well-targeted application which is more likely to be successful. More crucially it is about protecting the organisation's independence and building funding relationships that will work well for both parties. The fundraiser, therefore, has an important role to play in scrutinising the conditions of the funding arrangement at the outset, and communicating their views to other decision-makers in the organisation (see www.dsc.org.uk for more advice on terms and conditions for fundraisers).

DSC's Big Lottery Refund campaign

The National Lottery occupies a unique place in the grant-making world. Whilst the various distributors are statutory bodies which distribute what is, technically speaking, public money, their activities, aims and beneficiaries have much in common with charitable grant-making trusts.

DSC's campaign will therefore be of interest to fundraisers, fundraising charities, and anyone interested in the Big Lottery Fund in particular. The aim of the campaign is for the government to refund to the Big Lottery Fund £425 million of Lottery revenue which was diverted to help pay for the London 2012 Olympics. We argue that this decision, taken in 2007, was wrong in principle, as it should have been given out in grants to voluntary and community groups across the country, not to make up the budgetary shortfall of a one-off sporting event.

Both the previous and current government have committed to refund the Lottery using proceeds from selling Olympics assets after the Games, and there have been a series of agreements between the various agencies involved. However, it is unfortunately not straightforward: asset sales are expected to take decades, which is not acceptable in our view. Learn more and stay updated with developments at www.biglotteryrefund.org.uk.

References

ACF (2009), *ACF Survey of Trusts and Foundations: Trusts and Foundations Cautiously Optimistic Over Longer Term* [press release], London, Association of Charitable Foundations, 7 June

BLF (2011), *Annual Report and Accounts for the Financial Year Ended 31 March 2011*, Big Lottery Fund, London, The Stationery Office

Charity Commission (2009), *Firm Foundations: A Snapshot of How Trusts and Foundations are Responding to the Economic Downturn in 2009*, Liverpool, August

Charity Commission (2011), 'Facts and Figures' [web page], www.charitycommission.gov.uk/About_us/About_charities/factfigures.aspx, accessed 6 February 2012

DSC (2009), *Critical Conditions*, London, Directory of Social Change

Perspectives of the new researchers

Our experiences of working on the front-line of the voluntary sector before joining DSC and coming into contact with the people responsible for the serious-minded work of fundraising gave us a limited understanding of what this vital role entailed. We never doubted its importance: without funding to provide the necessary financial lubrication, the organisational cogs would quickly grind to a halt. However, there was, in our experience, always a distance from this process. It appeared to be opaque, taxing work that occurred 'upstairs' out of the way of the rest of the charity's activities.

Equipped with this natural curiosity, the research process for this book was enlivened by our analytical focus on how a fundraiser might approach and see the accounts, annual reports, guidelines and public pronouncements of these grant-making trusts. For the most part accessing the information itself was straightforward: the online register of the Charity Commission is a mine of information and the vast majority of trusts had submitted their accounts in a timely manner. Furthermore, the increasing use of websites by trusts is to be welcomed, with trusts such as John Lyon's Charity deserving particular praise for the depth and clarity of information provided. Nevertheless, it was shocking to find so many trusts without websites. In a world where we are accustomed to being able to use the Internet to discover almost anything it was disquieting to find such an absence of information on some trusts and foundations. This felt particularly relevant considering the emphasis that many trusts put on the overwhelming amount of applications they receive that are not eligible for funding. We felt that it was obvious that a small website outlining the eligibility criteria, perhaps including an online form, could vastly reduce the amount of wasted time spent by both the funder and the applicants on ineligible applications. That said, many of the trusts that do have websites also seem to encourage applicants to contact them informally to discuss an application, which was heartening.

Arriving rather late in the research process for this book our input into the surveying of the trust and foundations featured here was limited to collecting and analysing responses. This in itself, however, has conditioned how we have continued to approach the work of researching different trusts. In sampling the mood of the sector we were reminded of the need to pursue trusts for information, which is so vital to fundraisers and the publication of which upholds DSC's mission of helping to strengthen the independence of the voluntary sector and our campaign to reduce ineligible applications.

It was interesting to see the different strategies and criteria employed by various trusts and foundations that are aiming to fulfil their different charitable purposes, from trusts with a long pedigree to recently founded legacy trusts established for very specific purposes. We realised that many trusts are quite old-fashioned and in some cases do not appear to have changed for many decades. It was novel, but in some ways frustrating, to discover certain trusts that have been practically impervious to any outside influence since they were established, perhaps 100 years ago. It was also interesting to note that some trusts are explicit in defining the good outcomes that they want their funding to achieve whereas others illustrate their main areas of funding less directly by simply publishing lists of previous beneficiaries. It could be argued, in light of the sums distributed here, that there is a strong obligation upon trustees to make their areas of funding clear to ensure that applicants have the strongest possible chance of determining their fit to the trustees' criteria.

Our first foray into the world of trust funding has also been at a time of great change, as many grant-making trusts continue to feel the effects of the economic crisis. Therefore, it was with a certain amount of trepidation that we began to discover how the economic crisis has continued to impact upon the vital funding provided by these organisations. It has been distressing in many ways to find some trusts which state that they are unable to meet the needs of many of their applicants, and as a result many vital organisations are going unfunded. Alongside this it was surprising to find that, at a time when local authority cuts are really beginning to have an effect on communities, trusts which would consider replacing statutory funding were few and far between. Yet it has also become apparent that grant-making trusts have recognised this need and it has been the catalyst for many to think long and hard about how they carry out their work, and how they can make the biggest impact. As a result of such introspection what has been most interesting are the trusts that appeared to be doing something genuinely different – trusts which funded projects that were almost finished and had run out of funding, for example, or those which funded campaigning.

We hope that the results speak for themselves and that this book is as useful in its application as it has been fulfilling in its preparation.

Jude Doherty and Lucy Lernelius-Tonks

Frequently asked questions

How do you get your information?

In general we use the copy of the report and accounts on the public file at the Charity Commission. We then write a draft entry and send it to the trust via email, if necessary, inviting suggested additions as well as corrections or comments. New information provided by the trust, and not generally available, is usually put in the form 'The trust notes that... '. In cases where the trust or foundation has a website containing full information on its activities, including downloadable annual reports and accounts, this is the first port of call. In many cases the amount of information available on a trust's website is comprehensive, including guidelines for applicants and detailed information on current programmes, and this information is used extensively throughout this book.

Do you print everything the trusts say?

Generally yes, but there are two kinds of exceptions. First, if what the trust says is purely formal and could be said equally of most of the other trusts in this book, we do not feel it needs repeating. Second, some trusts, such as the Lloyds TSB foundations or the Esmée Fairbairn Foundation, now produce literature on such a scale that it has become impossible to reprint it all. Provided it is available there, we often refer to the availability of further material on the trust's website. This is particularly the case where guidelines or funding programmes are under review and liable to change soon after the publication of this book.

Do you investigate further when the information from a trust is inadequate?

No, we just report the fact that it is inadequate. We also try to ignore hearsay and anecdote, whether positive or negative.

What is your policy on telephone numbers?

When we know the telephone number we will normally print it, and will do so even if a trust doesn't want us to (provided it is an office rather than a private number). Where a trust has stated that it does not wish to receive telephone calls from potential applicants, or to have its number listed, this is noted in the text of the entry. However, when the available telephone number is simply the head office of a big professional firm that acts as a post box for the trustees, we generally leave it out.

Do you edit the 'applications' information?

No and yes. The content of this section generally comes from the trust if they have a specific document regarding making applications, and we will reproduce whatever they have available. However, we sometimes edit it to achieve a reasonable level of consistent presentation from one entry to another. If there is no specific application document available we collate information from annual reports, accounts and websites.

Why do you leave out the letters after trustees' names?

There are so many of them, and we try to present the entries in as simple and straightforward a way as we can. Besides, where do you draw the line? At Captain the Honourable A Anthony, DSO? Or going on to MBE, D Phil, AMCEEE and so on? The additional information might be helpful in identifying one A Anthony from another. However, we do see more and more trusts using simpler systems themselves: Arthur Anthony being more often happy nowadays to appear as such. Nevertheless, we do list titles – Lord, Lady, Dr, Professor and so on.

We are also sparing with capital letters. We use this minimalist style in the interests of clarity and correct editorial rules, but it does annoy some trusts, which go to considerable effort to try to change our usage back to what they see as proper. But reading about Trust after Foundation after Guideline after Application Form can get tiring.

Why don't the figures in the entries always add up?

There are a number of reasons.

▶ Unclear distinctions between grant commitments and grant payments.
▶ The fact that grants' lists and totals are often created by trusts quite separately from their audited figures.

▶ The fact that values for returned grants are included in some totals and not in others.
▶ The existence of small undisclosed grants: if the discrepancies are large, we go to some effort to clarify the situation. Where they are small, the figures are normally for illustration rather than being the basis for further calculation. If resources were spent on seeking perfect numerical consistency, they would have to be taken from the more useful task of trying to find out and reflect clearly what the trust is doing.
▶ Grant figures given in the entries are rounded up or down, which sometimes means that there may be a slight discrepancy between figures given individually and sum totals given elsewhere.

What's in a name? Trusts, foundations, funds, charities, settlements, companies, appeals: are they all the same?

The book covers organisations, usually charitable, that give grants to other charities. They may use almost any name; we judge them by what they do rather than what they are called.

Which trusts are in this book?

Roughly, those that give, or could give £300,000 or more in grants. Smaller trusts are covered in Volume 2 of this book as well as DSC's www.trustfunding.org.uk subscription website and the *Directory of Grant-Making Trusts*.

Why are some grant-making charities omitted?

This book does not generally seek to cover the following grant-making charities.

▶ **Company trusts:** if they are operated by company staff on company premises, we will usually regard this as a channel for giving by the company, to be reported in our *Guide to UK Company Giving* and on our www.companygiving.org.uk subscription website.
▶ **Specialised grantmakers:** those that operate in a narrow field where they are likely to be well known and accessible to most applicants. Examples include trusts only funding research on specific medical conditions (these are generally accessible through the excellent website of the Association of Medical Research Charities, www.amrc.org.uk) or only supporting projects designed by themselves.
▶ **Trusts or charities only making grants for work overseas:** while some trusts included here do make grants to organisations overseas, we do not list those which do so exclusively, such as Oxfam or Christian Aid.
▶ **Statutory funders, awarding public money:** these sources are covered in our *Government Funding Guide* and on our www.governmentfunding.org.uk subscription website.

What about lottery grants?

We have difficulties about deciding what we should include and have to make compromises. We include the Big Lottery Fund and Awards for All, but we do not cover the arts councils, the sports councils or the Heritage Lottery Fund. Although all Lottery grants are part of public expenditure, subject to review by the National Audit Office and the Public Accounts Committee of the

House of Commons, in many ways the Big Lottery Fund looks and acts like a grant-making trust, and a particularly big and interesting one at that.

... and community foundations?

Local community foundations are a rapidly developing part of the voluntary sector. Originally the idea was that they would build up endowments which would enable them to become important local grantmakers. They are still doing this, but only a few have generated enough income from their endowments to earn them a place in this book. However, most of them have also developed two new streams of income. Firstly, they have become a vehicle through which local philanthropists make their donations, usually using a named subsidiary fund. But this is still on a modest scale in most cases. Secondly and more importantly, they have become the vehicles for distributing local and central government money. We have included brief entries for those giving grants of £300,000 or more, even when most of this is coming from statutory sources. Contact details for all community foundations registered with the Community Foundation Network can be found at the back of this book (see page 408).

Finally...

The research for this book has been conducted as carefully as possible. Many thanks to those who have made this easier, especially the trusts themselves through their websites, their trust officers who provided additional information and the trustees and others who have helped us. Also thanks to the Charity Commission for making the annual reports and accounts available online.

We are aware that some of this information may be incomplete or will become out of date. We are equally sure we will have missed some relevant charities. We apologise for these imperfections. If you come across any omissions or mistakes, or if you have any suggestions for future editions of this book, do let us know. We can be contacted at the Liverpool Office Research Department of the Directory of Social Change either by phone on 0151 708 0136 or by email: research@dsc.org.uk

How to use this guide

The trusts are listed alphabetically and the indexes are at the back of the book. As well as an alphabetical index, there are subject and geographical indexes which will help you to identify the trusts working in your field and area.

At the front of the book (from page xviii) we have ranked the trusts by the amount of money they give. This list also shows their main areas of interest. If you are looking for grants for your charity, we recommend that you start with this listing and select those trusts which might be relevant, starting with the biggest.

When you have chosen enough to be getting on with, read each trust entry carefully before deciding to apply. Very often a trust's interest in your field will be limited and precise, and may demand an application specifically tailored to its requirements or often no application at all as it may not currently be accepting applications.

Remember to cover all parts of the guide: do not just start at the beginning of the alphabet. It is surprising, but still true, that trusts near the end of the alphabet receive fewer applications.

It is particularly important to show awareness of all the information available from the trust, to acquire up-to-date guidelines where possible, and to target your applications with respect to each trust's published wishes where such information exists.

Inappropriate and ill-considered approaches, especially those that show you have not read the published guidelines, antagonise trusts and damage your organisation's reputation. Of course, many trusts publish little of use. Unfortunately this may result in a waste of your time and theirs if they reject an application which they then deem to be ineligible.

We have included a chart to help with the timings of your applications (see page xv). It shows, for over 100 trusts, the months when trustee meetings are usually held, or when applications need to be submitted.

For those new to raising money from trusts, following the 'How to apply to a trust' guidelines overleaf is recommended as a starting point.

Classification

Serious applicants who will be fundraising from trusts in the long term do best, we believe, if they go to the most promising entries in this book and try to establish specific links between what the trust seems to be interested in and what their organisation is trying to do. The indexes and summary headings in this book are not likely to be enough on their own to identify the trusts that are most likely to have matching interests with a particular charity.

Notes on the entries

The entry headings

Grant total and financial year
The most up-to-date information available is given here. In a few cases the grants commentary in the main text is for the preceding year, as this information for the most recent year was unavailable or it was supplied at the last minute and was too late for inclusion in this guide. Sometimes the information received on a particular trust dates from two different years. For example, most of the entry may contain information from the latest published annual report, but may also include very recent information gained from consultations directly with the trust or taken from its website.

The main areas of funding
These categories have been chosen by the editors from an analysis of the trusts' funding. They are indicative rather than definitive, and useful in a preliminary trawl through the guide. They are no substitute for a close reading of each entry.

The correspondent
This is the lead person. Sometimes this is a solicitor or an accountant handling trust affairs solely on a 'postbox' basis. Other useful administrative contacts may also be given in the 'applications' section, or within the main body of text.

Beneficial area
This is the area or areas – when this is restricted – within which the trust operates, either legally or as a matter of policy or practice. When a trust with a UK-wide remit shows an interest in a particular locality, this is noted. While the information usually comes from the trust itself, it may also arise from a pattern of grantmaking seen by the editors.

Information available
This section notes the information available directly from the trust. If there is a website, this is usually the best starting point for information.

The main body of the entry
A summary of the trust's grantmaking usually prefaces the text. Trusts' policy notes and guidelines for applicants, where these exist, are normally reprinted in full. However, there are a few instances in which these are so lengthy that some abridgement has had to be undertaken. More trusts now analyse their own funding in their annual reports and, where

available, this material will also usually be quoted in full. Some analysis has also been carried out by the editors based on grants lists accompanying the accounts.

Exclusions and applications sections
These reproduce, where possible, the trust's own information or comments, though edited to suit the format of this book.

It would be useful to mention here why we include trusts and foundations which do not wish to receive unsolicited applications. These are included partly because this book is a survey of the grantmaking of the largest trusts and also to try and save the time and resources of organisations that may otherwise apply for funding in vain.

Common applicant mistakes
New to this edition, we have added comments from trusts provided to us though a survey we conducted in summer 2011. Not all trusts responded to this question but where they did this information is included in individual entries in their own words.

How to apply to a trust

Although there are complete books on this (for example *The Complete Fundraising Handbook* and *Writing Better Fundraising Applications*, both published by DSC), there is no need to be daunted by the challenge of making effective applications. If your charity's work is good – and of a kind supported by the trust in question – a very simple letter (of one uncrowded page or less, and backed by a clear annual report and set of accounts) will probably do 90% of everything that can be done.

If there is an application form and detailed applications requirements, just follow them. However, because these sorts of trusts make the process easier, they tend to get a lot of applications. You may have even better chances with the others.

1) Select the right trusts to approach
If they fund organisations or work like yours, and if you genuinely fit within any guidelines they publish, put them on your list.

2) Ring them
If the entry makes this sound sensible, ring the trust to check that the guidelines in this guide still apply and that the kind of application you are considering is appropriate.

3) Send in an application
Unless the trust has an application form (many do not), we suggest that the main part of this should be a letter that fits easily on one side of a sheet of paper (back-up materials such as a formal 'proposal' may be necessary for a big or complex project, but are usually, in our view, secondary). We suggest that the letter contains the following points.

▷ A summary sentence such as: 'Can your trust give us £10,000 to develop a training programme for our volunteers?'
▷ The problem the work will address: This should normally be the beneficiaries' problem, not your charity's problem: 'Mothers of children with learning disabilities in our area get very little help from the statutory services in coping with their children's day-to-day needs.'
▷ What you are going to do about this: 'Our volunteers, who have been in the same situations themselves, support and help them, but the volunteers need and want better training, especially on home safety.'
▷ Details of the work: 'We want to commission an expert from our sister charity Home-Start to develop and test suitable training materials that we will be able to use.'
▷ Information about your charity: 'We attach one of our general leaflets explaining what we do, and a copy of our latest annual report and accounts.'
▷ Repeat the request: 'We would be very grateful if your trust can give us this grant.'

And that is all. Keep the style simple and informal. Where you can, handwrite the date, salutation and signature. A charity is not a business and is not impressed by applicants trying to sound like one. The best letter comes from a person involved in the proposed activity.

Making the letter longer will often reduce rather than increase its impact, but attaching compelling material is fine. You are not saying that they have to read it through. A letter of endorsement might also be nice: your local bishop saying your work is wonderful, for example.

Appearance matters. It is a great help if you have a good quality letterhead on something better than photocopy paper, and if your report and accounts and literature are of appropriately high quality for your kind of organisation. However, you don't want to give the impression that your charity spends unnecessary money on expensive materials rather than on carrying out its work.

Good luck.

Dates for your diary

X = the usual month of trustees' or grant allocation meetings, or the last month for the receipt of applications.

Please note that these dates are provisional, and that the fact of an application being received does not necessarily mean that it will be considered at the next meeting.

	Jan	Feb	Mar	Apr	May	Jun	Jul	Aug	Sep	Oct	Nov	Dec
The 29th May 1961 Charitable Trust		X			X			X			X	
The H B Allen Charitable Trust		X										
The Architectural Heritage Fund			X			X			X			X
BBC Children in Need	X			X			X			X		
The Bedford Charity (The Harpur Trust)			X				X					X
Percy Bilton Charity			X			X			X			X
The Bluston Charitable Settlement			X									
The Bromley Trust				X						X		
The William A Cadbury Charitable Trust					X						X	
Calouste Gulbenkian Foundation			X				X				X	
Sir John Cass's Foundation			X			X					X	
CfBT Education Trust			X				X		X			X
The Childwick Trust					X							X
CHK Charities Limited			X							X		
Church Burgesses Trust	X			X			X			X		
The Church Urban Fund			X			X			X			X
Richard Cloudesley's Charity				X							X	
The Colt Foundation			X							X		
Colyer-Fergusson Charitable Trust			X							X		
The Ernest Cook Trust				X						X		
The D'Oyly Carte Charitable Trust			X				X				X	
Roald Dahl's Marvellous Children's Charity			X						X			
The Daiwa Anglo-Japanese Foundation			X						X			
Baron Davenport's Charity			X						X			

	Jan	Feb	Mar	Apr	May	Jun	Jul	Aug	Sep	Oct	Nov	Dec
The London Marathon Charitable Trust								X				
John Lyon's Charity			X			X					X	
The R S Macdonald Charitable Trust			X						X			
The Mackintosh Foundation					X					X		
The MacRobert Trust			X								X	
The Manifold Charitable Trust	X	X	X	X	X	X	X	X	X	X	X	X
Marshall's Charity	X			X			X			X		
The Henry Moore Foundation	X			X			X			X		
The Frances and Augustus Newman Foundation						X						X
The Ofenheim Charitable Trust			X									
The P F Charitable Trust	X	X	X	X	X	X	X	X	X	X	X	X
The Parthenon Trust	X											
The Dowager Countess Eleanor Peel Trust				X			X				X	
The Pilgrim Trust	X			X			X			X		
Polden-Puckham Charitable Foundation										X		
The Rank Foundation			X			X			X			X
The Joseph Rank Trust			X			X			X			X
The Sir James Reckitt Charity					X					X		
The Robertson Trust	X		X		X		X		X		X	
Joseph Rowntree Reform Trust Limited			X				X			X		X
The Saddlers' Company Charitable Fund	X						X					
The Francis C Scott Charitable Trust			X				X				X	
Seafarers UK (King George's Fund for Sailors)							X				X	
The Archie Sherman Charitable Trust	X	X	X	X	X	X	X		X	X	X	
The Henry Smith Charity			X			X			X			X
Sparks Charity (Sport Aiding Medical Research For Kids)			X							X		
St James's Place Foundation							X					X
The Steel Charitable Trust		X			X			X			X	
The Sir Halley Stewart Trust		X				X				X		
Stratford upon Avon Town Trust		X					X			X		
The Sir Jules Thorn Charitable Trust											X	
The Tolkien Trust				X								
The Trusthouse Charitable Foundation		X			X		X				X	
The Douglas Turner Trust		X			X				X			X
The Garfield Weston Foundation	X	X	X	X	X	X	X	X	X	X	X	X
The Will Charitable Trust	X						X					
The Harold Hyam Wingate Foundation	X			X			X			X		
The Wixamtree Trust	X			X			X			X		

The major trusts ranked by grant total

Trust	Grants	Main grant areas
☐ The Wellcome Trust	£551.5 million	Biomedical research, history of medicine, biomedical ethics, public engagement with science
☐ The Big Lottery Fund (see also Awards for All)	£374 million	Community, young people, welfare
☐ Awards for All (see also the Big Lottery Fund)	£61.55 million	General
☐ The Leverhulme Trust	£53.4 million	Scholarships for education and research
☐ BBC Children in Need	£41.7 million	Welfare of disadvantaged children
☐ The Football Foundation	£40.5 million	Grassroots football, community, education
☐ The Garfield Weston Foundation	£34.2 million	General
☐ The Gatsby Charitable Foundation	£33.1 million	General
☐ The Monument Trust	£32 million	Arts, health and welfare (especially AIDS) and general
☐ The Wolfson Foundation	£28.2 million	Medical and scientific research, education, health and welfare, heritage, arts
☐ Esmée Fairbairn Foundation	£27.6 million	Social welfare, education, environment, arts and heritage
☐ The Henry Smith Charity	£24.9 million	Social welfare, older people, disability, health, medical research
☐ Lloyds TSB Foundation for England and Wales	£23.4 million	Social and community needs
☐ The Sigrid Rausing Trust	£21.3 million	Human, women's and minority rights and social and environmental justice
☐ Comic Relief	£19.7 million	Social welfare
☐ The Tudor Trust	£19 million	Welfare, general
☐ Paul Hamlyn Foundation	£18.7 million	Arts, education and learning in the UK and local organisations supporting vulnerable groups of people, especially children, in India, social justice
☐ The City Bridge Trust (formerly known as Bridge House Trust)	£16.8 million	Social welfare in Greater London
☐ Age UK (formerly Help the Aged and Age Concern)	£16 million	Older people

☐ **Wales Council for Voluntary Action**	£14.8 million	Local community, volunteering, social welfare, environment, regeneration
☐ **The Northern Rock Foundation**	£12.4 million	Disadvantaged people
☐ **The Coalfields Regeneration Trust**	£12.1 million	General, health, welfare, community regeneration, education, young people, older people
☐ **The Trust for London (formerly the City Parochial Foundation)**	£10.4 million	Social welfare
☐ **The Shetland Charitable Trust**	£10.3 million	Social welfare, art and recreation, environment and amenity
☐ **The Robertson Trust**	£9.7 million	General
☐ **J Paul Getty Jr Charitable Trust**	£9.5 million	Social welfare, arts, conservation and the environment
☐ **Allchurches Trust Ltd**	£8.3 million	Churches, general
☐ **The Elton John Aids Foundation**	£7.4 million	HIV/AIDS welfare and prevention
☐ **The Prince of Wales's Charitable Foundation**	£6.8 million	Culture, the environment, medical welfare, education, children and youth and overseas aid
☐ **Achisomoch Aid Company Limited**	£6.6 million	Orthodox Jewish religious charities
☐ **The National Art Collections Fund**	£6.6 million	Acquisition of works of art by museums and galleries
☐ **Keren Association**	£6.5 million	Jewish, education, general
☐ **The Joseph Rank Trust**	£6.3 million	The Methodist Church, Christian-based social work
☐ **Mayfair Charities Ltd**	£6 million	Orthodox Judaism
☐ **The LankellyChase Foundation**	£5.8 million	Social welfare, community development, arts, heritage, penal affairs, mental health, prevention of abuse
☐ **The Joseph Rowntree Charitable Trust**	£5.8 million	Peace, democracy, racial justice, social justice, corporate responsibility, Quaker issues
☐ **The Nuffield Foundation**	£5.7 million	Education, child protection, law and justice, older people, African development, science and social science research, and capacity development
☐ **The Rank Foundation**	£5.7 million	Christian communication, youth, education, general
☐ **John and Lucille van Geest Foundation**	£5.7 million	Medical research, healthcare, general
☐ **The Linbury Trust**	£5.6 million	Arts, heritage, social welfare, humanitarian aid, general
☐ **Royal British Legion**	£5.6 million	Armed services
☐ **The Waterloo Foundation**	£5.5 million	Children, the environment, developing countries and projects in Wales
☐ **The Foyle Foundation**	£5.2 million	Arts and learning
☐ **The Kay Kendall Leukaemia Fund**	£5.2 million	Research into leukaemia and patient care
☐ **The Severn Trent Water Charitable Trust Fund**	£5 million	Relief of poverty, money advice, debt counselling
☐ **Voluntary Action Fund**	£5 million	General
☐ **The Clothworkers' Foundation**	£4.9 million	General charitable purposes, in particular social inclusion, young people, older people, disability, visual impairment, alcohol/substance misuse, prisoners, ex-offenders, homelessness and textiles
☐ **The Wolfson Family Charitable Trust**	£4.9 million	Jewish institutions and charities
☐ **Community Foundation Serving Tyne and Wear and Northumberland**	£4.8 million	Social welfare, general
☐ **The Westminster Foundation**	£4.8 million	Social welfare, military charities, education, environment and conservation
☐ **The Joseph Rowntree Foundation**	£4.7 million	Research and development in social policy and practice
☐ **The Underwood Trust**	£4.7 million	General charitable purposes, in particular, medicine and health, social welfare, education, arts, environment and wildlife
☐ **The Helping Foundation**	£4.6 million	Orthodox Jewish

☐ The Stewards' Company Limited (incorporating the J W Laing Trust and the J W Laing Biblical Scholarship Trust)	£4.6 million	Christian evangelism, general
☐ The Barrow Cadbury Trust and the Barrow Cadbury Fund	£4.5 million	Young adult and criminal justice, migration and Europe, and poverty and exclusion
☐ The Fidelity UK Foundation	£4.5 million	General, primarily in the fields of arts and culture, community development, education and health
☐ Forever Manchester (The Community Foundation for Greater Manchester)	£4.5 million	General
☐ John Lyon's Charity	£4.5 million	Children and young people in north and west London
☐ The Baily Thomas Charitable Fund	£4.4 million	Learning disability
☐ The Clore Duffield Foundation	£4.3 million	Arts/museums, Jewish charities, education, elderly and disadvantaged
☐ The Eranda Foundation	£4.3 million	Research into education and medicine, the arts, social welfare
☐ The John Ellerman Foundation	£4.2 million	National UK charities supporting health, disability, social welfare, arts and conservation and overseas projects
☐ The Hintze Family Charitable Foundation	£4.2 million	Education; Christian churches; museums, libraries and galleries
☐ The Birmingham Community Foundation	£4.1 million	General
☐ The Charles Wolfson Charitable Trust	£4.1 million	Medical research, education and welfare
☐ The Liz and Terry Bramall Charitable Trust	£4 million	General, social welfare
☐ The Jack Petchey Foundation	£4 million	Young people aged 11 – 25 in the London boroughs, Essex and the Algarve, Portugal
☐ The Variety Club Children's Charity	£4 million	Children's charities
☐ The Volant Charitable Trust	£4 million	General
☐ AW Charitable Trust	£3.9 million	Jewish causes through educational and religious organisations, general charitable purposes
☐ The Community Foundation for Northern Ireland	£3.8 million	Community, peace building, social exclusion, poverty and social injustice
☐ Euro Charity Trust	£3.8 million	Relief of poverty, education
☐ The London Marathon Charitable Trust	£3.8 million	Sport, recreation and leisure
☐ UnLtd (Foundation for Social Entrepreneurs)	£3.8 million	Social enterprise
☐ The 29th May 1961 Charitable Trust	£3.7 million	Social welfare, general
☐ The Headley Trust	£3.7 million	Arts, heritage, welfare, overseas development
☐ The Tolkien Trust	£3.7 million	General
☐ The Charles Dunstone Charitable Trust	£3.6 million	General
☐ The Goldsmiths' Company Charity	£3.6 million	General, London charities, the precious metals craft
☐ The Audrey and Stanley Burton 1960 Charitable Trust	£3.5 million	Jewish causes, health, arts, education and social needs
☐ Community Foundation for Merseyside	£3.5 million	Community development, regeneration, general
☐ The Sobell Foundation	£3.4 million	Jewish charities, medical care and treatment, education, community, environment, disability, older people and young people
☐ The Barclay Foundation	£3.3 million	Medical research, young people, the elderly, people with disabilities, the sick and the disadvantaged
☐ The Baring Foundation	£3.3 million	Strengthening the voluntary sector, arts and international development
☐ The M and R Gross Charities Limited	£3.3 million	Jewish causes
☐ St James's Place Foundation	£3.3 million	Children and young people with special needs, hospices
☐ The Alice Trust	£3.12 million	Conservation and education
☐ Rachel Charitable Trust	£3.1 million	General charitable purposes, in practice mainly Jewish organisations
☐ Action Medical Research	£3 million	Medical research, focusing on child health

☐ Entindale Ltd	£3 million	Orthodox Jewish charities
☐ Allan and Nesta Ferguson Charitable Settlement	£3 million	Peace, education, overseas development
☐ The Peter Harrison Foundation	£3 million	Sports for people in the UK who have disabilities or are disadvantaged, support for children and young people in the south east of England who are terminally ill, have disabilities, or are disadvantaged, and certain educational initiatives
☐ The Mercers' Charitable Foundation	£3 million	General welfare, elderly people, conservation, arts, Christian faith activities, educational institutions
☐ Quartet Community Foundation (formerly the Greater Bristol Foundation)	£3 million	General
☐ The Maurice Wohl Charitable Foundation	£3 million	Jewish, health and welfare
☐ The Wates Foundation	£2.9 million	Assisting organisations in improving the quality of life of the deprived, disadvantaged and excluded in the community
☐ The Dulverton Trust	£2.8 million	Youth and education, conservation, welfare, general
☐ The February Foundation	£2.8 million	Education, heritage, community-based charities, environment, animals, medical/welfare
☐ The Lord's Taverners	£2.8 million	Youth cricket, minibuses for organisations supporting young people with disabilities and sports and recreational equipment for young people with special needs
☐ The Sir Jules Thorn Charitable Trust	£2.8 million	Medical research, medicine, small grants for humanitarian charities
☐ The Samuel Sebba Charitable Trust	£2.8 million	General, covering a wide range of charitable purposes with a preference for Jewish organisations
☐ The Scottish Community Foundation	£2.7 million	Community development, general
☐ The Childwick Trust	£2.6 million	Health, people with disabilities and older people, welfare and research in connection with the bloodstock industry and Jewish charities in the UK, education in South Africa
☐ The Dollond Charitable Trust	£2.6 million	Jewish, general
☐ The Dunhill Medical Trust	£2.6 million	Medical research, elderly
☐ The London Community Foundation (formerly Capital Community Foundation)	£2.6 million	Community activities
☐ The Rufford Foundation	£2.6 million	Nature conservation, sustainable development, environment, general
☐ The Zochonis Charitable Trust	£2.6 million	General
☐ The Freemasons' Grand Charity	£2.5 million	Social welfare, medical research, hospices and overseas emergency aid
☐ The Jerusalem Trust	£2.5 million	Promotion of Christianity
☐ Maurice and Hilda Laing Charitable Trust	£2.5 million	Promotion of Christianity, relief of need
☐ Seafarers UK (King George's Fund for Sailors)	£2.5 million	The welfare of seafarers
☐ ABF The Soldiers' Charity (formerly the Army Benevolent Fund)	£2.4 million	Army charities
☐ CHK Charities Limited	£2.4 million	General charitable purposes
☐ The Peter Moores Foundation	£2.4 million	The arts, particularly opera, social welfare
☐ The Pilgrim Trust	£2.4 million	Social welfare and the preservation of buildings and heritage
☐ The Trusthouse Charitable Foundation	£2.4 million	General
☐ Cumbria Community Foundation	£2.3 million	General charitable purposes in Cumbria, in particular grant making to children and young people, older people and their carers, people with disabilities, the unemployed and people on low incomes
☐ Amabrill Limited	£2.3 million	Orthodox Jewish

THE MAJOR TRUSTS RANKED BY GRANT TOTAL

☐ The P F Charitable Trust	£2.3 million	General charitable purposes
☐ The Bernard Sunley Charitable Foundation	£2.3 million	General
☐ Calouste Gulbenkian Foundation	£2.2 million	Cultural understanding, fulfilling potential, environment, maximising social and cultural value
☐ The Duke of Devonshire's Charitable Trust	£2.2 million	General
☐ Global Charities (formerly GCap Charities)	£2.2 million	Disadvantaged children, young people and adults
☐ Hobson Charity Limited	£2.2 million	Social welfare, education
☐ Nominet Charitable Foundation	£2.2 million	IT, education, social welfare
☐ Cash for Kids Radio Clyde	£2.1 million	Children
☐ The Charities Advisory Trust	£2.1 million	General
☐ The DM Charitable Trust	£2 million	Jewish, social welfare and education
☐ The Eveson Charitable Trust	£2 million	People with physical disabilities, (including those who are blind or deaf), people with mental disabilities, hospitals and hospices, children who are in need, older people, homeless people, medical research into problems associated with any of these conditions
☐ The Gannochy Trust	£2 million	General
☐ The Hadley Trust	£2 million	Social welfare
☐ Hurdale Charity Limited	£2 million	Advancement of Jewish religion, relief of poverty and general charitable purposes
☐ The Lancaster Foundation	£2 million	Christian causes
☐ Shlomo Memorial Fund Limited	£2 million	Jewish causes
☐ The Souter Charitable Trust	£2 million	Christian evangelism, welfare
☐ The Vail Foundation	£2 million	General, Jewish
☐ The Gosling Foundation Limited	£1.9 million	Relief of poverty, education, religion, naval and service charities and general charitable purposes beneficial to the community
☐ The Helen Hamlyn Trust	£1.9 million	Medical, the arts and culture, education and welfare, heritage and conservation in India, international humanitarian affairs and 'healthy ageing'
☐ Hampton Fuel Allotment Charity	£1.9 million	Relief in need, health, education of children and young people and social welfare
☐ The Manoukian Charitable Foundation	£1.9 million	Social welfare, education, medical, the arts, 'Armenian matters'
☐ SHINE (Support and Help in Education)	£1.9 million	Education of children and young people
☐ Cripplegate Foundation	£1.8 million	General
☐ The Charles Hayward Foundation	£1.8 million	Heritage and conservation, criminal justice, hospices, older people, overseas, youth at risk
☐ Hexham and Newcastle Diocesan Trust (1947)	£1.8 million	Religion
☐ The South Yorkshire Community Foundation	£1.8 million	General
☐ Essex Community Foundation	£1.7 million	Social welfare, general
☐ Lloyds TSB Foundation for Northern Ireland	£1.7 million	Social and community need, education and training
☐ The Peacock Charitable Trust	£1.7 million	Medical research, disability, general
☐ The True Colours Trust	£1.7 million	Special needs, sensory disabilities and impairments, palliative care, carers
☐ Sir Siegmund Warburg's Voluntary Settlement	£1.7 million	Arts
☐ The Joron Charitable Trust	£1.67 million	Jewish, education, medical research, general
☐ The Vardy Foundation	£1.54 million	Christian causes, education in the north east of England, general
☐ The Leverhulme Trade Charities Trust	£1.6 million	Charities benefiting commercial travellers, grocers or chemists
☐ The Performing Right Society Foundation	£1.6 million	New music of any genre
☐ The Yorkshire Dales Millennium Trust	£1.6 million	Conservation and environmental regeneration
☐ The Nationwide Foundation	£1.55 million	Social welfare
☐ The Stone Family Foundation	£1.5 million	Relief-in-need, social welfare, overseas aid

☐ CAF (Charities Aid Foundation)	£1.5 million	Capacity building for small and medium sized charities
☐ Community Foundation for Calderdale	£1.5 million	General
☐ The Debmar Benevolent Trust	£1.5 million	Jewish
☐ The Sir Joseph Hotung Charitable Settlement	£1.5 million	General
☐ The Beatrice Laing Trust	£1.5 million	Relief of poverty and advancement of the evangelical Christian faith
☐ The Northwood Charitable Trust	£1.5 million	Medical research, health, welfare, general
☐ Ridgesave Limited	£1.5 million	Jewish, religion, education, general
☐ The Peter Cruddas Foundation	£1.48 million	Children and young people
☐ The Hugh Fraser Foundation	£1.4 million	General
☐ The Albert Hunt Trust	£1.4 million	Health and welfare.
☐ The Kirby Laing Foundation	£1.4 million	Health, welfare, Christian religion, youth, general
☐ The Roddick Foundation	£1.4 million	Arts, education, environmental, human rights, humanitarian, medical, poverty, social justice
☐ The Schroder Foundation	£1.4 million	General
☐ The Cadogan Charity	£1.3 million	General charitable purposes, in particular, social welfare, medical research, service charities, animal welfare, education and conservation and the environment
☐ CfBT Education Trust	£1.3 million	Organisations involved in education, particularly those concerned with the development and management of schools, managing and delivering effective learning and teaching, overcoming barriers to learning; and projects involving communication, language and multi-lingualism.
☐ The Ernest Cook Trust	£1.3 million	Educational grants focusing on children and young people for the environment, rural conservation, arts and crafts, literary and numeracy and research
☐ The Davidson Family Charitable Trust	£1.3 million	Jewish, general
☐ The Football Association Youth Trust	£1.3 million	Sports
☐ The Heart of England Community Foundation	£1.3 million	General
☐ The National Churches Trust (formerly the Historic Churches Preservation Trust with the Incorporated Church Building Society)	£1.3 million	Preservation of historic churches
☐ The Queen's Silver Jubilee Trust	£1.3 million	General, in practice grants to organisations supporting disadvantaged young people
☐ Sparks Charity (Sport Aiding Medical Research For Kids)	£1.3 million	Medical research
☐ Stratford upon Avon Town Trust	£1.3 million	Education, welfare, general
☐ The Three Guineas Trust	£1.3 million	Autism and Asperger's Syndrome, climate change
☐ The John Armitage Charitable Trust	£1.2 million	Medical, relief-in-need, education, religion
☐ Charitworth Limited	£1.2 million	Religious, educational and charitable purposes. In practice, mainly Jewish causes
☐ Church Burgesses Trust	£1.2 million	Ecclesiastical purposes, education, and other charitable purposes
☐ Clydpride Ltd	£1.2 million	Relief of poverty, Jewish charities, general charitable purposes
☐ Dunard Fund	£1.2 million	Classical music, the visual arts, environment and humanitarian causes
☐ Isle of Dogs Community Foundation	£1.2 million	Regeneration, general
☐ John James Bristol Foundation	£1.2 million	Education, health, older people, general
☐ Jerwood Charitable Foundation	£1.2 million	The arts
☐ Ernest Kleinwort Charitable Trust	£1.2 million	General purposes. In practice, mainly to wildlife and environmental conservation both nationally and overseas, disability, medical research, welfare of older and young people

☐ **The Edith Murphy Foundation**	**£1.2 million**	General, individual hardship, animals, children and the disabled
☐ **The John R Murray Charitable Trust**	**£1.2 million**	Arts and literature
☐ **The Parthenon Trust**	**£1.2 million**	International aid, medical research, assistance to the disadvantaged including people with disabilities, culture and heritage, medical treatment and care, education, promotion of civil society and research on current affairs
☐ **S F Foundation**	**£1.2 million**	Jewish, general
☐ **The Geoff and Fiona Squire Foundation**	**£1.2 million**	General
☐ **Derbyshire Community Foundation**	**£1.16 million**	Social welfare
☐ **The Leathersellers' Company Charitable Fund**	**£1 million**	General
☐ **The Ashden Trust**	**£1.1 million**	Environment, homelessness, sustainable regeneration, community arts
☐ **The Church Urban Fund**	**£1.1 million**	Welfare and Christian outreach in deprived communities in England
☐ **The Maurice Hatter Foundation**	**£1.1 million**	Jewish causes, general
☐ **The R S Macdonald Charitable Trust**	**£1.1 million**	Neurological conditions, visual impairment, children and animal welfare
☐ **The Medlock Charitable Trust**	**£1.1 million**	Education, health, welfare
☐ **The Rayne Foundation**	**£1.1 million**	Arts, education, health, medicine, social welfare
☐ **The Shirley Foundation**	**£1.1 million**	Autism spectrum disorders with particular emphasis on medical research
☐ **Tees Valley Community Foundation**	**£1.1 million**	General
☐ **The H B Allen Charitable Trust**	**£1 million**	General
☐ **The Breadsticks Foundation**	**£1 million**	Healthcare and education
☐ **Edward Cadbury Charitable Trust**	**£1 million**	General
☐ **The Carpenters' Company Charitable Trust**	**£1 million**	Education, general
☐ **Sir John Cass's Foundation**	**£1million**	Education in inner London
☐ **The R and S Cohen Foundation**	**£1 million**	Education, relief in need and the arts
☐ **County Durham Community Foundation**	**£1 million**	Tackling social disadvantage and poverty, general
☐ **The Djanogly Foundation**	**£1 million**	General, medicine, education, the arts and social welfare
☐ **The Grace Charitable Trust**	**£1 million**	Christian, general, education, medical and social welfare
☐ **GrantScape**	**£1 million**	Environmental and community-based projects
☐ **The Hertfordshire Community Foundation**	**£1 million**	General
☐ **The Gerald Ronson Foundation**	**£1 million**	General, Jewish
☐ **The Rose Foundation**	**£1 million**	General – grants towards building projects
☐ **Joseph Rowntree Reform Trust Limited**	**£1 million**	Promoting political and democratic reform and defending of civil liberties
☐ **Mrs L D Rope Third Charitable Settlement**	**£998,000**	Education, religion, relief of poverty, general
☐ **The Bowland Charitable Trust**	**£991,000**	Young people, education, general
☐ **The Steel Charitable Trust**	**£988,000**	Social welfare, culture; recreation, health, medical research, environment, and occasionally, overseas aid.
☐ **Sussex Community Foundation**	**£983,000**	Community-based projects, education, disability, health, and the relief of poverty and sickness
☐ **Lloyds TSB Foundation for the Channel Islands**	**£977,500**	General
☐ **The Archie Sherman Charitable Trust**	**£974,000**	Jewish charities, education, arts, general
☐ **The Grocers' Charity**	**£973,000**	General
☐ **Mercaz Torah Vechesed Limited**	**£965,500**	Orthodox Jewish
☐ **The James Dyson Foundation**	**£959,000**	Science, engineering, medical research and education
☐ **The Execution Charitable Trust**	**£958,000**	Mainly local multi-purpose community projects supporting social welfare

☐ Itzchok Meyer Cymerman Trust Ltd	£944,000	Advancement of the orthodox Jewish faith; education, social welfare, relief of sickness, medical research and general charitable purposes
☐ The Sir James Reckitt Charity	£925,000	Society of Friends (Quakers), social welfare, general
☐ Reuben Brothers Foundation	£916,000	Healthcare, education, general
☐ The Community Foundation for Wiltshire and Swindon	£913,000	Community welfare
☐ The Francis C Scott Charitable Trust	£907,000	Disadvantaged young people in Cumbria and North Lancashire
☐ The Joseph Levy Charitable Foundation	£899,000	Young people, elderly, health, medical research
☐ The Sir John Fisher Foundation	£896,000	General charitable purposes with a preference for the shipping industry, medicine, the navy or military and music and theatre
☐ The EBM Charitable Trust	£880,000	Children/youth, animal welfare, relief of poverty, general
☐ The Michael Uren Foundation	£880,000	General
☐ The Sir James Knott Trust	£874,000	General charitable purposes, in practice, support for people who are disadvantaged, the young, the elderly, the disabled, education and training, medical care, historic buildings, the environment, music and the arts and seafarers' and services' charities
☐ The Haramead Trust	£870,000	Children, social welfare, education, people with disabilities, homeless people, medical assistance, victims and oppressed people and religious activities
☐ The Sutton Trust	£867,500	Education
☐ Sutton Coldfield Municipal Charities	£867,000	Relief of need, arts, education, building conservation, general
☐ The Stobart Newlands Charitable Trust	£864,000	Christian religious and missionary causes
☐ The Henry Moore Foundation	£857,000	Fine arts, in particular sculpture, and projects and exhibitions which expand the definition of sculpture, such as film, photography and performance
☐ The Sir Halley Stewart Trust	£849,000	Medical, social, educational and religious activities
☐ Jewish Child's Day	£847,000	Charitable purposes of direct benefit to Jewish children who are disadvantaged, suffering or in need of special care
☐ The Donald Forrester Trust	£845,000	General charitable purposes
☐ The Equitable Charitable Trust	£843,000	Education of disabled and/or disadvantaged children under 25
☐ The Constance Travis Charitable Trust	£841,000	General
☐ The Drapers' Charitable Fund	£839,000	General charitable purposes including education, heritage, the arts, prisoner support and textile conservation
☐ Network for Social Change	£833,000	Developing world debt, environment, human rights, peace, arts and education
☐ The Barnwood House Trust	£830,000	Disability and old age
☐ The Bromley Trust	£825,000	Human rights, prison reform, conservation
☐ The Freshfield Foundation	£820,000	Environment, healthcare
☐ The Kennedy Leigh Charitable Trust	£815,000	Jewish charities, general, social welfare
☐ The Bedford Charity (The Harpur Trust)	£814,000	Education, welfare and recreation
☐ Devon Community Foundation	£807,000	General
☐ The Valentine Charitable Trust	£807,000	Welfare, the environment and overseas aid
☐ The D'Oyly Carte Charitable Trust	£804,000	Arts, medical welfare, environment
☐ The Sylvia Adams Charitable Trust	£802,000	Disability, welfare, poverty, children and young people, social disadvantage
☐ The Marcela Trust	£800,000	Medical research

☐ The Girdlers' Company Charitable Trust	£793,000	Medicine and health, education, welfare, youth welfare, heritage, environment, humanities and Christian religion
☐ The Reed Foundation	£793,000	General, arts, education, relief of poverty, women's health
☐ Peter De Haan Charitable Trust	£789,000	Social welfare, the environment, the arts
☐ 4 Charity Foundation	£786,500	Jewish
☐ The J J Charitable Trust	£765,000	Environment, literacy
☐ Oglesby Charitable Trust	£765,000	General charitable purposes
☐ The Hunter Foundation	£750,000	Education, young people, children, relief of poverty, community development
☐ The Hedley Foundation	£749,000	Youth and health
☐ The James Tudor Foundation	£749,000	Relief of sickness, medical research, health education, palliative care
☐ The Polonsky Foundation	£743,500	Arts, social science, higher education institutions
☐ Marshall's Charity	£743,000	Parsonage and church improvements
☐ John Moores Foundation	£738,000	Social welfare in Merseyside and Northern Ireland, emergency relief overseas
☐ The Alice Ellen Cooper Dean Charitable Foundation	£734,000	General
☐ St Katharine and Shadwell Trust	£734,000	Community development
☐ British Record Industry Trust	£725,000	Performing arts, music therapy, general
☐ ShareGift (The Orr Mackintosh Foundation)	£723,000	General
☐ The Allen Lane Foundation	£718,000	Charities benefiting asylum-seekers and refugees, gypsies and travellers, lesbian, gay, bisexual or transgender people, offenders and ex-offenders, older people, people experiencing mental health problems and people experiencing violence or abuse
☐ Community Foundation for Bournemouth, Dorset and Poole	£717,000	Community
☐ The Mary Kinross Charitable Trust	£699,000	Relief of poverty, medical research, community development, youth and penal affairs
☐ The H D H Wills 1965 Charitable Trust	£698,500	Wildlife, conservation and general
☐ The Harold Hyam Wingate Foundation	£695,500	Jewish life and learning, performing arts, music, education and social exclusion, overseas development, medical
☐ The William A Cadbury Charitable Trust	£693,000	Local welfare and disability charities, environment and conservation, Quaker charities and international development
☐ Rowanville Ltd	£693,000	Orthodox Jewish
☐ Achiezer Association Ltd	£691,000	The relief of elderly people and people in need, advancement of education, advancement of religion, and general charitable purposes
☐ The Sheepdrove Trust	£687,000	Mainly environment, education
☐ The AIM Foundation	£683,500	Healthcare, community development, youth, environmental matters and other charitable activities particularly related to influencing long-term social change
☐ The Fishmongers' Company's Charitable Trust	£682,000	General, in particular education, relief of poverty and disability
☐ Baron Davenport's Charity	£676,000	Almshouses; hospices; residential homes for the elderly; children and young people under the age of 25
☐ Rosetrees Trust	£676,000	Medical research
☐ The Burdett Trust for Nursing	£667,000	Healthcare
☐ The Balcombe Charitable Trust	£664,000	Education, environment, health and welfare
☐ The Richmond Parish Lands Charity	£663,500	General
☐ Lord Leverhulme's Charitable Trust	£660,500	Welfare, education, arts, young people
☐ The MacRobert Trust	£658,000	General

☐ The Band Trust	£655,000	People with disabilities, children and young people, scholarships, hospices and hospitals, education, older people and people who are disadvantaged
☐ The Ardeola Charitable Trust	£652,500	General
☐ The Wixamtree Trust	£652,000	General, in particular, social welfare, environment and conservation, medicine and health, the arts, education, sports and leisure and training and employment
☐ The Thompson Family Charitable Trust	£648,000	Medical, veterinary, education, general
☐ Investream Charitable Trust	£644,500	Jewish
☐ Heathside Charitable Trust	£640,000	General, Jewish
☐ Colyer-Fergusson Charitable Trust	£631,000	Social isolation, exclusion or poverty, community activity (often through churches), church maintenance, environment, the arts
☐ The Bluston Charitable Settlement	£630,000	Jewish, general
☐ The Golden Bottle Trust	£623,000	General with a preference for the environment, health, education, religion, the arts and developing countries
☐ Melow Charitable Trust	£621,000	Jewish
☐ The Lennox and Wyfold Foundation	£618,500	General
☐ The Mulberry Trust	£603,000	General
☐ The Will Charitable Trust	£592,000	Environment/conservation, people with sight loss and the prevention and cure of blindness, cancer care, people with mental disability
☐ The Jane Hodge Foundation	£585,000	Medical care and research, education and religion
☐ The Kathleen Hannay Memorial Charity	£581,500	Health, welfare, Christian, general
☐ Simon Gibson Charitable Trust	£579,000	General
☐ The G C Gibson Charitable Trust	£574,000	Art, music and education; health, hospices and medical research; community and other social projects; religion
☐ The Architectural Heritage Fund	£572,500	Loans and grants for building preservation
☐ The Triangle Trust (1949) Fund	£568,000	Social welfare, health, people with disabilities, integration and general
☐ The Welton Foundation	£564,000	Medical research, health, the arts, general
☐ Roald Dahl's Marvellous Children's Charity	£532,000	Haematology and neurology conditions affecting children and young people up to the age of 25
☐ The Daiwa Anglo-Japanese Foundation	£529,000	Anglo-Japanese relations
☐ The Jones 1986 Charitable Trust	£513,000	People with disabilities, welfare of older people, welfare of younger people, education and purposes beneficial to the community
☐ The Tajtelbaum Charitable Trust	£510,500	Jewish, welfare
☐ The Schreib Trust	£510,000	Jewish, general
☐ Closehelm Ltd	£506,000	Jewish, welfare, general
☐ The Church and Community Fund	£500,000	Church of England, social welfare
☐ The 1989 Willan Charitable Trust	£498,000	General, in practice mainly organisations supporting, children, older people, people with mental and physical disabilities and medical research
☐ The Arbib Foundation	£495,000	General
☐ The Manifold Charitable Trust	£495,000	Education, historic buildings, environmental conservation, general
☐ Mr and Mrs J A Pye's Charitable Settlement	£490,000	General
☐ Milton Keynes Community Foundation	£489,000	Welfare, arts
☐ The Privy Purse Charitable Trust	£489,000	General
☐ The Glass-House Trust	£484,000	Social housing and the urban environment, art and child development
☐ The Mark Leonard Trust	£483,500	Environmental education, youth, general

☐ Erach and Roshan Sadri Foundation	£574,500	Education, welfare, homelessness, Zoroastrian religion, general
☐ Sir Harold Hood's Charitable Trust	£482,000	Roman Catholic charitable purposes
☐ The Mackintosh Foundation	£476,500	Theatre and the performing arts, children and education, medicine, homelessness, community projects, the environment, refugees, and other charitable purposes
☐ The Dowager Countess Eleanor Peel Trust	£476,000	Medical research, the elderly, socially disadvantaged people and general
☐ Jay Education Trust	£471,000	Jewish
☐ The Sovereign Health Care Charitable Trust	£468,500	Health, people with disabilities
☐ The Sandra Charitable Trust	£461,000	Animal welfare and research, environmental protection, social welfare, health and youth development
☐ The Enid Linder Foundation	£460,500	Health, welfare, general
☐ The Staples Trust	£460,000	Development, environment, women's issues
☐ The Colt Foundation	£459,500	Occupational and environmental health research
☐ Fisherbeck Charitable Trust	£457,000	Christian, homelessness, welfare, education, heritage
☐ Impetus Trust	£455,000	The development of charities working with people who are economically disadvantaged
☐ Trustees of Tzedakah	£450,000	Jewish charities, welfare
☐ Richard Cloudesley's Charity	£446,000	Churches, medical and welfare
☐ The Hilden Charitable Fund	£438,000	Homelessness, asylum seekers and refugees, penal affairs, disadvantaged young people and overseas development
☐ Nemoral Ltd	£437,000	Orthodox Jewish causes
☐ The Neil Kreitman Foundation	£435,500	Arts and culture; education; health and social welfare
☐ The Jordan Charitable Foundation	£434,000	General
☐ The Maud Elkington Charitable Trust	£432,000	Social welfare, general charitable purposes
☐ Percy Bilton Charity	£428,000	Disabled, disadvantaged youth, older people
☐ Queen Mary's Roehampton Trust	£428,000	Ex-service support
☐ Gwyneth Forrester Trust	£425,000	General
☐ The Saddlers' Company Charitable Fund	£424,500	General
☐ Childs Charitable Trust	£414,500	Christian, general
☐ The Douglas Turner Trust	£409,500	General
☐ The William Leech Charity	£401,500	Health and welfare in the north east of England, overseas aid
☐ The Great Britain Sasakawa Foundation	£400,000	Links between Great Britain and Japan
☐ The Rubin Foundation	£400,000	Jewish charities, general
☐ The Campden Charities Trustee	£397,000	Welfare and education
☐ The Tompkins Foundation	£394,500	General
☐ The ACT Foundation	£385,000	Welfare, health, housing
☐ Lady Hind Trust	£382,000	General with some preference for health and disability related charities
☐ The Tedworth Charitable Trust	£380,500	Parenting, child welfare and development, general
☐ Brushmill Ltd	£374,000	Jewish causes, education, social welfare
☐ The Stafford Trust	£369,000	Animal welfare, medical research, local community, relief in need
☐ The Joffe Charitable Trust	£368,000	Alleviation of poverty and protection/advancement of human rights
☐ The Isle of Anglesey Charitable Trust	£357,000	General
☐ Mike Gooley Trailfinders Charity	£351,000	Medical research, general
☐ The George John and Sheilah Livanos Charitable Trust	£351,000	Health, maritime charities, general
☐ The Pilkington Charities Fund	£350,500	General, health, social welfare, people with disabilities, older people and victims of natural disaster or war

☐ The Frances and Augustus Newman Foundation	£347,000	Medical research and equipment
☐ The Charles and Elsie Sykes Trust	£341,500	General, social welfare, medical research
☐ The Madeline Mabey Trust	£337,000	Medical research, children's welfare and education
☐ The North British Hotel Trust	£336,000	Health, social welfare
☐ The Alliance Family Foundation	£333,500	Jewish, general
☐ The John S Cohen Foundation	£333,500	General, in particular music and the arts, education and environment
☐ North West London Community Foundation	£333,000	General
☐ Polden-Puckham Charitable Foundation	£333,000	Peace and security, ecological issues, social change
☐ Private Equity Foundation	£328,500	Children and young people, social welfare, education
☐ Summary Limited	£321,000	Education, religion, social welfare
☐ The Ofenheim Charitable Trust	£318,500	General, mainly charities supporting health, welfare, arts and the environment
☐ The Alan and Babette Sainsbury Charitable Fund	£316,500	General
☐ H C D Memorial Fund	£129,000	Health, education, environment and community action

The 1989 Willan Charitable Trust

General. In practice mainly organisations supporting, children, older people, people with mental and physical disabilities and medical research

£498,000 (2009/10)

Beneficial area

Worldwide, in practice mainly the north east of England.

Community Foundation Tyne & Wear and Northumberland, 9th Floor, Cale Cross, 156 Pilgrim Street, Newcastle upon Tyne NE1 6SU

Tel: 0191 222 0945

Fax: 0191 230 0689

Email: mp@communityfoundation. org.uk

Correspondent: Mark Pierce, Head of Policy, Projects and Programmes

Trustees: Francis A Chapman; Alex Ohlsson; Willan Trustee Ltd.

CC Number: 802749

Information available

Accounts were available at the Charity Commission, without a list of grants.

The trust was established in 1989 for general charitable purposes, with a preference for benefiting organisations in the north east of England. The trust's annual report states:

> In recognition of the origins of the trust fund and the economic impact that the decline of shipbuilding has had on the region, the trustees tend to concentrate their support towards causes which are active in Tyne & Wear and its immediate surrounds. The trustees favour causes which aim to ease social deprivation and/or enrich the fabric of the local community and the quality of life of individuals within that community.

In 2009/10 the trust had assets of £15.7 million and an income of £355,500. There were 152 grants made during the year totalling £498,000. The trust's accounts give the following breakdown of how the money was distributed by category, region and size of grant:

Improving health	£199,500
Taking part in community life	£124,500
Building our children's future	£119,000
Enjoying later life	£38,500
Caring for our environment	£11,500
Getting people into work	£5,000
Tyne and Wear	£253,500
Northumberland	£102,500
County Durham	£58,500
International	£57,000
North East general	£13,500
Teesside	£9,500
Other UK	£3,000
£1,001–£5,000	£288,500
£5,001–£10,000	£115,000
More than £10,000	£58,000
£1,000 or less	£36,000

Previous beneficiaries included: SAFC Foundation and Cancer Connexions (£10,000 each); Amble Multi Agency Crime Prevention Initiative (£6,000); Durham City Centre Youth Project, The Children's Society and the Calvert Trust (£5,000 each); Chester le Street Youth Centre (£4,000); Different Strokes North East, Northern Roots and People and Drugs (£3,000 each); Leukaemia Research and Coast Video Club (£2,000 each); Northumberland Mountain Rescue and the Association of British Poles (£1,000 each); and Healthwise and Newcastle Gang Show (£500).

Exclusions

Grants are not given directly to individuals. Grants for gap year students may be considered if the individual will be working for a charity (in this case the grant would be paid to the charity).

Applications

In writing to the correspondent at the Community Foundation Serving Tyne & Wear. Applications are processed, collated and shortlisted by the Community Foundation on a quarterly basis. The shortlist is then circulated to each of the trustees for consideration and approval.

The 29th May 1961 Charitable Trust

Social welfare, general

£3.7 million (2009/10)

Beneficial area

UK, with a special interest in the Warwickshire/Birmingham/Coventry area.

Ryder Court, 14 Ryder Street, London SW1 Y 6QB

Tel: 020 7024 9034

Email: enquiries@29may1961charity. org.uk

Correspondent: The Secretary

Trustees: Vanni Emanuele Treves; Andrew C Jones; Anthony J Mead; Paul Varney.

CC Number: 200198

Information available

Accounts were on file at the Charity Commission. A separate 'Grants Awarded' document was provided by the trust.

The trust gives the following concise description of its grantmaking policy, aims and objectives:

> The 29th May 1961 Charitable Trust is a general grant making trust. The policy of the trustees is to support a wide range of charitable organisations across a broad spectrum. Although for disclosure purposes grants are analysed into separate categories, the trustees are interested in funding initiatives which meet their selection criteria regardless of the charitable area into which the grant falls. Grants are made for both capital and revenue purposes. Some grants are one-off, some recurring and others spread over two or three years. Grants that cover more than one year are subject to annual review and the satisfaction of conditions. The majority of grants are made to organisations within the United Kingdom and preference is given, where possible, to charities operating in the Coventry and Warwickshire area. The policy of the trustees is to consider grants on an equal opportunities basis, regardless of gender, religion or ethnic background.

Grants range in size from hundreds to hundreds of thousands of pounds; most are between £1,000 and £5,000. About half appear to be for work in the Coventry and Warwickshire area.

Most grants are now on a three-year basis and will not be renewed without at least some interval.

In 2009/10 the trust had assets of £99.2 million, which generated an income of £3.1 million. Grants were made to 469 organisations totalling £3.7 million, and were categorised as follows:

Social welfare	£1.2 million
Arts and museums	£631,000
Leisure, recreation and youth	£488,000
Homelessness and housing	£422,000
Employment, education and training	£417,000
Offenders	£217,000
Medical	£189,000
Conservation and protection	£139,000

Midlands	£1.5 million
National	£1.1 million
London and the South	£901,000
North	£153,000
International	£31,000
Northern Ireland	£2,000

Beneficiaries across all categories included: University of Warwick (£251,000 in total), toward the running costs of the arts centre and sponsorship of the Coull Quartet; Hereward College (£125,000), towards the costs of improving various aspects of the college for disabled students in Coventry; Coventry & Warwickshire Awards Trust (£100,000), towards the running costs of a sports centre providing facilities for under-privileged communities in Coventry; RNIB (£100,000), towards the costs of building a new vision school and children's home in Coventry; Shelter (£85,000), towards the costs of a project to prevent ex-offenders becoming homeless upon release; The Prince's Trust (£75,000), towards the general costs of the trust's work in the West Midlands; Macmillan Cancer Support (£50,000), towards the core funding for the national cancer counselling telephone line; Saddlers Wells Trust (£40,000), toward the costs of subsidised tickets for under-privileged people; NACRO (£30,000), towards the core costs; Historic Royal Palaces (£25,000), towards the cost of conserving the White Tower at the Tower of London; Royal Geographical Society (£10,000), towards the conservation costs of Lowther Lodge in London; Sir Oswald Stoll Foundation (£10,000), towards the costs of building 18 homes for homeless ex-

service people in Chiswick; Wellchild Trust (£10,000), towards the costs of nurses providing cover to sick children; New Bridge (£5,000), towards the costs of assistance to prisoners both in prison and following their release; Justice First (£5,000), towards the costs of an organisation in Teeside supporting asylum seekers; and the National Council for One Parent Families (£3,000), towards core costs.

Exclusions

Grants only to registered charities. No grants to individuals.

Applications

To the secretary in writing, enclosing in triplicate the most recent annual report and accounts. Trustees normally meet in February, May, August and November. Due to the large number of applications received, they cannot be acknowledged.

Common applicant mistakes

'Failure to enclose annual report and accounts.'

4 Charity Foundation

Jewish

£786,500 (2009/10)

Beneficial area

UK and Israel.

UK I Ltd, 54–56 Euston Street, London NW1 2ES
Tel: 020 7387 0155
Correspondent: Jacob Schimmel, Trustee
Trustees: Jacob Schimmel; D Rabson; Mrs A Schimmel.
CC Number: 1077143

Information available

Accounts were on file at the Charity Commission, without a list of grants.

Set up in 1999, in January 2008, the charity changed its name from Les Freres Charitable Trust to 4 Charity Foundation. Grants are made to Jewish organisations for religious and educational purposes.

In 2009/10 the foundation had assets of £11.2 million and an income of almost £6.9 million, mainly from rents. Grants were made during the year totalling £786,500.

A recent list of grants was not available. Previous beneficiaries include: the American Jewish Joint Distribution Committee; the Millennium Trust; Keren Yehoshua V'Yisroel; Project Seed; World Jewish Relief; Menorah Grammar School; British Friends of Jaffa Institute; Friends of Mir; Heichal Hatorah Foundation; Chai Life Line Cancer Care; Jewish Care; and British Friends of Ezer Mizion.

Applications

This trust does not respond to unsolicited applications.

ABF The Soldiers' Charity (formerly the Army Benevolent Fund)

Army charities

£2.4 million to organisations
(2009/10)

Beneficial area

Worldwide.

Mountbarrow House, 6–20 Elizabeth Street, London SW1W 9RB
Tel: 0845 241 4820
Fax: 0845 241 4821
Email: pcummings@soldierscharity. org
Website: www.soldierscharity.org
Correspondent: Col. Paul Cummings, Director of Grants and Welfare
Trustees: Michael Brett Hockney; Maj. Gen. George Kennedy; Maj. Sir Michael Parker; Stephen Clark; Gen. the Lord Walker; Guy Davies; Maj. Gen. Peter Sheppard; Maj. Gen. Stephen Andrews; Brig. Andrew Freemantle; Mrs Allison M Gallico; Maj. Gen. Andrew Gregory; Ms Susan Ryan; Ross Martin.
CC Number: 211645

Information available

Accounts were available at the Charity Commission.

Grants are made for the support and benefit of people serving, or who have served, in the British Army, or their families/dependants. The fund states:

> The work of the [applicant] charity/ service concerned must be of direct benefit to a number of soldiers, former soldiers or their dependants. Not only should this number be considerable but it must also comprise an appreciable portion of the numbers of people who benefit from the work or service of the charity.

In 2009/10 the fund had assets of £42.8 million and an income of over £12.1 million from donations, legacies and investments. Grants to other charities totalled £2.4 million plus £2.7 million to regiments and corps for the benefit of individuals.

Around 100 organisations benefit from the fund each year. They include the Army Families Federation, Royal Commonwealth Ex-Services League, Officers' Association, Portland Training College, Royal Star and Garter Home, Thistle Foundation, Alexandra House, Queen Alexandra Hospital Home and the Royal Hospital – Chelsea.

Applications

Individual cases should be referred initially to the appropriate Corps or Regimental Association. Charities should apply in writing and enclose the latest annual report and accounts.

Achiezer Association Ltd

The relief of elderly people and people in need; advancement of education; advancement of religion; and general charitable purposes

£691,000 (2008/09)

Beneficial area

Worldwide.

130–134 Granville Road, London NW2 2LD
Tel: 020 8209 3880
Email: genoffice@dasim.co.uk
Correspondent: David Chontow, Trustee
Trustees: David Chontow; Sydney S Chontow; Michael M Chontow.
CC Number: 255031

Information available

The 2008/09 accounts were the most recent available from the Charity Commission. In January 2012 the trust's 2009/10 accounts were 1 year overdue.

The trust's objects are to:

▷ offer relief to the 'aged, impotent and poor'

▷ advance education, religion and purposes beneficial to the community.

In 2008/09 the trust had assets of £1.2 million and a consolidated income of £965,000. Grants were made totalling £691,000. The accounts for the year do not include the individual beneficiaries of the grants made. According to the trust, a list of grant beneficiaries is 'detailed in a separate publication which is available from the Registered Office'. A copy has been requested but is yet to be received.

In the past, the trust has mainly supported Jewish charities with a few small grants being given to medical and welfare charities. No further information was available.

Exclusions

No grants to individuals.

Applications

In writing to the correspondent.

Achisomoch Aid Company Limited

Orthodox Jewish religious charities

£6.6 million (2009/10)

Beneficial area

Unrestricted.

---

35 Templars Avenue, London NW11 0NU
Tel: 020 8731 8988
Email: admin@achisomoch.org
Website: www.achisomoch.org/
Correspondent: Isaac Mark Katz, Secretary
Trustees: Isaac M Katz; David Chontow; Jack Emanuel.
CC Number: 278387

Information available

Accounts were available at the Charity Commission.

The trust seeks to advance religion in accordance with the Jewish faith, and also supports Jewish education and young people. The following information about how the trust operates is given on the its website:

> Achisomoch is a charity voucher agency – it is like a bank. You open an account with us and then pay money into the account. You are given a cheque (voucher) book and can then make (charitable) payments by using these vouchers. As a charity in its own right, we can reclaim the tax rebate under Gift Aid to increase the money in your account and available for distribution to charities. Donations, via vouchers can be made only to registered charities. You get regular statements and can arrange to speak to client services for any help or special instructions.

In 2009/10 the trust had assets of just over £2 million and an income of £6.4 million, mainly from donations and Gift Aid receipts. Grants were made during the year totalling £6.6 million.

Previous beneficiaries have included: the Ah Trust, Beis Malka Trust, Chevras Maoz Ladol, Comet Charities Ltd, Davis Elias Charitable Trust, Havenpoint Ltd, Heritage Retreats, Jewish Educational Trust, Lolev Charitable Trust, Menorah Primary School, Michlala Jerusalem College, SOFT, Tomchei Cholim Trust and Yad Eliezer – Israel.

Applications

In writing to the correspondent.

The ACT Foundation

Welfare, health, housing

£385,000 to organisations
(2009/10)

Beneficial area

UK and overseas.

61 Thames Street, Windsor, Berkshire
SL4 1QW
Tel: 01753 753900
Fax: 01753 753901
Email: info@theactfoundation.co.uk
Website: www.theactfoundation.co.uk
Correspondent: The Grants Officer
Trustees: Paul Nield; John
J O'Sullivan; Michael Street; David
Hyde; Robert F White; Denis Taylor.
CC Number: 1068617

Information available

Accounts were on file at the Charity
Commission. The charity also has a
clear and helpful website.

The foundation was established in
1994, and it provides grants to
individuals and other charities,
principally in the UK, with the aim of
enhancing the quality of life for
people in need, (specifically the
mentally and physically disabled).

Grants generally fall into the
following areas:

▶ building – funding modifications
   to homes, schools, hospices etc.
▶ equipment – provision of
   specialised wheelchairs, other
   mobility aids and equipment
   including medical equipment to
   assist independent living
▶ financial assistance – towards the
   cost of short-term respite breaks at
   a registered respite centre.

Projects that intend to be a platform
for continuing services will be
expected to demonstrate
sustainability. ACT would be
concerned to be a sole funder of
projects that require ongoing support.
The foundation's annual report states:

> ACT's income is derived almost entirely
> from its investment portfolio and in any
> year we receive many more
> applications than we can fund. As our

funds are limited we have to prioritise.
Not all applications for grants will be
successful and some may be met only
in part.

In 2009/10 the charity had assets of
£38.2 million and an income of
£15.8 million, mostly from property
investments. Grants were made
during the year totalling £779,000
(£2.6 million in 2008/09), including
£385,000 to 48 organisations and
£394,000 to 385 individuals.

Grantmaking in 2009/10

The foundation's activities are
described in the chairman's report for
2009/10:

> Despite increasingly challenging market
> conditions I am pleased to report a
> resilient performance in the year which
> saw our balance sheet strengthened
> and our goal of maintaining our grant-
> making budgets fulfilled. For this I am
> grateful to my fellow directors, our staff
> and our professional advisers, for the
> time, experience and wisdom they
> dedicate in helping us achieve our all
> important goal of making a difference
> to the lives of people in need.
>
> In common with the majority of our not-
> for-profit sector colleagues, the
> uncertain economic climate, both
> globally and here in the UK, has had an
> impact on income streams, but we
> have maintained a strong financial
> platform through the proactive
> management of every property in our
> investment portfolio, which has
> minimised arrears, limited voids,
> extended income security and realised
> attractive gains.
>
> Looking forward, reduced occupier
> demand looks certain to continue
> across all sectors and this will continue
> to impact rental values and put
> pressure on income for some time to
> come, especially across the Basepoint
> portfolio operated for us by our wholly
> owned subsidiary, Basepoint Centres
> Limited (BCL). Basepoint provides
> commercial workspace on flexible
> terms to small and medium sized
> enterprises (SMEs) and its profits are
> gift aided to the charity. The SME
> sector is feeling the effects of the lack
> of available credit and extremely
> difficult trading conditions, and until
> there is more certainty in occupier
> markets new development projects
> within Basepoint will not be
> implemented, and internal resourcing
> has been reduced accordingly. [...]
>
> We remain committed to maintaining
> our grant-making budgets and fulfilling
> our pledges and are focused on our
> core mission of helping those most in
> need. Like our investment strategy, the
> relationships we have through our
> grant-making are long term, and we
> have successfully begun the process of

making good the pledges we made last
year following the completion of our
review of our grant strategy.

> Grant-making now focuses more
> strongly on the 'transition' that young
> physically and mentally disabled people
> make as they leave full time education
> and move into adulthood. As reported
> last year we have agreed to help fund
> important projects, over a 3 to 5 year
> timeframe, with 6 new strategic
> partners, providing grant pledges of
> £1.8 million plus a 10 year interest-free
> loan of £1 million. These funds will
> support innovative projects based
> around providing support networks, life
> skills, employment training and access
> to meaningful daytime activities for
> both physically and mentally disabled
> people as well as those in danger of
> being excluded from society. In the
> year we paid down £250,000 of the
> £1.8 million new grant pledges.
>
> The largest of our new pledges,
> £500,000 plus the £1 million interest-
> free loan, was made to Hollybank Trust.
> Hollybank, with strong support from
> their local authority, were able to obtain
> planning permission, on green belt land
> within their current site at Mirfield, West
> Yorkshire for a new care facility for
> disabled children. These new state of
> the art facilities will provide
> accommodation supporting their 'care
> for life' philosophy and work on site is
> scheduled to commence this summer
> [2010], when our pledge and loan will
> begin to be drawn down.
>
> We are immensely proud to be
> associated with our partner charities
> and are looking forward to seeing the
> outputs from our funding as well as
> further developing and strengthening
> these relationships over the coming
> years.
>
> The deteriorating economy and volatile
> markets we have experienced over the
> last two years may have had a
> significant negative impact on the value
> of the foundation's investments, but it
> is clear the impact on many of our
> beneficiaries has been even more
> severe and the need for us to maintain
> and even increase our grant budgets
> has never been so important. Whilst
> recognising our limitations, we will
> continue to meet as many needs as we
> can using the available income from
> our property investment portfolio, and I
> remain confident that, with the skills we
> have across the group, we will achieve
> this for many years to come.

Beneficiaries during the year (some of
whom received instalments of multi-
year awards) also included: The Dani
Taylor Memorial Fund (£21,300);
Thames Hospicecare and the Theatre
Royal Stratford East (£20,000 each);
Lifeworks (£17,000); Wherever the
Need – India (£15,000); Barrs Court

School, Hampshire Riding Therapy Centre, Seeability and Wessex Autistic Society (£10,000 each); Rainbow Centre for Conductive Education (£8,200); Searchlight Workshops (£6,700); Noah's Ark Trust (£5,000); Lunch on the Run (£2,500); Voice of Carers Across Lothian (£1,500); and Ferring Country Centres (£500).

Exclusions

The foundation will not make grants:

- which would replace statutory funding
- which would pay for work that has already commenced or equipment already purchased, deposits paid or goods on order
- towards the operating costs of other charities except in connection with setting up new services
- to charities that have not been registered for at least three years
- for projects which promote a particular religion or faith
- to Community Centres and Youth Clubs except where those served are in special need of help (e.g. the elderly or persons with special needs)
- to Local Authorities
- to umbrella or grant-making organisations except where they undertake special assessments not readily available from our own resources
- to universities and colleges, and grant-maintained, private or local education authority schools or their Parent Teacher Associations, except if those schools are for students with special needs
- for costs associated with political or publicity campaigns
- towards deposits for motobility vehicles.

Applications

Application by registered charities and overseas charitable organisations has to be by way of letter on the organisation's headed paper and should:

- give a brief description of your organisation including any statutory or voluntary registration
- provide a summary of the work you plan to undertake with the grant, together with a cost breakdown, plans and/or

specification if available and a summary of the key milestones for the work

- provide information on why you need to do this work and what would happen if you were unable to do it
- give details of any other UK-based support received or pledged for your project
- specify what you expect the results of the work to be and the number of beneficiaries helped
- explain how you plan to evaluate whether the work achieved its goals
- explain if the work will require capital and/or ongoing operational funding and if so how you plan to meet these costs
- in addition you need to attach the following financial information to the letter:
  - a cashflow projection of income and expenditure budget for the work
  - details of any income already raised for the work and income outstanding and where you plan to raise it from
  - your latest annual report and accounts.

The foundation's guidelines state:

When to apply

You can apply for a grant at any time. Trustees meet four times a year, but you do not need to time your application to coincide with these meetings. Procedures exist to give approvals between meeting dates, where necessary.

We do not publish the dates of Trustees' meetings.

What happens to your application

We will send you an acknowledgement letter within one week of receiving your application. If your proposal is either in an unacceptable form, or ineligible, or a low priority, we will tell you in this letter.

We will assess all acceptable applications and we may contact you for further information and/or make a personal visit. In the case of charitable bodies we may also ask for a presentation.

We aim to make decisions on grants of up to £50,000 within one month of receiving your application. Decisions on grants over £50,000 can take up to three months.

If the application is for an emergency you may request a faster timescale and we will do our best to assist.

Action Medical Research

Medical research, focusing on child health

£3 million (2010)

Beneficial area

UK.

Vincent House, 31 North Parade, Horsham, West Sussex RH12 2DP
Tel: 01403 210406
Fax: 01403 210541
Email: info@action.org.uk
Website: www.action.org.uk
Correspondent: Martin Richardson
Trustees: Valerie Remington-Hobbs; Mrs Karen Jankel; Charles Jackson; Prof. Andrew George; Richard Price; Sir John Wickerson; David Gibbs; Mark Gardiner; Katie Stringer.
CC Number: 208701

Information available

Accounts were available from the Charity Commission. The charity also has a helpful website.

The charity was originally set up in 1952 as the National Fund for Poliomyelitis Research, and evolved into Action Medical Research. Since 2009 the focus of the charity has been child health, including problems affecting pregnancy, childbirth, babies, children and young people.

The charity's website states:

We support a broad spectrum of research with the objective of:
- preventing disease and disability and
- alleviating physical disability

Please note that our emphasis is on clinical research or research at the interface between clinical and basic science. We pride ourselves that our research is both innovative and of a high standard as judged by rigorous peer review.

Within the above criteria, we also support research and development of equipment and techniques to improve diagnosis, therapy and assistive technology (including orthoses, prostheses and aids to daily living) and we encourage applications in the field of medical engineering.

In 2010 the charity had assets of £7.4 million and an income of almost £7.2 million. Grants were made totalling £3 million.

Grants were made to look at a number of childhood related illnesses, some projects included: Sickle cell disease: a new diagnostic test; Attention deficit hyperactivity disorder; and Prematurity and mathematics disabilities. Beneficiaries included: King's College London (£195,000); University of Nottingham and University of Edinburgh (£193,000); University College London and University of Leicester (£159,000); St Mary's Hospital – University of Manchester (£125,000); Queen's University Belfast (£113,000); University of Southampton (£83,000); and University of Leeds (£64,000).

Guidelines

The charity gives the following guidance on its project grants, taken from its website:

Grants are made to those in tenured positions in a UK university or institution. Research workers who require personal support from a project grant, and who have made a substantial intellectual contribution to the grant proposal, may be named as co-applicants with an established member of staff as the principal applicant.

Grants are provided for up to three years duration in support of one precisely formulated line of research. A two page outline of the proposed research is required before a full application can be invited. Successful applicants from the outline stage will be sent a link to our application form. Awards will be made following peer review.

Applications should be of the highest quality as the scheme is very competitive.

The average award we make is in the region of £125,000 and grants above £200,000 would rarely be given. We are happy to consider grant requests at a lower level of funding (below £50,000).

Support covers salary costs, consumables and items of dedicated equipment essential for carrying out the work. The application should not include any indirect costs such as administrative or other overheads imposed by the university or other institutions and we would not normally pay salary costs for those already employed on salaried positions.

A research team can only apply for one grant per grant round.

Please note that there will be a limit to the number of full application forms that we can send out. Where the work is considered peripheral to our aims, or in cases where demand on our funds is high, we will inform you of our decision not to pursue a full application.

Exclusions

The charity does not provide:

- grants towards service provision or audit studies
- grants purely for higher education, e.g. BSc/MSc/PhD course fees and subsistence costs
- grants for medical or dental electives
- grants specifically for PhD studentships (although researchers may independently register for a higher degree)
- grants for work undertaken outside the UK
- any indirect costs such as administrative or other overheads imposed by the university or other institution
- costs associated with advertising and recruitment
- 'top up' funding for work supported by other funding bodies
- costs to attend conferences and meetings (current Action Medical Research grantholders may apply separately)
- grants to MRC Units, other than RTF awards where the training/ facilities cannot be offered elsewhere
- grants to other charities
- grants for research into complementary/alternative medicine.

Applications

The charity's website states:

Outline proposal

All applicants should complete a two page outline proposal form [available from the charity's website] summarising the research and giving an estimation of costs, and email it to the Research Department. The details on the outline form should include the potential clinical application of the work, how it fits the remit of the charity and a description of the work proposed.

The purpose of the outline proposal is to establish that your proposed work clearly falls within the charity's remit and priorities.

If your work is considered peripheral to our aims, or clearly falls within the remit of another funding organisation, and in cases where demand on our funds is high, we may be unable to pursue an application from you.

Full application

If the outline proposal is acceptable, you will be invited to complete a full application form online and you will be advised of the timetable.

Applications are assessed by peer review, first by independent external referees and then by our scientific advisory panel.

The decision to approve a grant is made by the council on the recommendations of the panel.

Closing dates for proposals and applications are available on the charity's website.

The Sylvia Adams Charitable Trust

Disability, welfare, poverty, children and young people, social disadvantage

£802,000 (2009/10)

Beneficial area

Hertfordshire; work in the UK which has a national impact; and overseas (mainly Africa).

Sylvia Adams House, 24 The Common, Hatfield, Hertfordshire AL10 0NB
Tel: 01707 259259
Fax: 01707 259268
Email: info@sylvia-adams.org.uk
Website: www.sylvia-adams.org.uk
Correspondent: Jane Young, Director
Trustees: Richard J Golland; Mark Heasman; Timothy Lawler.
CC Number: 1050678

Information available

Accounts were on file at the Charity Commission. The trust also has a clear and simple website.

This trust was set up using the income from the sale of works of art, following Sylvia Adams' death. The trust's aim is to improve the quality of life of those who are disadvantaged, through the alleviation of disease, sickness and poverty.

Grants generally range from £5,000 to a maximum of £30,000, though occasionally a grant may be made for £50,000. Most grants will be for one or two years, although grants can be made for over three years.

Grants are made in the following categories:

- children and young people
- people with a disability
- people living in poverty or who are disadvantaged

The trust is particularly interested in helping people to become self-supporting and self-help projects. UK focus is on enabling people to participate fully in society. Worldwide, the focus is on primary healthcare and health education, access to education, appropriate technology and community enterprise schemes. Both UK causes providing a national benefit and causes local to Hertfordshire are supported, as well as UK charities working overseas. The trust funds specific projects but will also consider core funding.

The trust reviews its priorities each year within its overall guidelines and up to date information is available on its website. Interests in Hertfordshire and the UK currently include:

Children and young people
We wish to support organisations that will give socially excluded children and young people opportunities to become resilient and capable adults.

In particular we are interested in:
- work which addresses the problems of children at risk of neglect and a lack of appropriate parenting
- supporting looked after children and those leaving the care system
- addressing the needs of those children and young people who have missed out on mainstream educational and training opportunities
- challenging activities, sport and the arts.

People with a disability
We wish to support organisations that are working to empower people with a disability.

In particular we are interested in:
- cultural and sporting opportunities
- access into employment.

Those living in poverty or who are disadvantaged
We wish to support organisations that enable people living in poverty or who are disadvantaged to access a better long term future.

In particular we are interested in:
- access into employment
- initiatives for rural communities facing hardship
- cultural and sporting opportunities

During 2011/12 the trust's overseas focus was on making grants in Kenya, Tanzania and Uganda, with a particular interest in:

- educational initiatives, particularly for girls and women
- low /alternative technology initiatives to support economic activity and improve quality of life
- water/sanitation
- high impact health initiatives such as vaccines, prosthetic aids and simple surgical procedures.

Check the trust's website for current priorities.

Grantmaking in 2009/10
In 2009/10 the trust had assets of £10 million and an income of £271,000. Grants were made totalling £802,000, and were broken down as follows:

Overseas	£361,000
Capital grant	£250,000
UK	£181,500
Trustee grants	£10,000

The capital grant was awarded to Basic Needs UK Trust for its transition into a 'social franchise'.

UK beneficiaries included: Motor Neurone Disease Association (£30,000), towards the development of Year of Pathway; Volunteer Reading Help (£25,000), for the post of Head of Volunteering and Best Practice; Friends United Network (£23,000), part-funding the post of clinical manager to expand the befriending service into new boroughs; Tacade (£20,000), for health education resources for visually impaired young people; Volunteer Centre Dacorum (£10,000), for research into supported volunteering; Youth at Risk (£5,000), to cover some core costs of their work with young people; Chrysalis School for Autism (£2,000), for the provision of additional specialist software; and The Activate Forum (£2,000), towards supporting people with physical disabilities into sport and leisure.

Exclusions
The trust does not give grants to:
- individuals
- projects in the Middle East or Eastern Europe or the countries of the ex-Soviet Union

- work that solely benefits elderly people
- organisations helping animals, medical research or environmental causes.

Applications
There is a two stage application process: Stage 1 can **only** be made through the trust's website; applicants who successfully get through this stage will be asked to submit a fuller Stage 2 application.

Telephone queries about the guidelines and application process are welcome in advance of applications being made.

Common applicant mistakes
'Using out of date information and not consulting the trust's website – then applying from overseas countries that we are not working in and applying by post when all applications have to come through our website.'

Age UK (formerly Help the Aged and Age Concern)

Older people

£16 million (2009/10)

Beneficial area
UK and overseas.

York House, 207–221 Pentonville Road, London N1 9UZ
Tel: 0800 169 8787
Email: contact@ageuk.org.uk
Website: www.ageuk.org.uk
Correspondent: Grants Unit
Trustees: Dianne Jeffrey, Chair; Patrick Cusack; Dr Bernadette Fuge; Jeremy Greenhalgh; Timothy Hammond; Chris Hughes; Glyn Kyle; Prof Brendan McCormack; Jane Newell; Michael Vincent; Pauline Walsh; Jane Wesson; Prof John Williams; Hilary Wiseman; Prof James Wright.
CC Number: 1128267

Information available

Accounts were available online at the Charity Commission. The trust also has a useful website.

General

In 2009 Help the Aged and Age Concern joined together to create a new charity dedicated to improving the lives of older people. Now operating under the name 'Age UK' it aims to speak with one voice on behalf of all older people.

The Age UK website describes the trust's vision as:

A world in which older people flourish is a world in which older people will:

 be equal citizens with equal rights
 have enough money for a secure and decent life, and have access as consumers to the products and services they need at a price they can afford
 have access to the healthcare and social care they need
 have the opportunity to live healthier longer lives and to enjoy a sense of well-being
 live in homes and neighbourhoods that are safe and comfortable and which enable them to lead fulfilling lives
 have opportunities to participate and contribute as volunteers, active citizens, good neighbours, family members, and workers
 enjoy the benefits of longer life, wherever they are in the world.

To achieve this vision, the trust focuses on five core areas of work:

 money matters
 health and wellbeing
 travel and lifestyle
 home and care
 work and learning.

Age UK has continued the work of Help the Aged and Age Concern, providing several million pounds in grant funding each year for research relating to age and ageing, and organisations working with people in later life. The charity's annual report states:

General grants

The trust administers a variety of grant programmes funded from its own reserves and on behalf of external providers such as government and the national lottery. All the programmes are aimed at organisations working to make life better for older people, by addressing people's immediate needs or tackling the root causes of problems they are experiencing. To qualify for funding, applicant organisations must be independently constituted, not-for-profit and accessible to all people in later life.

For further information on grant programmes currently open to applications, please contact the trust directly.

Research grants

Age UK aims to improve outcomes for older people in a wide variety of areas that may affect their lives. First-class research, knowledge and research partnerships support this aim. We:

 carry out research ourselves to generate authoritative evidence on age and ageing to achieve change and development in policy and services for older people
 fund research carried out by others that will lead to positive solutions for later life
 are a hub for knowledge about older people and issues in ageing for ourselves and others
 work in partnership with others from a local to global level to support the promotion and generation of age-related research and the uptake of new knowledge

We are the only UK charity to focus research effort and funds exclusively on later life.

Our research supports Age UK's vision of a world in which older people flourish.

Commissioned research

We commission social, economic and health research, often by competitive tender, to generate evidence on issues that affect older people. The research is at the heart of our work to change public policy and attitudes on ageing for the better and has supported major successes, for example, abolition of the default retirement age, increasing pensioner income and legislative change for a more age equal society.

Grant-funded research

From 1976 to 2010, we have supported over 360 biomedical research projects into healthy ageing, the diseases and disabilities of ageing and the ageing process itself through grants made by Research into Ageing, a constituent charity of Age UK. As a result, significant advances have been made in the understanding, prevention, diagnosis, management and treatment of age-related health problems and in knowledge about healthy ageing.

From 2012, we will award grants through the Research into Ageing Fund for research to improve the health and wellbeing of older people.

[Potential research grant applicants should check Age UK's website for information on upcoming deadlines.]

The Research into Ageing Fund is a fund set up and managed by Age UK to support age-related research and is the name by which we will refer to the Research into Ageing research programme from November 2011. This does not affect the way in which we award research grants, nor the continuation or funding of current projects. Research into Ageing remains a constituent charity in Age UK.

Grantmaking in 2009/10

In 2009/10 the trust had assets of £34 million and an income of £161 million. Grants in the UK were made totalling £16 million were broken down as follows:

Support for organisations working with people in later life	£8.3 million
Well-being services	£2.9 million
Information and advice	£1.9 million
Research	£1.7 million
Services development programmes	£680,000
Home services	£39,000
Digital inclusion	£32,000
Engagement	£6,000

Note: A significant proportion of the grant total was given to local Age Concern and Age UK branches.

There are also extensive grantmaking programmes overseas, amounting to £6.3 million, which are not covered here.

Exclusions

No grants to individuals.

Applications

For further information on general grant programmes currently open to applications, please contact the grants team. Applicants interested in research funding should contact the research department at Tavis House, 1–6 Tavistock Square, London WC1H 9NA or email research@ageuk.org.uk.

The AIM Foundation

Healthcare, community development, youth, environmental matters and other charitable activities particularly related to influencing long-term social change

£683,500 (2009/10)

Beneficial area

Worldwide. In practice, UK with a preference for Essex.

Whittle and Co, 15 High Street, West Mersea, Colchester, Essex CO5 8QA
Tel: 01206 385049
Email: louisa@whittles.co.uk
Correspondent: Miss Louisa Tippett
Trustees: Ian Roy Marks; Mrs Angela D Marks; Nicolas Marks; Joanna Pritchard-Barrett; Caroline Marks; Phillipa Bailey.
CC Number: 263294

Information available

Accounts were available at the Charity Commission.

Set up in 1971 as the Ian Roy Marks Charitable Trust, this trust changed its name to the AIM Foundation in 1993. The foundation stresses that grant-making policy is highly proactive in seeking out potential partners to initiate and promote charitable projects principally in the fields of healthcare, community development, youth, environmental matters and other charitable activities particularly related to influencing long-term social change, both in the UK and overseas. Grants are made for core costs and salaries.

In 2009/10 the foundation had assets of £9.5 million and an income of over £1 million. Grants were made totalling £683,500 and were broken down as follows:

Youth: care and development	£225,000
Healthcare	£152,000
Influencing long-term social change	£120,000
Environment	£46,000
Miscellaneous	£21,000

Beneficiaries included: Variety Club Children's Charity, the College for Integrated Health and the New Economics Foundation (£100,000 each); Essex Community Foundation (£52,000); Kids Company (£30,000); Community Foundation Network (£25,000); Worshipful Company Carmen Benevolent Fund (£20,000); The Soil Association (£15,000); Action for Child and Friends of the Earth (£10,000 each); Wells for India (£5,000); Farm Africa (£4,000); and Westminster Befriend a Family (£3,000).

Exclusions

No grants to individuals.

Applications

It cannot be stressed enough that this foundation 'is proactive in its approach' and does not wish to receive applications. 'Unsolicited requests for assistance will not be responded to under any circumstance.'

The Alice Trust

Conservation and education

£3.12 million (2009/10)

Beneficial area

Buckinghamshire.

The Dairy, Queen Street, Waddesdon, Aylesbury, Buckinghamshire HP18 0JW
Tel: 01296 653235
Correspondent: Fiona Sinclair
Trustees: Lord Rothschild; Lady Rothschild; Sir Edward Cazalet; Hon. Beth Rothschild; Lord Cholmondeley; SJP Trustee Company Limited.
CC Number: 290859

Information available

Accounts were available at the Charity Commission.

The Alice Trust was founded in 1984. Its aims include the preservation, protection, maintenance and improvement of Waddesdon Manor in the Vale of Aylesbury, Buckinghamshire, its lands and contents for the benefit of the public generally, together with the advancement of education in matters of historic, artistic, architectural or aesthetic interest.

Waddesdon Manor was bequeathed to the National Trust in the will of the late James de Rothschild. The Alice Trust manages the activities at the manor on behalf of the National Trust under an agreement dated 3 October 1993. It is the current policy of the trustees to direct their grant making activity almost entirely to the needs of Waddesdon Manor. Grants are very occasionally made to other charitable organisations.

In 2009/10 the trust had assets of £119.7 million and an income of £40.4 million, which included £33.7 million in the form of shares, property and other donations.

During the year the trust gave £3 million towards the running costs, repair and refurbishment of Waddesdon Manor. The only other beneficiary in this year was the Prince's Charities Foundation, which received £125,000.

At the end of 2010 the trust received further substantial assets totalling around £47 million following the dissolution of the Rothschild Foundation (CC no. 230159), a connected charity which shared two trustees. Further details are expected in the trust's 2010/11 accounts.

Applications

Applications can be made for the advancement of education in matters of historic, artistic, architectural or aesthetic interest, but in view of the commitment of the trust to its principal beneficiary, Waddesdon Manor, it is unlikely that many applications will be successful. The trust states that the trustees meet twice a year to consider grant applications and that grants are occasionally made to other charitable organisations. However, in reality very few grants are made. We would suggest that an informal enquiry is made to the trust before undertaking the preparation of any grant application. The trust acknowledges postal enquiries.

Allchurches Trust Ltd

Churches, general

£8.3 million (2010)

Beneficial area

UK.

Beaufort House, Brunswick Road, Gloucester GL1 1JZ
Tel: 01452 873189
Fax: 01452 423557
Email: atl@ecclesiastical.com
Website: www.allchurches.co.uk

ALLCHURCHES

Correspondent: Rachael Hall, Company Secretary

Trustees: Michael Chamberlain; Rt Revd Nigel Stock; Fraser Hart; Bill Yates; Nick J E Sealy; The Ven. Annette Cooper; William Samuel.

CC Number: 263960

Information available

Accounts were available from the Charity Commission. The trust also has a helpful website.

The trust makes a large number of small grants each year. Around 600 are awarded to churches and cathedrals, and perhaps 50 go to other organisations, many of which also have Christian associations in the UK and overseas.

The trust's income is derived from its wholly-owned subsidiary company Ecclesiastical Insurance Office plc.

The trust describes its grants strategy as:

- Supporting deployment of clergy at parish level, particularly within deprived areas;
- Funding other staff to support the work of the clergy;
- Funding new initiatives ranging from supporting parishes to educational work in schools;
- Maintaining and repairing church and cathedral buildings;
- Funding to support the work of the clergy; and
- funding specific mission and outreach activities.

In 2010 the trust had an income of £20 million and held assets of £383 million. Grants were made totalling £8.4 million.

Grantmaking in 2010

The trust described its activities during the year in its annual report, including a list of sample beneficiaries:

Dioceses	120	£5.8 million
Cathedrals	158	£1.1 million
Parishes and other charities	830	£1.4 million

Dioceses and cathedrals

The majority of the trust's donations are used to support the dioceses and cathedrals of the Church of England. During the year, the trust made donations of £7 million to those beneficiaries (2008: £5.5 million).

Anglican churches, churches of other denominations and the Christian community

The trust has a general fund which responds to requests for financial assistance from Anglican churches, churches of other denominations, the Christian community and other charitable organisations in accordance with its grant making policy. In general, the trust supports appeals from churches for building and restoration projects, repair of church fabric, church community initiatives, religious charities and charities preserving the UK heritage.

Special project fund

The special project fund was established in 1999. Its purpose is to support a small number of projects on a larger basis. During the year, the Trust allocated funds to the Council for the Care of Churches, the Archbishops' Council, the Rural Life and Faith project at the Arthur Rank Centre, the University of Surrey and the Eastern Region Training Partnership

Overseas projects fund

This fund was established in 2005. During the year, the trust allocated funds amounting to £80,000 (2009: £20,000) to support Christian causes overseas.

Some of the grants made

Some examples of recent donations are listed below to give an illustration of the variety of uses to which the grants have been put.

Alton Methodist Church, Hampshire
Funding was given towards the alteration of the church after joining with local Anglican churches, including the improvement of disabled access and energy efficiency.

Saint Peter's Catholic Church, Hinckley, Leicestershire
A donation was given to build a new community centre in the grounds of the church to benefit both Church and community.

Memorial Community Church (Baptist), Plaistow, London
Financial assistance was given for high-level brickwork repairs to the exterior of the church, to repair flat roofs and to restore the bells.

Faith 4 Families, Auckland
Funding was given for the development and launch of the Faith Box, a contemporary devotional tool for families that will be delivered to homes in New Zealand.

Gracehill Moravian Church, Co. , Antrim
Funding was given to enable urgent repairs to the church's spire and original windows to be undertaken, to re-slate the roof and to replace decayed masonry.

The Anglican Church of Canada, Diocese of Niagara
A donation was made to assist with hosting the 2010 Justice Camp residential programme for adults and young people.

St Andrew's Church, Fulham Fields, London
A grant was made towards the redevelopment of the church's site to create three floors of new community space and a residential plot to assist a homelessness project.

Selby Abbey, North Yorkshire
Funding was given towards the cost of repairing and conserving the abbey's medieval north porch.

Community of the Holy Cross, Rempstone, Leicestershire
Funding was given towards the conversion and restoration of a farmhouse at a new convent into guest accommodation with facilities for disabled people and for stressed clergy, church workers and laity to renew themselves physically, spiritually and mentally.

The Anglican Church of Canada (Indigenous Ministries), Toronto, Ontario
A grant was made towards the creation of two pilot projects to address suicide prevention in indigenous communities of northern Canada.

Prison Fellowship, New Zealand
A grant was made to assist with the funding of co-ordinators who will help ex-prisoners not to re-offend through Christian principles. The programme will involve churches of all denominations.

Sheringham Baptist Church, Norfolk
A donation was given to support the building of a new community church centre to benefit both Church and community activities.

The Children's Trust, Tadworth, Surrey
A grant was made to redevelop a building on the Trust's site to enable parents to stay while visiting their disabled children.

Exclusions

The trust is unable to support:

- charities with political associations
- national charities
- individuals
- appeals for running costs and salaries.

Applications cannot be considered from the same recipient twice in one year or in two consecutive years.

Applications

Applications should be submitted in writing using the form available on the website.

The H B Allen Charitable Trust

General

£1 million (2010)

Beneficial area
Worldwide.

Homefield, Chidden Holt, Hambledon, Waterlooville, Hampshire PO7 4TG
Tel: 023 9263 2406
Email: mail@hballenct.org.uk
Website: www.hballenct.org.uk/
Correspondent: Peter Shone
Trustees: Helen Ratcliffe; Peter Shone.
CC Number: 802306

Information available
Accounts were available from the Charity Commission. The trust also has a clear and simple website.

Background
This trust was established in 1985 by the late Heather Barbara Allen, whose family produced the famous Beefeater gin. The trust benefited from just under £10.5 million from her estate and smaller grant-making trust in 2005 (following her death) and 2006. Miss Allen had maritime interests and was a supporter of Padstow lifeboat station, paying for the 'James Burrough' lifeboat (named after the creator of Beefeater gin in the early 1860s and founder of the company). Its replacement, 'Spirit of Padstow', was bought by the trust with a £2 million donation to the RNLI in 2006.

Grants, generally for amounts between £5,000 and £25,000, are made to a wide range of national and, occasionally, local charities. Most grants are to charities previously supported.

General
The trustees have no restrictions on them as to the kinds of project or the areas they can support, and are generally prepared to consider any field. They do not make grants to, or sponsorship arrangements with, individuals or to organisations that are not UK registered charities.

There is no typical grant size, though the trustees do make a large number at £5,000. Grants can be recurring or one-off, and for revenue or capital purposes. The trustees give priority each year to those organisations to which grants have been made in the past.

The trust notes that many charities do not carry out up to date research into its activities and hopes that potential applicants will read the guidelines carefully and, if necessary, make a preliminary call to check their eligibility. The trust's guidelines are available on its website and include the current status of all the grant categories.

Note: the trust has recently stated that the trustees, 'are now planning to support a major project over the next two or three years. As they are also anticipating a substantial reduction in income this year, they do not expect to be able to support many new applicants in the next year or so'.

Grantmaking in 2010
In 2010 the trust had assets of £29.6 million and an income of £1.1 million. Grants were made during the year to 81 organisations totalling just over £1 million.

Beneficiaries were categorised under a wide range of fields, including: children and young people, general community, medical research, disability, environment and overseas aid. The largest grant was made to Exeter Cathedral – Libraries & Archives (£250,000).

Other beneficiaries included: Wildlife Conservation Research Unit (£40,000); Deafness Research UK (£35,000); Brain Research Trust (£20,000); the Prince's Trust (£15,000); Fauna & Flora International, Woodlands Hospice and the Inspire Foundation (£10,000 each); Dogs for the Disabled, RSPB, Missing People, St Mungo's and Prospect Burma (£5,000 each); and the Rural Youth Trust (£3,000).

Exclusions
No grants to individuals, organisations which are not UK-registered charities or gap-year students (even if payable to a registered charity).

Applications
In writing to the correspondent: including a copy of the organisation's latest annual report and accounts. Applications should be submitted by post, not email, although enquiries prior to any application can be made by email.

Note the following comments from the trust on its website:

> Applicants should note that, at their main annual meeting (usually in January or February), the trustees consider applications received up to 31 December each year but do not carry them forward. Having regard for the time of year when this meeting takes place, it makes sense for applications to be made as late as possible in the calendar year so that the information they contain is most up to date when the trustees meet. It would be preferable, from all points of view, if applications were made only in the last quarter of the calendar year. Although, preferably not in December.
>
> The trustees receive a very substantial number of appeals each year. It is not their practice to acknowledge appeals, and they prefer not to enter into correspondence with applicants other than those to whom grants are being made or from whom further information is required. Only successful applicants are notified of the outcome of their application.

Common applicant mistakes
'Not reading the guidelines or apparently thinking that they don't apply to them.'

The Alliance Family Foundation

Jewish, general

£333,500 to organisations
(2009/10)

Beneficial area
Unrestricted, but mainly UK, with some preference for the Manchester area.

12th Floor, Bank House, Charlotte Street, Manchester M1 4ET
Tel: 0161 236 8193
Fax: 0161 236 4814
Email: jridgway@bluebolt.com
Correspondent: Miss J M Ridgway, Secretary

Trustees: Lord David Alliance; Hon. Graham Alliance; Hon. Sara Esterkin; Hon. Joshua Alliance.
CC Number: 258721

Information available
Accounts were available at the Charity Commission.

The trust's objectives are 'the relief of poverty, advancement of education, advancement of religion and any other charitable purpose'. Most grants are made to Jewish organisations.

In 2009/10 the trust had assets of £12.9 million and an income of £563,000. Grants were made totalling £515,500, of which £333,500 was given to organisations and £126,000 was distributed to individuals. The remaining £56,000 was classified as 'sundry general charitable donations'.

Six beneficiaries were listed in the accounts; they were: Centre for Special Studies – Israel (£63,500); Jewish Community Secondary School Trust and LR Jiao Research Fund Hammersmith Hospital (£50,000 each); Imperial College Trust and the Centre for the Study of Jewish-Muslim Relations (£25,000 each); and Norwood Ravenswood (£22,000).

Applications
The trust has previously stated that unsolicited applications will not be responded to.

Amabrill Limited

Orthodox Jewish
£2.3 million (2009/10)

Beneficial area
UK, with a preference for north west London.

1 Golder's Manor Drive, London NW11 9HU
Tel: 020 8455 6785
Correspondent: Charles Lerner, Trustee
Trustees: Charles Lerner; Frances R Lerner; Salamon Noe; Israel Grossnass.
CC Number: 1078968

Information available
Accounts were on file at the Charity Commission, without a list of grants.

The principal activity of this charity is the advancement of education and religious practice in accordance with the teachings of the Orthodox Jewish faith. The charity's annual report states:

> Grants are made both for capital purposes – which can include buildings, equipments and educational material – and towards the general running costs of the grantee institution. Other grants are made for the relief of poverty and these are only made after appropriate certification has been seen. (An independent organisation has been set up in North West London to verify the identity and means of Orthodox Jewish persons for this purpose.)

In 2009/10 the charity had assets of £3.8 million and an income of £2.2 million, mostly from donations. Grants were made totalling £2.3 million.

A list of grants was not included in the most recent accounts. Previous beneficiaries include: Kahal Chassidim Bobov; YMER; BFON Trust; Beth Hamedrash Elyon Golders Green Ltd; Friends of Shekel Hakodesh Ltd; Friends of Mir and Parsha Ltd; Cosmon Bels Ltd; United Talmudical Academy; British Friends of Mosdos Tchernobel; Mayfair Charities Ltd; Friends of Toldos Avrohom Yitzchok; Achisomoch Aid Company; the Gertner Charitable Trust; and Higher Talmudical Education Ltd.

Applications
Appeal letters are received from, and personal visits made by representatives of Jewish charitable, religious and educational institutions. These requests are then considered by the trustees and grants are made in accordance with the trustees decisions. 'All applications receive the fullest and most careful consideration.'

The Arbib Foundation

General
£495,000 (2009/10)

Beneficial area
Unrestricted.

The Old Rectory, 17 Thameside, Henley-on-Thames, Oxfordshire RG9 1BH
Tel: 01491 848890
Correspondent: Carol O'Neill
Trustees: Sir Martyn Arbib; Lady Arbib; Annabel Nicoll.
CC Number: 296358

Information available
Accounts were available at the Charity Commission.

The foundation's grant making is described as follows:

> The charity supports the philanthropy of Sir Martyn Arbib, one of the trustees, and his direct family. Much of the funds are donated to the River and Rowing Museum Foundation, and mainly charities with which the trustees have a connection.

In 2009/10 the foundation had assets of £99,000 and an income of £500,000, in the form a donation from the Arbib family. Grants were made to 20 organisations totalling £495,000.

Grants were made during the year under the headings of social welfare, medical, education, children's welfare and animal welfare and conservation. Major grants during the year were made to: Sheffield Institute Foundation for MND (£125,000); Institute of Cancer Research and the River and Rowing Museum Foundation (£100,000 each); and Barbados Community Foundation and Ramsbury Recreational Centre (£50,000 each).

Other beneficiaries included: Black Watch Museum (£20,000); Royal Opera House Trust (£11,400 in total); Henley Festival and the Royal Horticultural Society (£5,000 each); Wiltshire Wildlife Trust (£3,000); and Tavistock Trust for Aphasia and Henley and District Agricultural Association (£1,000 each).

Exclusions
No grants to individuals.

Applications
In writing to the correspondent, although please note that grants are largely made to organisations with which the trustees have a connection, and therefore unsolicited applications are unlikely to be successful.

The Architectural Heritage Fund

Loans and grants for building preservation

£572,500 (2009/10)

Beneficial area
UK (excluding the Channel Islands and the Isle of Man).

Alhambra House, 27–31 Charing Cross Road, London WC2H 0AU
Tel: 020 7925 0199
Fax: 020 7930 0295
Email: ahf@ahfund.org.uk
Website: www.ahfund.org.uk
Correspondent: Barbara Wright, Loans and Grants Manager
Trustees: Colin Amery; Malcolm Crowder; Roy Dantzic; Fionnuala Jay-O'Boyle; George McNeill; John Pavitt; Merlin Waterson; Thomas Lloyd; Liz Davidson; John Townsend; Michael Hoare; John Duggan.
CC Number: 266780

Information available
Accounts were available at the Charity Commission. The fund also has a helpful and informative website.

The Architectural Heritage Fund promotes the permanent preservation of historic buildings in the United Kingdom by providing financial assistance, advice and information to building preservation trusts (BPTs) and other charities and by disseminating information about the work of BPTs to statutory and non-statutory bodies, other organisations and the public at large. BPTs, (charities established to preserve historic buildings for the benefit of the nation), operate within defined geographical areas, usually a specific town or county.

The fund seeks to achieve its objects primarily by making grants and low-interest short-term loans to assist BPTs and other charities to acquire and repair buildings which merit preservation for re-use. The trust makes grants towards initial options appraisals and certain other costs, including the cost to BPTs of employing a project organiser. Refundable grants towards the cost of specific professional work to develop a project and to provide additional working capital are also available.

In 2009/10 the fund has assets of almost £13.1 million and an income of £776,500, which included grants from statutory sources totalling £358,500. Grants were made totalling £572,500; loans were made to the value of £25,000.

Projects supported included those initiated by: Highland Buildings Preservation Trust; Glasgow Building Preservation Trust; Heritage of London Operations Limited; Heritage Trust for the North West; Manchester Historic Buildings Trust; The Vivat Trust; West Midlands Historic Buildings Trust; Cadwgan Building Preservation Trust; and The Strawberry Hill Trust.

The AHF's website features a number of studies of projects that have received support over the years which potential applicants may find particularly interesting.

Guidelines
The AHF offers the following guidelines on its schemes:

Options Appraisal Grant
The AHF offers grants of up to 75% of the cost of an initial options appraisal of a project likely to qualify for an AHF loan. The maximum grant is normally £7,500, but in exceptional circumstances this can be raised to £10,000. In rare cases the AHF may offer grants for options appraisals which examine the feasibility of only one option, but the grant offered will be a maximum of £3,000.

An options appraisal eligible for an AHF grant will look at the key conservation issues affecting the building, examine all options and consider in outline the viability of the most beneficial option. It should also explore all possible sources of funding for the project. The charity must bring together the findings in conservation and financial terms, implementation strategy and the further work that needs to be carried out to develop the preferred option.

More detailed guidance is available from the AHF website:

Project Development Grant
The AHF's Project Development Grant scheme is only available to building preservation trusts that are on the AHF's Register of revolving fund BPTs or are members of the UK Association of Preservation Trusts. To qualify the trust must have demonstrated that the end use for the project is likely to be feasible and have decided to take the project forward.

Project development grants are intended to help BPTs with the costs and expenses of developing a project once its viability has been established, and take it towards the point at which work starts on site.

The maximum amount available per project from this grant scheme is £20,000 in total and could include, for example, a combination of:

Administration costs: any reasonable administrative costs relevant to the project (e.g. printing and copying, photography, telephone etc) may be claimed, up to a limit of £1,000.

The costs of a suitably qualified project organiser to develop and co-ordinate a viable project and take it towards the point at which work starts on site. The project organiser is usually someone appointed for a fee from outside, but could be an employee; the grant will not normally exceed 75% of the project organiser's total cost, up to a limit of £15,000;

Other development costs: a BPT can apply for assistance towards development costs of an eligible project that cannot be recovered from other funders, e.g. the fee cost of business plans. BPTs with paid staff may claim for their own staff time and overheads to produce such items at cost, up to a limit of £7,500;

The costs of a Mentor to work with a less experienced BPT to help them move their project forward up to a limit of £7,500; in some cases this help may be available before an options appraisal is commissioned. Please speak to a member of the AHF's Projects Team for more information.

There is additional grant funding available for projects in Scotland, please speak to a member of the AHF's Projects Team to find out if you are eligible for this extra funding.

Loans
The AHF loan scheme is intended to assist registered charities by making short-term, low-interest loans for acquisition and/or working capital to repair historic buildings. The recipient must have, or acquire, title or a long lease for the historic building to be repaired.

Amount
Loans are usually subject to a ceiling of £500,000 with interest charged at 5% for working capital and 7% for acquisition.

Duration
The normal loan period is three years, or until the building is sold, whichever is earlier. The AHF will always consider allowing extra time, if this is requested before the loan falls due for payment, but the AHF does not offer long-term finance.

Security
Security can be offered in the form of a repayment guarantee from a bank, local authority or other acceptable institution, or as a first charge over any property (including that for which the loan is required) to which the borrower has a free and marketable title.

Development loans
Development loans are available for any professional work required to take a project to the point of it being ready to go on site. The recipient must be able to demonstrate that the project is viable and able to attract funding.

Amount
Development loans are subject to a maximum ceiling of £50,000 with interest charged at 2.5% simple. Should a larger AHF working capital loan for the same project be contracted, the interest charged on the development loan will be waived.

Duration
A development loan will normally be for a period of up to eighteen months and will not be extended beyond its due date.

Security
A development loan must be secured by a repayment guarantee, preferably from a local authority.

More detailed guidance is available from the AHF website.

Exclusions
Applications from private individuals and non-charitable organisations. Applications for projects not involving a change of ownership or of use, or for a building not on a statutory list or in a conservation area.

Applications
Detailed notes for applicants for loans and grants are supplied with the application forms, all of which are available from the fund's website. The trustees meet in March, June, September and December and applications must be received six weeks before meetings.

The Ardeola Charitable Trust

General
£652,500 (2009/10)

Beneficial area
Worldwide.

Coutts & Co, Trustee Dept., 440 Strand, London WC2R 0QS
Tel: 020 7753 1000
Correspondent: The Trustees
Trustees: Graham Barker; Joanna Barker; Coutts & Co.
CC Number: 1124380

Information available
Accounts were available at the Charity Commission.

This trust was established in 2008 for general charitable purposes.

In 2009/10 it had assets of £3.1 million and an income of £1.9 million, most of which was in the form of a donation from the settlors. Grants were made to three organisations during the year totalling £652,500.

The beneficiaries were: Target Ovarian Cancer (£595,000); Non-Profit Enterprise and Self-Sustainability Team (NESST Inc) (£54,500); and RedR UK (£3,000).

Applications
In writing to the correspondent.

The John Armitage Charitable Trust

Medical, relief-in-need, education, religion
£1.2 million (2009/10)

Beneficial area
England and Wales.

c/o Sampson West, 34 Ely Place, London EC1N 6TD
Tel: 020 7404 5040
Fax: 020 7831 1098
Email: finance@sampsonwest.co.uk
Correspondent: The Trustees

Trustees: John C Armitage; Catherine Armitage; William Francklin.
CC Number: 1079688

Information available
Accounts were available at the Charity Commission.

Established in 2000, this is the trust of John Armitage, co-founder of Egerton Capital, the City-based hedge fund. 'The principal objective of the trust is to provide financial support for charitable and worthy causes at the discretion of the trustees in accordance with the trust deed.'

In 2009/10 the trust had assets of £37.6 million and an income of just £4,000 (£2.5 million in 2008/09, mostly from donations in the form of shares gifted to the trust). Grants were made to 34 organisations totalling £1.2 million.

Grants were broken down as follows:

Medical research and medical care	10	£369,000
Relief for the poor, people with disabilities and older people	10	£359,000
Other	6	£232,000
Advancement of education	5	£139,000
Religion	3	£105,000

Beneficiaries in all categories included: Royal Marsden Cancer Campaign and the Wallace Collection (£100,000 each); Marie Curie Cancer Care (£72,000); Hop Skip Jump and the Russian Revival Project (£60,000 each); Bibury Community Trust, Farmor's School, Hartlepool & District Hospice and the Youth Sport Trust (£36,000 each); Amos Trust (£30,000); Bibury School (£27,000); Juvenile Diabetes Research Foundation (£20,000); Westmonasterium Trust (£15,000); and the Foundation of Prince William & Prince Harry (£6,000).

Applications
Applications received by the trust are 'reviewed by the trustees and grants awarded at their discretion'.

The Ashden Trust

Environment, homelessness, sustainable regeneration, community arts

£1.1 million (2009/10)

Beneficial area

UK and overseas.

Allington House, 1st Floor,
150 Victoria Street, London
SW1E 5AE
Tel: 020 7410 0330
Fax: 020 7410 0332
Email: ashdentrust@sfct.org.uk
Website: www.ashdentrust.org.uk
Correspondent: Alan Bookbinder, Director
Trustees: Sarah Butler-Sloss; Robert Butler-Sloss; Miss Judith Portrait.
CC Number: 802623

Information available

Excellent annual report and accounts are available from the trust's website.

General

This is one of the Sainsbury Family Charitable Trusts, which share a joint administration. They have a common approach to grantmaking which is described in the entry for the group as a whole.

Sarah Butler-Sloss (née Sainsbury) is the settlor of this trust and she has been continuing to build up its endowment, with donations and gifts in 2009/10 of £961,500. Total income during the year was £1.8 million including investment income. Its asset value stood at £26.7 million. Grants were paid during the year totalling almost £1.1 million.

Grantmaking

This trust's main areas of interest are (with the value of grants paid in 2009/10, including support costs as listed in the accounts):

	% of total	
Ashden Awards for Sustainable Energy	37.7%	£406,000
Sustainable development: international	16.7%	£179,500
Preventing deforestation (low carbon fund)	11.6%	£125,000
Sustainable development: UK	10.7%	£115,000
People at risk	7.8%	£84,000
Arts and sustainability	6.4%	£69,500
Cultural shift (low carbon fund)	4.6%	£50,000
Sustainable regeneration	3.1%	£33,500

The following information about the trust's grantmaking in 2009/10 is taken from its helpful and descriptive annual report:

The Ashden Awards

The Ashden Awards for Sustainable Energy was founded in 2001. Since then it has helped 120 winning projects develop their work, improved the lives of 23 million people, saved 3 million tonnes of CO2 every year and leveraged £7.5 million of support for winners. Today the Awards are an internationally recognised yardstick for innovation, excellence and good practice in the field of sustainable energy.

The Ashden Awards' mission is to encourage the wider use of local sustainable energy by:

- raising awareness, celebrating and rewarding best practice
- encouraging the expansion and replication of this work
- acting as an advocate for local sustainable energy to relevant audiences.

The 2010 International winners were: D.light Design – India/global (Gold Winner); CRELUZ – Brazil; Ministry of Agriculture & Rural Development and SNV – Vietnam; Rural Energy Foundation – Sub-Saharan Africa; Sky Link Innovators – Kenya; and TECNOSOL – Nicaragua.

The 2010 UK winners were: Isle of Eigg Heritage Trust – Scotland (Gold Winner); Northwards Housing – Manchester; Okehampton College – Devon; St Columb Minor School – Cornwall; Suffolk County Council; and Willis Renewable Energy Systems – Belfast.

Full details on the Ashden Awards can be found at: www.ashdenawards.org

Sustainable Development – International

The trust continues to support community-based sustainable technology projects which aim to equip people with the knowledge and tools to help themselves in an environmentally sustainable way. These projects help to alleviate poverty by using sustainable technologies for the enhancement of income generation, agriculture, education and health.

Examples of grants approved this year include:

- a grant to BioRegional Development Group [£90,000 over 3 years] to develop eco-communities in China and South Africa. This will include tackling social problems associated with migrant workers and writing a blueprint for sustainable building. It will be the first working model of sustainable building in South Africa
- the trust's interest in the widespread adoption of appropriate technology is reflected in a grant to E&Co [£25,000], an organisation which provides business development services and investment capital for clean energy enterprises in Africa, Asia and Latin America. It supports and invests in solar PV, improved cook stoves, biomass gasification and small wind enterprises which preserve natural resources, expand income, reduce indoor air pollution and light rural households and businesses.

Preventing Deforestation

The trust recognises the vital role that forests play in not only sequestering and storing carbon but also in the provision of eco system services that regulate the planet's weather. Recognising the vital role that forests play combined with their concern over the rapid destruction of tropical forests and rainforest, the trust has made grants to projects which address the issues from a number of perspectives; from the land rights of indigenous people to the value of carbon in forests as part of the Reducing Emissions from Deforestation and Forest Degradation (REDD) programme to highlighting and spotlighting illegal forest clearances.

Sustainable Development – UK

The trust initiates and supports work that can reduce the speed and impact of climate change including energy efficiency and renewable energy technology, aviation and transport policy, and the wide ranging benefits of sustainable agriculture. In the area of climate change, sustainable energy and sustainable agriculture, the trust aims to take a broad approach supporting research, practical action, awareness-raising, education and organisations that aim to influence policy in the field.

Examples of grants approved this year include:

- a grant to Green Alliance [£40,000] to feed the recommendations of the Green Fiscal Commission into policy-makers. The final report of the Green Fiscal Commission published an important body of evidence regarding green fiscal reform and the implications of such a programme. The advocacy work by Green Alliance will focus on the period up until the general election and immediately after in an effort to propose a programme of green fiscal reform to the newly elected government.
- the trust funded a new position at Living Streets [£45,000 over 3 years]. The staff member will work with community groups, helping them to make their local environment a

better and safer place to walk. This will involve community networks developing effective working relationships with Local Authorities in order to voice their opinions and to secure funding and action on the ground.

People at Risk

Grants are made to organisations which help people at risk of homelessness to obtain support , secure permanent accommodation, regain economic independence and reconnect with important family and social networks.

Over the years the trust has provided considerable help to projects where housing is seen as only part of the solution, and where there is awareness of the value for people at risk of cultivating their sense of personal identity, of aspiration for life and livelihood, and of belonging among family and friends. SupportActionNet, the fruit of this outlook operated by the leading social researchers Lemos & Crane [£9,000], is a network of agencies working with people at risk, offering working examples of effective practice, new ideas, training and organisational development. The trust encourages agencies at work in this field with annual Awards for the most effective and innovative achievements.

In this and the Sustainable Regeneration category, the trust assists projects that pioneer fresh approaches in self-help and peer support, education and training, and opportunities leading to employment for people at risk, and other socially excluded groups, especially where social enterprise can lead to inspiration and achievement.

Arts and Sustainability

The trust continues to support the rapidly developing field of arts and sustainability. Within this category, the trust explores ways in which arts organisations can collaborate with one another to reduce their carbon footprint. The trust also supports initiatives that encourage artists, writers and arts organisations to engage with current environmental issues through their work.

The trust continues to fund the Ashden Directory of Environment and Performance [£20,000] (www.ashdendirectory.org.uk).

Cultural Shift (Low Carbon Fund)

Work in this funding stream recognises the need for low carbon lifestyles to become the normal way of living and to catalyse this shift in behaviour using arts and the media. [One grant of £50,000 was made to 10:10 UK towards web development and staff costs.]

Sustainable Regeneration

Funding in this category is for projects which promote sustainability and greater environmental awareness in deprived communities and among disadvantaged people that bring social, economic and environmental benefits. The key areas the trust makes grants in are as follows:

- connecting disadvantaged people with nature in recognition of the value this brings to people's health and wellbeing. For example, meaningful countryside experiences for disadvantaged children e.g. working on farms and projects that bring vulnerable people, such as offenders, into fruitful contact with the natural world
- encouraging deprived communities and schools to grow and eat their own food
- supporting people to improve their own environment and their community's amenities
- encouraging the development of sustainable enterprises such as recycling, cycling and energy efficiency initiatives.

Examples of grants approved this year include:

- Giroscope [£10,000] is a co-operative of homeless people, private and business tenants in Hull, consorting to secure their own permanent accommodation by taking on abandoned private and council-owned property. The trust's grant will increase the organisation's capacity to generate solar power, to meet energy and hot water needs, support business tenants and train members to install solar energy systems around Hull and the wider region. Giroscope's business park, Arthur Street, will provide a working example to schools, colleges and community groups of photo-voltaic cells on the roofs and solar heating systems. The project aims to make Giroscope a completely green organisation and Arthur Street a completely green social enterprise park.
- St Mary's Secret Garden [£1,000] is a community resource for well-being and learning, accessible to all, based in Hackney. The garden contains a herb and sensory space, food growing areas, herbaceous borders and a small woodland. Various activities take place at the garden including therapeutic and social horticultural sessions, courses for adults with learning and physical disabilities, training and support for local residents, work preparation programmes, activities for young people and volunteering opportunities. A grant from Ashden will support the delivery of horticultural training for residents of local housing estates, providing an opportunity to gain a qualification in horticultural skills, good quality food and a greener local environment.

Exclusions

The trustees generally do not make grants in response to unsolicited applications. However, see Applications:

Applications

The trust gives the following advice:

Who should apply?

If your organisation has a proven track record in supplying local, sustainable energy solutions in the UK or in the developing world then you should read the guidelines for the Ashden Awards for Sustainable Energy.

The Ashden Trust is one of the Sainsbury Family Charitable Trusts. Before applying to one of the trusts, please read the guidelines below.

1   The trust does not normally fund individuals for projects, educational fees or to join expeditions. If you apply for a grant in one of these categories, we are afraid the trustees are unable to help. If you are a registered charity or institution with charitable status applying for a grant we must warn you that only an extremely small number of unsolicited applications are successful.
2   Do not apply to more than one of the Sainsbury Family Charitable Trusts. Each application will be considered by each trust which may have an interest in this field.
3   All of the Sainsbury Family Charitable Trusts have pro-active grant-making policies and have chosen to concentrate their support in a limited number of activities. If you have read through the Ashden Trust's website and feel your project fits into the trust's priorities we would be very interested to hear from you by post.
4   The trustees generally do not make grants in response to unsolicited applications.

If you would like to apply to the trust you should send a brief description of the proposed project, by post only, to the director.

The proposed project needs to cover:

- why the project is needed
- how, where, when the project will be delivered
- who will benefit and in what way
- income and expenditure budget
- details of funding – secured, applied for
- description of the organisation.

Please do not send any more than 2–4 sides of A4 when applying to the trust, at this point additional material is unnecessary.

Autonomous Research Charitable Trust

General

Beneficial area
UK, mainly London, and Africa.

Moore Stephens, 150 Aldersgate Street, London EC1A 4AB
Tel: 020 7334 9191
Email: keith.lawrence@moorestephens.com
Correspondent: Keith Lawrence, Administrator
Trustees: Graham Stuart; Britta Schmidt; Nathalie Garner; Neeta Atkar.
CC Number: 1137503

Information available
Basic information was available from the Charity Commission.

This trust was established in 2010 for general charitable purposes. It is the charitable trust of Autonomous Research, a company that provides intelligence on banking and insurance companies. The focus of the trust appears to be making grants to organisations working with children and young people and older people.

According to the company's website, 5% of its annual profits are donated to charitable causes, presumably through the trust, although no information on how much this amounts to was available.

The trust's website states its aims as:

- to help disadvantaged people get a step up in life. Our focus is therefore upon people rather than wildlife conservation or ecology
- to empower people to improve the quality of their lives. We are therefore naturally drawn to projects based around education opportunities or helping with start-up business ventures
- to focus our resources upon a small number of key partner charities – both in London and abroad – where we feel we can make a difference and establish long-term relationships
- our involvement is not simply about giving money. The partners of Autonomous will also be active in mentoring, providing business and career advice and in a variety of other hands-on roles.

The trust currently has a partnership with three charities: the Tusk Trust, working in Kenya; Plan UK, in Uganda; and One Degree, in London. The correspondent states that the trust's policies and guidelines will develop in due course, but at the moment all applications are simply forwarded to the trustees for consideration.

Exclusions
Wildlife or environmental causes are unlikely to be supported.

Applications
In writing to the correspondent.

AW Charitable Trust

Jewish causes through educational and religious organisations; general charitable purposes

£3.9 million (2009/10)

Beneficial area
Unrestricted.

1 Allandale Court, Waterpark Road, Manchester M7 4JL
Tel: 0161 740 0116
Correspondent: Rabbi Aubrey Weis, Trustee
Trustees: Rabbi Aubrey Weis; Rachel Weis.
CC Number: 283322

Information available
Accounts were on file at the Charity Commission, with a list of grants.

This trust was established in 1981 for general charitable purposes. The trust's aims are 'to support all worthy orthodox Jewish causes' and it meets these objects by making grants mainly to Jewish education and religious organisations both in the UK and abroad. It is the charitable trust of Aubrey Weis, director of Aberdeen Estate Company, owners of land and property throughout the North West.

In 2009/10 the trust had assets of £73.3 million and an income of £7.3 million, most of which came from rental income. Grants were made totalling £3.9 million. A list of beneficiaries was not included in the accounts.

Previous beneficiaries include: TET; Asser Bishvil Foundation; Chevras Oneg Shabbos-Yomtov; Friends of Mir; CML; Toimchei Shabbos Manchester; British Friends of Kupat Hair; Purim Fund; Beenstock Home; and Zoreya Tzedokos.

Applications
In writing to the correspondent. The trust considers 'all justified applications for support of educational establishments, places of worship and other charitable actives.'

Awards for All (see also the Big Lottery Fund)

General

£61.55 million available in 2011/12 (England: £45 million; Northern Ireland: £3.5 million; Scotland: £10.15 million; Wales: £2.9 million)

Beneficial area
UK.

(See General section)
Tel: 0845 600 2040
Website: www.awardsforall.org.uk

Information available
All information is accessible through the Awards for All website.

Awards for All is a Big Lottery Fund grants scheme funding small, local community-based projects in the UK. Each country in the UK administers its own programme. The following information is reproduced from Awards for All's website:

England
Awards for All England is a simple small grants scheme making awards of between £300 and £10,000.

The programme aims to help improve local communities and the lives of people most in need.

To do this Awards for All England wants to fund projects that meet one or more of the following outcomes:

- people have better chances in life – with better access to training and

development to improve their life skills
- stronger communities – with more active citizens working together to tackle their problems
- improved rural and urban environments – which communities are better able to access and enjoy
- healthier and more active people and communities.

You can apply if:
- you are a not-for-profit, voluntary and community organisation, including both registered and unregistered charities, co-operatives, friendly societies, industrial and provident societies, companies that are not for profit businesses and unincorporated associations
- you are a parish or town council, school or health body
- you have a bank account that requires at least two unrelated people to sign each cheque or withdrawal
- you have a governing body with at least three unrelated members
- you can spend the grant within one year.

Contact details:

If you have a general enquiry or want an application form, please contact us on one of the following.

Tel: 0845 410 2030

Textphone: 0845 602 1659

Email: general.enquiries@ awardsforall.org.uk

If you need to contact Awards for All England about an application you have made or grant you have received, please use the details provided in correspondence to you or use the following:

For projects where the beneficiaries are based in the **Eastern, North East, North West, South East or Yorkshire and the Humber regions:**

Big Awards for All
2 St James' Gate
Newcastle Upon Tyne
NE1 4BE

Tel: 0191 376 1600

Textphone: 0191 376 1776

Fax: 0191 376 1661

For projects where the beneficiaries are based in the **East Midlands, West Midlands, London or South West regions:**

Big Awards for All
Apex House
3 Embassy Drive
Calthorpe Road
Edgbaston,
Birmingham
B15 1TR

Tel: 0121 345 7700

Minicom: 0121 345 7666

Fax: 0121 345 8888

Northern Ireland

This Programme is delivered and funded by the Big Lottery Fund in Northern Ireland and awards funds of between £500 and £10,000. You can now re-apply for funding up to a maximum of £20,000 in any 12-month period.

This means:
- You can only hold one award up to £10,000 at any one time
- You can reapply for funding if we have received your completed end of award report, but we cannot make a decision until we have approved the report together with any other monitoring requirements

We want our money to make a difference by helping:
- people to participate in their communities to bring about positive change
- people to develop their skills and widen their experiences
- people to work toward better and safer communities
- improve people's physical and mental health and well being.

We hope these awards will improve people's lives and will strengthen community activity.

You can apply if:
- you are a voluntary and community organisation, including both registered and unregistered charities, co-operatives, friendly societies, industrial and provident societies, companies that are not for profit businesses and unincorporated associations; or
- you are a statutory organisation.

And:
- you have a UK bank or building society account in the name of your organisation, which requires at least two unrelated signatures on each cheque or withdrawal
- you can meet our requirements for annual accounts
- you need an award of between £500 and £10,000
- you can spend the award within one year
- the people who will benefit from your project live in Northern Ireland
- you have adopted appropriate policies in line with your type of work
- your award will pay for your project-related costs.

Contact details:

If you have any questions, please contact us at the address or telephone number below.

Awards for All
1 Cromac Quay
Cromac Wood
Ormeau Road
Belfast
BT7 2JD

Tel: 028 9055 1455

Fax: 028 9055 1444

Textphone: 028 9055 1431

Email:enquiries.ni@awardsforall.org.uk

Scotland

Awards for All Scotland gives grants of between £500 and £10,000 for people to take part in art, sport and community activities, and projects that promote education, the environment and health in the local community.

We can fund a wide range of activities through the programme and want to support projects that meet our outcomes.

The outcomes for Awards for All Scotland are:
- people have better chances in life
- communities are safer, stronger and more able to work together to tackle inequalities
- people have better and more sustainable services and environments
- people and communities are healthier.

If your project could help us achieve one or more of these outcomes, Awards for All could be the right scheme for you.

You can apply if:
- you are a not-for-profit, voluntary and community organisation, including both registered and unregistered charities, co-operatives, friendly societies, industrial and provident societies, companies that are not for profit businesses and unincorporated associations
- you are a parish or town council, school or health body
- you have a bank account that requires at least two unrelated people to sign each cheque or withdrawal
- you have a governing body with at least three unrelated members
- you can spend the grant within one year.

Contact details:

For advice on completing the application form and any general queries you have about the scheme you can call the Information and Events Officers on 0870 240 2391 and you can also email them at scotland@ awardsforall.org.uk

Awards for All
4th Floor
1 Atlantic Quay
1 Robertson Street
Glasgow
G2 8JB

Tel: 0141 242 1400

Fax: 0141 242 1401

Textphone: 0141 242 1500

Wales

Awards for All Wales is a simple small grants scheme making awards of between £500 and £5,000.

The programme aims to help improve local communities and the lives of people most in need.

Awards for All Wales aims to fund projects that:

- support community activity – by helping communities to meet their needs through voluntary action, self-help projects, local facilities or events (by communities we mean people in a local area or people who share a common interest or need)
- extend access and participation – by encouraging more people to become actively involved in local groups and projects, and by supporting activities that aim to be open and accessible to everyone who wishes to take part
- increase skill and creativity – by supporting activities which help to develop people and organisations, improve skills and raise standards
- improve the quality of life – by supporting local projects that improve people's opportunities, health, welfare, environment or local facilities, especially those most disadvantaged in society.

You can apply if:

- you are a not-for-profit, voluntary and community organisation, including both registered and unregistered charities, co-operatives, friendly societies, industrial and provident societies, companies that are not for profit businesses and unincorporated associations
- you are a parish or town council, school or health body
- you have a bank account that requires at least two unrelated people to sign each cheque or withdrawal
- you have a governing body with at least three unrelated members
- you can spend the grant within one year.

Contact details:

Tel: 0845 410 2030

Textphone: 0845 602 1659

Fax: 01686 622 458

Email: enquiries.wales@biglotteryfund.org.uk

Exclusions

Generally, organisations with an income more than £20,000 a year (though there are exceptions to this, particularly for projects coming through schools and similar bodies).

Also:

- costs related to existing projects, activities or resources currently provided by your group, for example, ongoing staff costs and utility bills, regular rent payments, maintenance (including maintenance equipment) and annual events
- items which only benefit an individual, for example, scholarships or bursaries
- activities promoting religious beliefs
- activities that are part of statutory obligations or replace statutory funding, including curricular activity in schools
- endowments
- loan payments
- second hand road vehicles
- projects with high ongoing maintenance costs – unless your group can show that you have the funds/skills to maintain them once your Awards for All grant runs out.

Applications

Application forms are simple and straightforward and are available from Awards for All's website.

The Baily Thomas Charitable Fund

Learning disability

£4.4 million (2009/10)

Beneficial area

UK.

c/o TMF Management (UK) Ltd, 400 Capability Green, Luton LU1 3AE
Tel: 01582 439225
Fax: 01582 439206
Email: info@bailythomas.org.uk
Website: www.bailythomas.org.uk
Correspondent: Ann Cooper, Secretary to the Trustees
Trustees: Prof. William I Fraser; Prof. Anne Farmer; Toby N J Nangle; Suzanne Jane Marriott; Kenneth Young.
CC Number: 262334

Information available

Accounts were available from the Charity Commission. The trust also has a helpful website.

This is the largest trust featured here dedicated solely to the well-being of those with learning disabilities. It combines one or two major funding programmes with an extensive programme of generally one-off medium and smaller grants. These are divided between revenue and capital costs, and seemingly without the common requirement for applications to be dressed up in 'project' form.

The trust gives the following general guidance on its website:

The Baily Thomas Charitable Fund is a registered charity which was established primarily to aid the research into learning disability and to aid the care and relief of those affected by learning disability by making grants to voluntary organisations working in this field.

We consider under learning disability the conditions generally referred to as severe learning difficulties, together with autism. In this area, we consider projects concerning children or adults. Learning disability, thus defined, is our priority for funding. We do not give grants for research into or care of those with mental illness or dyslexia.

In 2009/10 the trust had assets of £75.7 million and an income of £3.7 million. There were 348 grants made during the year totalling over £4.4 million.

Beneficiaries receiving £50,000 or more were listed in the accounts and included: The Development Trust (£200,000 in 2 grants); University of Cardiff (£115,500); Exmoor Calvert Trust (£100,000); King's College London (£80,000); Hansel Foundation (£75,000); Rix-Thompson-Rothenberg Foundation (£70,000); Mental Health Foundation, the National Society for Epilepsy and St George's Association (£50,000 each).

Exclusions

Grants are not normally awarded to individuals. The following areas are unlikely to receive funding:

- hospices
- minibuses except those for residential and/or day care services for the learning disabled
- advocacy projects

- arts and theatre projects
- physical disabilities unless accompanied by significant learning disabilities.

Applications

Meetings of the trustees are usually held in June and early December each year and applications should therefore be submitted no later than 1 May or 1 October for consideration at the next relevant meeting. Late applications will not be considered. If your application is considered under the Small Grants procedure then this will be reviewed by the trustees ahead of the usual meetings in June and December. Following the meeting all applicants are contacted formally to advise on the status of their application. Submit your application whenever you are ready, rather than waiting for the deadline.

Applications can be made online via the trust's website.

General applications

Funding is normally considered for capital and revenue costs and for both specific projects and for general running/core costs.

Grants are awarded for amounts from £250 and depend on a number of factors including the purpose, the total funding requirement and the potential sources of other funds including, in some cases, matching funding.

Normally one-off grants are awarded but exceptionally a new project may be funded over two or three years, subject to satisfactory reports of progress.

Grants should normally be taken up within one year of the issue of the grant offer letter which will include conditions relating to the release of the grant.

The following areas of work normally fall within the fund's policy:

- capital building/renovation/ refurbishment works for residential, nursing and respite care, and schools
- employment schemes including woodwork, crafts, printing and horticulture
- play schemes and play therapy schemes

- day and social activities centres including building costs and running costs
- support for families, including respite schemes
- independent living schemes
- support in the community schemes
- swimming and hydro-therapy pools and snoezelen rooms.

Research applications

The guidelines state:

We consider under learning disability the conditions generally referred to as severe learning difficulties, together with autism. In this area, we consider projects concerning children or adults. Learning disability, thus defined, is our priority for funding. We do not give grants for research into or care of those with mental illness or dyslexia.

We generally direct our limited funds towards the initiation of research so that it can progress to the point at which there is sufficient data to support an application to one of the major funding bodies.

How to apply

Applications will only be considered from established research workers and will be subject to normal professional peer review procedures.

Applications, limited to 5 pages with the type no smaller than Times New Roman 12, should be in the form of a scientific summary with a research plan to include a brief background and a short account of the design of the study and number of subjects, the methods of assessment and analysis, timetable, main outcomes and some indication of other opportunities arising from the support of such research.

A detailed budget of costs should be submitted together with a justification for the support requested. Details should be included of any other applications for funding which have been made to other funders and their outcomes, if known.

We do not expect to contribute towards university overheads.

A one page Curriculum Vitae will be required for each of the personnel actually carrying out the study and for their supervisor together with a note of the total number of their peer reviewed publications and details of the 10 most significant publications.

Evidence may be submitted of the approval of the Ethics Committee of the applicant to the study and approval of the University for the application to the fund.

An 80 word lay summary should also be submitted with the scientific summary.

Any papers submitted in excess of those stipulated above will not be

passed to the Research Committee for consideration.

Before submitting a full application, researchers may submit a one page summary of the proposed study so that the trustees may indicate whether they are prepared to consider a full application.

The Balcombe Charitable Trust

Education, environment, health and welfare

£664,000 (2009/10)

Beneficial area

UK and overseas.

Information available

Accounts were available at the Charity Commission.

This trust generally makes grants in the fields of education, the environment and health and welfare. It only supports registered charities.

In 2009/10 it had assets of £27.8 million and an income of £678,000. Grants were made to 35 organisations totalling £664,000.

Grants made were broken down as follows:

Health and welfare – 25 grants totalling £459,500

Beneficiaries included: Oxfam (£50,000); the United Kingdom Committee for UNICEF (£36,000); Princess Royal Trust for Carers (£30,000); NSPCC and the Samaritans (£25,000 each); Amnesty International (£20,000); the Esther Benjamins Trust (£17,000); Breast Cancer Care and Mind (£10,000 each); Thai Children's Trust (£7,000); and Brook Advisory Centres Limited (£5,000).

Environment – 3 grants totalling £110,500

The beneficiaries were: Durrell Wildlife Conservation Trust (£86,500); the Andrew Lees Trust (£15,000); and Living Coasts (£9,000).

Education – 7 grants totalling £94,000

The beneficiaries were: Action Aid (£41,000); Money for Madagascar (£23,000); Emmaus UK (£12,000); Young People in Focus Limited (£10,000); the Theatre Royal Bath Limited (£5,000); Volunteer Reading Help (£2,000); and Age Exchange Reminiscence (£1,000).

Exclusions

No grants to individuals or non-registered charities.

Applications

In writing to the correspondent.

The Band Trust

People with disabilities, children and young people, scholarships, hospices and hospitals, education, older people and people who are disadvantaged

£655,000 (2009/10)

Beneficial area

Worldwide but in practice UK.

Moore Stephens, 150 Aldersgate Street, London EC1A 4AB
Tel: 020 7334 9191
Fax: 020 7248 3408
Email: richard.mason@ moorestephens.com
Correspondent: Richard J S Mason, Trustee
Trustees: The Hon. Lavinia Wallop; The Hon. Nicholas Wallop; Richard J S Mason; Bruce G Streather.
CC Number: 279802

Information available

Annual reports and accounts were available at the Charity Commission.

The trust was established in 1976 for general charitable purposes and beneficiaries are registered charities in the UK. The trust describes its policy as follows:

> The objects of the trust are to aid persons (primarily those who are residents of the United Kingdom) who are in need of education or care, whether wholly or partially, including those who are ill, disabled or injured, old and infirm or children with special needs. Such aid will be given through making grants to the providers of care such as institutions, homes and to the carers themselves.

In 2009/10 the trust had assets of £22.3 million and an income of £738,000. There were 78 grants were made during the year totalling £655,000, broken down as follows:

Disabled people	14	£174,000
Children and young people	11	£142,500
Disadvantaged	7	£95,000
Educational	7	£74,000
Scholarships*	2	£53,000
Medical	2	£30,000
Hospice and hospital	1	£30,000
Miscellaneous (up to £2,000)	28	£19,500
Elderly	4	£18,000
Ex-employees	1	£13,500
Arts	1	£5,000

Beneficiaries across all categories included: CLIC Sargent (£45,000); Explore (£30,000); Community Service Volunteers (£15,000); Livability (£10,000); Pakenham Water Mill Appeal (£7,500); West London Action for Children (£5,000); Barristers' Benevolent Fund (£2,000); and the NSPCC (£1,500).

* The scholarship funds were awarded to the Florence Nightingale Foundation (£28,000) and the Honourable Society of Gray's Inn (£25,000).

Exclusions

No grants are made to individuals.

Applications

'The trustees do not wish to receive unsolicited applications for grants as they themselves identify sufficient potential recipients of grants who fulfil their criteria from information that is in the public domain. If they require further information, they will request this from the potential candidates identified.' Trustees' meeting are held at least three times a year.

The Barclay Foundation

Medical research, young people, the elderly, people with disabilities, the sick and the disadvantaged

£3.3 million (2010)

Beneficial area

Not defined, in practice, UK.

3rd Floor, 20 St James's Street, London SW1A 1ES
Tel: 020 7915 0915
Email: mseal@ellerman.co.uk
Correspondent: Michael Seal
Trustees: Sir David Barclay; Sir Frederick Barclay; Lord Alistair McAlpine of West Green; Aidan Barclay; Howard Barclay.
CC Number: 803696

Information available

Accounts were available at the Charity Commission.

The foundation was established in 1989 by brothers, Sir David and Sir Frederick Barclay who provide all of the funds. The objects of the foundation are wide and the trustees distribute the income at their own discretion for general charitable purposes.

In 2010 the trust had assets of £50 million and an income of £3.3 million. Grants were made totalling almost £3.3 million, broken down as follows:

Medical research and aid for the young	£3 million
Aid for the sick, disabled and disadvantaged	£252,000

The largest grants during the year were made to: Great Ormond Street Children's Hospital (£1.2 million in total); and Alder Hey Children's Hospital (£1.1 million in total).

The other beneficiaries were: The Prince's Foundation (£275,000); University of Oxford (£160,000); The Healing Foundation (£100,000); The Prince's Trust (£60,000); CFS Research Foundation (£50,000); Wellbeing for Women (£20,000); Make-A-Wish Foundation (£18,000);

Autism Treatment Centre of America (£12,000); Dorset Orthopaedic Limited (£11,000); Barts and the London Charity (£10,000); Muscular Dystrophy Campaign and Evelina Children's Hospital (£5,000 each); and the Asda Foundation (£1,000).

Applications

Applications should be in writing, clearly outlining the details of the proposed project, (for medical research, as far as possible in lay terms). The total cost and duration should be stated; also the amount, if any, which has already been raised.

Following an initial screening, applications are selected according to their merits, suitability and funds available. Visits are usually made to projects where substantial funds are involved.

The foundation welcomes reports as to progress and requires these on the completion of a project.

The Baring Foundation

Strengthening the voluntary sector, arts and international development

£3.3 million (2010)

Beneficial area

England and Wales, with a special interest in London, Merseyside, Cornwall and Devon; also UK charities working with NGO partners in developing countries.

60 London Wall, London EC2M 5TQ
Tel: 020 7767 1348
Fax: 020 7767 7121
Email: baring.foundation@uk.ing.com
Website: www.baringfoundation.org.uk
Correspondent: David Cutler, Director
Trustees: Amanda Jordan, Chair; Mark Baring; Geoffrey Barnett; Prof. Ann Buchanan; David Elliott; Katherine Garrett-Cox; Janet Morrison; Andrew Hind; Ranjit Sondhi; Dr Danny Sriskandarajah;

Christopher Steane; Prof. Myles Wickstead.
CC Number: 258583

Information available

Accounts were available at the Charity Commission. Full details of the foundation's current programmes are available from its website.

Established in 1969, the Baring Foundation's purpose is to improve the quality of life of people suffering disadvantage and discrimination. Its main objective is to help build stronger voluntary organisations, which serve those people, directly or indirectly, both in this country and abroad. The foundation aims to achieve its objective through its three grant programmes which place a high priority on funding organisations through its core costs programmes, whilst continuing to support smaller pieces of work through project funding.

The foundation's stated values are:

We:

- Believe in the fundamental value to society of an independent and effective voluntary sector.
- Use our funds to strengthen voluntary sector organisations, responding flexibly; creatively and pragmatically to their needs and with a determination to achieve value for money.
- Put high value on learning from organisations and their beneficiaries. We seek to add value to our grants by encouraging the communication of knowledge through a variety of means, including influencing others.
- Seek to build positive, purposeful relationships with grant recipients, as well as with other grant makers.
- Aim to treat grant-seekers and recipients with courtesy and respect; being as accessible as possible within clear programme guidelines and maintaining consistently high standards of administrative efficiency.

Grant programmes

The foundation makes grants under the following programmes – potential applicants are advised to check the website for current guidelines and up-to-date information on deadlines for applications.

Arts programme: The programme is close to applications for 2012. Check the foundation's website for the deadline for 2013 applications and current themes.

Joint International Development grants programme (in collaboration with the John Ellerman Foundation): Currently closed – check the foundation's website for up-to-date information on the programme for 2012.

Strengthening the Voluntary Sector – independence programme: New guidelines are currently being developed and will be available on the foundation's website from April 2012.

Grants in 2010

In 2010 the foundation had assets of £62.3 million and an income of £1.3 million. Grants were made totalling £3.3 million, broken down as follows:

Strengthening the voluntary sector	£1.05 million
International programme	£742,000
Arts programme	£709,000
Special Initiatives	£358,000
Other work	£172,000

Beneficiaries across all programmes included: Children in Crisis (£165,500 over three years), to train teachers in South Kivu, Democratic Republic of Congo and develop the capacity of Eben Ezer Ministries; Law Centres Federation (£149,500 over 2 years), to develop a new business model for third sector agencies delivering specialist legal advice; Advice UK (£135,000 over 2 years), to secure evidence of effectiveness and economic value of the BOLD intervention, develop a sustainable method for it and secure support of central and local government; Art in Hospital – Scotland (£75,000 over 3 years), core funding, to enable the employment of an artist co-ordinator, and develop support documentation, evaluation and publication on website as an accessible resource for others and professional development for artists; Green Candle Dance Company (£45,000 over 3 years), core funding, towards core staff costs to underpin the projects that benefit a wide range of London based elders and many existing and emerging practitioners across the country; Legal Aid Practitioners Group (£20,000 over 2 years), to encourage parliamentary involvement and scrutiny of Legal Aid reform by supporting the development of the All Party Parliamentary Group on Legal Aid and developing a team of Legal Aid

Champions; DG Legal (£10,000), to carry out feasibility and planning work on a range of activities associated with the rescue and recovery of South West London Law Centres. Part funded with four other trust and foundations: City Bridge Trust, City Parochial Foundation, Esmée Fairbairn Foundation and Lankelly Chase Foundation; and British Association of Settlements & Social Action Centres (£2,000), to support the design and publication of the Shared Energy toolkit, reflecting lessons generated by the Climate Change Special Initiative.

Exclusions

See individual grant programmes on the foundation's website. Generally, the foundation does not accept applications from:
- appeals or charities set up to support statutory organisations
- animal welfare charities
- grant maintained, private, or local education authority schools or their Parent Teachers' Associations
- individuals.

Applications

On application forms available via the foundation's website. Potential applicants should check the foundation's website for current guidelines and application deadlines.

The Barnwood House Trust

Disability and old age

£830,000 to organisations (2010)

Beneficial area

Gloucestershire.

162 Barnwood Road, Gloucester
GL4 7JX
Tel: 01452 611292
Fax: 01452 372594
Email: gail.rodway@barnwoodtrust.org
Website: www.barnwoodtrust.org/
Correspondent: Gail Rodway, Grants Manager
Trustees: John Colquhoun; James Davidson; Anne Cadbury; Richard Ashenden; Simon Fisher; David A Acland; Clare de Haan; Sara Shipway; Roger Ker; Annabella Scott; Jonathan Carr; Revd John Horan.
CC Number: 218401

Information available

Accounts were available from the Charity Commission. The trust also has a detailed website.

General

Barnwood House Trust was established in its original form in 1792 and is now governed by a Charity Commission Scheme of the 17th April 2000. It is one of Gloucestershire's largest charities providing assistance to people with disabilities, including those with mental disorders, who live in the county. Its current endowment arises principally from the sale of the land upon which Barnwood House Hospital stood until 1966.

Since the sale of the hospital the trust has developed as a provider of facilities and funding for people with disabilities. It offers grants to individuals and organisations and provides supported accommodation and day care, all of which is focused on improving opportunities and quality of life for individuals and subsequently their carers.

The trust describes its aims as:

> The relief of persons who have a mental or nervous disorder or a serious physical disability and who are sick, convalescent, disabled, infirm or in need, hardship or distress by relieving their condition or assisting their recovery. Preference is given to those who live or formerly lived in Gloucestershire. The relief of persons in need by providing housing or other accommodation, care nursing and attention.

This is currently changing due to their 2010 strategic review (see below).

Strategic review

The trust completed a major strategic review and planning exercise in 2010. The result of this is their new mission: To act as a catalyst for durable change. To implement this over the next 10 years the trust will invest in a community based initiative called the community animation programme whereby they will work in partnership with people living with disabilities and mental health problems, the voluntary and community and public sectors, and employers to strengthen capacity. As a result of this, the grantmaking policy has changed, including the termination of grants for over £750 and the phasing out of the provision of sheltered housing. Consequently the trust will not provide services directly itself but will ensure that the services that it has provided will be provided by other suppliers.

Grant Schemes

Grants of less than £750
Grants for holidays and playschemes are available to organisations with a demonstrable track record of providing holidays, trips or play schemes for Gloucestershire people with a disability. These grants are fast-tracked and have a dedicated application form.

Small grants to organisations already known to the trust can be applied for using the form and guidelines available on the trust's website.

Grants for up to £750 are available to make village halls adaptable for people with disabilities. These must meet the eligibility criteria agreed with Gloucestershire Rural Community Council. Application details can be found on the website.

Grants of over £750
The trust no longer awards open application grants for sums over £750. They have decided instead to fund organisations that they proactively find rather than have open grants schemes.

They are however running a community animation programme which recruits local organisations to form partnerships. The trust will cover the costs of organisations to work as partners. Within this programme there will also be seed funds for community-based projects involving people with disabilities and mental health problems. The trust will also be making matched-funding grants available for other community-based initiatives that develop through their policy and influencing programme.

This strategy is part of the implementation of the trust's ten-year investment plan and applicants should check their website for recent updates concerning this plan.

Grantmaking in 2010

In 2010 the trust had assets of £69.3 million and an income of £2.2 million. Grants were made to organisations totalling £830,000. A further £249,000 was awarded in grants to individuals. Key beneficiaries included:

▪ The Butterfly Garden (£50,000) – educational gardening and land skills project set up in 2002 to help children and young adults with learning disabilities. Currently the garden is attended to by over 60 students a week. The grant was towards a new building to provide a wheelchair-accessible classroom with disabled toilet and kitchen facilities.

▪ Gloucestershire Rural Community Council (£30,000 over 3 years) – to sustain and extend the service 'People for You' a befriending scheme for people living in outlying villages of the South Cotswolds.

▪ Mindsong, Gloucester Three Choirs Festival (£30,000 over 2 years)- arts and health project delivering 'music for dementia', a community project offering music appropriately and in a sustainable way to people who have dementia and other neurodegenerative conditions such as Parkinson's disease, in care homes and day centres across the country. The grant was to allow them to consolidate their organisation, plan for a sustainable future and increase delivery of their services countywide.

▪ Active Gloucestershire (£21,000) – to set up Multi-sports Clubs and Learn to Swim lessons for disabled children and to produce a DVD to promote the Active Inclusion Project, which supports volunteers to engage in disability sport and physical activity development.

▪ GL Communities (£7,800) – to set up befriending circles for elderly people on some of the most deprived housing estates in Gloucester.

Other major grants to organisations included: Consortium of Mental Health Day Support Providers (£305,000); Crossroads Care – Cheltenham & Tewkesbury, Independence Trust and People & Places in Gloucestershire (£30,000 each); Whitefriars Sailing Club (£27,500); Stroke Association (£25,000); Forest of Dean Citizen's Advice Bureau and Hop, Skip & Jump (Cotswold) (£18,000 each); Art Shape LTD, Barnwood Residents Association and Watershed Riding for the Disabled (£10,000 each).

Grants of less that £10,000 amounted to £186,000.

Exclusions

Grants are not normally made in the following circumstances:

▪ to people or organisations outside Gloucestershire

▪ To people with problems relating to drugs or alcohol- unless they also have physical disabilities or a diagnosed mental illness

▪ To pay for funeral costs; medical equipment; private healthcare; counselling or psychotherapy; top-up nursing home fees; council tax; court fines; house purchase or rent; regular income supplements; needs of non-disabled dependants or carers

Grants will not be awarded retrospectively

Applications

The trust states the following on its website:

> As part of the development of Unlocking Opportunities, our ten year investment plan, we have reviewed the way we make grants and allocate funding to organisations. As from [early] 2011 we no longer award open application grants for sums over £750. For the foreseeable future, the trust will be making funding available to communities across Gloucestershire on a proactive, not a reactive basis. This means that the trust will be seeking to fund specific types of activity, not responding to requests from organisations.

BBC Children in Need

Welfare of disadvantaged children

£41.7 million (2009/10)

Beneficial area

UK.

PO Box 1000, London W12 7WJ
Tel: 020 8576 7788
Fax: 020 8576 8887
Email: pudsey@bbc.co.uk
Website: bbc.co.uk/pudsey
Correspondent: David Ramsden, Chief Executive
Trustees: Stevie Spring, Chair; Tim Davie; Beverley Tew; Sir Terry Wogan; Susan Elizabeth; Peter McBride; Nicholas Eldred; Phil Hodkinson; Bob Shennan; Danny Cohen.
CC Number: 802052

Information available

Accounts were available from the Charity Commission. Comprehensive information is also available from the charity's website.

The charity, registered in 1989, distributes the proceeds of the BBC's annual Children in Need appeal (first televised in 1980). Around 2,000 grants in total may be made in a year. These are allocated in four rounds, in January, April, July and October. Amounts range from a few hundred pounds to a normal maximum of about £100,000.

Grants are made for specific projects which directly help children and young people (aged 18 and under).

The trustees approve all grant awards on the basis of the assessment of applications by third party assessors and the recommendations of eight regional advisory committees. Grants are awarded to properly constituted not-for-profit organisations working with disadvantaged children in the United Kingdom (and The Isle of Man and Channel Islands). Grants are for periods of one, two or three years, apart from holiday projects with overnight stays that can only apply for one year of funding at a time.

Where a grant is awarded for a period of greater than one year each annual instalment is only released after the receipt of a satisfactory report on the prior year's expenditure.

The information in this entry is compiled from the excellent guidelines and annual report and accounts produced by the charity:

General Grants Programme

Within our general grants programme, you can apply for:

- Main Grants over £10,000 per year for up to three years
- Small Grants of £10,000 or less per year for up to three years

We give grants for...

Our focus is firmly on children and young people experiencing disadvantage. We fund organisations working to combat this disadvantage and to make a real difference to children and young people's lives.

Such disadvantage includes:

- illness, distress, abuse or neglect
- any kind of disability
- behavioural or psychological difficulties
- living in poverty or situations of deprivation.

Who can apply

BBC Children in Need funds not-for-profit organisations that work with disadvantaged children and young people of 18 years and under who live in the UK, the Isle of Man or the Channel Islands.

We accept applications from organisations that already have a BBC Children in Need grant providing the grant is coming to an end. You will need to be able to provide convincing evidence of the difference to children that your current grant has made.

How much to apply for...

Organisations can apply to our Small Grants programme or our Main Grants programme.

Small grant applications can be for any amount up to £10,000 a year and we are looking for projects where a relatively small grant can make a big difference for children and young people.

For main grant applications there is no upper limit but we make very few grants over £100,000 and most grants are for much less. The total amount of money requested each year is far more than we have available to give and requests for larger grants are always more competitive.

- Funding can be awarded for between one and three years, depending on the nature of the request. Grants can only be made for one year at a time for holidays/residentials.
- BBC Children in Need will consider funding support costs associated directly with a project, but we cannot fund organisational overheads and running costs where these are not integral to the project you are applying for.
- Only one application can be assessed in any 12 month period.

Comprehensive guidelines for completing both the Main Grant and Small Grant application forms are available on the charity's website – a detailed A-Z of policy advice and guidance can also be found there.

Grantmaking in 2009/10

In 2009/10 the charity had assets of £31.4 million and an income of £44.2 million, which included £40 million raised through the 2009 appeal. The charity made 1,285 grants across the UK totalling £41.7 million. Grants were broken down as follows:

London and South East England	£10 million
North England	£9.2 million
Scotland	£5.7 million
Central England	£5.3 million
South and West England	£3.8 million
Wales	£3.3 million
Northern Ireland	£3.3 million
UK-wide grants	£1.1 million

Poverty and deprivation	£14.1 million
Disability	£10.3 million
Marginalised groups	£5.4 million
Distress	£4.8 million
Behavioural difficulties	£2.9 million
Abuse/neglect	£2.4 million
Illness	£1.8 million

The following information from the 2009/10 annual report gives an interesting insight into how the charity operates and its achievements during the year:

The most important thing we do is to fund projects that make a difference to disadvantaged children and young people in the UK. The ultimate beneficiaries of our grants are the children and young people themselves, and we regularly review our grantmaking policies to ensure that we can continue to make a real change to their lives.

In our 2008/09 Trustees' Report, we set out our grantmaking aims for [2009/10]. We aimed:

- To fund a portfolio of quality projects, with an appropriate mix of size, need and geography.
- To better evaluate and learn from our projects via improved grant monitoring and reporting.
- To deliver two proactive funding programmes.
- To confirm a strategy for the use of intermediaries to disburse funds in support of individual children and young people.
- To use our knowledge and position to educate and to influence change.

The following [reports] on our activities and achievements in these areas.

Total Grants Awarded

From the money raised during Appeal 2009, we made 1,275 grants to the value of £39 million. We also awarded £2.7 million to 10 projects through our Fun and Friendship programme [check the charity's website for details of the current status of this programme].

Applications made for the final deadline of the financial year, 15 July 2010, were approved by trustees on 21 October 2010, just after our financial year end. These grants, totalling £7.8 million, are not therefore included in our financial statements at 30 September 2010 as we were not committed to them at the year end. At the balance sheet date these amounts were held in a separate designated fund as they were made out of funds raised by our 2009 Appeal, and they have been included in the analysis of grants for the year in the trustees' Report.

In common with many charitable funders we expect demand for funding will continue to rise over the coming months. Currently the success rate for applications is 30%, meaning that only 3 in 10 applications for a grant are successful. While this is due partly to the charity not having the funds to award grants to all the projects we would like, we also recognise that we need to focus on communicating as effectively as possible with potential applicants – through outreach to organisations in the field and through clear and helpful information materials. We would like to increase success rates, as we recognise that unsuccessful applications are not a good use of our time or that of applicants. In a climate of increased demand from the voluntary and community sector for funding, this will be even more difficult to achieve.

Small Grants

In January 2010, following a successful pilot in Scotland, we launched a new Small Grants Programme across the UK for applications of up to £10,000 a year. The programme was based on our experience of supporting smaller projects across the UK, where the investment of relatively modest sums can make all the difference to their ability to help disadvantaged children. These grants can, for example, help organisations to make very effective use of the efforts of local volunteers in their work with children and young people, and this in turn helps their work to be more sustainable over time.

Through the programme we hoped to extend our reach across the four nations and we have been pleased to see that numbers of small applications and small grants have risen appreciably this year, right across the UK. We had set a target of a 20% increase in small grants on the previous year and were able to achieve a 52% increase in these. Small Grants also have a higher success rate than larger grants.

Grant Process

In 2009, we moved to a fully online process for grant applications and introduced additional closing dates for applications to make it easier for organisations to apply at the right time for their project. We are pleased to see that this has resulted in a more even flow of applications across the year and more organisations are applying well in advance of the deadlines.

It is important for us to offer advice and information to organisations that are not very experienced, both in making grant applications and/or in using electronic processes to do so. We do this centrally through our Helpdesk and locally via our teams based in 12 offices across the UK. Our grant staff work with individual applicants and they also participate in outreach events and workshops to help people understand whether they are eligible to apply and how to go about it.

During the decision making process, grant applications are typically assessed by one of our freelance assessors and in a small number of cases, by one of our staff. Our assessors have professional experience in the field and may also have knowledge of the geographical area where the project is based. The assessment involves making individual personal contact with applicant organisations in order to understand more about their work and its impact on disadvantaged children and young people. The assessment reports are then considered by seven national and regional advisory committees who are made up of members of the public recruited on the basis of relevant specialist and local knowledge.

Decisions on grant awards are made four times a year, by our Board of Trustees and the advice of the national and regional committees is invaluable in the process.

In the course of this year we received 4,001 applications, representing a rise of 10% on last year and we believe this is primarily due to our increased accessibility and the launch of a new Small Grants Programme.

Grant Management and Monitoring

Our relationship with grant-holders is very important to us and we want to be close to the work our funding supports. We maintain contact in a number of ways but the most important interface is through visiting projects and this year we have carried out 1,076 visits to project across the UK. This provided a very good indication to us of the progress of the work, the impact for children and young people and what some of the key success factors were in different types of projects. These visits also help us to stay in touch with the issues and challenges experienced by children and young people and by the groups that work to support them.

Currently we provide training in self-evaluation for a significant proportion of the organisations we fund – this is to help them measure and demonstrate the difference their work makes to children and it also helps them to report more effectively to us. Next year we will review our grant reports with a view to creating an online reporting system that places a strong focus on ensuring that organisations give us clear information about the impact of the grant on children and young people.

Bringing Organisations Together

We see great value in bringing organisations together – it encourages them to learn from each other and share good practice. We also use the opportunity to broker contact with others, such as the BBC. This year we convened 24 events in various parts of the UK which brought organisations together from fields including mentoring and befriending, counselling, children affected by HIV/Aids and children in refuges. Two of the events brought young people together and, in collaboration with BBC staff, made use of creative media techniques for them to express their views about issues affecting their lives.

Knowledge Sharing

We have made great progress in 2010 in developing and sharing learning from our reviews of holiday play schemes and community-led youth clubs and we are now in a position to start to share knowledge from these reviews with confidence and authority.

A full report on holiday play schemes for disadvantaged children was written and a four-page briefing paper was published. The review produces some very strong messages about the importance of holiday play schemes for disadvantaged children. We have generated greater knowledge and understanding about their outcomes, delivery and effectiveness that will be useful to many interests. The core message from this review is that holiday play schemes are fundamentally important for children whose life opportunities are limited. They provide real opportunities for children who would otherwise be isolated over holiday periods, especially long summer breaks, to be safe, to connect with friends, have an ongoing structure in their lives, broaden horizons and develop memories to embrace. [The report is available on the charity's website.]

The writing of a report on community-led youth clubs is currently progressing. In addition to a literature review and interviews in the field with those running local youth clubs, young people's views have been gathered for inclusion in the report through an online survey of young people attending youth clubs funded by us.

The learning from both reviews and our reflections on the thematic review process overall, has placed BBC Children in Need in an exciting position. We are keen to make sure that this learning and the thematic review model itself can be of as much value as possible to funders, policy-makers and practitioners and we are disseminating this in a range of ways, from running workshops to individual meetings with key individuals and organisations, as well as using it as a basis for submitting evidence to relevant government enquiries.

A comprehensive list of funded organisations, broken down by region, is available from the charity's website.

Exclusions

Grants will not be given for:

- relief of statutory responsibility
- applications from local government or NHS bodies
- building projects which are applying to us for more than £20,000
- the promotion of religion
- trips or projects abroad
- medical treatment/research
- projects for pregnancy testing or advice, information or counselling on pregnancy choices
- general awareness-raising work
- bursaries, sponsored places, fees or equivalent
- individuals (unless an eligible organisation is applying on their behalf)
- distribution to another/other organisation/s, for example, PTAs applying on behalf of schools
- general appeals or endowment funds
- deficit funding or repayment of loans
- retrospective funding (projects taking place before the grant award date)
- projects unable to start within 12 months of the grant award date
- unspecified expenditure.

Applications

Straightforward and excellent application forms and guidelines are available from the charity's website or from the following national BBC Children in Need offices:

England (and general helpline): PO Box 1000, London W12 7WJ. Telephone Number: 020 8576 7788.

Northern Ireland: Broadcasting House, Ormeau Avenue, Belfast BT2 8HQ. Telephone Number: 028 9033 8221.

Scotland: BBC Scotland, G10, 40 Pacific Drive, Glasgow, G51 1DA. Telephone Number: 0141 422 6111.

Wales: Broadcasting House, Llandaff, Cardiff CF5 2YQ. Telephone Number: 029 2032 2383.

There are four closing dates for applications – 15 January, 15 April, 15 July and 15 October. Applicants should allow up to three months after each closing date for notification of a decision

Application forms must be completed online.

Note: Incomplete or late application forms will not be assessed.

The charity has previously expressed an interest in receiving more eligible applications from North West England. The charity is particularly interested in hearing from organisations that have not had funding from Children in Need in the past. Contact Philip Jeffery, Regional Officer on 0161 244 3442 or by email at: philip.jeffery@bbc.co.uk.

Common applicant mistakes

'Submitting application forms with missing information; not reading the guidelines for ineligible items; and not actually explaining what their project will do.'

BC Partners Foundation

General

Beneficial area
UK.

BC Partners Limited, 40 Portman Square, London W1H 6DA
Tel: 020 7009 4800
Email: bcpfoundation@bcpartners.com
Correspondent: The Trustees
Trustees: Nikos Stathopolous; Mike Twinning; Joseph Cronley.
CC Number: 1136956

Information available
Basic information was available from the Charity Commission.

Established in 2010 for general charitable purposes, this is the foundation of private equity firm BC Partners. One of the trustees, Nikos Stathopolous, is also a trustee of the Private Equity Foundation.

Unfortunately, few details are known about how this new trust will operate.

Applications
In writing to the correspondent.

The Bedford Charity (The Harpur Trust)

Education, welfare and recreation

£814,000 to organisations
(2009/10)

Beneficial area
The borough of Bedford.

Princeton Court, Pilgrim Centre, Brickhill Drive, Bedford MK41 7PZ
Tel: 01234 369500
Fax: 01234 369505
Email: grants@harpur-trust.org.uk
Website: www.bedfordcharity.org.uk
Correspondent: Lucy Bardner, Grants Manager
Trustees: Sally Peck, Chair; David Palfreyman; David W Doran; Sue Clark; Ian McEwen; Judith Bray; Rae Levene; Rosemary Wallace; Tony Wildman; John K S Mingay; Colleen Atkins; Jean McCardle; Tina Beddoes; Phillip Wallace; Prof. Stephen Mayson; Murray Stewart; Justin Phillimore; David Meghan; Elizabeth Fordham; Michael Womack; Deirdre Anderson; Gail Dennis; David Dixon; Vina Mayor; Peter Budeck.
CC Number: 204817

Information available
Accounts were available at the Charity Commission. The charity has an excellent website.

This charity is one of the oldest described in this resource, and probably one of the oldest in the country. Full details are provided by the charity:

The Bedford Charity, also known as the Harpur Trust, has been in existence since 1566 when it was founded by Sir William Harpur (1496–1573) a tailor from Bedford and later Lord Mayor of London, who created an endowment to sustain a school he had established in Bedford. The endowment also made provision for the marriage of poor maids of the town, for deprived children to be nourished and informed, and for any residue to be distributed to the poor of the town.

These ideals evolved over the years into the three charitable objects of the Bedford Charity today which are:
▶ the promotion of education;
▶ the relief of those who are sick or in need, hardship or distress;
▶ the provision of recreational facilities with a social welfare purpose.

Most grants are made to organisations, but there is a very small budget (less than 5% of the total grants budget) for grants to individuals under the education object.

Today, the activities of the trust are still inspired by the vision of William Harpur who saw the real value of education and the real needs to be addressed amongst the disadvantaged, poor and sick in his home town of Bedford.

The trust owns and runs four independent schools in Bedford – Bedford School, Bedford High School, Bedford Modern School and Dame Alice Harpur School. All four provide selective education for a total of over 4,000 children in the age range 7–18 years. It also owns and manages 40 almshouses which provide secure, affordable accommodation for a number of the borough's less advantaged, older citizens.

Grantmaking Policy
Our responsive programme
Approximately £500,000 is awarded from our responsive programme each year. Grants within this category cover education, relief and recreation.

Our themed grants programmes
An additional £500,000 per year is available from our themed grants programmes. These enable us to focus resources on topics of particular interest which still fit within our three objects of education, relief and recreation. Our aim is to increase the impact and benefits of our funding through specific, targeted interventions. Each of the themed programmes has its own specific criteria and all projects funded through this programme must be able to demonstrate the potential to influence policy and practice in the field or be replicated in other locations.

We reviewed our themed programmes following the publication of *Sinking and*

Swimming – understanding Britain's unmet needs, a report by the Young Foundation which the Charity co-funded.

As a result, we have maintained one of our previous programmes and launched three new themed programmes based on the report's recommendations. Our new programmes are broader in scope than the old ones, with the aim of being accessible to a wider range of Bedford projects.

The programme we have maintained is:

The Education Challenge Fund
This is a partnership programme for state schools in the Borough of Bedford wishing to conduct research in school. Please contact the Grants Manager for more information.

The three new programmes are:

Transitions
This programme is for projects which provide preparation, bridges and support for people undergoing difficult life transitions in Bedford.

Resilience or Psychological Fitness
This programme is for projects which will help Bedford residents manage and cope with traumatic changes positively, learning to adapt and prosper despite setbacks.

Isolation
A programme for projects which reduce loneliness and lack of social networks amongst Bedford's most vulnerable residents.

For detailed information about each programme and examples of the type of project it might fund, please contact the Grants Manager.

Grantmaking in 2009/10

In 2009/10 the charity had assets of £102.3 million and an income of £52.4 million, which included £46.8 million from school fees and £2.8 million from investments. There were 37 grants to organisations totalling £814,000; grants, awards and bursaries to individuals totalled £90,000.

Beneficiaries during the year included: All Saints Parish Church (£75,000); CAN – Drugs, Alcohol and Homelessness (£69,000); Home-Start Bedford Borough (£60,000); Bedford Race Equality Council (£38,000); Music in Detention (£21,500); Bedford Creative Arts (£20,000); John Bunyan Museum (£15,000); Methodist Homes for the Aged (£10,000); Philharmonia Orchestra (£9,000); Bedfordshire and Northamptonshire Multiple Sclerosis Therapy Centre (£5,000); Sharnbrook

Village Hall Management Committee (£2,500); All Saints PCC Renhold (£1,500).

In addition to the above, the charity also made a donation of £1 million to the endowment fund of the Bedford Academy.

Exclusions

Grants are not made:

- in support of commercial ventures
- for any project that relates primarily to the promotion of any religion
- in support of projects that do not benefit the residents of the borough of Bedford
- to cover costs already incurred, although exceptions are considered and this should be discussed with the trust prior to an application being submitted
- for services which are the responsibility of the local authority, for example, a school applying for a grant to cover the cost of employing a teacher is unlikely to be successful. However, the trust could consider an application from a school for a creative arts project that involved paying a voluntary organisation to deliver lunch time or after school workshops.

Applications

The charity clearly sets out its application procedure as follows:

Step 1 – Check
First, read our guidance notes to make sure your project is eligible. [These are available on the charity's website upon completion of a short eligibility questionnaire.]

Step 2 – Call
If you think your project is eligible for a grant, call us. It's always better if you do this before you fill in a preliminary proposal form.

Remember, some grant applications won't be successful so before you spend time filling in forms, please contact our Grants Manager, Lucy Bardner or our Grants Officer, Peta Frost on 01234 369500 to discuss your project in more detail.

It's really important for organisations based outside of the Borough of Bedford who run projects in the Borough to call us before applying.

Step 3 – Preliminary proposal form
The fastest and simplest way to apply is to complete and submit our online application form. This form asks you to create a password. Once you've submitted the form it goes straight to our grants database.

Alternatively you can apply by using one of the following two methods:
- Download and fill in a PDF version of Preliminary Proposal Form. You can email or post it back to us
- Request a hardcopy of the form and notes. Call or email Lucy on 01234 369500 or lbardner@harpur-trust.org.uk

Make sure your application form reaches us by the deadline.

This is the first stage of your application process. It will enable our grants team and our trustees to give you some initial guidance.

Step 4 – Feedback
We'll read and discuss your preliminary proposal and give you feedback. If you've been successful, we'll ask you to fill in a full application form.

Step 5 – Full application form
Please don't fill in a full application form unless we've asked you to. We'll do this in step four, above.

Online applications
If you used our online application process to send us your preliminary proposal, you can also use the online system to complete and submit your final application.

Offline applications
If you sent us your preliminary proposal as a PDF or hard copy, you can either:
- Download the PDF version of the Full Application Form. You can email or post it back to us
- Request a hardcopy of the form and notes. Call or email Lucy.

Make sure your application form reaches us by the deadline and that you attach all of the relevant documents we've asked you for on the form.

Step 6 – Acknowledgement
Our grants team will usually contact you by phone to let you know that we've received your full application. We may ask you to visit us to discuss your application in more detail.

Step 7 – Decision
We'll discuss your proposal at the next meeting of our grants committee. If your application is successful, we'll write to you and let you know. We usually do this within seven working days of the meeting.

The Big Lottery Fund (see also Awards for All)

Community, young people, welfare

£374 million (2010/11)

Beneficial area

UK and overseas.

(See below)

Tel: 08454 102030

Email: enquiries@biglotteryfund.org.uk

Website: www.biglotteryfund.org.uk

Trustees: Peter Ainsworth, Chair; Anna Southall; Nat Sloane; Frank Hewitt; Janet Reed; Alison Magee; Diana Whitworth; Judith Donovan; Roland Doven; John Gartside; Albert Tucker; Rajay Naik.

Information available

Full details of all programmes can be found on the fund's website, along with application information.

Information available

Details of all lottery funders can now be found on one website: www.lotteryfunding.org.uk.

Summary

The National Lottery (the Lottery) was launched in 1994 and rapidly established itself as a key funder of the voluntary sector. Since it began, over £25 billion has been raised and more than 350,000 grants given out for good causes. However, the assessment process is a rigorous and demanding one. Many organisations commit a substantial part of their fundraising resources in applying for grants from the various Lottery distribution bodies. The Lottery currently funds four good causes and funding is allocated as follows:

- charities, health, education and the environment (jointly) – 50%
- sports – 16.67%
- arts – 16.67%
- heritage – 16.67%.

General

Distribution bodies
Distribution bodies, sometimes referred to as Lottery funders, are the organisations that distribute the good causes' money to local communities and national and international projects. They cover arts, heritage, sport, community and voluntary groups as well as supporting projects concerned with health, education and the environment. They will also be contributing to the funding of the 2012 Olympic Games and Paralympic Games in London and until at least 2012, the diversion of Lottery funds to the Olympics means that there will be less new Lottery money available.

The funding bodies are:

- Arts Council England. Arts Council England is the national development agency for the arts in England, distributing public money from government and the Lottery.
- Arts Council of Northern Ireland. This is the lead development agency for the arts in Northern Ireland.
- Arts Council of Wales. This body is responsible for developing and funding the arts in Wales.
- Awards for All. Awards for All is a BIG Lottery Fund grants scheme funding small, local community-based projects in the UK. Each country in the UK runs its own programme.
- Big Lottery Fund. The Big Lottery Fund (BIG) is committed to improving communities and the lives of people most in need.
- Heritage Lottery Fund. The Heritage Lottery Fund uses money from the Lottery to give grants for a wide range of projects involving the local, regional and national heritage of the UK.
- NESTA. NESTA (the National Endowment for Science, Technology and the Arts) was a non-departmental public body investing in innovators and working to improve the climate for creativity in the UK – the government is now seeking to establish the organisation as a separate, independent charity.
- Olympic Lottery Distributor. The Olympic Lottery Distributor's remit is to support the delivery of the London 2012 Olympic and Paralympic Games. The Olympic Lottery Distributor is not currently running any open funding rounds.
- Scottish Arts Council. The Scottish Arts Council champions the arts for Scotland.
- Sport England. Sport England invests in projects that help people to start, stay and succeed in sport and physical activity at every level.
- Sports Council for Northern Ireland. 'Making sport happen for you.'
- Sportscotland – the national sport agency for Scotland. Working with partners, it is responsible for developing sport and physical recreational activity in Scotland.
- Sports Council for Wales. The Sports Council for Wales is the national organisation responsible for developing and promoting sport and active lifestyles.
- UK Sport. UK Sport works in partnership to lead sport in the UK to world-class success – the organisation has now been merged with Sport England.

The Lottery distribution bodies are independent; however, because they distribute public funds, their policies are subject to a level of statutory control from government. Their grantmaking is also under close public and media scrutiny and is often the subject of wide-ranging debate.

Big Lottery Fund

The Big Lottery Fund (BIG) was launched in 2004 and given legal status on 1 December 2006 by way of the National Lottery Act 2006. It was brought about by the merging of the Community Fund and New Opportunities Fund, and the transfer of residual activities and assets from the Millennium Commission.

There was much controversy surrounding the launch of BIG as the Community Fund had previously operated via 'open-grants' programmes. BIG introduced new programmes based on themes and outcomes set by the government. These were announced by the government, not by BIG itself, and before the relevant consultation period had ended, which led to fears that funds would be used to achieve government ends rather than those of applicant charities.

BIG is the largest of the Lottery distributors and is responsible for giving out 50% of the money for good causes raised from the Lottery, which provides a budget of around £600 million a year. Funding covers health, education, environment and charitable purposes. During 2010/11, £773.2 million (£740.2 million in 2009/10) was received in Lottery income directly from ticket sales. As stated, BIG normally receives half of the money raised for the good causes by the Lottery, however, government has directed that between February 2009 and August 2012, £638 million should be transferred from BIG to the Olympic Lottery Distribution Fund (OLDF). During 2010/11 a total of £171.7 million was transferred for this purpose. (N.B. DSC is campaigning for this money to be refunded, as promised, by the government. Visit www.biglotteryrefund.org.uk for more information.)

In October 2010 responsibility for the Big Lottery Fund was transferred to the Cabinet Office.

BIG's mission is to be 'committed to bringing real improvements to communities and the lives of people most in need'. To do this, it has identified seven values.

They are:
- fairness
- accessibility
- strategic focus
- involving people
- innovation
- enabling
- additional to government.

In response to complaints about the short-term nature of its funding, a number of BIG's programmes now provide funding for up to five years. Projects are required to provide a realistic exit strategy that plans out how the project will continue after the funding from BIG has finished. One effect of this is that requests for larger amounts and for longer periods are made, which, over time, might lead to BIG funding fewer projects.

Administration of non-Lottery funding

The Act of 2006 also includes powers for BIG to distribute non-Lottery funding and to make loans. Much of BIG's funding is given in grants made directly to successful applicants, particularly those in the voluntary sector, however, BIG also administers non-lottery funds.

Funding in 2010/11

During the year grants which are measured against the fund's outcomes framework were distributed as follows (excluding small grants programmes including Awards for All, Breathing Places and 2014 Communities and any awards made through award partners and other delivery partners including Big Local Trust and Parks for People programmes):

England	555	£127.5 million
Wales	189	£48 million
Scotland	40	£11 million
Northern Ireland	57	£4 million

Total funding through all streams, including those with partner organisations, amounted to £374 million in 2010/11 – a further £200 million slipped into the next financial year. (Taking this into account, funding levels were higher than the £558 million awarded in 2009/10.)

A full analysis of BIG's activities during the year can be found in its latest annual report.

BIG programmes

The following programmes were open in 2012 – check BIG's website for up-to-date information on current programmes.

England

Advice Services Fund

A £16.8 million fund administered on behalf of the Cabinet Office. Grants of between £40,000 and £70,000 are available for organisations providing debt, welfare benefits, employment and housing advice services.

Awards for All England

A simple small grants scheme making awards of between £300 and £10,000.

The Big Society Investment Fund

The fund will distribute £5 million from the Big Society Bank, which raises money from dormant bank accounts. The aim of the fund is to 'build the diversity and resilience of the social investment market by investing in well managed, ambitious and financially sound social investment intermediaries, so that charities and social enterprises are able to access capital that will enable them to work more effectively in our communities and together address the needs of our society'.

Fair Share Trust

A £50 million fund, delivered through the Community Foundation Network, which aims to: Build Capacity and Sustainability – by involving local communities in decision-making about lottery funding; Build Social Capital – by building links within and between communities to promote trust and participation; and Improve livability – by improving the living environment for communities.

International Communities

Grants of between £50,000 and £500,000 are available to UK based non-governmental organisations working with overseas partners in Africa, Asia (including the Pacific and Central Asian countries), the Middle East, Central and South America, the Caribbean, and parts of Eastern Europe.

Parks for People

£5 million allocated in 2011/12 and 2012/13 to provide funding for parks. The programme is run in partnership with the Heritage Lottery Fund, to whom further enquiries and applications should be made.

Reaching Communities

The programme has two strands: revenue and small capital – funding from £10,000 to £500,000 for revenue projects and/or smaller capital projects up to £50,000; buildings – funding of between £100,000 and £500,000 for large capital projects. Reaching Communities funds projects that help people and communities most in need. Projects can be new or existing, or be the core work of your organisation.

Wales

Awards for All Wales

A simple small grants programme making awards of between £500 and £5,000

BIG Innovation

Aiming to develop innovative approaches to tackling emerging and entrenched social problems. Grants of between £20,000 and £1 million are available.

Fair Share Trust

A £50 million fund, delivered through the Community Foundation Network, which aims to: Build Capacity and Sustainability – by involving local communities in decision-making about lottery funding; Build Social Capital – by building links within and between communities to promote trust and participation; and Improve livability – by improving the living environment for communities.

International Communities
Grants of between £50,000 and £500,000 are available to UK based non-governmental organisations working with overseas partners in Africa, Asia (including the Pacific and Central Asian countries), the Middle East, Central and South America, the Caribbean, and parts of Eastern Europe.

People and Places
Grants of between £5,000 and £1 million are available for capital and revenue projects that encourage co-ordinated action by people who want to make their communities better places to live.

Scotland

2014 Communities
Building a lasting legacy for communities across Scotland. The fund distributes £1 million each year, with grants of between £300 and £2,000 available.

Awards for All Scotland
A simple small grants scheme making awards of between £500 and £10,000

International Communities
Grants of between £50,000 and £500,000 are available to UK based non-governmental organisations working with overseas partners in Africa, Asia (including the Pacific and Central Asian countries), the Middle East, Central and South America, the Caribbean, and parts of Eastern Europe.

Investing in Ideas
A £1 million fund, renewed each year, which provides groups with an opportunity to spend time and money developing ideas that have a clear public benefit. Grants of up to £10,000 are available.

Investing in Communities
Awards of between £10,000 and £1 million are available. The 3 strands of the programme are: Growing Community Assets, which aims to

help communities have more control and influence over their own future through ownership of assets; Life Transitions, which aims to support projects that help people at key times of change, helping them to make their lives better for the future; and Supporting 21st Century Life, which aims to support projects that build stronger families and stronger communities.

Life Changes
A £50 million fund which aims to transform the life chances of young people leaving care and improving the lives of older people with dementia and their careers.

Northern Ireland

Awards for All Northern Ireland
This programme is delivered and funded by the Big Lottery Fund in Northern Ireland and awards funds of between £500 and £10,000 over a 12 month period.

Building Change Trust
A £10 million investment fund, delivered in partnership with the Community Foundation for Northern Ireland, Community Evaluation Northern Ireland, Rural Community Network, Volunteer Development Agency and Business in the Community Northern Ireland. Contact the Community Foundation for Northern Ireland for further information.

Energy Efficient Venues
The fund will pay for community organisations to carry out works to their venue to make them more environmentally-friendly and energy-efficient. As well as benefiting the environment, this programme will help community organisations save on their heating and lighting costs. Grants of between £2,000 – £10,000 and £15,000 – £50,000 are available.

Fair Share Trust
A £50 million fund, delivered through the Community Foundation Network, which aims to: Build Capacity and Sustainability – by involving local communities in decision-making about lottery funding; Build Social Capital – by building links within and between communities to promote trust and participation; and Improve livability – by improving the living environment for communities.

Impact of Alcohol
A £10 million fund which makes grants to statutory, voluntary and community organisations for a range of projects which aim to reduce the harm to individuals, families and communities directly affected by alcohol misuse.

International Communities
Grants of between £50,000 and £500,000 are available to UK based non-governmental organisations working with overseas partners in Africa, Asia (including the Pacific and Central Asian countries), the Middle East, Central and South America, the Caribbean, and parts of Eastern Europe.

Useful contacts
Regional offices
England Regional Offices

North East
2 St James Gate
Newcastle upon Tyne
NE1 4BE
Tel: 0191 376 1600
Textphone: 0191 376 1776
Fax: 0191 376 1661
Email: enquiries.ne@
biglotteryfund.org.uk

North West
10th Floor
York House
York Street
Manchester
M2 3BB
Tel: 0161 261 4600
Textphone: 0161 261 4647
Fax: 0161 261 4646
Email: enquiries.nw@
biglotteryfund.org.uk

Yorkshire and the Humber
3rd floor
Carlton Tower
34 St Paul's Street
Leeds
LS1 2AT
Tel: 0113 224 5301
Textphone: 0113 245 4104
Fax: 0113 244 0363
Email: enquiries.yh@
biglotteryfund.org.uk

East Midlands
4th Floor
Pearl Assurance House
Friar Lane
Nottingham
NG1 6BT
Tel: 0115 872 2950

Fax: 0115 872 2990
Email: enquiries.em@
biglotteryfund.org.uk

West Midlands
Apex House
3 Embassy Drive
Edgbaston
Birmingham
B15 1TR
Tel: 0121 345 7700
Textphone: 0121 345 7666
Fax: 0121 345 8888
Email: enquiries.wm@
biglotteryfund.org.uk

Eastern
2nd Floor
Elizabeth House
1 High Street
Chesterton
Cambridge
CB4 1YW
Tel: 01223 449000
Textphone: 01223 352041
Fax: 01223 312628
Email: enquiries.ea@
biglotteryfund.org.uk

London
5th Floor
1 Plough Place
London
EC4A 1DE
Tel: 020 7842 4000
Textphone: 0845 039 0204
Fax: 020 7842 4010
Email: enquiries.lon@
biglotteryfund.org.uk

South East
Chancery House
2nd Floor
11 – 17 Leas Road
Guildford
GU1 4QW
Telephone: 01483 462900
Textphone: 01483 568764
Fax: 01483 46291
Email: enquiries.se@
biglotteryfund.org.uk

South West
Beaufort House
51 New North Road
Exeter
EX4 4EQ
Tel: 01392 849700
Textphone: 01392 490633
Fax: 01392 491134
Email: enquiries.sw@
biglotteryfund.org.uk

Strategic Grants Office – England
1st Floor
Chiltern House
St Nicholas Court
25 – 27 Castlegate
Nottingham
NG1 7AR
Tel: 0115 934 2950
Textphone: 0115 934 2951
Fax: 0115 934 2952
Email: strategicgrants@
biglotteryfund.org.uk

Northern Ireland
1 Cromac Quay
Cromac Wood
Belfast
BT7 2LB
Tel: 028 9055 1455
Textphone: 028 9055 1431
Fax: 028 9055 1444
Email: enquiries.ni@
biglotteryfund.org.uk

Scotland Office
1 Atlantic Quay
1 Robertson Way
Glasgow
G2 8JB
Tel: 0141 242 1400
Textphone: 0141 242 1500
Fax: 0141 242 1401
Email: enquiries.scotland@
biglotteryfund.org.uk

Wales Offices
2nd Floor
Ladywell House
Newtown
Powys
SY16 1JB
Tel: 01686 611700
Textphone: 01686 610205
Fax: 01686 621534
Email: enquiries.wales@
biglotteryfund.org.uk

6th Floor
1 Kingsway
Cardiff
CF10 3JN
Tel: 029 2067 8200
Textphone: 0845 6021659
Fax: 029 2066 7275

Applications

Full details on current programmes, application forms and guidance are available via the BLF website or by calling 08454 102030.

Percy Bilton Charity

Disabled, disadvantaged youth, older people

£428,000 to organisations
(2009/10)

Beneficial area

UK.

Bilton House, 7 Culmington Road, Ealing, London W13 9NB
Tel: 020 8579 2829
Fax: 020 8579 3650
Website: www.percybiltoncharity.org.uk
Correspondent: Wendy Fuller, Charity Administrator
Trustees: Miles A Bilton, Chair; James R Lee; Stefan J Paciorek; Kim Lansdown; Hayley Bilton.
CC Number: 1094720

Information available

Accounts were available from the Charity Commission. The charity has a clear and concise website.

Background

The following information is taken from the charity's website:

> The Percy Bilton Charity was founded on 9th July 1962 by the late Percy Bilton originally to relieve poverty, advance education and other exclusively charitable purposes for the benefit of the community. Percy Bilton was an entrepreneur who in the 1920s and 1930s built up a group of successful property companies which in the 1970s was listed on the London Stock Exchange. He endowed the charity with a substantial parcel of shares in Percy Bilton Limited, which later became Bilton plc. This investment was sold in 1998 and the proceeds invested in a diversified investment portfolio.

> During his lifetime, Percy Bilton took a keen personal interest in the activities of the charity retaining his involvement until his death in 1982. In compliance with his wishes, the endowment is considered to be an expendable endowment. The directors of the charity, who are its trustees, have continued the charity's activities but redefined the grant making policies over time to suit changing social and economic needs. The charity now makes distributions in areas relating to

older people, people with disabilities or mental health problems and young people who are socially or educationally disadvantaged.

Guidelines

The charity's website provides the following details and guidance on its grantmaking:

This is a guide to the charity's current grant policies and procedures.

We would ask you to read these notes carefully to verify that both your organisation and your project are within our policies before applying. You are welcome to contact the Grants Office at any stage of your application for advice and guidance by telephone or in writing.

Who may apply

Only registered charities in the UK whose primary objectives are to assist one or more of the following groups:

- disadvantaged/underprivileged young people (persons under 25)
- people with disabilities (physical or learning disabilities or mental health problems)
- older people (aged over 60).

We do not respond to organisations who do not meet the above criteria.

Type of grants offered

We have 2 programmes for organisations:

1 Large grants – one off payments for capital expenditure of approximately £2,000 and over, i.e. furniture and equipment; building/ refurbishment projects. Please note that we do not fund running costs.
2 Small grants – donations of up to £500 towards furnishings and equipment for small projects. This programme is more suitable for smaller organisations.

Amount of grant

The amount offered will usually depend on the number of applications received in relation to the funds available for distribution. You may therefore not receive the full amount requested.

Major appeals

In the case of major appeals and minibuses please apply after 75% of the funding has been secured, as offers are conditional upon the balance being raised and the project completed within one year. We also require grants to be taken up within 12 months of the offer and it is essential to ascertain that your project is likely to be completed within this time scale before applying.

Who the charity will fund

The charity will consider capital funding for the following projects and schemes:

1 *Disadvantaged/underprivileged young people (persons under 25)*: supported housing schemes and educational and training projects to encourage disadvantaged young people who may be homeless and/ or unemployed away from crime, substance/alcohol misuse and homelessness; facilities for recreational activities and outdoor pursuits specifically for young people who are educationally or socially underprivileged or disadvantaged.

2 *People with disabilities (physical or learning disabilities or mental health problems)*: residential, respite care, occupational and recreational establishments for children, young people and adults with physical or learning disabilities or enduring mental health problems.

3 *Older people (aged over 60)*: day centres, nursing and residential homes, sheltered accommodation and respite care for the frail or sufferers from dementia or age related disorders; projects to encourage older people to maintain their independence.

General

In 2009/10 the charity had assets of £19 million and an income of £696,000. Grants were made totalling £584,000, of which £428,000 was given to organisations, £115,000 was donated to individuals and £41,000 was given in food parcels to older people.

Grants to organisations were categorised as follows:

Disability	£145,000
Young people with a disability	£96,000
Older people	£83,000
Disadvantaged young people	£55,000

Grants in 2009/10

Beneficiaries receiving **large grants** included:

Disability

Independent Options (Stockport) Limited (£12,000), to replace the central heating system at the Pines which is a centre providing services for children and adults with disabilities and mental health needs; St John's Hospice – London (£11,000), to purchase new furniture and equipment for the hospice including mattresses, armchairs, specialist cushions and footstools; Sussex Multiple Sclerosis Treatment Centre – Southwick (£7,000), for the renovation of the centre, which offers a range of services for people with MS; Wirral Society of the Blind and Partially Sighted (£5,000), for the construction of a two room extension to their premises to provide facilities for computer courses and art sessions for people with a visual impairment; Tunbridge Wells Mental Health Resource – Kent (£2,600); towards the refurbishment of the kitchen at a resource centre for people with mental health problems; and the Wheelyboat Trust – Cornwall (£2,000), for the construction of one Mark III wheelyboat which allows wheelchair users to access boating activities.

Young people with a disability

Hollybank Trust – West Yorkshire (£10,000), for the purchase of four Hi-Lo beds for Holmfirth Transitions Development, a residential home for fifteen young adults with profound disabilities; Quest School – Kent (£8,000), towards the purchase of computer equipment, an interactive whiteboard and desks for the school for young people with autism and learning disabilities; Finchale Training College – Durham (£6,500), for the purchase of furnishings for three study bedrooms being part of the refurbishment of residential accommodation for disabled students; Martha Trust – East Sussex (£4,000), to construct a hydrotherapy pool at Mary House, a residential home for young people with profound physical and learning disabilities; and Norman Laud Association – Sutton Coldfield (£2,000), towards the cost of installing soft padding to one bedroom at the respite centre for use by children who have seizures or are unsteady on their feet.

Older people

Family Support Brightlingsea – Essex (£10,000), for the purchase of a minibus to provide door to door transport for older people (average age of over 80) attending their lunch clubs; Peggy Dodd Centre – Bath (£6,000), towards the construction of an extension to the day centre at Brierley House to provide occupational therapy for older people with dementia; Greenock Medical Aid Society – Scotland (£5,000), for the replacement of the outdated boiler control panels at two nursing homes for frail older people; Age Concern – Exeter (£3,000), for the refurbishment of kitchen and dining facilities at their cafe which provides hot cooked meals for older people; and All Souls Clubhouse – London (£1,700), towards the purchase and installation of a sink for the kitchen which provides hot meals for local older people who attend the day centre.

Disadvantaged young people
Caldecott Foundation – Kent (£7,000), to purchase 'tough furniture' for residential accommodation for young people who have experienced neglect and abuse; Venture Trust – Edinburgh (£5,000), to purchase and install a second-hand portakabin to provide equipment storage at the outdoor residential centre which runs personal development programmes for disadvantaged young people; Local Solutions – Liverpool (£3,800), to purchase kayaking equipment for the not-for-profit watersports centre to provide activities for disadvantaged young people; Warwickshire Association of Youth Clubs (£2,200), for the purchase of tables, chairs, safety lighting and a magnetic whiteboard for the training room at their premises; and CHICKS – Devon (£1,700), to install external lighting for the play barn at Moorland Retreat providing respite holidays for disadvantaged children from inner city areas across the UK.

Small grant beneficiaries included: ENABLE NI – County Down and M13 Youth Project – Manchester (£500 each); Shopmobility – Sheffield (£475); KEEN – Oxford (£450); Body and Soul – London (£390); Thalia Theatre Company – Norwich (£350); Edenbridge Mencap – Kent (£330); Different Strokes – Newcastle (£270); Dipton Out of School Hours Club – County Durham (£250); and SeeSaw – Oxford (£75).

Exclusions

The charity will not consider the following (the list is not exhaustive):

- running expenses for the organisation or individual projects
- salaries, training costs or office equipment/furniture
- projects for general community use e.g. community centre and church halls
- disabled access to community buildings
- publication costs e.g. printing/distributing promotional and information leaflets
- projects that have been completed

- items that have already been purchased
- provision of disabled facilities in schemes mainly for the able-bodied
- general funding/circularised appeals
- pre-schools or playgroups (other than predominantly for disabled children)
- play schemes/summer schemes
- holidays or expeditions for individuals or groups
- trips, activities or events
- community sports/play area facilities
- consumables (e.g. stationery, arts and crafts materials)
- refurbishment or repair of places of worship/church halls
- research projects
- mainstream pre-schools, schools, colleges and universities (other than special schools)
- welfare funds for individuals
- hospital/medical equipment
- works to premises not used primarily by the eligible groups.

Applications

The charity's website gives the following guidance on making an application:

Large grants (£2,000 and over)
Please apply on your organisation's headed notepaper giving or attaching the following information. 1–6 must be provided in all cases and 7 as applicable to your appeal:
1. A brief history of your charity, its objectives and work.
2. Description of the project and what you intend to achieve.
3. A copy of your most recent annual report and audited accounts.
4. Details of funds already raised and other sources that you have approached.
5. Proposals to monitor and evaluate the project.
6. Any other relevant information that will help to explain your application.
7. The following additional information that applies to your appeal.

Building/Refurbishment appeals:
- a statement of all costs involved – please itemise major items and professional fees
- confirmation that the project has on-going revenue funding
- confirmation that all planning and other consents and building regulations approvals have been obtained

- details of ownership of the premises and if leased, the length of the unexpired term
- timetable of construction/refurbishment and anticipated date of completion.

Equipment appeals:
- an itemised list of all equipment with estimate of costs – please obtain at least 2 competitive estimates except where this is not practicable e.g. specialised equipment
- when you plan to purchase the equipment.

Contribution towards purchase of minibuses:
- please note that minibuses can only be considered if used to transport older and disabled people with mobility problems
- please give details of provision made for insurance, tax and maintenance etc. – we require confirmation that your organisation can meet future running costs.

Small grants (up to £500)
Please apply on your organisation's headed notepaper with the following information:
1. Brief details about your organisation and its work.
2. A copy of your most recent annual accounts.
3. Outline of the project and its principal aims.
4. Breakdown of the cost of item/s required.
5. If your organisation is not a registered charity, please supply a reference from a registered charity with whom you work or from the Voluntary Service Council.

Common applicant mistakes

'Either the applicant organisation does not fit our criteria or the item that they are requesting funding towards doesn't.'

The Birmingham Community Foundation

General

£4.1 million (2009/10)

Beneficial area

Greater Birmingham.

Nechells Baths, Nechells Park Road, Nechells, Birmingham B7 5PD
Tel: 0121 322 5560
Fax: 0121 322 5579

Email: team@bbccf.org.uk
Website: www.bhamfoundation.co.uk
Correspondent: Karen Argyle, Grants Officer
Trustees: David Bucknall, Chair; John Andrews; Kay Cadman; Angela Henry; Shamiela Ahmed; David Scard; Richard Harris; Peter Grace; John Matthews.
CC Number: 1048162

Information available

Accounts were available from the Charity Commission. Full details on the foundation's website.

Summary

The Birmingham Community Foundation was established in 1995 to help local people 'create, encourage and resource initiatives that would alleviate poverty and deprivation, and also promote employment within our community'.

The foundation's mission is to:
- help local people provide local solutions to local community needs
- build an endowment fund to provide long-term, on-going support
- stimulate new initiatives and partnerships within the community
- enable people and business with the opportunity to maximise their charitable giving.

The foundation aims to build up an endowment fund by encouraging local individuals, businesses and other organisations to give donations and consequently invest in the long-term future of their local community.

Like many community foundations, it administers individual funds which enable donors to direct their contributions to specific locations and/or target groups. The foundation also distributes money from statutory sources. Small grants are generally given to community based groups involved in activities that regenerate and build communities, however priority is given to those projects which:
- encourage community responsibility
- develop community capacity
- are unable to access other forms of funding
- do not duplicate other work being done within the area.

Grantmaking

The Birmingham Community Foundation manages a number of funds, which are summarised below. Though, it should be noted that grant schemes often change quickly and as such, potential applicants are advised to consult the foundation's website for the latest information before applying.

Fairshare

The Fair Share Fund is a ten-year project, which targets those areas that suffer considerable disadvantage and have previously received less than their fair share of National Lottery funding. The places in Greater Birmingham eligible for funding are: Dudley – St Andrews, Sandwell – Great Bridge, Walsall – Alumwell and North Solihull.

More information on the local priorities and how to apply is available on the foundation's website.

The Midcounties Co-operative Community Fund

This fund is designed to benefit the communities where the Midcounties Co-operative trades. The fund is keen to receive applications from voluntary and community organisations that are able to demonstrate that their project will build their capacity and bring benefit to the local community and in doing so meet at least one of the following criteria:
- encourage community responsibility
- develop community capacity
- demonstrate 'Co-operative Values'

Grants are up to a maximum of £2,000 and groups are advised to apply only for the amount they need to purchase an item of equipment or to fund a project.

Note: The foundation is administering this fund in the Black Country (Dudley, Sandwell, Walsall and Wolverhampton) but there are other areas taking part. Please see the foundation's website for further information and guidance on how to apply.

Letisha and Charlene Educational Awards

This fund was established in memory of Charlene Ellis and Letisha Shakespeare, who were innocent victims of a drive-by shooting in January 2003. The organisation consists of the families of the two girls and representatives from Aston Pride New Deal for Communities, the Birmingham Mail, Aston Manor School, Birmingham City University and Birmingham Community Foundation.

Each award offers support for one year for people living in North West Birmingham who are aged 16 or over and who need financial help to continue with their education. Awards are up to £2,000.

Further information is available on the foundation's website and from the information sheet provided by the fund.

Note: If none of the current funds are applicable, the foundation suggests that you complete a registration form so it can notify you of any relevant future funds. Registration forms are available directly from the foundation or to download from its website.

Exclusions

No funding is available for:
- projects operating outside the Greater Birmingham area
- general appeals or large national charities (except for local branches working specifically for local people)
- individuals, for whatever purpose
- organisations and individuals in the promotion of political or religious ideology.

Applications

Refer to the foundation's website for full details of how to apply to the various programmes currently being administered.

Blackheart Foundation (UK) Limited

General, health, education and sport

Beneficial area

UK.

10 Maresfield Gardens, London NW3 5SU
Tel: 020 7016 4848

Correspondent: Richard Lewis, Trustee
Trustees: Richard Lewis; Ilina Singh; Claire Heath.
CC Number: 1136813

Information available

Basic information was available from the Charity Commission.

The foundation was established in 2010 by Richard Lewis, chief executive of Tristan Capital Partners. Mr Lewis also serves on the board of several other charitable ventures, including the I I Foundation, Teach First and Eastside Young Leaders Academy.

The objects of the foundation are to support individuals and organisations primarily in the areas health, education and sport.

Applications

In writing to the correspondent.

The Bluston Charitable Settlement

Jewish, general

£630,000 (2010/11)

Beneficial area

Mostly UK.

c/o Prism, 20 Seymour Mews, London W1H 6BQ
Tel: 020 7486 7760
Correspondent: Martin Paisner
Trustees: Daniel Dover; Martin Paisner.
CC Number: 256691

Information available

Accounts were available at the Charity Commission.

The trust has general charitable purposes, although in practice most grants are given to Jewish organisations. The level of grantmaking has been increasing over recent years, and the trust states that it intends to maintain the current level in the near future.

It is the trust's policy to support the following:

▪ the education of children
▪ capital expenditure projects for schools and other educational establishments
▪ the welfare of the underprivileged
▪ hospitals and medical institutions
▪ universities for specific research projects.

In 2010/11 the trust had assets of just over £8.6 million and an income of £466,000. Grants were made during the year to 20 organisations totalling £630,000.

Beneficiaries included: Norwood (£100,000); Ohel Torah Beth David (£90,000); Our Children (£50,000); UK Friends of IDC (£32,000); Prisoners Abroad (£25,000); Cancerkin (£19,000); Holocaust Educational Trust (£15,000); JAMI (£10,000); and Maccabi GB (£5,000). The trust has a list of regular beneficiaries.

Exclusions

No grants to individuals.

Applications

In writing to the correspondent. The trustees meet annually in the spring.

Community Foundation for Bournemouth, Dorset and Poole

Community

£717,000 (2009/10)

Beneficial area

The county of Dorset, including the unitary authorities of Bournemouth and Poole.

Abchurch Chambers, 24 St Peter's Road, Bournemouth BH1 2LN
Tel: 01202 292255
Email: grants@dorsetcf.org
Website: www. dorsetcommunityfoundation.org/
Correspondent: Tina Baker
Trustees: Gary Bentham; Richard Cossey; Gordon Page; Christopher Morle; Michael Green; Jane Raimes; Gwyn Bates; Richard Dimbleby; Ashley Rowlands; Christopher Beale.
CC Number: 1122113

Information available

Accounts were on file at the Charity Commission. Information was available on the foundation's website.

'The Community Foundation for Bournemouth, Dorset and Poole is a charitable trust and was founded in 2000. It is managed by a board of trustees who represent the voluntary, statutory and business sectors across Dorset. It was formed to support community initiatives across the whole county of Dorset, including the unitary authorities of Bournemouth and Poole.'

A member of the Community Foundation Network, the foundation administers a variety of funding programmes for projects in Bournemouth, Dorset and Poole.

Programmes

Available funding changes on an ongoing basis, please see the foundation's website for up-to-date information. Some current programmes include:

Dorset County Community Fund
Grants of up to £7,500 are available to build the capacity of the voluntary and community organisations of all sizes working across Dorset to support local communities.

Surviving Winter Fund
Grants available to organisations for the provision of cold weather related services and support to elderly people within Dorset.

Bournemouth Communities Fund
Small grants are available for charities and organisations meeting the needs of local communities in Bournemouth.

Fair Share
A strategic funding programme benefiting the former Ward of Wallisdown in Bournemouth.

Comic Relief
Grants are available from £1,000 up to £10,000 for community groups/ organisations tackling economic and social deprivation in their local communities. Projects should be run by people directly affected by the issues they are dealing with and priority will be given to small, locally based groups or organisations in areas of disadvantage.

The Meggitt Fund

This fund is managed on behalf of local company Meggitt PLC who are an international aerospace, defence and electronics group based at Bournemouth International Airport. In partnership with the foundation this fund seeks to support small voluntary/community groups working to benefit local people in the Bournemouth, Poole and/or Dorset area. Grants of £50 to £500 are available.

Dorset Education Trust

Aims to support children and young people through education, training and personal development.

In 2009/10 the foundation had assets of £778,000 and an income of £898,000. Grants were made totalling £717,000.

Beneficiaries included: The Listening Ear (£69,000); Bournemouth Churches Housing Association (£43,000); Action for Children (£38,000); Coastal Credit Union Ltd (£37,000); Dorset Race Equality Council (£25,000); Family Matters (£17,000); AFCB Sports Trust (£14,500); Vita Nova (£10,000); South Coast Tigers (£5,000); Poole Sailability (£3,000); Treewise Co-operative Ltd (£2,500); Pulse (£1,400); and 1st Alderholt Brownies (£1,000).

Exclusions

Each fund has different criteria, please consult the website for up to date eligibility.

Applications

Contact the foundation for details of up-to-date programmes. An online contact form is available on the foundation's website.

Common applicant mistakes

'Not checking criteria for funds.'

The Bowland Charitable Trust

Young people, education, general

£811,000 (2010)

Beneficial area

North west England.

Activhouse, Philips Road, Blackburn, Lancashire BB1 5TH
Tel: 01254 290433
Correspondent: Carol Fahy, Trustee
Trustees: Tony Cann; Ruth A Cann; Carole Fahy; Hugh D Turner.
CC Number: 292027

Information available

Accounts were available from the Charity Commission.

Although its beneficial area covers the whole of the UK, in practice grants are mainly made in north west England. 'Projects may be funded over varying periods of time, but the majority are made as one off payments.'

In 2010 the trust had assets of £9.3 million and an income of £601,500. Grants were made totalling £811,000.

Beneficiaries of grants approved in the year included: National Maths Case Studies Project (£560,500); General Assembly of Unitarian and Free Christian Churches (£154,000); School of the Future (£103,000); Thwaites Empire Theatre (£50,000); The Foyer Foundation (£28,000); Ribcaged (£20,000); King Edward Street Chapel (£15,000); Home Start Hyndburn (£5,000); Ruskin Foundation; The Rossendale Trust (£2,500); and Cancer Research (£1,500).

Applications

The charity invites applications for funding of projects from individuals, charities and other charitable organisations. The applications are made directly to the trustees, who meet regularly to assess the applications.

The Liz and Terry Bramall Charitable Trust

General, social welfare

£4 million (2009/10)

Beneficial area

UK, in practice mainly Yorkshire.

c/o Gordons LLP, Riverside West, Whitehall Road, Leeds, West Yorkshire LS1 4AW
Tel: 0113 227 0100
Fax: 0113 227 0113
Correspondent: Terry Bramall, Trustee
Trustees: Terry Bramall; Liz Bramall; Suzannah Allard; Rebecca Bletcher.
CC Number: 1121670

Information available

Accounts were available at the Charity Commission.

Registered in 2007, this is the charitable trust of Terry Bramall, former chairman of Keepmoat, builders of social housing in northern and central England. It was reported that the Bramall family sold their stake in the company in 2007 for £563 million. Terry Bramall is also a director of Doncaster Rovers FC.

The specific objects and areas of interest noted in the trust's accounts are as follows:

In practice the normal areas of support are in respect of the Christian faith, for the benefit of the public in accordance with the statements of belief of the Church of England, and the promotion for the benefit of the public of urban or rural regeneration, in areas of social and economic deprivation. In the prior year, the objectives of the trust were updated during the year to include the relief of sickness and the advancement of health. On 30 December 2009 the objectives of the charity were broadened further to include education and health as well as support for arts and culture. [...] It is unlikely that the trustees would support the total cost of a project and applicants should be able to demonstrate that funds have been raised or are in the process of being raised from other sources.

In 2009/10 the trust had assets of £108 million and an income of £1.9 million. Grants were made to 59 organisations totalling £4 million, a significant increase on the previous year when grants totalled £822,000. Grantmaking is likely to continue at this new level in the near future as the trust is attempting to reduce its level of free reserves.

By far the largest grant of the year was given to the University of Birmingham (£2 million) for a new auditorium for music, opera, drama and lectures as well as state of the art rehearsal and practice rooms and recording facilities.

Other beneficiaries included: Royal Horticultural Society – Harlow Carr (£500,000); Sprotborough PCC (£250,000 in three grants); Yorkshire Air Ambulance (£200,000); PPR Foundation and St Michael's Hospice (£100,000 each); When You Wish Upon a Star – Grimsby (£50,000); Harrogate Theatre (£40,000); Bradford Cathedral (£35,000); Chicken Shed and Artlink East Yorkshire (£20,000 each); St Andrews Roundhay Church (£15,000); British Association for Adoption and Fostering (£10,000); Otley Deanery Youth and Children's Network (£6,000); Enterprise Education Trust (£4,000); and Beyond the Streets and Whizz Kids – London (£1,000 each).

Applications

In writing to the correspondent. The trust also states that 'unsolicited requests from national charities will generally only be considered if there is some public benefit to the Yorkshire region'.

The Breadsticks Foundation

Healthcare and education

£1 million (2009/10)

Beneficial area

UK, Africa and Asia.

35 Canonbury Square, London
N1 2AN
Tel: 020 7288 0667

Email: info@breadsticksfoundation.org
Website: www.breadsticksfoundation.org
Correspondent: Beatrix Payne, Trustee
Trustees: Beatrix Payne, Chair; Dr Yolande Knight; Dr Paul Ballantyne; Beatrice Roberts; Trevor Macy.
CC Number: 1125396

Information available

Accounts were available from the Charity Commission. The foundation also has a helpful website.

The foundation was established in 2008 to support organisations involved in improving the provision of healthcare and education. The foundation supports projects based in the UK, Africa and Asia.

The following information is taken from the foundation's website:

> The Breadsticks Foundation supports programmes aimed at improving the quality of life within marginalised communities and creating a platform for long-term economic independence. We have a particular interest in health, education and child and youth development. Where possible, we will help talented individuals within a community to become change-makers. Where necessary, we work directly with other grant-making foundations to achieve these aims.
>
> We aim to build close, long-term partnerships with the organisations we support. Where possible we aim to provide partner organisations with long-term core funding but will also provide project-related grants. Grant sizes vary.
>
> We participate closely in monitoring and evaluation with our partners and, in order to achieve this, require quarterly progress reports on each grant. In assessing a grant application, we will analyse each applicant's financial reports and accounts and will conduct telephone and face-to-face interviews.

In 2009/10 the foundation had assets of £341,000 and an income of £1.2 million, most of which came from the anonymous settlor of the foundation. Grants were made to 11 organisations totalling £1 million.

The beneficiaries were: Class Act Educational Services – Johannesburg (£377,500); Hope & Homes for Children (£200,000); The Medical Foundation (£153,000); Action on Disability and Development (£78,000); Kids in Need of Education

(£62,500); Lao Basic Needs (£61,500); Zisize Educational Team (£25,500); Lao Disabled Women (£22,500); Christine Revell Children's Home (£17,500); Raphael Support & Skills Development (£5,000); and Volunteer Reading Help (£1,200).

Applications

The foundation invites applications for core funding activities or project grants. Applications are invited through the foundation's website. Applicants submit an initial summary application outlining key activities, existing funding and intended use for the applied funding. Initial applications are reviewed by the Executive Committee [trustees] who then begin a second round of information-gathering interviews including scrutiny of financial reports. Grants are usually [awarded] on an annual basis , with some grants nominally committed for up to five years subject to successful monitoring, evaluation and trustee review. Progress reports are usually requested quarterly, with an additional annual report submission. After renewal, grant progress reports may be adjusted to biannual reporting. Funding agreements are mutually agreed and signed prior to the commencement of the grant.

British Record Industry Trust

Performing arts, music therapy, general

£725,000 (2010)

Beneficial area

Worldwide, in practice UK.

Riverside Building, County Hall, Westminster Bridge Road, London
SE1 7JA
Email: alaina.harris@bpi.co.uk
Website: www.britttrust.co.uk
Correspondent: Aliana Harris
Trustees: John Craig, Chair; Andy Cleary; Derek Green; Paul Burger; David Kassner; Rob Dickins; Tony Wadsworth; Jonathan Morrish; Geoff Taylor; David Bryant; Mervyn Lyn.
CC Number: 1000413

Information available

Accounts were available at the Charity Commission.

The BRIT Trust was established in 1989 and is entirely funded by the music industry. Its mission is to give young people a chance to express their musical creativity regardless of race, class, sex or ability and to encourage them in the exploration and pursuit of educational, cultural and therapeutic benefits emanating from music. This includes the BRIT School in Croydon – the only non-fee paying performing arts school in the UK.

The trust's main source of funding is the BRIT Awards and all profits from the awards go to the trust. The income of the trust is primarily distributed between the BRIT School for Performing Arts and Technology in Croydon and Nordoff-Robbins Music Therapy, although smaller donations are also made to a number of other charities.

The trustees have no direct control over the funding received from the BRIT Awards and as a result of this uncertainty in their long term funding, have established a policy to hold back a proportion of otherwise distributable income to ensure a reasonable and realistic level of reserves. This will be the subject of regular review.

In 2010 the trust had assets of £6.8 million and an income of over £1.3 million, including £860,000 from BRIT Awards Limited. Grants were made to six organisations totalling £725,000.

As in previous years, the beneficiaries of the largest grants were the BRIT School for the Performing Arts & Technology (£350,000) and Nordoff-Robbins Music Therapy (£300,000).

The other beneficiaries were: Kickz (£47,000); Drugscope (£25,000); Haiti Earthquake Appeal (£1,700); and the Paul Walter Award (£1,000).

Exclusions

No scholarships or grants to individuals. No capital funding projects are considered. Only registered charities in the UK are supported.

Applications

The trust considers all applications that meet its criteria within the mission statement 'to encourage young people in the exploration and pursuit of educational, cultural or therapeutic benefits emanating from music'. The trust has a long standing relationship with a number of organisations that receive funding each year and consequently is limited to the amount of resources it can offer. Applicants should visit the trust's website and complete the on-line application form or contact the correspondent for further information.'

Please note: the trust states that applications where the organisation or project is known to the UK music industry have an advantage. There is space to include an industry contact on the application form.

Common applicant mistakes

'Applicants not understanding the nature of the trust's funding.'

The Bromley Trust

Human rights, prison reform, conservation

£825,000 (2009/10)

Beneficial area

Worldwide.

Studio 7, 2 Pinchin Street, Whitechapel, London E1 1SA
Tel: 020 7481 4899
Email: info@thebromleytrust.org.uk
Website: www.thebromleytrust.org.uk
Correspondent: Teresa Elwes, Grants Executive
Trustees: Anne Elizabeth Lady Prance, Chair; Bryan Blamey; Dr Judith Brett; Peter Alan Edwards; Jean Ritchie; Anthony John Roberts.
CC Number: 801875

Information available

Accounts were available from the Charity Commission. The trust has a clear and helpful website.

General

In 1989 Keith Bromley set up the Bromley Trust which he termed 'the most important work of my life' committed to 'offset man's inhumanity to man'; he endowed the trust with much of his fortune. The trust supports charities concerned with human rights, prison reform and conservation and sustainability. This well organised and focused trust also offers other organisations with similar interests and objectives the chance to participate in a network of like-minded groups.

In later years, the settlor had been particularly concerned with the plight of prisoners in overcrowded prisons and the waste of public resources spent building more and more prisons. He understood the cycle of re-offending and saw the value of supporting offenders to learn a trade that would enable them to gain employment after release.

In 2004 the Bromley Trust set up three awards in memory of Keith Bromley. Three charities involved with prison reform, were chosen for this additional support. They were the Butler Trust, the Hardman Trust and the Prison Reform Trust.

Additionally, the Koestler Award Trust, which encourages and rewards a variety of creative endeavours culminating in an annual exhibition of work from prison, probation and secure psychiatric hospitals, has named a prize after Keith Bromley as he had been such a support to their work over the years. The Bromley Trust chose nature photography as this had been a great interest of the settlor's throughout his life. The Keith Bromley Award for Outstanding Nature Photography was presented for the first time at the Koestler exhibition in 2004.

In 2008 the trust held a series of meetings with other like-minded grantmakers to agree on how they could take action to directly bring about change in response to the government's Corston Report, which looked into issues affecting vulnerable female offenders and how they should be treated. The result was an unprecedented agreement to collectively develop and fund a post (for 18 months) to work with independent funders and the government with an aim of implementing the recommendations from the report. The Corston Independent Funders' Coalition was established and it continues to support a shift from imprisonment to community sentencing for vulnerable women offenders. For further information visit: www.corstoncoalition.org.uk.

Aims and guidelines

The aims of the trust are as follows:

Human rights

To combat violations of human rights and help victims of torture, refugees from oppression and those who have been falsely imprisoned; to help those who have suffered severe bodily or mental hurt through no fault of their own and if need be help their dependants; and to try in some way to offset man's inhumanity to man.

The trust supports charities campaigning for human rights with particular focus given to the protecting the 'least powerful': oppressed refugees, people who are discriminated against and persecuted, and women whose rights are routinely and systematically violated. Support is also given to charities working with individuals and communities in the areas of: trafficking and slavery, torture and abuse, persecution and cruel and unreasonable punishment.

Prison reform

To promote prison reform within the United Kingdom with particular emphasis on the reduction of re-offending.

The trust is committed to the reduction of overcrowding in UK prisons through the reduction of re-offending. It also supports the implementation of the Corston Report for women offenders. Campaigning charities and service providers are supported, particularly charities that aim to reduce the cycle of re-offending by the furtherance of education and skill training thereby helping the offender to engage more successfully in society on release. The trust is particularly interested in supporting offenders working in catering and the environment.

Conservation and sustainability

To oppose the extinction of the world's fauna & flora and the destruction of the environment for wildlife and for mankind worldwide.

The trust makes grants to charities involved in conservation, biodiversity and sustainability, particularly those working to protect the Mata Atlantica (Atlantic Rainforest), marine diversity and the Arctic and Antarctic. Innovative work to address climate change and sustainability may also gain support.

The trust is interested in human rights and the environment and the protection of land rights, especially for those who are marginalized and discriminated against.

Guidelines

The trust's criteria for awarding grants are listed on its website as follows:

- we can only accept completed application forms – we will not consider any other form of application
- we can only make grants to UK-registered charities, and are unable to accept any applications from other organisations
- we will only support charities that fall within our remit and focus areas
- we are happy to work with other grant-making foundations to support worthwhile work within our focus areas
- we particularly encourage crossover between our different funding streams and focus areas
- we tend to provide unrestricted support to organisations that fall wholly within our remit; if you feel that you do not entirely fit within these criteria, but wish to apply for a specific project or element of your work then please send an email to info@thebromleytrust.org.uk and we will advise you on making an application
- as we make unrestricted grants, please do not request a specific amount, the size of our grants is made at the discretion of the trustees
- we are a small grantmaker with limited funds and a high demand. We are only able to support a fraction of the applications that we receive.

The trust's website contains full information on recent grants to organisations, many of which are supported on a regular basis. One-off grants are occasionally made, but are infrequent. The trust prefers to give larger amounts to fewer charities rather than spread its income over a large number of small grants.

Grantmaking in 2009/10

In 2009/10 the trust had assets of £16 million and an income of £580,000. Grants were made to 68 organisations totalling £825,000 and were distributed as follows:

Human rights	31	£403,000
Sustainability and conservation	18	£215,000
Prison reform and prison awards	19	£207,000

Beneficiaries included: ECPAT UK, Redress Trust, Prison Reform Trust and Ashden Awards (£25,000 each); Marine Conservation, Cape Farewell, Eden and HMP Dartmoor, and Anti-Slavery International (£20,000 each); London Detainee Support Group, Butler Trust, Deptford Churches Centre and REGUA (£15,000 each); Buglife, Clink, Moor Trees and Womankind Worldwide (£10,000 each); World Land Trust, Corston Independent Funders Coalition and Centre for Applied Human Rights (£5,000 each); and the Sherriff's and Recorder's Fund (£4,500).

Exclusions

Grants are only given to UK registered charities. The following are not supported:

- individuals
- expeditions
- scholarships, although in certain cases the trust supports research that falls within its aims (but always through a registered charity)
- statutory authorities, or charities whose main source of funding is via statutory agencies
- overseas development or disaster relief
- local conservation projects or charities that work with single species
- drug rehabilitation programmes.

Applications

New applicants are directed, where possible, to the trust's website, where the trust's criteria, guidelines and application process are available.

An application form can be accessed from the website for charities that fit the trust's remit, and should be completed and returned via email to: applicant@thebromleytrust.org.uk. There is no strict page limit on completed application forms but the average length is approximately 8–10 pages. Applicants are asked not to return applications which are significantly larger than this.

The trust aims to notify applicants within four to six weeks as to whether or not they are eligible for the next stage of the process. All charities are visited before a grant is made. The trustees meet twice a year in April and October.

Please note: the trust asks that organisations who have previously submitted an application do not submit any further requests for funding. Applicant details are held on the trust's database and if any assistance can be provided in the future, they will make contact.

Common applicant mistakes

'Applicants not fully reading the criteria and guidelines on the trust's website.'

The Bruntwood Charity

General, social welfare

Beneficial area
UK.

Bruntwood Ltd, City Tower, Piccadilly Plaza, Manchester M1 4BT
Tel: 0161 237 3883
Correspondent: Sally Hill, Trustee
Trustees: Katharine Vokes; Andy Allan; Rob Yates; Sally Hill; Kathryn Graham.
CC Number: 1135777

Information available
Basic information was available from the Charity Commission.

The charity was established in 2010 for general charitable purposes. It is the charity of Bruntwood Ltd, a company which owns and manages commercial property and offices space in Birmingham, Leeds, Manchester and Liverpool. The founder of Bruntwood is Michael Oglesby of the Oglesby Charitable Trust.

Applications
In writing to the correspondent.

Brushmill Ltd

Jewish causes, education, social welfare

£374,000 (2009/10)

Beneficial area
Worldwide.

76 Fairholt Road, London N16 5HN
Correspondent: Mrs C Getter, Trustee
Trustees: C Getter, Chair; J Weinberger; Mrs E Weinberger.
CC Number: 285420

Information available
Accounts were available from the Charity Commission, without a list of grants.

Established in 1982, the trust gives grants for education, the relief of poverty and to Jewish causes.

In 2009/10 the trust had an income of £381,000, entirely from donations. Grants were made totalling £374,000, although a list of beneficiaries was not available.

Previous beneficiaries have included Bais Rochel, Friends of Yeshivas Shaar Hashomaim and Holmleigh Trust.

Applications
In writing to the correspondent.

The Burdett Trust for Nursing

Healthcare

£667,000 to organisations (2010)

Beneficial area
Mostly UK.

SG Hambros Trust Company, Norfolk House, 31 St James's Square, London SW1Y 4JR
Tel: 020 7597 3000
Fax: 020 7702 9263
Email: administrator@ burdettnursingtrust.org.uk
Website: www.burdettnursingtrust. org.uk
Correspondent: Shirley Baines, Administrator
Trustees: Alan Gibbs, Chair; Dame Christine Beasley; Jack Gibbs; Bill Gordon; Dr Khim Horton; Andrew Martin-Smith; Lady Henrietta St George; Eileen Sills; Jo Webber.
CC Number: 1089849

Information available
Accounts were available from the Charity Commission. The trust has a good website.

The Burdett Trust for Nursing is an independent charitable trust named after Sir Henry Burdett KCB, the founder of the Royal National Pension Fund for Nurses. The trust was set up in 2001.

The following is taken from the trust's helpful website and explains the grant making policy:

> Nurses, midwives and the allied health professions make up the majority of the healthcare workforce and play a pivotal role in direct care to patients. The trust targets its grants at projects that are nurse-led, using its funds to empower nurses and make significant improvements to the patient care environment.

> The Burdett Trust for Nurses makes grants to support the nursing contribution to health care within three key priority areas:
> - *Building nursing research capacity:* to support clinical nursing research and research addressing policy, leadership development and delivery of nursing care.
> - *Building nurse leadership capacity:* supporting nurses in their professional development to create a cadre of excellent nursing and allied health professionals who will become leaders of the future and foster excellence and capacity-building in advancing the nursing profession.
> - *Supporting local nurse-led initiatives:* to support nurse-led initiatives that make a difference at local level and are focused explicitly on improving care for patients and users of services.

> The Burdett Trust for Nursing makes grants through the following grant programmes:

> **1. The Empowerment Programme**
> The trust invites proposals from charities, non-profit and public organisations that wish to take advantage of opportunities that have arisen from recent developments in the health sector. The trust is interested in supporting projects that will:

- transform services at the hospital-community interface by empowering nurses and other health professionals to provide the right care, in the right place, at the right time
- empower health visitors to provide a comprehensive service by helping them to reassert their roles in promoting health and preventing ill health, particularly among vulnerable groups and communities.

Two levels of award are available: for projects likely to fall within the range of £25,000 – £50,000, and for more substantial projects which are likely to fall within the range of £100,000 – £200,000. More may be available for exceptional projects of national significance.

2. Burdett Bursaries

The Burdett Bursaries programme will make bursary awards of up to £5,000 to nurses, midwives and allied health professionals who wish to undertake post-graduate study. Applicants must read the programme guidance material carefully and applications must be submitted via the online application form.

3. Funding Partners

To maximise the impact of their grants the trustees have appointed the following charitable organisations to manage grants programmes on their behalf:

- Help the Hospices (www.helpthehospices.org.uk)
- Florence Nightingale Foundation (www.florence-nightingale-foundation.org.uk)
- Foundation of Nursing Studies (www.fons.org)
- Queen's Nursing Institute (www.qni.org.uk)
- Roald Dahl's Marvellous Children's Charity (www.roalddahlcharity.org)
- ICN Global Nursing Leadership Institute 2011 (www.icn.ch)

The trustees regularly review their funding partner arrangements and consider proposals from organisations that would like to become a Burdett Funding Partner. Trustees will publish information about becoming a Burdett Funding Partner on its website when they are considering appointing additional partners.

4. Proactive Grants Programme

Burdett Trust for Nursing aims to be more than a reactive grant-making charity. It strives to be a catalyst for change, an active player in improving the health and well-being of patients. To this end the trustees participate in dialogue and share new ideas with grantee organisations, service providers, other funders and government agencies. The trust aims to create opportunities to engage nursing stakeholders in collaborative problem-solving and program development.

Through the Proactive Grants Program trustees work with a wide range of public and private partners to advance the foundation's long-term goals. Proactive grants are initiated by the Burdett Trust for Nursing.

Please note: the trustees **do not** accept unsolicited applications for the Proactive Grants Programme.

Grants in 2010

In 2010 the trust had assets of £71 million and a consolidated income of £1.2 million. Grants committed during the year totalled £959,000, of which £667,000 was given to institutions and the remaining £292,000 to individuals.

Institutional beneficiaries were: International Council for Nurses, Junius S Morgan Benevolent Fund, Roald Dahl Foundation, and Florence Nightingale Foundation.

Exclusions

Consult the relevant programme guidance for information on the funding criteria.

Applications

See the trust's website for further information on how to apply for funding. Applicants interested in the 'Funding Partners' programme should consult the appropriate partner website (listed above).

The Audrey and Stanley Burton 1960 Charitable Trust

Jewish causes, health, arts, education and social needs

£3.5 million (2009/10)

Beneficial area

Worldwide. In practice, mainly UK with a preference for Yorkshire.

Trustee Management Ltd,
19 Cookridge Street, Leeds LS2 3AG
Tel: 0113 243 6466
Email: trustee.mgmt@btconnect.com
Correspondent: Keith Pailing, Trustee Management Ltd

Trustees: Amanda Burton; Raymond Burton; Jeremy Burton.
CC Number: 1028430

Information available

Accounts were available at the Charity Commission.

The trust was established for general charitable purposes at the discretion of the trustees by an initial gift from S H Burton who died in 1991.

In 2009/10 the trust had assets of £8 million and an income of £3.2 million, which included a donation of £3.1 million from the estate of Mrs A R Burton. Grants were made to 109 organisations totalling £3.5 million and were distributed as follows:

Jewish/Israel	21	£1 million
Health	23	£924,000
Third World and overseas	12	£594,000
Social and welfare	34	£515,000
Education and arts	19	£413,000

Beneficiaries included: Leeds Jewish Housing Association (£500,000); Medical Foundation Care Victims of Torture (£160,000 in two grants); Médecins Sans Frontières and Donisthorpe Hall (£150,000 each); Save the Children UK and UNICEF (£100,000 each); Northern Ballet Theatre (£80,000); Harrogate Theatre (£50,000); Crisis and Anne Frank Trust (£25,000 each); Brain and Spine Foundation (£11,000 in two grants); RHS (£10,000); Diabetes UK (£5,000); Harrogate CAB (£2,000); and Council of Christians and Jews (£1,000).

Exclusions

No grants to individuals.

Applications

In writing to the correspondent. Unsuccessful applicants are not always notified.

The James Caan Foundation

Social welfare, education

Beneficial area

UK and Pakistan.

Hamilton Bradshaw, 23 Grosvenor Street, London W1K 4QL

Tel: 020 7399 6700

Email: hanah@thejcf.co.uk

Website: www.thejcf.co.uk

Correspondent: Hanah Caan, Trustee

Trustees: James Caan; Deepak Jalan; Hanah Caan.

CC Number: 1136617

Information available

Information was available from the Charity Commission. The foundation also has a useful website.

Registered with the Charity Commission in 2010, this is the charitable foundation of James Caan, entrepreneur and former panellist on the Dragon's Den television programme. The objects of the foundation are broadly social welfare and education in the UK and Caan's native Pakistan.

The foundation is currently focused on the 'Build a Village Project' – constructing villages in Pakistan to help those who were affected by the 2010 floods. A full description of the project and details on the other individuals and organisations involved can be found on the foundation's website.

Previously, Caan, either personally or through the foundation, has supported organisations in the UK and Pakistan including: Prince's Trust; NSPCC; Care Foundation; BBC Children in Need; Big Issue; Comic Relief; Sport Relief; vInspired; Marie Curie Cancer Care; Mosaic; and the British Asian Trust.

Applications

Note the following statement from the foundation's website:

> We are currently not providing funding to other organisations, individuals or projects, as we are concentrating all our efforts and funds on the 'Build a Village Project' in Pakistan. We would therefore ask that you kindly consider this when thinking of sending an enquiry, as we are not in a position to offer financial support to other projects at the moment and are unable to respond to such requests.

The William A Cadbury Charitable Trust

Local welfare and disability charities, environment and conservation, Quaker charities and international development

£693,000 (2009/10)

Beneficial area

West Midlands, especially Birmingham and, to a lesser extent, UK, Ireland and overseas.

Rokesley, University of Birmingham, Bristol Road, Selly Oak, Birmingham B29 6QF

Tel: 0121 472 1464

Email: info@wa-cadbury.org.uk

Website: www.wa-cadbury.org.uk

Correspondent: Carolyn Bettis, Trust Administrator

Trustees: James Taylor; Rupert Cadbury; Katherine van Hagen Cadbury; Margaret Salmon; Sarah Stafford; Adrian Thomas; John Penny; Sophy Blandy; Janine Cobain.

CC Number: 213629

Information available

Accounts were available from the Charity Commission. The trust also has a clear and simple website.

This trust was established in 1923 for general charitable purposes. It describes its origins as follows:

> William was the second son of Richard Cadbury, who, with his younger brother George, started the manufacture of chocolate under the Cadbury name. He came from a family with strong Quaker traditions which influenced his whole life. It was this Quaker ethos which underpinned his commitment to the advancement of social welfare schemes in the city of Birmingham.
>
> William Cadbury established the trust soon after his two years as lord mayor of Birmingham from 1919 to 1921, wishing to give more help to the causes in which he was interested. One such was the building of the Queen Elizabeth Hospital, a medical centre with the space and facilities to bring together

> the small specialised hospitals scattered throughout Birmingham [...] He did much to encourage the city library and art gallery and a wide circle of Midland artists who became his personal friends. Through this charity, he also secured several properties for the National Trust.
>
> As time went on, members of his family were brought in as trustees and this practice has continued with representatives of the next three generations becoming trustees in their turn, so that all the present trustees are his direct descendants.

The trust's website outlines a clear grantmaking policy:

- requests for funding are invited from organisations registered with the Charity Commission for projects covered by one of the four grant programmes set out below
- grant applications can be submitted on-line via our website or if preferred by post
- applications are considered by trustees on a regular basis and small grants (up to a maximum of £2,000) are awarded monthly
- trustees meet every six months to award approximately twenty large grants of between £10,000 and £20,000 with an occasional maximum of £50,000
- trustees will consider applications for core costs as well as for development/project funding
- grants are normally awarded on a one-off basis and repeat applications are not usually considered within two years of the award
- feedback on project outcomes is appreciated in any case and is required in support of repeat applications
- bodies legally exempt from registration with the Charity Commission may also apply and small grants are sometimes made to unregistered groups in the West Midlands (who must nevertheless have a constitution, an elected committee and a bank account controlled by two or more committee members)
- all applicants will receive a response from the trust whether or not their application has been successful.

Birmingham and the West Midlands

- *community action* – community based and organised schemes (which may be centered on a place of worship) aimed at solving local problems and improving the quality of life of community members
- *vulnerable groups* – vulnerable groups include the elderly, children and young people, the disabled, asylum seekers and similar minorities

- *advice, mediation and counselling* – applicants must be able to point to the rigorous selection, training and monitoring of front line staff (particularly in the absence of formal qualifications) as well as to the overall need for the service provided
- *education and training* – trustees are particularly interested in schemes that help people of working age develop new skills in order to re-enter the jobs market
- *environment and conservation* – projects which address the impact of climate change and projects to preserve buildings and installations of historic importance and local interest
- *medical and healthcare* – covers hospices, self help groups and some medical research which must be based in and be of potential benefit to the West Midlands
- *the arts* – music, drama and the visual arts, museums and art galleries.

United Kingdom

- *the religious society of friends* – support for groups with a clear Quaker connection and support for the work of the Religious Society of Friends in the UK
- *penal affairs* – restorative justice, prison based projects and work with ex offenders aimed at reducing re-offending.

Ireland

- *peace and reconciliation*

International development

- *Africa* – the international development programme is concentrated on West Africa and work to reduce poverty on a sustainable basis in both rural and urban communities – schemes that help children access education are also supported
- *Asia and Eastern Europe*
- *South America.*

Note: The international development programme is heavily oversubscribed and unsolicited applications are unlikely to be successful.

Grantmaking

In 2009/10 the trust had assets of £25 million and an income of £1.8 million. Grants were made totalling £693,000. Grants were broken down by category as follows:

International development	£165,000
The arts	£70,000
Community	£61,000
Medical and health care	£51,000
Environment and conservation	£49,000
Society of Friends (Quaker)	£43,000
Mediation and counselling	£42,000
Education and training	£39,000
Disability	£38,000
Youth	£35,000
Penal affairs	£32,000

Care for the elderly	£22,000
Church: social	£18,000
Children	£15,000
Ireland	£13,000

Beneficiaries across all categories receiving £2,000 or more included: Concern Universal (£115,000 in total*); Birmingham Museum and Art Gallery – Staffordshire Appeal (£20,000); St Martin in the Bull Ring, Restore, Worgan Trust and the Centre for Alternative Technology (£15,000 each); Action for ME (£13,000); YWCA – Wolverhampton, Warwick Arts Centre, Herefordshire Primary Trust, Lench's Trust and Bournville Parish Church (£10,000 each); Dhaka Ahsania Mission (£8,300); the Haven – Wolverhampton (£7,000); SACDA Creche (£5,000); and Woodbrooke Quaker Study Centre (£3,000).

* the trust entered into a funding agreement with Concern Universal under which it will contribute £90,000 per year to specified projects in each of the three years commencing in March 2009. Emergency funding of £25,000 was also donated to the charity during the year.

Exclusions

The trust does not fund:

- individuals (whether for research, expeditions, educational purposes or medical treatment)
- projects concerned with travel, adventure, sports or recreation
- organisations which do not have UK charity registration (except those legally exempt).

Applications

Applications can be submitted via the trust's online application form. Alternatively, they can be made in writing to the correspondent, including the following information:

- charity registration number
- a description of the charity's aims and achievements
- the grant programme being applied to
- an outline and budget for the project for which funding is sought
- details of funds raised and the current shortfall
- if the organisation has received funding from the trust before, please provide brief details of the outcome of this project.

Applications are considered on a continuing basis throughout the year. Small grants are assessed each month. Large grants are awarded at the trustees' meetings held twice annually, normally in May and November. Applicants whose appeals are to be considered at one of the meetings will be notified in advance.

Edward Cadbury Charitable Trust

General

£1 million (2009/10)

Beneficial area

Worldwide, in practice mainly UK with a preference for the Midlands region.

Rokesley, University of Birmingham, Bristol Road, Selly Oak, Birmingham B29 6QF

Tel: 0121 472 1838
Fax: 0121 472 7013
Email: ecadburytrust@fsmail.net
Correspondent: Sue Anderson, Trust Manager
Trustees: Dr Charles E Gillett, Chair; Andrew Littleboy; Charles R Gillett; Nigel Cadbury; Hugh Marriott; Dr William Southall.
CC Number: 227384

Information available

Accounts were available at the Charity Commission.

The trust was established in 1945 for general charitable purposes. The main areas of grant giving cover education, Christian missions, the ecumenical movement and interfaith relations, the oppressed and disadvantaged, the arts and the environment.

Up to 100 grants a year are made, many of them small – between £500 and £5,000. These are normally awarded on a one-off basis for a specific purpose or part of a project. As well as its usual grantmaking, the trustees occasionally seek projects where a significant grant can make a real impact, and these grants can be very large. A few grants are awarded to UK groups working overseas and to overseas charities. Grants are rarely made to local charities outside the Midlands region.

In 2009/10 the trust had assets of £30 million compared with £21 million in 2008/09. This is largely due to the gradual recovery of the financial markets following the 2008 crash and the Kraft Foods Inc takeover of Cadbury plc in February 2010, which resulted in the disposal of the historically high weighting in Cadbury plc shares. The cash proceeds from the takeover are being held pending investment in what the trust hopes will be a more balanced and less risky portfolio. Income for the year totalled £827,000 and there were 73 grants made totalling just over £1 million. Grants were distributed as follows:

Education and training	£558,000
Conservation and the environment	£264,000
Community projects and integration	£80,000
Compassionate support	£67,000
Arts and culture	£51,000
Research	£31,000
Ecumenical mission and interfaith relations	£7,000

The trust gives the following description of the larger grants made during the year in its annual report:

Larger grants this year have included a grant of £500,000 to the University of Birmingham towards the completion of the Aston Webb Building, a project which will incorporate a concert hall providing resources not only for students but also a venue for musical events for the wider community; a £250,000 grant was given to the Ironbridge Gorge Museum Trust towards the tercentenary celebrations of the foundation of Coalbrookdale and for the restoration and sustainable development of many of the key buildings and historic monuments of the Ironbridge Gorge World Heritage Site; a £50,000 grant was awarded to Birmingham Museum and Art Gallery towards the acquisition costs of securing the Staffordshire Hoard and its ongoing conservation and research; a £25,000 grant was given to the Royal National Institute of Blind People to help rebuild Ruston School and Children's Home in Coventry, and a £50,000 grant to Middlemore Family Centre in Birmingham to help provide practical, emotional and social support in a community setting for children and families in crisis.

Other beneficiaries included: Responding to Conflict and Cancer Research UK (£25,000 each); St John of Jerusalem Eye Hospital and Trinity Christian Centre – Bournville (£10,000 each); Worldwide Volunteering, Plantlife, Sunfield Children's Home – Clent, and Love of Christ Ministries – South Africa (£5,000 each); Wolverhampton Interfaith Group, Transrural Trust and YMCA – Worcester (£2,500 each); and Birmingham Civic Society, No Panic, Prison Fellowship, Castle Bromwich Hall Gardens, Bookaid International and Deafness Research (£1,000 each).

Exclusions
Grants to registered charities only. No student grants or support for individuals.

Applications
In writing to the correspondent at any time and allowing three months for a response. Appeals should clearly and concisely give relevant information concerning the project and its benefits, an outline budget and how the project is to be funded initially and in the future. The organisation's latest annual report and accounts are also required.

Applications that do not come within the trust's policy may not be considered or acknowledged.

The Barrow Cadbury Trust and the Barrow Cadbury Fund

Young adult and criminal justice, migration and Europe, and poverty and exclusion

£4.5 million (2009/10)

Beneficial area
Unrestricted, with a preference for Birmingham and the Black Country (Wolverhampton, Dudley, West Bromwich, Smethwick or Sandwell).

Kean House, 6 Kean Street, London WC2B 4AS
Tel: 020 7632 9060
Fax: 020 7632 9061

Website: www.bctrust.org.uk
Correspondent: Asma Aroui, Programme Administrator
Trustees: Ruth Cadbury, Chair; Anna Southall; Anna Hickinbotham; Erica Cadbury; Nicola Cadbury; Tim Compton; Tamsin Rupprechter; Gordon Mitchell; Harry Serle.
CC Number: 1115476

Information available
Accounts were available online at the Charity Commission. The trust has an informative website.

Background
The Barrow Cadbury Trust was set up in 1920 as the Barrow & Geraldine S Cadbury Trust and merged with the Paul S Cadbury Trust in 1994. Barrow Cadbury was the eldest son of Richard Cadbury, one of the two brothers who established the Cadbury chocolate factory. His main interest lay in the Quakers, peacetime reconstruction and the relief of war victims after the First World War. He believed that the profits from industry should be diverted into social causes that would safeguard the true welfare of people. In later life, he took a great personal interest in the administration of his trust fund, personally overseeing accounts, writing cheques himself, and addressing envelopes in his own hand.

Barrow's wife, Geraldine Southall, was a thinker and innovator, descended from a family of inventors and entrepreneurs. She campaigned for reform of the penal system, and the treatment of children and young adults in the criminal justice system. Geraldine was an early believer in working with the policy-makers and opinion-formers of her day to achieve social change.

The trust aims to encourage a fair, equal, peaceful and democratic society. The income generated from the endowment left by Barrow Cadbury and his wife Geraldine is used to make grants to support groups, (usually registered charities) that are working to achieve the trust's objectives. Grants are made to enable groups to act as catalysts of social change.

The trust was incorporated as a company limited by guarantee in June

2006. In August 2006, the trustees of the unincorporated separate charity the Barrow Cadbury Trust (registered charity number: 226331) transferred the assets, subject to their liabilities, and activities of that charity to this trust.

The company, the Barrow Cadbury Fund, administered and managed by the trustees of the trust, is not a registered charity and supports non-charitable activity where this meets the trust's priorities. Please note: it is not possible to apply to the fund.

The trust aims to work in partnership with groups it funds to:

- build bridges between policy makers and grassroots activity
- find ways of identifying best practice from projects to help social change
- encourage new solutions to old problems.

General

The trust promotes social justice through grant-making, research, influencing public policy and supporting local communities. The following themes are prominent across the trust's work:

- supporting the independence and diversity of the voluntary sector
- addressing gender-based disadvantage
- addressing disadvantage based on race and ethnicity
- funding groups, projects and programmes in Birmingham and the West Midlands.

The trust seeks to develop partnerships with the many projects it supports and its main priority is to fund grassroots, user-led projects. Projects that are likely to have a high impact on social change at a policy or practice level are favoured. The trust looks for visionary proposals, often those that are considered radical or risky and great emphasis is placed on projects that are backed by strong leadership. Detailed examples of previously funded projects are available under each programme stream on the trust's website.

The average grant for grassroots projects is between £15,000 and £50,000 per year. The maximum grant is £50,000 per year for two years (£100,000 in total), though this size of award is usually only made to groups which have been funded previously. Around 30–40 grants of varying sizes are made each year.

The trust is willing to provide match-funding for projects. Organisations should make it clear in their initial proposal if they require match-funding or a contribution to a large project and state whether or not they have secured other funding already. If not, the trust may still consider the application but the final award may depend on securing all of the funding. Funding for core costs is considered but the amount applied for should reflect the amount of funding the organisation is applying for compared to the total organisational budget. Proposals must explain and justify what costs are being applied for. If the proposal passes the initial assessment the trust will work with the organisation to understand what the full cost of the project delivery will be, including a percentage of the overhead costs for the organisation.

The availability of funds generally dictates what grants the trust is able to make but it does try to ensure a fair geographic spread. The primary focus is on Birmingham and the West Midlands but applications from elsewhere are considered under some programmes. Please refer to the specific grant programme criteria below to see which geographic areas are covered.

The trust always receives more applications than it is able to fund. Even if the organisation is eligible and the project meets the criteria, the application may not be successful. Assessments are based on the grant criteria but decisions will be influenced by the finance available and the overall profile of the trusts grant making through the year.

Strategic objectives and programmes

The programme priorities are based on social objectives that are of particular concern to the trust. These are based on the existing strengths of work previously funded and current or possible areas of policy development. Projects will be chosen that the trust believes will help to achieve tangible shifts in policy and practice.

The trust aims to develop clusters of activity around each social objective. This means identifying complementary projects, that is, those that add value to the efforts of other groups supported by the trust. It also aims to find ways of connecting them across community sectors and with people involved at different levels of decision-making (including policy officials, practitioners and leaders of statutory and mainstream organisations). This approach means that it is unlikely that the trust will support more than one of the same type of project in any cluster.

The trust aims to stay flexible and respond to current circumstances and will monitor and regularly review its objectives. Any amendments will be highlighted on the trust's website and published each year but this should not affect any projects that it is already considering.

The trust's work is divided into three main areas of interest:

- criminal justice
- migration and Europe
- poverty and exclusion.

Funding is given through two key streams – policy and research grants and grassroots funding – under each area of interest.

The following information has been largely taken from the trust's detailed website:

Criminal justice

The trust's current criminal justice work includes:

- transition to adulthood (T2A) alliance
- young adults and criminal justice grassroots
- women offenders and women at risk of offending

Policy and research grants: Through this programme we will fund research or policy development work that cover issues relating to young adults in the criminal justice system.

Grassroots funding: We will consider projects that seek to reduce the risk of disadvantaged young people being involved in criminal activity, which are likely to provide one or more of the following:

- access to education, training or employment
- peer mentoring or access to positive role models
- work with young people to change their perspectives and behaviours

- development of young people's life skills and self esteem
- enabling of conflict resolution
- utilisation of restorative justice
- other activities, similar to the above, where part of a wider project intended to reduce offending.

Organisations funded through this programme must be able to show that they:

- have identified the barriers to inclusion faced by the individuals with whom they are working
- work with all sections of the community sharing those common barriers
- are working towards long-term resolution of the causes of offending
- seek to reduce offending
- are able to evaluate the impact of their work.

Our focus for grassroots funding is the Birmingham or the Black Country (Wolverhampton, Dudley, West Bromwich, Smethwick, Sandwell). However, by exception we will consider projects from outside this locality following discussion with the trust prior to application.

Migration and Europe

This programme aims to ensure that migration is managed in an equitable and socially just manner. The trust supports a number of projects that look to promote more balance and a greater diversity of perspectives in the migration debate. It also aims to explore what drives public concerns about immigration and how these concerns can be addressed.

Policy and research grants: We work with a wide range of think tanks, academics, politicians, campaigners and policy-makers on research and policy initiatives related to immigration and integration. This work is informed by the trust's commitment to reframing the debate on migration and asylum and to exploring ways in which immigration policy can be managed in a socially just and equitable manner.

Although our work is principally UK-focused, it is clear that national developments can only be accurately understood in a wider European or even global context. Hence we have also developed partnerships with organisations and counterparts in Europe and North America in order to share good practice at both policy and grassroots level.

Grassroots funding: We want to fund grassroots groups working with refugees, asylum seekers, undocumented migrants and other marginalised migrants. We seek to enable grassroots groups to support the most vulnerable migrants. We also seek to ensure that migrants are not excluded from the public debate on migration.

The types of projects and/or organisations we are likely to support include:

- those which help ensure that migrant, refugee and asylum seeker voices contribute to the public debate on migration
- those which seek to improve the lives of undocumented migrants or other groups facing extreme hardship
- those which promote a more balanced public debate on migration and asylum
- those which focus on addressing injustice or unequal treatment faced by some migrants
- those which address specific issues experienced by undocumented migrants, asylum seekers and refugees, such as the restriction of access to health care and education.

Grassroots funding for small organisations will focus on Birmingham and the Black Country (Wolverhampton, Dudley, West Bromwich, Smethwick, Sandwell).

Please note that we also support campaigning organisations and grassroots groups seeking to influence the public and policy debate on migration.

Poverty and exclusion

The trust's current work under this programme includes:

- policy development to explore how the UK's economic and financial systems could be changed to benefit poorer communities, increase financial inclusion and deliver social as well as economic outcomes
- providing grassroots grants to local community organisations in Birmingham and the Black Country (Wolverhampton, Dudley, West Bromwich, Smethwick, Sandwell) to strengthen communities so that they can and better cope with the changes they face
- building a body of evidence, through research work and grassroots grants, to show how new technology, community organising, community activism or other techniques can be used to strengthen communities in Birmingham and the Black Country and help them tackle local problems.

Policy and research grants: Through this programme we will fund research

or policy development work in two main areas:

- new ideas in economics – after the experience of the banking crisis and a world-wide recession, we are interested in the development of new economic policies for the UK that would [address] social injustice and economic inequalities
- community resilience – reductions in public spending and an emphasis on pushing power and responsibility for services down to the local level represents a major shift in the relationship between the individual and the state. We are interested in research and policy work that looks at how, in this context, communities can be strengthened and enabled to take part in and benefit from the policy changes.

We expect that, where possible, research projects will be based in or include a West Midlands element.

Grassroots funding: We want to fund projects that are rooted in local communities and that address the underlying causes of poverty and exclusion. We expect that projects that are funded through this programme will have a long-term impact on the individuals and communities they support: strengthening voices, increasing cohesion and helping ensure that deprived communities do not lose out as the control of public services shifts from national to local.

Organisations funded through this programme must be able to show that they:

- have identified the barriers to inclusion faced by the group with which they are working
- work with all sections of the community sharing those common barriers
- are working towards long-term resolution of the causes of exclusion
- have evidence to suggest that their approach will reduce barriers to inclusion
- are able to evaluate the impact of their work.

Types of project we might fund include:

- enabling local people to influence public policy
- equipping local communities with the skills to participate in the proposed shift towards local management and control of public services
- exploring new approaches to community development and community inclusion, such as co-production, harnessing the potential of new technology and community organising.

You can only apply for grassroots funding under this programme if your project is based in Birmingham or the Black Country (Wolverhampton,

Dudley, West Bromwich, Smethwick or Sandwell).

Grantmaking in 2009/10

In 2009/10 the trust had assets of £63 million and an income of £1.4 million. Grants made during the year totalled £4.5 million.

Previous beneficiaries include: Castle Vale Tenants' and Residents' Alliance (CVTRA), St Margaret's Community Trust, Young Foundation, IPPR, Centre for Crime and Justice Studies, Revolving Doors Agency, Stechford Youth Network, Key Birmingham, Migrants' Rights Network, Transatlantic Trends – Immigration Survey, Women for Refugee Women and Refugee Youth.

Detailed examples of funded projects are available under each programme stream on the trust's website.

Exclusions

The trust does not fund:

- activities that the public sector is responsible for
- animal welfare
- arts and cultural projects
- capital costs for building, refurbishment and outfitting
- endowment funds
- fundraising events or activities
- general appeals
- general health projects
- individuals
- housing
- learning disability
- medical research or equipment
- mental health
- children under 16 and older people
- physical disability
- the promotion of religion or belief systems
- schools
- sponsorship or marketing appeals
- unsolicited international projects.

The trust will not consider funding the following areas unless they are part of a broader project:

- *counselling drug and alcohol services* will only be considered under our criminal justice programme, and must be part of a broader project that meets the aims of the programme
- *environmental projects* will only be considered under the poverty and inclusion programme, and must be as part of a broader project that meets the aims of the programme

- *homelessness and destitution* will only be considered for those leaving the criminal justice system or in relation to our migration programme
- *IT training*
- *sporting activities*.

The trust asks that organisations planning a proposal that includes one of these services contact the grants team before submitting any application.

Colleges and universities can only apply under the policy and research funding streams.

Applications

The trust asks that potential applicants first contact the grants team, either by calling 020 7632 9068 or completing the online enquiry form.

Note: applicants for policy and research grants under the Criminal Justice and Migration and Europe categories are asked to email general@barrowcadbury.org.uk with their proposal or call 020 7632 9068.

If the trust is not able to support the project, it will notify the applicant within one month. It can take three to six months for proposals that the trust wishes to take forward to be assessed and presented to trustees, but the trust will be in contact during this period. Grants are approved by trustees at quarterly meetings throughout the year.

The Cadogan Charity

General charitable purposes, in particular, social welfare, medical research, service charities, animal welfare, education and conservation and the environment

£1.3 million (2009/10)

Beneficial area

Worldwide. In practice, UK with a preference for London and Scotland.

18 Cadogan Gardens, London SW3 2RP
Tel: 020 7730 4567
Fax: 0207 881 2300
Correspondent: P M Loutit, Secretary
Trustees: Earl Cadogan; Countess Cadogan; Viscount Chelsea; Lady Anna Thomson; The Hon. William Cadogan.
CC Number: 247773

Information available

Accounts were available at the Charity Commission.

The trust was established in 1966 for general charitable purposes and operates two funds namely, the general fund and the rectors' fund. The rectors' fund was created with a gift from Cadogan Holdings Company in 1985 to pay an annual amount to one or any of the rectors of Holy Trinity Church – Sloane Street, St Luke's Church and Chelsea Old Church. The general fund provides support for registered charities in a wide range of areas (see below).

In 2009/10 the trust had assets of £28 million and an income of £1.4 million. 41 grants were made totalling £1.3 million and were categorised as follows:

Social welfare in the community	27	£1.1 million
Military charities	6	£138,000
Conservation and the environment	1	£20,000
Medical research	3	£15,000
Animal welfare	3	£15,000
Education	1	£10,000

Beneficiaries included: NSPCC – Full Stop Campaign and Children's Trust – Tadworth (£300,000 each); St Paul's Cathedral Foundation (£250,000); In-Pensioners Mobility Fund (£100,000); Awareness Foundation (£50,000); Papal Visit (£25,000); London Playing Fields Foundation (£20,000); Rotalec – Life Education Centres (£15,000); Army Benevolent Fund, Animal Health Trust, Oatridge Agricultural College and Kippen Sports Development (£10,000 each); Royal British Legion (£6,000); British Heart Foundation and British Lung Foundation (£5,000 each); Focus – Kensington and Chelsea Foundation (£4,000); and Atlantic Salmon Trust (£1,000).

Exclusions

No grants to individuals.

Applications

In writing to the correspondent. However, please note that we have received information stating that the trust's funds are fully committed until 2016.

CAF (Charities Aid Foundation)

Capacity building for small and medium sized charities

Around £1.5 million

Beneficial area

Worldwide, in practice mainly UK.

25 Kings Hill Avenue, Kings Hill, West Malling, Kent ME19 4TA
Tel: 03000 123 000
Fax: 03000 123 001
Website: www.cafonline.org
Correspondent: Advisory Team
Trustees: Dominic Casserley, Chair; Sue Ashtiany; Robin Creswell; Philip Hardaker; Alison Hutchinson; Kim Lavely; Martyn Lewis; David Locke; Stephen Lovegrove; John Lorimer; Iain Mackinnon; Jenny Watson.
CC Number: 268369

Information available

Accounts were available at the Charity Commission.

In 1924, the National Council of Social Service (now the NCVO) set up a charities department to encourage more efficient giving to charity. In 1958 the charities department began administering deeds of covenant – the first ever means of charities receiving untaxed donations. The following year, the department was re-named the charities aid fund, the purpose of which was to distribute large sums of money for charitable purposes. In 1968, the fund published the first Directory of Grant Making Trusts – a pioneering effort to find new donors and new funding sources, (now researched and published by the Directory of Social Change).

The fund, under the new title, Charities Aid Foundation became an independent registered charity in 1974 and its objectives are to benefit any charitable organisation anywhere in the world. In practice, it works to raise the profile of charitable giving, lobby for tax breaks and provide an increasingly broad suite of services to charities and their supporters. The foundation helps both individual and company donors as well as charities.

CAF also provides banking and investment services to charities, as well as a fundraising support service to help organisations process and manage donations.

Guidelines

Main grant programme
Please note the following statement taken from the trust's website:

> CAF grant programmes support organisations working across all areas of charitable and civil society, including:
> - health and wellbeing (including sports and recreation)
> - children and youth
> - the elderly
> - education and training
> - social exclusion in the UK
> - international development
> - environment and conservation
> - culture (including arts and heritage)
> - animal welfare.
>
> We run funding programmes on a periodic basis with each programme having its own theme. We use our data, research and understanding of the sector to invite organisations who fit the programme theme and criteria to apply for grants. As we do not run open grant programmes we are unable to accept applications or appeals for support.
>
> [...] If you would like a list of grants that CAF have awarded, please contact the advisory team.

Venturesome
Venturesome, a social enterprise initiative, operates where a charity needs finance but its requirements may be too risky for a bank loan or outside the criteria of a grantmaker. It offers loans and investment support to charities and other social enterprises, to suit the needs of individual organisations. This support might take the form of underwriting, unsecured loans or equity type investments and it is anticipated that the money loaned will be repaid over time.

The programme will only invest in social purpose organisations that:
- are registered in the UK
- can clearly state their charitable purpose and social impact (organisations do not have to be registered charities but do need to be of charitable purpose)
- can provide evidence of at least one year of income (whether from donations or trading)
- are looking for between £25,000 and £250,000
- have a legal structure which allows them to take on debt/equity funding.

Venturesome manages a fund of £10 million on behalf of CAF and other external investors, including individual philanthropists, foundations and banks.

Technically, CAF made grants worth £366 million in 2009/10, but almost all of these are 'donor directed' payments where the foundation administers the funds of other donors who are using its financial services. These include separate trusts set up within CAF by donors seeking to use the administrative and grant payment services of CAF while keeping for themselves the decisions about where those grants should go.

Applications

In the first instance, applicants to Venturesome should contact the trust directly to discuss their requirements.

Community Foundation for Calderdale

General

£1.5 million (2009/10)

Beneficial area

Calderdale, with ability to manage funds outside of this area.

The 1855 Building (first floor), Discovery Road, Halifax HX1 2NG
Tel: 01422 349 700
Fax: 01422 350 017
Email: enquiries@cffc.co.uk
Website: www.cffc.co.uk
Correspondent: Danni Bailey, Senior Administrator

CC Number: 1002722

Information available

Accounts were on file at the Charity Commission. Additional information taken from the foundation's website.

General

The foundation, as a registered charity, was established for the support or promotion of any charitable purposes, the relief of poverty, the advancement of education (including training for employment or work), the advancement of religion or any other charitable purpose for the benefit of the community in the area of the Metropolitan Borough of Calderdale and its immediate neighbourhood and other charitable purposes in the United Kingdom with a preference for those which are in the opinion of the executive committee beneficial to the community in the area of benefit.

By raising money through its network of supporting 'members' and donors, and holding a long-term investment fund, the Community Foundation for Calderdale is able to address local need indefinitely – the interest gained on the invested money is given out in grants. This gives local people the opportunity to give to local causes, see where their money has gone and be able to contribute to a permanent pot of cash to benefit the community forever. The foundation also manages several external programmes, such as Grassroots Grants.

The focus of the Foundation is:
▷ effective stewardship
▷ strong leadership
▷ strategic partnerships

Grants have been given to support causes as varied as social clubs for elderly people, community recycling schemes, children's after-school clubs, community bands, sports clubs, refugee centres, and individuals in crisis.

In 2009/10 the foundation had an income of £2.3 million, assets of £6.7 million and made grants totalling £1.5 million.

Grants programmes

There are three types of grants and funding programmes:

Donor interest programmes
Awards from this are usually small, from £200 to £3,000. Donors specify their interests and areas of work so that applicants can read about them on the website, and apply via the community foundation if they feel they match their needs.

Priority issue programme
This programme invited voluntary and community organisations to take part in a scheme to help them develop long term strategies to allow them to become more sustainable and enterprising in the future. This fund was closed at the time of writing but may reopen in the future so applicants are advised to check the funds website for recent updates.

Managed programmes
The foundation delivers schemes on behalf of other bodies which currently includes:

Henry Smith Charity
Grants are available for work connected with health and social welfare. They have a General List and a Small Grants programme. The General List looks to fund specific budget costs such as salaries for up to three years. The small grants programme offers one-off grants of up to £10,000 to registered charities with an annual income of less than £150,000.

Reducing the Harm Of Alcohol and Drugs (Children and Young People)
Funded by NHS Calderdale this programme has a budget of £6,000 that they intend to distribute between two and three imaginative grassroots projects seeking to provide innovative ways of protecting children and young people from the harmful effects of drugs and alcohol.

Grants programmes open and close regularly, new programmes are added, some end and deadlines for applications vary. Therefore it is important to check the foundations website or contact them to find out recent developments.

Beneficiaries included: North Kirklees MIND (£40,000); Calderdale Carers Project (£30,000); Mediation Yorkshire; Noah's Ark Community Cafe and Counselling Centre (£20,000 each); Scope Calderdale Community Outreach Service (£11,000); Women's Active project (£5,000); Huddersfield Taekwondo Club (£5,000); Batley Young Peoples Club (£2,000); Whiteknights Emergency Voluntary Service (£900); Mixenden Parents Resource Centre (£800) and Kirklees Transgender Support Group (£600).

Exclusions

The foundation will not fund any of the following:
▷ general appeals
▷ projects which have already taken place or for retrospective funding
▷ projects which would normally be funded from statutory sources, i.e., Calderdale MBC, the Local Education Authority, Social Services or Central Government
▷ projects for the advancement of religion
▷ projects where the main beneficiaries are animals
▷ projects that do not directly benefit people living in Calderdale
▷ political activities
▷ applications made up entirely of core and/or running costs (exceptions may be made in extraordinary circumstances)

Applications

The foundation's website has details of the grant schemes currently being administered. Application packs for all of the programmes are also available to download from the website. Alternatively, contact the foundation directly and they will send a pack in the post.

If you wish to discuss your project before applying, the grants team are always happy to answer any queries. The foundation also runs a monthly drop-in, where groups can go for advice and support on their applications.

Common applicant mistakes

'Failure to read the conditions and requirements of the scheme they are applying to.'

Calouste Gulbenkian Foundation

Cultural understanding, fulfilling potential, environment, maximising social and cultural value

£2.2 million (2010)

Beneficial area

UK and the Republic of Ireland.

50 Hoxton Square, London N1 6PB

Tel: 020 7012 1400

Fax: 020 7739 1961

Email: info@gulbenkian.org.uk

Website: www.gulbenkian.org.uk

Correspondent: Andrew Barnett, Director – UK Branch

Trustee: The foundation's Board of Administration in Lisbon. UK resident trustee: Martin Essayan.

Information available

Excellent annual reports with full details of the foundation's thinking, policies and grants. The foundation also has an excellent website. As the foundation is not a charity registered in the UK there are no files at the Charity Commission.

Background

This is described as follows by the foundation:

> Calouste Sarkis Gulbenkian was an Armenian born in 1869. He became a British citizen, conducted much of his work in Britain, and finally settled in Portugal. The Calouste Gulbenkian Foundation was established in 1956, a year after his death.
>
> He was multicultural and multilingual and spent his career bringing together people from different cultures and nationalities. Our interests today lie in bridging divides and looking across issues.
>
> The headquarters of the foundation are in Lisbon and consist of the administration, which deals with grant-giving throughout the world, the Calouste Gulbenkian Museum, housing the founder's art collections, the Modern Art Centre, an Art Library, book shop, concert and conference halls. The foundation also maintains a Science Institute near Lisbon, a

Portuguese delegation in Paris, and a grant-giving branch in London for the United Kingdom and the Republic of Ireland.

There is one resident trustee in London. Grant requests for more than £15,000 are referred to the Lisbon board.

The purpose of the UK Branch is to help enrich and connect the experiences of individuals in the UK and Ireland and secure lasting beneficial change. We have a special interest in those who are most disadvantaged and we place a particular emphasis on maximising the beneficial impact of our work through encouraging cross-border exchanges of lessons and experiences.

The UK Branch of the foundation is concerned with three key issues:

▶ cultural understanding
▶ fulfilling potential
▶ environment

The values that characterise all the foundation's work include 'aspiring to be innovative, international, independent yet involving.

Funding Programme

The majority of our work is proactive. Funding is available to support a small number of truly exceptional ideas and/ or projects that contribute to meeting the identified objectives under our three main strategic aims (see website).

Guidelines

▶ Not-for-profit organisations (not individuals) can apply for R&D funding to scope a new idea which enables them to work together with other organisations or experts **outside their usual practice**, or to enable them to undertake active research into areas they would not normally have the time or money to explore.
▶ If projects are specifically local they must be of a kind that have not been implemented elsewhere and which can set a precedent for emulation in other places, or serve as a national pilot.
▶ Although the host applicant and prime beneficiaries should be resident in the UK or Republic of Ireland, we are also interested in proposals that may involve European partners or that emulate good practice in other countries.
▶ Although we may occasionally give further funding for projects that are developed as a result of an R&D grant, we stress that we do not guarantee continued support.
▶ The funds available are modest in scale and **competition is likely to be strong**.
▶ As a guide, it is expected that grants will average between £10,000 and £25,000.

Aims for 2012

During 2012 the foundation aims to continue to develop partnerships and activities under its core themes. 'Maximising the beneficial impact of our work continues to be at the heart of our strategy. We place an emphasis on evaluating the impact achieved and communicating the lessons to those who can take these forward and help exact a greater impact.

Cultural Understanding

To help improve people's perception of each other by providing opportunities for interaction *through* culture and *between* cultures.

Fulfilling Potential

To assist the most disadvantaged in society to fulfill their potential by building connections and developing opportunities.

Environment

To help in the development of a society which benefits from a more sustainable relationship with the natural world and understands the value of its resources.

Maximising Social and Cultural Value

To contribute to enhanced effectiveness of the organisations we work with, maintaining an interest in sectoral developments and seeking to influence others in maximising social and cultural value.

The foundation develops its own work, initiatives and partnerships, but funding is available to support a small number of truly exceptional ideas and/or projects that contribute to meeting the identified objectives under our three main strategic aims.

The following information is taken from the UK Branch's website:

Our approach

▶ To achieve a greater impact, we are supporting fewer organisations with larger amounts of money.
▶ We work proactively by identifying needs and collaborating with a number of key organisations to help meet them.
▶ We support projects, partnerships and, indirectly, people.
▶ These partnerships and activities are selected by the Foundation and are time-limited from one to four years.
▶ Occasionally, we will invite new funding proposals for specific initiatives.
▶ We place an emphasis on evaluating the impact achieved and communicating the lessons to those who can take these forward and help exact a greater impact.

We will work to achieve our aims by:

▶ Exploring Gathering evidence from research, identifying what works
▶ Exchanging Connecting to practical experience and building coalitions

- Explaining Advocating and communicating the outcomes of work to those who can effect change
- Exiting Ensuring a legacy and moving on when the time is right.
- The funding channelled through the UK Branch is exclusively intended for organisations based in the UK and Ireland.
- We will support projects outside London in preference to those based in the capital. Although funding at national,
- regional and local levels, we want to ensure that we support projects that have a benefit beyond the locality in which
- they are situated, and which have potential for future international application.

In 2010 the UK Branch of the foundation made grants totalling £2.2 million.

Beneficiaries included: The Photographers' Gallery (£100,000); Manchester International Festival (£75,000); Botanic Gardens Conservation International (£60,000); Homeless Link (£55,000); Climate Outreach and Information Network (COIN) (£50,000 each); Green Alliance (£40,000); Clore Duffield Foundation (£45,000); Beth Johnson Foundation (£40,000); Oxford Institute of Ageing (£30,000); Catch 22 (£25,500); Your Square Mile (£15,000); Social Innovation Camp (£8,000) Central Belfast CAB and Mead Gallery, Warwick Arts Centre (£5,000 each).

Exclusions

The UK Branch of the foundation gives grants only for proposals of a charitable kind, from registered charities or similar not-for-profit organisations in the UK or Ireland. It does not fund:

- work that does not have a direct benefit in the UK or the Republic of Ireland
- individuals
- curriculum based activities in statutory education
- student grants or scholarships for tuition and maintenance
- vocational training
- teaching or research posts or visiting fellowships
- educational resources and equipment
- gap year activities
- group or individual visits abroad, including to Portugal

- core services and standard provisions
- routine information and advice services
- capital costs for housing or the purchase, construction, repair or furnishing of buildings
- equipment, including vehicles, IT, or musical instruments
- scientific or medical research
- medicine or related therapies such as complementary medicine, hospices, counselling and therapy
- promoting religion or belief system
- publications
- website development
- sports
- holidays of any sort
- animal welfare

Historically we have supported the arts, arts and science and arts education but we will not any longer consider arts applications unless they meet our current strategic aims. We never make loans or retrospective grants, nor help to pay off deficits or loans, nor can we remedy the withdrawal or reduction of statutory funding. We do not give grants in response to any capital, endowment or widely distributed appeal.

Applications

How and when to apply:

Please use the 'Initial Enquiry Form' to submit your proposal [available on the foundation's website].

- Initial Enquiries can be submitted at any time of the year but please allow at least three months between submission and the proposed starting date.
- Proposals are assessed at monthly meetings in the context of other applications.
- If proposals are short-listed, fuller information will be requested and applicants invited to discuss their project.
- Final applications will be considered at one of our three annual trustee meetings.

Please email any queries to the Grants Administrator, Barbara Karch, at: bkarch@gulbenkian.org.uk

The Campden Charities Trustee

Welfare and education

£397,000 to organisations
(2009/10)

Beneficial area

The former parish of Kensington, London; a north-south corridor, roughly from north of the Fulham Road to the north of Ladbroke Grove (a map can be viewed on the website).

27a Pembridge Villas, London W11 3EP
Tel: 020 7243 0551
Fax: 020 7229 4920
Website: www.cctrustee.org.uk
Correspondent: Chris Stannard, Clerk to the Trustees
Trustees: Revd Gillean Craig, Chair; David Banks; Elisabeth Brockmann; Chris Calman; Dr Kit Davis; Steve Hoier; Susan Lockhart; Tim Martin; Terry Myers; Ben Pilling; Victoria Stark; Richard Walker-Arnott; Ms M Rodkina; C Williams.
CC Number: 1104616

Information available

Accounts were available at the Charity Commission.

Summary

The Campden Charities were founded by endowments in the wills of Baptist Viscount Campden and Elizabeth Viscountess Dowager Campden who died in 1629 and 1643 respectively. The endowments were 'for the good and benefit of the poor of the parish forever' and 'to put forth one poor boy or more to be apprentices'. The charities' area of benefit remains the old Parish of Kensington.

The current scheme interprets the original objects in terms of providing grants for the relief of need and for the advancement of education. Grants are made directly for the benefit of individuals and to organisations that assist individuals.

During the course of the financial year to 31 March 2006 the management of the assets of the Campden Charities was transferred to the Campden Charities Trustee. The Uniting Order granted by the Charity Commissioners in a letter dated 25 January 2005 came into effect on 1 April 2005. This order united the Campden Charities Trustee and the Campden Charities under the former's charity number. Since then there has been aggregated accounts and reporting.

The charity is focused on supporting relief in need and education in the former parish of Kensington and the former Royal Borough of Kensington. It must spend at least half of its income available for grant giving on relief in need and up to half on the advancement of education.

Grantmaking in 2009/10

In 2009/10 the charity had assets of £90 million and an income of £2.4 million. Grants to organisations totalled £397,000, with a further £1.6 million going to individuals.

The following extract from the 2009/10 annual report describes the current grantmaking policy:

The trustees have developed an innovative approach to grant giving over the last three years. Their objective is to help financially disadvantaged individuals and families towards financial independence. They seek to do this by identifying the needs of individuals and tailoring packages of support to help them overcome the obstacles they face in improving their circumstances. This help is not restricted to a single payment, trustees want to continue to help people until their circumstances change; this may mean making a number of grants, sometimes over a period of years.

The trustees make incentive payments to non-statutory not for profit organisations that refer and support individuals. After twelve months of receiving such referrals trustees may enter into partnership arrangements to fund work delivered by these organisations to enhance the support offered to individuals. The trustees do not accept unsolicited applications from organisations.

The trustees are guided in their grant giving by two fundamental principles:
1 Independence
  Grants will not be made to support statutory services; neither are the trustees party to local or central Government initiatives or political priorities. The trustees value their position as an independent local grant maker.
2 Fairness
  Trustees seek to make the application process fair to all potential beneficiaries. All grant applications are made and considered in the same manner. There are no privileged applicants and individual trustees are required to declare an interest where appropriate.

Distribution of grants
The scheme governing the charities directs the trustees to apply one half of the charities' income to the relief of need and the other half to the advancement of education save that if in so far as income in any one year is not required for application for the advancement of education, it may be applied to the relief of need.

The young people whom the trustees wish to assist with educational support are those from impoverished backgrounds. Often those young people in greatest need have at some stage become disenfranchised from formal education and they find it difficult to re-engage without extensive professional advice and support. Independent applications made by these young people to the charities are often inappropriate or ill advised. Whilst it is relatively straightforward to make substantial grants to academically able scholars, it is more challenging to provide appropriate financial support directly to those individuals who may need it most.

Similarly adults who have experienced long periods of unemployment often become demoralised; occasionally they find themselves in a 'benefits trap' where they would be financially worse off in low paid employment. Lone parents often cannot finance childcare that would enable them to train. Many of the poorest people have also accumulated significant debt. In recognition of these and many other issues, the trustees employ an unusually large Grants Officer team so that instead of funding individuals at arm's length, Grants Officers can build up a relationship with families in need and work with them to tailor individual packages of assistance. Grants Officers also actively seek ways to work with other not-for-profit partners to support the charities' beneficiaries.

The trustees believe that the resources of the charities' are well deployed not only in making grants but also in funding a team of Grants Officers that can bring 'added value' to the grants made.' The trustees recognise the importance of the role advice and mentoring in making their grant giving more effective. 'During the year Nova New Opportunities provided an advisor at the charities' offices on two mornings each week to support the charities' beneficiaries. Trustees intend to develop this work during 2010 by increasing the mentoring provided by the charities' own staff team.

Direct grants to individuals
Grants are made in response to direct applications from individuals responding to the charities' publicity and referrals are also welcomed and encouraged from all not for profit organisations and statutory agencies. This year 268 Grants totalling £301,000 were made in support of vocational education. 142 individuals and families of working age also received grants totalling £61,000 for child-care, fares, goods and services to assist them towards financial independence. In addition 60 grants totalling £173,000 were awarded to encourage academically able young people from disadvantaged backgrounds to attend university.

£493,000 was awarded to 466 pension age beneficiaries in a programme to assist the financially worst off. Many of them had transferred from the Campden Pensioners scheme; the number of beneficiaries remaining under this scheme reduced from 523 to 293 during the year and received a total of £362,000.

Grants to Organisations
The aim of funding not for profit organisations has been to direct funding to those that are supporting individuals receiving direct grants. The focus is on outcomes for individual beneficiaries rather than responding to organisation requests. In 2009/10 Grants Officers negotiated and renewed individual partnership agreements to support and train individuals with 9 organisations, £359,500 was awarded in this way.

Trustees have also continued to award £1,000 to other organisations for each successful referral of an individual; £38,000 was awarded for such referrals during the year. This referral funding is intended to help organisations working within the charities' objects with individual beneficiaries. Such funding may lead to partnerships in the future.

Beneficiaries of partnership funding included: Westway Community Transport (£112,000); Nucleus Legal Advice Centre (£52,000); My Generation (£42,000); Blenheim Project (£30,000); Earls Court YMCA (£30,000); and NOVA (£5,000).

Beneficiaries of referral funding included: London Cyrenians (£4,000); Bramley Sheltered Scheme and Christian Alliance Housing Association (£2,000 each); and Off the Streets and Into Work Sixty Plus (£1,000 each).

Exclusions

No grants for:
- UK charities or charities outside Kensington, unless they are of significant benefit to Kensington residents
- schemes or activities which are generally regarded as the responsibility of the statutory authorities
- UK fundraising appeals

- environmental projects unless connected with education or social need
- medical research or equipment
- animal welfare
- advancement of religion or religious groups, unless they offer non-religious services to the community
- commercial and business activities
- endowment appeals
- projects of a political nature
- retrospective capital grants.

Applications

The charity's website states:

The charity is trying to target its resources where they can be of the most direct benefit to financially disadvantaged individuals. The charity therefore **does not** receive unsolicited applications for funding from organisations. However the charity's officers are eager to meet with colleagues from other not-for-profit organisations to explore ways in which we can work together to help individuals to end dependency on benefits or improve a low wage.

If you have contact with individuals whom you would like to refer, please telephone the correspondent on: 020 7313 3797.

Common applicant mistakes

'Applicant organisations misunderstanding how the charity funds.'

The Carpenters' Company Charitable Trust

Education, general

£1 million (2009/10)

Beneficial area

UK.

Carpenters' Hall, 1 Throgmorton Avenue, London EC2N 2JJ
Tel: 020 7588 7001
Email: info@carpentersco.com
Website: www.carpentersco. com/charitable_ccct.php
Correspondent: The Clerk
Trustees: Peter A Luton; Malcolm R Francis; Michael I Montague-Smith; Guy Morton-Smith.
CC Number: 276996

Information available

Accounts were available at the Charity Commission.

The trust's income is derived from a capital sum gifted by the company's corporate fund, supplemented when warranted by further grants from the corporate fund. Charitable causes benefiting from grants include organisations supporting the elderly, people with disabilities, homeless people, youth and children, education, medical and museums. Craft causes receive a high priority when awards are considered.

Educational grants are also awarded to individuals, only for wood related courses undertaken in the UK.

In 2009/10 the trust had assets of £18.6 million and an income of an income of £954,000. Grants were made totalling £1 million.

Grants were broken down as follows:

Craft activities	£884,000*
Homeless and elderly people	£26,000
Youth and children's organisations	£26,000
City of London	£25,000
Welfare	£23,500
Medical, hospitals and hospices	£18,000
Religious organisations	£18,000
People with disabilities	£19,000
Museums	£6,000
Miscellaneous	£19,500

*The Building Crafts College received a grant of over £731,000.

Exclusions

Grants are not normally made to individual churches or cathedrals, or to educational establishments having no association to the Carpenters' Company. No grants (except educational grants) are made to individual applicants. Funds are usually only available to charities registered with the charity commission or exempt from registration.

Applications

In writing to the correspondent.

Cash for Kids – Radio Clyde

Children

£2.1 million (2009/10)

Beneficial area

Radio Clyde transmission area, i.e. west central Scotland.

Radio Clyde, 3 South Avenue, Clydebank Business Park, Glasgow G81 2RX
Tel: 0141 204 1025
Fax: 0141 565 2370
Email: cashforkids@radioclyde.com
Website: www.clyde1. com/cashforkids
Correspondent: Trust Administrator
Trustees: J Brown; Ewan Hunter; Ian Grabiner; Sir Tom Hunter; Ms B Ritchie; Ms T McNellan; G Bryce.
SC Number: SCO03334

Information available

Accounts were provided by the charity.

This is a Christmas appeal established by the radio station and CSV, a charity supporting media involvement in volunteering and in community support generally. Since 1981 it has helped to support children under 16 who are facing financial, emotional, physical or educational challenges.

The charity states:

Every single penny donated to the charity goes towards helping disadvantaged children and young people in the West of Scotland. We are able to make this promise because the charity uses an annual donation from the Hunter Foundation combined with its sponsorship income to cover all operational costs.

The charity funds individuals and community organisations in Inverclyde, Argyll and Bute, Dumfries and Galloway, East Ayrshire, South Ayrshire, North Ayrshire, East Dumbartonshire, West Dumbartonshire, Renfrewshire, East Renfrewshire, Glasgow City Council, North Lanarkshire and South Lanarkshire.

Cash for Kids awards grants in four different ways:
1 sustainable grants – small grants for children at Christmas
2 special grants – these are given to organisations throughout the year
3 family grants – these are dispensed to local authority social work departments that nominate children in need on their caseloads
4 group grants – donations are also dispersed to a wide variety of deserving children's groups and support agencies across west and south-west Scotland. The grant application process opens in

October. All grant applications must be submitted by the beginning of November.

In 2010 the charity piloted a successful summer grant making project offering assistance to vulnerable children and at greater risk during the summer holiday period.

Grants to organisations

The charity supports projects delivered by organisations working with disadvantaged children and young people, who are aged 16 years and under.

Disadvantages experienced by children and young people include:

- illness, distress, abuse or neglect
- any kind of disability
- behavioural or psychological difficulties
- living in poverty or situations of deprivation.

Grants help fund holidays, away-days and summer activities run by community groups and charities specialising in the welfare, education and social development of children and young people.

Any application should focus on the children the project will work with and how the project will change their lives for the better.

Projects must be able to demonstrate that they are community based, volunteer led and representative of the client group they seek to serve. They must demonstrate meaningful engagement and consultation with young people. They should also provide a cost effective approach to interventions and demonstrate good quality data collection systems that provide information on the tangible difference their project makes.

For further information, please contact the trust directly or go to its website.

In 2009/10 the charity had assets of £648,000 and an income of £2.1 million. Grants were made totalling almost £2.1 million.

Exclusions

The trust does not fund:

- trips or projects abroad
- medical treatment/research
- unspecified expenditure
- deficit funding or repayment of loans
- retrospective funding (projects taking place before the grant award date)
- projects unable to start within 6 months of the grant award date
- distribution to another/other organisation/s

- general appeals or endowment funds
- relief of statutory responsibility
- the promotion of religion

No funding for capital expenditure except in very special circumstances that must be made clear at the time of applying. Organisations whose administration costs exceed 15% of total expenditure will not be supported.

Applications

Application forms and guidelines are available from the trust's website.

Sir John Cass's Foundation

Education in inner London

£1 million to organisations
(2009/10)

Beneficial area

The inner London boroughs – Camden, Greenwich, Hackney, Hammersmith and Fulham, Islington, Kensington and Chelsea, Lambeth, Lewisham, Newham, Southwark, Tower Hamlets, Wandsworth, Westminster and the City of London.

31 Jewry Street, London EC3N 2EY
Tel: 020 7480 5884
Fax: 020 7488 2519
Email: contactus@sirjohncass.org
Website: www.sirjohncass.org
Correspondent: Richard Foley, Grants Manager
Trustees: Michael Bear; Kevin Everett; Mark Boleat; HH Judge Brian Barker; Revd Christopher Burke; Barbara Lane; Graham Forbes; David Turner; Mervyn Streatfeild; Helen Meixner; Dr Ray Ellis; Revd Nigel Kirkup; Sarah Dalgarno; David Hogben; Prof Michael Thorne; Inigo Woolf; Revd Laura Burgess.
CC Number: 312425

Information available

Accounts were available at the Charity Commission and guidelines for applicants were provided by the trust. Information is also available via the foundation's very informative website.

The principal objective of this foundation is the promotion of education of young people in attendance at Sir John Cass's Foundation and Red Coat Secondary School, Sir John Cass's Foundation Primary School, the London Metropolitan University or resident in the City of London, the Royal Borough of Kensington and Chelsea, and the London Boroughs of Camden, Greenwich, Hackney, Hammersmith and Fulham, Islington, Lambeth, Lewisham, Newham, Southwark, Tower Hamlets, Wandsworth and the City of Westminster.

The following information is taken from the foundation's annual report:

The Sir John Cass Foundation dates formally from 1748. The foundation takes its name from its founder who was born in the City of London in 1661 and, during his lifetime, served as both Alderman and Sheriff. He was also MP for the City and knighted in 1713. In 1710 Cass set up a school for 50 boys and 40 girls in buildings in the churchyard of St Botolph-without-Aldgate. Intending to leave all his property to the school, when he died in 1718 of a brain haemorrhage, Cass had only initialled three pages of his will. The incomplete will was contested, but was finally upheld by the Court of Chancery 30 years after his death. The school, which by this time had been forced to close, was re-opened, and the foundation established.

The history of the foundation touches upon education in and around the City of London at almost every level, ranging from primary education to postgraduate study and representing an historical microcosm of the development of English education over more than three centuries. Today, the foundation has links in the primary, secondary and tertiary sectors of education. It provides support to its primary school in the City of London and its secondary school in Tower Hamlets, as well as the Sir John Cass Department of Art, Media and Design (part of London Metropolitan University) and the Cass Business School (part of City University).

In addition, the foundation supports three academies; St Mary Magdalene and the City of London Academies in Islington, and St Michael and All Angels Academy in Camberwell. It has also awarded grants to 34 secondary schools across inner London towards their bids to become designated as Specialist Schools, including a grant to Elmgreen School in Lambeth, which is the first parent promoted school in the country.

The foundation gives its name to Cass Housing Estate located in and around Cassland Road in Hackney.

Grants are made to organisations for educational work with children and young people in inner London. The majority of grants are revenue funding for projects, though capital grants are occasionally made.

There is also a substantial programme of support for individual students with priority to those aged 19–24. (see *The Educational Grants Directory* also published by the Directory of Social Change).

The foundation continued to provide support in the form of rent free accommodation to the Sir John Cass's Foundation Primary and Secondary Schools, Cass and Claredale Halls of Residence and London Metropolitan University, equating to a significant benefit to each of these educational institutions.

The foundation will only consider proposals from schools and organisations that benefit:

▶ children or young people under the age of 25, who are permanent residents of named *inner* London boroughs (Camden, Greenwich, Hackney, Hammersmith and Fulham, Islington, Kensington & Chelsea, Lambeth, Lewisham, Newham, Southwark, Tower Hamlets, Wandsworth, Westminster and the City of London) and from disadvantaged backgrounds or areas of high deprivation.

Priorities

The foundation's website states:

The foundation has four areas of focus for grant giving, which are as follows:
▶ widening participation in further & higher education
▶ truancy, exclusion and behaviour management
▶ prisoner education
▶ new initiatives.

There are one or more priorities for each area of focus. Details of the priorities and our aims and objectives for each area of focus are:

Widening Participation in Further and Higher Education
Aim
To promote access to further and higher education for disadvantaged young people in inner London.

Objective
To increase the number of inner London students from disadvantaged

backgrounds successfully participating in further and higher education.

Priorities
Work with communities currently under-represented in further and higher education and/or hard to reach learners (e.g. care leavers or young people with learning difficulties). Applications could involve work with secondary school pupils as well as those in further education and universities.

Truancy, Exclusion and Behaviour Management
Aim
To encourage and support children and young people's attainment through initiatives that help them engage with, and stay in, education.

Objectives
▶ to reduce truancy levels amongst pupils attending primary and secondary schools
▶ to reduce levels of exclusions and expulsions
▶ to improve pupil motivation, behaviour and achievement through initiatives that promote children and young people's emotional well being and social development.

Priority
Work with primary and secondary schools in challenging circumstances and/or those with higher than average truancy, exclusion or expulsion rates. Challenging circumstances could include, for example, schools in areas of high social deprivation or in special measures, as well as schools that have higher than average rates of truancy, exclusion or expulsion.

Prisoner Education
Aim
To reduce re-offending through education and initiatives that promote employability.

Objectives
▶ to improve the literacy and numeracy skills of prisoners and ex-offenders
▶ to help prisoners and ex-offenders gain skills and education qualifications that will help them into employment.

Priority
Work with prisoners and ex-offenders that helps secure employment and prevent re-offending.

New Initiatives
Aim
To influence and improve education policy and practice, both within the foundation's area of benefit and more widely.

Objectives
i) To test new and ground breaking approaches to learning that have the potential to enhance and influence education policy and practice.

ii) To support work that focuses on identified needs and gaps in statutory provision.

Priorities
▶ projects that are pioneering and original in their approach to teaching or learning and are strategic (relates to objective i)
▶ projects addressing an identified need within a geographical area or learning establishment that are new and innovative in context i.e. must be a new initiative for the school or borough, but need not be a completely new approach to education (relates to objective ii)
▶ projects that focus on addressing under-achievement in literacy and numeracy in primary and secondary schools (relates to objectives i and ii)
▶ projects seeking to attract greater numbers of young people into the teaching profession (relates to objectives i and ii).

Applicants should say which priority their project addresses as well as describing how their project meets that priority. Applications need not meet more than one priority but, for those that do, applicants are welcome to describe how their application meets each of the priorities.

Grantmaking in 2009/10

The foundation gives the following summary in its annual report:

During 2009/10, the foundation continued to provide support in the form of rent free accommodation to the Sir John Cass's Foundation Primary and Secondary Schools, Cass and Claredale Halls of Residence and London Metropolitan University, equating to a significant benefit to each of these educational institutions.

The foundation has an active role in educational projects and an innovative grants strategy involving partnership working and funding to provide maximum assistance to the foundation's beneficiaries.

Also during the year, in partnership with the University of East London the foundation opened the new Sir John Cass School of Education. This is a new state-of-the art teaching and resource centre in Stratford, that will contribute towards both the quality and quantity of teachers in London for many years to come.

The foundation has also continued its leading edge programme work with the London Ambassador Scheme for Learners with Disabilities, a uniquely innovative highly successful Widening Participation Project, which saw those with physical and mental health difficulties assisted into further and higher education.

The foundation also hopes to be able to agree shortly to the establishment of a

£1.5 million five year Sir John Cass's Foundation Lord Mayor's Scholarship Programme, which will commence in 2010/11. This imaginative partnership programme will enable bright young Londoners from disadvantaged backgrounds to be assisted through their undergraduate studies. This programme will strengthen ties between the foundation and the City of London Corporation.

In 2009/10 the foundation had assets of £79 million and an income of £1.7 million. Just under £1 million in total was awarded/paid to organisations and schools and £41,000 was awarded in grants to 57 individuals. Grantmaking was broken down as follows:

Organisations	£371,000
Church of England academies programme	£300,000
Diocesan boards	£200,000
Foundation schools	£91,000
Individuals	£41,000

Beneficiaries included: Southwark Diocesan Board of Education – Christ Church Primary School Brixton and University of East London (Sir John Cass School of Education) (£200,000 each); Southwark Diocesan Board of Education – academy programme (£100,000); Sir John Cass's Foundation and Redcoats Church of England Secondary School (£60,000 each); East London Business Alliance (£40,000); Shaftesbury Young People (£25,000); Sir John Cass's Foundation Primary School (Cass Benefits) (£14,000); and Prisoners' Education Trust (£6,000).

Exclusions

There are many activities and costs that the foundation will not fund. The following list gives a sample of the type of activities the foundation does not support:

- projects that do not meet a foundation priority
- conferences, seminars and academic research
- holiday projects, school journeys, trips abroad or exchange visits
- supplementary schools or mother tongue teaching
- independent schools
- youth and community groups, or projects taking place in these settings
- pre-school and nursery education
- general fund-raising campaigns or appeals

- costs for equipment or salaries that are the statutory responsibility of education authorities
- costs to substitute for the withdrawal or reduction of statutory funding
- costs for work or activities that have already taken place prior to the grant application
- costs already covered by core funding or other grants
- curriculum enhancing projects
- capital costs, that are exclusively for the purchase, repair or furnishing of buildings, purchase of vehicles, computers, sports equipment or improvements to school grounds.

Applications

The foundation operates a two stage application process – an initial enquiry and a full application stage.

The following information has been taken from the foundation's website:

Stage 1

Complete and submit the initial enquiry form which is available from the foundation's website and on request from the correspondent. The form asks for:

- outline information about your proposed project
- information about how the project meets the foundation's priorities
- a summary of the project that includes the following information: the aims of the project including outputs and outcomes, how the project will be delivered; the duration of the project, including when and where it will take place; and a budget covering project costs.

We will consider your enquiry and inform you, within three weeks, whether or not you may proceed to Stage 2. If we have any queries we may contact you during this time to discuss details of your project submitted in the initial enquiry form. We receive a large number of applications. Unfortunately, this means that good projects sometimes have to be refused even if they meet a priority. If we invite you to proceed to Stage 2 and submit a full application, we will send you a copy of our Stage 2 application guidelines for schools and organisations.

Stage 2

Complete your detailed application and send it to us with copies of your memorandum and articles of association (or constitution) and your organisation's latest annual report and accounts.

Assessment and decision making process

On receipt of your application our staff may meet with you as part of our assessment process. After we have received responses to any queries and any further information requested, a report on your application will be considered by the foundation's grants committee, whose decision is final. The grants committee meets in March, June and November each year. It normally takes between two and four months from receipt of a full application until a decision is made.

Notification of the decision

All applicants will be sent formal notification of the outcome of their applications within two weeks of the committee decision.

Successful applicants

Those who are offered a grant will be sent a formal offer letter and copies of our standard terms and conditions of grant. Copies of our standard terms and conditions of grant are available on our website. Additional conditions are sometimes included depending on the nature of the grant.

Monitoring and evaluation

Staff will contact you to clarify and agree how the outputs and outcomes for your project will be monitored and evaluated. Your project will be visited at least once during the lifetime of the grant. If your grant covers more than one year you will be asked to submit a progress report for each year. Continuation of multi-year grants is dependent upon satisfactory progress towards agreed outputs and outcomes. At the end of the grant you will be asked to provide a final report. The foundation provides guidance on the structure and content of these reports.

Unsuccessful applicants

Applying for funding is a competitive process and the foundation's grants budget is limited. Because of the high volume of applications received, good projects sometimes have to be refused, even if they meet a priority. All applications are assessed on merit. If your application is refused you can apply again twelve months after the date you submitted your last application.

The Castanea Trust

General

Beneficial area
UK.

Brabners Chaffe Street, Horton House, Exchange Flags, Liverpool L2 3YL
Tel: 0151 600 3000
Email: mark.feeny@brabnerscs.com
Correspondent: Mark Feeny, Trustee
Trustees: Geoffrey Wall; Ian Duncan; Mark Feeny.
CC Number: 1136180

Information available
Basic information was available from the Charity Commission.

The trust was established in 2010 for general charitable purposes. Unfortunately no further information was available at the time of writing (September 2011) on the likely level of funding available from the trust.

Applications
In writing to the correspondent.

CfBT Education Trust

Organisations involved in education, particularly those concerned with the development and management of schools; managing and delivering effective learning and teaching; overcoming barriers to learning; and projects involving communication, language and multi-lingualism

£1.3 million (2009/10)

Beneficial area
Worldwide.

60 Queens Road, Reading, Berkshire RG1 4BS
Tel: 0118 902 1231
Fax: 0118 902 1434
Email: alawal@cfbt.com
Website: www.cfbt.com/
Correspondent: Ade Lawal, Board Secretary
Trustees: John Webb; John Harwood; Sara Hodson; Alison Macleod; Marion Headicar; Stuart Laing; Sue Hunt; Tim Walsh; Phillip Wood; Sir Jim Rose; Margaret Platts.
CC Number: 270901

Information available
Accounts were available at the Charity Commission.

The trust's core objective is to provide education and to influence others who provide education in order to enable individuals, institutions and communities to achieve their maximum potential. The trust states: 'We recognise that in education, as in other person-to-person services, clients and beneficiaries are often not the same people. We aim to meet the needs of beneficiaries and communicate those needs to our clients.' This is achieved in part through the following aims:

▶ to promote and assist teaching in educational or training establishments or other organisations throughout the world
▶ to carry out or commission educational research
▶ to provide counselling and guidance
▶ to provide advice and consultancy services on education matters
▶ to provide training and other support for educators, which enables them to improve the quality of education.

Every year CfBT invests more than £1 million in educational research projects that help to inform education policy and practice in the UK and overseas.

In 2009/10 the trustees stated they would concentrate on: Investing in an Evidence for Education Programme (EfE) which identifies, develops and disseminates evidence-based good practice.

Through the Evidence for Education research programme CfBT is investing in a coherent body of work that can be shown over time to have a positive impact on public policy and plans for education, both in the UK and internationally. The trust's research work supports collaboration between researchers, practitioners, service deliverers and policy makers, for the benefit of learners.

CfBT has commissioned, conducted and published a significant volume of research over the past-ten years. The research largely aims to provide evidence about effective interventions, strategies and policies in education with a view to impacting on or improving practice and policy. Research is divided into the following four topics:

▶ Evidence for Practice
▶ Evidence for Schools: compulsory education in the UK
▶ Evidence for Youth: advising young people
▶ Evidence for Government: local, national, international education policy.

In 2010 CfBT published 19 new research reports.

The publications included research on:
▶ early years education
▶ school management and school improvement
▶ education workforce development
▶ careers information, advice and guidance
▶ basic skills and employability
▶ education sector policy development.

More information on the Evidence for Education programme is available on the CfBT website and in the *Guide to Applicants* document. See also the information given here in 'Applications'.

In 2009/10 the trust had assets of £25.7 million and an income of £83.3 million. Please note: this is total trading income from teaching, consultancy, counselling and support for educators and does not reflect the amount available for grants. Grants awarded under the four research topics totalled £1.3 million.

Grants have previously been used to fund: Education in Conflict, Emergencies, Reconstruction and Fragile States (£302,000); Public Private Partnerships in Basic Education: An International Review (£234,000); Student Integration in the United World College, Bosnia and

Herzegovina (£55,000); Designing Educational Technologies for Social Justice (£52,000); How Effective are Bullying Prevention Programmes for Children with Special Educational Needs? (£31,000); English Language Teaching- Bridging Programmes for Further Education (£20,000); Programme scoping: Start-up phase for Gifted and Talented and Learning and Skills Programmes (£16,000); and Adult Skills and Higher Education: Separation or Union? (£12,000).

Exclusions

The trust will generally not consider funding for:
- business development
- funding an extension or expansion of current service delivery
- funding an extension of existing R&D projects which are funded by other sources
- projects which are only innovative because they are being carried out at a local rather than a national level
- buildings, equipment or capital costs
- staff salaries (apart from researcher/consultant fees)
- day-to-day running costs
- general appeals
- grants to replace statutory funding
- funding for individuals to undertake professional development, including those undertaking masters degrees or doctorates
- expeditions, travel, adventure/ holiday projects
- 'gap year' projects
- arts, religion, sports and recreation
- conservation, heritage or environmental projects
- animal rights or welfare
- educational exchanges between institutions

Applications

Applicants should first submit an outline proposal to the research manager, Karen Whitby who will advise whether the proposal meets the agreed criteria and also how to proceed. The outline should be no more than three sides of A4 and include the following information:
- the issue or problem to be addressed
- the reasons for addressing it
- the expected outcome(s)
- what happens in the course of the project
- the amount of funding required and how long it will be needed.

Full applications are considered at the meetings of trustees in March, July, September and December.

Further application information and upcoming deadline dates are available on the trust's website and in the *Guide to Applicants* document.

Please note: The 'Apply for funding' page of the trust's website currently states:

> We are proud to reinvest in research and development projects and we commission, or work with in partnership on, innovative educational research and development projects that promote and complement our operational work.
>
> **The trust is not accepting open channel research until further notice but going forward is tendering research specifications which when available will be posted on our website.**

Please contact: research@cfbt.com if you have any further queries.

The Charities Advisory Trust

General

£2.1 million (2009/10)

Beneficial area

UK and overseas.

Radius Works, Back Lane, London NW3 1HL
Tel: 020 7794 9835
Fax: 020 7431 3739
Email: people@charitiesadvisorytrust.org.uk
Website: www.charitiesadvisorytrust.org.uk
Correspondent: Dame Hilary Blume, Director
Trustees: Dr Cornelia Navari; Dr Carolyne Dennis; Brij Bhasin; Ms Dawn Penso.
CC Number: 1040487

Information available

Accounts were available at the Charity Commission.

Summary
The Charities Advisory Trust is a registered charity, with an eclectic portfolio of interests. It generates income for its projects through initiatives such as Card Aid, the Good Gifts Catalogue, the Green Hotel, Knit for Peace, Medical Student Electives and Peace Oil.

The trust is an innovative organisation, concerned with redressing inequalities and injustice in a practical way. It believes the method of generating funds should reflect the ethical concerns of the organisation.

The trust is self-financing. It earns its income through its activities. As a matter of policy, at the outset of any initiative, the sustainability of the venture is considered, and a plan put in place to ensure viability. Some activities are subsidised by others. The trust not only earns its income, it also gives around £500,000 a year in charitable donations.

The charity's main objectives for the year 2009/10 were:
- nurture Card Aid and Good Gifts Catalogue through difficult economic circumstances
- make sure charities (and their beneficiaries) continue to receive support
- establish UK Disaster Relief, a charity which provided a central body to which the public could donate in the event of a UK disaster
- scale back on costs so as to protect the amounts available for the beneficiaries.

General

In 2009/10 the trust had assets of almost £2.6 million and an income of £1.9 million. Grants payable and direct aid totalled £2.1 million.

The main beneficiaries listed in the accounts included: Survivors Fund (£274,500); Africa Education Trust (£85,000); Ashwini (£46,000); Sight Savers International (£45,000); IPPF (£38,000); Bamboo Bikes (£33,000); Parivarthana (£30,000); Rainforest Concern (£21,000); Mines Advisory Group (£20,000); War Child (£17,000); and Accord (£16,000).

Smaller grants were made to a wide range of institutions through the Card Aid and Good Gifts schemes.

As mentioned above, grantmaking is only part of the trust's work. The trust's annual report describes some its other interesting and diverse activities:

The Green Hotel: The Coffee Shop and Bakery were opened at the Green Hotel (October 2005). The staff were recruited from the bungi caste, and this caused enormous excitement and was covered in the front pages of the Indian newspapers and on television. It should be noted that the profits shown in the accounts for the Green Hotel are after making substantial donations for charitable and environmental causes.

Happy Givers: We initiated a 'giving circle' for young professionals, to encourage giving to charity. Events were held in September and March, and exceeded our expectations. We hope to build on this success.

Knit for Peace: Knit for Peace has continued. Helped by knowledge of a 2 year grant from the Esmée Fairbairn Foundation (which will not be drawn on till the next financial year), trustee Brij Bhasin organised a visit to hand spinners in Himachal Pradesh, to seek out Knit for Peace yarn.

The Scrooge Award: this award highlights the small amounts going to charity from 'charity' cards sold on the high street, received a great deal of publicity, both in the press and on television and radio.

UK Disaster Relief: The Cumbria Flood in 2009 highlighted the absence of a national charity to which the public could send funds in the event of a disaster in the UK. It is ironic that we have a charity to collect funds for disasters in the developing world, but none in the UK. We decided to fund the set up of such a charity. This work was started this financial year and funds have been earmarked for this purpose.

The trust hopes to expand its work on peace and reconciliation projects, and to continue to develop its IT systems. It is also exploring new marketing strategies [...]. The trustees also expect to invest in replacement and new point-of-sale equipment, and signage for our Card Aid shops in the next year or two.

Exclusions

Nearly all our grants are made because we have prior knowledge of the project or area of concern. In most cases the idea for the project comes from us; we work with suitable organisations to achieve our objectives. We rarely respond to unsolicited applications for projects of which we know nothing. In such cases where support is given, the amounts are usually £200 or less. We do not consider grants to individuals in need. Neither do we give to individuals going on gap year trips to the developing world. We are unlikely to give to large fund-raising charities. We do not give for missionary work.

Applications

The trustees are pro-active in looking for causes to support. They are, though: 'happy for charities to keep us informed of developments, as we do change our support as new solutions to needs emerge.'

Unsolicited applications for projects of which the trust know nothing are rarely responded to.

To apply, simply send details of your proposal (no more than two pages in length) in the form of a letter. You might try to include the following information:

▷ the aims and objectives of your organisation
▷ the project for which you need money
▷ who benefits from the project and how
▷ breakdown of the costs and total estimated costs
▷ how much money you need from us
▷ other funding secured for the project
▷ a summary of your latest annual accounts.

The trust states: 'If we refuse you it is not because your project is not worthwhile – it is because we do not have sufficient funds, or it is simply outside our current area of interest.'

Charitworth Limited

Religious, educational and charitable purposes. In practice, mainly Jewish causes

£1.2 million (2009/10)

Beneficial area

Worldwide, mainly UK and Israel.

Cohen Arnold and Co., New Burlington House, 1075 Finchley Road, London NW11 0PU
Tel: 020 8731 0777
Fax: 020 8731 0778
Correspondent: David Halpern, Trustee
Trustees: David Halpern; Reilly Halpern; Sidney Halpern; Samuel J Halpern.

CC Number: 286908

Information available

Accounts were on file at the Charity Commission, without a list of grants.

This trust was set up in 1983 and its objects are the advancement of the Jewish religion, relief of poverty and general charitable purposes. It is particularly interested in supporting Jewish charities.

In 2009/10 the trust had assets of £25.7 million and an income of just over £1 million. Grants were made during the year totalling just under £1.2 million.

Previous beneficiaries include: Zichron Nahum; British Friends of Tchernobil; Cosmon Belz; Chevras Maoz Ladal; Dushinsky Trust; Centre for Torah Education Trust; Finchley Road Synagogue; Friends of Viznitz; Beer Yaakov; and Beis Soroh Schneirer.

Applications

In writing to the correspondent.

The Checkatrade Foundation

Social welfare, the arts, health and disability

Beneficial area

UK.

5 Sherrington Mews, Ellis Square, Selsey, Chichester, West Sussex PO20 0FJ
Tel: 01243 608803
Email: foundation@checkatrade.com
Website: www.checkatrade.com/Charity/
Correspondent: Nadine Hermon, Trustee
Trustees: Kevin Byrne; Richard Spiceley; Nadine Hermon; Claire Hossell; Anna Byrne; Bridget Barnes.
CC Number: 1137878

Information available

Basic information was available from the Charity Commission.

Established in 2010, it is the charitable foundation of Checkatrade, a website that promotes reputable tradesmen. The objects of the foundation are supporting social welfare, the arts, health and disability causes, particularly those that work with children and young people and older people.

The foundation has existing connections with several charities that it supports.

The foundation's first annual report and accounts had yet to be produced at the time of writing (December 2011).

Applications
In writing to the correspondent.

The Childs Charitable Trust

Christian, general

£414,500 (2009/10)

Beneficial area
Worldwide.

3 Cornfield Terrace, Eastbourne, East Sussex BN21 4NN
Email: info@childstrust.org
Correspondent: Melanie Churchyard
Trustees: Derek N Martin; Robert H Williams; Andrew B Griffiths; Steve Puttock.
CC Number: 234618

Information available
Accounts were available from the Charity Commission, without a list of grants.

The objects of the trust are the furtherance of Christian Gospel, education, the relief of poverty and other charitable causes. The principal object is the furtherance of the Christian Gospel and the trustees are actively involved in supporting and encouraging Christian charities to achieve this goal. There is a preference for large-scale projects in the UK and abroad and ongoing support is given to some long-established Christian organisations.

In 2009/10 the trust had assets of £9.9 million and an income of £528,500. Grants were made totalling £414,500. No grants list was available from the latest accounts.

Previous beneficiaries include: Home Evangelism, ICC Mission Reserve, Latin Link, Mission Aviation Fellowship, Counties Evangelistic Work, Echoes of Service and Mustard Seed Relief, Scripture Union, Orphaids, LAMA Ministries, ELAM Ministries, Hour of Revival and University of Bristol.

Applications
In writing to the correspondent. The trust states that 'all applications are considered but, unfortunately, not all charitable causes can be supported'. Funds may also be committed for long-term projects.

The Childwick Trust

Health, people with disabilities and older people, welfare and research in connection with the bloodstock industry and Jewish charities in the UK; education in South Africa

£2.6 million (2009/10)

Beneficial area
UK; South Africa.

9 The Green, Childwick Bury, St Albans, Hertfordshire AL3 6JJ
Tel: 01727 844666
Email: karen@childwicktrust.org
Website: www.childwicktrust.org
Correspondent: Karen Groom, Trust Secretary
Trustees: John Wood, Chair; Anthony Cane; Peter Glossop; Sarah Frost; Peter Anwyl-Harris.
CC Number: 326853

Information available
Accounts were available at the Charity Commission.

The trust was established in 1985 by the settlement of assets of the late founder, Mr H J Joel. The principal objects of the trust under which grants are awarded are as follows:

- to assist older people in need including the former employees of the settlor and of companies associated with the settlor and the families of such former employees
- to make payments to charities or for charitable objects connected with horse racing or breeding within the United Kingdom or people involved with horse racing or horse breeding who shall be in need
- to make payments to Jewish charities within the United Kingdom or support Jews in need within the United Kingdom
- to support charities and charitable objects for the education and benefit of people and the families of people who intend to work, are working, or have worked in the mining industry in the Republic of South Africa
- to support the education of people resident in the Republic of South Africa
- to make payments for the benefit of charities for the promotion of health and relief of people with disabilities within the United Kingdom.

The Childwick Trust controls a subsidiary charity in South Africa, The Jim Joel Education and Training Fund, through which it conducts its South African based charitable objects. The bulk of the grants awarded each year are made to charities that promote health and relief of the disabled in the UK. The next largest proportion of grants goes to charities in South Africa via the subsidiary charity. Charities connected with thoroughbred racing and breeding are next in line and Jewish charities follow. These funding preferences were set by Mr Joel in the Trust Deed in 1985 and are not changed by the trustees.

A summary of the main grant categories is given below, alongside the percentage analysis of grants made per object in 2009/10. Summaries are taken from the trust's website:

Health
Around half of the funds distributed by The Childwick Trust are within this area and cover a wide range of charities supporting children and adults with disabilities plus care of the elderly. This includes hospices and those in the

Services, Mr Joel himself served in the First World War with the 15th Hussars. A small number of research grants are also considered.

The majority of grants given are typically between £2,000 and £10,000 with a handful of more sizeable amounts for larger projects. The trust is pleased to help both small local charities within Hertfordshire as well as larger national organisations throughout the United Kingdom.

Education in South Africa

This area of the trust's activity reflects the Joel family's long involvement in the mining industry in South Africa. The trust's grants are channelled through the Jim Joel Education and Training Fund based in Johannesburg. This fund which receives around a third of the funds distributed each year has achieved considerable success in funding Early Childhood Development projects in the poorer areas of South Africa. Applications should be made to Mrs G Bland (Fund Director) at jimjoel@iafrica.com.

The Racing World

This reflects Mr Joel's long standing connection with the racing industry and his huge success within the sport over many years. A major portion of the donations are for the welfare of those in need within the Newmarket area.

Jewish Charities

Mr Joel was Jewish and the trust continues his lifetime support for charities that promote the Jewish faith and care for Jewish people of all ages who are in need. Grants are made within the United Kingdom only.

Grants in 2009/10

In 2009/10 the trust had assets of £57 million and an income of £2.3 million. 183 grants were made totalling £2.6 million. Most grants were for under £10,000.

UK

Beneficiaries of the largest grants included: Racing Welfare – Newmarket (£200,000); Northwick Park Institute for Medical Research (£55,000); and Animal Health Trust – Newmarket (£50,000).

Other beneficiaries included: Kings College Hospital (£33,000); MOVE – London (£30,000); Alkaptonuria Trust – Liverpool, Deafblind UK – Peterborough, EACH Children's Hospice – Cambridgeshire, Great Ormond Street Hospital, Grove House Hospice – Hertfordshire and Hospice of St Francis – Hertfordshire (£20,000 each); Open Door – Hertfordshire, Spinal Injuries Association – Milton Keynes,

St Nicholas Hospice – Suffolk, University College London Hospitals and Scope – London (£15,000 each); Tommy's, London, Toynbee Hall, London and Women's Counselling Centre – Hertfordshire (£10,000 each); and Africana Library Trust, Sense – London, South East Cancer Help Centre and Starlight Children's Foundation – Berkshire (£5,000 each).

Grants of less than £5,000 were made totalling £128,000.

South Africa

Beneficiaries included: Ntataise Rural Pre-school Development Trust (£101,000); Sekhukhune Educare Project (£28,000); Thusanang Association (£18,000); and Jim Joel Music Scholarship – the Orchestra Company (£5,000).

Exclusions

Grants to registered charities only. No funding for:
- general appeals
- animal welfare charities
- students' individual education or gap year costs
- drug or alcohol related causes or HIV/Aids related charities
- organisations outside of the UK, apart from pre-school education in South Africa.

Applications

In writing to the correspondent. Please note: the trust welcomes initial enquiries by email or telephone, but asks that formal applications are sent by post.

There is no official application form but the trust does provide the following guidelines for potential applicants:
- applications should be made to Karen Groom (Trust Administrator) on the charity's official headed paper and include the email address of the writer
- letters should be no longer than two sides of A4 and describe 'fully, clearly and concisely' the project for which funding is being sought and who the beneficiaries will be
- detailed costing or a project budget should be included and, if possible, a copy of the latest annual report (accounts will be viewed via the Charity Commission website)

- details of other sources of funding and any funding applications currently being made are also helpful to include.

Applications can be submitted only between the months of January to March and between July and September. Send to Karen Groom after following the guidelines given in the PDF document 'Guidelines for Applicants' available from the trust's website. The trustees meet in May and December to consider applications. Applications are assessed before each meeting to check that they meet the trust's objectives. Applicants will be informed of the outcome within six weeks following the meeting.

N.B. Applications for funding in South Africa should be made to Mrs G. Bland (Fund Director) at jimjoel@iafrica.com.

Common applicant mistakes

'Applicants don't do their homework; don't read our website application guidelines; don't address the letter properly; don't sign the letter; and writing too late to be considered at a trustees' meeting.'

CHK Charities Limited

General charitable purposes

£2.4 million (2010/11)

Beneficial area

Worldwide, mainly UK, with a special interest in national charities and the West Midlands.

c/o Kleinwort Benson Trustees Limited, 14 St George Street, London W1S 1FE
Tel: 020 3207 7338
Fax: 020 3207 7655
Website: www.chkcharities.co.uk/
Correspondent: Nick R Kerr-Sheppard, Administrator
Trustees: David Peake; Charlotte Percy; David Acland; Joanna Prest; Katharine Loyd; Lucy Morris; Rupert Prest; Serena Acland; Susanna Peake.
CC Number: 1050900

Information available

Accounts were available at the Charity Commission. The trust has a very comprehensive website.

CHK Charities Limited was established in 1995. The origin of the charity derives from the wish of Sir Cyril Kleinwort and his descendants, who constitute the members of the company, to devote some of their time and resources to charitable activities. Preference is given to National or West Midlands charities

Grantmaking

The trust's set meetings are held twice a year. Consideration of appeals received is undertaken by small groups of trustees who have the authority to make grants in specific fields up to individual amounts of £25,000. These groups meet roughly bi-monthly, so appeals can be dealt with quickly and their decisions are reviewed and ratified at the next trustee meeting.

Ad hoc meetings of the trustees are convened as and when applications exceeding £25,000 have to be considered between regular meetings. The trust seeks to provide support to a significant number of charitable organisations working in the fields on which it concentrates its activities. Included in this are national or west midlands charities working in countryside matters, drug prevention, education, job creation, population control, culture, conservation, deafness, blindness, and the provision of treatment and care for people with disabilities. The trust's current policy is to consider all written appeals received within these broad guidelines.

Types of grant

One-off grants
The trust aims to 'make a difference'; it does not support individuals or very small and narrowly specialised activities but, on the other hand, it tries to avoid 'bottomless pits' and unfocused causes. Therefore grants made on a one-off basis will be towards core costs for a specific project.

Conditionally renewable grants
Grants made for more than one year can be towards start-up costs, for a specific item in the applicant's budget

(i.e. a salary) or towards the costs of a particular project. These are subject to annual progress reports.

Large grants (over £25,000)
These are approved as a result of close knowledge of specific charities by a trustee.

Further information on the trust's funding guidelines is available on its website.

In 2010/11 the trust had a total income of £1.9 million and assets of £79 million. Grants were made totalling £2.4 million and were broken down into the following areas:

Treatment and care for people with disabilities	£576,000
Education	£279,000
Youth care	£247,000
Conservation/preservation	£141,000
Miscellaneous	£128,000
Artistic causes	£127,000
General welfare and social problems	£115,000
Countryside matters and animal welfare and disease	£87,000
Medical care and research	£80,000
Drug prevention and treatment	£75,000
Care of the elderly	£63,000
Employment and job creation	£62,000
Blindness	£61,000
Hospital/nursing home building and equipment	£59,000
Hospices	£54,000
Reproductive healthcare control	£54,000
Crime prevention	£43,000
Homelessness/housing	£40,000
Deafness	£25,000
Total	**£2.4 million**

The largest beneficiaries were: Charities Aid Foundation (£105,000); Thomley Activity Centre (£100,000); Footsteps Foundation (£90,000); Royal Shakespeare Company; Endelienta Appeal; Gloucester Cathedral Trust; Cure Parkinson's Trust; National Playing Fields Association; Global Canopy Programme; Auditory Verbal UK; Canine Partners; Army Benevolent Fund; Coram Life Education; Cotswold School (£50,000 each).

Other beneficiaries included: Prince's Youth Business Trust (£30,000); County Air Ambulance Trust (£13,000); Deaf Blind UK; Sense; Carers UK; Princess Royal Trust for Carers; Academy of Ancient Music; Interact Worldwide (£10,000); Family Haven; Noah's Ark Children's Venture; Mentor Foundation UK; Shakespeare Hospice Trust; Shelter; Marie Curie Cancer Centre (£5,000

each); Dentaid (£4,000); String of Pearls Project; U Can Do It; Farming and Wildlife Advisory Group (£3,000); Clean Rivers Trust (£2,000); and City University London (£1,600).

Exclusions

The following will not normally be considered for funding:

- organisations not registered as charities or those that have been registered for less than a year
- pre-school groups
- out of school play schemes including pre-school and holiday schemes
- projects which promote a particular religion
- 'bottomless pits' and unfocused causes
- very small and narrowly specialised activities
- community centres
- appeals for places of worship
- local authorities
- umbrella or grant-making organisations
- universities and colleges and grant maintained private or local education authority schools or their Parent Teachers Associations, except if these schools are for students with special needs
- individuals or charities applying on behalf of individuals
- general requests for donations
- professional associations and training of professionals
- projects which are abroad even though the charity is based in the UK
- expeditions or overseas travel
- 'campaigning organisations' or citizens advice projects providing legal advice
- community transport projects
- general counselling projects, except those in areas of considerable deprivation and with a clearly defined client group.

Applications

The trust does not have an application form, but suggests that the following guidelines be used when making an application which should be in writing to the secretary:

- applications should be no longer than four A4 sides

- include a short summary of the organisation and its status, e.g., registered charity
- confirm the organisation has a Child Protection Policy and carries out CRB checks (if appropriate)
- provide a summary of the project and why a grant is needed
- explain how it will be monitored and evaluated
- state any funds that have already been raised/applied for
- explain where on-going funding (if required) will be obtained when the grant has been used
- state the amount needed if the request is for revenue funding for a specific item
- enclose a job description if the request is for a salary
- include the most recent audited accounts.

Applications can be submitted at any time during the year. Trustees usually meet every two months. Both successful and unsuccessful applicants are expected to wait at least one year before reapplying. Small groups of trustees have the power to make donations in specific fields up to £25,000.

Additional information on the application process can be found on the trust's website.

The Church and Community Fund

Church of England, social welfare

£500,000 (2010)

Beneficial area

England and Wales.

Church House, Great Smith Street, London SW1P 3AZ
Tel: 020 7898 1541
Email: ccf@churchofengland.org
Website: www.centralchurchfund.org.uk
Correspondent: Andrew Hawkings, Grants Manager
Trustee: The Archbishop's Council.
CC Number: 1074857

Information available

Accounts for the fund were available included in financial statement for the Archbishops' Council, of which the fund is a subsidiary. These were available at the Charity Commission or on the Archbishops' Council website. The fund also has its own useful website.

Established in 1915, the Church and Community Fund is an excepted charity but its trustee, the Archbishop's Council, is registered under the above number. The fund exists to promote the charitable work of the Church of England primarily by making grants to church and community projects. It encourages the church to engage with their local communities by funding effective and innovative community outreach projects.

The fund awards grants to community projects run by local Anglican Churches in England or other organisations who are working in close partnership with the Church of England on the ground.

The strategic funding themes for 2012 are:

- Significantly expand the Church's engagement with neighbourhood renewal
- Seek innovative ways of developing established community projects so that they either grow existing or evolve into new communities of Christian faith
- Replicate models of successful community engagement across the wider church

During 2010 the fund had assets of £16.3 million and an income of £1.3 million. Grants were made totalling £500,000.

These mainly consisted of funding for projects that equip the church to connect with their neighbourhood and beyond. Projects supported included the salary costs for youth, children's and community workers, the running costs for homeless centres, conversion of church buildings to enable use by the wider community and funding towards street outreach amongst other socially engaging initiatives.

Grants were distributed into the following areas:

	% of total
Building conversion	31%
Youth and children salary	24%
Social outreach	15%
Other, youth, children	8%
Community worker salary	7%
Basic facilities	7%
Other, salary	5%
Other	3%

The most recent beneficiaries included:

Emmanuel, West Gorton – £3,500 for kitchen and toilet improvements for the church to extend its work in the community

St Barnabas, Clarksfield – £3,000 for two youth clubs to help cooperation/cohesion between the white and Asian communities

St Barnabas with Christchurch, Worcester – £10,000 to establish a missional community into a deprived area and to help address social issues

St Andrew, Haughton-le-Skerne – £4,500 to fund a youth worker to deliver the 'Across the Boundaries'' project

Changing Attitude Sussex – £2,000 to provide a safe place of worship to help support lesbian, gay, bisexual and transgendered (LGBT) Christians

Hope's Place, Bristol- £2,000 to provide counselling and listening services for women and men for all pregnancy related issues

Exclusions

The fund will not support:
- projects that are essentially insular and inward looking
- projects which are primarily about maintaining the nation's architectural heritage
- projects which are primarily about liturgical reordering
- restoration works to bells or organs
- research projects or personal grants
- the repayment of debts or overdrafts
- projects which are not directly connected with the Church of England, ecumenical or other faith partnerships in which the Church of England element is small and projects which are predominantly secular in nature

anything for which the Church Commissioners' funds or diocesan core funding are normally available, including stipend support

feasibility studies (the fund is able to offer limited support towards the preliminary costs of projects, for example professional fees, but where a grant is awarded at this stage, no further funding will be available for the main body of the work).

Applications

The fund closed for applications in October 2011 to reopen with the new funding themes that replace the old grantmaking stream on the 3 January 2012. The trust usually has four funding rounds per year. The fund's website states:

New guidance notes that will contain specific criteria, examples of what type of projects will be funded and more detail about the new strategy will be available in mid-December 2011.

The fund illustrates the application process in a flow chart available on the website. The first part of the process takes two weeks in which applications will either be confirmed or sent back if they are incomplete. The second part of the process from confirmation that the application is complete to notification of the outcome takes on average three months. These timescales depend upon the submission date of the application and applicants should check the website to ensure the correct application deadlines.

Trustees meet four times a year.

Church Burgesses Trust

Ecclesiastical purposes, education, and other charitable purposes

£1.2 million (2010)

Beneficial area

Sheffield.

Sheffield Church Burgesses Trust, 3rd Floor, Fountain Precinct, Balm Green, Sheffield S1 2JA
Tel: 0114 267 5594
Fax: 0114 276 3176
Email: sheffieldchurchburgesses@ wrigleys.co.uk
Website: www. sheffieldchurchburgesses.org.uk
Correspondent: Godfrey J Smallman, Clerk
Trustees: D F Booker; Revd S A P Hunter; Nicholas J A Hutton; Julie Banham; Peter W Lee; J F W Peters; Prof.G D Sims; Ian G Walker; Mike R Woffenden; D Stanley; B R Hickman; Mrs S Bain.
CC Number: 221284

Information available

Accounts were available at the Charity Commission. The trust also has a very useful website.

The Sheffield Church Burgesses Trust is governed by the Charter of Queen Mary of 8 June 1554 as varied by a Scheme of the Charity Commission sealed on 23 August 1999 and a supplemental Royal Charter granted on 8 May 2003. The trust's income is divided 71.5% for ecclesiastical purposes, which includes Cathedral maintenance and the building and adaptation of churches and halls and the furthering of ministry in the four Sheffield Anglican deaneries; 10.7% for general charitable purposes in the city; and, the remaining 17.8% for educational purposes administered by a separate charity, the Church Burgesses Educational Foundation.

The trust's website states:

The trust seeks to respond to the needs of a large modern city through its support for: the parishes carved out of the ancient parish of Sheffield; organisations working for the needy, the deprived, the elderly and the marginalised; the work of Sheffield Cathedral and the revitalisation of inner city communities.

In 2010 the trust had an income of £2.4 million and held assets of £39 million. Grants were made totalling £1.2 million, distributed as follows:

Cathedral expenditure	£483,000
Ecclesiastical grants to institutions	£525,000
General grants to organisations	£193,000
Ecclesiastical grants to clergy	£5,600

Ecclesiastical grants included: St James Norton- grant for church army officer (£23,000); St Luke's Hospice (£20,000); St John's Chapeltown Youth Worker (£18,000); St Paul Wordsworth Avenue (£12,000); The Ascension Oughtibridge (£9,400); Area Deans support grant (£6,000); Church Army (£5,000); and St Mary's Handsworth-Ordinand in Training (£700).

General charitable grants included: St Luke's Hospice (£10,000); Voluntary Action Sheffield (£7,000); Sheffield Association for People with Cerebral Palsy (£5,000); The Oakes Holiday Centre (£2,500); Shopmobility; Manor Young People's Health; SAGE Greenfingers (£2,000 each); and Star Enterprise Work and Play (£1,000).

Applications

In writing to the correspondent. The trustees meet in January, April, July and October and at other times during the year through its various committees. The day to day administration of the trust, work in connection with its assets, liaison with outside bodies such as the Diocese of Sheffield, the administration of its grant programmes and the processing and handling of applications prior to their consideration by relevant committees is delegated to the Law Clerk and applications should be made to them.

The trust invites applications from Anglican parishes, from individuals involved in Christian work of a wide variety of types and from charities both national and local, involved in general charitable work within the trust's geographical area of remit.

Further information, guidelines for applying and application forms are available on the trusts website.

The Church Urban Fund

Welfare and Christian outreach in deprived communities in England

£1.1 million (2010)

Beneficial area

The most deprived areas of England.

Church House, 27 Great Smith Street, Westminster, London SW1P 3AZ

Tel: 020 7898 1647

Fax: 2078981601

Email: enquiries@cuf.org.uk

Website: www.cuf.org.uk

Correspondent: Lucy Palfreyman, Director of Finance and Resources

Trustees: Bishop Peter Broadbent; Patrick Coldstream; Michael Eastwood; Ven Paul Hackwood; Andrew Hunter Johnston; Rev Dennis Poole; Derek Twine; Betty Thayer; Rev David Walker; Brian Carroll.

CC Number: 297483

Information available

Accounts were available at the Charity Commission. The trust also has a very comprehensive website.

General

The Church Urban Fund was set up in 1988 in response to the Church of England's Faith in the City report which drew attention to the increasing levels of poverty in urban areas and to the widening gap between rich and poor. The report suggested that the church should set up a fund to help churches work more closely with their local communities to help people tackle poor housing, poor education, unemployment and poverty. An initial capital sum was raised from what was presented at the time as a one-off appeal.

The fund tackles extreme poverty in England and helps local people to restore relationships and transform lives in their own communities. They do this by supporting, resourcing and working alongside people in the most deprived parts of England. They identify churches, projects and local people already at work in their own communities to offer funding, collaboration, advice and support.

They are continuing to build a series of local networks (CUF Locals) to enable them to focus their activities and respond more effectively in order to bring sustainable change to the most deprived parts of England.

In 2010 the trust had an income of £2.5 million and held assets of

£2.9 million. Grants were made totalling £1.1 million.

Strategy

During 2011, Church Urban Fund has begun to implement a three-year plan that will see it complete its transformation from being solely a grant maker operating from an endowment to become a robust, developmental organisation that raises the money it spends and has a local presence in each of the Church of England's 43 diocese [...] Our strategic goal is to support this emerging network of Christian activists across England and provide direct support to enable them to be effective in their local work.

They now seek to achieve their aims in three ways:

- Funding others- making grants to churches and other faith groups to improve the lives of some of the poorest people in England
- Equipping others- providing guidance and advice about improving the lives of poor people to churches, faith groups and others involved in social action.
- Telling others- increasing awareness across the Church, within Government and amongst existing and potential supporters about the existence and nature of poverty and the unique role of local churches and the Church Urban Fund in tackling it.

The fund has been very concerned about the disproportionate effect that the recent government cuts have had on the poor. They have produced an excellent report detailing these effects which is available on the website.

Grantmaking

Mustard Seed Grants

This provides start-up money of up to £5,000 for individuals and new projects, enabling them to engage in social action, by supporting them to initiate or develop community work. This is a rolling programme therefore there are no deadlines.

The main grants programme is suspended indefinitely so check the website for the latest information.

The trust's plan is now to make no grants from the original endowment and fund all grants through income which is supported by major donors who have said that their support will continue. 2010 was the first year that this new strategy was implemented, hence the lower grants total (£1.1 million, 2009: £1.4 million).

Beneficiaries in 2010 included: Project Freedom Trust; Sussex Pathways; Faith Drama Productions; Housing Justice; Community Money Advice; Reading Refugee Support Group; The Bridge Pregnancy Crisis Centre; All Saints Hanley (£5,000 each); (£4,900 each); Church Action on Poverty; Bristol Inter Faith Group Keeping Health in Mind (£4,500) Youth Project @ Apostles and Cuthbert's (£4,200); St Andrews Community Network (£4,000).

Exclusions

Grants are not made for:

- projects outside England
- individuals
- projects not directly tackling profound poverty or specific issues caused by poverty
- organisations with an annual turnover of over £150,000 or with significant reserves
- projects without church or faith links
- existing salary costs except where there is a significant increase in hours in order to expand an existing project or begin new work
- ongoing revenue costs
- repeated activities (such as an annual summer camp)
- retrospective funding or loan repayment
- campaigning and fundraising activity
- revenue and capital funding for national voluntary/ community organisations and public and private sector organisations
- activities only open to church members
- evangelistic activity not part of a response to poverty
- clergy stipends including Church Army posts
- general repairs and refurbishment, internal re-ordering of churches for worship, church maintenance or DDA (Disability Discrimination Act compliance
- general appeals

Applications

The trust has produced a detailed and helpful grants policy and procedure manual and applicants are advised to read this before making an application. The manual is available from the trust's website. The trust offers this overview of the application procedure:

1 Review whether your project fits in with our criteria
2 If yes, contact your local Link Officer. Discuss your proposal, and if appropriate you will be offered an application form
3 Complete the application forma and return it with a budget outline and your latest accounts to your officer.
4 Your application will be reviewed locally before being forwarded to Church Urban Fund offices for final assessment.

The fund aims to assess applications and communicate a decision within one month of receiving the proposal in the central offices.

The City Bridge Trust (formerly known as Bridge House Trust)

Social welfare in Greater London

£16.8 million (2010/11)

Beneficial area

Greater London.

PO Box 270, Guildhall, London EC2P 2EJ
Tel: 020 7332 3710
Fax: 020 7332 3127
Email: citybridgetrust@cityoflondon.gov.uk
Website: www.citybridgetrust.org.uk/CityBridgeTrust/
Correspondent: Clare Thomas, Chief Grants Officer
Trustee: The City of London Corporation.
CC Number: 1035628

Information available

Annual report, accounts and guidelines are available from the trust or from its website.

Background

The City Bridge Trust is the grantmaking arm of Bridge House Estates. The purpose of the charity was, for many years, to maintain the bridges connecting the City of London to Southwark. It now puts its surplus revenue to charitable purposes for the benefit of Greater London, which it has chosen to do so far by making grants to charitable organisations. It has done so in an unusually open way, with detailed grants schemes and meetings that are open to the public. In all cases priority is given to projects which tackle deprivation or disadvantage. The values of the trust are independence, inclusion and fairness.

In 2010/11 the trust had an income of £40 million and assets of £828 million. 228 grants were made totalling £16.8 million. Figures given in the annual report were consolidated with the Bridge House Estates charity.

Main grants programme

Type of grants
Grants are given for either running costs or capital costs. Grants for running costs can be from one to three years. Projects of an 'exceptional or strategic nature' may then make an application for a further two years, a maximum total of five years in all. The trust will also consider supporting core costs incurred in providing services which meet the funding criteria.

Grants may be awarded for feasibility studies or disability access audits (up to £5,000 per grant) to help organisations obtain the best advice to develop their proposed projects.

The following guidelines are taken from the trust's extensive website. The trust frequently reviews its guidelines so please see its website for up-to-date details.

There are five themes under the main grants programme, each with its own specific aims and objectives.
▶ Access for disabled people
▶ London's environment
▶ Children and young people (those aged up to 25 years)
▶ Older people in the community (those aged 60 and over)
▶ Strengthening the voluntary and community sectors.

In all cases priority is given to projects which tackle the greatest deprivation or disadvantage. The trust's current programmes are:
▶ Accessible London
▶ Bridging Communities

▶ Improving Londoners' Mental Health
▶ London's Environment
▶ Older Londoners
▶ Positive Transitions to Independent Living
▶ Strengthening the Third Sector.

Accessible London
Aims: To reduce disadvantage experienced by disabled people by removing those barriers that prevent full participation in society. Particular emphasis is given to artistic and sporting activities and improving the accessibility of transport and community buildings. The trust's definition of disability is that contained in the Disability Discrimination Act 2005.

Objectives:
▶ To make third sector buildings and services more accessible.
▶ Ensure buildings are better designed, constructed and equipped to meet the needs of disabled people.
▶ Improve access to transport services.
▶ Support community transport schemes that can demonstrate they are more sustainable and financially independent.
▶ Increase access to new opportunities or report improved well-being as a result of participation in arts or sporting activities.

Funding priorities: Your application must address one of the following priorities:
1 **Accessible transport**
   ▶ Offers up to 50% of the capital cost of new accessible vehicles.
   ▶ Supports work which looks to generate new business and develop new income streams for community transport schemes, improving their longer-term financial sustainability.
   Please note: organisations applying for funding for an accessible vehicle need to demonstrate how many people will benefit and must take out membership of the Community Transport Association (for the life of the vehicle).

2 **Accessible buildings**
  - Supports work which improves access to buildings in the voluntary and community sector (including capital and related project management costs).
  - Offers funding for access audits, disability equalities training and related consultancy up to a maximum of £5,000.

  Applicants must show that an independent access audit has been undertaken.

  Please note: the trust produces a useful publication, *Opening Doors across London* for those interested in this area.

3 **Accessible arts and sports**
  - Projects which increase participation in arts and sports.

  Applicants should specify which of these themes they are applying under.

Bridging communities

Aims: This programme aims to strengthen links between communities by building on commonalities and encouraging groups to come together. It also supports improving access to services and increasing the confidence of minority groups to participate fully.

Objectives:
- To increase the number of leaders from different communities with better leadership skills, understanding and respect for each other.
- To have more people from different backgrounds working together on projects which have benefited the whole community and improved community relations.
- To raise the number of adults learning English and using it to increase their participation in the wider community/access services.
- More large, established mainstream and minority community organisations working together to deliver improved services.

Funding priorities:
- Leadership initiatives which bring people together two or more different communities (geographical, faith based, cultural, ethnic or communities of interest).

- Work involving different communities working together on volunteering or active citizenship projects.
- English Language skills for adults who are not accessing mainstream courses.
- New partnership work between mainstream and minority community organisations on specific issues.

London's environment

Aims: This programme is designed to improve the quality of London's environment and its sustainable development.

Objectives:
- To increase Londoners' knowledge of environmental issues and the principles of sustainable development.
- To enhance London's biodiversity.
- To reduce London's environmental footprint, i.e. the excessive use of natural or non-renewable resources.

Funding priorities: Applications must address one of the following priorities:
- projects to promote environmental education
- work to maintain and enhance London's biodiversity.

Please note: the trust also manages a 'Greening the Third Sector' programme which aims to share experience and best practice with regard to improving environmental performance. Grants are available to cover the costs of an eco-audit, training or consultancy provided by approved consultants. More information on this scheme is available on the trust's website.

Improving Londoners' mental health

Aims: To support work which meets a wide range of mental health needs and ensures that services are reaching marginalised communities.

Objectives:
- To have fewer older people with depression and more people reporting improvements in well-being.
- To increase the number of children and young people receiving specialist help.

- To have more homeless, transient people and rough sleepers in touch with mental health services.
- To increase the number of offenders receiving help and reduce the amount of prisoners with mental health problems inappropriately imprisoned.
- Improve access to mental health services for refugees and asylum seekers.
- Raise the number of people successfully managing to live independently or in supported accommodation.

Funding priorities:
- Projects combating depression amongst older people.
- Specialist services for children and young people (and families and carers).
- Helping homeless people, transient people and rough sleepers.
- Supporting prisoners, ex-prisoners and others in contact with the Criminal Justice System.
- Work amongst refugee and asylum seekers (particularly around trauma).
- Supporting resettlement for people with mental health issues living independently or in supported accommodation.

Older Londoners

Aims: To contribute to a London where people can enjoy active, independent and healthy lives in their old age.

Objectives:
- Have a greater number of older people over 75 years living healthier and more active lives.
- To have more older people actively contributing in their communities through volunteering.
- Improving the quality of life for those with dementia and Alzheimer's.
- To have fewer older people with depression and more people reporting improved well-being.

Funding priorities: Your application should address one of the following priorities:
- work with older people (75 years old and above) including social, cultural, educational, volunteering activities and projects encouraging healthy lifestyles

- projects which encourage healthy lifestyles with older people (65 and above)
- non-medical services that support older people of any age living with dementia and Alzheimer's.

Positive transitions to independent living

Aims: To improve the range of services for people who are going through difficult transitions and challenges.

Objectives:

- To have more disabled people reporting increased choice and control in their lives and living independently.
- Raise the number of young disabled people taking up educational or employment opportunities.
- Help disabled parents manage their parental responsibilities successfully.
- To have more care-leavers living independently and taking educational opportunities or employment.
- Increase the number of ex-offenders successfully resettled within the community and reduce re-offending.

Funding priorities:

- Services for people with a newly acquired disability.
- Projects assisting young disabled people, such as managing the move from residential care to independent living or supporting disabled school leavers into employment/college.
- Support for disabled people and young care leavers in managing independent living.
- Projects supporting disabled parents.
- Work with ex-offenders leaving custody.

Strengthening the Third Sector

Aims: To strengthen the Voluntary and Community Sector so that it can deliver effective, efficient and sustainable services helping reduce disadvantage.

Objectives:

- To have more people undertake volunteering and volunteering standards are raised.

- To help minority ethnic and/or refugee community organisations become more sustainable and work more collaboratively.
- To encourage more strategic approaches to ICT development in the sector.
- Increase the number of organisations with improved financial management, financial skills and evaluation systems.

Funding priorities: Your application must address one of the following priorities and please note this programme is for second-tier and membership organisations only.

- Increase and improve volunteering.
- Strengthening minority ethnic and refugee community organisations and encourages collaboration between them.
- New and strategic approaches to the use of Information Communication Technology (ICT).
- Improving financial management and skills services.
- Improving evaluation quality.

Greening the Third Sector

Aims: To make practical changes in behaviour to minimise unwanted environmental damage

Objectives:

- Make specific and measurable reductions in carbon and waste
- Establish the connections between environmental and social action
- Promote other environmental benefits
- Embedding and spreading good environmental practice throughout the sector

Funding priorities: The trust will cover the cost of an eco-audit, training or consultancy provided by their approved consultants. Please contact the trust in the first instance to discuss an application for this project.

Exceptional grants

The trust occasionally makes grants outside its priority areas. Consideration may be given to applications from organisations which demonstrate that they are:

- responding to new needs and circumstances which may have arisen since the trust fixed its priorities (e.g. a major catastrophe impacting upon London)

- projects that require short-term assistance to cope with unforeseen circumstances enabling them to adapt to change and move forward (need arising from poor planning will not be considered).

Note: the trust states that only a small number of grants are likely to be made in this category.

Strategic work

The trust is also working alongside other partners in several strategic initiatives including:

- reducing knife crime among young people
- improving the quality of impact measurement in the third sector
- improving communications skills in the third sector
- improving access advice for developing buildings
- reducing the third sector's carbon footprint.

More information on the trust's strategic work is available on its website.

Principles of good practice

The trust expects applicants to work to its principles of good practice. These include:

- involving beneficiaries in the planning, delivery and management of services
- valuing diversity
- supporting volunteers
- taking steps to reduce the organisation's carbon footprint.

Monitoring and evaluation

The trust requires all grants to be monitored and evaluated. Details of the trust's monitoring and evaluation policy can be found on its website.

Grantmaking in 2010/11

Of the 228 grants awarded during the year, 103 were three-year revenue funding. The trust has also decided to extend a number of grants for up to five years. They also state in the annual report that they intend to support more projects with core funding. This decision was made against the backdrop of the severe drop in public expenditure, with the view that it is a more effective way of supporting charities long term sustainability in the current economic climate.

Grants were distributed as follows:

Accessible London	£147,000
Accessible buildings	£1.1 million
Accessible arts and sport	£1 million
Bridging communities	£1.7 million
Improving Londoners' metal health	£1.4 million
London's environment	£2 million
Older Londoners	£1.8 million
Positive transitions to independent living	£3 million
Strengthening the third sector	£2.2 million
Exceptional grants	£2 million
Strategic initiatives	£421,000
Total	**£16.8 million**

Beneficiaries included: Barbican Centre Trust (£1.5 million); Mind in Camden (£150,000); Positively UK; Greening the Third Sector (£100,000 each); Cricklewood Homeless Concern (£95,000);City Centre for Charity Effectiveness Trust Ltd (£80,000); Good Food Matters (£50,000); Royal Horticultural Society (£49,000); Bromley Autistic Trust (£46,000); Arachane Greek Cypriot Women's Group (£35,000); Rampage Holiday Project (£15,000) and Amici Dance Theatre Company (£9,300).

Exclusions

The trust cannot fund:
 - political parties
 - political lobbying
 - non-charitable activities
 - work which does not benefit the inhabitants of Greater London.

The trust does not fund:
 - individuals
 - grant-making bodies to make grants on its behalf
 - schools, PTAs, universities or other educational establishments (except where they are undertaking ancillary charitable activities specifically directed towards one of the agreed priority areas)
 - medical or academic research
 - churches or other religious bodies where the monies will be used for religious purposes
 - hospitals
 - projects which have already taken place or building work which has already been completed
 - statutory bodies
 - profit making organisations (except social enterprises)
 - charities established outside the UK.

Grants will not usually be given to:
 - work where there is statutory responsibility to provide funding
 - organisations seeking funding to replace cuts by statutory authorities, except where that funding was explicitly time-limited and for a discretionary (non-statutory) purpose
 - organisations seeking funding to top up on under-priced contracts
 - work where there is significant public funding available (including funding from sports governing bodies).

Applications

Application forms are available from the trust or downloadable from its website, along with full and up-to-date guidelines. This is also available on disk, on tape and in Braille or large print formats. The application will be assessed by a member of the grants team and then considered by the grants committee, this may include a visit. The application process usually takes 3 months from receipt of the application.

Organisations may usually hold only one grant at a time however charities with branches or that are running distinct activities in different parts of London may be able to hold up to 3.

Applications for over £25,000 need to be accompanied by a detailed proposal and grants over £500,000 need the approval of the City of London Corporation's Court Common Council and are very exceptional.

Note: the trust will not consider applications sent by fax or conventional email.

'Having read our guidelines, applicants are welcome to contact the trust to discuss their proposal on the telephone before submitting their application.'

Common applicant mistakes

'Applicants not meeting the criteria of our programmes. Receiving applications from a brand new organisation without a track record (our guidelines make it clear that applicants need to have at least one set of accounts). Applications where the trust would be by far the biggest funder (our guidelines make it clear that we will not usually be the biggest funder).'

The Cleevely Family Charitable Trust

General, children and young people

Beneficial area
Worldwide.

Coutts & Co, Trustee Dept, 440 Strand, London WC2R 0QS
Tel: 020 7753 1000
Correspondent: Coutts & Co
Trustees: Dr David Cleevely; Rosalind Cleevely; Olivia Florence.
CC Number: 1137902

Information available
Basic information was available from the Charity Commission.

Established in 2010 for general charitable purposes, this is the charitable trust of Dr David Cleevely and his family. Dr Cleevely is the founding director of the Centre for Science and Policy at the University of Cambridge, and he has also had a distinguished career in communications technology.

As Dr Cleevely and his wife Rosalind are patrons of the Prince's Trust, it is likely that the trust has a preference for organisations working with children and young people. There may also be a preference for education and the Cambridge area.

The foundation's first annual report and accounts had yet to be produced at the time of writing (December 2011).

Applications
In writing to the correspondent.

The Clore Duffield Foundation

Arts/museums, Jewish charities, education, elderly and disadvantaged

£4.3 million (2010)

Beneficial area
UK, the larger grants go to London-based institutions.

Studio 3, Chelsea Manor Studios, Flood Street, London SW3 5SR
Tel: 020 7351 6061
Fax: 020 7351 5308
Email: info@cloreduffield.org.uk
Website: www.cloreduffield.org.uk
Correspondent: Sally Bacon, Executive Director
Trustees: Dame Vivien Duffield, Chair; Caroline Deletra; David Harrel; Michael Trask; Sir Mark Weinberg.
CC Number: 1084412

Information available
Accounts were available from the Charity Commission. The foundation also has a helpful website.

The foundation makes a small number of main programme grants, though they can sometimes be very large, mainly in the fields of:

- museums, galleries and heritage sites (particularly for learning spaces)
- the arts
- the performing arts
- heritage
- education
- literature
- leadership training
- health, social care and disability
- Jewish charities with interests in any of the above areas.

The foundation's website states that it has:

Two distinct grant-making strands: the Main Grants Programme and a new Small Grants Programme, the Clore Poetry and Literature Awards for children and young people. When making an application to either of these programmes, please make sure you read all the information and follow the guidelines carefully. We are a small team, and try to keep things simple: we have made the application process as straightforward as we can and all the information you need should be on this site.

Main grants programme
This offers grants ranging from below £5,000 to in excess of £1 million and the foundation continues to maintain a balance between supporting large-scale projects, with far-reaching effects, and small-scale community endeavours. All grants are awarded at a meeting of the trustees, held twice a year. As there is no fixed schedule for these meetings, applications are reviewed on an ongoing basis.

Whilst the foundation does occasionally make donations to the health and social care sectors, it should be noted that the majority of its support is directed towards the cultural sector, and in particular to cultural learning and to museum, gallery, heritage and performing arts learning spaces. Support for enhancing Jewish life is largely directed towards the new Jewish Community Centre for London.

Please note that organisations must be registered charities to be eligible for the Main Grants Programme.

The Clore Poetry and Literature Awards
These awards fund poetry and literature initiatives for children and young people, under the age of 19, across the UK. The Awards are worth a total of £1m over five years, 2011 to 2015, with individual awards ranging from £1,000 to £10,000. The Clore Duffield Foundation has created these Awards with the aim of providing children and young people with opportunities to experience poetry and literature in exciting and compelling ways, in and out of school. For full details, please download the guidance leaflet from the website.

General
In 2010 the foundation had assets of £80.7 million and an income of £4.4 million. Grants were made totalling £4.32 million, excluding support and governance costs, and were broken down as follows:

Arts, heritage and education	£2.2 million
Leadership training	£1.4 million
Health and social care	£351,000
Jewish support	£242,000

Beneficiaries in 2010 included: University of Oxford – Institute of Ageing (£1 million); Greenwich Foundation (£150,000); George Piper Dances and Imperial War Museum (£100,000 each); RF Creativity, Culture and Education (£90,000); Norwood (£55,000); Royal Opera House (£53,000); South London Gallery and University of Oxford – Ashmolean Museum (£50,000 each); Prince's Teaching Institute and Royal Shakespeare Company (£25,000 each); Marie Curie Cancer Care (£22,000); The Domnar Warehouse and Hampstead Theatre (£10,000 each); The Paul Hamlyn Foundation (£7,000); and British Library, English Touring Opera, Kneehigh Theatre, National Campaign for the Arts and Starlight Foundation (£5,000 each).

Exclusions
Potential applicants should note that their organisation must be a registered charity to be eligible. Unfortunately, the foundation does not fund projects retrospectively and will not support applications from the following:

- individuals
- general appeals and circulars.

It should also be noted that the following are funded only very rarely:

- projects outside the UK
- staff posts
- local branches of national charities
- academic or project research
- conference costs.

Applications
Please refer to the foundation's guidance leaflet which can be downloaded from its website. You are invited to contact the foundation, before making application if you have any queries regarding criteria set or the process itself.

Closehelm Ltd

Jewish, welfare, general

£506,000 (2009/10)

Beneficial area

UK and Israel.

30 Armitage Road, London
NW11 8RD
Tel: 020 8201 8688
Correspondent: Henrietta W Van Praagh, Secretary
Trustees: A Van Praagh; Henrietta W Van Praagh; Hannah R Van Praagh.
CC Number: 291296

Information available

Accounts were available from the Charity Commission, without a list of beneficiaries.

The trust supports the advancement of religion in accordance with the Jewish faith; the relief of poverty; and general charitable purposes.

In 2009/10 the trust had assets of £3.6 million and an income of £425,000. Grants were made during the year totalling £506,000. No further information was available.

Applications

In writing to the correspondent.

The Clothworkers' Foundation

General charitable purposes, in particular social inclusion, young people, older people, disability, visual impairment, alcohol/ substance misuse, prisoners, ex- offenders, homelessness and textiles

£4.9 million (2010)

Beneficial area

UK.

Clothworkers' Hall, Dunster Court, Mincing Lane, London EC3R 7AH
Tel: 020 7623 7041
Fax: 020 7397 0107
Email: foundation@clothworkers.co. uk
Website: www.clothworkers.co.uk
Correspondent: Mr A C Blessley
Trustees: John Stoddart-Scott, Chair; Maj Oliver Howard; Michael Jarvis; Richard Jonas; Michael Maylon; Christopher McLean May; Dr Carolyn Boulter; Melville Haggard; Anthony West; Christopher Jonas.
CC Number: 274100

Information available

Accounts were available at the Charity Commission. Good website with detailed annual report.

The Clothworkers' Company is an ancient City of London livery company, founded in 1528 and the twelfth of the 'Great Twelve' companies. One of the functions of livery companies was to support their members in times of need. As they grew wealthier, they were also able to benefit outsiders. The Clothworkers' Company acquired a number of trusts, established by individual benefactors for specific charitable ends. These totalled over 100 by the twentieth century. In addition, the company has always made payments to good causes from its own funds.

The Clothworkers' Foundation was set up in 1977 by the company as the independent arm for the whole of its charitable work.

The foundation's early income came from a leasehold interest in a City of London property, 1 Angel Court. Subsequent funding from the company, together with the sale of the long leasehold interest in Angel Court in 1994, represents the assets of the foundation which are substantially invested in stocks and shares. Income from these investments, together with unrestricted donations from the company, is given away each year to a wide range of charities. During its first 30 years, the foundation has made grants totalling around £73 million.

The objects of the foundation are for general charitable purposes and the foundation seeks to improve quality of life, particularly for people and communities that face disadvantage.

Grant programmes

The foundation has two programmes that are open to unsolicited applications: the Main Grants Programme and the Small Grants Programme.

Main Grants Programme is open to UK registered charities and other organisations which can demonstrate their not-for-profit status:

- with an annual operating income of under £15 million (exceptional income, such as money received for a major, one-off, fundraising initiative) can be deducted from the total income of the organisation, in order to calculate the operating income total).
- applying for a grant of over £1,000 for capital costs

Small Grants Programme is open to UK registered charities and other organisations which can demonstrate their not-for-profit status:

- with an annual turnover under £250,000. Total income must be less than £250,000, regardless of any exceptional income.
- applying for a grant of between £500 and £10,000 for capital costs
- for projects that cost less than £100,000 in total.

The 2011 annual review notes that the trust will consider applications from eligible charities for capital projects in the following areas:

Disadvantaged young people
Projects which support disadvantaged young people, particularly (but not limited to) those in or leaving care, or not in employment education or training (NEET).

Homelessness
Projects providing services for people who are homeless or at risk of becoming homeless.

Alcohol and substance misuse
Projects supporting people affected by, or at risk of, drug and/or alcohol dependency, and their families.

Domestic and sexual violence
Projects supporting people affected by domestic or sexual violence.

Prisoners and ex-offenders
Projects supporting prisoners and/or ex-offenders, or those at risk of offending, and their families.

Integration of disadvantaged minority communities
Projects providing services to disadvantaged minority communities, in particular projects which promote integration and access to mainstream services.

Elderly
Projects providing services for elderly people, in particular those living in areas of high deprivation and/or where rural isolation is an issue.

Disability
Projects providing services for people with physical and/or learning disabilities, and/or for people with mental health issues. (We will not fund projects which focus only on meeting the requirements of the Disability Discrimination Act.)

Visual impairment
Projects providing services for blind or visually impaired people.

Textiles
UK academic institutions involved in textiles, technical textiles, colour science, and needlework. Heritage appeals substantively involved with textiles, with particular emphasis on projects which we consider to be of national importance. These are considered separately from the Main and Small Grant Programmes, and may take longer to assess.

Grantmaking policy
We fund one-off grants for capital costs for UK registered charities with an annual turnover of under £10 million.

Capital costs include:
- building purchase and renovation
- equipment (including IT hardware)
- vehicles.

We do not fund revenue costs including:
- salaries
- overheads
- consumables
- training
- rent
- lease of equipment
- volunteer expenses
- professional fees
- websites
- databases
- any other running costs.

For charities which, by their nature, have no capital requirements, we will consider funding one-off projects such as production of publications (not regular newsletters etc) or the creation of training materials.

Textile Heritage Projects
- our primary interest is in supporting the cataloguing, indexing, storing, conserving, display and access to important UK textile collections and archives
- we wish to encourage access to past history in order to stimulate scholarly research and future design
- we are more interested in cloth and its manufacture than costumes
- our priority is British textiles
- we will not fund the purchase of art textiles.

Grantmaking in 2010
In 2010 the foundation and associated trusts had assets of £88.9 million and an income of £4.8 million. There were 313 grants made totalling £4.9 million. Of this total approximately £4.6 million was made in reactive grants in response to applications. The remainder was proactively contributed to areas of defined benefit selected by the trust, for which they do not accept applications.

The foundation's annual review notes that the value of the its investments increased in 2010 to £116 million, recovering substantially from a low of £89 million in 2008.

The foundation's own resources provide the core income for its grant-making, but this continues to be augmented by the contributions received from the Company. In 2010, these amounted to £2.4m, of which £0.3m was added to the endowment.

Grantmaking activity
In 2010, we made 313 grants, a significant increase on the previous year. The bulk of our resources continue to be deployed in smaller grants, with 60% being for £20,000 or below. The statistics were distorted by the major V&A commitment of £1 million.

The foundation also commented on the quality of applications received:

We hope our guidelines and advice are clear, but like many grant-makers, we continue to receive far too many ineligible approaches.

Proactive grants programme
Following a strategic review in 2006, the trustees established a Proactive Grants Programme, under which three areas would be allocated £1.25 million each over a five-year period. The areas are autism, mathematics and conservation, reflecting the Foundation's longstanding interest in disability, education and arts and heritage.

As these proactive programmes come to a close the trust notes:

We will be establishing a new proactive programme of £375,000 devoted to giving overseas. The Trustees are keen for this to be sufficiently focused to enable it to have an impact. We expect to decide the emphasis of this new programme by the end of 2011. We will subsequently be exploring areas for proactive programmes to replace maths education and autism when these end. The Trustees have agreed to allocate £1.25m to each of the two new programmes, which are unlikely to begin for a year or so.

Grants were distributed across all of the priority areas as follows:

Textiles	£1.4 million
Social inclusion	£891,000
Disability	£829,000
Encouragement of young people	£774,000
Mathematics	£624,000
Conservation	£165,000
Elderly	£163,000
Autism	£118,000
Other	£40,000
Visual impairment	£5,000
Returned/cancelled grants	(£121,000)

A sample of beneficiaries across all categories includes: Victoria & Albert Museum (£1 million); Maths in Education & Industry (£250,000); Manchester Deaf Centre and Oxford Association for the Blind (£50,000 each); Osmani Trust, Sedgefield and District CAB and UCL Medical School (£30,000 each); Newlife Foundation for Disabled Children and St John of Jerusalem Eye Hospital (£25,000 each); Sobriety Project (£20,000); Bradford College Textile Archive and Ley Community Drug Services (£15,000); ConstructionSkills (£13,000); Acceptable Enterprises (Larne) (£12,000); Age Concern Richmond-Upon-Thames (£11,000); Bexley Autism Support and Information

Centre (£10,000); and Royal Fusiliers Museum (£5,000).

Exclusions

The foundation does not make grants to:

- non UK-registered charities
- organisations with an annual turnover of over £10 million (charities working in textiles with an annual turnover of over £10 million, wishing to make an application, are requested to contact the foundation)
- non-capital costs i.e. running costs, salary costs
- organisations that have received a grant from the foundation in the last five years
- heritage projects (other than textiles)
- environment projects
- arts and education projects are unlikely to be funded unless they are predominantly focused on disadvantaged young people, the elderly or the disabled
- projects that do not fit in with one of our programme areas
- individuals
- general or marketing appeals
- educational establishments
- grant-makers
- overseas work/projects
- medical research or equipment
- political, industrial, or commercial appeals
- relief of state aid or reduction of support from public funds
- events
- pay for websites, databases, or other software. The charity no longer funds IT equipment unless it will be used primarily by service users (and not staff or volunteers)
- appeals from any organisation where the money will be used for religious purposes or projects which promote a particular religion.

Applications

There are separate application forms for the main and small grants programmes available from the foundation's website, which also gives full details of the application process and criteria for funding. Both programmes require the following information:

- completed application form
- full project budget
- latest accounts for the organisation as submitted to the Charity Commission
- copy of the correspondence confirming Northern Ireland charitable status if registered in NI.

Applications are accepted at any time, there are no deadlines. Decisions normally take eight weeks for the small grants programme and six months for the main grants programme. Applications can be submitted by post or email. Email applications will only be accepted if the entire application (including accounts, budget and any supporting information) is sent electronically. If any part of the application cannot be emailed, the entire application must be posted.

Any applicants who have specific queries after reading the foundation's guidelines should contact the grants assistant on 020 7623 7041. The foundation does not however, provide advice on matters which are covered on its website.

If your application is not successful, you must wait six months before re-applying.

A charity which has received a grant in either programme cannot apply again for at least five years.

Common applicant mistakes

'Applicants failing to fill out our application form; failing to read our guidelines; failing to provide a project budget.'

Richard Cloudesley's Charity

Churches, medical and welfare

£446,000 to organisations (2009/10)

Beneficial area

North Islington, London.

Reed Smith LLP, 26th Floor, Broadgate Tower, 20 Primrose Street, London EC2A 2RS

Tel: 020 3116 3624
Email: kwallace@reedsmith.com
Correspondent: Keith Wallace, Clerk
Trustees: Kevin A Streater, Chair; Cllr J Asato; Courtney Bailey; Miranda Coates; Cllr P Convery; John Durdin; Ms M Elliott; Kathleen Frenchman; Roger Goodman; Rev S Harvey; Pat Haynes; JR Trotter; M Maunsell; Ms V Mirfin; Ms D Reeves; David R Stephens; Rupert Perry; Dorothy Newton.
CC Number: 205959

Information available

Accounts were available at the Charity Commission.

Summary

The charity was founded in 1518 by the will of Richard Cloudesley. He left the rent from a 14 acre field in Islington, London, to be used for the benefit of residents of Islington parish. The field was in Barnsbury and its centre was what is now Cloudesley Square.

In the charity's previous annual report and accounts it stated that property owned by the charity in the area was being redeveloped to be sold, although this process was 'taking longer than expected.' However, in the 2009/10 annual report and accounts the trust decided to re-let the property rather than to re-sell it. In the same year the trust's investment income also dropped. These instances saw an overall increase in expenditure and a reduction in income, resulting in the trustee's decision to reduce grant expenditure; the charity stated in its 2009/10 annual report:

> Our investment income reduced both through the fall of dividend income and in deposit interest earned (£593,000 (2010) against £828,500 (2009)). Capital values of our investments again disappointed, thought not to such an extent as the previous two years

> Despite wanting to maintain the grants at the fullest level possible, a consequence was that the trustees felt that grants could not be maintained and the overall figure fell from £762,000 in 2009 to £647,500 this year.

Grants ranging from £100 to around £40,000 are given to Church of England churches and to charities supporting a range of beneficiaries, for the 'sick poor in the ancient parish of Islington'. As part of its help to the 'sick poor' the trust operates a welfare fund making quick and modest grants to needy individuals.

The charity can only assist in activities in the ancient parish of Islington which is now the northern part of the modern London Borough of Islington – roughly everything north of Chapel Market and City Road. 'It is clear that there are few bodies that confine their work to such a small area and the charity does help charities in Islington as a whole, or Islington and nearby London boroughs.' The charity requires applicants to provide an assessment of the proportion of what they do that can be said to be related to people living in the ancient parish. This limited geographical scope makes for difficulties in granting funds to nationally organised charities. Some of these have locally accounted branches – and others have locally identifiable projects – but without some restriction like this, the charity will be unable to assist.

The charity's policy tends to be to make grants that are free of conditions. Feedback from grantees suggest that this gives much needed flexibility in helping to fill gaps caused by the more rigid terms that other funders are constrained to adopt. The charity though is aware of the need for accountability and is able to exercise some monitoring through accounts, information, trustee contact and the occasional visit.

Most grants are given to charities previously supported, though the amounts are clearly reassessed each year as they frequently vary.

Grantmaking in 2009/10

In 2009/10 the charity had assets of over £22 million and an income of £943,000. Grants were made in three categories totalling £647,000 as follows:

Churches	19	£334,000
Medical and welfare needs	22	£112,000
Welfare fund grants	unknown	£205,000

The above welfare fund grants refers to grants made to individuals in need in the Islington area [see A Guide to Grants for Individuals in Need published by Directory of Social Change]. All other grants were made to churches and organisations totalling £446,000.

Grants included those made to: St Augustine – Highbury New Park (£35,000); St John's District Church (£28,000); St Mary – Ashley Road (£22,000); St Thomas – Finsbury Park (£17,000); CARIS – Islington (£7,000); Stuart Low Trust (£6,000); Choices Islington (£5,000); St George's – Tufnell Park (£4,000); Community Languages Support Services (£3,000); Angel Shed Theatre Company (£2,000); and Single Homelessness Project (£300).

Applications

Applicants should write to the correspondent requesting an application form.

Applications should be in time for the trustees' meetings in April and November and should be accompanied by the organisation's accounts. The following information should be supplied:

- details of the work your organisation undertakes
- how it falls within the geographical area of the trust
- details what the grant will fund.

If you would like acknowledgement of receipt of your application send an sae.

Block grants are considered twice a year, in late April, and early November, at a grants committee meeting. Recommendations are made by the grants committee at these meetings and are reviewed and authorised by the trustees two weeks later. The charity will give brief reasons with any application that is not successful.

Clydpride Ltd

Relief of poverty, Jewish charities, general charitable purposes

£1.2 million (2010)

Beneficial area

Unrestricted.

Tavistock House South, Tavistock Square, London WC1H 9LG
Tel: 020 8731 7744
Correspondent: L Faust, Secretary
Trustees: L Faust; M H Linton; Aron Faust.
CC Number: 295393

Information available

Accounts were available at the Charity Commission.

The objects of this trust are to advance religion in accordance with the Jewish orthodox faith, the relief of poverty and general charitable purposes. The main focus is to support the 'renaissance of religious study and to alleviate the plight of poor scholars'. For example, the trust has recently made grants to an institution for advanced Talmudical study and research.

In 2010 the trust had assets of £14.3 million and an income of £1.1 million. Grants were made totalling £1.2 million. This comprised: £982,000 to educational institutions to support the advancement of religion through education; £163,000 for the relief of poverty; and £14,000 which was donated to institutions that benefit the Jewish community in ways such as through medical facilities.

No list of beneficiaries was available but previously has included: Achiezer; Achisomoch Aid Company; Beis Chinuch Lebonos; Beis Soroh Scheneirer Seminary; Bnei Braq Hospital; Comet Charities Limited; EM Shasha Foundation; Friends of Mir; Gevurath Ari Torah Academy Trust; Mosdos Tchernobil; Notzar Chesed; Seed; Society of Friends of Torah; and Telz Talmudical Academy Trust.

Applications

The trust states that unsolicited applications are not considered.

The Coalfields Regeneration Trust

General, health, welfare, community regeneration, education, young people, older people

£12.1 million (2009/10)

Beneficial area
Coalfield and former coalfield communities in England (North West and North East, Yorkshire, West Midlands and East Midlands, Kent), Scotland (West and East) and Wales.

Silkstone House, Pioneer Close, Manvers Way, Wath Upon Dearne, Rotherham S63 7JZ
Tel: 0800 064 8560
Fax: 01709 765 599
Email: info@coalfields-regen.org.uk
Website: www.coalfields-regen.org.uk
Correspondent: Janet Bibby, Chief Executive
Trustees: Peter McNestry, Chair; Kenneth Greenfield; Jim Crewdson; Prof. Anthony Crook; Dawn Davies; John Edwards; Peter Fanning; Vernon Jones; Peter Rowley; Wayne Thomas; Fran Walker; Sylvia Wileman; Nicholas Wilson.
CC Number: 1074930

Information available
Accounts were available at the Charity Commission. The trust's website is informative and helpful to applicants.

Summary
Set up in 1999, the Coalfields Regeneration Trust is an independent charity dedicated to the social and economic regeneration of coalfield communities in England, Scotland and Wales. It was set up in response to a recommendation by the government's *Coalfields Task Force Report*. The report highlighted the dramatic effects that mine closures had, and continue to have, on communities in coalfield areas.

The trust provides advice, support and financial assistance to community and voluntary organisations which are working to tackle problems at grassroots level within coalfield communities. It is closely connected with the areas it serves, operating through a network of staff based at offices located within coalfield regions themselves.

The trust's mission is: 'Working closely with partners, the Trust is a key agency promoting and achieving social and economic regeneration in the coalfields of England, Scotland and Wales.' The aim is to make coalfields sustainable, and to work towards the point where they can be prosperous, viable and cohesive without support.

In addition to grant making, the trust has invested and acted strategically where a more structured intervention is necessary. In areas where mines have just closed or are under threat, such as in Selby, the trust has demonstrated that with government support it can act swiftly to ensure that the worst effects do not happen.

Many coalfields' wards continue to be the most deprived in the country. The trust works with people at a very grassroots level in order to build confidence and encourage them to actively participate in taking their communities forward. The trust believes in giving people aspirations for the long term sustainability of their communities and is committed to standing by them to achieve their goals. This is illustrated in the collaboration with English Partnerships in establishing Initiate, a roving team to ensure that local people are connected to the major site developments on former coalfield sites and the trust intends to continue to build on this work to ensure that it makes a contribution towards making that happen.

General
In 2009/10 the trust had an income of £20.5 million, assets of £4.4 million and made grants totalling £12.1 million.

The trust has offices in all of the coalfield areas of England, Scotland and Wales. Each office has at least one regeneration manager and one administrative worker. These teams continue to provide essential support, application forms, advice and guidance to help applicants with their project and represent the trust's ongoing commitment to grass-roots regeneration of coalfield communities.

Programmes
The following information is taken from the trust's website:

One of the major strengths of the Coalfields Regeneration Trust is the flexibility of our funding programmes. They're there to help people, not make them jump through hoops. At the one end of the spectrum we give grants from our 'community chest' to small organisations to help them develop, and at the other end we give large grants of up to £100,000 to bigger voluntary, community and statutory organisations.

Our grants programme is about helping groups who respond to local need. But we're also proactive in developing ideas and projects that address key issues such as worklessness, isolation, skills, sector development and sustainability.

In short, the Trust is always interested in working with partners to deliver projects and programmes that will contribute to the regeneration of coalfields communities.

We try to keep our application form as simple as possible. However, as we are using public money we will need quite a bit of information from you, for we must manage our funds in a proper way.

It is important that we can judge how effective our funding decisions are in contributing to the regeneration of the coalfields. It is also important that the activities we support fit in well with our own priorities and those of other regeneration programmes.

Coalfields Community Grants- level 1
This programme awards grants from £500–£5,000 and is targeted at voluntary and community organisations that will impact positively on people living in coalfield communities. Examples of projects that this programme could support include:

▷ improvements to a community facility
▷ a training project that teaches people a new skill or enables them to get a qualification
▷ setting up a new or supporting an existing social enterprise
▷ an activity that gets people involved in physical activity or addresses a local health issue

- the establishment of a much needed new service or activity in a community
- the provision of childcare places for nursery, pre school, after school activities and holiday schemes
- activities that promote volunteering and get new people involved as volunteers

To apply to this programme it is advised that you contact your local trust office to develop the application and refer to the very comprehensive information booklet that is available to download on the trusts website

Coalfields Community Grants- level 2
Level 2 grants are for £10,000 to £100,000 and can be applied to by:

- voluntary, community and social enterprise organisations
- community interest companies
- statutory organisations
- branches of national organisations

There are four key funding themes that respond to the needs of coalfield communities. Projects must address one or more of the themes.

Access to Employment
This theme aims to connect people living in deprived neighbourhoods to mainstream opportunities and seeks to fund forward thinking and locally designed approaches that offer a route for people to get back into work.

Education and Skills
This theme aims to support people in accessing learning opportunities and developing their skills through added value activity.

Health and Well Being
This theme aims to improve the health and lifestyles of people living in coalfield communities through community based approaches and preventative projects. These should be:

- community based and prevent ill health
- additional to statutory provision
- complementary to the trust's Healthy Lifestyles Programme

Access to Opportunities
This theme aims to improve access to services in coalfield communities recognising that limited community infrastructure and geographical

isolation can prevent people from taking up opportunities.

This level 2 grants scheme can fund both capital and running costs. Applicants should refer to the comprehensive information booklet available on the foundations website.

Bridging the Gap (BtG)
Applications from Dover and Cumbria continue to be delivered under this programme. the foundation advises potential applicants for this programme to contact their regional office, details of which can be found on the website.

Grantmaking in 2009/10
Grants were broken down in the annual report by country and amount:

England		
under £10,000	333	£1.4 million
£10,000–£30,000	46	£1.1 million
£30,000–£60,000	21	£931,000
£60,000–£300,000	50	£5.4 million
over £300,000	1	£1.4 million
Total	**451**	**£10.2 million**
Scotland		
under £10,000	76	£337,000
£10,000–£30,000	12	£231,000
£30,000–£60,000	5	£232,000
£60,000–£300,000	1	£72,000
over £300,000	–	–
Total	**94**	**£872,000**
Wales		
under £10,000	33	£252,000
£10,000–£30,000	4	£76,000
£30,000–£60,000	2	£86,000
£60,000–£300,000	6	£667,000
over £300,000	–	–
Total	**45**	**£1.1 million**

Beneficiaries included: Aylesham Neighbourhood Project (£210,000); Haswell and District Mencap Society- The Community Anchor (£98,000); Derbyside Rural Community Council- Wheels to Work (£89,000); The Cornforth Partnership- The Reach project (£75,000); Nottinghamshire Independent Domestic Abuse Link Workers (£66,000); Stoke On Trent and District Gingerbread Centre Ltd- Peer Mentoring (£37,000); St Johns Church- A Building in Which to Serve Our Community (£10,000); Mansfield and Dukeries Irish Association- Luncheon Club (£5,000); City of Durham Air Cadets- Achieving Duke of Edinburgh's Awards (£3,800); Thornycroft Art Club- Christmas Tree Exhibition (£520).

Exclusions
The following are not eligible to apply for the Level 2 programme:

- individuals
- private businesses
- organisations that the trust believes are in a poor financial position or whose financial management systems are not in good order. The trust bases its opinion on an organisation's financial position and management systems, an analysis of its accounts, other management information and interviews with the organisation itself
- voluntary and community organisations and groups who hold 'free reserves' that total more than 12 months' operating costs and who are not contributing enough funds to the project. The trust will assess how much money the organisation has available in free reserves using information from their accounts. (Free reserves are the amounts of money an organisation hold that are not restricted by any other funder for any other purpose and do not include fixed assets i.e. the value of buildings)
- organisations whose purpose is to raise funds for a specific project
- 'friends of' groups where the end beneficiary will clearly be a statutory body
- organisations not established in the UK
- pigeon (flying) clubs

The following are not eligible to receive support from the Bridging the Gap programme:

- individuals
- private businesses
- statutory bodies
- national organisations
- parish, town and community councils
- organisations with total income (from all sources) above £100,000
- organisations that the trust believes are in a poor financial position or whose financial management systems are not in good order
- organisations whose purpose is to raise funds for a specific project
- 'friends of groups' where the end beneficiary will clearly be a statutory body
- organisations not established in the UK
- pigeon (flying) clubs.

Applications

Application details are different for each programme. The trust has produced very comprehensive information booklets that should be read before applying to any fund. The application form for the first stage of applications to the level one programme is available on the foundation's website. Applicants are advised to contact their regional manager before making an application, details of which are also on the trust's website. The staff will be able to advise on the Trust's application process and an appointment can be made with a member of the development team to discuss the application in more detail. Applicants should be aware that the application process can take up to 23 weeks.

The John S Cohen Foundation

General, in particular music and the arts, education and environment

£333,500 (2009/10)

Beneficial area

Worldwide, in practice mainly UK.

PO Box 21277, London W9 2YH
Tel: 020 7286 6921
Correspondent: Mrs Diana Helme, Foundation Administrator
Trustees: Dr David Cohen, Chair; Ms Imogen Cohen; Ms Olivia Cohen; Ms Veronica Cohen.
CC Number: 241598

Information available

Accounts were available at the Charity Commission.

The objectives of the foundation are general charitable purposes in the UK or elsewhere and it is particularly active in supporting education, music and the arts and the environment, both built and natural.

In 2009/10 the foundation had assets of £6.9 million and an income of

£480,000. Grants were made to 88 organisations totalling £333,500. Grants are generally for £5,000 or less.

Larger grants were made to: Harris Manchester College, Oxford (£40,000); Wigmore Hall (£29,000); Holburne Museum (£25,000); and the National Gallery (£20,000).

More typical grants included those to: Aldeburgh Music (£10,000); Garsington Opera (£7,000); Centre for Children's Books, Presteigne Festival and the Stephen Spender Memorial Trust (£5,000 each); Jewish Music Institute and Tricycle Theatre (£4,000 each); Edinburgh International Book Festival, London Chamber Music Society and the Royal Exchange Theatre – Manchester (£3,000 each); Father Thames Trust, International Programme on the State of the Oceans and Shelter (£2,000 each); and Disasters Emergency Committee, Norfolk Wildlife Trust and Wallace Collection (£1,000 each).

Grants of less than £1,000 each included those to: English National Opera; Hampstead Counselling Service; Liberal Jewish Synagogue; RAF Benevolent Fund; and the Worshipful Company of Musicians.

Applications

In writing to the correspondent:

> Grants are awarded after the submission of applications to the trustees. The trustees review the application to judge if the grant falls within the charity's objectives and whether the application meets its requirements in terms of the benefits it gives. Each application is discussed, reviewed and decided upon by the trustees at their regular meetings.

Common applicant mistakes

'Applicants not specifying the amount sought.'

The R and S Cohen Foundation

Education, relief in need and the arts

£1 million (2010)

Beneficial area

Worldwide.

42 Portland Place, London W1B 1NB
Correspondent: Tess Housden
Trustees: Lady Sharon Harel-Cohen; Sir Ronald Cohen; Tamara Harel-Cohen; David Marks; Jonathan Harel-Cohen.
CC Number: 1078225

Information available

Accounts were available at the Charity Commission.

The foundation was established in 1999 by Sir Ronald Cohen, chair of Bridges Ventures Investment Company, for general charitable purposes.

The trust states that its objectives are:

- The advancement of education
- The relief of persons who are in conditions of need, hardship or distress as a result of local, national or international disaster or by reason of their social and economic circumstances
- In promoting and encouraging for the public all aspects of the arts, including painting, sculpture, theatre and music
- Other deserving causes as the trustees see fit.

In 2010 the trust had an income of £2 million, held assets of £8 million and made grants totalling £1 million.

The most significant beneficiary was the Portland House Trust who received a grant of £747,000.

Other beneficiaries included: UJIA (£50,000); Design Museum (£40,000); Muscular Dystrophy, Royal National Institute for the Blind (£25,000 each); Jewish Care (£20,000); Tel-Aviv University Trust (£15,000); British Museum (£13,000); New Israel Fund (£8,000); Tate Foundation (£5,000); Royal Academy of the Arts (£4,500); WLS Charitable Fund (£1,200).

Grants of £1,000 or less totalled £9,000.

Applications

In writing to the correspondent.

The Colt Foundation

Occupational and environmental health research

£459,500 to organisations (2010)

Beneficial area
UK.

New Lane, Havant, Hampshire
PO9 2LY
Tel: 023 9249 1400
Fax: 023 9249 1363
Email: jackie.douglas@uk.coltgroup.com
Website: www.coltfoundation.org.uk
Correspondent: Mrs Jacqueline Douglas, Director
Trustees: Prof. David Coggon; Clare Gilchrist; Prof. A J Newman Taylor; Juliette O'Hea; Peter O'Hea; Alan O'Hea; Jerome O'Hea; Natasha Lebus; Patricia Lebus.
CC Number: 277189

Information available
Accounts were available at the Charity Commission.

This foundation was established in 1978 and its primary aim is to promote and encourage research into social, medical and environmental problems created by commerce and industry.

The foundation considers applications for funding high quality research projects in the field of occupational and environmental health, particularly those aimed at discovering the cause of illnesses arising from conditions at the place of work. The work is monitored by the foundation's scientific advisers and external assessors to achieve the maximum impact with available funds. The trustees prefer to be the sole source of finance for a project.

The foundation also makes grants through selected universities and colleges to enable students to take higher degrees in subjects related to occupational and environmental health. PhD Fellowships are awarded each year, and the foundation is committed to support the MSc course

in Human & Applied Physiology at King's College, London. More than 80 students have been supported since the inception of the foundation and grants to students account for over one-quarter of the foundation's annual grants.

Donations to organisations vary from a few thousand pounds to over £100,000 and may be repeated over two to five years. Beneficiaries are well-established research institutes (awards to individuals are made through these). The foundation takes a continuing interest in its research projects and holds annual review meetings.

In 2010 the foundation had assets of £18 million and an income of £487,00. Grants were made during the year totalling £624,000, which included £459,500 to 17 organisations and £104,000 to students.

Some institutions received more than one grant during the year. Beneficiaries included: Edinburgh Napier University (£96,000); National Heart and Lung Institute (£69,000); ELEGI (£52,000); University of Aberdeen (£44,000); University of Edinburgh (£42,000); Swansea University (£18,000); EPICOH 2011 (£10,000); University of Central Lancashire (£3,000); British Occupation Health Research Foundation (£1,000); Royal Society of Medicine – United States (£900); and, Manchester – Jones and Scrutton (£260).

Exclusions
Grants are not made for the general funds of another charity, directly to individuals or projects overseas.

Applications
In writing to the correspondent. Initial applications should contain sufficient information for the scientific advisers to be able to comment, and include a lay summary for the trustees' first appraisal. This lay summary is regarded as important, as the majority of trustees do not have a medical or scientific background and this helps them with their decision making.

The trustees meet twice each year, normally in May and November. Applications should reach the

correspondent by 23rd March and 1st October in time for these meetings so that advice can be obtained from external assessors beforehand. However, applicants can submit a single sheet 'lay summary' at any time during the year, so that advice can be given on whether the work is likely to fall within the remit of the foundation, prior to working on a full application.

The foundation does not have application forms. Applicants are asked to read the following guidelines carefully and follow them when preparing an application:

- what is the work you would like to do?
- why does the work need doing?
- who is doing or has done similar work, and how will your work add to it?
- how do you intend to carry out the work, and why do you think this is the right approach?
- what resources will you need to do the work, and are these resources available?
- who will do the work, and how much time will each of the people involved devote to it?
- how long will the work take?
- how much money do you need to complete the work?
- when do you plan to start?

Applicants are advised to visit the foundation's helpful website.

Common applicant mistakes
'They do not take into consideration that our main area of interest is occupational and environmental health.'

Colyer-Fergusson Charitable Trust

Social isolation, exclusion or poverty, community activity (often through churches), church maintenance, environment, the arts

£631,000 (2009/10)

Beneficial area

Kent.

Hogarth House, 34 Paradise Road, Richmond, Surrey TW9 1SE

Tel: 020 8948 3388

Email: grantadmin@cfct.org.uk

Website: www.cfct.org.uk

Correspondent: Jacqueline Rae, Director

Trustees: Jonathan Monckton, Chair; Nicholas Fisher; Robert North; Ruth Murphy.

CC Number: 258958

Information available

Accounts and information on new priority areas were provided by the trust.

In 1969 Sir James Herbert Hamilton Colyer-Fergusson created the Colyer-Fergusson Charitable Trust with an initial settlement of £50,000. The trust aims to make grants to charities and churches in Kent to improve quality of life, tackle poverty, social isolation or exclusion and protect the natural resources and heritage of the local areas for their inhabitants. It also supports the sustainability of local churches.

Extra consideration is given to projects that encourage self help, involve users in their management, have built in evaluation procedures and will use funds to lever funding from other sources.

The trust requires all grant recipients to submit monitoring reports online to keep the trustees informed about the progress of the work supported by the grant. The following information is available from the trust's website:

Programme areas

The trustees are currently inviting applications from charities and other not-for-profit organisations that are working within one of the following six programme areas:

1   **Safer communities** – Projects should be focused on: reducing levels of crime; tackling anti-social behaviour; addressing the problems of drug and alcohol abuse in communities; reducing the incidence of re-offending or providing support for victims of crime.

2   **Protecting and supporting older vulnerable people** – Projects that improve the lives of older people in Kent and in particular, those that are vulnerable or isolated.

3   **Refugees and asylum seekers** – the trust is particularly interested to hear from projects that provide services for older refugees and asylum seekers, or those that provide services for young people and children, improving their education and sense of identity.

4   **Caring for carers** – the trust will fund projects that give carers practical or emotional support and help them manage the impact that caring has on their lives. Priority will be given to projects that address the needs of 'hard to reach' carers, such as young carers or those from ethnic minority or refugee communities.

5   **Transition to independence for young people leaving care** – projects may be focused on meeting young people's economic, educational or emotional needs as they make the difficult transition to independence.

6   **Encouraging active living** – funding is available for projects that make it easier for people to enjoy physical activity as part of their daily lives. Priority will be given to projects that increase opportunities for physical activity among children, adolescents or older people living in low-income communities.

Extra priority will be given to organisations:

- operating with low overheads
- using innovative approaches to tackle long-standing issues
- collaborating with other local voluntary organisations
- offering matched funding opportunities (we are particularly interested in working with other funders to deliver solutions)
- tackling work that is unattractive to the general public or unpopular with other funders
- able to demonstrate the effective use of volunteers.

Supporting Communities in Kent

Kent is a large and diverse county characterised by areas of affluence and pockets of deprivation. The trustees keep local needs under regular review and consider the work of other Kent funders to ensure that their grants are targeted where they can have the greatest impact. With this in mind the trustees have decided to focus their grants on the following six programme as listed above.

Supporting Churches in Kent

The trust has supported churches in Kent for over thirty years. The trustees are aware that churches in Kent are not only important local landmarks but also essential community resources at the heart of many villages. Dwindling congregation numbers means that it is increasingly difficult for parishes to raise the funds to maintain church buildings. This programme will make grants to support the fabric and maintenance of churches in Kent, improve and re-order church buildings and where possible encourage their sustainability.

Full details of the new priority areas are available from the trust's website.

Grantmaking 2009/10

In 2009/10 the trust had assets of £26.2 million and an income of £492,000. Grants were made totalling £5.1 million. This was an exceptional grant total as a single large donation of £4.5 million was made during the year to the University of Kent towards the cost of a new building for music rehearsal and performance; grants usually total around £600,000. In 2009/10 grants were broken down as follows:

Rural and coastal community	11	£235,000
Church fabric repair	12	£177,000
Safer communities	6	£101,000
Encouraging active living	3	£51,000
Caring for carers	2	£35,000
Young people leaving care	1	£20,000
Older vulnerable people	1	£10,000
Other	2	£2,200
Special grant	1	£4.5 million

Beneficiaries included: Minster Abbey (£75,000); Deal Town Football Club (£40,000); St Giles Trust (£30,000); Alkham Valley Community Project (£21,000); Capel-le-Fern Village Hall (£15,000); Thanington Neighbourhood Community Centre (£12,500); Betteshanger Social Club & Community Centre (£10,000); and Volunteer Reading Help (£5,000).

Exclusions

No grants are considered for the following:

- Individuals directly
- Animal welfare charities
- Events such as conferences, seminars and exhibitions.
- Expeditions and overseas travel
- Fee-charging residential homes, nurseries and care facilities
- Festivals, performances and other arts and entertainment activities
- Fund-raising events
- Hospitals, Health Service Trusts, medically related appeals and medical equipment
- Loans or repayment of loans
- Commercial ventures or publications
- National charities – unless they have a project located and operating within Kent
- Mini-buses other than community transport schemes
- Research – academic and medical
- Retrospective grants
- Schools other than pre-school and after school clubs
- Work that duplicates existing local provision
- Sponsorship – organisations and individuals
- Large capital, endowment or widely distributed appeals.

Applications

All applicants must complete the online application form. There is no deadline for applications and they will all be acknowledged. Trustees meet regularly during the year and decisions are usually processed within six months. All applicants will be notified in writing. The trust requests applicants, where possible, to submit any supporting material by email as scanned documents or files.

Comic Relief

Social welfare

£19.7 million in the UK (2009/10)

Beneficial area

UK and overseas.

5th Floor, 89 Albert Embankment, London SE1 7TP
Tel: 020 7820 2000
Fax: 020 7820 2222

Email: ukgrants@comicrelief.com
Website: www.comicrelief.com
Correspondent: Gilly Green, Head of UK Grants
Trustees: Peter Benett-Jones, Chair; Lenny Henry; Cilla Snowball; Claudia Lloyd; Colin Howes; Diana Barran; George Entwistle; Harry Cayton; Imelda Walsh; Jana Bennett; Jim Hytner; Joe Cerrell; Mike Harris; Richard Curtis; Suzi Aplin; Theo Sowa; Tristia Clarke; Robert Stopford Webb.
CC Number: 326568

Information available

Accounts are available from the Charity Commission. Full information is also available from the charity's excellent website.

Since 1985 Comic Relief has raised around £500 million to tackle poverty and social injustice in the UK, Africa, and more recently in some of the poorest countries in other parts of the world. This entry is primarily concerned with grant making in the UK.

In 2002, Comic Relief started a second initiative, Sport Relief. Half of its income goes to the International Children and Young People's programme, the other half to projects in the UK that are using sport to increase social cohesion and inclusion.

The charity also administers Robbie Williams' Give It Sum Fund for community-based projects in his home area of North Staffordshire.

The charity principally receives its income through the generosity of the public via its Red Nose Day fundraising event. This is held every two years in partnership with the BBC, and the extent of the grantmaking depends entirely on the success of the preceding event.

In 2009/10 grants across all programmes totalled almost £58.2 million (£47 million in 2007/08) – this includes £19.7 million of grants made in the UK. Red Nose Day 2011 raised over £102 million.

Grantmaking principles

The charity describes its UK grantmaking principles as follows:

> Our vision in the UK – across England, Scotland, Northern Ireland and Wales – is that people should be able to live free from poverty, where their rights and safety are protected, their needs provided for and where they can play a part in the communities in which they live.

We aim to treat all organisations applying to us fairly and efficiently. We try to make applying for a grant as simple as possible, while making sure that the money the public works so hard to raise is well spent.

What we look for in applications

We always get many more applications than we can fund, so we have to make some difficult choices. We want to make sure that our funding is spread around the UK and that we support some large-scale initiatives as well as smaller, community-based groups. We also want to see that your organisation is well managed, your project is well planned and that you have the skills and experience to carry out the work.

We will undertake various checks to establish the authenticity of your organisation.

When we come to consider your application in detail we will look at the extent to which you work within the following principles as we believe that working in this way will help deliver the best possible outcomes.

We have designed our application form to help us understand the extent to which you take account of these principles in the way you work. You may find it helpful to consider the information below as you complete your application.

These principles guide both the way in which we work and the expectations we have of the organisations we fund. We use the principles to help inform how we allocate our funds, and organisations applying to us for a grant will need to demonstrate how their work takes account of the following:

Understanding the context

Organisations need to demonstrate their understanding of the local or national context in which they are working, and the root causes of the issues they wish to tackle. This may include the diversity of local communities, local decision making structures, and the role of others in the field and issues relevant to the nation in which they are working.

Consulting with key players

We want to see that organisations are informed by the views of relevant stakeholders and where possible ensure that people who will benefit from projects are consulted at the outset and their views incorporated in project design. Including more marginalised groups in this process is important.

Building on good practice and considering new ideas and approaches

We want to see how organisations are drawing on 'good practice' and knowledge of 'what works' to inform the work they do. But we also welcome projects that wish to experiment with new ideas and approaches to familiar problems.

Involving users

Where possible, we want to see how people benefiting from the projects we fund actively participate in those projects – from membership of advisory groups and trustee boards to feeding back on the value of the services – to help inform future plans.

Valuing Diversity and Working with others

We expect organisations to demonstrate a commitment to diversity and show how this runs through their governance, service delivery and policy development. We recognise that some organisations will need help to develop their approach to diversity.

Working with others

Very few organisations can bring about lasting change on their own. We need to see how organisations work with others. This may be through sharing information and learning, joint influencing work and approaches that can help to make the work sustainable in the long term.

Evaluating and Learning

Organisations will need to show how they have learnt from past experience, how they capture the learning from the work they do, and how they will use the evidence they have built up to inform their future plans and influence the decisions of others, particularly policy makers and others in the field.

UK Grant programmes

For the period 2009–2012 the charity's UK grants programmes are focusing on the following areas:

Mental Health
Background

- mental health problems affect one in four people at some point in their lives.
- as well as dealing with the impact of living with mental ill-health, many people also have to cope with stigma, discrimination and social exclusion, and can find it hard to get their voices heard in the decisions which affect their lives.

Too many people continue to have little say in their treatment or the services they need. Comic Relief has had a long history of helping people get their voices heard and promote a fairer society, and since 2005 mental health has become a key focus of our work.

Aim of the programme

This programme aims to ensure people with mental health problems get access to the services they need, their rights are respected, and their voices heard. It also aims to reduce the stigma and discrimination surrounding mental health.

We believe that change will be most effective and sustainable if organisations working in this field are led by those with direct experience of mental ill health. We recognise that some groups may not currently be user led, but we will want to see organisations moving towards this over the lifetime of their grant.

Outcomes

The organisations we fund will need to show how their work will help deliver one or more of the following outcomes:

- greater involvement of people who have mental health problems in decisions that affect their lives
- a reduction in stigma and discrimination, and a positive change in people's attitudes towards mental health
- more inclusive and accessible mental health services and organisations, in particular for people from black and minority ethnic communities

Who will we fund?

This programme has a strong user-led ethos. By this, we mean that projects will need to show how people with direct experience of mental ill health are actively and meaningfully involved in and leading the work. In most cases, we will look for a majority of people with direct experience to make up the trustee board or governing body. Where this is not the case, we will seek a firm commitment to involving users in the running of the project and where appropriate, want to see a move towards becoming a user-led organisation.

We encourage applications using a variety of approaches including advocacy, the development of social enterprises, user or peer support groups and campaigning activities – although these are examples only and we will consider any work which meets the aims and outcomes above.

We are especially keen to support work which addresses the needs and rights of people from communities who are often overlooked, such as those from Black and minority ethnic communities or older people.

We will not fund therapeutic interventions (such as counselling) or helplines under this programme. We will not fund services for carers or people with learning disabilities or dementia under this programme.

Domestic and Sexual Abuse (Young People)
Background

- More than 750,000 children and young people witness violence in the home.
- Young women are almost four times more likely to experience sexual violence than older women.

Since the early 1990s, Comic Relief has worked to tackle domestic violence at a local and national level. This year we have widened our focus to include sexual abuse; this will allow us to more fully address the gendered nature of abuse and the cycle of power, control and victimisation. Our current funding strategy covers a spectrum of work from crisis, to development, through to prevention. This reflects both our long history within this sector and our understanding that while direct services are vital, the sector also needs core support.

Aim of the programme

We aim to fund work to support young survivors of domestic and sexual abuse aged 11–25.

How we define 'domestic and sexual abuse

Our criteria includes: young people who have grown up in homes where they witness violence and harm. It also includes young people directly affected by abuse caused by a family member, by an outsider such as a stranger or family friend, or as a result of their own dating experiences.

There are two strands to the open programme:

- Crisis Support: we will fund support services with the aim of helping young survivors to cope with the physical, emotional and mental harm that they have experienced. This could include services such as counselling, advocacy and group work. Applications should demonstrate how your support services will build a safer future for young survivors. This could include activities that help young people cope better or increasing their understanding of abuse.
- Young Voices: we will fund work that helps young people to heal through having a voice. This could include setting up a new survivors group or support for an existing group. This fund will also cover work which aims to build networks of young survivors who can speak out to policy makers, planners and the sector, so that their views and voices are directly heard.

Outcomes

The organisations we fund will need to show how their work will help deliver one or more of the following outcomes:

Young survivors aged 11–25 feel that support services have helped them to cope and improve their mental and emotional wellbeing, or helped to keep them safe and increase their resilience against future harm.

Young survivors aged 11–25 feel that having a voice and hearing from fellow survivors has helped to progress their healing process. Policy makers and planners are more aware of the needs of young survivors.

Policy makers and planners are more aware of the needs of young survivors.

Who will we fund?
We particularly welcome applications for work with boys and young men as well as girls and young women. We recognise the gendered nature of domestic and sexual abuse and ALL work must be grounded in an understanding about the dynamics of power and control

We will not fund work with children under the age of 11

We do not fund preventative awareness raising work under this funding programme.

Other important information
Defining domestic and sexual abuse in relation to young people is often complicated, with agencies working to different criteria (for example the government only defines domestic abuse survivors from the age of 16). If you would like to talk to us about whether your work meets our criteria please ring us for a chat.

Refugee and Asylum Seeking Women
Background
- according to the UN, refugee and asylum seeking women are more likely to be affected by violence than any other group of women
- women claiming asylum often go through the process voiceless and traumatized.

Comic Relief has a long commitment to supporting refugees and asylum seekers and over the last four years, we have paid special attention to the needs of women who have experienced rape, torture and other forms of violence in their home countries.

We appreciate that all women seeking refuge have support needs, but our funding is focused on those who are the most vulnerable, both in terms of the legacy of past abuses and the threat of future exploitation in the UK. We seek to work with organisations that understand the gendered nature of the violence and inequalities faced by these women.

There are two strands to the programme:
- Crisis Support: we will fund support services for refugee and asylum-seeking women that help them cope with the trauma they have experienced; this could include counselling or group work. We will

fund legal support that recognises past trauma and enables women to disclose the full stories behind their asylum claims. We will also support health initiatives that help women with the impact of trauma on their mental and physical wellbeing.
- Training: we are also interested in funding work to develop training and support packages that improve and embed knowledge and practice about how to work with this vulnerable group of women. Training can be targeted at refugee or mainstream organisations.

Outcomes
The organisations we fund will need to show how their work will help deliver one or more of the following outcomes:
- refugee and asylum seeking women will feel more able to cope with the trauma they have experienced
- women will get the specialist support they need to make successful applications for asylum around rape, violence and torture
- organisations will have increased knowledge of the needs of vulnerable refugee and asylum seeking women and be able to meet their needs more effectively.

Who will we fund?
We welcome applications from a range of agencies who can reach this vulnerable group of women. We will give priority to organisations with a strong track record of working with this group or who can demonstrate a broad understanding of services that are needed.

We will not consider applications focusing on integration work for refugee and asylum seekers. Ineligible activities include job-seeking programmes, volunteering initiatives, and befriending schemes to alleviate isolation.

Sport for Change
Background
- as well as the more obvious health and participation benefits, there has been growing awareness of the broader social, emotional and cohesion opportunities that sport can bring
- while sport alone will never be the solution to injustice or poverty, we believe it can bring about positive changes as part of a broader programme of work.

We have developed this new programme to support a range of innovative projects that are using sport as a tool for making a real difference in the communities in which they are based.

Aim of the programme
The aim of this programme is to understand more about how sport can play a part in delivering positive change within the lives of individuals and

communities, and to meet one or more of the outcomes listed below.

We also want to understand how sport can be used to tackle identified social issues as part of a broader programme to achieve a measurable social change.

By 'broader programme' we mean other activities that are seen as part of a coordinated approach to a social issue or concern that supports or links to sporting activity. This might be workshops, educational sessions, awareness raising, work experience, volunteering, or mentoring.

Outcomes
The organisations we fund will need to show how their work will help deliver one or more of the following outcomes:
- increased sense of inclusion and well-being by marginalised and disadvantaged people
- greater community involvement
- an increased understanding of how sport can help bring about positive changes in the lives of individuals and communities
- greater knowledge across the community and sports sectors about effective work which uses sport as a tool for social change.

Prior to submitting the application, we would expect applicants to have identified the social issue or need that they wish to address through their project, and to then have defined the most appropriate response to that need, explaining how sport will be part of the overall response (so how it fits with a broader programme of activities).

Examples of social issues or community concerns could include substance use, crime related problems, integration, exclusion of older people, community cohesion, gangs or knife crime, mental health, and young people at risk. These are examples only and we welcome applications for work tackling any social issue so long as the need for the work is clearly explained.

Who will we fund?
We welcome applications from not-for-profit organisations using sport as part of a broader programme of work to bring about change at an individual and /or community level. We particularly want to fund organisation working to support people from black and minority ethnic communities, older people and women/girls. We also want to receive applications from all parts of the UK. We will fund across all age ranges and within a broad range of communities.

We are happy to receive applications from consortia of agencies as long as there is a lead community-based organisation. Applicants will also need to:

- demonstrate how they are using sport as part of a broader programme to achieve a measurable social change or impact
- show how the work is based in community development principles
- have monitoring and evaluation systems in place to track the impact of the work.

What we won't fund

We cannot fund any building work, refurbishment, upgrades to playing surfaces, or any other capital works. As we are interested in understanding how sport can be used as part of a broader programme to achieve a measurable social change, we also cannot fund projects which aim only to increase participation in sport, projects aiming to develop sporting excellence, individual athletes or sports teams or one-off sporting events

Other important information

The maximum grant size in this programme is £100,000 in total. We will not award grants of less than £10,000 and if you apply for less than £10,000 the proposal will be rejected. Please apply to a small grant funder (such as the Community Foundation Network or Awards for All) for amounts of less than £10,000.

If you would like to talk to us about whether your work meets our criteria please ring us for a chat.

If your application is chosen for further consideration, you will be invited to submit a full proposal, again online. We are usually able to let you know the outcome of your first stage application within 3–4 weeks of the cycle deadline. You will then have 3–4 weeks to submit your second stage application.

Sexually Exploited and Trafficked Young People (aged 11 to 25)

Background

- young people are at risk of sexual exploitation. 75% of women working in prostitution started before they were 18; the majority want to get out.
- the UK is recognised as a significant transit and destination country for trafficked children and young people.
- sexual exploitation and trafficking puts young people at risk and damages their health, safety and wellbeing; this pushes vulnerable young people further into poverty.

Comic Relief has a long history of working with marginalised young adults. From homeless teenagers, to those leaving care, we have supported young people hidden from public view. Since 2005 our work around sexual exploitation and trafficking has formed a key part of this commitment to helping vulnerable young people.

Aim of the programme

This programme aims to reduce harm to young people who have been sexually exploited or trafficked.

We want to fund a wide variety of work including direct services for young people which meet both immediate and longer term needs, especially in areas where there are no services or which are aimed at young people who are poorly served (e.g. young men, minority ethnic groups).

We will also fund prevention work, training for workers and professionals, and work that raises awareness of the issues surrounding sexual exploited and trafficked young people.

Outcomes

The organisations we fund will need to show how their work will help deliver one or more of the following outcomes:

- fewer young people will be sexually exploited or trafficked
- more sexually exploited and/or trafficked young people and those at risk will know their rights, understand their situation and/or have access to the help and support they need
- more sexually exploited and/or trafficked young people will have increased choice to make positive decisions about their futures.

Who will we fund?

We welcome applications from a range of organisations supporting young people aged 11–25 – some set up specifically to support sexually exploited young people and those at risk; others with a wider young people's brief who want to target this group. We will also support other organisations working around sexual exploitation or trafficking who want to address young people's needs; or projects in other fields whose work includes these young people at risk, such as housing.

We recognise we need to be flexible around the age range of people supported. Some young people, for example, young men and some trafficked young people, may not come to the attention of professionals or realise their situation themselves until they are 'older'. Therefore, although we expect that most of the services we fund will be aimed at younger people we will consider supporting projects working with those over the age of 25 where the case for need is made.

Young People and Alcohol (aged 11 to 25)

Background

- the proportion of young people drinking has decreased in recent years; but the amount of 'frequent' teenage drinkers has risen sharply. This increase is widely acknowledged to contribute to social problems such as poor health, violence and anti-social behaviour.
- some young people, such as those living in deprived areas or leaving care, are seen as especially vulnerable to drink related problems, and alcohol use at this age is a significant factor in school exclusion, teenage pregnancy, and youth offending.
- services for young people who have got into difficulty with drinking are patchy and poorly funded.

This programme aims to provide support for young people aged 11–25 who are drinking excessively and meets one or more of the outcomes listed below.

We will fund services that aim to reduce the levels of young people's drinking, create greater awareness of the dangers of harmful drinking and provide direct support to young drinkers at the greatest risk – those drinking excessively and dangerously. This could include individual or group work sessions, or street-based outreach.

Outcomes

The organisations we fund will need to show how their work will help deliver one or more of the following outcomes:

- a reduction in alcohol consumption by young people
- a reduction in harm and increased access to help for young people who have alcohol problems
- closer working relationships between alcohol and young people's services
- an increase in relevant skills to deliver services targeted at young people who have alcohol problems.

Who will we fund?

We welcome applications from voluntary and community organisations working with young people with alcohol problems aged between 11 and 25.

We particularly welcome applications from agencies working with those who are vulnerable and at high risk of heavy drinking. We are also interested in funding services that target particular groups such as those from black and minority ethnic communities and young women, as these groups find it especially hard to access services. We also welcome applications for work supporting training that equips staff with specialist skills in working with young people with alcohol problems.

We particularly want to encourage joint applications from young people's agencies and alcohol agencies where expertise can be shared, innovative approaches developed and where the added value of working together can be shown.

We also recognise that some organisations will work with people around a variety of substances. In these circumstances we specifically want to support the alcohol element of the work and our funding is likely to reflect this.

Young People and Mental Health (aged 11 to 25)

Background

- for many young people adolescence is a confusing time of change; for those who experience additional difficulties with their mental health, this can be a frightening and isolating time.
- over the last twenty-five years rates of anxiety and depression amongst young people have increased by 70%.

Young people are often reluctant to seek help from mental health services for fear of being stigmatised, and despite the greater focus on children's and young people's well-being, the availability of support both within and outside mental health settings is still patchy. If left unsupported, the impact of ill health and stigma can be devastating. But with the right help at the right time, young people with mental health problems can make great improvements to their well being. We have a long history of supporting young people with mental health problems and we are committed to continuing to grow this area.

Aim of the programme

We aim to support work with young people aged 11–25 with current mental health problems.

There are two strands to the programme:

- Services for young people: we are keen to fund a range of services and approaches to help young people experiencing mental health problems make positive changes in their lives. This could include individual counselling, group work or peer support. We especially welcome applications where support is provided in settings in which young people feel comfortable, and do not fear being labelled or stigmatised.
- Training: we will also fund projects that ensure those working with young people with mental health problems, including youth workers, have access to good quality training to improve their skill base and confidence levels.

We will also fund work that ensures those working with young people with mental health problems, especially youth workers, have access to good quality training to improve their skill base and confidence levels.

Outcomes

The organisations we fund will need to show how their work will help deliver one or more of the following outcomes:

- increased access to appropriate services for young people with mental health problems, resulting in improved mental health

- a greater understanding and specialist skill base amongst practitioners working with young people with mental health needs.

Who will we fund?

We encourage applications from organisations working with young people aged 11–25 providing general counselling and therapeutic interventions, as well as specialist projects focused on particular issues such as eating disorders or bi-polar conditions.

What we don't fund

- projects for young people with learning disabilities, autism or attention-deficit hyperactivity disorder (ADHD), unless they are supporting these young people with mental health issues
- prevention projects targeting those at risk of developing mental health problems
- projects dealing with young people's general emotional wellbeing.

Other important information

We recognise the importance of strong local partnerships between voluntary and statutory agencies in delivering effective services to young people with mental health problems. We know that, in practice, this means that agencies from these different sectors may be sharing resources and working together on specific projects. We are interested in hearing how you work within the local strategies on young people and mental health and how our funds can help you achieve the best possible outcomes in this complex funding environment.

Please note we cannot support work seeking to improve young people's general well-being in this programme, as we target our funds towards those with recognised mental health problems with a need for specialist support.

Please note this is a very oversubscribed funding programme. We are specifically looking to reach young people with current mental health problems such as depression, obsessive compulsive disorder, hearing voices, self harm, eating disorders or suicidal feelings.

Managing Money Better – Comic Relief's New Older People's Programme

Background

We know that currently one in five older people are living below the poverty line and many lack access to good, independent financial advice. Many don't know what benefits they are entitled to as they struggle to get through the complex claims process. In these testing times, and with the rising cost of living and soaring energy prices, older people are being adversely affected.

Aim of the programme

- we have decided to open a grants programme in 2012 to help older people cope with the challenges of this particularly harsh financial climate and the resultant exclusion and hardship it is causing
- this programme will be aimed at supporting older people (65+) to build their knowledge and skills to manage their money more effectively, ensure access to good, independent financial advice, guard against financial scams and abuse and cope better with cold homes
- we are especially interested in how older people can be supported to manage the extreme rising fuel and food prices.

Outcomes

The work will need to deliver one or more of the following outcomes for older people to:

- manage their money more effectively
- increase their income
- experience less fuel poverty
- deal better with financial distress (such as abuse, scams and so on).

Other information

Inevitably we know we will receive many more applications than we can fund. So, in addition to meeting one or more of the outcomes listed above, we will be assessing the extent to which applications meet the following:

- older people have been involved in the design of the proposal and will be supporting their peers who are less active
- there are strategic partnership approaches with voluntary, private and public organisations and local people of all ages to meet the needs of older people
- new approaches are being tested and disseminated
- the most isolated older people and those who are traditionally hard to reach or live in the poorest and most deprived areas are being targeted.

Projects that do not meet the criteria specified above will not be considered

In addition, the programme aims to encourage partnerships with voluntary sector organisations and banks, building societies, credit unions, energy companies and others to recognise and respond better to the needs of older people.

There is no overall maximum grant and we expect to make awards of varying sizes. This programme will not make grants under £10,000. Grants of this size are managed through our Local Communities' Programme, run by the Community Foundation Network (www.communityfoundations.org.uk).

Our first grant making cycle for this programme [opened] on 16th January 2012. This is a two-stage application process If your application is chosen for further consideration, you will be invited to submit a full proposal. Sample application forms are available to view on the Comic Relief website.

If you would like to talk to us about whether your work meets our criteria, please email us at: ukgrants@ comicrelief.com or call us on 020 7820 2000 and ask to speak to a member of staff from the Older People's programme.

Local communities

Background
One in five people in the UK live in poverty.

Poverty in the UK today is much more complex than simply being a measure of homelessness or unemployment; it can affect old and young, families and single people, and many whole communities face deprivation. People living in disadvantaged communities face a range of issues such as poor employment opportunities and reduced levels of physical and mental health.

Comic Relief has made a longstanding pledge to place funding into disadvantaged communities. We believe that local people should have a say in the decisions that are made about where they live, and are often best placed to know what is needed to bring about change.

We want to enable groups to create strong, thriving communities; this could involve helping people of all ages to feel more included in their community, provide more accessible services, or supporting people to build new skills. We also want to make sure that communities are equipped to respond to challenging economic, social and cultural trends. Whether it is unemployment or older people living in isolation, many individuals need help coping with challenging times.

How to apply
The funding for our communities programme is devolved to the Community Foundation Network. [Contact your local community foundation to find out if they are administering this programme in your area – further information can be found on the Community Foundation Network's website.]

Comic Relief's full UK Grant Making Strategy up to 2012 is available from its website.

The Robbie Williams Give it Sum Fund

Background
Set up by Robbie Williams in 2000 the Robbie Williams Give it Sum Fund is open to a broad range of self-help projects, community groups and voluntary organisations based in North Staffordshire. The Fund aims to support local people to find solutions to local problems.

Who will we fund?
The Robbie Williams Give it Sum Fund welcomes applications from groups working in all sections of the community particularly those who have struggled to find funding in the past. All groups and projects will need to show how they are involving the people who use their services and facilities in planning, running and reviewing their work.

Any work we fund must be charitable and we can now consider applications from organisations with an annual income of up to £175,000. We give priority to local community groups, but we will also consider your application if you are a larger voluntary organisation that provides services to people in need.

Some examples of groups that Give it Sum has funded include:

- residents' associations and self-help groups working to improve their local communities
- projects offering help and support to those in need, for example, young people with drug and alcohol problems, homeless people, single parents, older people, children, and people from black and minority ethnic communities
- projects that help people who are often left out to have their say – for example groups campaigning for better services, and disabled people's rights groups.

Grants can be for core, project and capital funding. Please note that the fund does not make contributions towards large capital costs or building schemes, unless the majority of other funding for the work has already been secured.

The fund will not give grants for the following:

- academic research
- general appeals
- schools, colleges and hospitals
- individuals
- work that promotes religion
- services run by statutory or public authorities
- medical research or equipment
- minibuses
- contributions to large capital appeals.

Other information
Most grants awarded by the Give it Sum Fund are between £15,000 and £30,000 for up to two years, and we also make smaller grants of up to £5,000 over one year.

In exceptional circumstances the Trustees can consider funding up to £20,000 per year for up to 2 years, but you will need to show us why you need this amount of money to run your project.

How to apply
Separate application forms for grants above and below £5,000 are available on the comic relief website. The fund also has a guidelines document which applicants are encouraged to read before applying.

The Comic Relief website also has details of application deadlines.

Exclusions

There are certain types of work and organisations that Comic Relief does not fund. If your proposal falls into one of these categories, do not apply.

- grants to individuals
- medical research or hospitals
- churches or other religious bodies where the monies will be used for religious purposes
- work where there is statutory responsibility to provide funding
- projects where the work has already taken place
- statutory bodies, such as local authorities or Primary Care Trusts or organisations seeking funding to replace cuts by statutory bodies
- profit-making organisations, except social enterprises
- where your 'free' (unrestricted or designated) reserves are more than one year's running costs, the charity may not provide the full amount you ask for – or may not fund at all – if it feels you have enough to pay for the work yourself
- the charity is also unable to fund minibuses

Applications

The charity's guidelines state:

We receive many more applications than we are able to fund and we usually only support work which fits our current priorities, so before you apply for funding, please read through all the essential information carefully.

Who can apply?
We accept applications from the voluntary and community sector throughout the UK including: constituted voluntary and community groups, charities, social enterprises, co-operatives, faith organisations, and community interest companies.

What we fund
We make grants in the programme areas outlined. You can make only one application to one programme at a time.

Where we fund
We fund work in England, Scotland, Wales and Northern Ireland – and are

very keen to make sure that we reach all parts of the UK, especially areas which often miss out, such as rural communities.

How long we fund for
We usually make grants for between one and three years.

The type of grants we give
We can give grants for running costs and capital costs.

However, we give building costs a very low priority, and only fund these in exceptional circumstances. We do not fund capital costs where they are part of a much larger appeal.

We usually make grants to cover project costs, but we recognise that you may wish to include a contribution towards your organisational costs so that it reflects the true cost of running your project. This is sometimes known as full cost recovery. We are happy for you to do this, but you will need to show us how you have worked out these additional organisational costs.

How much we give
We can pay for all or some of your project costs, but we encourage you to get some of your funding from other sources if you can. There is no minimum or maximum grant in most of our programmes, but where there are limits, these are clearly stated in the programme guidelines. Our grants on average vary between £25,000 and £40,000 per a maximum of three years, and rarely exceed this upper limit.

We will not generally fund the full cost of applications made by charities with an annual income over £10 million.

If your work is regional, national or provides a model that could be widely replicated, we may be able to fund at a higher level. Please call us to discuss this before you submit an application.

The number of applications you can make
You can make only one application at a time. If your application is unsuccessful, we are happy to provide feedback on the reasons for this. However, you cannot reapply for the same or a different project for another 12 months.

If you currently hold a grant with us, you can apply again, for the same or a different piece of work, within the last nine months of your existing grant. We do not give automatic priority to work we have funded in the past.

The number of grants you can hold at any one time
You can usually only hold one grant at any one time. Sometimes, however, large, national organisations may hold more than one grant with us where they can demonstrate they are the only organisation able to deliver work in a specific location or the work is particularly groundbreaking. In this situation, please contact us before submitting your application.

Ensure that you have read the charity's *Grant Making Principles and Essential Information* for applicants. Comic Relief has a new application procedure whereby applicants apply online via the website.

The Ernest Cook Trust

Educational grants focusing on children and young people for the environment, rural conservation, arts and crafts, literary and numeracy and research

£1.3 million (2009/10)

Beneficial area
UK.

Fairford Park, Fairford, Gloucestershire GL7 4JH
Tel: 01285 712492
Fax: 01285 713417
Email: grants@ernestcooktrust.org.uk
Website: www.ernestcooktrust.org.uk
Correspondent: Mrs Ros Leigh, Grants Administrator
Trustees: Anthony Bosanquet, Chair; Harry Henderson; Andrew Christie-Miller; Patrick Maclure; Miles C Tuely; Victoria Edwards.
CC Number: 313497

Information available
Accounts were available from the Charity Commission. The trust also has an informative website.

The following information on the trust's background, interests and activities is taken from its annual report:

> Ernest Edward Cook, the founder of the trust which bears his name, died in 1955 at the age of 90. Following the sale of his family business (the travel agent Thomas Cook & Sons) in 1928, Mr Cook devoted his wealth and energy to the purchase of country houses and estates, and the collections of works of art which they contained, thus preserving them from fragmentation. Mr Cook made

significant bequests and donations to the National Art Collections Fund and to the National Trust; as a result of those donations, the National Trust turned its attention to country houses, at that time a new activity for the trust.

Mr Cook founded his trust in 1952 as an educational charity, initially deriving its income from the 14,462 acres of agricultural estate land he put into trust which still continues to form part of the endowment.

The aim of the Ernest Cook Trust is to make educational grants and to carry out other educational work so as to be highly effective in pursuit of its charitable objective whilst, subject to that, maintaining its investment in its estates in ways that ensure their value, excellence and preservation.

[The trust's grants policy] is influenced by Mr Cook's two great passions, namely art and country estates. Grants, which must always be for clearly educational purposes, aim principally to focus upon the needs of children and young people.

To that end the trustees are keen to support applications from registered charities or other not-for-profit organisations within the United Kingdom in three main areas of activity, being the environment and the countryside, the wide spectrum of arts, crafts and architecture, and literacy and numeracy. All applications are expected to link in with either the National Curriculum or recognised qualifications.

It is appreciated that sometimes a contribution will be required towards the salary of an education officer, but the ECT always expects to be a part-funder. Funds are not usually committed for more than one year; successful applicants are normally asked to wait three years before applying for further help. A few research grants are awarded if the work links in to the above interests; suitable projects which do not fall into any of the main categories are also considered.

Grants range from £100 to £4,000 in the small grants category, of which modest amounts for education resources for small groups form a large part – the Small Grants Programme always seems to bring great benefits. At the two main meetings grants are mostly in the range of £5,000 to £10,000, with only a few larger awards for projects closely connected to the trust's land holdings and educational interests. Main grants to arts, crafts and architecture projects are considered at the spring meeting; those relating to the environment are put forward at the autumn meeting.

Programmes

Small Grants Programme

The small grants programme supports state schools and small registered charities which would like to undertake projects which meet the trust's objectives and require a small amount of pump-priming in order for such projects to take place. The programme is a rolling one, with meetings at two-monthly intervals throughout the year: pressure on funds is high; it is therefore wise to think well ahead.

Large Grants Programme

The large grants programme is aimed at more comprehensive education programmes: these sometimes require support for the salary of an education officer; in such cases the ECT would always expect to be a part-funder. The range of the programme is wide; over the years education projects linked to theatres, art galleries and orchestras have been supported, as have those covering a wide range of environmental and countryside projects.

In 2009/10 the trust had assets of £84.8 million and an income of £3.2 million. There were 382 grants made totalling £1.3 million, categorised as follows:

Environment	£515,500
Arts, crafts and architecture	£433,000
Literacy and numeracy	£252,000
Other	£98,000

Details of individual beneficiaries were not included in the trust's 2009/10 annual report, however recipients of grants from the previous year were detailed on the trust's website at the time of writing, with more recent examples no doubt available in due course.

Beneficiaries previously listed here, and the purposes for which grants were made, include: Edward Barnsley Trust (£25,000), to cover the cost of an apprentice; Chetham's School of Music (£21,000), towards an early years music project; Year of Food and Farming (£20,000), towards educational work in the North East and South West; Engineering Education Scheme in Wales (£10,500), towards bursaries for the scheme; Rockingham Forest Trust (£8,000), towards the People in the Forest project; Groundwork London (£7,500), towards the cost of an education officer for the Eco Schools project; Yorkshire Agricultural Society (£7,000), towards the cost of the information boards, education adviser and information packs; Arable Group Ltd (£6,000), for bursaries for

students taking part in the TAG Asset programme; and Langham Arts Trust (£4,000), towards the cost of Proms Praise for Schools.

Exclusions

Applicants must represent either registered charities or not-for-profit organisations. Grants are normally awarded on an annual basis and will not be awarded retrospectively.

Grants are not made:

- to individuals, Agricultural Colleges, independent schools or local authorities
- for building work or refurbishment work
- for youth work, social support, therapy and medical treatment, including projects using the arts for these purposes
- for projects related to sports, outward bound type activities or recreation
- for overseas projects
- for Wildlife Trusts and for Farming & Wildlife Advisory Groups other than those which are based in counties in which the ECT owns land (Buckinghamshire, Dorset, Gloucestershire, Leicestershire and Oxfordshire)

Applications

The ECT aims to have a 'light-touch' application process with a view to enabling small regional or local organisations to apply for support. All applicant organisations must be based and working in the UK and should be either state schools, registered charities or other recognised not-for-profit organisations. It is very important however to read the exclusions before applying. Grants are normally awarded for one year only.

There are no application forms. All applicants are asked to post a covering letter on the official headed paper of the applicant organisation and also include:

- up to two additional sheets of A4 describing the organisation, outlining the project and specifying its educational elements and the way in which it fits in with the interests of the ECT
- a simple budget for the project, outlining the way in which the grant would be spent

- a list of any other funding applications
- the latest annual report and accounts for the organisation (schools are not required to send one)

Please do not send further supporting material or email applications, which are not accepted. Applications must be posted.

Questions (not applications) can be addressed to the Grants Administrator via email or telephone.

The Alice Ellen Cooper Dean Charitable Foundation

General

£734,000 (2009/10)

Beneficial area

Mainly local organisations in Dorset and west Hampshire as a top priority.

Edwards and Keeping, Unity Chambers, 34 High East Street, Dorchester, Dorset DT1 1HA

Tel: 01305 251333

Fax: 01305 251465

Email: office@edwardsandkeeping.co.uk

Correspondent: Rupert J A Edwards, Trustee

Trustees: John R B Bowditch; Mrs Linda J Bowditch; Rupert J A Edwards; Douglas J E Neville-Jones; Emma Blackburn.

CC Number: 273298

Information available

Accounts were available at the Charity Commission.

The foundation was established for general charitable purposes in 1977 with an initial gift by Ellen Cooper Dean and supplemented by a legacy on her death in 1984. Donations are only made to registered charities with a preference for local organisations in Dorset and west Hampshire. Grants usually range from £1,000 to £10,000 each.

In 2009/10 the foundation had assets of £22.7 million and an income of

£7.3 million, most of which was in the form of a legacy from the estate of the late Sylvia Bowditch, a former trustee of the foundation. There were 147 grants made totalling £734,000.

In addition to supporting local and national charities in the areas of health, social disadvantage, education, religion, community, arts and culture, amateur sport and disability, mainly on a regular basis, the foundation has made overseas grants to advance education, relieve poverty, sickness, and suffering caused by conflict and disasters.

Larger grants were made to: the West of England School and College (£20,000); Motor Neurone Disease Association (£14,000); and, Powerful Information, Blanford Youth Trust and Families for Children Trust (£10,000 each).

Other beneficiaries included: Project Harar Ethiopia (£8,000); ITACA – Ecuador (£7,500) Action for Kids and Devonshire and Dorset Military Museums Charity (£7,000 each); Help the Aged (£6,000); Link Community Development, Mseleni Children's Home, Inspire Foundation, Special Boat Service Association and Rethink (£5,000 each); Salvation Army – Bournemouth (£3,000); Special Toys Educational Postal Service (£2,000); Queen Elizabeth's Foundation for Disabled People (£1,000); and, Help for Heroes (£500).

Exclusions

No grants to individuals. Grants to registered charities only.

Applications

In writing to the correspondent. Telephone calls are not welcome. Applications are considered from both local and national charitable organisations, with local charities given top priority and national charities only supported occasionally as funds permit.

Each application should include:
- name and address of the organisation
- charity registration number
- details of the project
- details of the community, including area covered and numbers who will benefit from the project
- details of fund-raising activities and other anticipated sources of grants
- a copy of the latest financial accounts.

Common applicant mistakes

'Applicants not sending copies of their financial accounts; not being aware that the primary area of support is Dorset and West Hampshire.'

County Durham Community Foundation

Tackling social disadvantage and poverty, general

£1 million (2010/11)

Beneficial area

County Durham, Darlington and surrounding areas.

Victoria House, Whitfield Court, St Johns Road, Meadowfield Industrial Estate, Durham DH7 8XL
Tel: 0191 378 6340
Email: info@cdcf.org.uk
Website: www.cdcf.org.uk
Correspondent: Barbara Gubbins, Chief Executive
Trustees: Mark I'Anson, Chair; Sir Paul Nicholson; David Watson; Michele Armstrong; Ada Burns; George Garlick; Christopher Lendrum; Andrew Martell; David Martin; Lady Sarah Nicholson; Gerry Osborne; Kate Welch.
CC Number: 1047625

Information available

Accounts were available at the Charity Commission. The foundation's website is user-friendly and informative for those seeking grants.

The aim of the County Durham Foundation is to build up endowment funds so as to provide long-term income that is used to provide grants to approved projects within County Durham and Darlington (and in specified circumstances across the north east).

The foundation supports and promotes charitable purposes in these areas and has focused on combating social disadvantage and poverty in its grant distribution. It receives donations and manages funds for individuals, companies, trusts and government departments who want to support the local community.

The foundation currently holds over 140 different funds all of which have their own policy and criteria. The majority of endowment-based funds are now donor advised, where the foundation works with the fund holder to determine potential recipients.

Grant schemes change frequently. Consult the foundation's website for details of current programmes and their deadlines.

In 2010/11 the foundation had assets of almost £8.6 million and an income of £2.4 million. Grants were made from all funds totalling just over £1 million. The foundation categorised its grant making as follows:

Environment	£288,000
Sport and recreation	£160,500
Community support and development	£145,000
Education and training	£143,000
Health and wellbeing	£119,000
Art, craft and drama activities	£86,000
Disability and access issues	£43,500
Counselling/advice/mentoring	£27,500
Crime	£25,500
Poverty and disadvantage	£16,000
Supporting family life	£14,500
Social inclusion	£10,000
Rural issues	£3,000
Transport issues	£2,000
Employment and labour	£1,800
Volunteering	£1,000
Housing	£800

The following summary of activities within the foundation's main programmes is taken from the 2010/11 annual report:

County Durham Community Foundation held over 140 different funds during this financial year, all of which have their own criteria and included 102 endowment funds. The remainder are revenue or flow-through funds where the money is given out during the course of the year or a few years.

The majority of our endowment based funds are now donor advised where we work with the fund holder to determine potential recipients. For general community activity, we have a general application form and criteria, and mix and match contributions behind the scenes to fulfil fund holder requirements. All grants aim to combat poverty and disadvantage. Major programmes delivered during the year include:

Community Action
Supporting local voluntary and community groups that seek to improve the quality of life in County Durham and Darlington, using funding from contributions made by various private endowment and revenue fund holders. We distributed more than £65,400 from this fund last year, supporting 112 local community groups.

The Banks Group Community Fund
This fund provides capital support for the groups looking to improve or maintain their community buildings or places of worship. The funding comes from the landfill tax credit scheme, and so is subject to the regulations of ENTRUST. Last year we awarded more than £259,000 from this fund to 28 groups, making it our largest private revenue fund.

Grassroots [no longer running]
The year saw the continuation of the Government's initiative to boost grant making and endowment growth through its Grassroots Grants Programme. A total of £262,500 was awarded in Durham and almost £47,500 in Darlington, for projects taking place in 2010/11.

The three year programme which commenced in 2008 and was funded by Government through the Community Development Foundation, was worth £80 million nationally, supporting local community groups through its small grants programme, delivered by local funders. In the case of County Durham and Darlington Top Tier Local Authorities, the programme was delivered solely by the foundation, with allocations for the three year period of £749,500 for County Durham and £93,000 for Darlington.

Minimum and maximum awards were set at £250 and £5,000 respectively and were available to local community groups with a maximum annual income of £30,000 who had been working in their local community for at least twelve months.

The Foundation has been able to match 20% (62) of the awards (8% of the value) with other County Durham Community Foundation funds, a total of 24 funds in all and three awards were matched with new Grassroots endowment funds. The three issues that were most addressed through Grassroots Grants were Sport & Recreation, Community Support & Development and Arts & Culture – clearly those issues that are most easily addressed through small voluntary organisations that rely on volunteers. Full evaluation is available on request from Brenda Dye – Brenda@cdcf.org.uk

Fair Share
Darlington's Northgate and Central Wards are the beneficiaries of the Fair Share Trust funding, which is a ten year strategic grants programme (January 2003 to March 2012), funded by The Big Lottery, and targeting the areas in the country that had not received their fair share of Lottery funding. Approval of the grants is taken by local residents and stakeholders, which not only ensures that the projects meet the priorities for the area, but also that they can drive the programme forward and take ownership of the funding. This last year, the panel concentrated on setting out its objectives for the final three years of the programme, as well as awarding two small projects to a total value of £15,000.

Full details of grants distributed throughout the year can be found on the foundation's website.

Exclusions
The foundation will not fund:

⦿ projects outside County Durham and Darlington

⦿ national or regional charities with no independent office in County Durham or Darlington

⦿ groups that have more than one year's running costs held as free reserves

⦿ projects which should be funded by a statutory body

⦿ sponsored events

⦿ improvements to land that is not open to the general public at convenient hours

⦿ projects promoting political activities

⦿ deficit or retrospective funding

⦿ faith groups promoting religious, non-community based activities.

Funding is not normally given for:

⦿ medical research and equipment

⦿ grants for more than one year

⦿ school projects

⦿ general contributions to large appeals (but specific items can be funded)

⦿ building or buying premises and freehold or leasehold land rights

⦿ minibuses or other vehicles

⦿ overseas travel

⦿ animal welfare.

Some of the programmes have other exclusions. If your project is at all unusual please contact the foundation to discuss your application before submitting it.

Applications
The foundation's website states:

Community groups, non-registered charities and registered charities are all able to apply to our many funds using just one main application form. We mix-and-match applications to the most appropriate fund behind the scenes, so you don't need to worry about which fund is right for you.

With the exception of the Banks Community Fund, ESF Community Grants and Surviving Winter, which have their own bespoke application forms, all our funds can be accessed using our standard application form. Please choose one of the options below to be taken to the application form.

To apply for a grant you need to read our general guidelines before filling in an application form. [The full guidelines are available from the foundation's website.]

The Michael Cowan Foundation

Medical research and education, conservation in California, USA

Beneficial area
UK and the USA.

Farrer & Co, 65–66 Lincoln's Inn Fields, London WC2A 3LH
Tel: 020 3375 7000
Fax: 020 3375 7001
Email: bryony.cove@farrer.co.uk
Correspondent: Bryony Cove, Trustee
Trustees: Michael Cowan; Martin Foreman; Bryony Cove.
CC Number: 1137182

Information available
Basic information was available from the Charity Commission. Additional information was provided by the foundation.

Established in 2010, this is the foundation of Michael Cowan, co-founder and a director of Silchester International Investors.

The objects of the foundation are:

▶ medical research and teaching in the fields of bronchial disorders and/or heart disease

▶ conservation projects in Santa Barbara, California.

Unfortunately no further information was available at the time of writing (September 2011) on the level of funding available from the foundation.

Applications

In writing to the correspondent.

Cripplegate Foundation

General

£1.8 million to organisations
(2010)

Beneficial area

London borough of Islington and part of the City of London.

76 Central Street, London EC1V 8AG

Tel: 020 7566 3138

Fax: 020 7549 8180

Email: grants@cripplegate.org.uk

Website: www.cripplegate.org

Correspondent: Kristina Glenn, Director

Trustee: Cripplegate Foundation Limited – Sole Corporate Trustee

CC Number: 207499

Information available

Accounts were available at the Charity Commission. The foundation has an excellent website.

Summary

The first recorded gift to the Church of St Giles-without-Cripplegate was by the Will of John Sworder dated 2nd April 1500. Cripplegate Foundation was established in 1891 by a Charity Commission scheme which amalgamated all the non-ecclesiastical charitable donations previously administered as separate trusts. The early governors of the foundation built an institute on Golden Lane, containing reading and reference libraries, news and magazine rooms, classrooms, a theatre and even a rifle range. The institute was run until 1973, when it

was closed and the foundation became a grant giving trust.

The original beneficial area of the foundation was the ancient parish of St Giles, Cripplegate, to which was added in 1974 the ancient parish of St Luke's, Old Street. On 1 April 2008, the Charity Commission agreed a scheme which extended the foundation's area of benefit. This now covers the Parish of St Giles, Cripplegate in the City of London and the former parish of St Luke, Old Street (both as constituted by the Act of Parliament of the year 1732–3), and the London Borough of Islington.

Note: although the foundation's area of benefit has been extended to cover the whole of Islington, the governors have agreed that the foundation will need to develop partnerships and significantly increase its income before it can fully fund new initiatives in north Islington.

The following statement is taken from the foundation's website:

Our work in Islington is more than cash grant giving. We use our local knowledge to identify needs, to develop new ways of tackling poverty, and to contribute to the wider policy debate about disadvantage and inequality.

Staff give advice to organisations on project development and management, premises, other sources of funding and local networks. We meet all applicants and all funded projects are visited.

Because the Foundation operates in a small geographical area, its work differs from many trusts. We bring organisations and residents together to identify and promote new areas of work.

The Foundation's grants support training, development and project work. We provide core funding. Our grants programme aims to be flexible to encourage organisations to meet the changing needs of local residents.

Our grants for residents programme aims to ensure that applicants receive all state benefits and that residents are aware of services which can help them.

Programmes

The foundation currently administers six grants programmes which are:

▶ main grants programme

▶ pro-activity programme

▶ grants for residents

▶ Islington Community Chest and Grassroots Grants

▶ Richard Cloudesley's Charity health grants.

▶ Finsbury Educational Foundation grants to organisations

The following programme information is drawn largely from the foundation's detailed website:

Main Grants Programme
Current priorities

Three themes capture the foundation's priorities:

1 Reducing poverty: applications which work with the poorest sections of the community to help to reduce poverty are encouraged.

2 Increasing access to opportunities and making connections: this addresses access to opportunities by the most deprived residents and includes access to cultural and arts facilities as well as education and employment.

3 Social cohesion: applications are encouraged which promote integration of communities and active participation in society.

All applicants must show how their work will address one of these themes.

The foundation funds:

▶ core costs for key Islington organisations

▶ project funding

▶ salary costs

▶ capital costs.

Pro-Active Programme

Cripplegate Foundation identifies and targets important local needs. Around 30% of the Foundation's funding is currently allocated this way. This is central to the foundation's approach to funding.

In 2008 Cripplegate Foundation commissioned research to shine a light on the hidden poverty in Islington. The report 'Invisible Islington: Living in Poverty in Inner London' tells the stories of Islington's residents. It examines the inter-connected factors that makes their deprivation so entrenched. The report reveals that:

▶ debt is a fact of life for many residents

▶ that being out of work is the norm

▶ family, friends and community are crucial

▶ ill health causes isolation and unhappiness.

In response to these findings the foundation has helped to set up:

▶ *Help on Your Doorstep*, a charity to run the 'Connect' door-knocking services in Islington

▶ *Access to a Wider Life* – to link ESOL to wider opportunities

▶ *Catalyst*

▶ *Islington Debt Coalition*

Recent initiatives include:
- *Xaawaley,* a new domestic violence service for Somali women in 2007, run in partnership with 3 Somali organisations
- *One Canonbury* to help improve the quality of life for Canonbury residents
- *'TEXT'* writers in schools project
- Three *welfare benefits and money advice projects* in the borough
- *Islington Giving*, a new coalition of Islington charitable trusts.

Grants to individuals programme

Cripplegate Foundation provides grants to Islington residents living on a low income and includes grants made on behalf of St Sepulchre (Finsbury) United Charities and Richard Cloudesley's Charity.

The foundation employs a dedicated grants officer who is an experienced welfare rights adviser who also ensures that applicants receive the correct state benefits and services. Applicants are visited at home. Referrals are made to local services such as Children's Centres, training projects, counselling or advice services.

Grants are given on behalf of:

St Sepulchre (Finsbury) United Charities

This provides financial help to people facing hardship who are:
- over the age of 45 years and
- live in the old London Borough of Finsbury.

Application should be made on the Cripplegate Foundation Grants for Residents application form.

Richard Cloudesley's Charity

This is a grants programme for those affected by illness or disability who are living on benefits or a low income. See the Richard Cloudesley's Charity pages on the foundation's website for details about the programme and how to apply.

Grants of up to £500 can be made for:
- Essential household items and furniture
- Electrical goods such as cookers, fridges and washing machines
- Aids and adaptations for people with disabilities
- Start-up packages for newly housed homeless people
- Respite breaks (for those who have not had a respite break for five years).

This list is not exhaustive and the foundation can be flexible about the items grants are made towards – if the item or service you wish to apply for a grant towards is not on this list, please contact the foundation to discuss your application. Only one-off needs will be considered and grants cannot be made that would replace statutory funding.

Islington Community Chest

Islington Council, in partnership with Cripplegate Foundation, has launched a new Community Chest Fund for small groups. Islington Council's Community Chest is available to Islington organisations with a turnover of less than £100,000. This is a small grants fund open to local voluntary and community groups. It funds small groups who know their communities inside out, organising activities not offered by statutory and larger agencies.

Islington Council's Community Chest aims to:
- Provide opportunities for less advantaged neighbourhoods
- Promote a vibrant cohesive community
- Contribute to local regeneration
- Empower people to take an active part in their communities
- Develop trust between people and build confidence

Priorities in 2011/12

Priority is given to supporting applications from the most deprived areas of Islington.

Applications are invited which focus on:
- Improving local residents' mental and physical health and independence and choice for older and vulnerable people
- Improving the environment and quality of life in neighbourhoods
- Raising educational achievement
- Improving skills, encouraging volunteering and helping residents find work
- Contributing to safer communities: reducing antisocial behaviour and drug and alcohol related crime

Applications for Islington Community Chest are considered by a panel drawn from Islington Councillors, Islington Community Network and Cripplegate Foundation Governors. Final decisions will be agreed by the Executive Committee of Islington Council and Cripplegate Foundation Governors.

Richard Cloudesley's Charity health grants

Richard Cloudesley's Charity Health Grants are administered by Cripplegate Foundation. Final decisions on grants are made by the Grants Committee, who meet twice a year. Applicant organisations are encouraged to contact the foundation to discuss their proposal before making a full application. The foundation will advise on whether your group meets Richard Cloudesley's Charity's criteria.

Finsbury Educational Foundation Fund

Finsbury Educational Foundation provides funding of £20,000 a year to promote education in a small area of south Islington.

Grantmaking in 2010

In 2010 the foundation had assets of £31 million and an income of £2.46 million. Grants were made to organisations during the year totalling £2 million (including £203,000 to individuals). Grants to organisations were categorised as follows:

Social welfare and advice	£344,000
Accessing opportunities/adults	£230,000
Schools programme	£96,000
Community development	£72,500
Education and training	£70,500
Arts, leisure and environment	£48,000
Health and mental health	£45,000
Capacity building	£35,000

Grant programmes administered by the foundation on behalf of others included:

Islington Community Chest	£417,000
Richard Cloudesley	£289,000
Grassroots grants	£146,000

Beneficiaries across all themes included: Help on your Doorstep and Islington Giving (£150,000 each); Islington Law Centre (£45,000); Islington Bangladesh Association (£40,000); The Maya Centre (£30,000); The Little Angel Theatre (£25,000); The Women's Therapy Centre (£15,000); Inner City Films, Islington Dyslexia Support Group and Talking News Islington (£5,000 each); Hanover Primary School (£4,300); African Swahiliphone Community Project (£4,000); Islington Townswomen's Guild (£2,000); and Everything Is A Benefit and Arvon Road Allotments Group (£500 each).

Exclusions

In the main grants programme no funding is given for:
- national charities or organisations outside the area of benefit
- schemes or activities which would relieve central or local government of their statutory responsibilities
- grants to replace cuts in funding made by the local authority or others
- medical research or equipment
- national fundraising appeals
- advancement of religion unless the applicant also offers non-religious services to the community
- animal welfare
- retrospective grants
- commercial or business activities

grants for events held in the church of St Giles-without-Cripplegate

trips or outings.

In the individuals programme the following will not be funded:

- funeral costs
- the purchase of computers
- child care costs
- money that has been stolen
- items already bought or ordered
- housing costs or council tax
- repayment of debts
- education needs (apart from school uniforms)
- wheelchairs or disability vehicles and scooters
- grants for students not normally resident in the area of benefit.

The Islington community chest will not fund:

- political activities
- promotion of religion
- construction or acquisition of buildings
- general appeals
- debts
- events which have already taken place
- expenses already incurred
- national organisations with local branches in Islington
- statutory organisations.

Applications

Each programme has a different application form and deadline dates. Applicants are encouraged to telephone or email the foundation to discuss their project before making a full application.

Full details of the application process are available on the foundation's website.

Common applicant mistakes

'We only work in Islington and parts of the City but get applications from the whole of the UK and worldwide.'

The Peter Cruddas Foundation

Children and young people

£1.48 million (2009/10)

Beneficial area

UK, with a particular interest in London.

133 Houndsditch, London EC3A 7BX
Tel: 020 3003 8360
Fax: 020 3003 8580
Email: s.cox@pcfoundation.org.uk
Website: www. petercruddasfoundation.org.uk
Correspondent: Stephen D Cox, Administrator
Trustees: Lord David Young, Chair; Peter Cruddas; Martin Paisner.
CC Number: 1117323

Information available

Accounts were available from the Charity Commission. The foundation also has a clear and simple website.

Established in December 2006, this is the charitable foundation of Peter Cruddas, founder of City financial trading group CMC Markets, who has pledged to donate at least £100 million to good causes during his lifetime. It was incorrectly reported in the general press that the foundation would be building up an endowment, however this is not the case and there are no plans to do so in the foreseeable future. Since December 2006 in excess of £12m has already been donated and/or committed to numerous charitable causes.

The foundation provides the following information about its funding priorities:

The foundation gives priority to programmes calculated to help disadvantaged and disengaged young people in the UK towards pathways into education, training and employment. Preference will be given to the support of projects undertaken by charitable organisations.

Priority Funding Programmes of the Peter Cruddas Foundation will change from time to time and you are advised that applications meeting the criteria will receive priority. Details of the Priority Funding Programmes can be found on the [foundation's website].

Priorities in 2009 were:

- pathways/support for young disadvantaged or disengaged young people into education, training or employment
- crime diversion schemes
- work experience/skills projects for young people

- mentoring of young people in London
- general youth work in London.

These priorities are to remain in place for the foreseeable future and at the time of writing (November 2011, there was no indication that they had changed).

There is also a small grants scheme to help small and medium-sized organisations with the general theme of 'helping young people achieve more'. The foundation looks to make grants of around £500 to £2,000. An amount is allocation each month to this scheme and applications are not carried over.

In 2009/10 the foundation had assets of £2.3 million and an income of £40,000. Grants were made during the year totalling £1.48 million, categorised as Support of disadvantaged young people – £610,000; Other – £874,000.

Beneficiaries included: The Challenge Charity Network (£400,000); The Caudwell Charitable Trust (£225,000); Duke of Edinburgh Awards (£125,000); Policy Exchange Limited (£120,000); Sheffield Institute Foundation for MND (£50,000); Mentor Foundation UK and Wicked Weather Watch (£20,000 each); Jewish Care (£16,500); Corum, Chai Cancer Care and Flying Scholarships for the Disabled (£10,000 each); and Help the Heroes and Norwood (£5,000 each).

Applications

On an application form available to download from the foundation's website.

The foundation provides guidance on how to complete the application form, also available on the website.

Please note: the foundation states that it is currently receiving a very high number of appropriate applications.

Cumbria Community Foundation

General charitable purposes in Cumbria, in particular grant making to children and young people, older people and their carers, people with disabilities, the unemployed and people on low incomes

£2.3 million to organisations
(2010/11)

Beneficial area
Cumbria.

Dovenby Hall, Dovenby, Cockermouth, Cumbria CA13 0PN
Tel: 01900 825 760
Fax: 01900 826 527
Email: enquiries@cumbriafoundation.org
Website: www.cumbriafoundation.org/
Correspondent: Andrew Beeforth, Director
Trustees: Sir Brian Donnelly; W Slavin; S Snyder; Ms J Stannard; C Tomlinson; J Whittle; Ian Brown; June Chapman; David Brown; James Carr; Chris Coombes; Rob Cairns; Trevor Hebdon; Bob Mather; Robin Burgess; Heike Horsburgh; Sarah Dunning; Shirley Williams; Dick Raaz; Stewart Young; Peter Stybelski; Catherine Alexander; Mike Casson.
CC Number: 1075120

Information available
Accounts were available from the Charity Commission and further information was available from the foundation's website.

Established in 1999, with the funding support of the local authorities and a founding donation of £1 million from British Nuclear Fuels Ltd., the foundation focuses on improving the community life of people in Cumbria, and in particular those in need by reason of disability, age, financial or other disadvantage.

These wide charitable objects allow the foundation to support most local charities. The foundation also responds to local disasters, such as floods, storms and Foot and Mouth to help those people affected. Grant levels differ from programme to programme but awards are mostly under £10,000.

In 2006/07 the objects of the charity were extended to enable the foundation to make limited grants immediately outside the principal area of benefit (Cumbria), subject to the majority of funds being spent in Cumbria.

In 2010/11 the foundation had assets of £6.7 million and an income of £2.7 million. Grants were awarded totalling £2.3 million. Grants are normally made to small, local charities and voluntary groups but have also been made to individuals in response to community need. The total grant figure includes £735,000 paid to 1,070 individuals. A further £153,000 was spent in distributing flood bags to households and £145,000 was awarded from funds managed for others.

The foundation manages more than 30 separate funds, each with different criteria and geographical interests, and distributes around £1 million each year. Distribution of grant awards reflects the money available through the different funds – potential applicants should check the foundation's website for information on current funds.

The foundation is currently targeting its grants to meet the following strategic aims:

- rural community regeneration
- urban deprivation
- children and young people
- mental health
- hidden and emerging need
- other aims.

Total grants distributed through the funds operated by the foundation were as follows:

Flood Recovery Appeal	1,059	£1.2 million
Children and young people	211	£552,000
Rural generation	105	£237,000
Other aims	70	£209,000
Urban deprivation	65	£154,000
Hidden and emerging need	33	£53,000
Mental health	9	£27,000

In addition the foundation also provides administrative and assessment support services for another six funds and grants awarded from these were as follows:

Mary Grave Trust	£93,000
Joyce Wilkinson Trust	£41,000
Holehird Trust	£38,000
Cumberland Educational Foundation	£18,000
Edmund Castle Educational Trust	£8,400
Allerdale Sport Action Zone	£1,800

Beneficiaries of grants £5,000 and over included: Cockermouth Flood Action Group (£150,000); Lake District Search and Rescue Association (£35,500); Young Cumbria (£35,000); West Cumbria Trades Hall Centre (£33,000); Cockermouth Town Council, Phoenix Youth Project Cleator Moor and Whitehaven Harbour Youth Project (£25,000 each); Aspatria Dream Scheme (£21,000); Workington Town Rugby League Community Development Foundation (£12,000); Cumbria Starting Point Ltd., Distington Club for Young People, Egremont Rugby Union Football Club, Keswick Flood Recover Group and Workington Life Boat Station (£10,000 each); and Appleby Chamber of Trade, Bolton Parish Hall Committee, Hospice at Home West Cumbria, Keswick Fitz Park Bowling Club, Kirkbride Church Institute, Maryport Inshore Rescue Boat, Mind in West Cumbria and Thirlmere Recreational Hall (£5,000 each).

Exclusions
The following are not supported:
- animal welfare
- deficit funding
- general large appeals
- boxing clubs
- medical research and equipment
- non-Cumbrian projects
- sponsored events
- replacement of statutory funding
- projects that have already happened
- applications where a grant from that fund has been received within the last year (except Grassroots Grants)
- individuals (except for specific funds).

Please contact the foundation for further information on individual restrictions on any of the grant programmes.

Applications

Applications should include the following supporting information:

- a copy of the organisation's governing document (not required for registered charities)
- a copy of the latest accounts (or bank statements covering the last quarter, if the organisation has been operating for less than a year)
- details of an independent referee
- a copy of the organisation's child protection or safeguarding policy (if the project will involve working with children and/or young people).

The foundation prefers to receive applications via email, even if the supporting documents have to be sent by post.

Applicants are encouraged to contact the foundation prior to making an application in order to confirm their eligibility.

Applications are accepted throughout the year and decisions are usually taken within two months. Some programmes offer a faster process for small urgent projects.

Itzchok Meyer Cymerman Trust Ltd

Advancement of the orthodox Jewish faith; education; social welfare; relief of sickness; medical research and general charitable purposes

£944,000 (2009/10)

Beneficial area

UK and Israel.

497 Holloway Road, London N7 6LE
Tel: 020 7272 2255
Correspondent: I Heitner, Trustee
Trustees: Mrs H F Bondi;
M D Cymerman; Mrs R Cymerman;
Mrs S Heitner; L H Bondi; I Heitner;
S Cymerman.
CC Number: 265090

Information available

Accounts were available at the Charity Commission.

The trust was established in 1972 and its objectives are the advancement of the orthodox Jewish faith and general charitable purposes. Almost all the trust's grants are to Jewish charitable organisations although occasional grants to individuals in need are made. Many grants are made to the same organisations each year.

In 2009/10 the trust had assets of just under £2.3 million and an income of £869,000. Grants were made to 74 organisations totalling £944,000, and were categorised as follows:

Advancement of education	£685,500
Relief of poverty	£164,000
Medical care and research	£75,000
Advancement of religion	£19,500

Larger grants were listed in the accounts, with beneficiaries including: Friends of Ohr Arkiva Institute (£90,000); Vehodarto P'Nei Zoken (£50,000); Russian Immigrant Aid Fund (£44,000); Torah Supporters Fund (£25,000); and Pardes Chana Institutions (£15,000).

Applications

In writing to the correspondent.

The D'Oyly Carte Charitable Trust

Arts, medical welfare, environment

£804,000 (2009/10)

Beneficial area

UK.

1 Savoy Hill, London WC2R 0BP
Tel: 020 7420 2600
Correspondent: Jane Thorne, Secretary
Trustees: Jeremy Leigh Pemberton, Chair; Francesca Radcliffe; Julia Sibley; Henry Freeland; Andrew Jackson; Michael O'Brien.
CC Number: 1112457

Information available

Accounts were available at the Charity Commission.

Summary

The trust was founded in 1972 by Dame Bridget D'Oyly Carte, granddaughter of the founder of both the Savoy Theatre and the Savoy Hotel. Its distributable income increased significantly on her death in 1985, when it inherited her shareholding in The Savoy Hotel plc, and again in 1998 following the company's sale.

The trust supports general charitable causes connected with the arts, medical welfare and the environment. Certain charities in which the founder took a special interest continue to be supported on a regular basis.

Grants start at around £500. The majority are for amounts under £5,000 although some can be for larger amounts. Most funding goes to the arts and medical welfare.

The majority of grants made by the trust are on a one-off basis although term grants are also agreed from time to time for a maximum period of three years, particularly in respect of bursary funding for educational establishments, mainly in the arts sector, and to help newly created charities become established. Recipients of these grants are required to report regularly to the trust for monitoring purposes.

The trustees have continued their commitment to make grants to charities that do not enjoy a high profile in order to create significant impact on the work of the charity concerned, and, recognising the day-to-day funding needs of charities, the trustees continue to consider applications for core costs.

Guidelines for applicants

The following information is taken from the 'Grantmaking Priorities' section of the trust's annual report and accounts:

Notwithstanding the trust's overall charitable objectives for the public benefit, the trustees regularly review their policies, objectives and guidelines, and, following a full review in November 2008, determined that their grant-making priorities for the three years 2009–2012 would continue to focus on:

The Arts

- promotion of access, education and excellence in the arts for young people to increase their opportunities to become involved outside school and to build future audiences

- access to the arts for people who least have access to them
- performance development of graduates in the performing arts in the early stages of their careers and to encourage their involvement in the community through performances and workshops for the benefit of those with special needs and those who would otherwise have no opportunity to hear or participate in a live performance

Medical/Welfare

- promotion and provision of music and art therapy to improve the quality of life for the elderly and the disabled, and in the palliative care of children
- support for charities concerned with alleviating the suffering of adults and children with medical conditions who have difficulty finding support through traditional sources
- support and respite for carers with emphasis on the provision of holidays for those carers who wouldn't normally have a break from their responsibilities – and with special emphasis on projects and schemes that allow young carers to enjoy being children

The Environment

- preservation of the countryside and its woodlands -with emphasis on the encouragement of voluntary work and active involvement in hands-on activities
- protection of species within the United Kingdom and their habitats under threat or in decline
- conservation of the marine environment and sustainable fisheries
- heritage conservation within the United Kingdom based on value to, and use by the local community – the trust favours projects that seek to create a new use for fine buildings of architectural and historic merit to encourage the widest possible cross-section of use. (The trust does not normally support major restorations unless a specific element of the work can be identified as appropriate to the aims of the trust.)

Grantmaking in 2009/10

In 2009/10 the trust had assets of £40.1 million and an income of £972,000. There were 255 grants made during the year totalling £804,000. Grants were broken down as follows:

		Average	Total*
Arts	121	£3,299	£399,000
Medical welfare	100	£3,370	£337,000
Environment	34	£3,338	£113,500

*These amounts include support costs. The trust's annual report includes the following description of its grantmaking activities during the year:

> This year again the Arts took the largest proportion of trust spending at £399,000 compared to £485,500 in the previous year, whilst spending in the Medical Welfare sector amounted to £337,000 compared to £404,500 in the previous year. In the third sector, the Environment, £113,500 was distributed in grants compared to £145,500 in the previous year.

Beneficiaries included: Royal Academy of Dramatic Arts (£20,000), towards bursaries; Help the Hospices (£15,000), towards an education and training programme to develop the specialist skills and expertise of doctors, nurses and hospice managers throughout the United Kingdom; Royal Northern College of Music (£10,000), towards bursaries; Tate Gallery (£5,000), to support a visual arts project for young people in the care of local authorities; British Association of Adoption & Fostering (£5,000), towards the Health Programme for children in care; Surrey Care Trust (£5,000), towards the Swingbridge Community Boat Programme's conservation projects along the waterways of Surrey; Wildlife Trust Sheffield (£4,000), towards hands-on activities for children and young people; CHASE Hospice Care for Young Children (£3,500), second and final instalment of two-year commitment towards music project for life-limited children in collaboration with the Royal Philharmonic Orchestra; and Brighton Early Music Festival (£3,500), to provide opportunities for young professional musicians to work with leading music animateurs in two major education projects.

Exclusions

The trust is unlikely to support the following:

- animal welfare
- applications from individuals, or for the benefit of one individual
- charities requiring funding for statutory requirements
- charities operating outside the UK
- conferences or seminars
- exhibitions
- expeditions and overseas travel
- general appeals

- large national charities which enjoy widespread support
- maintenance of religious buildings
- medical research
- NHS Trust hospitals for operational or building costs
- recordings and commissioning of new works
- religious activities
- schools, nurseries and playgroups (other than those for children with special needs)
- support and rehabilitation from drug or alcohol abuse.

Due to the volume of appeals received, the trustees have decided not to consider requests from charities that have had an application turned down until two years have elapsed after the date of rejection.

Applications

Potential applicants should write to the correspondent with an outline proposal of no more than two A4 pages. This should cover the work of the charity, its beneficiaries and the need for funding. Applicants qualifying for consideration will then be required to complete the trust's application form.

The form should be returned with a copy of the latest annual report and accounts. Applications for specific projects should also include clear details of the need the intended project is designed to meet and an outline budget.

The majority of applications are considered in March, July and November. The trust states that it is happy to discuss potential applications on the telephone.

Roald Dahl's Marvellous Children's Charity

Haematology and neurology conditions affecting children and young people up to the age of 25

£532,000 (2009/10)

Beneficial area

UK.

81a High Street, Great Missenden, Buckinghamshire HP16 0AL

Tel: 01494 890465

Fax: 01494 890459

Email: grants@ marvellouschildrenscharity.org

Website: www. marvellouschildrenscharity.org

Correspondent: James Fitzpatrick, Director

Trustees: Felicity Dahl, Chair; Martin Goodwin; Roger Hills; Georgina Howson; Virginia Fisher.

CC Number: 1137409

Information available

Accounts were available from the Charity Commission. The foundation also has an informative website.

The charity was established in 2010 to supersede the Roald Dahl Foundation following a strategic review, although the focus of the charity remains the same. The charity provides excellent information about its work, much of which is reprinted here.

Guidelines

The following information is taken from the charity's guidelines:

Roald Dahl's Marvellous Children's Charity helps in two areas which were of great interest to Roald Dahl: neurology and haematology. Within these areas we are targeting our support at rare, life-limiting, long-term debilitating and underfunded conditions.

The charity makes grants to hospitals, charities and individuals in the UK. We are keen to help children living with the specific conditions listed below. In general, we aim to provide:

 ▹ help to organisations to which funds are not readily available. We prefer to help small or new organisations in favour of long-established, large or national organisations
 ▹ help to individual families by providing financial assistance to help them cope with difficulties they face in caring for a sick child.

Please read these guidelines carefully. If you have a query, are uncertain whether the application you hope to make comes within our current criteria, or if you would like to discuss an application informally before completing the application form, we are happy for you to telephone us.

1. Our Medical Areas of Interest

The charity makes grants to benefit children who have the following conditions:

Neurology

 ▹ acquired brain injury as the result of:
   ▹ benign brain tumour
   ▹ encephalitis
   ▹ head injury
   ▹ hydrocephalus
   ▹ meningitis
   ▹ stroke
 ▹ neuro-degenerative conditions, defined as conditions in which there is progressive intellectual and/or neurological deterioration
 ▹ rare and/or severe forms of epilepsy.

Haematology

Chronic debilitating blood diseases of childhood, excluding leukaemia and related disorders. Conditions include:

 ▹ sickle cell anaemia
 ▹ thalassaemia
 ▹ haemolytic anaemia
 ▹ bone marrow failure syndrome
 ▹ haemophilia
 ▹ thrombophilia
 ▹ Von Willebrand's Disease.

2. Our Age Range

The charity primarily makes grants to benefit children (i.e. up to the 18th birthday). However, we may consider supporting young people between the ages of 18 and 25 (i.e. up to the 26th birthday) where a case can be made that they have specific needs associated with their medical condition.

3. What We Will Fund

We are looking for applications that will clearly tackle the needs and challenges children face as a result of living with the conditions listed above. We are particularly interested in:

 ▹ pump-priming of new specialist Paediatric nursing posts, where there is an emphasis on community care, for a maximum of 2 years. We will only consider funding posts where the applicant organisation commits to taking over funding of the post for a minimum of 3 years after our grant ends. During 2010/11 we are particularly interested in applications for Acquired Brain Injury Paediatric Nurse Specialist posts and Haemoglobinopathy Paediatric Nurse Specialist posts
 ▹ the provision of information and/or support to children and their families
 ▹ specific projects within residential and day centres to benefit children within the above-mentioned criteria
 ▹ small items of medical equipment, not available from statutory sources, to enable children to be cared for in their own homes
 ▹ activities to disseminate good practice in support of children living with our priority conditions

 ▹ other projects which specifically benefit children and young people within the above mentioned medical criteria may be considered.

Although we prefer to fund specific projects, posts and activities, we will consider providing core funding particularly in the case of very small organisations.

The charity has a small research fund. However, this fund is **not** open to applications. Instead, each year the charity will invite one or more organisations to submit proposals for work that will have a significant and long-term impact in our areas of interest.

In general the charity will consider applications for up to £25,000 per year – and for a maximum of 2 years. The majority of grants we make are for 1 year and are for between £10,000 and £15,000.

In 2009/10 the charity had assets of £1.6 million and an income of £577,000 including £297,200 in general donations and £197,000 from the proceeds of the annual Readathon. Grants were made to organisations totalling £532,000 and were broken down as follows:

Neurology	£443,200
Haematology	£89,500

Beneficiaries included: Society for Muco-polysaccharide Diseases (£37,000), towards a Specialist Muco-polysaccharide Disease Advocacy Worker; Sickle Cell Society (£35,000), towards the Befriending Project for Young People with Sickle Cell to support them with the transition to adulthood; Southampton General Hospital (£30,000), to establish the new post of Roald Dahl Sapphire Epilepsy Nurse Specialist; National Society for Epilepsy (£17,500), for seven Paediatric Epilepsy Information Network points in hospitals in England; Scottish Epilepsy Initiative (£10,000), towards the Young People's Fieldworker post costs for 2 years; UK Thalassaemia Society (£5,000), towards the Patient and Family National Conference; The MedicAlert Foundation (£2,000), MedicAlert service for 40 children with neurological difficulties.

Exclusions

The charity will not fund:

 ▹ general appeals from large, well-established charities
 ▹ national appeals for large building projects

- arts projects
- any organisations which do not have charitable status or exclusively charitable aims (other than NHS organisations under our specialist nurses programme)
- statutory bodies (other than NHS organisations under our specialist nurses programme)
- school or higher education fees
- organisations outside the UK
- organisations for people with blood disorders which are cancer related due to the relatively large number of charities helping in the oncological field.

Applications

The foundation's guidelines state:

First, make sure that your project or application falls within the criteria listed [in the general section]. Then contact the charity's director to discuss your proposal. If your idea fits closely within our current areas of interest you will be sent an application form to complete and return.

Organisations wishing to apply for funding for specialist nurse posts must contact the charity to request a special application pack.

Applications for nurse posts will not be accepted on our standard application form.

Once you have completed it you should send the application form, and any attachments, together with a copy of your organisation's accounts and annual report for each of the last two years, to the address above.

Applications for posts should include a copy of the proposed job description and person specification.

When completing the form you should clearly demonstrate how your project fits our eligibility criteria and funding priorities. You should also clearly tell us what activities you would undertake with the funding, who will benefit (including the number of beneficiaries, their age ranges and whether they are from a specific area or community), how they will benefit (e.g. what the project will do to help, support or empower them) and how you will measure the outcomes of the project.

We aim to visit as many organisations applying for funds as possible, but we may simply telephone for more information.

Currently grant applications are being considered twice per year – March and September. Urgent applications may be considered between meetings – please contact the charity's director to discuss this if required.

If we award your organisation a grant, we will want to ensure that your project makes a positive impact on the need you have identified. We will want to learn from projects we fund and sometimes share that learning with others. We will also need to account for the money that we have invested.

Any organisation awarded a grant must therefore comply with our standard conditions of grant. These include:

- the successful organisation will provide the charity with reports on the project – generally at six monthly intervals during the period of the grant. The report will include:
    - the number and breakdown of beneficiaries (e.g. age, gender, area of residence, condition)
    - a brief summary of the activities carried out
    - the impact of the project, activity or post being funded (e.g. the outcomes for the children, young people and their families)
    - a brief account of how the funding has been spent
- for larger grants the charity reserves the right to undertake monitoring visits
- the charity will be able to use the name of the successful organisation, and details of the funded project, in our publicity
- the successful organisation will provide the charity with photographs and, where appropriate, case studies, to illustrate the work funded by the charity. The photos will be suitable for use in the charity's publicity material, in printed form or on the website. We will require confirmation, in writing, that those pictured, and the guardians of those under 18 years, have given written permission for their photograph to be used by us
- the successful organisation will seek appropriate local and national publicity for the grant and for Roald Dahl's Marvellous Children's Charity – and the support of the Roald Dahl's Marvellous Children's Charity will be acknowledged and our logo prominently displayed on any publicity material relating to the project.

Our requirements will be proportionate to the size of the grant – and we would expect most organisations to be collecting the information we require for their own monitoring and evaluation purposes anyway.

The Daiwa Anglo-Japanese Foundation

Anglo-Japanese relations

£529,000 (2010/11)

Beneficial area

UK, Japan.

Daiwa Foundation, Japan House, 13/14 Cornwall Terrace, London NW1 4QP
Tel: 020 7486 4348
Fax: 020 7486 2914
Email: marie.conte-helm@dajf.org.uk
Website: www.dajf.org.uk
Correspondent: Prof. Marie Conte-Helm, Director General
Trustees: Sir Michael Perry; Hiroaki Fujii; Takafumi Sato; Mami Mizutori; Sir John Whitehead; Mr Dozen; Mr Hara; Mr Everett; Merryn Somerset Webb; Sir David Brewer; Lord Brittan; Sir Peter Williams; Andrew Smithers; Akira Kyota.
CC Number: 299955

Information available

Accounts were available from the Charity Commission. The foundation also has a detailed website

The Daiwa Anglo-Japanese Foundation is a UK charity, established in 1988 with a benefaction from Daiwa Securities Co Ltd. The foundation's purpose is to support closer links between Britain and Japan. It does this by:

- making grants available to individuals, institutions and organisations to promote links between the UK and Japan in all fields of activity
- enabling British and Japanese students and academics to further their education through exchanges and other bilateral initiatives
- awarding of Daiwa Scholarships for British graduates to study and undertake work-placements in Japan
- organising a year-round programme of events to increase understanding of Japan in the UK.

In 2003 the foundation introduced its restructured grants policy to bring a greater focus to its funding activities and to give encouragement to collaborations between British and Japanese partners.

The foundation awards grants to individuals and institutions in the UK and Japan in all areas of the visual and performing arts, the humanities, the social sciences, science and engineering, mathematics, business studies and education, including schools and universities, and grass roots and professional groups.

The following information is taken from the trustees' annual report 2010/11:

Plans for the Future

The foundation continues to carry out its objectives through its four main areas of charitable activity. In addition, there are related initiatives that will set priorities for the next twelve months:

Following a comprehensive Strategy Review in 2009, the trustees of the foundation approved priorities for the next three years. In addition to its core programmes (Daiwa Scholarships; Grants, Awards and Prizes; and Japan House Events), a special annual focus on science, education or the arts was agreed. In practice, this is being realised through the awarding of Daiwa Adrian Prizes in 2010 and plans for a programme of educational support for Tohoku in 2011 and the Daiwa Foundation Art Prize in 2012.

Further development of the role of Daiwa Foundation Japan House as a cultural centre for Japan in the UK continues. The events programme is being enhanced with a gradual build up of daytime activities, including lectures, seminars and courses. A programme of work placements and internships has successfully been launched and will continue to be offered to provide training opportunities for British and Japanese students and young professionals.

The foundation plans to extend its Japan House programme beyond London in 2011/12 with the organisation of a seminar in Wales in June 2011.

The 2012 monthly seminar series will once again seek to highlight contemporary issues of common interest to the UK and Japan. The foundation will periodically invite leading speakers from Japan to take part in these and other events.

The foundation's annual accounts provide a useful summary of its grant-making programmes:

Daiwa Foundation Small Grants

Daiwa Foundation Small Grants are available from £3,000–£7,000 to individuals, societies, associations or other bodies in the UK or Japan to promote and support interaction between the two countries. They can cover all fields of activity, including educational and grassroots exchanges, research travel, the organisation of conferences, exhibitions, and other projects and events that fulfil this broad objective. New initiatives are especially encouraged.

Daiwa Foundation Awards

Daiwa Foundation Awards are available from £7,000–£15,000 for collaborative projects that enable British and Japanese partners to work together, preferably within the context of an institutional relationship. Daiwa Foundation Awards can cover projects in all fields of activity. (Support for scientific collaborations is separately provided through The Royal Society-Daiwa Anglo-Japanese Foundation Joint Project Grants scheme).

The Royal Society Daiwa Anglo-Japanese Foundation Joint Project Grants

These grants support travel, subsistence and research for collaborative projects between British and Japanese researchers in the field of science. They are funded by the Foundation and administered by The Royal Society.

Daiwa Adrian Prizes

Named to commemorate the late Lord Adrian, [Daiwa Adrian Prizes] are awarded every three years in recognition of significant scientific collaboration between Japanese and British research teams.

In 2010/11 the foundation had assets of £37 million and an income of nearly £543,000. Charitable expenditure totalled £1.2 million, including £536,000 given in scholarships and £529,000 given in grants, awards and prizes. Grants, awards and prizes approved for the following year totalled £338,000.

Grants were awarded as follows:

Daiwa Foundation Awards	£136,000
Daiwa Foundation Small Grants UK-side	£70,000
Daiwa Adrian Prizes	£60,000
Royal Society Joint Project Grants	£34,500
Daiwa Foundation Small Grants: Japan-side	£30,000
Daiwa Foundation Art Prize	£7,000

Beneficiaries include: Cardiff University, School of Medicine (£12,000); Hiroshima City Culture Foundation, Imperial College London and John Innes Centre, Sainsbury Laboratory (£10,000 each); King's College London, Centre for Computing in the Humanities (£3,750); and National Galleries of Scotland (£3,000).

Exclusions

Daiwa Foundation Small Grants cannot be used for:
- general appeals
- capital expenditure (e.g., building refurbishment, equipment acquisition, etc)
- consumables (e.g., stationery, scientific supplies, etc)
- school, college or university fees
- research or study by an individual school/college/university student
- salary costs or professional fees
- commissions for works of art
- retrospective grants
- replacement of statutory funding
- commercial activities.

Daiwa Foundation Awards cannot be used for:
- any project that does not involve both a British and a Japanese partner
- general appeals
- capital expenditure (e.g., building refurbishment, equipment acquisition, etc)
- salary costs or professional fees
- commissions for works of art
- retrospective grants
- replacement of statutory funding
- commercial activities.

Applications

Details of deadlines and criteria for grants, awards and prizes, together with the relevant application forms and guidelines are available on the foundation's website.

Common applicant mistakes

'Applicants applying for fees or salaries; asking for retrospective funding.'

Baron Davenport's Charity

Almshouses; hospices; residential homes for the elderly; children and young people under the age of 25.

£676,000 to organisations (2010)

Beneficial area

Warwickshire, Worcestershire, Staffordshire, Shropshire and West Midlands.

Portman House, 5–7 Temple Row West, Birmingham B2 5NY
Tel: 0121 236 8004
Fax: 0121 233 2500
Email: enquiries@ barondavenportscharity.org
Website: www. barondavenportscharity.org/
Correspondent: Mrs Marlene Keenan, Administrator
Trustees: Christopher Hordern, Chair; Sue M Ayres; William M Colacicchi; Paul Dransfield; Philip A Gough; Rob Prichard.
CC Number: 217307

Information available

Accounts were available from the Charity Commission. The charity also has a simple website.

Established in 1930 by Mr Baron Davenport, the charity is now governed by a Charity Commission Scheme dated 16th April 1998.

Of the income, 40% goes in grants for individuals, specifically for widows, spinsters, divorced women (of 60 years and over) and women deserted by their partners together with their children, who are under 25 and in financial need.

The remaining 60% of the income is distributed, in Birmingham and the counties of the West Midlands, equally to:

- almshouses, residential homes for the elderly and hospices;
- charities that assist children and young people under 25.

Grants are made to a large number of organisations each year – some organisations are funded in consecutive years, but every grant must be separately applied for each year; there is no automatic renewal.

In 2010 the charity had assets of £29.2 million and an income of £1.1 million. Grants were made to 394 organisations totalling £676,000.

Beneficiaries of the largest grants (£6,000 or more) included: Age Concern Kingstanding and Mary Stevens Hospice (£15,000 each); Age Concern Birmingham and Laslett's Charities (£10,000 each); Douglas Macmillan Hospice (£9,000); Coventry & District Free Church Homes (£7,000); ExtraCare Charitable Trust and James Lloyd Almshouses Trust (£6,000 each).

The charity also awarded grants to 1,667 individuals totalling £396,500.

Exclusions

There are no exclusions, providing the applications come within the charity's objects and the applying organisation is based within the charity's beneficial area, or the organisation's project lies within, or benefits people who live in, the beneficial area.

Applications

In writing to the correspondent, accompanied by the latest accounts and any project costs. Distributions take place twice a year at the end of May and November and applications should be received at the charity's office by 15 March or 15 September. All applications are acknowledged and those not within the charity's objects are advised.

The Davidson Family Charitable Trust

Jewish, general

£1.3 million (2010/11)

Beneficial area

UK.

c/o Queen Anne Street Capital, 58 Queen Anne Street, London W1G 8HW
Tel: 020 72241030
Email: ewiner@wolfeproperties.co.uk
Correspondent: Eve Winer, Trustee
Trustees: Gerald A Davidson; Maxine Y Davidson; Eve Winer.
CC Number: 262937

Information available

Accounts were available at the Charity Commission.

Established in 1971, this is the trust of Gerald Davidson, director of Queen Anne Street Capital and Wolfe Properties, and his family.

In 2010/11 the trust had assets of £801,000 and an income, mainly from donations from the Davidson family, of £2.1 million. After very low governance costs of just £359, grants totalled £1.3 million.

Grants were awarded as follows:

Welfare	£820,000
Arts	£314,000
Medical	£123,500
Educational	£63,000
International aid	£17,500
Religious	£7,000

Beneficiaries included: Jewish Care (£801,000); Holburne Museum (£175,000); Museum of London (£92,000); Friends of Israel Antiquities Authority (£25,000); United Synagogue (£21,000); Emunah Child Resettlement Fund and Magon David Adom UK (£10,000 each); Friends of Ohel Torah (£6,000); Friends of Bnai Akiva and Youth Aliyah Child Rescue (£5,000 each); UJIA (£4,000); and Eastside Youth Leaders Academy and Great Ormond Street Hospital (£1,000 each).

Applications

In writing to the correspondent.

Peter De Haan Charitable Trust

Social welfare, the environment, the arts

£789,000 to organisations (2009/10)

Beneficial area

UK.

Wool Yard, 54 Bermondsey Street, London SE1 3UD

Tel: 020 7232 5471

Email: sjohnson@pdhct.org.uk

Website: www.pdhct.org.uk

Correspondent: Simon Johnson

Trustees: Peter Charles De Haan; Janette McKay; Nikki A Crane; Dr Rob Stoneman; Carol Stone; Opus Corporate Trustees Limited.

CC Number: 1077005

Information available

Accounts were available from the Charity Commission website. The trust also has a clear and simple website on which it gives the following information:

The Peter De Haan Charitable Trust aims to improve the quality of life for people and communities in the UK through its work with arts, environmental and social welfare organisations.

Led by businessman and philanthropist Peter De Haan, The Trust operates under a venture philanthropy model, working closely with the organisations it supports financially and organisationally to increase their capacity and impact.

Since 1999 it has donated £18,963,000 to over 520 organisations and three years ago launched leading youth arts network IdeasTap.

The objects of the charity are wide-ranging and allow it to operate as a generalist grant-making charity. The charity will not exist in perpetuity and the reserves will gradually be spent over a 20 year period from the date of constitution. It is this policy which governs the annual level of donations.

The trust's grantmaking currently focuses on three areas:

- social welfare
- environment
- arts.

The trust also operates:

Under One Roof – an innovative new model of collaborative working for charities sharing premises, human and physical resources, and creative new ways of thinking and working.

The purpose of the Under One Roof model is to increase the capacity of organisations, through a more efficient and creative working environment, to both achieve their individual and collective goals and make a greater contribution to the wellbeing of their employees, the local community and society as a whole.

In 2010 philanthropist and businessman Peter De Haan pioneered a new Under One Roof project where a number of charities moved into a shared workspace in Southwark, London.

The Peter De Haan Charitable Trust, online youth arts charity IdeasTap, the National Youth Theatre of Great Britain, the National Student Drama Festival, Team London Bridge and Old Vic New Voices now operate some of their administration from the Under One Roof Building.

Organisations working Under One Roof receive increased office space and meeting rooms to facilitate their expanding programmes of work, IT and telephony infrastructure, all key office and real estate services, a flexible creative space, cafeteria and cycle-park.

In 2010/11 it had assets of almost £16.6 million and an income of £345,000. Grants totalled £1.13 million of which £789,000 were made to organisations and £340,000 to young adults.

Guidelines

The following information is taken from the trust's website:

Social welfare

PDHCT initially approached social welfare work by making traditional grants to organisations, before evolving to make more conditional grants as The Trustees narrowed the focus towards young people and projects which are aimed at early intervention. Projects providing continuity which sought to help beneficiaries back into mainstream society were given priority.

Today PDHCT continues to work with social welfare but now in long term partnerships with delivery organisations in a philanthrocapitalism model. This approach has evolved through years of work and investment in social welfare and enables The Trust to achieve a focused and sustainable impact.

One example of how The Trust is support social welfare outcomes through its philanthrocaptialism model is its support of the National Youth Theatre of Great Britain:

The Trust's substantial core support of NYT has enabled it to remove financial, social, cultural and geographical barriers that in the past may have prevented some young people from accessing a first rate arts education. Financial stability achieved through the support of The Trust has enabled NYT to expand its flagship social inclusion programme 'Playing Up' in London, the West Midlands and Glasgow. The Playing Up Programme engages young people who are not in education, employment or training (NEET) or who are considered to be at risk.

Environment

The PDHCT Environment Programme is informed by an over-arching theme of climate change whilst remaining sensitive to the needs of its four colloquium charities – the London, Leicestershire & Rutland and Yorkshire Wildlife Trusts and the John Muir Trust. The programme has also sought to align itself with the thinking behind the environmental trilogy of S'warm, SLICK and Flood that the National Youth Theatre is using to theme their cultural projects.

Arts

The PDHCT arts programme aims to create and support activities that:

- Provide positive role models through mentoring opportunities with industry leading experts
- Enrich young people's lives by equipping them with skills they might not develop through the formal curriculum
- Foster entrepreneurial and business instincts in the next generation of young artists preparing them to contribute to the creative economy with innovative ideas and successful new ventures.

The PDHCT arts programme is now delivered through IdeasTap – the leading online youth arts hub for young creative people, founded by PDHCT in winter 2008.

On 6 April 2010 the activities of IdeasTap were transferred to a wholly owned subsidiary company, IdeasTap Limited, that has charitable status (number 1132623.) The result of this hive down is to leave The Peter De Haan Charitable Trust as a traditional donor trust with all its charitable trading activities in a separate legal entity.

IdeasTap continues to work extremely closely with The Trust, as the major financial supporter and with Peter De Haan chairing The Trust and acting as IdeasTap Chief Executive.

In summer 2010 IdeasTap also launched a children's community arm called Ideas Club, to deliver the work with children aged 8–18 in Southwark, Lambeth and Deptford previously carried out by the charity and former IdeasTap partner L'Ouverture.

Exclusions

The trust states:

We will not accept applications for grants:

- that directly replace or subsidise statutory funding
- from individuals or for the benefit of one individual
- for work that has already taken place
- which do not have a direct benefit to the UK

- for medical research
- for adventure and residential courses, expeditions or overseas travel
- for holidays and respite care
- for endowment funds
- for the promotion of a specific religion
- that are part of general appeals or circulars
- from applicants who have applied to within the last 12 months.

In addition to the above, we are unlikely to support:

- large national charities which enjoy widespread support
- local organisations which are part of a wider network of others doing similar work
- individual pre-schools, schools. out-of-school clubs, supplementary schools, colleges, universities or youth clubs
- websites, publications, conferences or seminars.

Applications

In writing or via email to the correspondent. The following information is provided by the charity:

Grants may be for project-based applications or to subsidise core costs.

In all areas, the trustees will consider funding up for to a maximum of three years.

The following information should be included:

- a description of the charitable institution's aims and achievements
- charity registration number, where applicable
- an outline and budget for the project for which funding is sought and the amount of funding requested
- a description of how the issues which the trustees want to be addressed are satisfied
- a copy of the latest financial statements
- details of funds raised and the current shortfall.

Applications are considered on a continuing basis throughout the year, with major grants being awarded at the trustee meeting held quarterly in March, June, September and December.

However, potential applicants should note the information in the 'general' section which states that in the environment category, no applications can be considered from wildlife trusts, that the social welfare programme is closed to new applications until after 5 April 2011, and that funding for the arts is now delivered through IdeasTap.

The Debmar Benevolent Trust

Jewish

£1.5 million (2009/10)

Beneficial area

UK and Israel.

c/o Haffner Hoff LLP, 3rd Floor, Manchester House, 86 Princess Street, Manchester M1 6NP
Tel: 0161 236 4107
Correspondent: Hilary Olsberg, Trustee
Trustees: Gella Klein; Hilary Olsberg; Rosalind Halpern; Vivienne Lewin.
CC Number: 283065

Information available

Accounts were available from the Charity Commission, without a list of grants.

Grants are given towards the advancement of the orthodox Jewish faith and the relief of poverty.

In 2009/10 the trust had assets of £4.8 million and an income of £5.3 million, mostly from the sale of assets in the form of property. Grants were made during the year totalling £1.5 million. The trust also distributed almost £5.7 million to newly registered charities established by the trustees – further details of these were not available at the time of writing.

A list of beneficiaries was not provided by the trust in its accounts. Previous beneficiaries included: Beis Hamedrash Hachodosh, Chasdei Belz, Chevras Mauous Lador, Gevurath Ari, Telz Talmudical Academy, Friends of Assos Chesed, Pardes Chana, ATLIB, Bobov Institutions, Ohr Akiva Institute, Tomchei Shaarei Zion, Ponivitch Institutions, Yeshiva Shaarei Zion, Beis Yoel High School, Format Charity Trust and Manchester Kollel.

Applications

In writing to the correspondent.

Derbyshire Community Foundation

Social welfare

£1.16 million (2009/10)

Beneficial area

Derbyshire and the city of Derby.

Foundation House, Unicorn Business Park, Wellington Street, Ripley, Derbyshire DE5 3EH
Tel: 01773 514 850
Fax: 01773 741 410
Email: info@ derbyshirecommunityfoundation.co.uk
Website: www. derbyshirecommunityfoundation.co.uk
Correspondent: The Grants Team
Trustees: Dr Ranjit Virma; Michael Hall; Arthur Blackwood; David Coleman; Kjell Karlsen; Nick Mirfin; Matthew Montague; Clive Moesby; Lucy Palmer; David Walker; Robin Wood; Rt Rev. Alastair Redfern; Janet Birkin; Louise Pinder; Simon Ingham; Helen Bishop.
CC Number: 1039485

Information available

Accounts were available from the Charity Commission website. Further information is available from the foundation's website.

As stated in the foundation's 2009/10 accounts:

Derbyshire Community Foundation's vision is to revitalise local life by means of a fund for Derbyshire, provided for the good of the community by people with the commitment and means to give. By meeting visible needs today, and anticipated and unexpected future needs, we hope to make a difference to Derbyshire forever.

Our objectives are:
- to build an endowment fund for the people of Derbyshire, to provide a growing sum for grants to tackle disadvantage and to enhance the quality of life in our county

by making grants creatively on behalf of our donors and other funders, to create the bridge between people who care about the local community and the wide range of groups and individuals that need their help.

We have Local Decision Making Panels across the county, comprising over 50 volunteers who live in their panel area and are involved in (and have a strong understanding of) the voluntary and community sector and what running an organisation involves. This helps us to ensure that funding is directed where it is most needed and that all bids are considered in accordance with both the foundation's constitutional objectives and the criteria of our funders and donors. In addition to our four core panels (covering North East, North West and South Derbyshire and Derby City), the foundation also manages a number of fund specific panels.

Current grant programmes

The foundation distributes funds on behalf of companies, individuals and local, regional and national government agencies, through a variety of grantmaking programmes. There are 11 main grant programmes:

Comic Relief Fund

Comic Relief has partnered the foundation to help distribute some of its funds into the City and County. The funds available have been split into two distinct themes, one related to sports and the other one for general community groups carrying out certain types of work.

Groups can apply for up to £10,000, however given the limited sums available this means the foundation is only likely to fund around 3 groups per financial year should all applicants apply for the full amount.

Derbyshire Community Foundation General Fund

The foundation is building up a long-term fund with contributions from local companies and individuals. It will support applications for awards of up to £1,000. However, due to limitations of resources, applications of up to £500 are favoured.

The fund aims to support as wide a range of voluntary groups as possible, both in terms of where they are based and the work that they do. The overarching purpose of each grant made is to enhance the quality of life for people living in Derbyshire communities and to tackle disadvantages and inequalities they face.

Fair Share Sinfin & Austin Fund

This funding stream is administered by the foundation on behalf of the National Fair Share program and was devised to

tackle issues within the Sinfin & Austin wards of Derby City creating a stronger community and to improve opportunities for residents. The fund consists of three main strands: community and voluntary group support, children and young people and training and education. The maximum grant per stream is currently £10,000.

Firm Foundations Fund

Firm Foundations is a broad funding stream aiming to improve the quality of life for Derbyshire residents by supporting a thriving community and voluntary sector that offers a wide range of services and facilities to local communities. The maximum grant is currently £5,000 (preference is given to bids of c. £2,000).

The Hutchinson Music Award

Grants of up to £250 each are made to talented young musicians from Derby and Derbyshire, to help with the cost of their music education.

Jefford Weller Fund

This fund provides financial assistance to any community and voluntary organisation tackling homelessness issues and/or addressing housing problems. The maximum grant is £2,000.

John Weston Fund

This fund was set up by local benefactor John Weston in 2002 and has two strands.

- Strand one: support to individual young people with personal development.
- Strand two: financial assistance to community and voluntary groups tackling issues related to health and well-being or supporting young people within the community.

Community groups can apply for up to £2,500.

Southern Derbyshire Learning Fund

This fund was designed to support community and voluntary groups offering opportunities for people to gain new skills, which will ultimately allow people to enter or re-enter employment. The maximum grant is currently £2,000.

Tom Carey Fund

This fund has been set up to support new and existing community activity in the Abbey ward of Derby City. Its main purpose is to improve the quality of life for residents in this area. The maximum grant is currently £10,000 although preference will be given to applications of up to £5,000.

More information on all of the fund's listed above including, grant priorities, types of project costs funded, application documents and

deadlines, can be found on the foundation's website.

Grants in 2009/10

In 2009/10 the trust had assets of £6.3 million and an income of £1.45 million. Grants totalled £1.16 million.

During the year 36 grants were payable to community groups and voluntary organisations in excess of £7,000 amounting to £502,000, 43 grants were paid between £4,000 and £7,000 amounting to £206,000, and 382 grants of up to £3,999 amounting to £466,000.

Grants in excess of £7,000 included those made to: SNAP (Project Fairshare) (£133,000); Pakistan Community Centre (£37,000); Fairshare Derby Community Safety Officers (£34,000); Derby Women's Centre (£29,000); First Steps Derbyshire (£24,000); Derby City Mission, Mickleover Gymnastics Club and Viva Chamber Orchestra Ltd (£10,000 each); and Austin Community Enterprise (£7,500).

Exclusions

The foundation's general exclusions are:

- profit making organisations where individual members benefit financially (legitimate social enterprises and community interest companies can receive funding but the foundation asks that you read the additional guidelines related to this type of group structure)
- medical equipment
- animal charities
- any project which promotes faith or involves the refurbishment/ building of a place of worship
- statutory bodies including schools, hospitals, police etc
- any project which directly replaces statutory obligations
- any project which promotes a political party
- projects which benefit people outside of Derbyshire
- retrospective funding (grants for activities which have already taken place)
- sponsored events.

Applications

The foundation offers several different funds, each offering funding for a maximum of twelve months and each with a specific focus or set of criteria. Please visit the foundation's website for full details of the current grant programmes and the relevant application documents. If you require any further help in deciding which fund to apply for contact the grants team on 01773 514850.

Applicants should download and complete the appropriate application form from the website and send it to the correspondent with the following supporting documents:
▷ annual accounts
▷ bank statements
▷ group constitution
▷ management committee form (please download this from the website)
▷ minutes from the last management committee meeting.

Applications are passed to a member of the grants team for assessment and to prepare all of the information ready to present to the award making panel. During this time, applicants are likely to be contacted by the grants team for an informal chat about their application and their group, which helps the foundation to understand the background of the project and gives the best chance of a successful bid.

The decision on whether to award a grant is made by, either a panel of independent people from the local community, who meet every eight weeks, or by a panel set up by the fund-holder, who will usually meet once every three months. Please note: the grants team are entirely independent and will not make any funding recommendations to the panels.

Applicants will be informed of the decision date for their application and are invited to call the grants team or check the website to find out the decision two days after the panel date. You will also receive the panel decision in writing within one week of the panel date.

The foundation states that it is willing to provide full, honest feedback on all decisions and is happy to discuss any outcome with applicants.

Devon Community Foundation

General

£807,000 (2009/10)

Beneficial area

Devon.

The Factory, Leat Street, Tiverton, Devon EX16 5LL
Tel: 01884 235887
Fax: 01884 243824
Email: grants@devoncf.com
Website: www.devoncf.com
Correspondent: Martha Wilkinson, Correspondent
Trustees: David Stevens; Dr Katherine Gurney; Steve Hindley; Mike Bull; Mark Haskell; Arthur Ainslie; David Searle; Peter Keech; John Sunderland; John Glasby; Caroline Marks; Nigel Arnold.
CC Number: 1057923

Information available

Accounts were available at the Charity Commission.

Grants go to support a huge range of projects tackling social exclusion and building better communities.

Devon Community Foundation is an independent local charity that aims to promote and support local charitable and community organisations throughout Devon to tackle disadvantage. This is achieved by channelling funds to grass roots organisations within the community to support a wide variety of causes. The foundation acts as a conduit for a variety of funds, including those from the statutory, voluntary and corporate sectors, and for donations and income from its own endowed funds.

The foundation always has a variety of grant programmes running and new ones are regularly added. It supports groups and projects throughout Devon. Organisations can hold more than one grant at a time from the different funds available. It is not necessary be a registered charity to receive a grant from the foundation, but you must be a not-for-profit organisation that is benevolent, charitable or educational and established to alleviate disadvantage in your local community.

The foundation has a range of different funds designed for small community and voluntary groups working to help local people across Devon. Each scheme tends to have a different application procedure and size of award.

Grant schemes change frequently. Please consult the foundation's website for details of current programmes and their deadlines.

In 2009/10 the foundation had assets and an income of £2.1 million. During the course of the year, the foundation awarded grants totalling £807,000 (2008/09: £548,000) to 353 projects throughout the county. Details of all grants awarded are available on the foundation's website. The major increase in the number of grants awarded is due to the Grassroots Grants Programme because the grants are focused on smaller groups and a very large number of applications have been received. The Targeted Support Fund supported voluntary groups in Torbay which help people who were likely to be disadvantaged as a result of the recession. These grants were up to £40,000 and made a major difference to the sustainability of the organisations.

Beneficiaries for the year 2009/10 included: Accessible Coach Holidays, Appledore Hall Trust, Exeter Shilhay Community Limited, Exeter YMCA, Kingsbridge Playspaces Group, Refugee Support Group, Swilly Kids Club – Youth Matters and Timeout for All (£5,000 each); Turntable Furniture (£3,500); 2nd Bideford Scout Group, Children's Summer Club, Merry Go Round Toy & Leisure Library, St Budeaux Mental Health Community Group and Torbay Youth Sailing Trust (£3,000 each); Combe Martin Senior Citizens, Cullompton Family Centre, Get Changed Theatre Company, Kenn Cricket Club, Ladysmith Community Action Team and Okehampton & District Duke of Edinburgh (£2,000 each); and Exeter Blue Anchor Majorettes, Health and Local Food for Families, Key Stop Luncheon Club, Tamerton Foliot Football Club and Welcombe Children's Group (£1,000 each). There were various grants under £1,000 but these were not listed in the accounts.

Exclusions

The foundation does not fund:

- more than one application to the same fund in a 12 month period
- groups it has funded before but have not returned an evaluation form when requested
- no major building works associated costs
- organisations that are regional or national charities (unless locally led and run)
- organisations that have substantial unrestricted funds
- activities that promote political or religious beliefs (groups that are based in a religious building can apply, providing the activity / project is open to all people in the community)
- statutory bodies e.g. schools/ colleges, local councils. However, 'Friends of' or Parents' Associations may be eligible to apply
- organisations or activities that primarily support animals or plants
- contributions to a large project where the amount applied for is less than one fifth (20%) of the total project cost
- retrospective funding – this includes activities that have already taken place or repayment of money that you have already spent
- consultancy fees or feasibility studies
- sponsorship and/or fundraising events
- contributions to an endowment
- minibuses or other vehicle purchases
- activities or organisations that are for personal profit or are commercial
- grants for IT and associated equipment will be limited to no more than £400
- overseas travel
- never 100% of the project costs
- no funding individuals (except from the Devonian Fund).

Individual programmes may have further eligibility criteria. Please check the website or contact the foundation directly to confirm that your organisation is eligible to apply.

Applications

The foundation's website has details of the grant schemes currently being administered and how to apply.

Common applicant mistakes

'Not reading the guidelines correctly, not meeting the criteria of a fund and not fully considering their project budget. Applicants often also supply incorrect information.'

The Duke of Devonshire's Charitable Trust

General

£2.2 million (2010/11)

Beneficial area

UK.

Chatsworth, Bakewell, Derbyshire DE45 1PP
Correspondent: The Trustees
Trustees: Duke of Devonshire; Duchess of Devonshire; Earl of Burlington; Sir Richard Beckett.
CC Number: 213519

Information available

Accounts were available at the Charity Commission.

In 2010/11 the trust had assets of £11.3 million and an income of £235,500. Grants were made totalling £2.2 million, due to a large grant of just over £2 million to Chatsworth House Trust for renovation work; the trust also received a substantial grant in the previous year.

Other grants were made to registered charities involved in a wide variety of charitable activities, with a slight preference to those working in Derbyshire. Grants mainly ranged between £100 and £35,000.

There were 70 other grants made during the year, including those to: Devonshire Educational Trust (£25,000); Arkwright Society (£10,000); Fields in Trust and

Bradford Diocesan (£7,000 each); Staveley Town Council (£5,500); Mercian Regimental Fund and Age UK (£4,000 each); Derbyshire Dales District Council (£2,500); RAF Benevolent Fund and Roche Court Educational Trust (£2,000 each); and the Countryside Alliance Foundation and the Meningitis Trust (£1,000 each).

The trust informed us that there has been a 'marked increase in applications for core costs and salaries [which is does not support] due to reduction in local authority support and general charitable giving'.

Exclusions

Grants are only given to registered charities and not to individuals.

Applications

In writing to the correspondent.

Common applicant mistakes

'Applying for running costs and salaries – the trust avoids this as they do not want to fund a position that may become unsustainable in the future. Applying for funding for work overseas – the trustees have concerns over governance and accountability of work outside UK.'

The Djanogly Foundation

General, medicine, education, the arts and social welfare

£1 million (2009/10)

Beneficial area

UK and overseas.

3 Angel Court, London SW1Y 6QF
Tel: 020 7930 9845
Correspondent: Christopher Sills, Secretary
Trustees: Sir Harry Djanogly; Michael S Djanogly; Lady Carol Djanogly.
CC Number: 280500

Information available

Accounts were available at the Charity Commission.

The foundation was established in 1980 by Sir Harry Djangoly, a wealthy businessman from Nottingham who made his fortune in the textile industry. He is a well-known benefactor of the arts and has made substantial donations to art institutions from his personal fortune.

The foundation supports developments in medicine, education, social welfare, the arts, Jewish charities and welfare of older and younger people, and is particularly concerned with funding projects that are new and may require a number of years to become established. In such cases the grant making activity will be related to the development phases of these projects.

In 2009/10 the foundation had assets of £9.6 million and an income of £206,000. There were 45 grants made totalling just over £1 million.

Beneficiaries of the largest grants were: Victoria & Albert Museum (£258,500); Nottingham City Academy (£216,500); University of Nottingham (£201,500); and the Jerusalem Foundation (£201,000).

Smaller grants included those to: the Royal Collections Trust and the British Museums Development Trust (£25,000 each); Nottingham City Council (£18,500); Jewish Care (£13,500); Burlington Magazine Foundation (£5,000); Community Security Trust (£2,000); and the Chicken Shed Theatre Company (£1,000). There were also 15 grants made for £500 or less.

Applications

In writing to the correspondent.

The DM Charitable Trust

Jewish, social welfare and education

£2 million (2009/10)

Beneficial area

UK and Israel.

Ground Floor, Sutherland House, 70–78 West Hendon Broadway, London NW9 7BT

Tel: 020 8457 3258
Correspondent: Stephen J Goldberg, Trustee
Trustees: Stephen J Goldberg, Chair; David Cohen; Patrice Klein.
CC Number: 1110419

Information available

Accounts were on file at the Charity Commission, without a list of grants.

The trust was established in 2005 for the relief of poverty and sickness, educational purposes and the support of Jewish organisations.

In 2009/10 the trust had assets of £5.9 million and an income of £6.6 million, most of which came from donations. Grants were made totalling £2 million, however a list of beneficiaries was unavailable in this year's accounts. Previous attempts to obtain a list of grants have been unsuccessful.

Applications

In writing to the correspondent.

The Dollond Charitable Trust

Jewish, general

£2.6 million (2009/10)

Beneficial area

UK and Israel.

c/o FMCB, Hathaway House, Popes Drive, Finchley, London N3 1QF
Tel: 020 8346 6446
Email: gwz@fmcb.co.uk
Correspondent: Jeffery Milston, Trustee
Trustees: Adrian Dollond; Jeffery Milston; Melissa Dollond; Brian Dollond; Rina Dollond.
CC Number: 293459

Information available

Accounts were available at the Charity Commission.

'Although the constitution of the charity is broadly based, the trustees have adopted a policy of principally assisting the Jewish communities in Britain and Israel. The trustees will remain focused on [these] main objectives – in addition, the trustees are considering a number of infrastructure (building) projects. Research is in progress and discussions are on-going with the relevant institutions.'

In 2009/10 the trust had assets of £38.1 million and an income of £4.2 million, including donations totalling £3.5 million from the settlor, Arthur Dollond. There were 158 grants made totalling £2.6 million, broken down as follows:

Education/training	50	£1.34 million
Religious education	31	£666,000
Relief of poverty	35	£289,500
Medical/health/sickness	22	£162,000
Disability	9	£67,500
Religious activities	7	£46,000
General charitable purposes	4	£32,000

A more specific breakdown of grants was obtained from the trust, although this does not detail specific beneficiaries:

Boys' schools	£684,000
Girls' schools	£627,000
Seminaries	£447,500
Poverty	£184,000
Yeshivas	£115,000
Kollelim	£91,000
Kiruv	£70,000
Disabled people	£67,500
Chesed	£53,000
Hospitals	£37,500
Cancer relief	£35,000
Fertility	£30,000
Food distribution	£25,000
General charitable purposes	£22,000
Clothing for the poor	£20,000
College/training	£20,000
School support services	£20,000
Medical relief	£17,000
Anti-missionary	£10,000
Elderly	£10,000
Hachnosas Kalloh	£10,000
Mikvaos	£10,000
Youth projects	£1,000

Applications

In writing to the correspondent.

The Drapers' Charitable Fund

General charitable purposes including education, heritage, the arts, prisoner support and textile conservation

£839,000 (2009/10)

Beneficial area

UK, with a special interest in the City and adjacent parts of London and Moneymore and Draperstown in Northern Ireland.

The Drapers' Company, Drapers' Hall, Throgmorton Avenue, London EC2N 2DQ

Tel: 020 7588 5001
Fax: 020 7628 1988
Email: charities@thedrapers.co.uk
Website: www.thedrapers.co.uk
Correspondent: Andy Mellows, Head of Charities
Trustee: The Drapers' Company.
CC Number: 251403

Information available

Accounts were available at the Charity Commission. The charity also has a helpful and informative website giving full details of the trust.

The Drapers' Company is a City livery company, one of those descended from the guilds of London, and the trust has a trail of historical connections, the most important of which are with Queen Mary College, University of London and Bancroft's School in Essex, but which also includes Adam's Maintained Comprehensive School in Wem, Shropshire and various Oxford and London university colleges.

The trust aims to improve the quality of life and expectations of people and their communities within the UK, particularly those disadvantaged or socially excluded, through the award of grants in the fields of education and relief of need. It also aims to support organisations and institutions, particularly those with historic links to the Drapers' Company and the City of London, within the fields of education, heritage, the arts, prisoner support, and in Northern Ireland, to promote the company's textile heritage through support for technical textiles and textile conservation.

In directing its grant making, the trust applies criteria such as geographical area, particular types of project, beneficiary group or specific areas of charitable activity.

'The trust is a flexible grant maker, responding to a broad range of appeals from a wide variety of organisations. It supports many initiatives and projects which are traditionally outside the mainstream of grant making. The main themes for support are reviewed tri-annually and the annual objectives within the three year period remain the same, to distribute net income within the themes chosen for support in an efficient and effective manner.'

There is no minimum or maximum grant size, but the majority of grants awarded are normally for sums under £10,000. Awards are seldom made for sums in excess of £20,000. Funding may be given towards capital costs such as buildings and equipment provided that the overall scale of the project does not make the trust's grant seem insignificant. Appeals for the provision of core costs, which may include running costs such as staff salaries and overheads, are also accepted. Applicants will be expected to demonstrate that plans are in place to meet future funding requirements of these core costs.

The trust's current priorities for funding are:

Relief of need
Homelessness
▷ funding will only be considered for structured programmes aimed at breaking the cycle of homelessness
▷ area of operation should be inner city areas
▷ projects offering temporary outdoor relief will not be funded

Causes and effects of social exclusion
▷ beneficiaries should be young people under 25 years old
▷ projects are expected to be based in deprived inner cities areas. Preference will be given to such projects in inner city London
▷ projects should be focused on returning young people to education, employment or training

Prisoners
▷ preference will be given to projects assisting young offenders
▷ projects should aim to improve the opportunities for offenders on release or to reduce reoffending

Servicemen and women
▷ projects should support injured or incapacitated ex-services personnel; or
▷ charities should improve the welfare of ex-servicemen and women, particularly those disadvantaged by need, hardship or distress

Welfare, particularly the provision of care or support services to the following beneficiaries:
▷ elderly
▷ vulnerable people or those disadvantaged due to poverty
▷ carers, particularly young carers

Disability
▷ projects should ease the lives and reduce the suffering of disabled people or those suffering long term ill health
▷ support will be focused on less visible disabilities such as hearing impairment, dyslexia, mental health, chronic fatigue syndrome
▷ applicant charities should seek to improve the quality of life for adults with less visible disabilities
▷ charities addressing children's disabilities, physical disabilities or medical conditions will not be funded

Education and Training
Outreach programmes
▷ in particular encouraging young people from disadvantaged backgrounds to continue or further their education

Leadership and volunteering
▷ either in the UK or overseas and as part of a structured programme
▷ applications from individuals will not be considered

Promotion of the learning of science

Textiles
Technical Textiles
▷ projects which support the study of technical textiles or the encouragement of young people to pursue careers in the sector

Textile conservation

Northern Ireland
▷ Projects falling under the Company's other themes for support in the area of historic involvement for the Drapers' Company, particularly in and around Draperstown and Moneymore

Heritage and Arts
Support for the preservation of the nation's heritage and the provision of public access to the arts and heritage, particularly in Greater London, in one of the following areas:
▷ City of London and the Mayoralty
▷ museums, memorials and monuments related to former exploits of the armed forces, the history of London or the textile trade
▷ public access to the arts for young people.

Grantmaking in 2009/10

In 2009/10 the trust had assets of £29.9 million and an income of £6.1 million, which included a donation of just over £5 million from the Drapers' Company. Grants were made to 188 organisations totalling £839,000.

The trust's annual report provides a detailed analysis of how its funds were spent and what it has achieved with those funds during the year:

Education – £280,500 distributed in 62 grants

The support of education continues to be an integral part of the company's grant making. The trustee remains committed to providing recurring financial assistance to the schools, colleges and universities with which the company has strong historic links and to supporting a wide variety of new initiatives within the sector.

Five schools with a close association with the Company, Howell's School, Llandaff, John Taylor High School, Kirkham Grammar School, Sir George Monoux College and Thomas Adams School, Weill each received between £3,000 and £6,000 towards a hardship fund. These funds, used at the discretion of the headteacher or principal, enabled a number of pupils to access extra-curricular activities such as sports tours, summer courses and school visits that would otherwise not have been possible. £8,500 was awarded to 27 pupils at the Company's affiliated schools in the form of small prizes or travel awards for particularly noteworthy achievement during the academic year.

Further and higher education establishments with company links also benefited from awards. Pembroke College, Cambridge received £30,000 towards a Fellowship. Queen Mary, University of London, with which the company has been connected since its establishment, was awarded £50,000 towards research studentships, scholarships and prizes. St Anne's College Oxford received a total of £24,500 towards initiatives to enhance access and outreach at the College and to provide Graduate Development Scholarships.

£74,500 was awarded to 13 institutions and organisations for a wide variety of educational projects and initiatives. Within this sum, City and Guilds of London Art School received £11,500 to provide scholarships to two students undertaking a diploma in wood carving. Raleigh received the second of three annual grants of £15,000 towards its Youth Agency Access Programme which provides the opportunity for young people from disadvantaged backgrounds to volunteer overseas and presents them with the skills and qualities to change their lives and raise their expectations. Lattitude provides structured, monitored and supported overseas volunteer placements for young people from disadvantaged

backgrounds from across the UK. The first of three annual grants of £6,000 was awarded towards a bursary scheme for those individuals who would otherwise not have the opportunity to benefit from such an experience. IntoUniversity provides an out-of-school study and mentoring programme which targets young people who due to disadvantage are most at risk of failing to meet their potential to go to university. A grant of £3,500 was awarded towards core costs.

Relief of Need – £247,900 distributed in 56 grants

Within this broad category grants were awarded to organisations focusing on disability, homelessness, the causes and effects of social exclusion, prisoner support, welfare and support of ex-servicemen and women.

Disability – £53,500 distributed in 13 grants

The majority of grants awarded in the disability field were small grants of up to £5,000 towards the core costs of organisations aiming to improve the quality of life for adults with invisible disabilities. Typical of these awards were grants of £5,000 to the British False Memory Society, £4,000 to the National Rheumatoid Arthritis Society and £3,500 to British Tinnitus Association.

Help the Hospices, the Master Drapers' Charity of the year, received £10,000 towards its work in supporting hospice care throughout the United Kingdom.

Homelessness – £41,000 distributed in 7 grants

Grants were awarded to homeless charities working in inner city areas which deliver structured programmes aimed at breaking the cycle of homelessness by providing their beneficiaries with life skills, education and training opportunities, and information and support.

The second of three annual grants of £15,000 was awarded towards the running costs of the Broadway Centre which delivers a range of services to homeless people in west London. The Marylebone Project received £5,000 towards the core costs of supporting older women, aged over 60, who are in severe housing crisis including those who are rough sleepers. Winter Comfort, based in Cambridge, provides opportunities for homeless people to get involved with meaningful activity, training, education and employment which forms part of the action plan used to support individuals in moving forward. A grant of £4,000 was awarded towards core costs.

Social Exclusion – £62,500 distributed in 15 grants

Funding continued to be directed towards projects for young people in

deprived inner city areas whose lives are often blighted by the effects of social exclusion, and in particular projects which focused on returning young people to education, employment or training.

The Salmon Youth Centre received £5,000 towards the Salmon Young Leaders Programme which gives disadvantaged young people from Southwark, including young offenders, the opportunity to contribute positively to their communities, develop skills and qualifications, and return to education, employment or training through volunteering and structured training at the centre.

SkillForce provides support to young people who are being left behind in education or whose prospects are being adversely affected by truancy and permanent exclusion. Its programmes provide intensive support to groups of young people on an alternative curriculum, taught in the school environment. A grant of £5,000 was awarded towards the cost of delivering the SkillForce programme in Birmingham. YouthNet, an internet-based charity, received £4,000 to raise awareness of its Lifetracks.com programme which supports young people particularly those who are disengaged, from disadvantaged areas or socially excluded backgrounds to begin or re-enter education, training or employment. Southside Young Leaders Academy located in south east London, received a grant of £5,000 towards its support activities for young African and Afro-Caribbean boys who are at risk of being excluded from school.

Prisoner support – £59,300 distributed in 13 grants

Grants awarded in this category concentrated on supporting the education and rehabilitation of offenders.

Startuponline which supports the Startupnow project for women recently released from prison in London and the south east, giving them the opportunity to become self-employed, received a grant of £7,500. Kainos Community aims to reduce reoffending through Challenge to Change, a community-based rehabilitation programme for persistent offenders. A grant of £6,500 was awarded towards its programme in HMP Stocken in Rutland.

Surrey Jobmatch creates opportunities for employment and training in Surrey for offenders and ex-offenders, and provides ongoing support, training and guidance to the employer and employee once employment has been secured. A grant of £5,000 was awarded towards core costs. The Fair Trials Abroad Trust received the first of three annual grants of £3,500 towards its work in helping British citizens facing criminal charges abroad to obtain a fair trial and its work on behalf of those who have been unfairly convicted outside the United Kingdom.

Ex-Servicemen and women – £6,000 distributed in 2 grants
Gardening Leave received £3,000 towards its garden project at The Royal Hospital, Chelsea, providing ex-Servicemen, who suffer from Post Traumatic Stress Disorder, with horticultural therapy.

Welfare – £26,000 distributed in 6 grants
Grants were primarily awarded to charities which provide care or support to the elderly, carers, particularly young carers, or vulnerable people.

Centre 33 received £6,250 to enable young carers living in rural areas of Cambridgeshire to attend respite groups and meet other young people in a similar situation and take part in a variety of activities. Sheffield Young Carers provides support throughout the Sheffield area to young carers aged 8 to 21 aiming to reduce their feeling of isolation through residential breaks, group activities and one-to-one support. A grant of £4,000 was awarded towards core costs.

The Almshouse Association received the final of three annual grants of £5,000 towards the core cost of its work for the benefit of older people in need.

Textiles – £64,000 distributed in 6 grants
The Industrial Trust received £54,000, the second of three annual grants extending the partnership programme between the Drapers' Company and the Trust. The programme aims to meet the skill needs of the UK Technical Textiles sector and to help young people to find worthwhile and challenging careers. The Partnership activities will achieve this by educating and informing young people about the vital importance of the Technical Textiles sector in the UK economy and the exciting and challenging career opportunities that it offers. The programme continued to achieve excellent results during the year with an increased number of educational visits by young people to technical textiles companies, and a fourth annual competition for undergraduate, Key Stage 5 and Key Stage 3/4 pupils which produced innovative and well presented technical textile based entries.

Heritage and the Arts – £44,000 distributed in 11 grants
The Southbank Centre received £5,000 to support its free programme scheme which enables over 65,000 people every year to attend events, exhibitions, installations and performances across all art-forms. A grant of £5,000 was awarded to

support the Youth Forum at Tate Britain, a peer-led youth group providing access to the arts for young people, including hard-to-reach, marginalised youth, who are interested in pursuing an arts-based career.

Other – £159,500 distributed in 95 grants
Within this category 82 grants totalling £29,500, each of £1,000 or less, were made to various charitable causes at the discretion of individual members of the Court of Assistants.

A grant of £105,000 was awarded towards the endowment of The Foundation of Prince William and Prince Harry. Funds from the Foundation, which will be the vehicle for their future charitable works, will be directed towards three particular areas: young people; the environment; and the welfare of Armed Forces' veterans.

Restricted and Designated Funds
The Baroness de Turckheim Music Fund awarded scholarships of £35,000 to five young musicians enrolled on the Opera Programme at the Royal Academy of Music, Royal College of Music, Guildhall School of Music and Drama, Trinity College of Music and the Royal Northern College of Music.

A grant of £20,000 was awarded from the Gift and Legacy Fund to a charitable foundation established by the Welsh Guards to support the dependents of soldiers killed or injured in action.

Contributions to the capital of this Fund are made by members of the Company and charities selected for receipt of an award are those which particularly fit the Company's traditional areas of support.

Exclusions
Grants are not usually made for:
- individuals
- schools, colleges and universities (except in North Wales and Greenwich and Lewisham through the Thomas Howell's Education Fund for North Wales and Sir William Boreman's Foundation)
- churches
- almshouses
- animal welfare
- counselling or advocacy
- medical research/relief, hospitals or medical centres
- children's disabilities, physical disabilities or medical conditions
- holidays or general respite care
- organisations solely assisting refugees, asylum seekers or specific cultural or ethnic groups within the UK

- organisations that are not registered charities, unless exempt from registration
- funds that replace or subsidise statutory funding
- local branches of national charities, associations or movements
- work that has already taken place
- general appeals or circulars
- loans or business finance.

Applications
Applications can be made at any time during the year. The charities committee meets four times a year (October, January, April and July). Applicants should complete the 'application summary sheet' (available to download from the website) and submit it together with a document on proposed funding. This should include detailed information about the organisation and the project/activity to be funded; full costings and project budget for the proposed work for which the grant is requested, or the organisation's income and expenditure budget for the current year (whichever is appropriate); and the most recent audited financial statements and trustees report. Applications should be submitted by post only.

For full details of the application process and the trust's current priorities, applicants are advised to refer to the trust's website.

Common applicant mistakes
'Applicants not reading all the guidelines to determine eligibility; failing to provide all the information requested; applying for sums in excess of our stated grant size; and not applying in the format required.'

The Dulverton Trust

Youth and education, conservation, welfare, general

£2.8 million (2009/10)

Beneficial area
Unrestricted. Mainly UK in practice. An interest in the Cotswolds. Limited support to parts of Africa. Few grants

for work in London or Northern Ireland.

Information available

Accounts were available from the Charity Commission. The trust also has a clear and concise website.

Background

This is one of the trusts deriving from the tobacco-generated fortune of the Wills family. It has an endowment worth £72 million and a body of trustees which combines family members with others who have achieved distinction in public life.

The Dulverton Trust is unusual in saying that an application, outside its guidelines, may be accepted if it is supported by an individual trustee – most trusts say that their trustees decide their grantmaking intentions and policies first, and then stick to them.

There is a clear, reported family connection with the Cotswold area (though no longer apparently with Bristol, where many of the Wills factories were located). Sir John Kemp-Welch is a former Chairman of the London Stock Exchange; Sir Malcolm Rifkind, is also a former foreign secretary; and Lord Gowrie, best known for his interests in the arts (although the trust excludes the arts entirely from its grantmaking).

General

Apart from a few special programmes described below, the trust makes one-off grants and will not normally consider further applications until a period of at least two years has passed.

The trust supports national, regional and local charities operating in England, Scotland and Wales, especially in areas where there is a significant amount of deprivation, and particularly where a grant would make a real difference to the recipients. Grants are also made overseas, particularly in Eastern and Southern Africa.

The trust makes two types of grant:

▶ *Major* – for charities that operate nationally or across the geographical regions of the UK. Support will normally be restricted to charities whose annual income is below £50 million.

▶ *Minor* – for smaller charities working in the North East of England, Cornwall, Devon or Wales. **Note:** the trust no longer administers its minor grants. The scheme is administered by the local community foundations in these areas, namely: Community Foundation Tyne & Wear and Northumberland; Cornwall Community Foundation; Devon Community Foundation; and the Community Foundation in Wales.

Grants in 2009/10

In 2009/10 the trust had assets of £74.4 million and an income of almost £1.8 million. During the year the trust received 1,155 appeals for funding, 247 of which received a grant, making the success rate slightly less than one in five. Though there are wide areas of 'exclusion' these can be funded if an application is recommended by a trustee. Grants paid during the year totalled £2.8 million and were distributed amongst the following categories:

	% of total	
Youth and Education	40.0%	£1.1 million
General welfare	19.4%	£543,000
Minor appeals	9.8%	£275,000
Conservation	8.6%	£241,000
Africa	8.1%	£262,000
Miscellaneous	5.0%	£140,000
Peace and humanitarian support	4.5%	£126,000
Preservation	3.6%	£101,000
Local appeals (Cotswolds)	0.9%	£25,000

The following analysis of the trust's areas of interest and achievements during the year is provided by the trust in its excellent annual report (with grant figures added where necessary):

Youth & Education

Youth & Education continues to be the largest single category supported by the trust, accounting this year for 40% of the grants by value; the largest number of perennial grants also falls within this category. This reflects the priority placed by trustees on assisting the development of young people, particularly those suffering from disadvantage. The largest grant again went for the Dulverton & Michael Wills Scholarships [£150,000] which are awarded at Oxford University for Eastern European students; a formal agreement has been signed with the university to govern these scholarships more closely. The bursaries at Atlantic College [£33,500] continue, but are now allocated to two African students. In addition, trustees agreed to fund two bursaries for Zimbabwean students at Waterford School in Swaziland, starting in 2010; both Waterford and Atlantic College are members of the United World College network. Many of the projects supported under the Youth & Education Category help disadvantaged young people in different ways, including those run by the Army Cadet Force Association [£40,000], Fairbridge [£32,000], Joint Educational Trust [£30,000], Skill Force Development [£28,000], Clubs for Young People [£25,000], Aberlour Child Care Trust [£21,500], Taste for Adventure [£21,000], Depaul UK [£20,000], Volunteer Reading Help [£20,000], Street League [£15,000], Valleys Kids [£15,000] and the Wilderness Foundation UK [£13,500]. The trustees continue to believe that introducing young people to challenging experiences in the 'great outdoors' is important, hence the support for the Trinity Sailing Trust [£30,000], Tall Ships Youth Trust [£29,000], Brathay Hall Trust [£25,000], British Schools Exploring Society [£25,000], Ocean Youth Trust [£15,000], Outward Bound Trust [£15,000] and Raleigh International[£15,000]. The importance placed on the introduction of inner-city primary school children to the countryside was underlined by the grants to the Country Trust [£12,000], Jamie's Farm [£25,000], the Royal Highland Education Trust [£15,000] and Whirlow Hall Farm Trust [£10,000]. The trustees place emphasis on the encouragement of young people to consider a career in science and engineering, hence the grants to the Engineering Development Trust [£25,000], the Institute of Physics [£20,000], the Arkwright Scholarship Trust [£18,000] and the Industrial Trust [£15,000].

General Welfare

General Welfare is the next largest category, accounting this year for

19.4% of grant expenditure. As always, a very wide range of charitable activity falls under this heading. Support was provided for families through grants to After Adoption [£23,000], ATD Fourth World [£15,000], Grandparents Plus [£15,000], Scottish Adoption Association [£11,000], Grandparents' Association [£10,000] and One Plus One [£10,000]. The problems of homelessness persist, and help was provided for Move On [£29,000], Furniture Re-Use Network [£20,000], Church Housing Trust [£18,000] and Emmaus UK [£15,000]. Hard-pressed carers were assisted through awards to Who Cares? Trust [£30,000], Crossroads Association [£25,000], Princess Royal Trust for Carers [£22,000] and Kiloran Trust [£5,000]. Trustees have long been concerned about the very high recidivism rates in the United Kingdom, and supported several charities which work in various ways to reduce this problem, including Trail-Blazers [£25,000], Kids VIP [£22,000], Howard League for Penal Reform [£20,000], NEPACS [£10,000], Action for Prisoners' Families [£7,000] and the Clean Break Theatre Company [£7,000]. However, trustees decided to discontinue the Perennial grant to NACRO after 2009/10 because the charity is now larger than the normal upper limit for consideration specified in the guidelines.

Minor Appeals
The sum available for minor appeals continued to represent 10% of the grant target, with maximum individual grants limited to a maximum of £3,500 (although no grants of this size were awarded during the year). Trustees were again encouraged by the worthiness and variety of the appeals considered, and the ability of a modest grant to make a significant difference to a small charity. A total of 111 grants were awarded to organisations such as Scout Groups, Youth Clubs and community groups, with priority as always given to the more disadvantaged regions of the UK. [Please note that the trust no longer administers this scheme – see above.]

Conservation
Conservation charities were awarded 8.6% of the grants made in 2009/10, a higher-than-average proportion. Trustees' interest in trees and native woodlands was reflected by grants to the Woodland Trust [£30,000], Central Scotland Forest Trust [£21,000], Friends of Bedgebury Pinetum [£20,000] and the Forest Stewardship Council [£12,000]. Wildlife was supported through grants to the Game & Wildlife Conservation Trust [£20,000] (a two year grant), Pond Conservation [£20,000], Wildfowl & Wetlands Trust [£20,000] and the Scottish Wildlife Trust [£10,000]. The Perennial Grant to UK CEED [£23,000] was continued, to support their important work in demonstrating how environmental protection and economic development priorities can be reconciled; other environmental work was supported through the Bioregional Development Group [£10,000] and the Centre for Alternative Technology [£10,000]. The grant towards the Royal Botanic Gardens, Kew [£25,000] went towards their pioneering work with the Millennium Seedbank in the year in which the Seedbank celebrated the conservation of seeds from 10% of the world's flora.

Africa
Grants amounting to 8.1% of the awards went to projects in Africa. The largest grant was the perennial award for Book Aid International [£36,000], for its much-needed work in delivering books to East Africa. Book-Link [£26,500] was also supported for its remarkably cost-effective work in supplying books for schools in Ethiopia. Alleviation towards the continuing problems in Zimbabwe was provided through the grants to ZANE [£25,000], the Peterhouse Appeal [£10,000] and Pump Aid [£5,000], whilst a four-year grant was approved for Zimbabwean students at Waterford School in Swaziland. Trustees decided, reluctantly, to discontinue after 2009/10 the long-standing perennial grant to VSO, which was used to support eight placements in East Africa, because of the increasing focus on medical placements and the relatively large size of the charity. The excellent work of the Northern Rangelands Trust [£24,000], which has been highly successful in persuading rural communities in Kenya that it is in their own interests to help preserve the wildlife, was commended with a further grant towards a new conservancy area. Further support was also given to FARM Africa [£15,000] (by way of a Perennial grant) and AMREF [£28,000], both of which have been associated with the trust for many years.

Miscellaneous
This category accounted this year for 5.0% of the grants, well below the 10% ceiling set by trustees. It embraces charities which trustees consider to be worthy of support, despite being at the margins of the trust's guidelines, and also some which provide services for the benefit of the charitable sector as a whole. The largest grant was the final instalment of the three-year grant to Combat Stress [£40,000], and this was augmented by a grant to Gardening Leave [£9,000], a charity which offers horticultural therapy for veterans suffering from Post Traumatic Stress. The perennial grant to the RNLI [£25,500], for training probationary inshore lifeboatmen, appears in this category because the income of the charity puts it well above the normal limit specified in the guidelines. Charities which help other charities to be more effective also appear in this category; these include Pilotlight [£20,000], NCVO [£15,000] and Reach Volunteering [£12,000].

Peace & Humanitarian Support
This category absorbed 4.5% of the grants awarded, a rather higher proportion than in the past, reflecting the change in this category agreed as part of the 2008 Quinquennial Review. The grant to Article 25 [£25,000] reflected the innovative work of the architectural profession in supporting communities recovering from war and natural disasters. MapAction [£24,000] received further support to train its volunteers for their vital role in providing up-do-date mapping for disaster areas. The Mines Advisory Group [£23,500] received a grant to establish emergency response equipment to allow a team to deploy at short notice to a conflict zone. The smaller grant to RUSI [£20,000] reflected an advance of the 2008/09 perennial grant to fund an urgent study of the Zimbabwean Security Forces. The high-level international conference for which a conditional grant was awarded in 2008/09 to the Oxford Research Group could not take place; the grant was transferred to a consultation on UK Defence Policy and paid in March 2010.

Preservation
The Preservation category was awarded only 3.6% of the grants made. The trustees continued their policy of making one significant grant each year to a major ecclesiastical building, and this was awarded to Lichfield Cathedral [£40,000] for the preservation of the remarkable Herkenrode glass. The perennial grants to the National Churches Trust [£50,000] and Scottish Churches Architectural Heritage Trust [£6,000] continued, as a contribution towards the steadily increasing preservation problems faced by parish churches.

Local Appeals
Within the allocation of £25,000 for Local Appeals in the Cotswolds, Lord Dulverton approved a total of eight small grants, which were subsequently ratified by trustees.

Exclusions
The trust will not usually give grants for the following:

- individuals (grants are given only to registered charities or organisations with officially recognised charitable status)
- museums, galleries, libraries, exhibition centres and heritage attractions

- individual churches, cathedrals and other historic buildings (except for limited support under the preservation category)
- individual schools, colleges, universities or other educational establishments
- hospices, hospitals, nursing or residential care homes
- activities outside the stated geographical scope.

The trust rarely supports charities whose main beneficiaries live within Greater London or in Northern Ireland.

The trust will not normally support the following areas of activity:

- health, medicine and medical conditions including drug and alcohol addiction, therapy and counselling
- specific support for people with disabilities
- the arts, including theatre, music and drama (except where used as a means of achieving one of its funding priorities)
- sport, including sports centres and individual playing field projects
- animal welfare or projects concerning the protection of single species
- expeditions and research projects
- individuals volunteering overseas
- conferences, cultural festivals, exhibitions and events
- salaries for specific posts (however funding salaries in the context of a multi-year grant will be considered)
- major building projects, including the purchase of property or land
- endowments
- work that has already taken place (retrospective funding).

Applications

How to apply

Please read the guidelines carefully, making sure that none of the exclusions apply to your charity or project. If you believe that your appeal falls within the funding policy of the trust, you are welcome to apply as follows:

1 Send your application by post to the Grants Director. The trust reserves the right not to respond to appeals by email from unfamiliar sources.
2 There is no set application form, but you should restrict your application to two pages.
3 Make sure you include your organisation's full contact details,

together with an email address and telephone number. Also please confirm your charitable status, giving the registered charity number.

4 Include a brief description of the background, aims and objectives of the charity; details of the specific purpose for which funding is sought together with the funding target; and the balance of funding outstanding at the time of the application.
5 Finally, please enclose a copy of your most recent annual report and accounts if they are not available on the Charity Commission's website.

If you wish to make initial enquiries, establish eligibility, discuss time scales or need to seek further guidance about an application, please telephone the trust's office.

When to apply

The trustees meet four times a year to consider major appeals: in February, May, July and October. There are no deadlines or closing dates.

The selection procedure can take between three to six months so it is advisable to apply in plenty of time, especially if funding is required by a certain date.

Assessment process

Each application is considered on its merits and all will receive a reply as soon as possible, although research and consultation may delay a response from time to time. The trust will usually acknowledge receipt of your application by email, so please remember to include a current email address. If you do not have one, we will send you an acknowledgement by post. All rejected applications will receive notification and an outline explanation for the rejection will usually be given.

Applications that are listed for consideration for a Major Grant will normally receive a visit from one of the trust's directors who will subsequently report to the trustees.

Following the trustees' meeting, successful applicants will be notified of their award in writing. The trustees' decisions are final.

Common applicant mistakes

'Applicants not reading the guidelines to check eligibility or sending out mass-produced, untargeted applications.'

Dunard Fund

Classical music, the visual arts, environment and humanitarian causes

£1.2 million (2009/10)

Beneficial area

UK with a particular interest in Scotland.

4 Royal Terrace, Edinburgh EH7 5AB
Tel: 0131 556 4043
Fax: 0131 556 3969
Correspondent: Mrs Carol Colburn Høgel, Trustee
Trustees: Carol Colburn Høgel; Elisabeth Høgel; Dr Catherine Høgel; Erik Høgel; Colin Liddell.
CC Number: 295790

Information available

Accounts were available at the Charity Commission.

The charity, established in 1986, is funded annually by Marlowe Holdings Limited, of which the correspondent is both a director and a shareholder. The funds are committed principally to the training for and performance of classical music at the highest standard and to education in and display of the visual arts, also at international standard. A small percentage of the fund is dedicated to environmental and humanitarian projects. The charity is also registered with the Office of the Scottish Charity Regulator.

In 2009/10 the charity had assets of £5.4 million and an income of just over £1.5 million, most of which came from the charity's benefactor. Grants were made to 36 organisations totalling £1.2 million, broken down as follows:

Music	17	£544,000
Culture and the arts	8	£338,000
Humanitarian and environmental	11	£330,000

Beneficiaries across all categories included: Edinburgh International Festival (£510,000); NVA Kilmahew Woodland Cardross (£200,000); London Philharmonic Orchestra (£193,000); Scottish Chamber

Orchestra (£126,000); Rosslyn Chapel (£50,000); Ludus Baroque (£45,000); Academy of St Martin in the Field and Pitlochry Festival Theatre (£30,000 each); Penicuik House Preservation Trust (£25,000); Dunedin Consort (£16,000); Royal Welsh College of Music & Drama (£10,000); Sherborne Abbey (£5,000); New Town Concerts Society (£4,000); the Cockburn Association (£3,000); and Live Music Now (£1,000).

Exclusions

Grants are only given to charities recognised in Scotland or charities registered in England and Wales. Applications from individuals are not considered.

Applications

No grants to unsolicited applications.

The Dunhill Medical Trust

Medical research, elderly

£2.6 million (2009/10)

Beneficial area

UK.

3rd Floor, 16–18 Marshalsea Road, London SE1 1HL
Tel: 020 7403 3299
Fax: 020 7403 3277
Email: info@dunhillmedical.org.uk
Website: www.dunhillmedical.org.uk
Correspondent: Claire Large, Administrative Director
Trustees: Ronald E Perry, Chair; Prof Sir Roger M Boyle; The Rt Revd Christopher T J Chessun; Kay Glendinning; Prof Roderick J Hay; Prof James McEwen; Richard A H Nunneley; Timothy W Sanderson; Prof Martin P Severs.
CC Number: 294286

Information available

Accounts were available from the Charity Commission. Detailed information is available on the trust's website.

Summary

The Dunhill Medical Trust originated in a will trust left by Herbert Dunhill in 1950 to support medical research. The trust was formally registered as a charity in the 1980s was established in 1950 with charitable objects focused on medical research, care and facilities and specifically the research into care of the elderly and the provision of accommodation and care for older people.

Within these objects the trust supports four main areas of activity:
▷ the development of new and innovative projects
▷ support for pilot research studies that could establish whether major funding is justified
▷ pump-priming projects that have the potential to develop and attract other sources of funding
▷ developing research capacity within the medical, clinical and scientific community, particularly where this relates to issues of ageing and older people.

The trust's current priorities for support are:
▷ care of older people, including rehabilitation and palliative care
▷ research into the causes and treatments of disease, disability and frailty associated with ageing.

These priorities are reviewed every three years (or more often if deemed appropriate by the trustees), and may be changed in accordance with the trustees' view of the most effective application of available funds. As such, organisations are encouraged to consult the trust's website to confirm the latest information on funding priorities.

Applications can only be considered from organisations or groups which are charitable as defined by UK charity law. This includes UK registered charities and relevant exempt charities such as universities. Where deemed appropriate, applications from other not-for-profit organisations such as the NHS may be considered. To achieve a better balance in its distribution of funds the trust may occasionally actively seek out projects for support.

Grantmaking

During 2009/10 the trust had assets of £95 million and an income of £2.7 million. Grants were made to 40 organisations totalling £2.6 million.

The distribution of grants by category was broken down as follows:
▷ medical knowledge and research – 71%
▷ major initiatives – 14%
▷ services relating to medical care or care for older people – 12%
▷ provision of accommodation for older people – 3%

During the year the trust received approximately 330 grant applications of which 77% met the basic criteria for funding. Of these, 58% were either within the priority areas designated by the trustees, or were applications for Serendipity Awards (which may be in any area of medicine/medical science/health) or applications for Research Training Fellowships.

Grants are made through four main programmes. The following information is taken largely from the trust's very useful website:

Research grants
Research grants take five forms:
▷ project and programme grants
▷ research related infrastructure costs (i.e. buildings or equipment for specific research-related purposes)
▷ Joint Research Fellowships, which are awarded in partnership with Royal Colleges and other professional bodies
▷ DMT Research Training Fellowships, which are intended to provide training opportunities for clinicians, health professionals and scientists who wish to pursue a research career in ageing, rehabilitation or palliative care (see separate section below for further details)
▷ Serendipity Awards (see separate section below for further details).

Applications in the following areas are of particular interest to the trust:
▷ research that is concerned with: care of older people, including rehabilitation and palliative care; the causes and treatments of disease, disability and frailty associated with ageing
▷ initiatives aimed at evaluating and improving patient care or public health
▷ pilot studies which could establish whether major studies are justified.

DMT is keen to support high quality research and research-related projects and programmes on a smaller scale than can be managed by the major funders (e.g. Research Councils, Wellcome Trust). Priority will be given to:
▷ clinical and applied research
▷ health services research
▷ public health research

- research carried out on a multidisciplinary basis
- activities that will expand the research capacity in the above areas.

DMT will also consider applications related to the more qualitative end of the research spectrum (e.g. research related to modifiable risk factors for well-being and health: environmental factors, diet, stress, exercise, social participation, recreation etc.)

DMT will seek to achieve its aims through providing:

- research project and programme grants for amounts up to £500,000 to cover salaries, consumables, small dedicated pieces of equipment and (exceptionally) travel costs, but will not pay the Full Economic Costs (FECs) of research or research sponsorship costs
- research project grants will usually be awarded for a maximum of three years; research programme grants will usually be awarded for a maximum of five years
- building and/or equipment grants within the range £100,000 to £1 million (not exceeding 75% of the total cost) for innovative developments in the designated research areas
- research fellowships, studentships etc. aimed at expanding research capacity in the designated priority areas
- Serendipity Awards to enable the testing of an idea which comes from an unexpected clinical or laboratory observation or well grounded practice to obtain proof of concept
- exceptionally, endowments for innovative academic posts within the priority areas.

Note:

- research will normally be supported directly with the academic or NHS institution in which the research is being carried out, rather than through a third party (e.g. a fundraising charity supporting research)
- DMT will not support research in respect of medical areas such as heart disease and cancer which are already supported by large dedicated charities
- where appropriate, DMT will be happy to work in partnership with other not-for-profit organisations to maximise the effectiveness of its funding (e.g. joint research fellowships).

DMT will support research carried out by:

- clinicians from all health professions (including allied health professionals) with the relevant qualifications and experience to undertake the research

- academics/scientists working in health-related fields (including epidemiologists, social scientists, health economists etc.) with the relevant qualifications and experience to undertake the research
- clinicians and scientists in training and/or registered to study for a higher qualification and who are supervised by an appropriately qualified clinicians/scientists.

All applicants for research grants must be able to demonstrate that they are based in a strong research environment with a suitable skill mix in the research team.

Full guidelines on research and research-related grants can be found on the trust's website.

Serendipity awards

DMT Serendipity Awards are intended to fund the testing of an idea which comes from an unexpected clinical or laboratory observation, or from well-grounded practice, with the objective of obtaining 'proof of concept', and providing sufficient evidence to convince other funding bodies to take the idea forward.

These awards are not simply another form of pump priming for conventional research projects. The key points for potential Serendipity Award applicants to note are that:

- the idea/observation on which the proposal is based must be serendipitous in nature
- evidence of the validity of the idea/ observation must be demonstrated.

Unlike all other research funding provided by DMT (which must be related to ageing and older people) Serendipity Awards may be in any area of medicine/medical science/health.

For further information, please see the Serendipity Awards applicant guidelines, available to download from the trust's website.

General grants

General grants are to fund work that is not primarily research, or research-related (but may include evaluation and/or audit of the work being supported).

There are four categories of award:

- building grants
- equipment grants
- core costs/staffing grants
- small grants, usually under £10,000.

A key aim is that the trust's funding should encourage and support innovative applications. As a general rule, to qualify for consideration, grant applications must be for an activity with a focus on older people.

Applications that address the following are of particular interest to the trust:

- the care and environment of older people
- the delivery of solutions that address disability, disease and frailty related to ageing.

The trust will consider applications for direct costs such as staffing, buildings or equipment for specific purposes related to the above.

Although there is no lower limit for a grant, in practice no awards are for less than £1,000. Whilst there is no upper limit, grants in excess of £1 million are awarded only in the most exceptional circumstances. Grants are normally awarded for a maximum of three years. Special rules apply to small grants under £10,000 and to major initiatives.

Full guidelines for the general grants programme are available on the trust's website.

Research Training Fellowships

In October 2009 DMT launched a pilot scheme of Research Training Fellowships (RTFs) to provide talented clinicians, health professionals and scientists with the opportunity to undertake research training together with a practical research project leading to a higher degree, as a basis for a career in research in the fields of ageing, rehabilitation or palliative care. The RTFs are intended to be flexible and may be undertaken on either a full-time (three year) or part-time (up to 4 year) basis.

At present the trust has no plans to hold a further round of DMT Research Training Fellowships. However, a review of the scheme to date was due to be held in spring/ summer 2012 which will inform a decision on its future. As such, prospective applicants are advised to monitor the trust's website for updates.

Please note: all requests for funding are first appraised against criteria set out within DMT's Grant Making Policy, available to download from its website. The Dunhill Medical Trust is a member of the Association of Medical Research Charities.

Exclusions

The trust will not fund:

- organisations based outside the UK, or whose work primarily benefits people outside the UK
- large national charities, with an income in excess of £10 million, or assets exceeding £100 million
- issues that are already well-funded in the UK, such as heart disease, cancer or HIV/AIDS

- sponsorship of individuals
- sponsorship of conferences or charitable events
- services or equipment that would be more appropriately provided by the National Health Service
- grants to cover the revenue or capital costs of hospices*
- travel or conference fees (except where these items are an integral part of a project)
- new or replacement vehicles (unless an integral part of a community-based development)
- general maintenance
- institutional overheads associated with research activity (i.e. the trust will not pay the full economic cost of research activities)
- research via a third party (such as a fundraising charity supporting research)
- continuation/replacement funding where a project or post has been previously supported from statutory sources or similar.

*Although the trust does not award grants to cover the revenue or capital costs of hospices, research undertaken within a hospice setting is eligible for consideration.

Applications

Applicants to the Research, Research-related and Serendipity funding programmes should complete the appropriate online *outline application form* available in the 'policies and documents' section of the trust's website.

Applicants to the General Grants programme are asked to provide an initial outline (approximately two sides of A4) by post or email, including the following information:

- a brief description of the organisation and its status (e.g. whether it is a registered charity); who you are and what you do within the organisation
- a description of the project for which funding is being sought, where it will take place and who it will involve
- an outline of who will benefit from the work and why
- the key outcomes and timescales
- the total cost of the project/work and the specific amount being applied for from the trust.

Outline applications for all programmes can be submitted at any time and those which are eligible will be invited to submit a formal application.

The formal application requirements differ depending upon the type of grant being applied for and applicants are strongly advised to visit the trust's website before making an application to ensure that they have all the relevant information.

Full applications are considered by the Grants and Research Committee which meets quarterly (normally in February, May, July and November). The committee makes recommendations on whether applications should be supported and decisions are then referred to the board of trustees for approval at their quarterly meetings (normally held in March, June, September and December). Successful applicants are normally notified within two weeks of the meeting. Generally, decisions are made within three to four months.

The Charles Dunstone Charitable Trust

General

£3.6 million (2009/10)

Beneficial area
UK.

H W Fisher and Company, Acre House, 11–15 William Road, London NW1 3ER
Tel: 020 7388 7000
Correspondent: The Trustees
Trustees: Denis Dunstone; Adrian Bott; Nicholas Folland; John Gordon.
CC Number: 1085955

Information available
Accounts were available at the Charity Commission.

Established in 2001 for general charitable purposes, this is the charitable trust of Charles Dunstone, co-founder of the Carphone Warehouse.

The following information on future activities is taken from the trust's annual report:

> In September 2009 the trustees began funding the development and improvement of the Fulwood Academy in Preston, Lancashire. This represents a substantial commitment of time and funds over the coming 5 years at least and is likely to be the focus for much of the trust's work.
>
> The trustees will continue to make a small number of grants in the following areas:
>
> - making lasting improvements to the lives of children with disabilities and their families
> - improving the prospects of prisoners on release, especially through the provision of better opportunities and services whilst in prison
> - making lasting improvements to the education and wellbeing of those living in disadvantaged communities, particularly young people
> - improving the availability of support and service for young carers.
>
> Grants are likely to be made to a small number of organisations which have entrepreneurial leadership and have potential to create significant impact, either at local or national level.

In 2009/10 the trust had an income of £991,000, mostly from donations. Grants were made totalling £3.6 million, broken down into the following categories:

Education and training	£2.3 million*
Children and youth	£519,000
Community care and ethnic organisations	£464,000
Social welfare	£248,500
Sport	£68,000
Medical and disability	£17,500
Art and culture	£250
Conservation	£150

*This includes £2 million to the Fulwood Academy Endowment Fund, to be paid in instalments over 5 years as outlined above – Charles Dunstone is also a trustee of the Fulwood Academy (and the Prince's Trust).

Other beneficiaries included: Every Child a Chance (£225,000); St Giles Trust (£188,500); The Prince's Trust (£154,000); Shelter (£105,000); Community Links (£75,000); Greenhouse Schools (£50,000); Norfolk Community Foundation (£25,000); and Trinity Sailing (£18,000).

Exclusions
The trustees do not normally make grants to individuals.

Applications

'Proposals are generally invited by the trustees or initiated at their request. Unsolicited applications are not encouraged and are unlikely to be successful. The trustees prefer to support innovative schemes that can be successfully replicated or become self-sustaining.'

The James Dyson Foundation

Science, engineering, medical research and education

£959,000 (2009/10)

Beneficial area

Mainly UK, local community around the Dyson company's UK headquarters, in Malmesbury, Wiltshire.

Tetbury Hill, Malmesbury, Wiltshire SN16 0RP
Tel: 01666 827 205
Email: jamesdysonfoundation@dyson. com
Website: www. jamesdysonfoundation.com
Correspondent: Grants Administrator
Trustees: Sir James Dyson; Lady Deirdre Dyson; Valerie West; Prof. Sir Christopher Frayling.
CC Number: 1099709

Information available

Accounts were available online at the Charity Commission. The foundation also has a good website.

This company foundation was set up in 2002 to promote charitable giving, especially to charities working in the fields of science, engineering, medicine and education.

The primary objects of the foundation, as stated in its governing document, are as follows:

▶ to advance education and training, particularly in the fields of design and technology – this work can take a number of forms including the free provision of support resources for teachers of design and technology in schools, the running of design engineering workshops and lectures in schools and universities, as well as bursary schemes and collaborative projects
▶ to support medical and scientific research
▶ to support charitable and educational projects in the region in which the foundation operates (Malmesbury, Wiltshire).

Each year, the foundation donates a number of Dyson vacuum cleaners (for raffle prizes) to charitable causes which fall within its objectives. Small grants may also be made to charitable projects that share the philosophies and objectives of the foundation. Previously, large grants have been made but due to what the foundation terms its 'ambitious priorities in design and engineering education', it is not currently donating large grants.

In 2009/10 the trust had an income of £545,000, down from £1.3 million in 2008/09. This was largely due to a combination of a drop in cash donations from Dyson Limited (£849,000 in 2008/09: £360,000 in 2009/10) and a fall in investment income (£264,000 in 2008/09: £66,000 in 2009/10). Assets stood at £1.4 million. Grants totalled £959,000 and were distributed in three categories as follows:

Education and Training – £263,000

The foundation supports educational projects both in the UK and overseas by means of bursaries and awards, such as awards to the Royal College of Art's Industrial Design Engineering students. The foundation's support also extends beyond monetary funding: design engineers from Dyson host workshops at schools and universities across the country and the foundation provides free resources to Design and Technology teachers in the UK.

Beneficiaries included: James Dyson Award (£109,000); 21/21 Japanese Museum (£34,000); Pompidou Project (£32,000); Corpus Christi Bursary (£15,000); Conservative Taskforce (£12,000); D and T Show (£8,000); University of Bath – J Fry Scholarship (£5,000); Nerd Herd (£3,500); and Bath Technology Centre (£137).

Other grants of less than £1,000 each totalled £13,000.

Science and medical research – £689,000

The foundation has previously partnered with several medical charities, including CLIC and the Meningitis Research Foundation, and donated the sales of various limited edition vacuum cleaners to them. Grants are also made to general medical and scientific research organisations at the trustees' discretion.

During the year major donations were given to: 'Breast Cancer Campaigns in Various Countries' (£351,000); Bath Royal United Hospital – Neonatal Intensive Care Unit Fund (£333,000); and Sparks (£2,700).

A further £2,200 was given in grants of less than £1,000 each.

Social and community welfare – £7,000

The foundation seeks to support charitable projects local to Malmesbury, the town where Dyson is based. The trustees are especially keen to support organisations that work within the fields of design and engineering education and medical and scientific research.

Under this category all grants totalled less than £1,000 and were not listed in the accounts.

Applications

Applications in writing on headed paper to the correspondent. Organisations can also apply through the 'get in touch' section of the foundation's website.

The EBM Charitable Trust

Children/youth, animal welfare, relief of poverty, general

£880,000 (2009/10)

Beneficial area

UK.

Moore Stephens, 150 Aldersgate
Street, London EC1A 4AB
Tel: 020 7334 9191
Fax: 020 7651 1953
Correspondent: Keith Lawrence
Trustees: Richard Moore; Michael
Macfadyen; Stephen Hogg.
CC Number: 326186

Information available

Accounts were available at the
Charity Commission.

The trustees report, as has been the
case in previous years, stated simply
that 'beneficiaries included charities
involved in animal welfare and
research, the relief of poverty and
youth development'. Furthermore,
that resources would be maintained
at a reasonable level in order
continue funding general charitable
purposes.

In 2009/10 the trust had assets of
£39.3 million and an income of
£1 million. Grants were made to 35
organisations totalling £880,000.

The trust manages two funds, the
general fund and the Fitz' fund. The
Fitz' fund was established following
the death of Cyril Fitzgerald, one of
the original trustees of the charity
who left the residue of his estate to
the trust. The money is held as a
designated fund for animal charities
and gave £35,000 during the year.

Larger grants included those to:
British Racing School, the Royal
Hospital Chelsea – Chelsea
Pensioners Appeal and the Salvation
Army (£200,000 each); and Fairbridge
(£100,000).

Other beneficiaries included: Animal
Health Trust (£50,000); Calvert Trust
Exmoor (£40,000); Community Links
(£35,000); Action for Kids (£30,000);
The Connection (£20,000); Mayhew
Animal Home (£15,000); YMCA
Norfolk (£10,000); Wildlife Trust
(£7,500); and the Prostate Cancer
Charity (£5,000).

Applications

The following statement is taken from
the annual trustees' report for 2010:

Unsolicited applications are not
requested as the trustees prefer to
support donations to charities whose
work they have researched and which
is in accordance with the wishes of the
settlor. The trustees do not tend to
support research projects as research
is not a core priority but there are
exceptions. The trustees' funds are
fully committed. The trustees receive a
very high number of grant applications
which are mostly unsuccessful.

The Maud Elkington Charitable Trust

Social welfare, general charitable purposes

£432,000 (2009/10)

Beneficial area

Mainly Desborough,
Northamptonshire and Leicestershire.

c/o Harvey Ingram LLP, 20 New
Walk, Leicester LE1 6TX
Tel: 0116 257 6129
Fax: 0116 255 3318
Email: paula.fowle@harveyingram.
com
Correspondent: Mrs Paula Fowle,
Administrator
Trustees: Roger Bowder, Chair; Allan
A Veasey; Katherine Hall.
CC Number: 263929

Information available

Accounts were available at the
Charity Commission.

The principle aim of the trust is to
distribute grants, particularly, but not
exclusively in Desborough and
Northamptonshire; grants are also
made in Leicestershire. Grants are
made to rather small projects, where
they will make a quantifiable
difference to the recipients, rather
than favouring large national charities
whose income is in millions rather
than thousands. It is the usual
practice to make grants for the
benefit of individuals through
referring agencies such as social
services, NHS Trusts or similar
responsible bodies.

In 2009/10 the trust had assets of
£20.5 million and an income of
£582,000. Grants were made to 269
organisations totalling £432,000. Most
grants were for £5,000 or less.

Beneficiaries included:
Nottinghamshire County Council
(£29,200 in 79 individual payments);
Leicester Grammar School – Bursary
(£9,500); Bromford Housing
Association (£7,000 in 24 individual
payments); Cynthia Spencer Hospice
and Launde Abbey (£5,000 each);
Cancer Research UK (£4,900); CARE
Shangton (£4,600); Multiple Sclerosis
Society (£3,100); Elizabeth Finn Care
(£2,500); Voluntary Action Northants
(£2,000); and Phoenix Furniture
(£1,500).

There were 178 grants made of £1,000
or less.

Exclusions

No grants directly to individuals.

Applications

In writing to the correspondent.
There is no application form or
guidelines. The trustees meet every
seven or eight weeks.

The John Ellerman Foundation

National UK charities supporting health, disability, social welfare, arts and conservation and overseas projects

£4.2 million (2009/10)

Beneficial area

Mainly UK; East and Southern Africa.

Aria House, 23 Craven Street, London
WC2N 5NS
Tel: 020 7930 8566
Fax: 020 7839 3654
Email: enquiries@ellerman.org.uk
Website: www.ellerman.org.uk
Correspondent: Barbra Mazur,
Grants Manager
Trustees: Lady Sarah Riddell, Chair;
Sue MacGregor; Dominic Caldecott;
Peter Mimpriss; Tim Glass; Brian
Hurwitz; Hugh Raven; Diana
Whitworth.
CC Number: 263207

Information available

Accounts were available at the Charity Commission. The foundation has a helpful and informative website.

The foundation was established on the death of Sir John Ellerman in 1970 as a generalist grant-making trust. John Ellerman had inherited his substantial wealth from the business interests set up by his father, especially in shipping – the family business was called Ellerman Lines. Sir John and his wife Esther had throughout their lives developed a profound interest in philanthropy.

Today the foundation uses Sir John's legacy to make grants totalling around £4 million a year to about 150 different charities, mostly in the United Kingdom; The foundation makes grants to UK registered charities which work nationally, not locally. For historical reasons it continues to support a few charities operating in Southern and East Africa.

The foundation's mission is 'to be and be seen as a model grant-maker to the charitable sector.' It aims to achieve its mission by managing its funds in such a way that it can both maintain its grant-making capacity and operate in perpetuity, funding nationally-registered charities so as to encourage and support those which make a real difference to people, communities and the environment.

Guidelines

The following guidelines are taken from the foundation's website:

We know core funding is difficult to obtain and are especially open to receiving applications for this purpose. Charities which receive core funding will be expected to account for expenditure and identify what it has enabled them to do. On the other hand, requests for a contribution to capital appeals are not encouraged. We also incline towards supporting charities which:

- offer direct practical benefits rather than work mainly on policy or campaigning
- attract and involve large numbers of volunteers
- co-operate closely with other charities working in similar or related fields
- do innovatory work
- are small/medium sized (annual income more than £100,000 and less than £25 million).

Health and Disability

Focus

At present our funding is directed towards:

- the relief and support of those with complex conditions and disorders
- severe physical disabilities, including deaf and blind people
- mental illness and learning disabilities
- carers, including nurses and the families of sufferers of any of the above.

Themes

The foundation is particularly interested in charities which can demonstrate all or most of the following:

- practical benefits to patients/ sufferers and to the quality of their lives
- a particular commitment to the young and/or to older people
- the provision of expert information, advice and self-help initiatives.

Please note: the foundation does not support medical research or NHS Hospital Trusts.

Social Welfare

Focus

At present the focus of our funding is directed towards:

- elderly people – see special focus immediately below
- disadvantaged young people – including homeless young people
- parents, families and children in need.

Our special Social Welfare focus of interest for 2010/11 [was] support for charities working with isolated, poor and lonely older people, especially those over 75. These people may be living independently or in residential care and from either rural or urban communities. We welcome applications from national charities working with and for older people in utterly practical ways and specifically to:

- organise befriending schemes which use volunteers
- improve the quality of housing, security and residential care
- encourage family and inter-generational contact
- promote health and well-being.

Themes

The foundation is particularly interested in charities which can demonstrate:

- tangible benefits on a significant scale for the most disadvantaged/ vulnerable people
- sharing of good ideas and collaborative work with other charities
- recruitment, training and employment of a broad base of volunteers
- it encourages self-help and self-sufficiency.

Arts and Heritage

Focus

At present the focus of our funding is directed towards the following:

- music and opera
- museums and galleries
- theatre and dance.

Themes

The foundation is particularly interested in charities which can demonstrate:

- excellence at the national level
- youth participation, motivation and development
- commitment to attracting new audiences and wider public access
- originality and creativity in design, production and/or presentation.

Generally the foundation does not support educational projects, festivals or particular productions. We do exceptionally on occasion support cathedral and historic building restoration. (A cathedral awarded a grant is not eligible to reapply for funding for five years.)

Conservation

Focus

At present the focus of our funding is UK-based charities working throughout the UK and/or internationally in at least one of the following areas:

- protection of threatened animals, plants and habitats
- promotion of better understanding of and solutions to major environmental issues like climate change and biodiversity
- promotion of sustainable ways of living, including renewable energy technologies.

Themes

The foundation is particularly interested in charities which can demonstrate:

- practical and enduring benefits of significant scale
- collaborative work with others and the open sharing of ideas
- effective operation with or alongside local communities and cultures
- recruitment, training and employment of a broad base of volunteers.

Overseas

At present our funding has two elements:

- Joint International Programme with the Baring Foundation – almost all our overseas funding allocation now goes towards a joint programme in Africa administered by the Baring Foundation. For details and application guidelines, visit: www.baringfoundation.org.uk. This programme seeks to help refugees and displaced peoples in sub-Saharan Africa.
- South Africa – we confine support to charities set up by or closely connected with Sir John Ellerman in and around Cape Town, which we have helped to fund for many years.

These are specific charities with which we have a long-established relationship.

Please note: we are not currently accepting overseas applications other than from those charities working in conservation.

Grants in 2009/10

In 2009/10 the foundation had assets of £116.8 million and an income of just over £1.4 million. There were 165 made totalling £4.2 million, with some organisations receiving instalments of multi-year awards. Grants were broken down by category as follows:

Social welfare	46	£1.35 million
Health and disability	50	£1.27 million
Arts and heritage	28	£598,500
Conservation	21	£524,500
Overseas	20	£473,500

Beneficiaries across all categories included: Ashden Awards (£130,000), in two one-off payments towards the cost of one international award for a sustainable energy initiative in 2009 and 2010; Adoption UK (£50,000), a one-off payment towards developing Adoption UK's core work of regional support groups and to develop an accredited adoptive parent/training qualification; Fairtrade Foundation (£50,000), the second of two payments towards the cost of implementing the foundation's new strategy for 2008–12; Fostering Network (£42,000), a one-off payment towards the cost of supporting foster carers to set up and run voluntary foster care associations in their own localities; Combat Stress (£40,000), the first of two payments towards the core costs of supporting ex-Service men and women with psychological injuries; BioRegional Development Group (£30,000), the first of two payments towards the director's work of championing sustainable enterprise, forging new partnerships and directing strategic development across the UK; Bladder and Bowel Foundation (£30,000), the first of two payments towards core funding; Anti-Slavery International (£28,000*), first of three payments towards local partners being enabled to bring together different groups of displaced migrants in constructive problem-solving dialogue, while also advocating for their rights; One-World Action (£22,000*), second of three payments towards the cost of

strengthening the capacity of refugee communities to respond to sexual and gender-based violence; Action for ME (£20,000), second of three payments towards the cost of a telephone support line, which provides employment legislation advice support; World Association of Girl Guides and Girl Scouts (£19,000*), the second of three payments to recruit and train 35 volunteer guide leaders and to develop and deliver training programmes to refugees and displaced girls and young women in the Republic of Chad; Elephant Family (£12,000), second of three payments towards the cost of creating a structured internship programme; and the English Folk Dance & Song Society (£10,000), the second of two payments towards the cost of a national outreach programme.

*Joint funding with the Baring Foundation

The foundation's excellent annual report also provides informative case studies written by a selection of grant recipients which potential applicants may find interesting.

Exclusions

Grants are not made for the following purposes:

- for or on behalf of individuals
- individual hospitals and hospices
- local branches of national organisations
- mainstream education/ establishments
- purchase of vehicles
- direct replacement of public funding, or deficit funding
- drug or alcohol abuse
- charities with an annual income less than £100,000
- religious causes
- friends of groups
- medical research
- conferences and seminars
- sports and leisure facilities
- domestic animal welfare
- prisons and offenders
- military museums at regimental/ arm/corps level.

The following information is taken from the foundation's website:

The foundation will only consider applications from registered and exempt charities with a UK office. Most of our grants are for one and two years,

but we will give grants for three years if a very strong case is made. Our minimum grant is £10,000. We aim to develop relationships with funded charities.

We will only support charities that work – or have reach and impact – across England/UK. Those operating within a single locality, city, borough, county or region will not be considered. We believe other trusts and funders are better placed to help individuals and local or regional charities. For this reason also, applications operating exclusively in Wales, Scotland or Northern Ireland will NOT be considered.

Applications

The website gives the following information on applications:

Like most other foundations, we receive many more applications than we can possibly fund. On average, only one in four of all appeals within our guidelines is successful. We recognise that preparing good applications places heavy demands on the time and resources of charities, and diverts energies from their ultimate purpose. We therefore have a two-stage application process.

Stage 1

Please first read our *General Guidelines for All Applicants* and then category guidelines. Please ensure that you are eligible to apply, and do not appear in the list of exclusions. Then, please send us your latest annual report and audited accounts, (include financial forecasts or estimates for financial years ended since then), together with a letter – no more than two sides of A4. This should tell us about your charity. Please include:

- what you do, who your beneficiaries are and where you work
- examples of your work and illustrate how you match our guidelines
- an explanation of your need for funding – your turnover, reserves, main sources of income, why you need funds now, and, if you are requesting funds for a particular project, rough costings.

All letters are reviewed by the grants manager, director and at least one trustee who recommend whether your proposal should be taken to the next stage. If not we will tell you at this juncture, rather than ask you to complete a full application.

Stage 2

If your proposal is recommended to the next stage, we will send you by email, an application form. You should return this to us within one month. We do not have specific deadlines for applications, as our trustees meet regularly throughout the year. (The application form is also available on request in printed format, and we ask you to post us a printed version when applying.)

On receipt of your full application, we will organise to come and see you (or meet you) and this will involve staff and/or trustees. We do this as a matter of policy with all full applications. During or after a visit we may ask for additional information, or clarification of some issues. Your application will then be considered at the next available board meeting which take place every two months. We will write to you as soon as possible after that with a decision.

Entindale Ltd

Orthodox Jewish charities

£3 million (2009/10)

Beneficial area
Unrestricted.

8 Highfield Gardens, London NW11 9HB
Tel: 020 8458 9266
Fax: 020 8458 8529
Correspondent: Barbara Bridgeman, Secretary
Trustees: Allan Becker; Barbara Bridgeman; Stephen Goldberg.
CC Number: 277052

Information available
Accounts were available at the Charity Commission.

This trust aims 'to advance religion in accordance with the orthodox Jewish faith'.

In 2009/10 it had assets of £14.7 million and an income of £1.3 million derived mainly from rent. Grants were made to 182 organisations totalling £3 million.

Beneficiaries included: British Friends of Rinat Aharon (£480,000); BHW Limited (£200,000); Moreshet HaTorah and the Jewish Heritage Holocaust Remembrance Trust (£180,000); Menorah Grammar School (£135,000); Yesamach Levav Trust (£108,000); RS Trust (£91,000); Friends of Beis Yisroel Trust (£73,000); Telz Academy Trust (£50,000); Matono (£46,000); LTC Trust Company (£36,000); Yesodei Ha Torah Primary Girls' School (£20,000); Union of Orthodox

Hebrew Congregation (£10,000); Merkaz Torah Vochessed (£3,000); and Knesses Hatorah (£1,000).

Applications
In writing to the correspondent.

The Equitable Charitable Trust

Education of disabled and/or disadvantaged children under 25

£843,000 (2010)

Beneficial area
Mainly UK: overseas projects can sometimes be supported.

Sixth Floor, 65 Leadenhall Street, London EC3A 2AD
Tel: 020 7264 4993
Fax: 020 7488 9097
Email: jennielong@ equitablecharitabletrust.org.uk
Website: www. equitablecharitabletrust.org.uk
Correspondent: Jennie Long, Grants Officer
Trustees: Brian McGeough; Roy Ranson; Peter Goddard.
CC Number: 289548

Information available
Accounts were on file at the Charity Commission. The trust also has a very informative website.

This trust was established in 1984 to receive and distribute, for charitable purposes, a portion of the profits from a commercial school fee investment plan scheme. This scheme is now winding down therefore it is not anticipated that the trust will continue indefinitely. However the trust is currently able to make grants totalling around £1 million each year towards projects for young children and young people under the age of 25 who are from disadvantaged backgrounds or who are disabled.

The trust's funds are highly oversubscribed and the trustees have therefore identified three specific priorities for the types of projects they wish to support:

- education projects or services that support the learning and development of disabled children and young people in the UK
- formal education projects for disadvantaged children and young people in the UK that support delivery of the National Curriculum (i.e. curriculum enrichment projects) or that deliver accredited vocational learning that will increase employability
- Education projects that will help increase participation in, or improve the quality of, education for disadvantaged or disabled children and young people in developing countries.

Types of grant
Grants can be made for project costs, capital expenditure, equipment and/or the salary costs of a post.

Area of benefit
The majority of projects funded by the trust take place within the UK at local or regional level, though national projects and those benefiting children or young people overseas (in developing countries only) are also supported.

Please note that grants for overseas projects are only made through UK registered charities.

Types of organisations funded
We support a broad range of organisations; from small and medium sized not-for-profit organisations to large charities. However, priority is normally given to organisations and charities with annual incomes of under £5 million. You do not need to be a UK registered charity to apply unless you are applying for a grant towards a project or work that will take place outside the UK. For overseas projects, trustees particularly wish to support projects with potential to deliver benefits over the medium to long term.

Length of Grants
The length of funding can range from one to three years. Grants of more than one year are paid in annual instalments, with instalments beyond the first year dependent on receipt of progress reports that are satisfactory to the trustees.

Size of Grants
The size of grants ranges from £2,500 to £30,000. Most are for sums between £5,000 and £20,000. It is rare for a multi-year grant to exceed £10,000 per year and most multi-year grants will be for sums between £5,000 and £7,500 per year.

Grantmaking in 2010
In 2010 the trust had assets of £6 million and an income of £368,000. Grants were made totalling £843,000 to 97 organisations.

Beneficiaries included: Promoting Equality in African Schools (£23,000), years two and three of a three year grant towards the capital costs of building and equipping science laboratories in six new schools in Uganda; Ministry of Parenting (£22,000); a one year grant towards a pilot project in Essex that is developing and testing new ways of working with hard to reach and disabled pupils in a range of education settings; Africa Educational Trust (£17,000), a one year grant towards a programme of work that aims to increase the number of girls attending secondary school in two regions of Somalia; Kibble Education and Care Centre (£15,000), a capital grant towards a new Expressive Arts Centre at a residential unit for high-risk and high-dependency young people in Scotland; School-Home Support (£10,000), the final year of a three year grant towards the salary of the Hackney Service Delivery Manager; Oval House (£10,000), the final year of a three year grant towards an alternative curriculum project for young offenders and excluded young people in London Boroughs of Lambeth and Southwark; Kids (£9,000), year one of a two year grant towards an educational project for disabled young people in Gloucestershire; The Jamie Oliver Foundation (£7,500), the first year of a three year grant towards the salary costs of the Programme Coordinator for a project that provides vocational training and work experience to disadvantaged young people in London; The Michael Palin Centre for Stammering Children (£5,000), the final year of a three year grant towards an advice service for the families and teachers of children who stammer; The London Centre for Children with Cerebral Palsy (£5,000), the final year of a three year grant towards the salary of an Outreach worker at a conductive education centre in London for children with Cerebral Palsy; and, Hampstead Theatre (£2,000), a one year grant towards a scriptwriting project for young people with disabilities from the Royal Free Hospital School in London.

Exclusions

According to the trust's 'Guidelines for Applicants' published on its website, the trust does not make grants towards the following:

- general appeals or mail shot requests for donations
- informal education projects and those that are only loosely educational
- projects felt to be more akin to social work than education
- therapeutic treatments
- supplementary schooling and homework clubs
- mother tongue language classes
- state maintained or voluntary aided schools, colleges or universities, either directly or via another charity (e.g. Friends, PTAs)
- local authorities
- public schools or independent schools that are not specifically for children and young people with disabilities or special educational needs
- sports education, facilities or activities (e.g. playing fields, sports clubs, or projects that are delivered through the medium of sport)
- projects or work related to the Olympic Games or Cultural Olympiad
- salaries for posts that are not directly related to service delivery (we would not make a grant towards the salary of a fundraiser or book-keeper, for instance)
- minibuses
- pre-school education projects (unless these are solely for the benefit of children with disabilities or special needs)
- individuals
- bursary schemes
- projects that promote religious belief or practice
- holidays, recreational activities or overseas trips
- capital applications for equipment or facilities that will be only partly used for education or by under 25s from disadvantaged or disabled backgrounds (e.g. outdoor education centres that also deliver recreational activities, or that are not exclusively for the use of disadvantaged or disabled children and young people)
- Grassroots projects without a strategic element, such as those which support students by paying their school fees or purchasing school uniforms, are also unlikely to be funded.
- Projects which relate to PSHE and Citizenship subjects are unlikely to be funded as they are a low priority.

Applications

There is no form but there are very comprehensive application guidelines available on the trust's website. Accounts must be included. Trustees meet monthly.

Common applicant mistakes

'Not reading our guidelines properly or relying on partial information. Not telling the trust about the outcomes of previous work or projects, or providing unsubstantiated claims about their impact. Sending in general letters of appeal.'

The Eranda Foundation

Research into education and medicine, the arts, social welfare

£4.3 million (2009/10)

Beneficial area

UK.

PO Box 6226, Wing, Leighton Buzzard, Bedfordshire LU7 0XF
Tel: 01296 689157
Email: eranda@btconnect.com
Correspondent: Gail Devlin-Jones, Secretary
Trustees: Sir Evelyn de Rothschild; Renée Robeson; Leopold de Rothschild; Miss Jessica de Rothschild; Anthony de Rothschild; Sir Graham Hearne; Lady Lynn de Rothschild.
CC Number: 255650

Information available

Accounts were available at the Charity Commission.

Established in 1967, this is one of the foundations of the de Rothschild finance and banking family. The foundation supports the promotion of original research, and the continuation of existing research into medicine and education, fostering of the arts and promotion of social welfare.

In 2009/10 had assets of £83.2 million and an income of £5.3 million. There were 144 grants made during the year totalling almost £4.3 million.

Exclusions

No grants to individuals.

Applications

In writing to the correspondent. Trustees usually meet in March, July and November and applications should be received two months in advance.

Essex Community Foundation

Social welfare, general

£1.7 million (2009/10)

Beneficial area

Essex, Southend and Thurrock.

121 New London Road, Chelmsford, Essex CM2 0QT
Tel: 01245 355947
Fax: 01245 246391
Email: general@essexcf.org.uk
Website: www. essexcommunityfoundation.org.uk
Correspondent: Grants Team
Trustees: John Spence, Chair; Peter Blanc; Jason Bartella; John Barnes; Charles Clark; Carole Golbourn; Peter Heap; Rhiannedd Pratley; Martin Hopkins; Margaret Hyde; Jonny Minter; Owen Richards; Colin Sivell; Jackie Sully.
CC Number: 1052061

Information available

Accounts were available at the Charity Commission.

The foundation was set up in 1996 and manages funds on behalf of individuals, companies, charitable trusts and public agencies in order to give grants to voluntary and community organisations working to improve the quality of life for people living in Essex, Southend and Thurrock. Support generally falls under the broad heading of social welfare and can cover core costs/ revenue costs, new or continuing projects, one-off initiatives and capital costs. The foundation is

particularly interested in small grass-roots groups.

Applications should meet the following criteria:

- have clear project aims and objectives
- demonstrate that the grant will make a real difference to people in the community
- involve local participation and support self-help wherever possible.

Further information on the different funds that are available and the foundation's grant guidelines can be found on its website.

In 2009/10 the foundation had assets of almost £13.9 million and an income of £4.1 million. There were 659 grants made to 490 organisations from various funds to support all aspects of social welfare, totalling £1.7 million.

The foundation's accounts list the 50 largest grants made during the year. Beneficiaries included: London Bus Theatre Company (£86,000); Basildon, Billericay & Wickford CVS (£62,500); Inclusion Ventures Ltd (£60,000); Acorn Housing Association (£39,000); Chelmsford Women's Aid (£29,000); Crossroads Care Brentwood Basildon and Districts (£15,000); Hythe Community Centre Association (£11,000); Home-Start Brentwood (£10,000); Rural Community Council of Essex (£8,500); Debden Village Hall (£6,000); Essex Wildlife Trust (£5,500); and Dunmow Blind and Housebound Social Club and Severalls Concert Group (£5,000 each).

Exclusions

The foundation does not support the following:

- political or religious activities
- statutory bodies undertaking their statutory obligations (including schools and parish councils)
- general appeals
- activities which support animal welfare
- projects that operate outside of Essex, or benefit non-Essex residents
- retrospective funding.

Applications

Essex Community Foundation manages a number of funds, many of which are tailored to the individual wishes of the donors. However, with the exception of the four funds listed below, all you have to do is complete a general application form and the foundation will find the right fund for you.

Application forms are available from the foundation's office or can be downloaded from its website. Deadlines are usually twice a year on 9 January and 9 September; please contact the foundation for exact dates. Grants are awarded within three months of the deadlines.

If in doubt about the suitability of your project for funding, call the foundation's grants team on 01245 356018, or email: grants@ essexcf.org.uk

The four funds which use a specific application form are: Comic Relief; Thriving Third Sector Fund; High Sheriffs' Award; and the Marion Ruth Courtauld Educational Fund. They may also have different application deadlines. Further information about each of these funds is available from the foundation's website, or by contacting the grants team, as above.

Euro Charity Trust

Relief of poverty, education

£3.8 million (2010)

Beneficial area

Worldwide, mainly India, Africa, Bangladesh and the UK.

51a Church Road, Edgbaston, Birmingham B15 3SJ
Email: info@eurocharity.org.uk
Correspondent: Ahmed Omer, Trustee
Trustees: Nasir Awan; Abdul Malik.
CC Number: 1058460

Information available

Accounts were available at the Charity Commission.

The trust receives the majority of its income from Euro Packaging Holdings Limited. Donations are made to both organisations and individuals worldwide. Euro Packaging has grown from a small paper bag merchants into a large diversified packaging group. Paper bag production commenced in 1984 and today the firm is the UK's largest manufacturer. It has its own facilities for polythene bag manufacture, and also recycles both plastic and paper products.

The trust's objects are as follows:

- to assist in bringing relief to the poor, orphans and other vulnerable children, and families in need
- to assist individuals and organisations in providing education and training to underprivileged boys and girls, thereby enabling them to support themselves and to raise sound families which will strengthen their local communities, with particular emphasis on India
- charitable activity is focused on providing education to people situated in rural areas, where schools do not exist, and on providing food and accommodation to support the students' families and guiding the students with moral and ethical values. The ultimate aim is to make them self sufficient so they can support their families
- to support and provide those deprived of basic necessities such as water, food, accommodation and healthcare amenities
- to build partnerships with institutions that have the understanding and commitment to deliver and sustain projects which further the charity's objects
- to promote the work of those who share the same values as the trust.

In 2010 the trust had assets of £1.7 million and an income of £5.2 million, which included £2.8 million from Euro Packaging. Grants were made totalling £3.8 million. Over two thirds of the trust's grantmaking is concentrated in India. It is also likely grants are made to organisations in the local area around Euro Packaging sites (in the UK in Birmingham and in Malaysia) and Malawi, where the settlor is

originally from. Grants were broken down as follows:

Construction and land	£2 million
Welfare including the provision of food, water, clothing and healthcare	£1.2 million
Construction and running costs of educational institute in India	£465,000
Medical provision	£231,000
Education and sponsorship	£102,000
Other activities	£2,500

* this includes £128,000 to individuals.

The largest donations, listed in the trust's accounts, were made to: Nathani Charitable Trust (£1 million); Anjuman-I-Islam (£745,000); Moulana Hussain Ahmad Madani Charitable Trust and Charitable Society (£479,000); Jamia lsiamia lshaatul Uloom (£465,000); and Darul Uloom Deoband (£400,000).

Applications
In writing to the correspondent.

The Eveson Charitable Trust

People with physical disabilities, (including those who are blind or deaf); people with mental disabilities; hospitals and hospices; children who are in need; older people; homeless people; medical research into problems associated with any of these conditions

£2 million (2009/10)

Beneficial area
Herefordshire, Worcestershire and the county of West Midlands (covering Birmingham, Coventry, Dudley, Sandwell, Solihull, Walsall and Wolverhampton).

45 Park Road, Gloucester GL1 1LP
Tel: 01452 501352
Fax: 01452 302195

Correspondent: Alex D Gay, Administrator
Trustees: David Pearson, Chair; Bruce Maughfling; Rt. Revd Anthony Priddis, Bishop of Hereford; Martin Davies; Louise Woodhead; Bill Wiggin; Richard Mainwaring.
CC Number: 1032204

Information available
Accounts were available at the Charity Commission.

The trust was established in 1994 by a legacy of £49 million from Mrs Violet Eveson to support the following causes:

- people with physical disabilities (including those who are blind or deaf)
- people with mental disabilities
- hospitals and hospices
- children in need, whether disadvantaged or have mental or physical disabilities
- older people
- people who are homeless
- medical research in any of these categories
- general charitable purposes.

It is the policy of the trust to support many charities on an annual basis provided such beneficiaries satisfy the need for continued support. Many capital and specific projects are also supported.

Grants are restricted to the geographical areas of Herefordshire, Worcestershire and the county of West Midlands, as a policy decision of the trustees. The trust does not instigate programmes of its own, but responds to the applications which it receives. Grants vary in amount but the average size of grants is around £7,000 to £8,000.

In 2009/10 the trust had assets of £60.5 million and an income of £587,000. Grants were made to 266 organisations totalling £2 million and were categorised as follows:

Social care and development	175	£1 million
Health care	70	£824,000
Accommodation	21	£138,500

Social care and development
These grants go to organisations that provide human and social services to a community or target population, including services for children, young people, physically and mentally

disabled people, elderly people and homeless people.

Health care

Health-care grants go to organisations that focus on the prevention or treatment of specific diseases, the prevention or treatment of diseases generally and/or health problems, the rehabilitation of disabled individuals, residential nursing homes for the frail, elderly, severely disabled people and those offering terminal care.

Accommodation

These grants go organisations providing non-health related accommodation and respite/holiday accommodation.

Beneficiaries included: Acorns Children's Hospice Trust (£50,000), towards nursing services at their hospice in Selly Oak, Birmingham, that provides support to life limited and life threatened children and young people; Breast Cancer Haven (£50,000), a two-year grant towards running costs of Hereford Haven that benefits people with breast cancer; Megan Baker House – Leominster (£30,000), towards the running costs of this charity that provides a free conductive education service to disabled children; Coventry & District Free Church Homes for the Elderly (£25,000), towards building extension to provide more bedrooms with improved facilities to benefit older people; Society for Mucopolysaccharide Diseases (£15,000), towards their advocacy support programme that benefits children living in our area who suffer from MPS; Community Voluntary Action – Ledbury (£12,000), towards the running costs of the Mobility Centre service that benefits disabled people and older people with mobility problems; Family Drug Support – Herefordshire (£8,000), towards work benefiting those affected by drug, alcohol and substance abuse in their families; Music in Hospitals (£6,000), towards live music performances in hospitals, hospices, homes, day care centres and special schools in the area; and Norman Laud Association – Sutton Coldfield (£4,500), towards refurbishment of bedrooms at this respite care home for children with special needs.

Exclusions

Grants are not made to individuals, even if such a request is submitted by a charitable organisation.

Applications

The trustees meet quarterly, usually at the end of March and June and the beginning of October and January.

Applications can only be considered if they are on the trust's standard, but very simple, 'application for support' form which can be obtained from the administrator at the offices of the trust in Gloucester. The form must be completed and returned (together with a copy of the latest accounts and annual report of the organisation) to the trust's offices at least six weeks before the meeting of trustees at which the application is to be considered, in order to give time for necessary assessment procedures, often including visits to applicants.

Before providing support to statutory bodies (such as hospitals and schools for people with learning difficulties), the trust requires written confirmation that no statutory funds are available to meet the need for which funds are being requested. In the case of larger grants to hospitals, the trust asks the district health authority to confirm that no statutory funding is available.

Where applications are submitted that clearly fall outside the grantmaking parameters of the trust, the applicant is advised that the application cannot be considered and reasons are given. All applications that are going to be considered by the trustees are acknowledged in writing. Applicants are advised of the reference number of their application and of the quarterly meeting at which their application is going to be considered. The decisions are advised to applicants in writing soon after these meetings. Funded projects are monitored.

Common applicant mistakes

'Some applicants ignore the trust's guidelines, however the number of those doing this has decreased.'

The Execution Charitable Trust

Mainly local multi-purpose community projects supporting social welfare

£958,000 (2010)

Beneficial area

Worldwide, in practice mainly UK.

10 Paternoster Square, London
EC4M 7AL
Tel: 020 7375 2007
Email: info@executionlimited.com
Website: www.execution-noble. com/x/charitable-interests.html
Correspondent: Cheryl Mustapha Whyte, Trustee
Trustees: Jacky Joy; John R Moore; Cheryl Mustapha Whyte; Damien Devine; Peter Ward; Neil Strong.
CC Number: 1099097

Information available

Accounts were available at the Charity Commission.

This trust funds local multi-purpose community projects in deprived areas in the UK that tackle the root causes, as well as the symptoms, of poverty and isolation. It was established in 2003 by stockbrokers Execution Ltd as a means of distributing funds raised from their 'charity days', when all commission revenues generated on the day are donated to charity.

From the outset the trust established a relationship with New Philanthropy Capital (NPC), itself a registered charity, set up in 2001 by a team of ex-City financiers which provides research based advice to donors on where and how their philanthropic funds can be targeted most effectively. Since then a partnership has grown out of a mutual commitment to tackling deprivation, disadvantage and degradation in the UK and beyond. NPC also provides evaluation of results to monitor the effectiveness of grants.

The criteria by which NPC selects charities are determined by the trust. These criteria ensure that the trust is able to locate projects for funding that are:

- in deprived communities – mainly in the UK
- run by local people wherever possible
- Meeting local needs, respecting race and gender issues individual to those communities.

The trust looks to fund locally driven, successful, community projects which struggle to raise private funds due to a lack of a wider profile. The trust distributes its funds to organisations in all parts of the UK and is willing to consider funding organisations in disadvantaged communities for almost any purpose, from core funding and salaries, to project costs.

In 2010 the trust had an income of £855,000, assets of £1 million and made grants totalling £958,000. This included £239,000 to Absolute Return for Kids and the remaining £720,000 in 54 grants.

The largest grant beneficiaries included: ARK- local and international projects; Myeloma- UK; Peace One Day- Surrey; The Tullochan Trust- Dunbartonshire; Bryncynon Community Revival Strategy Limited- Wales; Family Action – London; South Side Family- Bedford.

Details of grants awarded were not included in the accounts.

Applications

The trust does not consider unsolicited applications for grants.

The trust has appointed New Philanthropy Capital (NPC) to proactively identify effective organisations on its behalf. If you believe your organisation matches the funding criteria listed here and you want to provide basic contact details and a short outline of your project, go to the Execution Charitable Trust's website and fill in the online form.

Esmée Fairbairn Foundation

Social welfare, education, environment, arts and heritage

£27.6 million (2010)

Beneficial area

UK.

Kings Place, 90 York Way, London N1 9AG
Tel: 020 7812 3700
Fax: 020 7812 3701
Email: info@esmeefairbairn.org.uk
Website: www.esmeefairbairn.org.uk
Correspondent: Dawn Austwick, Chief Executive
Trustees: Tom Chandos, Chair; Felicity Fairbairn; Beatrice Hollond; James Hughes-Hallett; Thomas Hughes-Hallett; Kate Lampard; Baroness Linklater; William Sieghart; John Fairbairn; Jonathan Phillips.
CC Number: 200051

Information available

Detailed guidelines for applicants and excellent annual report and accounts, all available on the clear and helpful website.

Background

Ian Fairbairn established the foundation in 1961 (renamed Esmée Fairbairn Foundation in 2000). He was a leading city figure and his company, M&G, was the pioneer of the unit trust industry. Ian Fairbairn endowed the foundation with the greater part of his own holding in M&G, and in the early years the majority of grants were for economic and financial education.

His interest in financial education stemmed from his concern that most people had no access to stock exchange investment, and were therefore precluded from investing their savings in equities and sharing in the country's economic growth. It was precisely this concern that had led him into the embryonic unit trust business in the early 1930s.

The foundation was set up as a memorial to Ian Fairbairn's wife

Esmée, who had played a prominent role in developing the Women's Royal Voluntary Service and the Citizens Advice Bureaux before being killed during an air raid towards the end of the Second World War. Her sons Paul and Oliver Stobart contributed generously to the original trust fund, as co-founders.

General

In 2010 the foundation had assets of £825.3 million (£795.7 million in 2009) and an income of £10.6 million, mostly from investments. Grants were made during the year totalling £27.6 million.

Guidelines

The following guidelines are provided by the foundation and published on its website:

The Esmée Fairbairn Foundation aims to improve the quality of life throughout the UK. We do this by funding the charitable activities of organisations that have the ideas and ability to achieve change for the better. We take pride in supporting work that might otherwise be considered difficult to fund.

Funding is channelled through two routes.

Main Fund

The Main Fund distributes about two-thirds of funding.

What areas do we support?

Our primary interests are in the UK's cultural life, education, the natural environment and enabling people who are disadvantaged to participate more fully in society.

We welcome your suggestions about how we can help your organisation. We are particularly interested in hearing about how the work you are proposing:

- addresses a significant gap in provision;
- develops or strengthens good practice;
- challenges convention or takes a risk in order to address a difficult issue;
- tests out new ideas or practices;
- takes an enterprising approach to achieving your aims;
- sets out to influence policy or change behaviour more widely.

You do not have to be a registered charity to apply but we can only fund work that is legally charitable. Your constitution must also allow you to carry out the work you propose.

What type of funding do we offer?

At Esmée Fairbairn we are happy to consider requests to fund core costs or project costs. These may include running costs such as staff salaries and overheads but generally not equipment costs. We dot fund capital costs for building work or refurbishment.

New and emerging organisations may apply and we are willing to help finance the early stages of developing a convincing new idea in order to test its feasibility and give it the best possible chance of success.

We occasionally fund research where we consider it is likely to have a practical impact.

If you ask for our assistance, you should tell us how much you need.

The trust allocates funding to specific areas known as streams. The following topics are identified for more detailed attention. These will develop over time, and allow the foundation to make a more focused contribution in an area of interest. Others may come on stream in due course. Check the foundation's website for up-to-date information.

Food – The aim of the Food Strand is to promote an understanding of the role of food in enhancing quality of life. It will prioritise the enjoyment and experience of food rather than its production and we seek to enable as many people in the UK as possible to access, prepare and eat nutritious, sustainable food. We are interested in work that influences policy and practice across a range of food-related areas. We expect to support a mix of practical projects that have wide significance, and some research and policy based work.

Esmée Fairbairn Collections Fund – This new fund, run by the Museums Association, has been developed from the Esmée Fairbairn Museum and Heritage Collections Strand and the MA's Effective Collections programme. It focuses on time-limited collections work outside the scope of an organisation's core resources. Through this fund the MA will award approximately £800,000 per year to museums, galleries and heritage organisations with two grant rounds per year. Organisations can apply for sums between £20,000 and £100,000. Like the Museum and Heritage Collections strand we are keen to fund projects at an early stage of development where it may be difficult to guarantee tangible outcomes, but like Effective Collections we want organisations that are funded to become part of a network to develop ideas, share knowledge and build a legacy. Projects that are eligible to apply to the Esmée Fairbairn Collections Fund include research into collections, conservation, collections review and initiatives to develop the use of collections.

The Museum & Heritage Collections fund has now closed, although the themes of its work are carried on through the new Collections Fund. The New Approaches to Learning and Biodiversity funds have also closed although the trust notes that it will continue to fund work in these sectors through the Main Fund. The trust's website also states that the trustees 'maintain an active interest in biodiversity which is likely to be the subject of a future theme which we expect to finalise during 2011. Please check the website for up-to-date information.'

Small Funds

In addition the trust also has the following small funds open:

Finance Fund – Aims to complement the Foundation's grantmaking with loans and other investments to charities and social enterprises in our areas of interest.

Development Fund – investigates new ideas and approaches, such as testing ideas for possible future funding areas.

TASK Fund - Trustees' Areas of Specialist Knowledge (TASK) Fund supports organisations known to individual trustees.

Grants in 2010

Citizenship or community development	78	£5.74 million
Arts, culture and heritage	66	£5.08 million
Environment	33	£3.05 million
Education	32	£2.39 million
Human rights and conflict resolution	23	£2.29 million
Prevention or relief of poverty	27	£2.04 million
Other charitable purposes	11	£935,000
Total	**270**	**£21.54 million**

The average grant size from the Main Fund was £79,800; there were a total of 2,330 applications made to the Main Fund, with 270 grants approved. The following is a sample of beneficiaries from the Main Fund and the purposes for which grants were given:

Bristol Old Vic Trust Ltd (£500,000), towards a five year programme to support emerging theatre artists; Family Rights Group (£300,000), towards core costs over three years for work with families of looked after children; Global Canopy Foundation (£150,000), towards the costs of surveys of forest footprint disclosure, helping companies understand their exposure to tropical deforestation; Prisoners' Education Trust (£105,000), towards the salaries of a strategic project manager, policy and communications officer and an administrator over three years; Crafts Council (£96,000), towards the costs over three years of a national project to improve ceramics education and facilities in schools; Belfast Interface Project (£90,000), towards the salary of the practice co-ordinator over three years to influence government policy regarding the regeneration of interface or 'peace line' areas, promote greater levels of sharing, address youth-led interface violence, and address membership needs; Blackburne house Group (£80,000), towards the cost of establishing a women's maintenance social enterprise, which will work closely with local housing associations, providing training opportunities and earned income; West End Refugee Service (£45,000), towards the salary of the project director over three years; Colchester and Ipswich Museum Service (£41,000), towards Out in the Open project costs which will explore perceptions of homelessness in Colchester; African Community Advice North East (£38,500), towards the salary of the development director and project costs over three years; Community Energy Practitioners Forum (£35,000), towards the costs of research and report production to map community action on climate change with a focus on the links between process and outcome; York Travellers Trust (£30,000), towards a women's education project over two years; The Men's Room (£16,000), towards the salary of a part-time arts sessional worker over two years; and Index on Censorship (£15,000), towards the core costs of the Artistic Expression and Self Censorship Programme.

New approaches to learning	20	£1.62 million
Biodiversity	17	£1.48 million
Museum and heritage collections	17	£1 million
Food	14	£924,000
Total	**68**	**£5 million**

The following is a sample of beneficiaries from the four Strands and the purposes for which grants were given: University of Swansea

(£146,000), towards research costs over three years into jellyfish populations and lifecycles in the Irish Sea; The People's Supermarket (£110,000) towards the recruitment and salary of a general manager to establish this first urban based community owned supermarket; Dorset Wildlife Trust (£80,000), towards the costs of achieving a greater understanding of Devon's sabellaria reefs; Torquay Museum (£55,000), towards the salaries of two documentation assistants and a contribution to project management to document the geology and palaeontology collections; Zest-Health for Life (£46,000), towards the costs over two years for the establishment of four additional fresh fruit and vegetable outlets in food deserts in east Leeds; and Oban War and Peace Museum (£9,000), towards the salary of a documentation officer.

Finance Fund (£3 million): Loans were made to the following organisations: Big Issue Invest (£750,000), an investment into the Social Enterprise Fund over ten years; Ethical Property Company Ltd (£500,000), purchase of shares to allow further growth of the Ethical Property Company, enabling it to provide office accommodation to more charities and social enterprises; and Social Impact Partnership (£107,000), the first instalment of a £1 million commitment to the first Social Impact Bond at Peterborough Prison, enabling the rehabilitation of short sentence ex-offenders to reduce re-offending.

TASK Fund (£705,000): The foundation also makes grants from its TASK (Trustees' Areas of Special Knowledge) Fund to support organisations known to individual trustees. There were 87 awards made totalling £705,000.

Development Fund (£471,000): The foundation continued its partnership with the Henry Smith Charity by contributing £446,000 to develop civil society leadership in Northern Ireland. Overall the Northern Ireland Development Programme made 5 grants totalling £891,000. This included grants made to: North West Play Resource Centre (The Playhouse) (£280,600), towards the salary of a finance director, the cost

of 15 international artist residencies based in Northern Ireland and a contribution to core costs; and Committee on the Administration of Justice (£164,000), towards the salary of a public affairs officer, a contribution to core costs and an events and publications budget. Other development fund grants included: Institute of Public Policy Research (£15,000), towards the costs of the first phase of a project to develop a new progressive economic policy framework; and Performing Arts Labs Ltd (£10,000), towards the costs of the Movement and Meaning project.

Exclusions

The following information is taken from 'Applying to the Main Fund' guidelines published on the foundation's website:

The foundation does not support applications for:

- individuals or causes that will benefit only one person, including student grants or bursaries;
- support for a general appeal or circular;
- work that does not have a direct benefit in the UK;
- the promotion of religion;
- capital costs, including building work, renovations, and equipment;
- work that is routine or well-proven elsewhere or with a low impact;
- healthcare or related work such as medical research, complementary medicine, counselling and therapy, education and treatment for substance misuse;
- work that is primarily the responsibility of central or local government, health trusts or health authorities, or which benefits from their funding. This includes residential and day care, housing and homelessness, individual schools, nurseries and colleges, supplementary schools and vocational training;
- projects that primarily benefit the independent education sector;
- environmental projects related to animal welfare, zoos, captive breeding and animal rescue centres;
- individual energy efficiency or waste reduction schemes;
- retrospective funding, meaning support for work that has already taken place;
- recreational activities including outward bound courses and adventure experiences
- We will not normally replace or subsidise statutory income although we will make rare exceptions where the level of performance has been

exceptional and where the potential impact of the work is substantial;
- retrospective funding;
- general appeals.

Applications
Applying for a grant from the Main Fund

The website gives the following guidance:

Please follow these three steps:
1 Read through the guidance notes, paying careful attention to the sort of work we support – and what we do not.
2 If you think your organisation's activities could attract Esmée Fairbairn funding, go through the self-assessment checklist for eligibility [available from the foundation's website].
3 If you can answer 'yes' to each of the self-assessment checklist questions, submit a first stage application [available from the foundation's website].

What happens next

We will then get back to you, aiming to acknowledge your first stage application within a week of receiving it. Within a month we will either suggest taking it to the second stage or decline to support it.

If you are invited to proceed to the second stage, we will ask you for some additional information that will depend on what you have already told us and the size and complexity of the work you would like us to support.

How we assess applications?

When considering your first stage application we are particularly interested in:
- how closely your application fits with one or more of our six priorities
- the importance of the issue you are seeking to address
- why you are the best organisation to undertake the work, including your track record
- the strength and feasibility of your idea, and
- the overall difference that your work is likely to make.

We receive many more applications than we can support.

Applications should be succinct and applicants are encouraged to highlight past successes. The foundation wishes to know if you intend to work with partners. Your application should demonstrate in tangible ways what you hope to achieve with our funding. Give examples if you think this will help us understand what the results will be.

The first stage application form and full guidance note is available from the foundation's website. There is a different application process for the funding strands. To learn more about the strands and how to apply, visit the foundation's website.

Common applicant mistakes

'Applicants not fully reading the application guidance and information on our website.'

The February Foundation

Education, heritage, community-based charities, environment, animals, medical/ welfare

£2.8 million (2009/10)

Beneficial area

UK and overseas.

Chantala, Wilby Road, Stradbroke, Suffolk IP21 5JN
Email: rps@thefebruaryfoundation. org
Website: www. thefebruaryfoundation.org/
Correspondent: Richard Pierce-Saunderson, Trustee
Trustees: Richard Pierce-Saunderson; James Carleton; The February Foundation (Cayman).
CC Number: 1113064

Information available

Accounts were on file at the Charity Commission, without a list of grants.

The foundation was established in 2006 for general charitable purposes and has a broad range of interests. This grant-making policy is taken from the foundation's accounts:

The foundation will consider the following organisations for the receipt of grants, equity investment or loans:

- charities which are for the benefit of persons who are making an effort to improve their lives
- charities which are for the benefit of persons no longer physically or mentally able to help themselves
- charities which have a long-term beneficial impact on the future of individuals, groups of individuals, or organisations
- charities which protect the environment

- small or minority charities where small grants will have a significant impact, and
- companies where the acquisition of equity would be in line with the Trust's charitable objectives.

In 2009/10 the foundation had assets of just over £8.1 million and an income of £421,000. There were 24 grants made to 17 organisations totalling almost £2.8 million, and were broken down as follows:

Education	5	£2.1 million
Heritage	5	£396,000
Life skills development	2	£151,000
End-of-life care	10	£88,000
Medical research	2	£12,500

Although no individual beneficiaries are listed in the accounts, the foundation does offer some insight into its grantmaking objectives:

Education
The foundation's objective in its education grant strategy is to enable universal access. However, it will focus on managing its existing grant commitments in this area rather than accepting applications for new grants.

Heritage
The foundation remains committed to preserving the legacy of British heritage in the UK and overseas. Although not making any new grants in this area, it is determined, through managing its existing matched funding commitments here, to enable children to learn about unique aspects of British history, and thus to encourage them to hold values of courage, dignity, respect, and endeavour.

Life skills development
The foundation will continue to manage its existing commitments in this area, and is not planning any new grants.

End-of-life care
The foundation remains committed to supporting end-of-life care at the grassroots level. It continues to monitor the government's End-of-Life Care Strategy and its implementation by hospices.

There were no further details for medical research, although the foundation's exclusions note that application will not be considered for medical research.

Exclusions

The foundation will not consider applications from the following:

- child care
- Citizens' Advice Bureaux
- community centres
- environmental projects
- heritage and building projects

- higher education
- housing associations
- individuals
- medical research
- minibuses
- NHS trusts
- non-departmental government bodies
- overseas projects
- previously unsuccessful applicants
- primary education
- Scouts, Guides, Brownies, Cubs, and similar organisations
- secondary education
- single-faith organisations
- sports clubs, unless for the mentally or physically disabled
- theatre groups
- village halls
- youth centres.

Applications

The following concise information is taken from the foundation's website:

The February Foundation makes grants to selected charities. It monitors and supports the effective management of grants made. The foundation is focused on managing its current commitments, although applications from some charities are still being accepted.

Email applications are preferred.

Please send details and budget of the proposed project, how many people would benefit, how those benefits might be measured (not just financially), and what the estimated cost of raising funds for the project is. It is important to include in your email application full accounts for your most recent completed financial year, and, if your accounts do not contain it, what your total fundraising costs annually are.

Please note that hardcopy applications take significantly longer to process than email applications. Please do not send DVDs, CDs, glossy brochures or other additional information.

It normally takes 12 weeks from application to applicants being informed of the trustees' decision. There are no application deadlines as trustees make grant decisions on a monthly basis.

Please note that less than 5% of all applications are successful.

The Allan and Nesta Ferguson Charitable Settlement

Peace, education, overseas development

£3 million to organisations (2010)

Beneficial area

Unrestricted, with a local interest in Birmingham and Bishop's Stortford.

Stanley Tee Solicitors, High Street, Bishops Stortford, Hertfordshire CM23 2LU

Tel: 01279 755200
Email: jrt@stanleytee.co.uk
Website: www.fergusontrust.co.uk/
Correspondent: Richard Tee, Trustee
Trustees: Elizabeth Banister; David Banister; Lesley Roff; Richard Tee.
CC Number: 275487

Information available

Accounts were on file at the Charity Commission. The trust also has a clear and simple website.

The Allan & Nesta Ferguson Charitable Trust was set up in memory of two generations of the Ferguson family to promote their particular interests in education, international friendship and understanding, and the promotion of world peace and development.

Grants are given to charitable organisations involved in projects supporting the interests of the trust, and also to individual students who are undertaking a gap year or studying for a PhD.

The trust gives the following information for organisations on its website:

Charitable organisations can be situated either in the UK or overseas but must be registered as a charity with the Charity Commission and will principally be educational bodies or aid organisations involved in projects supporting educational and development initiatives, including the promotion of world peace and development. All grants made by the trust are project based and must have an educational aim, element or content. In general the trustees will not consider applications for core funding or the construction of buildings in the UK. Overseas, however, the trustees will consider funding aid projects e.g. water treatment, food and medical supplies or the provision of basic facilities that are the pre-requisite of an educational or development initiative.

Grants made to charities during the year will vary both in size and amount, and will probably total between £5 million and £6 million. The amount of the grant is entirely at the discretion of the trustees and no reason for giving, withholding or offering a partial grant will be made.

Please note:

▷ Grants to charities will be on a matching funding basis only so that if the applicant has raised 50% of their budget the Trustees will consider awarding matching funding up to a maximum of 50%. However, if the applicant has raised less than 50% of their budget the Trustees will only consider awarding a maximum of 30% funding.

▷ Evidence of actively seeking funds from other sources is seen by the Trustees as being a beneficial addition to any application.

In 2010 the trust had assets of £28.4 million and an income of £800,000. Grants were made to organisations totalling over £3 million.

Grants were categorised as follows:

Overseas development	£1.9 million
Educational bodies	£1 million
Educational projects: world peace	£63,000

Beneficiaries included: AMREF (£313,000); Royal Shakespeare Company (£200,000); The Fairtrade Foundation (£112,000); Woodbrooke Quaker Study Centre (£110,000); Practical Action (£65,000); Save the Children (£35,000); Help2Read (£30,000); Amnesty International, Assist a Child to School Charity Trust, Listening Books and Stepping Stones Nigeria (£20,000 each); Care and Relief for the Young, Centre for Development & Community Welfare, and St Ethelburga's Centre for Reconciliation and Peace (£10,000 each).

Applications

When to apply

▷ Applications by charities for small to medium grants (up to a maximum of £50,000) may be submitted at any time and will be considered on a regular basis.

▷ Applications for larger grants will be considered at bi-annual meetings held in March and October and applications should be submitted at the very latest in the previous months i.e. February or September.

Please note: No repeat applications will be considered within three years of the conclusion of the grant term.

How to apply

▷ We prefer where possible that you complete and submit the on-line application form on this website and email it to us. Alternatively you may download and print out the application form, complete it and send it by letter post. See the Contact Us page for address details.

▷ Please do not extend the length of the forms, or add any attachments. Applications **MUST NOT** exceed 3 pages. Please use text size 12.

▷ Please do not apply for more than one project.

All applications by email will be acknowledged and considered by the Trustees within 6 to 8 weeks. If you do not hear further, after the acknowledgement, then unfortunately your application has not been successful. If the Trustees do decide to award you a grant then they will contact you. No progress reports will be given and no correspondence will be entered into in the meantime.

The Fidelity UK Foundation

General, primarily in the fields of arts and culture, community development, education and health

£4.5 million (2010)

Beneficial area

Particular preference is given to projects in Kent, Surrey, London and continental Europe.

Oakhill House, 130 Tonbridge Road, Hildenborough, Tonbridge, Kent TN11 9DZ

Tel: 01732 777364
Email: foundation@fil.com
Website: www.fidelityukfoundation. org
Correspondent: Susan Platts-Martin, Chief Executive

Information available

Accounts were available at the Charity Commission. The foundation also has a clear and simple website.

This foundation was established in 1988 to strengthen not-for-profit organisations primarily in regions surrounding Fidelity International's major corporate locations. Particular preference is given to projects in Kent, Surrey, London and continental Europe. Grants from the foundation are made only for charitable purposes and are designed to encourage the highest standards of management and long-term self-reliance in non-profit organisations. Taking an investment approach to grant making, it funds organisations where it can add lasting, measurable value. The aim is to support major initiatives that charitable organisations undertake to reach new levels of achievement.

The foundation's charitable giving is mainly in the areas of:

- arts and culture
- community development
- education
- health.

The following additional information is provided by the foundation on its website:

> We have found that our resources can be most productive with charitable organisations taking significant measures to reach greater levels of proficiency. Most often, this entails major projects such as:
> - capital improvements
> - technology upgrades
> - organisational development
> - planning initiatives.
>
> The trust assesses the organisation including the following factors:
> - the organisation's financial health
> - the strength of its management team and board
> - evidence of an overall strategic plan.

They also seek evidence of potential for success through:

> - institutional commitment to the project on behalf of the organisation's board
> - a realistic project budget
> - a thorough implementation plan, including a plan for performance measurement
> - net value to the organisation and the community it serves

> - significant support from other funders, among other criteria.

Grantmaking in 2010

During the year the trust had an income of £13 million and assets of £120 million. They made grants totalling £4.5 million which was broken down into the following areas (examples of the largest beneficiaries are given):

Arts & Culture (£2 million)

Sir John Soane's Museum (£390,000); Museum of London (£300,000); National Maritime Museum (£229,000); The Photographers' Gallery (£100,000).

Community development (£227,000)

In Kind Direct (£46,000); Ebony Horse Trust (£25,000); Youthnet UK (£15,000); Kidscape Campaign for Children's safety (£13,000).

Education (£1.3 million)

The Exeter University Foundation (£724,000); The Guildhall School Development Fund (£150,000); The National Centre for Young People with Epilepsy (£97,000).

Health (£737,000)

The Institute of Cancer Research (£264,000); The Children's Trust (£150,000); The University of Cambridge (£125,000).

Other (£9,000)

Given in one grant to Thames21.

The majority of grants approved were for capital or technological initiatives, including approximately 25 % towards improvements in information technology. The remainder of grants were largely for equipment and organisational development initiatives.

Exclusions

Grants are not generally made to:

- start-up, sectarian, or political organisations;
- private schools, and colleges or universities;
- individuals.

Grants are not made for:

- sponsorships or benefit events;
- scholarships;
- corporate memberships;
- advertising and promotional projects;
- exhibitions.

Generally grants are not made for running costs, but may be considered on an individual basis through the foundation's small grants scheme. Grants will not normally cover the entire cost of a project. Grants will not normally be awarded to an organisation in successive years.

Applications

To the correspondent in writing. Applicants should enclose the following:

- Fidelity UK Foundation summary form (form can be downloaded from the foundation's website)
- organisation history and objectives
- description of request and rationale, see below
- itemised project budget
- list of other funders and status of each request
- list of directors and trustees with their backgrounds
- current management accounts
- most recently audited financial statements.

When writing the description of your request and your rationale, please address the following questions:

- how the project fits into the larger strategic plan of your organisation
- what a grant will allow your organisation to achieve
- how a grant will change or improve the long-term potential of your organisation
- what the implementation plan and timeline for the project will be
- how the project will be evaluated.

There are no deadlines for submitting grant proposals. All applications will normally receive an initial response within three months. The volume of requests as well as the review process require a three to six month period, which should be factored into the applicant's funding plan.

The Sir John Fisher Foundation

General charitable purposes with a preference for the shipping industry, medicine, the navy or military and music and theatre

£896,000 (2009/10)

Beneficial area

UK, with a preference for charities in the Furness peninsula and adjacent area and local branches of national charities.

Heaning Wood, Ulverston, Cumbria LA12 7NZ

Tel: 01229 580349

Email: info@sirjohnfisherfoundation. org.uk

Website: www. sirjohnfisherfoundation.org.uk

Correspondent: Dr David Hart Jackson, Trust Secretary

Trustees: Daniel P Tindall, Chair; Diane S Meacock; Sir David Hardy; Rowland F Hart Jackson.

CC Number: 277844

Information available

Accounts were available from the Charity Commission. The foundation also has a clear and simple website.

The foundation was established by a deed of settlement made in 1979 by the founders, Sir John and Lady Maria Fisher. The foundation gives grants to charities concerned with the Furness peninsula and local branches of UK charities.

It supports charitable causes and projects in six main categories; these are:

- maritime
- medical and disability
- education
- music
- arts
- community projects in and around Barrow-in-Furness.

The foundation gives priority to applying its income to projects and causes based in Barrow-in-Furness and in the surrounding Furness area. Exceptionally, occasional community projects from the remainder of Cumbria and North Lancashire will be considered. Some projects are supported nationally, particularly maritime projects and some music and art projects. The foundation also supports nationally a limited amount of high quality medical research.

Capital and revenue funding is available for up to three years. Grants do not usually exceed £10,000.

In 2009/10 the foundation had assets of £34 million and an income of £1.2 million. During the year there were 137 grants made totalling £896,000. Grants were broken down as follows:

Local beneficiaries included: Lancaster University (£119,000 in total); Barrow District Scouts (£40,000); Cancercare (£35,000 in total); St Mathews Community Hall (£29,000); the Wordsworth Trust (£20,000); Blackwell Sailing (£15,000); Lakeland Art Trust (£12,000); Dance Resource Ltd (£10,000); Rumic Foundation Trust (£8,500); Citizens Advice – South Lakeland (£6,300); Resolve Mediation Service (£3,000); Kidsafe UK (£1,500); and the Ulverston Outsiders (£100).

National beneficiaries included: National Maritime Museum – Cornwall (£60,000 in total); University of Dundee (£25,000); London Handel Society Ltd (£15,000); Chemical Industries Education Centre (£12,000); Imperial War Museum (£10,000); Barnardo's (£7,500); Changing Faces (£5,000); British Wireless for the Blind Fund (£2,500); and Brain and Spinal Injury Centre (£500).

Exclusions

The trustees will generally not fund:

- individuals
- sponsorship
- expeditions
- promotion of religion
- places of worship
- animal welfare
- retrospective funding
- pressure groups

- community projects outside Barrow-in-Furness and the surrounding area (except occasional projects in Cumbria or North Lancashire or if they fall within one of the other categories supported by the foundation).

Applications

Applications should be made by submitting a completed application form, either by email or post, together with all relevant information (set out on the application form) to the secretary at least six weeks in advance of the trustees' meeting. The trustees meet at the beginning of May and the beginning of November each year.

Urgent grants for small amounts (less than £4,000) can be considered between meetings, but the trustees would expect an explanation as to why the application could not be considered at a normal meeting.

Applicants are welcome to contact the secretary for an informal discussion before submitting an application for funding.

The trustees expect to receive feedback from the organisations they support, to help in their decision making process. Organisations are asked to provide a brief one page report about nine months after receipt of a grant (or when the specific project assisted has been completed). A feedback form is available from the foundation's website.

Fisherbeck Charitable Trust

Christian, homelessness, welfare, education, heritage

£457,000 (2009/10)

Beneficial area

Worldwide.

Home Farm House, 63 Ferringham Lane, Ferring, Worthing, West Sussex BN12 5LL

Tel: 01903 241027

Email: ian@roffeyhomes.com

Correspondent: The Trustees

CC Number: 1107287

Information available

Accounts were available at the Charity Commission.

This trust was registered with the Charity Commission in December 2004, and it is the vehicle for the charitable activities of the Cheal family, owners of Roffey Homes developers.

> The charity's objects are to encourage charitable giving from the extended Cheal family and to apply these funds to the making of grants for the following charitable objects:
> - the advancement of the Christian religion
> - support the provision of accommodation for the homeless and meeting their ongoing needs
> - the relief of poverty
> - the advancement of education
> - to encourage conservation of the environment and the preservation of our heritage
> - such other charitable objects in such manner as the trustees shall from time to time decide.

In 2009/10 the trust had assets of £239,000 and an income of £492,000, mostly from donations and gifts. Grants were made to 71 organisations totalling £457,000, most of which went to organisations.

There were 21 grants of £5,000 or more listed in the accounts, with most beneficiaries receiving support each year. Beneficiaries included: Tear Fund (£48,000); Christian Viewpoint for Men (£45,000); Urban Saints (£40,000); Bible Society (£30,000); Evangelical Alliance (£21,000); Release International (£20,000); Hope for Lugazi (£15,000); Resource (£15,000); Church Pastoral Aid Society (£6,000); and St Peter's Church Appeal (£5,000).

Other grants to organisations of £5,000 and under totalled £60,000. One individual received a grant of £5,600.

Exclusions

Grants are only made to individuals known to the trust or in exceptional circumstances.

Applications

In writing to the correspondent, although please note that the trust states: 'We are a small family trust and having built up a portfolio of donees (who we access yearly), we rarely add or subtract more or less than about five changes.'

The Fishmongers' Company's Charitable Trust

General, in particular education, relief of poverty and disability

£682,000 to organisations (2010)

Beneficial area

UK, however this refers to charities whose objects extend throughout England. Special interest in the City of London and its adjacent boroughs.

The Fishmongers' Company, Fishmongers' Hall, London Bridge, London EC4R 9EL
Tel: 020 7626 3531
Fax: 020 7929 1389
Email: clerk@fishhall.org.uk
Website: www.fishhall.org.uk
Correspondent: Peter Woodward, Clerk
Trustee: The Worshipful Company of Fishmongers.
CC Number: 263690

Information available

Accounts were available at the Charity Commission.

The trust was established in 1972 for general charitable purposes and its focus is in the areas of education, relief of poverty and disability, almshouses, fishery related organisations, the environment and heritage.

The trust provides the following guidelines for applicants:
- applications will be accepted only from charities operating within the City of London and the boroughs of Camden, Hackney, Islington, Lambeth, Southwark, Tower Hamlets and Westminster
- applications will be accepted from charities concerned with education, the relief of hardship and disability, heritage and the environment. Preference will be given to education
- applications will normally be accepted only from charities whose annual income does not exceed £500,000
- preference will be given to applications where the Company's donation would make a significant impact
- preference will be given to charities seeking to raise funds for a specific project rather than for administration or general purposes
- applications from individual educational establishments will be accepted only if they are either of national importance or if their principal purpose is to cater for disabled students
- donations will normally be made on a one-off basis, although successful applicants may re-apply after three years.

In 2010 the trust had assets of £18.3 million and an income of £1.6 million. Grants were made to organisations totalling £682,000, and were broken down as follows:

Education	£381,000
Hardship	£199,500
Fishery	£73,500
Disability and medical	£21,500
Heritage and environment	£6,000

Beneficiaries included: Gresham's School (£281,000); Jesus Hospital Almshouses (£100,000); Harrietsham Almshouses (£50,500); Rivers & Fisheries Trusts of Scotland (£21,500); New Model School (£20,000); Salmon & Trout Association (£11,500); Bristol Charities (£10,000); Royal College of Music (£8,000); Royal National Mission to Deep Sea Fishermen (£7,000); Against Breast Cancer (£5,000); Bermuda Institute of Ocean Sciences (£4,000); Prostate UK and St Mungo's (£2,000 each); and the British Museum and Age Concern Westminster (£1,000 each).

The trust also made grants totalling £91,500 to individuals.

Exclusions

No grants to individuals except for educational purposes. Ad hoc educational grants are not awarded to applicants who are over 19 years old.

Applications

In writing to the correspondent. Meetings take place three times a year in March, June/July and October/November, and applications should be received a month in advance. No applications are considered within three years of a previous grant application being successful. Unsuccessful applications are not acknowledged.

Common applicant mistakes

'Submitting applications that do not meet the stated criteria.'

The Football Association Youth Trust

Sports

£1.3 million (2009/10)

Beneficial area

UK.

The Football Association, Wembley Stadium, London HA9 0WS
Tel: 0844 980 8200
Email: mike.appleby@thefa.com
Correspondent: Mike Appleby, Secretary
Trustees: Raymond G Berridge; Barry W Bright; Geoff Thompson; Jack Perks.
CC Number: 265131

Information available

Accounts were available at the Charity Commission.

The principal activity of the trust continues to be the organisation or provision of facilities which will enable pupils of schools and universities and young people under the age of 21 in the UK to play association football or other games and sports including the provision of equipment, lectures, training colleges, playing fields or indoor accommodation.

In 2009/10 the trust had assets of £1.3 million and an income of £37,500. Grants were made during the year totalling £1.3 million. Grants were broken down as follows:

Girls' Centre of Excellence	1	£1 million
Schools and universities	4	£204,500
County Football Associations	48	£77,500
Other	2	£1,300

Applications

In writing to the correspondent. Grants are made throughout the year. There are no application forms, but a copy of the most recent accounts should be sent.

The Football Foundation

Grassroots football, community, education

£40.5 million (2009/10)

Beneficial area

England.

Whittington House, 19–30 Alfred Place, London WC1E 7EA
Tel: 08453 454555
Fax: 08453 457057
Email: enquiries@footballfoundation.org.uk
Website: www.footballfoundation.org.uk
Correspondent: Robert Booker, Director of Finance
Trustees: Richard Scudamore; Roger Burden; Peter McCormick; Philip Smith; Clive Sterling.
CC Number: 1079309

Information available

Accounts were available from the Charity Commission. The foundation also has a clear and informative website.

The Football Foundation is the UK's largest sports charity funded by the Premier League, The FA, Sport England and the Government.

The foundation's objectives are:

- to put into place a new generation of modern facilities in parks, local leagues and schools
- to provide capital/revenue support to increase participation in grassroots football
- to strengthen the links between football and the community and to harness its potential as a force for good in society.

Programmes

According to the foundation's website, the foundation aims to achieve its objectives through the following programmes:

Facilities Scheme

The facilities scheme gives grants for projects that:

- Improve facilities for football and other sport in local communities.
- Sustain or increase participation amongst children and adults, regardless of background age, or ability.
- Help children and adults to develop their physical, mental, social and moral capacities through regular participation in sport.

The types of facilities we give money for include:

- grass pitches drainage/improvements
- pavilions, clubhouses and changing rooms
- artificial turf pitches and multi-use games areas
- fixed floodlights for artificial pitches.

We also provide development (revenue) grants to deliver football development associated with the new facility e.g. coaching, football development officer etc.

The maximum grant available from the foundation for each facilities project is £500,000. However, applicants must show they have tried hard to get other funding for the project and that there is no further money available.

Build the Game

The Build the Game scheme provides grants for small facility projects. We aim to assess applications to this scheme within 12 weeks (once we have all the information from you that we need).

The scheme has flexible criteria and there are many eligible items, so long as it is the right project for the right applicant. All projects must demonstrate they can support the growth and retention of grassroots football.

A project that is considered to be an annual running cost, does not have appropriate insurance or meet basic child protection or health and safety requirements will not be eligible for grant aid.

All applications must have security of tenure either by freehold or leasehold. A minimum of 10 year security of tenure is required by leasehold.

The maximum grant available is £50,000 and there is no limit to the total cost of a project this could contribute towards.

Applicants must demonstrate a financial need for grant aid and contribute all of their own available money to the project. Financial contributions from other funding organisations are also expected.

All applicants must receive advice and support from their County Football Association before applying, or they will be returned.

Grow the Game

Grow the Game provides funding for projects that use football to increase participation by both players and volunteers. This is done by supporting the costs associated with providing **new** activity.

Grow the Game is an extremely popular scheme and the assessment process is competitive, therefore we strongly recommend that before making an application you contact your local County Football Association's Development Manager to discuss your project.

Applications are welcome from organisations that are 'not for profit' and planning to set up two new football teams over the next two years. We will not fund individuals or educational establishments.

Organisations must have a signed constitution, child protection policy, equal opportunities policy and income/expenditure records.

Please note organisations that have an existing Community Small Grant or Grow the Game grant are not eligible to apply for a Grow the Game grant.

Organisations can only apply for one Grow the Game grant every four years.

Grow the Game provides funding to contribute towards a combination of the following essential costs associated with providing new football activity:
- facility hire
- hire of FA qualified coaches and referees
- CRB checks
- affiliation fees
- league entry
- first aid kits
- promotion and publicity
- FA coaching courses.

The foundation does not fund retrospectively and will not consider applications for costs that have already been made or are due before an offer of a grant has been awarded. There is no funding available for groups wishing to apply for charitable status. No partnership funding will be requested. Organisations are able to receive a £5,000 grant over two or three years with financial support being reduced in the second or third year of the project.

Please note: this scheme was closed at the time of writing (December 2011) – check the foundation's website for the current status of the scheme and application deadlines.

Corporate Partner Programme – Barclays Space for Sport

Barclays Spaces for Sports has delivered 200 sustainable sports sites, awarded more than 4,000 coaching packs and given more than half a million people across the UK the opportunity to benefit.

The Barclays Spaces for Sports scheme is a partnership between Barclays, Groundwork and the Football Foundation. Barclays has committed more than £37 million to Barclays Spaces for Sports since its inception, along with a further £30 million donated and raised by partners the Football Foundation

For further information contact James Taylor from the Barclays Spaces for Sports Programme at the Football Foundation on 0845 345 4555 ext: 4261, or visit the Barclays' Spaces for Sports website (group.barclays.com/Citizenship/Community-Investment/Community-programmes/Barclays-Spaces-for-Sports).

Football Stadia Improvement Fund

The Football Stadia Improvement Fund (FSIF) provides grant aid to clubs in the Football League, the Conference and the National League System, down to step 7 and below, that want to improve their facilities for players, officials and spectators.

There are two levels of funding: Football League Clubs and National League System Clubs

Please discuss your project with your FSIF Technical Advisor and Programme Manager before applying for a grant.

We have published eight technical data sheets that offer you step by step advice on planning your project and give detail minimum specifications on various aspects of facilities. It is essential that your project complies with these data sheets.

We have also published *Accessible Stadia*, a good practice guide to the design of facilities that meet the needs of disabled spectators and other users. The publication has been funded by the FSIF supporter of the Football Foundation, and the Football Licensing Authority (FLA).

Extra Time

Funded by the Football Foundation and Sport Relief, and supported by Age UK, the Extra Time programme uses the power of football to target older people aged 55 plus; and delivers social inclusion and physical activity projects nationwide through Premier League and Football League club community schemes.

Following the success of the two year pilot the Football Foundation and Sport Relief launched 'Extra Time: Phase two' in September 2010, Phase two extends the programme by a further two years funding activity; and will grow the programme to around 30 community schemes.

Objectives

Older people are a group that both the Football Foundation and Sport Relief wish to engage with and this project tackles two important issues for older people, physical health emotional wellbeing and social isolation. The main aims of this programme are:
- to provide exercise opportunities so as to increase physical activity. Physical activity improves both physical health and emotional wellbeing. It is one of the most important factors in maintaining a good quality of life
- to provide a programme that improves muscle strength, balance and mobility
- to provide social networking opportunities which can help address some of the social exclusion and isolation issues faced by older people
- to increase the target groups interest and connections with the professional game
- to create a local legacy of participation that will be carried forward for many years in the community.

Project progress

The Extra Time programme was launched in May 2008 and opened for applications from the Premier League and Football League club community schemes. The programme was oversubscribed and during the first year, 15 club community schemes were successful in obtaining grants of up to £10,000. Seven further clubs were successful in the second year of the pilot. Phase two sees a further five club community schemes granted funding in the first year and five more in the second year, making a total of 29 club community schemes.

Mayor of London: Facility Fund

The Mayor of London: Facility Fund is part of the Mayor's commitment to deliver a sporting legacy from the 2012 Olympic and Paralympic Games.

The overall aim of the Mayor of London: Facility Fund is to raise participation levels in sport in London through the funding of sports facilities. The fund will help to provide affordable, good quality local facilities within local communities.

The Facility Fund is an integral part of 'A Sporting Future for London', the Mayor's 2012 legacy plan, which was unveiled in 2009 by the London Mayor Boris Johnson and his Commissioner for Sport, Kate Hoey. The plan sets out four key goals:

1 to get more people active
2 to transform the sporting infrastructure
3 to build capacity and skills
4 to maximise the benefits of sport to our society.

As a means of achieving Goal Two, the Football Foundation is delighted to continue managing the Mayor of London: Facility Fund on behalf of City Hall. The overall aim of the Mayor of London: Facility Fund is to raise participation levels in sport in London through the funding of sports facilities.

The fund will have several objectives, namely:

▶ to provide investment to support the development of new sports facilities or the refurbishment of existing facilities with a particular focus on small, community, park or estate-based projects

▶ to increase the number and breadth of target groups engaged in sport

▶ to prioritise projects for funding that are clearly addressing shortfalls in provision

▶ to support the development of multi-sport facilities that are a clear priority for the relevant sports

▶ to support projects that are able to demonstrate their sustainability, long term viability (for example through the co-location of services) and offer good value for money

▶ to support projects that, in addition to increasing participation rates, seek to address specific retention issues that are affecting their club/organisation or that try to retain participants amongst certain target groups (e.g. women)

▶ to advocate and promote the protection of London's playing fields and other existing sports facilities against unnecessary loss

▶ to explore ways to increase the use of existing sports facilities, with a particular focus on community usage of school and FE/HE sports provision

▶ to encourage the use of London's parks as places in which to participate in sport.

From April 2010 – March 2013, a number of funding rounds will be available to which eligible organisations can apply. For further enquiries email: pslfacilityfund@ footballfoundation.org.uk

Grantmaking in 2009/10

In 2009/10 the foundation had a total income of £46.9 million, which included unrestricted income of: £15 million from Sport England; £12.2 million from the Football Association; and £12.2 million from the Premier League. Grants were made across all programmes totalling

£40.5 million (£54.7 million in 2008/09).

Beneficiaries of the largest 100 grants were listed in the accounts, including: London Borough of Hackney (£1.9 million); North East Lincolnshire Council (£1 million); Evesham United Football Club (£700,000); City of Wolverhampton College (£557,000); South Manchester Sports Club (£495,000); Stoke Gabriel Football Club (£453,000); Oakworth Juniors Football Club (£416,000); Tresham Institute of Further & Higher Education (£300,000); Welbeck Miners Welfare Trust (£259,500); London Borough of Hillingdon (£250,000); Mole Valley District Council (£198,000); Norfolk County FA (£157,000); Witchford Village College (£121,000); and Norton Parish Council (£100,000).

Applications

Application forms and guidance notes are available on request directly from the foundation or downloadable from the website. See the general section for details of each scheme.

You can also apply for a grant through the foundation's website.

Forever Manchester (The Community Foundation for Greater Manchester)

General

£4.5 million (2010/11)

Beneficial area

Greater Manchester.

5th Floor, Speakers House, 39 Deansgate, Manchester M3 2BA
Tel: 0161 214 0940
Fax: 0161 214 0941
Email: enquiries@ communityfoundation.co.uk
Website: www.forevermanchester. com

Correspondent: Nick Massey, Chief Executive Officer
Trustees: John Sandford; Chris Hirst; Richard Hogben; Tony Burns; Simon Webber; Jo Farrell; Han-Son Lee; Sandra Lindsay; Natalie Qureshi.
CC Number: 1017504

Information available

Accounts were on file at the Charity Commission. Full information is available on the foundation's website.

The foundation's income originates, as with many community foundations, from a range of mostly statutory sources and each fund has its own criteria and conditions. With over 60 funding streams the foundation distributes grants to community groups, projects and social entrepreneurs across Greater Manchester. Many of the groups supported by the foundation have never applied for funding before and are run by volunteers. For easy accessibility to the process, a dedicated grants team has been established. The team gives advice, processes applications and monitors the impact the foundation's grants have in the local community to ensure real needs are met and lives improved.

The foundation serves the metropolitan borough areas of Bury, Bolton, Manchester, Oldham, Rochdale, Salford, Stockport, Tameside, Trafford, and Wigan. This adds up to a total population of over 2.6 million and an estimated 20,000 voluntary and community groups operating throughout the area.

The foundation's medium to long term strategy objectives are:

▶ to continue to grow the endowment with a vision to building a permanent source of community capital in excess of £50 million

▶ to make grant making more effective

▶ to meet the present taxing economic situation

▶ to develop the Forever Manchester brand

▶ to maintain donor levels

▶ to continue to invest in the training and development of staff

The foundation gives priority to projects which:

- are run by local volunteers who wish to improve the circumstances of individuals and communities in economically/socially excluded and/or deprived areas of Greater Manchester
- have no access to a professional fundraiser and experience difficulty in attracting funding from other sources
- encourage involvement of local residents in improving, designing, identifying and implementing community activities
- promote voluntary participation and social inclusion as well as community involvement and self-help
- meet and demonstrate an emerging or immediate need and serve to build the community's awareness
- do not duplicate an existing provision or service (if the project resembles an existing provision, you will be expected to explain why your services are needed in addition to existing provision or clarify how they are different).

During the year, the foundation had an income of £8.6 million and assets of £9.4 million. Grants were made totalling £4.5 million

The foundation manages a large number of different funds, some of which cover the whole of Greater Manchester, such as the Seed Grants fund, and some of which are specific to the separate boroughs of: Bolton, Bury, Manchester, Oldham, Rochdale, Salford, Stockport, Tameside, Trafford and Wigan. Organisations should check that they fulfil the eligibility conditions before applying and contact the trust if they are unsure.

As there are so many different funds, and they are regularly opening and closing for applications or finishing, they are not detailed here. Instead, applicants should check the foundation's very detailed website which has straightforward details of each fund including the application processes, which are generally downloadable forms that are specific to each fund.

Grantmaking in 2010/11

During the year, the foundation distributed £4.5 million in grants to 872 community groups and projects with the average grant being £4,800. 64 % of funding was in the top 20% of areas in Greater Manchester identified as suffering from high levels of health deprivation and disability. Half of the grants went to groups which had not previously received funding and one third benefited young people aged 13–18 years old. They were also a Charity Award Winner for being the Best UK Grant-giver.

No grants list was included in the annual report which is disappointing, especially for a fund of this size, however some case studies were available on the website.

Beneficiaries included: Tindall Street Allotments (£40,000); Groundwork-Oldham and Rochdale (£22,000); Brinnington Samba band (£5,000); Men Behaving Dadly (£4,800); Hope Carr Morris Dancers (£3,700); Abraham Moss Warriors JFC (£2,500); Chorlton Park Regeneration Group; Have Your Say Community Publishing Project (£2000 each); Droylsden Amateur Boxing Club (£1,600); Caribbean Elders (£900).

Exclusions

The foundation will not support the following:

- organisations and projects outside the Greater Manchester area
- organisations trading for profit or intending to redistribute grant awards
- major capital requests, i.e. building and construction work
- requests that will replace or enhance statutory provision
- academic or medical research and equipment
- overseas travel
- promotion of religious or political beliefs
- retrospective grants
- projects that fall within statutory sector responsibility
- sponsorship or fundraising events
- contributions to large/major appeals (where the application sum would not cover at least 75% of the total project cost)
- holidays and social outings (except in cases of specific disablement or proven benefit to a community or group of people)
- local branches of national charities unless locally managed, financially autonomous and not beneficiaries of national marketing or promotion
- more than one application at a time for the same project.
- organisations with an income of over £150,000 per annum
- organisations without a governing document/constitution

Applications

The foundation's website provides full guidelines for each of the programmes for which organisations can apply. It also provides application and monitoring forms for each programme.

If you are applying for a grant for the first time, or if you would like advice before making an application, contact the foundation who will be happy to provide you with advice. Applications will only be accepted if submitted on the foundation's application form. All sections of the form must be completed even if the information is supplied in the form of a report, leaflet and so on. The foundation prefers not to receive applications by fax; completed forms should be returned by post. The decision of the foundation's trustees is final and no discussion will be entered into. The foundation will, however, try to provide helpful feedback to both successful and unsuccessful applicants.

Applicants are requested to provide copies of the organisation's constitution, and a copy of the latest, relevant annual accounts and the last two bank statements with their applications. Decisions are almost always given within three months but the exact time will often depend on a number of factors and not just when the appropriate committee next meets.

One of our grants administrators may contact you for further information or to discuss your application with you. Contact the foundation directly for up-to-date information on deadlines for programmes and the dates of panel meetings.

The Donald Forrester Trust

General charitable purposes

£845,000 (2009/10)

Beneficial area
UK and overseas.

Lancaster House, 7 Elmfield Road, Bromley, Kent BR1 1LT
Tel: 020 8461 8014
Correspondent: Christopher A Perkins, Trustee
Trustees: Wendy J Forrester, Anthony J Smee; Michael B Jones; Hilary J Porter; Christopher A Perkins.
CC Number: 295833

Information available
Accounts were available at the Charity Commission.

When Donald Forrester, a successful London businessman and company director, died in 1985, his widow Gwyneth set up the Donald Forrester Charitable Trust which was established in 1986. The trust's grantmaking now covers a wide range of categories. Most grants go to well known (and often, though not exclusively, national) charities.

The trust is, for the most part, reliant on income from Films & Equipments Limited and the increased gift aid and the maintained dividend from the company has allowed the trust to continue to increase total charitable giving.

In 2009/10 the trust had assets of over £7.7 million and an income of £889,000, both increases on the previous year. As a result, the trust increased grant expenditure during the year to £845,000 (£650,000 in 2008/09) awarded to 143 organisations.

Grants were broken down as follows:

Overseas	17	£110,000
Children and youth (social welfare and education)	14	£95,000
Community care and social welfare	17	£90,000
Physical and mental disability	15	£80,000
Medical research	14	£80,000
Medical relief and welfare	11	£60,000
Blind and deaf	8	£60,000
Older people's welfare	10	£55,000
Services and ex-services	9	£55,000
Hospitals and hospices	7	£40,000
Animals and birds	5	£30,000
Children and youth (medical)	5	£30,000
Culture, heritage, environment and sport	5	£25,000
Other	5	£25,000
Maritime	1	£5,000

Most of the beneficiaries received grants for £5,000. Beneficiaries across all categories included: Great Ormond Street Hospital Children's Charity and Disasters Emergency Committee (£15,000 each); RSPCA, NSPCC, and the Blond McIndoe Research Foundation (£10,000 each); and Battersea Dogs and Cats Home, Marine Conservation Society, National Deaf Children's Society, Foundation for the Study of Infant Deaths, Volunteer Reading Help, Housing the Homeless Central Fund, Moorfields Eye Hospital Development Fund, RNLI, Down's Syndrome Association, Psychiatry Research Trust, Mental Health Foundation, Friends of the Elderly, Médecins Sans Frontières, Royal British Legion and All Souls Clubhouse (£5,000 each).

Exclusions
No grants to individuals.

Applications
The trust supports a substantial number of charities on a regular basis. We are informed that regrettably, detailed applications, which place 'an intolerable strain' on administrative resources, cannot be considered. It is suggested that very brief details of an application should be submitted to the correspondent on one side of A4.

The trustees normally meet twice a year to consider and agree on the grants which are paid half yearly. There are no specific requirements under the trust deed and over the years the trustees have supported a wide range of national and international charities and endeavoured to achieve a balance between the large institutions and the smaller charities that experience greater difficulty in fund raising. The trustees have developed a fairly substantial list of charities that are supported on a regular basis, but new proposals, both regular and 'one-off' are considered at each meeting.

Common applicant mistakes
'Sending too much information: applications need to be brief and concise; wastage: sending annual reports and accounts when they are available online; and paying large letter rates for one piece of paper.'

Gwyneth Forrester Trust

General

£425,000 (2009/10)

Beneficial area
England and Wales.

Lancaster House, 7 Elmfield Road, Bromley, Kent BR1 1LT
Tel: 020 8461 8014
Correspondent: Christopher Perkins, Trustee
Trustees: Wendy J Forrester; Anthony J Smee; Michael B Jones; Christopher Perkins.
CC Number: 1080921

Information available
Accounts were available at the Charity Commission.

Established in May 2000, the trustees support a specific charitable sector each year.

In 2009/10 the trust had assets of £21.1 million and an income of £384,500. Grants were made to 8 organisations during the year totalling £425,000. During the year the trust focused on organisations involved with research into strokes and heart disease and charities helping sufferers of those conditions.

No information was available on the future focus of the trust's grant-making because, as the trust states: 'once the charitable sector is chosen, we research that sector and produce a list of possibles and then contact the individual charities to discuss with them their particular needs and any specific projects they have in hand. These are then discussed and the final grant list is decided'.

Exclusions
No grants to individuals.

Applications

The trust has previously stated that 'applications for aid cannot be considered'.

The Foyle Foundation

Arts and learning

£5.2 million (2009/10)

Beneficial area

UK.

Rugby Chambers, 2 Rugby Street, London WC1N 3QU

Tel: 020 7430 9119

Fax: 020 7430 9830

Email: info@foylefoundation.org.uk

Website: www.foylefoundation.org.uk

Correspondent: David Hall, Chief Executive

Trustees: Michael Smith; Kathryn Skoyles; Sir Peter Duffell; Roy Amlot.

CC Number: 1081766

Information available

Accounts were available from the Charity Commission. The foundation also has a clear and helpful website.

Summary

The foundation was formed under the will of the late Christina Foyle. She was the daughter of William Foyle who, with his brother, founded the family owned bookshop Foyles in Charing Cross Road, London, which she managed after her father's death. The foundation is an independent charity and there is no connection with Foyle's Bookshop.

The foundation makes around 200 grants each year, most of which are for between £10,000 and £50,000, in the fields of arts and learning.

Guidelines

The foundation has a main grants scheme and a small grants scheme, and provides the following guidelines:

Main Grants Scheme

Arts

The foundation seeks applications that make a strong artistic case for support in either the performing or visual arts. Our Arts programme has a twofold purpose to help sustain the arts and to support projects that particularly help to deliver artistic vision. We look for value for money and sustainability in projects that we support. Typical areas of support include:

- helping to make the arts more accessible by developing new audiences, supporting tours, festivals and arts educational projects
- encouraging new work and supporting young and emerging artists
- building projects that improve or re-equip existing arts venues (rather than construction of new facilities, although this will not be excluded)
- projects that reduce overheads or which help generate additional revenue.

Generally, we make grants for specific projects/activities. We will consider applications for core funding (but generally only from smaller organisations or from those not receiving recurrent revenue funding from the Arts Council or local authorities).

Please note that community arts activity will not generally be supported.

Learning

The foundation will support projects which facilitate the acquisition of knowledge and which have a long-term strategic impact. Key areas for support are:

- libraries, museums and archives
- special educational needs and learning difficulties
- projects that reduce overheads or which help generate additional revenue will also be considered.

For state funded schools our main initiative will be The Foyle School Libraries Scheme [special guidance notes are available from the foundation's website]. Dedicated schools catering for those with Special Educational Needs (SEN) may also be supported. Private schools will not generally be supported.

Citizenship, esteem-building, training, skills acquisition to aid employment, independent living, early learning projects or playgroups will not generally be considered.

Small Grants Scheme

Our Small Grants Scheme is designed to support smaller charities in the UK, especially those working at grass roots and local community level, in any field, across a wide range of activities. Please note we are not able to support individuals.

Applications are welcomed from charities that have an annual turnover of less than £100,000 per annum. Larger or national charities will normally not be considered under this scheme. Nor will the Scheme generally support charities that are able consistently to generate operational surpluses or which have been able to build up unrestricted reserves to a level equivalent to three months turnover.

If applying on behalf of a state school please refer to the state schools webpage on the foundation's website.

Please note that competition for funding is intense and we receive many more applications that we are able to fund.

Grantmaking in 2009/10

In 2009/10 the foundation had assets of £74.1 million and an income of £3.6 million. There were 207 grants made during the year totalling £5.2 million, broken down as follows:

Arts	76	£2.6 million
Learning	62	£2.1 million
Health*	2	£198,000
Small grants scheme	66	£313,500

* Please note that there is no longer a specific priority for health-related organisations in the main grants scheme and these are likely to have been previous commitments.

The foundation provides details of major grants on its website. The following beneficiaries received major grants in 2010 (some of which will have been made in the 2010/11 financial year).

Cheltenham Art Gallery & Museum Development Trust (£300,000), towards the £6.3 million development to expand the museum to show more of its collections and provide improved public and education facilities; Chetham's School of Music – Manchester (£250,000), towards the creation of a new state-of-the-art music and academic building; London Academy of Music and Dramatic Art (£250,000), towards the fundraising campaign to mark the 150th anniversary of LAMDA and the capital redevelopment of the Talgarth site; Royal Welsh College of Music and Drama – Cardiff (£250,000), towards their new facilities which include a new concert hall, theatre and drama rehearsal studios; Turner Contemporary Art Trust – Margate (£250,000), towards the new contemporary visual arts gallery; The Courtauld Institute of Art Fund – London (£150,000 over three years), towards cataloguing and combining its separate holdings to create and open up the Renaissance and Baroque Special Collections; City & Guilds of London Art School (£125,000), towards Phase 1 of work on the Kennington site, for the refurbishment and improvements to a row of six Grade 2 listed Georgian terrace houses; The National Gallery – London (£125,000), to purchase an ATR-FTIR imaging system to analyse the material components of paintings, inform conservation treatment and research how paintings were created; Scott Polar Research Institute – Cambridge (£125,000), towards the refurbishment of the Polar Museum and its associated curatorial and storage spaces; Museum of London (£112,000), towards creation of the new Inspiring London Gallery, part of the redevelopment of the lower floor galleries; Black Cultural Archives – London (£100,000), towards the Raleigh Hall Development Project to create a national black heritage and archive centre; The Cambridge Foundation – Cambridge (£100,000), towards the extension for Kettle's Yard Museum expanding their educational and outreach provision; English Heritage (£100,000), towards the conservation, digitisation and display of a collection of 95,000 images from the Aerofilms Collection; and Historic Royal Palaces – London (£100,000), towards the re-development of Kensington Palace and opening up its environs and the expansion of public access to the building.

Exclusions

No grants to individuals, organisations which are not registered charities or for international work. No retrospective funding.

Applications

The following guidance is taken from the foundation's website:

Please note that competition is intense; we receive many more applications than we are able to fund. Also the Foundation only supports charities and is not able to support individuals.

Guidelines and application forms are available [from the foundation's website]. Charities wishing to make an application for funding should download and read the appropriate guidelines for applicants before completing and signing the appropriate application form and sending this together with the supporting information requested.

Applications are acknowledged by email or by post within two weeks of receipt. If you do not receive this acknowledgement, please contact the foundation to confirm safe receipt of your request.

When to Apply
Applications are accepted all year round. We have no deadlines. Except for capital projects, it may take up to four months, occasionally longer, to receive a decision from the trustees, so please apply well in advance of your funding requirements.

Capital Projects
Please note for capital projects seeking more than £50,000 the foundation will now only consider these twice per year in the spring and autumn. Therefore it could be six months or more before we take a decision on your project.

Small Grants Scheme
How much can you apply for?
We plan to make one year grants of between £1,000 and £10,000 to charities which can demonstrate that such a grant will make a significant difference to their work. If you cannot demonstrate this, your application will be declined. No multi-year funding awards will be made.

Other Information
There are no deadlines for submission. Applications will be received at all times but it may take up to four months to obtain a decision from trustees. Please apply well in advance of your requirements.

All applications will be acknowledged but in order to reduce administration, usually we will not send declination letters. If you have not heard from the foundation within four months of your application being acknowledged, you should assume that your application has been unsuccessful.

The Hugh Fraser Foundation

General

£1.4 million (2009/10)

Beneficial area

UK, especially western or deprived areas of Scotland.

Turcan Connell WS, Princes Exchange, 1 Earl Grey Street, Edinburgh EH3 9EE
Tel: 0131 228 8111
Correspondent: Katrina Muir, Trust Administrator
Trustees: Dr Kenneth Chrystie; Belinda Ann Hanson; Patricia Fraser; Blair Smith.
SC Number: SC009303

Information available
Accounts were provided by the trust.

This foundation was established in 1960 with general charitable purposes. Its annual accounts give the following guidance on the general grant making policy:

The trustees' policy is to support a broad range of charitable projects particularly in Scotland but also elsewhere at the discretion of the trustees.

The trustees consider that grants to large, highly publicised national appeals are not likely to be as effective a use of funds as grants to smaller and more focused charitable appeals.

The trustees also consider that better use of the funds can be made by making grants to charitable bodies to assist them with their work, than by making a large number of grants to individuals.

The trustees are prepared to enter into commitments over a period of time by making grants in successive years, often to assist in new initiatives which can maintain their own momentum once they have been established for a few years.

The foundation makes donations to charities working in many different sectors principally hospitals, schools and universities, arts organisations and organisations working with the disabled, the underprivileged and the aged.

Note: In 2007 the Hugh Fraser Foundation merged with the Emily Fraser Trust, a related charity. As a result, the trustees will, in exceptional circumstances, help individuals and the dependents of individuals who were or are engaged in the drapery and allied trades and the printing, publishing, books and stationery, newspaper and allied trades in the UK.

In 2009/10 the foundation had assets of £54.4 million and an income of £1.6 million. Grants paid during the year totalled £1.4 million; this included £30,000 paid to 12 individuals.

The foundation provided the following analysis of grants to institutions which includes future commitments and pledges:

Education and training	42	£358,000
Disadvantaged and disabled people	114	£324,000
Medical research facilities	30	£223,000
Musical, theatrical and visual arts	51	£171,000

Elderly, homeless and hospices	29	£81,000
Youth organisations	24	£65,500
Conservation and environment	17	£35,000
Religion	8	£26,500
Miscellaneous	18	£82,500

The beneficiaries listed in the accounts were: Inspiring Scotland (£200,000); Marie Curie Cancer Care – The Big Build (£100,000); and Scottish Ballet and the Edinburgh University Development Trust – Royal School of Veterinary Studies (£50,000 each).

Exclusions

Grants are only awarded to individuals in exceptional circumstances (see 'general').

Applications

In writing to the correspondent. The trustees meet on a quarterly basis to consider applications.

The Freemasons' Grand Charity

Social welfare, medical research, hospices and overseas emergency aid

£2.5 million in non-Masonic grants (2009/10)

Beneficial area

England, Wales and overseas.

Freemasons Hall, 60 Great Queen Street, London WC2B 5AZ

Tel: 020 7395 9261

Fax: 020 7395 9295

Email: info@the-grand-charity.org

Website: www.grandcharity.org

Correspondent: Ms Laura Chapman, Chief Executive

Trustees: Grahame Elliott; Roderic Mitchell; Peter Griffiths; Sir Stuart Hampson; Paul Richards; Michael Turnbull; John Hornblow; Raymond Larkin; Ian MacBeth; Reginald Rivett; John Woolway; Dr David Mccormick; Raymond Lye; Charles Assad Akle; Tom Hedderson; Dr Richard Dunstan; Geoff Tuck; Terry Baker; Dr Kevin Williams; Laurie Justice; Roger Richmond; Nigel Buchanan; Nigel Pett; Anthony Wood; Timothy

Dallas-Chapman; Judge Hone; Roger Needham; Alexander Stewart.

CC Number: 281942

Information available

Accounts were available at the Charity Commission. The charity also has a clear website.

This is the central charity of all freemasons in England and Wales. It provides grants for four purposes:

- the relief of 'poor and distressed freemasons' and their dependants
- the support of other Masonic charities
- emergency relief work worldwide
- the support of non-Masonic charities in England and Wales.

Guidelines

The following guidance is provided by the charity:

The Freemasons' Grand Charity gives grants principally in the following areas:
- vulnerable people (for example, people with disabilities or healthcare needs, older people and babies)
- medical Research
- youth opportunities
- hospices.

Minor Grants

Core funding grants of between £500 and £5,000 are given to smaller charities whose annual income does not exceed about £1 million. [Minor grants] can be used for the general running or overhead costs of the charity.

Major Grants

Grants of between £5,000 and £50,000 are made only for a designated purpose and generally made to larger, nationwide charities. Funding may be granted for up to three-year periods in certain circumstances where there is evidence of an on-going need for charitable grant funding.
- the average grant size is likely to be between £10,000 and £25,000
- a very few major grants of over £50,000 may be approved each year
- the purpose might be to fund a salary or to deliver a specific project
- grants may be made for capital projects provided the application is for an identifiable element of the project.

Hospice Grants

- Grants are made, on an annual basis, towards the operating costs of hospice services for adults and/or children
- Hospice services in England and Wales that receive 60% or less of their funding from the NHS are eligible to apply

- Individual grants are calculated on the basis of the services provided and the number of beds operated by the hospice
- Grants are not given towards building costs or to hospices that are not yet operational
- Applications must be accompanied by a set of audited accounts, no more than 18 months old

Medical Research Grants

Preference is given to medical research applications from charities that are members of the Association of Medical Research Charities (AMRC). If a charity is not a member of the AMRC its research project should have been peer reviewed in accordance with the guidelines of the AMRC. We recommend that charities applying for a grant to fund medical research should read the AMRC guidance prior to submitting an application.

Youth opportunities

The projects we support provide stability for disadvantaged young people and encourage them to learn new skills and gain knowledge, which will help them towards a better future.

Grants for Religious Buildings

A small number of grants are awarded annually to religious buildings of national importance. Typically the grant will be for no more than £5,000. Please note that The Freemasons' Grand Charity does not accept direct approaches from applicants in this category. Applications are only considered following the recommendation of the Provincial Grand Lodge, which must also be supporting the appeal.

Grantmaking in 2009/10

In 2009/10 the charity had assets of £62.3 million and an income of £22.3 million. Grants were made to 102 non-Masonic charities totalling £2.5 million, and were broken down as follows:

Vulnerable people	£1.1 million
Hospices	£600,000
Medical research	£285,000
Youth opportunities	£253,000
Other small grants less than £10,000	£155,000
Emergency grants	£136,500

A sample of the beneficiaries included:

Medical Research – The Cambridge Foundation – to fund research into the use of alemtuzumab in treating multiple sclerosis (£100,000); Nortwick Park Institute for Medical Research – to fund colonoscopy training and research (£100,000); Association for Spina Bifida Hydrocephalus – to fund research into the use of in utero MRI (£40,000); Spinal Research – to fund research on chondroitinase to enable nerve regrowth at Cambridge University (£25,000).

Vulnerable People – Soldiers, Sailors, Airmen and Families Association (SSAFA)-Forces Help – to be distributed to each of the provinces for presentation locally (£250,000); Grants for Air Ambulances and similar rescue services – 22 grants across the UK and channel islands (£192,000); Beating Bowel Cancer – to fund a specialist nurse advisor and head of patient services (£50,000); Connect – to fund a newsletter for aphasia sufferers (£30,000).

Youth Opportunities – Clubs for Young People – to fund the Do Something Out of School project (£83,000); Centrepoint – to fund the roll-out of the partnering project with local youth homelessness charities (£50,000); Childhood First – to fund a family placement and support scheme in Norfolk (£20,000); and Kidscape – to fund workshops for children at risk of becoming bullies (£15,000).

Hospices – The fund awarded £600,000 to a total of 226 hospices across England, Wales, the Isle of Man and the Channel Islands. The majority of grants were between £1,000 – £3,000 with the largest single grant going to St Christopher's Hospice, London (£8,000).

Emergency grants – Pakistan Floods via British Red Cross (£50,000); Haiti Cholera epidemic via British Red Cross (£25,000); Chile Earthquake via British Red Cross (£20,000); and Haiti Earthquake via Save the Children (£1,500).

Grants less than £10,000 – Refuge and Children with Cystic Fibrosis Dream Holidays (£5,000 each); Disability Law Service and Sand Rose Project (£3,000 each); Duchenne Family Support Group and Survivors of Bereavement by suicide (£2,000 each); and London Narrow Boat Project (£1,500).

Exclusions

Local charities (i.e. serving an individual city or region) should apply to the provincial grand lodge of the region in which they operate,

(these are listed in telephone directories, usually under 'freemasons' or 'masons').

Those not eligible for a grant are:

- individuals (other than for the relief of 'poor and distressed freemasons and their poor and distressed dependants');
- charities that serve an individual region or city, for example, a regional hospital, local church, day centre or primary school;
- organisations not registered with the Charity Commission, except some exempt charities;
- activities that are primarily the responsibility of central or local government or some other responsible body;
- organisations or projects outside of England and Wales;
- animal welfare, the arts or environmental causes;
- charities with sectarian or political objectives;
- charities that are deemed to hold funds in excess of their requirements.

Applications

Application forms are available from the charity's office or from its website. This form must be completed in full accompanied by a copy of the latest annual report and full audited accounts; these must be less than 18 months old.

Hospice grant applications are made on a separate form, available from either the appropriate provincial grand lodge or the trust's office.

Applications may be submitted at any time throughout the year and are considered at meetings held in January, April and July. Acknowledgement of receipt will be made by post.

Applications are not accepted for 'emergency grants' which are made as 'the need arises' and at the trustees' discretion.

The Freshfield Foundation

Environment, healthcare

£820,000 (2009/10)

Beneficial area

UK.

2nd Floor, MacFarlane and Co., Cunard Building, Water Street, Liverpool L3 1DS
Tel: 0151 236 6161
Fax: 0151 236 1095
Email: paulk@macca.co.uk
Correspondent: Paul Kurthausen, Trustee
Trustees: Paul Kurthausen; Patrick A Moores; Mrs Elizabeth J Potter.
CC Number: 1003316

Information available

Accounts were available at the Charity Commission.

The foundation was established in 1991, and aims to support organisations involved in sustainable development, and increasingly, climate change mitigation. In previous years the foundation had a preference for organisations in Merseyside – it would appear that this is no longer the case as the foundation moves to tackle broader issues.

In 2009/10 the foundation had assets of almost £5.9 million and an income of £1.76 million, which included a donation of £1.6 million from the settlor, Patrick Moores. Grants were made to 12 organisations during the year totalling £820,000.

The beneficiaries were: Sustrans (£200,000); Friends of the Earth (£180,000); Formby Land Trust for the Formby Pool Project (£150,000); Forestry Stewardship Council (£60,000); Osteopathic Centre for Children and the New Economics Foundation (£40,000 each); Centre for Tomorrow's Company (£35,000); Afghan Connection and Cambridge University (£30,000 each); Campaign for Better Transport and the Soil Association (£20,000 each); and Cree Valley Community Woodland Trust (£15,000).

The foundation's annual report includes the following information about the trustees' plans for the future:

The following strategy was agreed to increase the level of grantmaking:
- maintain the donations to UK sustainable development at £500,000 per annum
- explore the idea of giving between £100,000 and £500,000 per annum to overseas disaster relief.

Other ideas for future giving were discussed [at the 2010 trustees' meeting], including:
- music education with a link to social and health benefits
- funding the fitting of improved insulation to the homes of disadvantaged families.

Applications

In writing to the correspondent, although the trust states that 'the process of grant making starts with the trustees analysing an area of interest, consistent with the charity's aims and objectives, and then proactively looking for charities that they think can make the greatest contribution'. With this in mind, a letter of introduction to your organisation's work may be more appropriate than a formal application for funding.

The Gannochy Trust

General

£2 million (2009/10)

Beneficial area

Scotland, with a preference for the Perth and Kinross area.

Kincarrathie House Drive, Pitcullen Crescent, Perth PH2 7HX
Tel: 01738 620653
Email: admin@gannochytrust.org.uk
Website: www.gannochytrust.org.uk
Correspondent: Fiona Russell, Secretary
Trustees: Dr Russell Leather, Chair; Mark Webster; Dr James H F Kynaston; Ian W McMillan; Stewart N Macleod; John Markland.
SC Number: SC003133

Information available

Accounts were available from the trust's website which provides the following information:

The Gannochy Trust was founded in 1937 by Arthur Kinmond Bell, known as A K Bell, for charitable and public purposes for the benefit of the community of Perth and its immediate environs as a direct result of his family's successful whisky distilling business.

A K Bell's philanthropy has been developed into one of the more substantial grant-making trusts in Scotland. Originally, the trust contributed to worthy charitable causes solely within Perth and its immediate environs. In 1967 a Scheme of Alterations was approved by the Court of Session to expand its grant-making footprint to the whole of Scotland, but with a preference for Perth and its environs. The trust has made significant contributions to a wide variety of projects across Scotland over many years, ranging from major national flagship projects to smaller, but nonetheless important, community projects.

The trust has four grant-making themes:
1. inspiring young people
2. improving the quality of life of the disadvantaged and vulnerable
3. supporting and developing community amenities
4. care for the natural and man-made environment.

NOTE: Themes 3 and 4 are restricted to Perth and Kinross.

In 2009/10 the trust had assets of £120 million and an income of £4.9 million. Grants were made totalling £2 million.

Beneficiaries of grants paid or agreed during the year included: Horsecross Arts Ltd – Perth (£3 million); Kibble Education and Care Centre (£300,000); Perth Festival of the Arts (£260,000); Erskine and Royal Scottish Geographical Society (£75,000 each); Madderley Community Association, Quality of Life Trust – Village Halls and William Simpson's Home (£50,000); and Church of Scotland Viewpark parish and Rollo Park Trust (£40,000 each).

Exclusions

The following information is taken from the trust's website:
- General applications for funds will not be considered – applications must be specific, and preferably for a project with a defined outcome, not general running costs.
- Donations will not be made to individuals.
- Donations will only be made to organisations which meet the OSCR Charity Test.
- Projects where the benefit of a donation will be realised outside Scotland.
- Donations will rarely be made to projects that do not demonstrate an element of self or other funding.
- Donations will not be made that contribute to an organisation's healthy reserves or endowments.
- Applications will seldom be considered for more than a 3-year commitment.
- Applications will not be considered for holidays, with the exception of those for the disabled and disadvantaged living in Perth & Kinross where the project has a tangible recreational or educational theme.
- Applications will not be considered for animal welfare projects, with the exception of wildlife projects within Perth & Kinross that meet the sub-themes within theme 4.
- Applications will not be considered from schools for recreational facilities unless there will be a demonstrable and sustained community involvement, preferably for the disadvantaged or vulnerable.
- Applications from pre-school groups, play schemes, after school clubs and parent-teacher associations.
- Applications will not be considered from cancer and other health-related charities unless they demonstrate that their project directly provides tangible relief from suffering and direct patient benefit.
- Applications from places of worship will not be considered unless there is a distinct community benefit through use as a community centre or village hall, and where there is not a similar facility nearby.
- Applications will not be considered from charities re-applying within a year of their previous appeal or award, or instalment thereof.
- Applications will not be considered where funding would normally be provided by central or local government.
- Waste disposal/landfill, pollution control and renewable energy projects will not be considered if they are the sole purpose of the project, and unless they meet the criteria within theme 4.

> Applications will not be considered for political or lobbying purposes.

Applications

Application are made on a form which can be downloaded from the trust's website. Full guidelines are also available there.

The Gatsby Charitable Foundation

General

£33.1 million (2009/10)

Beneficial area

Unrestricted.

Allington House, 1st Floor,
150 Victoria Street, London
SW1E 5AE
Tel: 020 7410 0330
Fax: 020 7410 0332
Email: contact@gatsby.org.uk
Website: www.gatsby.org.uk
Correspondent: Peter Hesketh, Director
Trustees: Bernard Willis; Sir Andrew Cahn; Miss Judith Portrait.
CC Number: 251988

Information available

Accounts were available from the Charity Commission. Excellent information is available from the foundation's website.

Summary

This is one of the Sainsbury Family Charitable Trusts, which share a joint administration. It supports organisations that aim to advance policy and practice within its selected areas.

The foundation is proactive and seldom responds to conventional short-term applications – 'trustees generally do not make grants in response to unsolicited appeals' – but it does expect organisations to respond to its published long-term priorities: 'the trustees identify first the areas where they sense that something needs to be done. They hope organisations will respond to these priorities and propose projects.'

Background

This is one of the largest and most interesting grantmaking trusts in the UK, with assets of £460 million and an income of £34.7 million in 2009/10 (£64.4 million in 2007/08), made up of significant donations from the settlor and Lady Sainsbury. It allocates large sums to long-term programmes and so the figure for yearly grant approvals fluctuates considerably. In 2009/10 *grant expenditure given in the statement of accounts,* totalled £33 million. The 2009/10 trustees' report states: 'Gatsby has significant unpaid forward commitments totalling £82.1 million. Trustees approved grants amounting to £21.7 million, but made payments of £71.1 million covering some of these grants, together with others approved in earlier years.'

The foundation was set up in 1967 by David Sainsbury, created life peer and Lord Sainsbury of Turville in 1997. He was a Labour minister with the Department of Trade and Industry until November 2006. He himself has never been a trustee of Gatsby but is still contributing massively to the endowment of the trust, and it is generally supposed that the trustees pay close attention to the settlor's wishes. Since leaving his ministerial office, Lord Sainsbury has been able to 're-engage' with the foundation. A substantial part of the foundation's investments are in the form of shares in the Sainsbury company. In over 40 years of grant-making the Gatsby Charitable Foundation has distributed around £700 million; Lord Sainsbury has stated his intention to give away £1 billion in his lifetime.

General

The following statement by the settlor, David Sainsbury, is taken from the foundation's 2010 annual review:

> With the dramatic reduction in the amount of government funding available to projects across all sectors of public life, it seems a good moment to reflect on the role of private foundations such as Gatsby. I think it is extremely difficult for charitable funding to be a substitute for government funds in core areas of public spending such as education and welfare. However, I have long believed that private foundations have an important role to play in stimulating innovation and testing new models and ideas.
>
> I grew up in a strong family climate of philanthropy and from an early age knew I wanted to establish a Trust of my own. But it was the ability of charitable funds to foster new thinking and back innovative ideas that really excited me and continues to do so to this day. I believe private foundations should see part of their role as being, in some sense, a Research and Development arm of government. It is extremely difficult for any government to truly innovate, and the caution needed when handling public funds often makes it difficult for government agencies to back higher-risk proposals, even when they have significant potential for public benefit if successful. It is for that reason that in many of Gatsby's areas of activity we seek to support innovative and more risky projects. One example of this which has shown excellent progress in 2010 is our work in the cotton sector in Tanzania.
>
> We have worked with the Tanzanian government and a wide range of industry partners to pilot a new model for the sector which, if successfully implemented industry-wide, could improve the way 400,000 farmers access financial support, buy inputs and market their crops.
>
> Partnership also continues to be key to the success of many other Gatsby programmes. The new Sainsbury-Wellcome Centre for Neural Circuits and Behaviour at University College London is, by far, the largest partnership project we have undertaken and – even three years before the Centre is due to open – our partnership with Wellcome is already demonstrating the significant added value that can be gained from two organisations with shared objectives working together.
>
> On a more modest scale, but equally as vital to success, is our partnership with the Wood Family Trust to transform the tea sector in Tanzania. Furthermore, our developing partnerships with the Nuffield and Edge Foundations will be important in efforts to strengthen the education and training of technicians.
>
> To secure progress in such work in science and engineering education, partnership with government will also be crucial, and I look forward to building on the constructive early discussions we have already had with the new Ministers at the Departments for Education, and Business, Innovation and Skills.
>
> Gatsby's work in the field of public policy in the last year has also shown the importance of constructive partnership with government. Our support for the Centre for Cities and Institute for Government (IfG) is based on a firm belief that pragmatic,

nonpartisan think tanks, funded from charitable sources, can make a real and positive contribution to informing government policy and improving the machinery of government. I am delighted in particular with the progress being made at the IfG, and know it will continue to go from strength to strength under the leadership of its new Director, Andrew Adonis.

Finally, I would like to say what enormous pleasure Gatsby continues to give me. It allows me to support many exciting and imaginative projects and make a difference in areas I care about. It also involves working with a remarkable group of people and I would like to take this opportunity to pay particular tribute to the three Gatsby Trustees who give so generously of their time. I would like also to thank the small team of dedicated staff who, with great energy and skill, continue to ensure that maximum impact is secured with the minimum of bureaucracy.

Objectives
The trustees' objectives within their current fields of interest include:

- **Plant Science** – to develop basic research in fundamental processes of plant growth and development and molecular plant pathology, and to encourage researchers in the field of plant science in the UK
- **Neuroscience** – to support world-class research in the area of neural circuits and behaviour, and in the area of theoretical neuroscience; and to support activities which enhance our understanding in this field
- **Science and Engineering Education** – to support improvement in educational opportunity in the UK for a workforce that can better apply technology for wealth creation, by incubating innovative programmes in the field of science and engineering education and promoting excellence in teaching and learning
- **Africa** – to promote economic development through support to key sectors and markets in selected African countries that benefits the poor
- **Public Policy** – to support an independent institute available to politicians and the civil service, focused on making government more effective; and to support practical research and policy advice that helps cities understand how they can succeed economically
- **The Arts** – to support the fabric and programming of institutions with which Gatsby's founding family has connections
- **Mental Health** – to improve the quality of life for people with long-term problems by improved delivery of services.

The trustees occasionally support other charitable work which falls outside their main fields of interest.

[NB] Choosing to focus our support on some areas inevitably means that, over time, we must withdraw from others. In 2009 we decided to bring gradually to a close our support for the Sainsbury Centre for Mental Health (since renamed the Centre for Mental Health). Our commitment to the Centre dates back to its foundation in 1985 and we will continue to support it for the next few years to help ensure its long-term future.

Within these categories the trustees make grants in support of work which they judge to have particular merit. Many of their grants fund projects which the foundation has helped to initiate. It is the policy of the trustees to evaluate programmes and projects rigorously and carefully, and to assess when the evaluations should most usefully take place.

Generally, the trustees do not make grants in response to unsolicited applications or to individuals.

Grantmaking in 2009/10
Specific areas of support come under the headings shown in the table (with payments from new and previous grants):

Plant science	£38.42 million
Science and engineering education	£6.13 million
Africa	£7.73 million
Neuroscience	£5.14 million
Public policy	£5.24 million
General	£327,000
The arts	£5.72 million
Mental health	£2.35 million

Beneficiaries included: University of Cambridge (£31 million); Sainsbury Laboratory – Norwich (£5 million); Institute for Government (£4.8 million); Gatsby Technical Education (£2.96 million); Royal Shakespeare Theatre and RSC (£2.25 million); Tanzania Gatsby Trust (£2 million); Frenchay Hospital (£1.2 million); Royal Society (£1 million); Two Blades Foundation (£939,000); New Engineering Foundation £740,000); Harvard University (£601,000); Centre for Cities (£400,000); Hebrew University of Jerusalem (£271,000); Chamber Orchestra of Europe £250,000); Kenya Gatsby Trust (£211,000); University of York (£201,000); Shakespeare Birthplace Trust (£100,000); and African Agricultural Capital (£75,000).

There are big annual fluctuations in the size of its new awards each year to different categories of work because of the large multi-year funding commitments decided by the foundation.

Exclusions
No grants to individuals.

Applications
See the entry for the Sainsbury Family Charitable Trusts. Generally, the trustees do not make grants in response to unsolicited applications, although a single application will be considered for support by all the trusts in the group.

J Paul Getty Jr Charitable Trust

Social welfare, arts, conservation and the environment
£9.5 million (2010)

Beneficial area
UK.

1 Park Square West, London NW1 4LJ
Tel: 020 7486 1859
Website: www.jpgettytrust.org.uk
Correspondent: Elizabeth Rantzen, Director
Trustees: Christopher Gibbs, Chair; Lady Getty; Vanni Treves; Christopher Purvis.
CC Number: 292360

Information available
Accounts were available from the Charity Commission. The trust also has a useful website.

Summary
The trust funds projects to do with poverty and misery in the UK, and unpopular causes in particular. Its main aim is to fund well managed projects which will 'help to relieve poverty, support disadvantaged people, and effect long-term change where help is not readily available from the public or private purse'. The trust also provides some funding for the arts, and towards the conservation of the natural and built environment.

Grants, usually for revenue or capital costs, are often for three-year periods and can be up to a maximum of £250,000. There are also a large number of small grants of £5,000 or less.

In accordance with the express wishes of Sir Paul Getty Jr, the trustees decided in 2011 to wind down the trust within the next five years. It is likely that the trust will close to new applications within the next two years, and at least 6 months notice will be provided on the website

In 2010 the trust had assets of £43.1 million and an income of £1.1 million. Grants were made totalling £9.5 million.

Background
The J Paul Getty Jr Charitable Trust began distributing funds in 1986. Since then nearly £38 million has been given to over 3,000 worthwhile causes all over the UK.

The trust was funded entirely by Sir Paul Getty KBE, who died in April 2003 in London, where he had lived since the 1980s. He took a close interest in the trust, but also continued to make major personal gifts to the arts and other causes in England. For example, he gave £50 million to the National Gallery, £3 million to Lord's Cricket Ground, £17 million to the British Film Institute, £1 million towards the Canova Three Graces and £5 million towards the restoration of St Paul's Cathedral. These were personal gifts and had no connection with this trust.

It is important to note that this trust does not have any connection with the Getty Trust in the USA, to which J. Paul Getty Senior left his money, and which finances the J. Paul Getty Museum in California.

Guidelines for applicants
The trust awards grants towards both revenue and capital costs, however, it will not normally make grants to cover more than 20% of a charity's entire annual running costs. Grantmaking is focused on supporting charities in England, however UK wide applications will be considered if the project is likely to be of nationwide significance. The

trust favours projects with a long-term focus.

Main grants
These can be between £10,000 and £250,000 over one to three years. It can take at least six to nine months to award a main grant.

Small grants
These can be up to £5,000 and applications are made in the same way as for the main grants programme. grants take around three to six months to be awarded.

Church Urban Fund
Faith-based community groups planning to apply for a grant of £5,000 or less can seek assistance through this fund's Mustard Seeds Programme to which the Paul Getty Jr trust makes a contribution. Applicants should refer to www.cuf.org.uk for further information.

Applications from the following categories are currently being invited:

Social welfare
- Reducing Reoffending
- Improving prospects
- Repairing communities
- Repairing lives

Arts and heritage
- Preserving heritage
- Sustaining the arts

The trusts website is extremely comprehensive and should be referred to for full information on grantmaking.

> We aim to ensure that our grants are made to charities which do not discriminate on the grounds of age, gender, disability, marital status, sexual orientation, religion, race, colour or nationality, and therefore we support organisations with a clear commitment to equal opportunities. However, we recognise that the sensitive nature of some of the work we fund means that appropriate restrictions on staff or participants may sometimes need to be applied.

Grantmaking in 2010
Grants in 2010 were distributed as follows:

	% of total
Offender projects	27%
Young people	25%
Drug and alcohol projects	9%
Refugees and asylum seekers	6%
Other social welfare	13%
Arts and heritage	20%

Grants were also distributed geographically:

	% of total
South East	28%
Northern England	27%
Central England	10%
South West England	10%
Eastern England	5%
National	17%

The charity stated in its annual report for 2010 that:

> Following the unusually low number of applications in 2009, caused by planned temporary closure while new software was installed, grant applications soared above their previous levels and reached 1,516 in 2010. More than £9.5 million was committed in new grants this year, more than double the level of 2009, reflecting the trustees' continuing aim to spend the trust's capital over the coming years. Most of this sum (£9.3 million) was for [109] grants over £5,000 [...] A further £182,000 was spent on grants of £5,000 or less, representing 73 new grants.

Significant beneficiaries included:

Social Finance (£300,000) to support the Social Impact Bond, a high profile initiative to reduce reoffending amongst a group of 3,000 prison leavers from Peterborough Prison over the next 6 years.

Women's Diversionary Fund (£175,000) to support and develop women's centres and help reduce reoffending.

Restorative Solutions (£200,000 to help introduce restorative justice practice in the North of England

Shannon Trust (£150,000) towards helping prisoners learn to read.

Kensington Palace (£250,000) for the restoration of the gardens.

Abbotsford (£150,000) for heritage work.

Beneficiaries of less than £100,000 included: War Memorials Trust (£25,000); National Cataloguing Scheme (£60,000); Infobuzz Ltd (£45,000); Cardboard Citizens (£90,000); Housing for Women (£80,000); Wells Cathedral (£75,000); Ethnic Minority Training Project (£60,000); The Civil Liberties Trust (£50,000); Trinity Winchester (£30,000); and Hackfall Trust (£7,000).

Exclusions

Grants are not given for:

- individuals
- organisations based outside of the UK
- schools, universities or public sector organisations
- routine maintenance, repairs, refurbishment or modernisation costs, or large-scale development projects, such as church restoration work or the construction of new village halls and local community centres
- medical care or general health and wellbeing programmes
- one-off events, residential or adventure trips.

Priority is likely to be given to projects in the less prosperous parts of the country, particularly outside London and the south east, and to those which cover more than one beneficial area.

Please remember this trust has no connection with the Getty Foundation in the USA.

Applications

Applications must be submitted using the online form accessible through the trust's website. There are no 'closing dates', and all applicants should receive an initial response within 12 weeks. The form will ask you to provide:

- information on the work of the organisation
- details of the organisation's size and income
- an overview of the project/work for which funding is required
- the daytime contact details of someone with whom the trust can discuss the application.

When starting an application for the first time applicants will be asked to complete a short 'eligibility quiz' to check that their project falls within the trust's criteria. If successful you will be able to begin the full application (guidance on completing the form is given within the form itself).

If the project is short-listed for a grant of over £5,000, the trust will request more detailed information about the charity and the specific project.

Full application guidelines are available on the trust's website.

Simon Gibson Charitable Trust

General

£579,000 (2009/10)

Beneficial area

UK, with a preference for East Anglia and South Wales.

Wild Rose House, Llancarfan, Vale of Glamorgan CF62 3AD
Tel: 01446 781459
Email: marsh575@btinternet.com
Correspondent: Bryan Marsh, Trustee
Trustees: Bryan Marsh; Angela Homfray; George Gibson; Deborah Connor; John Homfray.
CC Number: 269501

Information available

Accounts were available at the Charity Commission.

The Simon Gibson Charitable Trust was set up by a settlement in 1975 by George Simon Cecil Gibson of Exning, near Newmarket, Suffolk. The trust is a general grant-making charity and therefore makes grants to the full range of charitable causes, including religious and educational causes. Local charities applying are restricted to East Anglia and South Wales. Grants can vary from £1,000 to £10,000 but most grants fall in the range £3,000 to £5,000.

In 2009/10 the trust had assets of £12.8 million and an income of £544,500. Grants were made to 141 organisations totalling £579,000.

The largest grants were made to: Ely Cathedral Appeal Fund, Prostate Cancer Charity, Save the Children Fund, St Nicholas Hospice Bury St Edmunds and the Prince's Trust (£10,000 each).

Other beneficiaries included: New Astley Club Endowment Fund (£6,000); Addenbrooke's Charitable Trust, Campaign to Protect Rural England, Crimestoppers, Help For Heroes, National Ankylosing Spondylitis Society and the Welsh National Opera (£5,000 each); Action

for Children, Blue Cross Animal Centre Cambridge, Flying Scholarship for the Disabled, Listening Books and Save The Rhino (£3,000 each); and the Temple Trust (£1,000).

Exclusions

No grants or sponsorships for individuals or non-charitable bodies.

Applications

'There are no application forms. Charities applying to the trust should make their application in writing in whatever way they think best presents their cause.' It acknowledges all applications but does not enter into correspondence with applicants unless they are awarded a grant. The trustees meet in May and applications should be received by March.

Common applicant mistakes

'Applicants who have not read the criteria, for example, regarding our geographical area or individuals applying.'

The G C Gibson Charitable Trust

Art, music and education; health, hospices and medical research; community and other social projects; religion

£574,000 (2009/10)

Beneficial area

UK.

c/o Deloitte PCS LTD, 5 Callaghan Square, Cardiff CF10 5BT
Tel: 02920 260000
Email: kagriffin@deloitte.co.uk
Correspondent: Karen Griffin
Trustees: Simon Gibson; Jane M Gibson; Robert D Taylor; Martin Gibson; Lucy Kelly; Anna Dalrymple.
CC Number: 258710

Information available

Accounts were available at the Charity Commission.

The trust was established in 1969 by G C Gibson, now deceased, for general charitable purposes. Grants are given mainly for art, music and education; health, hospices and medical research; community and other social projects; religion.

Whilst the trust will consider donations for capital projects, the average donation of £3,000 is more suited for meeting the revenue commitments of an organisation. Applications are considered from charities working throughout the United Kingdom and preference is given to applications from charities who have already received donations from the trust as the trust recognises the importance of providing recurring donations wherever possible.

In 2009/10 the trust had assets totalling £11.7 million and an income of £503,000. Grants were made to 158 organisations totalling £574,000, categorised under the following headings:

Community and other social projects	73	£247,000
Health, hospices and other medical research	42	£165,000
Religion	23	£93,000
Art, music and education	20	£69,000

Beneficiaries included: St Nicholas Hospice (£14,000); Botanic Garden Conservation Ltd, Ely Cathedral and Royal Welsh College of Music and Drama (£10,000 each); Friends of Horsmonden Church, Haiti Appeal and Help for Heroes (£5,000 each); Anti-Slavery International and Northampton Hope Centre (£2,000 each); and Campaign to Protect Rural Hampshire (£1,000).

Exclusions
No grants to individuals.

Applications
In writing to the correspondent by October each year. Trustees meet in November/December. Successful applicants will receive their cheques during January.

Organisations that have already received a grant should re-apply describing how the previous year's grant was spent and setting out how a further grant would be used. In general, less detailed information is required from national charities with a known track record than from small local charities that are not known to the trustees.

NB 'Due to the volume of applications, it is not possible to acknowledge each application, nor is it possible to inform unsuccessful applicants.'

Common applicant mistakes
'Individuals apply and also charities outside of the UK or the perimeter of where the trustees donate. The trust only supports registered charities.'

The Girdlers' Company Charitable Trust

Medicine and health, education, welfare, youth welfare, heritage, environment, humanities and Christian religion

£793,000 (2009/10)

Beneficial area
UK, with a preference for City and East End of London, and Hammersmith and Peckham.

Girdlers' Hall, Basinghall Avenue, London EC2V 5DD
Tel: 020 7448 4851
Fax: 020 7628 4030
Email: john@girdlers.co.uk
Correspondent: John Gahan, Charities Manager
Trustee: Court of the Company of Girdlers.
CC Number: 328026

Information available
Accounts were available at the Charity Commission.

Established in 1988, the trust's main areas of interest are: medicine and health, education, welfare, youth welfare, heritage, environment, humanities and Christian religion, throughout the UK, with a preference for the City and East End of London, Hammersmith and Peckham. In 2009 the trust received the assets of the Geoffrey Woods Foundation and this was merged with The Girdlers' Company Charitable Trust.

To achieve its objectives the trust donations are made under the following headings:
- Principal, Selected Appeals, Hammersmith and Peckham and General Applications
- New Zealand Scholarship and Fellowship
- Irish Guards
- Jock French Charitable Fund
- Christmas Court Donations
- Master's Fund Donations.

The focus of the trust's donations is with its Principal Charities many of which it maintains longstanding and close relationships. This represents around half of the trust's donations.

Selected Appeals are one of donations to charities proposed by a member of the Girdlers' Company who has a close personal involvement.

The trust operates an open application process for circa £50,000 of its total grant making. Of this £30,000 is awarded to between 25 and 30 charities whose beneficiaries reside in Hammersmith or Peckham. Around 20 awards are made, of approximately £1,000, to charities in the UK where the charity has an annual income less than £1 million. The trust informed us that over 400 eligible applications are received each year.

The trust continues to support New Zealand undergraduate scholarships at Cambridge University and a medical research fellowship at Oxford University.

An annual donation goes to support the Irish Guards' Benevolent Fund and an amount is spent at the direction of the 1st Battalion's Commanding officer to support guardsmen's welfare, adventurous training and sporting activities.

The Jock French Charitable Fund encourages charitable donations from members of the Livery of the Company. The subscribing members are invited to nominate charities to receive donations.

The Master's Fund is allocated an amount each year for the Master to donate to charities of his own choice. A sum is also allocated to Christmas

Court Donations for members to nominate donations to charities of their individual choice at Christmas time.

In 2009/10 the trust had assets of £5.5 million and an income of £875,000. Grants were made totalling £793,000, and were broken down as follows:

Principal charities	£370,000
Jock French charitable fund	£99,000
New Zealand scholarships and fellowship	£97,000
Selected appeals	£49,500
Irish Guards	£30,000
Hammersmith or Peckham Charities	£29,000
General donations	£20,000
Other	£7,600

Beneficiaries included: Leyton Orient Community Sports Programme (£40,000); London Youth (£37,500); London Youth – 2012 Project (£20,000); Queen Elizabeth Foundation and Resource Information Service (£10,000 each); Bosence Farm Community (£8,000); Ashburnham Christian Trust and Haven House Foundation (£5,000 each); The Voices Foundation (£3,000); Alone in London, Barons Court Project, Children's Safety Education Foundation, Fulham Good Neighbour Service, Manton Village Hall and West London Action for Children (£1,000 each); Milford and Villages Day Care Centre (£800); Retired Greyhound Trust (£700); Back-up Trust, Chicken Shed Theatre Trust, The Cranston Library and Together for Sudan (£500); and The Parish Church of St Margaret the Queen – Buxted (£400).

Exclusions

Applications will only be considered from registered charities. Whilst it is extremely rare for grants to be made to individuals, the trustees will consider applications from, or on behalf of, a person who is disabled or disadvantaged needing financial support to enable their participation in a course of training or study leading to employment.

Applications

Applicants should write to the correspondent. To be considered for a donation please cover each of the following points:

▷ the beneficial area under which a grant is sought

▷ a brief summary of the organisation's background and aims

▷ the specific nature of the request, highlighting the change you wish to bring about

▷ how you will know if you have achieved these changes

▷ your charity registration number.

Applications from charities whose beneficiaries reside in Hammersmith or Peckham are considered annually. Donations are in the order of £1,000.

Each April and November the trustee considers general applications with 10 donations of approximately £1,000 being made on each occasion. The closing dates are the last Friday in January and August. Successful applicants are unlikely to be awarded a further donation within the following 5 years.

Successful applicants will be informed in May and December.

The Glass-House Trust

Social housing and the urban environment, art and child development

£484,000 (2009/10)

Beneficial area

Unrestricted, but UK in practice.

Allington House, 1st Floor, 150 Victoria Street, London SW1E 5AE
Tel: 020 7410 0330
Fax: 020 7410 0332
Website: www.sfct.org.uk
Correspondent: Alan Bookbinder, Director
Trustees: Alexander Sainsbury; Timothy Sainsbury; Jessica Sainsbury; Elinor Sainsbury; Miss Judith Portrait.
CC Number: 1017426

Information available

Accounts were available from the Charity Commission. Brief information is also available from the Sainsbury Family Charitable Trusts' website.

This is one of the Sainsbury Family Charitable Trusts, which share a joint administration. They have in common an approach to grantmaking which is described in the entry for the group as a whole.

It is the trust of Alexander Sainsbury and three of the four other trustees are his brother and sisters, who each have trusts of their own.

In 2009/10 the trust had assets of £11 million and income of £504,000. Grants were paid during the year totalling £484,000.

Grantmaking in 2009/10

The trust's main areas of interest are (with the number and value of grants made):

Built environment	1	£390,000
Child development	2	£60,000
Art	2	£60,000
Social policy	1	£50,000
Older people	1	£35,000
Overseas	3	£30,000
General	1	£1,500

Beneficiaries included: Glass-House Community Led Design (£390,000); A Space (£55,000); Transform Drug Policy Foundation (£50,000); Resonance FM (£45,000); HACT: The Housing Action Charity (£35,000); Akany Avoko, Madagascar (£15,000); and WAM Foundation (£5,000).

Exclusions

Grants are not normally made to individuals.

Applications

See the guidance for applicants in the entry for the Sainsbury Family Charitable Trusts. A single application will be considered for support by all the trusts in the group. However, in the case of this trust, 'trustees initiate proposals to be considered and do not encourage unsolicited approaches'.

Global Charities (formerly GCap Charities)

Disadvantaged children, young people and adults

£2.2 million (2010/11)

Beneficial area

Greater London; UK.

30 Leicester Square, London
WC2H 7LA
Tel: 020 7054 8391
Email: charities@thisisglobal.com
Website: www.thisisglobal.
com/charities/
Correspondent: Sophie Marks, PA to
MD, Charities and Communities
Trustees: Martin George, Chair; Nigel
Atkinson; Moira Swinbank; Paul
Soames; James Wilkins; Cary
Wakefield.
CC Number: 1091657

Information available

Information provided by the charity's
correspondent.

Capital Charities Limited was
incorporated on 23 January 2002 and
began trading on 29 June 2002. On
May 2006 the charity changed its
name to GCap Charities Limited. The
charity changed its name again to
Global Charities Limited on
16 October 2008 following the
acquisition of GCap Media plc by
Global Radio Limited in June 2008.

Global Charities is the grant giving
charity of Global Radio, the UK's
largest commercial radio company.
Its mission is to improve the lives of
the people in the communities in
which its radio stations broadcast.

Guidelines

The charity aims to achieve its
objectives through the distribution of
grants to charities running projects
that help to make a real difference to
the lives of children, young people
and adults who:
- experience poverty and
  disadvantage
- have/are experiencing abuse,
  neglect, homelessness, violence or
  crime
- have an illness or disability.

Global Charities has three charity
appeals:

Help a Capital Child

Across the Capital FM network, Help
a Capital Child will launch in regions
outside of London in the autumn –
there will be one national charity
delivering projects in the local
regions.

In London, 95.8 Capital FM's Help a
Capital Child (and 97.3 LBC's Help a
London Child) invites charities and
voluntary organisations (*not* statutory
bodies) working with less advantaged
children and teenagers, aged 18 or
under, in Greater London only to
apply for project based funding.
Groups can request grants of up to
£5,000. HACC in London also runs
bespoke large grants programmes
from time to time.

Have a Heart

Heart FM's Have a Heart will be
raising funds for Children's Hospices
UK in 2011, and support 28
Children's Hospices in the
communities Heart FM's radio
stations broadcast to by helping them
deliver at home care to seriously ill
children & their families.

The Classic FM Foundation

In 2011, The Classic FM Foundation
is supporting music therapy sessions
for children and young people
delivered by Nordoff Robbins.

The grant giving strategy has been to
focus on awarding small and major
grants to charities and voluntary
groups in London. The charity invites
applications for grants through
application forms which are regularly
reviewed and updated by the grants
panel to ensure applications comply
with the funding criteria.

The trustees have delegated to a panel
of experts from the voluntary sector,
and radio station representatives the
task of assessing application forms
and making recommendations on
what grants the charity should make.
They are guided in their
recommendations by a list of
conditions as to what the charity will
fund to ensure that the money is used
in the best interests of the intended
beneficiaries. Groups that are
successful with their applications are
required to complete a project report
form and provide receipts to show
how the grant money has been spent.

In London there are two rounds of
small grant giving in the year in order
to improve accessibility of funding
and cash management of the charity.
Operationally, in order to reduce the
pressure on the volunteer grant panel,
Global Charities staff have and will
continue to undertake more sifting of

applications prior to panel
consideration.
The charity's funding categories are:
- community, playgroups and toy
  libraries
- youth
- social and leisure
- disability, health, illness and
  counselling
- refuge and homeless projects
- language and literacy.

Grantmaking 2010/11

In this financial year the charity
awarded 497 grants throughout the
UK totalling £2.2 million and were
categorised as follows:

Disability, health, illness and counselling	169	£1.3 million
Youth	67	£176,000
Social and leisure	116	£337,000
Community, playgroups and toy libraries	96	£252,000
Refuge and homeless projects	27	£75,000
Language and literacy	22	£60,000

Previous beneficiaries included:
Prince's Foundation for Children and
the Arts (£100,000); Missing People
(£61,000); and Impact Initiatives
(£25,000); Sixth Sense Theatre
(£7,500); Cambourne Youth
Partnership (£5,000); Havens
Hospices – Essex (£3,000);
Bangladeshi Parents Association
(£2,100); Howbury Friends (£1,800);
and Centrepoint – Hammersmith and
Fulham (£1,600).

It is estimated by the charity that
nearly 604,000 disadvantaged,
disabled or ill children and young
people, or those affected by abuse,
crime, neglect or homelessness (and
another 23,000 disadvantaged adults)
will benefit from grants awarded
across the country making a real
difference and positive impact on
their lives.

Future plans

Help a Capital Child and LBC's Help
a London Child will continue to
administer a grants programme in
London whilst also working with a
national charity partner in the other
eight regions where Capital FM is
transmitted.

Have a Heart and The Classic FM
Foundation will continue to work
with a national charity partner which
delivers locally within the broadcast
the radio station's regions.

In addition, Global Charities supports other national charity and community activity through other radio stations within the Group; Choice FM, XFM and Gold.

Exclusions

Each individual branch has specific exclusions, generally however the charities will not fund:

▶ individual children or families
▶ retrospective funding
▶ statutory funding, such as schools and hospitals
▶ salaried posts
▶ deficit funding
▶ medical research
▶ purchase of minibuses
▶ trips abroad
▶ distribution to other organisations
▶ distribution to individuals
▶ religious activities
▶ political groups
▶ general structural changes to buildings
▶ projects which are part of a larger charity organisation and not separately constituted
▶ core funding for a national or regional charity.

Applications

The charity provides the following guidance on its website:

> If you have a general enquiry regarding any of our appeals funds please contact us (Tel: 020 7054 8391). We are always glad to answer questions from any organisation, charity or group on our grants process.
>
> Help a Capital Child in London has two annual small grants funding rounds. We attempt to fund as many eligible applications as possible, although this is always limited to the funds raised in the year. Details are given on www.capitalfm.com/charity, as well as how to apply for an application form. The form is reviewed and updated by our grants panel in conjunction with the overall Board to ensure the application process is as accessible as possible and to ensure applicants are guided though our funding criteria.

The Golden Bottle Trust

General with a preference for the environment, health, education, religion, the arts and developing countries

£623,000 (2008/09)

Beneficial area

Worldwide.

Messrs Hoare Trustees, 37 Fleet Street, London EC4P 4DQ
Tel: 020 7353 4522
Fax: 020 7353 4521
Email: enquiries@hoaresbank.co.uk
Correspondent: Miss J Moore
Trustees: Messrs Hoare Trustees (H C Hoare; D J Hoare; R Q Hoare; A S Hoare; V E Hoare; S M Hoare; A S Hopewell.)
CC Number: 327026

Information available

The most recent accounts available from the Charity Commission were for 2008/09.

The trust was established in 1985 for general charitable purposes, by C Hoare and Co. bankers, the oldest remaining private bank in the UK. The trust is managed by the company, Messrs Hoare Trustees, and continues to receive most of its income from C Hoare and Co.

The objective of the trust is the continuation of the philanthropic commitments and ideals of the Hoare family. Traditionally the charity has supported causes including the arts, religion, environment, health, education, the developing world and also many charities with whom the Hoare family is familiar.

Grants range from £250 to £10,000 with larger amounts occasionally being granted, usually to the same charities that the Hoare family has funded regularly.

The charity has invested £214,000 in 'Investisseur et Partenaire pour le Développment' which provides

microfinance loans to small business start ups in the developing world.

During the year 2008/09 the charity held assets of £7.6 million and had an income of £558,000. Grants were made totalling £623,000 and were distributed in the following areas:

Health and education	£243,000
Related charities*	£87,000
Religion	£106,000
Environment	£70,000
Staff match funding	£61,000
Children	£15,000
Arts	£30,000
Other	£10,500

*Related charities included: The Bulldog Trust and The Henry C Hoare Charitable Trust (£40,000 each); and West Country Rivers Trust (£7,000).

Other beneficiaries, receiving £5,000 or more, were: St Dunstan-in-the-West (£50,000); Hand and Hand International (£50,000); Exeter Cathedral; Find Your Feet; Jesus College Cambridge; Temple Music Foundation; Trinity Hospice; Warrior Programme (£10,000 each); and Opportunity International (£7,000).

Exclusions

No grants for individuals or organisations that are not registered charities.

Applications

In writing to the correspondent. Applications are considered from bank staff and external registered charities. The trust may, in certain circumstances, also undertake fund raising events to sponsor a specific cause.

The Goldsmiths' Company Charity

General, London charities, the precious metals craft

£3.6 million (2009/10)

Beneficial area

UK, with a special interest in London charities.

Goldsmiths' Hall, Foster Lane, London EC2V 6BN
Tel: 020 7606 7010

Fax: 020 7606 1511

Email: charity@thegoldsmiths.co.uk

Website: www.thegoldsmiths.co.uk/charities/

Correspondent: Miss H Erskine, Charity Administrator

Trustees: Goldsmith's Company Trustee: Tim Schroder; Scott Shepherd; Bruno Schroder; Sir John Rose; David Peake; Lord Stuart Sutherland; Bryan Toye; Henry Wyndham; Sir Alfred Wiggin; Michael Wainwright; Richard Vanderpump; Richard Helly; William Parente; Richard Came; Dame Lynne Brindley; The Hon. Mark Bridges; Richard Agutter; Lord Roger Cunliffe; Martin Drury; George MacDonald; Prof. Richard Himsworth; Rupert Hambro; Hector Miller; Arthur Galsworthy.

CC Number: 1088699

Information available

Accounts were available at the Charity Commission.

Each year the charity gives over 300 small grants of between £500 and £5,000. Most of these are in response to applications received, and can be for almost any purpose, including supporting core costs. A dozen or so large grants are also given annually, generally up to a maximum of £100,000. These are usually to organisations proactively sought out by the charity rather than as a result of applying for a grant.

The following information is taken from the charity's website:

General

- Grants are made to London and national charities with a turnover of less than £10 million. Where charities are members, branches or affiliates of an association, appeals are normally accepted from the governing body or head office only. In the case of church restoration, block grants are made to the National Churches Trust and therefore appeals from individual churches will not normally be considered. Similarly a block grant is made to Children's Hospices UK, and therefore appeals from individual hospices will not normally be considered.
- The Goldsmiths' Company Charity's normal policy is to give small grants: the average grant last year was approximately £3,000. Recurring grants are not normally given, however where grants are payable in stages over a period of more than

one year, then each payment will be considered on its own merit and payment cannot be assumed for subsequent years.
- Requests for financial assistance by individuals are only considered if they are members of the Goldsmiths' Company. The charity, however, does make grants to other trusts who administer grants to individuals on our behalf.
- Appeals for specific projects are preferred, but requests for core funding will be considered.

Education

- to foster aspects of education considered to be in most need of encouragement
- to fill gaps in educational provision
- to help in situations where the Company's limited finances can have most impact through the multiplier effect

The [charity] currently funds four major proactive projects:

Science for Society Courses
Providing science teachers with free residential courses, aimed at broadening their perspective on subjects allied to the A-level syllabus.

Goldsmiths' Grant for Teachers
Providing primary and secondary school teachers with the opportunity to take time out from the classroom for personal and professional development.

Primary School Projects
Assisting seven selected primary schools to raise their standards of literacy and numeracy.

Post-Graduate Medical Students
Providing bursaries to promising but needy students who have switched to medicine as their second degree. This is carried out through the BMA who have a close association with the [Goldsmiths'] Company. Please note that we do not offer medical grants for individual applications.

The Royal Geographic Society Goldsmiths' Teaching Grants are awarded to five teachers each year to support them in developing educational resources linked to five field projects/expeditions mounted by the RGS each year. This scheme is administered by the RGS.

Grants in 2009/10

In 2009/10 the charity had assets of £89.3 million and an income of £3.2 million, mainly from investments. Grants were made totalling £3.6 million, broken down as follows:

General charitable work	£1 million
Support of the craft: other	£1.2 million
Goldsmith's Centre	£900,000
Education	£311,000
Extraordinary grant*	£173,000

Grants for general charitable work were further categorised as follows:

General welfare	£387,000
Medical welfare and disabled people	£233,000
Culture	£166,000
Youth	£152,000
Church	£72,000

Beneficiaries included: *University of Cambridge – Department of Material Science and Metallurgy (£173,000); National Churches Trust (£50,000); London Borough of Lambeth – for the support of individuals (£25,000); Refugee Council and School Home Support (£15,000 each); Children's Hospices UK (£10,000); Royal Air Force Disabled Holiday Trust (£6,000); Changing Faces, The Young Vic and Country Holidays for Inner City Kids (£5,000 each); and New Horizon Youth Centre (£3,000).

Exclusions

Applications are not normally considered on behalf of:
- medical research
- animal welfare
- memorials to individuals
- overseas projects
- individual housing associations
- endowment schemes
- charities with a turnover of more than £10 million.

Applications

Applications should be made by letter, no more than two sides of A4 in length, highlighting the case for the company to give its support.

The letter should be accompanied by:
- the completed application form, which can be downloaded from the company's website. The form may be retyped, but should follow the same format and length (three sides of A4). All questions should be answered. Do not cut and paste information on the form. Legible handwritten applications are acceptable.
- the charity's most recent annual report and audited accounts (or financial report required by the Charities Act).

Applications are considered monthly, except in August and September, and there is usually a three to four month delay between receipt of an appeal and a decision being made.

Applications from any organisation,

whether successful or not, are not normally considered more frequently than every three years.

Any enquiries should be addressed to the correspondent.

Common applicant mistakes

'Applicants not checking who to send the appeal to – they are often addressed to staff members who have left years ago. Applicants asking for too much, illustrating that they have not read our guidelines.'

Mike Gooley Trailfinders Charity

Medical research, general

£351,000 (2009/10)

Beneficial area

UK.

Trailfinders Ltd, 9 Abingdon Road, London W8 6AH
Tel: 020 7938 3143
Fax: 020 7937 6059
Correspondent: Louise Breton, Trustee
Trustees: Mark Bannister; Michael D W Gooley; Bernadette M Gooley; Tristan P Gooley; Fiona Gooley; Louise Breton.
CC Number: 1048993

Information available

Accounts were on file at the Charity Commission, without a list of grants.

The charity supports medical research, community projects which encourage young people in outdoor activities and armed forces veteran organisations particularly the Soldiers, Sailors, Airmen and Families Association – Forces Help.

In 2009/10 the charity had assets of £9.4 million and an income of £104,500. Grants were made during the year totalling £351,000.

No beneficiaries were listed in the charity's accounts. Previous beneficiaries have included: Alzheimer's Society (£400,000); Prostate Cancer Charity (£100,000);

and the Second World War Experience Centre (£40,000).

Exclusions

Grants are not made to overseas charities or to individuals.

Applications

In writing to the correspondent.

The Gosling Foundation Limited

Relief of poverty, education, religion, naval and service charities and general charitable purposes beneficial to the community

£1.9 million (2009/10)

Beneficial area

Worldwide. In practice UK.

21 Bryanston Street, Marble Arch, London W1H 7PR
Tel: 020 7495 5599
Correspondent: Miss Anne Yusof, Secretary
Trustees: Sir Donald Gosling; Sir Ronald F Hobson; A P Gosling.
CC Number: 326840

Information available

Accounts were available at the Charity Commission.

The foundation was established in 1985 by Sir Donald Gosling, co-founder of NCP car parks and former seafarer. The foundation's endowment derives from his personal fortune and its objects are the relief of poverty, education, religion and general charitable purposes beneficial to the community. Grants are given each year to a wide range of charities, with naval and other service related charities receiving substantial support.

In 2009/10 the foundation had assets of £91.2 million and an income of £4.9 million. There were 216 grants made to 180 organisations totalling

£1.9 million, which were broken down into the following broad categories:

Advancement of education	44	£699,000
Relief of poverty	27	£326,000
Advancement of religion	4	£87,000
Other purposes beneficial to the community	141	£793,000

Beneficiaries included: Marine Society and Sea Cadets (£200,000); Duke of Edinburgh's Award (£103,000 in 2 grants); SSAFA Forces Help (£100,500); Great Steward of Scotland's Dumfries House Trust (£75,000); National Museum of the Royal Navy (£70,000); Britannia Association and St Martin-in-the-Fields (£50,000 each); Tennis Foundation (£42,000 in 3 grants); Annual National Service for Seafarers and the Foundation for Liver Research (£25,000 each); Queen Elizabeth Castle of Mey Trust (£20,000); Entertainment Artistes Benevolent Fund (£12,000 in 2 grants); Special Olympics Leicestershire (£10,000); Action for ME and the Nordoff-Robbins Music Therapy Centre (£7,000 each); Bud Flanagan Leukaemia Fund (£6,000); Hampshire & Wight Trust for Maritime Archaeology, Bobarth Children's Therapy Centre Wales and Hearing Dogs for Deaf People (£5,000 each); Cherubim Music Trust (£3,000); British Association for Adoption & Fostering (£2,000); and Game and Wildlife Conservation Trust (£1,000).

Applications

In writing to the correspondent. The grant making policies of the foundation are 'regularly reviewed' and currently are:
- applications should fall within the objects of the foundation
- there is no minimum limit for any grant
- all grants will be approved unanimously
- the charity will only make grants to individuals in exceptional circumstances.

The Grace Charitable Trust

Christian, general, education, medical and social welfare

£1 million to organisations
(2009/10)

Beneficial area
UK.

Swinford House, Nortons Lane, Great Barrow, Chester CH3 7JZ
Tel: 01928 740773
Correspondent: Mrs G J R Payne, Trustee
Trustees: Mrs G J R Payne; E Payne; Mrs G M Snaith; R B M Quayle.
CC Number: 292984

Information available

Accounts were available from the Charity Commission, but without a list of beneficiaries.

Established in 1985, the trust generally gives grants of £1,000 to £10,000 each with a preference for Christian organisations.

In 2009/10 the trust had assets of £2.4 million and an income of £850,000. Grants were made to organisations totalling £1 million, which were broken down as follows:

Education	£760,000
Christian-based activities	£192,000
Social and medical causes	£71,000
General charitable purposes	£1,000

Previous beneficiaries included Alpha, the International Christian College and Euroevangelism. A further £5,000 was given in grants to individuals.

Applications
The trust states: 'Grants are made only to charities known to the settlors and unsolicited applications are, therefore, not considered.'

GrantScape

Environmental and community-based projects

£1 million (2009/10)

Beneficial area
UK.

Office E, Whitsundoles, Broughton Road, Salford, Milton Keynes MK17 8BU
Tel: 01908 247630
Email: helpdesk@grantscape.org.uk
Website: www.grantscape.org.uk
Correspondent: Mr S Hargreaves, Contact
Trustees: Dave Bramley; Doug De Freitas; Shirley Baines; Alan Loynes; Alastair Singleton; Steven Henry.
CC Number: 1102249

Information available

Accounts were available from the Charity Commission. The charity also has a helpful website.

GrantScape is a company limited by guarantee and is enrolled with ENTRUST as a Distributive Environmental Body. Its vision is 'to improve the environment and communities by the channelling and management of charitable funding towards deserving and quality projects.'

Its generic grantmaking policy is as follows:
- GrantScape will only make grants in line with its charitable objectives.
- Grants will be made on a justifiable and fair basis to projects which provide best value.
- Grants will be made to projects that improve the life of communities and the environment.
- GrantScape will make available specific criteria for each of the grant programmes that it manages.
- All grants are subject to meeting the generic grant-making criteria as well as the specific grant programme criteria.

Programmes
Grants are available in specific geographical areas from the following programmes – please check the charity's website for up-to-date information on current programmes before applying:

Caird Bardon Community Programme
Grant amount:
- The Caird Bardon Community Programme usually has approximately £300,000 available per annum.
- Grants are awarded between £5,000 and £60,000.
- Match Funding is not required

Contributing Third Party Donation
A CTP Donation of 10% of any grant award made will be required

(If you require further information, please refer to the separate document 'Contributing Third Party (CTP) Guidance', which can be downloaded in the application pack from the charity's website. Alternatively, contact the Grant Support Team on 01908 545780)

Project location:
Projects must be located in West Yorkshire, specifically within 10 miles of the Caird Bardon Limited Peckfield landfill site (LS25 4DW).

Project purpose:
Grants will be available for community and environmental projects.

Projects must comply with the requirements of the Landfill Communities Fund (LCF). Details of the LCF can be found on ENTRUST's website (www.entrust.org.uk).

Public access requirements:
Projects must be available and open to the general public – as a minimum, for 4 evenings a week, or 2 days a week, or 104 days a year.

Ineligible applicants:
- Individuals
- Commercial organisations

Project exclusions:
Grants will not be available for:
- Single user sports facilities (e.g. bowls, golf clubs)
- Projects that are considered statutory requirements
- Projects that are solely aimed to meet the requirements of the Disability Discrimination Act
- Revenue funding and core cost funding
- Retrospective funding (i.e. projects that have already been completed)
- Projects at schools
- Bus services, minibus services, or vehicles
- Projects at hospitals, or hospices, or day care centres
- Any works to public highways
- Staff posts and costs where they are not based, or specifically undertaking works, at the actual project site
- Projects to deliver visual enhancements (i.e. 'a view'), as this does not improve, maintain or provide a general public amenity

- Village or town centre enhancements, such as walkways, street works or signage
- CD's, websites or remote interpretation about a site
- Public car parks, unless they are specific to the general public amenity
- Public conveniences
- Allotments, or fruit growing projects
- Charity buildings, offices of charities, Citizens' Advice Bureaux and advice centres
- Large scale perimeter / security fencing programmes that do not directly enhance the public amenity

Judging criteria:

The main criteria used when assessing applications received will be:

- The level of community support for and involvement in the project
- The local community benefit and enjoyment which will result from the project

Other factors will also be considered which must be demonstrated in the application:

- The ability of the applicant to deliver the project
- How the work will be continued after the project has been completed, i.e. its sustainability and legacy
- Value for money

CWM Community and Environmental Fund

Grant amount:

- The CWM Community and Environmental Fund has approximately £200,000 available per annum.
- Grants are awarded between £5,000 and £50,000.
- Match Funding is not required

Contributing Third Party Donation

A CTP Donation of 10% of any grant award made will be required

(If you require further information, please refer to the separate document 'Contributing Third Party (CTP) Guidance', which can be downloaded in the application pack from the charity's website. Alternatively, contact the Grant Support Team on 01908 545780)

Project location:

Projects must be located in Carmarthenshire and be within 10 miles of a licensed landfill site.

Project purpose:

Grants are available for community and environmental projects, particularly those which can demonstrate the enhancement of biodiversity.

Grants will be available for capital improvement works to public amenity projects, for example:

- Village halls
- Village greens
- Public playgrounds *(see note below)*
- Sports fields and facilities

- Nature reserves
- Community centres
- Cycle paths
- Country parks

(Applications involving playgrounds on Council owned land will only be funded if applicants can demonstrate significant community fundraising efforts to help financially support the project. Management, administration and professional costs will only be considered for funding if they form part of a wider application for a capital project and can only constitute a maximum of 10% in total of the amount applied for.)

Projects must comply with the requirements of the Landfill Communities Fund (LCF). Details of the LCF can be found on ENTRUST's website.

Priority:

Priority will be given to applicants that clearly understand and can demonstrate the social, economic and environmental benefits the project will provide.

Public access requirements:

Projects must be available and open to the general public – as a minimum, for 4 evenings a week, or 2 days a week, or 104 days a year.

Ineligible applicants:

- Organisations operating for the purpose of making and distributing profit
- Schools
- Individuals
- Single user sports facilities

Project exclusions:

Grants will not be available for:

- Projects that have already been completed (retrospective funding)
- Projects that are considered statutory requirements
- Projects that are solely aimed to meet the requirements of the Disability Discrimination Act
- Projects that are located on private land
- Revenue costs will not normally be funded

Judging criteria:

The main criteria used when assessing applications received will be:

- The level of community support for and involvement in the project
- The local community benefit and enjoyment which will result from the project

Other factors will also be considered which must be demonstrated in the application:

- The ability of the applicant to deliver the project
- How the work will be continued after the project has been completed, i.e. its sustainability and legacy
- Value for money.

Woodford Waste Management Services Ltd

Location: Cambridgeshire. Total Grants Available: £140,000 (approximately per year)

Fund Provided by: Woodford Waste Management Services Ltd through the Landfill Communities Fund (LCF). Grants of between £5,000 and £35,000 to fund community and environmental projects located within 10 miles of the Woodford Waste Management Services landfill site near Warboys, Huntingdon (PE28 2TX).

There are two funding rounds each year.

The Woodford Community and Environmental Fund uses an on-line application process. Applications in other formats will not, therefore, be accepted.

If your group is not able to complete an online application form due to specific communication requirements, please contact GrantScape so that we can help you with alternative arrangements.

On-line applications to each funding round must be submitted to GrantScape between the opening and closing dates stated above. Applications received after a closing date will be automatically submitted to the next funding round, if available.

Mick George

Location: Northamptonshire. Total grants available: Approximately £200,000 each year.

Fund provided by: Mick George Limited through the Landfill Communities Fund (LCF).

The Mick George Community Fund provides grants of between £5,000 and £50,000, although it is unlikely that individual grants over £35,000 will be made.

The Mick George Community Fund uses an online application process. Applications in other formats will not, therefore, be accepted. If your group is not able to complete an online application form due to specific communication requirements, please contact GrantScape so that we can help you with alternative arrangements.

Applications received after a closing date will be automatically submitted to the next funding round, if available.

Whitemoss Community Fund

Location: Skelmersdale, Lancashire. Total grants available: Approximately £50,000 each year.

Fund provided by: Whitemoss Landfill Limited through the Landfill Communities Fund (LCF).

This fund provides grants of between £5,000 and £20,000 to fund community and environmental projects located in the West Lancashire Borough Council area and that are within 5 miles of Whitemoss landfill site in Skelmersdale.

The fund uses an online application process. Applications in other formats will not, therefore, be accepted. If your group is not able to complete an online application form due to specific communication requirements, please contact GrantScape so that we can help you with alternative arrangements.

Applications received after a closing date will be automatically submitted to the next funding round, if available. The fund only operates an annual funding round and consequently there will be a period of 12 months between funding decisions.

New grant programmes are introduced from time to time – check the charity's website for up-to-date information.

In 2009/10 it had assets of £2.8 million and an income of £1 million. Grants were made across the following programmes, some of which have now closed. Grants were made totalling £1 million; grants approved were as follows:

Caird Bardon Community Programme	£440,000 pa
CWM Community and Environmental Fund	£263,000 pa
Woodford Community and Environmental Fund	£140,000
Waste Recycling Group: Joint with Church Urban Fund	£15,000
Waste Recycling Group: Inner London Nature Conservation Fund	£292,000
Waste Recycling Group: Working with Nature	£1.18 million

In addition to the programmes listed, the charity has continued to administer Landfill Communities Fund grants from earlier programmes.

Exclusions

Specific exclusions apply to each programme – see General for details.

Applications

Applications are made electronically via the charity's website.

The Great Britain Sasakawa Foundation

Links between Great Britain and Japan

£400,000 (2010)

Beneficial area

UK, Japan.

Dilke House, 1 Malet Street, London WC1E 7JN

Tel: 020 7436 9042
Fax: 020 7355 2230
Email: grants@gbsf.org.uk
Website: www.gbsf.org.uk
Correspondent: Stephen McEnally, Chief Executive
Trustees: Earl of St Andrew, Chair; Hiroaki Fujii; Prof Nozomu Hayashi; Michael French; Jeremy Brown; Prof. Harumi Kimura; Yohei Sasakawa; Prof. Shoichi Watanabe; Sir John Boyd; Prof. Peter Mathias; Prof. David Cope; Taysuya Tanami.
CC Number: 290766

Information available

Accounts were available at the Charity Commission. The foundation also has a helpful website.

The following information is taken from the foundation's website:

The Great Britain Sasakawa Foundation was established as a result of a visit to London in 1983 by the late Ryoichi Sasakawa during which he met a number of senior British figures to discuss the international situation and, in particular, UK-Japanese relations. It was agreed at these discussions that it would be in the interest of both countries if more could be done to enhance mutual appreciation and understanding of each other's culture, society and achievements and that a non-governmental, non-profit making body should be established for this purpose.

A donation of almost £10 million was subsequently made by The Sasakawa Foundation (now called The Nippon Foundation), founded in 1962, and the Great Britain Sasakawa Foundation was inaugurated in May 1985, in parallel with similar initiatives in Scandinavia, France and the United States.

The Chairman of The Great Britain Sasakawa Foundation is the Earl of St Andrews. The Trustees are drawn from distinguished individuals in the UK and Japan, including Mr Yohei Sasakawa, Chairman of the Nippon Foundation

Foundation aims
The foundation's aim is to develop good relations between the United Kingdom and Japan by advancing the education of the people of both nations in each other's culture, society and achievements.

It seeks to promote mutual understanding and cooperation through financial support for activities in the following fields:
- arts and culture
- humanities and social issues
- Japanese language
- medicine and health
- science, technology and environment
- sport
- youth and education.

Whilst encouraging applications in each of the above fields, the foundation particularly wishes to support activities/ projects in science and technology; medicine and health; environment and social issues; Japanese studies; and in the Japanese language.

The foundation's awards are intended to provide 'pump-priming' and not core funding of projects, but even small grants have enabled a wide range of projects to reach fruition, such as:
- visits between the UK and Japan by academics, professionals, creative artists, teachers, young people, journalists and representatives of civic and non-governmental organisations
- research and collaborative studies, seminars, workshops, lectures and publications in academic and specialist fields
- teaching and development of Japanese language and cultural studies in schools, further education colleges and universities
- exhibitions, performances and creative productions by artists, musicians, film-makers, writers and theatre groups.

Criteria for awards
- Grants are intended to be 'pump-priming' or partial support for worthwhile projects which would not otherwise be realised, and evidence of core funding should be available before any application is made for an award.
- There are no set budgets for any category of activity, but emphasis is placed on innovative projects and on those involving groups of people in both countries (especially young people) rather than individuals.
- Trustees greatly appreciate acknowledgment of the foundation's support in any published material resulting from a grant.
- Applications are not normally accepted from individuals seeking support for personal projects. However, an organisation may apply for a grant in support of the work of an individual which advances the aims of the foundation, and an application from an individual may be considered if there is clear evidence of organisational support.

- The foundation does not make grants for student fees or travel in connection with study for a qualification, but might do so for research purposes.
- Projects originating in the UK should be submitted through the London office and those originating in Japan through, the Tokyo office.
- Projects for UK-Japan collaborations or exchanges should be submitted as a single project through Tokyo or London, and not as separate applications from the UK and Japanese partners.
- No grants are made for consumables, salaries, for purchase of materials, nor for capital projects such as the purchase, construction or maintenance of buildings.
- For projects designed to extend over more than one year, the foundation is prepared to consider requests for funding spread over a period of not more than three consecutive years.
- We welcome applications from previous recipients for new projects.
- In assessing applications for awards, the trustees will take into account any unique or innovative aspects of the project and the extent to which it will have a wide and lasting impact.
- Awards average £1,500 to £2,000 and do not normally exceed £5,000–£6,000 for larger-scale projects.

In 2010 the foundation had assets of £23.1 million and an income of £1.1 million. There were 193 awards were made totalling £400,000, broken down in the following categories:

Arts and culture	87	£137,000
Medicine and health	14	£80,000
Youth and education	25	£67,000
Science, technology and environment	19	£44,000
Humanities and social issues	33	£38,000
Japanese language	10	£17,000
Sport	5	£17,000

Beneficiaries included: Japan Experience Study Tour – Westminster City School, London (£25,500), for the ninth year of the GBSF Japan Experience Study Tour to Kansai; Wilton Park (£4,500), for the 'Japan: Increasing its Global Role?' conference; University College London, Department of Epidemiology and Public Health (£4,000), towards a symposium at Osaka University on the social determinants of health in Japan; MU:Arts (£3,000), towards Japanese Music Week at London's Kings Place; Bradley Stoke Community School – Gloucestershire (£2,500), towards an exchange programme with Japanese high school for year 12 students and teachers;

Buddhist Society Trust (£2,000), towards the re-publication of the works of Buddhist scholar Suzuki Daisuke; University of Strathclyde, School of Applied Social Sciences (£1,500), towards research for a book on crime in Japan; East West Artists and Culture Club (£1,000), towards an exhibition of Anglo-Japanese art, design and film projects; and the Transport Research Laboratory (£750), for a UK researcher to attend symposium in Osaka on development of brownfield sites.

Exclusions

Grants are not made to individuals applying on their own behalf. The foundation will consider proposals from organisations that support the activities of individuals, provided they are citizens of the UK or Japan.

No grants are awarded for: the construction, conservation or maintenance of land and buildings; student fees or travel in connection with study for a qualification; consumables; salaries.

Applications

The foundation expresses a strong preference for emailed applications. A form will be emailed on request, and is also available from the foundation's website where detailed information is given about the foundation's grant giving and application procedures. Application forms are also available from both the London headquarters or from the Tokyo office at: The Nippon Foundation Bldg 4F, 1–2–2 Akasaka Minato-ku, Tokyo 107–0052.

The application form requires the following information:

- a summary of the proposed project and its aims, including dates, its likely impact and long-term sustainability
- the total cost of the project and the amount of the desired grant, together with a note of other expected sources of funds
- a description of what elements of the project grant funding has been requested for (the foundation prefers to support identifiable activities rather than general overheads).

Organisations should be registered charities, recognised educational institutions, local or regional authorities, churches, media companies, publishers or other bodies that the foundation may approve.

Telephone enquiries or personal visits are welcomed by the foundation's staff to discuss eligibility in advance of any formal application. The awards committee meets in London in February, May and October. Applications should be received by December, March and August. Awards meetings in Tokyo are held in April and October, with applications to be submitted by February and September.

School applicants are requested to first file an application with Connect Youth International, Japan Exchange Programme, 10 Spring Gardens, London SW1A 2BN (which is part of the British Council), to which the foundation grants external finance, aimed at encouraging exchanges (both ways) for schools in Great Britain and Japan, (their website is www.connectyouthinternational.com).

All applicants are notified shortly after each awards committee meeting of the decisions of the trustees. Those offered grants are asked to sign and return an acceptance form and are given the opportunity to say when they would like to receive their grant.

Please note: the foundation receives requests for two to three times the amount of money it actually has available for grants and many applicants receive much less than they asked for.

The Grocers' Charity

General

£973,000 (2009/10)

Beneficial area

UK.

Grocers' Hall, Princes Street, London EC2R 8AD
Tel: 020 7606 3113
Fax: 020 7600 3082
Email: anne@grocershall.co.uk
Website: www.grocershall.co.uk
Correspondent: Anne Blanchard, Charity Administrator

Trustee: The Grocers' Trust Company Limited administers the Charity and the Directors of that company are the Master and Second Warden of the Grocers' Company, together with the Chairmen of the Education and Charities Committee and the Finance Committee. The Master and Second Warden together with eight other Members of the Court of Assistants, all of whom are elected for a fixed term of office, form the Education and Charities Committee which is responsible for grant-making.

CC Number: 255230

Information available

Annual accounts; annual report with list of grants (for £1,000 or more), detailed narrative breakdown of grants/grantmaking and guidelines for applicants.

The Grocers' Charity was established in 1968, and has general charitable aims. It describes its work as follows in its 2009/10 accounts:

> The charity has wide charitable aims, with education continuing to be a high priority. A significant proportion of the charity's expenditure is committed to this category in the form of internal scholarships and bursaries at schools and colleges with which the Grocers' Company has historic links.

> The balance is spread across several areas of interest, namely medicine, relief of poverty (including youth), heritage, disability, the arts, churches, and the elderly.

> Each year, the charity sets a budget that establishes expected income for the period and sets a target for the distribution of income and reserves through grants to charities. There is a broad categorisation of the nature of the budgeted grants, but this is advisory, and does not restrict the types of grant allocated. Once the overall financial parameters have been set, the policy on awarding grants is flexible, allowing due consideration of the worthiness of applications received from charities during the year. Over a period of time, this may result in different categories of need attracting a greater level of support, although there are certain charities to which the charity contributes on a regular basis. Amongst these, education continues to be a high priority and a significant proportion of the charity's expenditure is committed to this category in the form of scholarships and bursaries at schools and colleges with which the Grocers' Company has historic links. Donations to churches under the patronage of the Grocers' Company and payments to their respective Parochial Church Councils also feature annually.

> The amounts awarded per grant vary considerably. Excluding the grants provided to institutions with which there is an historic connection, 173 (2009 – 148) grants were awarded in 2009/10 from a total of 980 (2009 – 1,138) applications received. Of these, 20 were for £1,000 or less and the remainder, with the exception of major grants, ranged between £1,500 and £20,000.

> Major grants are awarded each year. Each year a different area of charitable activity is chosen for major grant support, and every member of the Company has the opportunity to nominate a charity. The nominations are then reviewed and a short-list produced. Charities on the short-list are invited to give a presentation to the Education and Charities Committee, after which the awards are decided. This year, the chosen areas were relief of poverty with special consideration given to those concerned with assisting the elderly. Five major grants were awarded, totalling £120,000. The Matched Funding Scheme initiative launched in 2007 continued in 2009/10, with the Company sponsoring 34 members who raised a combined sum of £302,280. It is the Trustee's intention that this worthwhile scheme be encouraged to develop.

Grantmaking in 2009/10

During the year the charity had assets of almost £12.4 million and an income of over £965,000. Grants totalled £973,000 and were summarised as follows:

Education	£310,000
Relief of poverty (including youth)	£231,000
Elderly	£90,000
Disability	£82,000
Heritage	£75,000
Churches	£75,000
Medicine	£73,000
The arts	£35,000
Other	£3,000

Beneficiaries of grants of £1,000 or more are listed in the annual report and annual review. Some examples of recipients are given below.

Oundle School for bursaries (£154,000); Dementia UK and The FOCUS Kensington & Chelsea Foundation (£50,000 each); The Coldstream Guards (£34,000); the Elms – Colwall (£22,000); Samaritans (£20,000); Combat Stress (£11,000); the Concertina Charitable Trust (£10,000); St Mary, Bow – Mile End (£7,000); Reed's School (£6,500); Flintshire Mental Health Advocacy, the Forget Me Not Club, National Trust for Scotland and Starlight Children's Foundation (£5,000 each); New London Orchestra and SPECIAL (£3,000 each); Shakespeare at the Tobacco Factory (£2,000); and Cherry Trees (£1,500).

Grant guidelines

- The charity will consider requests to support both capital and revenue projects.
- It is usual practice for successful applicants to be advised that a further request for support will not be entertained until at least two years have elapsed from the date of the successful application.
- Unsuccessful applicants are advised that a further request will not be considered until at least one year has elapsed from the date of the relevant application.
- Donations are made by way of a single payment and are of a non-recurring nature (although occasionally a commitment to fund a project for a limited period will be agreed).
- Public acknowledgement of the charity's support is allowed, although it is preferred that it is undertaken in an unobtrusive manner.

Please note the following from the 2009/10 trustees' annual report:

> The current level of charitable giving has been reviewed given the uncertain economic climate and for 2010/2011 is expected to be in the order of £750,000 which represents a decrease of 23.0% on actual donations of £973,400 for 2009/2010. It is the intention that awards will be presented in a similar fashion as before, including £100,000 reserved for major grants.

Exclusions

Only UK-registered charities are supported. Individuals cannot receive grants directly, although grants can be given to organisations on their behalf. Support is rarely given to the following unless there is a specific or long-standing connection with the Grocers' Company:

- cathedrals, churches and other ecclesiastical bodies
- hospices
- schools and other educational establishments.

Applications

Applications for grants can be considered from UK registered charities only and must comply with current guidelines, including restrictions, as detailed in the Grocers' Charity Annual Review and on the Grocers' Company website: www.grocershall.co.uk The company's website states:

Before making an application, please read our Charity Policy and Guidelines.

Please complete the Initial Enquiry Form. You can either submit it online or print it out and send it to: The Charity Administrator, Grocers' Hall, Princes Street, London, EC2R 8AD.

Please do not send any further information at this stage. We will review your enquiry and contact you if we wish to take your application further. We regret we are unable to acknowledge receipt of enquiries.

The M and R Gross Charities Limited

Jewish causes

£3.3 million (2009/10)

Beneficial area

UK and overseas.

Cohen Arnold and Co., New Burlington House, 1075 Finchley Road, London NW11 0PU

Tel: 020 8731 0777

Fax: 020 8731 0778

Correspondent: Mrs Rivka Gross, Secretary

Trustees: Mrs Rifka Gross; Mrs Sarah Padwa; Michael Saberski.

CC Number: 251888

Information available

Accounts were available at the Charity Commission.

This trust makes grants to educational and religious organisations within the orthodox Jewish community in the UK and overseas.

In 2009/10 the trust had assets of £22.2 million and an income of £6.75 million. Grants were made totalling over £3.3 million. A list of recent beneficiaries was not included in the latest accounts.

Previous beneficiaries, many of whom are likely to be supported each year, include: Atlas Memorial Limited; United Talmudical Associates Limited, a grant making organisation which distributes smaller grants made by the trust; Chevras Tsedokoh Limited; Kolel Shomrei Hachomoth; Telz Talmudical Academy; Talmud Torah Trust; Gevurah Ari Torah Academy Trust; Friends of Yeshivas Brisk; Beis Ruchel Building Fund; Beth Hamedresh Satmar Trust; Kehal Chareidim Trust; Daas Sholem; Craven Walk Beis Hamedrash; Union of Orthodox Hebrew Congregations; and Yetev Lev Jerusalem.

Applications

In writing to the organisation. Applications are assessed on a weekly basis and many of the smaller grants are dealt with through a grant making agency, United Talmudical Associates Limited.

H C D Memorial Fund

Health, education, environment and community action

£129,000 to organisations in the UK (2009/10)

Beneficial area

Worldwide.

Knowlands Farm Granary, Barcombe, Lewes, East Sussex BN8 5EF

Tel: 01273 400321

Correspondent: Harriet Lear, Secretary and Trustee

Trustees: Nicholas Debenham, Chair; Bill Flinn; Harriet Lear; Joanna Lear; Jeremy Debenham; Catherine Debenham.

CC Number: 1044956

Information available

Accounts were available at the Charity Commission.

The trust was established in 1995 for general charitable purposes and principally makes grants to organisations in the UK and abroad engaged in the fields of health, education, environment and community action.

The grants policy is to make grants as determined by the trustees at twice-yearly meetings. The policy is flexible as regards donees, but currently:

- maintains a balance between home and overseas grants
- directs grants mainly towards (1) the relief of human need, whether due to poverty, ill-health, disability, want of education, or other causes, and (2) projects which aim to mitigate the effects of climate change
- prefers projects which are small or medium-sized
- permits the taking of risks in an appropriate case.

During 2009/10 the trust made grants to a variety of charitable organisations. The organisations concerned support work in the fields of development, health and education in Africa, Central and South America, India, Pakistan, Palestine, Sri Lanka, Timor and Belarus; work in the environmental field, particularly in relation to climate change and other work in the UK and Ireland for environmental and community projects, including refugees and prisoners.

The charity also owns a freehold woodland property in the Republic of Ireland which is held for charitable purposes, including amenity value and recreational access for the community.

In this financial year the trust had assets of £548,000 and an income of over £647,000. Grants were made to 25 organisations totalling £638,000. Grants ranged from £2,000 to £60,000.

Organisations operating overseas – 17 grants totalling £510,000
Beneficiaries included: Practical Action – Sudan (£60,000); CAFOD – Ethiopia (£57,000); Angels International – Malawi (£23,000); Donald Woods Foundation – South Africa (£50,000); Build IT and Concern in Africa (£20,000 each); Rwanda Aid and Target Tuberculosis – Timor (£10,000 each); and Leaves of Hope – Belarus (£5,000).

Organisations operating in the UK – 8 grants totalling £129,000

Beneficiaries included: Newhaven Community Development Association, for people with disabilities (£30,000); Dartington Hall Trust and Refugee Support Group Devon, for refugees (£20,000 each); Green Light Trust (£16,000); Refugee Women of Bristol (£5,000); and Thanington Neighbourhood Resource Centre (£2,000).

Exclusions

The following are not supported:

▶ evangelism or missionary work
▶ individuals
▶ nationwide emergency appeals
▶ animal, cancer and children's charities.

The fund stresses that it receives applications for gap year funding which are always unsuccessful as grants are never made to individuals.

Applications

In writing to the correspondent, although note that the trust has a preference for seeking out its own projects and only very rarely responds to general appeals.

'Unsolicited applications are not encouraged. They are acknowledged, but extremely rarely receive a positive response. No telephone enquiries, please.'

The Hadley Trust

Social welfare

£2 million (2009/10)

Beneficial area

UK, especially London.

Gladsmuir, Hadley Common, Barnet, Hertfordshire EN5 5QE
Tel: 020 8447 4577
Fax: 020 8447 4571
Email: carol@hadleytrust.org
Correspondent: Carol Biggs, Trust Administrator
Trustees: Janet Hulme; Philip Hulme.
CC Number: 1064823

Informations available

Accounts were available from the Charity Commission, without a full grants list.

The trust was established in 1997 for welfare purposes. Its annual report gives an overview of its objects and activities:

> [The objects of the trust] are primarily, but not exclusively, to assist in creating opportunities for people who are disadvantaged as a result of environmental, educational or economic circumstances, or [disability], to improve their situation, either by direct financial assistance, involvement in project and support work or research into the causes of, and means to alleviate, hardship.

> The trustees' approach is to further the trust's objects by engaging with and making grants to other registered charities. In general, the trustees prefer to work with small to medium-sized charities and establish the trust as a reliable, long-term funding partner.

> In recent years the trust has become increasingly focused on some core areas of activity where the trustees feel the trust is able to have the greatest impact. Consequently the trust has tended to establish more in-depth relationships with a smaller number of selected partners.

> The result of this policy is that the trust does not take on many new funding commitments. Nevertheless the trustees will always consider and respond to proposals which might enhance the effectiveness of the trust.

Grantmaking in 2009/10

In 2009/10 it had assets of £75.6 million and an income of £4.4 million, which included a donation of over £3.1 million from the settlor. Grants were made to 68 organisations totalling £2 million, and were broken down in the following categories during the year. The trust also provides further information about grantmaking within several categories, and a brief analysis of its relationship with the five largest recipients of grants during the year.

	% of total	
Social investment	34.5%	£698,000
Crime and justice	21.4%	£433,000
Young people	13.2%	£267,000
Medical	8.9%	£180,000
International	7.6%	£154,000
Disability	6.7%	£135,500
Hospices	4.3%	£87,000
Other	3.4%	£69,000

The following is taken from the 2009/10 annual report:

> The social investment category includes a substantial amount of research and policy work carried out with policy 'think tanks'. Two of these (New Economics Foundation and Policy

Exchange) are discussed in more detail below. This policy work has been categorised as social investment but in most cases it simultaneously furthers the objects of the trust in other areas. For example, in the present period it has included work on early intervention crime-reduction initiatives and programmes to reduce the number of young people in custody. In fact, taking this into account, crime and justice was the largest area of activity for the Hadley Trust in 2009/10. Other crime and justice related activities include funding of support for prisoners and their families such as advice and information, education and rehabilitation services. Social investment also includes support for a number of local community charities.

The trust's involvement with charities working with young people is focused on adoption and fostering policy and practice, looked-after children and young people at risk.

New Economics Foundation

The trust has been engaged with New Economics Foundation (NEF) for a number of years on a programme of work on social return on investment. The early phases of this work emphasised the application of SROI to social enterprises. In recent years the trust and NEF have pressed ahead to use the ideas to inform other areas of policy. This programme is called Measuring what Matters and the first phase addressed four main policy areas: Enterprise-led Regeneration, Community Development Finance, Alternatives to Imprisonment for Women, and Residential Care for Looked-after Children.

In the last year the trust has funded further projects on Youth Justice, on the Community Allowance (furthering our interest in welfare reform), and on the case for (and against) a third runway at Heathrow. The last of these was very topical but it also provided a valuable opportunity to test the applicability of SROI methodology to a very different type of policy decision.

The trust also funded a project with NEF called Income/Time/Carbon which explored how the welfare system might evolve in a post-financial crisis, energy-constrained and carbon-constrained world.

Prison Reform Trust

The Hadley Trust is the principle funder of the Prison Reform Trust's advice and information service. Each year the service provides support to over 5,000 prisoners and their families. In addition the information gathered by the service provides an important input to PRT's policy and lobbying activity including the submission of evidence to the parliamentary Justice Select Committee.

Because of the strong link between the advice and information service and policy development the Hadley Trust also supports PRT's policy work directly. In the current year PRT contributed to the debate on numerous topics including IPP sentences, the ever-growing prison population, overcrowding and Titan prisons. PRT has also focused its efforts on the problems of particularly vulnerable groups such as young offenders, women and elderly prisoners. For example, PRT worked with New Economics Foundation to research, publish and disseminate 'Unlocking value: How we all benefit from investing in alternatives to prison for women offenders.

Policy Exchange

The trust has continued to increase its involvement in policy work and our relationship with the think-tank Policy Exchange is part of this changing emphasis. In the current year most of our work with Policy Exchange was in the areas of welfare reform and criminal justice. The welfare report was the last in a series of three and focused on the barriers to leaving welfare. The programme complements work the trust has already done with Community Links and its Need not Greed campaign and springs from our earlier work on regeneration policy.

The crime and justice programme included recommendations on early intervention crime reduction initiatives and approaches to reducing the number of young people in custody.

Centre for Justice Innovation

About a year ago the trust funded Policy Exchange to produce a report on problem solving justice. The work was actually carried out by Aubrey Fox and Greg Berman of the Centre for Court Innovations in New York where they have a wealth of experience of problem solving techniques. In the current year the trust funded a feasibility project to look at setting up a Centre for Justice Innovations in the UK and Aubrey Fox relocated to London for this purpose.

Since the end of the year which is the subject of this trustees' report the Centre for Court Innovations and the trust have taken the decision to set up a centre in London.

The Hadley Centre

The trust has now completed its second five year agreement to provide core funding to the Hadley Centre for Adoption and Foster Care Studies in Bristol. The centre is part of the School for Policy Studies at Bristol University.

The Hadley Centre has established itself as a leading centre of expertise on all aspects of permanence and contributes widely to research, dissemination and policy deliberations. Studies are frequently carried out at the request of the government or local authorities. For example 'Pathways to Permanence for Children of Black, Asian and Mixed Ethnicity' was funded by the DCSF.

Going forward the trust expects to support the centre on a project-by-project basis.

Applications

In writing to the correspondent.

Paul Hamlyn Foundation

Arts, education and learning in the UK and local organisations supporting vulnerable groups of people, especially children, in India, social justice

£18.7 million (2009/10)

Beneficial area

UK and India.

5–11 Leeke Street, London
WC1X 9HY
Tel: 020 7812 3300
Fax: 020 7812 3310
Email: information@phf.org.uk
Website: www.phf.org.uk
Correspondent: Tony Davey, Information and Resources Officer
Trustees: Jane Hamlyn, Chair; Michael Hamlyn; Robert Boas; James Lingwood; Baroness Estelle Morris; Claus Moser; Anthony Salz; Peter Wilson-Smith; Tim Bunting.
CC Number: 1102927

Information available

Accounts were available at the Charity Commission. Detailed information is also available on the foundation's interesting website.

Paul Hamlyn was a publisher and philanthropist. He established the Paul Hamlyn Foundation in 1987 for general charitable purposes and on his death in 2001 he bequeathed the majority of his estate to the foundation so that it became one of the UK's largest independent grant-giving organisations. He was committed to opening new opportunities and experiences for the less fortunate members of society.

The foundation is one of the larger independent grant-making foundations in the UK. Grants are made to organisations which aim to maximise opportunities for individuals to experience a full quality of life, both now and in the future. In particular it is concerned with children and young people, and others who are disadvantaged. Preference is given to supporting work which others may find hard to fund, perhaps because it breaks new ground, is too risky or is unpopular. Initiatives are established by the foundation where new thinking is required or where it is believed there are important unexplored opportunities.

The following information is taken from the foundation's website:

Below are the values that underpin the Paul Hamlyn Foundation in how it operates as an independent grant-making foundation. They very much mirror the values of the founder. He believed there was a 'better way', that way being 'a society that is fair, allows people to realise their potential, fights prejudice, encourages and assists participation in and enjoyment of the arts and learning, and understands the importance of the quality of life for all communities.

  ▷ strategic – wanting to make changes to policy and opinion
  ▷ enabling – giving opportunities and realising potential
  ▷ courageous – fighting prejudice and taking risks
  ▷ focused and flexible – through targeted and open grants schemes
  ▷ supportive – giving advice to applicants who need help
  ▷ fair – clear application processes, equality of opportunity
  ▷ value for money – controlling costs and expecting money to be well used.

The foundation states that it will:

Continue to support organisations which have a constructive influence on the law and public policy affecting grant-making charities, argue for proportionate regulation and accountability of charities, share our experiences with other grant makers, learn from other grant makers and organisations with similar values, and encourage philanthropy. We will, where possible, influence policy, legislation and change public opinion in our desire to find a better way. We will also support charitable organisations by developing and sharing knowledge about the most effective way of helping people and communities reach their potential and have a better quality of life.

The funding programmes are: arts; education and learning; and social justice. The foundation also works in India supporting vulnerable groups of people, especially children.

The foundation's strategic aims (taken from its website) up to 2012 are:

1. Enabling people to experience and enjoy the arts.
2. Developing people's education and learning.
3. Integrating marginalised young people who are at times of transition.

In addition, we have three related aims:

- Advancing through research the understanding of the relationships between the arts, education and learning and social change.
- Developing the capacity of organisations and people who facilitate our strategic aims.
- Developing the foundation itself to be an exemplar foundation, existing in perpetuity.

Grantmaking in 2009/10

In 2009/10 the foundation had assets of £548.3 million and an income of £11.2 million. 162 grants were made totalling £18.7 million, exclusive of support costs and broken down in each area of interest as follows:

Social justice	£5.65 million
Education and learning	£5.33 million
Arts	£4.6 million
India	£1 million
Other grants	£2.21 million

The annual report gives an insight into the foundation's objectives in each area, summarised here along with a selection of beneficiaries:

Arts programme
This programme is primarily aimed at increasing people's experience, enjoyment and involvement in the arts, with a particular focus on young people.

We support organisations and groups through our open grants scheme, concentrating on work that is transformational at three levels: for the participants, for the funded organisations themselves and, more generally, for the sector in which they operate. We also give grants to talented individuals through our Special Initiatives: the Awards for Artists, JADE Fellowships and Breakthrough Fund.

This year, we have worked against a backdrop of challenging economic circumstances and uncertainty for artists and the arts sector, working closely with other public and private funding bodies to share expertise and develop a better understanding of the impact of the recession. The year has seen some important developments in the Arts programme's Special Initiatives.

Following an extensive and thorough consultation and research process started in 2008, trustees approved £1.47m from 2010/11 towards a new five-year action-research Special Initiative to support artists working in participatory settings. The initiative will develop and work closely with three to four collaborative pathfinders that will each span initial training, continuous professional development and employers' needs. We will be appointing a Project Director and a Steering Group during 2010/11.

Work on the Breakthrough Fund has continued to bring us into close contact with applicants and grantees. As per the Fund's original conception – as a three-year annual funding initiative to be followed by evaluation of its impact – this year we made the third and final round of grants. Over the three years of the Fund, PHF has identified 19 exceptional individuals at critical points in their development – whether they are an emerging talent, reaching full stride in their work or at the pinnacle of their career – to which we provide support that will make a significant difference to them and to the organisations in which they work.

We awarded the last of the five JADE Fellowships in 2009, to Independent Ballet Wales and Amy Doughty. With the awards made we have turned our attention to maximising the impact of the dissemination of our findings from the initiative. Together with the Clore Leadership Programme and Dancers' Career Development, we organised a symposium, held in May 2010, to explore what makes a good transition after a successful dance career. The event celebrated our Fellowships in the context of what else is available to dancers, providing a much wider legacy for the dance sector.

Beneficiaries included: Eastside Projects (£360,000), to develop and underpin Eastside Projects and programming costs – full funding will be determined on successful year one and the development of a sustainable business and fundraising plan for Eastside Projects; Contact Theatre Company (£200,000), support for 'Future Fires', an innovative programme using the best international practice to develop

creative young leaders who will design and deliver projects in their own communities; New Writing North (£150,000), to support an innovative programme of activities and new partnerships to engage North East readers with quality literature events and activities; Spitalfields Music (£97,000), to enable the commissioning, development and performance of two pieces of music for the 2010 and 2011 festivals with the local community; Gwent Ballet Theatre Limited – JADE fellowship for Amy Doughty (£50,000); and Stroud International Textiles (£8,500), support for a symposium that will encourage debate and discussion around alternative approaches to textiles, looking at areas such as sustainable fashion and new textiles from old and zero waste.

Education and Learning programme
This programme has a strong focus on supporting innovation and aims to achieve significant impact, ideally at a national level, across a range of education themes. Our work fosters the development and sharing of new practice, experiences and learning between and within schools, local authorities and voluntary organisations. This year the Education and Learning programme has seen strong progress in its existing Special Initiatives and created a new one. We have also reconsidered our approach to Open Grants and are soon to announce revised guidelines for one theme in order to help us maximise the impact of our support.

Beneficiaries included: Tutu Foundation UK (£200,000), for the creation and roll-out over three years of ubuntu-based tools to enable young people to plan, execute and evidence transformation in communities; Southside Young Leaders Academy (£150,000), to develop leadership potential and raise aspirations for young boys from the BME community who are at risk of exclusion from school; CEWC – Cymru (£58,000), to extend the use of a proven classroom method for developing speaking and listening skills through establishing whole-school practices and inter-school networks; and Al-Haqq Supplementary School (£3,300), for the use of facilities at Woodsley Multicultural Community Centre.

Social Justice programme

This programme aims to help tackle the social injustice faced by young people living in the margins of society, particularly those making critical transitions in their lives, and those whose voices are least well heard by decision makers in our society.

Since the programme began in 2006 we have assisted a wide range of inspirational individuals and organisations from across the UK to develop and sustain their work with marginalised young people. These young people include those excluded from employment and education opportunities, living in poverty, asylum seekers, refugees and migrants facing multiple barriers to integration, young offenders leaving prison, young people at risk of offending, those struggling with mental ill-health, victims of violence, exploitation, abuse, and intolerance, and those with complex needs, including disability.

Beneficiaries included: The LankellyChase Foundation (£200,000), a contribution to the Women's Diversionary Fund, a joint fund set up between the Corston Independent Funders' Coalition and Ministry of Justice to support development of community-based provision to divert vulnerable women out of offending and custody; Project Art Works (£150,000), a three-year grant for a project that enables artist film makers and young people with severe and complex disabilities to create biographical films, to be used in their ongoing care assessments and training a range of service providers; UK Drug Policy Commission (£60,000), funding for the first phase of a wider investigation into how stigma towards recovering drug users is a major barrier to re-integration and social inclusion. The first phase of research will provide concrete evidence on the extent and nature of stigma, explore the implications of this, and disseminate findings to inform development of policy and practice; and Council for Assisting Refugee Academics (£10,000), towards the publication and dissemination of a practical guide for higher education institutions in providing more effective support to refugee and at risk academics.

Exclusions

In the UK the foundation does not support:

- individuals or proposals for the benefit of one individual
- funding for work that has already started
- general circulars/appeals
- proposals about property or which are mainly about equipment or other capital items
- overseas travel, expeditions, adventure and residential courses
- promotion of religion
- animal welfare
- medical/health/residential or day care
- proposals from organisations outside the UK, except under our India programme
- proposals that benefit people living outside the UK, except under our India programme.

The foundation is unlikely to support:

- endowments
- organisations to use funding to make grants
- websites, publications, seminars unless part of a wider proposal.

In India, the foundation does not support:

- individuals or proposals for the benefit of one individual
- retrospective funding (for work that has already started)
- general circulars/appeals
- proposals that solely concentrate on the purchasing of property, equipment or other capital items
- overseas activities, including travel, expeditions, adventure and residential courses.

Applications

The foundation's guidance on its application procedure is particularly detailed and helpful:

Applicants should submit an application using the outline application form which can be completed online. It will be acknowledged automatically by email.

You will hear from us within four weeks whether or not we accept your outline application and wish to take it forward.

If we accept your outline application, a member of our staff will contact you to progress your proposal.

You will normally be asked to send further details about the proposed work which should include the following information – in this order and up to a maximum of eight pages in total:

- what do you aim to achieve? (please describe in approx 50 words)
- how will you achieve your aim(s)? (please describe in approx 50 words)
- how your specific objectives link with the aims of the scheme to which you are applying
- job description (if you are applying for funding for a post)
- anticipated problems and how you will address them
- start date and length of work
- who will undertake the work?
- number of beneficiaries
- total budget for this work
- exact breakdown of how PHF money would be spent
- other funders/fundraising
- monitoring and evaluation plans
- dissemination strategy
- sustainability/future funding
- independent referee
- appropriate letters of support.

Please ensure that the above information reaches us by email. You can send any additional supporting information by post if necessary.

In addition to the details requested above, we would also like you to send us:

- an annual report and audited financial statements or equivalent (ideally electronically)
- name of your organisation's Chief Executive or equivalent.

We will then assess your application. This may involve correspondence and meetings between our staff and your representatives, and may also include consultation with our trustees, advisers and independent referees.

We will normally complete the assessment within two to three months of receiving the further details as listed above. The assessed proposal will then go to a decision making meeting.

Applications for up to £10,000 are normally considered by staff.

Applications over £10,000 and up to £150,000 are normally considered by the relevant programme committee.

Applications for over £150,000, or applications which are novel or potentially contentious, are considered first by the relevant programme committee and then by the full board of trustees.

The programme committees and the full board of trustees meet four times a year. We do not publish meeting dates.

Please allow six months between making an outline application and the start date for the work you propose to carry out with our funding, or longer if the proposal is particularly large or complex.

We will not consider applications from organisations outside the UK, or applications to help people who live outside the UK. This does not apply to our India programme.

Common applicant mistakes

'Failure to fully understand our criteria for innovation, participation and impact.'

The Helen Hamlyn Trust

Medical, the arts and culture, education and welfare, heritage and conservation in India, international humanitarian affairs and 'healthy ageing'

£1.9 million (2009/10)

Beneficial area

Worldwide.

129 Old Church Street, London SW3 6EB

Tel: 020 7351 5057

Fax: 020 7352 3284

Email: john.rochekuroda@ helenhamlyntrust.org

Correspondent: John Roche-Kuroda, Trust Administrator and Secretary

Trustees: Lady Hamlyn; Dr Kate Gavron; Dr Shobita Punja; Brendan Cahill; Margaret O'Rorke; Anthony Edwards; Dr Deborah Swallow; Mark Bolland.

CC Number: 1084839

Information available

Accounts were available at the Charity Commission.

Registered with the Charity Commission in January 2001, in April 2002 the assets and activities of the Helen Hamlyn 1989 Foundation were transferred into this trust.

The following information is taken from the trustees' report of 2009/10:

The trust has wide powers to make grants. The trustees bring forward recommendations for projects to support and these recommendations are subject to approval by the board.

The current strategy for grant making is concentrated on the following areas of activity: medical, the arts and culture, education and welfare, heritage and conservation in India, international humanitarian affairs and healthy ageing. Within these areas of activity the trust

also supports a number of projects with a design focus which are undertaken by the Helen Hamlyn Research Centre at the Royal College of Art, London.

Additionally, small grants of up to £10,000 are made to a wide variety of small charities. All small grants support the trust's charitable objectives.

The trust's core aim is to initiate and support innovative medium to long term projects, which will effect lasting change and improve quality of life.

Individual projects aim to:

- support innovation in the medical arena
- increase access to the arts and support the professional development of artists from the fields of music and the performing arts
- increase intercultural understanding; provide opportunities for young people to develop new interests and practical skills which will contribute to their education and their future lives and to create opportunities for young offenders to acquire practical skills which will support their personal development for their future lives and reduce re-offending
- conserve heritage in India for public access and cultural activities
- support good practice in the humanitarian sector through educational programmes
- provide practical support to enable the elderly to maintain their independence for as long as possible.

In 2009/10 it had assets of £4.6 million and an income of £2.8 million, mainly from donations. Grants were made totalling £1.9 million. Grants awarded in 2009/10 were broken down into the following categories:

Medical	£1 million
Education and welfare	£919,000
Healthy ageing	£31,500
Heritage and conservation in India	£5,000
Arts and culture	Nil

Beneficiaries included: Imperial College, London (The Hamlyn Centre for Robotic Surgery) (£1 million); The Design Dimension Educational Trust (£275,000); The Royal Horticultural Society (£83,0000; The Society for the Advancement of Philosophical Enquiry and Reflection in Education (£64,000); Royal Opera House, Covent Garden (£48,000); Safe Ground (£10,000); St Wilfred's Care Home (£7,000); and INTACH UK (£5,000).

Applications

'The trustees bring forward recommendations for projects to support.'

Hampton Fuel Allotment Charity

Relief in need, health, education of children and young people and social welfare

£904,000 to organisations (2009/10)

Beneficial area

Hampton, the former borough of Twickenham, and the borough of Richmond (in that order).

15 High Street, Hampton, Middlesex TW12 2SA

Tel: 020 8941 7866

Email: info@hamptonfuelcharity.co. uk

Website: www.hfac.co.uk

Correspondent: M J Ryder, Clerk

Trustees: David Parish, Chair; Revd Derek Winterburn; Jonathan Cardy; David Cornwell; Stuart Leamy; Geoffrey Clarkson; Jamie Mortimer; P Williams; George Hunter; Marie Martin; Jane Young.

CC Number: 211756

Information available

Accounts were available at the Charity Commission. The trust also has a useful website.

General

The trust was created following the 1811 Enclosure Act by the granting of 10.14 acres of land for producing a supply of fuel for the poor of the ancient parish of Hampton. Subsequently the land was rented out for nurseries. In 1988 the land was sold for development and the sale proceeds formed the financial base for the current work of the trust.

Historically, the trust's area of benefit was the ancient town of Hampton, now the area covered by the parishes of St Mary's Hampton, All Saints Hampton and St James's Hampton Hill. In 1989 the area was widened so that where the trust's income was not required in the ancient town of Hampton, help could be provided elsewhere in the London borough of Richmond upon Thames. The current priority area after the ancient town of Hampton, is the remainder of the former borough of Twickenham and then the remainder of the present Richmond upon Thames. Grants to individuals are restricted to the first two areas.

As the name of the trust suggests, its original purpose was to make grants of fuel to those in poverty. The trust has continued to fulfil its original purpose, while assuming many other roles and tasks.

The objects of the trust are:

- the relief of need, hardship or distress of those within the area of benefit
- improving the conditions of life for the inhabitants in the interest of social welfare.

The trust funds the following:

- individuals, their social welfare and individual support
- young people, through youth training organisations and clubs
- education, through nurseries, play groups, schools and colleges
- the community, through community based organisations
- people with disabilities, as individuals and through disability organisations
- older people, through old people's welfare organisations and clubs
- housing, through housing associations and trusts
- caring for the sick, through hospitals and hospices
- recreation and leisure, through social and sporting clubs.

Grants are given towards fuel costs and essential equipment and to not for profit organisations which support those in need or education or social welfare. The charity undertakes regular reviews of the cost of fuel, state benefits and other needs of the beneficiaries. £500,000 has been set aside for the purpose of loans to not for profit organisations.

Grantmaking in 2001/10

During the year the trust held assets of £43.4 million and had an income of £1.8 million. Grants were made totalling £1.7 million.

During the year 2,196 grants were made to individuals including £689,000 in 1,789 fuel grants with an average of £386. Essential equipment was purchased for 371 individuals totalling £87,000 including refrigerators, cookers, washing machines, wheelchairs and special medical equipment. The charity also supported the vital safety communication system 'Careline' to 197 individuals (£21,000).

86 grants were awarded to organisations, distributed into the following categories:

Hospitals and hospices	3	£39,000
Organisations benefiting people with disabilities	31	£174,000
Social welfare	27	£275,000
Housing	1	£15,000
Education	12	£107,000
Community	12	£294,000

The trust states in its annual report:

> The majority of these grants were for the organisations continuing activities, which is vital if their services are to continue to support our community and those who gain from their activities. A few grants this year have been for building works, mostly extensions and improvements providing improved community access.

The most significant beneficiaries were: Richmond Citizens Advice Bureau Service (£60,000); Teddington Methodist Church & Community Centre- building improvements (£50,000); Age Concern Richmond (£50,000); St Stephen's Church- building extension (£50,000); and London Borough of Richmond upon Thames Early Years and Childcare, and Richmond Youth Partnership (£45,000 each).

Other beneficiaries included: Landmark Arts Centre (£17,000); National Autistic Society Richmond Branch (£6,000); Royal Hospital for Neuro-Disability (£4,000); Marble Hill Playcentres (£3,000); Mediation in Divorce (£2,000); Vietnamese Community Association in South West London (£1,800); Hampton Village Youth Football Club (£1,000); and Churches together in Teddington (£500).

Exclusions

The charity is unlikely to support:

- grants to individuals for private and post-compulsory education
- adaptations or building alterations for individuals

- holidays, except in cases of severe medical need
- decoration, carpeting or central heating
- anything which is the responsibility of a statutory body
- national general charitable appeals
- animal welfare
- advancement of religion or religious groups, unless offering a non-religious service to the community
- commercial and business activities
- endowment appeals
- projects of a political nature
- retrospective capital grants.

Applications

In writing to the clerk on the application form available from the trust or its website, local vicarages, the Greenwood Centre and Citizens Advice Bureaux together with guidelines for completing it. Health and social workers also have them for applying on behalf of their service users. Please do not send requests by email. On receipt of your application form the clerk will review it and may wish to ask further questions before submitting it to the trustees for consideration. All eligible applications will be considered.

The individual grants panel meets every 2 months to consider applications. In urgent cases grants may be given in between these meetings. The board meets annually to decide the following year grant and household income levels.

The general grants panel also meets every 2 months to consider applications from organisations. Communication concerning major projects is encouraged prior to application submission.

The Kathleen Hannay Memorial Charity

Health, welfare, Christian, general

£581,500 (2009/10)

Beneficial area

UK.

15 Suffolk Street, London SW1Y 4HG
Tel: 020 7036 5685
Correspondent: G Fincham, Administrator
Trustees: Jonathan F Weil; Simon P Weil; Christian Alison K Ward; Laura Watkins.
CC Number: 299600

Information available

Accounts were available at the Charity Commission.

The trust supports a wide variety of UK and overseas charitable causes. In furtherance of its objectives, the trust continues to make a substantial number of grants to charitable organisations both on a one off and recurring basis.

In 2009/10 the trust had assets of £12.9 million and an income of £184,000. Grants were made to 32 organisations totalling £581,500. Grants were broken down as follows:

Prevention or relief of poverty	1	£150,000
Advancement of religion	11	£109,000
People who are disadvantaged	7	£105,000
Arts, culture, heritage and science	4	£100,000
Health or the saving of lives	4	£80,000
Education	3	£27,500
Sport	1	£5,000
Promotion of religious or racial harmony	1	£5,000

The beneficiaries listed in the accounts were: The Pennies Foundation (£150,000); the Story Museum and the Save the Children Fund (£50,000 each); and the Children's Fire & Burn Trust (£40,000).

Exclusions

No grants to individuals or non-registered charities.

Applications

In writing to the correspondent. The trustees usually meet in March (applications should be submitted in February).

The Haramead Trust

Children, social welfare, education, people with disabilities, homeless people, medical assistance, victims and oppressed people and religious activities

£870,000 (2009/10)

Beneficial area

Worldwide, in practice developing countries, UK and Ireland, locally in the East Midlands.

Park House, Park Hill, Gaddesby, Leicestershire LE7 4WH
Correspondent: Michael J Linnett, Trustee
Trustees: Simon P Astill; Mrs Winifred M Linnett; Michael J Linnett; Robert H Smith; David L Tams; Revd Joseph A Mullen.
CC Number: 1047416

Information available

Accounts were available at the Charity Commission.

The Haramead Trust was established in 1995 for general charitable purposes. The trust focuses its grant giving on the relief of those suffering hardship or distress, children's welfare, the relief of suffering animals and education in relation to the advancement of health.

The trustees may visit funded projects, both in the UK and overseas, for monitoring purposes or to assess projects/organisations for future grants. Travel and administration costs are borne by the settlor; only audit costs are met by the trust.

In 2009/10 the trust had assets of £237,500 and an income of £645,000, most of which was in the form of a regular donation from the settlor. Grants were made to 118 organisations totalling £870,000, which were split geographically as follows:

Developing countries	£335,000
East Midlands	£286,000
UK and Ireland	£249,000

Grants of £10,000 or more were made to: Action Aid (£130,000); Leicestershire Leicester & Rutland Community (£60,000); Launde Abbey and Menphys (£50,000 each); and Brainwave, Concern Worldwide, De Paul Trust, Duke of Edinburgh's Award, Emmaus, International Childcare Trust, Laura Centre, Leicester Rape Crisis, Raleigh International, SCOPE and World Orthopaedic Concern (£10,000 each).

Grants between £5,000 and £9,999 totalled £436,500; grants of less than £5,000 totalled £33,700.

Applications

In writing to the correspondent. The trustees meet every two months.

The Peter Harrison Foundation

Sports for people in the UK who have disabilities or are disadvantaged; support for children and young people in the south east of England who are terminally ill, have disabilities, or are disadvantaged; and certain educational initiatives

£3 million (2010/11)

Beneficial area

UK; south east of England.

Foundation House, 42–48 London Road, Reigate, Surrey RH2 9QQ
Tel: 01737 228 000
Fax: 01737 228 001
Email: enquiries@ peterharrisonfoundation.org
Website: www. peterharrisonfoundation.org
Correspondent: John Ledlie, Director

165

HARRISON

CC Number: 1076579

Information available

Accounts were available at the Charity Commission. The foundation's website is informative and gives clear guidelines for applicants for grants.

The foundation was established for general charitable purposes by Peter Harrison in April 1999. The aims of the foundation are to:

- help disabled people or disadvantaged children/young people, principally through sport and education
- support charitable activities which are well planned and demonstrate a high level of community involvement
- fund projects where their grant will make a substantial difference to the charity funded
- support projects that are likely to have a sustainable impact.

Peter Harrison is a keen and active sportsman and believes that education and sport provide the key stepping stones to self-development, creation of choice, confidence building and self reliance. A pioneering and successful businessman, entrepreneur and sportsman he wishes to share his success by making these stepping stones more readily available to those who have disabilities or who are disadvantaged and who may not otherwise have the opportunity to develop their self potential.

In 2009 the foundation celebrated its 10th anniversary. At this point over £19.6 million had been distributed to 375 charities throughout the United Kingdom; this has been achieved through the foundation's grants programmes.

Grant programmes

The following information is taken from the foundation's website:

Opportunities through sport

This programme is nationwide and applications are accepted from charities throughout the United Kingdom. Sporting activities or projects which provide opportunities for people who have disabilities or who are otherwise disadvantaged are supported

in order to fulfil their potential and to develop other personal and life skills.

Grants will often be one-off grants for capital projects. The foundation will, however, also consider revenue funding for a new project or if funding is key to the continuing success or survival of an established project. Applications are welcomed for projects that:

- provide a focus for skills development and confidence building through the medium of sport
- have a strong training and/or educational theme within the sporting activity
- provide sporting equipment or facilities for people with disabilities or disadvantaged people
- have a high degree of community involvement
- help to engage children or young people at risk of crime, truancy or addiction.

Special needs and care for children and young people

This programme is for charities in the south east of England and applications are accepted only from charities in: Berkshire; Buckinghamshire; Hampshire; Isle of Wight; Kent; Oxfordshire; Surrey; East Sussex; and West Sussex. Applications from charities based in or operating in London are not accepted, but the foundation may consider funding charities based in London for a specific project taking place in the south east area that meets its criteria. Applications are welcomed for projects that:

- work with or benefit children with disabilities, chronically or terminally ill children or provide support for their parents and carers;
- help to engage children or young people at risk of crime, truancy or addiction;
- are organised for young people at risk of homelessness or that provide new opportunities for homeless young people.

Opportunities through education

This programme supports education initiatives, primarily in the south east of England, which are of particular interest to the trustees. Through this programme bursary places for children from the Reigate and Redhill areas in Surrey are funded.

Applications are not invited for this programme.

Trustees' discretion

This programme supports projects that are of particular interest to the trustees and external applications are not invited.

Guidelines for applicants

The foundation accepts applications from registered charities, community amateur sports clubs, friendly societies or industrial provident

societies and organisations in Scotland and Northern Ireland recognised by the Inland Revenue. The foundation also accepts applications from local branches of national charities but only if they are either a separate legal entity or have the endorsement of their national head office.

The foundation wishes to support those charitable activities that demonstrate an existing high level of voluntary commitment, together with well planned and thought out projects.

Grantmaking in 2010/11

In 2010/11 the foundation had assets of almost £53 million and an income of £2.6 million. Grants paid totalled £3 million, broken down as follows:

Opportunities through sport	30	£2.5 million
Special needs and care for children and young people	10	£308,000
Opportunities through education	5	£111,000
Trustees' discretion	9	£87,000

Beneficiaries included: British Paralympic Association (£75,000); the Orpheus Trust (£53,000); Reigate and Redhill YMCA (£50,000); the Rose Road Association and SeeAbility (£45,000 each); Lake District Calvert Trust (£40,000); Access Sport (£35,000); Royal Caledonian Curling Club (£30,000); Carers First (£21,000); Poole Sailability (£20,000); the National Autistic Society (£19,000); Brittle Bone Society (£11,000); Different Strokes (£9,800); and Sportability (£7,500).

A full list of grant awards can be found on the foundation's website.

Exclusions

The foundation does not fund:

- general fundraising appeals
- retrospective funding
- other grant-making bodies to make grants on the foundation's behalf
- projects that directly replace statutory funding or activities that are primarily the responsibility of central or local government
- individuals
- holidays or expeditions in the UK or abroad
- outdoor activity projects such as camping and outward-bound expeditions

- overseas projects
- projects that are solely for the promotion of religion.

Applications

The foundation has a two stage application process.

Step 1: Initial enquiry

Potential applicants are asked to first read the information on eligibility and grant programmes available on the foundation's website. If your project meets the criteria for one of the open programmes (i.e. Opportunities through Sport or Special Needs and Care for Children and Young People), then complete the online initial enquiry form. This can be found in the 'application process' section of the foundation's website.

Applications are processed as quickly as possible, but please be aware that the foundation receives a large number of applications and it may sometimes take up to two months for an initial enquiry form to be considered.

Applications are first assessed by the foundation's staff. If it is felt the project will be of interest, they will arrange either to visit the project or to conduct a telephone discussion with the applicant about it. Depending on the outcome of these discussions, you may then be invited to submit a full application.

If your initial enquiry is not successful you will be notified by email. The foundation receives many more applications than it is able to support and unfortunately have to turn down many good proposals, even though they meet the criteria. No feedback is given on unsuccessful applications.

Step 2: Full application

Applicants should only submit a full application form if their initial enquiry has been successful. Completed forms should be sent by post to the correspondent.

If an application is successful the applicant will normally be contacted by telephone followed by a grant offer letter. The letter will explain the conditions which apply to all grant awards and also set out any special conditions which apply to your

organisation. It will also confirm details of how and when you will receive the grant and how payment is made.

If an application is unsuccessful the applicant will be informed by letter. The main reason for not funding projects is the volume of applications received.

Organisations supported by the foundation are required to show how they have used the grant and, depending on the grant amount and the nature of the project, may be asked to undertake a review and evaluation of the project being funded. This will normally be on completion of the project, but for charities receiving their grant in several instalments, interim reports may be requested. Full details of the monitoring information required are given in the foundation's grant offer letter.

The foundation aims to ensure that all grant applications that are eligible for consideration within the foundation's grants criteria are given equal consideration, irrespective of gender, sexual orientation, race, colour, ethnic or national origin, or disability.

Common applicant mistakes

'Applicants make mistakes in the finance part of the application form, i.e. amounts do not add up to totals etc. Applicants do not think about the fact that the form is the selling tool for their charity and must therefore be very concise and yet descriptive about their specific project.'

The Maurice Hatter Foundation

Jewish causes, general

£1.1 million (2009/10)

Beneficial area

Unrestricted.

Smith & Williamson, 1 Bishops Wharf, Walnut Tree Close, Guildford, Surrey GU1 4RA
Tel: 01483 407100
Correspondent: Jeremy S Newman, Trustee

Trustees: Sir Maurice Hatter; Ivor Connick; Jeremy S Newman; Richard Hatter.
CC Number: 298119

Information available

Accounts were available at the Charity Commission.

The foundation was established in 1987 for general charitable purposes, mainly for Jewish causes.

In 2009/10 it had assets of £6.2 million and an income of £487,000. Grants were made during the year totalling almost £1.1 million.

Grants were categorised as follows:

Education	£764,500
Medical research	£138,000
Culture and environment	£82,000
Social welfare	£61,500
Religion	£30,500

Beneficiaries included: British Friends of Haifa University (£354,000); World ORT (£134,000); Ray Tye Medical Foundation (£68,000); University College London Intellectual Property (£50,000); Traditional Alternatives Foundation (£25,000); Norwood Ravenswood (£10,000); and Nightingales House (£5,000).

Applications

Unsolicited applications will not be considered.

The Charles Hayward Foundation

Heritage and conservation; criminal justice; hospices; older people; overseas; youth at risk

£1.8 million (2010)

Beneficial area

Unrestricted, in practice mainly UK with some overseas funding.

Hayward House, 45 Harrington Gardens, London SW7 4JU
Tel: 020 7370 7063/7067
Website: www. charleshaywardfoundation.org.uk
Correspondent: Dorothy Napierala

CC Number: 1078969

Information available

Accounts were available at the Charity Commission.

Sir Charles Hayward was born in 1893 in Wolverhampton, Staffordshire. In 1911 he started his own business making wooden patterns for the developing engineering trade. His early involvement in the motor industry proved to be a springboard for his later success culminating in the formation of Firth Cleveland Ltd. He was Chairman from its inception in 1953 until 1973 when he retired.

Sir Charles used his personal fortune to establish and endow two charitable trusts, the Hayward Foundation and the Charles Hayward Trust. The two charities were combined on 1st January 2000, to become the Charles Hayward Foundation.

In 2010 the foundation had assets of £49.3 million and an income of £1.9 million. Grants were made totalling £1.8 million, and were broken down as follows:

Young people	£369,000
Criminal justice	£284,000
Heritage and conservation	£263,000
Older people	£262,500
Hospices	£240,000
Overseas	£181,000
Small grants	£148,500
Miscellaneous	£23,000

The foundation currently has a focus on the following priorities:

Current categories:

- Heritage and conservation
- Criminal justice
- Hospices
- Older people
- Overseas

There is also a small grants scheme for grants up to £5,000.

Following a review the following categories have been discontinued:

- youth at risk (on hold while we evaluate currently funded projects)
- community facilities (except for small grants in north west region of England only)
- people with disabilities
- medical research
- early intervention and under fives.

Beneficiaries during 2010 included: Amber Trust Wiltshire (£200,000); St Gemma's Hospice (£30,000); Wells Cathedral and College of St Barnabas, Surrey (£25,000 each); Phoenix Cinema, London (£20,000); Women's Work, Derby (£16,000); SOVA – Supporting Others Through Volunteer Action (£15,000); Caledonia Youth (£10,000); Holderness Road Methodist Church (£4,000); Islington Somali Community (£3,000); Proteus Theatre Company Limited (£2,000); and Solihull Bereavement Counselling Service (£1,500).

The following details are provided on the foundation's website:

Activities to which funds may be allocated

We predominantly fund capital costs. Occasionally, project funding may be offered for start-up or development activities where these are not part of the on-going revenue requirement of the organisation.

We place great emphasis on funding projects that are developmental or new. We would like to enable things to happen that would not otherwise happen. We prefer funding a project in its early stages rather than finishing off an already well supported appeal. Our preferred area of impact is at the community and neighbourhood level.

We also value projects that are preventive or provide early intervention. Our preferred area of impact is at the community and neighbourhood level.

We also wish to promote good practice. We would like to help with the development of solutions to society's problems and help to expand the take-up of these solutions where they are most needed.

Organisations eligible to apply

We will normally make grants to UK registered and exempt charities only. New charities that are yet to be registered may be considered for start-up funding if they are able to demonstrate good governance and sound financial management.

Geographical targeting

Our area of operation for our main grants programmes is the United Kingdom. Except in our community facilities small grant scheme we do not target particular regions. We consider the quality of projects more important than their geographical location. Nevertheless, we also recognise that London organisations in particular are well served by charitable trusts.

We also have an overseas grants programme which makes grants to UK registered charities which undertake projects in the Commonwealth Countries of Africa, India and Pakistan.

Socio-economic targeting

Although we consider levels of socio-economic deprivation in an area are an important factor in determining the value of a project, more important criteria for our grant making are innovation, excellence and the development of new services and activities.

Size and scope of grants

The small grant scheme makes grants up to £5,000 only to charities with an annual turnover of less than £250,000.

In our other programmes, grant sizes are typically from £10,000 to £25,000 one-off grant. Where agreed, project funding may be granted for a maximum of three years in duration, and will be tapered downwards if appropriate. Project funding may be up to £15,000 per year over three years

Heritage and conservation

We would like to concentrate our grant making on the following:

- Industrial heritage
- Conservation and preservation of pictures, manuscripts, books and artefacts
- Purchase of land or reclamation of recently purchased land to be used for nature reserves or inner-city gardens, parks etc., where these will be maintained in perpetuity.

Exclusions are:

- Community arts troupes
- Community arts centres
- Endangered species
- Conservation of gardens
- Environmental conservation
- Animal rescue
- Art and history workshops
- Fellowships and academic education
- Opera and ballet
- Artistic productions
- Heritage railways

Criminal justice

We would like to support:

- Alternatives to custody
- Victim support services
- Schemes to help prisoners maintain links with their families and be better parents
- Accommodation and support for offenders on release
- Rehabilitation of offenders
- Help for families suffering from domestic violence.

We will continue to occasionally fund prison reform activities.

The following are excluded:

- Welfare of prisoners and their families

Hospices

We would like to support:

- Capital expenditure for day care and home care
- Start-up funding for domiciliary services

- Capital expenditure for organisations which provide care for people with terminal illness.

The following are excluded:
- Equipment and computers
- Training facilities and costs

Older People

In this policy area we wish to fund preventative and early intervention programmes allowing older people to stay in their own homes and remain independent. We are particularly interested in seeking out programmes which show some creativity in improving the quality of life of older people. We wish to focus on:

- Programmes aiming to alleviate isolation and depression in older people.
- Capital costs for informal day care or social and recreational activities – except those contracted by government.
- Setting up schemes which mainly use volunteers to give practical help, assistance and support for older people living in their own homes.
- Expansion or improvements to older persons' care homes, sheltered and supported accommodation.

The following areas are excluded:
- Almshouses
- Meals on wheels
- Lifelong learning
- Workshops, events and productions for older people

Overseas

We will accept applications for projects in India, Pakistan and the Commonwealth countries of Africa. We favour high impact projects that have immediate results. We will only fund overseas projects through UK registered charities, which must be able to provide an adequate local monitoring function for the grant. We will consider the following areas:

- Clean water and sanitation
- Basic health education programmes
- Cure and rehabilitation from disease and disability
- Youth at risk, orphans, street children
- Basic training in farming skills and income generation

The following are exclusions:
- Overseas disability awareness
- HIV and AIDS
- Victims of famine, war and disaster
- Basic education
- Gap years, electives, project visits overseas

Youth at risk

Trustees will, until further notice, not accept unsolicited applications for Youth at Risk projects but will continue their support through internally researched programmes.

Other areas

We may wish to consider projects outside our main areas of interest when such projects develop novel interventions into society's ills or address causes which are rare or unpopular.

Small grant scheme

We have a small grant scheme which makes more rapid grants to smaller organisations. The grants are valued up to £5,000 and are only available to organisations with a turnover of less than £250,000. Applications for small grants will be accepted for activities fitting any of our UK funding categories above, except youth at risk.

In addition, small grants valued up to £5,000 will be made towards community facilities in the south west of England and Wales. We will contribute up to £5,000 towards capital projects to accommodate community activities, where the project is a capital build or extension costing less than £250,000. The new facilities must accommodate new activities, which are at a demonstrably advanced stage in their planning. The activities must be designed to meet the basic needs of new clients and users.

- Capital costs of community centres and village halls
- Capital costs of community facilities provided by churches and faith groups
- Capital costs for CABx
- Capital costs for rescue organisations.

The following areas are excluded:
- Existing parks, playgrounds and recreation grounds
- Sports clubs and sports facilities
- Community transport
- Refugees and asylum seekers.

Grants are only offered towards expenditure not yet incurred. Grants are paid on evidence of expenditure such as receipts or invoices. For project grants, budgets and management accounts will be required. The grant offer may be withdrawn after 12 months if it is not taken up. We do not seek publicity for our grants.

Exclusions

The following types of recipients will be excluded:

- large national organisations, with substantial fundraising or income generating capacity
- organisations that have large reserves or endowment funds
- individuals
- voluntary sector development and support organisations
- organisations that restrict their benefit to one section of society
- other grant-making organisations.

The foundation will not fund:
- academic chairs
- animal charities
- bursaries
- church restoration
- computers
- education
- endowment funds
- environmental and animal sciences
- fund-raising activities
- general repairs
- academic research
- paying off loans
- revenue funding of core costs, general funding, continuing funding and replacement funding
- replacement of government or lottery funding or activities primarily the responsibility of central or local government or some other responsible body
- travel, outings, holidays and gap schemes
- expenditure that has already been incurred or will have been incurred by the time the application can be considered by our trustees.

Applications

There is no application form. Your initial application should be made in writing to the Administrator, Dorothy Napierala. It should provide the details listed below. You may add any enclosures that help to describe your organisation or the project. The foundation will advise you whether more information is required.

All applications will receive an acknowledgement. However, as there is often a waiting list, and the trustees meet only four times a year to consider applications, you may have a wait of several months before you receive a decision. **Note:** there are always many more applications than the foundation is able to fund out of its limited resources. You are advised to read these guidelines very carefully, as inappropriate applications waste time.

Details required in your application:

Name and location of organisation: The official name of your organisation and its location

Contact details: Give your name and position within the organisation, contact telephone number and address.

Description of organisation: Provide a description of your present work and the priorities you are addressing. Quantify the scale of your operation – how many people do you help and how?

Description of proposed project: Describe the project you are undertaking, detailing the number of people and groups who will benefit and how. Specify how life will be improved for the target group.

Project cost: For larger projects give a breakdown of the costs. Capital and revenue costs should be kept separate. For a capital project, include only information on the capital costs.

Funds raised and pledged: Give a breakdown of the funds raised to date towards your target, separating capital and revenue, where applicable. Include the amount of any of your own funds or reserves going into the project, and any money you intend to borrow.

Outstanding shortfall: Specify the amount of money you still need for capital and revenue separately.

Timetable: State the timetable for the project; when it will start and be finished.

Accounts: Include one set of your latest audited accounts.

Small grants: Note that applications for the small grant scheme need only be up to four pages plus accounts.

Common applicant mistakes

'Applicants not reading our guidelines fully to find out what categories we fund and the restrictions that apply to these. Also, applicants not being a UK-registered charity.'

The Headley Trust

Arts, heritage, welfare, overseas development

£3.7 million (2010)

Beneficial area
Unrestricted.

Allington House, 1st Floor,
150 Victoria Street, London
SW1E 5AE
Tel: 020 7410 0330
Fax: 020 7410 0332
Website: www.sfct.org.uk
Correspondent: Alan Bookbinder, Director
Trustees: Sir Timothy Sainsbury; Lady Susan Sainsbury; Timothy James Sainsbury; J R Benson; Judith Portrait.
CC Number: 266620

Information available

Accounts were available from the Charity Commission.

Summary

This is one of the Sainsbury Family Charitable Trusts which share a joint administration. Like the others, it is primarily proactive, aiming to choose its own grantees, and its annual reports state that 'proposals are generally invited by the trustees or initiated at their request'. The extent to which readers should in general be deterred by this is discussed in the separate entry, under the Sainsbury name, for the group as a whole.

In this particular case, the statement and the general sentiment that unsolicited applications are unlikely to be successful seems to be contradicted in the same document where, under the 'health and social welfare' heading the trust notes that '[the trustees] will consider applications which deal with educational and psychological support for pre-school families [and] homelessness projects'

The trust has a particular interest in the arts and in artistic and architectural heritage and has made large grants to museums, galleries, libraries and theatres.

There are ongoing programmes for the repair of cathedrals and medieval churches and other conservation projects in the UK and overseas. The trust also supports a range of social welfare issues. Its support for activities in developing countries is focused on sub-Saharan Anglophone countries and Ethiopia. There is also a small Aids for Disabled Fund. Like many of the others in the Sainsbury group, the Headley Trust prefers to

support 'innovative schemes that can be successfully replicated or become self-sustaining'.

The settlor of this trust is Sir Timothy Sainsbury. His co-trustees include his wife, eldest son and legal adviser. The trust's staff includes the director of the Sainsbury family's charitable trusts, Alan Bookbinder.

Funding priorities

The following information is taken from the trust's website:

Arts & Heritage UK
The trustees respond to a wide and eclectic variety of projects to conserve buildings and important aspects of the UK's cultural heritage. This may include:

- regional museums with revenue costs or the purchase of exceptionally important artefacts
- educational access to museums and galleries particularly for the disabled and disadvantaged
- projects to conserve the industrial and maritime heritage of the UK
- work to encourage arts outreach and musical opportunities for young people, the disadvantaged or disabled, and the elderly
- notable archaeological projects in the UK
- projects to encourage rural crafts and heritage maintenance skills
- applied arts and crafts.

Funding within this category also covers:

- repair work to the fabric of cathedrals and large ecclesiastical buildings of exceptional architectural merit (pre-18th century). Modern amenities, organ repair/restoration and choral scholarships are not normally eligible
- funding for fabric repair and restoration is considered for medieval parish churches (or pre-16thcentury churches of exceptional architectural merit) in rural, sparsely populated, less prosperous villages, through a process of review, diocese by diocese. Urban churches are not eligible, and funding is available for fabric only (including windows), not refurbishment or construction of church halls nor other modern amenities.
- the Headley Museums Archaeological Acquisition Fund which was established in 2004 to help regional and local museums purchase treasure items found in the UK. In 2008 it was extended to include other archaeological items which are more than 300 years old. It is delivered in partnership with the Museums, Libraries and Archives Council/Victoria & Albert Museum Purchase Grant Fund.

THE HEADLEY TRUST

			Average grant
Arts and heritage (UK)	35	£1.9 million	£54,000
Cathedrals Programme	5	£180,000	£36,000
Parish Churches Programme	59	£164,500	£2,800
Museums' Archaeological Acquisition Scheme	20	£49,000	£2,500
Arts and heritage (overseas)	12	£235,000	£20,000
Developing countries	12	£272,500	£23,000
Education	12	£324,000	£27,000
Health and social welfare	39	£597,000	£15,000
Aids for disabled people	34	£29,000	£850
Total	**228**	**£3.7 million**	**£16,400**

Please note: this scheme has its own application form, available from the Headley Museums Archaeological Acquisition Fund website: www.headley-archaeology.org.uk.

Arts & Heritage overseas
Trustees support conservation projects of outstanding artistic or architectural importance; particularly the restoration of buildings, statuary or paintings, primarily in the countries of South Eastern Europe. They seek out reputable local non-governmental organisations as partners in these countries. They are also willing to consider archaeological projects in the region. Trustees hope to raise local community awareness of heritage issues and increase the culture of philanthropy.

Developing Countries
Initiatives are primarily in sub-Saharan Anglophone Africa and Ethiopia, priority projects include:
- water and sanitation
- environment
- education and literacy
- healthcare
- emergency appeals.

Education
Bursaries for higher education courses and vocational training in the arts, conservation and skilled crafts. Support, which is principally for British students, is rarely available for secondary education, except bursary support for exceptional students at the specialist music and dance schools.

Health & Social Welfare
Trustees are interested in tackling the causes and effects of social exclusion. Priority areas include: carers; independent living projects for the elderly; access for disabled people; and occasional research projects on medical conditions.

Aids for Disabled Fund
The trustees make a number of small grants towards aids for people with varying disabilities, channelled through appropriate charities, agencies and local authorities. These are awarded for a range of equipment, including, but not limited to, the following: specially adapted computer systems; communication aids; wheelchairs; electric scooters; and stair-lifts.

Grantmaking in 2010
In 2010 the trust had assets totalling £76.4 million and an income of just over £2.4 million. Grants were made during the year totalling £3.7 million.

Grants approved in 2010 were categorised with the number of grants and their value as shown in the table above.

Beneficiaries of grants of £5,000 or more across all categories included: Tate St Ives (£1 million); University of Durham (£120,000); Alzheimer's Society (£75,000); Orbis International (£60,000); Interact Reading Service (£50,000); Coventry Cathedra and Sing for you Life (£40,000 each); British Library (£34,000); Croatian Conservation Institute (£25,000); Textile Conservation Centre Foundation (£24,000); Woodbridge Tide Mill Trust (£20,000); Diocese of Newcastle (£15,500); Venice in Peril Fund (£12,500); Save the Children UK (£10,000); Marie Curie Cancer Care (£7,500); and Shrewsbury Museum & Art Gallery (£6,000).

Exclusions
Individuals; expeditions.

Applications
The Museums' Treasure Acquisition Scheme has its own application form, available from the Headley Museums Archaeological Acquisition Fund website: www.headley-archaeology.org.uk. For information on the small Aids for Disabled Fund, ring the trust on 020 7410 0330.

Otherwise, see the guidance for applicants in the entry for the Sainsbury Family Charitable Trusts. A single application will be considered for support by all the trusts in the group. However, for this group of trusts, as is the case for many trusts:

The trustees take an active role in their grant-making, employing a range of specialist staff and advisers to research their areas of interest and bring forward suitable proposals. Many of the trusts work closely with their chosen beneficiaries over a long period to achieve particular objectives. It should therefore be understood that the majority of unsolicited proposals we receive will be unsuccessful.

Applications should be sent by post with a description (strictly no more than two pages please, as any more is unlikely to be read) of the proposed project, covering:
- The organisation – explaining its charitable aims and objectives, and giving its most recent annual income and expenditure, and current financial position. Please do not send a full set of accounts.
- The project requiring funding – why it is needed, who will benefit and in what way
- The funding – breakdown of costs, any money raised so far, and how the balance will be raised.

All applications will receive our standard acknowledgement letter. If your proposal is a candidate for support from one of the trusts, you will hear from us within 8 weeks of the acknowledgement. Applicants who do not hear from us within this time must assume they have been unsuccessful.

The Heart of England Community Foundation

General
£1.3 million (2009/10)

Beneficial area
The city of Coventry and Warwickshire.

Pinley House, Sunbeam Way, PO BOX 227, Coventry CV3 1ND
Tel: 024 7688 4386
Fax: 024 7688 4640
Email: info@heartofenglandcf.co.uk
Website: www.heartofenglandcf.co.uk

Correspondent: Ms Catherine Mulkern, Director

Trustees: John Atkinson, Chair; Brian Clifford Holt; Peter Deeley; Mrs Sally Carrick; David Green; Zamurad Hussain; Susan Ong; Peter Shearing; John Taylor; Paul Belfield; Derek Cake; Alan Kirby.

CC Number: 1117345

Information available

Accounts were available at the Charity Commission.

In general, the foundation seeks to promote any charitable purposes for the benefit of the community in the city of Coventry, the county of Warwickshire and, in particular, the advancement of education, the protection of good health, both mental and physical, and the relief of poverty and sickness.

The Heart of England Community Foundation has a portfolio of grant making programmes for use by local community and voluntary groups. This enables benefactors to support community projects according to their own geographical or thematic criteria, and to have as much or as little involvement as they like in the awarding process. This portfolio often changes, so it is worth checking the community foundation's website when applying for funding, to keep informed of which funds are available at any time.

Funds are held on behalf of individuals, families, trusts, companies and statutory bodies, investing them to get maximum returns. The foundation can engage with groups on behalf of the funders – promoting their criteria, making awards and collecting feedback.

Potential applicants should contact the foundation directly or check its website for details of current funds as these may change frequently.

In 2009/10 the trust had assets of £2.5 million and an income of £1.4 million. Grants totalled £1.3 million and were made to 380 projects across the beneficial area averaging around £3,421 each. Grants are broken down by subject and geographical area as follows:

	% of total
Education and training	30%
Community support and development	24%
Sport and recreation	14%
Health and well-being	13%
Other	19%

	% of total
Coventry	22.7%
Warwickshire	30.7%
West Midlands	46.5%

Beneficiaries included: Blaze Community Foundation and Metal Dog Media Ltd (£12,000 each); Ford Residents Association and Southam Gymnastics (£5,000 each); Coventry Jesus Centre (£3,000); Tile Hill Trojans Basketball Club (£2,700); Somali Youth Community (£2,500); Milan Group (£2,000); Breakaway Holiday Project and Coventry Action for Autism Group (£1,000 each); Sea Cadet Corps (Leamington & Warwick) (£750); Alzheimer's Society Coventry and the Children's Care Campaign (£500 each); The Abbeyfield Society and Charterhouse District Scout Council (£250 each); and Youth of 2Day – Leavers Care Group (£150).

Exclusions

Grants will not usually be considered for the following:

- statutory provision
- individuals
- activities that promote religious activity
- activities that are not socially inclusive
- organisations with a turnover of over £100,000 excluding restricted funding
- grantmaking bodies
- mainstream activities of schools and colleges
- medical research
- animal Welfare
- political activities
- organisations with substantial reserves
- general and Major fundraising appeals
- sporting clubs except when aimed at addressing disadvantage
- continuation funding.

Applications

Application forms may be downloaded from the foundation's website, or you can call on 024 7688 4386 and a copy will be sent it to you.

Although guidance on how to complete the application form is included within the form itself, you are encouraged to telephone the foundation to discuss your project in advance of applying. Grants Officers, who cover specific geographical areas and funds, will be pleased to assist you.

None of the foundation's grant programmes run to deadlines, however applicants should expect an answer within 12 weeks. Applicants to the grassroots programme should expect to hear within 15 days.

Heathside Charitable Trust

General, Jewish

£640,000 (2010)

Beneficial area

UK.

Hillsdown House, 32 Hampstead High Street, London NW3 1QD

Tel: 020 7431 7739

Correspondent: Sir Harry Solomon, Trustee

Trustees: Sir Harry Solomon; Lady Judith Solomon; Geoffrey Jayson; Louise Jacobs; Juliet Solomon; Daniel Solomon.

CC Number: 326959

Information available

Accounts were available at the Charity Commission.

This trust has general charitable purposes, with a preference for Jewish organisations. The trustees tend to identify organisations and projects they wish to support and this generally arises from direct contacts rather than speculative applications.

In 2010 the trust had assets of £3 million and an income of £378,000. It made grants totalling £640,000.

A list of beneficiaries was not given however previous beneficiaries have included: Joint Jewish Charitable Trust (£141,000); Jewish Education Defence Trust and Community Security Trust (£25,000 each); Jewish Care (£15,000); and British Friends of

Jaffa Institute, GRET and Motivation (£10,000 each).

Other previous beneficiaries have included Holocaust Educational Trust, First Cheque 2000, Royal London Institute, Royal National Theatre, Jewish Museum, Cancerkin, King Solomon High School, Babes in Arms, Marie Curie Cancer Care and Weitzmann Institute.

Applications

In writing to the correspondent, at any time. Trustees meet four times a year.

The Hedera Charitable Trust

General

Beneficial area

UK.

Trustee Dept, Coutts & Co,
440 Strand, London WC2R 0QS
Tel: 020 7663 6838
Correspondent: Coutts & Co
Trustees: Ross Brawn; Jean Brawn; Coutts & Co.
CC Number: 1139607

The trust was registered in December 2010 with general charitable purposes. The settlor of the trust is Ross Brawn, who has been involved in Formula 1 motor racing for many years, notably with the Brawn GP team, with whom he won the world championship in 2009. It was reported in early 2011 that he made around £100 million from the sale of the Honda F1 team, which he bought for £1. He is currently the head of the Mercedes GP team.

Applications

In writing to the correspondent.

The Hedley Foundation

Youth and health

£749,000 (2009/10)

Beneficial area

UK.

1–3 College Hill, London EC4R 2RA
Tel: 020 7489 8076
Email: pbarker@hedleyfoundation.org.uk
Website: www.hedleyfoundation.org.uk
Correspondent: Pauline Barker, Appeals Secretary
Trustees: John F Rodwell, Chair; Patrick R Holcroft; George R Broke; Lt Col. Peter G Chamberlin; Lorna B Stuttaford; Angus Fanshawe; Lt. Col. Andrew Ford; David Byam-Cook.
CC Number: 262933

Information available

Accounts were on file at the Charity Commission, but without a grants list (available on request).

Summary

The Hedley Foundation was set up in 1971 and endowed from a family trust of which the principle asset was the compensation received on nationalisation (of the family mining concerns).

The main objective of the trustees' grant-making is to assist and encourage development and change. Grants are for specific projects only and are mostly one off, though the trustees sometimes agree to help fund the introduction of new and innovative projects with a series of up to three annual grants. Few grants exceed £5,000 and most of them go to charities where they can make an impact. The foundation does not support large or national appeals or appeals from cathedrals and churches.

Currently about 70% of the foundation's budget goes towards supporting young people; specifically, their education, recreation, support, training and health. Its subsidiary objective is to support people with disabilities and the terminally ill through the provision of specialist equipment and support for carers.

Trustees individually have visited many charities to which the foundation might make or has made grants.

Grants in 2009/10

During the year the foundation had assets of £29.2 million and an income of almost £1.3 million. Grants were made to 357 organisations totalling nearly £749,000.

Beneficiaries included: Abbeyfield (Reading) Society, Aberlour Child Care Trust; Academy Performance Ensemble; Access 2 Watersports, Action Medical Research, Adventure Limited, Air Training Corp ATC, Brookside Primary School, Brunswick Boys' Club, Buckingham Army Cadet League, Cumbria Cerebral palsy, Cuttleslowe Community Association, Daisy Chain, Friends of Holbeach School, Goal Line Youth Trust, Godalming Band, Magdalen Village Hall- Norfolk, Myton Hospices, Northern Ireland Cancer Fund for Children, Ocean Youth Trust, Raleigh International, RASCAL, Scouts, Sea Cadets, Wells Town Tennis Club and Youth Create.

Exclusions

Grants are made to UK registered charities only. No support for individuals, churches and cathedrals, core revenue costs, salary or transport funding, or for very large appeals.

Applications

Application forms are downloadable from the foundation's website. Once completed in typescript, the form should be printed off and sent by post to the appeals secretary named above, accompanied by a recent copy of your accounts and your email address. **Note:** the foundation is unable to return any enclosures that are sent in with applications.

The trustees meet six times a year. The closing date for a meeting is three weeks beforehand. All applications will be acknowledged, but, in the case of those short-listed, not until after they have been considered by the trustees. The trustees usually meet in January, March, May, July, September and November. A list of meeting dates for the current year is published on the foundation's website.

The foundation receives many more applications than it can fund and urges that applicants should not be surprised, or too disappointed, if they are unsuccessful.

The Helping Foundation

Orthodox Jewish

£4.6 million (2010)

Beneficial area

Greater London and Greater Manchester.

1 Allandale Court, Waterpark Road, Salford M7 4JN
Correspondent: Benny Stone, Trustee
Trustees: Benny Stone; David Neuwirth; Rabbi Aubrey Weis; Mrs Rachel Weis.
CC Number: 1104484

Information available

Accounts were available at the Charity Commission.

Registered with the Charity Commission in June 2004, the objects of the charity are the advancement of education according to the tenets of the Orthodox Jewish Faith; the advancement of the Orthodox Jewish Religion and the relief of poverty amongst the elderly or persons in need, hardship or distress in the Jewish Community.

In 2010 the foundation had assets of £60 million and an income of £17.8 million, which include properties gifted to the foundation to the value of £12.2 million and investment income of £4.6 million. Grants were made during the year totalling £4.6 million.

The beneficiaries of the largest grants during the year were: Asser Bishvil Foundation (£2 million); British Friends of Ezrat Yisrael (£670,000); Notzar Chesed (£236,500); New Rachmistrivka Synagogue Trust (£201,000); TTT (£198,500); Emuno Educational Centre (£163,000); United Talmudical Associates (£160,000); BCG CT (£105,000).

Other beneficiaries included: Friends for the Centre for Torah Education Centre (£57,000); Toimchei Shabbos Manchester (£30,000); Gateshead Kollel (£20,000); Beis Naduorna (£10,000); and Law of Truth (£5,500).

Applications

In writing to the correspondent.

The Hertfordshire Community Foundation

General

£1 million to organisations and individuals (2009/10)

Beneficial area

Hertfordshire.

Foundation House, 2–4 Forum Place, Fiddlebridge Lane, Hatfield, Hertfordshire AL10 0RN
Tel: 01707 251 351
Email: grants@hertscf.org.uk
Website: www.hertscf.org.uk
Correspondent: Christine Mills, Grants Manager
Trustees: J Stuart Lewis, Chair; Kate Belinis; Jo Connell; Gerald Corbett; David Fryer; Pat Garrard; Mike Master; Caroline McCaffrey; Brig John Palmer; John Peters; Cllr Richard Roberts; Penny Williams.
CC Number: 299438

Information available

Accounts were available from the Charity Commission. The foundation also has a detailed website.

Launched in 1989, the foundation is one of a number of community trusts in the UK, which supports and provides funds to local charities and voluntary groups that serve the local community and benefit the lives of the people they serve. The foundation is able to support a wide range of charitable activities, in and around Hertfordshire. The foundation advises, therefore, that it is always worth contacting them to discuss the project, in case they can help or direct you to someone else who can.

Foundation Grants

Project grants – Grants of up to £5,000 on a one-off basis. These grants are designed to help 'make something happen', whether on their own or together with other income. Major purchases or specific projects may be financed under this category.

Small grants – Grants of up to £500 on a one-off basis – usually for small groups. The foundation can provide a quick response to requests for all sorts of purposes, such as, start-up costs for a new group or project, equipment, training programmes, printed materials and so on.

Individual Grants – for children – Grants of up to £300 on a one-off basis. These grants are only made following referral by a professional, such as a social worker or health visitor. **Note:** grants are only payable to third parties, such as a shop, in order to purchase a much needed item.

Other programmes

From time to time the foundation also administers external funds, such as the Comic Relief and Grassroots Grants programmes.

For further information on the grant programmes currently available consult the foundation's website.

In 2009/10 the foundation had assets of £4.9 million, an income of nearly £3 million and made grants totalling £1 million. This included 248 grants to organisations and 167 grants to individuals. The main area of the foundation's grant making activity is in the field of social welfare. Its priority areas are as follows:

- disadvantaged children and families
- activities and opportunities for young people
- access to education, training and employment
- the quality of life of older people
- other community needs.

The majority of grants awarded from the foundation's unrestricted funds are made to local charities and voluntary groups for work within these areas. The foundation may also manage funds on behalf of local donors.

Exclusions

No grants are made towards:

- political groups
- animal welfare
- projects that are solely environmental
- statutory agencies
- medical research
- religious activities
- individuals, except within the terms of certain funds.

Applications

Ideally, applications should be made online via the foundation's website. However, if it is not possible to apply online, contact the foundation and they will send an application pack by post or email. An initial telephone call or email to check eligibility is also welcomed.

Common applicant mistakes

'They do not read our guidance! We receive umpteen generic letters and emails addressed to 'dear foundation, pls fund us' [sic] from all over the place, not having read our name which gives a clue as to our area of interest!!'

Hexham and Newcastle Diocesan Trust (1947)

Religion

£1.8 million (2009/10)

Beneficial area

Diocese of Hexham and Newcastle, overseas.

St Cuthberts House, West Road, Newcastle upon Tyne NE15 7PY
Tel: 0191 243 3300
Fax: 0191 243 3309
Email: office@rcdhn.org.uk
Website: rcdhn.org.uk
Correspondent: Kathleen Smith
Trustees: Revd Canon Seamus Cunningham; Revd Gerard Lavender; Revd James O'Keefe; Revd Philip Quinn; Revd Martin Stempczyk; Revd Christopher Jackson; Revd John Butters.
CC Number: 235686

Information available

Accounts were available from the Charity Commission.

This trust supports the advancement of the Roman Catholic religion in the Diocese of Hexham and Newcastle and other charitable works promoted by the church outside of the diocese. Usually this is done by initiating its own projects, but occasionally grants are given to other organisations to

carry out this work. 'All of our work is underpinned and reflects the ethos of the Roman Catholic tradition through prayer, worship, a commitment to community and a sense of mission.'

The trust aims to achieve its objects through four main areas of charitable activity which are:

▶ to provide support to the clergy in their ongoing work
▶ to provide and support pastoral work in parishes and local communities
▶ to provide support and direct lifelong Christian education in parishes and schools
▶ to preserve and invest in the property infrastructure of the diocese and parishes, facilitating worship and pastoral care.

In 2009/10 the trust held assets of £63.2 million had an income of £19.9 million. Grants were made totalling £1.8 million, as a share of the £18 million in charitable expenditure.

Funds were distributed in the following areas:

Clergy support	£1.2 million
Pastoral work	
Diocese/parishes	£7.5 million
St Cuthbert's Care	£5.8 million
Education	£703,000
Property	
Diocese/parishes	£2.1 million
School building work	£823,000
Total	£18 million

Grants were distributed in the following areas:

Clergy support	£24,000
Pastoral	£1.7 million
Education	£45,000

Beneficiaries included: Bede Chair of Catholic Theology (£700,000); CAFOD Development and emergency aid (£259,000); Catholic Education Service (£45,000); Peru Mission (£60,000); Peter's Pence; Sick and Retired Priests (£25,000 each); Apostleship of the Sea (£18,000); Domestic grants (£13,000); Racial Justice (£8,000); Survive MIVA (£7,000); and Catholic Agency for Social Concerns (£2,000).

Applications

Contact the correspondent.

Common applicant mistakes

'Applications for projects that do not meet our aims or do not match the Catholic ethos.'

The Hilden Charitable Fund

Homelessness, asylum seekers and refugees, penal affairs, disadvantaged young people and overseas development

£438,000 (2009/10)

Beneficial area

UK and developing countries.

34 North End Road, London W14 0SH
Tel: 020 7603 1525
Fax: 020 7603 1525
Email: hildencharity@hotmail.com
Website: www.hildencharitablefund. org.uk
Correspondent: Rodney Hedley, Secretary
Trustees: J R A Rampton; Prof C H Rodeck; Prof M B H Rampton; Mrs E K Rodeck; A J M Rampton; Miss E J Rodeck; Ms C S L Rampton; C H Younger; Prof D S Rampton; Ms M E Baxter; Miss E M C Rampton.
CC Number: 232591

Information available

Accounts were available online at the Charity Commission. The trust also has a helpful website.

General

This grant making trust was established in 1963 by an initial gift from Anthony and Joan Rampton. Priorities in the UK are homelessness, asylum seekers and refugees, penal affairs and disadvantaged young people. For projects in developing countries, priorities are projects which focus on community development, education, and health. These priorities are reviewed on a three year cycle and may change from time to time, as dictated by circumstances. The trust has also allocated a small budget to help community groups run summer playschemes for the benefit of children from refugee and ethnic minority families. Grants from this scheme rarely exceed £1,000.

The aim of the fund is to address disadvantage, notably by supporting causes which are less likely to raise funds from public subscriptions. Both the UK and overseas funding policy is directed largely at supporting work at community level.

Whilst the trust's policy is to address needs by considering and funding specific projects costs, the trustees are sympathetic to funding general running, or core costs. In awarding these types of grants, they believe that great value can be added, as most charities find fund raising for core costs most difficult.

All grant recipients are expected to send a report on how they have made use of their grant. The trust's staff team ensure adequate grant monitoring. Feedback is given to the trustees via regular mailings as well as at the quarterly meetings. Similarly the secretary produces briefings on all aspects of grant-making and policy development within the priority areas.

In establishing a secretariat for the trust in 1992, the trust aimed not only to effectively administer the grant making process but also to provide a helpful service to applicants on funding and good practice and applicants are encouraged to telephone the trust's offices for this service. The trustees and the staff team look to network with other funding and voluntary sector organisations, to identify new needs, improve standards and to prevent duplication.

Guidelines

The following information is taken from the annual report 2009/10 and the fund's website:

UK grants

The main interests of the trustees of the Hilden Charitable Fund are:

 ▹ homelessness
 ▹ asylum seekers and refugees
 ▹ penal affairs
 ▹ disadvantaged young people aged 16 to 25.

Grants are rarely given to well funded national charities. Fund policy is directed largely at supporting work at a community level within the categories of interest stated above.

Preference is given to charities with an income of less that £200,000 per year. Priorities given to different types of work within the main categories may change from time to time, as dictated by circumstances. Capital or revenue grants rarely exceed £5,000.

Overseas grants

Funds are available for capital and revenue funding. The funding programme is designed to help small and medium size initiatives. Trustees will consider applications from any countries within the developing world. Trustees wish to fund community development, education and health initiatives. Trustees will particularly welcome projects that address the needs and potential of girls and women.

Trustees will be pleased to hear from UK Non Governmental Organisations/charities and hope that UK NGOs/charities will encourage their local partners, if appropriate, to apply directly to Hilden for grant aid.

Summer playscheme grants

The trust has allocated a small budget to help community groups run summer playschemes for the benefit of children from refugee and ethnic minority families.

Grantmaking

In 2009/10 the trust had assets of £11 million and income of £334,000. There were 107 grants made totalling £438,000, broken down as follows:

Asylum seekers and refugees	24	£126,000
Overseas	24	£119,000
Penal affairs	15	£59,000
Homelessness	13	£53,000
Scotland	1*	£33,000
Playschemes	24	£19,000
Disadvantaged young people	3	£15,000
Other	3	£14,000

*to the Scottish Community Foundation for onward distribution

Beneficiaries included: Tanzania Development Trust – Tanzania (£20,000 in two grants); Joint Council for the Welfare of Immigrants – London (£15,000); Tolerance International UK – London and Church Mission Society – Bangladesh

(£7,000 each); Foundation of the Simon Bolivar Experimental United World College of Agriculture – Venezuela (£6,800); Detention Advice Service – London (£6,000); BOAZ Trust – Manchester (£5,600); Barts and the London NHS Trust (£5,300); Soundmix – London and Shekinah Torbay – Torquay (£5,000 each); Congo Action – D R of Congo (£4,000); Littlehampton Churches Together Homelink (£3,500); Alternatives to Violence Project (£3,000); Food Skills Limited – London (£2,500); Francis Clarissa Charitable Foundation – Philippines (£1,500); Inter Care – Ghana (£1,200); and Bondo Fund – Kenya (£1,000).

Exclusions

Grants are not normally made for well established causes or to individuals, and overseas grants concentrate on development aid in preference to disaster relief.

Applications

When making an application, grant seekers should note the following guidance from the trust:

We expect all applicants to complete our application form. Your case for funds should be concise (no more than 2 sides of A4), but supporting documentation is essential. Please ensure your application includes enclosures of:
 ▹ your most recent independently inspected accounts
 ▹ your most recent annual report
 ▹ projected income and expenditure for the current financial year.

Please be clear in your application form about when the proposed work is to commence, and give the relevant timetable.

Your application for funds should cover the following:
 ▹ clear explanation about who is responsible for managing the project
 ▹ a coherent plan of how the work is going to be carried out together with relevant budgets – project budgets should be presented in the context of the overall income and expenditure of the applicant NGO/ charity
 ▹ a plan of how the work is going to be maintained and developed in the future by involving relevant agencies and attracting money and resources
 ▹ an explanation of why the local project seeks the help of a UK agency

- details of local costs (e.g. salaries of state-employed teachers and medical personnel, cost of vehicles, petrol etc) and notes of any problems over exchange rates or inflation
- an account of the political, economic, religious and cultural situation in the country/area
- a brief comment on the extent to which the project can rely on government and local state funding in the country concerned
- details of monitoring and evaluation.

Applicants from the UK applying for funds for their project partners must complete both the UK Application Form and the Overseas Partner Profile Form.

Application forms, including one for Summer Playschemes, are available from the trust's website or offices. Note that forms must be submitted to the secretary by post as hard copies; forms submitted by email or other electronic means are not accepted. Applicants are advised to ensure that they have read the application guidelines at the top of the form prior to completion.

Potential applicants in Scotland should contact the Scottish Community Foundation, 22 Carlton Road, Edinburgh EH8 8DP; Tel: 0131 524 0300; website: www.scottishcf.org.

Lady Hind Trust

General with some preference for health and disability related charities

£382,000 (2010)

Beneficial area

England with a preference for Nottinghamshire and Norfolk.

c/o Shakespeares Solicitors, Park House, Friar Lane, Nottingham NG1 6DN
Tel: 0115 945 3700
Fax: 0115 948 0234
Email: ladyhind@btinternet.com
Correspondent: John Thompson, Administrator

Trustees: Charles W L Barratt; Tim H Farr; Nigel R Savory.
CC Number: 208877

Information available

Accounts were available at the Charity Commission.

The trust was established in 1951 for general charitable purposes. In practice, the trust has a preference for health, disability, medical and social welfare charities, with churches and animal welfare charities also being supported.

In 2010 the trust had assets of almost £11.7 million and an income of £377,500. Grants were made totalling £382,000, with most being for £5,000 or less, and were broken down geographically as follows (grants of £1,000 or more):

Nottinghamshire	59	£171,500
Norfolk	38	£107,000
Elsewhere	61	£76,000

Smaller grants were also made in the above areas totalling £28,000.

Beneficiaries of larger grants were: Oliver Hind Club (£17,500); Maggie's Nottingham, Nottinghamshire Community Safety Trust, The Hamlet Centre Trust – Norfolk and Norfolk Family Mediation Service (£10,000 each); The Norfolk Churches Trust, Lincolnshire & Nottinghamshire Air Ambulance, Nottinghamshire Historic Churches Trust and NSPCC – Nottinghamshire (£7,500 each).

More typical grants of £5,000 or less included those to: Rutland House School for Parents, Nottinghamshire Deaf Society, RSPCA – Radcliffe Animal Shelter, Nottingham Pregnancy Crisis Centre, Nottingham Youth Orchestra, YWCA Nottingham, Norwich Cathedral Choir Endowment Fund, Norfolk Community Foundation, Buckingham Emergency Food Appeal, North Walsham Multisports Club, National Rheumatoid Arthritis Society, Rainbows Children's Hospice, British Trust for Ornithology, Orchid Cancer Appeal and Shelter.

Exclusions

Applications from individuals are not considered.

Applications

Applications, in writing and with latest accounts, must be submitted at least one month in advance of trustee meetings held in March, July and November. Unsuccessful applicants are not notified.

The following information is taken from the 2010 trustees' annual report:

The trustees consider all written applications made to them by charitable organisations. Such applications are reviewed by every trustee prior to the trustees' four-monthly meetings and are discussed at such meetings. Grants are awarded at such meeting to those organisations which the trustees collectively consider to be worthy of their support. Grants are awarded principally to institutions based on their level of need and with a geographical bias towards Nottinghamshire and Norfolk.

The Hintze Family Charitable Foundation

Education; Christian churches; museums, libraries and galleries

£4.2 million (2010)

Beneficial area

England and Wales.

5th Floor, 33 Chester Street, London SW1X 7BL
Tel: 020 7201 6862
Correspondent: Oliver Hylton, Trustee
Trustees: Michael Hintze; David Swain; Brian Hannon.
CC Number: 1101842

Information available

Accounts were available at the Charity Commission.

Set up in 2003, the main objects of the foundation are providing support for:

- Christian churches in England and Wales, particularly the Diocese of Southwark
- relief of sickness and people with terminal illnesses

resources and equipment for schools, colleges and universities (in particular to enable the acquisition and retention of antiquarian books to be used as a learning resource)

promoting access to museums, libraries and art galleries.

In 2010 the foundation had assets of £2.7 million and an income of £5.9 million, mostly from donations. Grants were made to 39 organisations during the year totalling £4.2 million, and were broken down as follows:

Education: cultural	£2.3 million
Education: core	£1.3 million
Religion	£559,000
Health	£14,000

The largest grant made during the year was awarded to the National Gallery (£2 million), which has also received substantial donations in previous years. Other beneficiaries listed in the accounts were: Ridley Hall (£900,000); Catholic Conference for England & Wales (£540,000); the Prince's Foundation for the Built Environment (£219,500); Victoria & Albert Museum (£200,000); Glyndebourne Arts Trust (£150,000); and the Institute of Economic Affairs (£100,000).

Applications

The trust offers the following application guidance in its latest accounts:

The foundation invites applications for grants or commitments from charities which serve the objects of the foundation. No specific format is required for applications. Applications, along with potential donations and commitments identified by the Chief Executive and the trustees, are considered in formal trustee meetings.

The Hobson Charity Limited

Social welfare, education

£2.2 million (2009/10)

Beneficial area

UK.

Hildane Properties Limited, 7th Floor, 21 Bryanston Street, Marble Arch, London W1H 7PR

Tel: 020 7495 5599

Correspondent: Deborah Hobson, Trustee and Secretary

Trustees: Deborah Hobson; Sir Donald Gosling; Sir Ronald F Hobson; Lady Hobson; J Richardson.

CC Number: 326839

Information available

Accounts were available at the Charity Commission.

Established in 1985, the Hobson Charity Limited is the charitable vehicle of Sir Ronald Hobson, founder of Central Car Parks and later co-owner of NCP car parks with business partner, Sir Donald Gosling, also a trustee (see also the Gosling Foundation). Both charities are administered from the same address.

In 2009/10 the charity had assets of £14.9 million (2007/08: £591,000), and an income of £17.1 million, mainly from donations. There were 91 grants made to 66 beneficiaries during the year totalling almost £2.2 million.

Grants were awarded in the following categories:

Advancement of education	33	£1.1 million
Other purposes beneficial to the community	42	£711,500
Advancement of religion	10	£296,000
Relief of poverty	6	£210,000

Beneficiaries during the year included: Westminster Abbey (£250,000 in 4 grants); Royal Opera House (£150,000); RNLI (£105,000 in 4 grants); SSAFA and Queenswood School (£100,000 each); White Ensign Association (£90,000 in 2 grants); Great Steward of Scotland's Dumfries House Trust (£75,000); Outward Bound Trust (£60,000 in 2 grants); Churchill Archives Centre, Tate Millbank and the Foundation for Liver Research (£50,000 each); STOP – Trafficking UK (£35,000 in 2 grants); Children in the Arts, White Lodge Redevelopment and the British School of Osteopathy (£25,000 each); Centrepoint and the Swan Sanctuary (£10,000 each); and the British Association of Adoption & Fostering, Jewish Lads' and Girls' Brigade and

Christian Youth Enterprise (£5,000 each).

Exclusions

No grants to individuals, except in exceptional circumstances.

Applications

In writing to the correspondent. The trustees meet quarterly.

The Jane Hodge Foundation

Medical care and research, education and religion

£585,000 (2009/10)

Beneficial area

Unrestricted, in practice UK with a preference for Wales.

Ty Gwyn, Lisvane Road, Lisvane, Cardiff CF14 0SG

Tel: 029 2076 6521

Email: dianne.lydiard@ janehodgefoundation.co.uk

Correspondent: Margaret Cason, Secretary

Trustees: Eric Hammonds; Julian Hodge; Joyce Harrison; Derek Jones; Ian Davies; Margaret Cason.

CC Number: 216053

Information available

Accounts were available at the Charity Commission.

The foundation was established in 1962 and its objective is to apply its income in the following areas:

the encouragement of medical and surgical studies and research, and in particular the study of and research in connection with the causes, diagnosis, treatment and cure of cancer, poliomyelitis, tuberculosis and diseases affecting children

the general advancement of medical and surgical science

the advancement of education

the advancement of religion.

In 2009/10 the foundation had assets of £28 million and an income of just over £559,000. The foundation described it's grantmaking in the 2009/10 accounts:

> From the applications for grants received in the year, applications in respect of £585,000 (2009: £935,000) met the criteria required and amounts were granted to the charities concerned. The level of grants made each year can vary since there is a process of assessment and approval before grants can be made and grants may cover a period of more than one year. [...] Actual donations paid in the year including amounts committed in prior years, amounted to £625,000.

Grants awarded during the year were distributed as follows:

Medical	£299,000
Education	£92,000
Religion	£38,000
Other	£157,000

Beneficiaries paid during the included: Cardiff University – Macro Economics (£137,000 in three grants); George Thomas Memorial Trust (£58,000 in two grants); Tenovus (£30,000); Cardiff University – Merit Prizes (£14,000 in two grants); Ty Hafan (£8,000); Age UK (£6,000); Great Western Society Ltd, Bobath Cymru, Race Equality First, Shelter Cymru and Archdiocese of Cardiff – St Mary's Priory (£5,000 each); Plan International UK (£4,000); the Owl Fund (£3,000); and Missionary Sisters of the Holy Rosary, British Heart Foundation and Corpus Christi Catholic High School (£2,500 each).

Exclusions

Applications are only considered from exempt or registered charities. No grants to individuals.

Applications

In writing to the correspondent. Applications for grants are considered by the trustees at regular meetings throughout the year. Applications are acknowledged.

Common applicant mistakes

'Applications from organisations which are not registered charities.'

Sir Harold Hood's Charitable Trust

Roman Catholic charitable purposes

£482,000 (2009/10)

Beneficial area

Worldwide.

Haysmacintyre, Fairfax House, 15 Fulwood Place, London WC1V 6AY
Tel: 020 7722 9088
Correspondent: Margaret Hood, Trustee
Trustees: Dom James Hood; Anne-Marie Blanco; Nicholas True; Margaret Hood; Christian Elwes.
CC Number: 225870

Information available

Accounts were available at the Charity Commission.

The trust was established in 1962 by the late Sir Harold Hood, who died in 2005. Sir Harold was an influential editor and director of several Catholic publications during his lifetime, a philanthropist who was involved in a number of charities and an early investor in an electronics company that later evolved into Vodafone. The trust supports Roman Catholic charities.

In 2009/10 it had assets of £24.8 million and an income of £518,000. Grants were made to 83 organisations totalling £482,000.

Beneficiaries included: Prison Advice & Care Trust (£30,000); Craig Lodge Trust (£25,000); Duchess of Leeds Foundation (£20,000); Diocese of Brentwood (£15,000); St Joseph's Pastoral Centre (£12,000); Venerable English College – Rome (£10,000); Maryvale Institute – Birmingham (£8,000); Apostleship of the Sea (£6,000); Catholic Children's Society – Westminster and Saint John of God Care Services (£5,000 each); San Jose Retreat Centre – Chile (£4,000); Young Christian Workers (£3,000); Ten Ten Theatre (£2,000); and the Dominican Sisters of St Joseph (£1,000).

Exclusions

No grants for individuals.

Applications

In writing to the correspondent. The trustees meet once a year to consider applications, usually in November.

Common applicant mistakes

'There are many more applications that do not fit criteria – applications from organisations that are not Roman Catholic, applications from individuals and applications that do not include financial accounts.'

The Sir Joseph Hotung Charitable Settlement

General

£1.5 million (2009/10)

Beneficial area

Worldwide.

c/o Alison Holmes, HSBC Private Bank (UK) Ltd, 78 St James' Street, London, SW1A 1JB
Correspondent: Sir Joseph Hotung, Trustee
Trustees: Sir Joseph E Hotung; Sir Robert D H Boyd; Victoria F Dicks; Michael Gabriel; Joseph S Lesser.
CC Number: 1082710

Information available

Accounts were available at the Charity Commission.

Set up in 2000, in 2009/10 this trust had assets of £2.3 million and an income of £2.6 million, mainly from donations from Sir Joseph Hotung. Grants totalled £1.5 million.

The following beneficiaries received grants during the year: British Museum (£1 million), to fund the relocation of the Percival David collection of Chinese ceramics; School of Oriental and African Studies (£180,000 in total), for the Sir Joseph Hotung Programme for Law, Human Rights and Peace Building in the Middle EastAtlantic College (£135,000); London Symphony Orchestra, the Council for Assisting

Refugee Academics and Yesh Din Volunteers (£50,000 each); Rushmore Healthy Living (£10,000); and International Spinal Research Trust (£1,200 in total).

Applications

The trust has previously stated that: 'the trustees have their own areas of interest and do not respond to unsolicited applications'.

The Albert Hunt Trust

Health and welfare

£1.4 million (2009/10)

Beneficial area

UK.

Coutts and Co., Trustee Department, 440 Strand, London WC2R 0QS
Tel: 020 7663 6825
Fax: 020 7663 6794
Correspondent: The Senior Manager
Trustees: Coutts and Co; Richard Collis; Breda McGuire.
CC Number: 277318

Information available

Accounts were available at the Charity Commission.

The Albert Hunt Trust was established in 1979 and its mission statement is 'to promote and enhance the physical and mental welfare of individuals, or groups of individuals, excluding research or the diagnosis and treatment of specific medical conditions, by the distribution of trust funds, at the sole and absolute discretion of the trustees, principally to charities registered in England and Wales that are actively engaged in that field of work.'

A very large number of modest grants are given to a wide range of organisations, both national and local, each year. Most grants are for between £1,000 and £2,000 and many seem to go to new beneficiaries. There are around 80 grants for £5,000 or slightly more each year and many of these tend to go to regularly supported, national charities. The grantmaking capacity of the trust has increased in recent years following

the death of Miss M K Coyle, a long-standing trustee, who bequeathed £17 million from her estate to the trust.

In 2009/10 the trust had assets of £45 million and an income of £1.3 million. Grants were made to 587 institutions totalling £1.4 million.

Beneficiaries of the largest grants were: Royal School for the Blind (£50,000); Chiltern MS Centre (£41,000); Marie Curie Cancer Care (£30,000); East Anglia Children's Hospice and Lorica Trust (£25,000 each); St Barnabus Hospice (£20,000); St Christopher's Hospice (£15,000); and Fiveways School (£11,000).

Beneficiaries of grants of £10,000 included: Little Sisters of the Poor – Dundee, St Gemma's Hospice, RNIB, Clock Tower Sanctuary, Garwood Foundation, SENSE, Katherine House, Leonard Cheshire Disability and Harris Hospiscare.

Beneficiaries of grants of £5,000 included: YMCA, West Sussex Learning Link, Wigtownshire Women's Aid, Trinity Hospice, the Salvation Army, Sons of Divine Providence, Sue Ryder Care, Southview School Fund, St Andrew's Hospice, Newham Renewal Programme, CLIC Sargent and British Limbless Ex-Servicemen.

Beneficiaries of grants of £2,000 or less included: Blind in Business, 1 Voice, Citizen's Advice Bureau – Calderdale, Oesophageal Patients Network, Abingdon Bridge, Family Action, Age Concern – Torbay, Camp Horizon, Beating Bowel Cancer, Community Drug Service, Polycystic Kidney Disease Charity, Disability North, Guidepost Trust Ltd, Headway – Cambridgeshire, London Jesus Centre, Queen Alexandra Homes, Support for Parents and Autistic Children, Teenage Cancer Trust Scotland and Northern Ireland and, Voice UK.

Exclusions

No grants for medical research or overseas work.

Applications

In writing to the correspondent. All appeals should be by letter containing the following:

- aims and objectives of the charity
- nature of appeal
- total target if for a specific project
- contributions received against target
- registered charity number
- any other relevant factors.

The correspondent has stated that no unsolicited correspondence will be acknowledged unless an application receives favourable consideration. Trustees meet in March, July and November although appeals are considered on an ongoing basis.

The Hunter Foundation

Education, young people, children, relief of poverty, community development

Around £750,000 (2009/10)

Beneficial area

UK and overseas.

Marathon House, Olympic Business Park, Drybridge Road, Dundonald, Ayrshire KA2 9AE
Email: info@thehunterfoundation.co.uk
Website: www.thehunterfoundation.co.uk
Correspondent: Sir Tom Hunter, Trustee
Trustees: Sir Tom Hunter, Chair; Lady Marion Hunter; Jim McMahon; Robert Glennie; Vartan Gregorian.
SC Number: SCO27532

Information available

Despite making a written request for the accounts of this foundation these were not provided.

The following information on how the foundation operates was previously available from its website:

Summary

The Hunter Foundation (THF) is committed to adventure philanthropy, investing capital and intellect into tackling the root causes of societal problems through holistic and systemic interventions.

Our focus in the developed world is to invest in national educational programmes that challenge stubborn, system wide issues that prevent children from achieving their potential.

In the developing world we largely invest in holistic developments that embed solutions within communities and countries, again with education being central to our programmes.

Our aim is to act as a catalyst for change by investing in pilot programmes with strategic partners and often alongside government that, if proven, are then adopted by government or the community for embedding nationally where possible.

Principles of investment
Objective
Effect positive, long-term cultural change to deliver a 'can do' attitude initially in Scotland via major investment in, largely, educational programmes.

Why?
The more enterprising the nation, the more economically stable it becomes providing the necessary funds to deliver for all. Education is the ultimate change agent in achieving this end goal.

Investment principles
- proactive identification of investments via definitive research and analysis
- active investment management against targets
- joint ventures and partnerships dominate
- measurable ROI via definitive analysis
- exit strategies predominate – invest against target adoption of programmes by government.

Investment profile
Four distinct profiles across short, medium or long-term objective impact:
- national educational programmes or pilots therein to deliver on our objective
- policy influence to support delivery and Government investment
- advocacy to secure extended investor base and support
- support for disenfranchised or suffering children.

Funding guidelines
By way of guidance to applicants some basic facts about our investments are as follows:

UK and Ireland
THF invests in programmes that embed a 'can do' spirit in children and that tackle the root causes of the problems that see children consigned to the 'Not in Education, Employment or Training' group (NEET Group).

We do not fund capital projects nor individual causes and we always look towards investing in programmes that are nationally scalable and capable of being embedded for systemic change.

Developing World
In the developing world we look towards investing in holistic programmes of intervention that support self-sustainable communities thriving. Often these combine health, education, agriculture and business creation and development interventions.

We are currently working with the Clinton Foundation on the Clinton-Hunter Development Initiative. This initiative is concentrating in Malawi & Rwanda on pilot projects that could be replicated throughout different countries. Until we have completed these pilot programmes we will are unlikely to be in a position to consider new project funding as we fundamentally believe in taking a very strategic investment approach and this will only come from testing out models of intervention.

Unlike the UK and Ireland we do consider capital projects and often fund, for example, schools development.

On occasion we also fund humanitarian causes as we have done in both Northern Uganda and the Niger, albeit we always aim to integrate our approach and build in as much sustainability as is possible under the circumstances.

Grantmaking in 2009/10
Since 2007/08 the trust's income has fallen from £11 million to £1 million. A grants total was not available but based on previous years, may have been around £750,000. However, as no recent information was available, it may be that the trust has suspended its grant giving programme.

Additionally, since the financial crisis of 2007/08 the investment company West Coast Capital went into administration which impacted on the trust as its income was partially tied to the profitability of that company. Following this the spokesperson for the founder of the trust, stated that:

> The foundation will be leaner and meaner going forward, but [...] hopefully he's got another 40 years to invest £1bn in the common good. He is not withdrawing that challenge

Previous beneficiaries include: Determined to Succeed, the Children's Charity, Make Poverty History, Band Aid for Village Reach Mozambique, Cash for Kids at Christmas Charitable Trust, Maggie Care Centre, Retail Trust, Variety Club, NCH Action for Children Scotland, Cancer Research, Prince's Scottish Youth Business Trust and Children in Need.

Applications
The foundation offers the following application guidance on its website:

The Hunter Foundation proactively sources programmes for investment, or works with partners to develop new programmes where a gap or clear need is identified. As such it is very rare indeed for THF to fund unsolicited bids, however if you wish to apply please complete a maximum two page summary outlining how your project fits with our aims and objectives and email it to info@thehunterfoundation.co.uk. This summary should include:
- summary of project
- impact of project
- any independent evaluation undertaken of your project/ programme
- if this is a local programme how it could be scaled to become a national programme
- current sources of funding
- funding sought from the Hunter Foundation

Please note: we do not have a large staff and thus we will not consider meetings in advance of this information being provided. If your project appears to be of initial interest, we will then contact you to discuss this further.

Hurdale Charity Limited

Advancement of Jewish religion, relief of poverty and general charitable purposes
£2 million (2009/10)

Beneficial area
Worldwide.

Cohen Arnold and Co., New Burlington House, 1075 Finchley Road, London NW11 0PU

Correspondent: Abraham Oestreicher, Trustee

Trustees: Mrs Eva Oestreicher; Pinkas Oestreicher; David Oestreicher; Abraham Oestreicher; Jacob Oestreicher; Benjamin Oestreicher.

CC Number: 276997

Information available

Accounts were available at the Charity Commission, without a list of grants.

The trust supports charitable activities mostly concerned with religion and education. Almost all of the support is given to Jewish organisations that are seen to uphold the Jewish way of life, both in the UK and overseas.

In 2009/10 the trust had assets of £18.8 million and an income of £2.4 million. Grants were made to organisations totalling £2 million, however a list of beneficiaries was unavailable with this year's accounts.

Previous beneficiaries include: Mesifta; Chevras Moaz Ladol; Yetev Lev Jerusalem Trust; Vyoel Moshe Trust; Beis Ruchel; Kollel Rabinow; Craven Walk Beis Hamedresh Trust; Ezras Bis Yisroel; Mosdos Belz Bnei Brak; Pesach Project Trust; Shaarei Chesed; Kehal Chasidei Bobov; Hachzakos Torah V'chesed; Medical Aid Trust; Yeshiva Law of Trust; and Zichron Yechezkal Trust.

Applications

In writing to the correspondent.

Impetus Trust

The development of charities working with people who are economically disadvantaged

£455,000 (2009/10)

Beneficial area

Worldwide, in practice, UK.

20 Flaxman Terrace, London
WC1H 9PN
Tel: 020 3384 3940
Email: info@impetus.org.uk
Website: www.impetus.org.uk
Correspondent: Claire Kelly
Trustees: Louis G Elson, Chair; Nat Sloane; Amelia Howard; Andy Hinton; Stephen Dawson; Stephen Lambert; Ian Meakins; Chris Underhill; Craig Dearden-Phillips.
CC Number: 1094681

Information available

Accounts were available online at the Charity Commission. The trust has a useful website.

Impetus Trust was set up in 2002 and is believed to be the UK's first general venture philanthropy charitable fund.

The trust's website describes its vision as:

> A world in which people are not trapped in economic and social disadvantage, but where they can get the help they need, to lead independent and fulfilling lives. Our aim is to break the cycle of economic disadvantage by helping distinctive charities and social enterprises to improve levels of education, skills and employability. We are enabling them to create transformational change and to become robust and sustainable.

Impetus aims to achieve this by:

- helping distinctive charities to scale up dramatically
- encouraging donors to give and give more
- encouraging people to contribute their skills and experience
- combining the best of the business and non-profit worlds
- demonstrating its brand of venture philanthropy is successful.

Impetus offers an integrated venture philanthropy package designed to enable the organisations they help to turn around more lives, and hence maximise their impact. This support comprises three elements:

- *strategic core funding* – usually from three-to-five years, to scale up social impact
- *hands-on management support* – executive overview and support in implementing agreed strategy, including monthly meetings with the charity's chief executive and other senior executives, providing a sounding board, challenge and support; monitoring progress against business plan objectives and agreed milestones
- *specialist expertise* – targeted on specific areas for development and growth; delivered on a project basis by the highly skilled Impetus pro bono expert pool.

The venture philanthropy approach has parallels with the venture capital industry where partnership and long-term collaboration help build the capacity of the organisations supported. Impetus aims to help ambitious charities who want to make a 'transformational change' (typically significant growth). The charities supported have to both want and need the integrated package of support the trust offers to make them stronger and more sustainable when that support is removed.

The trust adopts a two-phase approach to its investment in charities. Typically, in the first phase of the investment programme (business planning phase), grant payments are lower than in the second phase (scale up phase). As a result, total annual payments to charities can vary significantly depending on which phase of the investment programme charities are in.

In 2009/10 the trust had assets of £2.5 million and an income of £3.8 million, mainly from donations. Grants were made to 13 organisations totalling £455,000.

Beneficiaries were: Street League (£125,000); Fairtrade Foundation (£95,000); Blue Sky (£75,000); FRC Group (£38,000); COUI – Teens and Toddlers, IntoUniversity and Camfed International (£25,000 each); Keyfund (£17,000); St Giles Trust (£13,000); Speaking Up, Beat and NPL (£5,000 each); and Leap Confronting Conflict (£2,500).

Guidelines

The trust will only consider funding charities that meet the following criteria, as detailed on its website:

How we work

We do not, under any circumstances, offer funding alone. We only support charities and social enterprises through our venture philanthropy package of management support, strategic funding and specialist expertise.

What we fund

Please look carefully at our selection criteria, which applies to all applicants:

1 **Coverage:** Impetus backs charities and social enterprises that are working with significant numbers of economically disadvantaged people.
2 **Ambition:** We support charities and social enterprises that have the ambition to effect far-reaching change for the economically disadvantaged.
3 **Outcome focus:** We seek charities and social enterprises that deliver outcomes addressing challenging

issues such as long-term unemployment or reoffending. We focus on outcomes relating to increased educational attainment, skills and employment. Organisations we back have a commitment to monitoring and evaluating their outcomes.

4 **Talented chief executive**: We seek chief executives with the vision, energy, enterprise and determination to motivate their teams to deliver ambitious plans that aim to help more people move out of poverty. Quality of leadership is an important factor in our decision making.

5 **Distinctive and good prospects for sustainability**: We target our support at charities and social enterprises that are distinctive and have strong prospects for success and sustainability in their sector.

6 **Supporting the whole organisation**: We provide funding and expertise to support the development of a whole organisation and not just a particular project or activity.

Structural criteria

Organisations must:

- be a registered charity or social enterprise
- have a turnover of at least £250,000
- be operational and with audited accounts for at least three years
- have a HQ and significant portion of management in England (the majority of organisations supported by the trust operate only in the UK, though a small number operate internationally).

Exclusions

Grants are not made to organisations in the following areas:

- those focusing on animals, culture and heritage rather than people
- umbrella organisations/networks
- services that are conditional upon the acceptance, profession or observance of a particular religious position
- projects substantially/exclusively working in the areas of research or advocacy
- those seeking funding for a particular project/building.

Applications

In the first instance, applicants should complete the *eligibility checker* on the trust's website and submit a brief expression of interest. The trust will then be in contact if it wishes to

pursue the application any further. If so, the assessment process will include a detailed due diligence assessment covering all aspects of the charity's operations, including meetings with the organisation's trustees and management as well as site visits and analysis of financial data. The charity states: 'We ask all potential applicants to refer to the selection criteria on our website prior to contacting us to ensure that they are a good fit with Impetus objectives.'

Common applicant mistakes

'They have not ensured that their organisation meets all of the selection criteria.'

Investream Charitable Trust

Jewish

£644,500 (2009/10)

Beneficial area

In practice the UK and Israel.

Investream Ltd, 38 Wigmore Street, London W1U 2RU
Tel: 020 7486 2800
Correspondent: The Trustees
Trustees: Mark Morris; Graham S Morris.
CC Number: 1097052

Information available

Accounts were available at the Charity Commission.

Established in 2003, the trust's income is derived from Investream Ltd and its subsidiary undertakings.

The trustees intend for the foreseeable future, to continue their policy of distributing income within a short period of time from its receipt rather than accumulating reserves for future projects.

The trustees have adopted a policy of making regular donations to charitable causes, having regard to the level of the trust's annual income. They regularly appraise new opportunities for direct charitable expenditure and from time to time make substantial donations to support special or capital projects.

In 2009/10 the trust had assets of £374,000 and an income of £436,500. Grants were made during the year totalling just over £644,000, and were categorised as follows:

Education	£523,000
Poor, needy and others	£58,500
Medical	£31,500
Community and elderly care	£31,250

Beneficiaries included: Jewish Care, Moreshet Hatorah, Cosmon Belz, Chana, Project Seed, Menorah High School for Girls, Train for Employment and Woodstock Sinclair Trust. Individual grant amounts were not disclosed in the accounts.

Applications

In writing to the correspondent.

The Isle of Anglesey Charitable Trust

General

£357,000 (2009/10)

Beneficial area

The Isle of Anglesey only.

Isle of Anglesey County Council, County Offices, Llangefni, Anglesey LL77 7TW
Tel: 01248 752607
Fax: 01248 752696
Email: gvwfi@anglesey.gov.uk
Correspondent: David Elis-Williams, Treasurer
Trustees: E Schofield; R G Parry; David Bowles; David Elis-Williams; Lynn Ball.
CC Number: 1000818

Information available

Accounts were available at the Charity Commission

The trust, independent in law from, but administered by the Isle of Anglesey County Council was set up with an endowment from Shell (UK) Limited when the company ceased operating an oil terminal on Anglesey, according to the terms of the 1972 private Act of Parliament which had enabled the terminal to be set up in the first place.

The objects of the trust are:
- the provision of amenities and facilities
- the preservation of buildings
- the conservation and protection of the land
- the protection and safeguarding of the environment.

Grantmaking

Allocations of grants are made annually to the following categories of projects:
- community and sporting facilities (small capital projects)
- village halls (annual running costs)
- other grants (mainly one-off small grants).

In the year 2009/10 the trust held assets of £15.5 million and had an income of £429,000. £357,000 was given in grants to 47 organisations, including the continual funding of the Oriel Ynys Mon art gallery which received the majority of the funding with £270,000.

Other beneficiaries included: Menai Bridge Community Centre (£8,000); Brynteg Village Hall (£7,000); Llangoed Village Hall (£6,500); Llanddanielfab Community Centre (£6,000); Children's Park Newborough (£5,000); Holyhead Weightlifting Club (£4,000); Newborough Institute and David Hughs Community Centre Beaumaris (£3,000 each); Trearddur Bay Community Centre (£2,000); and Rhosneigr Evangelical Church and Amlwch Port Hall (£1,000 each); .

The trust's accounts provide information as to the distribution of its income to various organisations in Anglesey, however, it is not possible to ascertain from the accounts whether any of the grants awarded are used to subsidise the county council by providing facilities and/or services which should be provided by the local authority.

Exclusions

No grants to individuals or projects based outside Anglesey.

Applications

In writing to the correspondent with an application form, following advertisements in the local press in February. The trust considers applications once a year and states:

'we will take details of any prospective applicants during the year, but application forms are sent out annually in February'.

Isle of Dogs Community Foundation

Regeneration, general

£1.2 million (2009/10)

Beneficial area

London Borough of Tower Hamlets.

Jack Dash House, 2 Lawn House Close, Isle of Dogs, London E14 9YQ
Tel: 020 7345 4444
Fax: 020 7538 4671
Email: admin@idcf.org
Website: www.idcf.org/
Correspondent: Tracy Betts, Director
Trustees: Sister Christine Frost; Gabrielle Harrington; Mohammed Shahid Ali; Stella Bailey; Rita Bensley; Howard Dawber; Elizabeth Passey; Timothy Archer; Elizabeth Cowie; Muge Dindjer; David Edgar; Duke Chifiero; Gareth Stephens.
CC Number: 802942

Information available

Accounts were available at the Charity Commission.

Established in 1990, the Isle of Dogs Community Foundation (IDCF) aims to establish a permanent and independent source of local charitable funds and use them to make grants to local charities and voluntary groups for the benefit of the community. Support is focused on Millwall and Blackwall, which remain among the most deprived wards in the country. However, in January 2008, IDCF extended its area of benefit to include the wards of Limehouse, East India and Lansbury. Although funding priorities are reviewed regularly, the areas of training and employment, community development and education seem to receive regular support.

IDCF offers three main types of grants:
- *fast track grants* of up to £800 – intended for small items of equipment, social outings, events and other items of one-off expenditure
- *standard grants* of between £800 and £10,000 – for general purposes, capital items, or running costs
- *large grants* over £10,000 p.a. – for multiple years are also available to larger, well established organisations.

The foundation also manages the Community Safety and Capital Works programme, the Millwall Park Endowment and two programmes on behalf of Poplar Harca. Further details can be found on the foundation's website.

It should also be noted that grant schemes can change frequently. Please consult the foundation's website for details of current programmes and their deadlines.

Exclusions

IDCF will not fund:
- individuals
- projects with primarily religious activities
- projects with primarily political activities
- projects or activities that are a statutory service
- activities that are the responsibility of the local or health authorities
- activities that have already taken place.

Applications

The foundation's website has details of the grant schemes currently being administered. Please note: the foundation asks that grant seekers discuss their potential applications with the director, Tracey Betts, before any application is submitted.

The J J Charitable Trust

Environment, literacy

£765,000 (2009/10)

Beneficial area

Unrestricted.

Allington House, 1st Floor,
150 Victoria Street, London
SW1E 5AE

Tel: 020 7410 0330

Fax: 020 7410 0332

Email: info@sfct.org.uk

Website: www.sfct.org.uk

Correspondent: Alan Bookbinder, Director

Trustees: John Julian Sainsbury; Mark Sainsbury; Judith Portrait; Lucy Guard.

CC Number: 1015792

Information available

Accounts were available online at the Charity Commission. Brief information is also available from the Sainsbury Family Charitable Trusts' website.

Summary

This is one of the Sainsbury Family Charitable Trusts, which share a joint administration. They have a common approach to grantmaking which is described in the entry for the group as a whole.

A relatively small number of grants are made. Few of them are for less than £5,000 and occasional grants can be for more than £100,000. The trust has previously stated that: 'Proposals are generally invited by the trustees or initiated at their request. Unsolicited applications are discouraged and are unlikely to be successful, even if they fall within an area in which the trustees are interested. The trustees prefer to support innovative schemes that can be successfully replicated or become self-sustaining.'

The settlor of this trust is Julian Sainsbury and he is still building up the endowment, which included making a donation of £1.6 million in 2009/10.

Grantmaking in 2009/10

In 2009/10 the trust had assets of £32 million and a total income of £2.5 million, including the donation from the settlor. 29 grants were approved during the year totalling £765,000. They were distributed as follows:

Literacy support	17	£276,000
Environment: UK	6	£223,000
Environment: overseas	4	£230,000
General	2	£36,000

The following examples of grants approved are prefaced by the trust's description of its interests in that area, taken from its annual report:

Literacy support

The trustees aim to improve the effectiveness of literacy teaching at primary and secondary education stages, and the transition between them, for children with general or specific learning difficulties, including dyslexia. For the last five years they have supported the Every Child a Reader programme, a widely effective Reading Recovery intervention for struggling readers in the early years. It has also become more apparent in their grants in the world of education how much good work at primary key stages is undermined after the transition of children to secondary school. Overcoming this particular challenge will be a focus of the trustees' attention and research in the next years.

The trustees seek to target similar help on literacy at people who have become disaffected from education and who now find themselves homeless, without access to training and employment, in prison or at risk of offending. They are also concerned to ensure that interventions on literacy at different stages can link up, as they impinge on individuals in various situations of their experience. Recently this led the trustees to commission Lemos & Crane, the leading social researchers, to set up the Literacy Action Net (www.literacyactionnet.org.uk) for all the charities and public sector initiatives which address literacy at the various stages of people's needs. Launched in spring 2010 this is a both a virtual network and a regular meeting of organisations and practitioners for mutual learning, improved public and government awareness and the dissemination of the best ideas on literacy. It is also strongly focused on strengthening individuals' own aspirations for life, livelihood, enterprise and personal achievement.

The trustees' selection of projects to support takes account of relevant government initiatives in schools and on-going developments within education and training for people at risk and in prison. They seek projects that pilot new ideas for teaching and supporting people with specific learning difficulties, or that provide demonstrations that are likely to be of wider interest. Given budget constraints within the education and criminal justice sectors, the trustees seek to support projects aiming to deliver cost-effective solutions.

Beneficiaries included: London Libraries Development Agency, towards the expansion of Outside Story, promoting reading and library support among homeless people and others at risk (£124,000); British Dyslexia Association, towards the mentoring training and development scheme and the local association and membership development scheme (£98,000); the Ministry of Stories, towards the London replication of 826 Valencia, a creative reading and writing store for children in San Francisco (£30,000); and Haven Distribution, towards the purchase of books for prisoners (£24,000).

Environment – UK

Grants are made for environmental education, particularly supporting projects that display practical ways of involving children and young adults. The trustees do not support new educational resources in isolation from the actual process of learning and discovery. They favour projects which enable schools to take on the benefits of education for sustainable development across the whole school and beyond, into the local community.

The trustees are particularly interested in projects that progressively enable children and young people to develop a sense of ownership of the project over time, and that provide direct support to teachers to deliver exciting and high quality education in the classroom.

The trustees are also interested in the potential for sustainable transport, energy efficiency and renewable energy in wider society. In some cases the trustees will consider funding research, but only where there is a clear practical application. Proposals are more likely to be considered when they are testing an idea, model or strategy in practice.

In collaboration with several other Sainsbury Family Charitable Trusts, the trustees are exploring how to address some of their grant-making to projects which will help make low carbon economies feasible and sustainable.

Beneficiaries were: Sustainability and Environmental Education – SEEd, towards core costs (£90,000); the Ashden Awards, towards a UK award at the 2010 Ashden Awards (£70,000); Green Alliance, towards 'Ask the

Climate Question' in the run up to the UK General Election (£30,000); Global Action Plan, towards creating sets of environmental exhibits (£20,000); Public Interest Research Centre Ltd, for research on the value of the UK's offshore renewable resource (£10,000); and University College London, for research on Germany's pay-as-you-save loan schemes for domestic energy efficiency retro-fitting to inform the plans of the UK Department of Energy and Climate Change (£3,100).

Environment – Overseas
The trustees continue to support community-based agriculture projects, which aim to help people to help themselves in an environmentally sustainable way.

Beneficiaries were: St Matthew's Children's Fund – Ethiopia, to expand the urban gardening project (£90,000); Koru Foundation, to increase capacity for delivering more renewable energy projects in the developing world (£75,000); Movement for Ecological Learning and Community Action – MELCA Ethiopia, to expand work with communities as they protect their local environment (£60,000); and Mobile Art School Kenya, towards operating costs (£5,000).

General
The two beneficiaries were: the Mayhem Company, towards performance work with young people in Southwark through the South Bank Centre (£26,000); and UNICEF, towards earthquake relief in Haiti (£10,000).

Exclusions
No grants for: individuals; educational fees; or expeditions. The trust only funds registered charities or activities with clearly defined charitable purposes.

Applications
See the guidance for applicants in the entry for the Sainsbury Family Charitable Trusts. A single application will be considered for support by all the trusts in the group.

However, for this as for many of the trusts, the following statement from the trust's website should be noted:

The trustees take an active role in their grant-making, employing a range of specialist staff and advisers to research their areas of interest and bring forward suitable proposals. Many of the trusts work closely with their chosen beneficiaries over a long period to achieve particular objectives. It should therefore be understood that the majority of unsolicited proposals we receive will be unsuccessful.

John James Bristol Foundation

Education, health, older people, general

£1.2 million (2009/10)

Beneficial area
Worldwide, in practice Bristol.

7 Clyde Road, Redland, Bristol BS6 6RG
Tel: 0117 923 9444
Fax: 0117 923 9470
Email: info@johnjames.org.uk
Website: www.johnjames.org.uk
Correspondent: Julia Norton, Chief Executive
Trustees: Joan Johnson; David Johnson; Elizabeth Chambers; John Evans; Andrew Jardine; Andrew Webley; John Haworth.
CC Number: 288417

Information available
Accounts were available from the Charity Commission. The trust has a clear and useful website.

The foundation was established in 1983 and its objects are the relief of poverty or sickness, the advancement of education or other charitable purposes amongst the inhabitants of Bristol, and other charitable purposes with no defined beneficial area. The foundation's main aim is to benefit as many residents of the city of Bristol as possible by granting money as diversely as they can within the foundation's key focus areas of education, health and the elderly. This may include making grants to organisations carrying out the following work:

- encouraging young people, through grants to schools, youth organisations and other charities, to make the most of their educational opportunities
- improving health care through grants for medical research, equipment in hospitals, specialist equipment, holidays and care at home for individuals whose health needs are recognised by a registered charity
- assistance, through organisations, to older residents of Bristol in ways which will encourage them and help improve their quality of life.

In 2009/10 the foundation had assets of £51 million and an income of £1.3 million. Grants made totalling £1.2 million were categorised as follows:

Education	£559,000
Health	£464,000
Elderly	£126,000
General	£4,000

Beneficiaries included: Vassall Centre Trust (£151,000); Bristol Grammar School and the Red Maid's School (£33,000 each); St James Priory Project (£31,000); Barton Hill Settlement (£30,000); Barnardo's – Bristol BASE Project (£25,000); Jessie May Trust, Feed the Children and St Ursula's School (£20,000 each); Marie Curie Cancer Care (£19,000); Cotham School (£15,000); Motability (£10,000); Age Concern – Bristol (£9,000); Caring at Christmas (£5,000); St Dunstan's (£3,000); InterAct (£2,500); Relate – Avon (£1,500); and Canynges Society (£1,000).

Exclusions
No grants to individuals.

Applications
The trustees meet quarterly in February, May, August and November to consider appeals received by 15 January, April, July and October as appropriate. There is no application form and appeals **must be submitted by post**, to the chief executive on no more than two sides of A4. Supporting information, sent by the applicant with their appeal, is available to the trustees at their meeting.

All appeal applications are acknowledged, stating the month in which the appeal will be considered by the trustees. If further information is required it will be requested and a visit to the applicant may be made by a representative of the foundation. Grants are normally only given to charitable bodies who can clearly show that they are benefiting Bristol residents, and working within the foundation's key focus areas of education, health and the elderly.

Common applicant mistakes

'Applying for a need that does not benefit citizens of the city of Bristol.'

Jay Education Trust

Jewish

£471,000 (2009/10)

Beneficial area

Worldwide.

37 Filey Avenue, London N16 6JL
Correspondent: Rabbi Alfred Schechter, Trustee
Trustees: Rabbi Alfred Schechter; Gabriel Gluck; Shlomo Z Stauber.
CC Number: 1116458

Information available

Accounts were available at the Charity Commission.

'The objects of the charity are: the relief of poverty in the Jewish Community worldwide; the advancement of religious education according to the beliefs and values of the Jewish Faith worldwide and any charitable purpose at the discretion of the trustees for the benefit of the community.'

In 2009/10 the trust had assets of £2 million and an income of £1.46 million. Grants were made totalling £471,000, broken down as follows:

Religious institutions	£179,000
Educational establishments	£174,000
Relief of poverty	£118,000

Previous beneficiaries included: Mifalei Tzedoko Vochesed; United Talmudical Associates; British Friends Of Igud Hakolelim B'Yerushalayim; Lolev Charitable Trust; Toldos Aharon Israel; Edupoor Ltd;

Chachmei Tzorfat Trust; Heichel Aharon; Friends of Sanz Institutions; Yad Vochessed; Zedokoh Bechol Eis; Belz Yeshiva London; Jewish Seminary For Girls; and Comet Charities Ltd.

Applications

In writing to the correspondent.

The Jerusalem Trust

Promotion of Christianity

£2.5 million (2010)

Beneficial area

Unrestricted.

Allington House, 1st Floor, 150 Victoria Street, London SW1E 5AE
Tel: 020 7410 0330
Fax: 020 7410 0332
Email: jerusalemtrust@sfct.org.uk
Website: www.sfct.org.uk
Correspondent: Alan Bookbinder, Director
Trustees: Rt Hon. Sir Timothy Sainsbury; Lady Susan Sainsbury; Dr V E Hartley Booth; Phillida Goad; Dr Peter Frankopan.
CC Number: 285696

Information available

Accounts were available at the Charity Commission.

Summary

This is one of the Sainsbury Family Charitable Trusts, which share a joint administration. Their approaches to grantmaking have aspects in common which are described in the entry for the group as a whole. The trust is primarily proactive, aiming to choose its own grantees, and it discourages unsolicited applications.

The trust supports a wide range of evangelical organisations, across a broad though usually moderate spectrum of Christian activity. The number and value of grant approvals in 2010 were categorised as follows:

Evangelism and Christian mission in the UK	63	£874,000
Christian education	17	£676,000
Christian evangelism and relief work overseas	23	£490,000
Christian media	11	£415,000
Christian art	8	£69,000

Grantmaking in 2010

In 2010 the trust had assets of £85 million and an income of £2.7 million. Grants were paid during the year totalling £2.5 million, which included grants approved during previous years.

The following are examples of grants that were approved during the year, including a description of the trust's interests in each category based on information provided in the latest accounts:

Evangelism and mission work (UK)

Trustees are particularly interested in Christian projects that develop new ways of working with children and young people, particularly those who have little or no contact with the church. Support is also given to evangelistic projects, especially new and emerging evangelists and those that undertake Christian work with prisoners, ex-prisoners and their families.

Beneficiaries included: Kainos Community, towards the cost of the organisation's long term development programme (£100,000); University of Aberdeen, towards the Kairos Forum for Cognitive Disabilities and Spirituality (£60,000); Bible Reading Fellowship, towards the costs of employing a regional coordinator for Messy Church (£50,000); Fusion, towards the costs of 'love your uni' (£30,000); pubchurch.co.uk, towards the organisation's charitable activity (£23,000); and Innervation Trust, towards Pop Connection (£10,000).

Christian education

Funding is given for the development of Christian curriculum resource materials for schools in RE and other subjects; the support, training and retention of Christian teachers in all subjects; and lay training. Trustees are also interested in projects which support Christian teachers in leadership in schools.

Beneficiaries included: University of York, towards Christianity and Cathedrals, to include a DVD, four pilot projects in cathedrals and an app for mobiles (£177,000); Churches' National Adviser in Further Education, towards the costs

187

of 'All Faiths and None' working in further education colleges (£70,000); Stapleford Centre, towards the cost of providing small grants towards the cost of Christian resources for schools (£60,000); Religious Education Council, towards the administration and support costs of the organisation (£40,000); Walk Through the Bible Ministries, towards the salary of a volunteer coordinator (£20,000); and Biblical Frameworks, towards developing resources (£7,500).

Christian evangelism and relief work overseas

Trustees are particularly interested in proposals for indigenous Christian training centres, the provision of Christian literature in Central and Eastern Europe and Anglophone Sub-Saharan Africa. Grants are also made to Christian organisations developing work with marginalised groups.

Beneficiaries included: Tearfund, towards the costs of supporting the Kale Haywet Church's development programme in Ethiopia (£131,000); Barnabas Fund, towards the College of Theology and Education, Moldova (£50,000); Institute for Bible Translation, towards the costs of translation work for Russia and the Commonwealth of Independent States (£30,000); SAH Speranta, towards salary and project costs (£20,000); and Starfish Asia, towards the costs of their scholarship fund (£10,000).

Christian media

Trustees are interested in supporting media projects that promote Christianity, especially in North Africa and the Middle East. They are also interested in supporting training and networking projects for Christians working professionally in all areas of the media and for those considering media careers. The trustees have supported a number of projects using digital media and are interested in supporting a range of projects that use the internet creatively to promote Christianity.

Beneficiaries included: Jerusalem Productions Ltd, for disbursement by Jerusalem Productions during the calendar years 2010–2011 (£250,000); Lapido Media, towards core costs (£60,000); Arab World Ministries, towards the extension of the online Bible course 'Rooted in the Word' (£40,000); HCJB UK, towards the costs of Spotlight (£16,000); and Premier Christian Media, towards the transmission costs of Premier Christian radio (£10,000).

Christian art

Trustees focus mainly on a small number of commissions of works of art for places of worship.

The two main beneficiaries were: National Gallery, towards the interpretation and education costs of the Gallery's exhibition in 2011, Devotion by Design – Italian Renaissance Alterpieces before 1500 (£45,000); and Creative Foundation, towards the cost of the work by Hew Locke for the Folkestone Triennial (£10,000). A number of small grants were also made, including those to: Art and Sacred Places, Lantern Arts Centre and the Society of Portrait Sculptors.

Exclusions

Trustees do not normally make grants towards building or repair work for churches. Grants are not normally made to individuals.

Applications

See the guidance for applicants in the entry for the Sainsbury Family Charitable Trusts. A single application will be considered for support by all the trusts in the group.

However, for this as for many of the trusts, 'proposals are generally invited by the trustees or initiated at their request'.

Jerwood Charitable Foundation

The arts

£1.2 million (2010)

Beneficial area

UK.

171 Union Street, Bankside, London SE1 0LN
Tel: 020 7261 0279
Email: info@jerwood.org
Website: www. jerwoodcharitablefoundation.org
Correspondent: Shonagh Manson, Director
Trustees: Tim Eyles, Chair; Katherine Goodison; Juliane Wharton; Anthony Palmer; Sarah Vine; Thomas Grieve; Rupert Tyler; Phyllida Earle.
CC Number: 1074036

Information available

Accounts were available at the Charity Commission.

The Jerwood Charitable Foundation (the foundation) was established in 1998 with general charitable purposes. In 1999 it took over the administration of a number of initiatives of the Jerwood Foundation (the parent company), including the Jerwood Applied Arts Prize, Jerwood Choreography Award and Jerwood Painting Prize.

In 2005 the charitable foundation became completely independent after receiving the final endowment donation from the Jerwood Foundation. However, as the foundation has previously stated, it retains close ties with all of the Jerwood family:

We continue to see ourselves as closely linked with, and will continue to seek guidance from, the Jerwood Foundation on our activities and of course, as ever, will work closely with other Jerwood family members especially the Jerwood Space.' [The Jerwood Space is a major initiative of the company, offering affordable rehearsal spaces for dance and theatre companies to develop their work.]

The aims of the foundation are the distribution of funds to individuals and organisations for the promotion of visual and performing arts and education in the widest sense. It has four main objectives:

▷ to support artists in the early stages of their careers
▷ to support the wider infrastructure of arts organisations
▷ to respond positively to those taking artistic risks
▷ to explore the opportunity of identifying small programme related investment opportunities.

Funding policy

The foundation is a major sponsor of all areas of the performing and visual arts, particularly projects which involve rewards for excellence and the encouragement and recognition of outstanding talent and high standards, or which enable an organisation to become viable and self financing. It rarely sponsors single performances or arts events, such as festivals, nor does it make grants towards the running or core costs of established arts organisations.

The following information is taken from the foundation's website:

> We are dedicated to imaginative and responsible funding of the arts across the UK, with a particular focus on supporting emerging talent and excellence. We aim for funding to allow artists and art organisations to thrive; to continue to develop their skills, imagination and creativity with integrity.
>
> Where we are able, and it is appropriate, we may wish to be sole funder of a project, but we also provide partnership funding and run co-commissioned projects with other funders. We aim to monitor chosen projects closely and sympathetically, and are keen to seek visible recognition of our support.
>
> The JCF has the benefit of association with capital projects of the Jerwood Foundation. These include the Jerwood Space, the Jerwood Theatres at the Royal Court Theatre, the Jerwood Gallery at the Natural History Museum and the Jerwood Sculpture Park at Ragley Hall, Warwickshire. The support for these initiatives by the Jerwood Foundation will be a factor when considering any applications.
>
> The foundation will fund individuals, organisations and companies who are not registered charities (providing the project meets the foundation's charitable aims).

Types of grants
Grant levels vary between the lower range of up to £10,000 (often plus or minus £5,000) and more substantial grants in excess of £10,000. The foundation states that there should be no expectation of grant level as all applications will be assessed on merit and need.

Projects and awards
The foundation actively pursues and develops initiatives in the arts world as well as receiving unsolicited applications for funding. Projects and awards cover a wide range of arts activities currently in the following areas:

- music
- dance
- theatre
- literature
- visual arts
- film

- multi disciplinary
- Mission Models Money (action research programme).

The foundation will rarely commit to repeat funding over a number of years, preferring to make revenue donations on a one-off basis. However, it is prepared, in many cases, to maintain support if the partnership has been successful and consistency will help to secure better results.

> The JCF also provides 'challenge funding', whereby the foundation will make a grant provided the recipient or other interested party can match the remaining shortfall.
>
> **Jerwood Visual Arts** – a year round contemporary gallery programme of awards, exhibitions, and events at Jerwood Space, London, which then tours the UK. JVA is developed and run by the Jerwood Charitable Foundation; as a major initiative it represents about a third of our work and resources. The programme currently comprises the Jerwood Drawing Prize, Jerwood Makers Open, Jerwood Painting Fellowships and the Jerwood Encounters series. We also run a talks and events programme, host a writer in residence placement and support a rolling Traineeship in gallery management.
>
> **Large Grants** – grant partnerships made over a number of years, or single awards of £10,000 or more. These partnerships tend to be developed proactively or through ongoing conversation with potential applicants, responding to key needs and issues within arts sectors. This fund allows us to develop strategic approaches to supporting artists through nurturing or professional development programmes founded and run by established arts organisations. Through this fund we also support research and development initiatives supporting experimentation or to generate new work or new collaborations, investigation into sectoral or policy provision, and commissioning initiatives.
>
> **Small grants** – We also support a broader number of small grants for one-off projects, generally under £10,000. This fund allows us to explore new relationships, work directly with individual artists, take risks and support research or development of future ideas. At the heart of every small grant is a targeted or particular professional or sectoral development opportunity to be explored.
>
> Due to the limitations of our funding, we do not offer general support for production costs, touring or staging exhibitions.

The majority of our partnerships and initiatives are proactively sought and developed, however we do accept unsolicited proposals. Please note that we very rarely fund projects which are put forward in this way and are seeking specific, targeted, tangible professional development opportunities in the work that we take on.

Grantmaking in 2010
In 2010 the foundation had assets of £27 million and an income of £979,000. 43 grants were made totalling £1.2 million. Grants can be categorised as follows:

	% of total
Visual arts	36%
Theatre	14%
Music	13%
Dance	12%
Cross-disciplinary projects	10%
Small grants	8%
Literature	7%

Beneficiaries of large grants included: Sadler's Wells, Jerwood Studio and Artangel (£100,000 each); Royal Court and Jerwood New Playwrights (£75,000 each); Young Vic and Jerwood Assistant Directors Programme (£50,000 each); Dance UK and Dancers' Health and Take Five (£40,000 each); Royal Society of Literature and the RSL Jerwood Awards for Non-Fiction (£28,000 each); The Opera Group and Incubator (£22,000 each); and Performing Arts Labs – Movement and Meaning Lab (£15,000).

Beneficiaries of £10,000 or less included: Aurora Orchestra, Jerwood Commissions and Circus Space: Creative Exchanges (£10,000 each); PRS for Music Foundation and New Music 20 x 12 (£8,000 each); Wittering Productions: Where are they now? (£6,000); and Brian Lobel: Carpe Minuta Prima (£4,800).

£402,000 of funding was also spent across 13 initiatives in the Jerwood Visual Arts programme.

More information on the projects, initiatives and awards supported by the foundation can be found on the foundation's website.

Exclusions
The Jerwood charitable Foundation will not consider applications for:
- building or capital costs (including purchase of equipment)
- projects in the fields of religion or sport
- animal rights or welfare

- study fees or course fees
- general fundraising appeals which are likely to have wide public appeal
- appeals to establish endowment funds for other charities
- appeals for matching funding for National Lottery applications
- grants for the running and core costs of voluntary bodies
- projects which are of mainly local appeal or identified with a locality
- medical or mental health projects
- social welfare, particularly where it may be considered a government or local authority responsibility
- retrospective awards
- projects outside Great Britain
- schools which are trying to attain 'Special Schools Status'
- general touring, production or staging costs
- environmental or conservation projects
- musical instruments
- informal education or community participation projects
- education or participation projects for those who have not yet left formal education.

The foundation may, where there are very exceptional circumstances, decide to waive an exclusion.

Applications

Initial applications should include:

- a short proposal, not more than two sides of A4, outlining a description of the organisation's aims or a short biography for individuals, and a description of the specific project for which funding is sought and the opportunity it seeks to fulfil
- a detailed budget for the project, identifying administrative, management and central costs details of funding already in place for the project, including any other trusts or sources which are being or have been approached for funds, and
- if funding is not in place, details of how the applicant plans to secure the remaining funding.

The trustees may decide to contact the applicants for further information including:

- details of the management and staffing structure, including trustees

- the most recent annual report and audited accounts of the organisation, together with current management accounts if relevant to the project.

However, the foundation asks that this information is *not* sent unless it is requested.

Applications may be made online via the website. Alternatively applicants can send proposals by post. The foundation may wish to enter into discussions and/or correspondence with the applicant which may result in modification and/or development of the project or scheme. Any such discussion or correspondence will not commit the foundation to funding that application.

Applications are assessed throughout the year. Successful applicants will be invited to report to the foundation at the completion of their project and to provide photographs of the work or project supported.

As the foundation receives a large number of applications, it is not always possible to have preliminary meetings to discuss possible support before a written application is made.

Jewish Child's Day

Charitable purposes of direct benefit to Jewish children who are disadvantaged, suffering or in need of special care

£847,000 (2009/10)

Beneficial area

Worldwide. In practice, mainly Israel, UK and Eastern Europe.

5th Floor, 707 High Road, North Finchley, London N12 0BT
Tel: 020 8446 8804
Fax: 020 8446 7370
Email: info@jcd.uk.com
Website: www.jcd.uk.com/
Correspondent: Daniel Burger, Executive Director
Trustees: Joy Moss, Chair; June Jacobs; Stephen Moss; Virginia

Campus; David Clayton; Francine Epstein; Susie Olins; Amanda Ingram; Gaby Lazarus; David Collins.
CC Number: 209266

Information available

Accounts were available at the Charity Commission. The trust also has an informative website.

The trust was established in 1947 to encourage Jewish children in the UK to help less fortunate Jewish children who were survivors of the Nazi holocaust. The trust exists to improve the lives of Jewish children, in the UK, Israel or elsewhere overseas, who for any reason are suffering, disadvantaged or in need of special care.

In 2009/10 the trust had assets of £646,500 and an income of £1.3 million from donations and appeals. Grants were made to 144 organisations totalling £847,000.

Beneficiaries included: Federation of Jewish Services (£70,000); Givat Ada and Leeds Jewish Welfare Board (£60,000 each); Kol Israel (£20,000); Friends of Givat Ada's Children's Home (£18,000); Mantas Arava (£10,000); Nitzan (£8,000); Reut Sderot Association (£5,000); and Orr Shalom (£2,000).

Exclusions

Individuals are not supported. Grants are not given towards general services, building or maintenance of property or staff salaries.

Applications

If your organisation meets JCD's criteria, you could apply for a grant ranging from £500 to £5,000 towards the cost of small or medium size items of equipment or a project that will directly benefit children.

The committee considers applications in February, June and September each year. Completed application forms should be sent together with a set of audited accounts by 31 December, 30 April and 31 July accordingly.

To apply for a grant from JCD please contact Jackie Persoff on 020 8446 8804 or jackie.persoff@jcd.uk.com

The Joffe Charitable Trust

Alleviation of poverty and protection/ advancement of human rights

£368,000 (2009/10)

Beneficial area

The Gambia, Kenya, Malawi, Mozambique, South Africa, Tanzania, Uganda, Zambia and Zimbabwe.

Liddington Manor, The Street, Liddington, Swindon SN4 0HD

Tel: 01793 790203

Email: joffetrust@lidmanor.co.uk

Website: www.joffecharitabletrust.org

Correspondent: Linda Perry, Trust Manager

Trustees: Lord Joel Joffe, Chair; Lady Vanetta Joffe; Deborah Joffe; Nick Maurice; Mark Poston.

CC Number: 270299

Information available

Accounts were available from the Charity Commission. The trust has a clear and simple website.

The Joffe Charitable Trust was established in 1968 by the settlor, Lord Joffe and Vanetta Joffe. The objectives of the trust are widely drawn but in reality most grants are made for the relief of poverty and the advancement of human rights in the developing world.

The trust conducts its activities through grant making and the trustees have an ongoing relationship with a large number of charities, (the settlor is a former chair of Oxfam and the Giving Campaign). The decisions made as to which organisations/ projects to support are based on the trustees' assessment of the quality of leadership within an organisation and the impact that the initiatives which they support are likely to have.

Guidelines

The following information on funding policy is taken from the trust's website:

Focus areas

The Joffe Trust normally makes grants for work in two areas:

Campaigning work in the UK & EU
We fund campaigning work that presses UK & EU governments and major companies to act in the interests of poor people in Africa. Campaigns may be in a range of areas such as: trade, patent law and tax as well as government aid, human rights, corruption, holding governments to account and other issues.

Pro-poor private enterprises
We fund organisations that support small to medium sized, locally owned enterprises that sell goods and services to poor people that help them improve their lives. For instance, these include: renewable energy products, family planning products, water pumps and others. We also support efforts to strengthen markets and distribution networks in these areas. *Please note the trust does not support micro-credit initiatives.*

Exceptional Grants

Occasionally, the Trust considers proposals for exceptional grants that fall outside these two areas. These grants are made for work that has the potential to make a disproportionate impact on tackling poverty in the developing world. They include unproven innovations, start-up organisations and other new approaches.

The trust considers proposals for exceptional grants on a case by case basis, with a particular emphasis on potential impact and leadership. Exceptional grants are very rarely made to unsolicited proposals.

Our Approach

In all our grants, we aim to contribute to long term results that tackle issues at scale, for instance by:
- helping build strong, independent organisations
- funding work that is based on a strong understanding of relevant issues and related initiatives
- funding work that has a clear strategic purpose and realistic plans for contributing to long term changes at scale over five or more years.

The trust normally funds UK registered charities or organisations with equivalent not-for-profit status that have annual income of less than £5m per year.

We support initiatives where our limited funding can make a significant difference and that are hard to fund from other sources.

In addition to making grants, the Trust invests a proportion of its assets in social investments which generate jobs and social benefits in sub Saharan Africa as well as a financial return for investors.

Geographical Focus

The Trust primarily funds work in Anglophone countries in sub Saharan Africa.

Assessment Criteria

All grant applications are assessed against the following criteria:
- strong leadership
- capacity to deliver
- clear and focused objectives
- realistic budgets and fundraising plans
- strategic purpose and long term results
- measurable impact
- strong partnerships with African organisations and / or related initiatives
- value for money
- activities that are hard to fund from other sources.

Grant size

The trust makes [individual] grants of between £5,000 and £40,000 per year, and very occasionally more, for up to three years.

Grants in 2009/10

In 2009/10 the trust had assets of £12 million and an income of £386,000. Grants were made totalling £368,000.

Beneficiaries included: Ubulele (£51,000); Acid Survivors Trust and Global Witness (£30,000 each); Tourism Concern (£27,000); BUILD (£20,000); Centre for Innovation in Voluntary Action (£17,000); Transparency International (£15,000); APT Enterprise Development (£13,000); One Voice Europe (£10,000); and Tomorrow's Company (£7,500).

Exclusions

No grants for: emergency relief, the arts, conflict resolution, formal education, micro credit, work directly in the field of HIV/Aids, individuals, large charities with income of over £5 million per annum.

Applications

Firstly, applicants must complete an online application form available through the trust's website. The trust aims to respond to applicants within one month if they have been successful. If so, they will be asked to submit a more detailed proposal, including:

- objectives and specific targets
- information on how they will measure results
- information on the sustainability of the work planned
- CV of the chief executive or key person in the organisation
- evidence of demand and fit to other initiatives in the geographic area
- the latest audited accounts, sent as a hard copy
- the most recent annual review, if applicable, sent as a hard copy.

The trust aims to let all stage two applicants have a decision within four months of receiving their proposal.

The Elton John Aids Foundation

HIV/AIDS welfare and prevention

£7.4 million (2010)

Beneficial area
Unrestricted.

1 Blythe Road, London W14 0HG
Tel: 020 7603 9996
Fax: 020 7348 4848
Email: admin@ejaf.com
Website: www.ejaf.com
Correspondent: Robert Key, Executive Director
Trustees: Sir Elton John, Founder; David Furnish, Chair; Lynette Jackson; Frank Presland; Anne Aslett; Marguerite Littman; Johnny Bergius; James Locke; Rafi Manoukian; Scott Campbell.
CC Number: 1017336

Information available
Accounts were available at the Charity Commission. The trust also has an excellent website with clear grantmaking guidelines.

Summary
This foundation was established in 1993 by Sir Elton John to empower people infected, affected and at risk of HIV/AIDS and to alleviate their physical, emotional and financial hardship, enabling them to improve their quality of life, live with dignity and exercise self-determination. Their mission is to provide focused and sustainable funding to frontline programmes that help alleviate the physical, emotional and financial hardship of those living with, affected by or at risk of HIV/AIDS and continue to fight against this world pandemic.

Since its establishment the Elton John AIDS Foundation (EJAF) UK has raised over £91 million to provide grants in 15 countries over 4 continents to support more than 1,200 projects.

In 2010 the foundation held assets of assets of £26.7 million and had an income of £9.2 million. Grants were made totalling £7.4 million.

Areas of work
The foundation funds a range of services for those living with or affected by HIV/AIDS including education, peer support, medical care, income generation, counselling and testing. It supports operational research but not pure medical research. Particular emphasis is given to the most disadvantaged or high risk groups, both nationally and internationally, and to community driven programmes that place people living with HIV/AIDS at the centre of service provision. Its activities fall into three main areas:
1 grantmaking for:
    - funding UK projects
    - funding international projects
    - providing small grants
2 fundraising and promotional activities
3 management and governance activities.

The EJAF has five main areas of work:

Innovation
The trust aims to use its money in innovative and resourceful ways to maximise its impact on those infected and affected by the disease. This includes finding partnerships with other organisations and finding new ways of dealing with existing issue including innovative technologies. They also fund many pilot programmes that, once proved, can be replicated or expanded by larger funders or government services.

Livelihoods
The foundation addresses livelihood and food issues through programme areas including risk mitigation, home based care, support for positive people and vulnerable children. It is primarily aimed at empowering households to live independently with adequate nutrition, shelter, medical care and with children in school. This also includes providing emergency hardship grants and nutritious home delivered meals to people in the UK.

Positive lives
This tackles the myriad of problems that HIV positive people around the world face including:
- accessing appropriate treatment and care services
- managing and dealing with side effects of treatment
- loss of employment and income
- stigma and isolation.

Vulnerable groups
This refers to those communities who face a high risk of HIV infection but who have been marginalised by society including:
- men who have sex with men
- transgender communities
- sex workers
- detained/ prison populations
- injecting drug users.

Women and children
The trust support programmes which mitigate the impact of HIV/AIDS on women and children, from practical help with food supplies, infant feeding, income and housework to psychosocial support in managing a life threatening illness, the process of disclosure of HIV status between parents and children, and peer support and advocacy.

Grantmaking in 2010
£7.4 million was distributed in grants during the year which was illustrated on the website by country:

Cambodia	2	£758,000
India	3	£885,000
Kenya	1	£221,000
South Africa	11	£1.9 million
Tanzania	4	£827,000
Uganda	2	£114,000
UK	5	£1.4 million
Ukraine	3	£409,000
Zambia	1	£1 million

Beneficiaries included: The Food Chain (£116,000); Terrence Higgins Trust (£445,000); University of Liverpool (£23,000); CARE International UK (£143,000); Tamil Nadu Voluntary Health Association (£200); AIDS Foundation of South Africa (£15,700); Thohoyandou Victim Empowerment Trust (£6,000); Bwindi Community Hospital

(£97,000); Centre for Infectious Disease Research in Zambia (£26,000); Grassroots Soccer (£233,000); Johannesburg Child Welfare Society (£5,800); and UK Ukrainian AIDS Response (£31,000).

Exclusions

For both UK and international grants the foundation will not fund:

- academic or medical research
- conferences
- grants to individuals
- repatriation costs
- retrospective funding.

Applications

The foundation's website has an interactive map which you can use to select a country you are interested in. This will take you to a page containing an overview of the country and the foundation's work within it, some examples of previous projects, details of the current grant strategy for that country and the application procedure.

Organisations interested in applying should complete a 'concept note' (available to download from the relevant country page) and email it to grants@ejaf.com.

The Jones 1986 Charitable Trust

People with disabilities, welfare of older people, welfare of younger people, education and purposes beneficial to the community

£513,000 (2009/10)

Beneficial area

UK, mostly Nottinghamshire.

Smith Cooper, Haydn House, 309–329 Haydn Road, Sherwood, Nottingham NG5 1HG
Tel: 0115 960 7111
Fax: 0115 969 1313
Correspondent: David Lindley
Trustees: Robert Heason; Richard Stringfellow; John David Pears.
CC Number: 327176

Information available

Accounts were available at the Charity Commission.

The charity was established in 1986 with very wide charitable purposes. The trust primarily supports causes in the Nottingham area and much of its grant giving goes to charities assisting people with disabilities or for medical research into disabilities and the welfare of older people. The trust also supports charities supporting the welfare of the young, education and purposes beneficial to the community. The trust prefers to develop a relationship with the organisations funded over an extended period of time.

In 2009/10 the trust had assets of £19.5 million and an income of £567,500. Grants were made to 52 organisations totalling £513,000, and were broken down as follows:

Relief of sickness or disability: general	24	£185,500
Medical research	3	£102,000
Purposes beneficial to the community	9	£94,500
Relief of sickness or disability: young	3	£49,000
Welfare of the aged	3	£34,000
Education	4	£33,000
Welfare of the young	5	£15,000

Beneficiaries included: Queens Medical Centre Nottingham – University Hospital NHS Trust (£80,000); Cope Children's Trust (£40,000); The Ruddington Framework Knitters Museum (£26,000); Age Concern Nottingham and Nottinghamshire (£25,000); Winged Fellowship (£24,000); Nottinghamshire Hospice (£23,000); Framework Housing Association (£20,000); Rutland House School for Parents (£15,000); National Head Injuries Association (Headway) (£12,000); Nottingham Deaf Society and The Place2be (£10,000 each); Prince of Paste Anglers (£8,000); Elizabeth Finn Care and The Boys' Brigade : Nottinghamshire Battalion (£5,000 each); Nottingham Society for Autistic Children and Adults (£2,000); and Deafblind UK (£1,000).

Exclusions

No grants to individuals.

Applications

In writing to the correspondent. The trust invites applications for grants by advertising in specialist press. Applications are considered for both capital and/or revenue projects as long as each project appears viable.

The Jordan Charitable Foundation

General charitable purposes

£434,000 (2010)

Beneficial area

UK national charities, Herefordshire and Sutherland, Scotland.

Rawlinson & Hunter, 8th Floor, 6 New Street Square, New Fetter Land, London EC4A 3AQ
Tel: 020 7842 2000
Email: jordan@rawlinson-hunter.com
Correspondent: Ralph Stockwell, Trustee
Trustees: Sir George Russell; Ralph Stockwell; Christopher Jan Andrew Bliss; Simon Paul Jennings; David Geoffrey Barker; Anthony Brierley.
CC Number: 1051507

Information available

Accounts were available at the Charity Commission.

The Jordan Charitable Foundation was established in 1995. The grant making policies are guided by the original intentions of the founders. Grants are made to UK national charities and also to charities that are local to the county of Herefordshire, and in particular, charities operating within the city of Hereford and to a much lesser extent, charities in Sutherland, Scotland, as there is a connection between the founders and this area. The trustees assist towards funding of a capital nature and towards defraying revenue costs.

In 2010 the foundation had assets of £44.5 million and an income of £844,000. Grants were made to 53 organisations totalling £434,000.

Around 60% of funding was given to organisations working throughout the UK, 38% in Hereford and 2% in Sutherland. Most grants are for between £5,000 and £10,000.

Beneficiaries included: Taste for Adventure (£50,000); Headway – Herefordshire (£30,000); MIND – Herefordshire (£26,000); Martha Trust (£20,000); County Air Ambulance Trust (£15,000); Alzheimer's Research Trust, Brooke Hospital for Animals and the Samaritans (£10,000 each); Sutherland Schools Pipe Band (£6,000); RNLI, Atlantic Salmon Trust, National Trust for Scotland and Age Concern (£5,000 each); International Animal Rescue and Loth Helmsdale Flower Show Society (£2,000 each); and Northlands Creative Glass (£1,000).

Applications

In writing to the correspondent.

The Joron Charitable Trust

Jewish, education, medical research, general

£1.67 million (2009/10)

Beneficial area

UK.

115 Wembley Commercial Centre, East Lane, North Wembley, Middlesex HA9 7UR
Tel: 020 8908 4655
Correspondent: Bruce D G Jarvis, Chair
Trustees: Bruce D G Jarvis; Mrs Sandra C Jarvis; Joseph R Jarvis.
CC Number: 1062547

Information available

Accounts were available at the Charity Commission.

The trust's policy is to make grants to registered charities in the fields of education, medical research and other charities who can demonstrate that the grants will be used effectively.

In 2009/10 the trust had assets of £848,000 and an income of almost £1.3 million, largely in donations from Ravensale Ltd. Grants to 16 organisations totalled £1.67 million.

As in previous years, a grant of £1 million was made to the Roan Charitable Trust, apparently for the onward distribution in further grants to other organisations worldwide. Other beneficiaries included: The Princess Royal Trust for Carers (£150,000); the Wilderness Foundation (£137,000); Hammersmith Hospital (£110,500); Child's Dream Foundation (£64,000); St Christopher's Hospice (£25,000); and Great Ormond Street Children's Hospice (£5,000).

Applications

In writing to the correspondent. 'There is no formal grants application procedure. The trustees retain the services of a charitable grants advisor and take account of the advice when deciding on grants.'

The Kay Kendall Leukaemia Fund

Research into leukaemia and patient care

£5.2 million (2009/10)

Beneficial area

Unrestricted.

Allington House, 1st Floor, 150 Victoria Street, London SW1E 5AE
Tel: 020 7410 0330
Fax: 020 7410 0332
Email: info@kklf.org.uk
Website: www.kklf.org.uk
Correspondent: Alan Bookbinder, Director
Trustees: Judith Portrait; Timothy J Sainsbury; Christopher Stone.
CC Number: 290772

Information available

Accounts were available from the Charity Commission. The trust also has a clear and helpful website.

This is one of the Sainsbury Family Charitable Trusts, which share a joint administration. They have a common approach to grantmaking which is described in the entry for the group as a whole.

This trust is solely concerned with funding research into the causes and treatment of leukaemia, which is done on the advice of an expert advisory panel.

The trust's website offers a clear and simple summary of its grantmaking:

Project Grants

Research grants are normally awarded for projects of up to 3 years' duration. It is intended that the KKLF funding should not be the 'core' funding of any research group. Applicants should state clearly how their proposal relates to their core funding.

What will be funded

Grants will be awarded for research on aspects of leukaemia and for relevant studies on related haematological malignancies. Requests for support for basic science programmes may be considered. Phase 3 Clinical trials will not normally be supported but applications for phase 1 or 2 studies may be considered. Proposals which are closely related to the prevention, diagnosis, or therapy of leukaemia and related diseases are particularly encouraged.

Grants are usually awarded to give additional support to programmes already underway, the aim being to further strengthen activities which are already of high quality. It follows that the KKLF will accept proposals from groups which already have support from other agencies.

The trustees will consider proposals from both UK and non-UK based organisations where the work to be funded is based primarily within the UK.

A preliminary letter or telephone call to the administration offices of the Kay Kendall Leukaemia Fund, or to one of its scientific advisers, may be helpful to determine whether or not a proposal is likely to be eligible.

Research proposal

Applicants should complete the approved Application Form and include a research proposal (aims, background, plan of investigation, justification for budget.) The research proposal should be 3-5 single-spaced pages for project grants (excluding references, costings, and CVs). Applications should be submitted by email in addition to providing a hard copy with original signatures. The trustees will take account of annual inflation and of salary increases related to nationally negotiated pay scales and these should not be built into the application.

Salaries should generally be on nationally agreed scales.

Tenured or non time-limited appointments will not be supported.

The trustees may, from time to time, set special conditions for the award of a grant.

Final decision on the award of a grant is made by the trustees, having taken into account advice from their scientific advisers.

Other Awards

Capital funding
Requests for capital grants for leukaemia research laboratories or for clinical facilities for leukaemia will be considered either alone or in conjunction with proposals for the support of research and/or patient management. Capital requests must give a budget estimate of costs, together with a full justification.

Equipment grants
Requests for single large items of equipment will be considered. Requests must give detailed cost estimates and a full scientific justification.

Travel grants
Travel grants are available to KKLF grantees and staff funded by a KKLF grant to cover travel, conference fees and expenses. Specific application, in writing, is required for a travel supplement. Conference fees do not form part of the recurrent costs of a KKLF grant.

Clinical care
Requests for clinical support must give full costing and a detailed explanation of how this support will enhance the existing service and/or research activities.

The trust also describes future plans as follows:

The trustees previously agreed to a spend-out of the charity's capital which is expected to be completed by about 2022. As a result, trustees are planning to spend in total about £4.5 million per annum; £2.5 million on scientific research grants and £2 million on its patient care programme.

In 2009/10 it had assets of almost £40.1 million and an income of £1.7 million. Grants were paid during the year totalling £5.2 million.

Grants included those to: Cambridge Institute for Medical Research (£896,000); Institute of Cancer Research (£680,500); Imperial College London (£229,000); The Rayne's Institute (£180,000); Royal Bournemouth Hospital (£150,000); Doncaster & Bassetlaw Hospitals NHS Foundation Trust (£75,000); Paterson Institute for Cancer Research (£53,500); University Hospitals Morecambe Bay Hospitals NHS Trust (£35,000); Bolton Hospitals NHS Trust (£20,000); and Aintree University Hospitals NHS Foundation Trust (£18,500).

Exclusions

Circular appeals for general support are not funded.

Applications

A preliminary letter or telephone call to the administration offices of the Kay Kendall Leukaemia Fund may be helpful to determine whether or not a proposal is likely to be eligible. Application forms are available by contacting the trust's office.

The trustees consider proposals twice each year, normally May and October. To allow for the refereeing process, new full proposals for the May meeting should be received by 28 February and for the October/November meeting by 15 July. Late applications may be deferred for 6 months.

Keren Association

Jewish, education, general

£6.5 million (2009/10)

Beneficial area

UK.

136 Clapton Common, London E5 9AG
Correspondent: Mrs S Englander, Trustee
Trustees: E Englander, Chair; Mrs S Englander; P N Englander; S Z Englander; B Englander; J S Englander; Mrs H Z Weiss; Mrs N Weiss.
CC Number: 313119

Information available

Accounts were on file at the Charity Commission, without a list of grants.

The trust has general charitable purposes, supporting the advancement of education and the provision of religious instruction and training in traditional Judaism. Support is also given to needy Jewish people.

In 2009/10 the trust had assets of £35.5 million and an income of £7.5 million. Grants were made totalling £6.5 million. A list of grant

recipients was not included in the accounts.

Previous beneficiaries include: Beis Aharon Trust, Yeshivah Belz Machnovke, U T A, Yetev Lev Jerusalem, Lomdei Tom h Belz Machnovke, Friends of Beis Yaakov, Yeshlvat Lom dei Torah, Friends of Arad, Kupat Gmach Vezer Nlsuin, Clwk Yaakov and British Heart Foundation.

Applications

In writing to the correspondent.

The Mary Kinross Charitable Trust

Relief of poverty, medical research, community development, youth and penal affairs

£699,000 (2010/11)

Beneficial area

UK.

36 Grove Avenue, Moseley, Birmingham B13 9RY
Correspondent: Fiona Adams, Trustee
Trustees: Elizabeth Shields, Chair; Fiona Adams; Neil Cross; Jonathan Haw; Gordon Hague.
CC Number: 212206

Information available

Accounts were available at the Charity Commission.

This trust makes grants in the areas of medical research, community development, youth, penal affairs, health and mental health. Grants made under the heading 'youth' tend to be made with crime prevention in mind.

The trust prefers to work mainly with a group of charities with which it develops a close connection, led by at least one of the trustees. It describes its grant policy as follows:

Trustees wish to continue the policy of the founder which was to use the trust income to support a few carefully researched projects, rather than to make many small grants. The fields of work chosen reflect the particular interests and knowledge of trustees and at least one trustee takes responsibility for ensuring the trust's close involvement with organisations to which major grants are made.

When the trust makes a major grant core office costs are often included, which may enable the recipients to apply for other sources of funding. Unfortunately, the trust has to disappoint the great majority of applicants who make unsolicited appeals.

In 2010/11 the trust had assets of £28.4 million and an income of £711,000. Grants were made to 34 organisations totalling £699,000 and were distributed as follows:

Medical research	8	£351,500
Youth	8	£163,000
Health	2	£60,000
Penal affairs	5	£52,500
Mental health	2	£48,000
Community development	3	£43,000
Miscellaneous	5	£17,500

Beneficiaries included: Weatherall Institute of Molecular Medicine (£97,500); Centre for Regenerative Medicine – University of Edinburgh (£50,000); Prospex and Moseley Community Development Project (£40,000 each); Hepatitis C Trust (£30,000); Breakthrough Breast Cancer (£25,000); New Horizon Youth Centre (£20,000); The Children's Trust (£15,000); Pendrigg Trust (£12,000); Oxford Concert Party (£7,500); Birmingham Civic Society (£5,000); Prison Radio Association (£2,000); and Warstock Community Association (£1,000).

Exclusions

No grants to individuals.

Applications

'Because the trustees have no office staff and work from home, they prefer dealing with written correspondence rather than telephone calls from applicants soliciting funds.'
Note: unsolicited applications to this trust are very unlikely to be successful.

Common applicant mistakes

'Not reading that we don't consider unsolicited applications.'

Ernest Kleinwort Charitable Trust

General purposes. In practice, mainly to wildlife and environmental conservation both nationally and overseas; disability; medical research; welfare of older and young people

£1.2 million (2009/10)

Beneficial area

UK, in particular Sussex; overseas.

Kleinwort Benson, 14 St George Street, London W1S 1FE
Tel: 020 3207 7008
Website: www.ekct.org.uk
Correspondent: Nick Kerr-Sheppard, Secretary
Trustees: Sir Simon Robertson, Chair; Richard Ewing; Alexander Kleinwort; Lady Madeleine Kleinwort; Marina Kleinwort; Sir Richard Kleinwort; Sir Christopher Lever.
CC Number: 229665

Information available

Accounts were available at the Charity Commission.

The trust was established in 1964 by Sir Ernest Kleinwort, former chair of Kleinwort, Sons & Co. bank. He was actively involved in setting up what was to become the World Wildlife Fund UK, and the trust continues to provide support for conservation of wildlife and the natural environment, both nationally and internationally. More than half of the trust's funds go to Sussex based charities.

The following information on the types of grants made is provided by the trust:

> In general, the trust aims to 'make a difference'; it does not support individuals or very small and narrowly specialised activities and, equally, it tries to avoid unfocused causes. Charities considered for grants will be notified and asked to complete an 'Account Summary' form taking various

information from their latest Annual Accounts.

In approved cases, the trustees will provide one of the following four types of grant support:

One-off grants

Grants made on a one-off basis will be approved approximately every four months, and awarded to start up costs, core costs or for a specific project for which applicants have requested support. This could include a contribution towards a building/ refurbishment project, purchase of specialist equipment or other similar capital expenditure, or assistance with running costs.

Conditionally renewable grants

Applications for annual support are not encouraged, but conditionally renewable grants might be awarded in exceptional circumstances for up to three years, following which support may be withdrawn to enable resources to be devoted to other projects.

Grants can be towards start-up costs, or for a specific item in the applicant's budget such as a salary, core costs or towards the costs of a particular project. Such grants are subject to satisfactory annual progress reports and only released at the trustees' sole discretion.

Annual subscriptions

A proportion of the trustees' annual spend is currently set aside to pay annual subscriptions, predominantly to charities operating in Sussex. Charities added or removed from this list of payments will be notified accordingly, and all payments are subject to satisfactory annual progress reports and submission of annual accounts prior to being released at the trustees' sole discretion.

Large grants (over £10,000)

Large grants are approved by the full board of trustees twice a year (normally April and October), and are typically agreed upon when the trustees have a deep understanding and/or a close relationship with the charity, which may have developed over a period of several years.

General guiding principles are:

- the trustees should be satisfied with the purpose and objectives of the charity, and that they are able to deliver a superior/pre-eminent service
- the trustees have confidence in the trustees and management of the charity, and are therefore satisfied as to its quality, efficiency, financial stability and income/expense ratios.

In 2009/10 the trust had assets of just over £48.4 million and an income of almost £1.3 million. Grants were made to 162 organisations totalling

£1.2 million, and were broken down as follows:

Disabled people: treatment and care	63	£368,500
Wildlife and conservation	25	£321,000
Youth care	25	£177,500
General welfare and social problems	21	£92,000
Family planning	2	£72,500
Miscellaneous	2	£71,000
Hospices	3	£45,000
Care for the elderly	11	£34,000
Medical research	8	£9,000

Beneficiaries included: Tusk Trust (£100,000); Cheiley Heritage School (£75,000); The River Trust (£70,000); World Wildlife Fund UK (£50,000); 3 Towns Shopmobility (£30,000); Federation of London Youth Clubs (£21,500); East Sussex Disability Association (£17,500); Raleigh International (£15,000); Livability and City Gate Community Projects (£10,000 each); Disabilities Trust and Wildfowl and Wetlands Trust (£7,500 each); Buglife and Scope (£5,000); Treloar Trust and the Living Paintings Trust (£2,000 each); and Monkey Sanctuary, the Stroke Association and Sussex Chorus (£1,000 each).

Exclusions

The trust will not consider funding:

▷ large national charities having substantial fundraising potential, income from legacies and or endowment income
▷ organisations not registered as charities or those that have been registered for less than a year
▷ pre-school groups
▷ out of school play schemes including pre-school and holiday schemes
▷ projects which promote a particular religion
▷ charities not funded by any other charity
▷ very small and narrowly specialised activities
▷ local authorities
▷ individuals or charities applying on behalf of individuals
▷ general requests for donations
▷ expeditions or overseas travel
▷ campaigning organisations
▷ charities whose main aim is to raise funds for other charities
▷ charities with substantial cash reserves

Applications

In writing to the correspondent. Applications should be no longer than two A4 sides, and should incorporate a short (half page) summary.

Applications should also include a detailed budget for the project and the applicant's most recent audited accounts. If accounts show a significant surplus or deficit of income, please explain how this has arisen.

Applicants must also complete and include an Accounts Summary form, which is available on the trust's website.

The Sir James Knott Trust

General charitable purposes, in practice, support for people who are disadvantaged, the young, the elderly, the disabled, education and training, medical care, historic buildings, the environment, music and the arts and seafarers' and services' charities

£874,000 (2009/10)

Beneficial area

Tyne and Wear, Northumberland, County Durham inclusive of Hartlepool but exclusive of Darlington, Stockton-on-Tees, Middlesbrough, Redcar and Cleveland.

16–18 Hood Street, Newcastle upon Tyne NE1 6JQ
Tel: 0191 230 4016
Fax: 0191 230 2817
Email: info@knott-trust.co.uk
Website: www.knott-trust.co.uk
Correspondent: Vivien Stapeley, Secretary

Information available

Accounts were available at the Charity Commission.

This trust is established for general charitable purposes; in practice its primary objective is to help improve the conditions of people living and working in the North East of England.

Background

The following information is taken from the trust's website, with additional historical facts taken from: www.wrecksite.eu

James Knott was one of the merchant giants of the nineteenth century. The Prince Line Ltd was a major shipping company that was held in the highest regard by all who sailed in their ships and by passengers voyaging on the round the world service. The Prince Line gave Knott enormous wealth and over the years he and his wife became well-known on Tyneside for their philanthropy. In 1920 and in order that his charitable giving could continue after his death he provided funds for the James Knott Settlement. The focus of his charitable interest was to support charitable bodies and organisations mainly connected with the north east of England.

The Sir James Knott Trust aims to help improve the conditions of people living and working in the North East of England allocating grants to charities working for the benefit of the population and environment of Tyne and Wear, Northumberland and County Durham, including Hartlepool. The main donations are in the fields of community issues and events, service charities, historic buildings and heritage, education, arts and culture, health, environment, public services and housing.

General

Grants are normally only made to registered charities specifically operating in or for the benefit of the North East of England (Tyne and Wear, Northumberland, County Durham inclusive of Hartlepool but exclusive of Darlington, Stockton-on-Tees, Middlesbrough, Redcar and Cleveland).

The trustees have wide discretion on the distribution of funds and meet to consider grant applications three times a year. Grants totalling about £1 million a year are made, funded out of income. The trustees try to follow the wishes and interests of the trust's founder where this is compatible with the present day needs of the north east. Charitable works known to have been of particular interest to Sir James are given special consideration, for example, Army Benevolent Fund, Northumberland Playing Fields Association, Mission to Seafarers, Royal British Legion, the YMCA and YWCA, Barnardo's, RUKBA, Historic Churches Trust, schools and universities.

In recent years, grants have been given in support of the welfare of people who are disadvantaged, the young, the elderly, people with disabilities, education and training, medical care, historic buildings, the environment, music and the arts and seafarers' and services' charities.

In 2009/10 the trust had assets of £38.4 million and an income of £1.3 million. There were 364 grants made totalling £874,000, broken down into categories as follows:

Community issues/events	111	£240,500
Health/sport and human services	73	£153,000
Service charities	40	£105,500
Historic buildings/heritage	19	£80,000
Arts and culture	35	£79,000
Education/training	30	£72,500
Homeless/housing	25	£55,500
Public services	18	£50,000
Conservation/horticultural/ biodiversity/environmental	13	£38,000

Most grants were for £5,000 or less. Beneficiaries included: Diocese of Newcastle (£20,000 in total); Northumbria Historic Churches Trust (£17,500); Durham Association of Clubs for Young People and Puffin Appeal (£10,000 each); YMCA-North East, Yorkshire & NE Lincolnshire Regions (£8,000); Durham University (£7,500); Astley Community High School, Berwick upon Tweed Preservation Trust, Collingwood 2010 Festival Committee, Durham Wildlife Trust and Phoenix Futures (£5,000 each); Corbridge Youth Initiative (£4,000); Action Foundation, Berwick Youth Project and Sacriston Cricket Club (£3,000 each); Action for Children, BLISS Mediation Services, Bubble Foundation UK and Kidney Research UK (£2,000 each); and Bamburgh Castle Cricket Club and Cruse Bereavement Care -Tyneside Branch (£1,500 each).

Exclusions

Individuals, the replacement of funding withdrawn by local authorities or organisations that do not have an identifiable project within the beneficial area.

Applications

In writing to the correspondent, giving a brief description of the need, with relevant consideration to the following points:

- the type of organisation you are and how you benefit the community
- how you are organised and managed
- how many staff/volunteers you have
- if a registered charity, your registered number, if not you will need to submit the name and registered number of a charity which is prepared to administer funds on your behalf
- your relationship, if any, with similar or umbrella organisations
- your main funding source
- the project you are currently fundraising for, including the cost, the amount required and when the funds are needed
- please give details of who else you have approached and what response have you had
- please confirm whether you have you applied to the Big Lottery Fund (if not, state why not)
- please enclose a copy of your latest trustees' report and accounts (if you are a new organisation then provide a copy of your latest bank statement).

Not all of these points may apply to you, but they give an idea of what the trustees may ask when considering applications. Applicants may be contacted for further information.

Trustees normally meet in spring, summer and autumn. Applications need to be submitted at least three months before a grant is required. However, if your application is for a grant of less than £1,000, this can usually be processed outside meetings and usually within 1 month.

Common applicant mistakes

'The trust has a geographical restriction (North East England) and many national charities apply. Also, applicants don't include accounts.'

The Neil Kreitman Foundation

Arts and culture; education; health and social welfare

£435,500 (2009/10)

Beneficial area

Worldwide, in practice UK, USA and Israel.

Citroen Wells & Partners, Devonshire House, 1 Devonshire Street, London W1W 5DR
Tel: 020 7304 2000
Fax: 020 7304 2020
Email: gordon.smith@citreonwells.co.uk
Correspondent: Gordon C Smith, Trustee
Trustees: Neil R Kreitman; Gordon C Smith.
CC Number: 267171

Information available

Accounts were available at the Charity Commission.

The foundation was established in 1974 and makes grants to registered or exempt charities for the arts and culture, education, health and social welfare. The foundation has also given to Jewish charities in previous years. In 2005/06 the foundation received £15 million from the Kreitman Foundation when it ceased operating.

In 2009/10 the foundation had assets of £23.2 million and an income of £465,000. Grants were made to 20 organisations totalling £435,500, which were categorised as follows:

Arts and culture	£330,000
Health and welfare	£91,000
Education	£14,500

Beneficiaries included: University of Washington (£132,000); British Museum (£70,000); Independent Shakespeare Company (£39,000); Sierra Club Foundation (£32,000); The Ancient India and Iran Trust (£14,000); Royal Numismatic Society (£12,500); Los Angeles County Museum of Art and Save the Children (£10,000 each); International PEN

Foundation (£7,000); and Ziyaret Tepe Archaeological Trust (£5,000).

Exclusions
No grants to individuals.

Applications
In writing to the correspondent.

Maurice and Hilda Laing Charitable Trust

Promotion of Christianity, relief of need

£2.5 million (2010)

Beneficial area
UK and overseas.

33 Bunns Lane, Mill Hill, London NW7 2DX

Tel: 020 8238 8890

Correspondent: Elizabeth Harley, Secretary

Trustees: Andrea Currie; Peter Harper; Robert Harley; Ewan Harper; Charles Laing; Stephen Ludlow.

CC Number: 1058109

Information available

Accounts were available at the Charity Commission.

This trust was established in 1996 and is mainly concerned with the advancement of the Christian religion and relieving poverty, both in the UK and overseas. The trust is administered alongside the Beatrice Laing Trust, the Martin Laing Foundation and the Kirby Laing Foundation with which it shares members of staff and office space; collectively they are known as the Laing Family Trusts.

In practice grants awarded fall into three main categories:

- to organisations seeking to promote Christian faith and values through evangelistic, educational and media activities at home and overseas
- to organisations seeking to express Christian faith through practical action to help people in need, for example, those with disabilities, the

homeless, the sick, young people, prisoners and ex-offenders
- to organisations working to relieve poverty overseas, with a particular emphasis on helping children who are vulnerable or at risk. In most cases these grants to overseas projects are made through UK registered charities who are expected to monitor and evaluate the projects on behalf of the trust, providing progress reports at agreed intervals.

See the entry for the Laing Family Foundations for the work of the group as a whole.

In 2006 the trust made the decision to work towards winding up the trust over a 10–15 year period. As such, there will be a controlled increase in the level of future grant expenditure.

During the year 2010 the trust had assets of £34 million, an income of £1.5 million and made grants totalling £2.5 million which were broken down as follows:

Children and young people	£281,000
Overseas aid	£374,000
Religion	£775,000
Social welfare	£853,000
Miscellaneous	£205,000
Health and medicine	£25,000

The most significant beneficiaries were: United Learning Trust (£100,000); Anglican Centre, Doha, Qatar (£100,000); The 2011 Trust (King James Bible Trust) (£100,000); and The Salvation Army UK (£650,000).

Beneficiaries of under £100,000 included: Ethiopian Graduate School of Theology (£50,000); Credit Action (£40,000); YMCA UK National Council (£25,000); Launde Abbey (£30,000); Scripture Union (£25,000); Bible Reading Fellowship (£25,000); Tearfund (£50,000); Release International (£25,000); Mission Aviation Fellowship (£50,000); Christian Youth Enterprises Sailing Centre (£50,000); and St Madoc Christian Youth Camp (£43,000).

Exclusions

No grants to groups or individuals for the purpose of education, travel, attendance at conferences or participation in overseas exchange programmes. No grants towards church restoration or repair.

Applications
In writing to the correspondent. One application only is needed to apply to this or the Kirby Laing Foundation, Martin Laing Foundation or Beatrice Laing Charitable Trust. Multiple applications will still only elicit a single reply, even then applicants are asked to accept non-response as a negative reply on behalf of all these trusts, unless an sae is enclosed. After the initial sifting process, the Maurice and Hilda Laing Trust follows its own administrative procedures.

Each application should contain all the information needed to allow such a decision to be reached, in as short and straightforward a way as possible.

Specifically, each application should say:
- what the money is for
- how much is needed
- how much has already been found
- where the rest of the money is to come from.

The trustees meet quarterly to consider applications for grants above £10,000. In most cases the trust's administrators will have met with applicants and prepared reports and recommendations for the trustees.

Applications for smaller amounts are considered on an ongoing basis throughout the year. The administrators are authorised to make such grants without prior consent up to a maximum of £100,000 in each quarter, the grants to be reported to the trustees and approved retrospectively at the following quarterly meeting.

The Kirby Laing Foundation

Health, welfare, Christian religion, youth, general

£1.4 million (2010)

Beneficial area
Unrestricted, but mainly UK.

33 Bunns Lane, Mill Hill, London NW7 2DX

Tel: 020 8238 8890

Fax: 020 8238 8897

Correspondent: Elizabeth Harley
Trustees: Lady Isobel Laing; David E Laing; Simon Webley; Rev Charles Burch.
CC Number: 264299

Information available

Accounts were available at the Charity Commission.

Summary

Along with the other Laing family trusts, this is a general grantmaker, with a Christian orientation and awarding almost all kinds of grants, few of them very large. It is unusual in the group for having a small number of artistic and cultural grants. The foundation was established in 1972 for general charitable purposes.

General

The foundation is administered alongside, and shares its 3 staff with, the Beatrice Laing Trust, the Martin Laing Foundation and the Maurice and Hilda Laing Charitable Trust. An application to any one of these four trusts, collectively known as the Laing Family Trusts, is treated as an application to all, although, after the initial 'sorting' process, applications considered suitable for further consideration by the Kirby Laing Foundation follow the foundation's own administrative and decision-making process. The trust makes grants based upon applications but may occasionally adopt a more proactive approach where there is evidence of a particular need in an area of interest to the trustees.

The trust states that it intends to increase the level of grant expenditure with a view to the likely winding down of the foundation in 5–10 years.

Grants are made in the following areas:

- the promotion and expression of the evangelical Christian faith and values
- education (particularly in the fields of theology, science and engineering) and youth development
- medical research with a particular emphasis on dementia and stroke
- social and medical welfare projects particularly where the beneficiaries include people who are elderly or disabled and ex-servicemen
- the preservation of cultural and environmental heritage and improving access to the arts for young people and people who are disabled
- overseas development projects (supported by UK registered charities).

Grantmaking in 2010

In 2010 the trust had assets of £46.8 million and an income of £1.7 million. Grants were made totalling £1.4 million, and were broken down as follows:

Religion	11	£356,000
Health and medicine	24	£326,000
Education and youth development	14	£252,000
Cultural and environmental	18	£221,000
Charities Aid Foundation	1	£125,000
Social welfare	7	£85,000
Overseas aid	9	£80,000

Beneficiaries included: Leicester Cathedral (£100,000); Great Britain Trust (£65,000); Oriel College and the University of Hertfordshire (£50,000 each); Institution of Civil Engineers (£35,000); Youth for Christ and the National Hospital for Neurology and Neurosurgery (£25,000 each); Mines Advisory Group (£15,000); The Art Fund (£10,000); and UK Sailing Academy, St Christopher's Hospice and the British Limbless Ex service Men's Association (£5,000 each).

Exclusions

No grants to individuals; no travel grants; no educational grants. The foundation rarely gives grants for the running costs of local organisations.

Applications

One application only is needed to apply to this or the Beatrice Laing Trust or Maurice and Hilda Laing Charitable Trust. Multiple applications will still only elicit a single reply.

These trusts make strenuous efforts to keep their overhead costs to a minimum. As they also make a very large number of grants each year, in proportion to their income, the staff must rely almost entirely on the written applications submitted in selecting appeals to go forward to the trustees.

Each application should contain all the information needed to allow such a decision to be reached, in as short and straightforward a way as possible. Specifically, each application should say: what the money is for; how much is needed; how much has already been found; where the rest is to come from.

Unless there is reasonable assurance on the last point the grant is unlikely to be recommended. The trustees meet four times a year to consider the award of grants of over £20,000. Decisions on smaller grants are made on an ongoing basis.

For all grants above £5,000 the foundation asks for a report from the charity one year after the grant has been made, describing briefly how the grant has been spent and what has been achieved. For larger and multi-year grants more detailed reports may be required. Where a grant is paid in instalments the usual practice is not to release the second and subsequent instalments until a review of progress has been satisfactorily completed.

The Beatrice Laing Trust

Relief of poverty and advancement of the evangelical Christian faith

£1.5 million (2009/10)

Beneficial area

UK and overseas.

c/o Laing Family Trusts, 33 Bunns Lane, Mill Hill, London NW7 2DX
Tel: 020 8238 8890
Correspondent: Elizabeth Harley, Secretary
Trustees: Sir Martin Laing; David E Laing; Christopher M Laing; Charles Laing; Paula Blacker; Alexandra Gregory.
CC Number: 211884

Information available

Accounts were available at the Charity Commission. See the entry on the Laing Family Foundations for the work of the group as a whole.

This trust was established in 1952 by Sir John Laing and his wife, Beatrice, both now deceased. The trust's objects are the relief of poverty and the advancement of the evangelical Christian faith in the UK and abroad.

The Beatrice Laing Trust is administered alongside the Maurice and Hilda Laing Charitable Trust, the Martin Laing Foundation and the Kirby Laing Foundation with which it shares members of staff and office space; collectively they are known as the Laing Family Trusts. The Beatrice Laing Trust concentrates mainly on small grants for the relief of poverty in its broadest sense, both throughout the UK and overseas.

In the UK grant recipients include organisations working with children, young people and the elderly, the homeless and those with physical, mental or learning difficulties. Grants to projects overseas are concentrated on building the capacity to provide long-term solutions to the problems faced by countries in the developing world rather than providing emergency aid.

In addition to the trust's own funds, the trustees are invited to make nominations to the grants committee of the J W Laing Trust, for donations totalling 20% of that trust's income up to a maximum of £550,000 per annum. The trustees use these funds to support the advancement of the evangelical Christian faith through projects of new church building or extension or church mission activities.

Grants are usually only made to UK registered charities. A very small number of individuals are supported, mostly for retired missionaries who were known to the founders and who receive an annual grant.

The trust notes in its latest accounts:

> The grant-making process is largely reactive rather than proactive and it should be noted that any fluctuation in the level of grants funded across the categories shown [. . .] is therefore, a reflection of the applications received rather than a change in the trustees' priorities. This is also true of the geographical spread of grants made.

The vast majority of grants fall into the £500 to £5,000 range. Most of these represent either modest annual grants towards the core costs of

selected national organisations working with the trust's priority groups, or small capital grants to local organisations working to relieve poverty in their local communities.

Grants of over £5,000 are awarded by the trustees at meetings held three times a year. Grants of under £8,000 are made on a monthly basis by the trust director and are ratified at the trustees' meetings.

In the year 2009/10 the trust held assets of £41 million and had an income of £1.5 million. Grants were made totalling £1.2 million and were broken down as follows:

Children and youth	£185,000
Health and medicine	£303,000
Overseas development	£282,000
Social welfare	£412,000
Religion	£38,000

Beneficiaries included: Home Farm Trust (£50,000); National Star College, Wirral Autistic Society, Impact Foundation and Open Door St Albans (£25,000 each); Chailey Heritage School (£20,000); DEMAND (£15,000); Cumbria Community Foundation (£13,000); and Garwood Foundation, Oxfam, Book Aid International and Scottish Veterans' Garden City Association (£10,000 each).

Exclusions

No grants to individuals; no travel grants; no educational grants.

Applications

In writing to the correspondent. One application only is needed to apply to this or the Kirby Laing Foundation, Martin Laing Foundation or Maurice and Hilda Laing Charitable Trust. Applicants are asked to accept non-response as a negative reply on behalf of all these trusts, unless a stamped addressed envelope is enclosed. Applications are considered monthly.

Specifically, each application should say:
- what the money is for
- how much is needed
- how much has already been found
- where the rest of the money is to come from.

Unless there is reasonable assurance on the last point the grant is unlikely to be recommended.

Where larger grants are contemplated, meetings and visits are often undertaken by the trust's staff.

The Lancaster Foundation

Christian causes

£2 million (2009/10)

Beneficial area

UK and overseas, with a local interest in Clitheroe.

c/o Text House, 152 Bawdlands, Clitheroe, Lancashire BB7 2LA
Tel: 01200 444404
Correspondent: Rosemary Lancaster, Trustee
Trustees: Rosemary Lancaster; Dr John Lancaster; Steven Lancaster; Julie Broadhurst.
CC Number: 1066850

Information available

Accounts were available at the Charity Commission.

'The object of the charity is to financially support Christian based registered charities across the world. Grants are awarded at the absolute discretion of the trustees. Although many applications are received, the administrative structure of the charity does not allow for the consideration of unsolicited requests for grant funding.'

In 2007/08 the trust had assets of £50 million and an income of £1.8 million. Grants were made during the year totalling £2 million. There were 28 grants for £1,000 or more; small grants totalled £7,000.

As in previous years the largest grant was made to the Grand at Clitheroe (£868,000), of which Rosemary, John and Steven Lancaster are also trustees. Other beneficiaries included: The Message Trust (£325,000 in total); Open Arms International (£240,000); Sparrow Ministries (£130,000); Mission Aviation Fellowship (£62,000); Cross Polinate (£21,000); Christians Against Poverty (£18,000); Exstreet Kenya Musical Instruments (£5,500); Ignition (£2,500); and Open Doors UK (£1,000).

Applications

The trust has previously stated: 'We do not consider applications made to us from organisations or people unconnected with us. All our donations are instigated because of personal associations. Unsolicited mail is, sadly, a waste of the organisation's resources.'

The Allen Lane Foundation

Charities benefiting asylum-seekers and refugees, gypsies and travellers, lesbian, gay, bisexual or transgender people, offenders and ex-offenders, older people, people experiencing mental health problems and people experiencing violence or abuse

£718,000 (2010/11)

Beneficial area

UK.

90 The Mount, York YO24 1AR
Tel: 01904 613223
Fax: 01904 613133
Email: info@allenlane.org.uk
Website: www.allenlane.org.uk
Correspondent: Tim Cutts, Executive Secretary
Trustees: Clare Morpurgo; Lea Morpurgo; John Hughes; Christine Teale; Zoe Teale; Guy Dehn; Juliet Walker; Jane Walsh; Fredrica Teale.
CC Number: 248031

Information available

Accounts were available at the Charity Commission. The foundation has a helpful and informative website with detailed information on grant giving.

Summary

The Allen Lane Foundation is a grant-making trust set up in 1966 by the late Sir Allen Lane, founder of Penguin Books, to support general charitable causes. The foundation has no connection now with the publishing company, but five of the trustees are members of the founder's family.

The foundation wishes to fund work which will make a lasting difference to people's lives rather than simply alleviating the symptoms or current problems, is aimed at reducing isolation, stigma and discrimination and which encourages or enables unpopular groups to share in the life of the whole community.

As the foundation's resources are modest, it prefers to fund smaller organisations where small grants can have more impact. Organisations should be not-for-profit, but need not be registered charities (provided their activities are charitable) and work to benefit groups of people who are unpopular in UK society today. The foundation makes grants in the UK but does not make grants for work in London.

Guidelines for applicants

The following summary has been taken largely from the foundation's website.

The foundation will make grants for start-up, core or project costs. The grants are relatively small and are likely therefore to be appropriate for costs such as:
- volunteers or participants expenses
- venue hire
- part-time or sessional staffing costs
- work aimed at strengthening the organisation such as trustee or staff training.

Examples of the kind of activities which might be suitable for funding are:
- advocacy
- arts activities where the primary purpose is therapeutic or social
- befriending or mentoring
- mediation or conflict resolution
- practical work, such as gardening or recycling, which benefits both the provider and the recipient
- provision of advice or information
- self-help groups
- social activities or drop-in centres
- strengthening the rights of particular groups and enabling their views and experiences to be heard by policy-makers
- work aimed at combating stigma or discrimination
- work developing practical alternatives to violence
- research and education aimed at changing public attitudes or policy.

These lists are not exhaustive and there will be many other appropriate items/activities which could be funded.

While recognising (and being willing to support) on-going, tried and tested projects, the foundation is particularly interested in unusual, imaginative or pioneering projects which have perhaps not yet caught the public imagination.

Making an application

There is no formal application form, but there is a short registration form, available from the foundation's website. The registration form should accompany the application. An application should be no more than 4 sides of A4 but the project budget may be on extra pages. It should be accompanied by your organisation's last annual report and accounts if you produce such documents and the budget for the whole organisation (and the project budget if they are different) for the current year.

The application should include the following information:
- the aims of your organisation as a whole;
- how these aims are achieved;
- how your proposals make a lasting difference to people's lives rather than simply alleviating the symptoms or current problems;
- how the proposals reduce isolation, stigma and discrimination or encourage or enable unpopular groups to share in the life of the whole community;
- why your cause or beneficiary group is an unpopular one;
- what you want the grant to pay for;
- what difference a grant would make to your work;
- the cost of the work;
- whether you are asking the foundation to meet the whole cost of the work;
- details of any other sources of funding you are approaching;
- details of how you know if the work has been successful;
- details of how the work, and the way it is done, promotes equal opportunities. If you do not think equal opportunities are relevant to your work please say why.

If further information is needed this will be requested and a visit may be arranged when the application can be discussed in more detail.

All applications should be made to the Foundation's office and **not** sent to individual Trustees. If you have any queries about making an application you are encouraged to phone the staff for clarification.

Where grants are given

The foundation makes grants for work all over the United Kingdom but not where the beneficiaries of the work all live in London. Organisations which have their offices in London are eligible provided the people who benefit from their work are not only in London. The foundation does not make any grants overseas and has ceased its grant programme in the Republic of Ireland.

Size and length of grants
The grants are relatively modest. The foundation has no maximum grant, but most single award grants range from £500 up to £15,000, with the average grant in 2010/11 being around £6,400. Grants repeated for more than one year vary from about £500 per annum up to £5,000 per annum, for a maximum of three years.

The foundation will make single grants, or grants for two or three years. It is unlikely to make a second grant immediately after one has finished and if an application is refused, we ask applicants to wait a year before applying again.

Organisations who can apply
Registered charities and other organisations which are not charities but which seek funding for a charitable project.

To be eligible for a grant you should be able to answer yes to the following questions:
- Does your work benefit people from one or more of our priority groups?
- Are you confident that your application is not subject to any of the exclusions listed?
- If your work relates to a relatively local area – for example a town, village or local community, was your income last year less than about £100,000? or
- If your work covers a wider area – for example a county, region or nation, was your income last year less than about £250,000?
- Is it more than a year since you last applied?
- Does your work take place in the UK?
- Does your work take place outside London?

Allen Lane Lecture
Each year the foundation hosts a lecture in memory of Sir Allen Lane. Past lecturers have included Mary Robinson, former President of the Irish Republic, The Bishop of Oxford the Rt. Rev Richard Harries and The Rt. Hon. Frank Field MP. In 2009, Kathleen Duncan OBE was the guest lecturer with the title 'Hard Times, but Great Expectations' at the Ismaili Centre in London. Since 1999 the text of each lecture each year has been published on the foundation's website.

The Allen Lane Foundation is interested in funding work which

benefits people in the following groups, or generalist work which includes significant numbers from more than one such group:
- asylum-seekers and refugees (but not groups working with a single nationality)
- gay, lesbian, bi-sexual or transgender people
- gypsies and travellers
- offenders and ex-offenders
- older people
- people experiencing mental health problems
- people experiencing violence or abuse.

'If the beneficiaries of your work do not include a significant proportion of people from one or more of these groups it is very unlikely that your application will be successful.'

A recent review has concluded that people from black and minority ethnic communities should be removed as a separate priority. Groups and organisations working with BME communities are still encouraged to apply within the other priorities. The trustees are keen to make the foundation's criteria as clear as possible to save applicants from wasted effort and disappointment, although this does mean that the guidelines list an ever increasing list of exclusions.

Grants in 2010/11
In 2010/11 the foundation had assets of £16.7 million and an income of £480,000. Grants were made totalling £718,000, of which 114 were committed new grants with a total value of £724,000.

Beneficiaries, and the purposes for which grants were given, are summarised as follows:

Beneficiaries from more than one 'unpopular' group – 24 grants totalling £146,000
Beneficiaries included: Merseyside Refugee & Asylum Seekers Pre & Post Natal Group – towards cost core costs (£15,000); Restorative Justice Consortium – towards core costs of this national organisation (£15,000); Active Community Team – salary for van driver to assist with furniture recycling which increases revenue for advice and advocacy work (£11,000); Here 4 Women – core costs to support project for women offenders

and people suffering violence and abuse (£10,000); Communicare in Southampton – core costs for project supporting the elderly and those experiencing mental health issues (£10,000); Links Project – towards running costs of a project for asylum seekers, refugees and migrant communities (£7,500); Brighton & Hove Unwaged, Advice & Rights Centre – core costs (£7,500); Archway Foundation – core costs for an organisation supporting people hurt by loneliness (£7,500); Lost Chord – towards music sessions supporting people with dementia (£7,500); Broken Rainbow – core costs of national organisation for lesbian, gay, bisexual and transgender people who experience domestic violence (£6,000); Volunteer Centre Whitstable – community gardening project to support the elderly and those experiencing mental health problems (£5,000); North Manchester Black Health Forum – towards the active citizens project aiming to empower older people and those with mental health problems (£4,000); and One Voice 4 Travellers – single grant towards the cost of the 'Breaking the cycle of abuse' project in East Anglia (£3,000).

Asylum seekers and Refugees – 19 grants totalling £135,000
Grants included those to: Kent Refugee Help – core costs (£15,000); Student Action for Refugees – core costs of a national organisation (£15,000); Boaz Trust – advocacy project helping asylum seekers in Manchester (£12,500); Southampton & Winchester Visitors Group – administrative costs for this group supporting asylum seekers in South Hampshire (£12,000); City of Sanctuary National – towards salary of the National Coordinator (£10,000); Biasan – running costs of a women's group in Bradford (£9,000); Govan & Craigton Integration Network – towards a women's befriending project in Glasgow (£7,000); Refugee Women of Bristol – core running costs (£6,000); Warm Hut UK – towards venue hire for this group in Salford providing advice and activities to asylum seekers and refugees (£4,000); and English in the Community – towards English classes

for Muslim women in East Sussex (£3,000).

People experiencing mental health problems – 19 grants totalling £110,000
Grants included those made to: Rural Community Link Projects CIC – towards sessional workers to facilitate six self-help activity groups across Cornwall and the Isles of Scilly (£15,000); Root & Branch – core costs of a horticultural and craft organisation in Oxfordshire (£12,000); Allied Resource Community – running costs of the Tools for Self Reliance project in Middlesborough (£9,000); Triumph Over Phobia – costs of establishing new self-help groups across the UK (£7,500); Aylesbury Vale Advocates – towards the cost of providing advocacy in residential homes (£5,000); Mind Yourself – running costs of supporting me with mental health problems in Letchworth Garden City (£2,700); and Saddleworth Carers Group – running costs of a self-help group for people, and carers of people, with dementia (£500).

Offenders and Ex-offenders – 12 grants totalling £102,000
Beneficiaries were: SHARP – towards volunteer costs at this charity supporting family members of offenders in Shrewsbury (£13,000); Bradford Court Chaplaincy Service – to develop the chaplaincy service at Bradford's Crown Court (£10,000); Restoring Broken Walls Trust – to fund a support worker helping people released from HMP Doncaster (£10,000); Cumbria Reducing Offending Partnership Trust – towards costs of The Seagull newspaper project (£9,000); Margaret Carey Foundation – towards storage and transport costs of this organisation working with offenders in prisons in the North West (£7,000); Inspire Cornwall CIC – towards the cost of the Dad's Project working with offenders (£5,000); and Women's Community Support Network – core costs of this project supporting women offenders in Belfast (£5,000).

People experiencing violence or abuse – 14 grants totalling £98,000
Beneficiaries included: Karma Nirvana – towards the salary of a Project Manager for this organisation working nationally to support victims of forced marriages and honour based abuse (£15,000); Argyll and Bute Rape Crisis – towards salary of a Development and Support worker to run a volunteer support programme across Oban and Isle of Mull (£10,000); Stop the Traffik – to establish five local groups to raise awareness on Human Trafficking (£10,000); South Cheshire CLASP – towards the Walking Tall project supporting single parent families who have been traumatised by domestic violence (£8,000); Advocacy After Fatal Domestic Abuse – towards the core costs of this organisation helping families who have suffered a loss due to domestic abuse (£5,000); Network for Surviving Stalking – towards core costs (£5,000); and Meadows Children & Family Wing – towards the cost of running Freedom Programmes in Cambridge (£3,000).

Older people – 21 grants totalling £78,000
Beneficiaries included: Cross Gates & District Good Neighbours Scheme – towards the Centre Administrator post at this scheme in Leeds (£10,000); Mind Active – core costs towards this organisation which supports activities for older people in Northumberland (£9,000); Southern Befrienders Ltd – towards office rental costs at this organisation on the Isle of Man (£7,500); Wolverhampton Elder Asian & Disabled – towards outreach work and a part-time co-ordinator (£4,500); Citizens of Senior Years – towards volunteer expenses, training and activity costs for this organisation in Derry (£3,250); Good Companions – towards running costs of friendship groups at this organisation in Nottingham (£2,600); Dance Discovery – towards sessional fees of dance leaders for this group in Sale (£2,000); and HIPS – towards running costs of this national support group for victims of failed equity release schemes/Home Income Plans (£500).

Migrant workers – 4 grants totalling £19,000
Beneficiaries included: Lincolnshire Mediation – towards a pilot community mediation work with the migrant/settled communities in Boston (£8,000); Citizens Advice Bureau Ryedale – towards the immigration advice service at this CAB in North Yorkshire (£5,000); Polish Community Association Wakefield – towards the cost of weekend advice and provision (£4,500); and CAIRDE – towards an advice and information service for migrant workers in Armagh (£1,500).

Lesbian, Gay, Bi-sexual and Transgender – 4 grants totalling £16,500
Beneficiaries included: Manchester Lesbian Community Project – towards the salary of an Admin, Information and Finance worker to support the work of this project (£7,000); Gay-Glos – towards helpline costs at this organisation based in Gloucester (£6,000); Gay Advice Scotland – towards premises costs (£3,000); and LAFS – towards core costs of this group in Kirkby, Nottinghamshire (£500).

Specific group/other – 1 grant totalling £15,000
The sole beneficiary was Witness Confident – as a contribution towards the full-time development officer post.

Gypsies and Travellers – 1 grant totalling £4,000
One grant was made for work specifically benefitting gypsies and travellers, although support has also been made available through organisations within the 'Beneficiaries from more than one group' category. The single grant was awarded to Dorset based Kushti Bok towards core costs.

Exclusions

The foundation does not currently make grants for:
- academic research
- addiction, alcohol or drug abuse
- animal welfare or animal rights
- arts or cultural or language projects or festivals
- children and young people or families

- endowments or contributions to other grant-making bodies
- health and healthcare
- holidays or holiday play schemes, day trips or outings
- housing
- hospices and medical research
- individuals
- museums or galleries
- overseas travel
- particular medical conditions or disorders
- physical or learning disabilities
- private and/or mainstream education
- promotion of sectarian religion
- publications
- purchase costs of property, building or refurbishment
- refugee community groups working with single nationalities
- restoration or conservation of historic buildings or sites
- sports and recreation
- therapy e.g. counselling
- vehicle purchase
- work which the trustees believe is rightly the responsibility of the state
- work outside the United Kingdom
- work which will already have taken place before a grant is agreed
- work by local organisations with an income of more than £100,000 per annum or those working over a wider area with an income of more than £250,000.

The foundation will not normally make grants to organisations which receive funding (directly or indirectly) from commercial sources where conflicts of interest for the organisation and its work are likely to arise.

Applications

There is no formal application form, but when sending in an application the foundation asks that you complete the registration form (available on the foundation's website) and return it with your application. Applications should be no more than four sides of A4 but the budget may be on extra pages. It should be accompanied by your last annual report and accounts (if applicable) and the budget for the whole organisation (and the project budget if they are different) for the current year.

The foundation now no longer has application deadlines. Applications are now processed continually. When the foundation has received your application they will usually be in touch within two weeks either to:

- ask for any further information,
- to tell you whether the application will be going forward to the next stage of assessment and what the timetable for a final decision will be,
- or to inform you that they are unable to help.

The time it takes to process an application and make a grant is usually between two and six months.

Common applicant mistakes

'Organisations applying to carry out activity in the London area [which the foundation does not fund]. Also, applications from outside of the UK, from organisations that are too big and from organisations that don't fit within our priority groups.'

The LankellyChase Foundation

Social welfare, community development, arts, heritage, penal affairs, mental health, prevention of abuse

£5.8 million (2010/11)

Beneficial area

UK.

1 The Court, High Street, Harwell, Didcot, Oxfordshire OX11 0EY
Tel: 01235 820044
Fax: 01235 432720
Email: enquiries@lankellychase.org.uk
Website: www.lankellychase.org.uk
Correspondent: Peter Kilgarriff, Chief Executive
Trustees: Nicholas Tatman (Chair); Ann Stannard; Dodie Carter; Paul Cotterill; Leo Fraser-Mackenzie; Victoria Hoskins; Marion Janner; Andrew Robinson; Kanwaljit Singh;

Clive Martin; Peter Latchford; Morag Burnett; Alison Leverett-Morris.
CC Number: 1107583

Information available

Accounts were available at the Charity Commission. The foundation has an excellent website.

The Chase Charity and the Lankelly Foundation were established through the generosity of two separate entrepreneurs who successively developed a complex of property companies which operated in and around London. The Chase Charity was founded in 1962 and the Lankelly Foundation six years later and both reaching out to the most isolated in society.

As time went by the two trusts adopted similar grant-making policies and whilst recognising that their differences of scale and emphasis were positive qualities; they reflected, particularly in the case of the Chase Charity, the founders' love of England's heritage and the arts, and these differences caught the attention of different needy groups, enabling the trusts to be more effective together than if they operated separately.

After so many years of working together, jointly employing the staff team, in 2005 the two trusts resolved to take the next natural step and amalgamate to form the LankellyChase Foundation. The foundation is established for general charitable purposes and its mission is 'to promote change which will improve the quality of people's lives ... particularly on areas of social need to help the most disadvantaged in our society to fulfil their potential.'

Guidelines

The following is taken from a press release, which is available in full on the foundation's website:

> After many years of working to improve the quality of people's lives in the UK, the LankellyChase Foundation has decided to intensify its focus on social disadvantage. From April 2012, the foundation will concentrate exclusively on bringing about change to improve the quality of life of people who face severe and multiple disadvantage.
>
> It has become increasingly clear that a significant number of people have been failed by attempts to tackle disadvantage and social exclusion.

These are people who face a number of social disadvantages simultaneously, and who are poorly served by services and systems that are limited to individual needs and that struggle to provide effective or appropriate support for the whole person (sometimes called 'deep exclusion').

LankellyChase and many others have funded practice which shows that effective, sustainable and creative approaches to severe and multiple disadvantage are possible. In recognition of the scale and urgency of this challenge, the foundation has decided to place at the heart of its mission a single and sustained drive to bring about change that will improve the quality of life of people who face severe and multiple disadvantage.

We will therefore be developing a number of proactive special initiatives that will try to get under the skin of severe and multiple disadvantage, tackle systemic failure and promote solutions that are both preventative and transformational. These initiatives will be developed in close partnership with organisations and individuals in the field, and they will typically combine grant making, research, learning and policy development.

We also recognise that many organisations working with people who face severe and multiple disadvantage don't fit neatly into categories and require flexible funding in order to thrive. So we are moving away from our current programme approach, and are developing an Open Grants scheme that will offer funding to organisations that are working to build the capabilities of people who face severe and multiple disadvantage. We expect to launch this in summer 2012.

The foundation has been working in the criminal justice system for more than twenty years, and we have helped fund many innovative services that have gone on to be regarded as best practice. This work has convinced us that people who face severe and multiple disadvantage need to be supported to avoid the criminal justice system altogether, and that our efforts and resources need to be concentrated at an early stage in their lives and in the system. We have therefore decided that our first Special Initiative should focus on ways of addressing severe and multiple disadvantage before people are drawn into offending. Details will be announced in summer 2012.

Potential applicants are advised to consult the foundation's website for further news of the reorientation of grantmaking.

Grants in 2010/11

In 2010/11 the foundation had assets of £124 million and an income of £4.4 million. Grants were made totalling £5.8 million, broken down as follows:

Women's Diversionary Fund	£1.2 million
Local people, local places	£1.15 million
Breaking the cycles of abuse	£1.13 million
Custody and community	£1 million
Free and quiet minds	£818,000
Arts	£369,000
Annual grants	£188,500

Beneficiaries across all programmes included: Family Action – London (£135,000); Clean Break (£100,000); Bright – London (£75,000); Kirckman Concert Society – London (£70,000); Women's Support Network – Belfast (£60,000); East Kent Rapeline – Canterbury (£57,000); Gorebridge Community Development Trust – Scotland (£50,000);Calderdale CAB – Halifax (£48,000); Red Dog Productions – Stroud; and Walsall Street Teams – Walsall (£45,000 each); Asylum Welcome – Oxford; and Justice First – Stockton on Tees (£30,000 each); Signpost and Rite Direkshon – Bristol (£20,000); Lateef Social Enterprise – Birmingham (£15,000); and St Mary at the Quay – Ipswich (£5,000).

Exclusions

The foundation receives many more applications from worthwhile projects than it can hope to fund and as a consequence it does not support the following areas of work which are in addition to those specifically mentioned in the guidelines to the current programmes:

- access to buildings
- advancement of religion
- after school and homework clubs
- animal charities
- breakfast clubs
- bursaries and scholarships
- child befriending schemes
- circular appeals
- expeditions/overseas travel
- festivals
- formal education including schools, colleges and universities
- general counselling
- holidays/holiday centres
- hospitals and hospices
- individual youth clubs
- individuals – including students
- medical care and medical research

- mother and toddler groups/playgroups
- museums/galleries
- organisations working with particular medical conditions
- other grant making organisations
- research
- sport
- work that has already taken place
- work which is primarily the responsibility of central or local government, education or health authorities.

Applications

Application forms are available from the foundation's office or website. Please post your application form and attach an itemised income and expenditure budget for the work for which funding is requested, a supporting letter (no more than 2 sides of A4) and the organisation's most recent annual report and/or accounts.

Please note the foundation's revised programme focus. Applicants are encouraged to contact the foundation for advice if necessary.

The Leathersellers' Company Charitable Fund

General

£1 million to organisations
(2009/10)

Beneficial area

UK, particularly London.

21 Garlick Hill, London EC4V 2AU
Tel: 020 7330 1444
Fax: 020 7330 1445
Email: dmsantao@leathersellers.co.uk
Website: www.leathersellers.co.uk
Correspondent: Mr David Santa-Olalla, Administrator
Trustee: The Leathersellers Company.
CC Number: 278072

Information available

Accounts were available at the Charity Commission.

Summary

The following is taken from the fund's website and 2009/10 accounts:

The Leathersellers' Company is one of the ancient livery companies of the City of London, ranked fifteenth in the order of precedence. It was founded by royal charter in 1444 with authority to control the sale of leather within the City. The company no longer has this regulatory role, and instead devotes its energies to support for charity, education and the British leather trade.

The policy of the trustees is to provide support to a broad range of registered charities or educational establishments in the fields of education and sciences, relief of those in need, the disabled, children and youth, medicine and health, the arts, the church and environment. At the same time support is provided to registered charities associated with the Leathersellers' Company, the leather and hide trades, education in leather technology and for the welfare of former workers in the industry and their dependants. Of grants awarded in 2010, 83% were to registered charities or educational establishments and 17% were to individuals.

Charitable grants are made to registered charities and individuals and are one of two types; a single grant or a multi-year grant. All multi-year grants are subject to annual review.

The trustees receive appeals from a wide range of registered charities and its policy is based upon the principle of making sure the money goes to those areas most in genuine need and those decisions are based on thorough investigations, including visits to individual charities, coupled with common sense.

The trust's website lists the current areas of priority for funding as:

- Education
- Disability
- Children & Young People
- Relief of Need

Types of grant

Small grants programme
This is a fast track application process for small one-off grants. The value of the grant awarded could be up to a maximum of £3,000; however the average level of grant is £500 – £1,500. A decision should be made within 6 weeks of receiving your application.

Main grants programme
The Main Grants programme awards Multi-Year Grants for a period of up to four years and large Single Year Grants. Multi-Year Grants can be offered as unrestricted revenue, for core costs or for established projects. Large Single Year Grants are normally awarded for capital costs or to cover crucial short-term development costs.

Grants in 2009/10

In 2009/10 the trust had assets of £37.5 million and an income of £1.4 million. Grants were made totalling £1.2 million, of which £209,000 was paid to 107 individuals for education and science purposes.

Grants to organisations were broken down as follows:

Education and sciences	21	£221,000
Advice and support	39	£197,000
Disability	32	£123,000
Recreational	27	£104,000
Heritage and environment	24	£104,000
Creative arts	16	£64,000
Uniformed organisations	13	£60,000
Medicine and health	35	£48,000
Homeless	8	£44,000
Leather associated	6	£44,000

The largest grants were made to: Colfe's School (£60,000); Prendergast Hilly Fields College (£50,000); Chatham Historic Dockyard and SSAFA (£30,000 each); The Leather Conservation Centre (£28,000); Fitzwilliam College and St Catherine's College (£27,000 each); National Churches Trust and the Mary Rose Trust (£25,000 each); Rainbow Trust, Until the Violence Stops and Cancer & Bio-detection Dogs (£20,000 each); and the Kids' Cookery School, New Horizon Youth Centre, Michael Palin Centre for Stammering Children and Prison Advice & Care Trust (£15,000 each).

Other aggregate grants under £15,000 totalled £474,000.

Applications

Appeals must be from registered charities operating within the UK. Priority will be given to charities connected with leather, the leather trade, and the London area due to the company's long associations there. The fund will also consider charities that are based throughout the United Kingdom. Applications are online via the trust's website.

Successful applicants to the main grants programme will typically have to pass through a four stage process, which can take up to 9 months: Initial assessment – applicants will hear whether they have been successful or unsuccessful within 6 weeks; consideration by the grants committee; possible visit by committee working group for a detailed assessment; and grants committee final decision.

Common applicant mistakes

'Using very old information about our grant programme.'

The William Leech Charity

Health and welfare in the north east of England, overseas aid

£401,500 (2009/10)

Beneficial area

Northumberland, Tyne and Wear, Durham and overseas.

Saville Chambers, 5 North Street, Newcastle upon Tyne NE1 8DF
Tel: 0191 243 3300
Fax: 0191 243 3309
Email: enquiries@williamleechcharity. org.uk
Website: www.williamleechcharity. org.uk
Correspondent: Mrs Kathleen M Smith, Secretary
Trustees: Prof. Peter H Baylis; Cyril Davies; Adrian Gifford; Roy Leech; Richard Leech; N Sherlock; David Stabler; Barry Wallace; Prof. Chris Day.
CC Number: 265491

Information available

Accounts were available from the Charity Commission. The charity also has an informative website.

In 1972 Sir William Leech set up The William Leech Property Trust (now The William Leech Charity) and donated to it some 300 tenanted properties, the income from which was to be distributed in accordance with his guidelines.

The purpose of charity is to make grants for charitable purposes in line with the guidelines of the founder. The main fund remains unrestricted and continues to make grants and interest free loans to registered charities in the North East of England at the discretion of the trustees.

In 2009/10 the charity had assets of nearly £14 million and an income of £448,000. During the year there were 89 grants made totalling £401,500, allocated as follows:

The Main Fund – 75 grants totalling £368,000

The trustees are concerned with community welfare and medical care which accounts for more than 73% of the grants awarded, with a further significant amount distributed to youth projects, initiatives to assist people with disabilities and the maintenance of churches.

The largest grant during the year was awarded to University of Newcastle upon Tyne Cardiovascular Stem Cell Research Department (£200,000), towards lab refurbishment and equipment. Other beneficiaries of larger grants included: Diocese of Newcastle Hirst Academy (£50,000); County Durham Foundation Grass Roots Challenge (£25,000); and Northumberland County Blind Association and Partners in the Community (£10,000 each). More typical grants of £1,000 or less included those to: Action for Children; Audio Visual Arts North East; DeafBlind UK; Felling Male Voice Choir; Listening Books; The Woodland Trust; and YMCA Newcastle upon Tyne.

The Lady Leech Fund – 14 grants totalling £33,700

The Lady Leech Fund is used to make grants to overseas projects focusing primarily on the medical, educational and environmental needs of children in underdeveloped countries, and also emergency aid in response to natural disasters.

Beneficiaries included: Hexham & Newcastle Diocese Peru Mission (£7,000 in total); Mylambaverly Sri Lanka Playschool (£5,000); Mityana Community Development Foundation – Uganda (£4,000 in total); Jitegemee School Building Project – Tanzania (£2,000); Orskov Foundation (£1,000); and Monkseaton High School (£500).

Exclusions

The following will not generally receive grants. The chairman and secretary are instructed to reject them without reference to the trustees, unless there are special circumstances:

- community care centres and similar (exceptionally, those in remote country areas may be supported)
- running expenses for youth clubs (as opposed to capital projects)
- running expenses of churches – this includes normal repairs, but churches engaged in social work, or using their buildings largely for 'outside' purposes may be supported
- sport
- the arts
- applications from individuals
- organisations which have been supported in the last 12 months. It would be exceptional to support an organisation in two successive years, unless the charity had promised such support in advance
- holidays, travel, outings
- minibuses (unless over 10,000 miles per annum is expected)
- schools
- housing associations.

Applications

The following guidance is taken from the trust's website:

The Main Fund

As it is the intention of the trustees to favour support for those charities who help others by utilising the generous time and skills of volunteers, they accept applications in the short form of a letter, rather than expecting the completion of a complicated application form, which may seem daunting to some applicants.

In order to safe-guard our charity status, it is important that we are accountable for how funds are distributed. As such, the following protocols exist for making and investigating applications.

Please note we only accept applications from registered charities, and the registered charity address must be included in the application process. For large grants and multiple grants, trustees would like to see as much supporting information as possible, and in rare cases, they may wish to interview the applicant.

Your applications must include:

- a description of the project that the charity is undertaking, who it hopes to help, and any evidence which will support the need for this particular project
- how much the project will cost, capital and revenue, with an indication of the amounts involved
- how much the charity has raised so far, and where it expects to find the balance
- the type of support sought; i.e. small grant, multiple grant, loan, etc.

- how much does it cost to run the charity each year, including how much of the revenue is spent on salaries and employees. Where does the revenue come from? How many paid workers are there, how many volunteers are there.

The Lady Leech Fund

Applications to this fund should be submitted in a letter containing:

- the name, address and registration number of the charity
- the name and contact details of the person who is authorised by the charity to apply for funding
- a description of the project that the charity is undertaking, who it hopes to help, and any evidence which will support the need for this particular project
- how much the project will cost, capital and revenue, with an indication of the amounts involved
- how much the charity has raised so far, and where it expects to find the balance
- a description of the connection between the Developing World Project, and the people in the North East of England
- how much does it cost to run the charity each year, including how much of the revenue is spent on salaries and employees. Where does the revenue come from? How many paid workers are there? How many volunteers are there?

Application letters can be written and submitted on the charity's website.

Common applicant mistakes

'Requests for salary costs or replacement of statutory funding, or requests from outside our beneficial area.'

The Kennedy Leigh Charitable Trust

Jewish charities, general, social welfare

£815,000 (2009/10)

Beneficial area

Israel and UK.

ORT House, 126 Albert Street, London NW1 7NE
Tel: 020 7267 6500
Email: naomi@klct.org
Correspondent: Naomi Shoffman, Administrator

Information available

Accounts were available at the Charity Commission.

The trust's objects require three-quarters of its grant-making funds to be distributed to charitable institutions within Israel, with the remainder being distributed in the UK and elsewhere. The trust's 'mission statement' reads as follows:

> The trust will support projects and causes which will improve and enrich the lives of all parts of society, not least those of the young, the needy, the disadvantaged and the underprivileged. In meeting its objectives the trust expects to become involved in a wide range of activities. The trust is able to provide several forms of support and will consider the funding of capital projects and running costs. The trust is non-political and non-religious in nature.

In 2009/10 the trust had assets of £17.6 million and an income of £431,000. Grants were made totalling £815,000.

Beneficiaries included: Yemin Orde (£50,000); Weizmann Institute (£45,000); Oxford Centre for Hebrew Studies (£25,000); Hebrew University Rehovol Campus Library (£20,000); and Jewish Care and the Community Security Trust (£10,000 each).

Exclusions

No grants for individuals.

Applications

The trust stated in its 2009/10 accounts:

> The funds available for distribution outside of Israel are all but committed for the foreseeable future to several UK charities. The trustees are therefore unable to consider applications for funding from charitable organisations outside of Israel at this time.

The trust has more recently stated that funds are fully committed.

The Lennox and Wyfold Foundation

General

£618,500 (2009/10)

Beneficial area

Worldwide.

Fleming Family & Partners Ltd,
15 Suffolk Street, London SW1Y 4HG
Tel: 020 7036 5000
Fax: 020 7036 5601
Correspondent: G Fincham, Secretary
Trustees: Lennox Hannay; Adam Flemming; Christopher Fleming; Caroline Wilmot-Sitwell.
CC Number: 1080198

Information available

Accounts were available at the Charity Commission.

This foundation was established in 2000 for general charitable purposes and was formerly known as the Wyfold Foundation. In September 2005, the foundation received all the assets of the Lennox Hannay Charitable Trust which has now been wound up. Grants are made to a wide variety of UK registered charities ranging from medical research to welfare of the young and the old, from the arts to animal welfare and in some cases whilst the donations have been made to a relevant UK organisation, some of the ultimate beneficiaries are overseas.

In 2009/10 the foundation had assets of £34 million and an income of £314,000. Grants were made to 108 organisations totalling £618,500, and were categorised as follows:

Education	23	£235,500
Health or the saving of lives	26	£119,500
Relief of need	25	£87,500
Citizenship or community development	10	£61,000
Religion	8	£31,000
Arts, culture, heritage and science	5	£30,500
Human rights and equality	1	£20,000
Sport	1	£15,000
Armed forces and emergency services	5	£8,000
Animal welfare	2	£6,000
Environment	2	£4,500

The largest grants made during the year were to: Eton College (£100,000), toward its endowment fund; and Maggie's Centre (£25,000), towards the development of a new cancer centre at Churchill Hospital. Unfortunately, no other beneficiaries were listed in the accounts.

Previous beneficiaries included: Breakthrough Breast Cancer; Absolute Return for Kids; RNIB; DeafBlind UK; Amber Foundation; Tusk Trust; Elephant Family; St George's Chapel – Windsor; Bucklebury Memorial Hall; Chipping Norton Theatre and Friends Trust; Gloucestershire Air Ambulance; Mary Hare Foundation; and Reform Research Trust.

Applications

In writing to the correspondent.

The Mark Leonard Trust

Environmental education, youth, general

£483,500 (2009/10)

Beneficial area

Worldwide, but mainly UK.

Allington House, 1st Floor,
150 Victoria Street, London
SW1E 5AE
Tel: 020 7410 0330
Fax: 020 7410 0332
Website: www.sfct.org.uk
Correspondent: Alan Bookbinder, Director
Trustees: Zivi Sainsbury; Judith Portrait; John Julian Sainsbury; Mark Sainsbury.
CC Number: 1040323

Information available

Accounts were available at the Charity Commission.

This is one of the 18 Sainsbury Family Charitable Trusts, which collectively give over £60 million a year. It mostly supports environmental causes and youth work, although it also gives towards general charitable purposes. Grants are made to support innovative schemes through seed-funding with the aim of helping projects to achieve sustainability and successful replication. The following descriptions of its more specific work are taken from its annual report:

Environment

Grants are made for environmental education, particularly to support projects displaying practical walls of involving children and young adults. The trustees do not support new educational resources in isolation from the actual process of learning and discovery. They are more interested in programmes which help pupils and teachers to develop a theme over time, perhaps combining IT resources with the networks for exchanging information and ideas between schools.

The trustees are particularly interested in projects that progressively enable children and young people to develop a sense of ownership of a project, and that provide direct support to teachers to deliver exciting and high quality education in the classroom.

The trustees are also interested in the potential for sustainable transport, energy efficiency and renewable energy in wider society. In some cases the trustees will consider funding research, but only where there is a clear practical application. Proposals are more likely to be considered when they are testing an idea, model or strategy in practice.

Youth Work

Grants are made for projects that support the rehabilitation of young people who have become marginalised and involved in anti-social or criminal activities. Trustees wish to apply their grants to overcome social exclusion. They are also interested in extending and adding value to the existing use of school buildings, enhancing links between schools and the community, and encouraging greater involvement of parents, school leavers and volunteers in extra-curricular activities.

An essential part of the youth work which the trustees wish to support will be a sense of realising the personal choice and responsibility of young people, building identity through taking their views and plans seriously and offering the tools to translate their aspirations and talents into practice. Above all, grants will be made towards work which gives young people, with the support and guidance they need, the autonomy and permission to be themselves and to be creative and enterprising. The trustees believe that creating this culture in young people in contemporary Britain will be essential for the future health of society.

In 2009/10 the trust had assets of £12.3 million and an income of £1.1 million. There were 14 grants paid during the year totalling £483,500.

The beneficiaries were: Sustainable Restaurant Association (£100,000); Grow Organisation and the Ashden Awards (£50,000 each); Fight for Peace (£35,000); Sustainability and Environmental Education (£30,000); Worldwide Volunteering for Young People and Youth at Risk (£25,000 each); East Potential (£23,000); Federation of City Farms and Community Gardens (£22,500); Charles Darwin Trust and Green Alliance (£20,000 each); People and Planet (£17,000); and City University and Medical Relief and Emergency International (£10,000 each).

Exclusions

Grants are not normally made to individuals.

Applications

'Proposals are generally invited by the trustees or initiated at their request. Unsolicited applications are discouraged and are unlikely to be successful, unless they are closely aligned to the trust's areas of interest.' A single application will be considered for support by all the trusts in the Sainsbury family group.

The Leverhulme Trade Charities Trust

Charities benefiting commercial travellers, grocers or chemists

£1.6 million to organisations (2010)

Beneficial area

UK.

1 Pemberton Row, London
EC4A 3BG
Tel: 020 7042 9881
Email: pread@leverhulme.ac.uk
Website: leverhulme-trade.org.uk
Correspondent: Paul Read, Secretary
Trustees: Sir Michael Perry, Chair; N W A Fitzgerald; P J-P Cescau; A S Ganguly; P Polman.
CC Number: 288404

Information available

Accounts were available at the Charity Commission.

The Leverhulme Trade Charities Trust derives from the will of the First Viscount Leverhulme, who died in 1925. He left a proportion of his shares in Lever Brothers Ltd upon trust and specified the income beneficiaries to include certain trade charities. In 1983, the Leverhulme Trade Charities Trust itself was established, with its own shareholding in Unilever, and with grant making to be restricted to charities connected with commercial travellers, grocers or chemists, their wives, widows or children. The trust has no full-time employees, but the day-to-day administration is carried out by the director of finance at The Leverhulme Trust.

Grants are only made to:

- trade benevolent institutions supporting commercial travellers, grocers or chemists
- schools or universities providing education for them or their children.

In 2010 the trust had assets of £46 million and an income of £1.8 million. Grants to ten organisations totalled £1.6 million. A further £600,000 was given in undergraduate and postgraduate bursaries.

The largest single grant went to Royal Pinner School Foundation (£480,000) and the second largest to the Girl's Day School Trusts (£276,000). Other beneficiaries were: Caravan (£150,000); UCTA Samaritan Fund (£130,000); Pharmacy Practice Research Trust (£125,000); Provision Trade Benevolent Institution (£24,000); and Royal Wolverhampton School Orphan Foundation (£6,000).

Educational grants totalled just over £600,000. During the year 82 applications for undergraduate bursaries were received all of which were approved as grants. A further 25 postgraduate grants were approved.

Exclusions

No capital grants. No response is given to general appeals.

Applications

By letter to the correspondent. All correspondence is acknowledged. The trustees meet in February and applications need to be received by the preceding October.

Undergraduate and postgraduate bursary applications should be directed to the relevant institution

The Leverhulme Trust

Scholarships for education and research

£53.4 million (2010)

Beneficial area

Unrestricted.

1 Pemberton Row, London
EC4A 3BG
Tel: 020 7042 9881
Email: enquiries@leverhulme.org.uk
Website: www.leverhulme.org.uk
Correspondent: Paul Read
Trustees: Sir Michael Perry, Chair; Patrick J P Cescau; Niall W A Fitzgerald; Dr Ashok S Ganguly; Paul Polman.
CC Number: 288371

Information available

Accounts were available at the Charity Commission. Detailed annual 'Guide to Applicants', and an annual report, available from the trust. Excellent website with very detailed grants information.

This trust derives from the will of William Hesketh Lever, the first Viscount Leverhulme. A businessman, entrepreneur and philanthropist who supported a variety of educational, religious, civic, community and medical causes. On his death in 1925, Lord Leverhulme left a proportion of his interest in the company he had founded, Lever Brothers, in trust for specific beneficiaries: to include first certain trade charities and secondly the provision of 'scholarships for the purposes of research and education', thus the Leverhulme Trust was established. In November 1983 a redefinition of the trust's objectives was brought about and subsequently,

the Leverhulme Trust has concentrated its attention solely on research and education.

The trust continues to combine the direct initiatives of the trustees made in the light of specialist peer review advice with a portfolio of awards made by a research awards advisory committee, itself comprising eminent research colleagues drawn predominantly from the academic world.

The awarding of scholarships for research and education continues to be represented by awards for the conduct of research and awards and bursaries for educational purposes. In terms of support, there are five main patterns of award, namely:

▶ research grants
▶ fellowships
▶ academic collaboration
▶ prizes
▶ fine and performing arts.

Awards for education are predominantly bursaries for students in fine and performing arts although there is a small involvement with innovative educational approaches in these disciplines.

Programmes

The following guidelines on grant programmes are taken from the trust's website:

1. Research grants
(i) Research project grants
The aim of these awards is to provide financial support for innovative and original research projects of high quality and potential, the choice of theme and the design of the research lying entirely with the applicant (the Principal Investigator). The grants provide support for the salaries of research staff engaged on the project, plus associated costs directly related to the research proposed.

Proposals are favoured which:
▶ reflect the personal vision of the applicant
▶ demonstrate compelling competence in the research design
▶ surmount traditional disciplinary academic boundaries
▶ involve a degree of challenge and evidence of the applicant's ability to assess risk.

(ii) Research programme grants
In the one major departure from its policy of operating in the responsive mode, the trust selects on an annual basis two themes of research for which bids are invited. Normally one grant is awarded for each theme. The grants

provide funds to research teams for up to five years to enable them to explore significant issues in the social sciences, in the humanities and, to a lesser extent, in the sciences. The scale of the awards (each one at a sum of up to £1.75 million) is set at a level where it is possible for a research team to study a significant theme in depth by conducting a group of interlinked research projects which taken together can lead to new understanding. The themes are selected not to exclude particular disciplines from the competition but rather to encourage research teams to look upon their established research interests from a set of refreshing viewpoints. Themes in recent years have included Security and Liberty and Ceremony and Ritual.

[The themes for 2012 are: Conspiracies; Patronage; and Values.]

2. Fellowships
Full details on the range of fellowships available to individuals can be found in the trust's Guide for Applicants.

3. Academic collaborations
(i) International Networks
These collaborations enable a Principal Investigator based in the UK to lead a research project where its successful completion is dependant on the participation of relevant overseas institutions. A significant research theme must be identified at the outset which requires for its successful treatment international collaboration between one or more UK universities, and two or more overseas institutions (normally up to a maximum of seven institutions in total). Networks should be newly constituted collaborations. Full justification should be given for the involvement of all participants, with each participant bringing specific – and stated – expertise which can directly contribute to the success of the project. Details of the proposed methodology for the research project should be provided at the outset, as well as a clear indication of the anticipated outcomes (publications, websites), and of the dissemination strategy to be adopted.

Value and duration: The value of an award is normally up to £125,000, the activities involved lasting for up to three years.

Topics: Applications for research on any topic within the entire array of academic disciplines are eligible for support. However, an exception is made for areas of research supported by specialist funding agencies and in particular for medicine. In such cases, applicants should consider an application to these alternative funding bodies as being more appropriate. Specific attention is paid to the reasons given by applicants in justifying their choice of the trust as the most appropriate agency for the support of their project.

Institutions

The Principal Investigator should be employed at a university or other institution of higher or further education in the UK. The award is made to that institution, which must agree to administer the grant, for allocation among the participating institutions.

(ii) Visiting Professorships

The objective of these awards is to enable distinguished academics based overseas to spend between three and ten months inclusive at a UK university, primarily in order to enhance the skills of academic staff or the student body within the host institution. It is recognised that Visiting Professors may also wish to use the opportunity to further their own academic interests. The over-riding criteria for selection are first the academic standing and achievements of the visitor in terms of research and teaching, and secondly the ability of the receiving institution to benefit from the imported skills and expertise. Priority will be given to new or recent collaborative ventures.

Applicants:

- must be made by a member of academic staff, based in a UK university or other higher education institution, who will be responsible for co-ordinating the visit. The host academic's employing institution must also agree to administer the grant, if awarded, and to provide appropriate facilities for the Visiting Professor. Applications may not be submitted by the visitor.

Value: The sum requested should reflect the individual circumstances of the visitor and the nature and duration of the proposed activities. A maintenance grant up to a level commensurate with the salary of a professor in the relevant field at the receiving institution may be requested. Economy travel costs to and from the UK will also be met. Requests for associated costs, if justified by the programme, may include, for example, travel within the UK, consumables, and essential technical assistance.

4. Philip Leverhulme Prizes

Philip Leverhulme Prizes are awarded to outstanding scholars (normally under the age of 36) who have made a substantial and recognised contribution to their particular field of study, recognised at an international level, and whose future contributions are held to be of correspondingly high promise. Approximately 25 Prizes are available each year across the five topics which are offered.

The Prizes commemorate the contribution to the work of the trust made by Philip Leverhulme, the Third

Viscount Leverhulme and grandson of the Founder.

Topics: For the 2012 competition the selected disciplines are:

- Classics
- Earth, Ocean and Atmospheric Sciences
- History of Art
- Law
- Mathematics and Statistics
- Medieval, Early Modern and Modern History.

The disciplines selected are intentionally broad, and nominations will be considered irrespective of a nominee's departmental affiliation.

Value: Each Prize has a value of £70,000; use should be made of the award over a two or three year period. Prizes can be used for any purpose which can advance the Prize holder's research, with the exception of enhancing the Prize holder's salary.

Nominees: Nominees must hold a post (irrespective of the source of funding) in a UK institution of higher education or research and should normally be under age 36. However, nominations are accepted for those aged 36 to 39 inclusive if they have had a distinct career change or break.

5. Art Initiatives

Applicants should note that any activities supported under this strand should offer an opportunity for a fresh and original educational approach to be initiated in the proposed project/ activity:

(a) Innovative Teaching Activity Awards

Innovative and/or distinctive educational teaching activities may be supported. The proposed activity should support the artistic development of the students concerned, although the payment of expenses to professional artists acting in a tutorial capacity may be considered.

(b) Arts and Technology Awards

Applications are invited from one or more institutions able to initiate a project which promotes the creative use of technology within any area of the arts. It is likely that the outcome of such projects will be a performance or exhibition in which new or emerging technologies are implemented.

Grantmaking in 2010

In 2010 the trust had assets of £1.59 billion and an income of £59.1 million from investments. There were 218 grants made during the year totalling £53.4 million, broken down as follows:

Responsive mode projects	£30 million
Research Awards Advisory Committee	£9.6 million
Major Research Fellowships	£3.6 million
Designated programmes	£3.1 million
Visiting fellows and professors	£2 million
Arts bursaries	£1.9 million
Leverhulme prizes	£1.7 million
Academy fellowships/ scholarships	£1.3 million

Beneficiaries included the following institutions, all of whom received multiple awards: Oxford University (£4.8 million); Leicester University (£2 million); Warwick University (£1.4 million); Reading University (£1.2 million); Edinburgh University (£895,000); Southampton University (£762,000); York University (£692,000); Liverpool University (£592,000); University of East Anglia (£530,000); British Museum (£429,000); Sheffield University (£377,000); and the Natural History Museum (£348,000). Grants of £300,000 or less were made to 87 institutions.

Exclusions

When submitting an application to the trust, applicants are advised that the trust does not offer funding for the following costs, and hence none of these items may be included in any budget submitted to the trust:

- core funding or overheads for institutions
- individual items of equipment over £1,000
- sites, buildings or other capital expenditure
- support for the organisation of conferences or workshops, which are not directly associated with International Networks, Early Career Fellowships or Philip Leverhulme Prizes
- exhibitions
- contributions to appeals
- endowments
- a shortfall resulting from a withdrawal of or deficiency in public finance
- UK student fees where these are not associated with a Research Project Grant bid or with Fine and Performing Arts schemes detailed in the Guidelines for Applicants.

Applications

Each programme, scholarship and award has its own individual application deadline and procedure. Full guidelines and application procedures for each award scheme are available from the trust directly or via its website.

Lord Leverhulme's Charitable Trust

Welfare, education, arts, young people

£660,500 (2009/10)

Beneficial area

UK especially, Cheshire, Merseyside and South Lancashire.

Leverhulme Estate Office, Hesketh Grange, Manor Road, Thornton Hough, Wirral CH63 1JD
Tel: 0151 336 4828
Fax: 0151 353 0265
Correspondent: Mrs S Edwards, Administrator
Trustees: A E H Heber-Percy; Anthony H S Hannay.
CC Number: 212431

Information available

Accounts were available from the Charity Commission, without a full list of grants.

The trust was established in 1957 by the late Lord Leverhulme. There are two restricted funds within the trust. One generates income which is paid to National Museums and Galleries in Liverpool for the trustees of the Lady Lever Art Gallery. The second is Lord Leverhulme's Youth Enterprise Scheme; the income from this sponsors young people in the Wirral and Cheshire areas who receive support from the Prince's Youth Business Trust.

In 2009/10 the trust had assets of £24.6 million and an income of £653,500. Grants were made totalling £660,500 and were categorised as follows:

Education	£337,500
Health	£88,000
Religious establishments	£84,000
Community	£79,500
Arts	£52,500
Environmental	£16,000
Animal welfare	£3,000

Only grants of over £20,000 were listed in the accounts. The beneficiaries of these larger grants were: Bolton School (£320,000 in total); Lady Lever Art Gallery (£60,000 in total); Royal College of Surgeons (£50,000); and the Prince's Youth Business Trust (£21,500).

Exclusions

No grants to non-charitable organisations.

Applications

The trust states:

> Priority is given [...] to applications from Cheshire, Merseyside and South Lancashire and the charities supported by the settlor in his lifetime. Others who do not meet those criteria should not apply without prior invitation but should, on a single sheet, state briefly their aims and apply fully only on being asked to do so. A handful of charities have heeded this warning and telephoned our administrator but the continuing volume of applications from charities which plainly do not meet the stated criteria suggests that many applicants do not concern themselves with their target's policies.

The Joseph Levy Charitable Foundation

Young people, elderly, health, medical research

£899,000 (2009/10)

Beneficial area

UK and Israel.

1st Floor, 1 Bell Street, London NW1 5BY
Email: info@jlf.org.uk
Website: www.jlf.org.uk
Correspondent: Sue Nyfield, Director
Trustees: Mrs Jane Jason; Peter L Levy; Melanie Levy; Claudia Giat; James Jason.
CC Number: 245592

Information available

Accounts were available at the Charity Commission.

The foundation was established in 1965 by the late Joseph Levy, property developer and philanthropist, who helped to rebuild post-war London in the 1950s and 60s. The trust website notes:

> He worked tirelessly all his life for many charitable causes and in particular had a deep concern for the welfare of young people. His longstanding interest in youth began as a member and manager at Brady Boys' Club. He subsequently became a Vice-President of the London Federation of Boys' Clubs, now London Youth. In 1963 he became a Founder Trustee of the Cystic Fibrosis Research Trust, now the Cystic Fibrosis Trust, acting as Chairman for almost twenty years till his retirement in 1984. He was awarded the MBE in 1976 and the CBE eight years later for his dedication to charitable causes.

As noted below, the amount committed each year varies considerably.

In 2009/10 the foundation had assets of £16.7 million and an income of £795,000. Grants were committed during the year totalling £899,000 (2008/09: £132,000; 2007/08: £4 million; 2006/07: £869,000).

Beneficiaries included: Cystic Fibrosis Holiday Fund (£58,000); Cystic Fibrosis Trust (£47,000); English Blind Golf (£40,000); Jewish Council for Racial Equality (£20,000); London Youth (£10,000); Oxford Centre for Jewish Studies (£5,000); and University of St Andrews (£3,000).

In 2010/11, Dementia received £1 million as part of it multi-year commitment.

Exclusions

No grants to individuals, under any circumstances.

Applications

'The trustees wish to inform you that due to current commitments, the foundation is no longer able to accept unsolicited applications.'

The Linbury Trust

Arts, heritage, social welfare, humanitarian aid, general

£5.6 million (2009/10)

Beneficial area

Unrestricted.

Allington House, 1st Floor, 150 Victoria Street, London SW1E 5AE
Tel: 020 7410 0330
Fax: 020 7410 0332

LINBURY

Website: www.linburytrust.org.uk/
Correspondent: Alan Bookbinder, Director
Trustees: Lord Sainsbury of Preston Candover; Lady Sainsbury; Sir Martin Jacomb; Sir James Spooner.
CC Number: 287077

Information available

Accounts were available at the Charity Commission.

Summary

This is one of the Sainsbury Family Charitable Trusts, which share a joint administration. They have a common approach to grantmaking which is described in the entry for the group as a whole, and which is generally discouraging to organisations not already in contact with the trust concerned, but some appear to be increasingly open to unsolicited approaches.

Over time, much of the trust's money has gone in major capital projects. It also funds numerous revenue projects in the following fields:

- arts
- education
- environment and heritage
- medical
- social welfare
- developing countries and humanitarian aid.

Under each of these categories, the trust makes grants very selectively; it gives priority to charitable causes where it has particular knowledge and experience. In past years the trust has supported major capital projects such as the National Gallery and the Royal Opera House, as well as other museums and galleries. It also has a special interest in dance and dance education, Lady Sainsbury being the well known ballerina Anya Linden. However, while the trust is particularly associated with supporting the arts, it is worth noting that some 67 per cent of the value of grants made between 2000 and 2010 was to other causes.

General

The trust takes a proactive approach towards grant-making and, consequently, unsolicited applications are not usually successful. However, the trust will consider proposals which fall within its guidelines and gives grants to a wide range of charities. The sums awarded may be small or may amount to many millions, either on a once-only basis or as a commitment over a number of years.

Within the UK, priority is given to causes that are either national in scope, or that are based in regions of which trustees have a particular knowledge or interest. Preferred causes are as follows (not in order of priority):

1 Disadvantaged young people, including those who are homeless or are in danger of becoming so, or who are drug abusers.

2 Specific medical causes which the trustees have adopted and where, in the trustees' opinion, inadequate research is currently undertaken, or inadequate treatment and understanding exists; for example, Chronic Fatigue Syndrome. Medical causes to which these criteria do not apply are generally not supported. The trustees usually take specialist advice before making decisions.

3 Although general educational causes are not supported unless they cover the particular needs of those in 1 or 2, limited exceptions are made when the trustees have particular knowledge concerning specific educational appeals.

4 Appeals for the benefit of older people will be considered if the results can be shown to improve their quality of life directly and in a cost effective way, and particularly when the goal is to help people to continue living in their own homes.

5 National heritage appeals will be considered and, in particular, appeals for historic buildings and major arts institutions. Trustees occasionally make grants for initiatives to safeguard the natural environment.

6 Grants for the visual arts, the performing arts and for education in the arts will be favourably considered where, in the opinion of the trustees, the aim is to produce work of the highest standard, and where long term benefits will result. Arts festivals are generally not supported.

7 Grants for capital projects or 'one-off' grants for specific purposes will not normally be repeated or supplemented within four years of the original grant, and then only in exceptional circumstances.

Grantmaking in 2009/10

In 2009/10 the trust had assets of £151.3 million and an income of £6.2 million. Grants were paid during the year totalling over £5.6 million.

The trust gives the following review of each area of grantmaking during the year in its annual report, which highlights some key donations (including payments made during the year where available):

Education – £2.2 million

Trustees have over many years been stalwart supporters of arts education in the UK, particularly in the fields of dance and the visual arts. Their long-standing provision of scholarships at the British School at Rome [£58,000], and of support for the Dance Fellowship within the Clore Leadership Programme, exemplify this.

Trustees have supported Stowe for many years – both the School, and the restoration of Stowe House, the classical Grade 1 listed house which stands in important National Trust landscape gardens. As part of the general upgrading of facilities at Stowe, the Art School required a complete renovation; The Linbury Trust is the principal benefactor [£1.5 million in 2009/10].

Trustees also gave a major grant to the Royal Welsh College of Music and Drama [£250,000]; the College's redevelopment project will significantly enhance its provision of teaching, rehearsal and performance space as well as increasing its accessibility to the public.

Trustees also have a particular interest in the teaching of history. They continued their support for a research project whereby a team at the Institute of Historical Research, a part of the University of London, is undertaking a study of how the teaching of history in Britain at secondary level has changed over the last 100 years, with a view to making policy recommendations for future developments in the curriculum [£127,500].

Trustees initiated a grant over 2 years to the Shakespeare Schools Festival [£75,000], in order to allow more young people to have the experience of performing Shakespeare.

Arts – £2.15 million

The Linbury Trust has consistently supported excellence in the visual and

214

performing arts, principally through a series of major grants to a select number of the UK's most important cultural institutions, usually towards major capital projects. In recent years the Trust has been the lead private donor to the redevelopment of the Ashmolean Museum, giving considerable support since the inception of the project [£1.5 million in 2009/10]. The Museum, incorporating the new extension designed by Rick Mather, was re-opened to the public in November 2009 amid considerable critical acclaim.

The Trustees also made the final payment of their £1 million grant towards the redevelopment of the Holburne Museum in Bath; this will add a modern extension to the existing Georgian building, providing a considerably enlarged display area, as well as ancillary facilities. The first payment was made under a total grant of £250,000 towards the complete re-building of the Lyric Players Theatre in Belfast. Both the Holburne and the Lyric [...] re-opened in early 2011.

The Trustees also offered grants to a number of performing arts companies towards their continuing work. These included support for an innovative collaboration between the Young Vic and a Palestinian theatre company – the resulting work was shown in London, Israel and the West Bank; and The Opera Group's production of The Lion's Face, a new opera about Alzheimer's disease, developed with research support from the Institute of Psychiatry.

Developing Countries and Humanitarian Aid – £462,000
The Trustees maintained their interest in supporting organisations that work in Palestine, primarily in the medical field. [Major beneficiaries during the year were: St John of Jerusalem Eye Hospital and Save the Children (£100,000 each); and Palestine Association for Children's Encouragement of Sports (£50,000).]

Environment and Heritage – £421,000
The University of Buckingham is the UK's only private sector university. The university has for many years owned Prebend House, a listed building dating back to Queen Anne, but which had fallen into a dangerous state of disrepair. The restoration of Prebend House will form a key element of a major development of the university's campus [£90,000].

Nant Gwrtheyrn, located on the Lleyn peninsula of North Wales, is the site of a former granite quarry; many of the mining village buildings still remain. The Nant Gwrtheyrn Trust is in the process of revitalising the village, creating a museum dedicated to the quarrying industry, and creating a centre of

Welsh language and culture. The Trustees agreed a grant towards the refurbishment of the building that will be primarily used for educational purposes [£85,000].

Social Welfare – £318,500
The Trustees take particular interest in charities working with severely disadvantaged and under-achieving young people. They have long supported a range of programmes designed to help young people to break free from the nexus of low aspirations, anti-social behaviour, substance abuse, crime and, in all too many cases, re-offending, which are so often the product of long-term economic deprivation, failure to benefit from the opportunities provided by education, and family breakdown. They made a number of grants in this category; these included the grants to the Foundation Training Company [£50,000], towards its resettlement centre in Lambeth; the Coldingley Crime Diversion Scheme (now re-named KeepOut); and Trail-Blazers. Trustees also believe that the arts can be an effective medium through which to reach disadvantaged young people.

Trustees reserve a part of their grant-making within this category for support for charities working with the elderly.

Medical – £62,000
The Trustees' primary area of interest in the Medical category is in research into CFS / ME. Trustees no longer actively solicit research proposals; however in recent years they have supported a major study into paediatric issues in CFS / ME under the aegis of the University of Bristol. During the year they agreed a grant towards a further piece of research, by the same University of Bristol team; this study will get underway during 2010/11. [In 2009/10 a grant of £40,000 was made to the Royal Liverpool University Hospital towards specialist equipment for the Early Diagnosis Suite at the St Paul's Eye Unit.]

Exclusions
No grants to individuals.

Applications
See the guidance for applicants in the entry for the Sainsbury Family Charitable Trusts. A single application will be considered for support by all the trusts in the group.

Note: 'the trustees take a proactive approach towards grant-making; accordingly, unsolicited applications to the trust are not usually successful'.

The Enid Linder Foundation

Health, welfare, general

£460,500 (2010/11)

Beneficial area
Unrestricted.

Moore Stephens LLP, 150 Aldersgate Street, London EC1A 4AB
Tel: 020 7334 9191
Fax: 020 7248 3408
Email: martin.pollock@ moorestephens.com
Correspondent: Martin Pollock, Secretary
Trustees: Jack Ladeveze; Audrey Ladeveze; M Butler; C Cook; Jonathan Fountain.
CC Number: 267509

Information available
Accounts were available at the Charity Commission.

There are often no more than ten new grants each year, with most money going to a mixed group of regularly supported beneficiaries, mainly in the fields of health and social welfare, particularly of children and disabled people, medical education and research. Local (normally London and the south), national and international charities are supported.

The aims of the foundation are:

- to fund research and teaching related to all areas of medicine by way of medical electives and general support costs to students and chosen medical universities
- to assist in the funding of chosen research fellowship schemes which are of particular interest to the trustees
- to distribute in full, in accordance with the governing Trust Deed, all the income available each year
- to maintain resources at a reasonable level in order to continue to provide general charitable assistance in the foreseeable future.

The main objectives for the year are shaped by these strategic aims with a view to maintaining both a stable medical electives scheme at universities, to support the research fellowship schemes and to continue funding chosen general charitable causes.

In 2010/11 the foundation had assets of £13.7 million and an income of £471,000. Grants were made totalling £460,500, which included £389,500 for 'general charitable causes' and £71,000 to six teaching hospitals and universities, all of which were supported in the previous year.

Beneficiaries included: Royal College of Surgeons (£100,000); National Children's Orchestra (£65,000 in total); Victoria & Albert Museum (£30,000); Médecins Sans Frontières (£20,000); Bath University (£15,000); Bath Intensive Care Baby Unit and Help for Heroes (£10,000 each); Beatrix Potter Society (£7,000); Chauncy Maples Malawi Trust and the Stroke Association (£5,000 each); and the Prostate Society (£1,000).

Applications

In writing to the correspondent. Although unsolicited applications are accepted, the trust states that it prefers to support organisations whose work it has researched.

The George John and Sheilah Livanos Charitable Trust

Health, maritime charities, general

£351,000 (2010)

Beneficial area

UK.

Jeffrey Green Russell, Waverley House, 7–12 Noel Street, London W1F 8GQ

Tel: 020 7339 7000

Correspondent: Philip N Harris, Trustee

Trustees: Philip N Harris; Timothy T Cripps; Anthony S Holmes.

CC Number: 1002279

Information available

Accounts were available at the Charity Commission.

The trust gives grants from its income of about £200,000 a year but has also been making substantial awards from capital. Grants are widely spread and the previously reported interest in maritime causes, while still existing, is not as prominent as it was.

In 2010 the trust had assets of £2.7 million and an income of £118,000. Grants were made to 28 organisations totalling £351,000.

The trust continued to make long-term project payments of £50,000 and £47,500 to Diabetes UK and SPARKS respectively, although these sums had been previously committed in other yearly grant budgets.

The largest beneficiary was St Mary's Hospital (£90,000). Other beneficiaries of larger grants were: The Watts Gallery (£54,000); Parkinson's Disease Society (£50,000); University of Dundee – Child Health Studentship (£29,000); and Ekklesia Project Fakenham (£24,000).

Other beneficiaries included: Breakthrough Breast Cancer and London Youth (£10,000 each); Disasters Emergency Committee and Paul D'Auria Cancer Support Centre (£7,500 each); British Liver Trust, Crimestoppers, Demand, Langalanga Scholarship Fund and the Cirdan Sailing Trust (£5,000 each); Stubbers (£2,000); and Whitechapel Mission (£1,000).

Exclusions

No grants to individuals or non-registered charities.

Applications

'Unsolicited applications are considered but the trustees inevitably turn down a large number of applications.'

Lloyds TSB Foundation for England and Wales

Social and community needs

£23.4 million (2010)

Beneficial area

England and Wales.

Pentagon House, 52–54 Southwark Street, London SE1 1UN

Tel: 0870 411 1223

Fax: 0870 411 1224

Email: enquiries@ lloydstsbfoundations.org.uk

Website: www.lloydstsbfoundations. org.uk

Correspondent: Mrs Linda Kelly, Chief Executive

Trustees: Prof. Ian Diamond, Chair; Janet Bibby; Rob Devey; Pavita Cooper; Alan Leaman; Rosemary Stevenson; Philip Grant; Mohammad Naeem; Lord Sandy Leitch; Sir Clive Booth; Dame Denise Platt.

CC Number: 327114

Information available

The foundation provides comprehensive information on its activities and achievements, all of which is available on its excellent website, and much of which is reproduced here:

> We fund small and medium local, regional and national charities working at the heart of communities to tackle disadvantage and help empower people on the margins of our society.
>
> Our funding is always driven by communities' needs and we have a strong local knowledge and presence across England and Wales.
>
> In everything we do we aim to be:
> ▶ accessible to all
> ▶ approachable and supportive
> ▶ responsive and customer focused
> ▶ straightforward
> ▶ timely and transparent.
>
> *Who do we fund?*
> ▶ we support small and medium 'underfunded' registered charities (12 months reserves or less)
> ▶ we fund local or regional charities with an income of £1 million or under
> ▶ we fund national charities with an income of £5 million or under.
>
> The majority of our funding is given to organisations with an income of £1 million or less:
> ▶ more than three-quarters of funded charities have an income of less than £500,000
> ▶ almost a half of funded charities have an income of less than £100,000.
>
> *What do we fund?*
> In support of our Mission Statement, the foundation adopts the following grant-making approach:

we fund work that helps disadvantaged people to play a fuller role in the community

▶ we support both well established and new work across the voluntary sector

▶ we provide 'second stage funding' to support charities' development – we fund organisations that are looking to innovate, expand, improve or maintain their capacity, effectiveness or services

▶ we fund running costs, including salaries, to ensure that charities can continue to operate their core services

▶ we provide grants of up to three years appropriate to the charity's size.

Community Programme

The Community programme focuses on funding core work that helps disadvantaged people to play a fuller role in the community. We are particularly interested in work that achieves this through:

▶ improved social and community involvement

▶ improved life choices and chances

▶ helping people to be heard.

To be eligible:

▶ you must be an underfunded charity (12 months reserves or less)

▶ if you work locally or in a region you must have an income of £1 million or less

▶ if you work nationally you must have an income of £5 million or less

▶ your work must enable disadvantaged people to play a fuller role in the community in one or more of the following ways:

 ▶ improved social and community involvement

 ▶ improved life choices and chances

 ▶ helping people to be heard.

▶ you will need to be clear on the specific changes and benefits that your work will provide for your users/ beneficiaries

What type of funding do we provide?

We fund charities to continue and develop existing community-based work, or to develop the organisation or its services. We can support charities in a range of ways – examples include funding to:

▶ Enable the continued provision of services

▶ Support the expansion of services

▶ Help improve the quality of services

▶ Maintain and or improve their capacity and or effectiveness

▶ Encourage learning and best practice

▶ Lobby or campaign at a local, regional or national level.

We make grants of one to three years that are appropriate to the size and needs of each charity.

The foundation also has a matched giving scheme for Lloyds TSB Group staff. The foundation introduces new programmes from time to time – potential applicants should check the foundation's website for up-to-date details of current programmes.

Grantmaking in 2010

In 2010 the foundation had assets of £33.7 million and an income of £26 million, most of which was received under the deed of covenant from Lloyds Banking Group. There were 908 grants made during the year totalling £23.4 million.

During the year, grants made through the Community programme and the Mental Health and Criminal Justice programme (the latter of which is no longer accepting applications), were broken down geographically as follows:

Kent and South East London	77	£2.26 million
Essex and North East London	81	£2.20 million
Yorkshire	71	£2.13 million
West Midlands	63	£2.12 million
Lancashire and North Manchester	72	£2.0 million
South Central and South West London	67	£2.0 million
Lincolnshire and Nottinghamshire	68	£1.84 million
Cheshire and South Manchester	65	£1.62 million
Mid and South Wales	66	£1.49 million
North East and Cumbria	66	£1.45 million
South West Central	48	£1.15 million
Hertfordshire and North West London	35	£1.1 million
Devon and Cornwall	45	£740,000
East of England	38	£640,000
North West Midlands	30	£530,000
North Wales	16	£160,000

The following summary analysis of grantmaking is taken from the foundation's 2010 Annual Report, the full version of which is available from the foundation's website.

Investing where is counts

We remain committed to tackling disadvantage wherever it exists and our extensive geographical network means that we ensure we target and weight our support to the most deprived areas across England and Wales.

In the last three years, over 49% of our funding was targeted towards the top 20% most deprived areas.

[The following table lists funding given to the ten most deprived areas in England in the last three years.]

Liverpool	£1.8 million
Hackney	£650,000
Tower Hamlets	£950,000
Manchester	£1.4 million
Knowsley	£190,000
Newham	£900,000
Easington	£200,000
Islington	£920,000
Middlesbrough	£250,000
Birmingham	£1.62 million

In the same period, over £1.7 million has been awarded to 82 charities in Wales, with 14% of this total being spent in the most deprived areas of Merthyr Tydfil, Blaenau Gwent, Rhondda Cynon Taff and Neath Port Talbot.

In 2010, our top funded areas across all geographies in the Community programme were:

Children and young people	£3.1 million
Disability	£2.8 million
Health (including mental health)	£2.6 million
Advice, advocacy and outreach	£2.1 million
Geographically-based support	£1.6 million
Older people	£1.1 million
Family and relationships	£1.1 million
Training and education	£1 million

As in 2009, the top two funded issues were Children and Young People and Disability particularly learning disability. However, an increase in funding in health including mental health and training and education was seen in 2010.

Helping in hard times
Advice support

In 2010, unemployment figures remained high and cost of living expenses continued to rise with food, energy and petrol prices all contributing to rising inflation, adding increased pressure on those people already struggling with their financial situations.

Recent research found that, at any given time, up to five million people report arrears on consumer credit, failure to keep up with mortgage payments, or that meeting credit commitment is a heavy burden, and around 30% of over-55s have some form of unsecured debt that they are struggling to clear.

This has lead to around 1.4 million people, one in every 33 UK adults, seeking advice from charities such as National Debtline and Citizens Advice Bureau, which alone, dealt with 9,389 new debt problems every working day in England and Wales.

Supporting vulnerable groups remains one of our key focuses, including helping people with mental health problems, disabilities and the elderly, to avoid isolation from friends and family due to the financial circumstances they find themselves in.

In 2010 we provided £2.1 million support to charities offering advice including:

▶ one to one counselling and advice on debt and benefits

- outreach and information services to the hardest to reach groups
- workshops supporting good financial practice
- self advocacy, for users to speak out to improve their personal situation.

This funding has ensured that hundreds of vulnerable people are now receiving the support they need to cope with debt, manage their budgets better and avoid being taken advantage of by inappropriate lenders. This support has helped to restore and improve the quality of their lives.

Supporting charities

Charities tell us they are spending more time fundraising and submitting applications, which is particularly challenging for smaller charities with limited resources. Our process of supporting charities by giving advice at every stage of the application process has a positive impact for them by saving time through early indication of their chances of success when applying for funding. Even when we cannot award a grant we provide feedback and signposting to other sources where funding may be available.

This year with the use of our online eligibility tool, we have seen 4,757 enquiries, which has resulted in 2,529 eligible charities applying for funding. Feedback from these charities has highlighted that the advice from the foundation's team at every stage of the application has made a significant difference to the application process.

A comprehensive list of the grants made during the year is available from the foundation's website.

Exclusions

The foundation does not fund the following types of organisations and work:

Organisations

- organisations that are **not** registered charities
- second or third tier organisations (unless there is evidence of direct benefit to disadvantaged people)
- charities that mainly work overseas
- charities that mainly give funds to other charities, individuals or other organisations
- hospitals, hospices or medical centres
- rescue services
- schools, colleges and universities.

Types of work

- activities which a statutory body is responsible for
- capital projects, appeals, refurbishments

- environmental work, expeditions and overseas travel
- funding to promote religion
- holidays or trips
- loans or business finance
- medical research, funding for medical equipment or medical treatments
- sponsorship or funding towards a marketing appeal or fundraising activities
- work with animals or to promote animal welfare.

Applications

The trust states:

We aim to be accessible and supportive to charities that request funding from us.

Step 1 – Read our guidelines

Please check our guidelines and individual criteria for the programme you are interested in so that you are clear what is and is not funded.

Step 2 – Check if your charity is eligible

Before you apply you need to complete our short charity eligibility questionnaire which you can find on our website. If you don't have access to the internet or would prefer to talk to us first, please call 0870 411 1223.

Please note that charity eligibility does not mean that your work meets the criteria for all of our programmes.

Step 3 – We will contact you to discuss whether your work is eligible

If your charity is eligible, one of our team will contact you to discuss whether the work you are seeking funding for fits within our guidelines – and if it does to discuss the next steps.

Step 4 – Assessment

If your work is eligible for consideration and you are applying for a grant of over £5,000, your local Grant Manager will visit you to discuss your funding requirements. If you are applying for a grant of under £5,000, the Grant Manager will carry out a telephone assessment.

Assessment visits take one to two hours, and your local Grant Manager will discuss a range of issues relevant to your potential application, including: your governance; your finances; your evidence of need; your work; and the difference it will make to your users/ beneficiaries.

The Grant Manager will tell you whether or not to proceed with an application. If you are advised to apply, they will help you to make the best application.

Step 5 – Complete the application form

If your local Grant Manager recommends that you complete an application form, they will give you a copy of the form. You will need to read the accompanying guidance notes and include:

- a copy of your most recent annual report and full signed accounts. These should be signed as approved on behalf of your Management Committee or equivalent. You must make sure your charity annual returns are up to date and registered with the Charity Commission – we will check this when we assess your application. (If your records are not up to date this could delay your application being processed)
- a copy of your charity's most recent bank statement so that we can verify the account details
- the relevant job description if you are applying for funding towards the cost of a post, a copy of your equal opportunities policy or if you do not have one, information about your commitment to equal opportunities. We will also need to know about the other governance policies that you have in place that are relevant to your work.

Step 6 – Return your application form to us

You will need to submit a signed copy of the form together with the supporting documents to us.

Step 7 – The decision on your application

We respond to all applications that we receive and it takes from three to six months for a decision to be made on your application. Your local Grant Manager will tell you when you are likely to hear the decision.

Common reasons for unsuccessful applications

The foundation cannot fund all eligible applications even if they are of a high quality because each year the total amount requested by charities exceeds the money that we have available. Other reasons for the foundation not being able to make a grant include:

- charities' core work not being sufficiently focused on our mission
- applications not falling within our guidelines
- charities not filling in the application form properly
- charities not having up to date annual returns or accounts filed with the Charities Commission or other relevant regulatory bodies.

When can I reapply?

If you receive a grant, you will not be eligible to apply for another grant from the Community Programme for another two years from receipt of the grant (or from receipt of the final payment if it has been two or three-year funding). If your application is unsuccessful, you must wait for a year before you apply again.

Regional contact details	Tel
Cheshire and South Manchester	07500 787747
Devon and Cornwall	07770 925946
East	07912 798053
Essex and North East London	07770 925943
Hertfordshire and North West London	0870 411 1223
Kent and South East London	07872 031792
Lancashire and North Manchester	07734 973464
Lincolnshire and Nottinghamshire	07734 973060
Mid and South Wales	07802 540793
North East and Cumbria	07802 337481
North Wales	07500 787749
North West Midlands	07500 787751
South Central and South West London	07872 031793
South West Central	07500 787750
West Midlands	07500 787746
Yorkshire	07500 787745

Common applicant mistakes

'Organisations enquiring about funding [not] meeting our specific criteria, i.e. they are not registered charities or their work does not have a focus on tackling disadvantage or working with disadvantaged groups. Also, accounts not being filed with Charity Commission. On completing applications charities are not able to demonstrate the impact their work has on beneficiaries, normally because they lack systems to monitor or measure this.'

Lloyds TSB Foundation for Northern Ireland

Social and community need, education and training

£1.7 million (2010)

Beneficial area

Northern Ireland.

2nd Floor, 14 Cromac Place, Gasworks, Belfast BT7 2JB
Tel: 028 9032 3000
Fax: 028 9032 3200
Email: info@lloydstsbfoundationni.org
Website: www.lloydstsbfoundationni.org
Correspondent: Sandara Kelso-Robb, Executive Director

IR Number: XN72216

Information available

Full information on the foundation's helpful website, including the latest annual review.

Summary

The foundation allocates its funds in support of underfunded, grassroots charities that enable people, especially disabled and disadvantaged people, to be active members of society and to improve their quality of life.

Most donations are said to be one-off, with a small number of commitments made over two or more years. The trustees say that they prefer to make donations towards specific items rather than contributions to large appeals, though the trust will consider core funding for small local charities. Applications which help to develop voluntary sector infrastructure are encouraged. Donations are generally between £2,500 and £5,000.

Programmes

The foundation's main grant programme, the Standard Grant Programme, makes grants to underfunded, grassroots organisations with a total income of less than £1 million. The programme focuses on social and community welfare and education and training. Donations are generally in the region of £2,500 to £5,000 but there is no minimum amount set by the trustees. In 2010 the average grant from the Standard Grant Programme was £3,715.

The foundation also manages other short-running, ad-hoc programmes. In 2007, for example, the foundation ran a Creating Change pilot programme and in 2008, it announced a one year International Grant Programme. The 2010 annual report notes the success of the International programme, which was repeated in 2010. At present the programme is closed and it is not an ongoing programme. However, the foundation's website notes that any further international grants

programmes will be widely publicised there.

A Special Initiatives Programme was also established in 2008 to recognise the funding requirements of those organisations undertaking work of a strategic or Northern Ireland wide nature. Consequently, potential applicants are advised to visit the foundation's website or contact them directly to ensure that they keep up-to-date with the latest programme information.

Guidelines for applicants

The guidelines for applicants, detailed on the foundation's website, read as follows:

The overall policy of the charity is to support underfunded charities which enable people, especially disadvantaged or disabled people, to play a fuller role in the community.

The trustees are keen to encourage the infrastructure of the voluntary sector and welcome applications for operational costs. This may include a contribution toward salary costs, and training and education for managers and staff, with the exception of the pre-school sector. The trustees are also keen to support sector self-rationalisation.

The foundation has two main target areas to which it seeks to allocate funds:
▶ social and community needs
▶ education and training.

Social and Community Needs
A wide range of activities are supported and the following are meant as a guide only.

Community services
Family centres, women's centres, youth and older people's clubs, after school clubs, play schemes, help groups, childcare provision.

Advice services
Homelessness, addictions, bereavement, family guidance, money advice, helplines.

Disabled people
Residences, day centres, transport, carers, information and advice, advocacy.

Promotion of health
Information and advice, mental health, hospices, day care, home nursing, independent living for older people.

Civic responsibility
Juveniles at risk, crime prevention, promotion of volunteering, victim support, mediation, rehabilitation of offenders.

Cultural enrichment
Improving participation in and access to the arts and national heritage for disadvantaged and disabled people.

Education and Training
The objective is to enhance educational opportunities for disadvantaged people and those with special needs.

Projects which help socially excluded people develop their potential and secure employment. Employment Training (for disadvantaged people and those with special needs).

Promotion of life skills, independent living skills for people with special needs.

Enhancing education for disabled pre-school children and young people (where no other support is available).

Grantmaking in 2010
In 2010 the foundation held assets of £2.8 million and had an income of £1.9 million. 422 grants were made totalling £1.7 million. Most of the grants made were for social welfare purposes.

Grants were distributed across four programmes:

Standard grant programme	296	£1.1 million
Creating change programme	19	£364,000
International grant programme	15	£172,000
Special initiatives programme	1	£18,000

Grants within Northern Ireland were broken down geographically as follows:

Belfast	147
County Antrim	78
County Down	63
County Tyrone	29
County Londonderry	25
Derry	24
County Armagh	24
County Fermanagh	13
Great Britain	4

Grants approved by programme area in the Standard Grants Programme were as follows:

Community services	138
Advice services	32
Disability	25
Promotion of health	35
Civic responsibility	17
Cultural enrichment	16
Education and training	33

Beneficiaries of the standard grant programme included: Carntogher Community Association – towards the salary and travel expenses of a Volunteer Co-ordinator (£6,700); Positive Futures – towards purchasing equipment for people with learning difficulties (£6,700); CAB – Antrim District – towards the salary of an outreach information advice worker (£6,000); Chinese Welfare Association – towards the salary of the welfare rights officer (£6,000); Disability Action – towards the project co-ordinator post (£6,000); Reco (NI) Ltd – towards the salary of a workshop joiner (£5,000); Belfast Samaritans – to support the publicity campaign (£5,000); Strabane & Lifford Lesbian Gay Bisexual & Transgender Group – towards governance and strategic planning training (£3,300); Tandem Walking Group – physical activity programme for people with visual impairment (£3,000); Eskra Community Association – to purchase fitness suite equipment (£2,500); and Castlederg Childcare Services – towards security and CCTV (£1,000).

Beneficiaries of the international grant program included: Christian Aid Ireland – for farm equipment and training in Afghanistan (£20,000); Africare – towards improvements at a children's hospital in Uganda (£20,000); War on Want – irrigation projects and farmer training in Malawi (£12,500); Grooms-Shaftesbury – towards a spinal chord rehabilitation centre in Nepal (£10,000); Romanian Partnership Committee – to support young orphans in and out of orphanages in Romania (£5,000); and Camara Education UK Ltd – for computer facilities and teacher training in Zambia (£3,200).

The special initiatives programme provided one grant of £18,000 to NICVA to conduct research into the financial capabilities of small voluntary and community organisations

Exclusions
Grants are not usually given for:
- organisations that are not recognised as a charity by HM Revenue and Customs
- individuals, including students
- animal welfare
- environmental projects including those that deal with geographic and scenic issues – however, the trustees may consider projects that improve the living conditions of disadvantaged individuals and groups
- activities that are normally the responsibility of central or local government or some other responsible body
- schools, universities and colleges (except for projects specifically to benefit students with special needs)
- hospitals and medical centres
- sponsorship or marketing appeals
- fabric appeals for places of worship
- promotion of religion
- activities that collect funds for subsequent redistribution to others
- endowment funds
- fundraising events or activities
- corporate affiliation or membership of a charity
- loans or business finance
- expeditions or overseas travel
- construction of and extension to buildings
- salary or training costs for the pre-school sector.

Please note: organisations must have a total income of less than £1 million to be eligible to apply to the Standard Grant Programme.

Applications
From April 2011, in order for organisations to be eligible to apply, they must have an *income of less than £1 million* in the previous 12 months. For registered charities with a headquarters based outside Northern Ireland, the income of their Northern Ireland operation will be the figure used to assess eligibility. The trustees have taken this decision as there have been an increasing number of applications to the foundation which makes the decision process more difficult. Also the trustees are keen to ensure they stay in line with the overall aim of the foundation, 'to support *underfunded* charities that enable people, especially disadvantaged or people with special needs, to play a fuller role in the community.' There has been no change to the level of grant issued, with the average grant remaining between £3,000–£4,000. This new eligibility will stay in place for the foreseeable future.

The foundation offers the following advice on applying to the Standard Grant Programme on its website:

Who can apply?
The Standard Grant Programme is open to any organisation that is

registered as a charity with HM Revenue and Customs. Constituted groups with charitable purpose, but not registered as a charity and have an annual income of less than £2,000, may apply for a grant of up to £1,000.

How to apply?

The application pack should be downloaded from the foundation website. The downloaded application form is in Microsoft WORD format to enable it to be completed on screen before printing off a hard copy. The application form should then be signed and dated by the three required signatories, before attaching copies of the required supporting documents.

When to apply?

The closing dates for applications are normally the second Friday of January, April, July and October. Always check the website for the latest closing dates, as they may change due to statutory holidays. Applications will be accepted until 5pm on each closing date.

- Applicants are required to leave one year between applications whether they are successful or unsuccessful.
- Organisations who have received three years consecutive funding must leave two years before reapplying.
- All applicants will be informed in writing of the decision approximately ten weeks from the closing date for applications.

Unfortunately, demands made on the foundation always out-strip the funds available, and this means that many good applications, whilst meeting the criteria, will still be unsuccessful.

Please note: the application process for other programmes may differ. Organisations are advised to contact the foundation for details (as appropriate).

The foundation welcomes the opportunity to discuss projects with applicants before submission to the trustees in order to ensure that projects are within the criteria and also to afford applicants the opportunity to ask questions about the process. Applicants are invited to telephone the foundation should they wish to discuss.

Common applicant mistakes

'Failing to complete the application form and failing to enclose the required documents.'

Lloyds TSB Foundation for Scotland

Social welfare

Around £2 million

Beneficial area

Scotland.

Riverside House, 502 Gorgie Road, Edinburgh EH11 3AF
Tel: 0131 444 4020
Fax: 0131 444 4099
Email: enquiries@ ltsbfoundationforscotland.org.uk
Website: www. ltsbfoundationforscotland.org.uk
Correspondent: Karen Brown, Administrator and Secretary
Trustees: Christine Lenihan, Chair; Martin Cheyne; Prof. Sir John P Arbuthnott; Prof. Sandy Cameron; James G D Ferguson; Paul Hardie; Jane Mackie; Maria McGill; Ian Small.
SC Number: SC009481

Information available

Information was taken from the foundation's clear and helpful website.

The following information on the foundation's activities is taken from its excellent website:

Court ruling welcomed as great news – January 2012

We are delighted to start the year with the news of a court decision ordering Lloyds Banking Group to pay the foundation over £3.5 million. This is money due to the foundation for 2010, and is great news for Scotland's hard-pressed charities at a time when many are struggling.

The foundation had raised an action in the Court of Session against the Lloyds Banking Group, following a dispute over the money it was due from the group under the terms of a covenant entitling it to a share of the group's pre-tax profits. The group had claimed the foundation was due £38,920 in 2010, while the foundation maintained the correct sum was more than £3.5 million.

After the first hearing a judge – Lord Glennie – ruled against the foundation, but following an appeal hearing in November three appeal judges overturned that decision on

29 December [2011] and ordered Lloyds Banking Group to pay £3.5 million to the foundation for 2010. This clarity on the way our money is calculated also means that we are due a payment of £1.75 million for 2011.

The decision in favour of the foundation was taken by Scotland's senior judge, the Lord President, Lord Hamilton, sitting with Lord Carloway and Lord Kingarth.

The court's decision is extremely welcome and shows that the foundation's trustees were right not to accept the original finding. The money we are now due to receive will help us carry on with our work supporting charities throughout Scotland which are clearly focused on improving the quality of life for people who are disadvantaged or at risk of becoming so.

Programmes

The following programmes are available from the foundation:

Henry Duncan Awards

In 2010 our main grant programme was renamed the 'Henry Duncan Awards' in honour of The Reverend Henry Duncan who founded the first Trustee Savings Bank, which ultimately led to the establishment of the foundation, just over 200 years ago.

This programme was previously called the Standard Grants Scheme, so you will find that statistics and case studies from previous years refer to this name.

The majority of our grants are made through our Henry Duncan Awards, funding a huge variety of organisations to carry out an even wider range of work. Many of the organisations we fund are small grassroots charities working in their own local communities.

Registered charities with an annual income of less than £500,000 can apply to us for funding through this programme.

We have two application forms and accompanying guidance notes: one for amounts up to £2,500 for organisations with a turnover of up to £25,000, and one for grants over £2,500. You must choose which one of these forms you wish to submit, as we can only accept one application from you. We have designed these forms to try to make it easier for organisations to apply to us – any feedback would be gratefully received.

Partnership Drugs Initiative

The Partnership Drugs Initiative (PDI) promotes voluntary sector work with vulnerable children and young people affected by substance misuse. It has been running since 2000 and is funded by the foundation and the Scottish Government. Groups targeted are:

- children and young people in families in which parents misuse drugs or alcohol
- pre-teen children who are at higher risk of developing problems with substance misuse
- young people who are developing or who have established problems with substance misuse.

How the programme works

As we work with voluntary and statutory groups, the projects we fund gain strength from the partnership approach used.

We are also really interested in making sure the projects we fund will be accessible to the children and young people they are trying to help. So, a group of young people assess potential projects, making sure they are relevant to the children and young people who will be using them.

There are many different things to think about when we consider how effective projects will be at addressing issues around drugs and alcohol, and a steering group who have a wide range of expertise in this area gives us confidence that all aspects of projects have been looked at.

Alcohol & Drug Partnerships (ADPs) are a key group in co-ordinating work locally, and charities develop two-stage applications with them. This makes sure all the projects we fund are linked into other work going on locally.

How to apply

There is a two-stage application process for our Partnership Drugs Initiative (PDI) awards. You will need to work with your local Alcohol & Drug Partnership (ADP) to complete an initial outline application. Your ADP will send us the completed form, which needs to reach us by our deadline date [check the foundation's website for upcoming deadlines]. It will also be useful to read our 'Using the Learning to Develop a Proposal' document before you fill out your application form. If you would like to discuss your outline application before you submit it, call us on 0131 444 4020 and ask to speak to one of our PDI team.

You can also apply for funding for up to three years.

Once we have received your application form, it will be considered by an expert steering group and a panel of young people. If the proposal is successful at this stage you will be invited to develop a full application. Feedback from both groups is available to successful and unsuccessful projects.

You can find out more about what happens next or request us to send you one. If you would like to have a chat with someone about this award programme please call us on 0131 444 4020.

Capacity Building grants

At their recent board meeting, trustees agreed to review the Capacity Building Programme to identify the best way to deliver capacity building from 2012. [Potential applicants should check the foundation's website for current information on this programme.]

Recent financial information was not available at the time of writing, although it is expected that previous levels of grantmaking will be maintained, totalling around £2 million each year.

Exclusions

The foundation will not support:

- charities with an income of more than £500,000 per annum
- organisations which are not formally recognised as charities in Scotland
- charities which pay their board members or have paid employees who also hold a position as Director on the Board. This principle also applies to charities operating as collectives
- individuals – including students
- animal welfare
- initiatives that are focused on sport, the arts or the environment, except where the subject is being used as a vehicle to engage with at risk or disadvantaged groups to increase life skills
- conservation and protection of flora and fauna
- mainstream activities and statutory requirements of hospitals and medical centres, schools, universities and colleges
- sponsorship or marketing appeals
- establishment/preservation of endowment funds
- activities that collect funds for subsequent grant making to other organisations and/or individuals
- expeditions or overseas travel
- major building projects/capital appeals
- historic restoration/historic publications
- retrospective funding
- promotion of religion/church fabric appeals
- hobby groups
- one-off events such as gala days.

Applications

Application forms for all programmes, complete with comprehensive guidance notes, are available from the foundation. These can be requested by telephone, by email, or through its website. Foundation staff are always willing to provide additional help. Check the foundation's website for details of upcoming application deadlines.

Lloyds TSB Foundation for the Channel Islands

General

£977,500 (2010)

Beneficial area

The Channel Islands.

PO Box 160, 25 New Street, St Helier, Jersey JE4 8RG
Tel: 01534 845889
Email: john.hutchins@ lloydstsbfoundations.org.uk
Website: www.ltsbfoundationci.org
Correspondent: John Hutchins, Executive Director
Trustees: Sir Rocky Goodall; Advocate Susan Pearmain; Pauline Torode; John Boothman; Stephen Jones; Dr John Furguson; Patricia Tumelty; Martin Fricker.
CC Number: 327113

Information available

Accounts were available at the Charity Commission.

The foundation's mission is to 'support charitable organisations which help people, especially those who are disadvantaged or disabled, to play a fuller role in communities throughout the Channel Islands'.

The overall policy of the trustees is to support underfunded charities which enable people, especially disadvantaged or disabled people, to play a fuller role in the community. The trustees are keen to support organisations which contribute to local community life at the grass-roots level. The trustees are also keen to encourage the infrastructure of the voluntary sector and encourage applications for operational costs. This includes salary costs, which may be funded over two or three years, and training and education for managers and staff.

Donations for one-off projects are generally in the region of £2,500 to £25,000, but there is no minimum amount set by the trustees. Applications for larger amounts will be considered where there is a wider benefit. The trustees generally make donations towards specific items rather than making contributions to large appeals, for example, building costs. The majority of donations are made on a one off basis. Successful applicants are advised to leave at least one year before reapplying.

The foundation provides the following information on its website:

Social Partnership Initiative

In 2001 we launched the Social Partnership Initiative, designed to encourage real working partnerships to be set up between the voluntary sector and the relevant States departments' in the Islands, to stimulate the voluntary sector into seeking out opportunities to develop new services, increase knowledge and key skills.

Our funding goes mainly to charities working in Social and Community Needs and Education and Training. The trustees regularly review changing social needs and identify specific areas they wish to focus on within their overall objectives. Current priorities are:

- Creating Positive Opportunities for Disabled People – enabling people with either learning or physical disabilities to live independently
- Family Support – including the development of relationship skills for young people, and encouraging good relationships between generations
- Homelessness – in particular helping homeless people back into mainstream society, including support after temporary or permanent accommodation has been secured
- Promoting Effectiveness in the Voluntary Sector – Supporting the training of trustees, managers, staff and volunteers and encouraging the sector to communicate and work together
- Prevention of Substance Misuse – including both education and rehabilitation
- The Needs of Carers – for example, information and support services, and the provision of respite care
- Challenging Disadvantage and Discrimination – Promoting understanding and encouraging solutions which address disadvantage, discrimination or stigma.

In 2010 it had assets of £1.2 million and an income of £1.1 million, most of which was in the form of a covenant from Lloyds Banking Group. Grants were made totalling £977,500, broken down as follows:

Jersey	£520,000
Guernsey	£433,000
Matched giving	£24,000
Channel Islands-wide and UK	£1,000

Beneficiaries included: Action for Children Guernsey Youth Housing (£111,000); Autism Jersey (£105,000); Drug Concern (£98,000); Guernsey Women's Refuge (£60,000); Weston Health Care Foundation (£50,000); St Mark's Church (£30,000); Headway Jersey (£25,000); St Stephen's Community Centre Millennium Trust (£15,000); Jersey Army Cadet Force League (£10,000); Communicate Guernsey (£5,000); and Sailaway (£1,000).

Exclusions

No grants for:

- organisations which are not recognised charities
- activities which are primarily the responsibility of the Insular authorities in the Islands or some other responsible body
- activities which collect funds to give to other charities, individuals or other organisations
- animal welfare
- corporate subscription or membership of a charity
- endowment funds
- environment – conserving and protecting plants and animals, geography and scenery
- expeditions or overseas travel
- fabric appeals for places of worship
- fundraising events or activities
- hospitals and medical centres (except for projects which are clearly additional to statutory responsibilities)
- individuals, including students
- loans or business finance
- promotion of religion
- schools and colleges (except for projects that will benefit disabled students and are clearly additional to statutory responsibilities)
- sponsorship or marketing appeals
- international appeals – trustees may from time to time consider a limited number of applications from UK registered charities working abroad.

Applications

Applications are only accepted on the foundation's own form. These, along with guidelines, are available from its website or from the foundation's office in Jersey and can be returned at any time. They must be returned by post as the foundation does not accept forms that have been emailed or faxed.

All applications are reviewed on a continual basis. The trustees meet three times a year to approve donations. Decision-making processes can therefore take up to four months. Applications up to £5,000 are normally assessed within one month and all applicants are informed of the outcome of their application.

Applicants are encouraged to discuss their project with one of the foundation's staff before completing an application form. This will help ensure that your project is within its criteria and that you are applying for an appropriate amount. You will also be informed of when you should hear a decision.

The Trust for London (formerly the City Parochial Foundation)

Social welfare

£10.4 million (2010)

Beneficial area

Greater London.

6–9 Middle Street, London EC1A 7PH
Tel: 020 7606 6145
Fax: 020 7600 1866
Email: info@trustforlondon.org.uk
Website: www.trustforlondon.org.uk
Correspondent: Bharat Mehta, Chief Executive and Clerk to the Trustees
Trustee: Trust for London trustee.
CC Number: 205629

Information available

Accounts were available from the Charity Commission. Full information is also available on the trust's excellent website.

Summary

Trust for London is the new name for the City Parochial Foundation following the amalgamation of the foundation and its sister charity the Trust for London. The trust manages two funds – The Central Fund and The City Church Fund – and its assets are split between these two on a 60:40 basis. The central fund is used to tackle poverty in London by making grants to the voluntary and community sector. The money from the City Church Fund offers support to the Church of England in a defined area of benefit in London. There are six dioceses within the area of benefit: London, Southwark, Chelmsford, Rochester, St Albans and Guildford.

The trust's 2010 annual return describes its work as follows:

> We are one of the largest independent charitable foundations in London and we exist to reduce poverty and inequality in the capital. We do this by funding the voluntary and community sector and others, as well as by using our own expertise and knowledge to support work that tackles poverty and its root causes.
>
> Established in 1891, Trust for London is our new name following the amalgamation of City Parochial Foundation and the Trust for London in July 2010. We brought the two organisations together to make us more efficient, allow us to use our capital more flexibly, and to avoid any confusion to groups seeking funding from us.
>
> The Trust is independent of Government and special interest groups and we use this freedom to take risks. In 2010 we provided nearly £7 million helping Londoners tackle poverty and inequality. The funding programmes were designed to achieve social justice for people who need it most, tackling those important but unpopular causes such as human trafficking, domestic violence and the destitution of asylum seekers. This style of funding led us to invest in work addressing the problem of faith based abuse amongst London's African communities and an independent evaluation of this initiative was completed in 2010.
>
> Our aim is to enable and empower Londoners to tackle poverty and inequality, and their root causes; and to ensure that our funds reach those most in need. We achieve this by funding charitable work: making grants through our open programme; and funding special initiatives where we want to make a greater strategic impact on a specific issue.

A brochure provided by the trust describes their values:

> We are committed to working in an approachable and accessible way, listening to and learning from those that we fund. We believe that commissioning research can improve understanding of the causes and effects of poverty and inequality in London. We look to partnerships, particularly with other funders, to help us to increase the impact of our work.

Funding available

> We are one of the largest independent charitable trusts in London. Each year we expect to make available funds of approximately £6 million and award around 150 grants. There is no minimum or maximum size of grant and the amount you request should be the amount you need. However, the average grant under aims 1 – 4 is likely to be about £54,000 in total, although a number of grants will be for a lesser amount, while a few will be for more.
>
> Grants made to small community groups under Aim 5 will not normally exceed £30,000 with an average grant being £16,000 in total, although many grants will be less than this. You may apply over one, two or three years.
>
> We will not normally make grants that exceed £100,000. You may therefore need to apply to other funders to fund your proposal jointly with us and we encourage you to do this.

Funds are also distributed from the City Church Fund for the advancement of religion for the benefit of the public in accordance with the doctrines of the Church of England. Payments can be made within these aims for the repair, restoration and preservation of churches, the provision of church services, pastoral support and mission. The income from this fund is divided between the church commissioners, the six metropolitan dioceses and the city churches grants in accordance with the objects of the trust. Note that the applications procedure detailed here applies to the central fund *only*.

Who and what we will fund

> We fund voluntary and community organisations undertaking charitable activities. You do not need to be a registered charity. We will support work which meets our areas of work [...] This may be for a specific project or ongoing costs. This includes staff salaries and overheads. We encourage organisations to include a reasonable amount of core costs to cover their overheads when they apply for funding. The majority of our funding is for revenue costs, though we can also fund small capital items.
>
> We want to make sure that our funds reach the people who need them most, especially those who are excluded and are particularly disadvantaged and discriminated against. Some of our work benefits all those living in poverty, while other work targets particular groups. These may include women, black and minority ethnic communities, asylum seekers and refugees, lesbians and gay men, disabled people (including those with mental health issues), young men and white working class communities. We therefore welcome applications from these groups and others who can demonstrate that they are particularly affected by poverty.

Guidelines 2010–12

The trust's guidelines are summarised below. The full document is available from the trust's website.

> These funding guidelines provide information about us, what we will and will not fund, and how you can apply to us.

Open programme

> Our open programme has five priority areas. We aim to:
> - improve employment opportunities for disadvantaged people
> - to promote the inclusion of recent arrivals to the UK
> - to promote social justice
> - to strengthen the skills of the voluntary and community sector
> - support small community groups.
>
> We will also fund exceptional work to tackle poverty which falls outside our open programme. Organisations will need to demonstrate clearly how the work is genuinely exceptional or how you are addressing new and emerging needs. You will need to speak to us if you wish to apply under this heading. Generally we will only make a few grants under this category each year.
>
> Please read our funding guidelines to gain a better understanding of our priorities before making an application to us.

Special Initiatives

> In addition to the open programme, we also undertake proactive work by developing special initiatives where we want to make a more strategic impact and, where appropriate, influence the work of others. Details of our current special initiatives are available on our website. In some instances, we will commission an organisation to deliver a piece of work and in others we will invite applications from agencies working in the field we have decided to focus on.

Recent special initiative programmes have included: Fear and Fashion – a joint initiative of five funders, led by City Bridge Trust, to tackle young people carrying and using knives; Latin American Community in London – research into the size, profile and needs of this relatively new community in the capital; a partnership with Latin American Women's Rights Service; and Safeguarding Children's Rights – Community-based activity challenging child abuse linked to beliefs in spirit possession and witchcraft.

Further details of these and the other special initiatives and research commissioned by the trust is available on the trust's very comprehensive website.

Grantmaking in 2010

In 2010 the trust had assets of £226.9 million and an income of £8.3 million. Grants were made totalling £10.4 million.

Central fund

£5.7 million of total grants was made from the central fund. The following summarisation of grantmaking within the Open Programme is taken from the foundation's excellent annual report [including grants awarded]. The trust is ambitious about the priorities which it is pursuing and offers great detail on the projects and programmes funded during the year on its website. For a fuller insight into the work of the trust it is recommended that applicants consult the trust website; in particular the publications section which contains a lot of detail on previous grant programmes.

Promoting social justice	£1.7 million
Improving employment opportunities	£1.7 million
Promoting the inclusion of recent arrivals to the UK	£1.5 million
Supporting small community groups	£707,000
Strengthening the skills of the voluntary and community sector	£273,500

Beneficiaries within each category included:

Promoting social justice: London

Voluntary Service Council – towards policy work examining the impact of spending cuts on Londoners (£139,000); Disability Alliance – towards a tribunal support unit (£90,000); Eaves Housing for Women – to fund an Exiting Prostitution Development Officer to promote support for women who leave prostitution (£75,000); Anti-Slavery International – to fund campaigning work in relation to human trafficking to the UK, with a special focus on the risks association with the 2012 Olympics (£75,000); and Zacchaeus 2000 Trust – to fund a Parliamentary Researcher post to collect evidence relating to policy proposals on welfare reform (£64,000).

Improving employment opportunities: Hammersmith and

Fulham Law Centre – towards the salary of an employment lawyer (£116,000); Disability Times Trust – towards the salary of a job broker and a contribution to the costs of employers' engagement events (£60,000); Mind (The National Association for Mental Health) – for the Mind Workplace project, which helps employers to manage and support mental health in the workplace (£50,000); and Trees for Cities – towards funding for an accreditation in horticulture for black and minority ethnic groups with mental health issues in Tower Hamlets (£34,000).

Promoting the inclusion of recent arrivals to the UK: Bail for

Immigration Detainees – core costs for this campaigning group which operates to support immigration detainees in the UK (£140,000); Asylum Aid – towards salary and running costs for the Head of Law post (£100,000); Farsophone Association – towards a counselling and psychotherapy service for the Farsi speaking community in Barnet (£80,000); and Baobab Centre for Young Survivors in Exile – towards salary and project costs of this charity which offers a counselling and therapy service for young, unaccompanied migrants (£56,500).

Supporting small community groups: Kanlungan Filipino

Consortium – salary costs for this body which represents and campaigns for the Filipino community in the UK (£36,000); Waltham Forest Somali Women's Association – funding towards the salary costs of a part-time co-ordinator to manage activities aimed at improving the lives of Somali refugees (£21,000); Downright Excellent – towards salary costs of a sessional speech and language teacher for children with Down's syndrome (£18,000); and Barking and Dagenham Yu Hua Chinese Association – towards costs of a mother-tongue classes (£10,000).

Strengthening the skills of the voluntary sector: Evelyn Oldfield Unit – to fund the Unit's evaluation and learning capacity; and policy and research activities (£100,000); Sheila McKechnie Foundation – towards its annual award for campaigners working on social justice issues in London and towards training facilities (£70,000); and Co-ordinated Action Against Domestic Abuse (CAADA) – towards salary and costs of the London development manager's post (£48,500).

The trust continued to make payments to bodies connected to the trust's Special Initiatives programme. These are areas in which the trust wishes 'to make a greater strategic impact [...] and to which we commit additional resources, including significant staff time.'

£632,000 was awarded under the special initiatives programme in 2010. Some of the beneficiaries included: Changing Minds – towards the creation of a new social justice communications agency, which will work on changing public attitudes towards migrants and migration (£300,000); Africans Unite Against Child Abuse – towards funding for the Policy Officer, with a particular focus on abuse linked to spirit possession and witchcraft (£60,000); Africa Policy Research Network – towards the co-ordinator's post and new work to support 'agents of change' (£47,000); and Churches' Child Protection Advisory Service – towards child protection training and services with African churches in London (£40,000).

One grant of £10,000 was awarded under the 'exceptional cases/new and emerging needs' category to Naz Project London in response to a funding crisis which threatened the continuation of this project which addresses the sexual health and HIV/AIDS needs of Black and Minority Ethnic communities in London.

City Church Fund: £4.2 million of total grants was made from the City Church Fund. A City Church Fund report on the use of funding in the period 2008–10 shows that:

At the Church Commissioners' direction, a small portion of the monies available from the City Church Fund is paid to the Commissioners for direct use. In 2008–10 these payments totalled £296,400. From them, the Commissioners:

   ▶ made fixed grants totalling £2,179 in 2008–10 to a small number of City benefices. These grants date back to the terms of the City of London Parochial Charities Act, 1883; and

   ▶ met the cost of supporting the Office of the Dean at King's College London. In 2008–10, these payments totalled £294,585.

The remainder of the City Church Fund monies available in 2008–10 was allocated to the six dioceses, on the Commissioners' direction, on the basis of the size of their population within the area of benefit.

Three of these dioceses give out grant funding, they are: Chelmsford, Rochester and St Albans. Applicants should contact the relevant diocesan secretary directly for information on applying.

The Church of England, who are largely responsible for the fund, have produced a guide detailing the projects which benefitted from grants from the fund. It is available on the Church of England website. No further information was available on the church fund.

Aside from the central fund and city church fund the trust manages a number of smaller, historical subsidiary funds which make up the difference of around £0.5 million.

Exclusions

The foundation will not support proposals:

▶ which do not benefit Londoners
▶ that directly replace or subsidise statutory funding (including contracts)
▶ that are the primary responsibility of statutory funders such as local and central government and health authorities
▶ from individuals, or which are for the benefit of one individual
▶ for mainstream educational activity including schools
▶ for medical purposes including hospitals and hospices

▶ for the promotion of religion
▶ for umbrella bodies seeking to distribute grants on our behalf
▶ for work that has already taken place
▶ for general appeals
▶ for large capital appeals (including buildings and minibuses)
▶ from applicants who have been rejected by us in the last six months

The foundation is unlikely to support proposals:

▶ from large national charities which enjoy widespread support
▶ for work that takes place in schools during school hours
▶ where organisations have significant unrestricted reserves (including those that are designated). Generally up to six months expenditure is normally acceptable
▶ where organisations are in serious financial deficit.

Applications

The foundation's funding guidelines for 2010–12 are available to download from its website. Alternatively contact the foundation's office for hard copies. It is strongly recommended that potential applicants read the guidelines before making an application.

There is a three-stage application process:

Stage one

An initial proposal to be submitted by post. There are three closing dates for proposals to be submitted by – you may submit your proposal at any time but it will only be assessed once the next closing date has passed. Closing dates are:

▶ 7 February for the June Grants Committee
▶ 30 May for the October Grants Committee
▶ 5 October for the February Grants Committee.

Stage two

All organisations whose initial proposals are shortlisted will be visited by the foundation to assess their suitability for funding.

Stage three

The grants committee will make the final decision on all funding requests.

Applicants will be contacted within 10 days of the committee meeting.

The whole process can take approximately four and a half months from the closing date for successful applicants.

The London Community Foundation (formerly Capital Community Foundation)

Community activities

£2.6 million (2009/10)

Beneficial area

The London boroughs including the City of London.

357 Kennington Lane, London SE11 5QY
Tel: 020 7582 5117
Fax: 020 7582 4020
Email: enquiries@londoncf.org.uk
Website: www.londoncf.org.uk/
Correspondent: Gordon Williamson, Trustee
Trustees: Carole Souter, Chair; Gordon Williamson; Ade Sawyerr; Clive Cutbill; Michael Brophy; Nicholas Hammond; William Moore; Toni Cupal; Juliet Wedderburn; Stephen Jordan; Donovan Norris; Martin Richards; Grant Gordon; Davina Judelson.
CC Number: 1091263

Information available

Accounts were available from the Charity Commission. Full details of the foundation's current programmes are available from its website.

The London Community Foundation (formerly Capital Community Foundation) provides grants to non-profit groups (you do not need to be a registered charity) that are for community benefit. The foundation manages and distributes funds on behalf of several donors, including companies, individuals and government programmes and is able to offer a number of grant programmes which cover different areas and type of activity. Contact the foundation directly or visit its website for up-to-date information on current programmes.

During 2009/10 the foundation had assets of just under £5.4 million and an income of over £4.1 million. There were 459 grants made totalling nearly £2.6 million, broken down by programme as follows:

New Deal Communities:		
New Cross Gate	18	£258,000
Targeted Support Fund	8	£188,000
Lambeth First: Working		
Neighbourhoods Fund	24	£175,000
Grassroots Grants Lambeth	45	£165,000
Grassroots Grants Southwark	41	£148,000
Columbia Foundation Fund	13	£132,000
Grassroots Grants Lewisham	41	£128,000
Grassroots Grants Greenwich	43	£119,000
Grassroots Bromley	33	£119,000
Grassroots Grants Camden	30	£116,000
Grassroots Grants		
Westminster	26	£108,000
Comic Relief	12	£102,000
Grassroots Grants		
Kensington and Chelsea	24	£85,000
Grassroots Grants Bexley	29	£85,000
Land Securities Capital		
Commitment Fund	12	£75,000
Deutsche Bank Small Grants		
Fund	19	£61,000
Other Corporate Fund	6	£60,000
Other grants awarded	9	£49,000
Deptford Challenge Trust	10	£49,000
Pedlar's Acre Trust	10	£49,000
Russell Investment Fund	6	£20,000

Beneficiaries across all programmes included: Food Skills Ltd., (£50,000); Bench Outreach (£48,000 in total); Cystic Fibrosis (£33,000); Ilderton Foundation, Fresh Visions People Ltd., Mosaic Clubhouse and Springfield Community Flat After School Club (£25,000 each); Cricket for Change, Snow-Camp, Southwark Tigers Rugby Club and Tideway Sailability (£10,000 each); The Dodds Fund (£8,000); Latin American House and Highbury Roundhouse Youth & Community Centre (£7,000 each); Emmaus South Lambeth Community and Indoamerican Refugee and Migrant Organisation (£5,000 each); Centre Point Corporation CIC and Foundations UK (£4,000 each); Bounce Theatre Company (£2,000); Allianz Community Fund (£1,000); and The Capital Community Foundation Fund (£500).

Exclusions

Generally, no grants for individuals, political groups or activities which promote religion.

Applications

In order to qualify for a grant from the foundation your organisation must have:

- a management committee of at least three people who are not related and are not paid wages by your group
- a governing document (e.g. constitution or Memorandum and Articles of Association)
- a bank account with at least two unrelated signatories for transactions (Pass Book accounts or those which permit only cash withdrawals are not accepted)
- a child protection policy and procedures if the project will be working with children.

As the foundation offers funds on behalf of different donors, you may apply to each and every programme for which your group is eligible. However, the criteria do vary for each grant programme, so be sure to read the guidance carefully. If you are unsure about your eligibility, please call the grants team on Tel: 020 7582 5117 before making an application.

Application forms and guidance notes specific to each programme are available from the foundation and/or its website.

Each programme has its own set of closing dates. All applications must reach Capital Community Foundation by 5pm on that date.

The London Marathon Charitable Trust

Sport, recreation and leisure

£3.8 million (2009/10)

Beneficial area

London and any area where London Marathon stages an event (South Northamptonshire).

Kestrel House, 111 Heath Road, Twickenham TW1 4AH

Tel: 020 8892 6646
Fax: 020 8892 6478
Email: lmct@ffleach.co.uk

Correspondent: David Golton, Secretary

Trustees: Bernard Atha; Simon Cooper; Dame Mary Peters; Joyce Smith; John Graves; James Dudley Henderson Clarke; John Austin; John Disley; Sir Rodney Walker; John Bryant; Richard Lewis; John Spurling.
CC Number: 283813

Information available

Accounts were available at the Charity Commission.

The trust was formed to distribute the surplus income donated to the charity by its subsidiary, the London Marathon Limited, which organises the annual London Marathon and other such events each year. Funds are given for much-needed recreational facilities across the city, as well as in areas where London Marathon Limited stages an event. This currently includes South Northamptonshire – Silverstone. Recent achievements of the trust are noted in the 2009/10 accounts:

Projects once again include the provision of MUGAs (Multi Use Games Areas); improvements to existing children's play areas and the development of new ones; the refurbishment, upgrading and expansion of existing sports and community facilities both indoor and outdoor; contributions towards brand new sporting facilities; assistance to water activities by contributions to various organisations to provide new boats. The Trustees have also set aside a further sum towards their commitment to the maintenance of the legacy remaining after the London 2012 Olympics. As in previous years, the grants they have made will benefit both the able bodied and the disabled and include the sports of athletics, cricket, tennis, gymnastics and dance, sailing, football, boxing, climbing, BMX and skateboarding.

Note: the trust has no connection to the fundraising efforts of the individuals involved in the race, who raise over £40 million each year for their chosen good causes.

In 2009/10 the trust had assets of £15.4 million and an income of £4.8 million. Grants were made to 59 organisations totalling just under £3.8 million.

Most of the grants made during the year were in Greater London, with around half being made through borough councils. The largest beneficiary was Camden Community Football and Sports Association, whom the trust granted £732,000 for the purchase of Chase Lodge playing fields. This grant is in line with the trustees' principal objective: 'to provide facilities for recreation and leisure activities which will bring a lasting benefit to the communities in which they are established.'

Other grants included those to: LM Playing Field Mottingham – all-weather court (£256,000); Lee Valley Regional Park – indoor track upgrade at Lee Valley Stadium (£174,000); Jo Richardson Community School, Barking & Dagenham – dual use fitness suite (£150,000); London 2012 Legacy Stadia – development of pool lift for disabled (£90.000); and Liverpool Sailing Club – rebuild slipway (£25,000).

Exclusions

Grants cannot be made to 'closed' clubs or schools, unless the facility is available for regular public use. No grants are made for recurring or revenue costs. Individuals are not supported.

Applications

On a form available from the correspondent. Applications are welcomed from London Boroughs and independent organisations, clubs and charities. The trustees meet once a year; the closing date is usually the end of August.

Common applicant mistakes

'Applicant not reading our grant criteria.'

The Lord's Taverners

Youth cricket, minibuses for organisations supporting young people with disabilities and sports and recreational equipment for young people with special needs

£2.8 million (2009/10)

Beneficial area

Unrestricted, in practice, UK.

10 Buckingham Place, London SW1E 6HX
Tel: 020 7821 2828
Fax: 020 7821 2829
Email: foundation@lordstaverners.org
Website: www.lordstaverners.org
Correspondent: Nicky Pemberton, Head of Foundation
Trustees: John Ayling; John Barnes; Leo Callow; Mike Gatting; Robert Powell; Sally Surridge; Tom Rodwell; Robert Griffiths; David East; Christine Colbeck; Martin Smith.
CC Number: 306054

Information available

Accounts were available at the Charity Commission. The foundation has a helpful and informative website.

The Lord's Taverners started life as a club founded in 1950 by a group of actors who used to enjoy a pint watching the cricket from the old Tavern pub at Lord's. In the early days, the money raised each year was given to the National Playing Fields Association (now the Fields in Trust), whom the Taverners still support, to fund artificial cricket pitches. Since then the Taverners has developed into both a club and a charity. There are now three fundraising groups – Lord's Taverners, Lady Taverners and Young Lord's Taverners. The trust has 28 regional groupings (all volunteer) throughout the UK and Northern Ireland. The Lady Taverners has 24 Regions.

The principal activities and charitable mission continue to be 'to give young people, particularly those with special needs, a sporting chance'.

The trust has decided to distribute funding on the following basis: around 50% of the funds awarded by the trust are given to cricket projects for equipment and competitions for those young people playing the game at grass roots level in schools and clubs. £30,000 is to be granted to Fields in Trust, whose mission is to ensure that everyone across the country has access to outdoor space for sport, play and recreation. The balance of funds is then to be distributed as follows: 70% to supplying minibuses to special needs organisations; and 30% to provide sports and play equipment to organisations looking after young people with special needs.

The trust's mission is carried out by:
- encouraging participation in youth cricket, particularly in disadvantaged areas
- supporting recreational and sporting activities for youngsters with special needs.

The Lord's Taverners is recognised by the England and Wales Cricket Board (ECB) as the official national charity for recreational cricket. Most cricket grants are distributed in association with the ECB. An annual grant is also made to the English Schools Cricket Association.

Grantmaking

In 2010 the trust had assets of £3.4 million and an income of just under £6.8 million, including £4.5 million generated through fundraising activities. Grants totalled around £2.8 million from restricted and unrestricted funds.

The trust's charitable giving is channelled through five key funds:
- youth cricket at grass roots level
- the supply of specially adapted minibuses
- sports wheelchair sponsorship scheme
- sports and recreation facilities for young people with special needs (SRSN)
- the Brian Johnston Memorial Trust.

Youth cricket – grants totalling £1 million.

Each year the trust provides grants of more than £750,000 to encourage participation in cricket by young people.

Cricket equipment bags – the trust provides hard ball equipment bags with enough items to equip a full team (at u16, u13 and u11 levels and girls 15–18) at a cost of £25. Soft ball kit bags are provided free. 1,086 cricket bags were distributed in the period under review.

Applications are considered from cricket clubs affiliated to a National Governing Body, individual schools or other organisations directly involved in the organisation of youth cricket and which have a genuine need for assistance. Application forms are available on the trust's website and should be submitted to your local ECB Development Manager to be countersigned; a list of local boards is available on the trust's website. Completed applications are processed in batches approximately every 4–6 weeks, although the whole process may take around three to four months.

Chance to shine – the trust's aim is to give as many young people as possible a sporting chance and, therefore, it tries to distribute its limited resources as widely and as fairly as possible. In 2005, the trust pledged £1 million for the programme and as of 30 September 2010, £950,000 had been donated. To date, the programme is the single biggest sport for development programme in the UK, with one million children across 3,700 state schools involved, of whom 45% are girls.

Note: after lengthy discussions between the trust and Chance to shine, it has been agreed that any clubs and schools taking part in the Chance to shine programme will not be eligible to apply to either the Lord's Taverners Cricket Equipment Scheme or the Grant Aid Scheme for non-turf pitches/batting ends/nets.

Non-turf pitch grants – grants are made towards the installation of non-turf pitches, practice ends and nets. 118 schools and clubs benefited in the 2009–10 period. Applications will be considered from cricket clubs affiliated to a National Governing Body, individual schools or other organisations directly involved in the organisation of youth cricket and which have a genuine need for assistance. Applications will not be accepted from clubs or schools involved in the Chance to shine programme.

Awards do not normally exceed the following levels:
- non-turf match pitch – £3,000
- non-turf practice – £2,000
- outdoor nets – £1,000.

Application forms are available on the trust's website. Please note: all applications must be countersigned by the appropriate County Cricket Board (CCB) or Lord's Taverners Regional Chairman prior to submission. Contact details can be found on the website.

Citicricket – this was initially set up by Channel 4 in 2000 under the name of Street Cricket with the objective of giving children in deprived city areas the opportunity to experience the benefits of playing cricket. The Lord's Taverners has invested over £250,000 since it became involved in the project in 2002. In 2003 the trust took over the funding of the programme. In the summer of 2008 the project was re-launched under the name of CitiCricket to reflect the initiatives' core objectives.

The programme is now present in eight counties including Berkshire, Gloucestershire, Nottinghamshire, Warwickshire, Yorkshire, Lancashire, Leicestershire & Rutland and Oxfordshire.

Funding for other cricket projects – exceptionally, one-off grants are steered towards major projects designed primarily to assist in the furtherance of youth cricket. For further details please contact the trust on 020 7821 2828 or email them.

Applications will be considered for grants toward the cost of youth cricket festivals, tournaments, regional competitions and for youth special coaching schemes. Grants towards refreshments, trophies, overseas tours, clothing or individual/team sponsorship are not available. Application forms are available on the trust's website.

The trust also funds the National Table Cricket Competition; a game which provides young people who have severe physical disabilities with an opportunity to compete in a competitive game of cricket. In 2010, in partnership with Cerebral Palsy Sport, the trust appointed a national development officer, responsible for growing grass-roots participation. Further information about Table Cricket and how your school can get involved is available on the website.

Minibuses – 34 minibuses awarded totalling £1.2 million

The minibus scheme provides vital transport and mobility for youngsters with special needs, that is to say, those with physical, sensory or learning disabilities. Since 1975 the trust has provided over 950 minibuses.

Each minibus costs around £48,500 (depending on specifications). The trust asks that organisations make a minimum contribution of £10,000 for a standard minibus or £12,500 for a wheelchair accessible minibus. This is done for the following reasons:
- it demonstrates that the organisation is able to raise funds to maintain the vehicle once it has been received it (each minibus costs about £4,500 a year in running costs)
- it is hoped that if the organisation has invested in the vehicle, it will be treated with respect
- once the minibus has been received it belongs to the organisation, provided the vehicle's use falls within the trust's guidelines.

The trust states that there is currently a waiting list of two years for all applications on new minibuses. However, there is a FAST TRACK (6-month waiting list) option for organisations able to make a contribution of £20,000 for a standard minibus or £25,000 for a wheelchair accessible minibus.

The trust provides very detailed information regarding applications for minibuses including waiting lists, self help contributions, eligibility and terms and conditions. Application forms and guidelines are available to download from the trust's website.

Sport and recreation for young people with special needs – grants totalling £333,000

Since 1988 the trust has given grants towards sports & recreational equipment under a programme known as SRSN (Sport & Recreation for young people with Special Needs). Over 2,000 organisations have received help with many types of equipment from sports wheelchairs to special pool hoists, multi-sensory equipment to play ground equipment. The trust looks to encourage those youngsters with special needs, particularly those with mobility, sensory and mental disabilities, to participate in sporting and recreational activities within a group environment. In 2008, 33 grants were made under this programme.

Grants do not normally exceed £5,000. Examples of equipment which has been funded are specially adapted sports equipment, outdoor play equipment, soft play and multi-sensory equipment, riding equipment, pool hoists, water ski equipment and sports wheelchairs.

Application forms are available to download from the trust's website.

Disability Sports Appeal Grants – grants totalling £201,000

The Appeal Grants scheme aims to raise £1 million for disability sports by 2012, the year of the London Paralympic Games. The appeal aims to introduce young wheelchair users to sport and sustain their involvement through regular training, coaching and club development. The Lord's Taverners have employed a junior development officer for each of the sports adopted and in 2010 contributed £201,000 in grant funding.

Brian Johnston Memorial Trust – grants totalling £37,000

The Lord's Taverners is the sole corporate trustee of the Brian Johnston Memorial Trust, which raises funds to enable financial support to be given to young cricketers with potential to succeed in the game, as well as to cricket for blind people. More information is available on the trust's website.

Sport wheelchair sponsorship scheme – 60 grants

The trust assists with the purchase of manual chairs for those between 8 and 25 years of age. It will generally award funds of up to 50% of the cost of the wheelchair to those who apply through their sports club, association or school and whose application complies with the scheme guidelines. The grant will be paid directly to the wheelchair supplier. There is also a multi-sports wheelchair scheme which enables applicants to obtain a chair at a subsidised cost of £350.

Application forms are available on the trust's website.

Plans for the future

Through the trust's strategic review it is expected that the trust will continue to forge 'closer partnerships with complementary charitable organisations to increase [...] charitable impact and reach.' The trust continues to widen revenue streams in order to achieve a broader balance of income.

Exclusions

Youth cricket

Only one application in any 12 month period. The following is not normally grant aided:

- building or renovation of pavilions
- sight screens
- bowling machines
- mowers/rollers
- overseas tours
- clothing
- refreshments
- trophies.

Sport for young people with special needs

The following will not normally be considered for a grant:

- capital costs
- general grants
- running costs including salaries
- individuals (although applications will be considered for equipment to enable an individual to participate in a team/group recreational activity)
- holidays/overseas tours.

Minibuses

Homes, schools and organisations catering for young people with special needs under the age of 25 years, are entitled to only one minibus per location, although applications are accepted for a replacement.

Applications

The trust committee meets regularly to review applications for grant aid. All applications must be presented on the appropriate application forms and should be submitted to the secretary. Please see the grantmaking section for further information on individual programmes.

Application forms with detailed application instructions are available from the secretary or on the trust's website.

John Lyon's Charity

Children and young people in north and west London

£4.5 million (2010/11)

Beneficial area

The London boroughs of Barnet, Brent, Camden, Ealing, Kensington and Chelsea, Hammersmith and Fulham, Harrow and the Cities of London and Westminster.

45 Cadogan Gardens, London SW3 2TB
Tel: 020 7591 3330
Fax: 020 7591 3412
Email: info@johnlyonscharity.org.uk
Website: www.johnlyonscharity.org.uk
Correspondent: The Grants Office
Trustee: The Governors of Harrow School.
CC Number: 237725

Information available

Accounts were available from the Charity Commission. The charity also has a clear and helpful website.

This is one of the largest local educational charities in the country, supporting both formal and informal educational activities of every sort. Its budgets vary greatly from year to year for historical reasons, and from one part of its beneficial area to another. There are, however, significant cross-borough grants.

The charity began in the late 16th century when John Lyon donated his 48 acre Maida Vale farm as an endowment for the upkeep of two roads from London to Harrow and Kenton. In 1991, the charity was given discretion to use the revenue from the endowment to benefit the inhabitants of the London boroughs through which these roads passed.

The charity is an independent branch of the larger Harrow Foundation which also governs Harrow and the John Lyon schools. The charity makes over 60 substantial new grants a year, for amounts normally between £2,000 and £50,000 and there are a further 50 or so for amounts of £2,000 or less under its small grants programme. Larger awards may be for periods of up to three years.

Guidelines

The following guidelines are offered by the charity:

John Lyon's Charity gives grants to groups and organisations for the benefit of children and young people up to the age of 25 who live in nine boroughs in northwest London: Barnet, Brent, Camden, Ealing, Hammersmith & Fulham, Harrow, Kensington & Chelsea and the Cities of London and Westminster.

Grants from the charity are restricted to these areas and are made in accordance with certain rules covering allocation and consultation with these local authorities.

In general the charity only gives grants to groups and organisations which are registered charities or who have automatic charitable status. Occasionally grants are awarded to local authorities in the charity's beneficial area who are working with voluntary sector partners. The charity does not give grants to individuals.

We give grants to:

▶ support education and training, particularly for young adults
▶ broaden horizons and encourage an appreciation of the value of cultural diversity through activities such as dance, drama, music, creative-writing and the visual arts
▶ provide child-care, support for parents, help where parental support is lacking
▶ enhance recreation through sport, youth clubs and play schemes
▶ help young people achieve their full potential
▶ develop new opportunities for young people.

What we fund:

▶ core costs
▶ salary costs
▶ direct project costs
▶ apprenticeships
▶ equipment
▶ buildings & refurbishments

Main Grants Programme

Grants can be up to three years in length, subject to monitoring reports and the specific approval of the Trustee. There is no maximum grant amount. Applications for Main Grants are considered by the Trustee three times a year in March, June and November.

Access to Opportunity

All state schools within the charity's beneficial area are invited to apply to this new grants programme. Applications are invited from groups of schools, in partnership with local voluntary organisations where appropriate, for programmes aimed at supporting their most challenged pupils, strengthening links with home life and co-coordinating the support of other available professionals. We anticipate that a typical application might centre on a key worker, based at the lead school, whose brief would be to project manage support for a caseload of named individual young people. A typical proposal might cost £25,000–£50,000. Funding will be available for a **maximum of three years**. It is hoped that after the initial start-up period, the projects will be self-financing, having justified their continuation through their success. Details of how projects will seek to be self-financing will be an important part of applications submitted.

Small Grants Programme

There are no deadlines for applications made under the Small Grants Programme. Requests are considered up to six times per year. The maximum amount awarded under the Small Grants Programme is £5,000 for one year only. If a repeat request is expected in the following year applicants may be referred to the Main Grants Programme.

The John Lyon Access to the Arts Fund

The John Lyon Access to the Arts Fund is open to all state primary schools in the charity's nine boroughs.

Grants awarded under this programme are available to assist primary schools in accessing and taking part in arts activities at the many high class institutions in London. Activities could include visits to the theatre, a musical experience or to a museum or art gallery. To be eligible the school must provide a clear rationale for the activity, explain how it will add value to the school experience and demonstrate an existing commitment to the arts.

There is no restriction on which institution you can visit, but the activity must enhance the current activities of the class or year group and be the kind of experience that the children do not normally have access to. Suggestions for suitable requests include:

▶ travel costs (including coach costs) to venues within London
▶ match funding for ticket prices (i.e. if the school is paying for one class to participate in an activity the charity could be asked to support the costs of enabling a second class to also take part)
▶ a contribution towards the costs of participating in a venue-based education programme.

Successful applications must include the following:

▶ evidence that this activity is in addition to, and not a replacement of, existing annual arts activities
▶ a clear rationale for taking part in the activity
▶ details of how it will add value to the children's school experience

Grantmaking in 2010/11

In 2010/11 the charity had assets of £221.3 million and an income of £6.3 million. Grants were made during the year totalling £4.5 million, which included grants committed in previous years. Grants were broken down by programme area as follows:

Schools, Education and Training	£1.6 million
Arts in Education	£914,000
Youth Clubs and Youth Initiatives	£909,000
Child Care and Support for Families	£470,000
Emotional Wellbeing	£243,000
Special Needs and Disability	£232,000
Sports	£96,500
Other	£8,500

The charity also gives a helpful breakdown of its grants by the purpose for which they were made:

Project support	£1.7 million
Salaries	£926,000
Core costs	£784,000
Bursaries	£677,000
Buildings and refurbishment	£415,000
Other	£8,500
Arts fund	£3,000
Equipment	£1,600

The charity's website lists the beneficiaries of the 20 largest grants during the year. They were: London Diocesan Board for Schools (£250,000); Continyou (£80,000); City Literary Institute (£75,000); Phoenix Cinema Trust (£70,000); Harrow Club W10 (£54,000); Skill Force (£52,500); HAFPAC, Tate Gallery, Kentish Town Community Centre and London Jewish Cultural

Centre (£50,000 each); St Gregory's Catholic Science College (£48,000); HAFD (£36,000); Arts Depot, British Museum, Tricycle Theatre Company, Mousetrap Theatre Projects and Roxeth Primary School (£35,000 each); Unicorn Theatre (£33,000); Wigmore Hall and Urban Partnership Group (£30,000 each).

Exclusions

Grants are restricted to the London boroughs of Harrow, Barnet, Brent, Ealing, Camden, City of London, City of Westminster, Hammersmith & Fulham and Kensington & Chelsea.

Grants are not made:

- to individuals
- to national organisations
- to grant-giving organisations
- to not-for-profit organisations that are not registered charities
- to schools that have not yet been inspected by Ofsted
- to hospitals, hospices or primary care trusts
- to faith schools with a closed admissions policy
- for research, unless it is action research designed to lead directly to the advancement of practical activities in the community
- for lobbying or campaigning
- for endowment funds
- for mother tongue teaching
- for feasibility studies
- for medical care and resources
- in response to general charitable appeals, unless they can be shown to be of specific benefit to children and young people in one or more of the geographical areas listed
- as direct replacements for the withdrawal of funds by statutory authorities for activities which are primarily the responsibility of central or local government
- to umbrella organisations to distribute to projects which are already in receipt of funds from the charity
- for the promotion of religion or politics
- for telephone helplines
- for advice and information services
- to housing associations
- for school journeys or trips abroad
- for capital for educational institutions
- for IT equipment
- for bursaries for higher education
- for programmes which fall under PHSE, Citizenship or Social Enterprise
- for conservation, environmental projects and therapeutic gardens
- for core costs for umbrella bodies or second tier organisations
- for grants to registered charities that have applied on behalf of organisations that are not registered with the Charity Commission.

Applications

The charity's main and small grants programmes have a two stage application process:

Stage One – Initial Proposal

Write to the Grants Office with the following information:

- a summary of the main purpose of the project
- details of the overall amount requested
- the timescale of your project
- some indication of how funds from the charity would be allocated.

The charity has produced guidelines on how best to write the initial proposal which can be accessed on its website.

Trustees meet to decide three times a year in March, June and November. There is no stage two for small grants of less than £2,000. Applications are made by initial proposal letter and the grants team will be in touch if more information is required.

Stage Two – Application Form

If your Initial Proposal is assessed positively, you will be advised whether you will need to complete an application form. Forms are required for all applications to the Main Grants Programme, Access to Opportunity and for requests of over £2,000 to the Small Grants Programme.

If you qualify for Stage Two you will be advised by your Grants Officer when your application form must be returned.

Applications by fax or email will not be accepted.

The John Lyon's Access to the Arts Fund

The John Lyon Access to the Arts Fund has a single stage application process and requests are made by application form. Applications can be made at any time.

Application forms are available via the charity's website.

Common applicant mistakes

'They don't work or operate in our beneficial area. Making general charitable appeals.'

The Madeline Mabey Trust

Medical research, children's welfare and education

£337,000 (2009/10)

Beneficial area

UK and overseas.

Madeline Mabey Trust, Woodview, Tolcarne Road, Beacon, Camborne TR14 9AB
Tel: 0120 971 0304
Correspondent: Joanna Singeisen, Trustee
Trustees: Alan G Daliday; Bridget A Nelson; Joanna L Singeisen.
CC Number: 326450

Information available

Accounts were on file at the Charity Commission, but without a list of grants.

'The principal areas of benefit continue to be the education and welfare of children both in the UK and overseas, and medical research into the causes of and cures for life threatening illnesses. The trust favours identifying organisations itself, although it is willing to consider applications for grants. The intention is to fund organisations rather than individuals directly'.

During the year 2009/10 the trust held assets of £271,000 and had an income of £246,000. Grants were made totalling £337,000 to 152 charitable causes, an increase of over

£100,000 on the previous year. A list of beneficiaries was not available.

Exclusions

No grants to individuals.

Applications

In writing to the correspondent. **Note:** unsuccessful applications are not acknowledged.

The R S Macdonald Charitable Trust

Neurological conditions, visual impairment, children and animal welfare

£1.1 million (2009/10)

Beneficial area

Scotland.

21 Rutland Square, Edinburgh
EH1 2BB
Tel: 0131 228 4681
Email: secretary@rsmacdonald.com
Website: www.rsmacdonald.com
Correspondent: Richard K Austin, Secretary
Trustees: Richard Sweetman, Chair; Richard K Austin; Donald Bain; Fiona Patrick; John Rafferty.
SC Number: SC012710

Information available

Accounts were provided by the trust. Information was also taken from the trust's website.

Established in 1978, this is the trust of the late R S MacDonald, whose family founded the famous whisky distiller Glenmorangie plc in 1893. The value of the trust increased substantially in 2005/06 due to the realisation of shares in the company, which were sold to LVMH (Moët Hennessy Louis Vuitton), the proceeds of which having been reinvested.

The trust supports charities concerned with the following:
- neurological conditions
- visual impairment
- child welfare
- animal welfare.

Six organisations are mentioned in the trust deed and these are often, but not always, supported. The trust is prepared to give very large grants to enable organisations to carry out major projects or develop ideas.

In 2009/10 the trust had assets of £54.2 million and an income of £1.7 million. There were 83 grants made during the year totalling £1.1 million, with several organisations receiving more than one grant.

The chairman of the trust noted in the latest annual report that eligible applications to the trust have increased from 27 in 2008/09 to over 100 in 2009/10. The trust also notes that, up to and including 2013/14, the trustees plan to utilise the trust's reserves to maintain a constant level of grants in excess of the trust's net income.

Beneficiaries during the year (some of whom received part of a multi-year commitment) included: Children 1st (£70,000 in total), towards several projects; University of St Andrew's (£50,000), for research into neuro-degeneration caused by Alzheimer's disease and stroke trauma; University of Aberdeen (£42,000), for a Parkinson's disease research project; Sense Scotland (£30,000), for the TouchBase cafe; Scottish Spina Bifida Association (£20,000), to fund a post; Grampian Society for the Blind (£15,000), for a communication technology project; Safe Space (£10,000), towards revenue costs; Quarriers (£5,000), towards an initiative for children and young people affected by parental substance abuse; and the Greyhound Awareness League (£3,000), towards revenue costs.

Exclusions

Grants are not given to non-registered charities or individuals, or for projects which have already started or been completed.

Applications

Applicants are invited to apply by letter; there is no application form. The trustees request that, except in relation to medical or social research,

the application letter should not exceed two pages in length. It should explain (as appropriate) what and how the need to be addressed has been identified, the costs involved and the extent to which support has been sought from other sources, the outcome hoped for and how that outcome is to be measured. It should also demonstrate how the subject of the application meets the charitable objects of the trust. Where an application is for help with revenue costs for a particular service there should be an explanation of how this will continue following the expiry of the award.

> Along with your letter you may enclose separate papers, providing background information and/or more detailed financial information. If there is a current DVD providing an insight into the work of your organisation you may wish to submit this.
>
> **In addition to the application letter you are required to complete and submit (a) a copy of the applicant's most recently audited accounts and (b) an 'Organisation Information Sheet'. This can be downloaded from the trust's website or obtained from the trust's secretary.**

Common applicant mistakes

'Failure to read the trust's guidelines and deliver what is required.'

The Mackintosh Foundation

Priority is given to the theatre and the performing arts. Also funded are children and education; medicine; homelessness; community projects; the environment; refugees; and other charitable purposes

£476,500 (2009/10)

Beneficial area

Worldwide. In practice, mainly UK.

1 Bedford Square, London
WC1B 3RB
Tel: 020 7637 8866

Fax: 020 7436 2683

Email: info@camack.co.uk

Correspondent: Nicholas Mackintosh, Appeals Director

Trustees: Sir Cameron Mackintosh, Chair; Nicholas Mackintosh; Nicholas Allott; D Michael Rose; Robert Noble; Bart Peerless; Thomas Schonberg; F Richard Pappas.

CC Number: 327751

Information available

Accounts were available at the Charity Commission.

The foundation was established in 1998 by the settlor, Sir Cameron Mackintosh, to advance education in the arts, particularly the performing arts of music and drama; to establish and maintain scholarships, bursaries and awards for proficiency in drama, music or ancillary performing arts; and to relieve poverty, hardship and distress.

The foundation has endowed Oxford University at a cost of well over £1 million with a fund known as *The Cameron Mackintosh Fund for Contemporary Theatre,* part of which has been used to set up a Visiting Professorship of Contemporary Theatre at the university. It also provided a fund of £1 million over a period of 10 years, to the Royal National Theatre, for revivals of classical stage musical productions under the auspices of the RNT.

Partnership funding of £500,000 over five years, has been provided by the foundation in respect of theatres and other organisations under the Art Council's Arts for Everyone scheme.

The foundation has also provided financial support to a number of projects in the United States including a major grant of US$1.5 million over five years to The Alliance of New American Musicals to support the creation and production of new plays by American writers and artists.

In 2009/10 the foundation had assets of just over £9.9 million and an income of £80,000. Grants were made totalling £476,500, broken down as follows:

Theatre and the performing arts	
Theatrical training and education	£91,000
Promotion of new theatrical and musical works	£47,000
Theatre buildings	£15,000
Theatre company development	£15,000
Children's theatre	£11,000
Theatre related pastoral care	£4,000
	£183,000
Medical	
Medical: general	£52,000
Medical: cancer	£40,000
Medical: HIV/AIDS	£10,000
	£102,000
Community projects	**£76,500**
Children and education	**£63,500**
Environment	**£37,500**
Homelessness	**£14,500**

Beneficiaries during the year included: Sylvia Young Theatre School (£32,500); Charlton Musgrove Memorial Hall (£25,000); American Music Center (£17,000); Royal Academy of Music (£10,000); Kids Company (£6,000); Breakthrough Breast Cancer (£5,000); Marefat Education Centre (£4,500); Cambodian Child's Dream Foundation and Lochaber Fisheries Trust (£3,000 each); NSPCC (£2,500); and Afghan Connection (£2,000).

Exclusions

Religious or political activities are not supported. Apart from the foundation's drama award and some exceptions, applications from individuals are discouraged.

Applications

In writing to the correspondent outlining details of the organisation, details of the project for which funding is required and a breakdown of the costs involved. Supporting documentation should be kept to a minimum and an sae enclosed if materials are to be returned. The trustees meet in May and October in plenary session, but a grants committee meets weekly to consider grants of up to £10,000. The foundation responds to all applications in writing and the process normally takes between four to six weeks.

Common applicant mistakes

'The most common mistakes are: not reading the guidelines properly; not asking the administrator's advice before submitting an application; sending too much information; and asking for too much money'

The MacRobert Trust

General

£658,000 (2010/11)

Beneficial area

UK, mainly Scotland.

Cromar, Tarland, Aboyne, Aberdeenshire AB34 4UD

Tel: 01339 881444

Website: www.themacroberttrust.org.uk

Correspondent: Air Comm. R W Joseph, Administrator

Trustees: W G Morrison, Chair; S Campbell; C D Crole; K Davis; J D Fowlie; Group Capt. D A Needham; C W Pagan; J C Swan; H B Wood; J H Strickland.

SC Number: SC031346

Information available

Accounts were available from the trust's website.

Summary

Originally several trusts established by Lady MacRobert in memory of her three sons who were all killed as aviators, the eldest in a civil air accident in 1938 and the middle and youngest as officer pilots in the Royal Air Force on operational sorties in 1941.

This trust was established on 6 April 2001 when the assets of the no longer operating MacRobert Trusts, a collection of four charitable trusts and two holding companies were merged into the new, single MacRobert Trust. The merging of these trusts has led to a decrease in management and administration cost and a general increase in grantmaking.

The trust has assets comprising of Douneside House (a holiday country house for serving and retired officers of the armed forces and their families) and an estate of 1,700 acres of woodland and 5,300 acres of farmland and associated residential properties let by the trust. The surplus income generated from these assets, following management and administration costs, is donated in grants.

Guidelines

The following guidelines are taken from the trust's website:

Lady MacRobert recognised that new occasions teach new duties and therefore the new trust deed gives wide discretionary powers to the trustees. The trust is reactive so, with very few exceptions, grants are made only in response to applications made through the correct channels.

The trustees reconsider their policy and practice of grant giving every five years. The beneficial area is United Kingdom-wide but preference is given to organisations in Scotland. Grants are normally made only to a recognised Scottish Charity or a recognised charity outside Scotland.

Trust's Categories of Interest

Currently, the major categories under which the trustees consider support are:

- science and technology
- youth
- services and sea
- ex-servicemen's and ex-servicewomen's hospitals and homes
- education
- disability
- community welfare

The minor categories are:

- agriculture and horticulture
- arts and music
- medical care
- Tarland and Deeside

The trust offers a very detailed breakdown of these categories on a document available from the trust's website.

Most grants are between £5,000 and £10,000 but larger awards, including capital grants, are sometimes given. 'A small grants programme facilitates awards of up to £5,000. Occasionally recurring grants are made for periods of up to three years. The trust administrator also operates a small fund from which he can make immediate smaller donations with an upper limit of £1,000 per application.'

Donations are given only to organisations registered as charities and are always dependent on funding availability.

Grantmaking in 2010/11

In 2010/11 the trust had assets of £74.1 million and an income of £2.2 million. During the year the trust made grants totalling £658,000, broken down as follows:

Ex-service people's hospitals and homes	3	£134,000
Tarland and Deeside	11	£124,000
Youth	20	£91,000
Education*	11	£78,000
Disability	16	£57,000
Services and sea	9	£46,000
Science and technology	4	£27,000
Arts and music	9	£22,000
Agriculture and horticulture	6	£18,000
Medical care	5	£16,000

Beneficiaries across all categories included: Erskine Hospital (£120,000); Tarland Welfare Trust (£75,000); Mid Deeside Limited (£25,000); Cairngorms Outdoor Access Trust and Combat Stress (£20,000 each); The Trust for St John's Kirk of Perth (£15,000); Greenock Arts Guild Limited (£10,000); The Royal Institution of Great Britain (£9,000); The Royal Marines Association (£8,000); Glasgow Shettleston New Church of Scotland (£5,000); Orange Tree Theatre Limited (£3,000); Musically Active Dudes (£2,000); and Marie Curie Cancer Care (£500).

The education total includes £24,000 awarded to 14 students from 12 separate schools in educational grants.

Exclusions

Grants are not normally provided for:

- religious organisations (but attention will be given to youth/community services provided by them, or projects of general benefit to the whole community)
- organisations based outside the United Kingdom
- individuals
- general appeals or mailshots
- political organisations
- student bodies as opposed to universities
- fee-paying schools, apart from an Educational Grants Scheme for children who are at, or who need to attend, a Scottish independent secondary school and for which a grant application is made through the Head Teacher
- expeditions, except those made under the auspices of recognised bodies such as the British Schools Exploring Society (BSES)
- community and village halls other than those local to Tarland and Deeside
- retrospective grants
- departments within a university, unless the appeal gains the support of, and is channelled through, the principal.

Applications

The application form and full guidelines can be downloaded from the trust's website, although applications must be posted.

The trustees meet to consider applications twice a year in March and November. To be considered, applications must be received for the March meeting by 31 October previously and for the October meeting by 31 May previously.

Time bars:

- Unsuccessful applicants must wait for at least one year from the time of being notified before re-applying
- Successful applicants must wait for at least two years from the time of receiving a donation before re-applying
- When a multi-year donation has been awarded, the time bar applies from the date of the final instalment
- Withdrawn applications do not normally face a time bar

The trust stresses the importance of including an informative covering letter; completing all sections of the application form and asks that applicants maintain a process of dialogue with the trust: 'We deal with many hundreds of worthy applications each year. If we have to chase you for information, you will understand that our interest might wane.'

A further list of additional guidance and feedback on the application procedure is available on the trust's website.

Applicants are informed of the trustees' decision, and if successful, payments are made immediately after each meeting.

Common applicant mistakes

'They don't fully complete the application form or read the guidance which can be downloaded; they don't take the opportunity to provide an informative covering letter; they don't enclose annual reports and accounts or financial statements; and they don't follow up the application with regular 'status of fundraising' information.'

The Manifold Charitable Trust

Education, historic buildings, environmental conservation, general

£495,000 (2010)

Beneficial area

UK.

Studio Cottage, Windsor Great Park, Windsor, Berkshire SL4 2HP
Email: helen.niven@ cumberlandlodge.ac.uk
Correspondent: Helen Niven
Trustee: Manifold Trustee Company Limited.
CC Number: 229501

Information available

Accounts were available at the Charity Commission.

This trust was established in 1962 for general charitable purposes. It had previously focused much attention on the preservation of churches, however following the death in 2007 of its founder, Sir John Smith, the trust is now allocating most of its grants for educational purposes. Grants to Eton College, the largest beneficiary, are provided to 'enable boys whose families otherwise would not be able to support the fees to be educated at Eton College.' The trust still makes grants to the Historic Churches Preservation Trust for onward distribution to churches; however it would seem that the amount has been reduced on previous years.

As noted in the past, the trust continues to make grants in excess of its income, preferring to 'meet the present needs of other charities rather than reserve money for the future'.

In 2010 the trust had assets of £8.6 million and an income of £490,000. During the year grants totalled £495,000.

Grants were apportioned roughly as follows:

	% of total
Education, research and the arts	85%
Repairs to churches and their contents	13%
Other causes	2%

81% of grants were of £1,000 or less, and only 11% were for £10,000 by number.

Unfortunately a full list of beneficiaries was not included in the 2010 accounts. However, the trustees do acknowledge that 85% of the grant total (approximately £421,000) was received by Eton College. Eton College has also been a beneficiary in previous years and other past recipients have included: Historic Churches Preservation Trust (£140,000 in total); Thames Hospice Care (£50,000); Imperial College (£15,000); Berkeley Castle Charitable Trust and Maidenhead Heritage Trust (£10,000 each); Berkshire Medical Heritage Centre (£7,500); Gislingham PCC (£6,000); Household Cavalry Museum Trust (£5,000); Brompton Ralph PCC (£4,500); Morrab Library (£2,500); and Richmond Building Preservation Society, Askham PCC and Westray Heritage Trust (£1,000 each).

Exclusions

Applications are not considered for improvements to churches as this is covered by a block grant to the Historic Churches Preservation Trust. The trust regrets that it does not give grants to individuals for any purpose.

Applications

The trust has no full-time staff, therefore general enquiries and applications for grants should be made in writing only, by post or by fax and not by telephone. The trust does not issue application forms. Applications should be made to the correspondent in writing and should:

▶ state how much money it is hoped to raise
▶ if the appeal is for a specific project state also (a) how much it will cost (b) how much of this cost will come from the applicant charity's existing funds (c) how much has already been received or promised from other sources and

(d) how much is therefore still being sought
▶ list sources of funds to which application has been or is intended to be made (for example local authorities, or quasi-governmental sources, such as the national lottery)
▶ if the project involves conservation of a building, send a photograph of it and a note (or pamphlet) about its history
▶ send a copy of the charity's latest income and expenditure account and balance sheet.

Applications are considered twice a month, and a reply is sent to most applicants (whether successful or not) who have written a letter rather than sent a circular.

The Manoukian Charitable Foundation

Social welfare, education, medical, the arts, 'Armenian matters'

£1.9 million (2010)

Beneficial area

Worldwide.

c/o Berwin Leighton Paisner, Adelaide House, London Bridge, London EC4R 9HA
Tel: 020 7760 1000
Correspondent: Anthony Bunker, Trustee
Trustees: Mrs Tamar Manoukian; Anthony Bunker; Steven Press; Dr Armen Sarkissian.
CC Number: 1084065

Information available

Accounts were available at the Charity Commission.

Set up in 2000, the foundation has received donations from sources associated with the Manoukian family. The following extract is taken from the foundation's 2010 accounts:

The objects of the charity are the promotion of general charitable purposes; the trustees give particular emphasis to projects with medical, educational or cultural aspects and those that relate to Armenian matters, although they consider applications for other charitable purposes.

Applications are considered on the basis of whether they meet the general aims of the foundation and the nature of the project concerned. The foundation will consider providing assistance to projects that may be partly funded by others if this will enable the project to proceed. The trustees have tended to give greater consideration to educational and cultural projects as well as those which are intended to relieve poverty, illness and suffering.

In 2010 the foundation had an income of just over £1.5 million almost entirely from donations. Grants were made to 16 organisations totalling £1.9 million, and were broken down as follows:

Culture and the arts	£750,000
Religious causes	£599,000
Education and training	£192,000
Social services and relief	£188,000
Medical research and care	£102,000
Environmental	£55,500

Beneficiaries included: Royal Opera House – Thurrock (£750,000); Armenian Apostolic Holy Church (£589,000); Elton John AIDS Foundation (£102,000); Cherie Blair Foundation for Women (£100,000); Chronic Care Centre (£65,000); Action Innocence (£32,500); British Lebanese Association (£30,000); Jenkins Penn Haitian Relief Organisation (£17,000); and Our Lady of Lebanon Church (£10,000).

Applications

'Requests for grants are received from the general public and charitable and other organisations through their knowledge of the activities of the foundation and through personal contacts of the settlor and the trustees.' The trustees meet at least once per year.

The Marcela Trust

Medical research

£800,000 (2009/10)

Beneficial area

UK.

OMC Investments Limited, 2nd Floor, 14 Buckingham Street, London WC2N 6DF
Tel: 020 7925 8095
Correspondent: Josephine Paxton
Trustees: Brian Groves; Dawn Rose; Dr Martin Lenz; Mark Spragg.
CC Number: 1127514

Information available

Accounts were available at the Charity Commission.

The trust was established in 2009 for general charitable purposes. All of the trust's income comes from OMC Investments Limited – two of the trustees, Dawn Rose and Brian Groves, are also directors of OMC. Donations may be made to the trust by the company for restricted purposes, i.e. to then be awarded to specific organisations.

In 2009/10 the trust had an income of over £73.4 million, which included donated shares worth £69.2 million in Omarca Investment Holdings Limited, a dormant holding company which owns OMC Investments Limited.

Grants were made to three organisations during the year totalling £800,000. They were: Nuffield Orthopaedic Centre Appeal (£500,000), to fund an extension to the Botnar Research Centre; Consensus Action on Salt and Health (£200,000), for research; and the Open Eyes Foundation (£100,000), for research into the treatment of retinoblastoma.

Applications

In writing to the correspondent, although potential applicants should be aware that grant recipients may be pre-determined by the directors of OMC Investments Limited.

Marshall's Charity

Parsonage and church improvements

£743,000 (2010)

Beneficial area

England and Wales with preference for Kent, Surrey, Lincolnshire and Southwark.

Marshall House, 66 Newcomen Street, London SE1 1YT
Tel: 020 7407 2979
Fax: 020 7403 3969
Email: grantoffice@marshalls.org.uk
Website: www.marshalls.org.uk
Correspondent: Richard Goatcher, Clerk to the Trustees
Trustees: Anthea Nicholson, Chair; Colin Bird; David Lang; Michael Dudding; Colin Stenning; Stephen Clark; Gina Isaac; Bill Eason; Jeremy Hammant; John Heawood; Surbhi Malhotra; Revd Jonathan Rust; Ven. Christine Hardman; Tony Guthrie; Lesley Bosman.
CC Number: 206780

Information available

Accounts were on file at the Charity Commission. The charity has an informative website.

The charity supports parsonage buildings throughout England and Wales, helps with the upkeep of Anglican churches in Kent, Surrey and Lincolnshire (as the counties were defined in 1855), supports the parish of Christ Church, Southwark and makes grants for education to Marshall's Educational Foundation. Special consideration is given to parishes in urban priority areas. Further information on the types of grant available can be found on the charity's website.

Grants to churches are usually between £3,000 and £5,000, though they can be higher. The majority of grants to parsonages range from £1,000 to £4,000.

In 2010 the charity had assets of £15.6 million and an income of £1.2 million. Grants were made totalling £743,000, and were broken down as follows:

Parsonages	£493,000
Repair of churches	£158,500
Christ Church, Southwark	£57,500
Marshall's Educational Foundation	£34,500

Churches receiving grants included: St Lawrence – Aylesby; St Andrew – Deal; All Saints – Elsham; St Michael – Hernhill; St Bartholomew – Keelby;

Holy Trinity – Milton Regis; St Botolph's – Quarrington; and St Mary the Virgin – Swineshead. A full list of churches receiving grants can be found on the charity's website.

Exclusions

No grants to churches outside the counties of Kent, Surrey and Lincolnshire, as defined in 1855. No church funding for the following:

- cost of church halls and meeting rooms
- kitchens
- decorations, unless they form part of qualifying repair or improvement work
- furniture and fittings
- work to bells, brasses or clocks
- private chapels or monuments
- stained glass, although work to repair ferraments can be supported
- grounds, boundary walls and fences
- external lighting.

Applications

Applicants should write a letter or send an email to the correspondent, giving the name and location of the Church and a brief (30 – 40 words maximum) description of the proposed work. If appropriate the charity will then send out an application form. Applications for parsonage grants should be made by the relevant Diocesan Parsonage Board. Trustees usually meet in January, April, July and October. Application forms for 2012 are available from 1 January 2012.

Mayfair Charities Ltd

Orthodox Judaism

£6 million (2009/10)

Beneficial area

UK and overseas.

Freshwater House, 158–162 Shaftesbury Avenue, London WC2H 8HR
Tel: 020 7836 1555
Email: mark.jenner@highdorn.co.uk
Correspondent: Mark Jenner, Secretary

Trustees: Benzion S E Freshwater, Chair; D Davis; Solomon I Freshwater.
CC Number: 255281

Information available

Accounts were available at the Charity Commission.

Established in 1968, the trust makes grants to Orthodox Jewish colleges and institutions for the advancement of religion and education and to other organisations for the relief of poverty, in the UK and Israel. It largely appears to be a vehicle for the philanthropic activities of property investor Benzion Freshwater, who is closely connected with the management of some of the major beneficiary organisations.

> In recent years, the trustees have decided to support certain major projects which, during the year under review and subsequently, have received substantial financial grants from the company. At the present time the trustees have entered into commitments for the financial support of colleges and institutions which would absorb approximately £7 million over the next five years.

This statement has been in the trust's accounts for several years, presumably indicating that major commitments are made each year on a rolling basis.

In 2009/10 the trust had assets of £54.1 million and an income of £4 million. Grants were made to over 600 organisations totalling £6 million.

There are no set amounts for sizes of grants – several substantial donations were made during the year and many organisations received small grants for a little as a few hundred pounds. A list of beneficiaries was unavailable.

Previous beneficiaries include: SOFT; Beth Jacob Grammar School For Girls Ltd; Merkaz Lechinuch Torani; Ohr Akiva Institute; Kollel Chibas Yerushalayim; Mesivta Letzeirim; Chevras Maoz Ladal; Congregation Ichud Chasidim; Chaye Olam Institute; United Talmudical Association; Talmud Torah Zichron Gavriel; Friends of Bobov; Regent Charities Ltd; Comet Charities Ltd; Woodstock Sinclair Trust; Yesodei Hatorah School; Beis Aharon Trust; Ezer Mikodesh Foundation; Gateshead Jewish Teachers Training College; Edgware Foundation;

Heritage House; Kiryat Sanz Jerusalem; and PAL Charitable Trust.

Applications

In writing to the correspondent.

Common applicant mistakes

'We only support causes in the Jewish Orthodox community mainly in the relief of poverty or education. This kind of rules out the average church restoration appeal!'

The Medlock Charitable Trust

Education, health, welfare

£1.1 million (2009/10)

Beneficial area

Overwhelmingly the areas of Bath and Boston in Lincolnshire.

c/o Hebron & Medlock Ltd, St Georges Lodge, 33 Oldfield Road, Bath, Avon BA2 3ND
Tel: 01225 428221
Correspondent: Leonard Medlock, Trustee
Trustees: Leonard Medlock; Jacqueline Medlock; David Medlock; Peter Carr.
CC Number: 326927

Information available

Accounts were available at the Charity Commission.

The trust describes its grantmaking policy as follows:

> The trustees have identified the City of Bath and the borough of Boston as the principal but not exclusive areas in which the charity is and will be proactive. These areas have been specifically chosen as the founder of the charity has strong connections with the City of Bath, the home of the charity, and has family connections of long standing with the borough of Boston.
>
> To date the charity has supported and funded a number of projects in these areas by making substantial grants. These grants have been made to fund projects in the areas of education, medicine, research and social services all for the benefit of the local community. During the year, the trustees also receive many applications for assistance from many diverse areas

in the United Kingdom. These are all considered sympathetically.

In 2009/10 the trust had assets of £26.5 million and an income of £791,500. Grants were made to 141 organisations totalling £1.1 million.

The largest grants during the year were made to: The Well's Palace Appeal (£150,000), to make the palace more accessible to visitors and provide a new education centre and cafe; and Bath University (£100,000), to replace an old Astroturf facility with a modern state-of-the-art surface. Other large grants were made to: Quartet Community Foundation (£80,000); SS Great Britain Trust (£75,000); the Boshier-Hinton Foundation (£60,000); and the Forever Friends Appeal (£51,000).

Other beneficiaries included: The Prince's Trust (£25,000); Hayesfield School (£18,000); Somerset 500 Club (£15,000); Julian House, Southern Spinal Injuries Trust, Royal Air Force Benevolent Fund and Centrepoint Outreach (£10,000); John Cabot Academy (£8,000); Bristol Care & Repair (£7,000); St Saviour's Church of England Junior School (£6,000); Bath Preservation Trust, Boston and District Athletic Club, NSPCC and the Clara Cross Rehab Unit (£5,000 each); Bristol Children's Help Society (£3,000); The Anchor Society and the Thera Trust (£2,000 each); and Castle Primary School, Mid-Somerset Festival, Avon Outward Bound Association and Centre for Deaf People (£1,000 each).

Exclusions
No grants to individuals or students.

Applications
In writing to the correspondent.

The Melow Charitable Trust

Jewish
£621,000 (2010)

Beneficial area
UK and overseas.

21 Warwick Grove, London E5 9HX
Tel: 020 8806 1549

Correspondent: J Low
Trustees: Miriam Spitz; Esther Weiser.
CC Number: 275454

Information available
Accounts were available at the Charity Commission.

The trust makes grants to Jewish charities both in the UK and overseas. In 2010 the trust had assets of £9.7 million and an income of £1.4 million. Grants totalled £621,000 and were broken down as follows:

Religious institutions	£213,000
Needy persons	£185,000
Synagogues	£77,500
Education	£62,000
General	£38,000
Schools	£20,500
Talamudical colleges	£13,000
Publication of religious books	£11,400
Community organisation	£500

The largest grants were to: Friends of Kollel Satmar (Antwerp) Ltd (£107,000); Ezer V'Hatzalah Ltd (£81,000); Lolev Charitable Trust (£75,000); Tchaba Kollel (£50,000); and Rehabilitation Trust (£38,000).

Applications
In writing to the correspondent.

Mercaz Torah Vechesed Limited

Orthodox Jewish
£965,500 (2009/10)

Beneficial area
Worldwide.

28 Braydon Road, London N16 6QB
Tel: 020 8880 5366
Correspondent: Joseph Ostreicher, Secretary
Trustees: Jacob Moishe Grosskopf; Joseph Ostreicher; Mordche David Rand.
CC Number: 1109212

Information available
Accounts were available at the Charity Commission.

The charity was formed in 2005 for the advancement of the orthodox Jewish faith, orthodox Jewish religious education, and the relief of

poverty and infirmity amongst members of the orthodox Jewish community.

In 2009/10 the charity had an income of £1 million from donations. Grants were made totalling £965,500. Unfortunately further information was not available in the charity's accounts

Applications
In writing to the correspondent.

The Mercers' Charitable Foundation

General welfare, elderly people, conservation, arts, Christian faith activities, educational institutions
£3 million (2010/11)

Beneficial area
UK; strong preference for London and the West Midlands. The foundation is keen to stress that it currently has geographical restrictions on its welfare and educational grant making. Please see individual programme information for details.

Mercers' Hall, Ironmonger Lane, London EC2V 8HE
Tel: 020 7726 4991
Fax: 020 7600 1158
Email: mail@mercers.co.uk
Website: www.mercers.co.uk
Correspondent: The Clerk
Trustee: The Mercers' Company
CC Number: 326340

Information available
Accounts were available at the Charity Commission. The foundation also has an informative website.

The Mercers' Company has several trusts, the main one being the Mercers' Charitable Foundation. The foundation was established in 1983 to make grants and donations for the benefit of a wide range of charitable purposes including welfare, education, the arts, heritage and religion. Its primary source of income is gift aid donations from the Mercers' Company. On 1st August 2008 the Mercers' Company Educational Trust Fund transferred all of its assets and liabilities to the foundation.

The foundation seeks to support a range of organisations with the common theme of providing effective services and facilities to those in need and to strengthen communities. Whist continuing to support small grass roots organisations, the foundation has developed relationships with some much larger organisations, complementing work that is funded by statutory bodies.

The foundation runs a number of responsive grant-making programmes, each with agreed guidelines and each year identifies a small number of organisations working within the key programme areas who are then invited to submit proposals for the larger grants. In most cases the work takes place in London or the West Midlands. These proposals are subject to detailed scrutiny by the specialist committees and the executive staff. The grant-making committees each meet a minimum of four times a year to discuss applications and recommend grants to the trustees.

The company has several categories of grant making. The following descriptions of funding categories are taken from guidance available on the foundation's website.

Guidelines

The following guidelines are taken from the trust's website:

General Welfare

The Mercers' Company supports grassroots and front-line charities that work to improve the lives of disadvantaged and marginalised people.

The company does this by awarding grants to organisations that work in the following fields:

- reducing offending
- social and medical welfare
- special needs
- youth work
- care for the elderly.

Assistance in this area is restricted to a geographical area within the M25,

particularly the inner London Boroughs.

Education

The Company makes a number of grants to improve the availability and quality of education for children and young adults. These grants are focused on young people from the ages of 5–25, particularly in London, and in the West Midland areas of Walsall, Sandwell and Telford & Wrekin. Applicants must be UK registered charities, UK exempt charities, or state schools and colleges. Priority is given to work that:

- Encourages participation in science, maths and technology;
- Improves educational achievement, particularly for young people aged 5–19;
- Offers educational opportunities for underachieving groups;
- Enriches educational opportunity through innovative projects that use art, drama, dance, music and sport; and
- Builds students' social capital, confidence and life skills.

The trust may also support work that:

- Promotes the effective management of schools and colleges, for the direct benefit of pupils;
- Provides help for children and young adults with special educational needs, including the development of gifted and talented young people;
- Provides ways of increasing parental and community support for learning; and
- Encourages educational progression, the acquisition of vocational skills and participation in Higher Education.

Support for the Christian faith

In its work to advance and support the Christian faith, the Mercers' Company invites grant appeals from a wide variety of sources. These need not be exclusively from Anglican organisations, but we discourage appeals from overseas unless there is a UK charitable involvement. Appeals may be broadly grouped into those relating to buildings and those connected with people.

Buildings

We consider appeals from:

- Churches in the City of London.
- Churches with a Mercer connection – historic (church patronage) or a present Mercer closely involved.
- Cathedrals, specifically those with close links to Mercer churches

People

We aim to contribute to deepening understanding and acceptance of the Christian religion, and to developing its relationships between its denominations and with other world faiths. We seek appeals that:

- Help young people to learn about the Christian faith and develop their spiritual lives.
- Support clergy and help them to develop their outreach work.
- Provide spiritual training for clergy and lay people.
- Provide respite, recuperation and spiritual nourishment for clergy and their families.
- Improve the effectiveness of parish administration through support for core costs for key people.

Heritage and the arts

Heritage appeals are considered for:

- material or fabric conservation and refurbishment
- library/archive conservation
- wildlife/environment conservation.

Arts: 'We have a modest budget for the performing arts and priority is given to supporting young professional performers at the start of their careers. There is a preference for organisations based in London but occasionally we support national organisations that are centres of excellence.'

Grantmaking 2010/11

The annual report for 2010/11 stated that 'there is a current focus on supporting service delivery rather than new capital projects.'

In 2010/11 the foundation had assets of £10.1 million and an income of just under £6 million. Grants totalled £3 million. Grants are mostly in the range of £1,000 to £15,000 and those above £10,000 were listed in the accounts, and were broken down as follows:

Education – £1.1 million
Beneficiaries included: St Paul's School (£430,000); Every Child a Chance Trust (£35,000); Peter Symonds' College (£34,000); Sandwell Academy (£30,000); Southside Young Leaders' Academy (£20,000); First Story Ltd (£15,000); London Citizens (£11,000); Baxter College, London Philharmonic Orchestra, Tate Gallery and The Ethics Academy (£10,000 each).

Social, medical, youth and community welfare – £620,000
Beneficiaries included: Prior's Court Foundation (£50,000); Treloar Trust (£30,000); Maytree Respite Centre and Superkidz Community Trust (£15,000 each); Westminster Boating Base, Finsbury Park Homeless

Families Project and Blue Sky Development & Regeneration (£10,000 each).

Other – £386,000
Beneficiaries included Gresham College (£322,000); Masons Company Charitable Trust and St Dunstan's (£10,000 each).

Heritage and the arts – £300,000
Beneficiaries included: Water City Festival, Chichester Cathedral and St Alfege Church Greenwich (£10,000 each).

Church – £292,000
Beneficiaries included: Hexham Abbey (£21,000); National Churches Trust (£18,000); Ripon College, The Contextual Theology Centre and St Paul's Cathedral Foundation (£10,000 each).

Bursaries – £152,000
Beneficiaries included: Buttle UK (£50,000); Royal National Children's Foundation (£35,000); Emmott Foundation (£25,000); and Royal Ballet School (£12,000).

Care for the elderly – £81,000
Beneficiaries included: Age Concern Westminster (£12,000); Rotherfield St Martin and Tower Hamlets Friends and Neighbours (£10,000).

Exclusions

These should be read alongside the specific exclusions for the particular category into which an application falls.

- animal welfare charities
- endowment appeals
- projects that are primarily political
- activities that are the responsibility of the local, health or education authority or other similar body
- activities that have already taken place
- other grant making trusts
- sponsorship or marketing appeals
- loans or business finance
- general or mailshot appeals

Capital projects: 'This is restricted to appeals that are within the last 20 % of their target. No capital projects are funded under the Education programme.'

Applications

Applications can be made online via the foundation's website. In addition applicants are required to post:

- The organisation's most recent statutory report and accounts (produced not later than 10 months after the end of the financial year).
- A copy of the organisation's bank statement, dated within the last three months.

Grants officers are happy to give advice by telephone or email.

Applicants must submit applications four weeks prior to committee meetings. Applications will be acknowledged within 10 working days. Committees meet regularly throughout the year. For up to date committee meeting dates consult the foundation's website for each grant programme. Approval of successful applications may take up to four weeks from the date of the meeting at which your applications is considered.

According to the most recent accounts:

> Where possible, applicants awarded, or being considered for, a grant over £10,000 will receive a visit either from staff or from members of the Mercers' Company.

Note: This foundation is under the trusteeship of the Mercers' Company and one application to the Company is an application to all its trusts including the Charity of Sir Richard Whittington and the Earl of Northampton's Charity.

Common applicant mistakes

'Applicants not reading the latest available criteria on grant funding information on our website and, therefore, submit ineligible applications.'

Community Foundation for Merseyside

Community development, regeneration, general

£3.5 million (2010/11)

Beneficial area

Merseyside, Halton and Lancashire.

Third Floor, Stanley Building, 43 Hanover Street, Liverpool L1 3DN
Tel: 0151 232 2444
Fax: 0151 232 2445
Email: info@cfmerseyside.org.uk
Website: www.cfmerseyside.org.uk
Correspondent: Cathy Elliott, Chief Executive
Trustees: Michael Eastwood; Abi Pointing; Andrew Wallis; Robert Towers; William Bowley; Sally Yeoman; David McDonnell; Jayne Pugh.
CC Number: 1068887

Information available

Accounts were available at the Charity Commission. The trust also has a useful website.

The Community Foundation for Merseyside connects donors with local causes in Merseyside. By providing grants to local communities, the foundation helps them focus on building a better stronger Merseyside for future generations.

At present the foundation's main function of distributing grants to local communities is supported by distinct funds, confined to specific objectives within time-limited periods. However, its long-term vision is to be sustainable; to be the biggest funder of the voluntary sector on Merseyside and to have substantial endowment – enabling the foundation to utilise unrestricted funds in creative grant making.

Their aim over the coming years is to address long-term sustainability by engaging with high-value donors to build endowment, while developing and cementing their position as a community leader within the voluntary sector.

By increasing public awareness of their work, they will work with and advise donors who are passionate about their communities to establish endowment funds that will make a lasting impact on local lives.

In 2010/11 the foundation had assets of £5.5 million and an income of £6.5 million. During the year 806 grants were made to organisations totalling over £3.5 million.

Grant programmes 2010/11

The foundation delivers a range of grantmaking programmes across Merseyside, Halton and Lancashire. The number and type of grants available from the foundation can vary considerably over time.

According to the trust's annual report the social priorities of the trust in 2010/11 were as follows
- environment
- children & young people
- community development & cohesion
- employable communities
- health & well-being
- arts & culture.

At the end of 2011, the following funds were available for applications – as with other community foundations, funds may close and new ones open, so check the foundation's website for up-to-date information (smaller, unpublicised funds may also be open – see table below).

Liverpool ONE Foundation
The Liverpool ONE Foundation aims to help the lives of local people in Merseyside, especially Liverpool, by providing support for good causes in and around the city.

Each major borough of Merseyside has been assigned different priorities, but broad themes which projects should meet include the following
- education and skills – especially for young people
- social and community advancement
- health
- crime reduction.

Funding is available from two different fund programmes. The programmes are:

Programme 1: Up to £5,000 in any 12 month period may be offered for activity based projects. This programme is aimed at grassroots groups. The funders are keen to see evidence of a sustainability plan and it is expected that grants will primarily fund direct project costs, although certain staff costs may be considered where no statutory funding exists.

Programme 2: Between £5,001 and £10,000 may be awarded in any 12 month period for projects which

clearly demonstrate the applicant's capacity to deliver the project and evidence project sustainability. Priority will be given to new social enterprises or groups that have secured commissioned work from the public sector to deliver new services.

The trust is unable to accept simultaneous applications to both programmes.

Merseyside Police Property Act Fund
The Police Property Act Fund provides grants of up to £5,000 to support community organisations whose work has an impact on community safety and crime reduction within their neighbourhood.

Grants are available in the boroughs of Knowsley, Liverpool, Sefton, St Helens and Wirral conforming to the objects of the fund.

Every application must conform to the object of the fund which is:
- to promote for the public benefit in and around Merseyside a safer and increased quality of life through the prevention of crime and the protection of people and property from criminal acts.

Project costs must be clearly explained and best price evidenced. Core salaries cannot be supported though sessional fees may be considered. Applicants must clearly state when their project is taking place in order for the committee to assign the application to an appropriate meeting. Applications should be sent 6 weeks in advance of the meeting date.

Mersey Docks & Harbour Company 500 Fund
The Mersey Docks and Harbour Company 500 Fund provides funding of between £50 and £500 to registered charities, voluntary and community groups working in Sefton, Liverpool, Halton or Wirral, that can show local community involvement in the decision making of the organisation.

To be eligible for a grant your project must demonstrate a local community need and meet with your group's aims and objectives. Priority will be given to organisations working with disadvantaged areas of the community. Your project must:

- build the capacity of the community to help itself
- be based on real need
- demonstrate sustainability and long-term benefits
- show value for money.

Liverpool PCT Sexual Health & Well Being Fund
Grants of up to £5,000 are available for initiatives which improve awareness of sexual health issues within the Liverpool Primary Care Trust area. Grants of more than £5,000 may be awarded for innovative and well evidenced projects.

Priorities:
- reducing the rate of conception among under-18s
- increasing access to sexual health services and contraception for young people
- increasing chlamydia screening among under-25s.

In order to apply your group must:
- be based in the area covered by Liverpool PCT, or be able to prove that 95% or more of the beneficiaries of your proposed project are from this area
- have a formal constitution or governing document in the name of the group
- be meeting the needs of the local community and be able to evidence this
- be able to demonstrate the links or partnership working that you are undertaking with the contraception and sexual health agencies in Liverpool. Please see the website for guidance, including a list of suggested agencies.

Liverpool Mutual Homes Green Machine Fund
Grants ranging from £50 – £500, or higher for exceptional projects, are available for environmental projects which benefit residents living in Liverpool Mutual Homes housing in the Liverpool area.

In order to apply your group must:
- demonstrate sustainability and long-term benefit
- show volunteer involvement and wide community benefit.

The fund does not generally cover salary costs or trips/outings.

Sonae Green Machine

Grants ranging from £50 – £500, or higher for exceptional projects, are available for environmental projects in Knowsley and St Helens.

In order to apply your group must:

▶ demonstrate sustainability and long-term benefit

▶ show volunteer involvement and wide community benefit.

The fund does not generally cover salary costs or trips/outings. Examples of what may be funded include greening of urban areas, community clean ups or improving local wasteland.

Royal London Foundation

Launched in April 2011 the Royal London Foundation aims to help communities in Merseyside and Cheshire by providing grants to charities and projects nominated by Royal London mutual insurance or Royal Liver assurance members. Grants of between £1,000 and £10,000 are available.

Priorities:

▶ education – specifically, developing the skills of those who require assistance which they would not otherwise have access to

▶ elderly

▶ health.

In addition to the core grant programme the fund makes an annual Degge & Ridge Award of £25,000. For this award the fund may focus specifically on an individual priority in one year, so applicants are encouraged to regularly check the fund's priorities and guidelines on their website.

To be eligible for a grant your organisation must:

▶ be a registered charity or be clearly able to demonstrate that you are working towards a charitable cause

▶ have an annual turnover of less than £50,000 for standard grants and less than £150,000 for the Degge & Ridge Award.

The application must be made on behalf of a Royal London Mutual Insurance Society Limited member.

Applications must be made directly to the funder via their website.

John Goore Fund

The John Goore Fund has been established to support the residents of Lydiate, Sefton. This fund has been supported by the Grassroots Endowment Challenge. There are three elements to the fund:

▶ to support the advancement of higher education and training (grants of up to £250 available to individuals or £1,000 to community groups)

▶ grants for adults who may need to re-train after a period of unemployment or redundancy

▶ helping those with mental or physical disabilities (grants of up to £500 are available)

▶ to provide respite for local carers (grants of up to £250 are available).

In order to be eligible, organisations must:

▶ be a voluntary or community group with a constitution or set of rules in the group name

▶ demonstrate benefit to the community and a real need for the project.

Standard Merseyside Community Foundation guidelines apply for groups and individuals; these may be accessed on the trust's website.

Grantmaking in 2010/11

The following is a breakdown of the foundation's grant distributions by fund during the year:

Grassroots Grants	283	£1.2 million
Employable Communities	120	£665,000
Fairshare Trust	7	£514,000
Merseyside Police Authority	85	£352,200
Liverpool ONE Foundation	52	£180,000
Deutsche Bank	12	£146,000
Comic Relief	24	£102,000
Active @ 60 Fund	46	£95,000
Shop Direct	7	£43,000
23 Foundation	5	£37,000
St Helens Listen	33	£29,000
Wirral Third Sector Health Innovation	–	£25,000
Lancashire Community Foundation	12	£25,000
Bootle Flood Appeal	33	£21,000
Hill Dickinson	3	£15,000
Sefton Council	12	£14,400
Neighbourhood Learning in Deprived Communities	7	£14,200
Cobalt Housing	4	£13,500
Merseyside Young Transformers	11	£13,100
Mark McQueen Foundation	3	£12,400
Merseyside Police and High Sheriffs Trust	10	£12,300
Merseyside Docks and Harbour Company	22	£11,000
Villages Housing	2	£9,000
Rank Foundation	1	£8,000
Keepmoat Fund	6	£8,000
Jim Hosker Memorial Fund	16	£7,500
Liverpool Primary Care Trust	4	£7,100
Green Machine	14	£5,300
Lancashire Young Transformers	3	£5,200
Sefton Sports and Activity Alliance	7	£5,000
Merseyside 100	4	£1,000
Alliance & Leicester	–	£3,200
John Goore Trust	13	£2,700
Barnett Waddingham	1	£2,200
Joseph Harley Trust	6	£2,100
Leahy Foundation	1	£1,200
Rensburg Sheppard	2	£1,000

Beneficiaries included: Halton Voluntary Action – to promote youth volunteering in the Halton area (£7,000 from the Local Network Fund); JoJo Mind & Body – to provide educational classes for young people with learning difficulties (£7,000 from the Local Network Fund); The Zero Centre – to fund a drop-in centre for victims of domestic abuse (£6,600 from the Local Network Fund); Liverpool Academy of Art – to provide running costs for art exhibitions (£5,000 from the Arts & Culture Fund); Fire Support Network – to develop a community garden (£500 from Unilever Green Machine); and Liverpool Greenbank Wheelchair Basketball Club – to offer introductory sports sessions to people with disabilities (£500 from Alliance & Leicester).

Exclusions

Each of the separate funds has separate guidelines and exclusions, see the general tab for an outline. Full lists of exclusions are available with guidance notes from the trust's website.

Applications

Most of the trust's funds can now be applied for online using a standard form. Royal London fund applications must be submitted directly to the fund and the John Goore fund has a separate application form available on the trust website.

The trust's website states that, during the application process:

> You will be asked to give information on what your organisation needs. Information on our fund guidelines is

below, on submission of your application we will determine which fund your project proposal meets. If your project proposal does not fit one of our funds at the time of submission, your application will be WITHDRAWN. If your application is withdrawn, if your organisation needs change, or if our fund portfolio changes you can reapply after 12 weeks of your original submission, however there is no guarantee of funding.

Applications must also include the following documents:

- constitution
- accounts
- bank statement
- safeguarding policy (where applicable)

Unless your organisation has received a grant from the foundation in the last 12 months you *must* submit these documents, otherwise your application will not be considered.

The website also states: 'We ask you to identify a theme for your project and outcome indicators which will be compared when monitoring successful grants.' A list of themes and outcome indicators may be downloaded from the foundation's website.

Full guidelines and application forms for individual funds are also available from the foundation's website.

Milton Keynes Community Foundation

Welfare, arts

£489,000 (2010/11)

Beneficial area

Milton Keynes Unitary Authority.

Acorn House, 381 Midsummer Boulevard, Central Milton Keynes MK9 3HP
Tel: 01908 690276
Fax: 01908 233635
Email: information@ mkcommunityfoundation.co.uk
Website: www. mkcommunityfoundation.co.uk
Correspondent: Bart Gamber, Grants Director
Trustees: Judith Hooper; Fola Komolafe; Francesca Skelton; Jane

Matthews; Michael Murray; Peter Kara; Peter Selvey; Richard Brown; Roger Kitchen; Ruth Stone; Stephen Norrish.
CC Number: 295107

Information available

Accounts were available from the Charity Commission.

Established in 1986, the foundation is a local grantmaking charity that helps to improve the quality of life for people living within the unitary authority area of Milton Keynes. It awards around 150 grants each year to local voluntary organisations and charities, supporting projects that benefit the whole community, including; public health, the needs of children and young people, older people, people with special needs, arts and culture and projects providing services to the community.

The foundation helps to build stronger communities by encouraging local giving and raises a large part of its funds through a membership scheme, supported by local people and companies who make an annual donation.

The foundation has a range of different funds and accepts application from not-for-profit organisations working for the benefit of the community of Milton Keynes.

The foundation has three main grant programmes.

- *Small Grants* – up to £1,500. These grants are considered monthly.
- *Community Grants* – up to £5,000.
- *Arts/Crafts Bursaries* – varying amounts year on year.
- *Extraordinary Grants* – the trust states: 'We sometimes have the ability to fund projects that do not fit within our ordinary grant schemes, either because they require a larger amount than the normal maximum or because they arise with urgent need that cannot wait until the next deadline. We will only accept applications for Extraordinary Grants if we agree that the circumstances justify it, if we can identify potential funds available to make the grant should it be successful and if you have been given permission by our Grants Team to submit it.'

The foundation's website notes that it has:

A special interest in projects that are led and driven by local people, as well as projects that utilise partnerships between different organisations.

When reviewing grant applications, we look for projects that have been carefully thought through and planned.

Due to the limited funds available for grants, we also appreciate applicants who submit frugal applications – those that only ask for the minimum amount needed to deliver the intended impact.

Examples of what may be funded:

- start up costs
- extension of existing projects
- pilot projects and extension funding for successful pilots
- equipment & resources
- leverage
- conservation projects
- total core costs related to the wider project.

It is important to note that grant schemes can change frequently. For full details of the foundation's current grant programmes and their deadlines please consult its website.

In 2010/11 the foundation had assets of £6.1 million and an income of £1.9 million. Grants were made from various funds totalling £489,000.

Recent beneficiaries have included: Milton Keynes YMCA – towards a winter emergency accommodation service (£5,000 from the Koss Fund and Community Fund); Maybe Magazine – for a youth music project (£5,000 from thecentre:mk Fund and NHBC Fund); Hanslope Village Hall Trust – towards repairs (£3,000 from the Brighton Acorn Fund); SCOPE – for an IT project for people with disabilities (£2,400 from the Margaret Powell Fund); and AKOTA – to fund a pilot project offering a Bengali language course to children (£1,000 from the Grassroots Fund.)

Exclusions

No grants are made to the following types of organisation:

- statutory organisations – including schools, hospitals and borough councils (applications from parish councils for community projects are accepted)
- political parties or groups affiliated to a political party
- individuals.

Grants are normally not given for:

- sponsorship and fundraising events
- contributions to major appeals
- projects outside the beneficial area
- political groups
- projects connected with promoting a religious message of any kind
- work which should be funded by health and local authorities or government grants aid
- animal welfare
- medical research or treatment
- ongoing core costs not related to a particular service or activity
- retrospective grants, nor grants to pay off deficits.

Applications

Application forms and guidelines are available on the foundation's website or can be requested by telephoning the office. The grants staff can be contacted to assist with any queries or help with applications.

Deadlines for small grants programme is the last working Friday of each month and the community grants programme has five deadlines per year.

Small grant applications are usually processed within 2 weeks and community grants, 5 weeks.

The Monument Trust

Arts, health and welfare (especially AIDS) and general

£32 million (2009/10)

Beneficial area

Unrestricted, but UK and South Africa in practice.

Allington House, 1st Floor, 150 Victoria Street, London SW1E 5AE
Tel: 020 7410 0330
Fax: 020 7410 0332
Website: www.sfct.org.uk
Correspondent: Alan Bookbinder, Director
Trustees: Stewart Grimshaw; Linda Heathcoat-Amory; Sir Anthony Tennant; Charles Cator.
CC Number: 242575

Information available

Accounts were available at the Charity Commission.

Summary

This is one of the Sainsbury Family Charitable Trusts, which share a joint administration, but are otherwise independent of each other. They have a common approach to grantmaking which is described in the entry for the group as a whole. In this case the trust notes that: 'proposals are generally invited by the trustees or initiated at their request. Unsolicited applications are not generally encouraged and are unlikely to succeed, unless they closely match the areas in which the trustees are interested'.

In 2009/10 the trust had assets of £236.9 million and an income of £13.6 million, which included a further £6 million from the late Simon Sainsbury's estate. Grants were paid during the year totalling £32 million (£46.9 million worth of grants were approved, with £14.9 million to be paid in future years). The trustees anticipate continuing to make substantial grants over the coming years, in excess of the trust's income, which will be funded using the trust's expendable endowment.

The trust's main areas of interest are (with number and the value of grant approvals during the year, including support costs):

Arts and heritage	64	£30.1 million
Health and community care	69	£12.4 million
Social development	28	£4.2 million
General	3	£295,000

The trust gives the following indication of its current particular area of interest:

In the arts and heritage category [the trustees] particularly wish to be made aware of significant appeals. [They] continue to support a number of arts projects of national or regional importance. In other areas they prefer to help prove new ideas or methods that can be replicated widely and where possible become self-sustaining.

Grants in 2009/10

The following extract is taken from the 2009/10 accounts:

Arts and Heritage

Over time many of the UK's major arts and heritage institutions have received support from the trust for their work in bringing cultural treasures to a wide public. As well as the National Gallery, the British Museum, the Tate, the V&A, the Royal Opera House, the National Theatre and the National Trust, the list of beneficiaries includes many regional museums, galleries, gardens, theatres and heritage trusts. The trust has helped rescue exceptional pieces of fine art and sometimes whole houses and gardens for public enjoyment.

Grants paid during the year included those to: Fitzwilliam Museum – Cambridge (£2.4 million*), towards major exhibitions and selected other initiatives; The Great Steward of Scotland's Dumfries House Trust (£2 million), towards the further conservation and development of Dumfries House; Royal Academy of Arts (£1.5 million*), towards the entrance hall renovation; London Library (£1 million), towards a capital appeal; Victoria & Albert Museum (£660,000*); Public Catalogue Foundation (£500,000), towards the digitisation programme; Liverpool and Merseyside Theatres Trust Limited (£300,000), towards rebuilding the Everyman Theatre in Liverpool; Midhurst Town Trust (£200,000), towards improvements to the Midhurst market square and part of Church Hill; and the University of Cambridge Development Office (£150,000*).

Health and Community Care

The trust has long funded areas of public health and social care which struggled to find support elsewhere. During a period when AIDS was widely stigmatized, the trust helped organisations such as Body Positive, London Lighthouse, Crusaid and Red Admiral to establish themselves. The trust continues to fund leading HIV/AIDS charities, both in the UK and Southern Africa. Parkinson's Disease is also of special interest to the trustees. They also respond to appeals across a range of social issues where they believe they can bring significant benefit, such as homelessness, drug addiction and teenage pregnancy.

Grants paid during the year included those to: Parkinson's Disease Society (£1.5 million*), towards the research project 'Understanding the early pathological pathways in Parkinson's Disease' at the University of Oxford; Homerton University Hospital NHS Foundation Trust (£580,000*), towards the building refurbishment and running costs of the Hospital's HIV care centre; Sheffield Institute

Foundation for Motor Neurone Disease (£250,000), towards the capital appeal for the Sheffield Institute of Translational Neuroscience; South African HIV Clinicians' Society (£222,000*), for the development of a national nurse education programme in South Africa; Stonewall (£200,000*), towards 'Education for All', Stonewall's national programme to tackle homophobic bullying in schools in England and Wales; and Revolving Doors Agency (£150,000*), towards core costs.

Social Development

Criminal justice has been an abiding concern of the trustees, particularly the need to give offenders the chance to rehabilitate themselves and make a beneficial contribution to society. Arts in prison, education of offenders, employment schemes and sympathetic mentoring are of particular interest to the trustees. They also support projects which address the most troubled offenders, where the risk may be high but the potential public benefit is great. The trustees also take an interest in homelessness, especially projects which encourage the homeless to take an active role in management.

Grants paid during the year included those to: Inspiring Scotland (£350,000*); Khulisa – South Africa (£200,000*); Prison Radio Association (£200,000), towards the national syndication and programme production service; Bankside Open Spaces Trust (£180,000*), to support development of community gardening in north Southwark and Lambeth; Corston Independent Funders' Coalition (£175,000), towards the Women's Diversionary Fund, a collaborative fund to help organisations to develop one-stop-shop services for women offenders; Natural Justice (£150,000*), towards running costs; and Broadway (£140,000*), towards a resettlement worker and a property-landlord negotiator to expedite homeless people's moving on from hostel spaces to private tenancies.

General

The Ashden Awards (£250,000), towards the 2010 and 2011 Awards.

*part of a multi-year award, some of which were approved in previous years.

Exclusions

Grants are not normally made to individuals.

Applications

See the guidance for applicants in the entry for the Sainsbury Family Charitable Trusts. A single application will be considered for support by all the trusts in the group.

'Proposals are generally invited by the Trustees or initiated at their request. Unsolicited applications are not generally encouraged and are unlikely to succeed, unless they closely match the areas in which the Trustees are interested.'

The Henry Moore Foundation

Fine arts, in particular sculpture, and projects and exhibitions which expand the definition of sculpture, such as film, photography and performance

£857,000 (2009/10)

Beneficial area

UK and overseas.

Henry Moore Foundation, Dane Tree House, Perry Green, Much Hadham, Hertfordshire SG10 6EE
Tel: 01279 843 333
Fax: 01279 843 647
Email: admin@henry-moore.org
Website: www.henry-moore.org/
Correspondent: Charles M Joint, Grant Contact
Trustees: Marianne Brouwer; Greville Worthington; Dawn Ades; Simon Keswick; James Joll; Malcolm Baker; Duncan Robinson; Laure Genillard.
CC Number: 271370

Information available

Accounts were on file at the Charity Commission. The foundation also has an informative website.

The foundation was established in 1977 to promote the public's appreciation of the fine arts and in particular the works of Henry Moore. It concentrates most of its support on sculpture. The aims of the foundation are achieved through specific projects initiated within the foundation both at Perry Green and in Leeds, particularly exhibitions and publications, and by giving grant aid to other suitable enterprises.

The foundation's grant-making programme has been revised to provide additional financial resources to support the work of living artists and contemporary art practice. Special consideration is given to projects outside London and to venues with limited opportunities to show contemporary art. The foundation is willing to support projects in the UK which involve artists from another country but overseas projects must include a British component.

Grantmaking

In 2009/10 the foundation had assets of £97.4 million and an income of £1.8 million. £2.4 million was spent on funding the Moore institutions and their exhibitions, publications, library, the Perry Green estate, research and works of art acquisitions. Grants were paid totalling £857,000 in the following categories:

New projects
This includes exhibitions, exhibition catalogues and new commissions. Grants will be awarded as follows, up to a maximum of: £20,000 for a large museum exhibition; £10,000 for an exhibition catalogue; £30,000 for a commission.

Beneficiaries include: *Revealed: Turner Contemporary Opens*, Turner Contemporary, Margate (£20,000); Klaus Weber, *If you leave me, I'm not coming,* and *Already there!* Nottingham Contemporary (£12,000); and Liverpool Biennial 2010 – five commissions, *International 10: Touched* (£10,000).

Collections
This is designed to provide minor capital grants help public institutions acquire, display and conserve sculpture. The maximum grants available will be around £15,000 for acquisition, £20,000 for display and £20,000 for conservation and/or display.

Grants have been made to: Sculpture display in new and refurbished galleries, National Museum, Cardiff (£20,000); and the acquisition of Henry Moore, *Reclining Figure* for the Gropius House, Lincoln, Massachusetts (£7,000).

Research and development
For sculptural projects whether creative (e.g. contemporary commissions), academic (e.g. permanent collection catalogues of sculpture) or practical (e.g. a long-term conservation project) that require funding for more than one year. Maximum grants are likely to be in the region of £20,000 per annum.

Grants have been made to Penrose Film Productions, Sussex for an online collection database (£15,000).

Fellowships
For artists: grants of up to £6,000 each are available to artists, who are supported by host institutions, for fellowships or residences of 2–6 months.

Beneficiaries include: Artist's residencies Enschede, The Netherlands for Anthony Schrag (£3,000); and International Ceramic Research Centre, Guldagergaard, Denmark for Malgorzata Jablonska (£6,000).

For post-doctoral research: two year fellowships available to scholars who have recently finished their PhD to allow them to develop publications. Three or four fellowships will usually be awarded in the spring.
Applications must be supported by an appropriate UK university department.

Conferences, lectures and publications
Grants of up to £5,000 are available. Please note a publication can be a book or a journal but not an exhibition catalogue or a permanent collection catalogue. If applying for a publication, please specify within the application, how and where the publication will be distributed.

Beneficiaries include: *The Burlington Magazine*, London – sculpture coverage June 2010-July 2011 (£5,000); and FACT, Liverpool – conference: *The Future is Now: Media arts, performance and identity after Nam June Paik* (£3,000).

Exclusions
The foundation does not give grants to individual applicants (except in the fellowship category) or for revenue expenditure. No grant (or any part of grant) may be used to pay any fee or to provide any other benefit to any individual who is a trustee of the foundation.

Applications
Applicants should complete an application form which is available on the trust's website. Applications must be posted to the grants administrator. Applications will be acknowledged by letter.

The grants committee meets quarterly; please consult the trust's website for exact dates as the trust advises that applications received late will not be considered until the next meeting. It is advised to leave six months between the grants committee meeting and the project start date as funds cannot be paid for retrospective projects.

Applicants should also advise the foundation whether it is envisaged that any trustee will have an interest in the project for which a grant is sought.

John Moores Foundation

Social welfare in Merseyside and Northern Ireland, emergency relief overseas

£738,000 (2009/10)

Beneficial area
Primarily Merseyside (plus Skelmersdale, Ellesmere Port and Halton); Northern Ireland; and overseas.

7th Floor, Gostins Building, 32–36 Hanover Street, Liverpool L1 4LN
Tel: 0151 707 6077
Fax: 0151 707 6066
Email: info@johnmooresfoundation.com
Website: www.jmf.org.uk

Correspondent: Phil Godfrey, Grants Director
Trustees: Barnaby Moores; Kevin Moores; Nicola Eastwood; Alison Navarro.
CC Number: 253481

Information available
Accounts were on file at the Charity Commission. The foundation also has a very comprehensive website.

The foundation was established in 1964 with aims and objectives which were widely drawn at the beginning to allow for changing patterns of need. During the last twenty years the foundation has confined giving to four main categories:
- Merseyside – this is the priority area and receives 60–80% of the annual grant total
- Northern Ireland – usually receives around 15% of annual grants
- World crises – including man-made or natural disasters such as famine, flood or earthquake, which by definition require large one-off grants to prevent loss of life. These donations are usually made to major relief agencies
- One-off exceptional grants to causes that interest the trustees.

Please note: the foundation does not respond to unsolicited applications in the last two categories.

The foundation aims to enable people who are marginalised, as a result of social, educational, physical, economic, cultural, geographical or other disadvantage, to improve their social conditions and quality of life by way of making grants. It prefers to assist small, grass-roots and volunteer driven organisations and new rather than long-established groups, particularly those groups that find it more than usually difficult to raise money.

In line with the foundation's commitment to equal opportunities, it supports projects which aim to counter racism, sexism or discrimination of any kind. Projects which particularly focus on such anti-discrimination would be expected to have substantial input from the discriminated groups concerned.

Consideration is given to organisations working in the

foundation's target areas for giving, which are:

- grass roots community groups
- black and minority ethnic organisations
- women including girls
- second chance learning
- advice and information to alleviate poverty
- support and training for voluntary organisations.

And, in Merseyside only:

- people with disabilities
- carers
- refugees
- homeless people
- child care
- complementary therapies.

The foundation is an enabling funder and would like to help groups achieve their targets and outcomes in their own way. Groups can be given advice with setting up monitoring and evaluation systems that best meet their needs and capacity.

Guidelines

The guidelines for applicants, detailed on the foundation's website, read as follows:

We make grants towards:

- start up and running costs
- volunteer and programme costs
- education and training costs
- one-off project costs
- equipment
- salaries.

We will consider funding:

Local community groups

Local community groups/projects in disadvantaged areas, run by and for local people, including support and self-help groups, tenants' associations, and community action. Where there are unmet needs in the community we would support fresh approaches and new ideas for tackling them. We also encourage networking with groups doing similar work either locally or in other regions.

Black and minority ethnic organisations

Projects run by and for people from black and minority ethnic communities, including travellers and migrant workers, especially those which work towards redressing the disadvantage faced by such groups. Projects may be broad-based or concentrate on a particular group, e.g. women, elders, etc. We also support non-black community groups who are developing and implementing culturally sensitive policies, and cross-community trust-building initiatives.

Refugees

Projects working towards emergency support to incoming refugees (including legal advice) and helping their integration into community life including basic education, literacy, training, health and general social welfare. Schemes that target excluded people within the refugee community and initiatives that enable them to meet their own needs are also supported.

Women including girls

Projects which work towards redressing the disadvantages faced by women in society, including women's health and support groups, literacy and second chance learning.

Youth

Local groups running projects in disadvantaged areas which provide facilities or opportunities for children and young people (up to the age of 21), e.g. play-schemes, youth clubs, and detached youth work. We would particularly encourage projects which are, or which are working towards being, user-led.

Family support

Projects giving support to families to allow parents to access learning/ employment. This would also include parenting skills, mutual support/self help, families in crisis, and childcare. After school clubs and playgroups etc. might only be funded where there is a family support element.

Second chance learning

Projects run by non-statutory organisations which enable people who have little or no education to return to learning. Grants may be given to organisations towards the cost of courses (including tutors), childcare, advice and information services etc.

Homeless people

Projects to provide services for homeless people or to furnish accommodation including: provision of emergency food, shelter and clothing; support, advice and advocacy; and training and second chance learning.

Advice and information to alleviate poverty

Projects providing welfare rights, or other advice and information services, to alleviate poverty. Priority will be given to funding local independent advice projects, and we will not normally fund those which are part of a national network. Groups would be encouraged to hold or to be working towards a nationally-recognised quality standard in advice-giving.

Grassroots social health initiatives

Projects run by local non-statutory organisations which aim to improve people's physical and/or mental health. Priority will be given to projects in disadvantaged areas where health problems arise from social and environmental factors, and which work with vulnerable groups. Issues might include stress, HIV/AIDS, self-harm, substance misuse etc.

Support and training for voluntary organisations

Training for voluntary and community organisations to enhance the skills particularly of management committee members, but also of staff, to enable them to operate more effectively and improve the quality of the service they offer. Funding is also available for the recruitment and training of volunteers. We will consider applications from Credit Unions for the training of management committee members or the development of a new business plan.

People with disabilities

Projects for adults with disabilities, which would be expected to have substantial input from people with disabilities in the running of the project.

Carers

Projects which benefit carers by the provision of support services, advice, information or non-medical respite care.

Grants in 2009/10

During the year the trust held assets of £24.4 million and had an income of £876,000. 157 grants were made totalling £738,000. Of these 42 were revenue grants of more than one year. Approximately 63 % of grants given in Merseyside and 91% of grants given in Northern Ireland were for £5,000 or less, with the average in Northern Ireland being £4,117. Grants were broken down into areas as shown in the table at the top of the following page.

Beneficiaries in Merseyside included: Sefton Advocacy and St Joseph's Hospice Association (£9,000 each); Lyndale Knowsley Cancer Support Group (£8,000); Norris Green Community Alliance (£7,000); Croxteth Child Development Service (£6,000); Somali Umbrella Group (£5,400); One Vision Housing (£5,200); West Lancashire Crossroads Caring for Carers and Tranmere Action Group (£5,000 each); Bread of Life Community Project (£4,500); Sefton Women & Children's Aid (£2,600); Kenyan Community Liverpool (£2,000); The Bridge Project (£1,600); and Step Forward (£1,200).

Beneficiaries in Northern Ireland included: East Belfast Independent Advice Centre (£7,000); Homeplus

JOHN MOORES FOUNDATION

Area	Merseyside	Northern Ireland
Advice	£22,400	£7,000
Black and ethnic minority organisations	£52,000	£7,000
Carers	£11,000	
Childcare	£6,000	£23,000
Community organisations	£78,000	£71,000
Complementary therapy	£17,000	
Disabled people	£26,000	£1,000
Family support	£45,000	
Grassroots social health	£6,200	
Homeless people	£4,500	£8,000
Refugees/asylum seekers	£7,500	
Second chance learning	£19,000	
Social welfare	£42,000	£27,000
Training for community groups	£11,500	£5,000
Women	£10,000	£50,000
Young people	£48,000	£22,000
Total	**£407,000**	**£232,000**

(£5,500); Polish Abroad, Northern Ireland Anti-Poverty Network and Ballybeen Women's Group (£5,000 each); Threeways Community Association (£3,000); Pennyburn Community Playgroup and Belfast Interface Project (£2,000 each); Shopmobility Lisburn (£1,000); and Lettershandoney & District Youth Project (£840).

Two international donations of £50,000 were made to UNICEF (emergency relief in the Philippines, Sumatra and Samoa) and the Disasters Emergency Committee (Haiti earthquake).

Exclusions

Generally the foundation does not fund:

- individuals
- national organisations or groups based outside Merseyside even where some of the service users come from the area
- statutory bodies or work previously done by them
- mainstream education (schools, colleges, universities)
- faith-based projects exclusively for members of that faith, or for the promotion of religion
- capital building costs – except to improve access for disabled people
- festivals, carnivals and fêtes
- medicine and health – except under the headings listed above
- holidays, expeditions and outings
- gifts, parties etc
- sport
- vehicles
- animal charities

- arts, crafts, heritage, or local history projects
- conservation and environmental projects
- employment and enterprise schemes
- victims – except rape crisis and domestic violence projects
- academic or medical research
- uniformed groups (e.g. scouts, cadets, majorettes)
- sponsorship, advertising or fund-raising events.

Applications may be refused where the foundation considers that the organisation concerned is already well funded or has excessive reserves.

Unsolicited applications which fall outside the policy criteria are not considered. Unsolicited applications for the categories World Crises and One-off exceptional grants are not responded to.

Applications

Please refer to the foundation's website and make sure your project falls within the criteria. If you are unsure, or if you would like to discuss your application before submitting it, please telephone the foundation staff who will be happy to advise you.

Applications should be made by letter (no more than four sides of A4) accompanied by a completed application form. Application forms and guidance notes can be obtained by letter, phone or email or from the foundation's website.

Decisions about which projects to fund are made by the trustees who

meet five to six times a year to consider Merseyside applications and four times a year to consider Northern Ireland applications. As a general rule, Merseyside applicants should allow three to four months for a decision to be made, and applicants from Northern Ireland should allow four to five months. Applicants are welcome to telephone the foundation to find out at which meeting their application will be considered.

Common applicant mistakes

'Mistakes in adding up the budget; not including all the paperwork requested.'

The Peter Moores Foundation

The arts, particularly opera, social welfare

£2.4 million (2009/10)

Beneficial area

UK and Barbados.

c/o Wallwork, Nelson and Johnson, Chandler House, 7 Ferry Road, Riversway, Preston PR2 2YH
Tel: 01772 430000
Fax: 01772 430012
Email: moores@pmf.org.uk
Website: www.pmf.org.uk
Correspondent: Peter Saunders, Administrator
Trustees: Michael Johnson, Chair; Eileen Ainscough; Ludmilla Andrew; Nicholas Payne; Kirsten Suenson-Taylor; Joanna Laing.
CC Number: 258224

Information available

Accounts were available from the Charity Commission. The trust also has a website.

Summary

The foundation concentrates on supporting opera and other forms of music, and the opera-connected Compton Verney House project which receives up to one-third of the available funds. Education and health organisations have also been supported. Peter Moores himself worked professionally in opera.

General

The trust supports:

- the creation and staging of new operatic work in the UK
- student singers and young artists to maintain college studies and projects to expand their professional experience
- music organisations providing training and performance opportunities for young singers and conductors
- Compton Verney House, the new museum-art gallery opened in 2004
- health (especially AIDS), environmental, education and youth projects in the UK and Barbados.

In 2009/10 the trust held assets of £592,000 and had an income of £4.2 million. The large majority of funding comes from the Peter Moores Charitable Trust which serves only to fund the Peter Moores Foundation and, to a lesser extent, Compton Verney House. Grants were made totalling £2.4 million and were broken down as follows:

Musical performance	£111,000
Fine art	£1.9 million
Music education	£89,000
Heritage	£22,000
Youth and education	£49,000
Social	£93,000
Health	£149,000

Beneficiaries included: Compton Verney House Trust (£1.8 million); University of the West Indies (£52,000); Childline (£40,000); Opera Group (£44,000); Rossini in Wilbad (£16,000); Royal Opera House (£8,700); Compton Verney Collection Settlement (£15,000); National Opera Studio main scholarship (£17,000); Royal Philharmonic Society Main Scholarship (£14,000); Sunflowers Foundation (£15,000); and HIV/AIDS charities (£131,000).

Applications

In writing to the correspondent, but applicants should be aware that the foundation has previously stated that it 'will normally support projects which come to the attention of its patron or trustees through their interests or special knowledge. General applications for sponsorship are not encouraged and are unlikely to succeed.'

The Mulberry Trust

General

£603,000 (2009/10)

Beneficial area

UK, with an interest in Harlow, Essex and surrounding areas, including London.

Farrer and Co, 66 Lincoln's Inn Fields, London WC2A 3LH
Tel: 020 7242 2022
Correspondent: Ms Cheryl Boyce
Trustees: John G Marks; Mrs Ann M Marks; Charles F Woodhouse; Timothy J Marks; Chris Marks; Rupert Marks; William Marks.
CC Number: 263296

Information available

Accounts were available at the Charity Commission.

Around 70 grants are made each year, most being for amounts of £5,000 or less. Grants go to a wide range of causes, with both local institutions, including hospices and universities, and national charities receiving funding. Around half the grants seem to go to regularly supported recipients.

In 2009/10 the trust had assets of £6.7 million and an income of £186,000. Grants were made to 87 organisations totalling £603,000, broken down as follows:

Christian church and leadership	14	£169,000
Education and research	13	£152,500
Parenting, the family and children's work	12	£81,000
The disadvantaged	15	£74,500
Health	12	£52,500
The community and environment	7	£25,000
Debt relief and counselling	2	£25,000
The arts	2	£13,000
Homelessness	1	£5,000
Other material grants	3	£3,000
Grants of £500 or less	6	£2,800

Beneficiaries included: The Cambridge Foundation and the Foundation for Church Leadership (£100,000 each); Prison Dialogue (£30,000); Calm Centre Ltd (£25,000); NSPCC (£20,000); Stewardship (£15,000); Parents Like Us (£11,000); Credit Action and the Royal National Theatre (£10,000);

Home Start Witham (£9,000); Boston Stump Restoration Development Trust, Church Housing Trust and Victim Support Essex (£5,000 each); Royal Academy of Arts (£3,000); and the Williams Syndrome Foundation (£1,000).

Applications

The trust has stated that it 'will not, as a matter of policy, consider applications which are unsolicited'.

Common applicant mistakes

'Not reading the criteria for eligibility. Not reading the (very simple) application form, therefore not answering the questions adequately. Forgetting to say how much money they need over what period and waffling on for too long.'

The Edith Murphy Foundation

General, individual hardship, animals, children and the disabled

£1.2 million (2009/10)

Beneficial area

UK with some preference for Leicestershire.

C/o Crane and Walton, 113–117 London Road, Leicester LE2 0RG
Tel: 0116 2551901
Correspondent: David L Tams, Trustee
Trustees: David L Tams; Pamela M Breakwell; Christopher P Blakesley; Richard F Adkinson.
CC Number: 1026062

Information available

Accounts were available at the Charity Commission.

The foundation was set up in 1993 by the late Mrs Murphy in memory of her late husband, Mr Hugh Murphy, with the following objectives:

- to assist those who by reason of their age, youth, infirmity, disablement, poverty or social and economic circumstances are suffering hardship or distress or are otherwise in need

▸ to provide relief of suffering of animals of any species who are in need of care and attention and the provision and maintenance of facilities of any description for the reception and care of unwanted animals and the treatment of sick or ill-treated animals

▸ to make donations for general charitable purposes.

Following the death of Mrs Murphy in 2005, her will provided for the foundation to receive certain benefits including a proportion of the residue of her estate. The value of the benefits received the following year amounted to £28.2 million. A further £1.8 million was added in 2007. This has resulted in the level of grant giving increasing substantially in recent years.

In the year 2009/10 the foundation held assets of £31 million and had an income of £683,000. 132 grants were made totalling £1.2 million which were broken down as follows:

Welfare	£1 million
Education	£65,000
Children's charities	£64,000
Animal charities	£48,000
Help for disabled people	£29,000

The most significant beneficiaries were: University of Leicester – cardiovascular research centre (£375,000); Parish of Dromintee – new graveyard for St Patrick's Church, County Armagh, NI (£100,000); De Montford University – work on diabetes (£50,000); Vitalise – sufferers of Alzheimer's and their carers (£47,000); and University of Leicester – Student's Union building (£46,000).

Other beneficiaries included: The Stroke Association (£30,000); Motor Neurone Disease Association (£20,000); PDSA (£15,000); Rainbow Children's Hospice, Launde Abbey, Leicester Charity Link and RSPCA (£10,000 each).

£10,000 was made in grants to individuals through Leicester Charity Link.

Applications

In writing to the correspondent.

The John R Murray Charitable Trust

Arts and literature

£1.2 million (2010)

Beneficial area

UK.

50 Albemarle Street, London W1S 4BD
Correspondent: The Trustees
Trustees: John R Murray; Virginia G Murray; Hallam J R G Murray; John O G Murray; Charles J G Murray.
CC Number: 1100199

Information available

Accounts were available at the Charity Commission.

Established in 2003, the trust supports organisations promoting the arts and literature. The following extract is taken from the trust's 2010 accounts:

> The trustees will normally only make grants or loans to other registered charities in area in which the trustees have an interest in the arts an literature (although not strictly limited to such areas) and where the award of a grant will have an immediate and tangible benefit to the recipient in question.
>
> In the medium term the trustees' principal aim will be the continued support of the National Library of Scotland (as the ownership of the John Murray Archive) and its curatorial and preservation responsibilities for the archive as well as developing its support of the arts and in particular literature.

In 2010 the trust had assets of £25.1 million and an income of £784,000. Grants to 47 organisations totalled just over £1.2 million.

Beneficiaries included: National Library of Scotland (£322,000); Abbotsford Trust (£61,500); Friends of Highgate Cemetery Trust (£50,000); Save (£48,000); British School at Rome (£39,000); Kew Foundation (£25,000); College of Arms (£20,000); Historic Chapels Trust (£15,000); Anglo Peruvian Society (£10,000); South East Prisoner Forum Project (£7,500); Royal Society of Literature (£6,000);

Music Works (£5,000); and British Red Cross Haiti Appeal (£2,000).

Applications

The trustees will not consider unsolicited applications for grants.

The National Art Collections Fund

Acquisition of works of art by museums and galleries

£6.6 million (2010)

Beneficial area

UK.

Millais House, 7 Cromwell Place, London SW7 2JN
Tel: 020 7225 4800
Fax: 020 7225 4848
Email: grants@artfund.org
Website: www.artfund.org
Correspondent: Johnathan Guy Cubitt
Trustees: David Verey; Paul Zuckerman; Dr Wendy Baron; Prof. Michael Craig-Martin; Christopher Lloyd; Jonathan Marsden; Charles Sebag-Montefiore; Timothy Stevens; Dr Deborah Swallow; Prof. William Vaughan; Sally Osman; James Lingwood; Richard Calvocoressi; Caroline Butler; Prof Chris Gosden; Antony Griffiths; Lisa Tickner; Michael Wilson.
CC Number: 209174

Information available

Accounts were available from the Charity Commission. An annual review, with accounts, which gives a full illustrated record of all works assisted, is also available. Very comprehensive website.

Known simply as The Art Fund, this fundraising and membership charity believes that everyone should have the opportunity to experience great art at first hand, and it works to achieve this by:

▸ enriching museums and galleries throughout the UK with works of art of all kinds

▸ campaigning for the widest possible access to art

promoting the enjoyment of art through its membership scheme.

The Art Fund's grant-giving policy is to support applications for financial assistance towards acquisitions by fully or provisionally accredited museums, galleries and historic houses of works of art of all kinds, dating from antiquity to the present day. It also receives gifts and bequests of works of art for presentation to public collections and helps to secure works of national and international importance, and good quality works of great local interest.

The trust has a main grants scheme for applications of above £5,000. These are considered at board meetings which are held 6 times a year where the trustees will expect the work under consideration to be brought to the meeting and should be informed as soon as possible if this will not be the case.

There is also a small grants scheme for under £5,000 (usually). These may be submitted at any time and applicants can expect to wait 3–4 weeks for a decision. Works will need to be viewed but this can be arranged at a convenient location.

This fund can also fast-track applications for potential acquisitions coming up at auction. They need 7 working days for work at auction in London and 10 for work at auction outside London (including international auctions).

From time to time the Art Fund runs other funding initiatives; applicants should check the website for details of these.

Grantmaking in 2010

The trustees state in their 2010 annual report that:

The pressure on budgets and spending in museums had a noticeable impact on our grant giving this year. Fewer applications were received, a fall of 7% from 2009 but the average grant requested was significantly higher- £55,000 compared to £29,000 last year. As a result the average grant given rose to £36,000 compared to £26,000 in 2009.

During the year the fund held assets of £34 million and had an income of £10 million. Grants were made totalling £6.6 million.

The most significant beneficiaries were: Birmingham Museum and Gallery, Potteries Museum & Art Gallery- Staffordshire Hoard (£1.4 million each); Warwickshire Museum (£500,000); Glasgow Gallery of Modern Art (£425,000); and Nostell Priory (National Trust) – Brueghel Appeal (£419,000).

Other beneficiaries included: British Museum (£260,000); Cecil Higgins Art Gallery (£196,000); Dulwich Picture Gallery (£90,000); National Media Museum (£49,000); Powis Castle (£25,000); Whitworth Art Gallery (£24,000); Nottingham Castle (£5,000); Paisley Art Gallery and Observatory (£3,300); Museum of Transport (£2,000); and Potteries Museum and Art Gallery (£310).

Exclusions

- Applications where the applicant has already purchased or made a commitment to purchase the object, or made a financial commitment.
- Other costs associated with acquisitions such as the conservation and restoration of works, transport and storage costs, temporary or permanent exhibitions and digitisation projects.
- Applications from individuals, artist's groups, commercial organisations, hospitals, places of worship, schools or higher education institutions.
- Funding towards professional development, travel or research.

Applications

Firstly discuss the application with a member of the programmes office then register on the website to access the online application form. The Art Fund 'actively encourages strong applications from national and designated museums for objects which will enrich their collections and supports their effort s to expand into new collecting areas when appropriate. The Art Fund considers applications for whatever amount is needed. Applicants are expected also to apply for any public funding for which they might be eligible, and to raise funds from other sources if they can'. 'The Grants Office requires all applications to be made online. Please see our website for full details and contact the Grants team to discuss any potential application.'

The National Churches Trust (formerly the Historic Churches Preservation Trust with the Incorporated Church Building Society)

Preservation of historic churches

£1.3 million (2010)

Beneficial area

UK.

31 Newbury Street, London
EC1A 7HU
Tel: 020 7600 6090
Fax: 020 7796 2442
Email: info@nationalchurchestrust.org
Website: www.nationalchurchestrust.org
Correspondent: Miriam Campbell
Trustees: Charlotte Cole; Richard Carr-Archer; Michael Hoare; Anthony Wedgwood; John Readman; John Drew; Rev Nicholas Holtam; Jennifer Page.
CC Number: 1119845

Information available

Accounts were available at the Charity Commission. The trust also has an informative website.

Summary

The National Churches Trust was launched in 2007 as a national, non-profit organisation dedicated to supporting and promoting places of worship used by Christian denominations in the UK. The trust promotes the use of these buildings by congregations and the wider community. It also advocates the conservation of places of worship of historic value for the use and enjoyment of future generations.

The trust was formed to act as a catalyst within the sector and to consolidate and expand the role played by its two predecessor charities, the Historic Churches Preservation Trust and the Incorporated Church Building Society (see below).

Its key roles are to:

▶ encourage good management practices and regular maintenance by providing advice on access to funding, support and training and by developing and implementing practical solutions to the needs of the sector

▶ provide an annual grants programme of £2 million that allocates funds for both building restoration and modernisation

▶ encourage projects that benefit communities, integrate places of worship fully into their local areas and enable buildings to be open to the wider public

▶ work to enhance the public and governmental perception of and support for Christian places of worship.

General

In 2008 the Charity Commission appointed the National Churches Trust (NCT) as the sole trustee of the Historic Churches Preservation Trust (HCPT) and also granted a 'uniting direction'. Consequently, the NCT and HCPT are treated as a single charity for administrative, accounting and regulatory purposes. They will however, remain legally distinct so that the HCPT will operate as restricted funds within the NCT. A similar process is envisaged for the Incorporated Church Building Society (ICBS), which has been managed by the HCPT since 1983.

Founded in 1953, the HCPT, now the National Churches Trust (NCT), is the leading fundraising body involved in the restoration of architecturally and historically significant parish churches. Over the decades, work that was originally begun to reverse the neglect brought about by the socio-economic changes of the late 19th and early 20th centuries and to repair the damage of World War II has

become increasingly important and far-reaching.

The trust has helped virtually every church named in Simon Jenkins' 'England's Thousand Best Churches'. Whichever way the grants are analysed – by architectural style or importance, historical interest or significance, by geographical area, by rural or urban community, by denomination – the trust's net has been spread wide. Wales is the newcomer to the grants system, as the trust's remit was only extended to the Principality in 1987. With the support of the Esme Mitchell Trust, since 1984 a small number of churches in Northern Ireland have also been helped. Over £27 million in grants and loans to churches of all denominations has been awarded in the UK.

Spreading awareness of the needs of churches and encouraging participation in their restoration and revival at both national and local level is also an important part of the trust's remit. Six local county trusts – in Cheshire, Essex, Kent, Lincolnshire, Staffordshire and Wiltshire were active when the trust was established. Since then, most of England has been covered.

The trust has often helped with the first essential tranche of money to get things under way, but the county trusts are all individual and independent. Representatives from the local trusts have always been members of the trust's grants committee and their ground level knowledge is considered essential in understanding the situation and pressures facing the local area. At the time of writing, only Wales, Lancashire, Cumbria and the metropolitan districts of London, Birmingham and Merseyside have no local trust.

The NCT receives no government funding, other than via the Gift Aid scheme and relies entirely on voluntary giving. The majority of income comes from legacies and grant making trusts and foundations, with the remaining balance made up from donations from places of worship, members of the public, subscriptions from 'Friends' and investment income.

During 2010 the trust continued to review the structure, size and priorities of the annual grants programme.

Guidelines

To help those applying for grants, the trust has developed detailed guidelines on how to apply. The funds and the corresponding guidelines change frequently so it is advisable to check the trust's website before applying.

The trust advises that before applicants complete an application pack, it is important for them to make sure that their project will be eligible by checking it meets the following criteria:

▶ the building must be open for regular public worship – the trust does not currently have grants available for cathedrals, but any other Christian places of worship can apply if they meet the eligibility criteria

▶ it must be sited in England, Northern Ireland, the Isle of Man, Scotland or Wales

▶ the congregation must belong to a denomination that is a member or associated member of Churches Together in Britain and Ireland

▶ all projects must be overseen by an architect who is either ARB, RIBA or AABC accredited, or by a chartered surveyor who is RICS accredited.

The trust managed the following grants programmes during 2011, and their website states that: 'We envisage offering similar programmes during 2012. This is dependent on income and available resources.' Full details of these programmes will be published on the trust's website from January 2012; therefore applicants are strongly encouraged to check this for updated funding programmes and guidelines before applying. The following extract is taken from a guidance document, avalable in full on the trust's website:

Partnership Grants Programme – In 2011 to 2013 the trust is working with a number of partner organisations around the UK to help Christian places of worship with grants of £2,500 to £10,000 towards structural repair projects that will cost less than £50,000. These organisations are working in partnership with us, using their local knowledge and expertise to ensure that grants reach the places they are most needed. The grants are available through several County Churches Trusts in England and through the Scottish Churches Architectural Heritage Trust in Scotland. Applications should be made directly to the organisations involved and not to the National Churches Trust.

For a list of participating local organisations please consult the trust's website.

WREN (Waste Recycling Environmental Ltd) – The National Churches Trust is pleased to be working with WREN to administer a number of grants on their behalf. If your place of worship is sited within a 10 mile radius of a landfill site operated by Waste Recycling Group (WRG Ltd) you may qualify for one of these grants. A limited number of grants are available. These are for urgent structural repair projects (to Grade I or II∗ listed buildings only) with an estimated cost of at least £50,000. The work, or a significant portion of the work, must not begin before the WREN Board make their decision.

To apply please contact: grants@ nationalchurchestrust.org to receive the relevant forms.

The Repair Grants Programme – This programme offered the opportunity to apply for grants of £10,000 and above for urgent and essential structural repair projects. In addition to meeting other eligibility criteria, projects demonstrated estimated costs of at least £50,000 including VAT and fees to qualify. The trust's main priority in 2011 was repairs to roofs and rainwater goods. There were a small number of grants of £40,000 and above available.

The Community Grants Programme – This programme allowed places of worship to apply for grants of £5,000 to £25,000 towards projects enabling the wider use of places of worship. In 2011 the trust was particularly interested in new toilets and catering facilities but these could form part of a larger project. Applicants had to be able to demonstrate a need and local demand for the facilities. Projects had to demonstrate an estimated cost of at least £25,000.

Grantmaking in 2010

In 2010 the trust had assets of £3.4 million and an income of £1.5 million. There were 123 grants made totalling £1.3 million.

Grants in 2010 were awarded by denomination as follows:

Anglican	102
Methodist	6
Catholic	4
Presbyterian	4
Society of Friends	3
United Reformed	2

A full list of beneficiaries was unfortunately not included with the 2010 accounts. However, the trust website details some recent grant recipients, these include: Saltaire United Reformed Church – Yorkshire (£40,000) for repairs; St Patrick – Glasgow (£20,000) for repair and conservation of the building fabric, including repairs to the roof and gutters; Zion Baptist Church – Cambridge (£10,000) for building work to develop a vestibule used as a homeless shelter; St Mary's Parish Church – Carmarthenshire, Wales (£10,000) for urgent repairs to the tower and spire and repainting work; and St Leonard – Herefordshire (£5,000) towards the cost of incorporating community amenities within the Church.

Exclusions

Please be aware that the trust cannot make grants for certain purposes including:

▶ non-church buildings (such as church halls and vicarages)
▶ bell repairs
▶ organ repairs
▶ repairs to internal furnishings
▶ redecoration, other than after structural repairs
▶ clock repairs
▶ buildings that were not originally built as places of worship
▶ to congregations that are not members or associated members of Churches Together in Britain and Ireland
▶ monument repairs.

Applications

The trust is currently reviewing funding which will be available from 2012. Please check the trust's website for up-to-date guidelines.

Applicants are advised that each fund has different application procedures. In 2010/11 applications to the Partnership Grants Programme had to be made via local Church trusts, a list of which was made available in a funding guidance document available on the trust's website. Applications for the WREN scheme were made by contacting the trust via email, expressing interest.

The Nationwide Foundation

Social welfare
£1.55 million (2009/10)

Beneficial area
UK.

Nationwide House, Pipers Way, Swindon SN38 2SN
Tel: 01793 655113
Fax: 01793 652409
Email: enquiries@ nationwidefoundation.org.uk
Website: www.nationwidefoundation. org.uk/
Correspondent: Jennifer Thompson, Grants Officer
Trustees: John Kingston, Chair; Richard Davies; Lucy Gampell; Simon Law; Karen McArthur; Dr Michael McCarthy; Chris Rhodes; Ben Stimson; Fiona Ellis; Graeme Hughes.
CC Number: 1065552

Information available

Accounts were on file at the Charity Commission. Full information and guidelines are available from the foundation's website.

This foundation is funded principally from contributions from Nationwide Building Society.

It makes grants to registered UK charities (including those in Northern Ireland) which offer financial and/or housing related support to:
1 Survivors of domestic abuse.
2 Older people.

Further information on the foundation's funding priorities is available on its website.

The foundation's small grants programme, under the heading of *Money Matters, Homes Matter, Families Matter*, offers one-off grants of between £500 and £5,000 to registered charities with an income of under £750,000.

In 2009/10 the foundation had assets of £3.3 million and an income of just under £2.2 million. Grants were made totalling £1.55 million, which included £1.15 million through the Investor Programme, £42,500 as part of a bridging fund whilst the foundation undertook a strategic review, and £351,000 under the small grants programme. The Investor Programme has since closed and was due to re-open in early 2012, however no further information was available on this status so potential applicants are advised to check the foundation's website or contact the foundation directly.

Beneficiaries receiving grants under the small grant programme highlighted in the foundation's annual report include: Black Community Development Project – Scotland (£5,000), to help establish an outreach service and employ a caseworker for people aged 50yrs+ from black and minority ethnic groups, to assist them with advice, support and management of finances, debts and benefits; St Peter's Community Advice Centre – London (£5,000), for outreach housing support, advice and help for Bangladeshi women who have been affected by domestic abuse; and Independent Living North Lincolnshire (£5,000), to assist with salary costs for the Outreach Benefits Adviser who provides a home visiting service to older people in North Lincolnshire. This service enables older people to remain living independently in their own homes and maximise income entitlement.

Exclusions
The foundation will not fund the following:

For older people:
▷ transport schemes.

For survivors of domestic abuse:
▷ counselling for survivors of domestic abuse
▷ refurbishing, equipping or running costs of refuges
▷ help to find employment.

Other exclusions which apply to all applications:
▷ charities with 'unrestricted reserves' which exceed 50% of annual expenditure, as shown in their accounts
▷ charities which are in significant debt as shown in their accounts
▷ promotion of religion or politics
▷ charities which have been declined by the foundation within the last 12 months

▷ applications which do not comply with the foundation's funding criteria/guidelines.

Applications
On an application form available from the foundation's website. Applicants should expect to wait up to three months for a final decision.

Common applicant mistakes
'Not reading the guidelines carefully and not sending all relevant information.'

Nemoral Ltd

Orthodox Jewish causes

£1.2 million (2010)

Beneficial area
Worldwide.

c/o Cohen Arnold and Co., New Burlington House, 1075 Finchley Road, London NW11 0PU
Tel: 020 8731 0777
Correspondent: Rifka Gross, Secretary
Trustees: Ellis Moore; Rifka Gross; Michael Saberski.
CC Number: 262270

Information available
Accounts were available at the Charity Commission.

The trust supports the promotion of the Jewish religion, Jewish education and the relief of poverty in the Jewish community in the UK and abroad.

In 2010 it had assets of £2.2 million and an income of £200,000. Grants were made totalling almost £1.2 million. A list of grant beneficiaries was not included in the trust's accounts.

Applications
In writing to the correspondent.

Network for Social Change

Developing world debt, environment, human rights, peace, arts and education

£833,000 (2009/10)

Beneficial area
UK and overseas.

BM 2063, London WC1N 3XX
Tel: 01647 61106
Email: thenetwork@gn.apc.org
Website: thenetworkforsocialchange.org.uk/
Correspondent: Tish McCrory, Administrator
Trustees: Sue Gillie; Bevis Gillett; Sam Clarke; Monica Marian Sanders; Sara Robin; Tom Bragg; Anthony Stoll; Cathy Debenham.
CC Number: 295237

Information available
Accounts were on file at the Charity Commission. The trust also has a useful website.

Summary
Network for Social Change, formerly the Network Foundation, is a group of philanthropic individuals who have come together to support progressive social and ecological change. Grants, mainly for up to £15,000, typically go to organisations addressing such issues as environmental sustainability and economic and social justice.

Funding is given in the UK and overseas to projects which are likely to affect social change, either through research, public education, innovatory services and other charitable activities. The network tends to favour structural change, rather than relief work, but there is no set policy on the specific types of organisations it will fund.

In each year a new major and longer-term project may also be initiated.

Organisation
The network is unusual in its organisation and offers the following information about how it operates:

Network members are each personally active in sponsoring, assessing, selecting and commending projects to fellow members. Our funding processes are designed to encourage members to find worthwhile projects, assess their potential and evaluate their achievements. Those without previous experience of such an undertaking work alongside more experienced members.

Most network members are members of one of the six Funding Pools: Arts and Education for Change, Economic Justice, Green Planet, Health and Wholeness, Human Rights and Peace. They meet two or three times a year between the biannual conferences to assess the projects that have been submitted to that pool. Two pool members are appointed as assessors to examine each project in detail, and to obtain written references from external referees. Where possible the projects are visited by the assessors. In the case of overseas projects, Network can obtain advice from well-established charitable trusts: Ashoka, Right Livelihood, Gaia Foundation, and Practical Action (formerly Intermediate Technology Development Group). Funds are raised mainly at the network conferences in February and October each year. At the February conference, the pools present the projects that they have selected, invite questions from other members, and ask for funding.

While all members participate in the process, it is clearly understood that the legal responsibility for the distribution of funds raised at the Pools meeting remains with the trustees, and that the charitable monies are given for the general purposes of Network for Social Change. On the pledging forms, members can express a preference for certain pools, but they recognise that the trustees have the final responsibility for the allocation of funds.

Matters relating to the running of network are discussed at the biannual business meetings. All members are encouraged to contribute to the running of the organisation: as conference organisers, coordinators, convenors, links with specialist sub-groups, or as directors/trustees. The trustees have final responsibility for all decisions.

In 2009/10 the trust had assets of £72,000 and an income of £877,000. Grants totalled £833,000. Unrestricted funds were broken down into the following categories:

Arts and education for change	£37,000
Economic justice	£95,000
Green planet	£85,000
Health and wholeness	£67,000
Human rights	£63,000
Peace	£73,000
Unallocated	£21,000

Peace Direct and Climate Change were awarded £57,000 and £58,000 respectively under the Major Projects restricted fund. Two new major projects were awarded a one-off grant in the year: One society which aims to combat inequality (£86,000); and New Economics Foundation which aims to produce a great transition to a new economic system (£106,000).

Other beneficiaries included: The Joseph Rowntree Charitable Trust (£89,000); the Climate Movement (£59,000); War on Want (£30,000); Raw for Women and Girl survivors of War (£21,000); Citizens UK Charity and Medical Justice Network (£15,000 each); Traidcraft Exchange (£14,000); Friends of the Earth Trust Limited (£13,000); Life Mosaic (£11,000); and Partnership for Children and the International Security Information Service (£10,000 each).

Applications

The network chooses the projects it wishes to support and does not solicit applications. Unsolicited applications cannot expect to receive a reply.

However, the network is conscious that the policy of only accepting applications brought by its members could limit the range of worthwhile projects it could fund. To address this, the network has set up a 'Project Noticeboard' to allow outside organisations to post a summary of a project for which they are seeking funding. Members of the network can then access the noticeboard and, if interested, contact the organisation for further information with a view to future sponsorship. The network states that any posts will be available on the website for six to nine months.

The Frances and Augustus Newman Foundation

Medical research and equipment

£347,000 (2009/10)

Beneficial area
UK.

c/o Baker Tilly, Chartered Accountants, Hartwell House, 55–61 Victoria Street, Bristol BS1 6AD
Tel: 0117 945 2000
Fax: 0117 945 2001
Email: hazel.palfreyman@bakertilly.co.uk
Correspondent: Hazel Palfreyman, Administrator
Trustees: Sir Rodney Sweetnam, Chair; Lord Rathcavan; John L Williams.
CC Number: 277964

Information available

Accounts were available at the Charity Commission.

The foundation aims to advance the work of medical professionals working in teaching hospitals and academic units, mostly (but not exclusively) funding medical research projects and equipment, including fellowships of the Royal College of Surgeons. Grants range from £1,000 to £100,000 a year and can be given for up to three years.

In 2009/10 the trust had assets of £11.7 million and an income of £284,500. There were 18 grants made to 14 organisations totalling £347,000.

The beneficiaries during the year were: University of Cambridge – Next Generation Fellowship (£100,000 in total); Royal College of Surgeons (£70,000 in total); Peterhouse and the Stroke Association (£50,000 each); UCL Cancer Institute and the Alzheimer's Research Trust (£20,000 each); National Centre for Young People with Epilepsy (£10,000); St Peter's Hospice (£6,000); Royal College of Physicians, Women and Medicine and the Puffin Appeal (£5,000 each); Trinity Hospice (£4,500); Nyumbani UK (£4,000); War Memorial Trust (£2,000); and Dream Makers (£1,000).

Exclusions

Applications are not normally accepted from overseas. Requests from other charities seeking funds to supplement their own general funds to support medical research in a particular field are seldom supported.

Applications

Applications should include a detailed protocol and costing and be sent to the correspondent. They may then be peer-reviewed. The trustees meet in June and December each year and applications must be received at the latest by the end of April or October respectively. The foundation awards for surgical research fellowships should be addressed to the Royal College of Surgeons of England at 35–43 Lincoln's Inn Fields, London WC2A 3PE, which evaluates each application.

Nominet Charitable Foundation

IT, education, social welfare

£2.2 million (2009/10)

Beneficial area

UK and overseas.

Nominet, Minerva House, Edmund Halley Road, Oxford Science Park, Oxford OX4 4DQ

Tel: 01865 334000

Fax: 01865 332314

Email: enquiries@nominettrust.org.uk

Website: www.nominettrust.org.uk

Correspondent: Annika Small, Director

Trustees: Jonathan Welfare, Chair; Nora Nanayakkara; James Kemp; Vanessa Miner; Ian Ritchie; Dr Peter Gradwell.

CC Number: 1125735

Information available

Accounts were available from the Charity Commission. The trust also has a clear and helpful website.

Established in 2008, this is the charitable trust of Nominet, the company which runs the registry for all .uk domain names. The Nominet Trust, the working name of the foundation, was set up with a £5 million donation from the company.

The following information on its aims and objectives is taken from the trust's website:

Areas of focus

We will consider funding UK-based initiatives that contribute to a safe, accessible Internet used to improve lives and communities. Our current areas of focus are:

- web access – providing people with the motivation, skills and tools to get online in a meaningful and sustained way
- web safety – improving understanding about the risks of being online and reducing Internet crime and abuse
- web in society – imaginative applications of the Internet to address specific social problems.

Each year, we make a small number of investments in international projects which align with our areas of focus.

Selection criteria

Nominet Trust supports initiatives that can align with our areas of focus and can demonstrate significant social impact.

- We place a high value on models, tools and methodologies that can be replicated or scaled up.
- We are interested in amplifying existing good practice as well as supporting innovative, unproven approaches.
- We back projects which can scale and be replicated, and organisations who share this aim.
- We encourage knowledge sharing between applicants to reduce unnecessary duplication and to promote best practice.
- We value partnership and collaboration in order to increase the reach and impact of our social investments.
- We are interested in supporting research in our areas of focus.
- We do not finance hardware procurement projects.
- We only fund a proportion of overheads and core costs; project budgets should be detailed and transparent.

There is no minimum grant application and in some circumstances applications for more than £100,000 may require an interview. In addition we may request a meeting to discuss a grant application.

In 2009/10 the trust had assets of £5.3 million and an income of £3.1 million, the majority of which came in donations from Nominet UK (£3 million). Grants were made totalling £2.2 million.

Beneficiaries included: UnLtd (£500,000); the e-Learning Foundation (£282,000); Age UK (£185,000); Beatbullying (£175,000); Channel 4 (£100,000); Gemin-i.org (£82,000); Alzheimer's Society (£69,000); Busymummy Ltd and AbilityNet (£60,000 each); ENABLE Scotland (£59,000); and the Internet Watch Foundation, Gateshead College, Oxford Internet Institute, Citizens Online, Action for M.E. and UK Internet Crime and Disorder Reduction Partnership (£50,000 each).

A further £336,000 was given in grants of less than £50,000.

Exclusions

The trust will not fund the following:

- hardware infrastructure projects, e.g. a project to equip a school with PCs, or to install Wi-Fi for a community
- website improvements where no new functional or service delivery innovations are delivered
- website development unless the project and organisation delivers against one of our areas of focus and meets our funding guidelines
- organisational running costs per se.

Applications

Potential applicants should first read the *Self-Evaluation Checklist* then, if appropriate, complete an initial *Eligibility Questionnaire* – both of which are available on the trust's website.

Once submitted, the trust aims to respond by email within two weeks. If invited to make a full application, further details such as a project plan and budget will be required. Funding applications are reviewed quarterly.

The North British Hotel Trust

Health, social welfare

£336,000 (2009/10)

Beneficial area

Scotland.

1 Queen Charlotte Lane, Edinburgh EH6 6BL

Email: nbht@samuelston.com

Correspondent: Claire Smith, Clerk

Trustees: Ian C Fraser; Patrick Crerar; Graham Brown; Mrs Jeanette

Crerar; Mike Still; James Barrack; John Williams.

CC Number: 221335

Information available

Accounts were available at the Charity Commission.

The trust was established with shares from the North British Hotels Trust Company for general charitable purposes. Giving is concentrated in areas where the company operates, namely, mainly Scotland. There are also four hotels in England, with grants being made close to those in Scarborough, Harrogate and Barnby Moor in Yorkshire.

The trust's only source of income is from its investment in North British Trust Hotels Limited and the trust holds 50% of the voting rights in this company.

The trust has a non-trading subsidiary trust, the North British Hotel Cancer and Leukaemia in Childhood Edinburgh Trust.

In 2009/10 the trust had assets of £9.55 million and an income of £528,500. Grants were made during the year totalling £336,000.

Beneficiaries included: Euan MacDonald Centre of Motor Neurone Disease (£61,000); HIT Scotland (£25,000 in total); Scottish Outward Bound (£12,500); Circle (£10,000); the Prince's Trust (£7,500); Cosgrove Care Limited (£6,000); Stepping Stones and Pebbles Crèche, Autism Initiatives UK and the Teenage Cancer Trust (£5,000 each); Hearts & Minds Limited (£4,000); Parkinson's Disease Society (£2,000); and Age Concern Eastwood (£1,000).

Exclusions

No grants to individuals.

Applications

On an application form available from the correspondent.

North West London Community Foundation

General

£333,000 (2009/10)

Beneficial area

London boroughs of Barnet, Brent, Ealing, Enfield, Haringey, Harrow and Hillingdon.

Central Depot Unit 4, Forward Drive, Harrow, Middlesex HA3 8NT
Tel: 020 8909 2788
Fax: 020 8909 2730
Email: kath.s@nwlondoncf.org.uk
Website: www.
northwestlondoncommunityfoundati-
on.org.uk
Correspondent: Kath Sullivan, Grants Officer
Trustees: Natalie Forbes, Chair; Kanti Nagda; David Wood; Tajinder Nijjar; Howard Bluston; Malcolm Churchill.
CC Number: 1097648

Information available

Accounts were available from the Charity Commission, without a list of grants; information was also taken from the foundation's website.

Established in 2002, this community foundation makes grants from various funds to local organisations in the London boroughs of Barnet, Brent, Ealing, Enfield, Harrow, Haringey and Hillingdon, an area of around 1.3 million people. The foundation raises and distributes funds in order to improve the quality of life within local communities. Grants are made in the following areas:

▸ children and young people
▸ community development
▸ education, arts and the humanities
▸ relief of suffering, disadvantage or poverty
▸ health and special needs.

In 2009/10 the foundation held assets of £411,000, had an income of £734,000, and made grants totalling £333,000.

The foundation currently manages the following funding schemes:

North West London Community Foundation

Small grants for local organisations from funds donated by local donors.

Comic Relief Local Communities

Small grants for Barnet, Brent, Ealing, Enfield, Harrow and Hillingdon. This fund makes grants available for projects that address the issues of economic and social deprivation, particularly in the context of the current economic climate. Grants of £1,000–£10,000 are available to empower local people and enable them to create lasting change in their communities. Small, locally based organisations run by the people directly affected by the issues they are dealing with can apply for funding to:

▸ increase local services
▸ build skills of local people
▸ increase community cohesion
▸ respond to local economic needs
▸ increase access to sport and exercise for people who face social exclusion and isolation.

For examples of types of programmes that may be funded and exclusions, please see the relevant page on the foundation's website.

Fair Share

A grantmaking programme funded by the National Lottery. The funds priorities consist of:

▸ children, young people and families- providing extracurricular activities for children and young people to gain new skills, discipline, and divert from anti-social behaviour/ crime. Providing holistic support to families with education and healthy living advice
▸ community development- providing resources and support for community development and social enterprise to increase the capacity of community groups working for the benefit of local residents
▸ neighbourhood pride- promoting a sense of neighbourhood pride and raise a positive profile of the neighbourhood through working in partnership with residents, local police and local stakeholders.

Veolia Community Investment Fund

This company which provides water and wastewater management services has set up a fund to support environmental projects and voluntary/ community organisations within their water supply area. Bronze (up to £500), Silver (up to £1,000) and Gold (up to £2,500) grants can be applied for through the company's website. Projects must include activities which reflect at least one of the following areas:

- child welfare and education
- social inclusion
- environment
- quality of life for the disadvantaged

Please note that as with all community foundations, funds open and close for applications, new funds are established and other funds finish throughout the year. Therefore it is important to contact the trust or view their website for the most recent information.

No list of grant beneficiaries was included in the annual report but previously beneficiaries have included: Barnet Elderly Asian's Group; Harrow Young Achievers (£5,000 each); St Mary's Acorns Parent and Toddler Group; Community Link Up (£4,000 each); The Kilburn Festival; The Special Yoga Centre (£1,100 each); Somali Women Enterprise and Employment Project (£1,500); and Harrow in Leaf (£900).

Exclusions

No grants to individuals; organisations outside the area of benefit or statutory bodies and their agencies.

Applications

Application forms and further details are available from the correspondent or from the foundation's website. Different funds have different application processes and deadlines so please refer to the individual fund guidelines.

The Community Foundation for Northern Ireland

Community, peace building, social exclusion, poverty and social injustice

£3.8 million (2010/11)

Beneficial area

Northern Ireland and the six border counties of the Republic of Ireland.

Community House, Citylink Business Park, 6a Albert Street, Belfast BT12 4HQ
Tel: 028 9024 5927
Fax: 028 9032 9839
Email: info@ communityfoundationni.org
Website: www. communityfoundationni.org
Correspondent: Avila Kilmurray, Director
Trustees: Tony McCusker, Chair; Les Allamby; Mike Bamber; Barbary Cook; Sammy Douglas; Dr Jeremy Harbison; Noreen Kearney; Julie Knight; Dr Mike Morrissey; Dr Duncan Morrow; Stephanie Morrow; Conal McFeely; Tayra McKee; Anne McReynolds; Hilary Sidwell; Colin Stutt.
IR Number: XN45242

Information available

The foundation has a helpful and informative website where the annual report and accounts can be accessed.

The Community Foundation for Northern Ireland, formerly the Northern Ireland Voluntary Trust, was established in 1979 with a grant of £500,000 from government. It is an independent grantmaking organisation that manages a broad portfolio of funds and programmes, aiming to tackle social exclusion, poverty and social injustice, as well as developing communities and promoting peace and reconciliation.

Grant programmes

Programmes are subject to open and close for applications throughout the year. New funds are also established

and some end, therefore it is important to contact the foundation or check their comprehensive website for the most recent information.

Acorn Fund
To focus of this fund is to provide support for projects in Londonderry that are inclusive and promote the values of community, health and well-being and the environment.

Comic Relief Community Cash
This fund aims to support small local projects in Greater Belfast where there is a clear evidence of a sustained beneficial impact on people's lives that are excluded or disadvantaged through low income, rural or social isolation, age, disabilities, race, sexuality or gender.

Comic Relief and Sport Relief Community Grants
This fund shares its aims with the Comic Relief Community Cash fund however has allocated 50% of its available funds to support sports projects that further this aim, and 50% of funds to support community groups that: increase local services; build skills of local people; increase community cohesion and respond directly to local needs.

Community Arts Fund
The fund's priority is to support community arts groups that involve ethnic minority groups with the aim of integrating communities.

The David Ervine Foundation Grant Fund
The aim of this fund is to provide opportunities that enable children and young people from disadvantaged communities to reach their full potential

Eaga Community Fund
This fund has been created to support community projects that educate, raise awareness and demonstrate community involvement in addressing environmental issues at grassroots level.

McKibbin Fund
The aim of this fund is to improve the lives of young people with physical disabilities, learning disabilities or who are affected by illness. They will fund: equipment; outings; residentials and tutors.

One Small Step Grant Fund

The One Small Step grant fund encourages initiatives that stimulate people into action to build a peaceful future. It is about spreading the message that everyone is responsible for developing a peaceful society in Northern Ireland. The Fund will support small local projects organised by individuals – these projects should encourage people into action. 'The context is one of peace being an issue for each of us as individuals, for all of our organisations and for our communities.' Grants will range from £500 to £1,500. Partnership funding is encouraged.

Patrons Fund

This fund was established by Baroness Mary Goudie and will support small initiatives that are prioritised by the trustees of the Community Foundation as of particular importance to the foundation.

Rural Women's Fund

The focus of the fund is to provide support for women's projects particularly in isolated rural areas.

Social Justice Initiatives Fund

This small grants programme supports work in areas of social justice and human rights in Northern Ireland and the Irish border counties. They support self-help amongst minority groups affected by social need and initiatives that will enable people to overcome barriers to participation and that promote inclusive and resilient communities.

Telecommunity Programme

The Telecommunity Programme is an 'own name' fund set up with capital from BT, management and unions and matched by Community Foundation funds. The programme targets work with young people (teenagers) and people with disabilities in community based organisations in areas of disadvantage.

The Thomas Devlin Fund

This fund offers bursaries to young people for developing their career in the arts field, with priorities set each March for the following school/college year.

The Turkington Fund

The Turkington Fund is being established in recognition and celebration of the contribution of older people to our society. It aims to offer funding for locally based community projects that are run by, and for, older people. Grants will generally range between £200 and £3,000. The fund will allocate some £60,000 each year in a range of small grants. Priority will be given to those applications that show a clear involvement of older people in the design and delivery of a project. The project does not need to be new or particularly innovative in nature, but its programme must be realistic and clearly thought through. An emphasis will be placed on locally-based self-help groups that are working in disadvantaged areas.

Ulster Bank Sir George Quigley Community Award

The fund offers one grant to a project or initiative each year that promotes and demonstrates sustainability through practical action. Community organisations from throughout the island of Ireland are eligible to apply.

Workspace

This group provides business support services, recruitment, training and employment initiatives, energy efficiency, event management, childcare and recreational activities. These commercial activities are pursued to generate profits that are then used for the benefit of the local community.

Grantmaking in 2010/11

In 2010/11 the foundation had assets of £15.6 million and an income of £5.2 million. Grants were made totalling £3.8 million. Small grants range from £500 to £5,000 although they do not usually exceed £1,500. Main grants range from £5,000 to £10,000 although higher amounts may very occasionally be granted.

Beneficiaries included: Teach Na Failte (£202,500); SEEDS (£10,000); Justices for Magdalene's (£5,000); Council for the Homeless NI (£3,000); Multi-Cultural Senior Citizens Group (£2,500); St Patrick's Girls FC (£2,000); Suffolk Lenadoon Interface Group and Lesbian Advisory Services Initiative (LASI) (£1,500 each); Community Arts Forum and Village Focus Group (£1,000 each); Women 2 Gather (£900); and Music Theatre for Youth (£500).

Exclusions

The foundation will not fund:
- activities that duplicate existing services
- retrospective funding
- capital build projects or large equipment purchase
- promotion of religion
- dinners, fund-raising promotions or other ticketed events
- party political activity
- housing associations
- individuals- unless a fund is specifically aimed at helping individuals
- replacement of statutory funding
- projects where the foundation's contribution is a minor part of a larger funded initiative, except where it clearly contributes to the foundation's funding objectives
- projects beginning within 12 weeks of application
- organisations that did not comply with the reporting requirements of previous grant aid

Applications

Applications to any of the funds are made through the same online process. The foundation will match the application with the most suitable fund. There are comprehensive guidelines available on the website for applications. A turnaround time of 12 weeks should be allowed for all applications.

There are two parts to the application process:
- Part A: complete the short online form to answer the questions about the project, beneficiaries and budget
- Part B: you will be sent a unique link to your own application form in an email along with guidelines on how to fill it out. This part must be printed off and signed by two members of the organisation.

Both parts should then be posted to the foundation together with the following documentation:
- a copy of the governing document
- a copy of the most recent accounts or income and expenditure statement
- a list of the management committee members and their contact details
- a recent original bank statement for the organisation's bank account

The foundation will normally only fund groups located in Northern Ireland however some funds will make grants in the Republic as well. Applicants should check the fund specifications.

Applications are assessed by the foundation's staff and recommendations are considered by the trustee's grants sub-committee.

Successful applicants will be required to submit both qualitative and quantitative monitoring information for the benefit of both the grant holder and the foundation.

The Northern Rock Foundation

Disadvantaged people

£12.4 million (2010)

Beneficial area

Cumbria, Northumberland, Tyne and Wear, County Durham and the Tees Valley.

The Old Chapel, Woodbine Road, Gosforth, Newcastle upon Tyne NE3 1DD

Tel: 0191 284 8412

Fax: 0191 284 8413

Email: generaloffice@nr-foundation.org.uk

Website: www.nr-foundation.org.uk

Correspondent: Penny Wilkinson, Chief Executive

Trustees: Alastair Balls, Chair; David Chapman; David Faulkner; Jackie Fisher; Tony Henfrey; Chris Jobe; Lorna Moran; Frank Nicholson; Mo O'Toole; Julie Shipley.

CC Number: 1063906

Information available

Excellent report, accounts, newsletter, guidelines and application forms, all available on the foundation's website.

Summary

This foundation is funded by Northern Rock plc and aims to tackle disadvantage and improve quality of life in the North East and Cumbria. It gives grants to organisations which help people who are vulnerable, disadvantaged, homeless, living in poverty or are victims of crime and discrimination. They also support training, research and demonstration work and share what they learn from the activities they fund. The foundation is also involved in seeking to inform and influence wider regional and national policies.

Recent developments

In 2010, the publicly owned Northern Rock was spilt into two separate companies; Northern Rock (Asset Management) plc stated that it would not continue to support the Foundation. Northern Rock plc, the new retail bank, agreed to donate 1% of pre-tax profits for the next 2 years. In 2011 it was announced that Virgin Money would buy Northern Rock plc in 2012 and the agreement with the Northern Rock Foundation was extended to at least 2013 so the Foundation and Virgin could make a new agreement on how they could work together.

In the foundation's latest annual report (2010) there was major concern that following the end of the 1% agreement they would not receive any more significant funding and they therefore resolved to promote the value of the relationship with the foundation when Northern Rock returned to the private sector. At this point the trustees decided to use the capital over the next 5 years to make grants. Currently it remains to be seen whether Virgin, the new owners of Northern Rock, will sustain the funding to the foundation. If they do not, it is likely that the foundation will wind down. In this situation it is possible that Virgin Money Giving, the company's not for profit arm, would increase their giving or take on some of the aims of the Northern Rock Foundation.

General

The aim of the foundation is to help those who are disadvantaged and to improve quality of life in the North East of England (Northumberland, Tyne and Wear, County Durham and the Tees Valley) and Cumbria.

When talking specifically about disadvantage, the foundation means the problems people face because of:

- age – for example, young people and old people
- disability
- displacement – for example, refugees and asylum seekers
- a lack of employment opportunities
- geography – where people live may affect their ability to get basic services, to work together for mutual benefit or to enjoy a healthy and fulfilled life
- crime – for example, victims of domestic abuse
- prejudice and discrimination – for example, against lesbians and gay men or black and minority ethnic communities.

As described above, the foundation is also increasing its emphasis on projects which focus on homelessness from 2010 onwards in response to the current economic situation.

During the year 2010 the trust had assets of £43.5 million, an income of £15 million and made grants totalling £12.4 million.

Grant programmes

Independence and Choice

This aims to give people with mental health problems, people with learning disabilities, older people and carers a choice of excellent services that help them to become or remain independent.

This programme is designed to improve the amount and range of services for people that the foundation considers receive the least support from other sources. They are:

- people with mental health problems
- people with learning disabilities
- older people
- carers.

In this programme the foundation is also especially concerned to see that the people who use your services are involved in their development and delivery.

Safety and Justice

Reducing the incidence and impact of domestic abuse, sexual violence, prostitution, child abuse and hate crimes, by investing in better support for victims.

Examples of the kinds of work in which the foundation might invest include:

- advocacy and support
- crisis services
- schemes that encourage reporting of crimes

- prevention and education programmes with children and young people
- projects that encourage survivors to get involved in policy and practice development
- research that has a clear application to policy and practice.

Managing Money

Helps people who are in debt or have other financial problems and needs. The foundation is interested in receiving applications from organisations working to increase the supply of appropriate financial products. They are also interested in supporting the capacity of the third sector lenders to provide affordable credit and other financial products by funding improved governance, product development and marketing. The foundation wants to encourage leadership within the sector and is keen to help credit unions share costs, to grow their common bond and to merge together.

Having a Home

Helps vulnerable people who are homeless or are at risk of becoming homeless. The foundation invests in organisations that provide one-to-one support to vulnerable people to help them maintain a home or to help them find somewhere safe and secure to live. Applications are particularly encouraged from organisations working to:

- prevent homelessness
- help people in crisis
- develop day centre provision for homeless people
- provide training and employment opportunities
- make permanent accommodation available and sustainable.

Changing Lives

This programme helps young offenders and young people within the criminal justice system, refugees and asylum seekers and people who misuse drugs or alcohol. Organisations that are supported provide one-to-one support that helps people plan for a more fulfilling future such as:

- mentoring and befriending
- personal development programmes, including life skills and those that use the arts as a tool to engage people

- advice and support, including peer support groups
- crisis support.

Note: choose the programme whose description best fits the intended results of your work. Do not tick more than one box on the application form. Most importantly please do not apply if your plan does not really fit anywhere within our programmes.

Grantmaking in 2010

The foundation offers this overview of grantmaking in 2010:

- 147 grant applications were successful and £12 million was awarded
- 82 grants were made for a term of three years and one for four years, 22 were for two years and 42 for one year or under
- 74 % of the number of grants made were to organisations which had previously held a foundation grant
- the foundation dealt with 341 completed grant applications during the year
- 66 % of eligible applications were successful
- The foundation rejected 76 eligible applications and 118 applications were ineligible for funding or were withdrawn by the applicant
- by the end of December 2010, the foundation was managing new or ongoing grants totalling £27 million.

Grants were awarded under the following programmes:

Enabling independence and choice	£2.9 million
Changing lives	£2.4 million
Safety and justice for victims of abuse	£2.2 million
Managing money	£2.1 million
Having a home	£1.9 million
Exceptional	£380,000
Training and development grants	£91,000
Commissions	£285,000
Total	**£12.2 million**

The annual report also illustrated grants by geographical spread:

Cumbria	26	£1.7 million
Durham	11	£750,000
Northumberland	12	£905,000
Tees Valley	22	£1.9 million
Tyne and Wear	43	£2.9 million
North East wide	24	£1.7 million
North East and Cumbria	9	£2.1 million

Beneficiaries included: Citizens Advice- Northern Area (£1.5 million); Mind (£200,000); Regional Refugee

Forum North East (£150,000); North East Special Needs Network (£127,000); Equal Arts (£68,000); Homeless Link (£123,000); Barnardo's SECOS and ACE Projects (£270,000); Derwentside Domestic Abuse Service (£105,000); Gay Advice Darlington (£99,000); Rape Crisis England and Wales (£60,000); University of Bristol (£48,000); and Tony Mullin (£4,000).

Exclusions

There are certain organisations, projects and proposals that the foundation will not consider for grants. You should be aware that it costs the equivalent of several small grants to administer ineligible applications each year. If your organisation or your project falls into one of the categories below please **do not apply** to the foundation for a grant:

- activities which are not recognised as charitable in law
- applications for under £1,000
- charities which appear to us to have excessive unrestricted or free reserves (up to 12 months' expenditure is normally acceptable), or are in serious deficit
- national charities which do not have a regional office or other representation in North East England or Cumbria
- grant-making bodies seeking to distribute grants on our behalf
- open-ended funding agreements
- general appeals, sponsorship and marketing appeals
- corporate applications for founder membership of a charity
- retrospective grants
- replacement of statutory funding
- activities primarily the responsibility of central or local government or health authorities
- individuals and organisations that distribute funds to individuals
- animal welfare
- mainstream educational activity, schools and educational establishments
- medical research, hospitals, hospices and medical centres
- medical treatments and therapies including art therapy
- fabric appeals for places of worship
- promotion of religion
- expeditions or overseas travel

- minibuses, other vehicles and transport schemes except where they are a small and integral part of a larger scheme
- holidays and outings
- playgrounds and play equipment
- private clubs or those with such restricted membership as to make them not charitable
- capital bids purely towards compliance with the Disability Discrimination Act
- amateur arts organisations
- musical instruments
- sports kit and equipment.

Applications

The foundation provides comprehensive guidelines for applications on their website. As they have made a shift in their grantmaking to focus on sustainability they will encourage organisations working towards consolidation and increased collaboration, including reviewing organisational focus or restructuring. The focus will also be on organisations that the trust currently has a relationship with. If an applicant has not applied to the foundation previously it is advised that they get in contact before applying.

Guidelines available include specific instructions for applicants applying for salary costs or those applying from universities. There are also separate forms for applications for under £20,000 and for those that are over.

The foundation prefers online applications as they are quicker and easier but applications may still be submitted via post, providing they are on the correct forms.

The Northwood Charitable Trust

Medical research, health, welfare, general

Around £1.5 million (2009/10)

Beneficial area
Scotland, especially Dundee and Tayside.

William Thomson and Sons,
22 Meadowside, Dundee DD1 1LN
Tel: 01382 201534
Fax: 01382 227654
Email: bmckernie@wtandsons.co.uk
Correspondent: Brian McKernie, Secretary
Trustees: Brian Harold Thomson; Andrew Francis Thomson; Lewis Murray Thomson.
SC Number: SC014487

Information available
Brief annual report and accounts, with a list of the 50 largest donations only, available from the trust for £10.

The Northwood Trust is connected to the D C Thomson Charitable Trust, D C Thomson and Company and the Thomson family. It was established by Eric V Thomson in 1972 and has received additional funding from other members of the family.

The brief annual report notes that 'the trustees have adopted the principle of giving priority to assisting Dundee and Tayside based charities' and says 'unsolicited applications for donations are not encouraged and will not normally be acknowledged'. Other than this there is little indication of the trust's grantmaking policy, beyond what can be deduced from the partial, uncategorised grants lists, and there was no review of the trust's grantmaking in previous reports.

Grants total around £1.5 million each year. No recent information was available.

Previous beneficiaries include: Tenovus Medical Projects; Tayside Orthopaedic and Rehabilitation Technology Centre; Macmillan Cancer Relief Scotland; Brittle Bone Society; Dundee Repertory Theatre; Dundee Samaritans; Dundee Age Concern; Couple Counselling Tayside; and Tayside Association for the Deaf.

Applications
The trust has previously stated that funds are fully committed and that no applications will be considered or acknowledged.

The Nuffield Foundation

Education, child protection, law and justice, older people, African development, science and social science research, and capacity development

£5.7 million to organisations (2010)

Beneficial area
UK and Commonwealth.

28 Bedford Square, London WC1B 3JS
Tel: 020 7631 0566
Fax: 020 7232 4877
Email: info@nuffieldfoundation.org
Website: www.nuffieldfoundation.org
Correspondent: Clerk to the Trustees
Trustees: Prof. Genevra Richardson; Lord Krebs; Prof. Sir David Watson; Dr Peter Doyle; Prof. David Rhind; Mr Andrew Dilnot; Prof. Terrie Moffitt.
CC Number: 206601

Information available
Excellent annual report and accounts; detailed guidelines for applicants (summarised below, but all potential applicants should see a full copy).

Summary
The Nuffield Foundation is one of the UK's best known charitable trusts which was established in 1943 by William Morris (Lord Nuffield), the founder of Morris Motors. Lord Nuffield wanted his foundation to 'advance social well being', particularly through research and practical experiment. The foundation aims to achieve this by supporting work which will bring about improvements in society, and which is founded on careful reflection and informed by objective and reliable evidence.

The foundation's income comes from the returns on its investments. It does not fundraise, or receive money from the government. The foundation's financial independence and lack of vested interests helps to ensure an impartial and even-handed approach to problems in the projects it funds. Most of the foundation's income is spent on grants some of which are for research and others support practical innovation or development, often in voluntary sector organisations. In both cases the preference is for work that has wide significance, beyond the local or routine. The foundation looks to support projects that are imaginative and innovative, take a thoughtful and rigorous approach to problems, and have the potential to influence policy or practice.

The foundation's grant making reflects its aim of bringing about improvements in society through research and practical experiment. The wide range of activities supported by the foundation fall into two main categories:

- by funding research and innovation in education and social policy
- by increasing the proliferation and quality of research and professional skills – both in science and social sciences – through our capacity building programmes.

'Project grants' are made to organisations and institutions to support research, developmental or experimental projects that meet a practical or policy need.

The foundation has four grant programmes that support research and innovation; these are:

- Law in Society – promotes access to, and understanding of, the civil justice system.
- Children and Families – helps to ensure that the legal and institutional framework is best adapted to meet the needs of children and families.
- Open Door – for projects that advance social well being, but lie outside the main programme areas.
- Education - supports innovative research and development in specific priority areas.

The foundation offers very detailed breakdowns of specific funding priorities within each category on its website:

Grants are mainly for research (usually carried out in universities or independent research institutes) but are also made for practical developments or innovation, often in voluntary sector organisations.

As an independent foundation, we are well placed to deal with sensitive issues, to challenge fashions and tacit assumptions. We support people with creative ideas to identify change or interventions which will have a practical impact for researchers, policy makers and practitioners.

We do not fund the ongoing costs of existing work or services, or provide core funding for voluntary sector bodies.

Development of research and professional capacity

We believe policy and practice should be influenced by independent and rigorous evidence. We aim to ensure these qualities are maintained in the future by funding programmes to build research and professional capacity in science and social science.

In science and social science, the foundation's grants for the development of research and professional capacity are targeted mainly at people in the early stages of their career.

- Science Bursaries for Schools and Colleges – these enable sixth form students to take part in research at a university, research institute or in industry.
- Undergraduate Research Bursaries in Science – previously these have supported summer vacation research projects. This scheme is changing – more details will be available on the foundation's website from early 2012.
- Quantitative Methods for Undergraduate Social Scientists – this is a new funding programme aimed at improving the teaching, training and work experience of quantitative methods among social science undergraduates at a small number of UK universities.

The foundation runs the Oliver Bird Rheumatism Programme which makes grants to support PhD students in biosciences at five UK Collaborative Centres of Excellence in rheumatic disease control.

The foundation also sets up and runs projects of its own. The two largest are The Nuffield Council on Bioethics (which is jointly funded with the Wellcome Trust and the Medical Research Council), and The Nuffield Curriculum Centre. The most recent is The Nuffield Adolescent Mental Health Initiative – a specific programme of research on time trends in adolescent mental health, set up by The Nuffield Foundation in 2005 (see website for further details). None of these are covered in this entry. Extensive publicity and information work is also carried out directly by the foundation.

Grant programmes

The foundation currently has three grant programmes in areas of social policy. These are: Access to Justice; Children and Families; and Education. Support for these three areas is through project grants. Each area has separate criteria which are detailed below. Grants range in size from £5,000 to £150,000 and upwards and support research and/or innovative projects that will inform the development of policy or practice. The following details are taken from the foundation's website:

Access to Justice

We focus on three types of work:

- critical reviews to summarise what is known about how law functions in a particular area. These reviews are not solely doctrinal or conceptual, but evaluate empirical evidence, assessing findings and their robustness
- empirical research to establish descriptive information or look for evidence about causes
- evaluations of programmes or experiments. These may be formative evaluations or evaluations of outcomes, in which case a comparison group or randomised-design is likely to be needed.

Our work falls within seven different themes:

1. Administrative justice

We do not focus on public administration *per se* but on how dispute resolution may be improved. This may require acquiring better descriptive information or studying reforms or making comparisons between different practices. A comprehensive analysis of particular topics contained within this theme is available on the foundation's website.

2. Mental health and mental capacity law

We are interested in empirical and evaluative work on mental health and mental capacity law. This could include the workings of mental health tribunals, the Court of Protection and so on.

3. Aspects of human rights law

We fund only a limited number of projects in human rights and are particularly interested in those which seek to investigate the structures for human rights adjudication in Europe and elsewhere or that address issues like the margin of appreciation.

4. Family law and family courts

We are interested in legal policy issues like co-habitation, divorce and separation and child contact; issues in family courts (such as expert witnesses and transparency); and the use of other mechanisms to promote outcomes appropriate to promote child welfare.

5. Funding for civil justice

We are interested in the issue of how appropriate civil justice might be funded and believe the ultimate issue is what is best for citizens and society, rather than a particular profession. We would be particularly interested in work that includes expertise in behavioural economics in a multi-disciplinary approach and that might move the debate on and lead, for example to better allocation, appropriate triage, and consideration of proportionate costs.

6. Outcomes, enforcement and consequences

We are interested in outcomes across all these legal themes. What happens after adjudications or settlement? Are outcomes enforced? What do disappointed claimants do? Are family settlements adhered to? What other outcomes result? We would like to see more longitudinal work, both of a descriptive kind and that which is aimed at improving outcomes.

7. Cross national comparisons

In all our subject themes, we are interested in European comparisons, as well as those based on other common-law jurisdictions. How do other countries handle issues, compared to England and Wales, or Scotland, or Northern Ireland? What policy alternatives are revealed? We understand that findings from elsewhere are not necessarily applicable to the UK, but we are willing to fund comparative work that might shed light not only on the workings of law in the UK, but on underlying issues of commonality or difference.

The foundation will not fund:

- delivery of core or normal or local legal services including law centres
- criminal law, unless it relates to our other interests such as children and young people and considered under our Open Door programme
- projects on penal policy, drugs, policing, crime prevention, or environmental law
- doctrinal or jurisprudential analysis.

Children and Families

Our Children and Families programme supports work to help ensure that the laws and institutions governing family life in the UK are operating in the best interests of children and families.

Our interests include (but are not limited to):

- links between education and child development, either in the case of adolescent mental health or younger children
- consideration of policies relevant to child welfare in a broader institutional context: parents' paid working patterns; childcare and early years provision
- consideration of the well-being of children growing up in adverse conditions, and what institutional responses may be appropriate
- family law, including cohabitation, child contact and child support
- child protection and placement (adoption and fostering), but only when it raises significant issues.

Where a proposal is for a research study, the committee is interested in the dispassionate examination of evidence. It notes that evidence is likely to be different in different cases, for different types of children and families, and is more likely to support work that takes this approach.

In all its areas of interest the Foundation is interested in supporting work that has an international comparative dimension and is particularly interested in fostering work that considers European perspectives.

Education

We are committed to improving education opportunities and outcomes for all. We have supported innovative research and development in education for over 60 years.

We consider applications for education and research grants in the following areas:

- Foundations for learning – we are looking for proposals that will improve understanding about language, learning and development in early childhood (from birth to around eight years of age) addressing where possible the implications for policy and practice.
- Mathematics education – we are interested in supporting research and development projects designed to improve policy and practice in the teaching and learning of mathematics.
- Secondary education transitions – we are keen to improve understanding of the significance and impact of transitions into, through and out of secondary education. We are interested in proposals addressing issues of policy and practice relating to progression and movement through institutions and phases; the role of schools in supporting these transitions; and the value that can be added by other educational and local agencies.

- Student parents' and women's education – We are looking to fund research, development and pilot projects around this theme. We are particularly interested in the development and evaluation of pilot projects, run by intermediary organisations, aimed at improving opportunities for parents to access – and be successfully supported through – further and higher education.

For details of current themes and priorities within each area please consult the foundation's website before applying.

Open Door

The foundation keeps an 'open door' to proposals of exceptional merit for research projects or practical innovations that lie outside our main programme areas, but that meet trustees' wider interests. These must have some bearing on our widest charitable object – 'the advancement of social well-being.

Subjects of interest include, but are not limited to: work on poverty, disadvantage, social welfare, disability, the financial circumstances of the elderly, the UK and Europe, and work that crosses boundaries between our areas of special interest (for instance, learning and social provision; law and society; science and education).

The foundation is particularly interested in projects which identify change or interventions which will have practical implications for policy or practice, or that will improve the quality of research evidence in areas of public debate. Through the Open Door programme, the foundation may also identify emerging areas that justify more sustained attention.

Africa

The Africa Programme supports the development of research and professional expertise required for African countries to grow their economies and deliver health, education and other services.

We fund UK and African universities and/or NGOs working in partnership, often together with African government departments or quasi-government bodies such as training and research institutions, to develop training initiatives in science, technology and public service provision.

We also initiate funding collaborations with other foundations to support larger schemes to increase African research capacity.

Aside from the social policy, Open Door and Africa programmes detailed above the foundation also funded undergraduate vacation research projects (which are changing for 2012, see the 'Applying for a project grant' section below or the foundation's website). The foundation also provides up to 1,000 bursaries a year to enable post-16 students in the first year of a STEM course to take up a paid summer placement in a university, industry or research institution. The bursaries are administered by regional Nuffield representatives.

Applying for a project grant

Applicants should read the information in this section in conjunction with the information in the 'Grant programmes' section above.

Research and innovation

The following information has been extracted from *Grants for Research and Innovation Guide for applicants* available from the foundation's website. These guidelines detail very comprehensively the grant criteria, exclusions, frequently asked questions, terms and conditions, and application deadlines. In particular the guidelines give detailed instructions on every aspect of the application process including how to summarise the project, prepare a budget and plan the communication of the results. Key points are included here but to ensure the strongest application possible applicants are advised to consult the trust's website to ensure that they are accessing the most up-to-date guidelines available.

Types of project: The projects we fund involve at least one of three types of activity: research, practical experiments, or development work. About two-thirds of our funded projects have a significant research element. All projects must be self-contained: we do not fund centres or longer-term programmes of research except in our capacity-building programmes.

- **research** – projects must have implication for policy or practice in at least the medium term. Trustees do not normally support research that aims *only* to accumulate knowledge or to produce academic publications, which is properly the responsibility of the research councils.
- **practical experimental projects** – these involve trying something new and evaluating the outcomes. These projects must have significance beyond the local, with the potential for wide application and a significant evaluative component. We do not fund projects that simply involve 'rolling out' a well-known way of working to new local areas.

- **development projects** – involve development of something of practical value. Examples include new approaches or tools for the classroom, guidance about technical issues for a wider audience, or new service development where experimental results are not relevant. Funding of these projects is rare, and they must be of wide significance and in one of our areas of interest.

Occasionally the trust will fund research reviews in any areas of interest if there is a clear gap in the existing literature and it will inform policy makers or practitioners or result in a new research agenda that will do so.

Grant criteria:

- Your project must be innovative. We will not fund the ongoing costs of existing work or services, or routine research. The research must have implications beyond the academic and we welcome cross-disciplinary collaborations.
- The project should aim to have an impact beyond its immediate beneficiaries. It should be of more than local or regional interest.
- We will give preference to projects with outcomes which will be important and useful to practitioners and policy makers or result in some sort of social change.
- We will look for evidence that you have identified those to whom the outcomes of the project will be most relevant, and have engaged them where possible from the early stages of the project.
- Your project should include a discussion of how you will assess the success or otherwise of the project, and what outcomes might be relevant in judging whether the desired impact was achieved.

Capacity Building

Each individual scheme within this area has separate application processes. Some managed by the foundation and others by partner organisations.

Undergraduate research bursaries – The foundation is altering this scheme and will be working with other organisations who provide similar opportunities and will provide similar funding for some of these in 2012 and 2013. Full details of the application procedure will be available on the foundation's website from early 2012.

Science bursaries for schools and colleges - these are administered regionally throughout the UK. Applicants should contact their regional coordinator to register their interest and to find out more information about the scheme in their area. A full list of regional deadlines and contact details is available on the foundation's website.

Africa programme – the programme only supports projects within defined geographic and thematic areas. These include projects that:

- benefit Southern or Eastern Africa
- develop training initiatives that focus primarily on health or STEM subjects; proposals in education, law and social welfare may also be considered
- build expertise at research and professional level.

Only UK-based non-profit organisations – academic institutions and NGOs – can apply for funding from the Programme. These organisations must have well-established links with partner organisations in the country/region where the proposed work is to take place and must have developed the proposal together with these partners.

The Programme supports a range of project sizes, from small pilot projects of £5,000 to medium-sized projects or self-contained elements of larger projects of up to £150,000. In some circumstances we may consider funding subsequent stages or developments of projects we have previously supported. Applications for co-funding are welcome, for example, where the Programme would fund the training element of a larger project.

What we will fund:

- salary costs of partner UK and overseas staff and consultants
- rent and other premises costs in-country
- training costs – tuition fees, accommodation, living costs, travel etc. Please note that we will not contribute towards the salaries of trainees/participants or the salaries of their replacements, nor will we pay a per diem on top of actual living costs
- travel costs of partner staff both within country and between UK and project country
- internal monitoring and evaluation costs
- direct administrative and office expenses of UK and overseas partners. Please note that the Foundation does not pay a straight percentage overhead.

We won't fund:

- activities that are primarily about community development, advocacy and rights-based work
- work that has already begun, unless it is for an identifiably new phase
- applications primarily concerned with the career development of individuals
- support for in-country projects with no direct UK involvement
- support for the day to day running costs of existing organisations or services
- administrative costs that are not directly related to the application

other costs not listed above, such as capital costs of equipment etc, will be considered on a case by case basis.

Applicants should first contact Sarah Lock, Programme Head, by telephone (020 7631 0566) or email (slock@ nuffield.org), to talk through the proposal to get a preliminary view on its eligibility. The next stage is to send a written outline application. If the outline is suitable for consideration by the trustees we will ask you to submit a final detailed proposal. Applicants seeking large grants may be interviewed. Outline applications decisions will be made three times a year with the cut off dates usually falling in March, July and November. The exact dates will be published every year on the foundation's website. The foundation publishes a very useful guide detailing what to include in outline proposals and key features of successful applications which is also available on the website.

Oliver Bird Rheumatism Programme

This programme supports four year PhD training at five collaborative centres of excellence (University of Aberdeen; University of Glasgow; King's College London and Queen Mary University of London (joint centre); University of Newcastle; University College London).

Applications for the Oliver Bird Rheumatism Programme are managed by these centres and not by the foundation. As of winter 2011 all studentships were filled for the current round – check with the above institutions for future opportunities.

Grantmaking 2010

Project grants generally range in size from £5,000 to £150,000 although increasingly larger grants for over £200,000 are made. The preference is for work 'that has wide significance, beyond the local or routine. The foundation looks to support projects that are imaginative and innovative, take a thoughtful and rigorous approach to problems, and have the potential to influence policy or practice'.

There are three areas of special interest and they are described below. In addition, the Open Door programme is used to fund projects that lie outside these areas of interest – or span boundaries between them – and that address the general aims of the foundation.

During the year the foundation had assets of £232.4 million, an income of £4.7 million and awarded grants totalling £5.7 million to organisations and individuals. Aside from expenditure on grants the foundation spent an additional £6.3 million on support costs. This total includes staffing, hosting seminars and conferences, commissioned research and evaluations of research.

Grants were categorised/broken down in the annual report as follows:

Social policy	
Open Door	£1.5 million
Children and families	£1.4 million
Law in society	£321,000
Education	
Education grants	£892,000
Capacity Building	
Undergraduate research bursaries	£590,000
Africa programme	£519,000
School science bursaries	£368,000
Social science small grants	£177,000
New career development fellowships	£1,000

The five largest grant beneficiaries were: University College London (£371,000); University of Oxford (£304,000); London School of Economics (£273,000); Brunel University (£267,000); and Gingerbread (£260,000).

Other beneficiaries across all categories included: The Royal Statistical Society (£250,000); Department of Law, University of Sussex (£152,000); Liverpool School of Tropical Medicine (£118,000); Institute for Criminal Policy Research (£91,000); Council for Assisting Refugee Academics (£75,000); School of Education, Durham University (£50,000); British Association for Adoption and Fostering (£39,000); Refugee Council (£30,000); Law Centre Northern Ireland (£20,000); and School of Law, University of Edinburgh (£15,000).

Exclusions

The foundation normally makes grants only to UK organisations, and support work that will be mainly based in the UK, although the trustees welcome proposals for collaborative projects involving partners in European or Commonwealth countries.

Several of our funding programmes are open to applications. There are different exclusions for different programmes so please consult the full guidelines for each area before applying.

There are a number of things that **we do not fund under any of our funding programmes.** These include:

- general appeals
- buildings or capital costs
- applications solely for equipment – grants for equipment are allowed when they are part of a project that is otherwise acceptable
- support or attend conferences or seminars
- projects that could be considered by a government department, a Research Council or a more appropriate charity
- the establishment of Chairs, or other permanent academic posts
- grants for the production of films or videos, or for exhibitions
- funding for school fees, a university course, or a gap year project
- requests for funding for financial help from or on behalf of individuals in distress.

Applications

The application process for all research and innovation grants is the same, regardless of whether you are applying for Law in Society, Children and Families, Education or Open Door. All applicants must first submit an outline application of *no more than* three pages. If your application is successful at this stage you will be invited to submit a full application of *no more than* 10 pages.

The outline application should include:

- a general background needed to understand the application
- issues to be addressed and research questions if relevant
- what you will do to achieve your aims, including an outline of the methodology if it is a research project, or of the activities you will undertake. This should be the largest section of the outline
- the expected outcomes of the project, including identification of the relevant audiences and an explanation of how you will engage with them
- an outline of the budget and the timetable. The budget should include a rough allocation between staffing, research assistance and direct costs
- a short selected CV of the primary applicants. This should be no more than two pages in total, but it does not count towards the three page limit for the outline
- all outline and full applications need attach a front page summary sheet which can be downloaded from the foundation's website.

We welcome cross-disciplinary collaborations or applications that straddle our own areas of interest. If your application meets the criteria of more than one programme, then submit the outline to the most suitable category and note if you think there is an overlap. You do not need to submit it to more than one programme.

The foundation currently operates several different grant programmes. Each programme publishes a comprehensive guide on its aims, policies and process for application, together with expectations for evaluation. All applications are reviewed by independent referees. Extensive guidance on the preparation of full applications is available from the foundation and is published in the foundation's funding guideline document available on the trust's excellent website, where you will also find application timetables for project grants.

The Oliver Bird Rheumatism PhD studentships are managed by the foundation's partner universities. Contact the relevant university departments directly and not the foundation.

Applicants considering the Africa programme should contact the programme head, Sarah Lock, first to obtain a preliminary view on your outline proposals eligibility (see: 'Applying for a project grant').

Applications requesting sums of £200,000 or more may take up to six months for a decision.

The Ofenheim Charitable Trust

General, mainly charities supporting health, welfare, arts and the environment

£318,500 (2009/10)

Beneficial area

Worldwide, in practice UK with some preference for East Sussex.

Baker Tilly, The Pinnacle, 170 Midsummer Boulevard, Milton Keynes MK9 1BP

Tel: 01908 687800

Email: geoff.wright@bakertilly.co.uk

Correspondent: Geoffrey Wright

Trustees: Roger Jackson Clark; Rory McLeod; Alexander Clark; Fiona Byrd.

CC Number: 286525

Information available

Accounts were available at the Charity Commission.

Established in 1983 by Dr Angela Ofenheim, it is the policy of the trust to 'provide regular support for a number of charities in East Sussex because of the founder's association with that area'. High-profile organisations in the fields of health, welfare, arts and the environment are supported with many of the same organisations benefiting each year.

In 2009/10 the trust had assets of £11.4 million and an income of £343,500. Grants were made to 60 organisations totalling £318,500.

Beneficiaries included: Trinity College of Music (£13,000); Save the Children Fund (£12,000); National Art Collections Fund, Marie Curie Cancer Care and St Mungo's (£9,000 each); British False Memory Society, Greater London Fund for the Blind, Glyndebourne Arts Trust and Canine Partners for Independence (£5,000 each); Universal Beneficent Association, Hospice Care Kenya, Alzheimer's Research Trust and Game Conservancy Trust (£3,000 each); and Home Start UK, Benslow Music Trust Instrument Loan Scheme and Battersea Summer Scheme (£2,000 each).

Exclusions

No grants to individuals.

Applications

In writing to the correspondent. 'The trustees' policy has been to provide regular support for a number of charities and to respond to one-off appeals to bodies where they have some knowledge [...] They will consider all applications for grants and make awards as they see fit.'

Oglesby Charitable Trust

General charitable purposes

£765,000 (2009/10)

Beneficial area

The North West of England.

PO Box 336, Altrincham, Cheshire WA14 3XD

Email: oglesbycharitabletrust@bruntwood.co.uk

Website: www.oglesbycharitabletrust.co.uk

Trustees: Jean Oglesby; Michael Oglesby; Robert Kitson; Kate Vokes; Jane Oglesby; Chris Oglesby; Peter Renshaw.

CC Number: 1026669

Information available

Accounts were available from the Charity Commission. The trust also has a clear and helpful website.

The Oglesby Charitable Trust was established in 1992. The funding of the trust comes from annual contributions from Bruntwood Limited, part of a group of North West based property investment companies owned by the founding trustees that has a net worth of approximately £300 million. The trust has been established to support charitable activities across a broad spectrum, and these reflect the beliefs and interests of the founding trustee family.

The following information is taken from the trust's website:

It is accepted that the trust will be relatively modest in it resources and the trustees will be looking to place funds where they can make a real and measurable impact. They acknowledge that there already exists a large number of charitable and government backed organisations operating across all fields and it is not the trustees intention of compete with, or supplement, these. Although funding grants are made to organisations following unsolicited cold applications, increasingly these are reducing in number. The trustees are now making the majority of their grants based on areas of direct interest into areas of need which they have personally identified. [...]

When appropriate the trustees are looking to form associations with organisations over a number of years in order that a longer-term project can be supported and the trustees can better understand an individual charity. A maximum of three years is normally placed on their associations to avoid the funding becoming core of an organisation's activities.

Who do we help?
Primarily applicants whose activities are based in the North West of England.

Organisations that can demonstrate that the funds are making a real difference, rather than being absorbed into an anonymous pool, no matter how significant the end result may appear to be.

Organisations that demonstrate both the highest standards of propriety and sound business sense in their activities. This does not mean high overheads but it does mean focused use of funds, where they are needed.

Funding that is to be operated as an individual project that can be ring-fenced as far as possible. Although preferred activities will be those that do not form part of current core operations, and which can be demonstrated to make a real difference, it is accepted that, in certain cases, they may be considered in exceptional circumstances. It is most unlikely that a new start up project will be funded if it has already commenced.

Grants are made mainly in the following areas:

- artistic development, both on an individual and group level
- educational grants and building projects
- environmental improvement projects
- improving the life and welfare of the underprivileged, where possible, by the encouragement of self-help
- medical aid and research.

Acorn Fund

We do have a fund set aside each year for smaller donations, which we call our Acorn Fund and donations from this fund will be between £200 and £1,000. This fund is administered by the Community Foundation for Greater Manchester and applications can be obtained from the foundation's website at: www.communityfoundation.co.uk.

In 2009/10 the trust had assets of £847,000 and an income of £835,000. Over 50 main grants given totalling over £765,000, which included a donation of £12,500 for administration to the Community Foundation for Greater Manchester for the Acorn Fund.

Unfortunately a list of grant beneficiaries for the year was not available, however, a list of organisations previously supported taken from the trust's website include: Action for Kids, Alcohol Drug Abstinence Service, Centre for Alternative Technology, Cheadle Hulme School, Cheetham's School, Fairbridge – Family Contact Line, Halle Youth Orchestra, Manchester City Art Gallery, Manchester University Arts and Drama, Motor Neurone Disease, National Asthma Campaign, National Library For The Blind, Stroke Research, Whitworth Art Gallery.

Exclusions

The trust will not support:

- non registered charities
- those whose activities are for the purpose of collecting funds for redistribution to other charities
- animal charities
- charities whose principal operation area is outside the UK
- church and all building fabric appeals
- conferences
- continuing running costs of an organisation
- costs of employing fundraisers
- expeditions
- general sports, unless strongly associated with a disadvantaged group
- holidays
- individuals
- loans or business finance
- religion
- routine staff training
- sectarian religions
- sponsorship and marketing appeals.

Applications

To enable the trustees to assess all applications from a similar basis, they ask that every applicant complete the *Stage 1 Application Form*. The trustees undertake to respond to this in 6 weeks. If this response is positive, then applicants will be required to complete a more detailed form under Stage 2.

By Stage 2, wherever possible, the trustees will require a proper Financial Plan prepared by the applicant. This should contain clear and measurable goals, which will be reviewed at regular intervals by the parties. In cases where the applicant does not possess either the skills or the resources to prepare such a Plan, the Trust may be prepared to assist.

Finally, the trustees will want to interview the applicant(s) at their place of operation or project site, both prior to the granting of funds and during the lifetime of the project, to monitor its progress. In addition the trustees will expect regular communication from the applicant, either verbal or by letter, to keep them informed of how the project is moving forward.

The P F Charitable Trust

General charitable purposes

£2.3 million (2009/10)

Beneficial area

Unrestricted, with local interests in Oxfordshire and Scotland.

Fleming Family & Partners,
15 Suffolk Street, London SW1Y 4HG
Tel: 020 7036 5685
Correspondent: The Secretary to the Trustees
Trustees: Robert Fleming; Philip Fleming; Rory D Fleming.
CC Number: 220124

Information available

Accounts were available at the Charity Commission.

The trust was established in 1951 to assist religious and educational charities and for general charitable purposes. The trust makes grants to a wide range of causes and states that its policy is to continue to make a substantial number of small grants to charitable organisations both on a one-off and recurring basis.

In 2009/10 the trust had assets of £92.2 million and an income of £1.7 million. There were 371 grants made totalling £2.3 million, broken down as follows:

Health or the saving or lives	115	£770,000
Religion	13	£341,500
Arts, culture, heritage and science	48	£310,000
Education	47	£224,000
Relief of need	80	£218,000
Other charitable purposes	3	£150,500
Armed forces and emergency services	12	£89,000
Citizenship and community development	16	£83,000
Human rights, conflict resolution or the promotion of religious or racial harmony	7	£37,000
Environment	6	£33,000
Relief of poverty	10	£28,500
Animal welfare	9	£11,500
Amateur sport	5	£10,000

Beneficiaries of the largest grants of £50,000 or more, listed in the accounts, were: St Martin-in-the Fields Development Trust (£300,000), towards redevelopment of the church; Eton Collage Appeal (£100,000), towards the establishment of an endowment fund; Great Ormond Street Hospital Children's Charity (£100,000), towards continued development; Charities Aid Foundation (£93,000), for onward distribution to other charities; and Soldiers of Oxfordshire Trust, British Heart Foundation, Cicely Saunders International, Scottish Community Foundation and Royal Shakespeare Company (£50,000).

Grants of less than £50,000 each totalled almost £1.5 million.

Exclusions
No grants to individuals or non-registered charities.

Applications
Applications to the correspondent in writing. Trustees usually meet monthly to consider applications and approve grants.

The Parthenon Trust

International aid, medical research, assistance to the disadvantaged including people with disabilities, culture and heritage, medical treatment and care, education, promotion of civil society and research on current affairs

£1.2 million (2010)

Beneficial area
Unrestricted.

Saint-Nicolas 9, 2000 Neuchatel, Switzerland
Tel: 00 41 32 724 8130
Correspondent: J E E Whittaker, The Secretary

Trustees: Dr J M Darmady; J E E Whittaker; Mrs Y G Whittaker.
CC Number: 1051467

Information available
Accounts were available at the Charity Commission.

This trust was established in 1995 for general charitable purposes. The giving is international, with the organisations, as well as the activities, being based in a number of countries. Although geographically distant for UK charities, the trust is not unapproachable but applicants are urged to contact the secretary informally before submitting their applications. The trust is based in Switzerland, the home of the chair, Geraldine Whittaker and the secretary, her husband John Whittaker and is a UK registered charity.

The areas which the trust focuses on are:
- international aid organisations
- medical research
- assistance to the disadvantaged including people with disabilities
- cultural and heritage purposes
- medical treatment and care including supporting services, preventative medicine and assistance to those with disabilities
- education
- promotion of civil society and research on current affairs.

The annual report for 2010 noted that:

It has been decided that Parthenon will undertake no grant-giving or other charitable activities in 2011. However, the Elysium Foundation, a Swiss charitable foundation of which Mrs Whittaker is a trustee, will continue to undertake charitable activities in 2011 and there is an ongoing commitment by the Elysium Foundation to provide continued funding if and when required, so as to ensure that Parthenon's obligations can be met as they fall due.

In 2010 the trust had an income of £1.1 million, mostly from donations and gifts and assets stood at £131,000. there were 20 grants made totalling £1.2 million, broken down as follows:

Medical research	£522,000
International aid organisations	£284,000
Assistance to the disadvantaged	£220,000
Culture and heritage purposes	£150,000
Medical treatment and care	£138,000
Education	£50,000

Beneficiaries included: Cancer Research UK (£400,000); Friends of Diva Opera (£150,000); Mont Blanc Foundation (£125,000); Ungureni Trust (£117,000); International Committee of the Red Cross, UNICEF UK (£100,000 each); Ashoka Africa (£84,000); Downside Up (£75,000); Cecily's Fund (£40,000); Andover Young Carers (£10,000); Basingstoke-Hoima Partnership for Health, Esther Benjamins Trust, Leprosy Mission, North Hampshire Medical Fund, Trinity Winchester, United Aid for Azerbaijan (£5,000 each); Feet First World Wide, Kariandusi School Trust and Langalanga Scholarship Fund (£2,500 each).

In addition to direct charitable expenditure on grants the trust provided £122,000 of sponsorship expenses for an event at the Albert Hall to help raise funds for Asthma UK and José Carreras International Leukaemia Foundation.

Exclusions
No grants for individuals, scientific/geographical expeditions or projects which promote religious beliefs.

Applications
In writing to the correspondent. Anyone proposing to submit an application should telephone the secretary beforehand. Unsolicited written applications are not normally acknowledged. Most grants are awarded at a trustees' meeting held early in the new year, although grants can be awarded at any time.

The Peacock Charitable Trust

Medical research, disability, general

£1.7 million (2009/10)

Beneficial area
UK with a possible preference for London and the south of England. .

c/o Charities Aid Foundation, Kings Hill, West Malling, Kent ME19 4TA
Tel: 01732 520081
Fax: 01732 520001
Correspondent: The Administrator
Trustees: Charles Peacock; Kenneth Burgin; Bettine Bond; Dr Clare Sellors.
CC Number: 257655

Information available

Accounts were available at the Charity Commission.

This family trust was administered personally by Mr and Mrs Peacock for almost 35 years, with the assistance of Mr D Wallace who prepared reports on the majority of applicants to the trust for presentation to the trustees. Following the retirement of Mr Wallace the administration was taken over by the Charities Aid Foundation (CAF). No changes to grant making policy or practice have occurred with the main aims and objects being to advance the education of poor and deserving young boys and girls, and the relief of poverty, hardship, suffering and distress.

The trust has also previously commented that many of the repeated grants go towards the running costs of organisations, in recognition of the fact that charities need, and sometimes lack, continuity. It says its newer grants are often for capital purposes. Some of its recent grants have also helped organisations to pay off their debts.

The trustees rely on CAF to present charities requiring grants to them; although we note the majority of present beneficiaries are recipients of recurrent grants. As such, the opportunity for new applicants to be successful appears limited.

In 2009/10 the trust had assets of £40.7 million and an income of £2.9 million, half of which came from legacies. Grants were made to 93 organisations totalling almost £1.7 million. Grants ranged from £1,500 to £105,000, although the majority were for £10,000 or less. Just £80,500 in grants in total went to organisations not supported during the previous year.

The largest grants were made to: Cancer Research UK (£105,000); Macmillan Cancer Support (£103,000); Fairbridge (£100,000); Marie Curie Cancer Care (£82,000); Neuro Disability Research Trust (£70,000); Brain Research Trust and the Jubilee Sailing Trust (£50,000 each); and St Wilfred's Hospice (£47,000).

Other beneficiaries included: British Eye Research Foundation (£32,000); Mental Health Foundation (£30,000); Action for ME and the Parkinson's Disease Society of the UK (£25,000 each); Addaction (£20,000); Arthritis Care (£16,000); Listening Books and Motivation (£15,000 each); Combat Stress and the Salvation Army (£10,000 each); Not Forgotten Association (£8,000); Marine Conservation Society, RNLI and the Straight Talking Project (£5,000 each); the Endeavour Club and REMAP (£3,000 each); and the St Helier Kidney Patients' Association (£1,500).

Exclusions

No donations are made to individuals and only in rare cases are additions made to the list of charities already being supported.

Applications

In writing to the correspondent.

The Dowager Countess Eleanor Peel Trust

Medical research, the elderly, socially disadvantaged people and general

£476,000 (2009/10)

Beneficial area

Worldwide, in practice UK, with a preference for Lancashire (especially Lancaster and District), Cumbria, Greater Manchester, Cheshire and Merseyside.

Trowers & Hamlins LLP, Sceptre Court, 40 Tower Hill, London EC3N 4DX
Tel: 020 7423 8000
Fax: 020 7423 8001
Email: secretary@peeltrust.com
Website: www.peeltrust.com
Correspondent: Allan J Twitchett, Secretary
Trustees: Sir Robert Boyd; John W Parkinson; Michael Parkinson; Prof. Richard Ramsden; Prof. Margaret Pearson; Julius Manduell.
CC Number: 214684

Information available

Accounts were available at the Charity Commission. The foundation also has a helpful website.

The Dowager Countess Eleanor Peel Trust was established by trust deed in 1951 in accordance with the terms of her will. The objects of the trust are for general charitable purposes but with a preference for medical charities, charities for older people and those who are disadvantaged. There is a schedule to the trust deed listing 'scheduled charities' the trust may also support.

Grants are made to:
- medical charities including medical research
- charities in connection with old people
- charities assisting people who have fallen upon hard times through no fault of their own, and
- various charitable bodies specified in the Trust Deed

The trustees have a clear preference for supporting charities and projects in the North West of England, from where the trust fund monies originally emanated.

In each category, trustees will consider the following areas:
- medical charities – research and care specifically aimed at benefitting older people, to include Alzheimer's, macular disease, prostate cancer and Parkinson's disease
- charities in connection with old people – old age, homes, carers
- charities for people fallen upon hard times – those helping people with a disability, hospitals, hospices, ex services charities, relief

after natural or man-made disasters, mental health charities (including drug and alcohol addiction) and homelessness.

In 2009/10 the trust had assets of over £14.7 million and an income of £535,000. There were 56 grants made totalling £476,000, and were categorised as follows:

Medical charities (including medical research)	£145,000
Charities assisting people facing hardship	£130,500
Charities in connection with older people	£32,500
Charities listed in the trust deed	£20,000
Other charitable purposes	£148,000

Beneficiaries included: Peel Medical Research Trust (£91,500); The Healing Foundation (£75,000); University of Liverpool (£50,000); Wellbeing of Women (£40,000); Peel Studentship Trust – University of Lancaster (£34,000); British Red Cross (£15,000); Age UK (£12,500); Daniel Turnberg Trust Fund and the Calvert Trust (£10,000 each); Cumbria Flood Relief Recovery Fund (£7,500); Fareshare (£5,000); People's Dispensary for Sick Animals (£2,500); and the Olive Branch (£1,500).

Exclusions

Grants are not made to charities substantially under the control of central or local government or charities primarily devoted to children. Due to the number of applications received, the trust is usually unable to support small local charities with a gross annual income of less than £50,000, or those with substantial surpluses. Applications from individuals are not considered.

Applications

The trustees apply the following criteria in making grants:

1. There is no geographical limitation on applications; however applications from charities in the 'preferred Locations' of Lancashire (especially Lancaster and District), Cumbria, Greater Manchester, Cheshire and Merseyside will receive preference over applications from other geographical areas.

2. The trustees focus on small to medium sized charities where grants will make a difference. Applications from large well-funded charities (with income in excess of £2.5 million per annum) will normally be rejected, unless the project is a capital project.

3. The trustees aim to support fewer charities with larger average grants (£5,000 or more).

4. The trustees' preference is to support capital projects or project driven applications and not running costs, although the trustees are flexible to take account of the needs of smaller charities.

5. The trustees do make grants to disaster appeals which are considered on a case by case basis.

The trustees feel it is important to know the charities to which grants are or may be awarded. They will therefore from time to time arrange to visit the charity and/or arrange for the charity to make a presentation to a trustees meeting.

Applications for grants along with the required supporting information, should be forwarded by post.

The following information is required:

- a general outline of the reasons for the application
- the amount of grant applied for
- the latest annual report and audited accounts
- if the application is for a major capital project, details of the cost of the project together with information regarding funds already in hand or pledged.

A grant application form can be downloaded from the trust's website.

Print out the application form before filling it in and enclosing it with any other information that you may feel is relevant.

Applications for Medical Research Grants

Applications for medical research grants will be categorised as appropriate for a 'minor grant' (£10,000 or less) or a 'major grant' (greater than £10,000 per annum for a defined research project for 1–3 years). Applications to be considered for a major grant will be assessed en-block annually at the trustee's March meeting. Applications will be competitive and will be met from funds set aside for this purpose. The following additional information is required:

- aims, objectives and direction of the research project
- the institution where the research will be carried out and by whom (principal researchers)
- An outline of costs and of funding required for the project and details of any funds already in hand.

A brief (but not too technical) annual report on the progress of projects receiving major grants will be requested from the research team.

Common applicant mistakes

'Not fully considering the trustees' grant making strategy on our website before submitting an application, including applications from charities primarily concerned with children, which are prohibited by the terms of the trust deed from receiving funds from the trust.'

Pendragon Charitable Trust

Life sciences, medical research, social welfare

Beneficial area

UK and overseas.

Cadogan Trustees Limited, Royalty House, 32 Sackville Street, London W1S 3EA
Tel: 020 74345 6068
Fax: 020 74345 6001
Email: admin@ pendragoncharitabletrust.co.uk
Website: www.pendragoncharitable trust.co.uk
Correspondent: Cadogan Trustees Limited
Trustee: Cadogan Trustees Limited.
CC Number: 1139718

Information available

Information was taken from the trust's website.

Registered in January 2011, the trust provides the following information on its website about its objectives:

We are set up to support exclusively charitable projects, with a focus in the following 3 areas:

- to advance the education of the public in the life sciences and to promote medical research with the aim of improving human health by supporting research, training, public engagement and dissemination of knowledge
- to advance the Catholic values for the public benefit
- to relieve of those in need by reason of youth, age, ill-health, disability, financial hardship or other disadvantage.

We intend to focus within these three areas on the major barriers and challenges experienced by those in need or experiencing disadvantage or hardship. The Pendragon Charitable Trust intends to support and work closely with organisations in the UK or abroad, that share its vision to provide practical solutions in the areas above.

Applications

Applications can be made online using the form on the trust's website. Applications can also be made in writing to the trust via email, and must include full contact information and funding proposal fully describing the project. The following guidelines are taken from the trust's website:

> When describing the project, all applicants should include information about the organisation(s) running the project, the need the project is seeking to address, the activities that will be undertaken, and a project budget. We may contact you to request additional information or documentation needed to assess your application and the eligibility of the project under the law of England and Wales.
>
> Applications will be considered for decision at scheduled intervals throughout the year.
>
> In exceptional circumstances, it may be possible to assess an application on a more flexible basis to meet project timetables so please indicate any timing requirements clearly in your application.
>
> If your application is successful, you will be notified as soon as possible after the decision has been made on the contact details you provide.

The Performing Right Society Foundation

New music of any genre

£1.6 million (2010)

Beneficial area

UK.

29–33 Berners Street, London W1T 3AB

Tel: 020 7306 4233

Fax: 020 7306 4814

Email: info@prsformusicfoundation. com

Website: www. prsformusicfoundation.com/

Correspondent: Fiona Harvey, Applications Manager

Trustees: Prof Edward Gregson; Simon Platz; Michael Noonan; Baroness Morris of Yardley; Sally Millest; Paulette Long; Mick Leeson; Stephen McNeff; Lesley Douglas; Simon Darlow.

CC Number: 1080837

Information available

Accounts were on file at the Charity Commission. Further information is available on the foundation's detailed and helpful website.

The PRS for Music Foundation (PRSMF) is the UK's largest independent funder purely for new music of any genre. Its main aims are to support, sustain and further the creation and performance of new music in the UK and increase the public's appreciation of, and education in, new music. The foundation describes its work in the following way in its 2010 accounts:

> The foundation supports music creators, performers and promoters who are involved in creatively adventurous or pioneering musical activity. In particular, support is focused on music creators (composers / song-writers / producers) who live and work in the UK and on not-for-profit performers, festivals and promoters who are based in the UK. The foundation supports a huge range of new music activity – everything from unsigned band showcases to residencies for composers, from ground breaking commissions to live electronica, from the training of music producers to cross art form commissioning.

The foundation has a range of funding schemes and often works in partnership with other organisations to develop pioneering new programmes. In 2010 it was involved in the following activities:

- grant-giving schemes to provide core support for new music organisations
- project grants to stimulate the creation and performance of new music
- partnership programmes with other organisations to develop long-term support for new music and stimulate significant change e.g. in professional development, international showcasing and collaboration

- the New Music Award, to create a pioneering new work and raise the profile of new music.

Full details of the foundation's activities are available on its website, including grant-making policies, priorities for each scheme and application forms.

2010 marked the beginning of a new 3 year funding partnership between the foundation and PRS for Music, which is donating £1.5 million per year in the period 2010–2012.

In 2010 the foundation had assets of £440,000 and an income of £1.9 million. Grants were made totalling £1.6 million. The foundation offers the following analysis of its grantmaking during the year:

- 82% of our grants supported new work and infrastructure across all genres
- 18% was awarded to partnership programmes which supported professional development for emerging talent (e.g. British Music Abroad, Aftershock, Composer in the House, Take Five, scholarships and bursaries) and collaboration (e.g. Beyond Borders, international creative exchanges).

New music across the UK has been supported, with 9% of funding to Scotland, 6% to Wales, 2% to Northern Ireland and 83% to England or UK-wide.

Unrestricted grants were categorised as follows:

Organisations	£268,000
Festivals	£203,000
New works	£193,000
Performance groups	£181,000
Promoters	£143,000
Partnerships	£92,000
Prizes and awards	£68,000
Special projects	£10,000
Unsigned award	£2,300

Restricted grants developed with strategic partners were distributed in the following programmes:

New Music Plus ... North West	£126,000
British Music Abroad	£119,000
Beyond Borders	£105,000
New Music Plus ... London	£55,000
National Film and Television School PRSF/Alan Hankshaw scholarships	£10,000
New Music 20x12	£3,000

A list of grant recipients was not included in the accounts. However, details of previously funded projects are available on the foundation's website, although without information on the individual grant awards. They included: London

Sinfonietta, Way out West, Jazz North East, SXSW, Camden Crawl, Flavour Magazine, Punch Records, The Irene Taylor Trust, NU Century Arts, Youth Music Theatre: UK, The Opera Group, The Late Music Festival, Chimera Productions and Oh Yeah Music Centre.

Bands and artists supported include: James Blake, Jessica Curry, The Scottish Flute Trio, Matthew Bourne, Aaron Cassidy, Shiva Feshareki, Imogen Heap and Fuzzy Lights.

Exclusions

The foundation will not offer funding for:

- recordings/demos
- college fees
- musical equipment or instruments

Applications

Apply via the foundation's website. The application forms for each programme also include full guidelines for applicants. Only one scheme per calendar year can be applied for. Deadlines for applications vary from programme to programme. Contact the foundation or check its website for further information. The foundation stresses that it funds NEW music.

Common applicant mistakes

'Submitting applications for activities which the foundation does not support; a lack of new UK music in the programme of work; poor marketing plans; and a lack of focus or unclear project aims and objectives.'

The Jack Petchey Foundation

Young people aged 11 – 25 in the London boroughs, Essex and the Algarve, Portugal

£4 million (2010)

Beneficial area

London, Essex and the Algarve, Portugal.

Exchange House, 13–14 Clements Court, Clements Lane, Ilford, Essex IG1 2QY
Tel: 020 8252 8000
Fax: 020 8477 1088
Email: mail@jackpetcheyfoundation. org.uk
Website: www. jackpetcheyfoundation.org.uk
Correspondent: Trudy Kilcullen, Chief Operating Officer
Trustee: Jack Petchey Foundation Company
CC Number: 1076886

Information available

Accounts were available at the Charity Commission. The foundation's website includes guidelines, specific areas of benefit, application forms and good general information. Information was also provided by the foundation's staff.

This foundation was established in 1999 by Jack Petchey and gives grants to programmes and projects that benefit young people aged 11 – 25. Jack Petchey was born in July 1925 in the East End of London. From a background with very few advantages he became a prominent entrepreneur and businessman. The foundation is a rapidly expanding trust that is eager to help young people take advantage of opportunities and play a full part in society by broadening their horizons and strengthening their positive skills to grow into healthy and considerate citizens.

In the UK the foundation benefits all London boroughs and Essex. In 2004, the foundation introduced a programme in the Algarve, Portugal. It focused initially on the Albufeira District. In July 2005 the Loulé District was included and in January 2006, Silves District. The objectives of the work in Portugal are the same as those established in the UK. The following excerpt is taken from the 2010 accounts:

The Jack Petchey Foundation celebrated its 10th anniversary in 2009/10. The following has been achieved during the first 11 years:
- Grants totalling over £65 million have been given to youth and school projects.

- Over 12,000 Achievement Awards are made to young people each year contributing millions of pounds to support their youth organisation/school.
- The Jack Petchey Achievement Award Scheme operates in over 2,000 schools and youth groups.
- Over 75 presentation ceremonies each year highlight the achievements of young people and promote a positive perception of youth.
- Nearly all the uniformed youth organisations in London and Essex benefit from grants, including Army Cadets, Police Cadets, Sea Cadets, Air Cadets, Scouts, Guides, Boys' Brigades, Girls' Brigades and St John Ambulance.
- The "Jack Petchey Speak Out Challenge!" is now the largest speaking competition for young people in the world.
- The "Jack Petchey Foundation Step into Dance" programme in partnership with the Royal Academy of Dance now operates in 150 schools.
- Sponsorship of many overseas/community projects including: Fulcrum Challenge, Raleigh International, Groundwork East London, Schools Worldwide.
- The Foundation has assisted over 76 schools in raising funds to obtain Specialist School Status.
- approx. £5.5 million has been given to support "Out of School Hours" or "Study Support" programmes 'for example in Tower Hamlets, Barking & Dagenham, Newham and Waltham Forest.
- £500,000 given to establish the "Centre for Entrepreneurship" at the University of East London which opened in 2009.
- £1.7 million to support the Summer Uni programme in all London boroughs.
- £1 million given to enable the Sea Cadets to purchase a training ship 'TS Jack Petchey.
- £1 million to establish an accommodation lodge at Gilwell Park Scout Activity Centre.
- Sponsorship of the Petchey Academy in Hackney which had a very successful Ofsted monitoring visit in January 2009.
- Many millions of pounds given to support youth sports programmes, performing arts, training schemes, mentoring and counselling programmes across London and Essex.

In 2010 the foundation had an income of £5 million. Grants were made totalling £4 million.

Achievement Award Scheme
The Jack Petchey Achievement Award Scheme is run in almost 2,000

schools, colleges and clubs throughout London and Essex, contributing millions of pounds to youth organisations. The scheme is a reward and recognition initiative which enables schools and clubs to celebrate the achievements of young people AND receive additional funding for the organisation.

Over £2 million is allocated to this scheme each year. The benefits of these awards are that they:

- enable schools/colleges/youth clubs etc., to recognise the effort, endeavour and achievement of young people in a practical and positive way;
- provide additional funds for schools/colleges and youth clubs worth £2,300 plus, a year, including the leader awards' small grant scheme;
- enable young people to nominate an adult to win a leader award (for a youth worker, volunteer, teacher, non-teaching member of staff and so on).

Each month participating youth clubs, schools, colleges etc. select one young person to receive an achievement award. The month's winner receives a framed certificate and a cheque (payable to the school/college/club) to be spent on a school, club or community project of the recipient's choice.

There are two categories, one for youth or sports clubs or programmes operated outside schools and one for educational establishments.

Individual grants for volunteering

The foundation will consider sponsoring young people (11–25 years old) living in London and Essex who are undertaking voluntary projects that will benefit other young people or specific charities. The normal support from the foundation will be £300 (maximum of 50% of the costs).

A sponsorship form is available from the foundation's website. Applicants should check the following points:

- do you live in the foundation's area?
- does the project benefit other young people (charity/school/community project)?
- will each applicant raise at least half of the total amount?

- the form should be carefully completed by the young person concerned (not the adult leader or parent) and endorsed by the adult leader for the relevant organisation, club, school.

Petchey Academy

The Petchey Academy is a school in Hackney, which opened in September 2007. The Jack Petchey Foundation sponsors the Academy and made a £2 million contribution to the construction of the school. The state of the art building was completed on time and on budget. The school can accommodate 1,200 students. The specialism is 'Health, Care & Medical Sciences'.

The school is heavily oversubscribed with over 1,000 students chasing 180 places each year. The school does not select by ability but focuses on the local community. All the students come from within 2 kilometres of the school. For more information visit: www.petcheyacademy.org.uk

Jack Petchey's Speak Out Challenge!

The foundation sponsors the Jack Petchey's Speak Out Challenge! a public speaking competition run by SpeakersBank in schools throughout London and Essex. Jack Petchey's Speak Out Challenge! is the largest speaking competition for young people in the world. Almost 20,000 year 10 students from 32 boroughs in London and 14 districts in Essex participate in the challenge.

The students have the opportunity to talk openly and honestly on any subject they feel strongly about. Every student receives up to six hours of training in the skills of public speaking and effective communication from professional trainers. For more information visit: www.speakoutchallenge.com

Step Into Dance

Step into Dance is a fully inclusive, open access dance programme funded by The Jack Petchey Foundation and led by the Royal Academy of Dance. The programme offers weekly, extra-curricular dance classes to secondary schools in selected London boroughs. The programme aims to widen participation in dance for secondary school students aged between 11 and 16 years old.

The programme aims:

To provide a fully inclusive and sustainable dance programme.

To engage both students and in-school teachers in the benefits of dance and guide them to further training opportunities.

Aimed at 11–16 year olds, the programme runs over at least two terms, with dance teaching offered in 10 week blocks. Participation in the programme is free for schools and dance classes are offered as 2 – hour sessions per school, per week, on an extra-curricular basis, unless otherwise requested. For more information visit: www.stepintodance.org

Panathlon Challenge

The Panathlon Challenge seeks to inspire young people with disabilities to use competitive sport and fair play as a means of social and personal development.

Since 1996, Panathlon has provided training courses, coaching grants, free equipment and mini Paralympic type competitions to young people with disabilities in London, Kent, Essex and Merseyside. The organisation continues to expand in 2009/10.

Panathlon is the only organisation in England to offer young people with severe special needs the chance to compete in sport at both local and regional level. It is a unique social opportunity as well as a sporting one, allowing young people to meet outside of the school community, and providing opportunities both for friendship and heightened competition. For more information visit www.panathlon.com.

TS Jack Petchey

The Jack Petchey Foundation donated £1 million to enable The Marine Society & Sea Cadets to build a new power-training ship for young people. The 'TS Jack Petchey' has 16 berths and will train 16,000 young people over an anticipated lifespan of 25 years. For more information visit: www.ms-sc.org

Grants for 2010 were broken down as follows:

Schools	£1.3 million
Youth clubs/projects	£877,000
Sports clubs	£622,000
Uniformed organisations	£563,000
Training	£518,000

Disability	£70,500
Advice/support/counselling/ mentoring	£21,000
Volunteering	£17,000
General	£16,500
Housing/homelessness	£9,000
Medical/hospice/hospital	£4,600

During 2010 the Foundation supported many programmes in London and Essex and administered grants from £200 to £550,000.

Beneficiaries of the largest grants included: SpeakersBank Limited (£546,000); Royal Academy of Dance RAD (£440,000); School Planners (£80,000); ETTA (£70,500); Army Cadet Force (£67,000); Panathlon Challenge (£42,500); Boys' Brigade and Community Links (£19,000 each); YMCA and STEMNET (£10,000 each).

Exclusions

The foundation will not accept applications:

▶ that directly replace statutory funding

▶ from individuals or for the benefit of one individual (unless under the Individual Grants for Volunteering)

▶ for work that has already taken place

▶ which do not directly benefit people in the UK

▶ for medical research

▶ for animal welfare

▶ for endowment funds

▶ that are part of general appeals or circulars.

The foundation is also unlikely to support:

▶ building or major refurbishment projects

▶ conferences and seminars

▶ projects where the main purpose is to promote religious beliefs.

Applications

Application forms for each of the grant schemes can be downloaded from the foundation's website. There are no deadlines for applications but they should be made in 'good time' before the money is needed. The foundation holds monthly management meetings and aims to give a decision within six weeks.

Common applicant mistakes

'Applicants don't meet our criteria or fail to provide requested information.'

The Pilgrim Trust

Social welfare and the preservation of buildings and heritage

£2.4 million (2010)

Beneficial area

UK, but not the Channel Islands and the Isle of Man.

Clutha House, 10 Storeys Gate, London SW1P 3AY

Tel: 020 7222 4723

Fax: 020 7976 0461

Email: info@thepilgrimtrust.org.uk

Website: www.thepilgrimtrust.org.uk

Correspondent: Georgina Nayler, Director

Trustees: Lady Jay of Ewelme; Tim Knox; Paul Richards; Sir Mark Jones; Sir Alan Moses; John Podmore; James Fergusson; David Verey; Prof. Colin Blakemore; Lady Riddell; Sarah Staniforth; Michael Baughn.

CC Number: 206602

Information available

Accounts were available at the Charity Commission. The trust also has an excellent website.

The Pilgrim Trust was founded in 1930 by the wealthy American philanthropist Edward Stephen Harkness. Inspired by his admiration and affection for Great Britain, Harkness endowed the trust with just over £2 million. Harkness did not want the charity named after him, so the decision was taken to name the charity The Pilgrim Trust to signify its link with the land of the Pilgrim Fathers. It was Harkness's wish that his gift be given in grants for some of Britain's 'more urgent needs' and to 'promote her future well-being'. The first trustees decided that the trust should assist with social welfare projects, preservation (of buildings and countryside) and the promotion of art and learning. This has remained the focus of The Pilgrim Trust and the current Board of

Trustees follows Harkness's guidelines by giving grants to projects in the fields of Preservation and Scholarship and of Social Welfare. Trustees review these objectives every three years.

General

In 2010 the trust had assets of £56.6 million and an income of £1.2 million. Grants were made across both of the trust's programme areas totalling almost £2.4 million, broken down as follows:

| Preservation and scholarship | £1.3 million |
| Social welfare | £1.1 million |

Programmes

The following is taken from a funding guideline document available in full on the trust's website, with the main points reproduced here:

Preservation and scholarship

▶ Preservation of and repairs to historic buildings and architectural features. Special consideration is given to projects that give new use to buildings of outstanding architectural or historic importance.

▶ Conservation of monuments or structures that are important to their surrounding, including buildings designed for public performance.

▶ Conservation of works of art, books, significant ephemera, museum objects and records associated with archaeology, historic buildings and the landscape. Note: funding for such work is considered only if normal facilities are not available.

▶ Promotion of knowledge through academic research and its dissemination, including cataloguing within museums, galleries and libraries and institutions where historic, scientific or archaeological records are preserved. Note: funding is restricted to works for which public funds are not available. Costs for preparing the work for publication will be considered but not those for the publication itself.

▶ Cataloguing of archives and manuscripts: The Pilgrim Trust is currently funding the cataloguing of archives and manuscripts through the National Cataloguing Scheme administered through the National Archives. Please visit the National Archives website for more information: www.nationalarchives.gov.uk

▶ Conservation of manuscripts is funded through the National Manuscripts Conservation Trust. Please visit the National Archives website for more information

▶ Places of Worship. To apply under our block grant allocation scheme please contact the relevant administering organisation directly:

- The Pilgrim Trust is currently funding repairs to the historic fabric of cathedrals through a programme administered by the Cathedrals Fabric Commission for England (CFCE). For information on eligibility and how to apply, please visit the CFCE website: www.churchcare.co.uk
- Appeals for fabric repairs to churches in England and Wales should be sent to: National Churches Trust, 31 Newbury Street, London EC1A 7HU.
- Appeals for fabric repairs to churches in Scotland should be sent to: Scottish Churches Architectural Heritage Trust, 15 North Bank Street, The Mound, Edinburgh EH1 2IP.
- Appeals for fabric repairs to churches in Northern Ireland should be sent directly to the Pilgrim Trust.
- Appeals for historic contents of Church of England churches should be directed to: Church Buildings Council, Cathedral and Church Buildings Division, Church House, Great Smith Street, London SW1P 3NZ.
- Appeals for historic contents of non-Church of England establishments (including Northern Ireland, Scotland and Wales should be sent directly to the Pilgrim Trust.

Social Welfare

- Projects supporting people who misuse drugs or alcohol that fall within the following theme. Applications that fall outside this thematic area will not be considered.
  - Projects to support the families and/or carers of people who have been or are misusing drugs or alcohol, trustees include an interest in projects which assist the individual substance misuser where support for the family is integral part of the package or care delivered, as well as evidence led approaches to support the families and carers of substance misusers.
  - Projects to support substance misusers with complex social needs. Trustees have an interest in supporting projects which incorporate a robust, integrated approach to the treatment of

substance misuse where issues such as domestic violence, care for children, prostitution, or homelessness may feature as additional difficulties.
  - Evidence driven projects will be prioritised.
- Projects in prisons and projects providing alternatives to custody that fall within the following themes:
  - Projects that seek to reduce the use of custody for women. Trustees will include work with women with extreme vulnerabilities which are likely to lead to offending. Organisations applying in this area will be expected to have considerable experience and expertise in work with women with multiple and complex needs.
  - Projects that seek to support women who are leaving custody and that assist them to reintegrate with society and their families. Trustees have an interest in projects that assist female offenders and ex-offenders families, particularly their children.

Proposals for small academically robust research projects that meet the Trust's priority themes and that provide tangible outputs in either policy or practical terms will also be accepted. Projects that link to our priorities in both prisons and substance misuse are particularly welcome.

Please note that for all research projects that a full specification will need to be submitted at second stage.

Applications regarding the above will be considered for:

- revenue costs such as staff salaries but generally not equipment costs
- project costs
- the costs of initial exploratory work for organisations seeking to rescue important buildings, monuments etc.
- capital costs.

Grantmaking

Trustees committed £1.5 million for spending in 2010 with £733,000 and £259,000 forward commitments for 2011 and 2012 respectively. They awarded 91 grants with the main grants averaging just over £32,000.

The following table [see below] shows how the Pilgrim Trustees committed the trust's funds during 2010. Although trustees aim to spend 60% of their grant giving on preservation and scholarship and 40% on social welfare, their commitments must reflect the quality of the applications they receive. They are not bound by these percentages; they are an aim and trustees are free to vary the allocations.

Recent beneficiaries include: Toynbee Hall (£45,000); Prisoners' Advice Service (£30,000); The Paddocks Riding for All (£20,500); The Wallace Collection and the Jewish Museum (£15,000 each); and the Belfast Preservation Trust (£10,000).

Exclusions

Grants are not made to:

- individuals
- non UK registered charities or charities registered in the Channel Islands or the Isle of Man
- projects based outside the United Kingdom
- projects where the work has already been completed or where contracts have already been awarded
- organisations that have had a grant awarded by us within the past two years. Note: this does not refer to payments made within that timeframe
- projects with a capital cost of over £1 million pounds where partnership funding is required
- projects where the activities are considered to be primarily the responsibility of central or local government
- general appeals or circulars
- projects for the commissioning of new works of art
- organisations seeking publishing production costs
- projects seeking to develop new facilities within a church or the re-ordering of churches or places of worship for wider community use

THE PILGRIM TRUST

Grants committed by region and subject area (2010)	Preservation and scholarship	Social welfare	% by region	Total
National organisation	£513,000	£595,000	44.7%	£1.1 million
Scotland	£165,000	£30,000	7.9%	£195,000
Wales	£54,000	£0	2.2%	£54,000
Northern Ireland	£125,000	£20,000	5.9%	£145,000
London	£74,500	£171,500	9.9%	£246,000
'Home counties'	£81,500	£60,000	5.7%	£141,500
Rest of England	£347,000	£241,500	23.7%	£588,500
Total by subject area	**£1.3 million**	**£1.1 million**	**100%**	**£2.4 million**

- any social welfare project that falls outside the trustees' current priorities
- arts and drama projects – unless they can demonstrate that they are linked to clear educational goals for prisoners or those with drug or alcohol problems
- drop in centres – unless the specific work within the centre falls within one of the trustees' current priority areas
- youth or sports clubs, travel or adventure projects, community centres or children's play groups
- organisations seeking funding for trips abroad
- organisations seeking educational funding, e.g. assistance to individuals for degree or post-degree work or school, university or college development programmes
- one-off events such as exhibitions, festivals, seminars, conferences or theatrical and musical productions.

Applications

Main Grant Fund

As our primary grant outlet, this fund distributes approximately 90% of our annual grant budget. If the project fits our programme criteria, organisations can apply under this scheme for sums above £5,000.

Small Grant Fund

This fund is reserved for requests of £5,000 or less. Applications to this fund normally require less detailed assessment (though a visit or meeting may be required) but applicants should include the names of two referees from organisations with whom they work.

Full funding guidelines are available from the trust's website. Applications can also be made online or a form can be requested from the correspondent. The trustees meet quarterly.

The Pilkington Charities Fund

General, health, social welfare, people with disabilities, older people and victims of natural disaster or war

£350,500 (2009/10)

Beneficial area

Worldwide, in practice mainly UK with a preference for Merseyside.

Rathbones, Port of Liverpool Building, Pier Head, Liverpool L3 1NW
Tel: 0151 236 6666
Fax: 0151 243 7003
Email: sarah.nicklin@rathbones.com
Correspondent: Sarah Nicklin, Trust Administrator
Trustees: Neil Pilkington Jones; Mrs Jennifer Jones; Arnold Philip Pilkington.
CC Number: 225911

Information available

Accounts were available at the Charity Commission.

The trust was established in 1950 to assist employees or former employees of Pilkington's or any associated companies. It now mainly supports registered charities in the areas of social welfare, disability, health, medical research and overseas aid. A small proportion is reserved for the benefit of present or former employees of the Pilkington Glass Company.

Grants are awarded twice a year, in November and April. Most range from £1,000 to £8,000, though larger grants for up to £100,000 are sometimes made, and typically go to national or international charities.

In 2009/10 the trust had assets of £17.4 million and an income of £444,000. Grants were made to 100 organisations totalling £350,000.

As in previous years, the largest grant was awarded to the C & A Pilkington Trust Fund (£66,000). The more general distributions were for less than £5,000 each with the exception

of: Cancer Research UK and the Willowbrook Hospice – St Helens (£10,000 each); Home Farm Trust (£8,000); Shelter (£7,000); and Team Oasis (£6,000).

Other beneficiaries of £5,000 or less included: Alzheimer's Research Trust; Changing Faces; Foundation for the Study of Infant Death; Kidney Research UK; Missing People; Parents Against Drug Abuse; Somali Umbrella Group; Toxteth Town Hall Community Resource Centre; and Wirral Autistic Society.

Exclusions

Grants are only made to registered charities. No grants to individuals.

Applications

In writing to the correspondent. Applications should include the charity registration number, a copy of the latest accounts and details of the project for which support is sought.

Polden-Puckham Charitable Foundation

Peace and security, ecological issues, social change

£333,000 (2009/10)

Beneficial area

UK and overseas.

BM PPCF, London WC1N 3XX
Email: ppcf@polden-puckham.org.uk
Website: www.polden-puckham.org.uk
Correspondent: Bryn Higgs, Secretary
Trustees: Harriet Gillett; Linda Patten; Daniel Barlow; Bevis Gillett; Val Ferguson; Ben Gillett; Suzy Gillett; Jean Barlow.
CC Number: 1003024

Information available

Accounts were available at the Charity Commission.

Established in 1991, the foundation gives the following information about its areas of interest:

> In the limited areas described below we support projects that seek to influence

values and attitudes, promote equity and social justice, and develop radical alternatives to current economic and social structures.

Peace and Sustainable Security

We support the development of ways of resolving violent conflicts peacefully, and of addressing their underlying causes.

Environmental Sustainability

We support work that addresses the pressures and conditions leading towards global environmental breakdown; particularly national initiatives in UK which promote sustainable living.

Our resources are limited and we receive a huge number of applications. In order to make informed grant decisions we have to focus our grant-giving in a number of ways. For this reason we fund organisations in UK that are working to influence policy, attitudes and values at a national or international level. These may be single issue groups working to achieve a particular change, or organisations with a broader remit. We give particular consideration to small pioneering headquarters organisations.

We only support practical projects when they are clearly of a pioneering nature, with potential for influencing UK national policy.

Size of grants and supported organisations

We usually give grants of between £5,000 and £15,000 per year, for up to three years. We usually support organisations for whom this would represent between 5% and 50% of their annual income (organisations with an annual income of between £10,000 and £300,000 approximately).

In 2009/10 the foundation had assets of £12.7 million and an income of £459,500. There were 53 grants made to 51 organisations during the totalling £333,000. During the year there were 33 new organisations supported. Grants were broken down as follows:

Environmental sustainability	26	£168,600
Peace and security	21	£138,400
Other	5	£22,000
Quaker	1	£4,000

Beneficiaries during the year included: British American Security Information Council (£15,000); Climate Outreach Information Network and Scientists for Global Responsibility (MEDACT*) (£11,000 each); British Pugwash Trust, International Coalition to ban Uranium Weapons (Manchester Environmental Research Centre Initiative*), Peace and Security

Liaison Group (Lansbury House Trust Fund*) and Oxford Research Group (£10,000 each); Crisis Action UK (MEDACT*) (£9,000); Public Interest Research Centre and the Transition Network (£8,000 each); Apollo Gaia Project (Unit for Research into Changing Institutions*) (£7,000); Conflicts Forum (Street Theatre Workshop Trust*) and Oil Depletion Analysis Centre (£6,000 each); Airport Watch (Airfields Environment Trust*) and the UK Social Investment Forum (£5,000 each); Quaker Council for European Affairs British Committee (£4,000); Solar Aid and Women's International League for Peace and Freedom (MEDACT*) (£3,000 each); Be the Change (Gaia Foundation*) (£2,000); and World Court Project (Institute of Law and Peace*) (£1,400).

*The names in brackets are charitable organisations receiving the grants on behalf of campaign organisations for their educational and research work.

Exclusions

The foundation does not fund:

- organisations that are large (see general section)
- organisations that are outside UK (unless they are linked with a UK registered charity and doing work of international focus)
- work outside the UK (unless it is of international focus)
- grants to individuals
- travel bursaries (including overseas placements and expeditions)
- study
- academic research
- capital projects (e.g. building projects or purchase of nature reserves)
- community or local practical projects (except innovative projects for widespread application)
- environmental/ ecological conservation
- international agencies and overseas appeals
- general appeals
- human rights work (except where it relates to peace and environmental sustainability).

Applications

The trustees meet twice a year in spring and autumn. Application forms and guidance notes can be

downloaded from the foundation's website and must be submitted via email. Applicants are also asked to submit their latest set of audited accounts and an annual report, preferably via email.

Note: the foundation is happy to provide brief feedback on applications one week after the trustees have made a decision.

Common applicant mistakes

'Common applicant mistakes are: not reading our criteria; not applying using our application process; not reading current guidelines but assuming they have not changed for over five years; applying even though they know they are unlikely to fit our guidelines; reading our guidelines but not with sufficient care.'

The Polonsky Foundation

Arts, social science, higher education institutions

£743,500 (2009/10)

Beneficial area

UK, Israel and the USA.

8 Park Crescent, London W1B 1PG
Correspondent: The Trustees
Trustees: Dr Georgette Bennett; Dr Leonard Polonsky; Valarie Smith.
CC Number: 291143

Information available

Accounts were available at the Charity Commission.

Established in 1985, this is the foundation of Dr Leonard Polonsky, executive chairman of Hansard Global plc, a global financial services company based in the Isle of Man and listed on the London Stock Exchange. Its aims and objectives are as follows:

To support higher education internationally, principally in the arts and social sciences, and programmes favouring the study and resolution of human conflict. Much of this work is part of ongoing programmes being undertaken in conjunction with various Departments of the Hebrew University of Jerusalem and the Bezalel Academy of Art and Design, as well as other organisations within the United States and the United Kingdom.

In the 2009/10 the foundation had assets of £46.2 million and an income of £1.1 million. Grants were made to 23 organisations totalling £743,500.

Beneficiaries included: The Jewish Museum (£250,000); British Friend of Haifa University (£107,000); Royal Shakespeare Company (£81,000); Bezalel Academy of Art and Design (£60,500); New York University (£20,500); Yale University (£18,500); Port Regis School (£8,500); Lincoln College (£5,000); North Western Reform Synagogue (£2,000); and Whitechapel Foundation (£1,000).

Applications

In writing to the correspondent.

Porticus UK

Social welfare, education, religion

See below

Beneficial area

UK.

4th Floor, Eagle House, 108–110 Jermyn Street, London SW1Y 6EE
Tel: 020 7024 3503
Fax: 020 7024 3501
Email: porticusuk@porticus.com
Website: www.porticusuk.com
Correspondent: Nathan Koblintz
Trustees: Louise A Adams; Mark C L Brenninkmeyer; Stephen R M Brenninkmeyer.
CC Number: 1069245

Information available

Accounts were available from the Charity Commission. Further information was taken from the charity's website.

The charity was previously called Derwent Charitable Consultancy, which administered the Waterside Trust, whose grant making has now been succeeded by other sources in the Netherlands advised by Porticus UK.

It is believed to be one expression of the philanthropy of the Brenninkmeyer family, founders of the C&A clothing stores in Europe. Long-term fundraisers will remember organisations such as the Marble Arch Trust. The family always sought the minimum of publicity for their energetic and much admired work.

Though the family's Catholic interests were always apparent, the range of their philanthropic interests have been wide and enterprising over the years.

Porticus UK is not in itself a grantmaker – it advises and assesses grants on behalf of several foundations in the Netherlands, including Stichting Porticus.

Porticus UK has four areas of interest and recommends in the region of 170 grants each year. Grants are normally in the range £10,000 to £25,000 but occasionally larger projects are funded. Total funds available amount to around £4 million each year.

The following information on the charity's programmes and guidelines is taken from its website:

> Porticus UK's mission is to have solidarity with the poor and the marginalised, reflecting our Christian responsibility and support for the social teaching of the Roman Catholic Church. We do this through the provision of high quality charity advice, grant assessment and administration, and services to our donors and partners that promote organisational effectiveness.
>
> We aim to offer a dynamic service, providing both effectiveness and initiative whilst remaining an organisation in touch with people's needs.
>
> The success of our work is judged, ultimately, by how much long-lasting and tangible impact is made on people's lives; whilst producing changes which ensure the respect of our network partners, beneficiaries and donors.
>
> We have no set funding limits and instead prefer to fund at a variety of levels.
>
> Although our values are based in the Catholic faith, we welcome applications from all organisations, whether or not they have a faith basis.
>
> We understand that a charity's funding priorities are not always specific project costs, and so welcome applications for

developing policy, advocacy and research.

We put particular emphasis on organisations which have a proven model and wish to expand.

Strengthening Family Relationships

Encouraging and cherishing the family relationship that is so often central to people's lives, is at the centre of what we do. The support we offer aims to strengthen those family relationships that are most vulnerable and strained. We, therefore, look for applications which are focused on:

- building networks and connections that tackle family isolation, especially where there is disability or illness
- offering respite for families with a member who is terminally ill or disabled
- encouraging family cohesion through drop-in centres and intensive family support, particularly among families who have been under considerable stress from issues of violence and abuse
- tackling isolation of the elderly, especially through intergenerational work.

Enriching Education

We recognise that a well-rounded, holistic education is crucial in allowing a person to shape their future. Our funding, therefore, is aimed at educational projects which deal with the disadvantaged and vulnerable, with a particular interest in Catholic schools and education based on Catholic social teaching. We are particularly interested in projects which focus on:

- pastoral care in education focused on projects which deal with character building, conflict resolution and values
- educational opportunities for groups who have missed out on traditional learning, especially prisoners and ex-offenders
- the professional development of teachers.

Transformation through Faith

As the roots of our philanthropy are in the Catholic faith, we are keen to support projects which nourish and develop that faith in a complex world. We look to fund the following particular areas:

- the development of Church and lay leadership capacities
- projects which encourage ecumenical collaboration
- organisations and projects which focus on inclusion
- the promotion of exploration and discussion around difficult issues, both within the Christian family and in dialogue with other Faiths.

Ethics in Practice

Porticus UK sees moral formation and ethical decision making as crucially important in today's complex societies. We, therefore, support work guided by Catholic Social principles and directed at the development of the values and virtues of professionals and leaders. Since ethics cannot be considered in isolation, we are particularly interested in interdisciplinary and applied approaches. We will consider applications for:

- developing courses, case studies and training
- facilitating constructive public or private debates
- research projects on the ethical problems encountered in specific professions
- business ethics and medical ethics
- initiatives that enhance understandings of Catholic social teaching.

In 2010 Porticus UK assessed 488 applications which resulted in 129 new grants being made.

Exclusions

No grants to non-registered charities.

Applications for the following will not be considered:

- high profile appeals
- major capital projects or restoration of buildings
- grants to individuals
- endowment appeals
- overseas projects (including travel).

Applications

On an application form available from the charity's website. Applications can be submitted at any time.

The charity also says that: 'if you are unsure whether your project/ organisation fits in with our guidelines, you are welcome to submit an initial brief outline of your organisation and funding requirements'.

The Prince of Wales's Charitable Foundation

Culture, the environment, medical welfare, education, children and youth and overseas aid

£6.8 million (2009/10)

Beneficial area

Unrestricted.

The Prince of Wales's Office, Clarence House, St James's, London SW1A 1BA
Tel: 020 7930 4832 ext 4788
Fax: 020 7930 0119
Website: princeofwales.gov.uk
Correspondent: David Hutson
Trustees: Sir Michael Rake; Lord Rothschild; Leslie Jane Ferrar; Dame Amelia Fawcett.
CC Number: 1127255

Information available

Accounts were available at the Charity Commission.

The Prince of Wales's Charitable Foundation was established by trust deed in 1979 for general charitable purposes. The foundation principally continues to support charitable bodies and purposes in which the founder has a particular interest, including culture, the environment, medical welfare, education, children and youth and overseas aid.

The foundation makes small grants of up to £10,000 and 'major grants' – new guidance on how to apply for major grants will be available on the foundation's website from early 2012.

In 2009/10 the foundation had assets of £14.5 million and an income of over £4.8 million, most of which came from donations. Grants were made to 39 organisations during the year totalling almost £6.8 million, from both restricted and unrestricted funds, and were broken down as follows:

Environment	£3.7 million
Culture	£1.5 million
Medical welfare	£324,500
Education	£297,500
Overseas aid	£173,000
Children and young people	£14,200
Other	£731,000

There were 21 grants made over £10,000 each listed in the accounts. Many of the larger grants were awarded to other Prince of Wales charities.

Beneficiaries included: The Great Stewart of Scotland's Dumfries House Trust (£975,000); The Prince's Foundation for Integrated Health (£186,000); Mihai Eminescu Trust (£158,000); The Prince's School of Traditional Arts (£85,000); Wells for India (£52,500); Leprosy Mission England and Wales and English National Opera (£46,000 each); Great Ormond Street Children's Hospital (£39,000); Music in Country Churches (£20,000); and Peak Choice Ltd (£10,000).

Exclusions

No grants to individuals.

Applications

In writing to the correspondent:

- write a letter setting out brief details of the project for which you are seeking support and how it fits the foundation's criteria. You should include details of your beneficiaries, where you work and any other charities or agencies that work with you
- include the latest audited accounts for your charity and a note from your treasurer of your current financial position and how this award will help.

The Foundation of Prince William and Prince Harry

General, social welfare, children and young people

See below

Beneficial area

UK and overseas.

St James's Palace, London SW1A 1BS
Tel: 020 7024 5694

Information available

Information was available from the
foundation's website.

Registered in late 2009, the
foundation has broad, general
charitable purposes. Specific interests
include: children and young people;
health; the environment and
conservation; and the armed forces.

The following information is
provided by the foundation:

The Foundation of Prince William and
Prince Harry was set up in September
2009 to enable The Princes to take
forward their charitable ambitions. The
Duchess of Cambridge, now officially a
Patron of the foundation, shares similar
charitable interests to her husband and
Prince Harry and will also use her
position to help those in need. [...]

The foundation is the culmination of
The Princes' charitable lives so far.
Along with The Duchess of Cambridge
they intend to use the foundation as the
main vehicle for their future charitable
activities and through raising
sustainable sources of funds, the
foundation will be able to make
charitable grants and support projects
of particular interest. The foundation
has collaborated with two organisations
to date (Fields in Trust and ARK).

Areas of focus
Although their foundation is not limited
to these three areas of focus, The Duke
and Duchess of Cambridge and Prince
Harry aim to make the following their
early areas of focus:

- Young People – particularly those of
their own age and younger who are
disadvantaged or in need of
guidance and support at a crucial
time in their lives
- Sustainable development –
particularly to build on the growing
awareness of the need to find better,
more sustainable, models to balance
development and the conservation
of resources and the natural
environment
- Armed Forces – for the welfare of
those who serve their country in the
Armed Forces. Particularly looking
after those who return broken in

body or mind – or not at all – and
their families.

The Duke and Duchess and Prince
Harry will also aim to use their
foundation to respond to other needs
and opportunities although at this point
the foundation is unable to accept
unsolicited requests for support.

The trustees of the foundation also
include Anthony Lowther-Pinkerton,
private secretary to the princes, Guy
Monson, chief executive of
investment managers Sarasin and
Partners, Fiona Shackleton, the lawyer
who represented the Prince of Wales
in his divorce from Diana, Princess of
Wales, Sir David Manning, former
British ambassador to Washington,
and Edward Harley, president of the
Historic Houses Association.

The foundation's first annual report
and accounts for 2010, which became
available in late 2011, showed an
income of £629,000 and a total
expenditure of £164,000. All of the
money spent by the foundation went
on governance, staff and recruitment
costs associated with the getting the
foundation operational. It is
anticipated that the foundation will
begin making grants in 2012.

Applications

The foundation is not currently
seeking unsolicited applications
(October 2011). Check the
foundation's website for up-to-date
information.

Private Equity Foundation

Children and young people, social welfare, education

£328,500 (2009/10)

Beneficial area
UK and Western Europe.

Information available

Accounts were available from the
Charity Commission. The foundation
also has a helpful and informative
website.

The foundation was established in
2006 as the collective charity for the
UK private equity industry. Detailed
information on its activities is
provided by the foundation:

PEF is committed to enabling
disadvantaged children and young
people to reach their full potential. By
identifying the most effective
interventions and supporting charities
to deliver them more efficiently and
effectively, more young people can
reach their potential.

PEF matches the business skills of the
private equity community to charities in
order to enable them to achieve scale
and become more efficient and
effective in their work. As a result, PEF
makes invaluable contributions to the
portfolio of charities and to the lives of
thousands of young people. PEF's
unique model of venture philanthropy is
helping charities to reach their potential
and helping to change the lives of
individuals and communities.

PEF envisions a world in which every
individual achieves their full potential.
Our mission is to empower children and
young people to achieve this and to
enable the private equity industry to
reach its potential and give something
back to the community. In order to
achieve this, PEF has developed the
following strategy:

- to work with disadvantaged children
and young people, helping them to
engage with society and fulfil their
potential
- to enable charities to increase their
social impact and demonstrate clear
and measurable outcomes
- to make the private equity industry
leaders in venture philanthropy
- to become a leading expert on the
issue facing children and young
people by pursuing a rigorous and
innovative research and political
engagement programme
- to establish a reputation for rigour
and high impact social investment
- to develop a model for sustainable
revenue
- to develop a highly skilled, expert,
flexible, focused and results driven
team.

On an annual basis, the trustees formulate objectives against which the management team and the portfolio of charities are measured. These include fundraising targets, overheads budgets and strategic decisions over investment.

Grantmaking policy

The foundation's annual report gives an interesting insight into the process of selecting charities for its portfolio:

PEF's aim continues to be to build a small but powerful portfolio of charities to provide a range of interventions to help disadvantaged children and young people to fulfil their potential. PEF believes that, by identifying the most effective charities and helping to scale them up, it can shift the needle on the NEET issue and transform thousands of lives.

PEF primarily focuses on UK charities, but also aims to work across Europe and already works with three charities in Germany, applying the same rigorous model to help charities achieve step change in their activities and expanding their support to more children and young people.

Although the specific selection criteria for portfolio charities may change from year to year, PEF will select grantee charities primarily for the following criteria:

- the potential for the intervention to contribute to solving the problems of children and young people
- the ability of the charity's leadership and the organisation to develop their work to its full potential
- the alignment of the potential grantee to PEF's mission, funding, support resources and overall strategy.

Broadly, the process for sourcing and selecting new charity investments will be as follows:

1. Expressions of Interest – PEF publicises the opening of its grant round and invites interested organisations to lodge Expressions of Interest via [its] website. PEF also informs its partners, members and supported who might be able to refer suitable organisations to PEF.
2. Screening and initial research – PEF staff members scrutinise the list of interested parties, carrying out initial research with a view to arriving at a shortlist of potential charities.
3. Due Diligence – the shortlisted charities undergo due diligence by the PEF staff and pro bono supporters from the private equity community. Due diligence follows the model employed by private equity with the process having been specifically tailored to PEF's needs.

4. Selection and approval – following due diligence, suitable charities with the potential to join the portfolio are put to the PEF board. The board then makes the decision on which charities PEF should invest in and the level of any investment.
5. SWOT process and grant agreement – A SWOT [Strengths, Weaknesses, Opportunities and Threats] team is assembled to assess and identify the key challenges facing the charity as they look to achieve PEF's targets for growth. Headed by a 'deal captain' the team will work towards a grant agreement that will be agreed between PEF and the grantee charity. At this stage specific deliverables will be agreed, upon which the disbursement of funds contingent. Throughout the grant period and beyond, the grantee charity will benefit from the pro bono resources of PEF and the wider private equity community.

Grants are generally for a period of three years. Throughout, and beyond, the grant period, the grantee charity will receive close support and guidance from PEF and our pro bono supporters. By utilising the expertise and drive of the private equity community, PEF can help the portfolio of charities to scale up and reach more young lives and achieve social change in communities across the UK and Europe.

In 2009/10 the foundation had assets of £3.4 million and an income of almost £4 million, £3.5 million of which was in the form of donations from private equity firms. Grants were made to 5 organisations totalling £328,500 (£2.5 million in 2008/09). Support costs associated with grantmaking totalled £606,000, although this figure remained about the same as the previous year when total grants were considerably higher.

The beneficiaries during the year were: Place2Be (£160,000); Skill Force (£120,000); City Year (£25,000); Community Links (£21,500); and Cranfield Trust (£2,000).

Further information on the purposes for which grants were made can be found on the foundation's website.

Applications

Charities must first complete a form (letter of inquiry) to express an interest in being selected for support from the foundation. The form and further details for applicants are available from the foundation's website.

The Privy Purse Charitable Trust

General

£489,000 (2009/10)

Beneficial area

UK.

Buckingham Palace, London
SW1A 1AA
Tel: 020 7930 4832
Email: ian.mcgregor@royal.gsx.gov.uk
Correspondent: Ian McGregor, Trustee
Trustees: Ian McGregor; Sir Alan Reid; Christopher Geidt.
CC Number: 296079

Information available

Accounts were available at the Charity Commission.

This trust supports a wide range of causes, giving grants to UK-wide and local charities. 'The main aims of the trustees are to make grants to charities of which The Queen is patron and to support ecclesiastical establishments associated with The Queen.'

In 2009/10 it had assets of £2.3 million and an income of £532,000. There were 352 grants made during the year totalling £489,000 (with support costs amounting to just £106), and were broken down as follows:

Ecclesiastical	36	£229,000
Other	314	£156,000
Education	2	£104,000

Most grants were for relatively small amounts. Larger grants were made to: Hampton Court Palace Royal Chapel (£82,000); St James' Palace Royal Chapel (£57,500); Sandringham Group of Parishes (£54,500); Sandringham Church Organ (£20,000); Windsor Great Park Royal Chapel (£16,000); Royal Chapel Appeal Fund (£15,000); and the British Red Cross (£10,000).

Applications

The trust makes donations to a wide variety of charities, but states that it does not respond to unsolicited applications.

Mr and Mrs J A Pye's Charitable Settlement

General

£490,000 (2010)

Beneficial area

UK, with a special interest in the Oxfordshire region and, to a lesser extent, in Reading, Cheltenham and Bristol.

c/o Mercer and Hole Chartered Accountants, Gloucester House, 72 London Road, St Albans, Hertfordshire AL1 1NS

Tel: 01727 869141

Fax: 01727 869149

Email: pyecharitablesettlement@ mercerhole.co.uk

Website: www. pyecharitablesettlement.org/

Correspondent: David S Tallon, Trustee

Trustees: Simon Stubbings; David S Tallon; Patrick Mulcare.

CC Number: 242677

Information available

Accounts were available at the Charity Commission.

The trust was endowed in 1965 by the Pye family of Oxford for general charitable purposes. The trust emphasises that it is currently concentrating its funding in the Oxfordshire region.

The following information is taken from the trust's website:

> In making grants the trustees seek to continue the settlors' interests while expanding them to encompass other causes. Although the trustees have a wide discretion they will mainly entertain applications from causes in, or relating to, projects in Oxfordshire and its surrounds.
>
> The following list is by no means exhaustive and is given for guidance only:

Environmental

This subject particularly deals with organic farming matters, conservation generally and health-related matters such as pollution research and some wildlife protection.

Adult Health and Care

Especially causes supporting the following; post-natal depression, schizophrenia, mental health generally and research into the main causes of early death.

Children's Health and Care

For physical, mental and learning disabilities, respite breaks etc.

Youth Organisations

Particularly projects encouraging self-reliance or dealing with social deprivation.

Education

Nursery, Primary, Secondary or Higher/ Institutions (not individuals).

Heritage and the Arts

Under this category, the Trustees will consider applications relating to heritage and the arts generally.

The overall policy of the trustees is to support under-funded charities in their fields of interest in order to assist those charities to play a fuller role in the community. Unfortunately, due to the demands made it is not possible to support all applications even though they may meet the charity's criteria. However, the trustees particularly recognise the difficulty many smaller charities experience in obtaining core funding in order to operate efficiently in today's demanding environment.

In 2010 the trust had assets of £10.6 million and an income of £620,000. Grants were made to 203 organisations totalling £490,000, with many receiving a grant in the previous year.

Beneficiaries of larger grants included: Organic Research Centre (£135,000); Music@Oxford (£75,000); University College Oxford (£50,000); Harris Manchester College and Magdalen College School (£30,000 each); Association for Post Natal Illness and Oxford Brookes University (£20,000 each); BTCV (£15,000); and Headington School and ORH Children's Hospital Fund (£10,000 each).

Other beneficiaries included: Mansfield College (£6,000); Oxford University Tennis Foundation (£3,000); The Brain Research Trust (£2,000); and the Ashmolean Museum and the Dipex Charity (£1,000 each).

The majority of the trust's grants were for less than £1,000.

Exclusions

Applications will not normally be considered in relation to:

▶ organisations which are not registered charities

▶ individuals
▶ activities which are primarily the responsibility of central or local government
▶ appeals for funds for subsequent redistribution to other charities; this would also preclude appeals from the larger national charities
▶ endowment funds
▶ fabric appeals for places of worship, other than in Oxford, Reading, Cheltenham and Bristol
▶ fundraising events
▶ hospitals and medical centres (except for projects which are clearly additional to statutory responsibilities)
▶ overseas appeals
▶ promotion of religion.

Applications

All applications should be sent to the administrative office (and not to individual trustees). These are reviewed on a continual basis and the trustees meet quarterly to make their decisions. Any decision can therefore take up to four months before it is finally taken. However, all applicants are informed of the outcome of their applications and all applications are acknowledged. Telephone contact will usually be counter-productive.

There are no application forms but the following information is essential:

▶ the registered charity number or evidence of an organisation's tax exempt status
▶ brief description of the activities of the charity
▶ the names of the trustees and chief officers [NB more important than patrons]
▶ details of the purpose of the application and where funds will be put to use
▶ details of the funds already raised and the proposals for how remaining funds are to be raised
▶ the latest trustees report and full audited or independently examined accounts (which **must** comply with Charity Commission guidelines and requirements)
▶ details of full name of the bank account, sort code, and number into which any grant should be paid
▶ the charity's email address.

Common applicant mistakes

Applicants sending too much glossy material. Failure to identify officers and trustees (our guidelines emphasise that we are not influenced by patron's names). There are a regular number of private nurseries [applying] which do not cater for disabled or disadvantaged children and we therefore consider [that they do not have] charitable objects.

We have recently started a website and emphasised that we are concentrating on the Oxfordshire region. It will be interesting to see whether this has been noticed.

Quartet Community Foundation (formerly the Greater Bristol Foundation)

General

£3 million (2009/10)

Beneficial area

West England – Bristol, North Somerset, South Gloucestershire, Bath and North East Somerset.

Royal Oak House, Royal Oak Avenue, Bristol BS1 4GB

Tel: 0117 989 7700

Fax: 0117 989 7701

Email: info@quartetcf.org.uk

Website: www.quartetcf.org.uk

Correspondent: Helen Moss

Trustees: John Kane; Alexander Hore-Ruthven; Mary Prior; Peter Rilett; Alison Reed; Tim Ross; Anna Schiff; Gail Bragg; Prof. Murray Stewart; Cedric Clapp; William Lee; Gill Stobart; Richard Hall; Lin Whitfield.

CC Number: 1080418

Information available

Accounts were available from the Charity Commission.

Quartet Community Foundation supports small, community-based charities and voluntary groups in the West of England whose work benefits local people. It gives grants to a broad range of causes and welcomes applications from both new and established groups. Through their grants programme they aim to:

- help people who are most disadvantaged and isolated
- encourage people to get involved in improving their own community
- give people opportunities others take for granted
- respond to the needs and concerns of people living in local communities.

The foundation runs its own grants programme, the Express Programme. It also manages a range of other funds each with their own criteria, closing dates and maximum amounts (see grants programmes).

In the year 2009/10 the fund had assets of £16 million, an income of £3.2 million and made grants totalling £3 million.

Grant programmes 2009/10

During the year 1,077 grants were distributed to the value of £3 million, 226 of which were to organisations applying for the first time. At the time of writing there were 14 grants programmes available to Bristol, Bath & North East Somerset, North Somerset and South Gloucestershire however the fund's website should be checked for the most recent updates.

Bath Half Marathon Grants Programme

Grants are awarded to small, local voluntary and community organisations for activities involving sport, exercise or play. Priority is given to organisations with an annual income of less than £25,000. Grants can be made up to £5,000 and the average grant is £2,000.

Bristol Youth Community Action Grants Programme

Scheme 1: Grants are awarded to young people-led, community safety projects in Bristol. The maximum grant is £1,000 and the panel meets every 2 months to discuss applications.

Scheme 2: Grants are awarded for locally-based groups providing summer activities for young people.

Churngold Environment Fund Grants Programme

Grants are given to projects that aim to protect the environment in the area of benefit. The maximum grant available is £4,000.

Comic Relief Local Communities Grants Programme

Aims to empower local people, enabling them to make lasting change in their communities. Priority is given to locally based groups in areas of disadvantage that have a clear understanding of the needs of their community. The maximum grant awarded is £10,000 and the average is £5,000. Organisations can apply for funding to:

- increase local services
- build the skills of local people
- increase community cohesion
- respond to local economic needs
- increase access to sport and exercise for people who face social exclusion and isolation.

CYPS Aiming High for Disabled Children Small Grant Programme

This fund is for small voluntary and community sector organisations working in Bristol with 5–19 yr olds for the purpose of providing a quality short break service to children and young people who are disabled. Grants are awarded up to £5,000.

Express Grants Programme (Quartet Community Foundation's own programme)

Grants of up to £2,000 are awarded to small local voluntary and community organisations where a small amount of funding can make a difference in disadvantaged areas. The work of the organisation must benefit people who are disadvantaged or isolated (due to poverty, disability, age, location or culture). Priority is also given to groups that enable people to take opportunities that would not have otherwise been available to them and that reflect the concerns and priorities of people living and working in the area. They are currently welcoming applications for activities that tackle:

- homelessness
- disability
- the care and resettlement of offenders
- disadvantage among children and young people.

Localgiving.com

This online tool allows local charities and community groups to raise money awareness and support. It gives groups web pages that they can simply write and upload themselves; accept donations through and use extensive search facilities. It is free for the first three months then £72 annually thereafter.

Mall Foundation Fund Grants Programme

Grants of up to £1,000 are awarded to small voluntary and community organisations within a 25 miles radius of the Mall (including Weston-super-Mare and Newport, Stroud, Chippenham and Shepton Mallet) which help people in need.

R W Barnes Educational Fund Grants Programme

This programme offers bursaries of up to £2,000 to undergraduate students on programmes of study based around engineering, maths or physics, at certain criteria and exceptions. Applicants must live in certain postcodes.

Red Nose Day Community Cash Grants Programme

Support community groups that undertake work that helps people of all ages to feel more included in their community, build their skills and increase their sense of achievement. Groups must have an income of less than £50,000. Priority is given to groups that promote social cohesion, reduce isolation and help disadvantaged groups and less well supported causes. Grants are between £500 and £1,000.

Stoke Park Group Friends' Fund Grants Programme

Grants of up to £2,000 (average £500) are awarded to individuals and care groups working with people with learning disabilities. The fund intends to benefit clients who previously used the facilities at the now disbanded Stoke Park Hospital Group and its outreach provisions.

University of Bristol RAG Grants Programme

Grants up to £1,000 are awarded to local voluntary and community organisations which benefit people who are disadvantaged or isolated. It also supports people with long-term illnesses.

B&NES Healthy Lives, Healthy People Grants Programme

Please check the website for the latest details as they were not available at the time of writing.

B&NES Supporting Communities Grants Programme

Please check the website for the latest details as they were not available at the time of writing.

Grants to institutions were broken down into the following areas:

Black and minority ethnic groups	88	£253,000
Community	166	£562,000
People with disabilities	247	£681,000
Family	217	£485,000
People who are homeless	15	£107,000
Older people	172	£256,000
Young people	307	£608,000

Beneficiaries included: Voluntary Action North Somerset (£64,000); Amos Vale Cemetery Trust (£50,000); Society of Merchant Venturers (£42,000); Easton Community Children's Centre (£40,000); Big Issue Foundation (£27,000); Bristol Refugee Rights (£20,000); Restore Ltd (£15,000); L'Dub Race Club (£14,000); Epsom Riding for the Disabled (£10,000); St Margaret's Hospice Somerset (£9,000); Bath City Farm (£7,600); Dorset Blind Association (£7,400); and Pre-primary Education Centres in West Bengal (£5,100).

Exclusions

The foundation does not give grants to:

- individuals
- general appeals
- statutory organisations or the direct replacement of statutory funding
- political groups or activities promoting political beliefs
- religious groups promoting religious beliefs
- arts projects with no community or charitable element
- sports projects with no community or charitable element
- medical research, equipment or treatment
- animal welfare
- projects that take place before an application can be processed.

Applications

Before you apply to the Community Foundation check that your group or project meets the following requirements:

- you must be a small charity, community group or local voluntary organisation operating in the West of England i.e. Bath and North East Somerset, Bristol, North Somerset or South Gloucestershire
- you do not need to be a registered charity but you must be able to provide a copy of your group's constitution or set of rules
- your group must be managed by a board of trustees or management committee
- you must be able to provide the foundation with up-to-date financial information for your group.

Applicants should refer to the fund's website for details on how to apply to each grants programme. The funding team can be contacted for any help or advice concerning grants applications.

Queen Mary's Roehampton Trust

Ex-service support

£428,000 (2010/11)

Beneficial area

UK.

2 Sovereign Close, Quidhampton, Salisbury, Wiltshire SP2 9ES
Tel: 01722 501413
Email: qmrt@hotmail.co.uk
Correspondent: Col Stephen Rowland-Jones, Clerk to the Trustees
Trustees: Maj Gen Peter Craig, Chair; Lt Col Simon Brewis; Cathy Walker; James Macnamara; Dr Gordon Paterson; Colin Green; Col Paul Cummings; Ray Greenwood; Com Stephen Farringdon; Beverley Davies; Debbie Bowles; Stephen Coltman; Sir Barry Thornton.
CC Number: 211715

Information available

Accounts were available at the Charity Commission.

The trust is established for the benefit of people who served in the armed forces or services established under the Civil Defence Acts 1937 and 1939 who have suffered a disability in that service and their widows/widowers or dependants.

The trust's objectives are met by making grants to any charities or organisations whose objects include the reception, accommodation, treatment or after-care of persons who come within the charity's objects. Grants are also made in aid of medical or surgical research having particular regard to the needs of people with disabilities who served in the armed forces of the crown.

During 2010/11 the trust carried out a major review of its activities, as described in its annual report:

Against the background of a continuing fall in investment income and the high level of demand, a fundamental review was undertaken on the trust's Grant Making Policies and Strategy. The trustees concluded that the needs of a significant number of war pensioners would remain a high priority for the foreseeable future. It was decided to adopt a more robust approach to applications with due emphasis on the number of war pensioners assisted and the financial need of each organisation. Accordingly, the balance of grants between larger and smaller charities would be redressed in favour of the latter. Furthermore, the trustees would continue to give high priority to Service care homes and housing for the disabled. The trustees would also continue to consider applications for grants towards medical and surgical research which has a specific regard to the needs of disabled members of the Armed Forces. As a result of this review a new compilation of the trust's Working Practices and Policies was established with effect from January 2011.

In 2010/11 the trust had assets of £11.5 million and an income of £481,500. Grants were made to 34 organisations totalling £428,000. The majority of grants were made to ex-service charities concerned with the welfare, housing and care of war disabled ex-service men and women and war widows. Grants were categorised as follows:

Support: general	6	£119,500
Homes	9	£116,500
Housing	7	£97,000
Support: specific groups	5	£59,000
Support: specific needs	5	£27,000
Other	3	£9,000

Beneficiaries included: The Soldiers' Charity (£35,000), for welfare grants; Royal Naval Benevolent Trust (£30,000), for welfare grants; Combat Stress (£25,000); Scottish Veterans' Garden City Association (£20,000), to refurbish properties; Queen Alexandra Hospital Home (£15,000), towards core costs; British Ex-Services Wheelchair Sports Association (£13,000), Gurkha Welfare Trust (£10,500), towards pensions; Royal Alfred Seafarers' Society (£7,000), towards core costs; Council of British Service and Ex-Service Organisations (£5,000), towards administration costs; and Holidays for Heroes Jersey (£1,000).

Exclusions
No grants to individuals.

Applications
On a standard application form available from the correspondent. Representatives of the trust may visit beneficiary organisations.

The Queen's Silver Jubilee Trust

General, in practice grants to organisations supporting disadvantaged young people

£1.3 million (2009/10)

Beneficial area
UK, Channel Islands, Isle of Man and the Commonwealth.

The Prince's Trust, 17–18 Park Square East, London NW1 4LH
Tel: 020 7543 1234
Fax: 020 7543 1200
Email: nicola.brentnall@royal.gsx.gov.uk
Website: www. queenssilverjubileetrust.org.uk
Correspondent: Nicola Brentnall
Trustees: Rt Hon Christopher Geidt; Sir Fred Goodwin; Stephen Hall; Sir Alan Reid; Peter Mimpriss; Michael Marks.

CC Number: 272373

Information available
Accounts were available at the Charity Commission.

The Queen's Silver Jubilee Trust was established in 1977 and while its objects are wide, it is especially concerned with young people who are disadvantaged.

Specific details of the trust's grant programme for 2012 and beyond were unavailable at the time of writing. Check the trust's website for up-to-date information.

The trust gives the following general summary of its grantmaking activities, although potential applicants should note that this information may be subject to change:

The trust gives grants to youth projects based throughout the UK, Commonwealth, Channel Islands, and Isle of Man.

Subject to funds being available for grant-making, the trustees of The Queen's Silver Jubilee Trust will consider applications from registered charities that offer support to young people across the UK, Commonwealth, Channel Islands and the Isle of Man. The Queen's Silver Jubilee is particularly interested in those organisations that support disadvantaged young people or those that enable young people to volunteer in their local community, broadly defined.

The trustees will also consider a small number of applications from registered charities that offer general support to young people, along with applications from youth charities from the Isle of Man, the Commonwealth and the Channel Islands.

Further factors affecting eligibility:
⟩ the age-range for those supported is 14–30
⟩ grants can only be awarded to registered charities
⟩ grants cannot be awarded to individuals.

The trust's annual report provides further details of its objects:
⟩ the advancement of education
⟩ the relief of need, hardship or distress
⟩ the advancement of [the] physical, mental and spiritual welfare [of children and young people]
⟩ the provision of facilities for recreation or other leisure time occupation
⟩ other charitable purposes as the trustees see fit.

In 2009/10 the trust had assets of £35.5 million and an income of £465,000. Grants were made to 15 organisations during the year totalling £1.3 million. The main beneficiary, as in previous years, was the Prince's Trust, which received £1.2 million.

The other beneficiaries were: HMP Coldingley, Nightstop Teeside, Llynfi Valley Project, The Bridge Mentoring Scheme and Read International (£10,000 each); Surf Life Saving GB and Aberlour Children's Trust (£8,000 each); Warwickshire Clubs For Young People and Commonwealth Youth Exchange Council (£5,000 each); Young and Free (£4,000); Oxford Wheels and Clock Tower Sanctuary (£3,000 each); and Wester Hailes Youth Agency and Blue Horizon (£2,000 each).

Exclusions

Grants are only made to registered charities. No grants to individuals.

Applications

Potential applicants are advised to email the contact before making a formal application.

Applicants must ensure that:
- their organisation is eligible
- they have read the *Terms and Conditions* and other guidance notes
- they enclose their most recent annual report and accounts, or financial projections and previous income expenditure charts if the organisation is less that two years old
- they enclose their most recent annual review or a brief summary of what their organisation does
- retain a photocopy of all submitted materials.

In January 2012 the following information was on the trust's website:

The Queen's Silver Jubilee Trust now accepts solicited applications only. It works with charities that run programmes at scale, that enable young people to help others. Detailed guidance concerning our priorities will be published early in 2012, however we would be keen to receive summary information from established UK registered charities that provide this support, at regional or UK-wide level. We would also like to hear from you if you are an established, UK based and regulated charity supporting work of this nature in the Commonwealth, particularly Commonwealth countries in need.

Rachel Charitable Trust

General charitable purposes, in practice mainly Jewish organisations

£3.1 million (2009/10)

Beneficial area

Unrestricted.

F & C Reit Asset Management, 5 Wigmore Street, London W1U 1PB
Tel: 020 7016 3549
Correspondent: Robert Chalk, Secretary
Trustees: Leopold Noe; Susan Noe; Simon Kanter.
CC Number: 276441

Information available

Accounts were on file at the Charity Commission, without a list of grants.

This trust was established in 1978 for general charitable purposes and focuses on the relief of poverty and the advancement of religion and religious education. In practice the trust gives mainly to Jewish organisations.

In 2009/10 the trust had assets of £26.2 million and an income of £4.3 million which included a donation of £2.7 million from Leopold Noe. Grants were made totalling £3.1 million. A separate list of donations made during the year was available from the trustees for £25.

Previous beneficiaries include: British Friends of Shuut Ami, Children's Hospital Trust Fund, Cometville Limited, Encounter – Jewish Outreach Network, Chosen Mishpat Centre, Gertner Charitable Trust, Hertsmere Jewish Primary School, Jewish Learning Exchange, London Millennium Bikeathon, Manchester Jewish Grammar School, Project Seed, Shaarei Zedek Hospital, Shomrei Hachomot Jerusalem, Yeshiva Ohel Shimon Trust and Yeshiva Shaarei Torah Manchester.

Applications

In writing to the correspondent.

The Rank Foundation

Christian communication, youth, education, general

£5.7 million (2010)

Beneficial area

UK.

12 Warwick Square, London SW1V 2AA
Tel: 020 7834 7731
Email: jan.carter@rankfoundation.co.uk
Website: www.rankfoundation.com
Correspondent: Jan Carter, Grants Administrator
Trustees: Earl St Aldwyn; James Cave; Andrew Cowan; Mark Davies; Lindsay Fox; Joey Newton; Lucinda Onslow; Lord Shuttleworth; Hon. Caroline Twiston-Davies; Johanna Ropner; Rose Fitzpatrick; Daniel Simon; Nicholas Buxton; Jason Chaffer.
CC Number: 276976

Information available

Accounts were available from the Charity Commission. The foundation has an informative website.

Summary

This is a heavily proactive foundation, with offices around the country. It concentrates on:
- the promotion of Christian principles through film and other media
- encouraging and developing leadership amongst young people
- supporting disadvantaged young people and those frail or lonely through old age or disability.

Major grants are typically part of a three or five year commitment and very seldom result from an unsolicited application as the projects in this area are mainly identified by staff who have considerable experience and contacts within the field. Small grants (less than £7,500) are usually one off. Local charities are unlikely to get recurrent funding or multi-year awards.

General

The charity was established in 1953 by the late Lord and Lady Rank (the founders). It was one of a number established by the founders at that time and to which they gifted their controlling interest in The Rank Group plc (formerly The Rank Organisation plc), best known as a film production company, though this was but one of its commercial interests. The Rank trusts and foundations all share a Christian ethos.

In 2010 the foundation held assets of £221 million, had an income of £6.8 million and made grants totalling £5.7 million. These figures represent the consolidated accounts for the foundation including the subsidiary media arm, CTCV.

Major projects in 2010

Youth projects

To fund organisations that have the potential to:

- engage with young people in open, thoughtful and exciting ways that foster their all-round development
- deepen and extend the abilities of those who work with young people
- be 'pebbles in the pond' to act within local networks and communities, to collaborate with, and be examples to other groups and agencies.

The youth projects include a youth apprenticeship program and awards scheme, details of which can be found on a separate website: www.rankyouthwork.org

Special projects

In the majority of cases, these programmes are funded through pro-active, research driven activities. The category focuses on two main issues:

- reducing reoffending and community development projects
- building capacity and inspiring local people to do more to help themselves.

The budget for this category has been increased to build upon the foundations capacity to respond to new and emerging needs.

Community Care

The objective of this programme is to invest in projects that will help improve the quality of life and wellbeing of those who are disadvantaged, specifically:

- older people
- people with a physical or learning disability
- people who are mentally ill
- people with long term health conditions
- carers

Grants in this category range from £250 to £300,000 and can be awarded over up to five years.

Volunteering

This programme exists to identify and coordinate a network of young team leaders who will be able to utilise a budget of £1,000 for a campaign within 3 areas which have yet to be announced. Each team leader will also receive a £1,000 bursary upon completion of the programme for personal training or education.

The foundation also has a media arm, **CTCV** which produces content for broadcasters and also works with youth groups to develop technical, creative and life skills through the production of media.

Funding policy

Major grants

The majority of the foundation's grant giving is tied to their proactive, research driven programmes and they very rarely accept unsolicited appeals for major grants.

If you are interested in a major grant (over £7,500) you should contact the respective executive director. If you would like to submit an application for a major grant, in either the Special Project, Youth Project or Community Care category, then you should email a one page outline to the respective executive (see the 'Applications' section for further information). This arrangement is being reviewed and may change in 2012; please check the foundation's website for recent updates.

Small grants

Small general grants are available to encourage imaginative work at local community level. Applications are only accepted from UK registered charities or recognised churches –

there are no exceptions to this rule. Using another charity to bid for funds on behalf of a third party is not permitted.

In considering unsolicited appeals, the foundation prefers applications where there are relatively small, attainable targets and they place great importance on clear evidence of local support. The directors also take into account whether it is likely that any grant they make will be put to immediate use.

Grantmaking in 2010

Grants were distributed in the following areas:

	% of total
Promotion of Christian religion (CTVC)	24%
Youth programme	36%
Community service programme	40%

In the small appeals category, one third of applications were successful resulting in 250 grants being awarded, with amounts from £200–£7,500 mostly for small capital projects or activity costs.

Grants were also illustrated in the foundation's annual report as a geographical analysis:

	% of total	
Anglia	2.6%	£174,000
London	9.9%	£652,000
Midlands	5.3%	£347,000
North East	6.2%	£408,000
North West	8.5%	£558,000
South Central	3.3%	£214,000
South East	1.2%	£76,000
South West	5.9%	£387,000
Total	**43%**	**£2.8 million**

	% of total	
Northern Ireland	2.5%	£162,000
Scotland	7.3%	£479,000
Wales	3.1%	£206,000
Total	**13%**	**£848,000**

	% of total	
National	44%	£2.9 million

Beneficiaries included: YMCA George Williams College (£179,000); Help the Hospices (£100,000); Belfast Community Sports Development Network and Hemlington Detached Youthwork (£30,000 each); Meningitis Trust and St Pauls Church (£25,000 each); Community Foundation for Lancashire (£22,000); Countryside Alliance Foundation and Women in Prison (£20,000 each); Christians Against Poverty (£15,000); Kings School of Worcester (£575); and Tall Ships Youth Trust (£14,000).

Exclusions

Grants to registered charities only. Appeals from individuals or appeals from registered charities on behalf of named individuals will not be considered; neither will appeals from overseas or from UK-based organisations where the object of the appeal is overseas. In an endeavour to contain the calls made upon the foundation to a realistic level, the directors have continued with their policy of not, in general, making grants to projects involved with:

- agriculture and farming
- cathedrals and churches (except where community facilities form an integral part of the appeal)
- cultural projects
- university/school building and bursary funds
- medical research.

Unsolicited appeals are extremely unlikely to attract a grant for salaries, general running costs or major capital projects.

Applications

Major grants

If you would like to submit an application for a major grant (over £7,500), in either the Special Project, Youth Project or Community Care category, then you should email a one page outline to the respective executive, details of which can be found on the 'contact us' section of the website. This should contain the following information:

- organisation objectives, location and structure (staff numbers)
- outline of what you do and where
- what you are seeking support for – details of the specific programme including costs
- any evidence of partnership working or summary of existing evaluation.

Small grants

Complete the short eligibility quiz online to confirm your application is eligible. This takes you to a short online form to which you can attach supporting documentation.

The following information is required:

- charity name and registration number

- brief details about the project and the sum to be raised – please ensure you include a clear aim or list of objectives
- details of the amount raised so far towards the target and if relevant, briefly mention how you intend to raise the rest
- a copy of the last audited accounts and annual report.

There are two committees: appeals and community care, and education and youth which both meet quarterly. Please note: due to the overwhelming number of appeals, the foundation can only fund about 25% of current applications. If you are unsure whether your appeal is likely to succeed then please contact the grants administrator for further advice.

Due to overwhelming demand, unsolicited appeals are extremely unlikely to attract a grant in connection with salaries, general running costs or major capital projects.

The Joseph Rank Trust

The Methodist Church, Christian-based social work

£6.3 million (2010)

Beneficial area

Unrestricted. In practice, UK and Ireland.

Worth Corner, Turners Hill Road, Crawley RH10 7SL

Tel: 01293 873947

Email: secretary@ranktrust.org

Website: www.ranktrust.org

Correspondent: D J Sanderson, CEO/Director of grants and special projects

Trustees: Lindsay Fox, Chair; Joey Newton; Nicholas Buxton; James Cave; Jason Chaffer; Andrew Cowen; Mark Davies; Rose Fitzpatrick; Lucinda Onslow; Johanna Ropner; Lord Shuttleworth; Daniel Simon; Earl St Aldwyn; Hon Caroline Twiston-Davies.

CC Number: 1093844

Information available

Accounts were available at the Charity Commission. The trust also has a useful website.

This trust was established in 2002 for the advancement of the Christian faith and represents an amalgamation of a number of charities established by the late Joseph Rank, or members of his family, during the period from 1918 to 1942. The original trusts represented a practical expression of the strong Christian beliefs of their founder and his desire to advance the Christian faith and to help the less fortunate members of society.

The trust's three main areas of interest are:

- the adaptation of Methodist Church properties with a view to providing improved facilities for use both by the church itself and in its work in the community in which it is based
- work with young people
- projects that demonstrate a Christian approach to the practical, educational and spiritual needs of people.

The trust also owns CTCV which produces television and radio programmes, and the distribution of films and videos for Christian and educational purposes.

The trust also offers the following information on its grantmaking preferences:

> In considering all appeals, the trustees take into account the primary objective of the trust, which is to advance the Christian faith. After earmarking funds to support their main areas of interest the trustees are prepared to consider other unsolicited appeals, although resources remaining to support such appeals are limited. Unsolicited appeals are selected for consideration by the trustees that demonstrate, in their view, a Christian approach to the practical, educational and spiritual needs of people.

There are two committees dedicated to grant applications- appeals and community care and education and youth.

In 2010 the trust held assets of £225 million (this includes funds from CTCV) and had an income of £6.8 million. Grants were made totalling £6.6 million. £1.6 million was given to the promotion of

Christian religion including the CTVC media company.

The trust gives a geographical breakdown of its grants:

	% of total	
North West England	8%	£558,000
North East England	6%	£408,000
London	10%	£652,000
Midlands	5%	£347,000
South West England	6%	£387,000
Northern Ireland	2%	£162,000
Anglia	3%	£174,000
South Central	3%	£214,000
South East	1%	£76,000
Wales	3%	£206,000
Scotland	7%	£479,000
National*	44%	£2.9 million

*organisations working across the UK rather than regionally

The trust gives a breakdown of the various projects they have funded:

Youth work

Investing in success	£119,000
Key workers	£209,000
Youth/adult (YAP)	£1.2 million
Skills apprentice scheme	£261,000
Bursaries: Rank leadership award	£55,000
Bursaries: other	£44,000
Gap year project	£325,000
General	£157,000
Total	£2.4 million (36%)

Beneficiaries in this area included: Gap Year Project (£325,000); Volunteer Development East Lothian (£73,000); Belfast Community Sports Dev. Network (£30,000); Community Action Placement and Outward Bound (£17,000 each); Ocean Youth Trust (£11,000); and Rugby School (bursary) (£4,000).

Community service programme

Carers	£163,000
Disability	£650,000
Elderly	£340,000
Community care	£160,000
Community development	£268,000
Community service	£273,000
Reoffending	£305,000
Homelessness	£12,000
Special projects	£132,000
General	£327,000
Total	£2.6 million (40%)

Beneficiaries in this area included: Help the Hospices (£100,000); Mentoring Mediation and Communication (£65,000); Forgiveness (£25,000); Winchester Young Carers Project, Liverpool Community Spirit and Cornwall Music Therapy Trust (£20,000 each); Christians Against Poverty (£15,000); Smartmove Exeter (£12,000); and Cricket Foundation (£10,000).

Exclusions

No grants to individuals, for charities on behalf of individuals, or for unregistered organisations.

Applications

On-going commitments, combined with the fact that the trustees are taking an increasingly active role in identifying projects to support, means that uncommitted funds are limited and it is seldom possible to make grants in response to unsolicited appeals.

If applicants consider that their work might fall within the areas of interest of the trust the following basic information is required:
- charity name and charity registration number
- an outline of the project for which funding is sought
- details of the total amount required to fund the project in its entirety
- details of the amount already raised, or irrevocably committed, towards the target
- a copy of the most recent annual report and audited accounts.

Applicants should endeavour to set out the essential details of a project on no more than two sides of A4 paper, with more detailed information being presented in the form of appendices. Applications must be sent in hard copy. If a Methodist Church is applying funding they should read the further information on the trust's website.

In normal circumstances, papers received before the middle of February, May, August and November may be considered in March, June, September and December respectively. Visits to appeals may be made by the secretary and trustees.

All appeals are acknowledged and the applicants advised that if they do not receive a reply by a specified date it has not been possible for the trustees to make a grant.

The Sigrid Rausing Trust

Human, women's and minority rights and social and environmental justice

£21.3 million (2010)

Beneficial area
Unrestricted.

12 Penzance Place, London W11 4PA
Tel: 0207 313 7727
Fax: 020 7908 9879
Email: info@srtrust.org
Website: www.sigrid-rausing-trust.org/
Correspondent: Sheetal Patel, Administrator
Trustees: Dr Sigrid Rausing; Joshua Mailman; Susan Hitch; Andrew Puddephatt; Geoff Budlender.
CC Number: 1046769

Information available
Accounts were available at the Charity Commission.

Summary
The trust was set up in 1995 by Sigrid Rausing and takes as its guiding framework the United Nations' Universal Declaration of Human Rights. Its vision is 'A world where the principles of the Universal Declaration of Human Rights are implemented and respected and where all people can enjoy their rights in harmony with each other and with the environment.'

The trust made its first grants in 1996 and, from the beginning, has taken a keen interest in work that promotes international human rights. It was originally called the Ruben and Elisabeth Rausing Trust after Sigrid's grandparents. In 2003 the trust was renamed the Sigrid Rausing Trust to identify its work more closely with the aims and ideals of Sigrid Rausing herself.

General
The trust has four funding categories which provide a framework for its activities:

- civil and political rights
- women's rights
- minority rights
- social and environmental justice.

Each programme has a number of sub-programmes, which can be found on the trust's website.

The trust has five main principles which guide its grantmaking:

- the essential role of core funding
- good and effective leadership
- flexibility and responsiveness to needs and opportunities
- the value of clarity and brevity in applications and reports
- long term relationships with grantees.

The following is taken from the trust's 2010 accounts and explains the trust's grantmaking policy in further detail:

The trust supports sub-granting organisations as an effective way of ensuring funds reach small grassroots organisations. £845,000 was distributed in this way in 2010. The following is taken from the trust's 2010 accounts:

The trust continued to implement its commitment to long-term relationships with its grantees through the introduction of three year grants. A successful applicant will usually receive initially a one year grant, followed by up to three terms of three year grants. Long-term core support is particularly valued by grantees, [as it] provides increased certainty for the organisations funded, and allows the trust to be more realistic in assessing the impact of the work it funds.

In late 2010, the trust discontinued the open enquiry system for applications. **It no longer accepts unsolicited applications for funding**. The trust has limited resources and enters into long term relationships with its partners. There is, therefore, a limit to how many new organisations the trust can take on.

Organisations invited to apply are allocated to one of the trust's sub programmes. Each sub-programme is considered once a year at one of the trustees' meetings held usually in February, June and October.

Types of grant

Grants may be ear-marked, or given as general support. There is no minimum or maximum level for a grant; however, it would be unusual for the trust to support more than 25% of the costs of an organisation or a project.

The trust may also exceptionally consider supporting existing grantees with an advancement grant, designed to support a major infrastructure change for an organisation.

Emergency funding is available in response to a sudden human rights crisis, or for the protection of human rights defenders. Emergency grants must be given via an existing or previous grantee, who can apply directly to their programme officer.

A detailed breakdown of grantees under each funding stream is available on the trust's website.

Grantmaking in 2010

In 2010 the trust had assets of £7.9 million and a total income of £18.5 million. Grants totalled £21.3 million, some of which will be paid in 2011 and 2012 as part of multi-year commitments. Grants can be broken down as follows:

Civil and political rights	£8.4 million
Women's rights	£4.2 million
Social and environmental justice	£5.7 million
Minority rights	£2.6 million

Beneficiaries across all categories included: Interights – UK (£750,000); The Global Witness Trust – UK (£600,000); International Lesbian and Gay Association European Region – Belgium (£555,000); BTselem – Israel (£450,000); European Roma Rights Centre – Hungary (£375,000); Sisters in Islam – Malaysia (£300,000); Legal Resources Centre – South Africa (£300,000); Mani Tese – Italy (£240,000); Journalists for Human Rights – Canada (£240,000); Memoria Abiert – Argentina (£180,000); NGO Platform on Shipbreaking – Philippines (£150,000); and Zimbiala – UK (£100,000).

Exclusions

No grants are made to individuals or faith based groups. Funds are not normally given for building projects.

Applications

The trust does not accept unsolicited applications for funding. The trust's website does, however, offer the following advice:

From time to time, we may request proposals from organisations working in particular fields. Details of requests will be made available on the trust's website.

If you have not been invited to apply, but wish to let the trust know about your work, you can send an email describing your organisation to: research@srtrust.org. Programme staff review emails regularly, but are unlikely to be able to meet with you in person.

The Rayne Foundation

Arts, education, health, medicine, social welfare

£1.1 million (2009/10)

Beneficial area

UK.

Carlton House, 33 Robert Adam Street, London W1U 3HR
Tel: 020 7487 9650/9630
Email: info@raynefoundation.org.uk
Website: www.raynefoundation.org.uk
Correspondent: Morin Carew, Grants Administrator
Trustees: The Hon Robert Rayne, Chair; Lord Claus Moser; Lady Jane Rayne; Lady Hilary Browne-Wilkinson; Prof. Dame Margaret Turner-Warwick; Prof. Anthony Newman Taylor; The Hon Natasha Rayne; The Hon Nicholas Rayne; Sir Emyr Jones Parry.
CC Number: 216291

Information available

Accounts were available from the Charity Commission. The foundation also has a helpful and informative website.

The foundation provides the following description of its activities on its excellent website:

Background
The Rayne Foundation was established in 1962 by Lord Rayne, who was Life President of London Merchant Securities plc, a diversified property and venture capital business, which he built up and of which he was chairman for forty years until 2000. Lord Rayne was also chairman, trustee or council member of numerous arts, education, medical and social welfare charities. These included Chairman of the National Theatre and St Thomas' Hospital. He remained chairman of the Rayne Foundation until his death in 2003.

Over more than forty years at the Rayne Foundation we have given to many different causes and organisations. As well as being a traditional philanthropist, Lord Rayne took great efforts to ensure that the Rayne Foundation was actively engaged with the needs of society. Examples of the foundation's early work along these lines are the Rayne Institutes – created in London, Edinburgh and Paris in the 1960s and 1970s to build a bridge between medical research and hospitals. Lord Rayne worked with the government, universities and hospitals, drew on his property development expertise and experience and, with contributions from the foundation, he encouraged this new approach and provided buildings where medical researchers and doctors could work alongside each other. This kind of active engagement is now being revived.

Summary
Here at the Rayne Foundation our theme is bridge building. The aims and outcomes of our work are of utmost importance to us, and we measure the success of our own work, our partnerships and our investments by the degree to which they satisfy these two areas:

The 'bridge building' outcomes of our work such as:
- 'enlarged sympathies' – increased understanding and/or tolerance
- reduced exclusion
- reduced conflict
- new productive relationships which benefit the public.

The aims of our work:
- it can have wider than just local application or is of national importance
- it helps the most vulnerable or disadvantaged
- it provides direct benefits to people and communities
- it tackles neglected causes
- it levers other funds and encourages the involvement of other organisations
- it strives to achieve excellence.

Guidelines
We work within four sectors:
- arts
- education
- health and medicine
- social welfare and development.

The 2009/10 annual report also notes that:

As well as its general grant-making across the arts, education, health and medicine, and social welfare and development, the foundation will have at any one time a number of Areas of Special Interest. In each case, the foundation aims to develop a depth, of knowledge and, if appropriate, do more than respond to grant applications.

Our areas of special interest
Within our four sectors we encourage applications which apply to our evolving list of areas of special interest, which are listed below. Excellent applications outside these areas are also welcomed.
- achieving learning outcomes through the work of artists and arts organisations
- improved quality of life for older people
- improved numeracy skills.

During the year over 65% of social investments were outside Areas of Special Interest. This reflects the foundation's interest in supporting innovation and development in many different areas.

What we support
These are the specific types of costs the foundation will fund:
- salaries and all types of project costs plus a reasonable contribution to overheads (there is no fixed percentage)
- general running or core costs (normally for a maximum of three years)
- capital costs of buildings and equipment (unless specifically stated in certain sectors).

We do not specify minimum or maximum amounts [for grants]. You can apply for a specific amount or a contribution to the total cost. Please note we are rarely able to fund a project completely and urge you to approach others to part-fund alongside The Rayne Foundation.

You can apply for a grant towards a programme of any duration, although a period of greater than three years is rare.

Please check the foundation's website for full details and up-to-date information.

Grantmaking in 2009/10
In 2009/10 the foundation had assets of £58.6 million and an income of £1.4 million. Grants paid in the year totalled £1.1 million. The average award was around £14,500 and the maximum award was £50,000.

Grants were distributed as follows:

Arts	£235,000
Education	£98,000
Health and medicine	£146,000
Social welfare and development	£594,000

Beneficiaries included: London Borough of Tower Hamlets (£50,000); Institute for Voluntary Action Research (£40,000); Wigmore Hall (£30,000); Carers UK (£24,000); Tenovus – Youth Cancer Charity (£20,000); Bath Festivals and Watford Grammar School for Boys (£15,000); and Dyslexia Action, Newlife Foundation for Disabled Children and Compassion in Dying (£10,000 each.)

Exclusions
Grants are not made:
- to individuals
- to organisations working outside the UK
- for work that has already taken place
- for repayment of debts
- for endowments
- to those who have applied in the last twelve months.

  Generally speaking, we do not support organisations whose levels of free reserves are higher than 75% of annual expenditure. However, we may make an exception if your organisation makes a contribution from free reserves to the area of work for which you are seeking funding – and if this reduces your free reserves to below 75% of your annual expenditure.

Please do not send 'round robin' or general appeals.

Applications
Applying for a grant is a two-stage process. First you must fill in the Stage One Application Form available from the foundation's website, which you can complete and email to: applications@raynefoundation.org.uk, or print out and post. If it is not possible for you to access the first stage application online you should call the trust on 020 7487 9650.

If you can demonstrate that the foundation's aims will be met, the foundation will contact you to make a more detailed application. They aim to respond to all Stage One proposals within one month of receipt.

Continuation funding – if you have previously received a grant from the foundation, you must complete a satisfactory monitoring report before reapplying. Organisations can only hold one grant at a time. Use the two-stage process for all applications, even if you are asking the foundation to continue funding the same project.

Common applicant mistakes
'Not reading the guidance on our website; not completing the application form fully; and trying to shoehorn their project into our guidance.'

The Sir James Reckitt Charity

Society of Friends (Quakers), social welfare, general

£925,000 (2010)

Beneficial area

Hull and the East Riding of Yorkshire, UK and occasional support of Red Cross or Quaker work overseas.

7 Derrymore Road, Willerby, East Yorkshire HU10 6ES

Tel: 01482 655861

Email: jim@derrymore.karoo.co.uk

Website: www. thesirjamesreckittcharity.org.uk

Correspondent: James McGlashan, Administrator

Trustees: William Upton; James Harrison Holt; Caroline Jennings; Philip James Harrison Holt; Robin James Upton; Sarah Helen Craven; Martin Dickinson; Charles Maxsted; Simon J Upton; Simon E Upton; James Marshall; Edward Upton; Rebecca Holt; Dr Karina Mary Upton.

CC Number: 225356

Information available

Accounts were available from the Charity Commission. The trust also has a useful website.

The charity was founded in 1920 by Sir James Reckitt, who endowed trust with a large number of shares in the family manufacturing business of Reckitt and Sons Ltd.

Summary

The charity gives grants to a wide range of local charities in Hull and the East Riding of Yorkshire as well as to some national charities. Quaker organisations and those in line with Quaker beliefs are supported, and there is an emphasis on those concerned with current social issues. Some of the charity's grants are awarded over a period of years and many organisations are regular recipients. It has a list of regular beneficiaries which it supports on an annual basis, although the recipients

are informed that the grant may end at any time at the discretion of the trustees. Most grants are for £5,000 or less.

Guidelines

The following grant guidelines are taken from the charity's useful website:

> The trustees give support to a wide range of charitable causes. However, in accordance with the wishes of the founder, they give priority to purposes connected with the Society of Friends (Quakers) and those connected with the city of Hull and the East Riding of Yorkshire.
>
> Beyond those two priority areas, the trustees will consider support for national and regional charities, particularly those concerned with current social issues and whose work extends to the Hull and East Yorkshire areas.
>
> Like most other grant makers, the trustees of the Sir James Reckitt Charity prefer to make grants to registered charities. Grants may be made to local non-registered organisations provided they are known to the local Council for Voluntary Service through whom grants may be channelled.
>
> Grants to individuals are very occasionally made depending on the circumstances. Appeals from individual Quakers need the support of their local Monthly Meeting. Appeals from other individuals are normally only considered from residents of Hull or the East Riding of Yorkshire.
>
> Trustees will not normally make grants to support activities for which central or local government are responsible. Neither are they likely to support activities which collect funds to be passed on to other organisations, charities or individuals.
>
> International causes are considered only in exceptional circumstances, such as major disasters, with support usually being channelled through the Society of Friends or the British Red Cross Society.

Grantmaking in 2010

In 2010 the trust had assets of £28 million and an income of £896,000. Grants were made totalling £925,000, and were distributed as follows:

Children	£35,000
Education	£189,000
Elderly	£18,000
Environment	£5,300
Medical	£104,000
Religion	£94,000
Social work	£428,000
Youth	£51,000

There were 184 grants to individuals made totalling £40,000, constituting

£39,000 of the social work figure and £850 of the youth work figure.

Beneficiaries across all categories included: Britain Yearly Meeting (£50,000); Dove House Hospice (£30,000); British Red Cross (£23,000); The Mount School, York (£22,000); Friends School Saffron Walden (£19,000); ZANE Zimbabwe National Emergency (£17,000); Cat ZERO (£15,000); North Humberside Hospice (£10,000); International Rescue Committee UK (£8,500); RAPT Rehabilitation for Addicted Prisoners (£6,000); Hull Pre-School Learning Alliance (£5,500); Tweendykes Special Needs School (£5,000); Barnardo's (£4,000); Farm Africa (£3,000); and Children & Family Action in Withernsea, Tall Ships Youth Trust and Northern Ballet Theatre (£2,000 each)

Exclusions

Grants are normally made only to registered charities. Local organisations outside the Hull area are not supported, unless their work has regional implications. Grants are not normally made to individuals other than Quakers and residents of Hull and the East Riding of Yorkshire. Support is not given to causes of a warlike or political nature.

No replacement of statutory funding or activities which collect funds to be passed on to other organisations, charities or individuals.

Applications

In writing to the correspondent.

The charity provides a checklist of information on its website which should be included in any letter of application:

- the nature of your organisation, its structure and its relationship with other agencies and networks
- the aims of your organisation and its mission statement
- the purpose of the project, the need which has been identified and evidence of the need
- exactly what the grant will be used for
- the total cost of the project and how you intend to raise any balance
- who will benefit from the project, the outcomes and how you will know if the project is successful

- whether your organisation is a registered charity or, if a small local group, it is known to a local CVS
- your bank account payee name to whom the cheque can be made payable
- a set of the latest accounts or a record of income and expenditure which has been subject to independent scrutiny
- your contact details, i.e. address, telephone number and email.

Applications are measured against the charity's guidelines and decisions are taken at a twice-yearly meeting of trustees in May and October. Applications should be submitted by mid-April and mid-September respectively.

Common applicant mistakes

'Applicants who haven't read, or have ignored, our stated criteria; lack of precision over essential details such as date of the project, the funding required or the details of the bank account payee for grant.'

The Reed Foundation

General, arts, education, relief of poverty, women's health

£793,000 (2010)

Beneficial area

UK and developing countries.

6 Sloane Street, London SW1X 9LE
Tel: 020 7201 9980
Email: reed.foundation@reed.co.uk
Correspondent: The Secretary
Trustees: Alec Reed; James A Reed; Richard A Reed; Mrs Alex M Chapman.
CC Number: 264728

Information available

Accounts were available at the Charity Commission.

This trust has general charitable purposes. There has historically been an interest in women's causes in developing countries. The settlor is

Alec Reed, entrepreneur, philanthropist and founder of several successful and high profile charitable ventures.

The Reed Foundation donated £50,000 as a loan in 2007 to set up The Big Give, an online charity comparison site for high-level donors. A further £245 was donated in 2009 to continue and develop the site. During the year the Reed Foundation again sponsored a challenge fund on The Big Give which raised over £8.5 million from an initial Reed pledge of £1.5 million.

In 2010 the trust had assets of £14.8 million and an income of £787,000 (£266,000 in 2009). Grants were made to 185 organisations totalling £793,000 (£2 million in 2009).

Beneficiaries included: World Wildlife Fund – UK (£83,000); Promoting Equality in African Schools (£28,000); The Prince's Trust (£25,000); Self Help Africa and the One Voice Movement (£20,000 each); Friends of the Earth (£15,000); In Kind Direct (£13,500); Activiteens, Refugee Council and British Youth Opera (£10,000 each); Dulwich Picture Gallery (£8,500); The Wildlife Trust for Lancashire, Manchester and North Merseyside (£5,000); and Camden Arts Centre (£1,000). Numerous grants for less than £1,000 were also made.

Applications

In writing to the correspondent. The trust states that it does not respond to unsolicited applications.

Reuben Brothers Foundation

Healthcare, education, general

£916,000 to organisations (2010)

Beneficial area

UK and overseas.

Millbank Tower, 21–24 Millbank, London SW1P 4PQ
Tel: 020 7802 5000
Fax: 020 7802 5002

Email: contact@reubenfoundation.com
Website: www.reubenfoundation.com
Correspondent: Patrick O'Driscoll, Trustee
Trustees: Richard Stone, Chair; Simon Reuben; David Reuben; Malcolm Turner; Michael Gubbay; Annie Benjamin; Patrick O'Driscoll; James Reuben; Dana Reuben; Debra Reuben.
CC Number: 1094130

Information available

Accounts were available at the Charity Commission.

This relatively new trust was established in 2002 as an outlet for the charitable giving of billionaire property investors David and Simon Reuben. The foundation was endowed by the brothers with a donation of $100 million (£54.1 million), with the income generated to be given to a range of charitable causes, particularly to healthcare organisations and for educational purposes. It is likely that organisations in India and Iraq, where the brothers have their roots, may benefit as well as organisations in the UK and Israel.

In 2010 the foundation had assets of £66.3 million and an income of £3 million. Grants were made to 363 organisations totalling £916,000.

One of the foundation's major projects is outlined on its website:

The Reuben Foundation, through a multi-million pound endowment has launched Team London in partnership with the Mayor of London and with the strategic help of New York Mayor Michael Bloomberg.

Based on a programme initially developed by McKinsey & Company for the Mayor of New York, Michael Bloomberg, Team London is an ambitious vision for volunteering which encourages individuals, organisations, public, private and voluntary to work more effectively together to transform communities and the lives of Londoners, particularly in priority need areas.

Introducing the concept of 'impact volunteering' in which existing voluntary community organisations are mobilised to develop strategies to target London's most urgent community needs, Team London will increase the number of voluntary efforts and will set clear outcomes and measurements to judge progress.

Team London will focus on three key areas – crime, improving quality of life and increasing youth opportunities.

The programme was launched to the voluntary community in March 2011 with the official public launch held on 30 June 2011 in City Hall along with the Mayor of London, Boris Johnson, and the Prime Minister's wife, Samantha Cameron. The Mayor, Mrs Cameron and James Reuben each gave speeches to mark the launch of the Team London programme.

The foundation has allocated £2 million to this project, to be paid by the end of 2012, with £230,000 awarded during 2010.

Other beneficiaries during the year included: The Prince's Charities Foundation, Great Ormond Street Hospital's Tick Tock Club and the Community Security Trust (£25,000 each); and Jewish Care (£10,000).

Grants were also made to 16 individuals totalling £54,000.

Applications

In writing to the correspondent, although the trust has stated that applications are by invitation only.

Grant applications are processed with all requests for funds being put before the trustee meetings and the merits of each application being considered. Unsuccessful applicants are notified by post. Donations are sent out to the successful applicants having regard to the current reserves and the long-term policy of the foundation. Trustees meetings are held every month.

The Richmond Parish Lands Charity

General

£663,500 (2009/10)

Beneficial area

Richmond, Kew, North Sheen, East Sheen, Ham, Petersham and Mortlake.

The Vestry House, 21 Paradise Road, Richmond, Surrey TW9 1SA

Tel: 020 8948 5701

Fax: 020 8332 6792

Website: www.rplc.org.uk

Correspondent: Jonathan Monckton, Director

Trustees: Colin Craib, Chair; Ashley Casson; David Marlow; Janet Kingston; Jeffery Harris; John Wylie; Margaret Marshall; Margaret Saunders; Niall Cairns; Rita Biddulph; Robert Guy; Sue Jones; Susan Goddard; Vivienne Press.

CC Number: 200069

Information available

Accounts were on file at the Charity Commission. The charity also has a helpful and informative website.

Established in 1786, the charity supports a wide range of causes in specified parts of the borough of Richmond-upon-Thames, as outlined under 'Beneficial area'.

The charity describes its objectives as:

▶ the relief of poverty in the London Borough of Richmond upon Thames
▶ the relief of sickness and distress in the borough
▶ the provision and support of leisure and recreational facilities in our beneficial area
▶ the provision educational facilities and support for people in Richmond wishing to undertake courses
▶ any other charitable purpose for the benefit of the inhabitants of Richmond.

Strategic priorities are reviewed periodically – from July 2011 the charity's priority for strategic funding was social inclusion. Check the charity's website for current priorities.

In 2009/10 the charity had assets of £59.6 million and an income of £1.4 million. Grants were made to 86 organisations totalling £663,500. Grants were also made to individuals totalling £198,500.

The charity's annual report describes its impact in the local community, and also its focus on core grants which make up over 63% of funding to organisations:

The charity's commitment to the voluntary sector in Richmond has again been demonstrated through grants towards core costs of groups operating in our benefit area. Voluntary groups active in the arts, the environment, health, youth work, care for the elderly and the vulnerable in our community

received core grants in excess of £420,000 to meet a wide variety of need. Such grants gave continuity and security to groups, especially during the recent financial crisis. Each year these grants are reviewed to ensure that they still reflect the profile of need in our benefit area and that the level of the grant reflects this.

Beneficiaries included: RB Mind – Vineyard Project (£53,000 in total); Cambrian Community Centre (£40,000); MiD Mediation and Counselling (£21,000 in total); Brentford Football Community Sports (£20,000); Age Concern (£19,500); Richmond Youth Partnership (£18,000); Richmond Music Trust (£15,000); Latchmere House (£11,000); Ham Youth Centre (£9,000); Off The Record (£7,500); Environment Trust Richmond (£6,000); Furniture Scheme (£5,000); FiSH Neighbourhood Scheme (£4,500); Royal Hospital for Neuro-Disability (£3,000); Crossway Pregnancy Crisis Centre (£2,000); Young Science Events Richmond (£1,000); Greycourt School (£500).

Exclusions

Projects and organisations located outside the benefit area, unless it can be demonstrated that a substantial number of residents from the benefit area will gain from their work. UK charities (even if based in the benefit area), except for that part of their work which caters specifically for the area.

Applications

Organisations receiving core grants from the charity must apply by the deadlines set out in the document available on the charity's website.

If you are applying for a grant that is new or a one-off application, and it does not fall within the charity's recent strategic priorities (see 'General' section) your application will not be considered until January each year.

How to apply

If you would like some clarification on whether your organisation would qualify for a grant, please contact the charity on 020 8948 5701 for guidance.

An application form can be downloaded from the charity's website.

Please be sure that you have filled in all sections and that you have enclosed all the documents requested.

For applications seeking £500 or less there is a different form, which can also be downloaded from the charity's website. These applications are usually considered from November to May.

When your application is received, it will be evaluated and any queries arising from it will be followed up. you may be assured that all eligible applications will be put before the trustees.

There are currently 15 trustees all of whom live within the benefit area. three of them are nominated by the borough council, five are nominated by local voluntary organisations and the remainder are co-opted from the community. the mayor is an ex officio member of the board of trustees.

Eligible applications must be received at least ten working days before the meeting at which they will be considered – check the charity's website for upcoming deadlines.

You will be advised by letter within fourteen days of the meeting whether or not your application has been successful. Following agreement for a grant you will be sent a conditions of grant form setting out the terms and conditions of the grant. Payment will be arranged on receipt of a signed agreement. A monitoring and evaluation form will also be required on completion of your next application form.

Ridgesave Limited

Jewish, religion, education, general

£1.5 million (2009/10)

Beneficial area
UK and overseas.

141b Upper Clapton Road, London E5 9DB
Correspondent: Zelda Weiss, Trustee
Trustees: Joseph Weiss; Zelda Weiss; E Englander.

CC Number: 288020

Information available
Accounts were available from the Charity Commission, without a list of grants.

The trust is largely focused on supporting organisations engaged in education, the advancement of the Jewish religion and the giving of philanthropic aid.

In 2009/10 the trust had assets of £3.8 million and an income of almost £2 million, most of which came from donations. Grants were made totalling £1.5 million. Information on recent beneficiaries was not available.

Previous beneficiaries include: Keren Associates Ltd, BAT, UTA, CM L, TYY, Square Foundation Ltd, Ateres Yeshua Charitable Trust, Side by Side, My Dream Time, British Friends of Rinat Aharon, Chanoch Lenaar, and All in Together Girls.

Applications
In writing to the correspondent.

The Robertson Trust

General

£9.7 million (2009/10)

Beneficial area
Scotland.

85 Berkeley Street, Glasgow G3 7DX
Tel: 0141 221 3151
Fax: 0141 221 0744
Email: enquires@therobertsontrust.org.uk
Website: www.therobertsontrust.org.uk
Correspondent: Lesley Macdonald, Assessment Manager
Trustees: Sir Ian Good, Chair; Richard Hunter; Dame Barbara Kelly; Shonaig Macpherson; David Stevenson; Ian Curle; Fiona McBain.
SC Number: SC002970

Information available
Accounts were provided by the trust; there is also an excellent website.

Summary
A wide range of organisations are supported each year, with grants of all sizes. There are four priority areas:
- health
- care
- education and training
- community arts and sport.

The trust also has a small grants programme for one-off donations of up to £10,000 for a particular project or activity. Outside this programme, there is no set minimum or maximum grant size.

General
The trust was established in 1961 by the Robertson sisters, who inherited a controlling interest in a couple of whisky companies (now the Edrington Group) from their father and wished to ensure the dividend income from the shares would be given to charitable purposes. In 2009/10 the trust had an income of £19 million, assets of £364 million and made grants totalling £9.7 million.

Guidelines
In August 2009 the trust adopted revised guidelines for its priority areas as follows:

Health
This category includes activities which promote health, as well as those which seek to prevent or treat sickness and disease. Examples include projects which work with children who are at risk of misusing drugs or alcohol or are affected by parental substance misuse, and with people recovering from addictions to assist them in rebuilding their lives.

Care
This category is broadly defined. Examples include palliative care, care for older people, people with disabilities, people with mental health issues, people who are homeless and offenders and their families. Support is given to charities working at both local and national level. The category includes sports and arts projects which have a specifically therapeutic purpose.

Education and training
This category includes support for community-based education activities, capital projects at Universities and F.E. Colleges and provision for people with special educational needs. The trust is particularly interested in supporting projects, which increase access and opportunity, develop recognised Centres of Excellence and contribute to the growth of the Scottish economy.

Community arts and sport

This category is primarily aimed at encouraging young people to participate in artistic and sporting activities within their local community. Projects should demonstrate that they provide access and opportunity and/or support emerging talent. The trust is particularly interested in supporting activities which increase the use of existing facilities; however, capital projects which seek to widen opportunity, access and participation, as well as improve provision, will also be considered.

These priority areas account for approximately two-thirds of the trust's expenditure each year. However, applications will be considered from most other areas of charitable activity, including:

- work with children, young people and families
- preservation of the environment
- the strengthening of local communities
- the development of culture, heritage and science
- animal welfare
- the saving of lives.

It should be noted that overall priority will be given to those projects and posts which relate to direct service delivery.

The Robertson Trust currently disburses around £9 million a year. There are no minimum or maximum donations. Donations are classified according to four main types, to which different guidelines apply.

Small Donations comprise revenue donations of up to £5,000 and capital donations of up to £10,000. The application process is designed to be straight-forward and this is an ideal starting points for charities who have done little fundraising before or those with one-off funding appeals.

Main Donations comprise revenue donations in excess of £5,000 and capital donations of between £10,000 and £100,000. Revenue grants rarely exceed £15,000 a year and may be for core or project funding for a maximum initial period of three years. Capital donations will be for a maximum of 10% of the total project cost.

Major Capital Donations comprise capital donations in excess of £100,000, for which the overall project costs will normally be in excess of £1 million. Major capital donations will contribute specifically to one of the trust's priority areas other than where an exceptional case is made. Applications will be considered three times a year, in January, May and September, to allow the trustees to compare the merits of different applications. Organisations considering applying for a major donation are advised to telephone the trust beforehand for an informal discussion.

Development Donations are given under the trust's current special development areas, a list of which can be found in the Development section of the trust's website. Applications for a donation under one of these headings will only be considered after prior discussion with Christine Scullion, the Assessment Manager.

Grants in 2009/10

The trust mentions in its annual review that it is a challenging time for the charitable sector given the budget cuts and their impact upon frontline services. Consequently the trustees decided to concentrate giving on smaller and medium sized charities and so increased the proportion of funds for the small and main categories. The average small donation was £3,500 and the average main was £25,000 over three years. Donations were distributed among the categories as seen in the table below.

Of the priority areas, funding was distributed as follows:

	% of total	
Care	23%	£2.2 million
Education and training	17%	£1.7 million
Community art and sport	15%	£1.5 million
Health	16%	£1.5 million

Beneficiaries included: FARE – new centre for families (£170,000); Marie Curie Cancer Care – new hospice in Stobhill Hospital (£150,000); Girvan Youth Trust (£45,000 over three years); Community Connections – developing entrepreneurial skills and business practices in young people; Bobath Scotland – support of children with Cerebral Palsy (both £42,000 over three years); Edinburgh Community Food initiative – community food co-ops (£36,000 over three years); Royal Caledonian Curling Club – National Disability Officer (£33,000 over three years); The Accord Hospice – palliative care and support; Breast Cancer Care (£30,000 over three years); Independent Living Support – vulnerable individuals affected by homelessness and associated problems (£26,000 over three years); TechFest – Set Point – promotion of science, technology, engineering and mathematics, annual festival (£3,000); Action for Children – supporting young offenders; Outward Bound Metro – outdoor education for inner city young people; Mentor UK – alternatives to drinking; Alcohol Focus Scotland.

Exclusions

The trust does not support:

- individuals or organisations which are not recognised as charities by the Office of the Scottish Charity Regulator (OSCR)
- general appeals or circulars, including contributions to endowment funds
- local charities whose work takes place outside Scotland
- generic employment or training projects
- community projects where the applicant is a housing association
- core revenue costs for playgroups, nurseries, after school groups etc
- projects which are exclusively or primarily intended to promote political beliefs
- students or organisations for personal study, travel or for expeditions whether in the United Kingdom or abroad
- medical research

THE ROBERTSON TRUST

			% of total	Average grant
Small	232	£808,000	8%	£3,500
Main	261	£6.7 million	70%	£26,000
Major capital	8	£1.1 million	11%	£136,000
Development	17	£1 million	11%	£60,000
Total	518	£9.7 million	100%	£19,000

organisations and projects whose primary object is to provide a counselling, advocacy, advice and/ or information service.

The trust is unlikely to support:
- charities which collect funds for onward distribution to others
- umbrella groups which do not provide a direct service to individuals e.g. CVS
- feasibility studies and other research
- charities already in receipt of a current donation from the trust.

Applications

Applicants are advised to read the guidelines available to download on the trust's website.

There are two ways to apply:

By application form which is available on the trusts website, to be returned with the supporting documents, or by letter which should include the following details:
- a brief description of the organisation, including past developments and successes
- a description of the project – what you want to do, who will be involved, where will it take place and how it will be managed
- how you have identified the need for this work
- what you hope will be the outputs and outcomes of this work and the key targets you have set
- how you intend to monitor and evaluate the work so that you know whether or not you have been successful
- the income and expenditure budget for this piece of work
- How you propose to fund the work, including details of funds already raised or applied for
- the proposed timetable.

In addition the trust will also require three supporting documents. These are:
1. A completed copy of the 'Organisation Information Sheet', which is available from the trust's website or the trust office.
2. A copy of your most recent annual report and accounts. These should have been independently examined or audited.

3. A job description, if you are applying for salary costs for a specified worker.

The trust requests that applicants do not send a constitution or memorandum and articles. If there is any other bulky information which you feel may be relevant, such as a feasibility study, business plan or evaluation, then you should refer to it in your application, so that the assessment team can request it if required.

Small and main donations form the bulk of the donations made by the trust and are assessed on a rolling programme with recommendations made to the trustees six times a year.

Applications for major capital donations are considered three times a year in January, May and September.

The Roddick Foundation

Arts, education, environmental, human rights, humanitarian, medical, poverty, social justice

£1.4 million (2009/10)

Beneficial area
Worldwide.

PO Box 112, Slindon Common, Arundel, West Sussex BN18 8AS
Tel: 01243 814788
Email: karen@theroddickfoundation.org
Website: www.theroddickfoundation.org/
Correspondent: Karen Smith
Trustees: Justine Roddick; Samantha Roddick; Gordon Roddick; Christina Schlieske.
CC Number: 1061372

Information available

Accounts were available at the Charity Commission.

The foundation was established in 1997 by the late Dame Anita Roddick, founder of the Body Shop. It has the following objects:

- the relief of poverty.
- the promotion, maintenance, improvement and advancement of education for the public benefit.
- the provision of facilities for recreation or other leisure time occupations in the interests of social welfare provided that such facilities are for the public benefit.
- the promotion of any other charitable purpose for the benefit of the public.

In 2009/10 the foundation had assets of £23.8 million and an income of £488,000. Grants were made to 34 organisations totalling just over £1.4 million. Grants were broken down as follows:

Human rights	14	£560,500
Educational and media	5	£329,000
Poverty and social justice	5	£295,500
Arts and culture	4	£160,000
Environmental	3	£61,000
Humanitarian	1	£30,000
Medical and health	1	£10,000

Beneficiaries included: Mother Jones Anita Fund: A Global Justice Journalism Project (£267,500); Body & Soul (£100,000); Organic Marketing (£99,000); Helen Bamber Foundation (£70,000); New Economic Foundation, World Development Movement and Reprieve (£50,000 each); David Suzuki Foundation (£30,000); Chichester Festival Theatre, Foundation Rwanda and Protect Local Globally (£25,000 each); Crisis Action (£13,000); and Iasis (£10,000).

Exclusions
The trust states that it is 'particularly not interested in the following:'
- Funding anything related to sport
- Funding fundraising events or conferences
- Sponsorship of any kind

Applications
The foundation does not accept or respond to unsolicited applications. 'Grants made by the foundation are at the discretion of the board of trustees. The board considers making a grant and, if approved, notifies the intended recipient.'

The Gerald Ronson Foundation

General, Jewish

£1 million (2009/10)

Beneficial area

UK and overseas.

H W Fisher & Company, Acre House, 11–15 William Road, London NW1 3ER

Tel: 020 7388 7000

Email: jtrent@hwfisher.co.uk

Correspondent: Jeremy Trent, Secretary

Trustees: Gerald Maurice Ronson, Chair; Dame Gail Ronson; Alan Irving Goldman; Jonathan Simon Goldstein; Lisa Debra Ronson; Nicole Julia Ronson Allalouf; Hayley Victoria Goldenberg.

CC Number: 1111728

Information available

Accounts were available at the Charity Commission.

The foundation was registered with the Charity Commission in September 2005. 'The trustees' grant making policy is to make donations to registered charitable organisations undertaking a wide range of charitable activities.' It is the foundation of businessman and philanthropist Gerald Ronson, chief executive of Heron International, a UK-based property developer.

In 2009/10 the foundation had assets of £11.4 million and an income of £150,000. Grants were made totalling just over £1 million, and were broken down as follows:

Education	£414,000
Community and welfare	£370,000
Medical and disability	£117,000
Arts and culture	£82,500
Overseas aid	£28,000
Religion	£17,000
General	£5,000
Relief of poverty	£1,000

The largest grants were made to: Jewish Care (£202,000); The Jewish Community Secondary School Trust (£200,000); United Jewish Israel Appeal (£155,000); The Community Security Trust (£105,000); Great Ormond Street Hospital Children's

Charity (£50,000); Roundhouse Trust (£33,500); and the Royal Opera House (£28,500). A number of grants are made to organisations with which the trustees have a connection.

Applications

In writing to the correspondent. 'The trust generally makes donations on a quarterly basis in June, September, December and March. In the interim periods, the Chairman's Action Committee deals with urgent requests for donations which are approved by the trustees at the quarterly meetings.'

Mrs L D Rope Third Charitable Settlement

Education, religion, relief of poverty, general

£998,000 to organisations (2009/10)

Beneficial area

UK and overseas, with a particular interest in Suffolk.

Crag Farm, Boyton, Near Woodbridge, Suffolk IP12 3LH

Tel: 01473 333 288

Correspondent: Crispin Rope, Trustee

Trustees: Crispin Rope; Jeremy Heal; Anne Walker; Ellen Jolly; John Wilkins; Catherine Scott; Paul Jolly.

CC Number: 290533

Information available

Accounts were available at the Charity Commission.

This charity is based near Ipswich, and takes a keen interest in helping people from its local area. Most of the funds are already committed to projects it has initiated itself, or to ongoing relationships. Unfortunately, only about one in ten applications to this trust can be successful.

Guidelines

The charity offers the following distinction between projects initiated by itself and unsolicited applications:

In practice, the work of the charity may be divided into two distinct categories. Firstly it initiates, supports and pursues certain specific charitable projects selected by the Founder or known to be generally in accordance with her wishes. Secondly, it approves grants to unsolicited applications that fall within the Founder's stated objectives and that comply with the set of grant-making policies outlined below, specifically for this second element of its work. The trustees devote more of the charity's resources to self-initiated projects as compared to pure grant making to unsolicited requests. In terms of grants funded during the year [2009/10], roughly £678,000 was given towards projects where the charity had either initiated the work or where a long-standing relationship over a number of years gave rise to new or continued assistance.

Successful unsolicited applications to the charity usually display a combination of the following features, as outlined in the charity's 2009/10 accounts:

Size
The trustees very much prefer to encourage charities that work at 'grassroots' level within their community. Such charities are unlikely to have benefited greatly from grant funding from local, national (including funds from the National Lottery) or European authorities. They are also less likely to be as wealthy in comparison with other charities that attract popular support on a national basis. The charities assisted usually cannot afford to pay for the professional help other charities may use to raise funds.

Volunteers
The trustees prefer applications from charities that are able to show they have a committed and proportionately large volunteer force.

Administration
The less a charity spends on paying for its own administration, particularly as far as staff salaries are concerned, the more it is likely to be considered by the trustees.

Areas of interest
Charities with the above characteristics that work in any of the following areas:

▶ helping people who struggle to live on very little income, including the homeless
▶ helping people who live in deprived inner city and rural areas of the UK, particularly young people who lack the opportunities that may be available elsewhere
▶ helping charities in our immediate local area of south east Suffolk
▶ helping to support family life

- helping disabled people
- helping Roman Catholic charities and ecumenical projects.

Grants made to charities outside the primary beneficial area of south east Suffolk are usually one-off and small in scale (in the range between £100 and £1,000).

Unlike many trusts, the charity can consider helping people on a personal basis. The trustees give priority, as they do with charities, to people struggling to live on little income, within the primary beneficial area. Grants are rarely made to individuals living outside the primary beneficial area. Of the individuals assisted, most are referred by field professionals such as housing or probation officers, on whose informed advice the trustees can place some reliance [for further information, see *The Guide to Grants for Individuals in Need*, published by the Directory of Social Change].

Grantmaking in 2009/10

In 2009/10 the charity had assets of £49.1 million and an income of £1.7 million. Grants were made totalling £1.1 million, including £102,000 to individuals. Of the total disbursed to organisations £323,000 was awarded in unsolicited grants while £674,000 was awarded to projects identified and selected by the trust itself.

The charity made grants in the following areas (including the amount given in grants to organisations) in 2009/10:

Relief of Poverty – £415,000 (£221,000 of which to organisations)
Support for a number of causes and individuals where the Trustees have longer term knowledge and experience, particularly those both in the UK and in the Third World who are little catered for by other charities or by grants or benefits from governments or other authorities, or are in particularly deprived areas and, for overseas work, only through established links.

General Charitable Purposes – £546,000 (£544,000 to organisations)
Public and other charitable purposes in the general region of south east Suffolk and in particular the parish of Kesgrave and the areas surrounding it, including Ipswich.

Advancement of Religion – £152,000 (£151,000 to organisations)
Support for the Roman Catholic religion and ecumenical work, both generally and for specific institutions connected historically with the families of William Oliver Jolly and his wife Alice and their descendants.

Advancement of Education – £86,000 (£82,000 to organisations)
Support for educational projects connected with the Founder's family. Support for a proposed airship museum; support for Catholic and other schools in the general area of Ipswich; and projects relating to the interaction of mathematics and physical science with philosophy.

Beneficiaries of major grants during the year included: EACH (East Anglian Children's Hospices) (£251,000); Worth Abbey (£175,000); International Refugee Trust (£90,000); Mrs L D Rope Second Charitable Settlement (£72,000); Norfolk Venda Project (£65,000); Medical Missionary Sisters (£40,000); New Dawn India (£37,000); St Albans RC High School – Ipswich (£10,500); RC Parish of St Joseph (£10,000); Cafod – Haiti Appeal (£10,000); IHAG (Ipswich Housing Action Group) (£7,500); and Disability Advice Service – East Suffolk (£5,000).

Exclusions

The following categories of unsolicited applications will not be successful:
- overseas projects
- national charities
- requests for core funding
- buildings
- medical research/health care (outside of the beneficial area)
- students (a very limited amount is available for foreign students)
- schools (outside of the beneficial area)
- environmental charities and animal welfare
- the arts
- matched funding
- repayment of debts for individuals.

Applications

Send a concise letter (preferably one side of A4) explaining the main details of your request. Always send your most recent accounts and a budgeted breakdown of the sum you are looking to raise. The charity will also need to know whether you have applied to other funding sources and whether you have been successful elsewhere. Your application should say who your trustees are and include a daytime telephone number.

Common applicant mistakes

'Insufficient information supplied with applications and unsolicited applications from individuals outside our priority geographical area.'

The Rose Foundation

General – grants towards building projects

£1 million (2009/10)

Beneficial area

In and around London.

28 Crawford Street, London W1H 1LN
Tel: 020 7262 1155
Website: www.rosefoundation.co.uk
Correspondent: Martin Rose, Trustee
Trustees: Martin Rose; Alan Rose; John Rose; Paul Rose.
CC Number: 274875

Information available

Accounts were on file at the Charity Commission. The foundation has a clear and simple website.

Established in 1977, the foundation supports charities requiring assistance for their building projects, giving small grants to benefit as large a number of people as possible rather than large grants to small specific groups. The foundation applied to the Charity Commission to modernise its trust deed in 2002, which was to make it more applicable to how the foundation operates rather than to change how it works.

Grants are made towards small self-contained schemes (of generally less than £200,000) based in or around London and usually range from £5,000 to £10,000 each. Previously the trust has given up to £30,000, but has reduced this figure to keep to its spirit of giving a large number of smaller grants despite the decline of the stock market in recent years. Projects should commence between January and August or have started earlier but still be ongoing during that period.

The trustees' policy is to offer assistance where needed with the design and construction process, ensuring wherever possible that costs are minimised and the participation of other contributing bodies can be utilised to maximum benefit.

In 2009/10 the foundation had assets of £21.3 million and an income of £358,500. Grants were paid during the year to 75 organisations totalling £1 million.

As in previous years, the largest grant made during the year was given to St John Ambulance, which received £555,000 as part of a continuing programme of support. Other larger grants were made to the New Amsterdam Charitable Foundation (£104,000), a connected organisation based in the US and the Fred Hollows Foundation (£46,000).

Other beneficiaries included: Qazi Foundation (£15,000); Central Synagogue General Charities Fund (£12,000); Friends of St Mary's Association (£10,000); Old Vic Theatre (£7,000); Training Ship Broadsword (£6,000); Community Links (£5,000); Massey Shaw and Marine Vessels Preservation Society (£4,000); Help the Hospices (£3,500); and Hampstead Theatre (£1,200).

Exclusions

The foundation can support any type of building project (decoration, construction, repairs, extensions, adaptations) but not the provision of equipment (such as computers, transportation and so on). Items connected with the finishes, such as carpets, curtains, wallpaper and so on, should ideally comprise a part of the project not financed by the foundation. Funding will not be given for the purchase of a building or a site or for the seed money needed to draw up plans.

Applications

In writing to the correspondent including details of the organisation and the registered charity number, together with the nature and probable approximate cost of the scheme and its anticipated start and completion dates. Applications can be submitted anytime between 1 July and 31 March (the following year). The foundation

hopes to inform applicants of its decision by the second week in July.

Rosetrees Trust

Medical research

£676,000 (2009/10)

Beneficial area

UK.

Russell House, 140 High Street, Edgware, Middlesex HA8 7LW
Tel: 020 8952 1414
Email: richard@rosetreestrust.co.uk
Website: www.rosetreestrust.co.uk/
Correspondent: Richard Ross, Chief Executive and Trustee
Trustees: Richard Ross; Lee Portnoi; Clive Winkler; Steve Rosenbaum.
CC Number: 298582

Information available

Accounts were on file at the Charity Commission. The trust also has an informative website.

Registered as the Teresa Rosenbaum Golden Charitable Trust, the trust was established in 1987 to support medical research leading to early improved treatments or new therapies covering many medical conditions. The trust is currently supporting over 100 research projects. Its intention is to increase the amount given to medical research and to find like minded charities with which to co-fund valuable research projects.

The trust's main objectives are:
- seed corn funding for outstanding research
- encouraging outstanding young researchers with the potential to become professors and leaders in their field
- diagnostic testing or testing of existing drugs for additional benefits to help or cure illnesses for relatively little cost
- helping clinicians test bright ideas arising out of their everyday work to improve procedures and treatments.

The trust usually starts with relatively small grants, but as the reporting progresses and a good working relationship develops between the trust and the researchers, these grants

are steadily increased and over a period of years can build up to substantial sums. The vast majority of grants are made through university and medical schools.

Note: the trust is very keen to share the expertise it has developed over 20+ years, which is available to co-donors at no cost. Organisations interested in sharing this knowledge should contact the trust directly.

Grants in 2009/10

During 2009/10 the trust's assets increased to just over £32.2 million (2008/09: £448,000) following the transfer of company shares in from the settlor's estate. Income in the form of donations has been around £850,000 each year, although this may increase in future years as a result of this bequest. Grants were made totalling almost £676,000 and were distributed in the following categories:

Cancer	£104,500
Coronary and lung disease and strokes	£79,500
Brian research	£76,500
Tissue engineering and regenerative medicine	£57,500
Rheumatology and tissue disorders	£56,500
Eye and hearing disorders	£43,500
Immunology, transplantation and infections	£30,000
Maternity and children	£28,000
Digestive and urinary disorders	£24,500
Miscellaneous	£175,000

Exclusions

No support for individuals or for non-medical research.

Applications

In writing to the correspondent. Applicants must complete a simple pro forma which sets out briefly in clear layman's terms the reason for the project, the nature of the research, its cost, its anticipated benefit and how and when people will be able to benefit. Proper reports in this form will be required at least six-monthly and continuing funding will be conditional on these being satisfactory.

The trust has previously stated: 'The trustees are not medical experts and require short clear statements in plain English setting out the particular subject to be researched, the objects and likely benefits, the cost and the time-scale. Unless a charity will undertake to provide two concise progress reports each year, they should not apply as this is a vital requirement. It is essential that the trustees are able to follow the progress and effectiveness of the research they support.'

Rowanville Ltd

Orthodox Jewish

£693,000 (2009/10)

Beneficial area

UK and Israel.

8 Highfield Gardens, London NW11 9HB
Tel: 020 8458 9266
Correspondent: Ruth Pearlman, Secretary
Trustees: Joseph Pearlman; Ruth Pearlman; Michael Neuberger.
CC Number: 267278

Information available

Accounts were available at the Charity Commission.

The objectives of the trust are 'to advance religion in accordance with the orthodox Jewish faith'. The trust provides grants to charitable institutions and free accommodation for educational use.

In 2009/10 the trust had assets of £4.8 million and an income of £1.1 million. Grants were made totalling £693,000.

Beneficiaries included: Chevras Mo'oz Ladol (£35,500); Yeshivas Shaarei Torah (£27,000); Friends of Beis Yisroel Trust (£20,500); Telz Academy Trust (£15,000); Union of Orthodox Hebrew Congregation (£10,000); Project Seed (£7,000); Pinto Talmudical College (£5,000); Akiva School Foundation (£3,000); and Made in Heaven (£1,000).

Applications

The trust has previously stated that applications are unlikely to be successful unless one of the trustees has prior personal knowledge of the cause, as this charity's funds are already very heavily committed.

The Joseph Rowntree Charitable Trust

Peace, democracy, racial justice, social justice, corporate responsibility, Quaker issues

£5.8 million (2010)

Beneficial area

Unrestricted, in practice mainly UK, Republic of Ireland and Europe.

The Garden House, Water End, York YO30 6WQ
Tel: 01904 627810
Fax: 01904 651990
Email: jrct@jrct.org.uk
Website: www.jrct.org.uk
Correspondent: Stephen Pittam, Trust Secretary
Trustees: Beverley Meeson; Christine Davis; Emily Miles; Margaret Bryan; Marion McNaughton; Peter Coltman; Susan Seymour; Helen Carmichael; Imran Tyabi; Stan Lee; Michael Eccles.
CC Number: 210037

Information available

Accounts were available at the Charity Commission. Detailed and up-to-date information on funding programmes is available on the trust's excellent website.

Background

The Joseph Rowntree Charitable Trust (JRCT) is established for general charitable purposes and benefits people and organisations mainly within Britain. Outside Britain, the trust makes grants for work towards peace, justice and reconciliation in both jurisdictions in the island of Ireland and, increasingly, in relation to influencing the policies of the European Union.

This is a Quaker trust and the value base of the trustees, as of the founder Joseph Rowntree (1836–1925), reflects the religious convictions of the Society of Friends. In the original founding trust deed of 1904 (from which the present deed is derived)

Joseph Rowntree gave the trustees power to spend the trust fund and its income on any object which is legally charitable. In a memorandum written at the same time, which is not part of the trust deed and therefore not binding, he expressed a clear vision of how he hoped the fund would be used, while urging that 'none of the objects which I have enumerated, and which under present social conditions appear to me to be of paramount importance, should be pursued after it has ceased to be vital and pressing'.

There are three Rowntree trusts, each of which is independent of the others. Joseph Rowntree Foundation (JRF) is one of the largest social policy research and development charities in the UK and seeks to better understand the causes of social difficulties, and to explore ways of overcoming them. The JRF is also involved in practical housing and care work through the Joseph Rowntree Housing Trust.

Joseph Rowntree Reform Trust Limited (JRRT) promotes democratic reform, constitutional change and social justice, both in the UK and elsewhere. It is a non-charitable limited company and is therefore free to give grants for political purposes. The JRRT and JRCT have collaborated on various initiatives combating racism and encouraging democratic renewal, including research into voting behaviour in towns in the North of England, and the Power Inquiry.

Regular reviews are undertaken to reassess how it is appropriate to interpret the founder's vision in today's conditions. The trust continues to operate an ethical investment policy, aiming to ensure that, as far as possible, the trust's income is earned in ways which are compatible with its Quaker values and its grant making policy. As Quakers, they share a belief in the equal worth of all members of the human race, together with a recognition and appreciation of diversity.

Grantmaking

The trust tries to maintain an adventurous approach to funding. Where appropriate, risks are taken and unpopular causes funded, which

303

may not always fall neatly into one of the programme areas listed above. The trust does not usually respond to proposals which can be funded by public appeals.

The work the trust supports is about removing problems through radical solutions, and not about making the problems easier to live with. Joseph Rowntree was always very clear on one thing: for your efforts to have any lasting benefit, you must tackle the roots of a problem. If you only treat the 'superficial manifestations' of poverty, or social injustice, or political inequality, then you will ease the symptoms for a time, but make no lasting difference. The trust seeks to engage in philanthropy which changes the existing power imbalances in society to effect real change.

The trust makes grants to individuals and to projects seeking the creation of a peaceful world, political equality and social justice. There should be a clear sense of objectives and details of how to achieve them. The work should be both innovative and imaginative and there should be a clear indication that the grant has a good chance of making a difference.

Though the trust has policies for all of its grant programmes, it is not prescriptive in its grantmaking. Its programme areas are widely drawn and the trustees are open to persuasion about applications which fall outside these areas. Occasionally the trust will initiate projects which it directly manages itself. The 'Visionaries for a Just and Peaceful World' project falls into this category.

The trust deliberately places itself at the cutting edge of difficult and contentious issues and believes in creating a dialogue across difference and supporting change towards a better world. It also recognises that this change can take many years to achieve and is willing to take the long view, and to take risks. In doing so, the trust tries to be flexible enough to respond quickly to the changing needs and demands of our world.

The trustees are Quakers, and decision-making and practice are based on Quaker values. Trust meetings are based on Quaker business methods. Each trust meeting starts and ends with a period of silent worship, no voting takes place and they trust that they are guided to the right decision.

The trust generally funds work under one of the following five programmes:

- peace
- racial justice
- power and responsibility
- Quaker concerns
- Ireland

A programme of funding for South Africa is no longer open to new applicants, with all commitments relating to it being fulfilled by 2012.

Programmes

The following policy summaries have been drawn from the trust's highly informative website:

Peace

Joseph Rowntree hoped that his trust would 'sound a clear note with regard to the great scourges of humanity, especially with regard to war'. As part of the Quaker tradition, the JRCT is committed to the creation of a peaceful world, and the creation of a culture of peace.

The trust recognises that complex phenomena create peace and war and that new drivers of conflict, such as climate change and access to water, are constantly emerging. Joseph Rowntree wanted to seek out the underlying causes of weakness or evil rather than remedying 'more superficial manifestations'. The trust believes that long-term approaches to create peace are usually more effective than short-term fixes. We are idealistic, but recognise that pragmatism is often more effective than purity.

Much of our work on corporate responsibility, racial justice and democracy, in Ireland (North and South) and South Africa, is already aimed at these underlying causes in order to create a culture of peace, accountability and democracy. Under the heading of 'Peace', we anticipate funding groups or organisations that are working to influence the behaviour and thinking of the public, and of people in powerful positions including those working in the military, national governments and international organisations.

We wish to support organisations or individuals who promote values similar to our own when working towards peace. We do not fund those who advocate aggressive military solutions to conflicts.

We wish to fund organisations or individuals who can identify the strategic steps needed towards achieving peace. We hope to evaluate grant applications in terms of the extent to which the work proposed will ultimately advance the cause of peace and nonviolence.

We are particularly interested in funding organisations or individuals who are working on:

- control or elimination of specific forms of warfare and the arms trade
- influencing appropriate agencies to take or promote peaceful choices to prevent violent conflict or its recurrence
- improving, through practical measures, the effectiveness of peacebuilding and conflict resolution
- bringing nonviolent and non-military responses to conflict into the mainstream amongst NGOs, decision-makers and the wider public
- pacifism and conscientious objection to military service
- initiatives which strengthen the peace sector's ability to effectively promote the issues above.

We will not fund:

- work on interpersonal violence, domestic violence, or violence against children
- work focused solely on specific local or regional conflicts
- work which focuses on the immediate effect of conflict on victims
- research which is more theoretical than practical, or which is not aimed at making change happen
- work focused more exclusively on other governments' policy than on that of the UK, unless the work is on pacifism or conscientious objection to military service
- work which seems only to 'preach to the converted.

Location of work:

- we are most likely to fund individuals and organisations working in the UK and (if the organisation is working on influencing an international institution such as the EU, NATO or the UN) the rest of Europe.

Racial Justice

The trust seeks to promote racial justice and equality of opportunity as a basis for a harmonious multi-racial, multi-ethnic society in Britain. The trust seeks to work towards this aim through all its grant making fields, but particularly through its racial justice programme.

The Racial Justice programme area works at three levels:

- Local – West Yorkshire
- National – focusing on England, Wales, Scotland and the UK (work specific to Northern Ireland is funded through a separate programme)
- European

An important test of all applications to this programme area is whether they are promoting racial justice. The Racial Justice programme recognises racial injustice focuses on racial justice in its broadest sense, including black and minority ethnic communities; migration including refugee and asylum; and Islamophobia.

JRCT is keen to encourage communication and co-operation between different racial groups.

The trust welcomes applications from black and ethnic minority groups and from multi-racial groups working in these areas. The trust encourages and looks for involvement of black and ethnic minority people at all levels of the projects and organisations it supports. Applications for work to tackle Islamophobia should describe where the work is positioned in the context of the UK's diverse Muslim communities, and explain how it will engage with and address the needs of young people and women.

In West Yorkshire, JRCT aims to promote the full participation of racially disadvantaged groups in community life. This includes members of black and minority ethnic communities and newly arrived communities. The trust supports local projects working for equality, social justice and civil rights.

Forthcoming changes to the West Yorkshire Racial Justice Programme
After a period of careful reflection, including listening to grantees, trustees have decided to make some significant changes to the shape of the West Yorkshire Racial Justice Programme. We hope these changes will create a more focused, dynamic programme for addressing racial injustices in West Yorkshire. [Details of the revised programme will be available on the trust's website from early 2012.]

At both national and European level, JRCT is keen to support organisations developing and disseminating policy proposals, and advocating policy improvements. The emphasis is on organisations with good access to policy makers. The committee is also willing to make relatively small grants to some marginal and under-supported organisations doing campaign work.

At National level, JRCT supports projects working to:
- promote issues of racial justice with policy shapers, decision makers and opinion formers
- encourage black and ethnic minority people/black-led organisations to contribute to policy development on the basis of their experience in meeting needs; and to participate at planning and decision making levels
- monitor and challenge racism and racial injustice whether relating to colour or culture
- tackle Islamophobia

- promote rational and humane migration and asylum policies benefitting both migrant and settled communities
- explore and advocate ways to eliminate racial violence and harassment.

At European level, the trust expects that work undertaken on an EU-wide basis will be funded from sources in several EU member states. The priority is to fund work which has direct relevance to communities living in the UK, although the work may also impact on communities elsewhere in Europe. JRCT supports projects working to:
- promote awareness amongst policy makers and within the European institutions of the need to protect the human rights of minority communities, asylum seekers and migrants
- research and disseminate information concerning current EU policies and their impact on minority communities
- provide a forum for NGOs from all EU countries to share experiences on matters relating to race and immigration and to build alliances on shared interests
- work for a more accountable and open process for developing EU policy in relation to race and migration.

What we do not fund
In relation to the Racial Justice programme, JRCT does not make grants for:
- local projects, except in West Yorkshire
- projects that provide services or training to members of BME communities, refugees or asylum seekers
- academic research, except as an integral part of policy and campaigning work
- work which we believe should be funded from statutory sources, or which has been in the recent past
- work which tries to make a problem easier to live with, rather than getting to the root of it.

Please also note the general exclusions.

Power and responsibility
The responsible use of power was important to Joseph Rowntree. He saw business and politics as forms of public service to be used to promote social justice, equality and a spirit of citizenship. Whilst being fully aware that corporate and government power can be used to the detriment of individuals and communities, he recognised their potential for good and for building the kind of society he was interested in. Much has changed since 1904, but Rowntree's concern about 'the power of selfish and unscrupulous wealth' still rings true 100 years later.

The ways corporate and political institutions operate continue to concern the trust. Though the context is different, the trust's Quaker values remain constant and are expressed in a concern for social justice. We believe that greater social responsibility, accountability, openness, and responsiveness within political and corporate institutions will benefit everyone.

The nature of the world today means that it is harder for people to know where, and by whom, decisions affecting their lives are taken, let alone have a chance to influence them. There is a need to strengthen the democratic process, to enhance corporate accountability, and to build confidence in the way decisions are taken.

What we will fund
This area of concern builds upon the trust's experience in the corporate responsibility and democracy fields. The Trust will consider applications from organisations and individuals which:
- encourage accountability, openness and responsiveness in government, local government, government agencies, and the private sector; or which explore an appropriate role for the media in achieving this
- foster understanding of, and respect for, human rights in government, business and civil society as a means to promote social justice
- explore appropriate relationships between people, their communities and the institutions that affect them – whether these be local and central government, quangos, or companies
- explore whether and how political participation and involvement can be increased and deepened within Britain, as a means to promote a socially just society
- promote ideas to nurture the democratic process and to counter the misuse of power
- explore how government and business might change their planning, evaluation and reward systems from their current short-term outlook to a longer-term one
- promote a relationship between government and business that works in the public interest.

Other factors
The trust wants to support initiatives which make a difference. We are interested in changing the agenda and willing to consider radically challenging models that demonstrate new and different thinking. The limited size of our resources, together with our interest in influencing policy, tends to lead us towards supporting organisations working at the national level.

Issues of social responsibility, corporate governance, accountability,

305

openness and responsiveness are equally relevant to the European Union and global institutions to which the UK belongs. In this programme we will consider applications from organisations working at a European Union level. We will also consider applications aimed at increasing the accountability of the UK government and other UK bodies for the impact of the policies and practices that they pursue within global institutions.

The ways in which business and government can be held accountable for the impact of their policies and practices differ significantly. Applications may address either or both of these sectors.

The trust believes that our care for future generations morally compels us to play a part in tackling climate change. This programme will look carefully at applications that address the inter-relationship between climate change and the national public policy agenda; citizens' participation and 'voice' in the climate change debate; and climate change as an issue of corporate accountability and as a symptom of our unsustainable and unjust global economic system.

What we will not fund
The interests of this programme are broad and funds are limited. In order to maintain a focus the Trust has to be selective and generally will not fund work that:
- is about participation in service provision eg education and health
- focuses on international development issues
- is limited to a particular business sector eg tourism or supermarkets (unless it has wider application)
- engages in public education about climate change.

Please also note the general exclusions.

Quaker
The Quaker Concerns programme supports work relating to the Religious Society of Friends.

What we will fund
Through this programme the trust seeks to foster the development, within the liberal or unprogrammed tradition of the Society of Friends, of what Joseph Rowntree called a 'powerful Quaker ministry'. This is interpreted as widely as possible and includes practical ways to deepen the spiritual life of Friends and to develop Quaker responses to problems of our time. Trustees see the lives of individual Friends and Meetings, and their work in the wider community, as interdependent.

At this time, trustees are particularly interested in:
- Bringing Quaker values to the wider community.

- Trustees want to encourage Friends to take forward innovative and practical work that brings Quaker values and beliefs to the world around them.
- Strengthening Quakers' shared identity.
- Trustees want to support projects which will promote Friends' understanding of Quakers' shared history, theology and spirituality, as trustees believe this will strengthen Quaker faith and practice. Trustees are particularly interested in this area of work because they recognise that many people now come to Quakerism as adults.

We are looking for exciting initiatives and for new ideas and approaches.

Size of grants
JRCT can make grants ranging from a small amount for one-off projects, to more than £100,000 over three years (in the case of larger institutions). The Trust is unlikely to offer more than £2,000 towards theatre productions.

Who can apply
Trustees will consider applications from Quakers in Britain and the rest of Europe. This includes Yearly Meetings, local Meetings, other Quaker organisations and individuals.

How applications will be considered
Each application will be considered carefully, in the light of the general application requirements.

In addition, Trustees will consider:
- the way in which a Concern has been developed and tested
- the prospective benefit of the project to Friends and to wider society
- the relationship between the proposed project and other work within the Society of Friends
- other funds available to the applicant.

What we will not fund
Trustees will generally not make grants:
- for the core administration and management of the Society of Friends, either nationally or in local Meetings
- to maintain or resurrect work, where a decision has been made to lay it down
- to cover an individual's personal income while they research or write a book, film or play.

Please also note the general exclusions. There are also additional guidelines available for Quaker applicants – please see the trust's website for details.

Ireland
The Joseph Rowntree Charitable Trust's Ireland Committee oversees the organisation's funding in Northern Ireland and the Republic of Ireland.

Following a consultation process in 2010, the trust has developed a new funding policy to cover the period from 2011–2016. The trust has decided to focus primarily on work related to the Northern Ireland conflict. This includes work that takes place in Northern Ireland, the Republic of Ireland, on a cross-border basis, and in Britain.

Northern Ireland Conflict
The Joseph Rowntree Charitable Trust aims to fund work which will contribute to the ongoing transformation of the Northern Ireland conflict. Its vision is of a Northern Ireland with the following characteristics:
- a constitutional settlement which takes account of the range of political views of the people of Northern Ireland, Britain and the Republic of Ireland and which is underpinned by the principles and values of participation, human rights and equality
- a non-sectarian political culture which is inclusive, transparent, responsive and accountable
- effective processes and mechanisms for managing societal and political conflict without recourse to violence
- a respectful and inclusive public discourse about the Troubles, which promotes a shared understanding of the root causes of past violence, and a public policy framework which facilitates truth, justice and reconciliation
- a vibrant, pluralist and activist civil society, responsive to the needs of the most vulnerable and able to hold the government to account.

What we will fund
The trust is interested in funding work which:
- addresses the root causes of violence and injustice, rather than alleviating symptoms
- cannot be funded from other sources; and
- is likely to make a long-term, strategic difference.

With effect from 5 April 2011, the trust will operate a new 5-year programme of responsive grantmaking within the following priority areas:
- Strengthening 'new politics' in Northern Ireland – this includes work to promote democratic reform, more inclusive and participatory governance, anti-sectarian political leadership and policy-making, and the demilitarisation of politics. Work that addresses Northern Ireland's politics from a broader perspective (North-South, East-West, or in the context of the European Union) is also of interest.
- Fostering a culture of human rights, equality and civil liberties – this includes work which fosters cross-community consensus on and support for human rights, equality

and civil liberties in Northern Ireland, or which encourages the governments in Dublin, Belfast and Westminster to adopt policies which strengthen a culture of human rights in Northern Ireland.

- Encouraging and enabling marginalised groups to play a full part in the political process and in civil society – this includes work to enable politically or socially marginalised groups to effectively and non-violently articulate their interests, engage in processes of demilitarisation and participate in the political process.
- Dealing with the past – the trust is concerned primarily with work that promotes a shared understanding of the root causes of past violence, or which encourages government to implement initiatives to address the legacy of violence at a societal level.
- Strengthening civil society – the trust is concerned primarily with work that facilitates strategic thinking about, and new approaches to, strengthening citizens' engagement with government on social justice issues.

The trust is particularly interested in receiving applications related to women's participation in all of these areas. It is also interested in supporting racial justice dimensions to all of the above areas. In addition to applications from Northern Ireland, it is open to receiving applications from Britain and the Republic of Ireland for work related to the above areas, and for work with an all-Ireland focus. Local work will be supported only where it is likely to have a wider impact, for example if it is testing a model which can then be replicated, or is addressing a local issue that has wider social or political implications.

In exceptional cases, the trust is willing to make small grants for crisis-response work that has the potential to contribute to wider change. For further details, please contact the trust's office.

The trust is also exploring possible pro-active initiatives in the above priority areas during the five-year period from 2011–2016.

Exclusions
In addition to the trust's general exclusions, the following types of work will not be funded:

- the delivery of basic services to people in need, including welfare advice, women's refuges, basic skills training etc.
- the core costs of community centres, local women's groups, local voluntary sector infrastructure organisations or similar community level groups
- work with or for children and young people

- work related to health or disability
- community development or community relations projects that do not relate directly to the priority interests outlined above
- any form of personal healing or therapeutic work, including counselling
- historical research, documentation or archival work
- work related to the past which is primarily concerned with particular events during the conflict.

Grantmaking in 2010

In 2010 the trust had assets of £166.2 million and an income of £4.4 million. During the year there were 119 grants made totalling £5.8 million, which included £136,000 to individuals. Grants were broken down by category as follows:

Power and responsibility	£1.53 million
Peace	£1.24 million
Racial justice	£1.15 million
Ireland	£944,000
Quaker	£525,000
New Leadings*	£365,000
South Africa	£39,000

*Joseph Rowntree encouraged future trustees to be alert to new openings and opportunities. A review of our work has emphasised the importance of New Leadings, and we expect to invest more resources in the area in future years.

The trust's website features a database of grants awards by the trust – the following is a sample of beneficiaries across all programmes from 2010:

JUST – West Yorkshire (£200,000 over 3 years), towards core costs; Community Foundation for Northern Ireland (£203,000 over 3 years), towards a Transitional Support Co-ordinator for the Dialogue Programme; British American Security Information Council (£180,000 over 2 years), towards 'Getting to Zero' and 'Trident Commission'; British Institute of Human Rights (£120,000 over 3 years), towards core costs; Compass (£100,000), toward the High Pay Commission; Campaign for Freedom of Information (£80,000 over 2 years), towards core costs; Black Training and Enterprise Group (£75,000 over 3 years), towards core costs; Envision (£54,500 over 3 years), towards 'Building on Success', which promotes community participation for more racially disadvantaged young people; Foundation for Democracy and Sustainable Development (£45,000 over 3 years),

towards core costs; Moyallon Centre Management Committee (£28,500 over 3 years), towards a Vision and Outreach worker; Travellers Aid Trust (£16,500), towards a panel review of government policy on Gypsies and Travellers; Bradford Muslim Women's Council (£10,000), towards development costs; and 38 Degrees (£1,500), towards engaging with the Iraq war enquiry.

Exclusions

Generally, the trust does not make grants for:

- the personal support of individuals in need
- educational bursaries
- travel or adventure projects
- medical research
- building, buying or repairing buildings
- business development or job creation schemes
- general appeals
- providing care for elderly people, children, people with learning difficulties, people with physical disabilities, or people using mental health services
- work which has already been done
- work in larger, older national charities which have an established constituency of supporters
- work in mainstream education
- academic research, except as an integral part of policy and campaigning work that is central to our areas of interest
- work on housing and homelessness
- the arts, except where a project is specifically concerned with issues of interest to the trust
- work which the trust believes should be funded from statutory sources, or which has been in the recent past
- work which tries to make a problem easier to live with, rather than getting to the root of it
- local work in Britain (except Racial Justice work in West Yorkshire)
- work outside the UK, Ireland and South Africa (except for groups working elsewhere within Europe at a European level).

Further specific exclusions are included for individual programmes. Within its areas of interest, the trust makes grants to a range of organisations and to individuals. It is not necessary to be a registered charity to apply to the trust. However, it can only support work which is legally charitable as defined in UK law.

Applications

The trust expects all applicants to have made themselves familiar with the relevant funding programmes, summarised here but set out in full on the trust's website and available in leaflet form.

They then require an application letter (including budget, accounts and equal opportunities policy) and a completed registration form. The details expected in the letter are set out in detail on the website and in the leaflet. Applications can be submitted either online or by post. Organisations submitting an application by post can download a registration form from the website to complete. For those submitting their applications online, the registration details are included in the initial steps.

There is a deadline for receipt of applications of around ten weeks before the meeting of trustees. It is very helpful if applications arrive well before the deadline. The period immediately after the deadline is the trust's busiest time, so it cannot normally consider applications that arrive late until the following funding round. The trust has three grant-making rounds each year. Contact the trust or go to the website for the latest information on application deadlines.

Please note: for organisations applying to the West Yorkshire Racial Justice Programme, there is a slightly different application process. Full details are available on the trust's website.

Common applicant mistakes

'They don't do enough research, not only on our criteria, but also on what our current priorities are by studying recent grants (we publish details of all grants made).'

The Joseph Rowntree Foundation

Research and development in social policy and practice

£4.7 million (2010)

Beneficial area

UK, with some preference for York and Bradford.

The Homestead, 40 Water End, York YO30 6WP
Tel: 01904 629241
Fax: 01904 620072
Email: info@jrf.org.uk
Website: www.jrf.org.uk
Correspondent: Julia Unwin, Chief Executive
Trustees: Don Brand; Debby Ounsted; Ashok Jashapara; Bharat Mehta; Tony Stoller; Dame Mavis McDonald; Steven Burkeman; Graham Millar; Prof Dianne Willcocks; Tony Stoller
CC Number: 210169

Information available

Accounts were available from the Charity Commission. Detailed information is available from the foundation's informative website.

General

This is not a conventional grantmaking foundation. It supports research, of a rigorous kind, usually carried out in universities or research institutes, but also has a wide range of other activities not necessarily involving grants of any kind.

The Joseph Rowntree Foundation works in collaboration with the Joseph Rowntree Housing Trust to understand the root causes of social problems, identify ways of overcoming them, and show how social needs can be met in practice.

The purpose is to influence policy and practice by searching for evidence and demonstrating solutions to improve:

- the circumstances of people experiencing poverty and disadvantage

- the quality of their homes and communities
- the nature of the services and support that foster their well-being and citizenship

The foundation initiates, manages and pays for an extensive social research programme. It does not normally respond to unsolicited applications and many of its programmes issue formal and detailed requests for proposals. However modest proposals for minor gap-filling pieces of work in the foundation's fields of interest may sometimes be handled less formally and more rapidly.

They also make some grants locally in and around York and Bradford (where the foundation has made a 10 year commitment), and directly manage or initiate housing schemes.

In 2010 the foundation had assets of £202 million and an income of £6.9 million. It spent £4.7 million on grant commitments.

Areas of work

Poverty

Examining the root causes of poverty, inequality and disadvantage and identifying solutions. The key objectives are:

- to monitor child poverty and propose policy solutions to help end it
- to provide authoritative annual statements on poverty and social exclusion
- to explore how poverty affects people and families in different ways at different times
- to implement an anti-poverty strategy within the foundation
- to explore the nature of contemporary slavery in order to develop practical solutions and influence policy
- to collect and use evidence that will help to stop or reverse negative drinking patterns in the UK

Place

Contributing to the building and development of strong, sustainable and inclusive communities. The key objectives are:

- to inform the debate about affordable housing

- to provide authoritative annual statements on housing and neighbourhoods
- to understand the housing needs of young people and how policy can best meet them
- to assess how community assets can contribute to a thriving civil society
- to develop a new 'model' community for the design and management of 21st century homes and neighbourhoods
- to deliver excellent services and effective management of our land and buildings

Empowerment

Finding ways in which to have control of their own lives. The key objectives are:

- to contribute to the debate about a fairer, more transparent system of funding long-term care
- to support groups of people whose voices are seldom heard to be involved in policy, planning and practice
- to deliver excellent services that encourage people to stay healthy and lead active lives
- to develop the evidence base on housing with care for older people, focusing on outcomes and cost-effectiveness
- to improve the experience of people who use services and live and work in different social care settings
- to influence society and services to reflect what service users want in their own lives

Research programmes

The foundation describes its programmes in considerable depth on its website. They all fall under a main area of work, or cover more than one.

How the foundation works

The foundation does not make grants: those supported are considered partners in a common enterprise. The foundation takes a close interest in each project from the outset, often bringing together an advisory group to give guidance on a project, and taking an active role in the dissemination of the project's findings to bring about policy and practice change. Foundation staff oversee the progress of individual projects within the programme and act as a point of contact throughout.

As a general rule, the foundation aims to provide full financial support rather than being one of a number of funders. However, where the involvement of another organisation would help the project achieve its aims, joint funding may be considered.

How work gets funded

The foundation is keen to fund a variety of different kinds of projects, depending on the state of knowledge about a particular topic.

- The majority of proposals are canvassed under broad programme themes, or through specific briefs using the JRF website, email notification, direct mail, and, occasionally, advertisements.
- In addition, JRF sometimes commissions work directly.
- Occasionally they will consider proposals arising from an unsolicited approach.

The foundation does not have a preference for methodology but it must be appropriate for the question.

The foundation likes to be outward looking in its approach and encourages user groups and community-based groups to apply for funding where appropriate. If the proposal is for a research project the project team must include people with knowledge, experience and research skills to carry out a successful research project.

Who decides which projects are approved?

For proposals which have been received in response to a programme-based call for proposals:

1. Programme Manager and lead Assistant Director (Policy and Research) scrutinise all proposals to sift out proposals which are methodologically weak and which do not meet the foundation's brief.

2. Promising proposals are then further scrutinised by at least one independent external assessor who has relevant expertise, alongside the Programme Manager and lead Assistant Director, and the Director of Policy and Research.

3. Based on rigorous internal and external assessments, recommendations are made to the Director of Policy and Research (who makes the final decision for proposals which cost less than £100,000) and to the Trustee Board (who make the final decision for proposals which cost more than £100,000).

In some circumstances (e.g. when commissioning short evidence reviews or think-pieces, or commissioning pieces of work which are highly specialist and where the field is very limited), the foundation will use a 'limited competitive tender' or 'direct commission' approach.

Programmes and projects

Programmes use different approaches to secure the advice and scrutiny they require for good governance. Programmes often have a programme advisory group or network to draw in expertise from relevant fields, to advise on priorities and progress of the programme as a whole, and on issues concerning influence and impact. Programme advisory groups and networks do not make funding decisions.

York Committee

The York Committee makes grants to organisations to help improve the general quality of life in York, with particular regard for those who are in any way disadvantaged. Grants typically range from £100 to £5,000. trustees prefer to support specific needs rather than general running costs. Grants are given to charities and other not-for-profit organisations in the area covered by the City of York Council.

Funding in 2010

Funds committed to the main programmes during 2010:

Poverty	£1.1 million
Place	£580,000
Empowerment	£752,000
Bradford	£282,000

In addition to these programmes of work under the foundations core themes, re-active grant funding was also provided.

Research beneficiaries of over £25,000 included: Spending cuts: mitigating risks for Scotland's disadvantaged communities – Glasgow Caledonian University (£97,000); Designing carbon taxation to protect low income households – Policy Studies Institute (£95,000); How can Universities support disadvantaged communities- Durham University (£88,000); Building a sustainable quality part-time recruitment market – Women Like Us; Development Manager post- York Young Peoples Trust (£60,000); Modelling poverty – Institute for Fiscal Studies (£28,000); and Funding of the Rowntree Society (£25,000).

Exclusions

The foundation does not generally support:

- projects outside the topics within its current priorities
- development projects which are not innovative
- development projects from which no general lessons can be drawn
- general appeals, for example from national charities
- conferences and other events, websites or publications, unless they are linked with work which the foundation is already supporting
- grants to replace withdrawn or expired statutory funding, or to make up deficits already incurred
- educational bursaries or sponsorship for individuals for research or further education and training courses
- grants or sponsorship for individuals in need.

Grants from the York Committee are not given to:

- animal welfare groups
- archaeological work
- individuals
- routine maintenance or construction of buildings
- medical research
- overseas visits or overseas holidays

Applications

The foundation does not respond to unsolicited applications. Instead, it issues 'calls for proposals' and invites submissions to them. Detailed information, including guidance and a proposal registration form, is available from the foundation's website.

The York Committee has its own application guidelines and form, available on the foundations website. Meetings to decide grants are held

four times a year, usually February, May, August and November.

Joseph Rowntree Reform Trust Limited

Promoting political and democratic reform and defending of civil liberties

£1 million (2010)

Beneficial area

UK.

The Garden House, Water End, York YO30 6WQ
Tel: 01904 625744
Fax: 01904 651502
Email: info@jrrt.org.uk
Website: www.jrrt.org.uk
Correspondent: Tina Walker, Trust Secretary
Trustees: Dr Christopher Greenfield, Chair; Tina Day; Mandy Cormack; Dr Peadar Cremin; Archy Kirkwood; Andrew Neal.

Information available

Helpful website for applicants but little financial information was available.

Joseph Rowntree was a Quaker businessman with a lifelong concern for the alleviation of poverty and the other great social ills of his day. He made a considerable fortune from the chocolate company which bore his name, and in 1904 transferred a large part of this wealth to three trusts, each designed to reflect and develop different aspects of his thinking about contemporary social problems. Known today as the Joseph Rowntree Foundation, the Joseph Rowntree Charitable Trust and the Joseph Rowntree Reform Trust (JRRT), all three continue to build upon the founder's original vision, applying it in their different ways to the problems of present-day society, however, they have always been separately administered and are totally independent of each other.

JRRT differs from the other Rowntree Trusts, and from almost every other trust in the UK, in that it is not a charity. Charities must not have political objectives and whilst they may engage in political activity in pursuit of their charitable aims, those aims must not in themselves be political. By contrast, this trust is a limited company which pays tax on its income. It is therefore free to give grants for political purposes; to promote political and democratic reform and defend civil liberties. It does so by funding campaigning organisations and individuals who have reform as their objective, and since it remains one of the very few sources of funds of any significance in the UK which can do this, it reserves its support for those projects which are ineligible for charitable funding.

The trust's main aims are to:

- correct imbalances of power
- strengthen the hand of individuals, groups and organisations who are striving for reform
- foster democratic reform, civil liberties and social justice.

The following is taken from the trust's website:

> The trust is not committed to the policies of any one political party although it has been a long term funder of the Liberal Democrats (and predecessor parties) in order to redress the balance of financial inequality between parties and to foster political developments central to a healthy democratic process. It has also supported individual politicians or groups promoting new ideas and policies from all the major parties in the UK.

> The trust has also helped a large number of non-party pressure groups needing short-term assistance: however, the trust will not normally provide long-term funding. Such groups need not be national organisations, but the national relevance of local campaigns is a crucial factor that Directors will consider.

Currently, the trust has assets of around £30 million. Each year a potential grant budget of around £1 million is allocated which excludes administrative expenses and tax.

Information about grants is published on the trust's website once the grant has been ratified at a subsequent trust meeting. The list is not necessarily complete as the trust may decide that to achieve a particular grant's purpose or to protect the personal safety of those undertaking the work, it is not appropriate to make available the information.

Beneficiaries in 2010 included: Yes To Fairer Votes (£500,000), towards the campaign for a Yes vote in the AV Referendum; Liberal Democrats (£350,000), towards the cost of campaigning in target seats; Institute for Government (£50,000 over 2 years), towards their 'Methods of Selection of Candidates' project; Hope Not Hate Yorkshire (£40,000), to campaign against far right groups over 1 year; Action on Rights for Children (£33,000), to continue to campaign on children's rights issues; Compass (£23,000), to campaign for economic and banking reforms; Operation Black Vote (£10,000), towards their General Election campaign; and Alliance for Choice Northern Ireland (£5,000), to raise awareness amongst women of existing abortion law in Northern Ireland and begin the process of redressing both the misinformation and the fear among women in talking about abortion.

Exclusions

The trust is not a registered charity and provides grants for non-charitable political and campaigning activities. Examples of work for which the trust does not make grants are:

- the personal support of individuals in need
- educational bursaries
- travel and adventure projects
- building, buying or repairing properties
- business development or job creation
- general appeals
- academic research
- work which the trust believes should be funded from statutory sources, or which has been in the recent past
- administrative or other core costs of party organisations.

Applications

Applicants should email a one page outline to the correspondent before making a formal application. If accepted, a full application can then be made.

The trust does not have a standard form, but applications should include:

- an Application Registration Form (available to download from the trust's website)
- up to four pages setting out the proposal
- a full budget for the project
- the most recent audited accounts
- a CV, if applying as an individual.

Trust staff make an initial assessment of applications and are authorised to reject those that are clearly inappropriate. All staff rejections are reported to the directors at their next meeting, when they consider all remaining applications. The meetings take place at quarterly intervals in March, July, October and December and the deadline for applications is approximately four or five weeks prior to the trust meeting. Applications for small grants of up to £5,000 can, however, be considered at any time and applicants should hear of the decision within two weeks.

Common applicant mistakes

'Not contacting the trust before applying and not reading the grants application guidelines.'

Royal British Legion

Armed services

£5.6 million to organisations
(2009/10)

Beneficial area

UK, excluding Scotland.

Haig House, 199 Borough High Street, London SE1 1AA
Tel: 08457 725 725
Fax: 020 3207 2218
Email: info@britishlegion.org.uk
Website: www.britishlegion.org.uk
Correspondent: External Grants Officer
Trustees: John Farmer, Chair; John Crisford; Una Cleminson; Dennis Compton; Eddy Dixon; Noel Duston; Denise Edgar; John Fisher; Eddie Hefferman; Bill Parkin; Keith Prichard; Martyn Tighe; Peter Twidle; Terry Whittles; Adrian Burn; Dr

Diana Henderson; Ian Lindsay; Anthony Macauley; Jenny Rowe; Rev Mike Williams; Wendy Bromwich.
CC Number: 219279

Information available

Accounts are on file with the Charity Commission and detailed information is available on the Legion's website. The following is taken from the 'guidelines on applying for external grants' available on the charity's website:

The Royal British Legion was formed in 1921 as a caring organisation for people in need from the Service and ex-Service community. We aim to safeguard the welfare, interests and memory of those who have served in the Armed Forces including, under certain circumstances, other support and defence organisations and the Mercantile Marine (beneficiaries).

We can also give grants to any ex-Service charity that shares this aim.

We may also give grants to non-ex-Service organisations provided that the grant will directly benefit ex-Service personnel.

We give grants to any charitable organisation in England, Wales, Ireland and the Isle of Man that shares one or more of our objects, namely:
- to relieve need and to further the education of beneficiaries and their spouses, children and dependants
- to relieve need and protect the mental and emotional health of families left by those who have died in service
- to relieve suffering, hardship and distress to spouses and dependants caused by the absence of those serving in the Royal Navy, Army and Royal Air Force on Regular, Reserve or Auxiliary engagements and, under certain circumstances, other support and defence organisations and the Mercantile Marine
- to promote and support schemes for the resettlement, rehabilitation, retraining and sheltered employment, of beneficiaries and their spouses, children and dependants.

Grants may be for:
- projects, for example, a particular time-limited activity that benefits ex-Service personnel
- services, for example, to provide a support or welfare service
- capital, for example, to build a facility or to purchase equipment.

Grants are awarded at the following levels:
- Level 1 – up to £25,000
- Level 2 – £25,000 – £500,000
- Level 3 – over £500,000.

Detailed guidelines for each funding level are available on the trust's website.

In 2009/10 the trust had assets of £290.1 million and an income of £115.2 million. Total charitable expenditure was £85.3 million, most of which was spent on its own services. Grants to 28 organisations totalled just over £5.6 million, with a further £19.6 million given in grants to individuals (further information can be found in *A Guide to Grants for Individuals in Need*, also published by the Directory of Social Change).

The largest organisational grants during the year were made to: St Dunstan's (£2.6 million); and the Officers' Association (£1.6 million). Other beneficiaries included: SPEAR Housing Association Ltd (£239,000); English Churches Housing Group (£150,000); Poppyscotland (£112,000); Veterans Aid (£60,000); Skill Force (£40,000); and Gardening Leave (£25,000).

Smaller grants of less than £25,000 each were made to 10 organisations totalling £52,000.

Exclusions

Grants are not made for:
- memorials
- commercial ventures, or any potential commercial ventures, for example clubs.

Grants are not normally given for core costs, for example, administration or running costs of an organisation that is supporting ex-Service personnel. However, there may be exceptions to this, and the Royal British Legion aims to respond flexibly to applications, and is prepared to negotiate if there are special circumstances, for example, if the withholding of grant would harm the interests of ex-Service personnel.

Applications

In the first instance you should contact Scarlet Harris, External Grants Officer (Tel. 020 3207 2138 or Email: externalgrants@ britishlegion.org.uk) in order to explore whether you may be eligible for a grant, and at what level, so that you can be advised further on the detailed requirements.

Following this, you will be sent an application form which will explain on it the information you need to submit depending on the size of grant you are asking for.

Successful applicants, depending on the level of grant applied for, can expect to receive an award in between two and six months of sending in a correctly completed application form.

The Rubin Foundation

Jewish charities, general

Around £400,000 (2009/10)

Beneficial area

UK and overseas.

The Pentland Centre, Lakeside House, Squires Lane, Finchley, London N3 2QL
Tel: 020 8346 2600
Email: amcmillan@pentland.com
Correspondent: Allison McMillan, Secretary
Trustees: Alison Mosheim; Angela Rubin; R Stephen Rubin; Andrew Rubin; Carolyn Rubin.
CC Number: 327062

Information available

Information was available from the Charity Commission.

This foundation is closely connected with Pentland Group Ltd (see *The Guide to UK Company Giving*, published by Directory of Social Change), with three trustees being on the board of directors of that company. The foundation's income comes from donations from the company and interest on its bank deposits.

In 2009/10 it had an income of £21,000 and a total expenditure of £467,000. Unfortunately, due the low income of the foundation during the year accounts are not required by the Charity Commission. Based on figures from previous years, grants are likely to have been made totalling in the region of around £400,000.

Previous beneficiaries included ULIA; Jewish Community Secondary School

Trust; Jewish Museum; Civitas; Peace and Sport; Weidenfeld Institute for Strategic Dialogue; South Bank Centre; Board of Deputies of British Jews; Royal Opera House Foundation; the Roundhouse; Cancer Backup; and Maccabiah Football Bursaries.

Applications

The foundation has previously stated that 'grants are only given to people related to our business', such as charities known to members of the Rubin family and those associated with Pentland Group Ltd. Unsolicited applications are very unlikely to succeed.

The Rufford Foundation

Nature conservation, sustainable development, environment, general

£2.6 million (2009/10)

Beneficial area

Developing countries, UK.

6th Floor, 248 Tottenham Court Road, London W1T 7QZ
Tel: 020 7436 8604
Email: simon@rufford.org
Website: www.rufford.org
Correspondent: Simon Mickleburgh, Grants Manager
Trustees: Charles Barbour; Anthony Johnson; John Laing; Col. Iain Smailes; Robert Reilly.
CC Number: 326163

Information available

Accounts were available at the Charity Commission website and useful information can be found on the trusts website.

Summary

The foundation is another trust deriving from the Laing building fortune, though it does not share a common administration with the other Laing trusts. The original trust was established in 1982 by John Hedley Laing, who is also a trustee of the Whitley Laing Foundation (now the Whitley Fund for Nature) and has previously been a trustee of WWF-UK, Conservation International and the Wildlife Protection Society of India.

The trustees maintain a strong interest in nature conservation, the environment and sustainable development projects in developing countries where funds are most scarce. A number of projects aimed primarily at helping young people with HIV/AIDS in the developing world are funded via the Elton John Aids Foundation. A limited number of grants (of £15,000 or less) are made to UK organisations supporting health, medicine and social welfare. These may be one-off or recurring and are made at the discretion of the trust director.

Funding policy
The trust concentrates on funding nature conservation projects in developing countries undertaken by small to medium organisations. A small amount of funding (grants up to £5,000) is available for projects that focus on overseas development or social welfare issues in the UK.

To be considered for support by the foundation organisations should fulfil the following criteria:

- all applicants should be UK registered charities
- projects must fall within the foundation's main areas of funding
- there are only limited funds currently available due to existing commitments therefore only projects that meet the criteria in full are eligible, so organisations should ensure that this is the case before they apply
- the minimum grant awarded is £1,000 – there is no set maximum for nature conservation projects
- grants to projects focusing on either overseas development or social welfare issues in the UK will not normally exceed £5,000

A number of grants (£15,000 or less) are made to UK Organisations working outside of the foundations main area. These may be one-off or recurring and are made at the discretion of the trust director on the basis of the application and are reviewed and ratified by the Trustees at the next meeting

Grant making between £15,000 and £30,000 follows the same procedure but a visit or meeting may be arranged, also a progress report will be required.

If a grant of over £30,000 is being considered there will be a visit to the project, or a meeting. Alternatively an organisation may be invited to a trustee meeting to make their proposal in person. Applications may be referred to experts known by the trust. Grants of this size must be approved by the settlor and a majority of the trustees. A full progress report, annual return and accounts will be required.

The Rufford Small Grants Foundation
The Rufford Small Grants Foundation was established in 2007 due to the success of the Rufford Small Grants facility, to award the Rufford Small Grants in perpetuity. More information on RSGF can be found on its website: www.ruffordsmallgrants.org.

Grants in 2009/10
In 2009/10 the trust had assets of £63 million and an income of £2.7 million. Grants were made totalling £2.6 million. The sharp drop in grants paid during the year was due to the implementation of the trusts' new grant giving policy which aims to ensure the future sustainability of the Rufford Foundation and the Rufford Small Grants Foundation and ensure that future capital is not used for grant giving. A grant of £5 million has been allocated to WWF-UK for its new headquarters. The £2.6 million paid in grants during the year was distributed as follows:

	% of total
Nature conservation projects in developing countries	84%
Overseas development projects	3%
Health and medicine projects in the UK	5%
Social welfare projects in the UK	8%

Grant expenditure was outlined in the accounts as:

The Rufford Small Grants Foundation	£850,000
Nature conservation	£1.2 million
Health and medicine	£127,000
Social welfare	£194,000
Overseas aid	£67,000

Beneficiaries of over £1,000 included: University of Southampton

(£115,000); EIA Charitable Trust and Zoological Society of London (£100,000 each); RSPB (£75,000); Whitley Fund for Nature and the Environmental Justice Foundation (£50,000 each); Wildlife Protection Society of India (£40,000); International Animal Rescue and Wildlife Conservation Nepal (£25,000); Botanic Gardens Conservation International and Ocean Youth Trust South (£20,000 each); St Albans High School for Girls (£13,000); Bat Conservation Trust and the Samaritans (£10,000 each); Canine Partners for Independence, Farm Africa and the University of Surrey (£5,000 each); British Council for the Prevention of Blindness and the 3H Fund (£3,000 each); Dogs for the Disabled and International Childcare Trust (£2,500 each); and, Wells for India (£2,000).

Exclusions
The foundation will not generally fund the following:

- building or construction projects
- donations to individuals or projects that directly benefit one individual
- loans
- endowment funds
- student/gap year conservation expeditions
- general appeals or circulars.

Applications
The trust considers all applications which meet its criteria but states:

With limited funds available it is neither possible to give detailed reasons why applications are not successful nor to enter into any dialogue or correspondence regarding projects which have been refused funding. In all cases, organisations are only able to make a single application for funding from the foundation during any one-year period.

All applications must be received by post [addressed to the correspondent]. All new applicants must be charities registered in the UK. There is no deadline for applications as they are accepted throughout the year.

There is no set form but applications must include:

- a covering letter with contact details

- a comprehensive plan outlining the project for which funding is being sought, including measurable objectives (4–6 pages max)
- a full budget – with details of funding secured to date, other funding applications being made and the amount being requested from the foundation
- a copy of the charity's most recent accounts
- a copy of the latest annual report (if available).

Please note, the foundation does not accept applications for funding by email and is unable to discuss the suitability of an application by telephone.

Applications are accepted throughout the year. The foundation strives to respond to all applications within 6 weeks of receipt and asks that applicants do not telephone to check on their application, as they will be contacted in due course.

Common applicant mistakes

'Applicants do not read the guidelines that are available on our website. Our main focus is nature conservation and we still get a significant number of applications that fall outside this main remit.'

S F Foundation

Jewish, general

£1.2 million (2009/10)

Beneficial area

Worldwide.

143 Upper Clapton road, London E5 9DB
Tel: 020 8802 5492
Correspondent: Rivka Niederman, Secretary
Trustees: Hannah Jacob; Rivka Niederman; Miriam Schrieber.
CC Number: 1105843

Information available

Accounts were on file at the Charity Commission. Charitable donations made by the foundation are detailed in a separate publication: *SF Foundation – Schedule of Charitable Donations*. The accounts stated that the publication is available by writing

to the Secretary. Despite requesting this publication, including an SAE, no reply was received.

Set up in 2004, this trust gives grants towards the 'advancement and furtherance of the Jewish religion and Jewish religious education and the alleviation of poverty amongst the Jewish community throughout the world.'

In 2007/08 the foundation had assets of just over £15.1 million and an income of £3.7 million. Grants were made totalling £1.2 million.

Applications

'The charity accepts applications for grants from representatives of various charities, which are reviewed by the trustees on a regular basis.'

The Saddlers' Company Charitable Fund

General

£351,000 (2010/11)

Beneficial area

UK.

Saddlers' Hall, 40 Gutter Lane, London EC2V 6BR
Tel: 020 7726 8661/6
Fax: 020 7600 0386
Email: clerk@saddlersco.co.uk
Website: www.saddlersco.co.uk
Correspondent: Nigel Lithgow, Clerk to the Company
Trustees: Campbell Pulley; D J Serrell-Wattes; David Hardy; David Snowden; Edward Pearson; Hugh Dyson-Laurie; Iain Pulley; John Vant; Jonathan Godrich; Michael Bullen; Michael Laurie; Peter Laurie; Peter Lewis; Tim Satchell; William Dyson-Laurie; Mark Farmar; David Chandler; Paul Farmar; Petronella Jameson; Charles Barclay; John Robinson; Hugh Thomas; James Welch.
CC Number: 261962

Information available

Accounts were available from the Charity Commission. The trust also has a website.

General

The Saddlers' Company Charitable Fund was formed in 1970. Over time, the objects of the fund have been refined to provide support for education, the British saddlery trade, the equestrian world, the City of London and general charitable activities. The decisions regarding the company's charities are taken by the Charities and Education Committee with regular reports back to the full trustee body.

The fund supports many of the same charities each year such as Alleyn's School and Riding for the Disabled. After making such allocations, and allowing for the agreed level of reserves, about one quarter of the remaining funds is allocated to major national charities working in all charitable sectors and the remaining three quarters are held for charitable appeals which are received throughout the year. The trustees have formulated a policy to focus on smaller charities assisting people with disabilities.

For grants targeted to be paid in July, members of the Livery are asked to visit a charity local to them and to report on the charity's suitability to receive a grant. The Liveryman prepares a report on the charity's purpose, budgetary and financial control, administration and general viability, together with a recommendation as to whether the charity should be supported and at what level. These reports are considered by a grant committee whose recommendations are passed to the trustees.

For grants targeted to be paid in January, a points- based system is used whereby a charity will accumulate points according to various criteria. The total amount of funds available is then distributed amongst the charities based upon how many points they have.

R M Sturdy Charitable Trust

A Past Master of the Worshipful Company of Saddlers and former trustee of the fund, Mr R M Sturdy, died in 2006. By a letter of wishes, he expressed the desire that the R M Sturdy Charitable Trust, of which he was the benefactor, be administered by the Worshipful Company of

Saddlers after his death. The Court of Assistants, the governing body of the Worshipful Company of Saddlers, and whose members are the trustees of the fund, concluded that the most expeditious way of fulfilling this desire would be to create a restricted fund within the Saddlers' Company Charitable Fund. In 2007/08 a transfer of £550,000 was made from the R M Sturdy Charitable Trust to the Saddlers Company Charitable Fund to establish the new fund.

Diamond Jubilee Fund

The trustees have re-affirmed their intention to make a significant charitable grant to mark the diamond jubilee of Her Majesty Queen Elizabeth II in 2012 and have determined to continue to transfer the sum of £5,000 each year into a designated fund – the Diamond Jubilee Fund – with the aim of achieving a total of £75,000 by 2012. During 2007/08 the trust added £30,000 to enable the fund to reach its target ahead of schedule. The trustees have agreed that they should apply the income from this Designated Fund to support the British Equestrian Paralympic Teams taking part, initially, for the 2012 Paralympic Games (the year of Her Majesty's diamond jubilee) and, thereafter, for each succeeding four-yearly Games.

Grantmaking in 2010/11

In 2010/11 the charity had an income of £393,000, assets of £9.3 million and made grants totalling £351,000. The designated charity for the year was CLIC Sargent, which received £4,000. Grants were distributed in the following categories:

Education (£161,000)
Including: Alleyn's School- Saddlers' scholarships and bursaries (£130,000); Royal Veterinary College (£4,000); University of Liverpool (£3,900).

Support for people with disabilities (£62,000)
Including: Riding for the Disabled Association (£28,000); Autism Sussex (£1,400); RoRo Sailing Project (£1,400).

Equestrian world (£23,000)
The trustees intend that young people will be given the opportunity of self-development, whether through formal education or activity-based events, when lack of finance may otherwise deprive them. Two grants were made in this area: British Horse Society (£22,000) and British Equestrian Vaulting (£1,300).

Service charities (£21,000)
Grants are made to service benevolent funds and cadet forces for the purposes of support for service or ex-service personnel and/or their families and the training of cadets, including: The Royal British Legion – Pedal to Paris (£7,300); Army Cadet Force – Middlesex and north west London (£2,000); Royal Navy Officers Charity (£1,000).

British saddlery and leathercraft trades (£7,000)
Beneficiaries included: Leathercraft Conservation Centre (£4,000); the Museum of Leathercraft (£2,000); Walsall Leather Museum (£1,000).

City of London (£8,800)
Including: Lord Mayor's Appeal; Mansion House Scholarship Appeal (£5,000 each); City of London Police Widows & Orphans Fund (£1,500); City of London Corporation- literacy project (£1,300); St Paul's Cathedral (£1,000).

General Charitable Activities (£33,000)
Including: Birmingham Cathedral (£5,000); Salisbury Cathedral (£3,000); St Christopher's Hospice (£1,800); The Firefighters Charity (£1,000).

Exclusions

No grants to individuals.

Applications

In writing to the correspondent. Grants are made in January and July, following trustees' meetings. Charities are asked to submit reports at the end of the following year on their continuing activities and the use of any grant received.

Erach and Roshan Sadri Foundation

Education, welfare, homelessness, Zoroastrian religion, general

£574,500 (2010/11)

Beneficial area

Worldwide.

10a High Street, Pewsey, Wiltshire SN9 5AQ
Email: markcann@ersf.org.uk
Website: www.ersf.org.uk
Correspondent: Mark Cann, Administrator
Trustees: Margaret Lynch; Shabbir Merali; Darius Sarosh; Jehangir Sarosh; Sammy Bhiwandiwalla.
CC Number: 1110736

Information available

Accounts were on file at the Charity Commission. Detailed information is available on the foundation's website.

The main objects of the foundation are:

▶ providing financial assistance for education and welfare purposes
▶ relieving poverty by alleviating homelessness
▶ assisting members of the Zoroastrian religious faith.

The trustees also consider grant applications which fall outside the main criteria but have particular appeal to them. Grants are in the range of £2,000 and £100,000. 'Pump-priming' donations are offered – usually given to new organisations and areas.

In 2010/11 the foundation had assets of £4.1 million and an income of £109,500. Grants were made to 44 organisations during the year totalling £574,500, and were broken down as follows:

Education and welfare	£436,500*
Homelessness	£70,500
Zoroastrian	£50,000
General	£22,500

* the figure also includes a grant of £5,000 to an individual.

Many of the foundation's beneficiaries received multiple grants during the year. Beneficiaries included: The British Forces Foundation (£25,000); On Course (£22,000); Honeypot (£18,000); World Federation (£12,500); Bobby Van Trust (£10,000); Manthan (£9,000); The Passage (£5,000); Calcutta Rescue (£3,500); and Charlie's Charity (£1,500).

Exclusions

Applications are unlikely to be successful if they:

- involve animal welfare or heritage
- are a general appeal from large UK organisations.

Applications

On a form which can be downloaded from the foundation's website, along with full and detailed guidelines. Forms can be returned by post or email. Meetings are held four times a year.

Please note: 'Unsolicited material sent in addition to the clear and concise requirements of the application form is very likely to prove detrimental to your application. The trustees insist that additional items such as annual reports, glossy brochures, Christmas cards and accounts are not sent unless specifically requested.'

Common applicant mistakes

'Not reading our website clearly.'

The Alan and Babette Sainsbury Charitable Fund

General

£316,500 (2009/10)

Beneficial area

Worldwide.

Allington House, 1st Floor, 150 Victoria Street, London SW1E 5AE
Tel: 020 7410 0330
Fax: 020 7410 0332
Website: www.sfct.org.uk

Correspondent: Alan Bookbinder, Director
Trustees: The Hon. Sir Timothy Sainsbury; Judith Portrait; John Julian Sainsbury; Miss L M H Anderson.
CC Number: 292930

Information available

Accounts were available at the Charity Commission.

This is one of the Sainsbury Family Charitable Trusts, which share a joint administration and have a common approach to grantmaking.

'The trustees concentrate their resources on a small number of programmes which build on themes in the trust's earlier grantmaking.' During 2009/10 the trust concentrated on civil liberties, scientific and medical research, youth work, overseas projects and general charitable purposes.

In 2009/10 the trust had assets of £12.9 million and an income of £411,000. Grants totalling £316,500 were paid during the year and were categorised as follows:

Overseas	6	£85,000
Youth work	6	£77,000
Civil liberties	5	£65,000
Scientific and medical research	1	£50,000
General	4	£39,500

The beneficiaries during the year were: Juvenile Diabetes Research Foundation (£50,000); Canon Collins Educational Trust for South Africa (£40,000); Citizen Organising Foundation, Jewish Association of Business Ethics and Blue Elephant Theatre (£30,000 each); Cubitt (£20,000); Female Prisoners Welfare Project Hibiscus and Refugees Into Jobs (£15,000); Islington Music Centre (£14,000); King's College London, Minority Rights Group, Anglo-Israel Association and Arab-Jewish Center for Equality, Empowerment & Cooperation (£10,000 each); Council of Christians & Jews, World Jewish Relief, Lion Ballroom Ltd and Theatre Peckham (£5,000 each); The Sainsbury Archive and Toppesfield Community Village Shop Association Ltd (£4,300 each); Get Sorted Academy of Music (£3,000); and Vernon House School (£1,000).

Exclusions

Grants are not normally made to individuals.

Applications

The trust states that: 'proposals are likely to be invited by the trustees or initiated at their request. Unsolicited applications will only be successful if they fall precisely within an area in which the trustees are interested'. A single application will be considered for support by all the trusts in the Sainsbury family group.

The Sainsbury Family Charitable Trusts

See individual trusts

£89.6 million (2009/10)

Beneficial area

See individual trusts.

Allington House 1st Floor, 150 Victoria Street, London SW1E 5AE
Tel: 020 7410 0330
Fax: 020 7410 0332
Website: www.sfct.org.uk
Correspondent: Alan Bookbinder, Director

These trusts, listed below, each have their own entries. However they are administered together and it is said that 'an application to one is taken as an application to all'.

Their grantmaking ranges from the largest to the smallest scale, including massive long-term support for major institutions such as the National Gallery or the Sainsbury Centre for Mental Health as well as for a range of specific issues ranging from autism to the environmental effects of aviation. There is an office with over 30 staff and a large number of specialist advisers.

However, even collectively, the trusts do not form a generalist grantmaking organisation; though active in most fields of charitable activity, it is usually within particular and often quite specialised parts of each sector.

Most of the trusts use a similar formula to describe their grantmaking:

> The trustees take an active role in their grant-making, employing a range of specialist staff and advisers to research their areas of interest and bring forward suitable proposals. Many of the trusts work closely with their chosen beneficiaries over a long period to achieve particular objectives. It should therefore be understood that the majority of unsolicited proposals we receive will be unsuccessful. As a rule the Gatsby, Glass-House, Linbury, Staples and Tedworth trusts do not consider unsolicited proposals.

A typical programme might have the following elements:

▶ support for a major, long-term research initiative, whether academic or in the form of an action research programme;
▶ support for specialised national groups promoting good practice in the field concerned;
▶ grants for a few service delivery organisations, often small and local, and addressing the most severe aspects of the issues involved.

In these editors' view, charities that are indeed developing new ideas and approaches would be most unwise to assume that the Sainsbury trusts will automatically get to hear of this.

'Applications' are probably not the best way forward and may perhaps be best avoided except where specifically requested. More sensible might be to write briefly and say what is being done or planned, on the assumption that, if one or more of the trusts is indeed interested in that area of work, they will want to know about what you are doing. A telephone call to do the same is fine. Staff are polite, but wary of people seeking to talk about money rather than issues.

More generally, the trusts are involved in a number of networks, with which they maintain long-term contact. Charities doing work relevant to the interests of these trusts may find that if they are not a part of these networks (which may not be inclusive and most of which are probably London-based) they may get limited Sainsbury attention.

The most inappropriate approach would often be from a fundraiser. Staff, and in many cases trustees, are knowledgeable and experienced in their fields, and expect to talk to others in the same position.

Most of the trusts do fund ongoing service delivery, but generally infrequently and usually on a modest scale. For such grants it is not clear how they choose this play scheme or that wildlife trust. To them, these may be small and relatively unimportant decisions, and they may rely on trustees or staff simply coming across something suitable, or on recommendations through what they have called their 'usual networks'.

The Sainsbury Family Trusts (with totals of grant payments or approvals for the most recent year available):

Gatsby Charitable Foundation	£33.1 million
Monument Trust	£32 million
Linbury Trust	£5.6 million
Kay Kendall Leukaemia Fund	£5.2 million
Headley Trust	£3.7 million
Jerusalem Trust	£2.5 million
True Colours Trust	£1.7 million
Three Guineas Trust	£1.3 million
Ashden Trust	£1.1 million
J J Charitable Trust	£765,000
Glass-House Trust	£484,000
Mark Leonard Trust	£483,000
Staples Trust	£460,000
Tedworth Trust	£380,500
Alan and Babette Sainsbury Trust	£316,000
Indigo Trust	£270,000
Woodward Charitable Trust	£240,000
Total	**£89.6 million**

Collective support

The trusts sometimes act collectively, with support for the same organisations from a number of the trusts. Organisations that occasionally appear in more than one grants list include the Royal Ballet School and National Portrait Gallery, and also Ashden Awards for Sustainable Energy.

It is not clear to the outsider whether such cross-trust support is the result of interaction at trustee or at officer level, or both. However it does seem that there is such a thing as being 'in' with the group of trusts as a whole – a cause of occasional resentment by those who see the Sainsbury trusts, perhaps entirely wrongly, as being something of a closed shop.

Exclusions

No grants are normally given to individuals by many of the trusts (though a number of them fund bursary schemes and the like operated by other organisations). Grants are not made for educational fees or expeditions.

Applications

Please do not send more than one application. It will be considered by all relevant trusts.

The trusts only fund registered charities or activities with clearly defined charitable purposes.

The trustees take an active role in their grant-making, employing a range of specialist staff and advisers to research their areas of interest and bring forward suitable proposals. Many of the trusts work closely with their chosen beneficiaries over a long period to achieve particular objectives.

It should therefore be understood that the majority of unsolicited proposals the trust receives will be unsuccessful. As a rule the Gatsby, Glass-House, Linbury, Staples and Tedworth trusts do not consider unsolicited proposals.

The other trusts will consider exceptional proposals which fit closely their specific areas of interest.

There are no application forms, except in a small number of clearly defined areas:

▶ The Woodward Charitable Trust
▶ The Kay Kendall Leukaemia Fund
▶ The Headley Museums Archaeological Acquisition Fund

Applications to all other trusts should be sent by post, with a description (strictly no more than two pages please, as any more is unlikely to be read) of the proposed project, covering:

▶ the organisation – explaining its charitable aims and objectives, and giving its most recent annual income and expenditure, and current financial position. Please do not send a full set of accounts
▶ the project requiring funding – why it is needed, who will benefit and in what way
▶ the funding – breakdown of costs, any money raised so far, and how the balance will be raised.

At this stage please do not send supporting books, brochures, DVDs, annual reports or accounts.

All applications will receive our standard acknowledgement letter. If your proposal is a candidate for support from one of the trusts, you will hear from us within 8 weeks of the acknowledgement. Applicants who do not hear from us within this time must assume they have been unsuccessful.

The Sandra Charitable Trust

Animal welfare and research, environmental protection, social welfare, health and youth development

£461,000 to organisations (2009/10)

Beneficial area
UK with slight preference for south east England.

Moore Stephens, 150 Aldersgate Street, London EC1A 4AB
Tel: 020 7334 9191
Fax: 020 7651 1953
Email: keith.lawrence@ moorestephens.com
Correspondent: Keith Lawrence, Secretary
Trustees: Richard Moore; Michael Macfadyen.
CC Number: 327492

Information available
Accounts were available at the Charity Commission.

The trust was established in 1987 for general charitable purposes, with the main aim of the charity also being:

▷ to support a wide variety of beneficiaries including nurses and charities involved in animal welfare and research, environmental protection, relief of poverty and youth development

In 2009/10 the trust has assets of £15.4 million and an income of £417,000. Grants were made totalling £538,000, of which £461,000 was donated to 121 organisations and just over £77,000 to 127 individuals.

Beneficiaries of the largest grants included: Kids (£40,000); The Florence Nightingale Foundation (£25,000); Leander Club (£15,000); Oxfordshire Victoria County History Trust (£11,000); River Thames Society (£10,500); and the Royal Horticultural Society and SCOPE (£10,000 each).

More typical grants included those to: Barnardo's, Crisis, Mercy Ships and Wessex Heartbeat (£5,000 each); DEC Haiti Earthquake and Plantlife (£4,000 each); Alone in London and Deafness Research UK (£3,000 each); Friends of Shakespeare's Church and Thames Valley Air Ambulance (£2,000 each); and the 9th Chelsea Scout Group and Woodland Heritage (£1,000 each).

Exclusions
No grants to individuals other than nurses.

Applications
The trust states that 'unsolicited applications are not requested, as the trustees prefer to support charities whose work they have researched ... the trustees receives a very high number of grant applications which are mostly unsuccessful'.

The Schreib Trust

Jewish, general

£510,000 (2009/10)

Beneficial area
UK.

147 Stamford Hill, London N16 5LG
Tel: 020 8802 5492
Correspondent: Mrs R Niederman, Trustee
Trustees: A Green; Mrs R Niederman; J Schreiber; Mrs I Schreiber.
CC Number: 275240

Information available
Basic accounts were on file at the Charity Commission, without a list of grants or a full narrative report.

It is difficult to glean an enormous amount of information about this trust's grant-giving policies as only

brief accounts were on file at the Charity Commission. Although the trust's objects are general, it lists its particular priorities as relief of poverty and the advancement of religion and religious education. In practice, the trust only supports Jewish organisations.

In 2009/10 the trust had assets of £492,500 and an income of £567,500. Grants were made totalling £510,000.

Previous beneficiaries have included: Lolev, Yad Eliezer, Ponovitz, Craven Walk Charity Trust, Shaar Hatalmud, Beis Rochel, Beth Jacob Building Fund, Toiras Chesed and Oneg Shabbos.

Applications
In writing to the correspondent.

The Schroder Foundation

General (see below)

£1.4 million (2010/11)

Beneficial area
Worldwide, in practice mainly UK.

81 Rivington Street, London EC2A 3AY
Correspondent: Sally Yates, Secretary
Trustees: Bruno Schroder, Chair; Edward Mallinckrodt; Nicholas Ferguson; Charmaine Mallinckrodt; Leonie Fane; Claire Howard; Richard Robinson; Philip Mallinckrodt.
CC Number: 1107479

Information available
Accounts were available at the Charity Commission.

Set up in 2005, this foundation shares a common administration with Schroder Charity Trust (Charity Commission Number 214060). It does not respond to unsolicited applications.

The foundation's grant-making policy, described in its 2008/09 accounts, reads as follows:

The objects of the foundation are to apply the income and capital for the benefit of any charitable object or purposes, in any part of the world, as the trustees think fit. The trustees have a policy of supporting a broad range of activities within the areas of the environment, education, arts, culture and heritage, social welfare, the community and international relief and development.

At their quarterly meeting the trustees consider what grants they will make and receive reports from grant recipients. The trustees travel widely in the UK and abroad and use the knowledge gained to support the work of the foundation and to inform grant-making policy. The foundation's policy is to focus on charitable causes with a previous track record or in organisations in which the foundation has a special interest. Organisations identified by the trustees for potential support are normally invited to submit a formal application outlining the project, its beneficiaries and how the funds will be applied according to the guidance for applicants to The Schroder Foundation. It is generally the trustees' policy to make only one-off grants. However, grants over a number of years are occasionally awarded.

In 2010/11 the foundation had assets of £11.9 million and an income of £477,000. Grants were made to 77 organisations totalling almost £1.4 million.

Beneficiaries included: Household Cavalry Operational Casualties Fund (£75,000); Courtauld Institute of Art and Great Ormond Street Hospital Children's Charity (£50,000 each); Beat Bullying and Priors Court Foundation (£40,000 each); School Home Support (£35,000); London Youth Support Trust (£30,000); Ashden Awards for Sustainable Energy (£25,000); Melanoma Focus – National Melanoma Database (£20,000); Hertford College – Oxford (£15,000); University of Cape Town Trust (£10,000); and the Cranleigh Foundation (£4,000).

Applications

This trust **does not** respond to unsolicited applications. 'The trustees identify projects and organisations they wish to support and the foundation does not make grants to people or organisations who apply speculatively.'

The Francis C Scott Charitable Trust

Disadvantaged young people in Cumbria and North Lancashire

£907,000 (2010)

Beneficial area

Cumbria and north Lancashire (comprising the towns of Lancaster, Morecambe, Heysham and Carnforth).

Suite 3, Sand Aire House, New Road, Kendal, Cumbria LA9 4UJ
Tel: 01539 741610
Fax: 01539 741611
Email: info@fcsct.org.uk
Website: www.fcsct.org.uk
Correspondent: Chris Batten, Director
Trustees: Susan Bagot, Chair; Joanna Plumptre; Alexander Scott; Madeleine Scott; Don Shore; Clare Spedding; Peter Redhead; Melanie Wotherspoon.
CC Number: 232131

Information available

Accounts were on file at the Charity Commission. The trust also has an extremely comprehensive website.

Summary

The trust was created in 1963 by Peter F Scott CBE, then Chairman of the Provincial Insurance Company. Peter Scott, together with his parents Francis and Frieda Scott and his sister Joan Trevelyan, endowed the trust with a significant holding of Provincial Insurance Company shares.

It supports registered charities addressing community deprivation in Cumbria and north Lancashire, and is principally concerned with meeting the needs of young people from 0–19 years. It seeks to target its funds where they can be most effective and can make a real difference to people's lives.

The trust's helpful website gives the following overview of its grantmaking policy:

What we fund

The trust focuses on four main areas of work:

- early years/ family support work (0–5 year olds and those responsible for their care)
- junior youth work (issues that attend the primary to secondary school transitions)
- targeted youth work (adolescents' concerns re discrimination, pregnancy, homelessness, abuse and substance misuse)
- transition to adulthood (prioritising those who are homeless and leaving care/ youth justice to go into training, employment and/or education).

The majority of our grants are multi-year revenue grants (i.e. salaries and running costs), however trustees will also fund capital projects that make a tangible difference to a local community.

Whilst we prefer to fund organisations that are registered charities, we will consider offering grants to organisations who are pursuing charitable objectives providing their aims/constitution are clearly not-for-profit. We will only consider applications from national organisations where the beneficiaries and project workers are based within our beneficial area.

Please note that charities should not apply to both the Frieda Scott and Francis C Scott Charitable Trusts at the same time and we would encourage you to seek guidance from the staff if you are unsure.

FCSCT Community Leadership Programme

In partnership with the Brathay Trust and University of Cumbria, the trust has launched the Aspiring Leaders Programme which gives local young adults the opportunity to achieve a foundation degree, leadership development training and 1:1 mentoring support over a 3-year period. Refer to the website or contact the charity for further details.

8-year Funding Model

The trustees have adopted the following approach to revenue funding [shown in the table overleaf] for those projects/organisations they believe require extended investment in order to become established. Appeals for capital or bursary funding are considered separately.

Grants in 2010

In 2010 the trust held assets £28 million and had an income of £655,000. There were 51 grants made totalling £907,000, including £871,000 in 36 main grants (average £24,000) and £36,000 in 15 small grants (average £2,400). During the year,

THE FRANCIS C SCOTT CHARITABLE TRUST

Phase	Year	Focus	Objective
1	up to 1 year	Research	Define area of need and then seek organisations to address it.
2	1–3	Core funding	Provide running costs (some or all) and actively support with staff time to ensure the project's early success.
3	4–6	Project funding	Foster a more strategic approach to funding and target project development.
4	7–8	Scale down funding	Withdraw funding over an agreed time period and attract other funders (especially statutory).
5	8+	Cease funding	Remain a background advocate for the project, but move on.

96% of grants were to benefit the 0–21 year old age group at the heart of the trust's grant giving policy and 94% of grants were awarded to charities working in the top 25% most deprived regions in the trust's beneficial area.

Grants were distributed into the following areas:

Young people	53	£547,000
Families and children, women and men	31	£256,000
Disabled, chronically ill and elderly people	10	£158,000
Communities and charity support	8	£87,000
Other	3	£59,000

Beneficiaries included: Young people, including: Champ's Camp (£20,000); Self Harm Awareness for the Furness Area and Eden Community Outdoors (£15,000 each); and Practical Alternatives to Custody (£10,000).

Families & children, women & men, including: Safety Net Advice & Support Centre – West Cumbria (£20,000); Barrow Dad's Group (£18,000); New Rainbow Pre-School (£15,000); and Christ Church Night Shelter (£2,000).

Communities & charity support, including: Marsh Community Centre (£20,000); St Matthew's Community Halls (£10,000); and Morecambe Brass Band Association (£5,000).

Disabled, chronically ill & elderly, including: Calvert Trust- Keswick (£100,000); South Cumbria Dyslexia Association (£10,000); and Centre for Complementary Care (shootings) (£5,000).

Other, including: Thomas Gane Estate (FST beneficiaries) (£40,000); and University of Cumbria (£15,000).

It should be noted that these figures represent grants paid in the year, not the total committed to each beneficiary. As the trust funds many long-term projects many of these grants only represent one year of long term funding.

Exclusions

The trust does not consider appeals:
- from individuals
- from statutory organisations
- from national charities without a local base/project
- from charities with substantial unrestricted reserves
- from medical/health establishments
- from schools/educational establishments
- from infrastructure organisations/second-tier bodies
- for projects principally benefiting people outside Cumbria/north Lancashire
- for retrospective funding
- for expeditions or overseas travel
- for the promotion of religion
- for animal welfare.

Applications

The trust is always pleased to hear from charities that need help. If an organisation thinks that it may come within the trust's criteria it is encouraged to contact the director for an informal discussion before making an application.

Application forms are available to download from the trust's website or can be requested by phone, email or post. Applications should be completed and returned with the latest set of accounts (via email or post).

Applications for over £4,000 should be submitted at least 4 weeks before the trustee's meetings in late February, June, October and November. Please check the website for the latest deadlines.

Applications for grants of less than £4,000 will be considered at small grants meetings every 3–4 weeks.

Applicants should refer to the trusts website which is very comprehensive and covers all aspects of the grantmaking process.

Common applicant mistakes

'Not focusing on the needs of their client group and how their service will positively impact on them.'

The Scottish Community Foundation

Community development, general

£2.7 million (2010/11)

Beneficial area

Scotland.

Empire House, 131 West Nile Street, Glasgow G1 2RX
Tel: 0141 341 4960
Fax: 0141 341 4972
Email: nick@scottishcf.org
Website: www.scottishcf.org/
Correspondent: Alice Dansey-Wright, Programmes Administrator
Trustees: Bob Benson; Gillian Donald; Beth Edberg; Colin Liddell; Ian McAteer; Jimmy McCulloch; John Naylor; Ella Simpson; Lady Emily Stair; Tom Ward.
SC Number: SC022910

Information available

Accounts were provided by the foundation. Information was also taken from the foundation's detailed website.

In common with other community foundations, the Scottish Community Foundation makes grants from various sources – both public and private – as well as having its own endowment with which it distributes money. They provide administration and management support services to make charitable giving easy and tax-efficient. They also offer advice on charitable giving and a professional grant-making service which links them to exceptional charities that are seeking funding. They aim 'to be the leading philanthropy organisation in Scotland for stronger communities [and] to inspire giving for Scotland – to improve lives'.

The foundation makes small grants, usually up to £5,000, for charities and community groups in Scotland, particularly those which are helping to build and sustain local communities.

There are two broad programmes, under which there are a range of different funds.

Scotland-wide programmes: includes express grants (up to £2,000); grants for women's projects; and comic relief local communities grants.

Local grants programmes: there are a variety of programmes which benefit people in specific areas of Scotland. Each has different grant levels, deadline dates and decision making practices. A list of local programmes is available on the foundation's website.

Please note that grant schemes change frequently and potential applicants should consult the foundation's website, which is extremely comprehensive, for details of current programmes and their deadlines.

In 2010/11 the trust held assets of £14.5 million and had an income of £8.7 million. Grants were made totalling £2.7 million with an additional £69,000 also given for community development.

Beneficiaries in the year included: LifeScan Scotland, Judy Russell Fund for Women, Fairshare trust, Evelyn Jamieson Memorial, Poles Apart Trust, Our Community Our future, Elizabeth Montgomerie Appeal, Eaga (Scotland-wide), Al Maktoum Institute, ABO Wind Lairg Community Benefit, Clary Jack and Edinburgh Arts Prize.

Exclusions

The foundation does not usually fund:

- individuals or groups which do not have a constitution
- groups other than not-for-profit groups
- groups whose grant request is for the advancement of religion or a political party (this means the foundation won't fund grant requests to support the core activities of religious or political groups)
- the purchase of second hand vehicles
- trips abroad
- the repayment of loans, payment of debts, or other retrospective funding (the foundation will consider replacement of statutory funding for non-statutory activities on a case by case basis)
- payments towards areas generally understood to be the responsibility of statutory authorities
- groups who will then distribute the funds as grants or bursaries
- applications that are for the sole benefit to flora and fauna. Applicants are invited to demonstrate the direct benefit to the local community and/or service users in cases where the grant application is concerned with flora and fauna
- projects which do not benefit people in Scotland.

Please note different grant programmes may have additional restrictions.

Applications

The foundation has a comprehensive website with details of the grant schemes currently being administered. Organisations are welcome to contact the grants team to discuss their funding needs before making any application. Trustees meet at least four times a year.

Common applicant mistakes

'They fail to have their accounts independently inspected as we require. New groups fail to provide a projection of income and expenditure for their first year of operation. Bank accounts, constitution and/or annual accounts not in the name of the organisation given on the application form.'

Seafarers UK (King George's Fund for Sailors)

The welfare of seafarers

£2.5 million (2010)

Beneficial area
UK and Commonwealth.

8 Hatherley Street, London SW1P 2YY
Tel: 020 7932 5984
Fax: 020 7932 0095
Email: dennis.treleaven@seafarers-uk.org
Website: www.seafarers-uk.org
Correspondent: Dennis Treleaven, Head of Grants
Trustees: Frank Welsh; Barry Miller; Maj Patrick Dunn; Anthony Lydekker; Capt David Parsons; James Watson; Michael Acland; Peter Mamelok; Timothy Warren; John Thompson; Christine Gould; Christian Marr; Simon Rivet-Carnac; Vice Admiral Peter Wilkinson.
CC Number: 226446

Information available

Accounts were available from the Charity Commission. The charity also has a helpful and informative website.

Summary

This trust supports people who have served at sea in the Royal Navy, Royal Marines, Merchant Navy and fishing fleets, their equivalents in the Commonwealth and their dependants. The fund makes grants, often recurrent, for a wide but little-changing range of seafarer's charities. Grants range from a few hundred pounds to several hundred thousand.

General

The charity gives grants to other charities that help with all aspects of seafarers' welfare including accommodation, medical services, disability services, financial aid, childcare, education and training and youth activities. They describe their four main objectives as:

- to ensure that all former UK and Commonwealth seafarers over normal retirement age and their dependants can live life free of poverty and with access to all reasonable health care and domestic assistance

▶ to ensure that serving UK and Commonwealth seafarers have access to reasonable shore amenities and communication with their families and financial help where appropriate

▶ to ensure that the dependent families of UK and Commonwealth seafarers can have access to a reasonable quality of life including adequate accommodation, clothing, education and holidays

▶ to assist those UK and Commonwealth citizens in maritime youth organisations training for a seagoing careers, including the Sea Cadets, with the cost of facilities.

The fund was set up in 1917 as a central fundraising organisation to support other seafarers' charities. A few years ago the charity underwent a structural overhaul to address its extremely high fundraising costs (35 % of income). It succeeded in bringing this figure down to 21 % in 2008 and in the process modernised the fund to make it more relevant, including adopting the operational name Seafarers UK. However in 2010 fundraising costs had again risen to 36 %. In the annual report the charity stated that a large part of the increase was due to one-off costs and they hoped to bring this down following a restructure of the fundraising department.

In the annual report for 2010 the trust stated that in future years they will be focusing on raising public awareness of seafarers and the hardship and danger that they face on a daily basis. They intend to do this by holding 'Seafarers Awareness Week'. The trust is also increasingly interested in research and following work with the British Legion intended in 2011 to set up and maintain a maritime research database that all maritime charities can use.

In 2010 the trust held assets of £41 million and had an income of £3 million. 77 grants were made to 74 organisations totalling £2.5 million.

Main grants
These are for over £5,000 and can be up to 3 years in length.

Small grants
This scheme awards grants of up to £5,000, it is permanently open.

Marine Society and Sea Cadets
The trust makes a substantial contribution towards the Sea Cadets 'annual fund' which allocates money to units needing repairs, maintenance or new equipment. Any sea cadet unit should apply to that fund and will not be considered under the other programmes.

Emergency grants
In exceptional circumstances, it may be possible for the trust to authorise payments of up to an agreed limit where applications from organisations or individuals are too urgent to wait for the normal cycle of distribution.

Grantmaking in 2010
Grants were made in the following areas:

	% of total	
Older and ex-seafarers	43%	£1.1 million
Seafarers' dependants and families	28%	£697,000
Seafarers of working age	22%	£550,000
Maritime youth groups	5%	£100,000

Beneficiaries included: Shipwrecked Fishermen and Mariners' Royal Benevolent Society (£256,000); Royal Navy and Royal Marines Charity (£166,000); Royal Alfred Seafarers Society (£125,000); Royal National Mission to Deep Sea Fishermen and Ex-Services Mental Welfare Society-Combat Stress (£100,000 each); Nautilus Welfare Funds (£91,000); International Seafarers Assistance Network (£67,000); Maritime Charities Funding Group Seafarers Projects (£40,000); Centres for Seafarers and KIDS (£35,000 each); Apostleship of the Sea (£30,000); Douglas Haig Memorial Homes (£11,000); Handicapped Children's Pilgrimage Trust (£7,500); Felixstowe Sea Cadets Corps (£6,600); Peterhead & District Fisherman's Benevolent Fund and Spinal Injuries Association (£5,000 each); and Scottish Shipping Benevolent Association (£1,200).

Exclusions
The fund does not make any grants directly to individuals except in very exceptional cases but rather helps other organisations which do this. However, the fund may be able to advise in particular cases about a suitable organisation to approach.

Applications
Applications to the main grants scheme should download the form available on the trust's website and use the guidance notes also available. There is a deadline for this scheme each year which is published on the website.

Applications to the Marine Society and Sea Cadets scheme should use the specific form and guidelines available on the website.

Applications to the small grants scheme should download the small grants form and guidelines available on the website. There are no closing dates for the schemes that awards grants of up to £5,000. Only one application from an organisation can be considered in any 12 month period.

The Samuel Sebba Charitable Trust

General, covering a wide range of charitable purposes with a preference for Jewish organisations

£2.8 million (2009/10)

Beneficial area
UK and Israel.

25–26 Enford Street, London
W1H 1DW
Tel: 020 7723 6028
Fax: 020 7724 7412
Correspondent: David Lerner, Chief Executive
Trustees: Leigh Sebba; Stanley Sebba; Victor Klein; Clive M Marks; Lady Winston; Sallie Tangir; Yoav Tangir.
CC Number: 253351

Information available
Accounts were available at the Charity Commission.

This trust was established in 1967 for general charitable purposes. The trust focuses on the areas of education, community, children and youth, medical, hospice and older people, arts, interfaith, medical, people with disabilities, mental health, health, asylum seekers and preventative medicine. The trust hopes to expand on its present grant giving and from time to time respond to environmental concerns and international aid.

Key areas for funding in the UK are palliative care, refugees, Jewish education, welfare and communal infrastructure. In Israel, the focus is on the environment, human rights and social justice, disability and youth at risk.

In 2009/10 the trust had assets of £39.9 million and an income of £705,000. There were 143 grants made totalling £2.8 million, consisting of grants of £15,000 or more to 75 institutions totalling £2.3 million and grants of less than £15,000 to 68 institutions totalling £572,000. These were categorised as follows:

Welfare/disability	£1 million
Human rights and social justice	£447,000
Education	£404,000
Community	£253,500
Youth at risk	£132,000
Environment	£123,500
Arts	£93,000
Health and medical	£83,000
Palliative care	£67,500
Disability	£61,000
Student	£60,000
Research	£45,000
Interfaith	£29,500

Beneficiaries across all categories included: Sulam School – Jerusalem (£296,000); New Yeruham Fund (£67,000); Tel Aviv university Trust (£60,000); Medical Foundation for the Care of Victims of Torture (£45,000); Music of Remembrance (£33,000); Alzheimer's Association of Israel (£32,000); Association for Civil Rights in Israel (£30,000); North London Hospice and Union of Jewish Students Hillel (£25,000 each); JDC Israel and Reuth- Women's Social Services (£20,000 each); Elem- Youth in Distress (£19,000); and DeafBlind UK, Cystic Fibrosis Trust, The Parents Club- Bereaved Families Forum and Jewish Association for Business Ethics (£15,000 each).

Exclusions
No grants to individuals.

Applications
Organisations applying must provide proof of need; they must forward the most recent audited accounts, a registered charity number, and most importantly a cash flow statement for the next 12 months. All applications should have a stamped addressed envelope enclosed. It is also important that the actual request for funds must be concise and preferably summarised on one side of A4. The trustees meet quarterly.

However, because of ongoing support to so many organisations already known to the trust, it is likely that unsolicited applications will, for the foreseeable future, be unsuccessful.

The Seneca Trust

Social welfare, education, children and young people

Beneficial area
UK.

Blick Rothenberg, 12 York Gate, London NW1 4QS
Tel: 020 7486 0111
Email: colin.lehmann@ blickrothenberg.com
Correspondent: Colin Lehmann, Trustee
Trustees: Tatjana May; Adam Sweidan; Colin Lehmann; Angela Beech.
CC Number: 1137147

Information available
Basic information was available from the Charity Commission.

The trust was established in 2010 to support social welfare and education, with a particular emphasis on children and young people who are disadvantaged through disability, ill health or lack of education. The settlors of the trust are Kevin Gundle, co-founder of Aurum Funds Limited and also a trustee of Absolute Return for Kids (ARK), and his wife Deborah, who amongst other things has been involved in publishing and film production – her most recent venture is NetBuddy (www.netbuddy.org.uk), an online resource offering tips, help and advice for parents and carers of children with learning disabilities.

Applications
In writing to the correspondent.

The Severn Trent Water Charitable Trust Fund

Relief of poverty, money advice, debt counselling
£500,000 to organisations
(2009/10)

Beneficial area
The area covered by Severn Trent Water Ltd, which stretches from Wales to east Leicestershire and from the Humber estuary down to the Bristol Channel.

FREEPOST RLZE-EABT-SHSA, Sutton Coldfield B72 1TJ
Tel: 0121 355 7766/ 01213211324
Email: office@sttf.org.uk
Website: www.sttf.org.uk
Correspondent: Gay Hammett, Operations Manager, Auriga Services Limited
Trustees: Dr Derek Harris, Chair; Elizabeth Pusey; David Vaughan; Alexandra Gribbin; Lowri Williams.
CC Number: 1108278

Information available
Accounts were available at the Charity Commission.

The trust was established by Severn Trent Water Ltd in 1997 with a donation of £2 million.

The main objects of the trust are to help people out of poverty and debt by helping needy individuals to pay their water bills and making grants to organisations to support debt and money advice. Assistance may also be given with other household costs if it can be demonstrated that it will help towards future financial stability or make a significant improvement to the recipient's circumstances.

Small grants to individuals are available up to £1,500.

Organisational grants are available in three main areas:

- ▶ **revenue funding:** normally for money advice/debt counselling services
- ▶ **capital grants:** a maximum of £1,500 is available for small capital items
- ▶ **continuation funding:** organisations can apply for further funding in the final 6 months of the project (*please note*: this type of funding is not designed to continue current projects indefinitely but to enable other funding to be sourced and agreed, if appropriate).

Grants can be for up to three years. Organisations seeking revenue funding of more than one year must be able to prove that the project will be able to continue to achieve its objectives and deliver a quality service with no additional funding. The continuation of funding beyond one year will always be subject to satisfactory project performance and availability of funding. Recipients will be required to report on the progress of the project. The funding will be made quarterly in advance. Capital purchases must normally be made within three months of the grant award.

Prospective applicants should note that each year the trust decides on areas of special interest in order to target funding, e.g. a social group or geographical area. It is a good idea, therefore, to contact the trust to find out what these areas are before applying.

All recipient organisations will be required to provide an end of year report detailing project achievements. The trust may require the provision of further information to help publicise the work of the trust.

In 2009/10 the trust had an income of £6.7 million and assets of £1.4 million. Grants were made totalling £5 million including £4.5 million to 7,500 families plus £500,000 in grants to organisations. Grants to individuals were broken down as follows in the accounts:

Water debt (to Severn Trent)	£4.3 million
Water debt (to others)	£5,400
Council tax	£400
Rent	£5,300
Gas	£19,000
Electricity	£57,000
Telephone	£1,100
Other household	£148,000
Bankruptcy orders	£53,000

In 2009/10 organisations which received revenue funding included: ASHA/ Worcester CASH; Birmingham Disability Resource Centre; CARES Sandwell; Castle Vale Tenants & Residents Alliance; Citizens Advice Leicester; Community Focus; Coventry CAB; Edas; Forest of Dean CAB; IMA; Ladywood Project; Life Matters; Sherwood Forest Community Church; South Birmingham Young Homeless Project; Telford & Wrekin CAB; Wood End Advice and Information Centre.

ARC Addington Fund, South Leicester CAB, Melton Mowbray CAB and North West Leicestershire CAB have all previously received capital funding. Grant amounts were not available.

Exclusions

Only applications from organisations within the Severn Trent Trust Fund area will be considered. A map of this area can be found on the trust's website.

Applications

If you would like to apply for a grant on behalf of your organisation you can email the trust at: office@ sttf.org.uk. A reply within 48 hours can be expected.

Alternatively, initial interest can be lodged by posting no more than two A4 sheets outlining your proposed project.

ShareGift (The Orr Mackintosh Foundation)

General, but see below

£723,000 (2010/11)

Beneficial area

UK.

2nd Floor, 17 Carlton House Terrace, London SW1Y 5AH
Tel: 020 7930 3737
Fax: 020 7839 2214
Email: help@sharegift.org.uk

Website: www.sharegift.org
Correspondent: Lady Mackintosh
Trustees: Matthew Orr; Stephen Scott; Baroness Goudie.
CC Number: 1052686

Information available

Accounts were available at the Charity Commission.

Summary

Creating an entirely new flow of money to charities, this unique organisation is entirely unlike other Trusts included in this book. ShareGift creates its income each year by pooling and selling donations of shares, principally those which are uneconomic to sell by normal methods because they are too small or otherwise inconvenient or unwanted. The funds released from this ongoing process are used to make donations, on a regular basis, to a wide range of other UK charities each year.

The charity makes donations at its own discretion, but is guided in doing so by information gathered in the course of its work about the charities and causes which are of interest to people who donate shares or help ShareGift in other ways. Since its inception, ShareGift has generated over £14m for 1,700 charities, from major household names to tiny local initiatives, covering a vast area of national and international work.

Grants are normally made to the general funds of the charity concerned, rather than for specific projects. ShareGift is cause neutral and there are no restrictions on the kind of charitable work it can support, or where in the world it takes place, so long as the charity receiving the donation is UK-registered. No grants are given in response to applications by charities.

General

Launched in 1996, this charity was developed by Claire Nowak, a former city investment manager, now Viscountess Mackintosh of Halifax and Chief Executive of the charity, and Matthew Orr, a stockbroker whose firm, Killik and Co., provides free of charge many of the technical and support services required to operate ShareGift.

ShareGift's success as a charity is based on the fact that many people own small parcels of shares, for a variety of reasons, such as popularly advertised flotations of companies and as the result of take-overs and mergers. In what is still largely a paper-based share registration system, small shareholdings are often a considerable nuisance, needing some know-how to handle but being of too little value to justify paying professional fees to sell or manage. ShareGift's funds are mainly generated by working either directly with companies or with individual shareholders.

ShareGift accepts the relevant share certificates, with minimum hassle for the donor, transfers the shares into the charity's name, and, once sufficient shares in any given company have been collected by bulking together batches of similar donations from a number of donors, sells them. Donors who are UK taxpayers may also be able to claim tax relief on the gift.

Fundraising charities also work with ShareGift, primarily as a solution for donors who offer them small holdings of shares which are not viable for the charity to accept themselves. In the case of larger donations and major gifts, ShareGift generally encourages charities to accept and handle these themselves, as it is unable to act as a charitable stockbroker or as a direct conduit for donations to other charities. However, it will advise and assist charities which are having problems or are unfamiliar with dealing with a gift of shares, and, in some cases, may be able to facilitate a larger donation.

Grants in 2010/11

During the year the charity had assets of £343,000 and an income of nearly £1.1 million. Grants were made to 281 charities totalling £723,000. Individual donations ranging from £100 to £37,500 were made across the spectrum of UK charities.

Larger grants included: Great Ormond Street Hospital Children's Charity (£37,500); Daily Telegraph Christmas Appeal (£30,000); British Heart Foundation (£23,000); Breast Cancer Campaign (£20,000); Alzheimer's Society and River &

Rowing Museum Foundation (£15,000 each).

Smaller grants of £10,000 or less included: Marie Curie Cancer Care (£10,000); Sense International (£7,500); The Prince's Foundation for Children & the Arts (£6,000); World in Need International (£5,000); Cats Protection (£1,000); and Essex Women's Advisory Group (£250).

The foundation previously placed £100,000 of cash balances as a deposit with Charity Bank, so that this capital sum can be used for the wider benefit of the charity sector through Charity Bank's loan programme. Interest on this amount is waived as a donation towards Charity Bank's work. In 2010/11 this amounted to £2,000.

Exclusions
Grants to UK registered charities only.

Applications
Applications for funding are not accepted and no response will be made to charities that send inappropriate applications. ShareGift's trustees choose to support UK registered charities which reflect the broad range of charities which are of interest to the people and organisations that help to create the charity's income by donating their unwanted shares, or by supporting the charity's operation in other practical ways.

However, charities wishing to receive a donation from ShareGift's trustees can increase their chances of doing so by encouraging their supporters to donate unwanted shares to ShareGift and to make a note of their charitable interests when so doing, using the regular donation form provided by ShareGift.

In addition, ShareGift is willing to use its extensive experience of share giving philanthropically to help charities which wish to start receiving gifts of shares themselves. Charities are, therefore, welcome to contact ShareGift to discuss this further. ShareGift advises that, as basic training on share giving is now available elsewhere, charities wishing to benefit from their advice should ensure that they have first researched share giving generally and put some

thought into how their charity intends to initiate and run a share giving appeal or strategy. Further information on this and other issues is available on the charity's website.

The Sheepdrove Trust

Mainly environment, education

£687,000 (2010)

Beneficial area
UK, but especially north Lambeth, London, where applicable.

Sheepdrove Organic Farm, Lambourn, Berkshire RG17 7UN
Tel: 01488 674726
Correspondent: Juliet E Kindersley, Trustee
Trustees: Juliet E Kindersley; Peter D Kindersley; Harriet R Treuille; Barnabas G Kindersley.
CC Number: 328369

Information available
Accounts were available at the Charity Commission.

The trust is endowed with money made by the Dorling Kindersley publishing enterprise, but the trust's holding of shares in the company was sold in 2000, when the endowment was valued at £18 million. The trust has general charitable purposes but has a particular interest in supporting initiatives involved in sustainability, biodiversity and organic farming. Grants are also made in other areas including educational research and spiritual care.

In 2010 the trust had assets of £20.2 million and an income of £501,000. Grants were made to organisations totalling £687,000.

The largest beneficiary during the year was the Slow Food UK Trust, which received £472,000 in total over 5 years.

Other beneficiaries included: City & Guild London Art School (£70,000 in total); British Trust for Ornithology (£57,000); Homoeopathy at Wellie Level (£30,000); Ibiza Preservation Fund (£20,000); Newbury Spring

Festival (£17,000); New Economics Foundation and the Wildlife Conservation Partnership (£15,000 each); UK Pesticides Campaign (£10,000); Future of Farming (£7,500); Agrarian Renaissance (£6,000); King Alfred School – Five Court Building Appeal (£2,000); and Education Business Partnership (£1,200).

Grants were also made to individuals totalling £16,500.

Applications

In writing to the correspondent.

The Shekinah Legacy

Education, relief of poverty

Beneficial area

UK, Israel and Romania.

Caladine Accountants, 1A The Avenue, Eastbourne, East Sussex BN21 3YA
Tel: 08456 216666
Email: info@caladine.co.uk
Correspondent: Neville Smith, Trustee
Trustees: Kevin Byrne; Richard Spiceley; Neville Smith.
CC Number: 1137846

Information available

Basic information was available from the Charity Commission.

The trust was established in 2010 to support organisations involved in education and also the relief of poverty. Two of the trustees are also trustees of the Checkatrade Foundation (Charity Commission no. 1137878).

The trust's priorities are education and the relief of poverty. Unfortunately no further information was available at the time of writing (December 2011).

Applications

In writing to the correspondent.

The Archie Sherman Charitable Trust

Jewish charities, education, arts, general

£974,000 (2009/10)

Beneficial area

UK and Israel.

27 Berkeley House, Hay Hill, London W1J 8NS
Tel: 020 7493 1904
Email: trust@sherman.co.uk
Correspondent: Michael Gee, Trustee
Trustees: Michael J Gee; Allan H S Morgenthau; Eric A Charles.
CC Number: 256893

Information available

Accounts were available at the Charity Commission.

Most of the funds go to Jewish causes, many of which receive ongoing support of typically more than £20,000 a year each. A few arts organisations are similarly supported, although the level of donation varies year to year.

The trust states that it reviews all commitments on a forward five-year basis so that a few new projects can be undertaken and income is made available.

In 2009/10 the trust had assets of £22.4 million and an income of just over £1.3 million. Grants were made to 30 organisations totalling £974,000, broken down as follows:

General charitable causes	14	£546,000
Overseas aid	6	£313,000
Health	7	£76,000
Education and training	3	£25,000

Large grants to organisations in Israel and the UK included those to: Yemin Orde Therapeutic Centre (£129,000); Jacqueline and Michael Gee Charitable Trust and the Rosalyn and Nicholas Springer Charitable Trust (£125,000 each); Neve Ilan Ashkelon (£117,500); Belsize Square Synagogue (£100,500); and the Diana and Allan Morgenthau Charitable Trust (£95,000).

Other beneficiaries included: Jewish Care (£37,500); Nightingale House

(£30,000); Royal National Theatre (£25,000); The Tel Aviv Foundation (£20,000); Community Security Trust (£15,000); The London Jewish Cultural Centre (£10,000); Yad Vashem UK Foundation (£5,300); Combat Stress (£2,000); and Glyndebourne Arts Trust (£1,500).

Applications

In writing to the correspondent. Trustees meet every month except August and December.

The Shetland Charitable Trust

Social welfare; art and recreation; environment and amenity

£10.3 million (2010/11)

Beneficial area

Shetland only.

22–24 North Road, Lerwick, Shetland ZE1 0NQ
Tel: 01595 744994
Fax: 01595 744999
Email: mail@shetlandcharitabletrust. co.uk
Website: www. shetlandcharitabletrust.co.uk
Correspondent: Ann Black, General Manager
Trustees: William Manson; James Henry; Leslie Angus; Laura Baisley; James Budge; Alexander Cluness; Alastair Cooper; Adam Doull; Allison Duncan; Elizabeth Fullerton; Florence Grains; Robert Henderson; Andrew Hughson; Caroline Miller; Richard Nickerson; Valerie Nicolson; Frank Robertson; Gary Robinson; Joseph Simpson; John Scott; Cecil Smith; Jonathon Wills.
SC Number: SC027025

Information available

Accounts and annual reports were available from the trust's website.

The original trust was established in 1976 with 'disturbance receipts' from the operators of the Sullom Voe oil terminal. As a clause in the trust deed prevented it from accumulating income beyond 21 years from its inception, in 1997 most of its assets were transferred to a newly established Shetland Islands Council Charitable Trust, which is identical to the old trust except for the omission of the prohibition on accumulating income. This has now been renamed Shetland Charitable Trust.

The trust was run by the Shetland Islands Council until 2002. The trust is currently administered by its own separate staff.

The trust is generally a strategic funding body providing funding for other organisations to carry out their activities and only undertakes a small amount of 'direct' charitable activity in the Shetland community itself. The trust aims to provide public benefit to and improve the quality of life for the inhabitants of Shetland; ensure that people in need receive a high standard of service and care; protect and enhance Shetland's environment, heritage, culture and traditions; provide facilities that will be of long-term benefit to the inhabitants of Shetland; build on the energy and initiatives of local groups, maximise voluntary effort and input and assist them to achieve their objectives; support a balanced range of services and facilities to contribute to the overall fabric of the community; support facilities and services and jobs located in rural areas and maintain the value of the funds in the long term to ensure that future generations have access to similar resources in the post oil era.

In 2010/11 the trust had assets of £219.8 million and an income of £9.2 million. Grants were made totalling £10.3 million.

The funds are used to create and sustain a wide range of facilities for the islands, largely by funding further trusts including: Shetland Recreational Trust (£2.5 million); Shetland Amenity Trust (£1.1 million); and Shetland Arts Development Agency (£696,000).

Other organisations and local projects receiving grants during the year included: Support to Rural Care Model (£2.5 million); Planned Maintenance Scheme (£1.3 million); Xmas grant scheme (£578,000); COPE Limited (£330,000); Shetland Youth Information Service (£189,000);

Voluntary Action Shetland (£144,000); Citizens Advice Bureau (£132,000); Community Support Grants scheme (£73,000); Shetland Churches Council Trust (£54,000); Buses for Elderly and Disabled (£52,000); Shetland Link Up (£48,000); Festival Grants (£30,000); Sheltered Housing Heating scheme (£25,500); VAS – ICT replacement (£20,000); and Couple Counselling Shetland (£12,000).

Exclusions

Funds can only be used to benefit the inhabitants of Shetland.

Applications

Applications are only accepted from Shetland-based charities. The trustees meet every two months.

The trust has different contact points for different categories of grant:

▶ Christmas grants – contact the trust on 01595 744994

▶ arts grants, development grants, senior citizens club grants and support grants – contact Michael Duncan on 01595 743828

▶ social assistance grants – contact the duty social worker at duty@shetland.gov.uk

SHINE (Support and Help in Education)

Education of children and young people

£1.9 million (2010/11)

Beneficial area

Greater London and Manchester.

1 Cheam Road, Ewell Village, Surrey KT17 1SP
Tel: 020 8393 1880
Email: info@shinetrust.org.uk
Website: www.shinetrust.org.uk
Correspondent: Paul Carbury, Chief Executive
Trustees: Jim O'Neill, Chair; David Blood; Gavin Boyle; Mark Heffernan; Mark Ferguson; Cameron Ogden; Krutika Pau; Richard Rothwell; Caroline Whalley.
CC Number: 1082777

Information available

Accounts were available from the Charity Commission. The charity also has a detailed website.

The following description of the charity's work is taken from its 2010/11 annual report:

SHINE supports educational projects that work with disadvantaged, disengaged and challenged children and young people (6 – 18 years), mostly in Greater London and Manchester. We provide grants to fund educational programmes which give these young people the extra support and attention they need to learn the basic but essential tools for life. SHINE also supports projects that help talented children from poor neighbourhoods to recognise and then realise their full potential.

SHINE projects include intensive one-to-one literacy and numeracy support, Saturday learning programmes, homework clubs and computer-assisted study projects – all specifically designed to make a meaningful difference to the children and young people who need it most. We work in partnership with primary and secondary state schools, the independent sector and world-class universities to get more from existing facilities and resources.

SHINE operates as a business, working closely with potential grant recipients to make sure their projects can be delivered. Most importantly, early monitoring and evaluation planning with those organisations which receive grants establishes the quantitative methods by which the success of these projects will be judged. When the projects are up and running, we then monitor and evaluate them rigorously to ensure they are efficient and have only the most positive effect on the young lives they help. This research means that we can prove what works, how and why. This allows us to replicate the most effective projects and help spread good practice.

The SHINE trustees take decisions on grant applications based on the recommendations of the grant-making team. Prior to each full board meeting, these recommendations are considered in detail by the grant-making trustee cluster group. We spend a significant amount of time and energy in order to find, fund and support projects which will have a measurable impact on the educational attainment of disadvantaged children and young people.

Types of grant

SHINE funds and develops educational programmes to help disadvantaged children make the most of their time at school. These include specialist after school clubs, complementary classes on Saturdays, intensive literacy and numeracy support sessions and help for children with special educational needs, underachievers, and gifted children.

SHINE wishes to fund projects that have the following key elements:

- the main focus is on educational subjects, especially promoting literacy, numeracy and science
- content and methodology that will excite and engage participants, making creative use of IT where appropriate
- there are clear and measurable target educational outcomes. Principally this will mean linking to standardised tests (at primary level) and GCSEs or a recognised equivalent (at secondary level)
- a significant number of children / young people will be supported
- these children / young people themselves want to improve their situation
- the project will be sufficiently long term to support sustainable improvement
- families of participants are linked to the project in a way which supports their child's learning
- there is appropriate use of volunteers
- the project budget represents value for money.

SHINE wishes to build long term relationships and partnerships with the organisations it funds, so the majority of grants are in excess of £20,000. It funds new start ups, pilots and development or replication of projects. It also funds core costs.

The trust has used their research and experience over the past 10 years to allow them to concentrate their funding on four key areas. These are described below. For more information on any of the programmes or their associated projects, please go to the charity's website.

SHINE on Saturdays – a core programme helping underachieving children at both primary and secondary schools by injecting 150 hours of additional and creative learning every year, accelerating and complementing their classroom achievements. Each project is based at a school and runs for 30 Saturdays a year, working with 60 primary or secondary school children. The trust is particularly keen to fund clusters of primary schools in Greater London.

Serious Fun on Saturdays – top independent schools open their superb facilities to enrich and expand the core curriculum for local state school children unlikely to receive extra educational support at home. The trust is keen on hearing from independent schools that are interested in hosting a

Serious Fun project and can identify potential partner schools in the state sector.

Other Saturday Programmes – most of these projects offer study support, structured learning and extra-curricular activities to students preparing for GCSEs – a crucial hurdle that can often determine a teenager's path in life. They work with students of all abilities; some need an extra push to avoid underperforming just when it matters most, while Brunel Urban Scholars stretches gifted students and encourages them to raise their game and take their education all the way. These programmes are: Stepladder, Climbing Higher, Windsor Fellowship and Brunel Urban Scholars.

Innovation – funding for non-Saturday projects that take a fresh approach to closing the attainment gap. The trust are particularly interested in projects with potential for future growth and are amenable to partnership funding in order to address the trust's priorities on a bigger scale. Some of the projects under this category have included: Digismart, Lyric, IntoUniversity, City Year, Reach Out!, The Latin Programme, and Finish Line Tutors.

Additional Grants – this category includes projects which take a fresh approach to literacy, speaking and thinking skills; others involve summer schools and after-school programmes. The help they provide takes many different forms but each one has a common goal: to help students to improve their grades so that they can start to fulfil their potential, whatever it may be and wherever it may take them. Some of the projects under this category have included:

- Ocean maths – an intensive programme of support for 100 students and their parents in Tower Hamlets
- Debate mate – uses formal, structured argument to help secondary students develop their reasoning skills, communication and confidence.
- Civitas – summer schools for children who have limited access to both enrichment activities and ongoing learning support over the summer.

Guidelines

The charity's website states:

We will consider funding organisations that can demonstrate that they are:

- well managed;
- in a healthy financial position;
- working with other local agencies, particularly schools and local authorities;
- providing venues and services which are open and accessible to all; and
- led by staff who have a high level of experience and competency.

We wish to fund projects that have the following key elements:

- the main focus is on educational subjects, especially promoting literacy, numeracy and science;
- content and methodology will excite and engage participants, making creative use of IT where appropriate;
- there are clear and measurable target educational outcomes: principally this will mean linking to standardised tests (at primary level) and GCSEs or a recognised equivalent (at secondary level);
- a significant number of children / young people will be supported;
- these children / young people themselves want to improve their situation;
- the project will be sufficiently long term to support sustainable improvement;
- families of participants are linked to the project in a way which supports their child's learning;
- there is appropriate use of volunteers; and
- the project budget represents value for money.

These guidelines should be read in conjunction with the charity's current priorities, listed above and on the charity's website.

Grants in 2010/11

During the year the charity had assets of £6.1 million and an income of £3.3 million. Grants were made totalling £1.9 million and were distributed as follows:

Lift for Learning: DigiSmart	£592,000
SHINE @ Kingswood	£180,000
IntoUniversity	£120,000
Watford Grammar School	£112,000
SHINE @ St Stephen's	£90,000
SHINE @ Clapham and Larkhall	£82,000
SHINE @ Sebright	£82,000
Children's Discovery Centre	£70,000
Stepladder	£60,000
Serious Fun Forest School	£43,000
Entrepreneurs in Action	£42,000
SHINE @ Hillyfield	£40,000
Reach Out	£35,000
Serious Fun Skinners and Tonbridge	£35,000
Brunel University Urban Scholars	£33,000
Eastside Young Leaders Academy	£30,000
Serious Fun Eltham	£30,000
PiXL Club	£25,000
Serious Fun Highgate	£18,000
Serious Fun Latymer Upper-Science	£17,000
Serious Fun Winchester	£17,000
Serious Fun Sheffield High	£16,500
Story Museum	£16,000
Serious Fun Lady Eleanor Holles	£13,000
SHINE @ Richard Atkins	£9,000
National Literacy Trust	£7,500
Serious Fun Latymer Upper: Design	£6,000

Exclusions

SHINE will not fund:

▶ individuals
▶ the direct replacement of statutory funding
▶ schools or other educational establishments, except where funding is for activities which are clearly additional
▶ short term programmes
▶ programmes targeted at specific subject or beneficiary groups
▶ parenting programmes, where the primary focus is the parent rather than the child
▶ activities promoting particular political or religious beliefs
▶ projects taking place outside Greater London, except projects that are part of SHINE's replication programme.

Applications

All potential applicants must initially speak to a member of the grants team by telephoning 020 8393 1880. The trustees meet about three times a year, but not at fixed intervals.

Common applicant mistakes

'Applicants not meeting our eligibility criteria, or applying for projects with no clearly defined outcomes.'

The Shirley Foundation

Autism spectrum disorders with particular emphasis on medical research

£1.1 million (2009/10)

Beneficial area

UK.

North Lea House, 66 Northfield End, Henley-on-Thames, Oxfordshire RG9 2BE
Tel: 01491 579004
Fax: 01491 574995
Email: steve@steveshirley.com
Website: www.steveshirley.com/tsf
Correspondent: Anne McCartney Menzies, Trustee
Trustees: Dame Stephanie Shirley, Chair; Prof. Eve Johnstone; Michael

Robert Macfadyen; Anne McCartney Menzies.
CC Number: 1097135

Information available

Accounts were available at the Charity Commission.

The foundation, (formerly known as the Shirley Foundation Charitable Trust), was established in 1996 by Dame Stephanie Shirley, a business technology pioneer and the current Chair. Dame Stephanie is a highly successful entrepreneur turned ardent philanthropist. Having arrived in Britain as an unaccompanied child refugee from Germany in 1939, she started what is now Xansa on her dining room table with £6 in 1962. In 25 years as its chief executive she developed it into a leading business technology group, pioneering new work practices and changing the position of professional women (especially in hi-tech) along the way.

The foundation is established for general charitable purposes and the main areas of interest are information technology and autism (not excluding Aspergers Syndrome) which occasionally extend to learning disabilities in general. The foundation's mission is 'the facilitation and support of pioneering projects with strategic impact in the field of autism spectrum disorders, with particular emphasis on medical research'.

In 2009/10 the foundation had assets of £3.3 million and an income of £94,000. Grants were made totalling just over £1.1 million, which included £1 million pledged to Balliol College, Oxford during the previous year for the Historic Collections Centre in St Cross Church, Holywell.

The other beneficiaries during the year were: The World Health Organisation (£100,000); Mental Health Foundation (£4,900), for research for an Autistic Spectrum Disorders report; and a publication on the history of autism (£3,400).

The foundation's 2009/10 annual report stated that at the end of 2010 there were no major projects or grants under consideration at that time, and that the trustees will continue to review grant requests and possible future projects as they arise.

Exclusions

No grants to individuals, or for non autism-specific work. The foundation does not make political donations.

Applications

Trustees currently meet annually but applications for support are received throughout the year. Only those within the foundation's mission are considered; applicants are reminded that projects should be innovative in nature with the potential to have a strategic impact in the field of Autism Spectrum Disorders. Research proposals should be aimed ultimately at determining causes of autism. Researchers should refer to the 'Guidance: Application for a medical research grant' [downloadable from the foundation's website].

In the first instance a simple letter with outline proposal should be sent to Dame Stephanie Shirley at the registered address or emailed.

Shlomo Memorial Fund Limited

Jewish causes

£2 million (2009/10)

Beneficial area

Unrestricted.

Cohen Arnold and Co., New Burlington House, 1075 Finchley Road, London NW11 0PU
Tel: 020 8731 0777
Fax: 020 8731 0778
Correspondent: Channe Lopian, Secretary
Trustees: Amichai Toporowitz, Chair; Hezkel Toporowitz; Eliyah Kleineman; Channe Lopian; Chaim Y Kaufman.
CC Number: 278973

Information available

Accounts were available at the Charity Commission.

This trust was established in 1978 to advance the orthodox Jewish religion, relief of the poor and general charitable purposes.

In 2009/10 the trust had assets of £36.4 million and an income of £6.4 million. Grants totalling just over £2 million were made to religious, educational and other charitable institutions. A list of grant beneficiaries was not included in the trust's accounts.

Previous beneficiaries include: Amud Haolam, Nachlat Haleviim, Torah Umesorah, Beit Hillel, ZSV Charities, Layesharim Tehilla, British Friends of Tashbar Chazon Ish, Chazon Ish, Mei Menuchos, Mor Uketsio, Shoshanat Hoamakim, Millennium Trust, and Talmud Torah Zichron Meir.

Applications
In writing to the correspondent.

The Henry Smith Charity

Social welfare, older people, disability, health, medical research

£24.9 million to organisations
(2010)

Beneficial area
UK. Specific local programmes in east and west Sussex, Hampshire, Kent, Gloucestershire, Leicestershire, Suffolk and Surrey.

Applications, 6th Floor, 65 Leadenhall Street, London EC3A 2AD
Tel: 020 7264 4970
Fax: 020 7488 9097
Website: www.henrysmithcharity.org.uk
Correspondent: Richard Hopgood, Director
Trustees: Carola Goodman-Law; James Hambro; Anna McNair Scott; Merlyn Lowther; Noel Manns; Anne Allen; Rt Hon Claire Countes; Diana Barran; Marilyn Gallyer; Mark Newton; Peter Smallridge; Tristan Millington Drake; Nicholas Acland; Miko Geidroyc; Vivian Hunt; Bridget Biddell; Patrick Maxwell; Sir Richard Thompson.
CC Number: 230102

Information available
Accounts available from the Charity Commission. The charity also has an excellent and informative website.

The Henry Smith Charity was founded in 1628 with the objects of relieving and where possible releasing people from need and suffering. These objects continue in the grant making policy today. The Henry Smith Charity makes grants totalling around £25 million per annum for a wide range of purposes across the UK, funded from investments.

Grant programmes
The charity provides a number of grant programmes and offers the following details:

We strongly recommend that you download and read the full guidelines for the type of grant you wish to apply for before making your application. [Comprehensive guidelines are available from the charity's website.]

The types of projects and services you can apply for a grant towards through our Main and Small Grants Programmes [are listed below].

Main Grants Programme
Our Main Grants Programme is for grants of £10,000 per annum or over. There are two types of main grant:
- Capital Grants: one off grants for purchase or refurbishment of a building or purchase of specialist equipment.
- Revenue Grants: grants of up to three years for things like core costs (including salaries and overheads), or the running costs of a specific project (including staffing costs).

Small Grants Programme
Our Small Grants Programme is for grants of under £10,000 per year. There are two types of small grant:
- County Grants: grants of £500 – £20,000 for small organisations working in the counties with which we have an historical association, i.e., Gloucestershire, Hampshire, Kent, Leicestershire, Suffolk, Surrey, East Sussex and West Sussex. To be eligible to apply for a County Grant, your annual income must be below £250,000, unless you are working county-wide, in which case your income must be below £1 million.
- Small Grants: grants of £500 – £20,000 for small UK registered charities working in any UK county not listed above. To be eligible to apply for a Small Grant, your annual income must be below £150,000.

Medical Research
Grants of up to three years for research undertaken by recognised 'Centres of Excellence.

Priority areas of support are:
- Alzheimer's/dementia
- child health
- bowels/gastroenterology
- diseases of the lung (excluding TB)
- neurology

- pancreatic disease (excluding diabetes)
- spinal conditions
- urinary and faecal incontinence
- engineering and medicine.

Further guidelines and an application form are available from the charity's website.

Holiday Grants for Children
One off grants of up to £3,000 for organisations, schools, youth groups etc specifically for holidays or outings for children under the age of 13 who are disabled or who live in areas of high deprivation.

There are currently no Major Grants open for applications.

Through the Main Grants Programme and Small and County Grants Programmes, grants are made in the following categories (with examples of the type of work funded under each category):

Areas of funding
Black, Asian and Minority Ethnic (BAME)
Projects that provide culturally appropriate services to Black, Asian and Minority Ethnic communities; this includes those that promote integration and access to mainstream services.

Carers
Projects that provide advice and support; this includes respite services for carers and those cared for. Work can include educational opportunities for young carers.

Community Service
Projects that provide support for communities in areas of high deprivation; this includes projects providing furniture recycling services, debt advice and community centres.

Disability
Projects that provide rehabilitation, training or advocacy support to people who are disabled; this includes learning disabilities as well as physical disabilities.

Domestic and sexual violence
Projects that provide advice, support and secure housing for families affected by domestic violence or sexual violence. Perpetrator programmes can be considered where organisations have secured, or are working towards, Respect accreditation.

Drugs, alcohol and substance misuse
Projects supporting the rehabilitation of people affected by, or at risk of, drug and/or alcohol dependency, and projects supporting their families.

Ex-service men and women
Projects that provide services or residential care to ex-service men and women and their dependents.

Family services
Projects providing support to families in areas of high deprivation.

Healthcare
Projects that provide residential care, health care or outreach services, such as home care support. Services operated by the NHS will not normally be funded. In the case of applications from hospices, priority is given to requests for capital expenditure.

Homelessness
Projects that provide housing and services for homeless people and those at risk of homelessness.

Lesbian, Gay, Bisexual and Transgender
Projects providing advice, support and counselling for people who are Lesbian, Gay, Bisexual or Transgendered.

Mental health
Projects that promote positive mental health or provide advice and support to people experiencing mental health problems.

Older people
Projects that provide residential care, health care or emotional support, such as befriending services and day care centres. Priority will be given to projects in areas of high deprivation and those where rural isolation can be demonstrated.

Prisoners and ex-offenders
Projects that help the rehabilitation and resettlement of prisoners and/or ex-offenders; including education and training that improve employability, and projects that support prisoners' families.

Prostitution and trafficking
Projects that provide advice and support to sex industry workers; including advice on housing support and personal health, escaping exploitation and exiting prostitution.

Refugees and asylum seekers
Projects that provide advocacy, advice and support to refugees and asylum seekers, and those promoting integration.

Young people
Projects that maximise the potential of young people (including young people in, or leaving, care) who experience educational, social and economic disadvantage.

Grantmaking in 2010

In 2010 the charity had assets of £701.5 million and an income of £14.3 million. Grants were made totalling over £25.5 million, broken down as shown in the table below.

£447,000 worth of grants were withdrawn or returned in 2010, explaining the discrepancy between total grant figures and the category totals.

The following is taken from the trust's 2010 annual report:

> The number of applications to our main grants programme increased by 17% in 2010, reversing a sharp fall in 2009.

> The number of grants awarded was almost 20% higher than 2009, with most of the grants awarded for three years funding of revenue costs; as in previous years we dealt with around five applications for every award we made.

> Around 26% by number of the awards were given as continuation funding, following the completion of previous awards.

> The average size of grant awards was slightly smaller than previous years. Grants of between £50,000 and £70,000 are still most typical, but there was a significant decrease in the number of grants over £100,000.

> The largest amounts of grant funding continue to be made for work in London, however as we do not target particular regions the mix of funding varies significantly year by year.

Funding towards Young People increased significantly and was the area of highest funding in 2010, whilst Medical Research funding fell sharply Community Service, Mental Health and Young People continue to be the programme areas receiving the highest levels of funding.

The following are a sample of organisations which received a grant in 2010:

Cripplegate Foundation(£300,000), towards funding local community projects which target vulnerable and hard to reach groups in Islington; Cool Recovery (£120,000), towards running costs of support services for people in south Devon affected by mental health problems; Bethel Community Church (£94,500), towards three years' salary of a co-ordinator at a community cafe and night shelter in Newport; Choir With No Name (£75,000), towards running costs; Dudley Christian Fellowship (£70,500), towards running costs of a charity for homeless people and substance misusers; Action Medical Research (£70,000), towards the second and third year of a project to research Rett Syndrome; Headway Belfast(£60,000), towards three years' salary of a Neuro Physiotherapist for an exercise project for people affected by brain injury; British Refugee Council (£50,000), towards one year's running costs of the Therapeutic Casework Unit based in London; Age Concern Cardiff and the Vale of Glamorgan (£45,000), towards running costs; Cutteslowe Community Association (£33,000), towards one year's salary of two part-time community workers at a community centre in Oxford; Mildmay Mission Hospital (£28,000), towards continued funding of the running costs of an occupational

---

THE HENRY SMITH CHARITY

Grant expenditure: organisations	2010	2009
Main grant programme (grants above £10,000)	£21.7 million	£19.4 million
Small grants (up to £10,000)	£1.7 million	£1.6 million
Major grants	£447,000	£210,000
Grant to historic parishes (Estates Fund distributions)	£468,000	£520,000
Grants for Christian projects	£460,000	£222,000
Holiday grants	£151,000	£94,000
Total grants to organisations	**£24.9 million**	**£22 million**

Grant expenditure: individuals	2010	2009
Grants to clergy	£518,000	£605,000
Grants to poor kindred	£520,000	£502,000
Total grants to individuals	**£1 million**	**£1.1 million**

therapy service in London for people with AIDS; Gargaar Somali Welfare Association (£15,000), towards running costs of a luncheon club for older people from London's Somali and East African community; Powerful Partnerships (£15,000), towards the core costs of an advocacy service in Edinburgh for people with learning disabilities; Suffolk Punch Trust (£2,500), towards equipment purchase for a centre in Suffolk that provides training to young offenders; and African Sub-Saharan Development Partnership (£1,400), towards a trip to Butlins for 15 Congolese children from a refugee background in London.

Exclusions

Grants are not made towards the following:

- local authorities and areas of work usually considered a statutory responsibility
- state maintained schools, colleges, universities and friend/parent teacher associations, or independent schools not exclusively for students with special educational needs
- organisations not providing direct services to clients such as umbrella, second tier or grant-making organisations
- youth clubs, except those in areas of high deprivation
- uniformed groups such as Scouts and Guides, except those in areas of high deprivation
- community centres, except those in areas of high deprivation
- community transport organisations or services
- professional associations or projects for the training of professionals
- start up costs or organisations unable to demonstrate a track record
- individuals, or organisations and charities applying on their behalf
- projects that promote a particular religion, or capital appeals for places of worship
- arts projects, except those which can clearly demonstrate a therapeutic or rehabilitative benefit to disabled people, prisoners or young people who experience educational, social and economic disadvantage, including young people in, or leaving, care
- education projects except those which can clearly demonstrate a rehabilitative benefit to disabled people, prisoners or young people who experience educational, social and economic disadvantage, including young people in, or leaving, care
- leisure, recreation or play activities, except those exclusively for disabled people or those which can clearly demonstrate a significant rehabilitative benefit to people with mental health problems or that significantly improve opportunities and maximise the potential of young people who experience educational, social and economic disadvantage
- overseas trips
- projects taking place or benefiting people outside the UK
- residential holidays for young people (except those that qualify under the Holiday Grants scheme)
- counselling projects, except those in areas of high deprivation and with a clearly defined client group
- environmental projects where the primary purpose is conservation of the environment
- Citizens Advice Bureau or projects solely providing legal advice
- core running costs of hospices
- feasibility studies
- social research
- campaigning or lobbying projects
- projects where website development or maintenance is the focus of the bid
- IT equipment (unless as direct support costs for a funded staff member)
- capital projects to meet the requirements of the Disability Discrimination Act
- applicants declined within the previous six months
- Organisations that do not have charitable aims (e.g. companies limited by shares and commercial organisations are not eligible to apply)
- mailshots or general appeals.

Applications

Each of our grant programmes has a slightly different application and assessment process.

You will find information about how to make your application in the guidelines for each type of grant. Some of our grants require you to fill in an application form. For others there is no application form; instead we provide guidance about to structure your application and what supporting documents you need to send us.

Please ensure you send us all the supporting documents we ask you to include with your application. Incomplete applications will be returned unread.

We strongly recommend that you download and read the guidelines of the relevant grant programme carefully before you start your application. It is important that you follow our guidance on how to apply.

Guidelines for each programme can be downloaded from the Grant Programmes section of the charity's website.

The Sobell Foundation

Jewish charities, medical care and treatment, education, community, environment, disability, older people and young people

£3.4 million (2009/10)

Beneficial area

Unrestricted, in practice, England and Wales, Israel and the Commonwealth of Independent States (CIS).

PO Box 2137, Shepton Mallet, Somerset BA4 6YA
Tel: 01749 813135
Fax: 01749 813136
Email: enquiries@sobellfoundation.org.uk
Website: www.sobellfoundation.org.uk
Correspondent: Penny Newton, Administrator
Trustees: Susan Lacroix; Roger Lewis; Andrea Scouller.
CC Number: 274369

Information available

Accounts were available at the Charity Commission.

The Sobell Foundation was established by the late Sir Michael Sobell in 1977 for general charitable purposes and is a grant-making trust with which he was actively involved until shortly before his death in 1993. Funding is generally restricted to small national charities in England and Wales or local charities working in the following fields:

▶ medical care and treatment (including respite care and hospices)
▶ care and education for children and adults with physical and/or mental disabilities
▶ homelessness
▶ care and support for the elderly
▶ care and support for children from disadvantaged backgrounds.

The following information comes from the foundation's 2009/10 annual report:

> In addition, in Israel only, the foundation supports higher education, co-existence projects and projects relating to immigrant absorption.

> The trustees aim to achieve a reasonable spread between Jewish charities (operating principally in the UK, Israel and the CIS) and non-Jewish charities operating in the UK, with between a third and a half generally being allocated to the former category. Grants are only made to, or through, UK registered charities.

> The trustees visit Israel annually, seeing new projects and paying visits to projects which have been supported in the past. Many of the charities supported send reports of their activities to the trustees on a regular basis and, where possible, the trustees pay follow-up visits.

In 2009/10 the foundation had assets of £62.7 million and an income of £5.5 million, which included £3.5 million in the form of capital from the settlor's estate. During the year grants were made to 428 organisations totalling £3.4 million, with awards ranging from £450 to £300,000. Of these, 29 grants were made of amounts ranging from £20,000 to £50,000.

Approximately 53% of grants made were to UK non-Jewish charities, 31% to Israeli charities and charities in the CIS, 15% to UK Jewish charities and 1% to other overseas charities. This allocation is within the ranges set by the trustees for grant allocation.

Grants were categorised as follows:

UK non-Jewish

Medical (care and treatment)	133	£974,500
Hardship alleviation	69	£338,000
Community	61	£295,700
Education	20	£102,700
Medical research	2	£50,000
Cultural and environmental	8	£49,200

Israel

Education	35	£392,000
Medical (care and treatment)	38	£317,000
Community	24	£196,000
Hardship alleviation	17	£155,000
Cultural and environmental	1	£5,000

UK Jewish

Medical (care and treatment)	5	£335,000
Community	8	£91,000
Education	2	£45,000
Cultural and environmental	1	£20,000
Hardship alleviation	2	£15,000

Overseas

Hardship alleviation	1	£25,000
Community	1	£1,600

The largest grants during the year were made to: Jewish Care (£300,000), the second instalment of a 3-year grant towards the building a new day care centre at their Golders Green campus; and Leonard Cheshire Disability (£85,000), the first instalment of a 3-year grant to expand Sobell Lodge care home in Kent.

Exclusions

No grants to individuals. Only registered charities or organisations registered with the Inland Revenue should apply.

Applications

'Due to the enormous number of appeals the trustees are now receiving they have had to limit their support within the UK to charities operating in England and Wales.'

Applications should be made in writing to the administrator using the application form obtainable from the foundation or printable from its website.

The application form should be accompanied by:

▶ current year's summary income and expenditure budget
▶ most recent annual report
▶ most recent full accounts
▶ Inland Revenue certificate of exemption (if required).

The trustees receive a large number of applications for funding from registered charities during the year

and support as many as possible of those which fall within the foundation's objectives. They aim to deal with requests within three months of receipt and to respond to each application received, whether or not a grant is made.

Trustees meet every three to four months and major grants are considered at these meetings. Requests for smaller amounts may be dealt with on a more frequent basis. Most applications are dealt with on an ongoing basis, and there are no deadlines for the receipt of applications. Organisations should wait 12 months before reapplying.

The Souter Charitable Trust

Christian evangelism, welfare

About £2 million.

Beneficial area

UK, but with a preference for Scotland; overseas.

PO Box 7412, Perth PH1 5YX
Tel: 01738 450408
Email: enquiries@soutercharitabletrust.org.uk
Website: www.soutercharitabletrust.org.uk
Correspondent: Andy Macfie, Secretary
Trustees: Brian Souter; Betty Souter; Ann Allen.
SC Number: SC029998

Information available

Information was taken from the trust's website. Accounts are available from the trust for £10.

This trust is funded by donations from Scottish businessman Brian Souter, one of the founders of the Stagecoach transport company. It gives the following account of its policies:

> Our stated policy is to assist 'projects engaged in the relief of human suffering in the UK or overseas, particularly those with a Christian emphasis'. We tend not to get involved with research or capital funding, but would be more likely to provide a contribution towards the revenue costs of a project. Grants

333

are generally given to charitable organisations and not to individuals or in support of requests on behalf of individuals. Applications for building projects, personal educational requirements or personal expeditions are specifically excluded.'

Most grants are one-off payments of £1,000 or less; a small number of projects receive support over three years. Previous grants indicate an interest in the support of marriage and parenting issues. There is a preference for funding revenue rather than capital costs. In 2009/10 the trust received 1,800 applications for funding.

In 2009/10 the trust had an income of £2.8 million. Grants totalled around £2 million. No further information was available.

Previous beneficiaries include: Alpha International (an Anglican evangelical movement based in London), Highland Theological College, Operation Mobilisation, Prince's Trust – Scotland, Sargent Cancer Care, Scripture Union and Turning Point Scotland.

Exclusions

Building projects, individuals, personal education grants and expeditions are not supported.

Applications

In writing to the correspondent. Please keep applications brief and no more than two sides of A4 paper: if appropriate, please send audited accounts, but do not send brochures, business plans, DVDs and so on. The trust states that it will request more information if necessary. The trustees meet every two months or so, and all applications will be acknowledged in due course, whether successful or not. A stamped addressed envelope would be appreciated. Subsequent applications should not be made within a year of the initial submission.

The Sovereign Health Care Charitable Trust

Health, people with disabilities

£468,500 (2010)

Beneficial area

UK with a preference for Bradford.

Royal Standard House, 26 Manningham Lane, Bradford, West Yorkshire BD1 3DN
Tel: 01274 729472
Fax: 01274 722252
Email: cs@sovereignhealthcare.co.uk
Website: www.sovereignhealthcare.co.uk
Correspondent: The Secretary
Trustees: Mark Hudson, Chair; Michael Austin; Dennis Child; Michael Bower; Russ Piper; Kate Robb-Webb; Robert Dugdale; Stewart Cummings.
CC Number: 1079024

Information available

Accounts were available at the Charity Commission.

The Sovereign Health Care Charitable Trust is funded by donations received under the Gift Aid scheme from the investment income of The Hospital Fund of Bradford. Its objects are to provide amenities for hospital patients and to make grants to charitable organisations 'for the relief and assistance of needy, sick and elderly persons'.

In 2010 the trust had assets of £23,500 and an income of £510,000. Grants were made to organisations totalling £468,500.

Larger grants included those to: Yorkshire Air Ambulance (£29,000); Hospital Heartbeat Appeal (£18,500); Bradford Soup Run and Heart Research UK (£15,000 each); Community Cougars Foundation and Positive Lifestyles (£10,000 each); and the Samaritans (£7,500).

Other beneficiaries included: Christians Against Poverty (£5,000); Changing Faces (£4,000); Harrogate & District NHS Trust (£3,500); Kirkwood Hospice and Prostate UK

(£2,000 each); Listening Books (£1,500); and the Firefighters Charity (£1,000).

Exclusions

No grants to individuals.

Applications

In writing to the correspondent.

Common applicant mistakes

'Applicants not making clear how the money will be used, and also what other steps they are taking to raise funds.'

Sparks Charity (Sport Aiding Medical Research For Kids)

Medical research

£1.3 million (2010/11)

Beneficial area

UK.

Heron House, 10 Dean Farrer Street, London SW1H 0DX
Tel: 020 7799 2111
Fax: 020 7222 2701
Email: kirti@sparks.org.uk
Website: www.sparks.org.uk
Correspondent: Dr Kirti Patel, Medical Research Manager
Trustees: Sir T Brooking; Hugh Emeades; Michael Higgins; Roger Uttley; Simon Waugh; Julian Wilkinson; Floella Benjamin; Jonathon Britton; Victoria Glaysher; Guy Gregory; Gabby Logan; David Orr; Frank van den Bosch.
CC Number: 1003825

Information available

Accounts were on file at the Charity Commission. Information was also provided by the charity.

Sparks is one of the few charities that funds research into the wide range of conditions that can affect babies and children. It supports vital medical research that will:

▸ increase the life expectancy of new born babies

- reduce the health risks for babies born prematurely
- combat common conditions such as spina bifida and cerebral palsy
- develop more effective treatments for conditions affecting babies and young children.

The following is taken from the charity's guidelines for research grant applications, available on its website:

The charity will only support research which is likely to have a clear clinical application in the near future. Therefore grant applications for routine basic research which is unlikely to have clinical application within ten years will not be considered.

Sparks funded research takes the form of project grants of up to three years in length with a clearly definable subject area and outcome, equipment grants for use within a specific research proposal as previously defined, programme grants for researchers who have a sustained track record of successful grant awards from Sparks and fellowship grants. Pilot projects of short duration to test a concept in preparation for a full application will also be considered (see website). Grants are only made to projects where the principal applicant is in a tenured position at a university or research institution.

Researchers who are making a substantial intellectual contribution to the project and require personal support from the grant may apply as co-applicants with a tenured member of staff as the principal applicant.

In 2010/11 the charity had assets of £478,000 and an income of over £3.5 million, mainly from fundraising events. The charity made six new research grants and four supplementary grants to hospitals, universities and research institutions totalling just over £1.3 million.

The beneficiaries during the year were: St Michael's Hospital – Bristol (£229,500); University of Bristol (£200,000); The Institute of Cancer Research (£197,000); University of Birmingham (£149,000); University of Cambridge (£137,500); University College London – Institute of Child Health (£137,000 in total); Imperial College – London (£118,000); University College London Hospitals NHS Foundations Trust (£100,000); and Newcastle University Medical School (£69,500).

Exclusions

The charity is unable to consider:

- grants for further education, for example, MSc/PhD course fees
- grants towards service provision or audit studies
- grants for work undertaken outside the UK
- grants towards 'top up' funding for work supported by other funding bodies
- grants to other charities.

Applications

Sparks funds project grants up to the value of £200,000, Research Training Fellowships and Programme grants. Prior to submitting a full application, all applicants are required to complete an outline proposal form which is available for download from the charity's website in Word format. Completed outlines and any queries should be sent to: Dr Kirti Patel, Medical Research Manager, email: Kirti@sparks.org.uk, direct Tel/Fax 020 7799 2111/020 7222 2701. Please refer to the Sparks website for outline closing dates. Applicants with suitable research projects will be sent an application form (by email in Word format) and a copy of the relating terms and conditions. Closing dates for full applications are generally March and October; please refer to the Sparks website.

The Geoff and Fiona Squire Foundation

General

£1.2 million (2009/10)

Beneficial area

UK.

The North Canonry, 60–61 The Close, Salisbury SP1 2EN
Correspondent: Fiona Squire, Trustee
Trustees: G W Squire; Fiona Squire; B P Peerless.
CC Number: 1085553

Information available

Accounts were available at the Charity Commission.

Registered with the Charity Commission in March 2001, in 2009/10 the foundation had assets of £1.2 million and an income of £599,000. Grants were made to 32 organisations totalling £1.2 million.

The largest grants included those made to: Wessex Children's Hospice – Naomi House (£277,000); the Stars Appeal – Salisbury District Hospital (£200,000); Teenage Cancer Trust (£156,000); Changing Faces (£152,000); Information Technologists' Company (£100,000); SENSE Holiday Fund (£83,000); and, Stable Family Home Trust (£50,000).

Other grants included those made to: the Children's Trust (£10,000); Music for Youth (£7,500); Friends of Shepherds Down School (£6,000); Canine Partners for Independence (£5,000); Strong Bones Children's Charitable Trust (£2,500); Three Choirs Festival (£1,500); and, Dressability (£500).

Applications

The trust has previously stated: 'the trustees have in place a well-established donations policy and we do not therefore encourage unsolicited grant applications, not least because they take time and expense to deal with properly.'

St James's Place Foundation

Children and young people with special needs, hospices

£3.3 million (2010)

Beneficial area

UK.

1 Tetbury Road, Cirencester, Gloucestershire GL7 1FP
Tel: 01285 878 562
Email: sjp.foundation@sjp.co.uk
Website: www.sjp.co.uk/foundation
Correspondent: Mark Longbottom
Trustees: Malcolm Cooper-Smith, Chair; David Bellamy; Mike Wilson; Andrew Croft; Hugh Gladman; David Lamb.
CC Number: 1031456

Information available

Accounts were available at the Charity Commission. Information is also available on the foundation's website.

This foundation was established in 1992, when it was known as The J. Rothschild Assurance Foundation. St James's Place is a wealth management group. Employees and Partners (members of the St James's Place Partnership, the marketing arm of St James's Place) contribute to the foundation throughout each year and the sums raised are matched by the company. The combined amount is distributed each year to causes determined by the contributors.

The focus of the foundation has been widened in recent years to include: children with illnesses and disabilities; people with cancer; disadvantaged young people in the UK and overseas; hospices; returning service personnel; and disaster appeals.

The foundation operates two main grant programmes and three smaller charitable initiatives which are detailed in the trust's annual accounts:

Small grants programme

The small grants programme is open to charities that work in the UK with children and young people under the age of 25 who are disadvantaged either economically or socially, have physical and/or mental conditions, a life threatening or degenerative illness. The maximum grant under this programme is £10,000 and it is open to charities with a turnover of under £750,000 pa. This income restriction does not apply to special needs schools or mainstream schools with a special needs unit.

Hospices are also able to apply under this programme, irrespective of both the age of their patients and the turnover of the hospice.

Major grants programme

Note: as of winter 2011 the major grants programme was closed for new applications. Please consult the foundation's website before embarking upon an application.

The major grants programme:

Is open to UK registered charities that work in the UK and overseas with children and young people under the age of 25 who are disadvantaged either economically or socially, have physical and/or mental conditions or a life threatening or degenerative illness. Grants are often made over more than

one year and there is no maximum grant under this programme and it is open to charities with a turnover of under £8 million pa.

Local office allowance

£20,000 is available for each of the St James's Place locations to use for any local registered charity, at the discretion of the offices' foundation sub-committee, by way of grants of no more than £2,500 individually.

In addition to these grantmaking schemes the company runs a pound-for-pound matching of monies raised by partners and staff. Staff or partners who are involved 'hands on' with a charity that matches the themes of the trust can apply to the foundation for funding.

Grantmaking in 2010

In 2010 the foundation had assets of £603,000 and an income of £2.9 million. Grants totalling £3.3 million were made to over 400 charities.

Grants were categorised as follows:

Helping disadvantaged young people: £1.1 million was awarded to charities in this category. The foundation's annual report uses the example of New Horizon Youth Centre (London) which was awarded £96,000 over three years to fund an ICT Life Skills Project.

Helping children with illnesses and disabilities: £969,000 was donated to help make a difference to the day-to-day lives of children and their families. The foundation funds both capital items and revenue costs, including, for example, specialist equipment which will make a real difference to the mobility of a child with a disability or funding the cost of a therapist who works with children to alleviate physical or mental health issues. In 2010 the foundation awarded Cerebral Palsy Sport £39,000 to fund the salary of a specialist athletics coach.

Overseas: £772,000 was awarded to organisations alleviating child poverty and the aftermath of disasters overseas. In 2010 a significant portion of this income was donated to charities helping those affected by the earthquake in Haiti and floods in Pakistan. £75,000 was granted to the Philippine Community Fund who work to alleviate poverty in the Philippines.

Hospices: £239,000 was donated to Hospices in the UK. Donations have gone towards equipment, buildings, staff costs and general patient support. £30,000 was awarded to St Cuthbert's Hospice to fund a specialist bereavement service for young people.

Exclusions

The foundation has a policy of not considering an application from any charity within two years of giving a grant.

The foundation does not provide support for:
- charities with reserves of over 50% of income
- administrative costs
- activities primarily the responsibility of statutory agencies
- replacement of lost statutory funding
- research
- events
- advertising
- holidays
- sponsorship
- contributions to large capital appeals
- single faith charities
- social and economic deprivation
- charities that are raising funds on behalf of another charity.

Applications

Application forms are available from the foundation's website and can be returned by email or post. Applications will only be considered if accompanied by a signed copy of the most recent audited accounts and annual report. An initial enquiry should be made before applying for a major grant.

Applications will be assessed against a number of criteria, including user involvement, sustainability, maximum benefit and volunteer involvement. Assessment visits will normally be made and applications for major grants will either receive a visit or be invited to present to the foundation committee.

The whole procedure can take between three to six months (sometimes longer if many applications are received) so it is advisable to apply in good time if funds are required for a certain date.

There must normally be a two year gap between applications.

Common applicant mistakes

'They do not read the criteria and do not match their application to the criteria; ignore the exclusions regarding reserves etc.'

St Katharine and Shadwell Trust

Community development

£734,000 (2010)

Beneficial area

The London boroughs of Tower Hamlets, Hackney, and City of London.

11–29 Fashion Street, London E1 6PX
Tel: 020 7782 6962
Email: enquiries@skst.org
Website: www.skst.org
Correspondent: The Director
Trustees: Eric Sorensen; Rev P David Paton; Cllr Denise Jones; Angela Orphanou; Dan Jones; David Hardy; Mark Gibson; Rosemary Ryde; Ian Fisher; Dr Tobias Jung; Christopher Martin; Jonathan Norbury.
CC Number: 1001047

Information available

Accounts were available at the Charity Commission.

The trust's website introduces the trust as follows:

A community foundation, raising funds and awarding grants to run and support a wide range of projects in East London. We have been actively working in Tower Hamlets for 18 years and in 2006 extended our work into Hackney, Newham and the City of London.

Our knowledge of the area and the relationships we have developed enable us to support and sustain positive change. Our aim is to ensure that the ideas and aspirations of local people for improving their area can be realised.

We run our own grant programme called St Katharine and Shadwell that has been ongoing since the trust began as well as manage other programmes.

The grant programmes and projects may vary from year to year so please check the trust's website for up-to-date information. Grant programmes administered in 2010 included:

Comic Relief

For voluntary and community and not for profit groups in the City of London, Hackney, Newham and Tower Hamlets.

Grassroots Grants

For very small community and voluntary organisations and groups in the City of London, Hackney, Newham and Tower Hamlets.

Société Générale UK Group Charitable Trust Fund

For small social and community enterprises in the City of London, Hackney, Newham and Tower Hamlets.

St Katharine & Shadwell

The trust's own grants programme, available to benefit residents of the former wards of St Katherine or Shadwell in the London Borough of Tower Hamlets.

In 2010 the trust held assets of £9.2 million and had a total income of just over £1.1 million. Grants disbursed totalled £734,000. Throughout the year when allocating grants from direct investment income, 'priority was given to applications to promote education and learning. This category also included training and development support for the voluntary sector'. Different priorities applied to other grant programmes, such as the Société Générale Social and Community Enterprise Fund, which are administered according to the priorities agreed with the funding organisations.

Grants are available to voluntary and community organisations. Some grants may be made to statutory organisations such as schools.

Recipients of large grants included: Common Ground East, Futureversity, Shadwell Basin Outdoor Activity Centre and Tower Hamlets Education Business Partnership (£10,000 each).

Other beneficiaries of smaller grants included: London Borough of Tower Hamlets (summer holiday programme) (£8,500); Summer Holiday Programme for Pensioners (£7,000); Wellington Way Sports Project, Somali Development Association, Kudu Arts Project and Banglatown Association (£5,000 each); ADEEG Community Centre (£4,000); Providence Row (£2,000); Vital Arts (£1,500) and Science in Schools – Hermitage Primary School and Mulberry School for Girls (£1,000 each).

Exclusions

Individuals.

Applications

Please see the trust's website or contact the trust directly for details and criteria of up-to-date schemes.

The Stafford Trust

Animal welfare, medical research, local community, relief in need

£369,000 (2009/10)

Beneficial area

UK, with a preference for Scotland.

c/o Dickson Middleton CA, PO Box 14, 20 Barnton St, Stirling FK8 1NE
Tel: 01786 474718
Fax: 01786 451392
Email: staffordtrust@dicksonmiddleton.co.uk
Website: www.staffordtrust.org.uk
Correspondent: Margaret Kane or Craig Clinton
Trustees: A Peter M Walls; Hamish N Buchan; Gordon M Wyllie; Angus Morgan.
SC Number: SC018079

Information available

Information was on file at OSCR and at the trust's website.

The Stafford Trust was set up in 1991 by the late Mrs Gay Stafford of Sauchie Estate near Stirling. During her lifetime, Mrs Stafford made substantial gifts to the trust and on her death in 2005, the residue of her estate was bequeathed to the trust. Over £10 million was received in the financial year 2006/07. The trust makes grants to charities from the income generated from the trust fund.

Grants vary, but most are for between £500 and £10,000. Occasionally the trustees make a recurring grant of up to three years.

Between 1991 and 2010, grants totalling £2.1 million were made in the following areas:

	% of total
Adult welfare	24%
Medical research	21%
Animal welfare	18%
Child welfare	14%
Local community projects	13%
HM services personnel	5%
Overseas appeals	3%
Sea rescue	2%

In 2009/10 the trust had an income of £362,000 and made grants to 51 organisations totalling £369,000.

Beneficiaries included: Strathcarron Hospice (£25,000); Citizen's Advice Edinburgh and Orcadia Creative Learning Centre (£15,000 each*); Crossroads Clackmannon (£11,000); Alzheimer's Research Trust and Seafarers UK (£10,000 each); Independent Resource Centre (£9,000*); Kidney Kids Scotland (£8,000); Alman Dramatic Club, Eric Liddel Centre and SANDS Lothian (£5,000 each); Link Living (£3,000); Borders Forest Trust and Scotland Seabirds Centre (£2,000 each); Care & Learning Alliance (£1,500); and REACT and West of Scotland Football Club for the Disabled (£1,000 each).

*Payable over more than one year.

Exclusions

The trust does not support:
- religious organisations
- political organisations
- retrospective grants
- student travel or expeditions.

Applications

The trust has a short application form which can be downloaded from its website. Applicants are invited to complete the form using their own words without the restrictions of completing set questions. Please also supply the following, where appropriate:
- a brief description of your charity
- a copy of your most recent annual report and accounts
- a description of the project/ funding requirement – what do you want to achieve and how will it be managed. The trustees look

for clear, realistic and attainable aims
- what is the expenditure budget for the project and the anticipated timescale
- what funds have already been raised and what other sources are being approached
- the need for funding must be clearly demonstrated
- what will be the benefits of the project and how do you propose to monitor and evaluate whether the project has been successful
- if applicable, what plans you have to fund the future running costs of the project.

The trustees usually meet twice per annum to consider applications. Applicants may be contacted for more information or to arrange an assessment visit. Successful applicants must wait at least two years from the time of receiving a grant before reapplying. In the case of a two or three year recurring grant this applies from the time of receiving the last instalment.

The Staples Trust

Development, environment, women's issues

£460,000 (2009/10)

Beneficial area

Overseas, UK.

Allington House, 1st Floor, 150 Victoria Street, London SW1E 5AE
Tel: 020 7410 0330
Fax: 020 7410 0332
Website: www.sfct.org.uk
Correspondent: Alan Bookbinder, Director
Trustees: Jessica Frankopan; Peter Frankopan; James Sainsbury; Alex Sainsbury; Judith Portrait.
CC Number: 1010656

Information available

Accounts were available at the Charity Commission.

Summary

The Staples Trust is one of the Sainsbury Family Charitable Trusts,

which share a joint administration. They have a common approach to grantmaking which is described in the entry for the group as a whole. The trust's main areas of interest are overseas development, environment, gender issues, the Frankopan Fund and general charitable purposes.

The trust is that of Jessica Frankopan (née Sainsbury), and its trustees include her husband and her two brothers who lead the *Tedworth* and *Glass-House* trusts (see separate entries).

The trust offers the standard Sainsbury description of its grantmaking practice: 'Proposals are generally invited by the trustees or initiated at their request. Unsolicited applications are discouraged and are unlikely to be successful, even if they fall within an area in which the trustees are interested. The trustees prefer to support innovative schemes that can be successfully replicated or become self-sustaining'. There is probably a special interest in Croatia, but this does not dominate grantmaking in central and Eastern Europe.

Grantmaking in 2009/10

During the year the trust had assets of £11.6 million and an income of £441,000. There were 28 new grants approved during the year amounting to £166,000, with payments made, including those approved in previous years, totalling £460,000. Grants paid during the year were categorised as follows, which includes a description of where the trust focuses its efforts in each area:

Grants in 2009/10 were distributed as follows:

Gender	£274,000
General	£112,000
Overseas development	£40,000
Environment	£18,000
Frankopan Fund	£16,000

Gender
Trustees are committed to raising awareness of gender and how the diverse understanding and experiences of men and women have an impact on the structures of society. Trustees are willing to consider projects in the UK and overseas, focusing mainly on domestic violence and women's rights.

General

Other grants which do not naturally fit within the other categories.

Overseas development

Trustees' priorities in this category are projects which contribute to the empowerment of women, the rights of indigenous people, improved shelter and housing, income-generation in disadvantaged communities and sustainable agriculture and forestry. Trustees are particularly interested to support development projects which take account of environmental sustainability and, in many cases, the environmental and developmental benefits of the project are of equal importance.

Environment

Projects are supported in developing countries, Central and Eastern Europe and the UK. Grants are approved for renewable energy technology, training and skills upgrading and, occasionally, research.

Frankopan Fund

Trustees have established a fund to assist exceptionally talented postgraduate students primarily from Croatia to further or complete their studies (in any discipline) in the UK.

Beneficiaries across all categories included: Gender Studies Institute – London School of Economics and Political Science (£250,000); St Paul's Girls' School (£50,000); Latin American Mining Monitoring Programme and the University of Oxford (£30,000 each); Victoria & Albert Museum (£20,000); Karuna Trust – India (£15,000); Oxford Centre for Byzantine Research (£10,000); Lifeline Network Association (£5,000); University of Cambridge Development Office (£3,000); and Survive (£1,000).

Exclusions

Normally, no grants to individuals.

Applications

See the guidance for applicants in the entry for the Sainsbury Family Charitable Trusts. A single application will be considered for support by all the trusts in the group.

However, for this, as for many of the family trusts, 'proposals are generally invited by the trustees or initiated at their request. Unsolicited applications are discouraged and are unlikely to be successful, even if they fall within an area in which the trustees are interested'. See also the text above.

The Steel Charitable Trust

Social welfare; culture; recreation; health; medical research; environment; and occasionally, overseas aid

£988,000 (2010/11)

Beneficial area

Mainly UK with 30% of all grants made to organisations in the Luton and Bedfordshire areas.

Holme Farm, Fore Street, Bradford, Holsworthy, Devon EX22 7AJ
Tel: 01409 281403
Email: administrator@steelcharitabletrust.org.uk
Website: www.steelcharitabletrust.org.uk
Correspondent: Carol Langston, Administrator
Trustees: Nicholas E W Wright; John A Childs, Chair; John A Maddox; Anthony W Hawkins; Paul Stevenson; Wendy Bailey; Mary Briggs; Philip Lawford.
CC Number: 272384

Information available

Accounts were on file at the Charity Commission. The trust also has a clear and simple website.

The trust was established in 1976 for general charitable purposes. Grants are made for social welfare, culture, recreation, health, medical research, environment, overseas aid and other general purposes. Grants are made at regular intervals during the year and the total level of grants is approximately £1 million per annum. Grants are generally made as single payments between £1,000 and £25,000. It is the trust's policy to distribute 30% of all grants in the Luton and Bedfordshire areas.

In 2010/11 the trust had assets of £21.9 million and an income of £1 million. There were 205 grants made totalling £988,000, broken down in the table below (including the number of applications received within each category).

Beneficiaries included: The National Society for Epilepsy (£50,000); Keech Hospice Care (£40,000); SSAFA Forces Help and Moorfields Eye Hospital Development Fund (£25,000 each); Luton Town Centre Chaplaincy and Cancer Research UK (£20,000 each); Bournemouth University (£15,000); South London Fine Art Gallery and Library (£10,000); Polka Children's Theatre Limited (£9,500); Bournemouth Symphony Orchestra (£8,000); Bedfordshire African Community Centre Limited and Refresh Limited (£5,000 each); Family Tree – Wirral (£4,000); Worcester YMCA (£3,000); Blind in Business Trust (£2,000); and War Memorials Trust (£1,000).

THE STEEL CHARITABLE TRUST

	Applications received	Grants made	Total amount
Ill-health, disability or other disadvantage	399	72	£328,000
Arts, culture, heritage or science	141	38	£154,000
Health	98	22	£146,000
Education	115	19	£103,500
Citizenship or community development	78	11	£77,000
Religion	38	5	£41,000
Poverty	67	12	£38,500
Environmental protection or improvement	43	11	£29,000
Armed forces, police or all rescue services	4	2	£26,000
Animal welfare	17	3	£16,500
Amateur sport	9	1	£4,000
Human rights, racial harmony or equality	19	1	£3,000
Other charitable purposes	28	8	£22,000

Exclusions

Individuals, students and expeditions are not supported.

Applications

All applicants must complete the online application form. Applications submitted by post will not be considered. There is no deadline for applications and all will be acknowledged. Trustees meet regularly during the year, usually in February, May, August and November. All successful applicants will be notified by email and will be required to provide written confirmation of the details of the project or work for which they are seeking a grant. Payment is then made in the following month.

To comply with the Data Protection Act 1998, applicants are required to consent to the use of personal data supplied by them in the processing and review of their application. This includes transfer to and use by such individuals and organisations as the trust deems appropriate. The trust requires the assurance of the applicant that personal data about any other individual is supplied to the trust with his/her consent. At the point of submitting an online application, applicants are asked to confirm this consent and assurance.

The Stewards' Company Limited (incorporating the J W Laing Trust and the J W Laing Biblical Scholarship Trust)

Christian evangelism, general

£4.6 million (2010/11)

Beneficial area

Unrestricted.

124 Wells Road, Bath BA2 3AH
Tel: 01225 427236
Fax: 01225 427278

Email: stewardsco@stewards.co.uk
Correspondent: Brian Chapman, Secretary
Trustees: Brian Chapman; Alexander McIlhinney; Dr Alexander Scott; Douglas Spence; Paul Young; Dr John Burness; William Adams; Andrew Griffiths; Prof Arthur Williamson; Philip Page; Denis Cooper; Alan Paterson; Glyn Davies; Ian Childs; James Crookes; John Gamble; Philip Symons; William Wood; Andrew Street; Keith Bintley; John Aitken.
CC Number: 234558

Information available

Accounts, listing the top 50 grants, were available from the Charity Commission.

The charity supports Christian evangelism, especially but not exclusively that of Christian Brethren assemblies. Its work is described as follows in their 2010/11 accounts:

> The principal activities of the charity are to act as owner or as custodian trustee of various charitable properties, mainly used as places of worship and situated either in the United Kingdom or overseas, and to act as administrative trustee of a number of Christian charitable trusts, including The J W Laing Trust and The J W Laing Biblical Scholarship Trust.

> The trust describes its objectives as being '[...] the advancement of the religion in any matter which shall be charitable, and in particular by the furtherance of the gospel of God and education in the Holy Scriptures as contained in the Old and New Testaments, and the relief of the poor.

Its grantmaking policy is described as follows:

> The trust takes into account the financial resources of the benefiting charities, the efforts made by members of such charities to maximise their own funding, including where appropriate sacrificial giving by themselves and their supporters, and the assessed value of the work of such charities consistent with the objective of the main grant-making charities [i.e. Stewards Company, Laing Trust and Laing Scholarship].

In 2010/11 the trust had assets of £128 million and an income of £4.3 million. Grants were made to organisations totalling almost £4.6 million and were broken down as follows:

Overseas	£2.3 million
Home	£2.2 million

Only the largest 50 grants were listed in the accounts. Beneficiaries included: Echoes of Service (£864,000); Beatrice Laing Trust (£465,500); UCCF (£435,500); Retired Missionary Aid Fund (£200,000); European Leadership Forum (£165,000); Interlink (£140,000); International Fellowship of Evangelical Students (£130,000); and Bright Hope World and Tearfund (£100,000 each).

Applications

In writing to the correspondent.

The Sir Halley Stewart Trust

Medical, social, educational and religious activities

£849,000 (2010/11)

Beneficial area

UK and some work in Africa.

22 Earith Rd, Willingham, Cambridge, Cambridgeshire CB24 5LS
Tel: 01954 260707
Fax: 01954 260707
Email: email@sirhalleystewart.org.uk
Website: www.sirhalleystewart.org.uk
Correspondent: Sue West, Administrator
Trustees: Lord Stewartby, President; Prof. Philip Whitfield, Chair; Prof. John Lennard Jones; Dr Duncan Stewart; William P Kirkman; George Russell; Prof. Phyllida Parsloe; Barbara Clapham; Prof. John Wyatt; Michael Ross Collins; Joanna Womack; Revd Lord Griffiths; Dr Caroline Berry; Prof. Gordon Willcock; Caroline Thomas; Brian Allpress; Theresa Bartlett; Louisa Macantab; Amy Holcroft.
CC Number: 208491

Information available

Accounts were available at the Charity Commission. The trust has a helpful website for applicants.

The trust was established in 1924 by Sir Halley Stewart who endowed the charity and established its founding principles.

During the course of his life Sir Halley Stewart was a non-conformist Christian minister, an MP, a pioneering industrialist and a philanthropist. When he founded the trust he specified four objects, to advance religion and education, to relieve poverty and to promote other charitable purposes beneficial to the community. He was concerned with the prevention and removal of human misery and in the realisation of national and worldwide brotherhood. He wished the trustees to have the fullest discretion in applying the income of the trust within its objects, but not for dogmatic theological purposes. A tradition of supporting medical research into the prevention of human suffering, not its relief, was established during his lifetime. He died in 1937.

The trust has a Christian basis and is concerned with the development of body, mind and spirit, a just environment, and international goodwill. To this end it supports projects in religious, social, educational and medical fields, mainly in the UK. The trust aims to promote and assist innovative research activities or pioneering developments with a view to making such work self-supporting.

The three principles by which the trustees are guided in administering the trust are:

▷ furthering for every individual such favourable opportunities of education, service and leisure as shall enable him or her most perfectly to develop the body, mind and spirit

▷ securing a just environment in all social life whether domestic, industrial or national

▷ in international relationships to fostering good will between all races, tribes, peoples and nations to secure the fulfilment of hope of 'peace on earth'.

Grants are usually in the form of salary and there is a preference to support innovative and imaginative people, often 'promising young researchers with whom the trust can develop a direct relationship.' Sometimes a contribution towards the expenses of a project is given. Grants are normally limited to two or three years but are sometimes extended. Small individual grants are sometimes given. In general, the trustees do not favour grant-giving to enable the completion of a project initiated by other bodies.

The trust's website states that during the coming year the trust plans to make grants up to a budget limit of £800,000. The effectiveness of grants made in previous years will be assessed on the basis of reports by grantees, published work and personal contacts. Grants will continue to be made to further the aims of the trust in the religious, social and medical fields.

In 2010/11 the trust had assets of £24.3 million and an income of £831,000. Grants were made totalling £849,000.

Current priorities

The current priorities of the trust are in the form of three programmes, namely, medical, religious and social and educational. Details are taken from the trust's website:

Medical

Projects should be simple, not molecular, and capable of clinical application within 5 – 10 years. They may include a social or ethical element. Non-medical trustees should be able to understand the application and appreciate the value of the work. Projects may be of a type unlikely to receive support from research councils or large research-funding charities. Projects must have ethics committee approval where needed. The trust welcomes applications direct from researchers at UK medical institutions or university departments concerned with:

▷ projects which aim to improve the quality of life of the elderly suffering from physical or psychological disorders

▷ the prevention of disease and disability in children

▷ the prevention, diagnosis and treatment of tropical infectious and parasitic diseases

▷ innovative projects, involving any discipline, which are likely to improve health care

▷ research focusing on developments in medical ethics

▷ innovative medical projects caring for the needs of disadvantaged groups.

Religious

The trust is committed to advancing the Christian religion and has a particular interest in innovative practical ecumenical projects in the UK; and also those in countries outside the UK where there is special and specific need. The trustees seek to support groundbreaking projects proposed by inspirational individuals who have proven track records, or those evidencing energy, enthusiasm and imagination.

Current priorities are:

▷ to encourage Christian people to develop their skills in upholding and communicating their faith in the public domain

▷ to support and encourage the innovative teaching of Christianity within the United Kingdom

▷ to encourage specific groups of people to explore their experience of spirituality and their spiritual needs and strengths, and to help others to understand these

▷ to support innovative projects which aim to facilitate a better understanding between faiths

Social and educational

Applications are welcomed for the feasibility or piloting stage or the dissemination / practical implementation stage of projects that are likely to improve the conditions of a particular group of people, as well as having wider implications. Trustees will normally expect that the beneficiaries of a development project will have been involved in the design of the project and its continuing governance, They will also wish to see how the work will continue after a grant from the trust has finished (I.e. sustainability plans).

In the UK the trust seeks to support innovative projects, which attempt to:

▷ prevent and resolve conflict, promote reconciliation and/or encourage re-connection between family members of all ages

▷ help people 'move beyond disadvantage' – such projects might be concerned with the social and family aspects of unemployment, crime, imprisonment, homelessness and migration

▷ address the needs of elderly people and those of all ages who may be vulnerable or exploited

▷ accept responsibility for disseminating results to practitioners in a form which is likely to result in changes in their way of working.

Overseas: the trust applies the same criteria as above to proposals from UK-based charities which operate through local organisations in the poorest politically stable African countries. (NB. for the foreseeable future the trust will fund overseas work in the field of education, water and healthcare through those organisations with which they have had previous partnerships or which trustees themselves identify. Please do not make general submissions).

Grants in 2010/11

Social and educational – grants totalling £323,000
Beneficiaries of grants over £10,000 included: UNSEEN UK (£57,000); Feltham Community Chaplaincy Trust (£50,000); Headway East London (£40,000); RECOOP – Resettlement of older prisoners (£27,000); KORI Arts (£25,000); PLAN UK – Burkina Faso (£24,000); Most Mira (£20,000); and Clapham Pottery (£14,000).

Medical – grants totalling £283,000
Beneficiaries of grants over £10,000 included: University of Wales Institute (£40,000); Health Action Leicester for Ethiopia (HALE) (£33,000); Medic to Medic (£30,000); Sightsavers (£24,000); University College London (£24,000); LSH&TM Fellowships (£18,000); and Southampton University (£17,000).

Religious – grants totalling £226,000
Beneficiaries of grants over £10,000 included: Wythenshawe Oasis (£50,000); St Ethelburga's Centre for Peace – London (£39,000); Art Beyond Belief (£25,000); Council on Christian Approaches to Defence & Disarmament (£20,000); Awareness Foundation (£16,000); and LICC (£10,000).

Across the three categories grants of less than £10,000 – including those to individuals – totalled £52,000.

Exclusions

The trust will be unable to help with funding for any of the following:

- general appeals of any kind
- the purchase, erection or conversion of buildings
- capital costs
- university overhead charges
- the completion of a project initiated by other bodies.

The trust does not normally fund:

- projects put forward indirectly through other 'umbrella' or large charities
- educational or 'gap' year travel projects
- running costs of established organisations
- climate change issues

personal education fees or fees for taught courses-unless connected with research which falls within current priority areas. Applications for such research work are normally made by a senior researcher seeking support for a student, or if coming directly from the student it should have project supervisor's written support; the trust does not favour grantmaking to enable the completion of a project or PhD.

Applications

The following applicant guidelines are taken from the trust's website:

- applications will not be accepted by fax or email
- applicants should make sure that their project fits the trust's objects and falls within its current priority areas
- initial telephone enquiries to the trust's office are welcomed to discuss the suitability of an application. Please note there is only one member of staff so please be patient and try again if there is no one in the office when you telephone.

The trust does not have an application form. Applicants should write to the administrator always including a one-page lay 'executive' summary of the proposed work. The proposal should state clearly:

- what the aims of the project are and why it is believed to be innovative
- what the overall budgeted cost of the project is and how much is being requested from the trust
- what the grant will be used for and how long the project will take to have practical benefits
- how the project/research results will be disseminated
- personal medical applications should be accompanied by a letter of support from a senior colleague or research supervisor
- development projects should indicate where they would hope to obtain future funding from
- where appropriate it is helpful to include a CV; job description, set of audited signed accounts and annual report.

There are no set application deadlines. When the trust has received your application they will make contact (normally within two weeks) either to ask for further information; to tell you the application will be going forward to the next stage of assessment and what the timetable for a final decision will be; or to tell you that they are unable to help. The 2010/11 accounts also note: it is a deliberate policy of the trust to maintain as much personal and

informal contact with applicants as possible, to keep paper work to the minimum consistent with efficient administration, and to make decisions on applications within four months.

The trust imposes terms and conditions on each award. Please note that the trust receives many applications for support, and although an application may fit the objects of the trust, it may not necessarily be able to help.

Common applicant mistakes

'Seeking funding for overseas work not within our priority area, e.g. Asia, when we only do Africa. Other common mistakes are: asking for too much; large established charities applying; using fundraisers; and, individuals applying who are looking for personal tuition fees.'

The Stobart Newlands Charitable Trust

Christian religious and missionary causes

£864,000 (2010)

Beneficial area

UK.

Mill Croft, Newlands, Hesket Newmarket, Wigton, Cumbria CA7 8HP
Tel: 0169 7478 531
Correspondent: Ronnie Stobart, Trustee
Trustees: Richard Stobart; Margaret Stobart; Ronnie Stobart; Peter Stobart; Linda Rigg.
CC Number: 328464

Information available

Accounts were available from the Charity Commission.

This family trust makes up to 50 grants a year, nearly all on a recurring basis to Christian religious and missionary bodies. Unsolicited applications are most unlikely to succeed.

The trustees are directors and shareholders of J Stobart and Sons Ltd, which is the source of almost all of the trust's income. In 2010 the trust had an income of £695,000 and made grants totalling £864,000. Its assets stood at £141,000.

As in previous years, the two beneficiaries of the largest grants were World Vision (£250,000); and Operation Mobilisation (£175,000).

Other beneficiaries of larger grants of £10,000 each or more included: Castle Sowerby Chapel (£70,000); Bible Society (£41,000); Tear Fund, Every Home Crusade (£35,000 each); London City Mission, Open Air Mission (£26,000 each); Keswick Convention (£25,000); Logos Ministries (£23,000); and Living Well Trust (£20,000).

Smaller grants went to: Release International, Spurgeons (£10,000 each); Way to Life (£8,000); Trinitarian Bible Society (£5,000); Caring for Life (£3,000); and Cancer Research UK (£2,000).

Grants of £1,000 or less totalled £1,700.

Exclusions
No grants for individuals.

Applications
Unsolicited applications are most unlikely to be successful.

Common applicant mistakes
'Applications by individuals.'

The Stone Family Foundation

Relief-in-need, social welfare, overseas aid

£1.5 million (2010)

Beneficial area
Worldwide.

Coutts & Co, 440 Strand, London WC2R OQS
Tel: 020 7663 6825
Correspondent: The Clerk
Trustees: Coutts & Co; John Kyle Stone; Charles H Edwards; Sophie Edwards.
CC Number: 1108207

Information available
Accounts were available at the Charity Commission.

Registered with the Charity Commission in February 2005, the foundation's objects are to relieve hardship or distress worldwide, particularly where this hardship is as a result of natural disasters or war.

In 2010 the trust had assets of £47.1 million and an income of £2.2 million. Grants were made totalling £1.5 million.

Beneficiaries included: Opportunity International (£464,000); WaterAid (£398,000); Hope and Home for Children (£219,000); Aid India (£54,000); Zamcog (£50,000); Rainforest Saver Foundation (£41,000); LSCDPA (Laos) (£32,500); Maytree Respite Centre (£32,000); Cult Information Centre (£29,000); and University of Oxford Development Trust (£3,500).

Loans are also available.

Exclusions
No grants to individuals.

Applications
'Applicants for grants and loans must be in writing, and trustees seek the completion of formal terms and conditions.'

Stratford upon Avon Town Trust

Education, welfare, general

£1.3 million (2010)

Beneficial area
Stratford upon Avon.

14 Rother Street, Stratford-upon-Avon, Warwickshire CV32 6LU
Tel: 01789 207111
Fax: 01789 207119
Email: admin@stratfordtowntrust.co.uk
Website: www.stratfordtowntrust.co.uk
Correspondent: Richard Eggington, Chief Executive
Trustees: John Lancaster, Chair; Cllr Jenny Fradgley; Jean Holder; Rosemary Hyde; Cllr Juliet Short; Carole Taylor; Tim Wightman; Clarissa Roberts; Rob Townsend; Charles Bates; Cllr Ian Fradgley.
CC Number: 1088521

Information available
Accounts were on file at the Charity Commission. The trust also has a clear and simple website.

The Town Trust distributes the money generated by the Guild and College Estates in accordance with the Charity Commission Scheme of October 2001. The objects of the charity are:

- helping people who are in need – for example because they are elderly, disabled, poor, physically or mentally ill, lonely or frightened
- providing facilities (such as buildings and equipment) or services to give people more opportunity for:
  - education and personal development
  - taking part in recreation, leisure pursuits or amateur sport
  - taking part in, or enjoying, arts, culture and science
- Supporting things which benefit the people of Stratford. For instance:
  - protecting the environment
  - preserving our heritage
  - promoting human rights and social harmony
  - promoting Christianity and other religions
  - preventing crime
  - civic pride.

The trust's priority areas are:
- Welfare and wellbeing – projects addressing need, suffering whether caused by poverty, sickness, disability, inequality, isolation, or being left out. Those promoting physical mental and spiritual wellbeing, healthy living and improving opportunities to live a full and active life.
- Strengthening communities – projects that help to bring and bind people together to have a voice, help one another, get involved and make their community stronger.

▶ Young people – projects that are led by young people for young people; helping them to access what's already available, grow into responsible citizens, meet their full potential and deal with the challenges and threats of life.

The main beneficiaries are the residents of the town of Stratford-upon-Avon, although those studying or working in the town may also benefit. As well as being a grant-maker, the trust owns a civic hall, bandstand, chapel and a fountain which commemorates the town's 800th anniversary. The trust makes both discretionary and non-discretionary grants.

In 2010 the trust had assets of £51.6 million and an income of just under £3.3 million. Grants were made totalling £1.3 million, which included £742,000 in discretionary grants and £655,000 in non-discretionary grants. The non-discretionary grants were awarded to King Edward IV Grammar School (£617,000); 24 almshouses (£30,500); and Holy Trinity Church (£7,000).

There were 170 discretionary grants made during the year. Those of £25,000 or more, listed in the accounts, were made to: Shakespeare Hospice and VASA (£50,000 each); Warwickshire Police Authority – Community Support Officers (£42,000); CAB (£40,000); Stratford High School (£39,500); Stratford upon Avon College (£31,500); and Stratford upon Avon Christmas Lights Co. (£30,000).

Exclusions
No grants to organisations outside Stratford upon Avon.

Applications
Application forms can be completed online at the trust's website. Awards are made on a quarterly basis. The latest application deadlines are also listed on the trust's website.

Summary Limited

Education, religion, social welfare

£321,000 (2010)

Beneficial area
UK, with a preference for Hertfordshire.

The Field House Farm, 29 Newlands Avenue, Radlett, Hertfordshire WD7 8EJ
Tel: 01923 855727
Correspondent: John Apthorp, Trustee
Trustees: John Apthorp; Duncan Apthorp; Justin Apthorp; Kate Arnold.
CC Number: 1102472

Information available
Accounts were available at the Charity Commission.

Established in 2004, the objects of the charity are the advancement of education, the advancement of religion and the relief of poverty and suffering.

In 2010 the charity received a donation to the value of £4.3 million from the Milly Apthorp Charitable Trust, which is in the process of spending out and shares two trustees from the Apthorp family. As a result of this, the grant-making capacity of this charity has increased significantly.

In 2010 the charity had assets of over £8 million and an income of £4.5 million (with both figures including the £4.3 million donation). Grants were made to 16 organisations during the year totalling £321,000 (2008/09: £80,000).

The beneficiaries were: Berkhamsted School (£75,000 in total); Purcell School of Music and Berkhamsted Raiders Community Football Club (£50,000 each); The Stroke Association to provide support services within Hertsmere District Council (£28,000); Radlett Music Club (£20,000); The Radlett Centre (£14,000); Aldenham Parish (£12,000); Walton & Frinton Yacht Club, Peace Hospice Watford, Shooting Stars Hospice, Milton Keynes Hospital and Aldenham School (£10,000 each); RAFT (£6,000); Radlett Centre Trust Art Society (£5,600); and St John's Church and Caister Lifeboat (£5,000 each).

Applications
In writing to the correspondent.

The Bernard Sunley Charitable Foundation

General

£2.3 million (2009/10)

Beneficial area
Unrestricted, but mainly southern England.

20 Berkeley Square, London W1J 6LH
Tel: 020 7408 2198
Fax: 020 7499 5859
Email: office@sunleyfoundation.com
Correspondent: John Rimmington, Director
Trustees: Joan M Tice; Bella Sunley; Sir Donald Gosling; Brian W Martin; Anabel Knight; William Tice.
CC Number: 1109099

Information available
Accounts were available at the Charity Commission.

Summary
This is one of the few big trusts that will, in principle, fund any kind of charitable activity in the UK, and which offers no information on the criteria by which one application is preferred to another. No doubt as a consequence of this, the charity receives many applications, only about one in five of which can be funded. Grants range in size from £250,000 down to less than £1,000, although most grants will be for less than £10,000. The long-noted bias towards the southern half of England continued in 2009/10, particularly amongst the larger grants.

As well as making grants for capital purposes, donations are also made for endowments, scholarship funds, research programmes and for core funding.

Joan Tice, Bella Sunley, Anabel Knight and William Tice are all members of the founding family. The external trustees are Sir Donald Gosling, founder of NCP car parks and one of Britain's wealthiest men [see also the Gosling Foundation

Limited], and Dr Brian Martin, former director of the foundation.

Guidelines

The following guidelines are provided by the foundation to potential applicants, which detail the foundation's current priorities, exclusions and application procedures:

The trust deed of the foundation allows the trustees to give to charitable causes at their discretion. The current trustees have decided that for the immediate future they will concentrate their interests under a number of broad headings, with limiting factors. Please read these carefully before making any application, as it will save you time and help to eliminate unnecessary work. [...] [The categories of applications that will be considered are as follows:]

Education

In education, those with disabilities continue to be an area of focus for the trustees, and their principle desire is to assist those with special educational needs. They will not normally support mainstream schools with either capital building or day-to-day core costs.

Capital funding
Areas of consideration: building projects, specialised equipment and specialised transport.

Revenue funding
Literacy assistance will be considered.

Arts

Trustees have built up a history of assistance to a small number of art based charities, where grants are usually in support of capital building projects. They will not support short term festivals, theatre productions or touring ensembles.

Capital funding
Areas of consideration: building and refurbishment for galleries, museums and theatres where there is an emphasis on education for the whole community.

Revenue funding
Areas of consideration: outreach programmes for special needs groups involving dance, music and drama; outreach programmes giving access to children who would not normally have the opportunity to experience art activities.

Religion

Trustees have given support to a few specific religious institutions, about which they have personal knowledge. They will not support applications from churches, where the needs are purely for repair and refurbishment of the church.

Capital funding
Areas of consideration: amenities within a church building for use by the whole community, including toilets, kitchen facilities, disability access and re-organisation of internal space.

Revenue funding
None.

Community

Trustees are strong believers that every community needs a focus on which to build the cohesion of that community. They are therefore advocates of the 'village hall', particularly in making buildings accessible for all, but also supporting isolated rural areas where other support is often very limited. They support capital projects including refurbishment and repairs, but expect halls to be self sufficient thereafter.

Capital funding
Areas of consideration: new build, refurbishment and improvement of village halls, often including access for the disabled, modernised kitchens, new storage space and updated toilets in line with Health and Safety regulations and the Disability Discrimination Act; new equipment; specialised transport.

Revenue funding
None.

Children & youth

One of the trustees' main themes is to assist young people to attain their full potential and take their place within society as responsible citizens. To this end, they support and advocate Youth Activities Centres, Scout & Guides Groups, Sea Cadet Units, and other uniformed youth groups, but also seek to help those who are young ex-offenders, at risk, or are in danger of exclusion.

Capital funding
Areas of consideration: capital building projects, plus refurbishment where appropriate, for youth clubs, outward bound and adventure training centres, scout groups, guide groups, sea cadet units, other uniformed youth groups, YMCA centres; equipment for the above organisations; IT, adventure training equipment including special needs equipment, playgrounds; minibuses; mobile youth club and play facility vehicles.

Revenue funding
Adventure training, and support and training for disadvantaged children will be considered.

Elderly

Trustees consider grants towards capital projects, which range from residential care housing to community centres, and seek to encourage inclusion and combat isolation.

Capital funding
Areas of consideration: new build and refurbishment of residential and day care centres; specialised equipment; specialised transport.

Revenue funding
None.

Health

While the foundation has given much support to research in the past, the trustees' current interests centre on provision of equipment to enhance medical treatment, and on capital projects to improve hospices and treatment centres.

Capital funding
Areas of consideration: improvements to hospices; injury recovery clinics; special needs residential care; new equipment such as research medical equipment, specialist transport and specialist mobility equipment.

Revenue funding
None.

Social welfare

Applications for capital projects are considered by trustees ranging from residential housing for the homeless, many of whom will be suffering from drug/alcohol abuse and mental health issues, to day centres giving support, training and rehabilitation, with a view to people recovering their health and self-esteem, and resuming their place in society. Prisoner rehabilitation and support comes within this category, and community schemes such as furniture recycling projects are sometimes considered.

Capital funding
Areas of consideration: new build and refurbishment of residential premises for rehabilitation and the relief of homelessness; 'move on' support facilities; day care / drop-in-centres; community household furniture recycling projects; care facilities for young people and those with special needs.

Revenue funding
Areas of consideration: rehabilitation of the homeless and those at risk; training and support for those with special needs.

Environment

Trustees support educational environmental projects, including building education and visitor centres at wildlife sites. They will also consider projects aimed at the preservation and stability of the natural world.

Capital funding
Areas of consideration: building education and visitor centres.

Revenue funding
Areas of consideration: information and teaching aids; children's educational visits; conservation awareness.

Animal welfare

Trustees support the welfare of working and farm animals.

Capital funding
Areas of consideration: hospital facilities for working animals.

Revenue funding
Areas of consideration: welfare of working and farm animals.

Amateur sport
Support is sometimes given to sports club capital projects, encouraging the community to take part in physical activities across all ages for health wellbeing, teamwork and community cohesion.

Capital funding
Areas of consideration: building and refurbishment of amateur sports facilities.

Revenue funding
Areas of consideration: physical activity projects.

Emergency & armed services
Trustees support the welfare needs of uniformed personnel and their families, particularly servicemen with health and mental issues resulting from their service to the Crown.

Capital funding
Areas of consideration: building and refurbishment of residential and rehabilitation centres.

Revenue funding
Areas of consideration: welfare services.

Grantmaking in 2009/10

In 2009/10 the foundation had assets of £80.8 million which generated an income of £2.8 million. There were 440 grants made during the year totalling £2.3 million.

Grants approved were classified as follows:

Category	2009/10	1960 to 2010
Community	£567,000	£15.7 million
Children and youth	£552,000	£10.4 million
Education	£274,000	£17.2 million
Social welfare	£212,000	£1.6 million
Health	£172,000	£19.7 million
Religion	£161,000	£4.3 million
Arts	£128,000	£8.7 million
Elderly	£116,000	£7.6 million
Emergency and armed services	£76,000	£217,000
Animal welfare	£39,000	£61,000
Amateur sport	£11,000	£59,000
Overseas	Nil	£2.4 million
Total	**£2.3 million**	£91.1 million

NOTE: 'Social welfare' was added as a new category in 2002. 'Animal welfare' grants have been added as a separate category since 2007, leaving 'environment' as a separate category. 'Amateur sport' and 'emergency and armed services' have been added as categories since 2007.

Beneficiaries across all categories receiving £5,000 or more included: Godmersham and Crundale Recreation Hall – Kent (£150,000); Royal Parks Foundation (£100,000); Wye College (£75,000); Fynvola Foundation (£60,000); St Clements Church – Sandwich and Anchor House East London (£50,000); Alzheimer's Society (£30,000); Royal Geographical Society (£25,000); Fight for Sight, Childhood First, Imperial War Museum and St John Ambulance (£10,000 each); Animal Health Trust (£7,000); and Kids Company and Bowel Cancer UK (£5,000 each)

Exclusions

The trust's guidelines outline the following exclusions:

> We would reiterate that we do not make grants to individuals; we still receive several such applications each week. This bar on individuals applies equally to those people taking part in a project sponsored by a charity such as VSO, Duke of Edinburgh Award Scheme, Trekforce, Scouts and Girl Guides, and so on, or in the case of the latter two to specific units of these youth movements.

Applications

The trust's guidelines give the following information about applications:

> Appeals are considered regularly, but we would emphasise that we are only able to make grants to registered charities and not to individuals. There is no application form, but the covering letter to the director should give details as to the points below, and should be accompanied by the latest approved report and accounts.
>
> The details requested are as follows:
>
> ▶ the purpose of the charity and its objectives
> ▶ the need and purpose of the project, for which a grant is requested, and who will benefit and how
> ▶ the cost of the project – a breakdown of costs is sometimes helpful
> ▶ the amount of money already raised and from whom, and how it is planned to raise the shortfall
> ▶ if applicable, how the running costs of the project will be met, once the project is established
> ▶ any other documentation that the applicant feels will help to support or explain the appeal.
>
> Be precise and to the point – one person is dealing with up to 200 applications each month.

Grant applications may be sent to the foundation at any time during the year, and you will be advised of the outcome of the application within a period of three to four months. Please do not reapply for at least twelve months, as it will not be accepted.

Primarily we are a capital projects focused grant maker, not a substitute for lack of Government revenue funding.

Common applicant mistakes

'Failing to read our guidelines or even make enquiries before submitting an application (i.e. wasting their time and ours!).'

Sussex Community Foundation

Community-based projects, education, disability, health, and the relief of poverty and sickness

£983,000 (2009/10)

Beneficial area

East Sussex, West Sussex or Brighton and Hove.

Suite B, Falcon Wharf, Railway Lane, Lewes BN7 2AQ
Tel: 01273 409 440
Email: info@sussxgiving.org.uk
Website: www.sussexgiving.org.uk
Correspondent: Kevin Richmond, Administrator
Trustees: Trevor James; John Peel; Kathy Gore; Neil Hart; Steve Manwaring; Sharon Phillips; Lesley Wake; Mike Simpkin; Humphrey Price; Richard Pearson; Margaret Johnson; Michael Martin; Charles Drayson.
CC Number: 1113226

Information available

Accounts were available at the Charity Commission.

The charitable objects of the foundation are:

> The promotion of any charitable purposes for the benefit of the community in the counties of East Sussex, West Sussex and the City of

Brighton and Hove and in particular the advancement of education, the protection of good health both mental and physical and the relief of poverty and sickness. Other exclusively charitable purposes in the United Kingdom and elsewhere which are in the opinion of the trustees beneficial to the community including those in the area of benefit.

We are particularly interested in supporting smaller community based groups where a small grant can make a really big difference.

Most of our grants are in the region of £1,000 to £5,000. In exceptional cases larger grant applications may be considered. Small applications of less than £1,000 are encouraged.

In 2009/10 the foundation had assets of £2.4 million and an income of £2.5 million. 540 grants were awarded totalling £983,000. The average grant award during the year was £1,820. The foundation notes its success in reaching small, local organisations with 75% of the organisations funded having an annual turnover of less than £18,000.

Grants were categorised according to the following themes, which the trustees intend to research and develop in future years in order to guide and inform donors:

Exclusion and isolation	179
Arts/culture/sports	155
Children and young people	94
Older people	64
Environment	41
Other	7

Recent beneficiaries have included: Danehill Memorial Hall (£5,000); Battle Town Band and Furnihelp Mid Sussex (£4,500 each); Age Concern Rye & District Day Centre (£4,000); Crawley Black History Foundation and The Biglove Association (£2,500 each); Friday Club at Concordia, Bosham Youth Centre, Stumped and Hope G (£2,000 each); Kinderoo (£1,500); Brighton Pebbles (£900); and Earthy Women and Kids (£750).

Funds available

As with all community foundations funds regularly open and close so it is worth consulting the foundation's website prior to embarking upon an application. At the end of 2011 15 funds were available (see the table below).

Each fund has different closing dates which are available on the foundation's website.

Exclusions

No support for:

- individuals (with the exception of the Paul Rooney Fund and the Westdene Fund)
- organisations that are part of central, local or regional government
- major capital appeals
- fundraising events
- projects with limited wider community benefit.

Applications

Applicants must have a signed copy of their constitution or set of rules; signed accounts; a copy of a recent bank statement; estimates for proposed purchases (if applicable) and copies of relevant policies (child protection, vulnerable adults, health

SUSSEX COMMUNITY FOUNDATION

Fund	Criteria	Amount you can apply for	Application form to use
Comic Relief Local Communities programme	Small locally based groups addressing disadvantage; groups using sport to relieve deprivation are welcome	Up to £10,000	CR application form (available on line)
Marit and Hans Rausing Fund	Charities/groups across Sussex addressing the root causes of disadvantage	Up to £5,000	SCF application form
Goldsmiths Charity Fund	Charities/groups across Sussex addressing disadvantage	Up to £5,000	SCF application form
American ExpressFund	Charities in Brighton and Hove or Burgess Hill	Up to £5,000	SCF application form
Cullum Family Trust	Charities/ groups operating between Brighton and Worthing and addressing homelessness or supporting children	Up to £5,000	SCF application form
William Reed Fund	Charities /groups working in the Crawley area and addressing social welfare issues.	Up to £3,000	SCF application form
Southern Water Fund	Community Garden and allotment projects across Sussex	£500–£2,000	SCF application form
Paul Rooney Fund	Children with life limiting illnesses; both individuals and groups working with children with disabilities or with special needs in Sussex may apply	Up to £5,000	Groups apply on SCF form; individuals contact us directly
SCF Grassroots Endowment Funds	Small volunteer led community groups in Brighton and Hove, East and West Sussex	Up to £2,000	SCF application form
Lisbet Rausing Fund	Hospices and groups working with people affected by terminal illness	Up to £5000	SCF application form
Westdene Fund	Grants to individual young people in Sussex with outstanding musical talent	Up to £800	Westdene Fund application form
Little Cheyne Court Wind Farm	Charities/community groups based within 10km radius of the Wind Farm	Up to £5,000	LCCWF application form
The Rainbow Fund	Charities/community groups in Brighton and Hove involved with LGBT issues	Up to £5000	SCF application form
Live Lewes Fund	Groups in Lewes building on community spirit and addressing climate change	Up to £2000	SCF application form
Rye Fund	Charities/ community groups operating in Rye and surrounding villages	Up to £500	Rye Fund application form

& safety, etc). Applicants have to be able to show that they are not-for-profit, but do not always have to be a charity.

Each of the funds listed under 'General information' are open to applications. As the criteria and application form differs for each you are advised to refer to the foundation's website.

Please note that you may only apply to one programme at a time.

Common applicant mistakes

'Not returning all of the background information requested on the form before the closing date.'

Sutton Coldfield Municipal Charities

Relief of need, arts, education, building conservation, general

£867,000 to organisations
(2009/10)

Beneficial area

The former borough of Sutton Coldfield, comprising three electoral wards: New Hall, Vesey and Four Oaks.

Lingard House, Fox Hollies Road, Sutton Coldfield, West Midlands B76 2RJ
Tel: 0121 351 2262
Fax: 0121 313 0651
Website: www. suttoncoldfieldmunicipalcharities.com
Correspondent: Andrew MacFarlane, Clerk to the Trustees
Trustees: Dr Freddie Gick, Chair; Rodney Kettel; Sue Bailey; John Gray; Cllr Susanna McCorry; Alfred David Owen; Jane Rothwell; Cllr David Roy; Michael Waltho; Cllr James Whorwood; Carole Hancox; Cllr Margaret Waddington; Dr Stephen C Martin; Cllr Malcolm Cornish; Neil Andrews; Linda Whitfield.
CC Number: 218627

Information available

Accounts were on file at the Charity Commission, without a list of grants.

The charity, which is one of the largest and oldest local trusts in the country, dates from 1528.

The charity states that its objectives are:

▷ to help the aged, the sick, those with disabilities and the poor
▷ to support facilities for recreation and leisure occupations
▷ to promote the arts and advance religion
▷ the repair of historic buildings
▷ the advancement of education of persons under the age of 25 through grants to schools and individuals for fees, maintenance, clothing and equipment.

Grantmaking to organisations is described as follows:

Priority is given to local organisations (large and small) that provide benefits for children and adults coping with the impact of disadvantage, sickness, old age or disability. Grants are made, for example, to local hospitals, hospices and charities. Some of these, such as St Giles Hospice, are large organisations with considerable clinical and care expertise. Others are locally organised support groups, dealing, for example, with complementary care therapies, eating disorders, prostate or breathing difficulties. Christmas lunches and summer trips are funded for local elderly groups.

Sutton's schools and colleges receive grants to purchase extra facilities and equipment that they cannot fund from their normal budgets. Charitable playgroups and nurseries are supported. SCMC does not fund independent schools and nurseries.

The charity makes awards to religious organisations, especially where these serve the wider community, for example through their centres. It also promotes art, music and drama (for example, concerts at the Town Hall and the local Theatres). Recreation and leisure are supported, including some amateur sport. Where there is significant public benefit, the charity makes grants to preserve historic buildings and improve the environment.

With a few exceptions, grants are not made to groups based outside Sutton.

In 2009/10 the charity had assets of £43.3 million and an income of £1.4 million. Grants were made to 68 organisations totalling £867,000.

A recent list of beneficiaries was not included in the charity's latest accounts, although due to the amount of local charities that receive support, it is likely that the list remains fairly similar each year, with Good Hope Hospital and St Giles Hospice receiving continued support.

Exclusions

No awards are given to individuals or organisations outside the area of benefit, unless the organisations are providing essential services in the area.

Applications

To make a grant application:

▷ contact the charity, either by letter, or by telephoning: 0121 351 2262
▷ outline your needs and request a copy of the charity's guidelines for applicants
▷ if appropriate, seek a meeting with a member of staff in making your application
▷ ensure that all relevant documents, including estimates and accounts, reach the charity by the requested dates.

Receipt of applications is not normally acknowledged unless a stamped addressed envelope is sent with the application.

Applications may be submitted at any time. The grants committee meets at least eight times a year. The board of trustees must approve requests for grants over £30,000.

At all stages, staff at the charities will give assistance to those making applications. For example, projects and applications can be discussed, either at the charity's office or on site. Advice about deadlines for submitting applications can also be given.

(There are application forms for individuals, who must obtain them from the charity.)

The Sutton Trust

Education

£867,500 (2010)

Beneficial area

UK only.

111 Upper Richmond Road, Putney, London SW15 2TJ

Tel: 020 8788 3223

Fax: 020 8788 3993

Website: www.suttontrust.com

Correspondent: The Trust Administrator

Trustees: Sir Peter Lampl; David Backinsell; Glyn Morris.

CC Number: 1067197

Information available

Accounts were available from the Charity Commission. The trust also has an informative website.

The Sutton Trust was established in 1997 with the aim of providing educational opportunities for children and young people from non-privileged backgrounds. It has funded a large number of access projects in early years, school and university settings, and now plans to focus primarily on research and policy work, as well as a small number of innovative pilot initiatives.

In 2008 the trust adopted a revised funding policy:

During the course of [2008] the trustees decided to move away from large scale initiatives and refocus on research and policy work – attempting to prompt wider change in the educational system by looking into an issue, proposing and testing a solution, and advocating evidence based reform. In keeping with this model, the trust will continue to fund small scale demonstration projects which will, as before, span the early years, school and college settings and into higher education and the professions.'

The trust provides recent further clarification:

Research and practical projects funded by the trust are commissioned from partners within our existing network of contacts in universities, schools and voluntary organisations.

We do not accept unsolicited grants, but if you have a project in line with our current priorities and approach please contact us to discuss whether it is likely to receive support.

Please be aware that we can only fund a small number of projects each year, even when proposals are in line with our aims and current priority areas.

The trust's current priorities are as follows:

- parents as first educators – narrowing gaps in school readiness and boosting cognitive development for non-privileged children
- free schools and equity
- encouraging the most effective teachers to serve in the most challenging schools
- boosting provision for gifted and talented students from non-privileged backgrounds
- access to highly selective universities and courses and the professions
- understanding the drivers of social mobility.

While we recognise that there are other areas which are relevant to our over-arching agenda of reducing educational inequality, all our work and funding will be related to the above specific priorities.

Grants in 2010

In 2010 the trust had assets of £892,500 and an income of £1.4 million, which included a donation of £1.1 million from Sir Peter Lampl. Grants totalled £867,500 and were broken down as follows:

University projects	£438,000
Research projects	£203,500
Early Years learning	£133,000
Schools/colleges	£93,500

Individual grant amounts were not listed in the accounts. Beneficiaries included: Cambridge University (various projects); Imperial College Maths Summer Schools; Felltham Community College; Family Links Teach First; SHINE Trust; Peers Early Education Partnership; London School of Economics (research project); UCAS (research projects); and Durham University (research projects).

Applications

The trust states that it, 'is now focusing on research and policy work, and will only be funding a select handful of small scale pilot projects. We envisage that most of these projects will be developed through existing contacts and partnerships'. As such, unsolicited applications are unlikely to be successful.

The Charles and Elsie Sykes Trust

General, social welfare, medical research

£341,500 (2010)

Beneficial area

UK, with a preference for Yorkshire.

Barber Titleys Solicitors, 6 North Park Road, Harrogate, Yorkshire HG1 5PA

Tel: 01423 817238

Fax: 01423 851112

Website: www. charlesandelsiesykestrust.co.uk

Correspondent: Mrs Judith M Long, Secretary

Trustees: John Ward, Chair; Mrs Anne E Brownlie; Martin P Coultas; Michael G H Garnett; R Barry Kay; Dr Michael W McEvoy; Peter G Rous; Dr Rosemary Livingstone; Sarah Buchan.

CC Number: 206926

Information available

Accounts were available at the Charity Commission.

Charles Sykes started his career as a twelve year old office boy, and became a successful businessman in the West Riding knitting wool trade with his own four-storey mill at Princeville, Bradford. He achieved his life ambition in his eighty-second year when he launched the Charles Sykes Trust on 16th December 1954.

In 2010 it had assets of £12.8 million and an income of £424,000. Grants were made to 112 organisations totalling £341,500.

A wide range of causes are supported, and the trust has sub-committees to consider both medical and non-medical grants.

The following is a breakdown of the total amounts awarded in each category:

Social and moral welfare	16	£80,000
Medical research	26	£78,000
Physical disability	14	£43,000
Children and youth	15	£31,500
Medical welfare	10	£23,000
Cultural and environmental heritage	5	£16,000
Old people's welfare	4	£15,500
Mental health and disability	6	£15,000

Hospices and hospitals	3	£13,000
Miscellaneous	7	£9,500
Deaf, hard of hearing and speech impaired	2	£8,000
Services and ex-services	1	£5,000
Blind and partially sighted	2	£3,500
Sundry	1	£280

Beneficiaries included: Alzheimer's Research Trust – Cambridge (£25,000); Age Concern – Leeds (£12,500); Sobriety Project – Goole (£9,000); Bowel Disease Research Foundation, Music and the Deaf – Huddersfield and Wakefield & District Carers' Association (£5,000 each); St John's Under 5's Pre-School – Bradford (£4,000); Harrogate Citizen's Advice Bureau and the Pain Relief Foundation – Liverpool (£3,000 each); and Clothing Solutions – Bradford and Kidney Research UK (£2,000 each).

Exclusions

Unregistered charities and overseas applications are not considered. Individuals, local organisations not in the north of England, and recently-established charities are unlikely to be successful.

Applications

The following information is available on the trust's website:

> To request funding you should download and fill in the application form [available on the trust's website]. Send it to the trust along with any other relevant information, particularly enclosing a copy of your latest audited or examined accounts to the present year, together with the annual report. It is more favourable for the application if the accounts are current. If the donation is required for any particular project, please provide full details and costings.

> Your request will be considered by the appropriate subcommittee, which for medical projects currently includes two doctors. The subcommittee then makes a recommendation to the next full meeting of the trustees. Please note it is the trustees' policy only to support applications from registered charities with a preference for those in or benefiting the geographical area of Yorkshire.

> Applications from schools, playgroups, cadet forces, scouts, guides, and churches must be for outreach programmes, and not for maintenance projects.

> Each application will be answered by letter to state if they have been rejected, or put forward for further consideration. Those that are rejected after further consideration will be duly informed. The trustees are under no obligation to state the reasons why any particular application has been rejected, and will not enter into correspondence on the matter. Successful applications will receive a donation which may or may not be subject to conditions.

> All applications are dealt with at the discretion of the trustees who meet quarterly.

The Tajtelbaum Charitable Trust

Jewish, welfare

£510,500 (2009/10)

Beneficial area

Generally UK and Israel.

17 Western Avenue, London NW11 9HE
Tel: 020 8202 3464
Correspondent: Ilsa Tajtelbaum, Trustee
Trustees: Ilsa Tajtelbaum; Jacob Tajtelbaum; Emanuel Tajtelbaum; Eli Jaswon.
CC Number: 273184

Information available

Accounts were on file at the Charity Commission, without a grants list.

The trust makes grants in the UK and Israel to orthodox synagogues, Jewish educational establishments, homes for older people and hospitals.

In 2009/10 the trust had assets of £4 million and an income of £539,000. Grants were made totalling £510,500. A list of grant beneficiaries was not included in the trust's accounts.

Previous beneficiaries include: United Institutions Arad, Emuno Educational Centre, Ruzin Sadiger Trust, Gur Foundation, Before Trust, Beth Hassidei Gur, Comet Charities Limited, Delharville, Kupat Gemach Trust, Centre for Torah and Chesed, Friends of Nachlat David and Friends of Sanz Institute.

Applications

In writing to the correspondent.

The Tedworth Charitable Trust

Parenting, child welfare and development, general

£380,500 (2009/10)

Beneficial area

Unrestricted, but UK in practice.

Allington House, 1st Floor, 150 Victoria Street, London SW1E 5AE
Tel: 020 7410 0330
Fax: 020 7410 0332
Website: www.sfct.org.uk
Correspondent: Alan Bookbinder, Director
Trustees: Alex J Sainsbury; Margaret Sainsbury; Jessica M Sainsbury; Timothy J Sainsbury; Judith S Portrait.
CC Number: 328524

Information available

Accounts were available at the Charity Commission.

This is one of the Sainsbury Family Charitable Trusts, which share a joint administration and have a common approach to grantmaking.

This trust's main areas of interest are parenting, family welfare, child development, arts and the environment; the trust also makes grants for general charitable purposes.

'Proposals are generally invited by the trustees or initiated at their request. Unsolicited applications are discouraged and are unlikely to be successful, even if they fall within an area in which the trustees are interested. The trustees prefer to support innovative schemes that can be successfully replicated or become self-sustaining.'

In 2009/10 the trust had assets of £10.5 million and an income of £393,500. Grants were paid during the year totalling £380,500, and were broken down as follows:

Arts and the environment	14	£236,000
Parenting, family welfare and child development	4	£104,000
General	4	£40,500

Beneficiaries included: Ashden Awards (£55,000); Best Beginnings (£45,000); Resurgence Magazine (£35,000); Worcester College – Oxford (£25,000); Tipping Point (£20,000); House of Illustration and the CarbonSense Foundation (£10,000 each); Women's Environmental Network (£7,500); and Platform (£5,000).

Exclusions

Grants are not normally made to individuals.

Applications

'Proposals are likely to be invited by the trustees or initiated at their request. Unsolicited applications are unlikely to be successful, even if they fall within an area in which the trustees are interested.' A single application will be considered for support by all the trusts in the Sainsbury family group. See the separate entry for the Sainsbury Family Charitable Trusts.

Tees Valley Community Foundation

General

£1.1 million (2009/10)

Beneficial area

The former county of Cleveland, being the local authority areas of Hartlepool, Middlesbrough, Redcar and Cleveland and Stockton-on-Tees.

Wallace house, Fallon Court, Preston Farm Industrial Estate, Stockton-on-Tees TS18 3TX

Tel: 01642 260860

Fax: 01642 313700

Email: info@teesvalleyfoundation.org

Website: www.teesvalleyfoundation. org

Correspondent: Hugh McGouran

Trustees: Alan Kitching; Peter Rowley; Christopher Hope; Pamela Taylor; Craig Monty; Rosemary Young; John Irwin; Marjory Houseman; Keith Robinson; Neil Kinley; John Harrison; Wendy Shepherd; Brian Beaumont.

CC Number: 1111222

Information available

Accounts were on file at the Charity Commission. Information on current schemes was available from the foundation's website.

The foundation's main aim is the promotion of any charitable purpose for the benefit of the community in the Tees Valley and neighbouring areas. Particular focus is given to the advancement of education, arts, the environment, the protection of good health (both mental and physical) and the relief of poverty and sickness.

Support is given to local registered charities and constituted community groups run for and by local people. The foundation always has a variety of grant programmes running and new ones are regularly added.

Funds Available

The foundation has a range of different funds designed for small community and voluntary groups working to help local people across Tees Valley.

As with all community foundations grant schemes change frequently. Please contact the foundation or check their website for details of current programmes and their deadlines.

Each scheme tends to have a different application procedure and size of award. A selection of some of the main programmes open at the end of 2011 is listed below:

Tees Valley Foundation Fund
The fund prioritises projects that address the issues of disadvantage, projects fulfilling a need not already being met and projects aimed at improving the social environment. Grants of up to £5,000 are available.

The Teesside Power Fund
This was set up in 1994 to make grants in support of charitable projects in the nine wards in the vicinity of Teesside Power Station. Applications are welcomed from registered charities or community groups resident in the nine wards or which benefit people who live in those wards. The wards are: Eston; Dormanstown; Kirkleatham; Teesville; Newcomen; Coatham; Grangetown; South Bank; Normanby. Grants of up to £5,000 are available to enable local people to launch or run initiatives to benefit their local community.

Northumbrian Water Fund
Grants of up to £1,000 are available for community projects or environmental

projects which improve any public space, facility or building.

Goshen Grassroots Fund
Small grants up to a maximum of £5,000 are available for local groups working to support those suffering disadvantage or social exclusion in the community in Tees Valley. Available in Darlington as well as the other common areas (see below).

Comic Relief
Grants of between £1,000 and £10,000 are available for projects which create lasting change in communities. Projects should be run by people directly affected by the issues they are dealing with and priority will be given to small, locally based groups or organisations in areas of disadvantage that have clear understanding of the needs of their community. Funding may be used to:
- increase local services
- build skills of local people
- increase community cohesion
- respond to local economic needs
- increase access to sport and exercise for people who face social exclusion and isolation.

European Social Fund Community Grants
ESF Community Grants will provide awards of up to £12,000 to small, voluntary community groups undertaking activities including help with basic skills, work experience, training advice and guidance, job search assistance, confidence building, personal development and support to overcome barriers to training and employment. The target group is unemployed and economically inactive people over 18, with particular priority given to black and minority ethnic groups, people over 50, women, lone parents and those with health conditions or disabilities.

Making a Difference Fund
Grants of up to £2,500 are available for projects that address the issues of disadvantage, projects fulfilling a need not already being met and projects aimed at improving the social environment.

Stockton Borough Community Fund
Small grants of up to £500 are available to support community projects and activities. Some of the listed examples include: arts & crafts, educational trips, keep-fit classes, walking trips, new equipment and social activities. Funds are available in the borough of Stockton-on-Tees.

Unless otherwise specified all of the above grant schemes are available in the following areas: Hartlepool, Middlesbrough, Redcar and Cleveland and Stockton-on-Tees.

In 2009/10 it had assets of £9.8 million and an income of £1.9 million. Grants from all funds totalled just over £1.1 million.

Beneficiaries included: Tees Credit Union Limited and Blindvoice UK (£40,000 each); My Sister's Place Women's Advice Centre (£32,000); Elm Tree Community Association (£13,000); Cultures (CIC) (£7,500); Acklam Rugby Club and The Silhouettes Jazz Band (£5,000 each); Redcar Literary Institute (£4,000); Whale Hill Community Association (£3,600); Sir William Turner's Hospital (£3,100); and Pig Pen Festivals (£1,000).

Exclusions

No grants for:

- major fundraising appeals
- sponsored events
- promotion of religion
- retrospective funding
- holidays or social outings
- existing operating costs, e.g. salaries, rent, overheads
- groups with excessive unrestricted or free reserves
- groups in serious deficit
- replacement of statutory funding
- meeting any need which is the responsibility of central or local government
- religious or political causes
- fabric appeals
- animal welfare.

Each fund has separate exclusions which are available on the trust's website.

Applications

Application forms are available on the trust's website. Applicants can received a maximum of £5,000 in any 12 month period from one or a combination of funds.

Common applicant mistakes

'Common applicant mistakes include: not providing requested supporting documents; badly worded or ineligible constitutions; and not completing the application form.'

The Thompson Family Charitable Trust

Medical, veterinary, education, general

£648,000 (2009/10)

Beneficial area

UK.

Hillsdown Court, 15 Totteridge Common, London N20 8LR
Correspondent: Katherine P Woodward
Trustees: David B Thompson; Patricia Thompson; Katherine P Woodward.
CC Number: 326801

Information available

Accounts were available at the Charity Commission.

This trust has general charitable purposes. There appears to be preferences for educational, medical and veterinary organisations, particularly those concerned with horses and horseracing.

In 2009/10 the trust had assets of £75.4 million and an income of £4.2 million. Grants were made to 32 organisations totalling £648,000. It regularly builds up its reserves to enable it to make large donations in the future, for example towards the construction of new medical or educational facilities. 'It is the policy of the charity to hold reserves which will enable [it] to make major donations for capital projects in the near future (for example, to fund the construction and endowment of new medical or educational facilities) and appropriate projects are currently being investigated. [...] In addition to such capital projects it is envisaged that grants to other charities will in future be made at a higher annual level than in recent years.'

The major beneficiary during the year was the Home of Horseracing Trust, which received £500,000. Other beneficiaries included: English PEN (£30,000); BBC Children in Need (£20,000); Multiple Sclerosis Society (£15,000); Cambridge Women's Aid and the North London Hospice (£10,000 each); British Horseracing Education and Standards Trust and Headway (£5,000 each); Cancer Research UK (£3,000); Addenbrooke's Charitable Trust and the Richard Dunwoody 1,000 Mile Challenge Trust (£1,000 each); and Girlguiding UK and the Injured Jockey Fund (£500 each).

Exclusions

No grants to individuals.

Applications

In writing to the correspondent.

The Sir Jules Thorn Charitable Trust

Medical research, medicine, small grants for humanitarian charities

£2.8 million (2010)

Beneficial area

UK.

24 Manchester Square, London W1U 3TH
Tel: 020 7487 5851
Fax: 020 7224 3976
Email: info@julesthorntrust.org.uk
Website: www.julesthorntrust.org.uk
Correspondent: David H Richings, Director
Trustees: Mrs Elizabeth S Charal, Chair; Prof Sir Ravinder N Maini; Sir Bruce McPhail; Nancy V Pearcey; Christopher Sporborg; William Sporborg; John Rhodes; Prof David Russell-Jones.
CC Number: 233838

Information available

Accounts were available at the Charity Commission. The trust also has a clear and helpful website.

The trust was established in 1964 for general charitable purposes and its primary interest is in the field of medicine. The founder of the trust, Sir Jules Thorn, made his fortune through his company Thorn Electrical industries. Grants are awarded to universities and hospitals in the United Kingdom to support medical research, with modest donations provided also for medically related purposes. It is a member of the Association of Medical Research Charities. Outside of medicine some funds are allocated for donations to humanitarian appeals and to special projects but on a lesser scale than the commitment for medical research.

Programmes

The trust gives the following information on its programmes:

Medical Research

The trust's main objective is to fund translational research which will bring benefit to patients through improved diagnosis or by assisting in the development of new therapies for important clinical problems. It recognises also the importance of encouraging young scientists to pursue a career in clinical research. Its two grant schemes have been designed with those objectives in mind.

(1) The Sir Jules Thorn Award for Biomedical Research

One grant of up to £1.25 million is offered annually to support a five year programme of translational biomedical research selected following a competition among applicants sponsored by the leading UK medical schools and NHS organisations.

UK medical schools and NHS organisations are eligible to submit one application annually.

[Full guidance notes are available from the trust's website.]

(2) The Sir Jules Thorn PhD Scholarship Programme

Three grants are available annually to support high quality postgraduate research training in UK medical schools under the supervision of a Senior Clinical Lecturer. A scholarship meets the cost of a stipend, tuition fees and consumables over a 3 year course of study leading to a PhD degree.

Scholarships are available only through medical schools invited to participate.

The Ann Rylands Special Project

This grant programme is associated with the name of Ann Rylands, daughter of Sir Jules Thorn, who chaired the Trust for 24 years following the death of her father, and was responsible for introducing the concept of the Special Project in 1980.

It is the trust's major humanitarian grant scheme, offering charities the opportunity to bid for funding at a level which could have a significant beneficial impact on their work.

Funds are allocated annually to one charitable theme determined by the trustees. The total award may be for up to a maximum of £500,000, but may be spread between several projects related to the same theme.

This programme is available by invitation only from the trust. When the trustees have chosen the annual theme, they select and invite individual charities that work in the appropriate area to submit an application.

Medically-related donations

The trustees endeavour to allocate some funds each year for medicine generally, in addition to their primary commitment to medical research. They keep in mind Sir Jules Thorn's concern to alleviate the suffering of patients and to aid diagnosis.

The resources available are limited and depending on the appeals received the Trustees may allocate the total fund in any one year to just one project, or divide it between several deserving appeals. Grants are awarded for a wide range of purposes. They may be linked to a very large appeal to expand important facilities for research in medical schools or to enhance patient care in hospitals. Other grants go to charities whose work is devoted to the care and comfort of patients with distressing clinical conditions. Grants under this programme are not provided for medical research.

Humanitarian

Sir Jules Thorn was a great humanitarian and whilst his endowment was provided primarily for medicine and medical research, he was content for some funds to be allocated to appeals of a humanitarian nature. Accordingly, the trustees earmark some resources each year for such purposes. The trust receives many more appeals than it can support with a grant. Each case is treated on its merits and the trustees' policy is to spread the funds as widely as possible.

The trust has two programmes:

(1) Small Grants Programme

The trust receives numerous appeals from fund-raising charities. Those which are successful are awarded grants of up to £1,500. Many charities have received grants over a number of years. Requests are considered for contributions to core funding or for specific projects, but this programme does not provide substantial sums for capital appeals.

(2) Larger Humanitarian Grants

Although this programme is not a major part its grant-making activities, the trust has been a consistent supporter of the humanitarian work of a limited number of charities who have received funding over a period of years.

These are restricted currently to special schemes initiated by the trust.

Grantmaking in 2010

In 2010 the trust had assets of £106.4 million and an income of over £2.4 million. There were 442 grants made during the year totalling £2.8 million, with most grants by number being small grants. Grants were broken down as follows:

The Ann Rylands Special Project*	£759,000
Other humanitarian grants	£658,000
Medical research	£655,500
Medically-related	£443,000
Small grants	£320,500

Large grants included those to: *Combat Stress (£759,000), over 3 years for a new Community Outreach team providing practical as well as therapeutic assistance for veterans suffering psychological injuries attributable to their military service; The Queen's University of Belfast – School of Medicine, Dentistry and Biomedical Sciences (£500,000), for 'Vascular stem cell therapy for ischaemic retionopathies' research project; The National Society for Epilepsy (£300,000), towards the cost of a new Epilepsy Research Centre to be built at the society's Chalfont campus; National Star College for Disabled Youth (£200,000), to assist with a new Therapies Centre to enhance the facilities provided for young people aged 16 – 25 with severe or complex physical disabilities or acquired brain injuries; and the Children's Trust – Tadworth (£200,000), towards the charity's appeal for funding to create new facilities to extend residential education for those aged 19 – 25 with profound and multiple learning difficulties.

Small grants of £1,000 included those to: Barnet and Chase Farm Hospitals NHS Trust; Children's Country Holiday Fund; Hampshire and Isle of Wight Air Ambulance; Hospice of the Valleys; Medical Foundation for the Care of Victims of Torture; NSF Scotland; Rainbow Trust; Royal Hospital for Neuro-disability; The Children's Foundation; The Police Rehabilitation Trust; Wessex Autistic Society; and the Variety Club.

Exclusions

The trust does not fund:

▶ research which is considered unlikely to provide clinical benefit within five years

▶ research which could reasonably be expected to be supported by a disease specific funder, unless there is a convincing reason why the trust has been approached

▶ research into cancer or AIDS, for the sole reason that they are relatively well funded elsewhere

▶ top up grants for ongoing projects

▶ research which will also involve other funders

▶ individuals – except in the context of a project undertaken by an approved institution which is in receipt of a grant from the trust

▶ research or data collection overseas

▶ research institutions which are not registered charities

▶ third parties raising resources to fund research themselves.

Applications

Medically-related grants

Appeals are considered annually by the trustees, usually in November.

There is no specific application form. Proposals should be submitted to the trust's director and should cover:

▶ the background to the appeal, including any brochures and feasibility assessment

▶ information about the applicant, which must be an institution having charitable status. Applications from individuals cannot be considered

▶ details of the appeal, including the total sum being raised, donations or pledges already received, and the plans for securing the remainder. Time scales for implementation should be given

▶ The latest trustees' report and audited financial statements should be provided.

Potential applicants who wish to establish whether their appeal would fit the criteria should contact the trust.

Small grants

On an application form available from the trust's website or by contacting the office.

There are no specific dates for submitting applications. Appeals may be made at any time and will be considered by the trustees as soon as possible, depending on volumes.

Common applicant mistakes

'Applying for purposes which are outside [the trust's stated] geographical area; providing a lack of information.'

The Three Guineas Trust

Autism and Asperger's Syndrome, climate change

£1.3 million (2009/10)

Beneficial area

Worldwide, in practice mainly UK.

Allington House, 1st Floor, 150 Victoria Street, London SW1E 5AE
Tel: 020 7410 0330
Fax: 020 7410 0332
Website: www.sfct.org.uk
Correspondent: Alan Bookbinder, Director
Trustees: Clare Sainsbury; Bernard Willis; Judith Portrait.
CC Number: 1059652

Information available

Accounts were available at the Charity Commission.

This is one of the Sainsbury Family Charitable Trusts, which share a joint administration. They have a common approach to grantmaking which is described in the entry for the group as a whole.

Clare Sainsbury established the Three Guineas Trust in 1996 for general charitable purposes. The trust's focus is in the area of autism and the related Asperger's Syndrome, and more recently, significant grants have been awarded for research into climate change.

There is a specific fund to enable people in developing countries to hire autism practitioners from the UK to deliver practical, one-off training courses for professionals and parents in countries which have little current provision for autistic children and adults.

In 2009/10 the trust had assets of £12.1 million and an income of £291,500. Grants were made to 21 organisations totalling almost £1.3 million.

The largest grant during the year was made to the University of Cambridge (£874,000), for a project to construct a new global economic model of a world free from dependence on carbon.

Other beneficiaries included: Bexley and Bromley Advocacy (£105,000); Autism Concern (£90,000); Jigsaw Group – Staffordshire (£9,000); and Sheffield Autistic Society (£5,000).

Exclusions

No grants for individuals or for research (except where it has an immediate benefit).

Applications

See the guidance for applicants in the entry for the Sainsbury Family Charitable Trusts. A single application will be considered for support by all the trusts in the group.

> The trustees do not at present wish to invite applications, except in the field of autism and Asperger's syndrome, where they will examine unsolicited proposals alongside those that result from their own research and contacts with expert individuals and organisations working in this field. The trustees prefer to support innovative schemes that can be successfully replicated or become self-sustaining. They are also keen that, wherever possible, schemes supporting adults and teenagers on the autistic spectrum should include clients/service users in decision-making.

The Tolkien Trust

General

£3.7 million (2009/10)

Beneficial area

UK, with some preference for Oxfordshire, and overseas.

Manches LLP, 9400 Garsington Road, Oxford Business Park North, Oxford OX4 2HN
Tel: 01865 722106
Fax: 01865 201012
Email: cathleen.blackburn@manches. com

Correspondent: Cathleen Blackburn
Trustees: Christopher Reuel Tolkien; Priscilla Mary Anne Reuel Tolkien; Michael Reuel Tolkien; Baillie Tolkien.
CC Number: 273615

Information available

Accounts were available at the Charity Commission.

The trust's main assets are the copyrights in relation to certain works written by the late J R R Tolkien including Smith of Wootton Major, Tree and Leaf, Roverandom and Mythopoeia. Although the trust has no permanent endowment, there should always be an income from book royalties during the period of copyright.

There are no specific guidelines for applicants. Grants are made to charities and charitable causes supporting children and young people, families, older people, the homeless and the socially disadvantaged, overseas aid and development, refugees, medical aid, research and education. Grants are also made to religious and arts organisations.

In 2009/10 the trust had assets of £26.3 million (2007/08: £6.8 million) and an income of £2 million (2007/08: £578,000). The significant increase in the trust's finances is due to an out-of-court settlement with New Line Cinema in September 2009 regarding the trust's entitlement to its share of the profits from the hugely successful *Lord of the Rings* trilogy of films. As a result, the trust has also been able to significantly increase its grantmaking, with grants to 150 organisations totalling £3.7 million (2007/08: £1.3 million).

The beneficiary of the largest grant during the year was Oxfam's East Africa Appeal, which received £1 million. Beneficiaries of other large grants included: Action Against Hunger, Médecins Sans Frontières and UNICEF, which received £200,000 each to support their work following the earthquake in Haiti.

Other beneficiaries included: University of Manitoba – Canada (£180,000 in total); Rebuild Sri Lanka (£80,000); WaterAid (£50,000); Practical Action (£45,000);

Breakthrough Breast Cancer (£35,000); Rochdale Special Needs Cycling Club and Ty Hafan Children's Hospice (£30,000 each); National Deaf Children's Society (£24,000); Trust for Research and Education on the Arms Trade and the City of Birmingham Symphony Orchestra (£20,000 each); Christian Peace Education Fund and West London Churches Homeless Concern (£15,000 each); British Red Cross, Friends of Cardigan Bay and Oxford Playhouse Trust (£10,000 each); Cancer Research UK, Lincoln Clinic and Centre for Psychotherapy and Woman for Women International UK (£5,000 each); and the Poetry Trust (£3,000).

Applications

In writing to the correspondent. The majority of donations are made to charities or causes selected by the trustees. There are no guidelines for applicants and the trust does not enter into correspondence with applicants in the interests of controlling administrative costs. Decisions about donations annually at the end of March/ beginning of April. Therefore, any applications should be timed to reach the trust by no later than 15 December in the preceding year.

The Tompkins Foundation

General

£394,500 (2009/10)

Beneficial area

UK, with a preference for the parishes of Hampstead Norreys, Berkshire and West Grinstead, West Sussex.

7 Belgrave Square, London
SW1X 8PH
Tel: 020 7235 9322
Fax: 020 7259 5129
Correspondent: Richard Geoffrey Morris
Trustees: Elizabeth Tompkins; Peter Vaines.
CC Number: 281405

Information available

Accounts were available at the Charity Commission.

The foundation was established in 1980 primarily for the advancement of education, learning and religion and the provision of facilities for recreation and other purposes beneficial to the community. However, most beneficiaries tend to be medical or health-related organisations. 'The trustees aim to respond to need and therefore consider that more specific plans [for the future] would be too restrictive.'

In 2009/10 the foundation had assets of £10.7 million and an income of £409,000. Grants were made to 20 organisations totalling £394,000, with 15 of the beneficiaries having received donations in the previous year.

The beneficiaries were: The Foundation of Nursing Studies and the Hesperus Foundation (£50,000 each); Right to Play (£30,000); Chicken Shed Theatre, Great Ormond Street Hospital Children's Charity, St Johns Hospice and the Passage (£25,000 each); Leonard Cheshire Foundation, Order of Malta Volunteers, The Place 2 Be and the Police Foundation (£20,000); Help for Heroes, Longview and Toynbee Hall (£10,000 each); CTBF Enterprises (£9,000); and the Anna Freud Centre, Gayfields Home of Rest, Maggie's Centre and Variety Club Children's Charity (£5,000 each).

Exclusions

No grants to individuals.

Applications

In writing to the correspondent, although applications from organisations unknown to the trustees are unlikely to be successful..

Common applicant mistakes

'Not recognising that unsolicited applications with whom the trustees have no connection are almost certain to be rejected.'

The Constance Travis Charitable Trust

General

£841,000 (2010)

Beneficial area

UK (national charities only); Northamptonshire (all sectors).

Quinton Rising, Quinton, Northampton NN7 2EF
Tel: 01604 862296
Correspondent: Earnest R A Travis, Trustee
Trustees: Mrs Constance M Travis; Earnest R A Travis; Peta J Travis; Matthew Travis.
CC Number: 294540

Information available

Accounts were available at the Charity Commission.

Established in 1986, the trust has general charitable purposes, supporting local organisations in Northamptonshire as well as organisations working UK-wide and internationally. During 2010 the trust merged with the Anthony Travis Charitable Trust, a charity with similar objectives.

In 2010 the trust had assets of £60.3 million and an income of £16.3 million, the majority of which was carried over from the merger with the Anthony Travis Charitable Trust. Grants were made during the year totalling £841,000, and were categorised as follows:

Medical and health	£239,000
Economic and community development	£161,500
Education and training	£78,000
Arts and culture	£72,000
Overseas aid	£62,000
Religion	£57,500
Disability	£45,000
Relief of poverty	£34,000
Environment and conservation	£30,500
Housing	£29,000
Animals	£17,000
General	£15,000
Sports and recreation	£1,000

The largest grants were made to: British Red Cross and Oxfam(£50,000 each); and Royal Academy of Music (£47,500).

Other beneficiaries included: Northants Association of Youth Clubs and Volunteer Reading Help (£15,000 each); Gateway School, The Institute of Cancer Research and National Tremor Foundation (£10,000 each); St Mary The Boltons (£7,500); Wootton Parish Church Council (£6,000); Royal National Institute of the Blind, Peoples Dispensary for Sick Animals and Prisoners Abroad (£5,000 each); Royal Marines Charitable Trust Fund (£3,000); Theatre Is and Northamptonshire Museum (£2,000 each); and Countryside Alliance (£1,500).

Exclusions

No grants to individuals or non-registered charities.

Applications

In writing to the correspondent. Trustees meet at least quarterly. The trust's 2010 accounts note that 'though the trustees make grants with no formal application, they may invite organisations to submit a formal application.'

The Triangle Trust (1949) Fund

Social welfare, health, people with disabilities, integration and general

£568,000 to organisations (2009/10)

Beneficial area

Worldwide. In practice UK.

32 Bloomsbury Street, London WC1B 3QJ
Tel: 020 7299 4245
Email: lesleylilley@triangletrust.org
Website: www. thetriangletrust1949fund.org.uk
Correspondent: Lesley Lilley, Secretary to the Trustees
Trustees: Melanie Burfitt, Chair; Dr Robert Hale; Mark Powell; Bruce Newbigging; Kate Purcell; Jamie Dicks; Helen Evans; Andrew Pitt.
CC Number: 222860

Information available

Accounts were available at the Charity Commission.

The trust was set up in 1949 by Sir Henry Jephcott, a pharmaceutical industrialist and former managing director of Glaxo Laboratories Ltd.

The following guidelines are taken from the trust's website:

The objects of the trust are:
- the education and alleviation from poverty of past or present employees, and their dependants, of the pharmaceutical industry
- the promotion of a good standard of health in the community, including recreational facilities and medical welfare
- such charitable purposes as the trustees may determine.

Trustees have established the following priorities within these objects:
- grants to individuals in need who are or have been employed in the pharmaceutical industry for a minimum of 2 years and resident in the UK, or their dependants
- grants to individuals in need made through block grants to a number of selected agencies
- grants to registered charities in the UK for activities which improve the well-being and health of communities.

The trust's current areas of interest for support are:
- carers
- community arts and education (where no statutory sources of funding)
- disability
- older people (particularly projects which maintain independence)
- poverty
- integration and rehabilitation.

Successful projects will either:
- maintain an open, inclusive society, or
- promote integration (or reintegration) of individuals or groups into society.

In general, priority is given to:
- smaller charities
- charities which serve a locality or region of the UK, rather than national charities
- causes which find it more difficult to raise funds from the general public
- activities where the Trust's financial contribution will have an identifiable impact
- new activities, provided there is evidence of these being sustainable in the longer term if they demonstrate success in meeting a need.

Grants are normally in the range £1,000 to £10,000, with the majority of grants around £4,000 to £5,000. Trustees either make one-off grants, or offer funding for up to 3 years, sometimes on a tapering basis. In the case of multi-year funding, an annual report is required to confirm funding for the second and third years.

Grants in 2009/10

In 2009/10 the trust had assets totalling £15.7 million and an income of £609,000. Grants were made to 75 organisations totalling £568,000, broken down as follows:

Poverty	21	£161,500
Community arts and education	17	£127,000
Rehabilitation and integration	22	£100,500
Disability	15	£84,500
Older people	12	£53,000
Carers	10	£41,500

Beneficiaries included: Family Action Education (£45,000); Leicester Charity Link (£35,000); Mobility Trust (£20,000); Dundee City Council (£16,000); South Yorkshire Probation (£14,000); Aberdare Town Centre Project, Bristol Care & Repair and Leukaemia CARE (£10,000 each); Right Employment (£9,000); Asperger East Anglian (£8,000); The Trust Women's Project (£7,000); Relate Brighton & Hove (£6,000); National Youth Orchestra, Storybook Dads and Threshold Housing Advice (£5,000 each); Sudden Productions and St Wilfred's Centre (£3,000 each); St Luke's Family Centre – Belfast and Crossroads Care North Somerset (£2,000 each); and Carers' Forum Stirling (£1,000).

The trust also gives a proportion of its money to individuals in need, mostly former employees of the pharmaceutical industry or their dependants. In 2009/10 this amounted to £43,000.

Exclusions

Generally, only registered charities are funded. In addition the trust will not fund the following:

- direct applications from individuals
- overseas charities or projects outside the UK
- charities for the promotion of religion
- medical research
- environmental, wildlife or heritage appeals
- applications funded in the last two years, unless at the trustees invitation.

Applications

Organisations should apply using the trust's application form, available from its website. Guidelines are also provided by the trust. Application hardcopies should be typed, and applicants should include their latest report and accounts with the application form (if submitting an online application, applicants should send their latest report and accounts separately as soon possible).

The trustees meet quarterly in February, June, October and December to award grants. Applications should be submitted in the preceding month (January, May, September and November). Please note: applicants may be asked to present their project(s) to the trustees.

The True Colours Trust

Special needs, sensory disabilities and impairments, palliative care, carers

£1.7 million (2009/10)

Beneficial area

UK and Africa.

Allington House, 1st Floor,
150 Victoria Street, London
SW1E 5AE
Tel: 020 7410 0330
Fax: 020 7410 0332
Email: truecolours@sfct.org.uk
Website: www.truecolourstrust.org.uk/
Correspondent: Alan Bookbinder, Director
Trustees: Lucy A Sainsbury; Dominic B Flynn; Bernard J C Willis; Tim Price.
CC Number: 1089893

Information available

Accounts were available from the Charity Commission. The trust also has a clear and helpful website.

Established in 2001, this is one of the newest of the Sainsbury family charitable trusts. The following detailed information on the trust's interests and activities is taken from its website:

The True Colours Trust has always been passionate about making a difference to the lives of children with special needs and their families. We believe that all children and their families should be able to live happy, fulfilled lives with opportunities for play, friendship and education without the burdens of poverty, exclusion and discrimination.

We are currently focusing our grant making in the following three areas:

- improving the geographical spread and range of palliative care services available for children and young people in the UK
- improving the service delivery and support offered to children with complex disabilities and their families and siblings in the UK
- promoting and developing the palliative care sector in sub-Saharan Africa.

The True Colours Trust aims to focus on the major barriers and challenges expressed by families, children and young people with complex disabilities and/or life-limiting and life-threatening conditions. We work closely with organisations that share our ambitions to provide imaginative, practical and often ground-breaking services in addition to delivering programmes that bring about sustained change both at a policy or practice level.

The trust has so far sought to bring about better lives for children and their families through a broad mix of research, advocacy, service delivery and innovation.

Children with complex disabilities in the UK

Trustees care passionately about making life better for children and young people with profound disabilities and their families.

In 2004, trustees commissioned research into the needs of children with profound and complex disabilities and their families in the UK. The results of the research were stark: 55% of families with a disabled child live on the poverty line, primarily because of the costs of raising a disabled child. The research also highlighted the emotional strain that the majority of families live with and the desperate need for respite care and appropriate child care provision. It was also apparent that there were very few accessible activities or services for these children.

On the basis of this research, trustees decided to concentrate their grant-making in three main areas:

- support for organisations leading the way in developing services and opportunities for children and their families

▶ raising the profile of the siblings of disabled children and services to meet their needs

▶ raising the profile of disabled children and their families with central and local government.

Trustees have been delighted by the success of the *Every Disabled Child Matters Campaign* which has been very successful in raising the profile of disabled children and securing additional Government funding. They continue to support the work of the campaign in the challenge of ensuring that national policy becomes local practice.

Other major achievements include the increasing recognition of the needs of siblings, the successful piloting of specialised, targeted financial and benefits advice and the growing importance being placed on the need for fun and friendship in the lives of disabled children.

Over the coming three years, trustees will focus much of their attention in this area on finding solutions to the negative impact of Health and Safety Legislation and on researching and piloting solutions to the very high debt levels amongst families with children with complex needs and the impact on already stressful lives.

Palliative care for children and young people in the UK

The trust believes that everyone with a life-limiting or life-threatening illness has the right to affordable palliative care.

The understanding and provision of Palliative Care for children and young people in the UK is inconsistent. Although there are some excellent service providers, too few families receive the help they need during a very difficult time in their lives. Families need support to enable their children to live their lives to the full with the minimum of pain and discomfort, and to die with the highest degree of dignity. There should be a range of services available to allow children and families to choose how and where they receive support. There should also be specific support available to help parents and siblings through a very emotional and challenging time in their lives.

Over the past four years, trustees have supported the development of the children's palliative care sector through a mixture of grants, which have been used for a variety of different purposes, from influencing national policy to demonstrating best practice at local, regional and national levels. The first national strategy for England and Wales, *Better Care, Better Lives* was published by the Department of Health in March 2008, the culmination of much of this work.

The challenge now is to make the strategy and statements of best practice a reality for all families regardless of their geographical location, on a day-to-day basis. After significant consultation with those working in the palliative care sector, trustees have decided to focus on the following areas for the next three years:

▶ creation of the UK's first Professorial Chair in Palliative Care for Children and Young People to lead the development of best practice across the country

▶ creation of a pilot regional, 24 hour support service for children with Palliative Care needs, bringing together the full range of specialists and agencies. We expect this to incorporate a complete set of clinical and social services and be replicable for any region of the UK

Alongside these two key pieces of work, trustees will continue to focus on building the infrastructure of the palliative care sector, influencing policy at a national and local level, and supporting a small number of organisations which demonstrate excellence and innovation at a local level.

Palliative care in Africa

The trust believes that everyone with a life-limiting or life threatening illness has the right to affordable palliative care.

The need for palliative care is particularly acute in sub-Saharan Africa where it is estimated that there are 22 million people living with HIV and that the number of people with cancer will increase by 400% in the next fifty years. The widespread introduction of anti-retroviral drugs has increased the need for palliative care as patients are living longer but still suffering from symptoms of HIV and side effects of the medication.

Trustees are committed to improving access to affordable palliative care in sub-Saharan Africa. The trust's strategic programme is focused on increasing access to opioids in Zambia. It has also launched a small grants programme which is administered by the African Palliative Care Association (www.apca.org.ug). This programme provides grants, of between £1,000 – £2,500, to organisations offering palliative services across the continent.

Small grants in the UK

The trustees are committed to supporting a large number of excellent local organisations and projects that support disabled children and their families on a daily basis. The trust has a small grants programme, open to application at any time, which provides grants of up to £10,000, usually for one-off purposes, to help smaller organisations develop and deliver

programmes for children, their siblings and families.

The trustees are particularly keen to support:

▶ Hydrotherapy pools
▶ Multi sensory rooms
▶ Mini buses
▶ Young carers projects
▶ Sibling projects
▶ Bereavement support

In 2009/10 the trust had assets of almost £8.5 million and an income of £2 million, mostly from donations. Grants were paid to around 100 organisations during the year totalling £1.7 million, and were broken down as follows:

Children with complex disabilities in the UK	£714,500
Palliative care in Sub-Saharan Africa	£460,000
Palliative care for children and young people in the UK	£320,500
Small grants in the UK	£168,000

Beneficiaries during the year (of both paid and approved grants) included: Great Ormond Street Hospital Children's Charity (£750,000 over 3 years), towards the True Colours Chair in Palliative Care for Children and Young People; African Palliative Care Association (£330,000 in total), most of which going towards the True Colours Trust African small grants programme for the period 2008–2013, which APCA administers; Palliative Care Association of Zambia (£231,000 over 2 years), towards the pilot of morphine in Zambia's hospices; Heart'n Soul (£150,000 over 3 years), towards its work with young people; Social Finance (£75,000), towards phase two of the Disabled Children's Credit Facility; and the Dance Art Foundation (£20,000), towards core costs.

Small grants to UK organisations included those to: Hope House (£10,500), towards refurbishment works; Guy's Gift (£10,000), towards core costs; Birtenshaw Hall Children's Charitable Trust (£8,000), towards the costs of a sensory garden; Break All About Caring, towards its holiday programme, Demelza House Children's Hospice, towards its bereavement service, and Mosaic, towards core costs (£5,000 each); and Kent Kids (£4,000), towards refurbishment works.

Exclusions

The trust does not give direct support for:

- individuals
- educational fees
- expeditions

Applications

The following information was taken from the trust's website:

Programme Grants

The trust only funds registered charities or activities with clearly defined charitable purposes.

The trustees take an active role in their grant-making, employing a range of specialist staff and advisers to research their areas of interest and bring forward suitable proposals. The trust works closely with its chosen beneficiaries over a long period to achieve particular objectives. It should therefore be understood that the majority of unsolicited proposals we receive will be unsuccessful.

Applications should be sent by post to The Sainsbury Family Charitable Trusts, Allington House (1st Floor), 150 Victoria Street, London SW1E 5AE, with a description (strictly no more than two pages please, as any more is unlikely to be read) of the proposed project, covering:

- the organisation – explaining its charitable aims and objectives, and giving its most recent annual income and expenditure, and current financial position. Please do not send a full set of accounts
- the project requiring funding – why it is needed, who will benefit and in what way
- the funding – breakdown of costs, any money raised so far, and how the balance will be raised
- at this stage please do not send supporting books, brochures, DVDs, annual reports or accounts.

All applications will receive our standard acknowledgement letter. If your proposal is a candidate for support, you will hear from us within 8 weeks of the acknowledgement. Applicants who do not hear from us within this time must assume they have been unsuccessful.

Small Grants

The small grants programme is broken down into two categories: UK and Africa.

UK

The UK small grants programme is to fund local organisations and projects that support disabled children and their families. No direct support will be given for salaries and the grants are usually on a one-off basis.

Key areas of particular interest to the trustees are:

- hydrotherapy pools
- multi sensory rooms
- mini buses
- young carers projects
- sibling projects
- bereavement support.

Applications for small grants should be made using our online application form.

Africa

The Africa small grants programme is administered by the African Palliative Care Association (www.apca.org.ug). This programme provides grants, of between £1,000 – £2,500, to organisations offering palliative services across the continent.

Trustees favour support for items which directly improve the patient experience and the standard of palliative care services. Priority is given to the following, in no particular order:

- equipment for patients (beds, wheelchairs etc)
- innovative projects for paediatric services (this could include purchasing toys)
- medicines
- capital improvement costs (such as adapting buildings to improve the patient experience)
- developing small palliative care projects

Applications should be sent directly to APCA at: TrueColoursSmallGrants@apca.co.ug.

See the guidance for applicants in the entry for the Sainsbury Family Charitable Trusts. A single application will be considered for support by all the trusts in the group. However, please see comments regarding the selection of beneficiaries.

The Trusthouse Charitable Foundation

General

£2.4 million (2009/10)

Beneficial area

Unrestricted, but mainly UK.

6th Floor, 65 Leadenhall Street, London EC3A 2AD
Tel: 020 7264 4990

Website: www. trusthousecharitablefoundation.org. uk
Correspondent: Judith Leigh, Grants Manager
Trustees: Sir Jeremy Beecham; Baroness Sarah Hogg; The Duke of Marlborough; Anthony Peel; The Hon. Mrs Olga Polizzi; Sir Hugh Rossi; Lady Janet Balfour of Burleigh; Sir John Nutting; Mr Howell Harris-Hughes; Rev. Rose Hudson-Wilkin; Lady Hamilton.
CC Number: 1063945

Information available

Accounts were on file at the Charity Commission. The foundation also has a helpful website.

The Trusthouse Charitable Foundation was formed out of a trust operated by the Council of Forte plc which inherited investments in the Granada Group. Its objects are such general charitable purposes as the trustees in their discretion may from time to time determine.

The foundation is administered on a day-to-day basis on behalf of the trustees by the Henry Smith Charity, although each charity is entirely independent.

Guidelines

The foundation gives the following information about its grantmaking objectives and policies on its website:

Trusthouse gives grants for running costs or one-off capital costs to charities and not-for-profit organisations in accordance with criteria that are regularly reviewed and decided by the trustees.

In July 2008, the trustees reviewed its grants policy and decided to concentrate on projects addressing Rural Issues and Urban Deprivation.

Rural Issues

We accept applications from organisations which are addressing issues in rural areas. 'Rural' in this context means cities, towns, villages and areas with 10,000 or less inhabitants. We are interested in, for example, projects providing transport for the elderly, disabled or disadvantaged; contact networks for the young disabled; projects which encourage a sense of community such as community centres and village halls;

employment training schemes especially those promoting local, traditional crafts; projects addressing issues such as drug/alcohol misuse or homelessness.

Urban Deprivation

We will accept applications from local or national charities or not-for-profit organisations which are working with residents of urban areas (i.e. more than 10,000 inhabitants) which are classified in the latest government Indices of Multiple Deprivation as being in the lowest 20%. We are interested in, for example, youth clubs; training schemes to help people out of unemployment; drop in centres for the homeless.

Applicants must clearly show in their appeal how their project fits into one or both of these categories.

Within these overarching themes, we are interested in three areas:

Community support
Community

Projects supported: the support of carers; projects in deprived communities; projects addressing financial exclusion; the provision of sporting facilities or equipment in deprived areas.

Drugs and alcohol

Projects supported: rehabilitation of substance and alcohol misusers.

Elderly

Projects supported: those addressing isolation and loneliness (e.g. befriending schemes); domiciliary support (e.g. respite for carers), residential improvements/ adaptations.

Ex-offenders

Projects supported: those working with prisoners and ex-offenders to improve their life skills and reduce reoffending.

Young people

Projects supported: those which build the confidence, life skills and employment skills of young people in need.

Disability and Healthcare
Physical and mental disability

Projects supported: those involving rehabilitation, (including related arts and sport programmes); projects particularly for ex-service men and women (including former employees of the emergency services); projects for children (including holidays); and respite care.

Palliative care

Areas supported: the provision of domiciliary care; support for volunteers and carers; outreach services; the refurbishment of premises; the provision of equipment (excluding in all cases services or costs which are normally funded from statutory sources).

Medicine

Areas supported: special equipment (not available on the NHS) for the chronically or terminally ill at home. (Medical research projects are ineligible.)

Arts, Education and Heritage
Arts

Projects supported: those which enable the disabled people and people living in areas of need and poverty to participate in the performance arts and to experience artistic excellence in the performing arts; projects which encourage and give opportunities to young talented people whose circumstances might otherwise deny them (but not bursaries or fees).

Education

Projects supported: those which help children at risk of exclusion or with exceptionally challenging behaviour to realise their educational potential; projects which encourage and give opportunities to young talented people whose circumstances might otherwise deny them access to further/higher education.

Heritage

Projects supported: smaller heritage projects, with a particular interest in industrial and maritime projects in areas of deprivation, which provide employment and/or volunteering opportunities for the local community and contribute to the regeneration of the area.

Types of grant

The trust details the types of grant it gives on its website. The table below also details eligibility.

What type of grant you apply for depends on:
- the annual income of your organisation
- the grant amount you are looking for
- whether you are looking for capital costs or for running (i.e. core, salary or project) costs.

Please note:
- All grants are for 1 year only. Trusthouse prefers not to make grants in successive years.
- Organisations with an income over £300,000 are not eligible for Small Grants or Fast Track grants.
- Organisations with an income over £5 million are not eligible under any of the grant schemes.

- Capital projects are only eligible where the total cost is £1 million or less.
- Hospices are eligible for capital grants even if their income is over £5 million and the total project cost is over £1 million.

Grants in 2009/10

During the year the foundation had assets of £59.6 million and an income of £1 million. There were 307 grants paid totalling £2.4 million and were distributed as follows (including support costs):

Disabilities	£396,000
Youth	£298,500
Community centres	£243,000
Community service	£190,500
Overseas	£172,000
Hospices	£169,000
Arts	£157,000
Themed grant (mental health)	£153,000
Homeless	£132,000
Themed grant (rural elderly)	£80,000
Family support services	£79,500
Sport	£62,500
Aged	£44,000
Counselling	£36,500
Rehabilitation of offenders	£35,000
Heritage	£34,000
Ethnic minorities	£28,500
Domestic violence	£21,000
Education	£18,500
Medical	£16,000
Carers	£14,000
Substance misuse	£14,000
Churches	£9,500
Ex-services	£3,000
Refugees and asylum seekers	£1,000

The foundation's annual report gives an interesting and informative summary of its achievements and activities during the year:

The trustees received 1,460 applications during the year, as compared with 1,836 in 2008/09. Much of the decrease can be attributed to the effects of the more focussed grants policy in 2008, with 2009 seeing the full effects of the new policy after the transition during 2008. The decrease was a planned and expected outcome of the revised policy to enable larger grants to be awarded to the smaller number of applicants. Some of the fall was due to a decrease in the number of applications for capital appeals under the Large Grants scheme, with charities deciding to defer or cancel capital projects until fundraising prospects look more positive. Trustees are

---

THE TRUSTHOUSE CHARITABLE FOUNDATION

Your organisation's annual income	Grant amount sought	What is the grant for?	Grants available*
Under £300,000	£5,000 and under	Capital and/or running costs	Fast track
Under £300,000	£5,001 to £9,999	Capital and/or running costs	Small grant
Under £300,000	£10,000 to £30,000	Capital costs only	Large grant
Over £300,000, less than £5 million	£10,000 to £30,000	Capital costs only	Large grant

concerned at the poor quality of many appeals which require additional investigation by the office team to ascertain if they are suitable for support. Feedback is given to unsuccessful applicants on how they may improve their application if they wish to reapply in the future. (All applicants, except those who are ineligible, may reapply six months after the date of an unsuccessful application.) The success of the new policy was reviewed throughout the year, and it was noted that applicants for rural projects were much fewer and of poorer quality than those for urban projects. A mailshot and explanatory leaflet to community foundations working in rural areas, rural community councils and other rural project umbrella organisations was made, and the results are positive to date.

307 grants were paid (360 in 2008/09) totalling £2.4 million (£1.95 million in 2008/09), while grants were awarded totalling £2.7 million, net of grant repayments of £17,000. Not all grants are paid within the financial year when the grantee is continuing to fundraise before the start of a project. The amount awarded was significantly higher than the previous year following a return to a larger budget, plus the allocation of grants for the whole three years of the new thematic programme for projects addressing mental health issues in the criminal justice system. [...] Most of the grants were under £10,000, with an average value of £9,687 (£5,394 in 2008/9). This increase in average grant size was a planned aim of the new policy.

The current grants policy means that where possible, applications under the Large Grants scheme are awarded the full amount recommended by the Visitor, with Small Grants being allotted funds from the remaining budget for each meeting of the Grants Committee. The average Large Grant in 2009 was £20,572 (£18,991 in 2008/09).

Seven grants of £30,000 were awarded under the Large Grants scheme including:

- Pilsdon Community: towards the cost of creating 20 en-suite rooms at a farm community for homeless, vulnerable and otherwise excluded people
- Options for Life: towards the cost of a hydrotherapy pool, hoist system and sensory equipment at a centre for people with learning difficulties
- Artlink, West Yorkshire: towards the cost of repairing and upgrading the venue for a community arts project.

In addition to the above, 21 grants of between £6,000 and £29,200 were awarded under the Large Grants Scheme (26 grants in 2008/09).

98 Small Grants recipients received on average £8,016 (£5,989 in 2008/09), again demonstrating the results of the revised grants policy to enable the trustees to make bigger grants with a more significant impact for the grantee. Several grantees have commented that the grants helped them to leverage other funding, gave them a breathing space to allow them to arrange longer term funding, and generally helped them to reach more people through their work.

The trustees considered a number of possible candidates for the Super Grants Scheme. Two grantees were finally selected: Emmaus Burnley (towards the cost of setting up a new scheme for homeless adults in Burnley) and Calvert Trust Lake District (towards the cost of a new Water Centre for use by disabled people). Each of the two charities were awarded a grant of £100,000 following visits by the chairman of the Grants Committee and assessment reports. The grant of £125,000 agreed in principle at the end of the financial year 2009 to Hearing Dogs for the Deaf, for its new centre at Bielby, East Yorkshire, was confirmed during the year.

The 'Fast Track' Accelerated Grants scheme, for grant applications of £5,000 and under, remained popular and 76 projects received a total amount of £237,500 between them following the return to the standard budget after the decrease in 2008 (when 68 projects received £188,000).

Most of the grants awarded by the foundation are for relatively modest amounts and therefore it is not practical to attempt a detailed analysis of impact either for individual grants or across sectors.

[...] The largest categories by value were Disabilities (16%), Youth (12%), and Community Centres (10%). The geographical incidence (by value) was highest in London. The foundation does not set budgetary limits on particular categories or regions apart from overseas, where the maximum is 10%.

The trustees had individual budgets of £20,000 during the financial year to award to the projects of their choice (subject to the approval of a quorum of the Grants Committee) reflecting their personal interests and local knowledge, which may fall outside the guidelines for the standard grants. [...]

The trustees agreed a special sum of £100,000 for the retiring Chairman, Sir Richard Carew Pole, to recommend to the Grants Committee the award of larger grants. The Grants Committee approved three grants on Sir Richard's recommendation: the Cornwall Community Foundation (towards the endowment fund of the Caradon Area Fund); the Merlin Project of the Cornwall MS Therapy Centre (towards

the building of a new multi-purpose centre) and, just after the end of the financial year Trelya (towards the purchase of a building to provide a permanent home for a youth club in Truro).

Exclusions

The foundation will not normally consider supporting the following:

- animal welfare
- applications for revenue funding for more than one year
- capital appeals for places of worship
- grant making organisations or umbrella groups
- grants for individuals (including bursaries through a third party organisation)
- feasibility studies and evaluations
- local authorities
- Local Education Authority schools or their Parent Teachers Associations, except if those schools are solely for students with Special Needs
- medical research projects
- office IT equipment including software costs
- organisations that have received a grant for three consecutive years from the foundation
- projects involving the start-up or piloting of new services
- projects where the primary objective is environmental or conservation
- projects where the primary objective is the promotion of a particular religion
- renovation or alteration projects to make a building compliant with the Disability & Discrimination Act
- revenue funding for organisations with an income of over £300,000 per annum
- services operated by the NHS
- social research
- training of professionals within the UK
- universities.

Under normal circumstances, the foundation is not currently funding projects which are for:

- the purchase of computers, other electronic equipment or software for delivery of the charity's work (e.g. for an IT suite in a youth centre)

▶ PR or other awareness raising campaigns, including the publication of leaflets or events calendars, websites.

Applications

On an application form available from the foundation's website, accessed following the completion of a brief eligibility questionnaire, which also identifies which type of grant may be most suitable. Details of additional information to be included with the application are given on the form. Applications must be made by post.

Common applicant mistakes

'Not providing information stated as required in our guidelines; not explaining the reason for late submissions to Charity Commission; applying before they have raised 50% of total funds needed; and, not explaining how their project fits our overarching themes.'

The James Tudor Foundation

Relief of sickness, medical research, health education, palliative care

£749,000 (2009/10)

Beneficial area

UK and overseas.

WestPoint, 78 Queens Road, Clifton, Bristol BS8 1QU
Tel: 0117 985 8715
Fax: 0117 985 8716
Email: admin@jamestudor.org.uk
Website: www.jamestudor.org.uk
Correspondent: The Secretary
Trustees: Martin G Wren, Chair; Richard R G Esler; Malcolm R Field; Roger K Jones; Cedric B Nash.
CC Number: 1105916

Information available

Accounts were available from the Charity Commission. The foundation also has a helpful website.

The foundation was established in 2004. It makes grants for charitable purposes, usually in the UK, across six programme areas:
▶ palliative care
▶ medical research
▶ health education, awards and scholarship
▶ the direct relief of sickness
▶ the UK independent healthcare sector
▶ the fulfilment of the foundation's charitable objects by other means.

In line with the principal objective, the foundation seeks to help small charities stay on their feet; to significantly improve the financial position of medium to large charities and to contribute to medical research where there is a probability of positive clinical outcomes.

Types of funding

Direct project support
This is the most successful area for funding requests.

Research
We will fund research where its aims match our objects and where we consider that it is likely to have a beneficial impact.

Awards and scholarships
We will occasionally fund awards and scholarships where they demonstrate that they contribute to the foundation's areas of benefit.

Building or refurbishment projects
The foundation is less likely to make grants towards capital projects (i.e. buildings and refurbishment costs). However, capital projects will be supported where clear benefit and good management are demonstrable.

Equipment
Items of equipment may be funded, particularly if part of a wider proposal. You should contact us first if your proposal includes requests for equipment funding.

Staffing
Staffing is occasionally supported. We would normally expect to see a proposal where self-financing is indicated within three years.

In 2009/10 the foundation had assets of £25.1 million and an income of £725,000. There were 63 grants made totalling £749,000, broken down as follows:

Medical research	£196,500
Direct relief of sickness	£194,000
Palliative care	£156,000
Health education	£62,500
Other	£142,500

The foundation gives the following analysis of the applications received during the year in its annual report:

309 full written, postal applications were received, a 7% increase over the previous year (2009: 288). Of the 309 received, 256[83%] were eligible (2009:220[76%]). 29 have already resulted in grants being awarded, 130 were declined (2009: 130) and 2 were withdrawn. 44 are in progress (2009: 34) and 51 applications are held awaiting further information. One grant of £45,000 was approved in favour of the University of Nottingham but has not been paid.

As a result of the foundation's excellent analysis of its grantmaking in its annual reports, it is possible to look at the figures for applications received over the past few years in the table below.

Grantmaking in 2009/10

The foundation's annual report gives the following analysis of grantmaking during the year:

Medical research
The directors continue to demonstrate support for medical research with an aim of ultimately providing a benefit to the public and stipulate all applications in this category must have a high potential of a positive clinical outcome.

Seven grants were awarded in this category totalling £196,500 (2009: £131,300). The most significant was a grant of £45,000 to the University of Nottingham to fund a James Tudor Foundation Research PhD Studentship at the Centre for Hospital Acquired Infection. This grant is payable when the successful applicant is appointed and has not yet been paid [at the time of writing].

The University of Bristol received £37,000 to extend the tenure of a research doctor working in the field of stem cell research. The University of East Anglia received £29,000 to continue research into post capsular opacification. The University of Liverpool received £26,000 for research

THE JAMES TUDOR FOUNDATION

	2005/06	2006/07	2007/08	2008/09	2009/10
Applications received	108	226	386	288	309
No. of ineligible applications	20	63	87	50	53
No. of successful applications	75	36	43	56	63

into cell metastatis. The Brain Research Trust received £20,500 towards epilepsy research. The University of Southampton received £20,000 for research into bladder cancer and Wellbeing for Women received £19,500 for research into womb rupture.

Five payments honouring constructive obligations made in previous periods were made totalling £65,000.

Direct relief of sickness

The relief of sickness is the principal objective of the foundation and the direct relief of sickness is a major classification of grants. The 20 grants approved in this category were the result of careful screening. They represent a broad range of causes, both thematically and geographically. Seven of the grants were for work conducted overseas.

The gross amount awarded in this category was £208,000 (£194,000 net), almost double that granted in the previous year (2009: £104,500).

One award was for a period greater than 1 year; The Cornwall Society for the blind was granted £7,000 to support their hospital helpdesks over 2 years. £3,500 has been paid and a further £3,500 will fall due within 12 months.

One discretionary grant of £2,500 was made to the Red Cross Appeal for Disaster Relief in Pakistan.

The most significant award was a grant of £50,000 to the World Health Organisation. This, second donation to the Human Reproductive Programme was aimed towards the achievement of the Millennium Development Goal of improving maternal health. This award was used for a Stage 2 project in Moldova. Under the guidance of Professor Comendant a national programme for comprehensive abortion care is being put in place in this Eastern European country.

Palliative care

Palliative care is a major area of funding for the foundation. In common with all awards, those made in this category have been tested against the requirement for public benefit. Ten grants (2009: 5) were awarded, all of which demonstrate clear benefits that match the foundation's aims. Furthermore, awards in this category show a wide distribution across the United Kingdom and have not been restricted geographically or by age of ultimate benefactor. The awards covered a spectrum of services.

In the year ended 30 September 2010, £156,000 (2009:£66,500) was awarded to ten grant recipients. The most significant grants were: £41,000 granted to the Tapping House Hospice to match fund a bereavement counselling service; £30,000 granted to the Children's Hospice – South West so

that an addition bed could be opened in the hospice at Wraxall; £17,000 was granted to Help the Hospices for a project to collate, for the first time ever, data on the size and scope of hospices and range of services provided; £15,000 was granted to the Beacon of Hope hospice towards their hospice-at-home services; £15,000 was granted to the Rainbow Hospice to refurbish their bereavement suite; £14,500 was granted to the Princess Alexandra Hospice for triage nursing and £10,000 was granted to Cornwall Hospice Care for lymphoedema training. Three other awards of less than £10,000 were made.

Health education – scholarships and awards

Health Education is a principal theme for the James Tudor Foundation and the directors seek to achieve its aims of contributing to the relief of sickness through the medium of health education. This category attracts a broad spectrum of applications. In this year 9 grants (2009:6) were made totalling £62,500 (2009: £13,000).

Two grants in this category were for periods greater than 1 year. The Anglo-French Medical Society was granted £12,000 as continuity of funding for the annual James Tudor Prize and travel bursaries. £3,000 will fall due within 12 months and £9,000 will fall due at a time greater than 12 months. The Florence Nightingale Foundation was granted £15,000 for student nurse bursaries. £5,000 has been paid, £5,000 will become due within 12 months and £5,000 will fall due at a time greater than 12 months.

One payment honouring a constructive obligation made in a previous period was made totalling £2,600.

Other

The directors recognise that not all applications which contribute to the fulfilment of the foundation's objects neatly fit into one of the previously mentioned categories. It was not intended to restrict applications by applying narrow criteria and therefore this additional category was provided. The inclusion of this category has enabled the directors of the foundation to approve an additional 17 awards in this year.

It is to be expected that proposals in this category cover a wide range of interpretations and uses and, although populous, awards in this category tend to be smaller in magnitude. The average grant in this category was £9,000 whereas the overall average was £11,500.

Seventeen grants were awarded with a net value of £140,500 (2009: £145,000). A grant of £8,500 was approved in favour of Forget-Me-Not but not paid due to changes in the application.

The highest value grant was awarded to Crossroads Caring for Carers South West. This organisation received a two-year grant of £54,000. £27,000 has been paid for first year costs and £27,000 will fall due within 12 months. This award was for an innovative proposal for the provision of support and signposting for carers in the South West of England.

Konnect9, a Leicester-based charity, received a grant of £16,500. This is the fourth occasion that the Foundation has provided support for this exciting and dynamic organisation. £11,500 was granted to Generate who used the money to provide a much-needed healthcare website for people with disabilities. The Chailey Heritage School was granted £10,000 as a contribution to a new multi-sensory room. The Harbour was awarded a two-year grant of £10,000. £5,000 has been paid and £5,000 will fall due within 12 months.

There were 12 grants of less than £10,000 awarded ranging from £30 to £8,000. These awards included £500 for a charity golf event that went on to raise £9,000 for charitable causes in the Bristol area and £8,000 granted to the Meningitis Trust towards core costs.

Three discretionary awards were made totalling £1,000.

Exclusions

The foundation will not accept applications for grants:

- that directly replace, or negatively affect, statutory funding
- for work that has already taken place
- for endowment funds
- for economic, community development or employment use
- for adventure or residential courses, expeditions or overseas travel
- for sport or recreation uses, including festivals
- for environmental, conservation or heritage causes
- for animal welfare
- from applicants who have applied within the last 12 months.

Applications

On an application form available from the foundation's website. Comprehensive guidelines for applicants are also available from there.

Common applicant mistakes

'Common mistakes include: not reading guidelines correctly; not contacting the foundation before requesting funding for equipment; and, confusing us with another charitable trust.'

The Tudor Trust

Welfare, general

£19 million (2010/11)

Beneficial area

UK and sub-Saharan Africa.

7 Ladbroke Grove, London W11 3BD
Tel: 020 7727 8522
Fax: 020 7221 8522
Website: www.tudortrust.org.uk
Correspondent: The Trustees
Trustees: Mary Graves; Helen Dunwell; Desmond Graves; Penelope Buckler; Christopher Graves; Catherine Antcliff; Louise Collins; Elizabeth Crawshaw; Matt Dunwell; James Long; Ben Dunwell; Francis Runacres; Monica Barlow; Vanessa James.
CC Number: 1105580

Information available

Excellent annual report and accounts are available from the trust. The trust's website also includes full, clear guidelines for applicants.

The trust meets a range of both capital and revenue needs for voluntary and community groups. Grants can be of all sizes, very often to be paid over a period of two or three years. There is no maximum or minimum grant amount. The trust supports work which addresses the needs of people at the margins of society – applications will only be considered if they have a strong focus on supporting and empowering disadvantaged people and communities.

Grants for work outside the UK are targeted and proactive, and therefore applications are not sought for this aspect of the trust's work.

Background

The trust was founded in 1955 by Sir Godfrey Mitchell who endowed it with shares in the Wimpey construction company (making this one of the extraordinary number of major trusts with their origins in the building industry) for general charitable purposes.

The trust spends from both income and capital, and has so far maintained its levels of grantmaking despite reductions in both income and, to a greater extent, in the value of its investment portfolio.

The staffing is modest for an organisation spending this amount of money and giving around 340 grants a year. The 'support costs' of the grantmaking activity represent around 5% of the grant total. In part this may be made possible by a substantial degree of voluntary input from trustees. In 2011 trustees and staff reduced the list of areas that the trust cannot fund, they made a decision that they wished to be as open and inclusive as possible and to open the fund's scope even further. During the year, 31% of grants were made to new beneficiaries.

What can be funded

The trust focuses on smaller forward-looking groups, led by capable and committed people. Characteristics that they look for in an organisation include:

▶ organisations working directly with people who are on the margins of society
▶ a focus on building stronger communities by overcoming isolation and fragmentation and encouraging inclusion, connection and integration
▶ organisations which are embedded in and have developed out of their community- whether the local area or a 'community of interest'
▶ high levels of user involvement, and an emphasis on self-help where this is appropriate
▶ work which addresses complex and multi-stranded problems in unusual or imaginative ways
▶ organisations which are thoughtful in their use of resources and which foster community resilience in the face of environmental, economic or social change.

They are more likely to fund groups with an annual turnover of less than £1 million however do sometimes make grants to larger groups, particularly for work which could be influential or which a smaller organisation would not have the capacity to deliver. The trust supports work which is untried and has uncertain outcomes but also recognises the need for sound, practical work which seeks to bring stability and wellbeing into difficult places and situations.

Types of funding

Grants are made in four categories:
▶ core funding
▶ project grants
▶ capital grants
▶ grants to help strengthen an organisation.

The trust may consider making a loan if this could be a helpful solution (one loan was made in 2010/11). There is no maximum or minimum grants and they can be made up to 3 years. They may fund over a longer period which usually involves a re-application.

Grantmaking in 2010/11

In 2010/11 the trust had an income of £7.6 million and assets of £239.8 million. Grants were made to 338 organisations totalling £19 million, with the average amount being £56,000. Grants were distributed into the following areas:

		% of total	
Community	123	35%	£6.6 million
Youth	51	16%	£3 million
Relationships	36	14%	£2.3 million
Criminal justice	23	8%	£1.6 million
Mental health	22	7%	£1.3 million
Housing	28	6%	£1.1 million
Learning	11	4%	£708,000
Overseas	22	4%	£706,000
Older people	10	3%	£526,000
Substance misuse	7	2%	£418,000
Financial security	5	1%	£193,000

The trust's annual report also included the distribution of grants by geographical spread which can be seen in the table on the following page.

In order to tackle deep-rooted problems which can take time, their aim is to commit funding over a sustained period of time. In 2011, 40% of grants were being made over 3 years or via continuous funding.

THE TUDOR TRUST

			% of total	% of UK population	Grant per head
London	55	£2.8 million	14%	12%	£0.38
North West	42	£2.4 million	13%	11%	£0.36
South West	36	£1.9 million	10%	8%	£0.38
Yorkshire and the Humber	28	£1.7 million	9%	9%	£0.35
Wales	17	£1.3 million	7%	5%	£0.45
South East	18	£939,000	5%	14%	£0.12
Scotland	20	£922,000	5%	9%	£0.18
North East	14	£829,000	4%	4%	£0.33
East Midlands	12	£737,000	4%	7%	£0.18
Eastern	12	£730,000	4%	9%	£0.14
West Midlands	10	£507,000	3%	9%	£0.10
Northern Ireland	5	£323,000	2%	3%	£0.19
National/multi-regional	45	£3.1 million	16%	n/a	n/a
Overseas	24	£826,000	4%	n/a	n/a

The trust gives the following information in its annual report:

2011 was a year of continuing economic and social volatility and it is clear that this instability will continue into 2012 and beyond. Voluntary and community organisation are entering unchartered waters and charitable funders will continue to have an important, if necessarily limited, role to play in supporting the sector as it navigates new territory. Tudor's trustees have therefore decided to maintain their grant making at current levels over this financial year, subject of course to close and regular review by the board.

A grant of £1.35 million was made to the Family Centre Trust to finance the construction of a new family and visitors' centre at HMP Wormwood Scrubs. Other beneficiaries included: Bail for Immigration Detainees (£150,000 over 3 years), as continuation funding for this national advice and campaigning charity, based in East London, for people held in immigration detention centres; New Futures Corner House Ltd (£124,000 over 3 years), towards the salary of a therapeutic support worker to work in a new residential home for young women who are at risk of or who have experienced sexual exploitation; A Way Out (£90,000 over 3 years), towards the core running costs for working with vulnerable and hard to reach young people in Stockton on Tees and the Tees Valley; Outside Chance (£90,000 over 3 years), towards the core costs of an organisation working with young people at risk of offending across England; Doncaster CVS (£90,000 over 3 years), for the Give Us A Voice project for Gypsy/Traveller people; Salisbury Trust for the Homeless (£70,000), towards the conversion of a disused almshouse in Salisbury into 12 move-on flats for single homeless people; Centre for Complementary Care, Eskdale (£60,000 over 3 years), towards the running costs of an organisation in Cumbria which provides healing and complementary therapies for local people; Llynfi Valley 11–25 Project (£10,000), towards the running costs of a youth project in Maesteg; Sikh Resource and Community Development Centre (£2,500): as a development grant towards an external consultancy scoping exercise; Heads Together Productions Ltd (£2,100), as development funding to provide peer learning for staff and young volunteers; and Community Rehabilitation & Environmental Protection Programme (£270), to cover additional costs relating to a 2-day capacity building visit to SACDEP in Kenya.

Exclusions

The trust does not make grants to:
- individuals, or organisations applying on behalf of individuals
- larger charities (both national and local) enjoying widespread support
- statutory bodies
- hospitals, health authorities or hospices
- medical care, medical equipment or medical research
- universities, colleges or schools
- academic research, scholarships or bursaries
- nurseries, playgroups or creches
- one-off holidays, residentials, trips, exhibitions, conferences, events etc
- animal charities
- the promotion of religion
- the restoration or conservation of buildings or habitats (where there isn't a strong social welfare focus)
- work outside the UK. The trust runs a targeted grants programme promoting sustainable agriculture in sub-Saharan Africa. They do not consider unsolicited proposals from groups working overseas
- endowment appeals
- work that has already taken place.

Applicants are encouraged to call the information team for advice concerning applications.

Applications

The following information on the two-stage application process is available on the trust's website:

The first-stage proposal

A first-stage proposal must include:
1. An introductory letter, of no more than one side of A4, on your organisation's letterhead.
2. A completed organisation details sheet [available from the trust's website].
3. Your answers to the following questions, on no more than two sides of A4:
   - What difference do you want to make, and how will your organisation achieve this?
   - Why are you the right people to do this work?
   - Tell us about the people you are working with, and how you know there is a need for your work.
   - How would you use funding from Tudor?
4. A copy of your most recent annual accounts, and annual report if you produce one. If your organisation is too new to have annual accounts please send a photocopy of a recent bank statement instead. Please don't send any other supporting documents.

Address the proposal to 'The Trustees' and send it via post. Proposals should be acknowledged within a few days of it being received. It will then go through an assessment process which involves trustees and staff. The trust aims to let applicants know within a month whether or not they will be invited to make a second-stage application.

The second-stage application

Applicants who are successful at the first stage proposal will be sent more information about the second-stage proposal process. A member of the trust's staff will be designated as the applicants grants manager in order to develop the application and manage the grant, if it is made. This stage may involve a detailed 'phone conversation or a visit. Trustees and staff meet every

3 weeks to consider applications and it usually takes around 3 months for an applicant to receive a final decision at this stage.

Any interested applicants should refer to the trust's very comprehensive website which outlines in detail all stages of the grantmaking process. This trust has an extremely good track record for applications, with 100 % of applicants thinking that the application process was good or excellent, including those who had been unsuccessful.

Common applicant mistakes

'Not sending all info we ask for; not relating their application to what they say we are looking for; and, not providing any financial information or a sense of the scale of their work.'

The Douglas Turner Trust

General

£409,500 (2009/10)

Beneficial area

UK and overseas; however, in practice, there is a strong preference for Birmingham and the West Midlands.

3 Poplar Piece, Inkberrow, Worcester WR7 4JD
Tel: 01386 792014
Email: timpatrickson@hotmail.co.uk
Correspondent: Tim J Patrickson, Trust Administrator
Trustees: John M Del Mar, Chair; James M G Fea; Peter J Millward; David P Pearson; Stephen L Preedy.
CC Number: 227892

Information available

Accounts were available at the Charity Commission.

The trust was established in 1964 by Douglas Turner, a West Midlands industrialist who died in 1977. Grants are made to registered charities, mainly in the West Midlands, and around 53% by value of the grants awarded in 2009/10 were made to charities that are supported on an annual basis. These beneficiaries are visited every other year by the administrator and must satisfy the

trustees of the need for continuing their support. Most of these charities are situated in, or working in, the West Midlands. The remaining grants are awarded to charities, principally in the same geographical area, many of which are seeking funds for single projects. The trustees also give consideration to national appeals, especially where these can show a local application, and to overseas appeals.

In 2009/10 the trust had assets of £14.1 million and an income of £351,000. Grants were made to 113 organisations totalling £409,500, broken down as follows:

Youth and children	£93,000
Disabled people and health	£72,500
Work in the community	£67,000
Older people	£52,000
The arts	£39,000
Hospices	£32,000
International aid	£20,500
Social Support	£16,000
Environment and heritage	£9,000
Medical research	£9,000

In addition to the above, a residential property with the value of £215,000 was donated to the R D Turner Charitable Trust, a connected charity.

The only beneficiaries listed in the 2009/10 accounts were to connected charities; these were: St Mary's Hospice Ltd (£17,000); Birmingham Boys' & Girls' Union (£10,000); and Multiple Births Foundation (£5,000).

Previous beneficiaries included: 870 House Youth Movement; Gingerbread; Listening Books; Dial Walsall; Compton Hospice; Gracewell Homes Foster Trust; Cotteridge Church Day Centre; Busoga Trust; Birmingham Botanical Gardens; Midlands Actors' Theatre; and Action Medical Research.

Exclusions

No grants to individuals or non-registered charities.

Applications

In writing to the correspondent, 'on applicant letterhead, two pages or less, and preferably not stapled together', with a copy of the latest annual report and accounts. There are no application forms. The trustees usually meet in February, May, August and December to consider applications, which should be submitted in the month prior to each

meeting. Telephone enquiries may be made before submitting an appeal.

Community Foundation Serving Tyne and Wear and Northumberland

Social welfare, general

£4.8 million (2010/11)

Beneficial area

Tyne and Wear and Northumberland.

Cale Cross, 156 Pilgrim Street, Newcastle upon Tyne NE1 6SU
Tel: 0191 222 0945
Fax: 0191 230 0689
Email: grants@ communityfoundation.org.uk
Website: www. communityfoundation.org.uk
Correspondent: The Grants Team
Trustees: Ashley Winter, Chair; Prof Chris Drinkwater; Colin Seccombe; John Clough; Alastair Conn; Roger Kelly; Gev Pringle; Fiona Cruickshank; Betty Weallans; Kate Roe; Sue Winfield; Jamie Martin; Jo Curry; Charles Harvey; Dean T Huggins;
CC Number: 700510

Information available

Accounts were on file at the Charity Commission. Further information was taken from the foundation's excellent website.

General

Established in 1988, the Community Foundation Serving Tyne and Wear and Northumberland is one of the largest community foundations in the UK. Its helpful website contains comprehensive information on all of its activities and the programmes from which grants are available.

Funds are set up by individuals, families and companies to help donors support their chosen interests. The Community Foundation manages over 200 such funds with most grants being for under £5,000 and for one off costs.

The majority of grants are made to groups, many of which are small and volunteer led, but the trust also funds larger organisations seeking smaller grants to support particular activities or developments. Applicants do not have to be registered charities but must be undertaking charitable work. Occasionally 'Trademark Grants' are made which are larger awards combining contributions from different funds. Some funds do support individuals.

Grants can be made for most types of community activity or projects. In the past support has been given to:

- projects run by and for disabled people
- community groups
- children and Young Peoples' groups
- projects run by and for people from minority ethnic communities
- sports groups
- older peoples' groups
- environmental projects
- arts projects
- training
- women's groups.

Grant programmes

As these funds can open and close to applications regularly it is advised that potential applicants check the community foundation's website for the most recent information. The following are currently detailed on the foundation's website:

General Community Foundation grants

These can be applied to using the general online application process.

Northumberland High Sheriff

Established to give awards to community groups that encourage useful and beneficial pursuits for young people aged 10–25, helping them to be upstanding citizens and steer them away from crime and anti-social behaviour. There is an annual awards ceremony.

Northumberland Group Fund

Provides grants of up to £1,000 to individuals aged 16–25, residing in Northumberland who are accessing employment, a vocational training course or a further educational college course in Northumberland for the first time and who need funding for training fees, materials or equipment to enable them to take up the opportunity.

Sammy Johnson Memorial Fund

Established by actors Tim Healy and Jimmy Nail in memory of their friend and colleague Sammy Johnson with whom they appeared in Auf Wiedersehen Pet. The biennial Sunday for Sammy concerts feature local, national and international music, comedy and acting stars, raising money to support talented performers from the region.

Young Musicians Fund/ Alan Hull Award

Established in 1996 by Kathryn Tickell to develop the musical skills of children and young people in Tyne & Wear, Northumberland and Durham under the age of 18 who are struggling to pay for tuition fees or want help to purchase an instrument.

Brian Roycroft Fund

Established to mark the retirement of the late Brian Roycroft, former Social Services Director in Newcastle, to help young people who have been in local authority care who are entering adult life.

Dulverton Trust Fund

Grants of £500–£5,000 are available to community and voluntary groups with an annual income under £200,000 in Northumberland, Tyne & Wear, County Durham and Tees Valley that provide youth opportunities; address disadvantage and improve the natural and built environment. This can be applied to via the standard Community Foundation form, as long as applicants mention the Dulverton Trust Fund.

Surviving Winter

Working with National Energy Action to bring people out of fuel poverty. Community and voluntary groups will also benefit from a hardship grant that can be distributed to individuals.

Fogo Grassroots Fund

Applications for up to £5,000 are being invited to support community development in disadvantaged areas of Newcastle.

Survive to Thrive

A new fund to support voluntary and community organisations that are facing reductions in public funding that threatens their useful existence.

John D Fund

For community and voluntary groups that encourage young people to achieve and raise their aspirations. Grants of up to £2,500 are available.

European Social Fund Community Grants

Provides grants of up to £12,000 to small, third sector voluntary and community organisations to engage with local communities to deliver a range of skills and employment support to enable people from the hardest to reach communities, experiencing multiple disadvantages to make progress towards the labour market.

Grantmaking in 2010/11

In 2010/11 the trust had assets of £50.8 million, an income of £6.7 million and made grants totalling £4.8 million, given in 1,600 grants broken down as follows:

Charities and voluntary organisations	1,389	£4.7 million
Individuals	214	£110,000

Grants were distributed in the following categories:

Community Foundation Funds	1,198	£3.2 million
Henry Smith Charity	30	£693,000
Grassroots Grants	335	£636,000
Fair Share	7	£190,000
Active at 60	13	£36,500

The annual report states:

The majority of grants continued to be for amounts of under £5,000 and to provide practical support for small voluntary and community groups [...] The Community Foundation works with outreach partners to ensure that grants are available to new and grass roots projects. There was a slight increase in the value of grants made from Community Foundation funds during the year and this figure includes an exceptional grant of £446,000 made to the Stuart Halbert Foundation.

There continued to be good levels of new donations during the year, with six new endowment funds established including 2 new acorn funds [...] In addition to new funds, a number of other endowment funds saw additional gifts [...and] there were seven new revenue funds.

Exclusions

Grants are not normally given for:

- non charitable activities
- sponsorship and fundraising events
- small contributions to major appeals
- large capital projects

- endowments, loan repayments or for activities bought or ordered before the foundation makes a grant
- grants which will be used to make grants to a third party
- political activities
- acts of religious worship
- work which could be funded by health and local authorities or government grant aid
- work which only benefits animals.

Exceptions may be made to this at the request of the donors.

Applications

There is one application form for the general Community Foundation grants and generally, separate forms for the other rolling grants programmes and one-off funds. All of these plus application guidelines are available on the website under the 'apply' section.

Some of the programmes have deadlines and some do not; also, programmes change regularly so the trust's website should be checked for the most recent information.

If a grant is approved, there are terms and conditions that must be adhered to and a project report to be submitted.

Trustees of Tzedakah

Jewish charities, welfare

Around £450,000

Beneficial area

Worldwide, in practice mainly UK and Israel.

Brentmead House, Britannia Road, London N12 9RU
Tel: 020 8446 6767
Correspondent: Michael Lebrett
Trustee: Trustees of Tzedakah Ltd.
CC Number: 251897

Information available

Limited information was available from the Charity Commission.

The objectives of this trust are the relief of poverty; advancement of education; advancement of religion;

and general charitable purposes. The trust makes over 300 grants to organisations in a year ranging from around £25 to £35,000.

The charity has an income of around £500,000 each year, most of which is usually given in grants. Up-to-date information is usually unavailable as accounts are consistently filed late with the Charity Commission.

Previous beneficiaries include: Hasmonean High School Charitable Trust; Gertner Charitable Trust; Society of Friends of the Torah; Hendon Adath Yisroel Synagogue; Medrash Shmuel Theological College; Torah Temimoh; Willow Foundation; Tifferes Girls' School; Sage Home for the Aged; Wizo; and Torah Movement of Great Britain.

Exclusions

Grants only to registered charities. No grants to individuals.

Applications

This trust states that it does not respond to unsolicited applications.

The Underwood Trust

General charitable purposes, in particular, medicine and health, social welfare, education, arts, environment and wildlife

£4.7 million (2009/10)

Beneficial area

Worldwide. In practice UK with a preference for Scotland and Wiltshire.

Fourth Floor South, 35 Portman Square, London W1H 6LR
Tel: 020 7486 0100
Website: www.theunderwoodtrust.org.uk
Correspondent: Antony P Cox, Trust Manager
Trustees: Robin Clark, Chair; Jack C Taylor; Briony Wilson.
CC Number: 266164

Information available

Accounts were available at the Charity Commission.

The Underwood Trust was established in 1973. The name derives from Underwood Lane, Paisley, Scotland, which was the childhood home of one of the founders. It currently supports registered charities and other charitable organisations which benefit society nationally and locally in Scotland and Wiltshire.

The general aims of the trust are to cover a wide spectrum of activities so as to benefit as many charitable causes as possible and to make donations to organisations where its contribution really can be seen to make a difference. The trust does not wish to be the principal funder of a charity and medium sized bodies are more likely to receive grants than either very small charities or well known large national ones.

Grants are categorised under the following headings:
- medicine and health
- social welfare
- education and the arts
- environment and wildlife.

The allocation between these headings varies from year to year. Currently the specific interests are the environment and welfare, specifically, crime prevention, victim support and the re-education of offenders.

In 2009/10 the trust had assets of £32.2 million and an income of £586,000. A total of 41 grants were paid amounting to £4.7 million. The trust provides the following summary of grantmaking during the year in its annual report:

Medicine and Health
The trust made a special donation of £1.2 million from the expendable endowment to endow the Underwood Trust Chair for Language and Communication Impairment at The University of the West of England. This follows on from the support for the Speech & Language Therapy Research Unit at Frenchay Hospital in Bristol given by the trust over many years. Indeed a final donation of £93,000 was made to the unit during the year.

Other large donations in this category included £100,000 given to the Shooting Star Children's Hospice and two donations totalling £65,000 given to the Living Paintings Trust. A donation of £25,000 was made to the

Accord Hospice in Paisley in memory of the late Andrew Woods, who served as one of their trustees and was formerly employed by Taylor Clark Limited. Four other donations totalling £60,000 were made.

Education and the Arts

Three special large donations were given in this category to the Royal Scottish Academy Of Music and Drama in Glasgow of £1 million to fund scholarships for Scottish students, £1 million to the Glyndebourne Arts Trust as a major donation to their New Generations Programme and £500,000 to endow the annual music competition of the Royal Over-Seas League.

Other donations included two donations to the Chamber Orchestra of Europe, £50,000 of which was to fund their Academy programme and £25,000 given to Stage One to give bursaries to trainee theatre producers. Four other donations were made totalling £47,000.

Social Welfare

The largest donation was £85,500 to Restorative Solutions for their Restorative Approaches in Neighbourhoods scheme, being the third contribution towards this project. This helps the expansion of this project which aims to arrange structured meetings between perpetrators and victims of crime. Initial studies show this can significantly reduce re-offending rates and can be a very cost effective approach to reducing crime.

The trust gave £50,000 towards the CEOP programme of the NSPCC and £44,000 to Prisoners Abroad. Eight other donations totalling £106,000 were made. Most of these were for £15,000 to charities where the trust has given long term support.

The Environment and Wildlife

The two largest donations in this category were £50,000 to the Wiltshire Wildlife Trust for work to combat litter, and £50,000 to the Friends of the Earth Trust to assist with their campaign leading up to the Copenhagen Climate Change Conference in December 2009. The former was in addition to regular core funding donations. Other major donations included £30,000 to the Wilts & Berks Canal Trust as a contribution towards a canal officer post, £25,000 to the Greenpeace Environmental Trust towards their anti-whaling work, and £25,000 to Wildscreen for their ARKive educational website. Five other donations, each of £15,000 were made during the year.

Exclusions

No grants are given to:

- individuals directly
- political activities
- commercial ventures or publications
- the purchase of vehicles including minibuses
- overseas travel, holidays or expeditions
- retrospective grants or loans
- direct replacement of statutory funding or activities that are primarily the responsibility of central or local government
- large capital, endowment or widely distributed appeals.

Applications

Do not apply to the trust unless invited to do so.

The trust's website states that:

Due to the current economic situation and the reduction in interest rates our income has been greatly reduced. As such there are currently no free funds in the trust and therefore THE TRUST IS UNABLE TO ACCEPT UNSOLICITED APPLICATIONS. This position is expected to continue for the foreseeable future, but any changes to this will be posted on [its] website at the time.

Please note: the trust is unable to deal with telephone or email enquiries about an application.

UnLtd (Foundation for Social Entrepreneurs)

Social enterprise

£3.8 million to social entrepreneurs (2010/11)

Beneficial area

UK.

123 Whitecross Street, Islington, London EC1Y 8JJ
Tel: 020 7566 1100
Fax: 020 7566 1101
Email: info@unltd.org.uk
Website: www.unltd.org.uk
Correspondent: Raymond Tran, Director of Finance, IT and Human Resources
Trustees: Rich Benton, Chair; John Brown; Norman Cumming; Anthony Freeling; Rodney Stares; Alastair Wilson; Martin Wyn Griffith; Richard Tyrie; Rajeeb Dey; Natalie Campbell; Andrew Croft; Dr Alison Fielding; Judith McNeill.

CC Number: 1090393

Information available

Accounts were available form the Charity Commission. The foundation has a detailed and informative website.

Summary

UnLtd is unique here in that it exists to make grants to individuals to undertake social initiatives. In effect it makes grants for the start-up costs of new organisations and community groups to enterprising individuals who need support to implement their ideas and projects for improving their communities.

It was established in 2000 by seven partner organisations: Ashoka (since resigned), Changemakers, Comic Relief, Community Action Network, Scarman Trust, School for Social Entrepreneurs and Senscot. In 2003 the Millennium Commission invested £100 million in the organisation after a competitive process in which UnLtd was successful.

Its prime objective is to distribute Millennium Awards to social entrepreneurs. These awards are funded by the income generated from the endowment which is held by the Millennium Awards Trust of which UnLtd is the sole trustee. Award winners receive a complete, tailored package of money, training and advice at every stage of their project. Networking opportunities are also provided by UnLtd, along with intensive business support and mentoring to the most promising social entrepreneurs.

The foundation also manages several other schemes, including the UnLtd 4ip Awards and the UnLtd Sport Relief Awards. Further information on the different schemes can be found on the foundation's website.

UnLtd awards are for people:

- over the age of 16
- living in the UK
- who are applying as an individual or informal group
- who want to run projects that: benefit the public or a community in the UK, need an UnLtd award to ensure its success, offer a learning opportunity for the applicant(s), are a new initiative.

A short eligibility questionnaire is available on the foundation's website.

Grants in 2010/11

In 2010/11 the foundation had assets of £2.3 million and an income of £8.8 million. (The initial investment of £100 million from the Millennium Commission was allocated under 'group assets' and is used to generate income for UnLtd. In 2008/09 the value had fallen to £88.5 million; in 2009/10 it had increased to £111.6 million; in 2010/11 the value stood at £113.5 million.)

Grants were made under Millennium Trust Awards totalling almost £3.8 million, and were distributed as follows:

Level 0	0	–
Level 1	1,265	£2.9 million
Level 2	76	£832,000
Level 3	3	£60,000

A comprehensive analysis of the activities and achievements of the foundation can be found in the latest annual report.

Applications

Applicants are advised to read the guidelines on its website carefully to check that they meet the criteria and then contact the nearest UnLtd office (see below) to discuss their ideas.

Regional offices

Head office/London office: 123 Whitecross Street, Islington, London EC1Y 8JJ. Telephone: 020 7566 1100; Fax: 020 7566 1101/1139; Email: info@unltd.org.uk.

Birmingham office: Unit G2, The Ground Floor, The Arch, 48–52 Floodgate Street, Birmingham B5 5SL. Telephone: 0121 766 4570.

Bradford office: 15 Halfield Road, Bradford BD1 3RP. Telephone: 01274 750630.

Northern Ireland office: Room 55–57, Scottish Mutual Building, 16 Donegal Square South, Belfast BT1 5JG. Telephone: 028 9024 4007.

Scotland UnLtd office (Glasgow): Tobacco Merchants House, 42 Miller Street, Glasgow G1 1TD. Telephone: 0141 221 2322.

Scotland UnLtd office (Edinburgh): Cornerstone House, 2 Melville Street, Edinburgh EH3 7NS. Telephone: 0131 226 7333.

Wales office: Fourth Floor, Baltic House, Mount Stuart Square, Cardiff CF10 5FH. Telephone: 029 2048 4811.

The Michael Uren Foundation

General

£880,000 (2009/10)

Beneficial area

UK.

Haysmacintyre, Fairfax House, 15 Fulwood Place, London WC1V 6AY
Email: agregory-jones@haysmacintyre.com
Correspondent: Anne Gregory-Jones, Trustee
Trustees: Michael Uren; Anne Gregory-Jones; Janis Bennett; Alastair McDonald.
CC Number: 1094102

Information available

Accounts were available at the Charity Commission.

The foundation was established in 2002 with general charitable purposes following an initial gift from Michael Uren.

'The trustees are particularly keen on making grants for specific large projects. This could mean that, to satisfy this objective, no significant grants are paid in one year. With the resultant reserves retained a large grant could be made in the following year.'

In 2009/10 the foundation had assets of £60.1 million and an income of £3.3 million, which included a donation of £1.8 million from the settlor. Grants were made to seven organisations during the year totalling £880,000.

The largest beneficiary during the year was King Edward VII Hospital in Marylebone, which received £570,000 for the new Michael Uren Critical Care Unit. The other beneficiaries were: The City of London Royal Fusiliers Volunteers Trust (£125,000); UK Trust for Nature Conservation in Nepal (£75,000); International Animal Rescue (£50,000); Friends of St Mary's Kenardington (£30,000);

Magdalen and Lasher Trust (£20,000); and Street Child of Sierra Leone (£10,000).

Applications

In writing to the correspondent.

The Vail Foundation

General, Jewish

£2 million (2009/10)

Beneficial area

UK and overseas.

5 Fitzhardinge Street, London W1H 6ED
Tel: 020 7317 3000
Correspondent: Michael S Bradfield, Trustee
Trustees: Michael S Bradfield; Paul Brett; Michael H Goldstein.
CC Number: 1089579

Information available

Accounts were available at the Charity Commission.

This foundation was set up in 2001. 'The trustees receive applications for donations from a wide variety of charitable institutions including those engaged in medical ancillary services (including medical research), education, helping the disabled and old aged, relieving poverty, providing sheltered accommodation, developing the arts etc.'

In 2009/10 the foundation had assets of £9.2 million and an income of £282,500. There were 69 grants made to organisations totalling £2 million.

As in previous years, the organisations receiving the largest grants were: Jewish Care (£575,000 in 3 grants); KKL Charity Limited (£470,000 in 5 grants); United Jewish Israel Appeal (£150,000); London School of Jewish Studies (£125,000); and the Jewish Community Secondary School (£100,000).

Other beneficiaries included: Project Seed (£50,000); Jewish Learning Exchange (£30,000); UNICEF UK (£25,000); Anne Frank Trust (£15,000); Jewish Leadership Council (£10,000); Langdon Foundation and the Old Vic Theatre Trust 2000

£5,000 each); and the Roundhouse Trust and the Jewish Volunteering Network (£1,000 each).

Applications

In writing to the correspondent. 'The trustees consider all requests which they receive and make such donations as they feel appropriate.'

The Valentine Charitable Trust

Welfare, the environment and overseas aid

£807,000 (2009/10)

Beneficial area

Unrestricted, but mainly Dorset, UK.

Preston Redman LLP, Hinton House, Hinton Road, Bournemouth, Dorset BH1 2EN

Tel: 01202 292424
Fax: 01202 552758
Email: valentine@prestonredman.co.uk
Correspondent: Douglas J E Neville-Jones, Trustee
Trustees: Douglas J E Neville-Jones; Roger A Gregory; Mrs Shiela F Cox; Mrs Susan Patterson; Mrs Patricia B N Walker; Peter Leatherdale; Mrs Diana Tory; Donald Jack.
CC Number: 1001782

Information available

Accounts were available at the Charity Commission.

The trust was founded by the late Miss Ann Cotton in 1990. The trust was established for general charitable purposes but in particular for the provision of amenities and facilities for the benefit of the public, the protection and safeguarding of the countryside and wildlife and the control and reduction of pollution. Miss Cotton lived most of her life in Dorset and involvement in local projects appealed to her. The present trustees do not set a limit on what they consider to be local, but when dealing with charities with limited areas of interest, they will be likely to give preference to those which operate in Dorset.

The trust offers an interesting and informative insight into its grantmaking policy and the wishes of the trust's settlor in its annual report, which is reproduced here:

Grants to local charities

Miss Cotton lived most f her life in Dorset, first at Broadstone and latterly at Canford Cliffs in Poole. Involvement in local projects appealed to her as she demonstrated while she was a trustee of the charity. The trustees do not propose to set a physical limit on what they consider to be local but when dealing with charities with a limited area of interest, they will be likely to give preference to those which operate in Dorset.

The trustees also consider making grants to charities which, while not based in the local area, operate there.

Grants to charities which have traditionally received small grants

Over the years the charity has been in the habit of making relatively small grants to a number of charities on a regular basis. Many of these originated in Miss Cotton's time or are a direct reflection of her thoughts. The trustees propose to continue these subject to appropriate review at the time each is considered to be repeated. The trustees do however appreciate that circumstances change so the mere fact that a charity has received grants on a regular basis in the past does not mean there is an automatic decision to continue to do so.

Grants to objects in other parts of the world

The charity under Miss Cotton's influence developed the tradition of making relatively large donations to help in areas of the world devastated by natural or other disasters. These have normally been made through organisations, such as the British Red Cross and UNICEF, which are involved in huge scale aid programmes in such areas.

In addition the charity has supported a small number of initiatives in the third and developing world. The trustees particularly like to look for projects which offer sustainability to local communities.

Grants to one-off appeals

There are regularly one-off appeals to provide funding for specific projects the trustees have regularly made donations to such appeals where they are for local facilities. However the trustees are not keen on village halls or the fabric of church buildings.

Grants for medical research and hospitals

The charity has made regular donations in these areas but, as a matter of policy, the trustees look for guarantees that any donations the charity makes to bodies or objects related to the NHS are projects or equipment which have no likelihood or being provided out of central funds in the foreseeable future.

Grants for core funding

One of the themes of comments made to trustees by applicants concerns the problems of raising core funding. Apparently many grant-making trusts avoid providing core funding. The trustees appreciate that a one-off appeal for a particular project may be much more appealing than a general request for funds just to keep a charity functioning. They therefore make regular donations to the core funding of charities. However this is always subject to review. The trustees do occasionally make it clear that such funding is only for a set period of time but in many cases they are prepared to consider such funding on an indefinite basis. They take the view that if it has been right to support a particular charity once then, unless something changes, that motive can be followed continuously.

Matched funding and pledges

The trustees regularly use the device of offering funding to a project conditional upon the applicant raising other funds before the donation will be forthcoming. Similarly offers of donations are sometimes made on the basis that they will only be made once the project actually proceeds. All such offers are subject to review up until the time they are actually made.

Social investment funding

Following Miss Cotton's death the charity's assets were invested in a very narrow range of investments. To assist with diversification the trustees developed what they term social investment funding. This involves either the purchase of premises which are then leased to an operating charity for its use, the lease is usually at a modest or nominal rent and for a relatively limited term, or the provision of a loan with an interest rate of between 0% and base rate to an operating charity to allow it to acquire property.

In 2009/10 the trust had assets of £25.1 million and an income of £830,000. Grants were made to 141 organisations totalling £807,000.

Beneficiaries during the year included: Special Boat Service Association (£25,000); Wessex Autistic Society (£20,000); Bournemouth Symphony Orchestra (£15,000); Disability & Development Partners (£11,000); Action on Addiction, Combat Stress and Victoria Education Centre & Sports College (£10,000 each); Rainbow Trust (£7,000); Brainwave Centre (£6,000); British Liver Trust, Dorset

MS Therapy Centre and the Jubilee Sailing Trust (£5,000 each); Bournemouth Town Centre Detached Youth and Live Music Now (£4,000 each); Breakthrough Breast Cancer and MOVE Europe (£3,000 each); Donald Woods Foundation (£2,000); and Self Help Africa and Farming & Wildlife Advisory Group (£1,000 each).

Exclusions

No grants to individuals. The trust would not normally fund appeals for village halls or the fabric of church buildings.

Applications

In writing to the correspondent. The trust provides the following insight into its application process in its annual report:

All applications will be acknowledged with standard letters, even those that are not appropriate for receiving a grant. This responsibility is delegated to Douglas J E Neville-Jones who then provides a report to the next trustees' meeting.

The following general comments summarise some of the considerations the trustees seek to apply when considering applications for funding.

The trustees look for value for money. While this concept is difficult to apply in a voluntary sector it can certainly be used on a comparative basis and subjectively. If the trustees have competing applications they will usually decide to support just one of them as they believe that to concentrate the charity's donations is more beneficial than to dilute them.

Regular contact with the charities to which donations are made is considered essential. Reports and accounts are also requested from charities which are supported and the trustees consider those at their meetings.

The trustees take great comfort from the fact that they employ the policy of only making donations to other charities or similar bodies. However they are not complacent about the need to review all donations made and the objects to which those have been given.

The trustees are conscious that, particularly with the smaller and local charities, the community of those working for and with the charity is an important consideration.

The trustees regularly review the classifications to which donations have been made so that they can obtain an overview of the charity's donations and assess whether their policies are being implemented in practice. They are conscious that when dealing with individual donations it is easy to lose sight of the overall picture.

John and Lucille van Geest Foundation

Medical research, healthcare, general

£781,000 (2009/10)

Beneficial area

UK, with some interest in south Lincolnshire and adjoining areas; occasionally overseas.

108 Pinchbeck Road, Spalding, Lincolnshire PE11 1QL
Email: trustees@ johnandlucillevangeestfoundation.org
Website: johnandlucillevangeestfoundation.org
Correspondent: Brenda Ruysen, Clerk to the Trustees
Trustees: Hilary P Marlowe; Stuart R Coltman; Tonie Gibson.
CC Number: 1001279

Information available

Accounts were available at the Charity Commission.

The foundation was founded by the late John van Geest and his wife, the late Lucille van Geest in 1990. John van Geest founded Geest Plc, producer and distributor of fresh chilled foods to the UK and Western Europe.

The objects of the foundation are general charitable purposes but the grant making policy is for grants usually to be awarded for the purpose of medical research and for welfare purposes.

Grants for the purpose of medical research are directed towards research into:

▸ brain damage e.g. Alzheimer's disease, Huntington's disease, Parkinson's disease and strokes
▸ cancer
▸ heart disease
▸ lung disease
▸ sight and/or hearing loss.

The trust has recently stated:

It is the trustees' intention that for the foreseeable future grants for medical research purposes shall be made in the main direct to a limited number of selected research establishments involved in one or another of such areas of research. It should be noted that the trustees already have in place a grant expenditure programme for cancer research for the years 2008 – 2012 (inclusive).

Grants for welfare purposes are directed towards people in need through illness, infirmity or social circumstances and in particular the welfare of older people and of children resident in South Lincolnshire and adjoining areas who:

▸ suffer from brain damage/mental illness
▸ suffer from cancer
▸ suffer from heart disease
▸ suffer from lung disease
▸ suffer from sight and/or hearing loss
▸ suffer from disfigurement through injury
▸ are physically disabled
▸ are bedridden
▸ are terminally ill
▸ are at risk.

Grants are also occasionally made towards victims of natural disasters and man-made disasters.

The trustees' aim is that approximately 75% of grant expenditure will be for the purpose of medical research (with grants, where possible, being made direct to the research establishment) and 25% of grant expenditure will be for welfare purposes (with the emphasis being on grants to locally based charitable institutions with minimal overheads).

In 2009/10 the foundation had assets of £31.5 million and an income of £831,000. Grants were made to 22 organisations totalling £5.7 million.

The major beneficiary during the year was Nottingham Trent University, which received a total of £4.9 million comprising of a capital grant and instalments of a five-year grant for a cancer research programme. Excluding this substantial donation, grants totalled just over £781,000.

Other beneficiaries included: Royal National Institute for Deaf People (£247,500); University of Leicester (£134,000); University of Cambridge

Brain Repair Centre (£112,000); Lincolnshire & Nottinghamshire Air Ambulance (£24,000); East Anglia Children's Hospice (£20,000); British Heart Foundation (£15,000); St Barnabas Hospice Trust (£12,000); Action for Children (£10,000); Headway Cambridgeshire (£5,000); and the Dystonia Society (£2,000).

Exclusions
No grants to individuals.

Applications
In writing to the correspondent. Please note that only charities engaged in areas of work to which the trust's policy extends are considered (and in the case of healthcare grants, only charities providing services in South Lincolnshire and adjoining area). Telephone calls are not welcome. The trustees meet two to three times a year to consider applications, but there are no set dates. Every applicant will receive a reply.

Common applicant mistakes
'The most common error is applying for a welfare grant for projects operating outside the foundation's stated geographic area of benefit.'

The Vardy Foundation

Christian causes, education in the north east of England, general

£1.54 million to organisations (2009/10)

Beneficial area
UK with a preference for north east England, overseas.

Venture House, Aykley Heads, Durham DH1 5TS
Tel: 0191 374 4727
Email: foundation@regvardy.com
Website: vardyfoundation.com
Correspondent: Victoria Spencer
Trustees: Sir Peter Vardy; Lady Margaret Barr Vardy; Peter D D Vardy; Richard Vardy.

CC Number: 328415

Information available
Accounts were available from the Charity Commission. The foundation also has a clear and simple website.

The foundation was set up in 1989 with general charitable objectives. It makes grants to registered charities, social enterprises and individuals, and also considers the payment of vehicle leasing costs and other expenses to third parties where these services can be obtained at better rates through the foundation than would be available to the beneficiaries themselves. Sir Peter Vardy made his fortune in the motor retail business through his company, Reg Vardy plc, founded by his father.

> One of the major activities [of the foundation] is the establishment of secondary schools (11–18 yrs), providing an education with a distinctly Christian ethos. The Emmanuel Schools Foundation [which will receive future support from the Vardy Foundation] currently runs 3 schools with a fourth under construction. The goal is to have 10,000 children educated to the highest possible standards making a significant impact not only on the students, but also on the parents and the wider community.
>
> The schools are among the top performing in the UK with children, coming from disadvantaged backgrounds, achieving outstanding success.
>
> The foundation also supports initiatives in other countries, principally Africa. In Zambia the foundation has funded a Hydro Electric plant which was switched on in July 2007.
>
> The foundation has helped hundreds of projects large and small both in the UK and worldwide. It looks for people who are doing tremendous and very worthwhile projects and seeks to support them. Support is invariably financial but management expertise is also called on in many instances.

In 2009/10 the foundation had assets of £22 million and an income of £907,000. Grants were made totalling £1.65 million, of which £1.54 million was distributed to 86 organisations and £112,500 to 45 individuals.

Grants were categorised as follows:

Religion	59	£769,000
Welfare	32	£423,000
Education	20	£277,000
Arts	6	£97,500

The largest beneficiaries during the year, listed in the accounts, were:

Thana Trust (£200,000); Youth for Christ (£144,000); Bede Academy (£140,000); The Message Trust (£112,500); and the University of Sunderland (£100,000).

Exclusions
The foundation will not fund:

- applications for more than a 3 year commitment
- animal welfare projects
- health related charities
- projects normally provided by central or local government
- individuals (including requests for educational support costs) (NB: the foundation does award grants to individuals, however these are likely to already be connected to the foundation or one of the educational institutions that receive funding from the foundation
- projects that do not demonstrate an element of self funding or other funding
- contribute to an organisation's healthy reserves or endowments.

Applications
Please note that as of 1 July 2011 the foundation is undertaking an internal review of its activities and **will not** be accepting any funding applications until further notice.

The Variety Club Children's Charity

Children's charities

£4 million to organisations (2010)

Beneficial area
UK.

Variety Club House, 93 Bayham Street, London NW1 0AG
Tel: 020 7428 8100
Email: grants@varietyclub.org.uk
Website: www.varietyclub.org.uk
Correspondent: Stanley Salter
Trustees: Kenneth R Mustoe; Keith Andrews; John E Barnett; Gary Beckwith; Anthony Blackburn; Malcolm Brenner; Laurence Davis; Alan Fraser; Lionel Rosenblatt; John Sachs; Jonathan Shalit; Pamela

Sinclair; Anne Wadsworth; Norman Kaphan; Russell Kahn; Ronnie Nathan; Anthony Harris; Stephen Crown; Jarvis Astaire; Tony Hatch; Nicholas Shattock; Ronald Sinclair; Richard Freeman; Grant Lewis; Lloyd Barr; Philip Burley; Robert Beecham; Stanley Salter; Joseph Williams.

CC Number: 209259

Information available

Accounts were available at the Charity Commission.

Summary

Variety Club Children's Charity aims to improve the lives of children and young people who are disabled and disadvantaged throughout the UK through a variety of inspirational programmes. Our vision is that every child or young person who is disabled or disadvantaged should be given the hope, independence and mobility to reach their full potential.

The charity raises money and then provides Sunshine Coaches, mobility aids or general grants to help those:

》 with mental, physical or sensory disabilities;
》 with behavioural or psychological disturbances;
》 suffering through distress, abuse or neglect.

Applications can be made from non-profit making groups and organisations working with children under the physical age of 19. In general, consideration is given to funding specific items of equipment that are for the direct use of sick, disabled and disadvantaged children.

There is no upper or lower limit on the level of grant, but most grants are for less than £5,000. Many requests are for small sums under £500.

Grantmaking

In 2010 the charity had assets of £3.5 million and an income of £10 million. Grants and donations paid out during the year totalled just over £4 million. Of this total, just under £4 million was granted to organisations and £93,000 was granted to individuals

As well as purchasing the familiar white Variety Club minibuses for schools, youth clubs, hospices etc., the charity also operates the Easy Riders Wheelchair Programme, which donates custom-designed wheelchairs, trikes and buggies to children who are contending with a wide range of disabilities, and Variety at Work, a special part of the charity which exists purely to give children wonderful experiences, rather than raise money. Its aim is simple – to bring happiness to as many youngsters as possible, so that they can look forward to magical moments. This is achieved by providing entertainment and experiences for them through all sorts of spectacular events throughout the country, all year long.

The 2010 accounts provide an analysis of some of the services provided by the trust through the year:

》 Gave 177 electric wheelchairs.
》 Provided 1010 sunshine coaches to schools, homes and other organisations.
》 Almost 34,000 children enjoyed days out, at no cost to the charity.

Charitable expenditure was broken down as follows:

Sunshine coaches	£2.9 million
Appeals	£553,000
Electric wheelchairs	£550,000

Organisations who received grants of over £5,000 included: Leeds Teaching Hospitals NHS Trust (£125,000); Sports Aid (£108,000); Martin House, Amateur Swimming Association (Loughborough), King's College Hospital (£50,000 each); Stepping Stones (Lancashire), Charlie Chaplin Adventure Playground (London) (£37,000 each); Oakwood School (Manchester), Butterwick Hospice Care (Stockton-on-Tees) (£36,000 each); Heath Park Business & Enterprise Co. (Wolverhampton) (£26,000); East Muir School (Glasgow) (£24,000); Linden Lodge School (London) (£10,000); and Kenth Youth (Gillingham) (£5,000).

A total of £45,000 was disbursed in grants of less than £5,000.

The history of the Variety Club

The club's website has the following interesting account of the origins of the charity:

> The roots of the Variety Club of Great Britain go back to 1927 when, in Pittsburgh, United States, a group of 11 men-all friends-and involved in show business set up a social club. They rented a small room in the William Penn Hotel for their new club, which they named the Variety Club, as all its members were drawn from various branches of the show business world.

> On Christmas Eve 1928 a one-month-old baby was abandoned on a seat in the Sheridan Square Theatre in Pittsburgh, Pennsylvania, with a note pinned to her dress, which read as follows:

> Please take care of my baby. Her name is Catherine. I can no longer take care of her. I have eight others. My husband is out of work. She was born on Thanksgiving Day. I have always heard of the goodness of show business people and pray to God that you will look after her' (signed, 'A heartbroken mother').

> When all efforts by the police and local newspapers failed to locate the parents, the theatre's 11 club members decided to underwrite the infant's support and education.

> The subsequent publicity surrounding Catherine and her benefactors attracted many other show business people anxious to help. Before long Catherine had more clothes and toys than any child could possibly need. Naturally the Club members had no trouble finding other disadvantaged children to benefit from the extra gifts and while the generous show business world donated presents to Catherine, the Club continued to supply a growing number of children with much-needed presents. As a result, by the time Catherine was adopted at the age of five, the Club that she had effectively started was well on the way to becoming a recognised children's charity.

> It was not long before the Variety Club decided to actively raise funds for its adopted cause of disadvantaged children. The first fund-raising event of the Club was held under a Circus Big Top, which is why the circus vernacular is used within the Club structure world-wide.

> The Variety Club of Great Britain – or Tent 3 6- was set up by two Americans: Robert S Wolff, chairman of RKO, who became the club's first Chief Barker, and C J Latta of ABC Cinemas/Warner Brothers. It was formed at an inaugural dinner at the Savoy in October 1949 and by the end of 1950 had already raised nearly £10,000.

> From the start, Tent 36 – like the Variety Club as a whole – consisted of a group of charitable individuals and companies, the majority of whom were related to show business and were happy to give large sums of money for the cause-sometimes as straightforward cash donations and sometimes through their support for the Club's auctions and raffles with donated items. The Club numbered a formidable array of film producers, agents and celebrities within its ranks,

all of whom were eager to give their time and services – free of charge – to help towards making the increasingly varied and wide ranging fundraising events as successful as possible.

Variety Club of Great Britain, along with the other members of Variety Club International, has long been characterised as 'the Heart of Show Business'. Its membership over the years is drawn in large measure from the multi-faceted world of entertainment and the leisure industries.

Exclusions

For grants to organisations: trips abroad; medical treatment or research; administrative or salary costs; maintenance or ongoing costs; repayment of loans; distribution to other organisations; computers; education/tuition fees; garden adaptations; basic cost of a family vehicle; hire, rental costs or down payments; and non-specific appeals.

Applications

There are application forms for each programme, available – with application guidelines – from the charity or through its website.

The Volant Charitable Trust

General

£4 million (2009/10)

Beneficial area

UK, with a preference for Scotland, and overseas.

PO Box 8, 196 Rose Street, Edinburgh EH2 4AT

Email: admin@volanttrust.com

Website: www.volanttrust.com/

Correspondent: Christine Collingwood, Administrator

Trustees: J K Rowling; Dr N S Murray; G C Smith; R D Fulton.

SC Number: SC030790

Information available

Accounts were provided by the trust.

This trust was established in 2000 by the author J K Rowling for general charitable purposes. In recent years the trust has refined its objects and now has two broad areas of funding:

- research into the causes, treatment and possible cures of Multiple Sclerosis (the trust is not considering further applications for funding in this area at the present time).
- charities and projects, whether national or community-based, at home or abroad, that alleviate social deprivation, with a particular emphasis on women's and children's issues. (At present the trustees consider the funding of major disaster appeals and this is the focus of the trust's international support; therefore, applications for other projects overseas are not being considered for the foreseeable future.)

Check the trust's website for up-to-date information on any changes to the above circumstances.

The trust has simple guidelines:

- the trustees' principal objective is to support charitable organisations whose purpose is to alleviate poverty and social deprivation with particular emphasis on children's and women's issues. All charities should be registered with the relevant national charity commission or equivalent body
- the trustees are prepared to support a charity by way of regular annual payments but only in exceptional circumstances would grants exceed three years. In addition, even if the activities of a charity appear to fall within the guidelines this does not automatically mean that it will receive a grant. All grants are at the discretion of the trustees
- the trustees will as and when appropriate, support disaster appeals but will not support applications from individuals who are seeking assistance, for a specific project or charitable work which that individual may be carrying out, or to relieve a need due to illness or similar circumstances.

The trust also states that grants can be made to appropriate projects that fall outside these guidelines at the trustees' discretion.

In 2009/10 the trust had assets of £49.1 million and an income of £5.6 million, a substantial amount of which included donations from the settlor. Grants were made during the year to 66 organisations totalling £4 million, and were broken down as follows:

International aid	£2 million
Support and protection of women, children and young people	£1.2 million
Provision of social benefit to the community	£547,000
Relief of poverty and social deprivation	£147,000
Social welfare (total)	£1.9 million
Medical research/relief	£135,000
International aid	£2 million
Support and protection of women, children and young people	£1.2 million
Provision of social benefit to the community	£547,000
Relief of poverty and social deprivation	£147,000
Social welfare (total)	£1.9 million
Medical research/relief	£135,000

Beneficiaries of the largest grants were listed in the accounts; these were: Unicef – Ethiopia Children's Appeal (£1 million); British Red Cross Society – Darfur Appeal and DEC – Haiti Earthquake Appeal (£500,000 each); The Kids Company (£225,000); University of Edinburgh (£125,000); Royal Blind and Sacro (£90,000 each); and Young Enterprise (£82,500).

Exclusions

No grants to individuals.

Applications

Applications for funding requests of up to and including £10,000 per annum, for those projects based in **Scotland** only, are dealt with by the appointed agents, the Scottish Community Foundation (www.scottishcf.org).

All other requests for funding are dealt with via an application form available from the trust's website.

Complete and return the application form, plus any supporting materials by post. Applications should not be hand delivered. If an application is hand delivered, management at Mail Boxes are not in a position to discuss applications and will not be expected to provide any form of receipt.

Voluntary Action Fund

General

£5 million (2009/10)

Beneficial area

Scotland.

Dunfermline Business Centre, Unit 14, Izatt Avenue, Dunfermline, Fife KY11 3BZ

Tel: 01383 620780

Fax: 01383 626314

Email: info@voluntaryactionfund.org.uk

Website: www.voluntaryactionfund.org.uk

Correspondent: Keith Wimbles, Chief Executive

Trustees: Ron Daniel, Chair; Dorothy MacLauchlin; ; Michael Cunningham; Julie Hogg; Pam Judson; Caron Hughes; John McDonald; Douglas Guest.

SC Number: SC035037

Information available

The fund has an informative website, with detailed guidance and application forms.

Summary

Formed in 2003 this organisation evolved from the former Unemployed Voluntary Action Fund (UVAF) which was established in 1982. In response to the changing nature of their work and the evolving economic and social environment in Scotland, the mission and objectives of the fund were updated and it became a charity called Investing In Social Change and Community Action: The Voluntary Action Fund (VAF). They are an independent grant-making body which invests in voluntary and community based organisations across Scotland. Organisations and projects that challenge inequalities and overcome barriers to active participation in community life are supported.

General

The fund's website provides the following overview of its values, aims and objectives:

Our vision is for a fair society in which strong, resilient communities can flourish, and people can achieve their own potential through active participation, volunteering and working together to tackle inequality and discrimination.

We believe in:
- the ability of individuals and communities to create positive social change through volunteering and collective action
- equality of opportunity, diversity, eliminating discrimination and the protection of human rights
- promoting learning and continuous improvement through action and evaluation
- working co-operatively with others and developing positive relationships to achieve mutual objectives

- listening to our stakeholders and adopting a flexible and responsive approach to achieve success
- fairness, transparency and rigour in our policies, processes and decision making
- sustainable policies and practices in all aspects of our work.

Our mission is to promote equality and social justice to enable communities to thrive. We achieve this through investing grants and providing customised support to build the capacity of voluntary and community organisations. We also work collaboratively with government, other funding bodies and development agencies to promote best practice in grant making, and with the sector to promote volunteering and community action as a force for social change.

Grants programmes

The fund currently runs one small grants programme:

The Community Chest

Aimed at small community groups across Scotland, this fund provides grants of up to £1,000 to help small community groups across Scotland with an income of under £25,000 fund their activities. Recipients of grants also have the opportunity to attend various free workshops covering topics relevant to charities. The fund is particularly keen to support community groups who work with:

- disability or health related issues
- people who are excluded due to their ethnic origin, disability, gender, sexual orientation or gender identity
- families and young people
- older people.

There are also two main grants programmes:

The Volunteering Scotland Grant Scheme (VSGS)

Supports organisations to develop high quality volunteering opportunities that attract harder-to-reach volunteers and volunteers who want to gain work-relevant skills. VSGS grants in 2011/12 [were] invested either in projects that encourage the development of partnership working between clusters of volunteer-engaging organisations, or in extending volunteering projects that are already funded.

The Equality Grants Programme (EGP)

The EGP incorporates 4 separate streams funded by the Scottish Government. The programme aims to combat inequality, foster integration and promote dialogue and understanding between communities:

- Race Religion and Refugee Integration Fund
- Grants through the Gender funding stream
- Grants through the LGBT funding steam
- Grants through the Disability funding stream

These main grants funds open and close to applicants throughout the year so it would be wise to check the fund's website for the most recent information.

Grantmaking in 2009/10

In 2009/10 the fund had an income of £5.3 million, assets of £179,000 and made grants totalling £5 million, distributed through the following funds:

Equality Grants Programme	£3.9 million
Volunteering Scotland Grant Scheme	£813,000
Community Chest Programme	£198,000
Small grants	£26,000

Exclusions

See the fund's website for details of any individual exclusions for each fund.

Applications

Application forms and guidance notes for open programmes are available on the fund's website. The fund recommends that interested parties contact them to discuss the project before making any application. Funds may open and close so applicants should check the website for the most recent updates.

Wales Council for Voluntary Action

Local community, volunteering, social welfare, environment, regeneration

£14.8 million (2009/10)

Beneficial area

Wales.

Baltic House, Mount Stuart Square, Cardiff CF10 5FH

Tel: 0870 607 1666

Fax: 029 2043 1701

Email: help@wcva.org.uk

Website: www.wcva.org.uk

Correspondent: Helen Wilson, Grants Manager

Trustees: Win Griffiths, Chair; Louise Bennett; Nerys Haf Biddulph; Mike Denham; Walter Dickie; Eurwen Edwards; Paul Glaze; Simon Harris; Margaret Jervis; Efa Gruffudd Jones; Harri Jones; John R Jones; Liza Kellet; Joy Kent; Mike Lewis; Marcella Maxwell; Mark McLean; Judy Owen; Chad Patel; Martin Pollard; Jaswant Singh Jas; L Mair Stephens; Anne Stephenson; Hilary Stevens; Fran Targett; Nick Taylor; Alan Underwood; Mal Williams; Michael Williams; Catriona Williams; Wendy Williams; Victoria Winckler; Clive Wolfendale; Shirley Yendell; Pauline Young.

CC Number: 218093

Information available

Accounts were available from the Charity Commission. The charity has a detailed website, although not all funds are listed.

Wales Council for Voluntary Action (WCVA) represents, supports and campaigns for the voluntary sector in Wales by undertaking research on policy, providing information and training, and administering a range of grant programmes on behalf of various bodies including charitable trusts, the Millennium Commission, the National Assembly for Wales, the Big Lottery Fund and the European Structural Funds. Although it only administers funds for other bodies and has no funds of its own, it merits inclusion here due to the diverse nature of the schemes and the amounts of money involved.

WCVA administers a variety of grant programmes (17 in 2009/10) in a similar way to a community foundation. Below is one of the largest (and probably most over-subscribed) funds – check WCVA's website for up-to-date information on current programmes and deadlines.

Communities First Trust Fund

The CFTF aims to support small voluntary organisations that are based in a Communities First area, in activities that involve local people and provide a positive benefit in their community.

Enabling small voluntary organisations to make a difference in their community is the emphasis of the CFTF and is part of the eligibility criteria.

Applications are welcome from a range of community projects including music and the arts. However, the activities must provide some measure of economic, environmental, social or cultural benefit for people living in a Communities First area.

There are over 180 areas across Wales eligible for support from the CFTF.

The CFTF is a scheme funded by the Welsh Assembly Government aimed at small community led organisations in Communities First areas in Wales. The fund is administered by WCVA.

Who can apply to the fund?
Priority will be given to new groups who have NOT received funding from the CFTF or Music Trust Fund previously.

Your group can apply if you:

- are a small community led organisation and /or are a not-for-profit group with an annual income under £150,000
- are working in and involving people from a communities First area, or if you are based outside the area, the beneficiaries must be living in a Communities First area
- have a governing document/ constitution, dated and signed as 'adopted' by the chair, or other senior office holder on behalf of the group
- have a bank account, in the name of your group, which requires at least two signatures and can provide a copy of a recent bank statement
- can provide a copy of your most recent audited annual accounts or a statement of income and expenditure. These documents must be audited or signed as approved by your chair or other senior office holder

- can spend and account for the grant within six months of receipt or return it, or part of it, to the fund. (Previous grant accountability will be taken into consideration for the assessment process e.g. late submission of the end of project report, unapproved changes to costs, inappropriate receipts etc.).

Full guidelines are available from WCVA's website.

Grantmaking in 2009/10

In 2009/10 the charity had assets of £12.4 million and an income of just over £30.7 million, including £23 million from the Welsh Assembly (£15.9 million in 2008/09) and £2.5 million from European Structural Funds. Grants were made to 1,785 organisations across Wales totalling £14.8 million.

The following is a breakdown of the charity's grant distributions by programme during the year:

Mental Health*	146	£3.8 million
Local Volunteering Services	19	£3 million
Communities First Fund	1,054	£2.8 million
Volunteering Enhancement Initiative	38	£1.6 million
Active Community	25	£943,000
Environment Wales	151	£868,500
Volunteering in Wales Fund	54	£643,000
Gwir Vol	56	£312,500
Russell: Youth Volunteering	40	£220,000
Millennium Volunteers	48	£198,000
Advice Training Network	13	£193,000
Partnership Council	27	£122,000
Russell: Youth Led	17	£85,000
Gold Star	32	£50,000
Volunteering	19	£44,000
Strategic Recycling: ERDF	2	£40,000
Age of Stupid	44	£10,500

*This fund is no longer administered by WCVA

Exclusions

Grants are made to constituted voluntary organisations only. Check for specific exclusions for individual funds.

For the Communities First Trust Fund, the following are not supported:

- applications for a project on behalf of another group/organisation/ Communities First Partnership/ statutory body/school

- Communities First Partnerships
- organisations whose annual income exceeds £150,000
- national organisations – unless the group is a local branch with local management/accountability arrangements and its own bank account
- political organisations
- individuals– applications must come from a community organisation
- private businesses
- Communities First Trust Fund Referees – however the group the referee is associated with may apply provided they use a different nominated referee
- town and community councils
- schools
- other statutory organisations, e.g. local authorities, local education authorities
- local authority music services – the Friends of the Music Service may apply to the trust fund providing the costs are not revenue costs (e.g. staff costs & running costs).

Groups are not eligible to apply if there is a previous CFTF project that has been 'deemed closed' because it has not been completed as per the terms and conditions of grant award. Groups are not eligible to apply to the CFTF if they have an outstanding End of Project report from a previous CFTF or Music Trust Fund grant. The previous grant award must be completed and accounted for before a new application is submitted.

Applications
There are separate application forms for each scheme. Contact WCVA on 0870 607 1666, or visit its website, for further information.

Sir Siegmund Warburg's Voluntary Settlement

Arts

£1.7 million (2010/11)

Beneficial area
UK, especially London.

19 Norland Square, London
W11 4PU
Email: applications@sswvs.org
Correspondent: The Secretary
Trustees: Hugh Stevenson; Doris Wasserman; Dr Michael Harding; Christopher Purvis.
CC Number: 286719

Information available
Accounts were available at the Charity Commission.

This trust is a general grant-maker, which is currently focused on providing support for the arts. Both revenue funding and capital projects will be considered. The trust states that it is 'likely to make only a small number of grants a year; the intention being to identify arts institutions and projects of the highest quality and to make grants which are likely to 'make a difference'. Therefore, while the trustees consider unsolicited applications, they are likely to be able to support only a small proportion of those received.'

In 2010/11 the trust had assets of £10.5 million and an income of £234,000. Following the trustees decision to start planning for the eventual wind-down of the trust, they have begun withdrawing larger amounts from the invested portfolio and distributing this in grants. During the year grants were made to 32 organisations totalling £1.7 million.

Beneficiaries included: Royal Shakespeare Company (£125,000); Academy of Ancient Music and the National Children's Orchestra (£100,000 each); Chickenshed Theatre Company and the Royal Welsh College of Music and Drama (£50,000 each); Cheltenham Festivals (£40,000); Paintings in Hospitals (£30,000); British Youth Opera (£25,000); Jewish Book Week (£10,000); and Oxford Playhouse (£5,000).

Exclusions
No grants to individuals.

Applications
Registered charities only are invited to send applications by email to applications@sswvs.org. It is

requested that initial applications should be no more than four sides of A4 and should be accompanied by the latest audited accounts.

Applications sent by post will not be considered.

The Waterloo Foundation

Children, the environment, developing countries and projects in Wales

£5.5 million (2010)

Beneficial area
UK and overseas.

c/o 46–48 Cardiff Road, Llandaff, Cardiff CF5 2DT
Tel: 029 2083 8980
Email: info@waterloofoundation.org.uk
Website: www.waterloofoundation.org.uk
Correspondent: Janice Matthews, Finance Manager
Trustees: Heather Stevens; David Stevens; Janet Alexander; Caroline Oakes.
CC Number: 1117535

Information available
Accounts were available from the Charity Commission. The foundation also has a helpful website.

The foundation was established in early 2007 with a substantial endowment of £100 million in shares from David and Heather Stevens, co-founders of Admiral Insurance.

Who can apply?
We welcome applications from registered charities and organisations with projects that have a recognisable charitable purpose. Your project has to be allowed within the terms of your constitution or rules and, if you are not a registered charity, you will need to send us a copy of your constitution or set of rules.

We make grants for all types of projects; start-up, initial stages and valuable ongoing funding. This can include running costs and overheads as well as posts; particularly under the World Development and Projects in Wales. We do not have any upper or lower limit on the amount of grant we offer but it is unlikely that we would offer a grant of more than £100,000 in any one year.

In 2010, the foundation had assets of over £121 million a total income of £4.2 million. Grants were made totalling £5.5 million. Grant expenditure can be broken down across the following areas:

World development	87	£2 million
Environment	57	£1.6 million
Child development	47	£1 million
Other	74	£472,000
Wales	29	£460,000

Programmes

The foundation makes grants under four programmes, the following information is taken from the trust's very detailed website:

World Development

We are currently not accepting new funding applications for our World Development fund. We have received significantly more funding proposals than we are able to support this year. We hope to accept new applications for the World Development fund in early 2012.

The Waterloo Foundation aims to support projects or organisations which help the economically disadvantaged build the basis of sustainable prosperity. We have three main themes of interest, as described below.

The Waterloo Foundation is committed to providing support to developing countries which will be used in a sustainable way with lasting impact, and which avoids promoting a culture of aid-dependency. All applicants should be able to demonstrate the impact of their programmes, and show how they meet the Foundation's objectives.

Funding priorities

1) Enterprise development

The foundation believes that development of commercial activity is at the heart of ensuring a country's prosperity and independence. The foundation is keen to support organisations which encourage economically disadvantaged individuals or communities to develop enterprise and business growth. This could be achieved through a variety of interventions. The Foundation's main interests are in the following:

- enterprise facilitation activities which have a proven track-record of leading to the establishment or growth of sustainable and profitable enterprises
- providing investment support to enterprises which have the potential to remain profitable and which will benefit a large number of relatively

disadvantaged individuals. The foundation is only interested in providing investment to support enterprises which cannot obtain funding from other sources.

Applicants must provide evidence that their enterprise initiative has genuine potential to lead to a significant financial return (for the enterprise or programme beneficiaries) given the total level of financial investment made in the enterprise or programme.

For further details on presenting a business case to the foundation, please consult the foundation's website before applying.

2) Education

The foundation believes that educating children is key to ensuring a country's long-term development, prosperity and independence. An educated population will help bring about a more vibrant civil society, as well as increase the numbers of people available to offer their skills, knowledge and expertise to support the development of their communities.

The foundation's two key aims are:

- to increase access to education
- to increase the quality of education.

The foundation recognises that there are a large number of approaches that can be taken to meet these aims. Our priority is to fund projects or programmes which can demonstrate that they meet these aims in a highly cost-effective manner with long-term impact. Applicants are encouraged to use evidence from previous work undertaken, or other relevant research, to indicate the effectiveness of their project's approach. Relevant evidence would include:

- indicators of improved student or school performance
- data related to an increase in school enrolment, or reduction in absenteeism/ school drop-out rates
- any other facts or data which demonstrate the effectiveness of the project in comparison to similar programmes.

In exceptional circumstances the foundation will also consider providing support for other stages of education if you can demonstrate that these approaches are particularly effective.

3) Water, sanitation and hygiene

The foundation believes that access to sanitation, hygiene and clean water is one of the core requirements to support the sustainable development of a community. Without access to these basic resources people can spend a huge amount of time every day collecting water, whilst water-borne diseases will remain prevalent. This can significantly restrict an individual's ability to gain an education or contribute towards household income-

generation. This has a particular impact on women and girls because of their traditional household role in many cultures.

The foundation is concerned about the rapid growth of urban slums, which frequently lack basic sanitation facilities. In 2009, the foundation will prioritise projects which aim to deliver improved sanitation and hygiene to these areas.

The Foundation is keen to support programmes which take an integrated approach to addressing both sanitation and access to clean drinking water.

Your application must demonstrate the following:

- evidence from previous work undertaken to indicate that your organisation has a history of delivering successful integrated water and sanitation programmes
- evidence that your improved water sources have remained operational a number of years after your original programme was completed
- evidence that improvements in sanitation practices have been sustained since your original programme was completed.

Geographical priorities

It is unlikely that the foundation will provide support to an organisation working outside a country ranker as either 'low human development' or towards the bottom of the 'medium human development' list [in the United Nations Development Programme's *Human Development Index* rankings.]

The foundation is committed to the principle that development work should have long-term impact, and believes that stable national and local government plays an important role in achieving this. The foundation is therefore unlikely to provide support to conflict-affected regions.

The foundation supports the twinning of Wales and Lesotho, and therefore prioritises support for organisations working in Lesotho. Priority is also given to organisations operating in the Republic of Congo, as a reflection of this country's importance as the location of one of the key rainforest areas of the world.

What we will not fund

It is not our intention to provide financial support to organisations seeking to alleviate the suffering resulting from high-profile natural or man-made disasters, including the delivery of food aid or shelter.

It is also not our intention to fund projects with a principle aim to deliver increased access to improved health care.

Child Development

The foundation is keen to support research designed to give us a better understanding of the psychological and behavioural development of our children. The foundation is particularly interested in research into childhood neuro-developmental conditions and the factors that influence them.

The main priority of the foundation is to fund research, while dissemination of research and intervention projects are funded to a lesser extent.

Funding priorities

We are most interested in the following neurodevelopment topics:

- Autistic spectrum disorders
- Dyslexia
- ADHD
- Rolandic epilepsy (also called BECCTS or BECTS)
- Development Co-ordination Disorder
- Trauma

The foundation's website offers a detailed breakdown of the current particular priorities of the foundation:

We run an annual call for research applications to the Child Development Fund. For the first time, with funding in 2012 we will have single deadlines for two of our key topics [please check with the foundation for current details].

Environment

For the first time in Earth's history humans are altering the natural equilibrium of the environment. We hope through this fund that we can help mitigate the damaging effects that humans are causing and contribute to a positive change both now and in the future.

Funding priorities

We want to support projects which can help mitigate the damaging effects that humans are having on the environment and contribute to a positive change both now and in the future. The fund has two main themes:

1) Tropical forests

Under our Forests programme, preference will be given to initiatives working to protect **tropical** forests for their value to the climate, communities and biodiversity, principally through avoided deforestation or to a lesser extent, through reforestation of degraded forest areas. We will consider both practical local projects, and strategic initiatives.

Applications for practical local projects that we will consider would typically be working on a specified tropical forest area, defined in hectares. Applicants will need to demonstrate how their project involves:

- Exposing and addressing the local drivers of deforestation
- Management of the specified area
- Methods to measure and monitor the protected area
- Sustainable livelihoods for forest-dependent communities

We will consider applications for strategic projects that are working on addressing the drivers of deforestation on a wider or international scale. These could include:

- Working on international or regional forest policy
- Campaigning for improved practices in commerce
- Innovative ways of reducing deforestation e.g. financial systems or solutions based on the value of forest ecosystem services

2) Marine

Applications for local projects should demonstrate that they will positively impact upon the marine resource they are working to protect, and could include:

- Development of marine protected areas or sustainable fisheries management
- Addressing local causes of over-exploitation of fish stocks and other seafood
- Creation of sustainable livelihoods for coastal and seafood dependent people

We will consider applications for strategic projects that are working on addressing marine issues at a wider or international scale. These could include:

- Working on international or regional marine policy
- Campaigning for improved practices in commerce
- Exploring different fishing practices and techniques
- Maintaining or improving fish stocks to a sustainable level

Other interests

In addition to our forest and marine programmes foundation may occasionally support water and energy projects.

3) Wales

The foundation will support small-scale, community benefit renewable energy projects with financial support of £10,000 or less.

What we will not support

Under the Environment Fund, foundation does not support:

- Animal conservation or biodiversity projects, except as an adjunct to work funded under our forest or marine goals
- Standalone tree-planting projects that are not part of a wider tropical forest protection or management programme

Projects in Wales

Although the funding priorities for the foundation are the Environment and World Development, the original founders of the foundation live and work in Wales. To support our local community, we have two funding programmes for Wales: *Caring Wales* and *Working Wales.*

1) Working Wales

When the UK economy was expanding, Wales continued to be the least prosperous region of the UK, with economic activity lower than the UK average. On top of this, the Welsh labour market has been affected slightly more by the recession than the rest of the UK, experiencing relatively large falls in its employment rate during the first third quarter of 2008 and second and third quarters of 2009.

Our Working Wales funding programme focuses on employment and business in Wales. We assess Working Wales applications on the basis of paid employment or business start-up outcomes.

A strong application for support would:
- demonstrate how effective their programme is at getting people into paid work,
- provide evidence of past success in terms of numbers of people who have got into paid work or started their own profitable business as a result of their specific approach,
- provide more long-term evidence that their employment or business has been sustained over a period of time,
- give details of the types of employment their beneficiaries have secured or
- show that the businesses set up have become profitable.

Therefore we tend to favour supporting established programmes that have been evaluated to show their effectiveness in achieving and sustaining these outcomes over a length of time.

2) Caring Wales

It is estimated that 1 in 10 people in Wales is providing unpaid care for a family member, a total of some 340,000 people. Of these, 7,000 are likely to be children aged 5 to 15 (source: *National Office of Statistics*). There are an estimated 90,000 people providing unpaid care for family members, for more than 50 hours per week.

The Caring Wales funding programme is open to applications from organisations working to support long-term carers, especially young carers or carers of people with the conditions prioritised in our Child Development research fund. The strongest applications to this fund have been from organisations that:

- provide a range of carer-centred support services,
- reach a substantial number of individuals,
- proactively identify and work with the most isolated and vulnerable carers,
- offer sufficient levels of support,
- proactively monitor and evaluate their work to shape services and demonstrate impact, and
- promote participation of service users in shaping their services.

Other information and advice

- Applicants should note that the funding priorities for the foundation are World Development and the Environment.
- Applications from project/ organisations in Wales that fall within the other areas of the foundation's core interests, particularly in the areas of economically disadvantaged people in poorer countries and climate-change related issues, should be made, in the first case to the World Development fund and in the latter, to the Environment Fund.
- Although there is no upper or lower limit, awards made under the Working or Caring Wales programmes have ranged from £5,000 – £20,000.

The trust will occasionally fund:

- research, where its aims and objectives match our priorities particularly under our Environment and Child Development programmes
- the cost of disseminating information obtained from projects supported by the foundation
- the cost of evaluating and writing up a project.

Previous beneficiaries across all programme areas have included: WaterAid (£175,000); Link Community Development (£150,000); Microloan Foundation (£100,000); and The Fairtrade Foundation (£20,000)

Other organisations awarded funding were listed without figures, these included: University of Bristol; Crossroads Care Mid & West Wales; The Forest Trust; Kids Company; Food and Behavioural Research; The Prince's Trust Wales; Blue Ventures and The National Autistic Society.

Exclusions

The foundation will not support:

- applications for grants for work that has already taken place
- applications for grants that replace or subsidise statutory funding.

We will not consider applications for grants in the following areas:

- the arts and heritage, except in Wales
- animal welfare
- the promotion of religious or political causes
- general appeals or circulars.

We are unlikely to support projects of the following kind:

- from individuals
- for the benefit of an individual
- medical charities (except under certain aspects of our 'Child Development' programme, particularly mental health)
- festivals, sports and leisure activities
- websites, publications, conferences or seminars, except under our 'Child Development' programme.

Applications

We hope to make applying for a grant fairly painless and fairly quick. However it will help us a great deal if you could follow the simple rules below when sending in an application (there are no application forms).

Email applications to applications@ waterloofoundation.org.uk (nowhere else please!) Include a BRIEF description (equivalent to 2 sides of A4) within your email, but NOT as an attachment, of your project or the purpose for which you want the funding, detailing:

- your charity's name, address and charity number
- email, phone and name of a person to reply to
- a link to your website
- what it's for
- who it benefits
- how much you want and when
- what happens if you don't get our help
- the programme under which you are applying.

Don't write long flowery sentences – we won't read them.

Do be brief, honest, clear and direct. Use abbreviations if you like!

Don't send attachments to your email – your website will give us an introduction to you so you don't need to cover that.

Who can apply?

We welcome applications from registered charities and organisations with projects that have a recognisable charitable purpose. Your project has to be allowed within the terms of your constitution or rules and, if you are not a registered charity, you will need to send us a copy of your constitution or set of rules.

We make grants for all types of projects; start-up, initial stages and valuable ongoing funding. This can include running costs and overheads as well as posts; particularly under the

World Development and Projects in Wales. We do not have any upper or lower limit on the amount of grant we offer but it is unlikely that we would offer a grant of more that £100,000.

If you are an organisation not based in the UK, then you must send us contact details for a named person **preferably from a UK registered entity** who is willing to provide us with a reference for your work. This could be:

- A current or former donor
- A partnership organisation
- A fundraising group
- An academic institution or think tank
- A government department or agency

They must have visited your organisation and be able to feed back on the quality of your work. Please state the **name, contact details** and **relationship to the referee** (i.e. past funder) at the beginning of your application. If you do not have a UK referee, please contact us to discuss a suitable alternative. **Only applications with references will be considered**.

The Wates Foundation

Assisting organisations in improving the quality of life of the deprived, disadvantaged and excluded in the community

£2.9 million (2009/10)

Beneficial area

Berkshire; Bristol, Avon & Somerset; Buckinghamshire; Cambridgeshire; Dorset; Gloucestershire; Hampshire; Middlesex; Nottinghamshire; Oxfordshire; Surrey; Sussex; Warwickshire (not including the Greater Birmingham area) and the Greater London Metropolitan Area as defined by the M25 motorway.

Wates House, Station Approach, Leatherhead, Surrey KT22 7SW

Tel: 01372 861000

Fax: 01372 861252

Email: director@watesfoundation.org.uk

Website: www.watesfoundation.org.uk

Correspondent: Brian Wheelwright, Director

Trustees: Annabelle Elliott; Christopher Agace; Richard Wates;

Emily King; Kate Minch; William Wates.

CC Number: 247941

Information available

Accounts were available at the Charity Commission. Excellent reports and accounts, including guidance for applicants, all on the particularly clear and simple website.

In 1966, three brothers Norman, Sir Ronald and Allan Wates of the Wates building firm (now the Wates Construction Group), amalgamated their personal charitable trusts into the single entity of The Wates Foundation.

In 2009/10 the trustees adopted a committee approach to deciding grants in each of the area of the foundation's interests.

Guidelines

The foundation has published new guidelines for applicants for the year from April 2011 to March 2012. Three former programmes have been retained, two closed and one new one opened. Minor changes have been made to the retained programmes. The foundation's website gives the following guidance for applicants:

The foundation aims to alleviate conditions of distress, deprivation and disadvantage that lead to social exclusion by funding charitable work across a broad range of social priorities that will bring about positive change. The foundation's current priorities are summarised in our programmes.

Organisations supported by the foundation tend to share these features:

- there is a clear sense of objectives and how to achieve them
- the work is about providing solutions to problems, not about making them more bearable
- an award has a good chance of making a difference to the organisation and to its clients and having an impact in the longer term
- the work may be a new imaginative approach, something in a new area of need, or something that is risky or sensitive
- every effort is made to comply with statutory requirements such as the Statement of Recommended Practice: Accounting and Reporting by Charities 2005
- recognised quality assurance and accreditation schemes and training for trustees and staff are used as tools to improve the organisation's effectiveness.

Grants Programmes

Foundation awards are made to work in four programmes areas which have specific aims and priorities set by the trustees. These are the criteria against which the trustees assess the relevance and potential impact of outcomes that applicants propose to achieve with the help of a foundation grant.

Under the general theme Foundations of Society, the objective of The Wates Foundation in 2011 is to promote work that builds social values and responsibility and provides access to opportunities that address disadvantage.

Following this summary, each programme is explained in detail.

Building Family Values

Aim

To promote and reinforce the role of the family unit as a safer more caring environment, fostering social and civic values, responsibility and behaviour, and encouraging the young to take up opportunities for education, training and employment.

Priorities

- promoting the family unit
- domestic abuse
- supporting children and young people at risk
- opportunities for children and young people 5–25 years of age.

Typical Activities

- family advocacy and advice; training and mentoring schemes for parents
- community volunteering
- vocational training for young people, especially those not in education, employment or training (NEET)
- support to children in care or adoption
- domestic abuse
- activity schemes for disadvantaged children
- urban streets youth projects
- literacy & out of school tuition.

Likely Outcomes

- people are confident in their parenting skills
- reduction in violence and abuse in the home
- more people contribute actively to their communities
- more young people have access to training for employment
- more volunteer support available to disadvantaged families.

Community Health

Aim

To provide avenues for an improved quality of life for those people with addictions, those disadvantaged by reason of mental or physical disability and their carers and those who are living less healthy or active lives by virtue of age or infirmity.

Priorities

- addiction
- mental health
- disabilities
- aged and infirm
- alternative and complementary practice.

Typical Activities

- community-based substance abuse therapy and rehabilitation
- volunteering and placement schemes
- advocacy and advice for the disabled; schemes assisting the disabled into independent living
- training, employment and access opportunities for the disabled
- young carer schemes
- promotion of healthy and active life styles for the aged and infirm
- schemes promoting inclusion of the disabled in the community including public awareness, employment, education and leisure
- schemes specifically for disabled ex-Service personnel including those with mental disabilities such as post traumatic stress syndrome and related substance abuse
- palliative care schemes
- neo-natal intensive care
- medical research
- mental health.

Likely Outcomes

- more people in addiction therapies
- more opportunities of all kinds for those disadvantaged by reason of mental or physical disability
- improved well-being amongst older people over 70 years
- more people in independent living including the disabled and young carers
- more young carers able to access education, training and employment
- better quality of life for long term adult carers
- more volunteers in community health work.

Life Transitions

Everybody experiences transitions during their life: in early childhood; passing through stages of schooling; into and out of employment; leaving military service; entering retirement and older age. People have to cope with bereavement, the onset of illness or disability and transitions through parenthood; others have to negotiate more unusual transitions, out of prison or mental health. Through relationships and support in the home and at school, through work provision and shaping of responsible attitudes, people can weather these transitions better and acquire the ability to sustain change and access improved life chances.

Aim

To prepare individuals and groups for the key physical, psychological and environmental change points in life that can affect significantly the development of personal attitudes and behaviour, and promote the ability for them to sustain change and access better life chances.

Areas of Specific Interest
This programme has the following areas of interest:
- Early Years Interventions – supporting families and children
- School Years Interventions – supporting young people at schooling change points
- Mental Health – supporting individuals to whole person recovery
- Interventions for Older People – supporting individuals into retirement, through loss of a partner and into old age
- Former Service Personnel – supporting those that leave military service to make a successful transition into civilian life.

Priorities
- preparing client groups for key transitions to facilitate informed and accessible changes in life circumstances
- addressing failure to deal adequately with key transitions, leading to negative outcomes in the short term and potentially in later life
- promoting personal resilience, allowing beneficiaries to access life opportunities better, having achieved a key transition successfully

Typical Activities
- building parent and baby relationships – physical, mental and social
- early years family support work: families struggling to cope with children; support to single parent families
- supporting single parents with the skills to raise responsible children
- development of social responsibility in children
- navigating key change points into and out of education
- addressing the needs of former Service personnel in areas of employment, mental health, addiction, criminal justice and homelessness
- addressing the wellbeing needs of mental health suffers to promote whole person recovery
- addressing the advent of disability or long term illness.

Likely Outcomes
- reinforcement of parent-children relationships as the basis for better life opportunities
- children grow up as responsible citizens
- fewer young people at risk of anti-social behaviour and exclusion from education
- facilitation into mainstream life of mental health sufferers

- reduction in numbers of former Service personnel in disadvantaged circumstances
- increased well being in old age.

Safer Communities
Aim
To promote initiatives contributing to the reform of the criminal justice system, a fairer and more appropriate penal system, the effective rehabilitation of offenders, particularly females, and the promotion of family contacts to reduce chances of re-offending on release.

Priorities
- crime in communities
- alternatives to custody
- preparing offenders for release
- resettlement of offenders after release
- female offenders.

Typical Activities
- crime diversion and prevention schemes especially with young people
- work around community sentences
- peer and other mentoring schemes
- 'through the gate' resettlement schemes encompassing physical and mental health, housing, training, education and employment
- substance abuse therapy and rehabilitation
- sexual abuse and violence in the home
- female offender and children work
- support to families of offenders
- parenting skills for offenders
- advocacy and advice schemes
- occupational therapy work
- volunteering and placements under licence
- trafficking.

Likely Outcomes
- a reduction in re-offending
- more opportunities pre and post-release for training, education and employment
- more opportunities pre and post-release for mental, physical and substance abuse support services
- fewer female offenders
- more offenders released into a family context
- greater resort to alternatives to custody
- more effective alternatives to custody.

Full guidelines are available from the foundation's website.

Grantmaking in 2009/10
In 2009/10 the foundation had assets of £20.4 million and an income of £159,500. There were 112 grants made during the year totalling almost £2.9 million.

The director's report for the year, which is reprinted here with the

addition of grant amounts received during the year where necessary, gives an interesting insight into the foundation's activities:

There was a visible shift in the types of awards made this year. Historically, a large proportion of the foundation's grants have gone to support the core costs of applicants; in some years these have been in excess of 60% of the total of awards by value. In 2008–2009 the level was lower at 40%, not least because our programmes closed over the period of our Next Steps restructuring review. This last year, however, the level of core costs awards dropped dramatically to just 22% by value.

On the other hand, it seems that the pressure of the economic downturn led many organisations to focus their applications on salaries, in order to retain experienced and highly valued staff. Our awards solely towards salaries rose from just 1% last year to 18% in 2009. Project-specific awards at 43% were largely in line with previous years (51%) as were capacity building awards at 8% (10%). Strategic awards comprised 7% of the whole.

Trustee Awards
The foundation has often been a generous supporter of improvements to the infrastructure of the voluntary sector. This may be either through direct capacity building awards to charities or to second tier organisations that provide services of training, mentoring or other forms of learning. The trustees added The Cranfield Trust [£15,000] to our portfolio of award winners this year with a grant that enables the trust to give priority in its support services to foundation beneficiaries. The trust joins Charities Evaluation Services and the London Advice Services Alliance (LASA) both of which have similar arrangements with us.

The trustees have supported the pioneering work of the Croydon Family Justice Centre [£20,000] on a number of occasions since its inception, where a range of charities combine to offer a multi-faceted service to victims of domestic violence and their families. To reinforce the success of the post set up by an earlier Wates award, the trustees have made a new contribution to the salary of the front line Health Worker.

Strategic Programme
The trustees supported four pieces of work this year that have strategic potential for the voluntary sector with awards valued at £190,000. The first was an award of £50,000 to the Prison Radio Association towards the costs of establishing a national radio station serving every prisoner in England and Wales. NOMS expects to have the

radio service installed across 30 prisons by the end of April 2010.

The second award, of £89,750 to Circles UK , was agreed in principle last year, but only came to fruition this year. Circles UK specialises in intense therapeutic mentoring support to sex offenders. Circles UK acts as the national infrastructure organisation for what are essentially local projects aligned to prisons regionally. By the end of 2009 there will be 48 Circles projects in UK. The award is towards strategic research to generate evidence on the UK Circles model; presently, the only Circles data relates to dated Canadian research that has only limited relevance to the UK experience.

In 2007 the foundation sponsored a Royal Society of Arts Commission looking at attitudes and practice around drug use in communities. The report made a significant contribution to the drugs debate and was widely acclaimed in UK and overseas. The foundation concluded that there are elements of the report's recommendations that are worthy of field testing. Consequently, the trustees made an award of £70,000 towards a user-focused trial of service access conducted by the Drug & Alcohol Action Team in West Sussex. Additional funding has come from the RSA and Tudor Trust. The trial aims to find alternative paths to treatment for substance abusers other than through the criminal justice system.

The foundation has a long record of supporting work to benefit women in the criminal justice system. We were therefore pleased to be an early contributor to the Corston Independent Funders Coalition of funders which is committed to seeing the recommendations of Baroness Jean Corston's influential review put into practice. Last year we made a small award towards the infrastructure costs of setting up an advocacy post. However, the availability of a Ministry of Justice (MoJ) £1 million under-spend on its diversionary funding for women's centres provided the opportunity for a more significant involvement in Corston work. Our award of £50,000 has contributed to the Consortium's match funding of the MoJ money to create a £2 million Women's Diversionary Fund , dedicated in three grant rounds to support work diverting women from offending.

Family Committee Awards
All the awards made by the three Family Grants Committees this year were under applications to the Foundation's five main programmes: Building Family Values; Community Health; Safer Communities; Sustaining the Environment; and Strengthening the Charitable and Voluntary Sectors. In all,

the Family Committees made 106 awards valued at £2.6 million.

The two most popular programmes were Community Health with new awards valued at £898,500 and Building Family Values at £748,000. Both of these reflect the Wates Foundation's continuing commitment to benefit the ideals that form the building blocks of a healthy, just and informed society.

In keeping with the foundation's overall aspiration to build the effectiveness of organisations to enable them to deliver greater impact, awards to strengthen the voluntary sector amounted to almost £500,000 in the year.

The Safer Communities programme's £433,000 in new awards reflects the transition of Wates awards from work purely inside prisons to that supporting the transition between custody and resettlement in the community. A particular emphasis of these awards is employment and training.

Although the foundation does not take applications for support to work overseas, two awards sponsored by Wates Family committees were made to school projects overseas. These were the Hope School at Kurche in the Sudan and the Baale Mane School at Gopalapura in India, both of which members of the Wates Family had visited previously.

Norman Wates Family Committee
Awards by the Norman Wates Family Committee were focused in three main areas: Family Values, Community Health and strengthening of the voluntary sector.

Mental health featured several times in the Committee's support of Community Health including an award to Sydenham Garden Community [£40,000] which provides horticultural therapy to people suffering from mental ill-health. A more strategic award was made to Social Spider [£30,000], a social enterprise promoting awareness in mental health through a quarterly magazine, One in Four. Other awards under this theme went to Dorset Reading Partners [£22,000], providing specialist reading support in schools, the Catalyst Trust [£30,000] to support skills training for mentors and Volunteer Reading Help [£38,500] to help the delivery of a new business plan for an expansion of services around literacy. In keeping with the Committee's support of arts-based approaches to addressing needs, an award was also made to the London Chamber Orchestra [£30,000] for its schools outreach programme in conjunction with Barnardo's.

In the Family Values programme, the Committee focused on education and training awards as a contributor to the foundations of an informed society. Beneficiaries included Caboodle

Theatre in Education [£5,000] for the Mother Earth project; and IntoUniversity [£40,000], which facilitates tertiary level education opportunities for children from disadvantaged backgrounds.

Other beneficiaries in the Community Health category were REACT [£39,500], which provides domestic and medical equipment to families with terminally-ill children; the Frank Barnes School for the Deaf [£9,500] for a Home Communication Programme to support the teaching of British Sign Language in the homes of deaf children; and Croydon Carers Centre [£30,000] with whom the foundation has had a relationship for many years.

Three other are organisations with a long-term relationship with the foundation were also beneficiaries of the Committee's awards in the year. These were Montage Theatre Arts [£40,000] which has been going through some major restructuring changes to reflect its growing profile as a provider of modern dance in communities; Southall Black Sisters [£40,000] who have also restructured to provide even better support to the causes of women in ethnic communities; and London Citizens [£40,000], whose work has done so much to promote community-level democracy and champion the employment rights of lower-paid workers in the Capital.

Several awards from the Safer Communities programme are worthy of mention. The Committee has developed a strong connection with HMP Downview in Surrey. Two awards were made to organisations in this prison: one for the printing of booklets concluding the Seeds of Forgiveness project; and one to Time for Families , sustaining the excellence work that strengthens bonds between offenders and their families to improve chances of successful resettlement on release.

Finally, under Sustaining the Environment, which includes heritage and archive work, the Committee was able to confirm its award to a new organisation, the Community & Youth Music Library [£34,500]. After a particularly long gestation period, CYML will be the new custodian of the archive library of sheet music originating with the former London County Council music service and the bequest of the Alan Cave Trust. The new organisation will now be well placed to continue to support the work of scholars and loan requests from amateur music organisations nationwide.

Ronald Wates Family Committee
The main thrust of the Ronald Wates Family Committee has been Community Health, particularly in North Surrey and Sussex.

Notable awards in support of people with disabilities were made to Axess Film for work that enables peoples with disabilities to make virtual tours of UK's heritage sites; the Sussex Association for Spina Bifida [£30,000], and DownsEd [£40,000], a centre pioneering language techniques for children with Down's syndrome. The Committee also made the latest in a series of awards to the Ebbisham Association [£40,000], which supports people with mental health difficulties, displaced from long stay psychiatric hospitals to care in the community in Surrey.

The Committee made a large grant to Cool2Care [£50,000], a community interest company. The founder has combined his business expertise with his own family's experience of a disabled child to set up a volunteer support service to families of disabled children.

Three medical units have benefited. At the British Home & Hospital for Incurables in Streatham [£10,000], the Committee supported the costs of a sensory garden for residents. The Princess Alice Hospice in Esher [£9,000] had an award towards its day patient care service, while children in a number of hospitals will benefit from an award to the Theodora Children's Trust [£4,000] that provides clown doctor visits to children's wards.

Long before the present public interest in the welfare of our Armed Services personnel, the foundation was committed to projects supporting former members of the Services. The Committee's awards to Combat Stress [£1,000] and Gardening Leave [£20,000] reflect this on-going commitment. Gardening Leave, which provides horticultural therapy support to former Service personnel and also works in partnership with Combat Stress, was established with the help of the Wates Foundation in 2007. The current joint award with the Wates Family Enterprise Trust will help establish a permanent gardening centre in Stovehouse, Scotland.

The Committee was also pleased to make a large award to the charity Forward [£50,000], which works to promote public awareness and change in relevant ethnic communities about the persisting practice of female genital mutilation.

Under the Sustaining the Environment programme, the Ronald Wates Committee made two important awards. The first was to the London Playing Fields Association [£25,000] which recently celebrated the 120th anniversary of its continuing work to sustain public sports grounds in London. From these facilities LPFA delivers projects for local communities. The second award was to the 10:10 campaign that seeks to bring about a ten percent reduction in carbon emissions in 2010.

The Committee made several important awards in the Safer Communities programme. The Ashiana Network in East London [£40,000] is a previous beneficiary of the foundation for their residential services for victims of domestic abuse. This new award was in support of work in schools to raise awareness amongst younger people of domestic abuse.

Four awards went to organisations supporting offenders on release. Those to the Apex Charitable Trust [£40,000] and Surrey Job Match [£6,000] support offenders in the London and Surrey areas. The others, to Startup Now for Women, a new initiative in response to the recommendations in the Corston Report, and Working Chance , offer employment opportunities specifically to women offenders on release.

Finally in this section are a number of awards made by the Ronald Wates Family Committee to the programme that aims to strengthen the voluntary and charitable sector. Several were to second-tier organisations such as Lambeth Voluntary Action [£40,000] and Ealing Resource Centre [£30,000] to improve the effectiveness of the many small community organisations that are the life blood of the sector. The award to the Small Charities Coalition [£36,000] is more strategic in nature given its national remit. We have been particularly pleased to assist the Calthorpe Project at King's Cross in London [£25,000] develop its multi-purpose community services and facilities site.

Allan Wates Family Committee

In common with the other Family committees, the Allan Wates Family Committee focused mainly on awards under the Family Values and Community Health programmes with Safer Communities awards coming in third.

The Committee's awards cover a broader geographical area than their peers with awards in Bristol & Avon, Gloucestershire, Oxfordshire, Berkshire and Buckinghamshire. A number of awards were also made in London.

Beneficiary organisations in the Bristol area include the Ideal charity's Domino Effect programme [£30,000], run by former substance abusers for abusers; the Jesse May Trust [£45,000] that provides a dedicated home visit service for terminally-ill children, but also supports their siblings; One25 [£30,000], a previous foundation beneficiary working with female workers in the sex industry; the Wheels Project [£40,000] which uses a graduated series of motor skills and safety training programmes to support young offenders and others involved in anti-social behaviour; and the Avon Riding Centre, one of the leaders in riding for the disabled in UK.

In Gloucestershire the Committee supported the work of Noah's Ark which provides short stay residential breaks to children from disadvantaged areas and those with disabilities. It also supported the Fairshares scheme operating in several prisons using the Time Bank model to support offenders and their families.

In Oxfordshire, the Committee continued its strong relationship with voluntary organisations on the Blackbird Leys and Rose Hill Estates; an award was made to The Art Room [£30,000] which offers high quality counselling to disadvantaged and troubled children through art work in schools. Work around literacy is represented with an award to ARCh [£29,500]. Other children's charities benefiting include Children in Touch [£30,000], which supports autistic children and their families, and the Oxfordshire Parent Infant Project [£30,000]. Two support schemes were funded: The Listening Centre [£30,000] that provides a community counselling service; and the eponymous Oxfordshire Befriending Network [£20,000], an end of life project to help the terminally ill plan for and approach death on their own terms.

Berks and Bucks had awards for a number of excellent organisations. Utulivu provides a support service to the large local Kenyan community in Reading. In Buckinghamshire Mothers4Mothers [£30,000] delivers a counselling and support programme for mothers of sexually abused children, while Wycombe MIND [£30,000] is being assisted with the setting up costs of a new drop in centre.

The Committee also made a number of awards in the London area, reflecting its interests in young people and their needs. Amongst the beneficiaries was the highly recommended Superkidz [£29,000] project on the Ferrier Estate, Shooter's Hill; to enable the project to replicate its model working with families to other estates in the Greenwich area. Also supported were Linden Lodge Charitable Trust [£5,000], in South London, which provides piano lessons for children who are visually impaired and profoundly disabled; and the Rugby Portobello Trust which works with disaffected young people in West London. The Committee also took the opportunity to reinforce the success of the charity Mediation in Divorce with renewal of an earlier award towards a project assisting children in families facing break-up.

Exclusions

See 'applications'.

Applications

Note the following statement from the foundation:

> The Wates Foundation reviewed its grant making policy in November 2011 in the light of a range of factors, including finance and levels of demand for support.
>
> As a result of this review, the foundation has adopted a wholly pro-active grant making strategy and will no longer take applications or bids for support from external organisations. Any unsolicited applications or bids will be rejected automatically.
>
> This strategy will be in place for three years until 31 March 2015.

Common applicant mistakes

'Not reading the guidelines!'

The Wellcome Trust

Biomedical research, history of medicine, biomedical ethics, public engagement with science

£551.5 million (2009/10)

Beneficial area

UK and overseas.

Gibbs Building, 215 Euston Road, London NW1 2BE

Tel: 020 7611 8888

Fax: 020 7611 8545

Email: grantenquiries@wellcome.ac.uk

Website: www.wellcome.ac.uk

Correspondent: Grants Information Officer

Trustees: Sir William Castell; Prof. Dame Kay Davies; Prof. Christopher Fairburn; Prof. Richard Hynes; Roderick Kent; Baroness Eliza Manningham-Buller; Prof. Peter Rigby; Prof. Peter Smith; Prof. Anne Johnson; Peter Davies.

CC Number: 210183

Information available

Extensive information is available from the trust and is accessible through its excellent website.

Summary

The Wellcome Trust is one of the world's leading biomedical research charities and is the UK's largest non-governmental source of funds for biomedical research. It is also the UK's largest charity.

The trust's mission is to foster and promote research with the aim of improving human and animal health.

Funding from the trust has supported a number of major successes including:

- sequencing of the human genome
- development of the antimalarial drug artemisinin
- pioneering cognitive behavioural therapies for psychological disorders
- establishing UK Biobank
- building the Wellcome Wing at the Science Museum.

The trust's major activities in 2009/10 are described by its chair, Sir William Castell, in its annual review as follows:

> In his will, Wellcome noted that: 'With the enormous possibility of development in chemistry, bacteriology, pharmacy and allied sciences [...] there are likely to be vast fields opened for productive enterprise for centuries to come.' The trust's first 75 years [celebrated in 2011] have indeed been highly productive. Through our investment in research, we have made major contributions to science and medicine, technology transfer, medical humanities and public engagement.
>
> *Our strategic approach*
>
> How can we ensure that the coming years are just as fruitful? In February 2010 we launched our new Strategic Plan to guide our activities. Unlike our previous five-year plans, this new framework covers the decade 2010–20. It takes a long time to make scientific discoveries, so we want to empower researchers to ask difficult and challenging questions and give them the confidence that they will have the time to find the answers. As part of the Plan, we set out five research challenges: maximising the health benefits of genetics and genomics; understanding the brain; combating infectious disease; investigating development, ageing and chronic disease; and connecting environment, nutrition and health. These are areas where we already fund many talented researchers and activities, but we are now setting out a vision of how our funding can have a significant impact over the next ten years and beyond.
>
> We have launched a major new funding scheme, Wellcome Trust Investigator Awards, to accompany the new Strategic Plan. These extend our ethos of funding talented and innovative researchers, and giving them the freedom and resources they need. The first successful recipients of Investigator Awards will be announced in 2011.
>
> During 2010 we celebrated the tenth anniversary of the completed first draft of the human genome sequence. This landmark in biomedical science was the starting point for a decade of discoveries in how variation in the genome influences health and disease. The Wellcome Trust Sanger Institute has been at the forefront of this research, and one of its many achievements during the year was to produce the first comprehensive analyses of cancer genomes. The studies reveal, for the first time, almost all of the mutations in the genomes of a lung cancer and a malignant skin melanoma. This research will aid the development of new drugs that target specific mutated cancer genes and help to determine which patients would benefit from such treatments.
>
> The Wellcome Trust Sanger Institute will also take the lead on the ambitious UK10K project, launched in June. This aims to decode the genomes of 10,000 people over the next three years, enabling an unprecedented level of study of individual human genomes and disease. Professor Mike Stratton took the helm of the Institute this year; his strategy is to build on the Institute's leadership in large-scale genome analysis to explore human and animal biology, and provide new insights into how disease develops.
>
> While some projects – such as UK10K – we fund alone, for others we can be even more effective if we work in partnership. For example, an exciting new development is a £37 million partnership with the UK government, the Technology Strategy Board, the East of England Development Agency and GlaxoSmithKline. This will build on 'open innovation' models to create a world-leading hub in Stevenage for early-stage biotech companies to translate research into health benefits. In addition, working with the Indian government's Department of Biotechnology, we launched a new £45 million partnership to support the development of innovative healthcare products. India's biotechnology sector is extremely vibrant, and we hope this new scheme will catalyse the development of new healthcare products at an affordable cost.
>
> *Medicine and culture*
>
> A rather different partnership led to Wellcome Collection's first major overseas exhibition, which took place

in Japan. Medicine and Art, co-curated by Wellcome Collection and the Mori Art Museum in Tokyo, considered the fundamental question of the meaning of life and death from the parallel perspectives of science and art.

Back in London, Wellcome Collection has continued to go from strength to strength, with the major exhibitions Skin and Identity. The latter formed part of the Trust's Identity Project, a season of activities focused on the captivating topic of human identity. This included our first major performance arts production – Pressure Drop, a passionate new play from acclaimed writer and theatre director Mick Gordon, with music and songs by Billy Bragg. I would also like to highlight the success of the film The English Surgeon. Made by film maker Geoffrey Smith and part-funded by the Trust, the film won the 2010 Emmy for Outstanding Science and Technology Programming.

Investments

The scale of our support for research is entirely driven by the health of our investment portfolio. I am delighted to report that, in 2009/10, our broadly based positive return of 11.1%, equating to £1.45 billion on a portfolio value of £13 billion at the start of the year, has propelled our investment returns to all-time record levels and provided a net endowment value of £13.9 billion at year end. This progress is due to our actions to reduce risk ahead of the financial crisis and to acquire assets at distressed prices in late 2008 and 2009.

Since September 2008, we have invested directly in a long-term basket of global stocks, principally in shares of 32 companies that each have a market capitalisation above $75 billion. To date, we have returned 25% on these direct investments, valued at £2.1 billion. A further £1.8 billion of our £6.6 billion public equity portfolio is invested in markets in the fast-growing economies of Africa, Asia, Latin America and the Middle East; in 2009/10, these investments delivered returns in excess of 20%. During the past two years, our total public equity assets have outperformed global stock markets by 12%. [...]

Grantmaking

In 2009/10 the trust had assets of over £13.9 billion and an income of £230.3 million. Grants were made during the year totalling £551.5 million.

Amongst the many grants awarded during the year were those to universities and other institutions, mainly in the UK, but also elsewhere (these figures represent the total amount awarded during the year, and may comprise many grants):

University of Oxford	£79.4 million
University of Cambridge	£51.7 million
University College London	£37.9 million
University of Edinburgh	£28 million
University of Dundee	£26.6 million
Kenya Medical Research Institute	£24.1 million
Imperial College London	£18 million
London School of Hygiene and Tropical Medicine	£14.4 million
University of Manchester	£13.7 million
UK Biobank Ltd	£12.5 million
King's College London	£12.3 million
University of Bristol	£12 million
University of Newcastle Upon Tyne	£11 million
University of Glasgow	£9.8 million
Structural Genomics Consortium Ltd	£8 million
Cardiff University	£7.3 million
University of York	£6.3 million
University of Liverpool	£6.2 million
Stevenage Bioscience Catalyst Limited	£6 million
Wellcome Trust–Department of Biotechnology India Alliance	£5.6 million
University of Birmingham	£5.1 million
Diamond Light Source Ltd	£5 million
University of Leeds	£4.6 million
Institute of Cancer Research	£4.1 million
St George's, University of London	£4.1 million
University of Leicester	£3.3 million
University of Sheffield	£3.2 million
Keele University	£3.1 million
Grants to other institutions	£62.5 million

Grantmaking Policy

The trust supports high-quality research across both the breadth of the biomedical sciences and the spectrum of proposals from 'blue skies' to clinical to applied research, and encourages the translation of research findings into medical benefits.

Although the majority of grants are awarded to United Kingdom recipients, there are also a number of schemes designed specifically for overseas applicants.

For the most part grant funding is channeled through a university or similar institution in response to proposals submitted by individual academic researchers. Applications are peer reviewed using referees selected by trust staff from the United Kingdom and international research communities. Expert committees, which also include members from outside the United Kingdom, make most funding decisions, with external experts also brought into Strategic Award Committee meetings to assist in the decision-making process.

Grant awards are made to the employing institution, which is then required to take responsibility for administering a grant in accordance with its purpose and with the terms and conditions attached to the award. Only a limited number of small-scale awards are made directly to individuals. Grant funding is available via a range of schemes including:

- short-term awards for between a few months and three years, and longer-term project and programme grants for research, usually for up to five years
- awards for research training and career development where support is provided for individuals at all stages of their careers
- strategic awards to provide outstanding research groups with significant levels of support.

The trust is aware of the profound impact biomedical research has on society and in its grant making also seeks to raise awareness of the medical, ethical and social implications of research and to promote dialogue between scientists, the public and policy makers.

The trust also undertakes activities in and funds research into the history of medicine. The Wellcome Library, which forms part of Wellcome Collection, provides access to resources that support its activities, and the trust also provides grant funding for improved access to and preservation of other medical history collections in the United Kingdom.

In addition to the above, the Trust funds its own research institute, the Wellcome Trust Sanger Institute, channelling support through a wholly-owned subsidiary, Genome Research Limited. Led by Allan Bradley, the Director of the Sanger Institute, its researchers are engaged in research programmes using large-scale sequencing, informatics and analysis of genetic variation to further understanding of gene function in health and disease and to generate data and resources of lasting value to biomedical research.

Strategic plan 2010–2020

The trust publishes its strategic plan 2010–2020 on its website:

For over 70 years, the Wellcome Trust has supported research of the highest quality with the aim of improving human and animal health. In our Strategic Plan for 2010–20, we present a vision that describes how we will work with our communities to evolve our support to be even more effective in achieving this aim. Our decision to develop a ten-year Plan reflects the long-term view we take in supporting research and the complex and global nature of the challenges that we face.

During the last five years, we have introduced several new approaches to our grant making. Strategic Awards enable outstanding research teams to take forward large and ambitious programmes of work. Our support for technology transfer to enable the practical applications of research has expanded, with the introduction of new schemes such as Seeding Drug Discovery. We have launched major initiatives to build individual and institutional research capacity in low- and middle-income countries. Wellcome Collection has opened as an innovative public venue for exploration and debate of medicine, life and art.

We have supported the work of thousands of individuals and teams leading to many important outcomes. Pioneering research at the Wellcome Trust Sanger Institute and in universities has transformed our understanding of the role of genetic variation in health and disease. The work at our Major Overseas Programmes has played a significant role in the fight against global diseases. Our support for the National Science Learning Centre in the UK has enhanced the professional development of science teachers in schools.

Looking ahead, we identify five major challenges for our partners in the research community. Each of these challenges contains many important research questions and opportunities. These range across the broadest spectrum of research, from structural biology to public health. We recognise that each of the challenges is enormous and complex and will require ambitious approaches to make progress. We will work in partnership to provide the funding and support to tackle these challenges. We will build on our key at tributes; these are our scale, our long track record, our independence, our dedication to research excellence, our ability to work in partnership, and the unique breadth of our funding activities.

We will provide talented and innovative researchers with the freedom and resources that they need to generate the discoveries that are essential to overcome these challenges. Our funding philosophy is to support the brightest researchers at all stages of their careers and to create the environments that they need for their research. We will support a wide range of activities to accelerate the application of research that can benefit health. We will maximise opportunities to engage diverse audiences with medical science and the questions that science raises for society.

This Plan for the next decade provides the basis on which we will develop our funding strategies. It sets out how we will assess progress towards our goals, so that we can help to realise extraordinary improvements in health.

Our vision is to achieve extraordinary improvements in human and animal health.

Our mission is to support the brightest minds in biomedical research and the medical humanities.

Our funding focuses on:
1 Supporting outstanding researchers
2 Accelerating the application of research
3 Exploring medicine in historical and cultural contexts.

Our five major challenges are:
1 Maximising the health benefits of genetics and genomics
2 Understanding the brain
3 Combating infectious disease
4 Investigating development, ageing and chronic disease
5 Connecting environment, nutrition and health.

Exclusions

The trust does not normally consider support for the extension of professional education or experience, the care of patients or clinical trials.

Contributions are not made towards overheads and not normally towards office expenses.

The trust does not supplement support provided by other funding bodies, nor does it donate funds for other charities to use, nor does it respond to general appeals.

Applications

eGrants: online application

The eGrants system enables applicants to apply for grants online. The system provides workflow to steer the application through head of department and university administration approval steps until final submission to the Wellcome Trust.

Most applicants for Science Funding and Medical Humanities grants are required to submit their applications via our eGrants system. However, Word forms are still available for:
▶ preliminary applications
▶ Public Engagement grants
▶ Technology Transfer grants
▶ for applicants who have limited/ unreliable access to the internet – please email the eGrants helpdesk: ga-formsupport@wellcome.ac.uk.

If you haven't applied using eGrants before, here is what you need to do:
▶ make sure your institution (or the institution that would be administering the grant, if you are not already based there) is registered with us and fill in a

home page for yourself (this will include your personal details that can be downloaded onto future application forms).

Other people – such as coapplicants – will need to fill in details too.

The benefits of our eGrants system include:
▶ better functionality
▶ clear sign off process through the host institution
▶ reduced administration at the Trust
▶ helping us to capture management information (useful for us and useful for you).

How to register

You can register with eGrants through the log-in page. Further information on the registration process, help and guidance notes are available by accessing this page.

Registration status of institutions

If you wish to register with eGrants but are not sure whether your institution is registered, you can check the list of registered institutions. If your institution is not on this list you should contact your administration office directly for further information.

Frequently asked questions

A list of frequently asked questions for eGrants is available from the trust's website.

The Welton Foundation

Medical research, health, the arts, general

£564,000 (2009/10)

Beneficial area

UK and overseas.

Old Waterfield, Winkfield Road, Ascot, Berkshire SL5 7LJ
Correspondent: The Trustees
Trustees: D B Vaughan; H A Stevenson; Dr Michael Harding.
CC Number: 245319

Information available

Accounts were available at the Charity Commission.

Registered in 1965, the objective of the foundation is 'to provide financial support to other charities at the absolute discretion of the trustees. As a discretionary trust the foundation has no fixed policy for making grants. The current policy of the trustees is in the main to support charitable causes in the fields of health and medicine, but they can exercise their discretion to make donations to any other charities'.

In 2009/10 the foundation had assets of £6.4 million and an income of £268,000. Grants were made to 23 organisations during the year totalling £564,000, categorised as follows:

Health and medicine	11	£443,500
Culture and the arts	3	£105,000
Education and training	6	£14,000
Caring for the elderly	1	£5,000
Community development	1	£3,000
Disability	1	£3,000

Beneficiaries included: University of Cape Town (£150,000); Royal Marsden Cancer Campaign, Great Ormond Street Children's Charity and the Royal Academy (£100,000 each); Wellbeing of Women (£50,000); Combat Stress and the Speech, Language and Hearing Centre (£10,000 each); Elizabeth Finn Care and St Andrew's Club (£5,000 each); Court Based Personal Support (£3,000); One to One Children's Fund (£2,500); and Paintings in Hospitals (£2,000).

Exclusions

Grants only to registered charities, and not in response to general appeals.

Applications

The foundation has previously stated that 'due to the number of appeals received, the foundation only replies to those that are successful'. However the foundation now also states that grants are not made to unsolicited applicants.

The Westminster Foundation

Social welfare, military charities, education, environment and conservation

£4.8 million (2010)

Beneficial area

Unrestricted, in practice mainly UK. Local interests in central London (SW1 and W1 and immediate environs), North West England, especially rural Lancashire and the Chester area, and the Sutherland area of Scotland.

70 Grosvenor Street, London
W1K 3JP
Tel: 020 7408 0988
Fax: 020 7312 6244
Email: westminster.foundation@grosvenor.com
Website: www.grosvenorestate.com/charity
Correspondent: Mrs J Sandars, Administrator
Trustees: The Duke of Westminster, Chair; Jeremy H M Newsum; Mark Loveday.
CC Number: 267618

Information available

Accounts were available at the Charity Commission.

The foundation was established in 1974 for general charitable purposes by the fifth Duke of Westminster and continues to make grants to a wide range of charitable causes. In 1987 the Grosvenor Foundation, a separately registered charity, transferred all its assets to The Westminster Foundation. This is assumed to be a largely personal trust, created by the present duke. He is well known in the charity world for his active personal involvement in many organisations, and no doubt a significant number of the regular beneficiaries are organisations with which he has developed a personal connection that goes beyond grantmaking.

The foundation makes over 100 grants a year, mainly for welfare and educational causes but with significant support for the environment and conservation.

Grants can be for very large amounts, but generally, all but a handful are usually for amounts of not more than £60,000 and most are between £5,000 and just a few hundred pounds. About half of the beneficiaries were also supported in previous years. The foundation has significantly increased its grantmaking in recent years, and in 2010 it spent over 150% more on its charitable activities than the previous year.

The foundation provides the following information on its website:

The Westminster Foundation aims to address human welfare and environmental issues in certain geographic areas only (see below) by supporting appropriate registered charities. Projects and activities which tackle social, educational and welfare issues have been a priority of the foundation since 1974.

Grants are made to charities whose work is both:
- within our three key funding categories, and
- in key communities local to businesses and land owned by the Grosvenor Estate. In the UK this means areas such as London W1 & SW1, the North West of England (specifically Chester and the surrounding area and rural Lancashire around the Trough of Bowland), the Sutherland and Edinburgh areas of Scotland and any areas where the property company 'Grosvenor' is undertaking large development projects.

The foundation only gives grants to groups and organisations that are registered with the Charity Commission of England and Wales or Office of the Scottish Office Regulator, or where the grant is for an exclusively charitable purpose.

Social Care and Education
- Social care – registered charities that support, for example, homeless people; prison offenders (with an emphasis on assisting return to gainful employment); those with learning difficulties; facial disfigurements; elderly people; relief for those with chronic or terminal illness.
- Education – in topics relevant to Grosvenor's core business activities (property, land management, historic buildings, construction); development of skills to help disadvantaged people, especially young people.

Military Welfare
Registered charities that support serving and former members of the armed services.

Environment and Conservation
Registered charities that support protection of rural or specific habitats in areas of geographical relevance to the Grosvenor Estate.

In 2010 the foundation had assets of £37.8 million and an income of £3.9 million, which included donations of £1.5 million and £1.3 million from the Grosvenor Family and Grosvenor Group Limited respectively. Grants were made to 151 organisations totalling £4.8 million (£2.1 million in 2009), and were broken down as follows:

Social care and education	115	£2.1 million
Military welfare	20	£1.5 million
Environment and conservation	16	£1.2 million

The beneficiaries of the largest grants during the year were: Combat Stress (£1 million over 4 years), for an initiative to develop and deliver a tailor made programme as part of the Enemy Within Appeal for veterans of the Territorial Army suffering from Post Traumatic Stress Disorder; Bray Fellowship (£1 million over 3 years), towards the capital costs over of major restoration work required at St George's Chapel – Windsor; and the North Highland Initiative (£300,000 over 3 years), towards the third phase of a project to bring together the farming community, local businesses and the tourism industry to try to address some of the challenges facing rural communities in the Scottish Highlands.

Other beneficiaries included: St Mungo's (£117,000 over 3 years), for a salary and core project costs; Community Foundation for Merseyside (£105,000), towards the grants programme of the Duke of Westminster's Liverpool ONE Foundation; Land Aid Charitable Trust (£101,000 over 4 years), towards its grants programme; Radicle (£75,000 over 3 years), towards salaries and running costs; The Clink (£66,000), for the salary of the chief executive; Kidscape (£55,500 over 3 years), towards the charity's rent; Start-Up Online (£45,000 over 3 years), towards staffing and running costs; NSPCC (£30,000), towards the

costs of recruitment and training for 15 volunteer counsellors for ChildLine North West; UK4U (£25,000), towards the cost of Christmas boxes for armed services personnel serving overseas; and Macmillan Cancer Support (£20,000), towards the salary costs of a Macmillan Nurse Consultant at the Royal Marsden Hospital.

Exclusions
Only registered charities will be considered. No grants to individuals, 'holiday' charities, student expeditions, or research projects.

Applications
In writing to the correspondent, 'as succinctly as possible and including only the most relevant details relating to the application'. The trustees meet four times a year.

Details of current application deadlines are published on the foundation's website.

The Garfield Weston Foundation

General
£34.2 million (2009/10)

Beneficial area
UK.

Weston Centre, 10 Grosvenor Street, London W1K 4QY
Tel: 020 7399 6565
Website: www.garfieldweston.org
Correspondent: Philippa Charles, Administrator
Trustees: Camilla H W Dalglish; Catrina A Hobhouse; Jana R Khayat; Sophia M Mason; Eliza L Mitchell; W Galen Weston; George G Weston: Melissa Murdoch.
CC Number: 230260

Information available
Excellent descriptive annual report and accounts with an analysis of a selection of grants, large and small, and a full list of beneficiaries.

Summary
This huge foundation makes about 1,500 one-off grants a year, typically for amounts anywhere between £3,000 and £1 million. It was established by Willard Garfield Weston, a Canadian businessman and philanthropist whose many companies included Associated British Foods. Awards are regularly made in almost all fields except overseas aid and animal welfare.

Probably more than 85% of the money, and an even higher proportion for the largest grants, is for capital or endowment projects.

The published 'criteria' for grantmaking, reported below, are in the most general terms. Compared to the general run of trusts described elsewhere, there are relatively few grants to unconventional causes, or for campaigning or representational activities, and more for institutions such as independent schools and charities connected with private hospitals. Nevertheless, almost all kinds of charitable activity, including the radical, are supported to some extent. Grants are rarely given to major charities with high levels of fundraising costs. The foundation is one of the few which can consider very large grants.

The foundation's trustees are backed by a very modest staff, but nevertheless the foundation aims to deal with applications within four months of them being received.

Grantmaking criteria
This application guidance is available on the trust's website:

What are the trustees looking for in an application?
Applications are considered individually by the Foundation trustees. In assessing applications, the following issues are taken into consideration so please bear this in mind to ensure your application is able to address these things.

1. The financial viability of the organisation:
Organisations that are relatively stable financially tend to be in a better position to run effectively and deliver the quality of services for which the charity was created. Therefore the trustees look for signs that the organisation is likely to remain running – these signs include, but are not limited to, past history, local support,

an appropriate level of reserves, statutory and local council funding.

2. The degree of need for the project requiring funding
There are many ways to evaluate this, however indicators include the level of local commitment to the project, evidenced by such things as fundraising activity, volunteer effort, local authority support, numbers who will benefit etc.

3. The amount spent on administration and fundraising as compared to the charitable activities
The Charity Commission indicates a target of 10% for administration

4. The ability to raise sufficient funding to meet the appeal target
The trustees are keen to assist projects where they can have a high degree of confidence that the necessary funds can be secured from relevant sources, therefore it is important to demonstrate the level of funds already secured and from what sources; as well as the likely targets to address any shortfall.

5. Whether the organisation has appropriate priorities and plans in place to manage its activities.
This includes ensuring that core services are adequately resourced and stable before expanding into new projects, locations or services. It also refers to the ability of an organisation to secure appropriate funding for key projects & services and that necessary capabilities are available for operational success.

In 2009/10 the foundation had assets standing at £4.1 billion and an income of just over £60 million. There were 1,529 grants made during the year totalling £34.2 million. For more information on the trust's grantmaking figures see the table below.

Grants in 2009/10

National, London and 'other'	£18 million
South East England	£3.1 million
South West England	£2.4 million
Eastern England	£2.2 million
North East England	£1.7 million

West Midlands	£1.4 million
North West England	£1.3 million
Scotland	£1.2 million
Wales	£1.2 million
East Midlands	£760,000
Yorkshire and the Humber	£600,500
Northern Ireland	£313,500

The following detailed analysis of grantmaking is taken from the foundation's 2009/10 annual report:

Arts
In the Arts category, the largest grant was made to the Royal Opera House (ROH) for £1 million. The ROH has continued to develop since its major refurbishment and has been especially focused on widening participation and on education work to engage a broad range of audiences. The organisation has an ongoing challenge to balance the high fixed cost base required to maintain a quality repertoire with variable revenue, and is developing wider income streams from commercial activity. The grant was made to support work across the range of ROH's activities in acknowledgement of the excellence of its work and of the importance of having a sustainable financial base.

There were three grants made of £500,000; the first was to Sadler's Wells for the development of a new studio theatre through the acquisition of an adjacent building. The second £500,000 grant was to the Royal Shakespeare Company in Stratford-upon-Avon for the final phase of its new theatre and visitor facilities which are nearing completion and in the final stages of fundraising. The third grant was a pledge to the Rambert Dance Company for their new building.

Four grants of £250,000 were made to: The Royal Welsh College of Music & Drama; Chetham's School of Music in Manchester, Bristol Old Vic Trust and the London Academy of Music & Dramatic Art. The Royal Welsh College of Music & Drama provides specialist practical and performance-based training for 600 students a year. The grant was towards a new building to house a new recital hall, theatre, four acting and movement studios, an exhibition space and a renovated television studio.

A grant of £200,000 was made to The Art Fund towards the purchase of the Staffordshire Hoard for the nation. With the discovery of 1,662 artefacts, the Hoard is the largest collection of Anglo-Saxon objects ever found in England and includes over 5kg of gold and 1.5kg of silver. It is comprised solely of war-related items including gold crosses, helmet fixtures and sword pommels. The Hoard will be managed jointly by the Potteries Museum in Stoke-on-Trent and the Birmingham Museum and Art Gallery, ensuring the artefacts are conserved appropriately and are available for public viewing.

The Midlands Arts Centre, 'mac', received £100,000 for a major refurbishment and renovation project. The centre is an arts venue in Birmingham offering a wide range of activities for all ages, including theatre, music, dance, pottery, films and exhibitions. The revived spaces provide improved access, a new performing arts studio, double height gallery, café and bar area, larger non-gallery exhibition spaces, refurbished pottery studios, a digital media studio and improved visitor facilities.

Community
In general this category is notable for a high volume of grants. The trustees remain aware that relatively small grants can have a transformational effect in this category as they are proportional to the size of projects. Another feature of this category is the fact that grants are spread widely across all parts of the UK as activity is not necessarily concentrated in the major cities and urban areas – grants include the smallest hamlets and villages in remote areas.

The largest grant in this category was for £100,000 to the Bishopsgate Institute near Liverpool Street Station in London. Each year the Institute has nearly 80,000 visitors who use the facilities and library and attend courses and events. The library holds over 110,000 items and includes unique book and archive collections which provide a focus for research into the history of London, in particular the East End, and the freethought, early labour, humanist, and co-operative movements. A major renovation project is transforming the Institute into a fully refurbished and vibrant centre. The refurbishment will include updating the Great Hall into a state-of-the-art performing arts venue, creating a dedicated learning space, a café, a specialist Library archive store, disabled access and modern studios. The project will also clean, repair and illuminate the striking façade of the building.

Other examples of grants in this category include the North London Muslim Community Centre and Credit Action.

THE GARFIELD WESTON FOUNDATION

	£20,000 and over		Less than £20,000		Total amount	Total no. of grants
Arts	£5.3 million	44	£350,000	52	£5.7 million	96
Community	£470,000	12	£1.3 million	272	£1.8 million	294
Education	£11.5 million	60	£473,500	76	£12 million	136
Environment	£2.1 million	16	£111,000	14	£2.3 million	30
Health	£3.7 million	44	£472,000	64	£4.2 million	108
Religion	£1.1 million	16	£1.7 million	420	£2.8 million	436
Welfare	£1.8 million	43	£1.1 million	181	£2.9 million	224
Youth	£1.5 million	33	£821,000	167	£2.3 million	200
Other	£250,000	7	£39,000	8	£289,000	15

Education

This category received the highest proportion of funds granted this financial year and it is notable that this sector includes a broad range of activities, from museums and science centres to special schools and education in specialist subjects such as ballet. The largest grant made was to the British Museum which received £3 million towards the new Research Institute for Science and Conservation – while based in central London it is anticipated that work conducted in this Centre will benefit galleries and museums across the country for the research and preservation of precious historical artefacts. The existing facilities are not fit for purpose with difficult-to-access spaces and lack of light, the new Centre will provide state-of-the-art research and conservation laboratories as well as a special exhibition gallery to engage the public in conservation activity.

There were five grants made of £500,000; one such was made to the Centre for Life in Newcastle which provides hands-on science education that cannot be replicated in the classroom, along with workshops for all ages, a planetarium and a series of permanent exhibition galleries with spaces aimed at different audiences and age groups. The grant was towards the refurbishment of a permanent exhibition space called 'Curiosity' which is designed to encourage experimentation and interactive learning. Exeter University also received £500,000 as part of a major campus refurbishment, as did the Royal Society for the development of Chicheley Hall, a residential centre for science and learning near Milton Keynes. The Historic Royal Palaces received £500,000 towards the upgrade of public spaces at Kensington Palace, enabling a more interactive accessible and vibrant experience for visitors. The fifth grant of £500,000 was to the Science Museum in London for a major new gallery on Climate Change.

The grant of £350,000 for Wells Cathedral School was towards their capital campaign to build a new music hall with performance and teaching spaces along with quality recording facilities.

There were ten grants of £250,000 which included the Scott Polar Research Institute at Cambridge University, and Edinburgh Napier University. All grants made of £250,000 were for capital purposes. The Scott Polar Research Institute, which is the UK's only dedicated polar museum and is a national repository for archives recording some of the most memorable episodes in the exploration of the Arctic and Antarctic, is creating a suite of new galleries which will exhibit many unseen items as well as enabling wider educational outreach.

Donations of £100,000 included Cheltenham Museum, Reading University, the Royal National College for the Blind in Hereford and the Museum of East Anglia.

Religion

As with previous years, this category received the highest volume of grants and, as with the Community category, a feature of this sector is the wide geographical spread of grants across the UK, reflecting the position of many churches in remote and rural areas. Many grants in this category are made to support fabric repair projects to listed church buildings across the country which are an important part of the UK's heritage and which also perform a vital function as community meeting spaces, especially for those requiring support such as the elderly and those with young families. The foundation has supported such projects since its inception over 50 years ago and the trustees are delighted to continue this work.

There were two grants of £250,000 in this category; one to the Cathedral and Abbey Church of St Alban for fabric repair and restoration works and the other to St Mellitus College. The Cathedral and Abbey Church of St Alban is documented from early times and the building has the longest nave in the UK, along with magnificent views from the top of the tower. The building has a wealth of ancient features and an active congregation – the work of the cathedral is supported by over 1,000 volunteers. The grant was to support the most urgent repairs including replacement wiring, stonework repairs in the nave, new guttering and refurbishment to the West of the Cathedral.

St Mellitus is a theological training college of the Church of England based in the dioceses of London and Chelmsford. A key part of their approach is to offer practical hands-on training in communities combined with academic theological study to provide a thorough and realistic preparation for full-time ministry. The grant was made towards the fit-out costs of new library and teaching facilities, spaces for filming lectures and seminars, and web-enabled technology to allow courses to be transmitted to colleges across the world.

Other significant grants in this category include grants of £100,000 to the Norwich Cathedral Trust and to St Patrick's in Soho Square in London, both for refurbishments to community and congregation facilities.

Welfare

The largest grant in this category was to Methodist Homes for the Aged for £250,000 towards a new residential dementia care and nursing centre in Harwich which will complement existing services for the elderly on the site. The project will provide care and accommodation for over 70 people with 24-hour expert assistance available while enabling maximum possible independence for the residents.

There were five grants of £100,000 in this category which included Human Rights Watch, The Mayor's Fund, Lench's Trust, ExtraCare and Erskine. The grant to Human Rights Watch was for general operational costs and both grants to ExtraCare and Lench's Trust were for supported accommodation for the elderly.

Other recipients in this category included the Sir Oswald Stoll Foundation for homes for ex-Service personnel; the Forgiveness Project for their work with offenders and victims in running restorative justice programmes and to St Cuthbert's Centre in West London for practical support to the homeless with the provision of healthy hot meals, washing facilities and advice.

Youth

As in previous years, the activities in one category may overlap with others and this is especially true for the youth category where much good work with young people is also undertaken by community and church groups across the country. The items noted in the Youth sector have been specifically dedicated to the benefit of young people and range from organisations such as Scouting and Boys' Brigade to mentoring and support for training and employment.

The largest grant made in this category was to Fairbridge and was for £250,000. Fairbridge runs personal development courses for young people, especially the 'NEET' population, addressing the issues of long term unemployment, crime, drugs, abuse and antisocial behaviour. Over 3,000 young people participate in their programmes annually across 13 centres operating in the most disadvantaged areas of the UK.

Three grants of £100,000 were made to the The British Sports Trust, the Outward Bound Trust (OBT) and The Challenge Network. The grant to the OBT was towards the costs involved in engaging disadvantaged children with outdoor adventure and learning programmes – over half the participants receive some level of financial assistance each year and around 26,000 young people benefit from OBT programmes annually.

The Sports Leaders grant was towards core costs; the organisation runs courses across the UK enabling young people to achieve awards and qualifications in tandem with leading community groups in sporting activity.

These awards enable young people to learn essential skills of leadership, including communication, organisation and motivation, as well as developing into good volunteers. Sport Leaders has identified 25 key locations across the country in the most deprived areas and is placing particular emphasis on working in these areas.

Environment

The largest grant in this category was a pledge made to English Heritage for £1 million towards the Stonehenge project to create a visitor centre with appropriate facilities, including re-routing the busy road that drives traffic right through the stones of this World Heritage site. The importance of this particular site to the UK's environmental heritage is incomparable and the project combines excellent facilities for the large number of visitors to the site while ensuring low impact on the important landscape and archaeological sites surrounding Stonehenge.

Other significant grants in this category include £250,000 to Oceana UK which aims to protect and restore the oceans of the world which are suffering from pollution, over-fishing and damaging practices such as bottom-trawling. The grant was for a range of projects aimed at delivering benefits to marine biodiversity in the UK, including the preservation of coral reefs along the Scottish coast and of algae and marine seagrass species at risk from over-fishing and damaging practices.

A grant of £100,000 was made to the Durrell Institute for Conservation Education (DICE) which undertakes research, training and the management of international biodiversity projects. This grant was towards bursaries for DICE's highly successful Masters degree in Conservation Biology which aims to educate students in the key issues (especially political, legal and social) required to generate change in behaviour and practice.

Health

In the health category the largest grant was for £1 million to the Royal Marsden Hospital towards a fully updated Critical Care Unit (CCU). The hospital experienced a fire in January 2008 and is using the resulting repairs as an opportunity to upgrade facilities as insurance covers only like-for-like replacement. The new CCU will include spaces for younger patients, a seminar room for staff development and private areas for discussion with patients and their families. The unit has also been designed to maximise the availability of natural light, a key factor in recovery and wellbeing. With the creation of updated spaces will also come the implementation of a highly sophisticated information system which will allow staff to monitor patient progress on a real-time basis, as well as to provide data on patient trends, a system which will contribute to research as well as to patient care on a more immediate basis.

The second most significant grant in this category was for £500,000 to Cancer Research UK for the new clinical trials unit at The Christie Hospital in Manchester, the largest cancer hospital in Western Europe with around 34,000 new cases annually. The current unit within the hospital is housed on a temporary basis in prefabricated accommodation but lacks space and flexibility, despite receiving around 10,000 patient visits annually. The new unit will provide state-of-the-art laboratories, consultation and treatment rooms and a chemotherapy suite. These new facilities will double the number of patients; once completed the unit will be able to accommodate 2,400 patients participating in 750 trials.

A grant of £250,000 was made to the Royal United Hospital in Bath (Friends Forever Appeal) towards the new neonatal Intensive Care Unit which cares for nearly 500 fragile babies annually. The existing unit is old and cramped and the new centre will provide more space for cots and incubators, privacy for parents and teaching space for professional staff.

Eight grants of £100,000 were made which included grants to the University of Dundee, Birmingham Children's Hospital and the Motor Neurone Disease Association. The grant to the University of Dundee was for the new Institute of Academic Anaesthesia which will focus on developing more effective approaches to pain relief and safer anaesthetic drugs.

Other

There are relatively few grants that do not fit easily within the foundation's existing categories, but some examples include a donation of £30,000 to New Philanthropy Capital towards the core costs of providing advice to charities and for conducting research. A grant of £10,000 was made to Transparency International for their research and information work.

Exclusions

What the foundation is unlikely to fund:

We cannot consider any funding request made within 12 months of the outcome of a previous application, whether a grant was received or not.

- The foundation only considers applications from UK registered charities and your registration number is required (unless you have exempt status as a church, educational establishment, hospital or housing corporation).
- The foundation does not typically fund projects outside the UK, even if the organisation is a registered charity within Britain
- The foundation is not able to accept applications from individuals or for individual research or study.
- The foundation does not support animal welfare charities.
- Typically the foundation does not fund one-off events, galas or festivals, even if for fundraising purposes
- The foundation does not fund specific salaries and positions (though we will consider contributing to the core operating costs of charitable organisations).
- The foundation does not make funding commitments over several years – grants made are typically for a single year.
- It is unusual for the foundation to consider making a grant to organisations who cannot demonstrate significant progress with fundraising, so please bear this in mind when considering the timing of your application. In general, the trustees look for organisations to have raised the majority of funding through local or statutory sources before an approach is made.
- The foundation does not place limits on information sent, however we ask that applications are concise and include only the most relevant details relating to the application.

Applications

In writing to the correspondent. A basic details form is available to download from the foundation's website and must be included with a letter of application.

All applications are considered on an individual basis by a committee of trustees. From time to time, more information about a charity or a visit to the project might be requested. Trustees meet monthly and there is no deadline for applications, which are considered in order of receipt. It normally takes three or four months for an application to be processed. All applicants are notified of the outcome by letter.

Grants are normally made by means of a single payment and the foundation does not normally commit to forward funding.

All applications are asked to include the following information:

- the charity's registration number
- a copy of the most recent report and audited accounts

- an outline description of the charity's activities
- a synopsis of the project requiring funding, with details of who will benefit
- a financial plan
- details of current and proposed fundraising.

The Will Charitable Trust

Environment/ conservation, people with sight loss and the prevention and cure of blindness, cancer care, people with mental disability

£592,000 (2009/10)

Beneficial area

UK and overseas.

Grants Office, Sunbury International Business Centre, Brooklands Close, Sunbury on Thames, Middlesex TW16 7DX

Tel: 01932 724148

Email: admin@willcharitabletrust.org.uk

Website: willcharitabletrust.org.uk

Correspondent: Christine Dix, Grants Administrator

Trustees: Mrs Vanessa A Reburn; Alastair J McDonald; Ian C McIntosh; Rodney Luff.

CC Number: 801682

Information available

Accounts were available at the Charity Commission.

The trust provides financial assistance to charities, mainly in the UK, supporting the following categories:

- care of and services for blind people, and the prevention and cure of blindness
- care of people with learning disabilities in a way that provides lifelong commitment, a family environment and the maximum choice of activities and lifestyle
- care of and services for people suffering from cancer, and their families

- conservation of the countryside in Britain, including its flora and fauna.

The trust provides the following additional information on its grantmaking:

A small proportion of the trust's income may be allocated to assistance in other fields, but this is rare and reserved for causes that have come to the attention of individual trustees. It is therefore only in very exceptional circumstances that the trustees will respond favourably to requests from organisations whose activities fall outside the categories listed above.

General

Grants are awarded only to UK registered or exempt charities which must have proven track records of successful work in their field of operation or, in the case of newer charities, convincing evidence of ability. Grants will only be awarded in response to direct applications from the charity concerned.

The trust will consider grants to charities of all sizes. Accordingly, grants vary in amount, but generally fall within the range of £5,000 to £20,000. The total amount awarded varies from year to year according to available funds. [...]

In the current financial climate, commitments to make future payments are rarely given, with grants normally being one-off annual grants. Charities which have received a grant are encouraged to apply in the next and subsequent years, but should note that only rarely will grants be given to the same charity for four successive years. This does not however mean that a charity that has received three successive grants will not be eligible in future years, just that we would not generally award a grant in year four.

Exceptional grants

The trustees may occasionally consider larger exceptional grants, but this is unusual and generally confined to charities that we know well and have supported for some time. There is no separate application process for this, and contenders will be identified from the normal grant round.

In 2009/10 the trust had assets of £16.9 million and an income of £574,500. There were 43 grants made during the year totalling £592,000, broken down as follows:

Care of cancer patients	15	£161,000
Care of people with learning disabilities	12	£151,000
Care of and services for blind people, and the prevention and cure of blindness	12	£150,000
Wildlife and other conservation	3	£30,000

Beneficiaries in the above categories included: Sightsavers (£20,000); Lakelands Day Care Hospice and Aspire Living Limited (£15,000 each); Essex Wildlife Trust (£14,000); DGSM YourChoice (£13,000); Focus Birmingham (£12,000); South Lakes Society for the Blind (£10,000); Music in Hospitals (£7,000); Gwent Wildlife Trust (£6,000).

In addition to the above, an exceptional grant of £100,000 was made to Maggie's Cancer Caring Centres.

Exclusions

Grants are only given to registered or exempt charities. 'It is unlikely that applications relating to academic or research projects will be successful. The trustees recognise the importance of research, but lack the resources and expertise required to judge its relevance and value.'

Applications

Applications in writing to the correspondent. There are no application forms – the trust offers the following advice on its website on how applications should be presented:

We are not necessarily looking for glossy professional bids and understand that your application to us will vary according to the size of organisation you are, and the size of the proposed project. It can be a professionally prepared presentation pack, but can equally be a short letter with supporting information. Both will receive equal consideration.

Whatever the presentation, the following is a guide to the main areas that we like to see covered. This is however intended only as a guide to assist you in preparing an application, it should not be seen as a prerequisite for applying for a grant – we understand that some small organisations will not have the sort of project(s) that need detailed treatment. Generally, we expect most applications will contain the following:

- An overview of your organisation. Please tell us in a nutshell who you are and what you do.

- Tell us what you want a grant for/ towards. Give us a full description of your project. For instance, what do you hope to achieve/who will benefit from the project and how?
- Costs. Tell us what your project is going to cost, giving details of the main items of expenditure. Tell us how you intend to fund it, and how much you have raised so far.
- A contingency plan. What will you do if you do not raise the funds you need?
- A timetable. Tell us your timescale for raising funds and when you aim to have the project up and running.
- A copy of your latest audited Annual Accounts must be included. A copy of your Annual Review is also useful if you have one.
- Other information. Please include any other information which you feel will assist us in judging your application. This could include for example a copy of any newsletter you produce, or short promotional/ advertising leaflets. Such publications often help give a flavour of an organisation.

Deadlines

Blind people and Learning disabilities

- Applications should be submitted from November and by 31 January at the latest. Decisions are made in the following March and successful applicants will be notified by the end of the month.

Cancer care and Conservation

- Applications should be submitted from June and by 31 August at the latest. Decisions are made in the following November and successful applicants will be notified by the end of the month.

The H D H Wills 1965 Charitable Trust

Wildlife, conservation and general

£698,500 (2009/10)

Beneficial area

Mainly UK.

Henley Knapp Barn, Fulwell, Chipping Norton, Oxfordshire OX7 4EN

Tel: 01608 678051
Email: hdhwills@btconnect.com
Website: www.hdhwills.org/
Correspondent: Wendy Cooper, Trust Secretary
Trustees: John Carson; The Lord Killearn; Lady E H Wills; Dr Catherine Wills; Liell Francklin; Martin Fiennes; Thomas Nelson.
CC Number: 1117747

Information available

Accounts were available at the Charity Commission.

The trust has been endowed by the family of Sir David Wills, from a fortune derived largely from the tobacco company of that name.

The trust runs two separate funds, with each having specific criteria:

General Fund

- grants are only made to registered, exempt or excepted charities
- grants are not generally made to organisations that have been supported within the previous eighteen months
- no grants to individuals
- donations are made to charities which are small enough in size, or which apply for support for a modest project, to benefit substantially from a donation of £250 or £500, though it will consider grants of up to £5,000
- grants may be made towards revenue, capital or project expenditure
- grants are made on a rolling basis and there is no deadline for applications.

The Martin Wills Fund

- grants are only made to registered, exempt or excepted charities
- grants may be made towards revenue, capital or project expenditure.
- grants are distributed after the end of each financial year. The trust's financial year runs from 1 April to 31 March
- applications must be received by the trust before the end of the appropriate financial year
- grants are made between £2,000 and £25,000

- grants are made for the conservation and protection of wildlife or the conservation, protection and improvement of the physical and natural environment to promote the biodiversity of fauna.

In 2009/10 the trust had assets of £53.5 million and an income of £2.6 million. Grants were made from both funds during the year totalling £698,500.

Grants from the Martin Wills Fund are made in a seven year cycle. Check the trust's website for current priorities.

Exclusions

No grants to individuals or national charities.

Applications

In writing to the correspondent. The trust considers small appeals monthly and large ones bi-annually from the Martin Wills Fund. Only one application from a given charity will be considered in any 18-month period.

The Community Foundation for Wiltshire and Swindon

Community welfare

£913,000 (2009/10)

Beneficial area

Wiltshire and Swindon only.

48 New Park Street, Devizes, Wiltshire SN10 1DS
Tel: 01380 729284
Fax: 01380 729772
Email: info@wscf.org.uk
Website: www.wscf.org.uk
Correspondent: Chan Chitroda, Grants Officer
Trustees: Richard Handover, Chair; Elizabeth Webbe; Denise Bentley; Christopher Bromfield; Clare Evans; David Holder; Andrew Kerr; Angus Macpherson; Dame Elizabeth Neville; Tim Odoire; Alison Radevsky; John Rendell; Dr Fiona Richards; Ram

Thiagarajah; Sarah Troughton; John Woodget; Simon Wright.

CC Number: 298936

Information available

Information was taken from the foundation's website.

The Community Foundation was set up in 1991 and is 'dedicated to strengthening local communities by encouraging local giving'. Grant funding is placed where it will make a significant difference to those most in need. The primary focus is on disadvantage including, supporting community care, tackling isolation and investing in young people.

The foundation states:

The Community Foundation for Wiltshire and Swindon has particular strengths as a grant-making organisation. We are local. We understand what life is really like for the groups we support – especially the smaller 'grass-roots' groups. We can also offer help with problems, ideas for development, and regularly put groups in touch with other organisations that can offer specialist advice or assistance.

Grants range in size from £50 to £5,000 and are awarded for up to three years.

The foundation manages a wide range of grant programmes and can provide access to a range of funds.

The foundation's website states that its two main programmes are:

Main Grants Fund
At the heart of our grant making is the Main Grants Fund. Groups can apply to Main Grants to support a wide variety of project, core and ongoing costs.

The Community Foundation for Wiltshire and Swindon will give grants to benefit local communities and to improve the lives of disadvantaged people in Wiltshire and Swindon.

We aim to fund projects which:
- reduce isolation
- improve access to skills development
- provide access to social & recreational opportunities
- improve opportunities for employment
- help people move on with their lives.

We do not make contributions to large building projects under Main Grants, but can help where our grant will help increase accessibility and you cannot get the funding elsewhere.

Small Grants Fund
Grants of up to £500 are available to small projects that have an annual income of no more than £10,000 per annum. This is a fast track programme and applications can be turned around within a month.

Please note: grant schemes can change frequently. Please consult the foundation's website for full details of current programmes and their deadlines.

In 2009/10 the foundation had assets of £7.7 million and an income of £1.8 million. Grants were made totalling £913,000, and were broken down as follows:

Young people	£301,000
Community development	£201,000
Advice/advocacy and specialist service	£182,500
Disability and mental health	£128,000
Older people and their carers	£36,500
Family support	£27,500
Homelessness	£18,500
BME groups	£18,500

Exclusions

The foundation will not fund:
- groups that have more than 12 months running costs in unrestricted (free) reserves
- projects operating outside the County of Wiltshire / Borough of Swindon
- organisations delivering services in Wiltshire or Swindon who do not have a local management structure
- sponsored events
- general large appeals
- the advancement of religion
- medical research and equipment
- animal welfare
- party political activities.

Applications

The foundation describes its application process as follows:

1. To ensure that you do not waste time unnecessarily, we strongly recommend that you read the [exclusions] carefully before you start your expression of interest form.
2. If after step 1, you feel that your project is eligible, fill in our 'Expression of Interest Form'. We will let you know if you are eligible and send you an application pack. We make our application forms as straightforward and as short as possible. If your project is not eligible to apply to one of our funds, we will aim to put you in touch with someone who can help you.
3. Complete the form and return it, within the deadline shown on the front of the pack. If you have any problems completing it, call us for assistance.
4. A member of the Grants Team will assess your application and will either visit or telephone you. This meeting also provides the opportunity to discuss the application further and answer any questions.
5. Your application and our assessment report go forward to the relevant Local Grants Committee. The committee then makes the decisions and these are ratified by our Trustees.
6. If we turn you down, you will get details in writing of the reason why. Contact us by telephone or email and we will let you know if you can re-apply.
7. If you are awarded a grant, you will be asked to report back to us on how the money is spent and has been achieved.

The Harold Hyam Wingate Foundation

Jewish life and learning, performing arts, music, education and social exclusion, overseas development, medical

£695,500 to organisations (2009/10)

Beneficial area
UK and developing world.

2nd Floor, 20–22 Stukeley Street, London WC2B 5LR
Website: www.wingatefoundation. org.uk/
Correspondent: Karen Marshall, Trust Administrator
Trustees: Roger Wingate; Tony Wingate; Prof. Robert Cassen; Prof. David Wingate; Prof. Jonathon Drori; Daphne Hyman; Emily Kasriel; Dr Richard Wingate.
CC Number: 264114

Information available
Accounts were available at the Charity Commission.

The foundation was established in 1960 and aims to support Jewish life and learning, performing arts, music, education and social exclusion, developing countries and medical organisations. The trust also administers the Wingate Scholarships which makes grants to young people with outstanding potential for educational research. The foundation provides the following information on its website about its areas of interest:

Jewish Life and Learning

Jewish Life and Learning are subjects that account for a significant part of the foundation's annual budget.

By their selection of projects, institutions and activities which they would support, the trustees' aspiration is to encourage Jewish cultural, academic and educational life in a manner that enhances the Jewish contribution to the life of the wider community.

In particular, applications are invited from academic institutions specialising in Jewish subjects and from bodies promoting Jewish culture, including museums, libraries and literary publications.

Applications are also welcomed from organisations able to demonstrate a record in inter-faith dialogue, in the promotion of reconciliation between Jews in Israel and their Arab neighbours and the encouragement of liberal values in both communities.

Performing Arts (excluding music)

The foundation has been a consistent supporter of the performing arts. The trustees intend to maintain that policy with particular emphasis on financial support for not-for-profit companies with a record of artistic excellence that require additional funding, not available from public sources or commercial sponsorship, to broaden their repertoire or develop work of potentially outstanding interest which cannot be funded from usual sources.

Assistance will also be considered for training and professional development for creative talent or the technical professions.

Funding to stage productions is not available.

Music

The trustees recognise that music is seriously under-funded in the UK and will consider applications for support in those areas of music performance and education which do not readily attract backing from commercial sponsors or other funding bodies, or which are not eligible for public funding. Priority will be directed towards supporting the work or education of musicians based in, or wishing to study in, the UK, but by no means exclusively so. An important criterion will be whether, in the opinion of the trustees, the funding sought will make a significant difference to the applicant's prospects.

The foundation will be prepared to consider applications for support for on-going expenses and will be willing to consider such support for a period up to three years. Priority will be given to those organisations which give opportunities to young professionals and to education projects for young people as well as for new adult audiences. This would include direct assistance as well as funding for organisations which promote their work or performance, and support for Master Classes.

The foundation reserves the right to draw up particular priorities for a given year such as support for aspiring conductors, young composers, amateur choral work, or the musical education of young people and/or adults.

Education and Social Exclusion

The foundation recognises that there are already considerable public resources allocated to these two areas. However, it will be willing to consider support for projects which may not qualify for public funding or attract other major funding bodies. Contributions towards the running expenses of projects for a strictly limited period will be considered.

Eligible projects would ideally:

▶ be innovative
▶ focus on the disadvantaged
▶ have lasting effects.

Alternatively they should consist of work (e.g. action research, pilot schemes) that would lead to such projects, and preferably they should also be capable of replication if successful.

UK projects which the foundation has supported in the past include those providing for vulnerable and disturbed children, the education of the autistic, homeless children, deaf adults, disabled artists, outreach work of arts organisations and help for ex-offenders.

Please note that we do not fund school capital projects.

Developing Countries

Applications are welcome from organisations working in developing countries for projects in any of the foundation's priority fields, including music and the arts. It will be willing to consider support for projects which may not qualify for public funding or attract other major funding bodies. However the foundation would welcome applications which address the particular problem of water supply.

Projects supported in the past have included education for scheduled castes in India, training for classical musicians in South Africa and water supply in Africa.

In 2009/10 the foundation had assets of £10 million and an income of just over £378,000. Grants were made to organisations totalling £695,500. The ratio of the value of grants made to organisations during the year were categorised as follows:

	% of total
Medical research	19%
Education and social exclusion	12%
Jewish life and learning	8%
Music	8%
Development projects	7%
Performing arts	5%
Literary prizes	1%

Beneficiaries of the largest grants were: Queen Mary & Westfield College (£142,000); Whitechapel Society for the Advancement of Knowledge of Gastroenterology (£79,500); World Ort Union (£28,000); Oxford Centre for Hebrew & Jewish Studies (£25,000); and the Soho Theatre (£18,000).

Smaller grants included those to: London Sinfonietta and the Who Cares? Trust (£10,000 each); Childhood First (£9,000); Springboard for Children (£8,000); The Jewish Museum – London (£7,500); Brandon Centre and London Master Classes (£6,500 each); Bush Theatre, Dhaka Ahsania Mission and The Place2Be (£5,000 each); Cardboard Citizens and the Busoga Trust (£3,000 each); Young Concert Artists Trust (£2,500); and the London School of Medicine & Dentistry (£1,000).

The Scholarship Fund awarded grants totalling £472,600 (40% of the foundation's total grants). For more information on the foundation's scholarship fund, visit: www.wingatescholarships.org.uk.

Exclusions

No grants to individuals (the scholarship fund is administered separately). The foundation will not normally make grants to the general funds of large charitable bodies, wishing instead to focus support on specific projects.

Applications

Applicants are advised to write to the trust administrator with full details, including the most recent financial accounts. Applications are only acknowledged if a stamped addressed envelope is enclosed or if the application is successful.

The administrator of the foundation only deals with enquiries by post and it is hoped that the guidelines and examples of previous support for successful applicants, given on the foundation's website, provides sufficient information. There is no email address for the foundation. Trustee meetings are held quarterly and further information on upcoming deadlines can be found on the foundation's website.

Common applicant mistakes

'Requesting support for individuals; asking for capital funding; being politically correct and ticking boxes appropriate for public funding rather than making the application individual and independent.'

The Wixamtree Trust

General. In particular, social welfare, environment and conservation, medicine and health, the arts, education, sports and leisure and training and employment

£652,000 (2009/10)

Beneficial area

UK, in practice mainly Bedfordshire.

148 The Grove, West Wickham, Kent BR4 9JZ
Tel: 020 8777 4140
Email: wixamtree@ thetrustpartnership.com
Website: www.wixamtree.org
Correspondent: Paul Patten, Administrator
Trustees: Sam C Whitbread; Mrs J M Whitbread; H F Whitbread; Charles E S Whitbread; Geoff McMullen; I A D Pilkington.
CC Number: 210089

Information available

Accounts were available at the Charity Commission.

The trust was established in 1949 for general charitable purposes. It considers requests from registered charities based or operating within Bedfordshire. A small number of national charities with a focus on family social issues are also supported. The trustees are also sympathetic towards applications received from organisations of which the late Humphrey Whitbread was a benefactor.

The trust has a formal agreement with Bedfordshire and Hertfordshire Historic Churches Trust (BHHCT), which uses its specialist knowledge to review applications received by the Wixamtree Trust from Bedfordshire churches seeking funds for repairs to the fabric of their buildings and other projects. BHHCT visits the projects, assesses the need and makes grant recommendations to the trustees on a quarterly basis.

The trust has set aside an annual sum of £100,000 for such applications, £90,000 of this is to be used to make grants to Bedfordshire churches and the remaining £10,000 is to be donated to BHHCT to establish an endowment fund, subject to an annual review. The usual amount of grant for a church in any one year will be £10,000 and will not normally exceed 10% of the project cost.

In 2009/10 the trust had assets of £22.5 million and an income of £746,500. Grants were made to 126 organisations (many being annual or bi-annual recipients) totalling £652,000. They were categorised as follows:

Social welfare	£306,000
Medicine and health	£123,000
Environment and conservation	£113,000
Arts	£72,500
Education	£25,000
Sports and leisure	£12,500

Beneficiaries were not listed in the accounts but could be viewed on the trust's website: though individual grant awards were not included. Beneficiaries included: Bedfordshire & Northamptonshire Multiple Sclerosis Therapy Centre; Motor Neurone Disease Association; Prostate Research Campaign UK; Keech Hospice Care; Hospice at Home

Volunteers Bedford; Leighton Linslade Homeless Service; British Association for Adoption and Fostering; Prince's Trust – Bedfordshire Programme; Help the Aged – Luton Your Money Matters Project; and Scope – Response Service in Bedfordshire.

Exclusions

No grants to non-registered charities or individuals.

Applications

Application forms can be downloaded from the trust's website or requested via email or post. The trust prefers completed forms to be returned by email so that any amendments can be made before they are presented to the trustees for consideration at their quarterly meetings. Future meeting dates and application deadlines are listed on the trust's website. All requests for support should be accompanied by a current report and accounts.

Common applicant mistakes

'Not having done their research as to what we support.'

The Maurice Wohl Charitable Foundation

Jewish, health and welfare

£3 million (2009/10)

Beneficial area

UK and Israel.

Fitzrovia House, 2nd Floor, 153 - 157 Cleveland Street, London W1T 6QW
Tel: 020 7383 5111
Email: josephhouri@wohl.co.uk
Correspondent: Joseph Houri, Secretary
Trustees: Mrs Ella Latchman; Prof. David Latchman; Martin D Paisner; Daniel Dover; Sir Ian Gainsford.
CC Number: 244519

Information available

Accounts were available at the Charity Commission.

Support is given to organisations in the UK with particular emphasis on the following areas:

▶ the care, welfare and support of children (including education)
▶ the promotion of health, welfare and the advancement of medical services
▶ the relief of poverty, indigence and distress
▶ the care, welfare and support of the aged, infirm and disabled
▶ the support of the arts.

In 2009/10 the foundation had assets of £80.8 million and an income of £5.4 million. Grants were made totalling almost £3 million, broken down as follows:

Health, welfare and the advancement of medical services	£1.5 million
Promotion of religion	£900,000
Care, welfare and support of children (including education)	£600,000
Care of the elderly	£9,000
Relief of poverty	£5,000

Grants included those to: Birkbeck University of London (£950,000), towards building molecular biology laboratories; Jewish Museum London (£750,000), towards building a religion gallery; Chai Cancer Care (£500,000), towards building a new wing of the building; WST Charity Limited (£150,000), towards onward assistance for the relief of poverty; Community Security Trust (£75,000), towards their Streetwise Project; Medical Aid Trust (£10,000); and the Jewish Volunteering Network (£5,000).

Exclusions

The trustees do not in general entertain applications for grants for ongoing maintenance projects. The trustees do not administer any schemes for individual awards or scholarships and they do not, therefore, entertain any individual applications for grants.

Applications

In writing to the correspondent. The trustees meet regularly throughout the year.

The Charles Wolfson Charitable Trust

Medical research, education and welfare

£4.1 million (2009/10)

Beneficial area

Unrestricted, mainly UK.

129 Battenhall Road, Worcester WR5 2BU
Correspondent: Cynthia Crawford, Administrator
Trustees: Lord David Wolfson of Sunningdale; Hon. Simon Wolfson; Dr Sara Levene; Hon. Andrew Wolfson.
CC Number: 238043

Information available

Accounts were available at the Charity Commission, without a list of grants.

The trust was established in 1960 for general charitable purposes with special regard to the encouragement of medical and scientific research and facilities, education or child welfare, the advancement of any religion and the relief of poverty. Particular regard is given to the Jewish community. Grants are mostly for capital or fixed term projects. The trustees tend to support a few large projects over two to three years and make a number of smaller annual grants to other projects.

The bulk of the trust's income derives from grants received from Benesco, which is a registered charity whose investments are held in property. Benesco is in effect controlled by the trust and the annual accounts present both trust and consolidated financial statements including the combined assets, liabilities and income of the trust, Benesco and its subsidiary companies as a group.

In 2009/10 the trust had assets of £137.6 million and an income of £9.2 million. Over 100 grants were made totalling £4.1 million and were categorised as follows:

Education	£1.8 million
Welfare	£1.2 million
Medicine	£1.2 million

Previous beneficiaries included: Addenbrookes Charitable Trust and Yavneh College Trust (£500,000 each); Jewish Care (£350,000); Cure Parkinson's Trust (£200,000); Huntingdon Foundation (£125,000); Royal Marsden Cancer Campaign (£50,000); Sir George Pinker Appeal (£30,000); Zoological Society of London (£25,000); Priors Court Foundation (£10,000); Tavistock Trust for Aphasia (£5,000); and the Roundhouse Trust (£1,000).

Exclusions

No grants to individuals.

Applications

In writing to the correspondent. Whilst all applications will be considered, the trustees do not notify all unsuccessful applicants because of the volume of appeals received.

The Wolfson Family Charitable Trust

Jewish institutions and charities

£4.9 million (2009/10)

Beneficial area

UK; mostly Israel.

8 Queen Anne Street, London W1G 9LD
Tel: 020 7323 5730
Fax: 020 7323 3241
Website: www.wolfson.org.uk
Correspondent: Paul Ramsbottom, Secretary
Trustees: Sir Eric Ash; The Hon. Janet Wolfson de Botton; Lord Turnberg; Lord Wolfson of Marylebone; Martin D Paisner; Sir Bernard Rix; Lady Wolfson; Sir Ian Gainsford; The Hon. Laura Wolfson Townsley.
CC Number: 228382

Information available

Accounts were available at the Charity Commission.

The trust gives a relatively small number of often very large grants, mostly to institutions in Israel, in the fields of science, medical research, health, welfare and, to a lesser extent, arts and humanities. The trust has previously stated that much of its future income is already committed to long-term projects. Offices and administration are shared with the much larger Wolfson Foundation, and an application to one may be considered by the other.

The trust operates on a large scale and over an extended time frame, often having sharp changes in the level of new commitments each year.

There is a 'three year rolling plan of grants' which, as a general policy, 'are given to act as a catalyst, to back excellence and talent and to provide support for promising future projects which may currently be underfunded, particularly for research, renovation and equipment'.

In 2009/10 the trust had assets of £31.2 million and an income of £1.2 million. Grants were paid during the year totalling £4.9 million, including commitments from previous years, and were broken down as follows:

Science, technology and medical research	£4.5 million
Health and welfare	£394,000
Education	£25,000
Arts and humanities	£4,000

Most grants were paid to Israeli institutions, the largest of which included those to: Weizmann Institute of Science – Israel (£265,000); Bar-Ilan University – Israel (£250,000); and Tel Aviv University – Israel (£235,000). Other beneficiaries include: Rochdale Special Needs Cycle Club (£20,000); Jewish Lads' and Girls' Brigade – London (£5,000); Center for Blind and Deaf Persons (£3,500); and the Temple Music Foundation (£1,500).

Exclusions

Grants are not made to individuals.

Applications

The trust shares its application procedure with the Wolfson Foundation. However, as most grants are made in Israel the following information is particularly relevant:

Our funding programmes in Israel are currently focused on universities and hospitals.

Awards for these organisations are normally made under the umbrella of designated programmes in which relevant organisations are invited to participate.

Over the past few years, funding for universities has been for equipment supporting nationally co-ordinated programmes on important research themes including nanotechnology, desalination, quantum information and solar energy.

Funding for hospitals in Israel is mainly for medical equipment.

Awards are also made for cultural institutions with a national importance, as well as for smaller organisations working with people with special needs.

In the first instance, all applications from Israel should be sent to the Advisory Committee:

Professor Haim Ben-Shahar
Chairman
WFCT Advisory Committee
The Eitan Berglas School of Economics
Tel Aviv University
Tel-Aviv 69978
Israel

Email: wfct@post.tau.ac.il

The Wolfson Foundation

Medical and scientific research, education, health and welfare, heritage, arts

£28.2 million (2009/10)

Beneficial area

Mainly UK, but also Israel.

8 Queen Anne Street, London W1G 9LD
Tel: 020 7323 5730
Fax: 020 7323 3241
Website: www.wolfson.org.uk
Correspondent: Paul Ramsbottom, Executive Secretary
Trustees: Hon. Janet Wolfson de Botton, Chair; Hon. Laura Wolfson Townsley; Sir Eric Ash; Sir David Cannadine; Hon. Deborah Wolfson Davis; Prof. Hermione Lee; Lord McColl; Sir Michael Pepper; Lord Turnberg; Sir David Weatherall; Lady Wolfson of Marylebone.

CC Number: 206495

Information available

Accounts were available from the Charity Commission. The foundation also has a detailed website.

Set up in 1955, it is endowed from the fortune created by Sir Isaac Wolfson through the Great Universal Stores company. Grants are for buildings and equipment, but not for revenue or project costs, in four main areas:

- science and technology
- education
- arts and humanities
- health and welfare.

Grants can be very large; few are for amounts of less than £5,000.

The foundation shares offices and administration with the smaller Wolfson Family Charitable Trust, and an application to one may be considered by the other. The foundation provides excellent information on its activities, objectives and achievements, much of which is used in this entry.

The foundation's 2009/10 annual report outlines recent developments and the current grant-making process and policy:

Trustees make awards twice each year and are advised by panels comprising trustees and specialists which meet before the main board meetings. During the year Sir Michael Pepper was appointed as a member of the Science and Medicine Panel and Ms Sandra Robertson was appointed as a member of the Investment Committee. As well as assessing the merits of the applicants' proposals and their congruence with the foundation's aims and priorities, appraisal criteria include: the anticipated outcome of the project (including public benefit); financial viability; value for money; adequate provision for ongoing costs and maintenance and the aesthetics of any building project.

Priorities [...] are grouped around four funding areas: Science and Technology, Education, Arts and Humanities and Health and Welfare. Funding is made through a number of programmes, including preventive medicine, people with special needs, historic buildings, libraries, the visual arts and education. Grants are made to universities for student accommodation, equipment for research, new buildings and renovations. Awards for university research are normally made under the umbrella of designated programmes in which vice-chancellors are invited to participate.

All applications are assessed by expert external reviewers, and applicants are given an opportunity to respond to queries raised during the review process.

Guidelines

The foundation provides more specific details about individual elements within its broader categories:

Scientific and Medical Research

Over the past decade this area has received the highest proportion of the Wolfson Foundation's funding. Grants are made for capital infrastructure supporting internationally competitive research of the highest standard. This includes new buildings, refurbishment and/or research equipment.

As with all applications from universities, initial approaches should come via the Vice-Chancellor's office (or equivalent) and be a priority for the institution. The foundation prefers to have a direct funding relationship with universities rather than allocating through conduit research charities. The foundation funds both physical and biological sciences.

Royal Society Wolfson Laboratory Refurbishment Programme

Since 1998 the Wolfson Foundation has worked in partnership with the Royal Society to provide funding for the refurbishment of laboratory space at British universities. The aim is to improve the existing physical infrastructure in UK universities to promote high quality scientific research.

The programme is based on an annual theme which has previously included bioinformatics, nanotechnology and medical materials. The current theme is reduction in carbon emissions.

[Full details of the programme, including how to apply, are available from the Royal Society website.]

General enquiries should be directed to the Royal Society.

Royal Society Wolfson Research Merit Awards

Since 2000, the Wolfson Foundation has committed £20 million to funding the Wolfson Merit Awards. The programme is jointly funded by the Department for Business, Innovation and Skills and is administered by the Royal Society.

Funding allows universities to increase academic salaries to internationally competitive levels. The intention is to enable British universities to attract to this country (or to retain) outstanding research scientists. By 2010 over 200

researchers had received this prestigious award.

[Full details of the programme, including how to apply, are available from the Royal Society website.]

General queries should be directed to the Royal Society.

Special Needs

Throughout its history the Wolfson Foundation has not only funded medical research but has made awards for people with particular health needs or disabilities, often through smaller charities doing excellent work in a specific local community. Over the past three years some £7.5 million has been allocated to nearly 150 different projects.

Grants are made for new buildings, major refurbishment work, equipment or vehicles. Charities are encouraged not to apply more than once every five years.

Palliative Care & Hospices

The Wolfson Foundation has funded palliative care since the early days of the modern hospice movement in the 1960s. The foundation's grants have helped to fund the capital infrastructure underpinning the expansion of the movement, as well as research and teaching, encouraging high quality palliative care both generally and within hospices.

Grants are made to adult and children's hospices for new buildings, major refurbishment work, equipment or vehicles. Projects funded relate either to patient care or to training. Over the past three years nearly £4 million has been allocated to over forty projects. Under this programme, hospices are generally encouraged not to apply more than once every five years.

Occasional grants are made to fund research into palliative care. These should be submitted under the foundation's programme for funding medical research in the usual way.

The foundation also has a programme of funding for the training of palliative care medical staff, administered by Help the Hospices. This recognises the importance of ongoing training and also that many palliative care organisations struggle to find the necessary funding for this important, core cost.

Wolfson Bursaries for Palliative Care Staff

Since 2003 the Wolfson Foundation has provided Wolfson bursaries for the training of palliative care medical staff. Staff at organisations providing palliative care are eligible to apply (including, but not limited to, adult and children's hospices).

The scheme is administered by Help the Hospices as part of their 'professional development grants' and more information is available on their

website (www.helpthehospices.org.uk). General queries should be directed to Help the Hospices.

Museums & Galleries

Support for museums and galleries reflect the Wolfson Foundation's strong interest in the country's heritage. From assistance in the acquisition of works of art to improvements to gallery space, the foundation's work in this area has sought to preserve the country's inheritance and enhance appreciation of collections.

The foundation has three funding programmes in this area.

First, it has since 2000 provided the majority of its funding through a partnership programme with government (the Department for Culture, Media and Sport). The programme funds the refurbishment of gallery space at eligible museums and galleries.

Secondly, museums and galleries with major capital projects that have a national significance may apply to the foundation directly.

Thirdly, the acquisition of works of art at galleries and museums has been supported since the 1970s through a joint programme with the Art Fund.

Historic Buildings & Landscapes

An interest in history informs much of the Wolfson Foundation's funding of the arts and humanities, whether through refurbishment of museums, support of academic research or the acquisition and display of works of art.

This interest is also expressed through support for conservation of historic buildings – the physical embodiment of the country's past. From churches to castles, cathedrals to stately homes, the foundation has contributed to the conservation of many architectural treasures across the country, great and small.

Eligible buildings should normally be listed grade II* or above, and the project should involve conservation or refurbishment work to the historic fabric of the building. The building should be accessible to the public for the majority of the year. Support is also given, on occasion, to landscapes and gardens where these are of exceptional historic significance.

Applications from cathedrals, churches and war memorials are considered through designated programmes.

Grants are also awarded through other partnership programmes, including with the National Trust.

Churches (Church Buildings Council)

The Wolfson Foundation has a programme providing small grants to Anglican churches for the conservation of the historic fabric of the building. Since this programme started, grants have been made to nearly 600 churches, generally up to the level of £4,000 each.

Eligible churches must be listed (Grade I or Grade II∗) and pre-date 1850. Specific exclusions include work to bells and organs as well as the provision of heating or other modern facilities, The programme is administered by the Church Buildings Council on behalf of the foundation and enquiries should be sent directly to the Council at the following address: The Conservation Officer, The Church Buildings Council, Church House, Great Smith Street, London, SW1P 3AZ.

Buildings belonging to other denominations that otherwise meet the above criteria may be eligible under the general historic buildings programme.

Cathedrals

The Wolfson Foundation currently funds repair to the historic fabric of English cathedrals through a programme administered by the Cathedrals Fabric Commission for England (CFCE). Awards made in the first round of the programme are detailed [on the Wolfson Foundation's website].

For information on eligibility and how to apply, please visit the CFCE website: www.churchcare.co.uk.

Grants for War Memorials (English Heritage)

The Wolfson Foundation's funding for war memorials is based on more than an interest in history. It also reflects the importance to communities of these silent monuments to lives lost in conflict.

Since 2003 the Wolfson Foundation has funded a joint programme with English Heritage and the War Memorials Trust, providing grants for the conservation of war memorials.

The programme is administered by the War Memorials Trust. For enquiries and eligibility please contact the Trust directly.

Performing Arts

The Wolfson Foundation supports the performing arts through the provision of infrastructure. Funding is usually in the form of refurbishment of buildings as well as, more occasionally, for the construction of new buildings and assistance in the acquisition of specialist equipment.

Funding tends to be focussed on theatres and concert halls housed in buildings of historic significance, or on ballet and opera companies with a national reputation.

Music education is supported through the Wolfson Music Awards. This programme, which has run since the late 1980s, provides scholarships for young (secondary school-age) musicians in the junior departments of musical conservatories – a rare

example of non-capital funding. It also funds the purchase of instruments for undergraduates, particularly those with an interest and aptitude for a performing career. Individuals should apply through the relevant conservatoire.

Education

Education is one of the Wolfson Foundation's central themes and underpins the majority of projects funded.

An important part of the Foundation's educational activity is the support of secondary schools, primarily for what was the 'maintained' sector (now foundation/voluntary aided/voluntary controlled schools) though not excluding independent schools, sixth form colleges and high performing community schools [see below].

Funding for the higher education sector is also described elsewhere [...] (notably under Scientific & Medical Research). The foundation has, in addition, smaller programmes for the funding of higher education buildings, particularly for libraries and student accommodation. In 2009 a programme, in partnership with the British Academy, to fund Wolfson Research Professorships was launched. This programme supports outstanding researchers in the arts and social sciences.

A particular focus throughout the Wolfson Foundation's history has been medical education, including the various learned societies supporting the medical profession and intercalated awards for students. Within universities, capital grants have often been made for medical school buildings and medical training facilities. As with all applications from universities, initial approaches should come via the Vice-Chancellor's office (or equivalent) and be a priority for the institution.

In a wider sense, public engagement with science and medicine is an important part of the foundation's remit. This theme cuts across a number of programmes areas.

Secondary Schools

The Wolfson Foundation currently allocates approximately £1.5 million each year, funding schools that have achieved a level of excellence or can demonstrate progressive improvement in their results.

Grants are made for science and technology, particularly providing suitable spaces for laboratories and helping towards the purchase of IT equipment.

Schools that may be eligible to apply are foundation, voluntary-aided and voluntary-controlled, independent schools and sixth form colleges. Grants do not normally exceed £40,000,

although higher grants may be offered to large sixth form colleges.

Grantmaking in 2009/10

In 2009/10 the foundation had assets of £652.8 million and an income of £24.4 million. There were 267 grants made during the year totalling £28.2 million, broken down as follows:

Science, technology and medical research	27	£16.8 million
Arts and humanities	104	£5.5 million
Education	80	£4.7 million
Health and welfare	56	£2.3 million

The foundation's annual report gives the following summary analysis of grantmaking during the year (headings overlap the foundation's main categories):

Medical research and health care

Trustees continued their policy of investing in infrastructure supporting high quality research at British universities.

The largest award under this heading was £3 million for the construction of a new Robotic Assisted Microsurgery Laboratory at Imperial College London. Two grants were made for research in the general area of neuroscience: a new Centre for Neuropsychiatric Genetics and Genomics at Cardiff University (£1.75 million) and equipment for the Sheffield Institute for Translational Neuroscience (£600,000). Other major awards included laboratories in the new Centre for Molecular Pathology at the Royal Marsden (£1.5 million) and a Centre for Mechanochemical Cell Biology at the University of Warwick (£1 million).

Internationally, trustees supported a new building for the School of Public Health at the University of Witwatersrand and equipment for Israeli hospitals.

The trustees continued their programmes in the fields of special needs and hospices. Grants totalling over £2.25 million were awarded for new buildings, refurbishment work and equipment.

Science education and research

The major investments in this area were toward new buildings for two outstanding university departments: for Materials Science and Metallurgy at the University of Cambridge (£2.25 million) and for Earth Sciences at the University of Oxford (£1.25 million).

Other major projects included awards for engineering at Loughborough and Coventry Universities and a programme for equipment for energy research at Israeli universities.

During the year the programme for refurbishment of research laboratories at UK universities was renewed. The programme, which is in partnership with the Royal Society, aims to improve the existing physical infrastructure in UK universities to promote high quality scientific research. The programme has been renewed for a further year at the level of £2 million, to be administered by the Royal Society. The commitment was made following a review of the existing programme undertaken by the Royal Society. The theme for 2010 [was] 'reduction in carbon emissions' and awards made under this programme will be reported in future annual reports.

Arts and humanities
The largest award during the year of £2 million went to the British Museum toward the creation of new conservation and scientific research laboratories in the proposed Centre on Montague Place.

A number of other significant awards were made to museums and galleries, including £500,000 to the National Maritime Museum for renovation work to create gallery space in the Alexander Wing and £200,000 to Historic Royal Palaces for the redevelopment of Kensington Palace.

Other awards for museums and galleries were made under the eighth and final year of the joint programme with the Department for Culture, Media and Sport for the renovation of museums and galleries. A review of this programme [was] undertaken during 2010. [The renewal of the programme for a further two funding rounds was announced in February 2011 – check the foundation's website for current information on any future renewals.]

In the field of music and the performing arts, a grant of £200,000 was made toward the recital hall in the major new building at Chetham's School of Music in Manchester. Smaller awards were made for a range of other organisations, including for major performance venues (such as St John's Smith Square and Glyndebourne) and facilities at musical conservatories (notably the Guildhall School of Music and Drama and the Royal Welsh College of Music and Drama).

The largest number of awards were made for the conservation of historic buildings, landscapes and monuments, including a grant of £100,000 for the conservation of Stowe House in Buckinghamshire. Other historic buildings funded included several dozen historic Anglican churches through the scheme administered by the Church Buildings Council. At the end of 2009, the joint programme with the Church Buildings Council completed its tenth year of funding. During the decade £2.4 million has been invested in some 600 churches.

During the year the programme for the conservation of war memorials was renewed for a further three years. This is jointly funded with English Heritage and administered by the War Memorials Trust.

It was also agreed, in principle, to establish a joint programme with the Cathedrals Fabric Commission for the conservation of English cathedrals.

Education
The largest awards were again made to learned societies promoting scientific education and research, notably £1.5 million for the Royal Society toward the creation of meeting rooms at Chicheley Hall in Buckinghamshire – which is to become a venue for science seminars and conferences. Other grants included £400,000 for a new lecture theatre for the Royal Academy of Engineering at 3–4 Carlton House Terrace and £180,000 for a seminar room as the final phase of the creation of new training facilities at the Royal College of Surgeons.

Grants of some £1.6 million were awarded as part of the ongoing programme funding equipment and building projects for the teaching of science and technology at secondary schools. Trustees recently extended the programme to include sixth form colleges and the largest award was for the College of Richard Collyer in Horsham.

Exclusions

Grants are not made directly to individuals or conduit organisations. The following are also ineligible for funding:

▶ overheads, maintenance costs, VAT and professional fees
▶ non-specific appeals (including circulars), and endowment funds
▶ costs of meetings, exhibitions, concerts, expeditions, etc.
▶ the purchase of land or existing buildings (including a building's freehold)
▶ film or website production
▶ repayment of loans
▶ projects that have already been completed or will be by the time of award.

Applications

The Wolfson Foundation has a two stage application process. Note that, under some funding programmes, applicants are asked to submit via partner organisations. The information below refers to applications submitted directly to the Wolfson Foundation.

Stage 1
In the first instance, please write with an outline of your project. As well as a brief description of the project, the outline should contain the total cost, the current funding shortfall and the proposed timetable. The letter need not be longer than 1–2 pages. It is important, however, that the initial application comes with the full backing of the institution and is therefore signed by the Chief Executive, Vice Chancellor or equivalent.

Statutory accounts for the past two years should be submitted at this initial stage. Our Finance Officer may be in contact if there are any queries – so it is helpful to provide contact details for this purpose.

The aim of the first stage is to determine whether a project is eligible. We respond to all enquiries, whether or not we are able to invite a further proposal.

Stage 2
Once an application has been invited, guidelines are issued for a full application. The deadlines this year for full, second stage, applications are 1 March and 1 September.

Please note that Stage 1 applications can be submitted at any time but in any case not less than 6 weeks in advance of these deadline dates.

All second stage applications are sent to expert reviewers and are also considered by a specialist panel, who make recommendations to the trustees. Details of panel membership are given here. If questions or queries are raised by expert reviewers or by the panel, applicants are given a chance to respond.

Please note that match funding is generally expected to be in place before a Stage 2 application is submitted.

Schools application process
Please note this information does not apply to special schools, who should apply under the special needs programme.

Some 50 applications are invited each year. They are considered first by the Schools Panel whose recommendations are then decided by trustees at their meetings in June and December. Members of the panel visit applicant schools. This means that the lead-in time from initial enquiry to an application being invited and considered is rather longer than for other programmes. It is also a popular programme which may mean an invitation to apply has to be deferred to the next meeting if the allocation for the first is already subscribed.

The timetable leading to each meeting of Trustees is as follows:

For the June meeting. Initial enquiries will have been received the year before and the schools put on a list for invitation. In about September letters of invitation are sent, enclosing a Method of Application guidance note. The deadline date for receipt of applications is 31 January the following year. Schools are visited between February and April, applications considered by the Education Panel in May and recommendations made to the June meeting of Trustees.

For the December meeting. Following initial enquiries and listing, letters of invitation are sent early in the year. The deadline date for application is mid June and schools are visited at the end of the summer term or early in the autumn term. The Education Panel meets in late October/early November and its recommendations go forward to the December meeting of Trustees.

The following points may be relevant to making an initial enquiry:

Excellence
The main thrust of the schools programme has been to provide support to schools that already have a proven record of excellent performance. However, the trustees will also help schools which, whilst not yet in the upper reaches of the performance tables, have a clear record of continuing improvement. Schools should cite their place in The Financial Times list of the top 1000 schools; refer to a recent 'excellent' Ofsted/ISI report; or provide information on academic attainments (full results of GCSE examinations for the preceding academic year presented in the form required by the Department for Children, Schools and Families, together with summary results for the last five years)

Eligible projects
These may be capital or equipment projects. A bid for both may be included in a single application. Grants are not made retrospectively so work on a project for which support is sought must be ongoing at the time of the trustees' meeting. Grants are made for the support of the teaching of science and technology for students taking A level or GCSE examinations. A music technology project may be considered on occasion, but the main focus of the schools programme is science and technology.

Ineligible projects
Examples of ineligible projects are those relating to performing or creative arts centres, dance studios, theatres, sports facilities, libraries and projects exclusively for junior pupils in the school.

Denominational schools
In making application, schools are asked for confirmation of non-discriminatory entry policies in respect of religious allegiance. Schools that are predominantly denominational may be supported but assurance should be provided that a significant number of pupils of other faiths, or of none, are admitted and that the school sees such a group as a positive asset for all the pupils in the school. An indication of the relevant numbers of such pupils should be provided.

Independent schools
Only schools with a sixth form of at least 50 students may be invited.

Previous grant(s)
It is usual to allow some five years to elapse before another application from the same organisation may be considered.

Common applicant mistakes
'Failing to follow the published guidelines.'

The South Yorkshire Community Foundation

General

£1.8 million (2009/10)

Beneficial area
South Yorkshire wide, with specific reference to Barnsley, Doncaster, Rotherham, Sheffield.

Unit 3 - G1 Building, 6 Leeds Road, Attercliffe, Sheffield S9 3TY
Tel: 0114 242 4294
Fax: 0114 242 4605
Email: grants@sycf.org.uk
Website: www.sycf.org.uk
Correspondent: Sandra Mullins, Operations Manager
Trustees: Jonathan Hunt, Chair; David Moody; Sir Hugh Neill; Peter W Lee; Martin P W Lee; Peter Hollis; Isadora Aiken; Frank Carter; Jackie Drayton; Galen Ives; Christopher Jewitt; Michael Mallett; Sue Scholey; Maureen Shah; Allan Sherriff; Lady R Sykes; R J Giles Bloomer; Timothy M Greenacre; Allan Jackson; Jane Kemp; Jane Marshall.
CC Number: 517714

Information available
Accounts were on file at the Charity Commission. The foundation also has a helpful and informative website.

The South Yorkshire Community Foundation, launched in 1986, specialises in funding small community and voluntary groups within the south Yorkshire area. Priority is given to small and medium-sized groups which find it hard to raise money elsewhere. Projects funded include those which help local people in need, such as people who may be homeless, ill, disabled or older, and community life, such as nursery care, arts and culture, nature and heritage and sport.

Applicants do not have to be a registered charity but do have to have a charitable purpose. As well as running its own programme, the foundation also makes grants on behalf of its donors.

The foundation is particularly interested in supporting groups or projects which:

- support people in greatest need
- are locally led and run
- involve people who face particular discrimination or disadvantage e.g. young people, people with disabilities or facing mental health issues, black and minority ethnic communities and so on
- respond to local communities' needs
- work well with other local community initiatives
- are innovative
- will benefit from relatively small amounts of funding
- give real value for money.

Grant programmes 2011/12
As with other community foundations, funds may close and new ones open, so check the foundation's website for up-to-date information:

SYCF Small Grants Fund
These grants are intended for small, developing and less well-resourced groups and organisations from across South Yorkshire, where small amounts of funding can make a real difference.

Organisations/groups do not have to be a registered charity and the majority of grants are one-off payments of between £50 and £1,500.

We welcome applications from all community and voluntary groups and organisations operating for the benefit of South Yorkshire communities. Groups must therefore have beneficiaries who live in South Yorkshire and be locally led and run. This includes locally constituted and managed branches of national or large charities.

Which groups or activities will be prioritised for funding?

Higher priority will be given to those applications that can demonstrate how they will address some of the following needs. If your group or activity will not meet these priorities then you can still apply but it is less likely that you will receive funding from us:

- groups that respond to their communities' needs
- activities or projects that will support people whose needs can be clearly demonstrated
- groups whose main activities focus upon the advancement of education, promotion of good health or the relief of poverty and sickness
- groups that work in collaboration with other local community groups
- activities or projects that will engage people who face discrimination or disadvantage
- activities or projects that will produce a wide range of benefits and provide good value for money.

How to apply?

To apply for a grant, simply download the Small Grants Fund overview sheet [from the foundation's website] for more information on eligibility and how the application process works.

Then download both the *Guidelines for Completing Forms* and the *Standard (SYCF) Application Form* and return the completed application form to the South Yorkshire Community Foundation to get the process underway.

Grassroots Grants – Small Grants

Small grants aims to reach out to those in our local communities who need assistance most. The foundation is able to distribute grants of £250–£5,000 to grassroots community groups throughout Barnsley, Rotherham and Sheffield.

By downloading the forms below you can make your application for assistance from the fund.

If you are thinking of applying for a Grassroots Grant you must read the *Overview and Criteria* sheet to check your eligibility for the scheme. If you are eligible and wish to apply, you need to complete both the standard *Grant Application Form* and the *Grassroots Grants Application Form*. [All of the forms are available from the foundation's website.]

If your group or project is not eligible to apply to Grassroots Grants small grants, you can still apply to the SYCF Small Grants scheme using the standard Grant Application Form.

It will help us to process your application efficiently if you provide as much detail as you can when completing the form(s), particularly when describing the project you would like funded and the costs of the items you intend to spend the grant on.

NB: Doncaster Central Development Trust will be administering the fund in Doncaster and prospective applicants should contact Katie Wall on 01302 735766 for an application pack and further information.

Third Sector ERDF Access Fund

Register your interest for the Third Sector ERDF Access Fund by emailing: admin@sycf.org.uk.

Yorkshire Forward has created the Third Sector ERDF Access Fund, offering grants of between £2,000 and £10,000, which will be delivered locally throughout the county by the Yorkshire Community Foundations.

The funding has been made available to help Third Sector organisations prepare themselves to make bids for larger sums from the European Regional Development Fund (ERDF).

Through ERDF, Yorkshire Forward is offering projects costing £1 million and above the chance to apply for a grant to cover up to 50% of the total cost.

Malcolm Taylor, who manages the ERDF Programme for Yorkshire Forward, said: 'We want to give Third Sector organisations throughout the region as great a chance as possible to be successful with bids for funding from ERDF. Support from the Third Sector Access Fund will enable organisations to improve the quality of bids they submit for ERDF funding.

The smaller grants from the Access Fund will help with preparatory tasks such as the carrying out of feasibility studies, exploring possibilities of collaborative working with other local organisations and gaining expert advice on the preparation of bids.

Successful bids for the larger sums from ERDF must be based upon the Fund's Priority 3 objectives:

- part capital (buildings/ refurbishment), part transport
- business support
- social enterprise support
- IT development/knowledge.

The grants come from the ERDF operational programme for the Yorkshire and Humber 2007–2013, which had over £500 million available for investment in the region. Over £100 million of which was earmarked to support the Programme's third priority of Sustainable Communities which is of

particular relevance to Third Sector organisations..

The Community Foundations for South Yorkshire, Leeds, Calderdale, Wakefield and District and York and North Yorkshire (including the Humber) will be delivering the Access Fund locally for their respective areas.

You can register your interest in the Access Fund by emailing SYCF on the email address above.

Comic Relief

The South Yorkshire Community Foundation has teamed up with Comic Relief to bring almost £80,000 in grants to local community groups over the next two years.

In the past, SYCF has delivered Sports Relief funding, but this new pot will provide much needed funding for non-sporting groups as well with grants of up to £10,000 [check the foundation's website for upcoming deadlines].

At least 50% of the funding will be delivered to sporting projects in the region, with the remainder distributed amongst other worthwhile groups.

Successful applications for sporting projects will show how the group increases access to sport and exercise for people who face social exclusion and isolation, and to help people who are experiencing difficulties in their lives.

Non-sporting projects should increase local services, build skills of local people, increase community cohesion or respond to local economic needs.

Further information, including eligibility criteria and application forms will appear on our website [...]

Sir Samuel Osbourne Deed of Gift

The Sir Samuel Osborn Deed of Gift provides grants ranging from £250 to £1,000 for applications that fall in to two main categories: education and special needs.

Sir Samuel Osborn headed one of Sheffield's great tool steelmaking families, who at their peak virtually monopolised the world's manufacture of tool steel back in the 19th century.

The fund has previously only been available to former employees or their dependants of the Osborn company (which ceased to exist in 1978), although now the fund is open to any individual resident in the city of Sheffield.

However due to the current high level of demand, applications received where there is no family connection to a former Samuel Osborn employee [may not be considered].

To find out more information about the fund and eligibility download the information sheet [from the foundation's website].

If you want to make an application to the fund then download the Grant Application form and return it to Karen Alsop at the foundation.

In 2009/10 the foundation had assets of £4.1 million and an income of £3.8 million. Grants were made totalling £1.8 million.

A wide range of organisations across all of the foundation's areas of operation were supported under various programmes, some of which may no longer be running. Many organisations received grants from more than one fund.

Exclusions

The following exclusions apply to all funds administered by the foundation:

- groups that have substantial unrestricted funds
- national charities
- activities promoting political or religious beliefs or where people are excluded on political or religious grounds
- statutory bodies e.g. schools, local councils, colleges
- projects outside of South Yorkshire
- endowments
- small contributions to large projects
- projects for personal profit
- minibuses or other vehicle purchases
- projects that have already happened
- animals
- sponsorship and fundraising events.

Applications

Applications are made by completing a simple form, available for download from the foundation's website. See the General section for additional application information for each fund.

Initial enquiries can be made by email, telephone or fax. Staff at the foundation are happy to talk to you, and can:

- talk through your project idea to assess eligibility and give advice
- provide support in putting together your application
- let you know about other useful support and advice services
- provide more detailed information on all our funds.

All applications are submitted to a grant assessment panel which meets every 6 weeks. The frequency of meetings means the foundation does not operate an advertised deadline system and applicants are invited to apply at any point during the year. The foundation endeavours to provide applicants with a decision within 8 weeks of a completed application form being received.

Common applicant mistakes

'Applicants make a variety of common mistakes that all would have been avoided if they had read the guidance notes or made contact with us prior to applying.'

The Yorkshire Dales Millennium Trust

Conservation and environmental regeneration

£1.6 million (2009/10)

Beneficial area

The Yorkshire Dales.

The Old Post Office, Main Street, Clapham, Lancaster LA2 8DP
Tel: 01524 251002
Fax: 01524 251150
Email: info@ydmt.org
Website: www.ydmt.org
Correspondent: Sue Musgrave, Finance & Administration Manager
Trustees: Joseph Pearlman; Carl Lis; Colin Speakman; Dorothy Fairburn; Dorothy Fairburn; Hazel Cambers; David Sanders Rees-Jones; Jane Roberts; Peter Charlesworth; Stephen Macare; David Joy; Thomas Wheelwright; Margaret Billing; Michael Ackrel; Andrew Campbell; David Shaw; Wendy Hull; Karen Cowley.
CC Number: 1061687

Information available

Accounts were available from the Charity Commission. The trust also has an informative website detailing current and previous projects.

This trust's patron is HRH The Prince of Wales and the role of the trust is to distribute money to organisations, communities and individuals in the Yorkshire Dales. Grants are made towards the conservation and regeneration of the natural and built heritage and community life of the Yorkshire Dales. It supports, for example, planting new and restoring old woods, the restoration of dry stone walls and field barns, conservation of historical features and community projects.

The trust has adopted the following aims:

1. to conserve or restore the natural, built, scenic and cultural heritage features which together make up the special landscape of the Dales
2. to develop and encourage opportunities for wider access to and understanding of the Dales
3. to improve understanding of and wider use of countryside and traditional skills
4. to support the people and communities of the Dales to live and work in harmony with this special and protected landscape.

The trust raises and distributes its own funds and manages programmes on behalf of external funders, such as the Heritage Lottery Fund and the Learning and Skills Council. Details of the trust's current funding schemes can be found on its website.

The trust makes grants to applicants for up to 70% of their project costs. For every project it supports the trust can pull in matching funding from other sources.

In 2009/10 it had assets of £614,500 and an income of just under £1.8 million, made up almost entirely from grants and donations. Grants were made to 47 projects during the year totalling £1.6 million, including grants from the following restricted funds:

North Yorkshire Aggregates Grant Scheme	£269,000
Grass Roots	£247,000
Settle Riverside	£236,000
YDNPA Sustainable Development Fund	£121,000
Dales Woodland Restoration	£103,500
Ribble Crayfish	£71,500

Nidderdale AONB Sustainable Development Fund	£44,000
Nidderdale SITA Woodlands	£32,500
Haytime	£24,500
People and the Dales	£5,000
Community Wardens	£1,000

Applications

In writing to the correspondent.

The Zochonis Charitable Trust

General

£2.6 million (2009/10)

Beneficial area

UK, particularly Greater Manchester, and overseas, particularly Africa.

c/o Cobbetts LLP, 58 Mosley Street, Manchester M2 3HZ
Tel: 0845 165 5270
Fax: 0845 166 6733
Email: ruth.barron@cobbetts.com
Correspondent: Ruth Barron
Trustees: Sir John Zochonis; Christopher Nigel Green; Archibald G Calder; Joseph J Swift.
CC Number: 274769

Information available

Accounts were available at the Charity Commission.

Established in 1977, this is the trust of Sir John Zochonis, former head of PZ Cussons, the soap and toiletries manufacturer. It has general charitable objectives but tends to favour local charities with a particular emphasis on education and the welfare of children. Grants do not appear to be ongoing, but local charities with an established relationship with the trust are supported intermittently, if not regularly, over many years.

In 2009/10 the trust had assets of £137.7 million (£76.3 million in 2008/09) and an income of £4 million (£2.6 million in 2008/09). Grants were made to 168 organisations totalling £2.6 million.

Beneficiaries included: Cancer Research UK and Concern Worldwide – Haiti Emergency Appeal (£150,000 each); Bolton School and the Smile Train (£100,000 each); Greater Manchester High Sheriff's Trust (£77,500); Withington Girl's School (£75,000); The Police Foundation (£60,000); CAFOD (£50,000); Manchester YMCA (£35,000); KIDS (£30,000); Barnabus (£20,000); The Missing Foundation (£15,000); Children's Safety Education Foundation and After Adoption (£10,000 each); Action for Children and the Royal Veterinary College (£5,000 each); Welfare Ambulance Association (£3,000); and the Wildlife Trust (£2,000).

Exclusions

No grants for individuals.

Applications

In writing to the correspondent.

Community Foundation Network

Community foundations are charitable trusts which work in specific geographical areas as endowment builders, grantmakers and community leaders. They channel funds on behalf of individuals, organisations, companies and other agencies which recognise that their detailed knowledge of local needs puts them in an ideal position to distribute funding.

In England, in particular, many community foundations have been the local agents for government programmes such as Grassroots Grants. They also manage large funds such as the Big Lottery funded Fair Share Trust programme. The foundations are increasingly called on to help deliver short-term programmes and emergency assistance on behalf of other grantmakers.

Community foundations already exist in most parts of the UK and new ones are being established all the time. In 2010/11 grants totalling £61.4 million were made by community foundations and their total assets stood at £280 million, an increase of 25% on the previous year. Statutory funding has decreased rapidly, reflecting the economic climate with only 21% of new funds being from statutory sources, down from 44% in 2008/9. However, the average value of newly set up funds rose from £50,000 in 2009/10 to £95,000 in 2010/11 (CFN 2011).[1]

A list of all current community foundations, with basic contact details, follows below. Many are still at early stages of development, while others are well-established grant-making foundations.

Contacts that are in italics have their own separate entries in this book. The list is ordered alphabetically either by area or the name of the foundation (when the name does not contain an area). For ease of navigation the area or name is marked in bold.

Bedfordshire and Luton Community Foundation
The Smithy
The Village
Old Warden
SG18 9HQ
Tel: 0176 7626 459
Fax: 0700 6006 800
Contact: Mark West (Chief Executive)
Email: administrator@blcf.org.uk
Website: www.blcf.org.uk

Berkshire Community Foundation
1650 Arlington Business Park
Theale
Reading
RG7 4SA
Tel: 01189 303021
Fax: 01189 304933
Contact: Andrew Middleton (Chief Executive)
Email: info@berkshirecf.org.uk
Website: www.berkshirecommunity foundation.org.uk

Birmingham & Black Country *Community Foundation*
Nechells Baths
Nechells Park Road
Nechells
Birmingham
B7 5PD
Tel: 0121 322 5560
Fax: 0121 322 5579
Contact: Zoe Keens (Development Director)
Email: team@bbccf.org.uk
Website: www.bhamfoundation.co.uk

---

[1] CFN (2011), 'Network Statistics 2010–2011: Community Philanthropists Continue to Support Local Causes Despite Austerity and Cuts in Public Spending' [web page], www.communityfoundations.org.uk/media/network_stats2010, accessed 6 February 2012.

Community Foundation for
Bournemouth, Dorset and Poole
Abchurch Chambers
24 St Peters Road
Bournemouth
BH1 2LN
Tel: 01202 292255
Contact: Tina Baker (Chief Executive)
Email: grants@dorsetcf.org
Website: www.dorsetcommunity
foundation.org

Bradford District Community
Foundation
11 Broad Street
Manor Row
Bradford
BD1 4QT
Tel: 01274 809790
Contact: John Corbishley (Chief
Executive)
Email: john@cnet.org.uk

Buckinghamshire Community
Foundation
Foundation House
119a Bicester Road
Aylesbury
HP19 9BA
Tel: 01296 330134
Fax: 01296 330158
Contact: Richard Dickson
(Development Director)
Email: info@buckscf.org.uk
Website: www.thebucksfoundation.
org.uk

Community Foundation for
Calderdale
The 1855 Building (First Floor)
Discovery Road
Halifax
HX1 2NG
Tel: 01422 349700
Fax: 01422 350017
Contact: Steve Duncan (Chief
Executive)
Email: enquiries@cffc.co.uk
Website: www.cffc.co.uk

Community Foundation Network
(UK-wide)
12 Angel Gate
320–326 City Road
London
EC1V 2PT
Tel: 020 7713 9326
Fax: 020 7278 9068
Email: network@
communityfoundations.org.uk
Website: www.community
foundations.org.uk

Cambridgeshire Community
Foundation
The Quorum
Barnwell Road
Cambridge
CB5 8RE
Tel: 01223 410535
Contact: Jane Darlington (Chief
Executive)
Email: jane@cambscf.org.uk
Website: www.cambscf.org.uk

Capital *Community Foundation*
357 Kennington Lane
London
SE11 5QY
Tel: 020 7582 5117
Fax: 020 7582 4020
Contact: Sonal Shah (Director)
Email: enquiries@capitalcf.org.uk
Website: www.capitalcf.org.uk

Cornwall Community Foundation
Suite 1
Sheers Barton
Lawhitton
Launceston
Tel: 01566 779333
Contact: Linda Whittaker (Executive
Director)
Email: office@cornwallfoundation.
com
Website: www.cornwallfoundation.
com

The **Craven** Trust (Keighley,
Sedbergh, Grassington, Barnoldswick
and the Trough of Bowland)
4 Halsteads Way
Steeton
Keighley
BD20 6SN
Tel: 01535 653373
Email: enquiries@craventrust.org.uk
Website: www.craventrust.org.uk

Cumbria *Community Foundation*
Dovenby Hall
Dovenby
Cockermouth
CA13 0PN
Tel: 01900 825760
Contact: Andrew Beeforth (Director)
Email: enquiries@cumbriafoundation.
org
Website: www.cumbriafoundation.org

Dacorum Community Trust
Cementaprise Centre
Paradise
Hemel Hempstead
HP2 4TF
Tel: 01442 231396
Contact: Margaret Kingston
(Administrator)
Email: mk@dctrust.org.uk
Website: www.dctrust.org.uk

Derbyshire *Community Foundation*
Foundation House
Unicorn Business Park
Wellington Street
Ripley
DE5 3EH
Tel: 01773 514850
Fax: 01773 741410
Contact: Rachael Grime (Chief
Executive)
Email: info @derbyshirecommunity
foundation.co.uk
Website: www. derbyshirecommunity
foundation.co.uk

Devon *Community Foundation*
The Factory
Leat Street
Tiverton
EX16 5LL
Tel: 01884 235887
Fax: 01884 243824
Contact: Martha Wilkinson (Chief
Executive)
Email: info@devoncf.com
Website: www.devoncf.com

County ***Durham*** *Foundation (includes*
Darlington)
Victoria House
Whitfield Court
St John's Road
Meadowfield Industrial Estate
Durham
DH7 8XL
Tel: 0191 378 6340
Fax: 0191 378 2409
Contact: Barbara Gubbins (Chief
Executive)
Email: barbara@cdcf.org.uk
Website: www.cdcf.org.uk

Essex *Community Foundation*
121 New London Road
Chelmsford
CM2 0QT
Tel: 01245 355947
Fax: 01245 346391
Contact: Bob Reitemeier (Chief
Executive)
Email: general@essexcf.org.uk
Website: www.essexcommunity
foundation.org.uk

European Foundation Centre
78 Avenue de la Toison d'Or
1060 Brussels
Belgium
Tel: 0032 2 512 8938
Fax: 0032 2 512 3265
Contact: Gerry Salole (Chief
Executive)
Email: efc@efc.be
Website: www.efc.be

Fermanagh Trust
Fermanagh House
Broadmeadow Place
Enniskillen
BT74 7HR
Tel: 028 6632 0210
Fax: 028 6632 0230
Contact: Lauri McCusker (Director)
Email: info@fermanaghtrust.org
Website: www.fermanaghtrust.org

Gloucestershire Community
Foundation
c/o EDF Energy
Barnett Way
Barnwood
Gloucester
GL4 3RS
Tel: 01452 656385
Fax: 01452 654164
Contact: Sally Booth
Email: sally.booth@edf-energy.com
Website: www.gloucestershire
communityfoundation.co.uk

*Community Foundation for Greater
Manchester*
5th Floor
Speakers House
Deansgate
Manchester
M3 2BA
Tel: 0161 214 0940
Fax: 0161 214 0941
Contact: Nick Massey (Director)
Email: enquiries@
commmunityfoundation.co.uk
Website: www.communityfoundation.
co.uk

Community Foundation for
Hampshire and the Isle of Wight
Community Foundation
Sun Alliance House
Wote Street
Basingstoke
Hampshire
RG21 1LU
Tel: 01256 776101
Contact: Toni Shaw (Chief Executive)
Email: info@hantscf.org.uk
Website: www.hantscf.org.uk

*Heart of England Community
Foundation (Coventry and
Warwickshire)*
Pinley House
Sunbeam Way
Coventry
CV3 1ND
Tel: 024 7688 4386
Contact: Kate Mulkern (Director)
Email: info@heartofenglandcf.co.uk
Website: www.heartofenglandcf.co.uk

Herefordshire Community
Foundation
The Fred Bulmer Centre
Wall Street
Hereford
HR4 9HP
Tel: 01432 272550
Contact: David Barclay (Director)
Email: info@herefordshirecommunity
foundation.org
Website: www. herefordshire
communityfoundation.org

Hertfordshire Community Foundation
Foundation House
2–4 Forum Place
Fiddlebridge Lane
Hatfield
AL10 0RN
Tel: 01707 251351
*Contact: David Fitzpatrick (Chief
Executive)*
Email: office@hertscf.org.uk
Website: www.hertscf.org.uk

Community Foundation for **Ireland**
32 Lower O'Connell Street
Dublin 1
Ireland
Tel: 00 353 1874 7354
Fax: 00 353 1874 7637
Contact: Tina Roche (Chief
Executive)
Email: info@foundation.ie
Website: www.communityfoundation.
ie

Kent Community Foundation
Office 23
Evegate Park Barn
Evegate
Smeeth
Ashford
TN25 6SX
Tel: 01303 814500
Contact: Carol Lynch (Chief
Executive)
Email: admin@kentcf.org.uk
Website: www.kentcf.org.uk

Community Foundation for
Lancashire
Chorley House
Centurion Way
Lancashire Business Park
Leyland
PR26 6TT
Tel: 0177 264 2387
Fax: 0151 232 2445
Contact: Cathy Elliott (Chief
Executive)
Email: info@lancsfoundation.org.uk
Website: www.lancsfoundation.org.uk

Leeds Community Foundation
51a St Paul's Street
Leeds
LS1 2TE
Tel: 0113 242 2426
Fax: 0113 2422432
Contact: Sally-Anne Greenfield (Chief
Executive)
Email: info@leedscommunity
foundation.org.uk
Website: www.leedscommunity
foundation.org.uk

Leicestershire, Leicester and Rutland
Community Foundation
20a Millstone Lane
Leicester
LE1 5JN
Tel: 0116 222 2206
Contact: Katy Green (Director)
Email: katy.green@llrcommunity
foundation.org.uk
Website: www.llrcommunity
foundation.org.uk

Lincolnshire Community Foundation
4 Mill House
Carre Street
Sleaford
NG34 7TW
Tel: 01529 305825
Contact: Gordon Hunter (Director)
Email: lincolnshirecf@btconnect.com
Website: www.lincolnshirecf.co.uk

East **London** Community Foundation
Unit G12
Office 7 (Upper Floor)
Chadwell Heath Industrial Park
Kemp Road
Dagenham
RM8 1SL
Tel: 0300 303 1203
Contact: Anja Beinroth (Acting Chief
Executive)
Email: enquires@elcf.org.uk
Website: www.elcf.org.uk

*North West London Community
Foundation*
Central Depot (Unit 4)
Forward Drive
Harrow
HA3 8NT
Tel: 0208 909 2788
Fax: 0208 909 2730
Email: kath@nwlondoncf.org.uk
*Website: www. nwlcommunity
foundation.org.uk*

*Community Foundation for
Merseyside*
Third Floor
Stanley Building
43 Hanover Street
Liverpool
L1 3DN
Tel: 0151 232 2444
Fax: 0151 232 2445
*Contact: Cathy Elliott (Chief
Executive)*
Email: info@cfmerseyside.org.uk
Website: www.cfmerseyside.org.uk

Milton Keynes Community
Foundation
Acorn House
381 Midsummer Boulevard
Central Milton Keynes
MK9 3HP
Tel: 01908 690276
Fax: 01908 233635
Contact: Julia Upton (Chief Executive)
Email: info@mkcommunityfoundation.
co.uk
Website: www.mkcommunity
foundation.co.uk

Norfolk Community Foundation
St James Mill
Whitefriars
Norwich
NR3 1SH
Tel: 01603 623958
Fax: 01603 230036
Contact: Graham Tuttle (Director)
Email: grahamtuttle@
norfolkfoundation.com
Website: www.norfolkfoundation.com

Northamptonshire Community
Foundation
19 Guildhall Road
Northampton
NN1 1DP
Tel: 01604 230033
Fax: 01604 636303
Contact: Victoria Miles (Chief
Executive)
Email: enquiries@ncf.uk.com
Website: www.ncf.uk.com

Community Foundation for Northern
Ireland
Community House
Citylink Business Park
6a Albert Street
Belfast
BT12 4HQ
Tel: 028 9024 5927Contact: Avila
Kilmurray (Director)
Email: info@communityfoundationni.
org
Website: www.communityfoundationni.
org

Nottinghamshire Community
Foundation
Cedar House
Ransom Wood Business Park
Southwell Road West
Mansfield
NG21 0HJ
Tel: 01623 636365
Fax: 01623 620204Email: enquiries@
nottscf.org.uk
Website: www.nottscf.org.uk

One Community Foundation
(Kirklees)
c/o Chadwick Lawrence Solicitors
13 Railway Street
Huddersfield
HD1 1JS
Tel: 01484 468 397
Fax: 01484 544 099
Contact: Ian Brierley (Director)
Website: www.one-community.org.uk

Oxfordshire Community Foundation
3 Woodins Way
Oxford
OX1 1HD
Tel: 01865 798666Contact: Jayne
Woodley (Chief Executive)
Email: ocf@oxfordshire.org
Website: www.oxfordshire.org

Quartet Community Foundation
(Bristol, Bath and North East
Somerset, North Somerset and South
Gloustershire)
Royal Oak House
Royal Oak Avenue
Bristol
BS1 4GB
Tel: 0117 989 7700
Fax: 0117 989 7701
Contact: Ronnie Brown (Development
Director)
Email: info@quartetcf.org.uk
Website: www.quartetcf.org.uk

St Katharine and Shadwell Trust
(East End and City of London)
Unit 1.4
11–29 Fashion Street
London E1 6PX
Tel: 020 7422 7523
Fax: 020 7247 2938
Contact: Jenny Dawes (Director)
Email: enquiries@skst.org
Website: www.skst.org

Scottish Community Foundation
22 Calton Road
Edinburgh
EH8 8PD
Tel: 0131 524 0300
Fax: 0131 524 0329
Contact: Giles Ruck (Chief Executive)
Email: info@scottishcf.org
Website: www.scottishcf.org

Community Foundation for
Shropshire and Telford
Academy House
1 Brassey Road
Old Potts Way
Shrewsbury
SY3 7FA
Tel: 01743 343 879
Email: contact@cfst.co.uk
Website: www.cfsat.org.uk

Solihull Community Foundation
Block 80
Land Rover
Lode Lane
Solihull
B92 8NW
Tel: 0121 700 3934
Contact: Sharon Pinnock (Manager)
Website: www.solihullcf.org

Somerset Community Foundation
Yeoman House
Royal Bath and West Showground
Shepton Mallet
BA4 6QN
Tel: 01749 344949
Contact: Justin Sargent (Chief
Executive)
Email: info@somersetcf.org.uk
Website: www.somersetcf.org.uk

South Yorkshire Community
Foundation
Unit 3 – G1 Building
6 Leeds Road
Attercliffe
Sheffield
S9 3TY
Tel: 0114 242 4857
Fax: 0114 242 4605
Contact: Pauline Grice (Chief
Executive)
Email: admin@sycf.org.uk
Website: www.sycf.org.uk

Staffordshire Community
Foundation
Dudson Centre
Hope Street
Hanley
Stoke-on-Trent
ST1 5DD
Tel: 01782 683000
Fax: 01782 683199
Email: info@staffsfoundation.org.uk
Website: www.staffsfoundation.org.uk

Stevenage Community Trust
Unit B
Mindenhall Court
High Street
Tel: 01438 525390
Contact: June Oldroyd (Manager)
Email: info@sct.uk.net
Website: www.sct.uk.net

Suffolk Foundation
Old Reading Rooms
The Green
Grundisburgh
Woodbridge
IP13 6TT
Tel: 01473 734120
Contact: Stephen Singleton (Chief
Executive)
Email: Stephen.singleton@
suffolkfoundation.org.uk
Website: www.suffolkfoundation.org.
uk

Community Foundation for **Surrey**
1 Bishops Wharf
Walnut Tree Close
Guildford
GU1 4RA
Tel: 01483 409230
Contact: Wendy Varcoe (Executive Director)
Email: info@communityfoundation surrey.org.uk
Website: www.surreycommunity foundation.org.uk

Sussex Community Foundation
Suite B
Falcon Wharf
Railway Lane
Lewes
BN7 2AQ
Tel: 01273 409440
Contact: Kevin Richmond (Chief Executive)
Email: info@sussexgiving.org.uk
Website: www.sussexgiving.org.uk

Tees Valley Community Foundation
Wallace House
Falcon Court
Preston Farm
Stockton-on-Tees
TS18 3TX
Tel: 01642 260860
Contact: Hugh McGouran (Chief Executive)
Email: h.mcgouran@ teesvalleyfoundation.org
Website: www.teesvalleyfoundation.org

Two Ridings Community Foundation (North Yorkshire, York, East Yorkshire and Hull)
Primrose Hill
Buttercrambe Road
Stamford Bridge
York
YO41 1AW
Tel: 01759 377400
Contact: Jackie McCafferty (Office Manager)
Email: office@tworidingscommunity foundation.org.uk
Website: www.tworidingscommunity foundation.org.uk

*Community Foundation serving **Tyne and Wear** and Northumberland*
Cale Cross
156 Pilgrim Street
Newcastle upon Tyne
NE1 6SU
Tel: 0191 222 0945
Fax: 0191 230 0689
Contact: Rob Williamson (Chief Executive)
Email: general@communityfoundation. org.uk
Website: www.communityfoundation. org.uk

Wakefield District Community Foundation
Suite 5
Vincent House
136 Westgate
Wakefield
Tel: 01924 239 181
Email: info@ communityfoundationwakefield.co.uk
Website: www.communityfoundation wakefield.co.uk

Community Foundation in **Wales**
9 Coopers Yard
Curran Road
Cardiff
CF10 5NB
Tel: 02920 536590
Fax: 02920 342118
Contact: Liza Kellett (Chief Executive)
Email: info@cfiw.org.uk
Website: www.cfiw.org.uk

*Community Foundation for **Wiltshire** and Swindon*
48 New Park Street
Devizes
SN10 1DS
Tel: 01380 729284
Contact: Rosemary MacDonald (Chief Executive)
Email: info@wscf.org.uk
Website: www.wscf.org.uk

Worcestershire Community Foundation
Foley Grove
Goley Business Park
Kidderminster
DY11 7PT
Tel: 01562 733000
Contact: Vikki Morris (Director)
Email: vikki@worcscf.org.uk
Website: www.worcscf.org.uk

Subject index

The following subject index begins with a list of categories used. The categories are very wide-ranging to keep the index as simple as possible. DSC's subscription website (www.trustfunding.org.uk) has a much more detailed search facility on the categories. There may be considerable overlap between the categories – for example, children and education, or older people and social welfare.

The list of categories is followed by the index itself. Before using the index, please note the following points.

How the index was compiled

1) The index aims to reflect the most recent grant-making practice. Therefore, it is based on our interpretation of which areas each trust has actually given to, rather than what its policy statement says or its charitable objects allow it to do in principle. For example, where a trust states that it has general charitable purposes, but its grants list shows a strong preference for welfare, we index it under welfare.

2) We have tried to ensure that each trust has given significantly in the areas under which it is indexed (usually at least £15,000). Thus small, apparently untypical grants have been ignored for index purposes.

3) The index has been complied from the latest information available to us.

Limitations

1) Policies may change, and some more frequently than others.

2) Sometimes there will be a geographical restriction on a trust's grantgiving which is not shown in this index, or the trust may not give to the area and the heading under which your specific purposes fall. It is important to read each entry carefully.

You will need to check that:

- the trust gives in your geographical area of operation
- the trust gives for the specific purposes you require
- there is no other reason to prevent you from making an application to this trust.

3) It is worth noting that one or two of the categories list almost half the trusts included in this guide.

Under no circumstances should the index be used as a simple mailing list. Remember that each trust is different and that the policies or interests of a particular trust often do not fit easily into the given categories. Each entry must be read individually before you send off an application. Indiscriminate applications are usually unsuccessful. They waste time and money and greatly annoy trusts.

The categories are as follows:

Arts, culture, sport and recreation *page 414*

This is a very wide category including: performing, written and visual arts; crafts; theatres, museums and galleries; heritage, architecture and archaeology; and sports.

Children and young people *page 415*

This is mainly for welfare and welfare-related activities.

Development, housing and employment *page 416*

This includes specific industries such as leather making or textiles.

Disability *page 416*

Disadvantaged people *page 417*

This includes people who are:

- socially excluded
- socially and economically disadvantaged
- unemployed
- homeless
- offenders
- educationally disadvantaged
- victims of social/natural occurrences, including refugees and asylum seekers.

Education and training *page 418*

Environment and animals *page 419*

This includes:

- agriculture and fishing
- conservation
- animal care
- environment and education
- transport
- sustainable environment.

General charitable purposes *page 419*

This is a very broad category and includes trusts that often have numerous specific strands to their programmes a well as those that will consider any application (subject to other eligibility criteria).

Arts, culture, sport and recreation

The 29th May 1961 Charitable Trust
The Alice Trust
Allchurches Trust Ltd
The Architectural Heritage Fund
The Ashden Trust
The Baring Foundation
The Bedford Charity (The Harpur Trust)
The Big Lottery Fund
Blackheart Foundation (UK) Limited
The Liz and Terry Bramall Charitable Trust
The Audrey and Stanley Burton 1960 Charitable Trust
Edward Cadbury Charitable Trust
The William A Cadbury Charitable Trust
The Barrow Cadbury Trust and the Barrow Cadbury Fund
Calouste Gulbenkian Foundation
The Carpenters' Company Charitable Trust
The Checkatrade Foundation
The Clore Duffield Foundation
The John S Cohen Foundation
The R and S Cohen Foundation
Colyer-Fergusson Charitable Trust
The Ernest Cook Trust
The D'Oyly Carte Charitable Trust
The Daiwa Anglo-Japanese Foundation
Peter De Haan Charitable Trust
The Djanogly Foundation
The Drapers' Charitable Fund
The Dulverton Trust
Dunard Fund
The John Ellerman Foundation
The Eranda Foundation
Esmée Fairbairn Foundation
The February Foundation
The Sir John Fisher Foundation
Fisherbeck Charitable Trust
The Fishmongers' Company's Charitable Trust
The Football Association Youth Trust
The Football Foundation
The Donald Forrester Trust
The Foyle Foundation
The Hugh Fraser Foundation
The Gannochy Trust
The Gatsby Charitable Foundation
J Paul Getty Jr Charitable Trust

Simon Gibson Charitable Trust
The Girdlers' Company Charitable Trust
The Glass-House Trust
The Goldsmiths' Company Charity
The Gosling Foundation Limited
The Great Britain Sasakawa Foundation
The Grocers' Charity
Paul Hamlyn Foundation
The Helen Hamlyn Trust
The Peter Harrison Foundation
The Charles Hayward Foundation
The Headley Trust
The Hintze Family Charitable Foundation
Hobson Charity Limited
Jerwood Charitable Foundation
The Sir James Knott Trust
The Neil Kreitman Foundation
The Leathersellers' Company Charitable Fund
The Leverhulme Trust
Lord Leverhulme's Charitable Trust
The Joseph Levy Charitable Foundation
The Linbury Trust
The George John and Sheilah Livanos Charitable Trust
Lloyds TSB Foundation for Northern Ireland
The London Marathon Charitable Trust
The Lord's Taverners
John Lyon's Charity
The Mackintosh Foundation
The MacRobert Trust
The Manifold Charitable Trust
The Manoukian Charitable Foundation
Marshall's Charity
The Mercers' Charitable Foundation
Milton Keynes Community Foundation
The Monument Trust
The Henry Moore Foundation
The Peter Moores Foundation
The John R Murray Charitable Trust
The National Art Collections Fund
The National Churches Trust
Network for Social Change
Nominet Charitable Foundation
The Northern Rock Foundation
The Northwood Charitable Trust
The Ofenheim Charitable Trust
Oglesby Charitable Trust
The Parthenon Trust
The Performing Right Society Foundation
The Pilgrim Trust

Children and young people

Development, housing and employment

Disability

Disadvantaged people

Education and training

Environment and animals

General charitable purposes

The H D H Wills 1965 Charitable Trust

The Community Foundation for Wiltshire and Swindon

The Harold Hyam Wingate Foundation

The Wixamtree Trust

The Charles Wolfson Charitable Trust

The South Yorkshire Community Foundation

The Zochonis Charitable Trust

Illness

The Sylvia Adams Charitable Trust

Roald Dahl's Marvellous Children's Charity

The John Ellerman Foundation

Esmée Fairbairn Foundation

The February Foundation

The Hugh Fraser Foundation

The Gatsby Charitable Foundation

J Paul Getty Jr Charitable Trust

The Girdlers' Company Charitable Trust

The Gosling Foundation Limited

The Hadley Trust

Hampton Fuel Allotment Charity

The Peter Harrison Foundation

The Heart of England Community Foundation

The Hedley Foundation

The Hintze Family Charitable Foundation

Impetus Trust

The Elton John Aids Foundation

The Jones 1986 Charitable Trust

The Mary Kinross Charitable Trust

The Kirby Laing Foundation

The Beatrice Laing Trust

The Allen Lane Foundation

The LankellyChase Foundation

The Joseph Levy Charitable Foundation

The Linbury Trust

Lloyds TSB Foundation for Northern Ireland

Lloyds TSB Foundation for Scotland

John Lyon's Charity

The Mackintosh Foundation

The Mercers' Charitable Foundation

The Monument Trust

John Moores Foundation

The Northern Rock Foundation

The Northwood Charitable Trust

The Pilgrim Trust

Mr and Mrs J A Pye's Charitable Settlement

The Robertson Trust

The Seneca Trust

The Sovereign Health Care Charitable Trust

St James's Place Foundation

The True Colours Trust

The James Tudor Foundation

John and Lucille van Geest Foundation

The Will Charitable Trust

Medicine and health

The 1989 Willan Charitable Trust

The ACT Foundation

Action Medical Research

Age UK (formerly Help the Aged and Age Concern)

The AIM Foundation

The Alliance Family Foundation

The John Armitage Charitable Trust

The Baily Thomas Charitable Fund

The Balcombe Charitable Trust

The Band Trust

The Barclay Foundation

The Barnwood House Trust

The Big Lottery Fund

Blackheart Foundation (UK) Limited

The Liz and Terry Bramall Charitable Trust

The Breadsticks Foundation

The Burdett Trust for Nursing

The Audrey and Stanley Burton 1960 Charitable Trust

The William A Cadbury Charitable Trust

The Charities Advisory Trust

The Checkatrade Foundation

The Childwick Trust

The Clothworkers' Foundation

Richard Cloudesley's Charity

The Coalfields Regeneration Trust

The Colt Foundation

The Michael Cowan Foundation

The Peter Cruddas Foundation

The D'Oyly Carte Charitable Trust

Roald Dahl's Marvellous Children's Charity

Baron Davenport's Charity

The Djanogly Foundation

The Dunhill Medical Trust

The James Dyson Foundation

The EBM Charitable Trust

The John Ellerman Foundation

The Eranda Foundation

The Eveson Charitable Trust

The Sir John Fisher Foundation

The Fishmongers' Company's Charitable Trust

The Donald Forrester Trust

The Hugh Fraser Foundation

The Freemasons' Grand Charity

The Freshfield Foundation

The Gatsby Charitable Foundation

J Paul Getty Jr Charitable Trust

Simon Gibson Charitable Trust

The G C Gibson Charitable Trust

The Girdlers' Company Charitable Trust

The Golden Bottle Trust

The Goldsmiths' Company Charity

Mike Gooley Trailfinders Charity

The Great Britain Sasakawa Foundation

The Grocers' Charity

H C D Memorial Fund

The Helen Hamlyn Trust

Hampton Fuel Allotment Charity

The Kathleen Hannay Memorial Charity

The Haramead Trust

The Maurice Hatter Foundation

The Charles Hayward Foundation

The Headley Trust

The Hedley Foundation

Lady Hind Trust

The Hintze Family Charitable Foundation

The Jane Hodge Foundation

The Albert Hunt Trust

John James Bristol Foundation

The Elton John Aids Foundation

The Jones 1986 Charitable Trust

The Joron Charitable Trust

The Kay Kendall Leukaemia Fund

The Mary Kinross Charitable Trust

Ernest Kleinwort Charitable Trust

Maurice and Hilda Laing Charitable Trust

The Beatrice Laing Trust

The Leathersellers' Company Charitable Fund

The William Leech Charity

The Joseph Levy Charitable Foundation

The Linbury Trust

The Enid Linder Foundation

The George John and Sheilah Livanos Charitable Trust

Lloyds TSB Foundation for Northern Ireland

Lloyds TSB Foundation for the Channel Islands

The Trust for London (formerly the City Parochial Foundation)

The Lord's Taverners

The Madeline Mabey Trust

Older people

Science and technology

Social sciences, policy and research

Social welfare

Voluntary sector management and development

Women

Geographical index

The following geographical index aims to highlight when a trust gives preference for, or has a special interest in, a particular area: a county, region, city, town or London borough. Please note the following points.

1) Before using this index please read the following information and the introduction to the subject index on page 413. We must emphasise that this index:

   ▶ should not be used as a simple mailing list
   ▶ is not a substitute for detailed research.

   When you have identified trusts using this index, please read each entry carefully before making an application. Simply because a trust gives in your geographical area, this does not mean that it gives to your type of work.

2) Most trusts in this list are not restricted to one area; usually the geographical index indicates that the trust gives some priority for the area or areas.

3) Trusts which give throughout England or the UK have been excluded from the index, unless they have a particular interest in one or more locality.

4) Each section is ordered alphabetically according to the name of the trust. The categories for the overseas and UK indexes are as follows:

England

We have divided England into the following nine categories:

North East *page 428*

North West *page 428*

Yorkshire and the Humber *page 428*

East Midlands *page 428*

West Midlands *page 428*

Eastern England *page 428*

South West *page 428*

South East *page 428*

Greater London *page 428*

Some trusts may be found in more than one category due to them providing grants in more than one area, such as those with a preference for northern England.

Channel Islands *page 428*

Wales *page 428*

Scotland *page 429*

Northern Ireland *page 429*

Republic of Ireland *page 429*

Europe *page 429*

Overseas categories

Developing world *page 429*

This includes trusts which support missionary organisations when they are also interested in social and economic development.

Individual continents *page 429*

The Middle East has been listed separately. Please note that most of the trusts listed are primarily for the benefit of Jewish people and the advancement of the Jewish religion.

England

North East
The 1989 Willan Charitable Trust
The Coalfields Regeneration Trust
County Durham Community
  Foundation
Hexham and Newcastle Diocesan
  Trust (1947)
The Sir James Knott Trust
The William Leech Charity
The Northern Rock Foundation
Tees Valley Community
  Foundation
Community Foundation Serving
  Tyne and Wear and
  Northumberland

North West
The Bowland Charitable Trust
The Coalfields Regeneration Trust
Cumbria Community Foundation
Forever Manchester (The
  Community Foundation for
  Greater Manchester)
The Helping Foundation
Community Foundation for
  Merseyside
John Moores Foundation
The Northern Rock Foundation
Oglesby Charitable Trust
The Pilkington Charities Fund
The Francis C Scott Charitable
  Trust
SHINE (Support and Help in
  Education)
The Yorkshire Dales Millennium
  Trust
The Zochonis Charitable Trust

Yorkshire and the Humber
The Audrey and Stanley Burton
  1960 Charitable Trust
Community Foundation for
  Calderdale
Church Burgesses Trust
The Coalfields Regeneration Trust
The South Yorkshire Community
  Foundation
The Yorkshire Dales Millennium
  Trust

East Midlands
The Coalfields Regeneration Trust
Derbyshire Community Foundation
The Maud Elkington Charitable
  Trust
The London Marathon Charitable
  Trust
The Wates Foundation

West Midlands
The Birmingham Community
  Foundation
The William A Cadbury Charitable
  Trust
The Coalfields Regeneration Trust
Baron Davenport's Charity
The Eveson Charitable Trust
The Heart of England Community
  Foundation
The Jordan Charitable Foundation
The London Marathon Charitable
  Trust
Stratford upon Avon Town Trust
Sutton Coldfield Municipal
  Charities

Eastern England
The Bedford Charity (The Harpur
  Trust)
Essex Community Foundation
The Hertfordshire Community
  Foundation
The Jack Petchey Foundation

South West
The H B Allen Charitable Trust
The Barnwood House Trust
Community Foundation for
  Bournemouth, Dorset and Poole
Devon Community Foundation
John James Bristol Foundation
Quartet Community Foundation
  (formerly the Greater Bristol
  Foundation)
The Valentine Charitable Trust
The Wates Foundation
The Community Foundation for
  Wiltshire and Swindon

South East
The Alice Trust
The Arbib Foundation
The Coalfields Regeneration Trust
Colyer-Fergusson Charitable Trust
Milton Keynes Community
  Foundation
Sussex Community Foundation
The Wates Foundation

Greater London
ABF The Soldiers' Charity
  (formerly the Army Benevolent
  Fund)
Amabrill Limited
The Campden Charities Trustee
Sir John Cass's Foundation
The City Bridge Trust (formerly
  known as Bridge House Trust)
Richard Cloudesley's Charity
The R and S Cohen Foundation
Cripplegate Foundation

The Girdlers' Company Charitable
  Trust
The Glass-House Trust
The Goldsmiths' Company Charity
The M and R Gross Charities
  Limited
The Helping Foundation
The Sir Joseph Hotung Charitable
  Settlement
Hurdale Charity Limited
Isle of Dogs Community
  Foundation
The J J Charitable Trust
The Jerusalem Trust
Jewish Child's Day
The Trust for London (formerly the
  City Parochial Foundation)
The London Community
  Foundation (formerly Capital
  Community Foundation)
The London Marathon Charitable
  Trust
John Lyon's Charity
Mayfair Charities Ltd
Nemoral Ltd
North West London Community
  Foundation
The Nuffield Foundation
The Jack Petchey Foundation
The Richmond Parish Lands
  Charity
ShareGift (The Orr Mackintosh
  Foundation)
SHINE (Support and Help in
  Education)
St Katharine and Shadwell Trust
The Wates Foundation
The Will Charitable Trust

Channel Islands

The Freemasons' Grand Charity
Lloyds TSB Foundation for the
  Channel Islands

Wales

The John Armitage Charitable
  Trust
The Baring Foundation
The Church and Community Fund
The Coalfields Regeneration Trust
The DM Charitable Trust
The James Dyson Foundation
Gwyneth Forrester Trust
The Freemasons' Grand Charity
Lady Hind Trust
The Hintze Family Charitable
  Foundation

Middle East

Alphabetical index